EVANGELION DA-MEPHARRESHE

EVANGELION DA-MEPHARRESHE

The Curetonian Version of the Four Gospels, with the readings of the Sinai Palimpsest and the early Syriac Patristic evidence edited, collected and arranged by

F. CRAWFORD BURKITT, M.A.
University Lecturer in Palaeography.

VOLUME I

TEXT

WIPF & STOCK · Eugene, Oregon

Wipf and Stock Publishers
199 W 8th Ave, Suite 3
Eugene, OR 97401

Evangelion Da-Mepharreshe
Volume 1
By Burkitt, F. Crawford
ISBN 13: 978-1-5326-0861-2
Publication date 10/30/2016
Previously published by Cambridge University Press, 1904

TO THE MEMORY OF

ROBERT LUBBOCK BENSLY

SOMETIME LORD ALMONER'S PROFESSOR OF ARABIC

IN THE UNIVERSITY OF CAMBRIDGE

I DEDICATE THIS BOOK

PREFACE.

Scripturis sanctis ubi et uerborum ordo mysterium est.

HIERON., *Ep.* lvii.

THE present volume contains the text of the *Evangelion da-Mepharreshe*, or Old Syriac Version of the Four Gospels, with such variants as I have been able to collect and with literal translations of text and variants into English. In the second volume I have described the MSS at length, discussed the grammatical style of the version, examined the relation of the *Evangelion da-Mepharreshe* to the Peshitta and to the Diatessaron of Tatian, and attempted to estimate its place and value in the textual criticism of the Gospels. In this Preface I only wish to say a few words in explanation of the plan and arrangement of the present volume and in defence of the method of translation which I have adopted.

First of all I must express my lasting regret that the name of the late Professor Bensly should appear in the Dedication instead of on the Title-Page. Professor Bensly had been for many years contemplating a new issue of the 'Curetonian Gospels,' and on the discovery of the Sinai MS it seemed as if the man most fitted for the work of preparing a critical edition of our greatly increased material was on the spot and ready to do it. But to the grief of all students of Oriental Literature he died immediately after his return from Sinai in 1893, and when the present Dean of Westminster entrusted me with the work which Professor Bensly had undertaken for *Texts and Studies* I found that I had to begin from the very beginning. Of Professor Bensly's long projected edition of the 'Curetonian' nothing tangible remained after his death but his copy of Cureton's edition containing an incomplete recollation of the MS. There were no notes, no specimens of a new translation, no sketches of *Prolegomena*. Bensly's unrivalled familiarity with Syriac literature and the methods of Syriac translators would have given his edition, had he lived to complete but a portion of it, a unique value. But so far as we can discover, this store of learning perished with him. It was therefore impossible to place his name on the title-page of this book; but in dedicating it to his memory I wish to express the hope that my work may have attained some measure of the thoroughness and accuracy which Biblical and Oriental scholars have so justly associated with his name.

The reason that this book of mine does not after all appear among the Cambridge *Texts and Studies* is its size. Such books as Dr Abbott's edition of Codex Usserianus or Mr Horner's edition of the Bohairic Coptic, in which the Four Gospels are distributed into two volumes, are practically inconvenient for purposes of reference. It was important to place the English translation opposite the Syriac text, and to do this in the size of *Texts and Studies* would have resulted in a book of nearly a thousand pages, even if the Introduction was reserved, as here, for a second volume. The plan of incorporating this edition of *Evangelion da-Mepharreshe* into the Cambridge Series was therefore reluctantly abandoned, and I have to thank the generous enterprise of the Syndics of the University Press for undertaking it as a separate work.

It was clear from the first that no attempt should be made to reconstruct an ideal text. The need of Syriac and Biblical students is to have the evidence set before them in such a way that one may see at a glance what authorities are extant for any given passage and what reading our several authorities preserve. To print our two MSS *S* and *C* in full would swell the bulk of the volume, already large, to unmanageable dimensions; moreover such a course would obscure the fundamental agreement of the two MSS, which is as important a feature as their perpetual divergence. One of the two therefore had to be printed in full, with the other exhibited in the form of various readings, and the question arose which was to be promoted to the place of honour.

In many ways it would have been more interesting to have printed *S* in full, with the variants of *C* in the notes, but I was advised by Dr Armitage Robinson and by the ever-regretted Professor Robertson Smith to adopt the opposite course. I feel sure they were right even now; nine years ago, when the decision had to be made, the case was still clearer. In the first place there is no other readily available means of getting at the continuous text of *C*. Cureton's edition has been long out of print, and it does not contain the Berlin leaves: I hope the text of *C* is printed in this volume with sufficient accuracy to be and to remain the definite edition of the 'Curetonian' MS. But *S* was printed in full in 1894 (the "*Syndics' Edition*"), and a glance at that book will shew that it is not very well suited to be the basis of an apparatus of variants. Since that date, it is true, our knowledge of the text of *S* has been greatly increased by the publication of Mrs Lewis's *Some Pages* (1896). The additional readings there supplied, together with the corrections published for the first time in this volume[1], leave but a comparatively small harvest for the future decipherer of the Palimpsest to gather. But when I started on my work these subsidiary sources of information did not exist.

When *C* fails us, as in the whole of S. Mark, *S* is placed in the text. In any case it will be understood that the readings printed in the notes are of the same importance as those printed in the text. I have only aimed at collecting together the materials, not at a reconstruction of the original form of the Version. At the same time I ought to state at once my conviction, which I believe to be that of every other Syriac scholar, that *S* is on the whole a better representative of the *Evangelion da-Mepharreshe* than *C*, although there are not a few instances where *S* fails to maintain its habitual superiority.

A few words must now be said about the translation. I venture to think that I need hardly apologise that the translation is in English. A reconstruction of the Greek text underlying the 'Old Syriac' would be most unsatisfactory, as can be seen from Baethgen's attempt in *Evangelienfragmente*. It is unsatisfactory, because it seeks to establish what from the nature of things cannot be ascertained, *viz.* the continuous Greek text underlying the Syriac. Syriac is a language of very different genius to Greek, and the translator of the *Evangelion da-Mepharreshe* was far more careful to reproduce the sense of the original than to express Greek idioms in a foreign tongue. This makes his work more natural and animated, while it does not seriously interfere with its value as a critical witness in matters of importance. But in many minor points the evidence of the Syriac is really ambiguous, and

[1] These corrections are incorporated into the text of *S* as here given and are also collected together in *Appendix* III: they are about 300 in number.

in such cases to give a re-translation into Greek introduces an appearance of definiteness, where no such definiteness is justified.

Similar arguments may be urged against a Latin rendering of the Syriac. A most important branch of the critical study of the Syriac is a comparison of its readings with the Latin Versions; for this purpose, the adoption of a particular Latin style or vocabulary in translation would inevitably make the agreement of the Syriac and the Vulgate, or the Syriac and some branch of the 'Old Latin,' greater (or less) than the ascertainable facts actually warrant.

I therefore decided upon an English translation, and here again a choice of alternatives had to be made. The first and most obvious course was to take either the Authorized Version of 1611 or the Revised Version of 1881 as a basis, and make only such changes as faithfulness demanded. The chief objection to this method is the same that has been urged against a Greek or Latin rendering, that it gives an appearance of agreement in detail when perhaps no agreement exists: moreover the inevitable occasional disagreement between a faithful translation executed on these principles and the English Bible in either form would produce a patchwork, open to more objection than the course I have actually followed. Another method would have been to try and copy the freedom of the *Evangelion da-Mepharreshe* itself, to give an English rendering as idiomatic and nervous as the Syriac. The first and most decisive reason for not attempting this lies in the certainty of failure. The combination of scholarship and literary gift which would be required could scarcely be united in a single individual. But even if it were well done, we may fairly ask what use would such a translation serve? For purposes of edification indeed it might be valuable. It might shew to the English reader how well the *Evangelion da-Mepharreshe* had caught the fresh and unaffected spirit of the Gospel story. But people do not read the translation of a Syriac Version for purposes of edification. They require a translation as an aid in reading the Syriac text, or in comparing the text attested by the Syriac with other critical authorities.

A knowledge of the letter rather than of the spirit is what is required by the readers of an ancient Biblical translation, and it is this that I have attempted to supply. I have tried to be as pedantically literal as possible, to render the same Syriac word by the same English word, and to make a distinction in the English where a distinction is made in the Syriac, whatever the underlying Greek may have been. The distinctions made in the Greek are not always represented in the Syriac, although on the other hand the Syriac sometimes makes a distinction where there is none in the Greek. For example, ἀγορὰ and πλατεῖα are represented indifferently in Syriac by *shûqâ*, i.e. 'street' or 'bazaar,' consequently we cannot tell whether the Syriac supports ἀγοραῖς or πλατείαις in Mk vi 56. On the other hand *S* in Matt vi 2, and both *S* and *C* in Lk xiv 21, are careful to render ῥύμη by the special term *sh'qâqâ*, i.e. 'lane.' Again, the Syriac *shanneq* corresponds exactly to βασανίζειν 'to torment,' and accordingly we find μή με βασανίσῃς in Matt viii 29 and Lk viii 28 appropriately rendered by *lâ θ'shann'qan*, as in the Peshitta. But in Mk v 7, a passage absolutely parallel to the others, *S* has *lâ θeshtannaδ bî*, a rendering which gives the same sense, but uses another verb. There is no trace of any various reading in the Greek, but the variation in the Syriac is interesting from the light it throws upon the methods of the translator: I have therefore tried to mark the difference in the English rendering of Mk v 7 by using 'torture me not,' instead of 'torment me not' as in the parallels.

The examples quoted above are of importance only as they help us to gauge the standard of accuracy aimed at by the Syriac Version, but occasionally distinctions are introduced or obliterated which have some exegetical significance. In such cases it becomes especially necessary to reproduce the peculiarities of the Syriac in our English rendering. Thus the somewhat rare word *eθ'azzaz* 'to be excited,' properly used of water *stirred up* by a storm, and then by a metaphor applied to personal feeling, occurs three times, and in each case it corresponds to a different Greek word. In Lk xxii 59 it is used of the indignation of S. Peter's interlocutor (διισχυρίζετο), in Mk viii 12 it is used of our Lord's indignation at the crass materialism of the Pharisees (ἀναστενάξας); while in Joh xi 33, 38 it is used of His emotion at the grave of Lazarus (ἐνεβριμήσατο, ἐμβριμώμενος). It seems therefore that the translator understood this emotion as indignation against the murmurs of the Jews rather than as expressing some inner conflict, but in any case it is clear that the Syriac word should be translated in all three passages by the same expression in English.

Again, the Holy Spirit, in the *Evangelion da-Mepharreshe* as in the Peshitta, is commonly called *Rûḥâ δ'Quδshâ*, lit. "Spirit of

Holiness." But in Mk xiii 11, Lk ii 25, 26, xi 13 (*C*), Joh xx 22, we find *Rûḥâ Qaddîshtâ*. We are scarcely justified in assuming that the two expressions were regarded as equivalent in Syriac because they equally represent [τὸ] πνεῦμα [τὸ] ἅγιον in Greek. But when we look at the context in which *Rûḥâ qaddîshtâ* occurs, especially Lk ii 26 which speaks of "that *Rûḥâ qaddîshtâ*," it is evident that it is definitely *not* used in the sense of a Divine Hypostasis. I have retained "the Holy Spirit" as on the whole the best equivalent for *Rûḥâ δ'Quδshâ*; but this would be misleading for *Rûḥâ qaddîshtâ*, which I have uniformly rendered 'a holy Spirit.' I did not adopt "the Spirit of Holiness" for *Rûḥâ δ'Quδshâ*, because I venture to think that also would have conveyed a wrong idea. *Quδshâ* is much nearer *sanctum* than *sanctitas*: in Matt iv 5 *M'δînaθ Quδshâ* does not mean what "City of Holiness" would mean in English, but simply and solely ἡ ἁγία πόλις, as in the Greek.

To sum up, my aim in the translation has been to give the reader who knows little or no Syriac such help as will enable him, by the exercise of reasonable care and intelligence, to understand the meaning of the Syriac on the opposite page, and also to compare the renderings of this Version in any given passage with its renderings elsewhere. To use the translation of a text for critical purposes instead of the original is always somewhat unsafe, but I have endeavoured to diminish the risk as much as possible. In this matter I cannot hope to please: I shall be content if my rendering is found to be serviceable.

It only remains to express my very warm thanks for the kind help which has been extended to me from various quarters during the preparation of this work. Mr T. R. Glover, of S. John's College, gave me a line-for-line transcript of the three Berlin leaves of Codex *C*, which cleared up several doubtful points not ascertainable from Wright's printed text. Mrs Lewis was good enough during her last visit in 1902 to examine the Sinai Palimpsest for me in several passages where the photograph was illegible. The two illustrations of the MS (see vol. ii, pp. 28, 257) are made from her photographs, for one of which she kindly lent the original film. It cannot be out of place here to repeat what I have said on p. 18, that it is by her enterprise and liberality in presenting complete sets of her photographs to the Cambridge University Library that we are able satisfactorily to control the original transcripts of the decipherers of the Palimpsest. To

Mrs Pattrick, of Cambridge, I am indebted for the excellent likeness of her father, Dr Cureton. Dr G. Mercati, of the Vatican Library, has more than once kindly verified references to the reading of MSS in the Vatican, and to the ever-ready kindness of Prof. Ignazio Guidi I owe an accurate transcript of the Genealogy in the Borgian MS of the Arabic Diatessaron (Ciasca's Cod. B). The chapter on the linguistic characteristics of the Old Syriac version (vol. ii, chap. ii) was read throughout by my friend Professor R. H. Kennett, who thereby did the book a service which is but inadequately represented by the Notes actually signed with his initials. Finally, I should be indeed ungrateful if I did not shew my appreciation of the intelligence and skill of the Compositors and Readers of the Cambridge University Press. Only those who have practical experience of the difficulties of setting up Notes, partly written in English which runs one way, and partly in Syriac which runs the other, can have any idea of the difficulties which had to be surmounted both in composition and in correction.

F. C. BURKITT.

CAMBRIDGE,
December, 1904.

ERRATA AND CORRIGENDA.

ܦܪܘܫܐ ܠܗܘ ܗܘ ܪܚܡ. ܠܟܬܒܐ ܕܓܪܝܕ ܘܡܒܚܪ.
ܣܟܠܐ ܗܘ ܪܚܡ ܠܟܬܒܐ. ܕܠܐ ܓܪܝܕܐ ܒܗ ܐܬܘܬܐ.

The careful scholar loves to look
Where faults are marked and variants collected;
Only a fool prefers a book
Where not one single letter is corrected.

Isaac of Antioch xxvii 1852 f.
(Bickell's Edition, vol. ii, p 348).

S. Matthew.

P. 9	Matt ii 18	*Notes*	*add*	will not] would not *S*		
p. 11	,, ii 23	*txt.*	*for*	spoken	*read*	said
	,, iii 6	,,	,,	their sins	,,	his sins
	,, iii 7	,,	,,	publicans	,,	toll-gatherers
p. 13	,, iii 13	*txt. & Notes*	*for*	to John	,,	unto John
p. 26	,, v 42	*Notes*	*add*	ܬܫܠܡܘܗܝ] ܬܫܠܡܝܗ *S*		
p. 27	,, v 47	*txt.*	*after*	pagans	*add*	also
pp. 38, 39		(*margin*)	*for*	(*S*)	*read*	[*S*]
p. 39	,, viii 3	*txt.*	,,	his leprosy	,,	the leprosy
	,, viii 4	*Notes*	*add*	*Beware* lest] *cf* Matt xvii 9		
p. 41	,, viii 21	*txt.*	*for*	the disciples	*read*	his disciples
p. 43	,, viii 24	,,	,,	broken in	,,	covered by
p. 45	,, ix 9	,,	,,	came	,,	went
	,, ix 18	,,	,,	ruler	,,	chief
p. 47	,, ix 22	,,	,,	the woman	,,	that woman
	,, ix 23[a]	,,	,,	the ruler	,,	that chief
	,, ix 23[b]	,,	,,	that was making	,,	that they were making
p. 48	,, ix 36	,,	,,	ܠܗܘܢ	,,	ܠܗܝ̈
p. 53	,, x 27	*Notes*	*add*	light] daylight *A*		
	,, x 28	*txt.*	*for*	but (1°)	*read*	and
p. 55	,, xi 8	,,	,,	clothed	,,	clad
p. 57	,, xi 16	,,	,,	unto	,,	to
p. 59	,, xi 23	*Notes*	,,	hath been	,,	hast been

p. 65 Matt. xii 33 *Notes*	*read*	*plur. in C; sing. in S*		
,, xii 36 *txt.*	*for*	speak	*read*	say
,, xii 36 *Notes*	,,	speak] say *S*	,,	say] speak *S*
p. 67 ,, xii 42 ,,	*add*	guilty] *see Notes*, vol. ii, p. 268		
,, xii 48 ,,	*for*	him which *S*	*read*	to him which *S*
p. 68 ,, xiii 8 ,,	*after*	ܘܝܗܒܬ] ܘܝܗܒ *S*	*add*	: *cf A* 301, *where* ܘܝܗܒܬ *is taken as a participle*
pp. 68, 69 ,, xiii 12 ,,	*delete*	(*cf* Mt xviii 9)		
p. 69 ,, xiii 8 *txt.*	*for*	some sixty	*read*	and some sixty
,, xiii 12 ,,	*delete*	even *and in Notes delete* even] *om. S*		
p. 71 ,, xiii 13 ,,	*for*	in no wise	*read*	never
p. 77 ,, xiii 51 ,,	,,	the disciples	,,	his disciples
p. 79 ,, xiv 9 ,,	,,	but	,,	and *yet*
pp. 82, 83 Matt xiv 24 *Notes*		*A reference to* syr.vg[loc] *shews that a more probable restoration of S would be* ܘܐܬܛܪܦܬ ܡܢ ܓ̈ܠܠܐ ܕܝܡܬܐ, i.e. 'and it (*sc.* the boat) was agitated by the waves of the lake'		
p. 85 Matt xv 7 *txt.*	*for*	said	*read*	had said
,, xv 8 ,,	,,	their lips....their heart	,,	its lips....its heart
p. 87 ,, xv 21 ,,	,,	and Sidon	,,	and of Sidon
p. 89 ,, xv 28 *Notes*	,,	that hour	,,	this hour
p. 91 ,, xv 36 ,,	,,	those seven	,,	these seven
,, xv 39 *txt.*	,,	went away	,,	came away
p. 95 ,, xvi 20 ,,	,,	these same	,,	those same
p. 156 ,, xxvi 24 *Notes*	,,	*pr.* ܕ S^{ed}	,,	*so also S*
pp. 160, 161 Matt xxvi 50 ,,	,,	S^{ed}	,,	*S* (*see* p. 544)
p. 160 Matt xxvi 60 ,,	,,	ܠܣܗܕܘܬܐ ܫܪ̈ܝܪܬܐ	,,	ܠܟܐܢܫ ܫܪ̈ܝܪܬܐ
p. 167 ,, xxvii 25 *txt.*	,,	and they said	,,	and said
,, xxvii 34 *txt. & Notes*	*for*	myrrh	,,	gall
p. 169 ,, xxvii 48 *txt.*	*for*	dipped	,,	moistened

S. Mark.

p. 190 Mk vi 49 *txt.*	*for*	ܫܘܢܗܝ	,,	ܫܘܘܗܝ
,, vi 49 *Notes*	*add*	49 ܫܘܘܗܝ] ܫܘܢܗܝ $S^{ed\,(mea\ culpa)}$		
p. 207 ,, ix 50 *txt.*	*for*	one	*read*	we
p. 226 ,, xiii 25 ,,	,,	ܫ̈ܠܘܬܗ	,,	ܫ̈ܠܘܬܐ
,, xiii 27ª ,,	,,	ܪ̈ܘܚܐ	,,	ܪܘܚܗ
,, xiii 28 ,,	,,	ܗܪ̈ܟܘ	,,	ܗܪ̈ܟܘ

S. Luke.

p. 249	Lk i 50	*Notes*	*add*	unto the age...fear him] *or,* unto ages and for generations to them that fear him		
p. 277	,, vi 30	,,	*for*	Cf *A* 270	*read*	*Cf A* 270
p. 297	,, viii 49	*txt.*	,,	house	,,	household
	,, viii 49	*Notes*	*after*	they came *S*	*add*	household] house *S*
p. 302	,, ix 18	,,	*immediately under* ܒܫܠܝܐ	*for* ܟܕ	*read*	ܘܟܕ
p. 304	,, ix 24	,,	*after*	ܒܚܠܝܬܘܢ] *om. S*	*add*	: *see Notes,* vol. ii
p. 310	,, x 6	,,	*omit* "& 2°" *and add* ܘܐܠܐ ܕܡ ܠܐ] ܐܠܐ ܕܠܐ *S* (*sic*): *see* p. 550			
p. 311	,, x 6	,,	*after*	If *S*	*add*	but] *om. S* (*sic*)
p. 318	,, xi 8	,,	*for*	ܚܝ ܡܚܘܬܐ *S*	*read*	ܚܝ ܡܚܬܐ *S* (*sic*)
p. 329	,, xii 18	,,	,,	should	,,	should *S*
p. 331	,, xii 20	,,	,,	senseless *A*	,,	senseless *A Ephr*
	,, xii 21	,,	,,	*S*	,,	*A*
p. 391	,, xxi 15	,,	,,	that all your	,,	such that your
	,, xxi 15	,,	,,	conquer	,,	conquer you
p. 415	,, xxiv 12	*txt.*	,,	went away	,,	went unto his *house*
p. 419	,, xxiv 43, 44[a]	*txt.*	*read*	[43]And while he took *and* was eating before their eyes, and took up that which was over *and* gave to them, [44]he saith to them:		
	(*see* vol. ii, p. 305)					

S. John.

p. 470	Joh vii 45	*Notes*	*for*	ܟܗܢܐ	*read*	ܟܢܫܐ
	,, vii 48	,,	,,	ܪ̈ܫܢܐ *S*[ed]	,,	ܪ̈ܫܢܐ *S* (*sic*)
	,, vii 49	,,	,,	ܥܡܥܐ *S*[ed]	,,	ܟܕ̈ܒܐ *S*[vid]
	,, vii 51	,,	,,	ܕܢܫܡܥ *S*[ed]	,,	ܢܫܡܥ *S* (*sic*)
p. 471	,, vii 45	,,	,,	priests	,,	multitudes
	,, vii 49	,,	,,	the mob] *S illegible*	,,	the mob] praters *S*[vid] : *but see Notes,* vol. ii, *and* Mk iv 11
p. 520	,, xviii 6	*txt.*	,,	ܠܒܣܦܪܗܘܢ	*read*	ܠܒܣܬܪܗܘܢ

TABLE OF ABBREVIATIONS USED IN THE TEXT AND NOTES.

Syriac MSS and Writings.

A = Aphraates' Homilies, cited by the pages of Wright's edition.

A^a = Wright's Codex A (= B.M. Add. 14619, *saec.* vi).

A^b = „ „ B (= B.M. Add. 17182, *foll.* 1—99, A.D. 474).

A^{b} = „ „ *B* (= B.M. Add. 17182, *foll.* 100—175, A.D. 512).

C = Cureton's MS of the *Evangeliôn da-Mĕpharrĕshê.*

C^* = the original reading of *C*, where there has been some alteration.

C^1 = the corrected reading, if made by the original scribe.

C^{corr} = a corrected reading made by a later hand.

E = Ephraim's Commentary on the Diatessaron, cited by the pages of Dr Moesinger's Latin translation of the extant Armenian text. The Gospel quotations are regularly taken from Dr Armitage Robinson's English translation of the Armenian in Hamlyn Hill's *Earliest Life of Christ*, pp. 334—377, but where it seemed advisable the renderings have been recompared with the Armenian.

S = the Sinai Palimpsest of the *Evangeliôn da-Mĕpharrĕshê.*

S^{ed} = the reading of *S* as hitherto published, where some error may be suspected.

S^{vid} = the apparent reading of *S*, where the photograph is not clear.

S^{nunc} = the reading of *S*, where some correction appears to have been made.

S (*sic*) = the reading of *S* as definitely ascertained from the photograph.

so also S = a reading ascertained from the photograph, where *S* agrees with the text of *C*.

Syr.vg = the Peshitta.

Syr^{palest} = any text of the Palestinian Bible or Lectionary.

Syr.vt is occasionally used for the text of the *Ev. da-Mepharreshe*, especially where *S* and *C* are agreed.

$Diat^{ar}$ = Ciasca's Arabic Diatessaron, cited by the chapter and verse numeration given in Hamlyn Hill's *Earliest Life of Christ.* The two extant MSS are called A and B, as in Ciasca.

ASD = Cureton's *Ancient Syriac Documents.*

Addai = Phillips's *Doctrine of Addai.*

Cyrill = Bickell's *Cyrillona* (ZDMG xxvii 566—598).

Ephr = S. Ephraim, cited by various editions. Ephr. v 166 E means p. 166 of the 2nd vol. of the Roman Edition, the three *Syriac* volumes being reckoned as the 4th, 5th and 6th of the whole six volumes: this is also Mr F. H. Woods's notation. The *Carmina Nisibena* are quoted as *Nis.*, otherwise the editor's name is given.

$Ephr^{arm}$ = Ephraim's Commentary on the Pauline Epp., cited by the pages of the Mechitarists' Latin translation.

Eus. HE = the Syriac translation of Eusebius' Ecclesiastical History.

Eus. Theoph^{syr} = Eusebius on the *Theophania.*

Jul = the *Romance of Julian* (the Apostate), as edited by Hoffmann.

Thos = the Acts of Judas Thomas in the original Syriac, cited by the Syriac pages of Wright's edition (*Apocryphal Acts of the Apostles*, 1871). Wright's MS is occasionally quoted as cod. a, and the Cambridge transcript (*C.U.L.* Add. 2822) as cod. c. The ancient palimpsest fragments at Sinai are quoted wherever extant.

Harris = Dr Rendel Harris's *Fragments of the Commentary of Ephrem Syrus on the Diatessaron* (Cambridge, 1895), containing extracts from the unpublished Commentary of Îshô'dâd the Nestorian.

Other Authorities.

Greek :—ℵ = Tischendorf's Codex Sinaiticus, *saec.* iv.
B = Codex Vaticanus, *saec.* iv.
D = „ Bezae, *saec.* v.
L = „ Regius, *saec.* viii.
ς = the so-called *Textus Receptus.*

Latin :—*c* = Codex Colbertinus, *saec.* xi.
e = „ Palatinus, *saec.* v.
k = „ Bobiensis, *saec.* iv.
vg = the Latin Vulgate.
fuld = Victor of Capua's *Diatessaron,* A.D. 546.

Arm (*or,* arm.vg) = the Armenian version of the N. T.
Aeth = the Ethiopic version of the N. T.
Boh = the Bohairic Coptic version of the N. T.
Arab^{sin} = the Arabic version of the Pauline Epp. at Sinai, published by Mrs Gibson (*Studia Sinaitica* II).

General Abbreviations.

§ (in the text and margins)	= here begins the text of such and such an authority.
¶	= here ends that text.
§ (in the Notes)	= *S* or *C* here begins a paragraph.
[ ]	indicate words supplied wholly by conjecture.
⌜ ⌝	indicate illegible words or letters supplied by conjecture, in accordance with the demands of space.
†	indicates a suspected corruption.
S (in the margin)	indicates that Codex *S* is extant for this page.
(*S*)	indicates that it is extant at the beginning but not at the end.
[*S*]	indicates that it is extant at the end but not at the beginning, the actual place of the change being indicated by § or ¶.

Italics are used, as in the English Bible, to indicate words supplied to eke out the sense in English, but not needed in the Syriac.

NB. Where "*See Introd.* vol. ii" occurs in the Notes, look out the Note on the passage at the end of vol. ii to find the Cross-reference.

EVANGELION DA-MEPHARRESHE

C S
fol 1 v

…ܐܘܢܓܠܝܘܢ . ܕܡܦܪ̈ܫܐ[·]ܕܡܬܝ…

1ܟܬܒܐ ܕܬܘ̈ܠܕܬܗ ܕܝܫܘܥ ܡܫܝܚܐ. ܒܪܗ ܕܕܘܝܕ ܒܪܗ ܕܐܒܪܗܡ.
§¶*A*464 2ܐܒܪܗܡ ܐܘܠܕ ܠܐܝܣܚܩ. §ܐܝܣܚܩ ܐܘܠܕ ܠܝܥܩܘܒ.¶ ܝܥܩܘܒ
ܐܘܠܕ ܠܝܗܘܕܐ ܘܠܐܚ̈ܘܗܝ. 3ܝܗܘܕܐ ܐܘܠܕ ܠܦܪܨ ܘܠܙܪܚ ܡܢ ܬܡܪ.
§*A*465 §ܦܪܨ ܐܘܠܕ ܠܚܨܪܘܢ ܚܨܪܘܢ ܐܘܠܕ ܠܐܪܡ. 4ܐܪܡ ܐܘܠܕ
¶*A* ܠܥܡܝܢܕܒ. ܥܡܝܢܕܒ ܐܘܠܕ ܠܢܚܫܘܢ¶ ܢܚܫܘܢ ܐܘܠܕ ܠܫܠܡܐ.
§¶*A*465 §*A*466 §5ܫܠܡܐ ܐܘܠܕ ܠܒܥܙ¶ ܡܢ ܪܚܒ. §ܒܥܙ ܐܘܠܕ ܠܥܘܒܪ ܡܢ ܐܪܥܘܬ.
¶*A* ܥܘܒܪ ܐܘܠܕ ܠܐܝܫܝ. 6ܐܝܫܝ ܐܘܠܕ ܠܕܘܝܕ¶ ܡܠܟܐ. ܕܘܝܕ ܐܘܠܕ
ܠܫܠܝܡܘܢ ܡܢ ܐܢܬܬܗ ܕܐܘܪܝܐ. 7ܫܠܝܡܘܢ ܐܘܠܕ ܠܪܚܒܥܡ.
col 2 ܪܚܒܥܡ ܐܘܠܕ ܠܐܒܝܐ. *ܐܒܝܐ ܐܘܠܕ ܠܐܣܐ. 8ܐܣܐ ܐܘܠܕ
ܠܝܗܘܫܦܛ. ܝܗܘܫܦܛ ܐܘܠܕ ܠܝܗܘܪܡ. ܝܗܘܪܡ ܐܘܠܕ ܠܐܚܙܝܐ.
ܐܚܙܝܐ ܐܘܠܕ ܠܝܘܐܫ. ܝܘܐܫ ܐܘܠܕ ܠܐܡܘܨܝܐ. ܐܡܘܨܝܐ
ܐܘܠܕ ܠܚܘܙܝܐ. 9ܚܘܙܝܐ ܐܘܠܕ ܠܝܘܬܡ. ܝܘܬܡ ܐܘܠܕ ܠܐܚܙ.
ܐܚܙ ܐܘܠܕ ܠܚܙܩܝܐ. 10ܚܙܩܝܐ ܐܘܠܕ ܠܡܢܫܐ. ܡܢܫܐ ܐܘܠܕ
ܠܐܡܘܢ. ܐܡܘܢ ܐܘܠܕ ܠܝܘܫܝܐ. 11ܝܘܫܝܐ ܐܘܠܕ ܠܝܘܟܢܝܐ
ܘܠܐܚ̈ܘܗܝ، ܒܓܠܘܬܐ ܕܒܒܠ. 12ܡܢ ܒܬܪ ܓܠܘܬܐ ܕܝܢ ܕܒܒܠ.
§*A*472 ܝܘܟܢܝܐ ܐܘܠܕ ܠܫܠܬܐܝܠ. §ܫܠܬܐܝܠ ܐܘܠܕ ܠܙܘܪܒܒܠ.
13ܙܘܪܒܒܠ ܐܘܠܕ ܠܐܒܝܘܪ. ܐܒܝܘܪ ܐܘܠܕ ܠܐܠܝܩܝܡ. ܐܠܝܩܝܡ
fol 2 r ܐܘܠܕ ܠܥܙܘܪ. 14ܥܙܘܪ ܐܘܠܕ ܠܨܕܘܩ. ܨܕܘܩ *ܐܘܠܕ ܠܐܟܝܢ.
ܐܟܝܢ ܐܘܠܕ ܠܐܠܝܘܪ. 15ܐܠܝܘܪ ܐܘܠܕ ܠܐܠܝܥܙܪ. ܐܠܝܥܙܪ ܐܘܠܕ

Title. *The brackets correspond to holes in C; no title is legible in S*
1 ܕܬܘ̈ܠܕܬܐ *S*   2 ܐܝܣܚܩ] *C S*; *pr.* ܘ *A* (*and so throughout vv.* 2—16)
ܘܠܐܚ̈ܘܗܝ] *so also S*   5 ܠܥܘܒܪ....ܥܘܒܪ] *C* (*A*[a]); ܠܥܘܒܕ....ܥܘܒܕ *S*[ed];
ܠܥܘܒܝܕ. ܘܥܘܒܝܕ *A*[b]   ܪܥܘܬ *S A*   6, 7 ܠܫܠܝܡܘܢ....ܫܠܝܡܘܢ *S*
8 ܠܝܘܫܦܛ ܘܝܘܫܦܛ *S* (*A*[b])   ܠܝܘܪܡ ܝܘܪܡ *S*   ܠܐܚܙܝܐ....ܠܚܘܙܝܐ] *C A*;
ܠܚܘܙܝܐ *S* (*om. rel.*)   11 ܝܘܟܢܝܐ] ܘܝܘܟܝܡ *A*   12. § *in S*   ܫܠܬܐܝܠ *A*[b]
13 ܐܒܝܘܕ *A*   14 ܙܕܘܩ *A*   ܐܟܝܡ *A*[a]   14, 15 ܐܠܝܘܕ *S A*

EVANGEL OF THE SEPARATED [BOOKS.] MATTHEW. *C S*

i 1 The book of the genealogy of Jesus the Messiah, the son of David
2 the son of Abraham. Abraham begat Isaac. §Isaac begat Jacob.¶ §¶*A*464
3 Jacob begat Judah and his brethren. Judah begat Perez and Zerah
4 of Tamar. §Perez begat Hezron. Hezron begat Aram. Aram begat §*A*465
Amminadab. Amminadab begat Nahshon.¶ Nahshon begat Shala. ¶*A*
5 §Shala begat Boaz¶ of Rahab. §Boaz begat Ober of Ruth. Ober §¶*A*465 §*A*466
6 begat Jesse. Jesse begat David¶ the king. David begat Solomon of ¶*A*
7 the wife of Uria. Solomon begat Rehoboam. Rehoboam begat Abia.
8 Abia begat Asa. Asa begat Jehoshaphat. Jehoshaphat begat
Jehoram. Jehoram begat Ahazia. Ahazia begat Joash. Joash begat
9 Amozia. Amozia begat Uzia. Uzia begat Jotham. Jotham begat
10 Ahaz. Ahaz begat Hezekia. Hezekia begat Manasse. Manasse begat
11 Amon. Amon begat Josia. Josia begat Jechonia and his brethren
12 in the captivity of Babylon. Now after the captivity of Babylon,
13 Jechonia begat Shealtiel. §Shealtiel begat Zorobabel. Zorobabel §*A*472
14 begat Abior. Abior begat Eliacim. Eliacim begat Azor. Azor
15 begat Sadoc. Sadoc begat Achin. Achin begat Elior. Elior begat

---

TITLE. *The brackets in the Syriac correspond to holes in C; no title is legible in S* 2—16 *Actual quotations in Aphraates are indicated in the margin, but all the male proper names of the genealogy occur in order* *A* 463—472 2 Isaac 2°] *C S*; and Isaac *A* (*so throughout, rendering* δέ) 5 Obed A^b; *the diacritic point is not clear in S* 8 Joshaphat (*bis*) *S* Joram (*bis*) *S* Jehoram....... Uzia] *C A*; Jehoram begat Uzia *S* 11 Joiachin *A* (*? from O. T.*) 13 Abiud *A* 14 Zadoc *A* Abin A^a 14, 15 Eliud *S A*

C S ܠܡܬܢ ܂ ܡܬܢ ܐܘܠܕ ܠܝܥܩܘܒ. 16 ܝܥܩܘܒ ܐܘܠܕ ܠܝܘܣܦ. ܗܘ
ܕܡܟܝܪܐ ܗܘܬ ܠܗ ܡܪܝܡ ܒܬܘܠܬܐ. ܗܝ ܕܝܠܕܬ ܠܝܫܘܥ
¶A ܡܫܝܚܐ.¶

17 ܟܠܗܝܢ ܗܟܝܠ ܫܪܒܬܐ ܡܢ ܐܒܪܗܡ ܘܥܕܡܐ ܠܕܘܝܕ. ܗܘܝ
ܫܪܒܬܐ ܐܪܒܥܣܪܐ· ܘܡܢ ܕܘܝܕ ܘܥܕܡܐ ܠܓܠܘܬܐ ܕܒܒܠ·
ܫܪܒܬܐ ܐܪܒܥܣܪܐ· ܘܡܢ ܓܠܘܬܐ ܕܒܒܠ ܥܕܡܐ ܠܡܫܝܚܐ·
ܫܪܒܬܐ ܐܪܒܥܣܪܐ ܀

18 ܡܘܠܕܗ ܕܝܢ ܕܡܫܝܚܐ ܗܟܢܐ ܗܘܐ· ܟܕ ܡܟܝܪܐ ܗܘܬ ܡܪܝܡ
ܐܡܗ ܠܝܘܣܦ. †ܒܕ† ܠܐ ܢܬܩܪܒܘܢ ܚܕ ܠܘܬ ܚܕ: ܐܫܬܟܚܬ
col 2 ܒܛܢܐ ܡܢ *ܪܘܚܐ ܕܩܘܕܫܐ· 19 ܝܘܣܦ ܕܝܢ ܡܛܠ ܕܓܒܪܐ ܗܘܐ
ܟܐܢܐ. ܠܐ ܨܒܐ ܗܘܐ ܕܢܦܪܣܝܗ ܠܡܪܝܡ. ܐܬܚܫܒ ܗܘܐ
ܕܡܫܠܝܐܝܬ ܢܫܒܩܝܗ. 20 ܟܕ ܗܠܝܢ ܕܝܢ ܐܬܚܫܒ. ܐܬܚܙܝ ܠܗ ܠܝܘܣܦ
ܡܠܐܟܐ ܕܡܪܝܐ ܒܚܙܘܐ ܕܠܠܝܐ ܘܐܡܪ ܠܗ. ܝܘܣܦ ܒܪܗ
ܕܕܘܝܕ ܠܐ ܬܕܚܠ ܠܡܕܒܪ ܠܡܪܝܡ ܡܟܝܪܬܟ· ܗܘ ܓܝܪ ܕܡܬܝܠܕ
ܡܢܗ ܡܢ ܪܘܚܐ ܗܘ ܕܩܘܕܫܐ ܟܝܢ· 21 ܬܐܠܕ ܠܟ ܕܝܢ ܒܪܐ.
ܘܢܬܩܪܐ ܫܡܗ ܝܫܘܥ. ܗܘ ܓܝܪ ܢܚܝܘܗܝ ܠܥܠܡܐ ܡܢ ܚܛܗܝܗܘܢ.
22 ܗܕܐ ܕܝܢ ܕܗܘܬ. ܕܢܬܡܠܐ ܡܕܡ ܕܐܬܐܡܪ ܡܢ ܡܪܝܐ ܒܦܘܡ
ܐܫܥܝܐ ܢܒܝܐ ܕܐܡܪ ܗܘܐ· 23 ܗܐ ܒܬܘܠܬܐ ܬܒܛܢ ܘܬܐܠܕ

16 ܝܥܩܘܒ ܐܘܠܕ ܠܝܘܣܦ ܝܘܣܦ ܕܡܟܝܪܐ ܗܘܬ ܠܗ ܡܪܝܡ ܒܬܘܠܬܐ. ܐܘܠܕ ܠܝܫܘܥ ܕܡܬܩܪܐ ܡܫܝܚܐ .:. .:. S; ܘܝܥܩܘܒ ܐܘܠܕ ܠܝܘܣܦ. ܘܝܘܣܦ ܐܬܡܢܝ ܐܒܐ ܠܝܫܘܥ ܡܫܝܚܐ. A (cf Lk iii 23) 17 ܗܟܝܠ] ܗܠܝܢ S ܘܥܕܡܐ (bis)] ܥܕܡܐ S (bis) ܗܘܝ] om. S 18 ܒܕ ܠܐ] Eus. HE^{syr} 60; ܒܕ ܠܐ C; *the* ܒ *is illegible in S: see Notes*, vol. ii 19 ܕܝܢ]+ ܒܥܠܗ S ܡܛܠ ܕܟܐܢ ܗܘܐ S ܗܘܐ 2°] om. S^{ed} 20 ܠܝܘܣܦ *and* ܕܠܠܝܐ] om. S ܠܡܕܒܪ] ܠܡܣܒ S ܡܟܝܪܬܟ] ܐܢܬܬܟ S ܟܝܢ] om. S 21 ܘܢܬܩܪܐ] ܘܬܩܪܐ S ܠܥܠܡܐ] ܠܥܡܗ S 22 ܕܐܬܐܡܪ] ܕܐܬܡܠܠ S ܒܦܘܡ] om. ܒܦܘܡ S

16 Eleazar. Eleazar begat Matthan. Matthan begat Jacob. Jacob *C S*
begat Joseph, him to whom was betrothed Mary the Virgin, she
who bare Jesus the Messiah.¶ ¶*A*

17 All the generations therefore from Abraham even unto David
are fourteen generations; and from David even unto the captivity
of Babylon fourteen generations; and from the captivity of Babylon
unto the Messiah fourteen generations.

18 Now the birth of the Messiah was thus: When Mary his mother
was betrothed to Joseph, †before ever† they drew near one to the
19 other, she was found with child of the Holy Spirit. Now Joseph,
because he was an upright man, was not willing that he should expose
20 Mary and had meditated that quietly he should divorce her. Now
when he meditated these things there appeared to him, to Joseph, an
angel of the LORD in a vision of the night and said to him: "Joseph
son of David, fear not to take Mary thy betrothed, for that which
21 is being born from her is conceived from the Holy Spirit. Now
she will bear thee a son, and his name shall be called Jesus, for
22 he shall save alive the world from its sins." Now this that came to
pass *happened* that that might be fulfilled which was said by the
23 LORD through the mouth of Isaiah the prophet who had said: "Lo,

---

16 Jacob begat Joseph. Joseph, to whom was betrothed Mary the virgin, begat Jesus that is called the Messiah *S*; 'and Jacob begat Joseph, and Joseph was called father to Jesus the Messiah' *A*: *see Notes*, vol. ii
17 All...therefore] All these generations *S* 18 'The generation of Jesus the Christ was on this wise: When his mother Mary was betrothed to Joseph, and before she was given to a husband, she was found with child of the Holy Spirit' *E*[20] 19 Now Joseph] + her husband *S* because he was upright *S* 'Joseph, because he was a just man, was not willing to make Mary a public example, and was minded to put her away quietly' *E*[22] 20 to Joseph] *om. S* of the night] *om. S* take (*lit.* 'lead')] take *S* (*both words commonly used for 'marry'*) betrothed] wife *S* conceived] *om. S* '(the) angel appeared unto him and saith, Fear not to take Mary' *E*[23]
21 thee] *cf* Lk i 13, Joh iv 16 his name shall be called] thou shalt call his name *S* the world] his people *S*: *cf* Joh xviii 20 *in* syr.vg *and Notes*, vol. ii, p. 287 22 said 1°] spoken *S* the mouth of] *om. S*

C S fol 2v *ܒܪܐ· ܘܬܩܪܐ ܫܡܗ ܥܡܢܘܐܝܠ· ܕܡܬܬܪܓܡ ܐܠܗܢ
ܥܡܢ. ܀
24 ܟܕ ܩܡ ܕܝܢ ܝܘܣܦ ܡܢ ܫܢܬܗ· ܥܒܕ ܐܝܟܢܐ ܕܦܩܕ ܠܗ
ܡܠܐܟܐ ܕܡܪܝܐ· ܘܕܒܪܗ ܠܡܪܝܡ· 25 ܘܒܕܟܝܘܬܐ ܥܡܪ ܗܘܐ
ܥܡܗ. ܥܕܡܐ ܕܝܠܕܬܗ ܠܒܪܐ· ܘܩܪܬ ܫܡܗ ܝܫܘܥ ܀
1 ܘܟܕ ܐܬܝܠܕ ܝܫܘܥ ܒܒܝܬ ܠܚܡ ܕܝܗܘܕܐ. ܒܝ̈ܘܡܝ ܗܪܘܕܣ
ܡܠܟܐ. ܘܗܘܐ ܡ̈ܓܘܫܐ ܐܬܘ ܡܢ ܡܕܢܚܐ ܠܐܘܪܫܠܡ. 2 ܘܐܡܪܝܢ
ܐܝܟܐ ܗܘ ܡܠܟܐ ܕܝ̈ܗܘܕܝܐ ܕܐܬܝܠܕ. ܐܚܙܝܢ ܓܝܪ ܚܙܝܢ
ܟܘܟܒܗ ܒܡܕܢܚܐ. ܘܐܬܝܢ ܠܡܣܓܕ ܠܗ..
3 ܟܕ ܫܡܥ ܕܝܢ ܗܪܘܕܣ ܡܠܟܐ ܐܬܬܙܝܥ· ܘܟܠܗ ܐܘܪܫܠܡ ܥܡܗ·
col 2 4 ܘܟܢܫ *ܠܟܠܗܘܢ ܪ̈ܒܝ ܟܗ̈ܢܐ ܘܣ̈ܦܪܐ ܕܥܡܐ ܘܐܡܪ ܠܗܘܢ·
ܐܝܟܐ ܡܬܝܠܕ ܡܫܝܚܐ· 5 ܐܡܪܝܢ ܠܗ ܒܒܝܬ ܠܚܡ ܕܝܗܘܕܐ. ܗܟܢܐ
ܓܝܪ ܟܬܝܒ ܒܢܒܝܐ. 6 ܐܦ ܐܢܬܝ, ܒܝܬ ܠܚܡ ܕܝܗܘܕܐ· ܠܐ
ܗܘܝܬܝ, ܒܨܝܪܐ ܡܢ ܡܠܟܘܬܐ ܕܝܗܘܕܐ. ܡܢܟܝ ܓܝܪ ܢܦܘܩ ܡܠܟܐ
ܕܗܘ ܢܪܥܝܘܗܝ, ܠܥܡܝ ܐܝܣܪܝܠ· 7 ܗܝܕܝܢ ܗܪܘܕܣ ܒܛܫܝܐܝܬ ܩܪܐ
ܠܗܘܢ ܡ̈ܓܘܫܐ. ܘܡܒܥܒܥ ܗܘܐ ܠܗܘܢ. ܕܢܕܥ ܒܐܝܢܐ ܙܒܢܐ
ܐܬܚܙܝ, ܠܗܘܢ ܟܘܟܒܐ. 8 ܘܫܕܪ ܐܢܘܢ ܠܒܝܬ ܠܚܡ. ܘܐܡܪ
ܠܗܘܢ ܙܠܘ ܒܥܘ ܥܠܘܗܝ, ܥܠ ܛܠܝܐ ܚܦܝܛܐܝܬ. ܘܡܐ
fol 3r ܕܐܫܟܚܬܘܢܝܗܝ, ܬܘ ܚܘܐܘܢܝ. ܕܐܦ ܐܢܐ *ܐܐܬܐ ܐܣܓܘܕ ܠܗ·
9 ܗܢܘܢ ܕܝܢ ܟܕ ܫܡܥܘ ܡܢ ܡܠܟܐ ܐܙܠܘ· ܘܐܬܚܙܝ,
ܠܗܘܢ ܟܘܟܒܐ ܗܘ ܕܚܙܘ ܗܘܘ ܒܡܕܢܚܐ ܐܙܠ ܗܘܐ ܩܕܡܝܗܘܢ·
ܥܕܡܐ ܕܐܬܐ ܘܩܡ ܠܥܠ ܡܢ ܒܪ ܕܐܬܝܗ ܗܘܐ ܛܠܝܐ. 10 ܗܢܘܢ
ܕܝܢ ܟܕ ܚܙܘܗܝ, ܠܟܘܟܒܐ ܚܕܘܬܐ ܪܒܬܐ ܚܕܝܘ. 11 ܘܥܠܘ ܠܒܝܬܐ
ܘܚܙܘܗܝ, ܠܛܠܝܐ ܥܡ ܡܪܝܡ ܐܡܗ. ܘܢܦܠܘ ܣܓܕܘ ܠܗ. ܘܦܬܚܘ

---

23 ܘܬܩܪܐ] ܘܢܩܪܘܢ S ܕܡܬܪܓܡ S 24. No § in S ܐܝܟ S
ܘܕܒܪܗ to end of ver. 25] ܘܕܒܪ ܠܐܢܬܬܗ ܘܝܠܕܬ ܠܗ ܒܪܐ ܘܩܪܐ ܫܡܗ ܝܫܘܥ S
2 ܘܐܡܪܝܢ] ܘܐܡܪܘ S ܐܝܟܐ] ܐܝܠܟܐ S ܠܟܘܟܒܗ S ܡܢ ܡܕܢܚܐ S
3. No § in S ܐܬܬܙܝܥ] ܐܬܕܠܚ S 4 ܥܡܐ] ܕܥܠܡܐ S^vid
6 ܘܐܦ S ܗܘܝܬ S ܡܠܟܘܬܐ] ܡ̈ܠܟܐ S 8 ܚܦܝܛܐܝܬ] om. S
ܚܘܘܢܝ S 9 ܘܩܡ] ܩܡ S ܠܥܠ ܡܢ ܒܪ] ܐܬܪ S 11 ܘܦܬܚܘ S

the virgin shall conceive and shall bear a son, and his name *C S*
shall be called Emmanuel, which is interpreted 'Our God with
us.'"
24 Now when Joseph arose from his sleep, he did as the angel of the
25 LORD commanded him, and he took Mary, and purely was dwelling
with her until she bare the son; and she called his name Jesus.
ii 1 And when Jesus was born in Beth Lehem of Judah in the days
of Herod the king, lo, Magians came from the east to Jerusalem.
2 And they say: "Where is the king of the Jews that hath been born?
For we ourselves have seen his star in the east, and have come to
worship him."
3 Now when Herod the king heard he was troubled, and all
4 Jerusalem with him, and he gathered together all the chief priests
and scribes of the people and said to them: "Where is the Messiah
5 born?" They say to him: "In Beth Lehem of Judah, for thus it
6 is written in the prophet: 'Thou also, Beth Lehem of Judah, art
not less than the kingdom of Judah; for from thee shall go forth the
7 king that shall tend my people Israel.'" Then Herod secretly called
those Magians, and was enquiring of them that he might know at what
8 time the star appeared to them. And he sent them to Beth Lehem,
and said to them: "Go enquire about this same lad eagerly, and what
time ye have found him, come *and* shew me, that I may go myself
9 also *and* worship him." Now they, when they received command
from the king, went *away*, and there appeared to them that star
which they had seen in the east going before them, until it came
10 and stood over where the lad was. Now they, when they saw the
11 star, rejoiced with a great joy, and entered the house and saw the
lad with Mary his mother, and fell down *and* worshipped him, and

---

23 his name shall be called] they shall call his name *S*: *cf vv.* 23, 25 24 and he *to end of* 25] and he took his wife and she bare him a son, and he called his name Jesus *S*; '..he took her...he dwelt purely with her until she bare the first-born' E^{23} 2 say] said *S* from the east *S* 3 troubled] perturbed *S* 6 kingdom] kings *S* 8 eagerly] *om. S* 9 and stood] *and* stood *S* over where] in the place where *S* 11 *and*] and *S*

C S ܣܝ̈ܡܬܗܘܢ ܘܩܪܒܘ ܠܗ ܩܘܪܒܢܐ. ܕܗܒܐ ܘܡܘܪܐ ܘܠܒܘܢܬܐ.
[12]ܘܐܬܚܘܝ ܠܗܘܢ ܒܚܠܡܐ ܕܠܐ ܢܗܦܟܘܢ ܠܘܬ ܗܪܘܕܣ. ܘܗܢܘܢ
ܒܐܘܪܚܐ ܐܚܪܬܐ ܐܙܠܘ ܗܘܘ ܠܐܬܪܗܘܢ܆ [13]ܘܡܢ ܒܬܪܗܘܢ
col 2 ܐܬܚܙܝ ܠܝܘܣܦ *ܡܠܐܟܐ ܕܡܪܝܐ ܒܚܠܡܐ ܘܐܡܪ ܠܗ. ܩܘܡ
ܫܩܘܠ ܠܛܠܝܐ ܘܠܐܡܗ ܘܥܪܘܩ ܠܡܨܪܝܢ. ܘܬܡܢ ܗܘܝ ܥܕܡܐ
ܕܐܡܪܢܐ ܠܟ܂ ܡܛܠ ܕܥܬܝܕ ܗܘ ܗܪܘܕܣ ܠܡܒܥܝܗ ܠܛܠܝܐ
ܐܝܟܢܐ ܕܢܘܒܕܝܘܗܝ. ܀

[14]ܝܘܣܦ ܕܝܢ ܩܡ ܘܫܩܠܗ ܠܛܠܝܐ ܘܠܐܡܗ ܒܠܠܝܐ ܘܐܙܠ ܠܗ
ܠܡܨܪܝܢ. [15]ܘܗܘܐ ܬܡܢ ܥܕܡܐ ܕܡܝܬ ܗܪܘܕܣ ܡܠܟܐ. ܕܢܬܡܠܐ
ܡܕܡ ܕܐܬܐܡܪ ܡܢ ܡܪܝܐ ܒܝܕ ܢܒܝܐ ܕܐܡܪ ܗܘܐ. ܕܡܢ
ܡܨܪܝܢ ܩܪܝܬ ܠܒܪܝ. ܀

[16]ܗܝܕܝܢ ܗܪܘܕܣ ܟܕ ܚܙܐ ܕܒܙܚܘ ܒܗ̇ ܗܢܘܢ ܡ̈ܓܘܫܐ. ܐܬܚܡܬ
ܠܗ܂ ܘܫܕܪ ܩܛܠ ܠܟܠܗܘܢ ܛ̈ܠܝܐ ܕܐܝܬ ܗܘܘ ܒܝܬ ܠܚܡ.
fol 3 v *ܘܒܟܠܗܘܢ ܬܚܘ̈ܡܝܗ. ܡܢ ܒܪ ܬܪ̈ܬܝܢ ܫ̈ܢܝܢ ܘܠܬܚܬ. ܠܙܒܢܐ
ܕܒܥܐ ܕܐܡܪܘ ܠܗ ܗܠܝܢ ܡ̈ܓܘܫܐ. [17]ܗܝܕܝܢ ܫܠܡܬ ܡܠܬܐ ܗܝ
ܕܐܡܪ ܐܪܡܝܐ ܢܒܝܐ. [18]ܩܠܐ ܐܫܬܡܥ ܒܪܡܬܐ. ܐܠܝܐ ܘܒܟܝܐ
ܘܐܘ̈ܠܝܬܐ ܣܓܝ̈ܐܬܐ. ܪܚܝܠ ܕܒܟܝܐ ܥܠ ܒ̈ܢܝܗ. ܘܠܐ
ܨܒܝܐ ܠܡܬܒܝܐܘ. ܡܛܠ ܕܠܐ ܐܝܬ ܐܢܘܢ܂ [19]ܟܕ ܡܝܬ ܕܝܢ
ܗܪܘܕܣ ܡܠܟܐ. ܐܬܚܙܝ ܠܝܘܣܦ ܒܡܨܪܝܢ ܡܠܐܟܐ ܕܡܪܝܐ
§A405 ܒܚܠܡܐ [20]ܘܐܡܪ ܠܗ. §ܩܘܡ ܕܒܪ ܠܛܠܝܐ ܘܠܐܡܗ ܘܙܠ ܠܐܪܥܐ
ܕܐܝܣܪܐܝܠ܂ ܡܛܠ ܕܡܝܬܘ ܠܗܘܢ ܗܢܘܢ ܕܒܥܝܢ ܗܘܘ ܢܦܫܗ

---

12 ܠܘܬ] ܠܗ S ܘܗܘܘ] om. S 13 ܡܛܠ S (and so often) 14. No § in S ܩܡ ܫܩܠܗ S 15 ܘܬܡܢ ܗܘܐ S ܕܐܬܐܡܪ] ܕܐܬܡܠܠ S ܒܝܕ] ܒܦܘܡ ܐܫܥܝܐ S ܕܡܢ] ܡܢ S 16. No § in S ܗܢܘܢ] om. S ܠܟܠܗܘܢ ܛ̈ܠܝܐ] ܟܘܠ ܛ̈ܠܝܐ S (sic) ܗܘܘ] om. S ܘܒܟܠܗܘܢ ܬܚܘ̈ܡܝܗ] ܘܒܬܚܘ̈ܡܝܗ S (sic) ܠܗ] so also S^{nunc}; ܟܠܗ S^{*vid} (sic) ܗܠܝܢ] om. S 17 ܗܝ] om. S ܕܐܡܪ] + ܗܘܐ S 18 ܘܒܟܝܐ] + ܗܘܬ S ܨܒܝܐ] + ܗܘܬ S ܐܝܬ ܐܢܘܢ] ܐܝܬܝܗܘܢ S 19. § in S ܘܐܡܪ ܠܗ ܒܚܠܡܐ S 20 ܕܒܪ] ܫܩܘܠ S A ܘܠܐܡܗ] om. A ܘܐܙܠ S ܕܐܣܪܐܝܠ S (sic) ܗܢܘܢ] ܐܝܠܝܢ S (sic) A

opened their treasures and offered him an offering, gold and myrrh C S
12 and frankincense. And it appeared to them in a vision that they
should not return unto Herod, and they by another road went away
13 to their own country. And after their *visit* the angel of the LORD
appeared to Joseph in a dream and said to him: "Arise, take up
the lad and his mother and flee to Egypt, and there be until I
say to thee, because Herod is about to seek for the lad, so that he
may destroy him."

14 Now Joseph arose and took up the lad and his mother by night
15 and went away to Egypt, and he was there until Herod the king died,
that that might be fulfilled which was said by the LORD through the
prophet, who had said "From Egypt I have called my son."

16 Then Herod, when he saw that those Magians had mocked at
him, was furious exceedingly, and sent *and* killed all the lads that
were in Beth Lehem and in all its borders, from two years old and
under, according to the time that these Magians said to him.
17 Then was accomplished the word which Jeremiah the prophet said:
18 "A voice was heard in Ramtha, wailing and weeping and much
groaning, the voice of Rachel who weepeth over her sons and will
19 not be comforted, because they are not!" Now when Herod the
king was dead there appeared to Joseph in Egypt the angel of the
20 LORD in a dream, and said to him: "§Arise, take the lad and his §A405
mother and go to the land of Israel, because those have died who

---

12 unto] to *S* 13 after their *visit*] *lit.* 'after them' *S C*: *cf on* Mt xi 7 14 and took] *om.* and *S* 15 and there he was *S* said] spoken *S* by the mouth of Isaiah the prophet *S* said: From *S* 16 those] the *S* all the lads] the lads, all *S*; every lad E^{33} all 2°] *om.* *S* these] the *S* 17 had said *S* 18 'In Rama a voice was cried' E^{33} weepeth] was weeping *S* E^{33} 19, 20 and said to him in a dream *S* 20 take up *S A* and his mother] *om.* *A* those] they *S A*

C S ¶A ܕܓܠܝܠܐ ܠܟܦܪܢܚܘܡ¶. [21]ܗܘ ܕܝܢ ܟܕ ܫܡܠܗ ܠܓܠܝܠܐ ܘܠܐܬܪܗ. ܘܐܬܐ
ܠܗ ܠܐܪܥܐ ܕܐܝܣܪܝܠ ܀

col 2 [22]*ܟܕ ܫܡܥ ܕܝܢ ܝܘܣܦ ܕܐܪܟܠܐܘܣ ܗܘܐ ܡܠܟܐ ܒܝܗܘܕ. ܒܕܘܟܬ
ܗܪܘܕܣ ܐܒܘܗܝ. ܕܚܠ ܕܢܐܙܠ ܠܬܡܢ. ܘܐܬܚܙܝ ܠܗ ܒܚܠܡܐ
ܕܢܐܙܠ ܠܗ ܠܐܬܪܐ ܕܓܠܝܠܐ. [23]ܘܐܬܐ ܠܬܡܢ. ܘܥܡܪ ܗܘܐ
ܒܡܕܝܢܬܐ ܚܕܐ ܕܡܬܩܪܝܐ ܢܨܪܬ. ܘܐܬܬܡܠܝܬ ܡܠܬܐ ܕܐܡܝܪܐ
ܒܢܒܝܐ. ܕܢܨܪܝܐ ܢܬܩܪܐ ܀

[1]ܘܒܗܘܢ ܝܘ̈ܡܬܐ. ܐܬܐ ܝܘܚܢܢ ܡܥܡܕܢܐ. ܘܡܟܪܙ ܗܘܐ
ܒܡܕܒܪܐ ܕܝܗܘܕ. [2]ܘܐܡܪ ܗܘܐ. ܬܘܒܘ. ܡܛܠ ܕܩܪܒܬ ܠܗ
ܡܠܟܘܬܐ ܕܫܡܝܐ. [3]ܗܢܘ ܓܝܪ ܕܐܬܐܡܪ ܥܠܘܗܝ, ܒܐܫܥܝܐ ܢܒܝܐ
ܕܐܡܪ ܗܘܐ. ܩܠܐ ܕܩܪܐ ܒܡܕܒܪܐ. ܛܝܒܘ ܐܘܪܚܐ ܠܡܪܝܐ.
fol 4r ܘܬܪܘܨܘ ܫܒܝܠܘܗܝ, *ܕܐܠܗܢ̈. [4]ܗܘ ܕܝܢ ܝܘܚܢܢ ܠܒܝܫ ܗܘܐ ܠܒܘܫܐ
ܕܣܥܪܐ ܕܓܡ̈ܠܐ. ܘܐܣܝܪ ܗܘܐ ܚܨܘܬܐ ܒܚܨ̈ܘܗܝ. ܘܡܐܟܘܠܬܗ
ܐܝܬܝܗ ܗܘܬ ܩܡ̈ܨܐ ܘܕܒܫܐ ܕܒܪܐ. [5]ܗܝܕܝܢ ܐܬܝܢ ܗܘܘ ܠܘܬܗ
ܟܠܗ ܐܘܪܫܠܡ ܘܟܠܗ ܝܗܘܕ. ܘܟܠܗ ܒܪܝܐ ܕܝܘܪܕܢ, ܡܥܡܕܝܢ ܒܢܗܪܐ.
[6]ܘܡܥܡܕ ܗܘܐ ܠܗܘܢ ܒܝܘܪܕܢ ܢܗܪܐ. ܟܕ ܡܘܕܐ ܗܘܐ ܐܢܫ
ܐܢܫ ܒܚܛ̈ܗܘܗܝ. [7]ܟܕ ܚܙܐ ܕܝܢ ܟ̈ܢܫܐ ܕܦܪ̈ܝܫܐ ܘܙܕ̈ܘܩܝܐ ܕܐܬܝܢ
ܠܡܥܡܘܕܝܬܗ. ܐܡܪ ܠܗܘܢ. ܝܠܕ̈ܐ ܕܐܟܕܢܐ ܡܢܘ ܚܘܝܟܘܢ
ܠܡܥܪܩ ܡܢ ܪܘܓܙܐ ܕܐܬܐ. [8]ܥܒܕܘ ܗܟܝܠ ܦܐܪ̈ܐ ܕܫܘܝܢ

ܠܟܦܪܢܚܘܡ] C A; om. S   21 ܗܘ ܕܝܢ] ܘܗܘ S (sic)   ܠܗ] om. S
ܕܐܝܣܪܐܝܠ S (sic)   22. No § in S   ܒܝܗܘܕ] om. S   ܕܢܐܙܠ] ܠܡܐܙܠ S
ܘܐܬܚܙܝ ܠܗ] ܘܚܙܐ S (sic)   ܒܚܠܡܐ] ܒܠܠܝܐ S   23 ܢܨܪܬ] om. S
1. No § in S   ܒܗܘܢ S   ܕܝܗܘܕܐ S   3 ܗܢܘ ܓܝܪ] ܗܢܐ S
ܩܠܐ...ܛܝܒܘ] ܕܛܝܒܘ S   ܘܬܪܘܨܘ...ܕܐܠܗܢ̈] om. S   4 ܒܣܥ̈ܪܐ ܕܓܡܠܐ S
ܐܝܬܝܗ ܗܘܬ] om. S   ܕܒܪܐ.] ܕܛܘܪ[.]ܐ S; cf Îshô'dâd (Harris, p. 17,
ܕܐܝܟ ܡܐܟܘܠܬܗ ܕܒܪܐ ܘܠܚܡܐ ܕܛܘܪܐ) and see also Lk xii 28   5 ܝܗܘܕܐ S
ܡܥܡܕܝܢ] ܕܫܡܥܝܢ ܡܥܡܕܝܢ S   6 ܡܥܡܕܝܢ ܗܘܘ S   7 ܟ̈ܢܫܐ.....ܐܡܪ]
ܕܣ̈ܓܝܐܐ ܕܐܬܝܢ ܠܡܥܡܘܕܝܬܗ ܡܢ ܦܪ̈ܝܫܐ ܘܙܕܘ̈ܩܝܐ ܐܡܪ S   ܕܐܬܐ]
ܕܥܬܝܕܐ ܠܡܐܬܐ S

21 were seeking the lad's life to snatch away¶." Now he arose *and* *C S*
took the lad and his mother, and came to the land of Israel. *¶A*
22 Now when Joseph heard that Archelaus was king in Judaea in
the room of Herod his father, he feared to go thither, and it appeared
23 to him in a vision that he should go to the country of Galilee; and
he came thither and was dwelling in a certain city called Nazareth,
and the word was fulfilled that was spoken by the prophet, that he
should be called a Nazarene.
iii 1 And in those days came John the Baptist, and was preaching
2 in the wilderness of Judaea and saying "Repent, because the king-
3 dom of heaven hath drawn nigh." For this is he of whom it is
written in Isaiah the prophet, who had said: "A voice that calleth
in the wilderness, 'Make ready a way for the Lord, and direct the
4 paths of our God!'" Now John was clad with clothing of camels'
wool, and was girt with a thong upon his loins, and his meat was
5 locusts and honey of the waste. Then were coming unto him the
men of Jerusalem and all Judaea and all the other side round
6 about the river Jordan, and he was baptizing them in the river
7 Jordan, each one confessing their sins. Now when he saw publicans
and Pharisees and Sadducees coming to his baptism, he said to
them: "Offspring of vipers, who is it hath shewed you to flee from
8 the wrath that is coming? Bring forth therefore fruits meet for

---

to snatch away] *C A*; *om. S* 21 Now] And *S* (*sic*) 22 in Judaea] *om. S* it appeared to him] he saw *S* (*sic*) vision] dream *S* 23 certain] *om. S* 1 And in] In *S* Judaea] Judah *S* 3 For this is he] This is *S* A voice...wilderness] *om. S* and direct...God] *om. S* 4 camels' wool] 'hair' $E^{40,101}$, *but cf* Îshô'dâd (*Harris*, p. 22: 'Mar Ephrem only reads wool'): *the word* ba'wâ '*wool*', *used here in S C* (*but not in* Syr. vg) *means the soft under-hair of camels. Cf also* وبر الجمال Diat^{ar} iv 12 (cod. B). upon his loins with a thong *S* honey of the waste] honey of the hills *S*; *cf* Îshô'dâd (*Harris*, p. 17: 'The Diatessaron says, His meat was honey and milk of the hills'). *See* Lk xii 28 *S C*, *and* Syr^{palest} *passim.* 5 Judaea] Judah *S* round about] *om. S* 7 Now when he saw many coming to his baptism from the Pharisees and Sadducees *S* coming 2°] about to come *S*

C S ܠܬܝܒܘܬܐ. §9ܘܠܐ ܬܬܐܡܪܘܢ ܒܢܦܫܟܘܢ ܕܐܒܐ ܐܝܬ *ܠܢ
§A 331 (cf 63) ܐܒܪܗܡ. ܐܡܪܢܐ ܠܟܘܢ ܓܝܪ ܕܡܫܟܚ ܐܠܗܐ ܡܢ ܗܠܝܢ ܟܐ̈ܦܐ
col 2 ¶A ܠܡܩܡܘ ܒ̈ܢܝܐ ܠܐܒܪܗܡ¶. ¹⁰ܘܗܐ ܡܟܝܠ ܠܗ ܢܪܓܐ ܥܠ
§'Julian' ܥܩܪܗܘܢ ܕܐܝ̈ܠܢܐ. §ܟܠ ܐܝܠܢܐ ܗܟܝܠ ܕܦܐ̈ܪܐ ܛ̈ܒܐ ܠܐ
29 ¶'Jul.' ܥܒܕ. ܡܬܦܣܩ ܘܠܢܘܪܐ ܐܙܠ¶. ¹¹ܐܢܐ ܕܝܢ ܗܐ ܡܥܡܕ ܐܢܐ
ܠܟܘܢ ܒܡ̈ܝܐ ܠܬܝܒܘܬܐ. ܗܘ ܕܝܢ ܐܢܐ ܕܐܬܐ ܒܬܪܝ، ܚܣܝܢ
ܗܘ ܡܢܝ. ܘܠܐ ܫܘܐ ܐܢܐ ܡܣܐܢ̈ܘܗܝ ܠܡܫܩܠ. ܗܘ ܢܥܡܕܟܘܢ
ܒܪܘܚܐ ܕܩܘܕܫܐ ܘܒܢܘܪܐ. ¹²ܗܘ ܕܐܚܝܕ ܪܦܫܐ ܒܐܝܕܗ ܘܡܕܟܐ
ܐܕܪܗ. ܘܚܛܐ ܢܟܢܫ ܒܐܘܨܪ̈ܘܗܝ· ܘܬܒܢܐ ܢܘܩܕ ܒܢܘܪܐ ܕܠܐ
ܕܥܟܐ.܀

fol 4 v ¹³ܗܝܕܝܢ ܐܬܐ ܝܫܘܥ ܡܢ *ܓܠܝܠܐ ܠܝܘܪܕܢܢ. ܠܘܬ ܝܘܚܢܢ
ܕܢܥܡܕܝܘܗܝ، ¹⁴ܘܟܠܝܗ، ܝܘܚܢܢ ܘܐܡܪ ܠܗ. ܐܢܐ ܐܢܐ ܣܢܝܩ ܐܢܐ
ܕܐܢܬ ܬܥܡܕܢܝ. ܘܐܢܬ ܠܘܬܝ ܐܬܝܬ. ¹⁵ܐܡܪ ܠܗ ܝܫܘܥ ܫܒܘܩ
ܗܫܐ. ܗܟܢ ܕܝܐܐ ܘܠܐ ܠܢ ܕܢܡܠܐ ܟܠܗ̇ ܟܐܢܘܬܐ. ܗܝܕܝܢ
ܫܒܩܗ ܠܡܥܡܕ. ¹⁶ܘܡܥܡܕ ܗܘܐ ܝܫܘܥ. ܘܟܕ ܥܡܕ· ܒܗ̇ ܒܫܥܬܐ
ܕܣܠܩ ܝܫܘܥ ܡܢ ܡ̈ܝܐ. ܘܗܐ ܐܬܦܬܚܘ ܫܡܝܐ. ܘܚܙܐ ܪܘܚܐ
ܕܐܠܗܐ ܕܢܚܬܬ ܐܝܟ ܝܘܢܐ ܘܫܪܬ ܥܠܘܗܝ، ¹⁷ܘܩܠܐ ܐܫܬܡܥ
ܡܢ ܫܡܝܐ ܕܐܡܪ ܠܗ. ܐܢܬ ܗܘ ܒܪܝ، ܘܚܒܝܒܝ ܕܒܟ ܐܨܛܒܝܬ.
¹ܗܝܕܝܢ ܝܫܘܥ ܐܬܕܒܪ ܡܢ ܪܘܚܐ ܕܩܘܕܫܐ ܠܡܕܒܪܐ.

---

9 ܠܐ ܬܚܫܒܘܢ ܫܒܝܩܝܢ ܘܐܒܪܗܡ A ܒܢܦܫܟܘܢ] om. S A ܐܡܪܢܐ...ܓܝܪ] ܡܟܝܠ A ܕܡܢ ܗܠܝܢ ܟܐ̈ܦܐ ܡܫܟܚ ܐܠܗܐ A²/₂ ܟܐܦܐ S 10 ܒܥܩܪܗܘܢ S ܘܟܠ S ܗܟܝܠ] om. S Jul ܕܠܐ ܥܒܕ ܦܐ̈ܪܐ Jul ܛ̈ܒܐ] om. S Jul ܘܠܢܘܪܐ ܐܙܠ] C Jul; ܘܒܢܘܪܐ ܢܦܠ S 11 ܗܐ] om. S ܡܥܡܕܢܐ S ܚܣܝܢ] ܪܒ S ܘܠܐ] ܐܢܐ ܕܠܐ S ܫܘܐ S (and so generally) ܒܪܘܚܐ ܘܒܢܘܪܐ ܕܩܘܕܫܐ S 12 ܒܐܘܨܪ̈ܗ S 13 ܠܝܘܪܕܢܢ] om. S ܕܢܥܡܕܝܘܗܝ] + ܒܝܘܪܕܢܢ S 14 ܠܘܬ] C sic (end of line); ܠܘܬܗ S 15 ܥܢܐ ܝܫܘܥ ܘܐܡܪ ܠܗ S ܘܠܐ] ܐܠܐ S ܒܟܠܗ S (and so often) ܠܡܥܡܕ] ܕܢܥܡܕ S 16 ܘܡܥܡܕ ܗܘܐ ܝܫܘܥ] om. S ܒܗ̇....ܝܫܘܥ] ܘܣܠܩ S ܐܝܟ ܝܘܢܐ] ܒܕܡܘܬܐ ܕܝܘܢܐ S *For the additions to ver.* 16 *in the Diatessaron, see Introd.*, vol. ii 1. § *in S* ܕܩܘܕܫܐ] om. S

9 repentance ; §and do not say in yourselves 'For a father we have *C S*
Abraham,' for I say to you that God is able from these stones to §*A* 331 (*cf* 63)
10 raise up sons to Abraham.¶ And lo, the axe hath arrived at the root ¶*A*
of the trees ; §every tree therefore that bringeth not forth good fruits §'*Julian*' 29
11 is hewn down and goeth unto the fire.¶ Now I, lo, I baptize ¶'*Jul.*'
you with water to repentance, but the one which cometh after me
is stronger than I, and I am not worthy to take up his shoes ; he
12 shall baptize you with the Holy Spirit and with fire, who holdeth a
fan in his hand and cleanseth his threshingfloor, and the wheat
he storeth into his barns, and the chaff he burneth with fire
unquenchable."
13 Then came Jesus from Galilee to the Jordan to John that he
14 might baptize him. And John forbad him and said to him: "I am
fit that thou shouldest baptize me, and thou unto me hast come?"
15 Jesus saith to him: "Suffer *it* at present, because thus it behoves
us to fulfil all uprightness." Then he suffered him to be baptized.
16 And Jesus had been baptized; and when he was baptized, in the same
hour that Jesus came up from the water, lo, the heavens were
opened, and he saw the Spirit of God that came down as a dove
17 and rested upon him. And a voice was heard from heaven, saying
to him: "Thou art my son and my beloved in whom I have been
iv 1 pleased." Then Jesus was led by the Holy Spirit into the wilderness,

---

9 Be not boastful and saying *A* in yourselves] *om. S A* for I say ...that] because *A* from these stones God is able *A* $^2/_2$ *E*[40] 10 hath arrived] *C S E*[39]: *cf* Jn iv 35 roots *S* and every tree *S* therefore] *om. S Jul* good] *om. S Jul* goeth unto] *C Jul*; falleth into *S* 11 lo] *om. S* stronger] greater *S* and...shoes] one whose shoes I am not worthy to take up *S* with fire and with the Holy Spirit *S* 12 his barn *S* 13 from Galilee to John that he might baptize him in the Jordan *S* 15 saith] answered and said *S* it behoves us] it beseemeth us *S* 'Suffer it now, that we may fulfil...' *E*[41, 42] 16 And Jesus had been baptized] *om. S* in the same hour...came up] and came up *S* as] in the likeness of *S*: *cf E*[99] 17 'This is my beloved Son' *E*[99] 1 Holy] *C E*[42]; *om. S*

C S ܕܢܬܢܣܐ ܡܢ ܣܛܢܐ. *2 ܘܟܦܢ ܒܬܪ ܐܪ̈ܒܥܝܢ ܝܘ̈ܡܝܢ ܕܨܐܡ ܗܘܐ
col 2 ܒܗܘܢ· 3 ܘܩܪܒ ܠܘܬܗ ܗܘ ܕܡܢܣܐ ܘܐܡܪ ܠܗ. ܐܢ ܒܪܗ
ܐܢܬ ܕܐܠܗܐ ܐܡܪ ܕܗܠܝܢ ܟܐ̈ܦܐ ܢܗܘܝܢ ܠܚܡܐ. 4 ܥܢܐ ܝܫܘܥ
ܘܐܡܪ ܠܗ· ܟܬܝܒ ܗܘ ܕܠܐ ܗܘܐ ܒܠܚܡܐ ܒܠܚܘܕ ܚܝܐ ܒܪܢܫܐ.
ܐܠܐ ܒܟܠ ܦܬܓܡ ܕܢܦܩ ܡܢ ܦܘܡܗ ܕܡܪܝܐ. 5 ܗܝܕܝܢ ܕܒܪܗ
ܐܟܠ ܩܪ̈ܨܐ ܘܐܝܬܝܗ ܠܡܕܝܢܬ ܩܘܕܫܐ. ܘܐܩܝܡܗ ܥܠ ܩܪܢܐ
ܕܗܝܟܠܐ. 6 ܘܐܡܪ ܠܗ ܐܢ ܒܪܗ ܐܢܬ ܕܐܠܗܐ ܐܪܡܐ ܢܦܫܟ
ܠܬܚܬ. ܟܬܝܒ ܓܝܪ ܕܠܡ̈ܠܐܟܘܗܝ ܢܦܩܕ ܥܠܝܟ. ܕܥܠ ܕܪ̈ܥܝܗܘܢ
fol 5 r ܢܫܩܠܘܢܟ. ܕܠܐ ܡܬܘܡ ܬܬܩܠ ܪܓܠܟ ܒܟܐܦܐ. 7 ܬܘܒ *ܐܡܪ
ܠܗ ܝܫܘܥ· ܟܬܝܒ ܗܘ ܕܠܐ ܬܢܣܐ ܠܡܪܝܟ ܘܐܠܗܟ· 8 ܬܘܒ
ܕܒܪܗ ܐܟܠ ܩܪ̈ܨܐ ܠܛܘܪܐ ܐܝܟܐ ܕܪܡ ܛܒ. ܘܚܘܝܗ ܟܠܗܝܢ
ܡ̈ܠܟܘܬܐ ܕܥܠܡܐ ܘܫܘܒܚܗܝܢ· 9 ܘܐܡܪ ܠܗ ܗܠܝܢ ܟܠܗܝܢ ܐܬܠ
ܠܟ ܐܢ ܗܘ ܕܬܦܠ ܘܬܣܓܘܕ ܩܕܡܝ. 10 ܗܝܕܝܢ ܐܡܪ ܠܗ ܝܫܘܥ·
ܙܠ ܠܟ ܠܒܣܬܪܝ ܣܛܢܐ. ܟܬܝܒ ܗܘ ܓܝܪ ܕܠܡܪܝܟ ܐܠܗܟ
ܬܣܓܘܕ· ܘܠܗ ܒܠܚܘܕܘܗܝ ܬܦܠܘܚ· 11 ܗܝܕܝܢ ܫܒܩܗ ܐܟܠ ܩܪ̈ܨܐ
§¶A 385 ܥܕ ܙܒܢܐ. §ܘܗܐ ܡ̈ܠܐܟܐ ܩܪܒܘ ܘܡܫܡܫܝܢ ܗܘܘ ܠܗ ܠܝܫܘܥ¶ ·܀·
12 ܟܕ ܫܡܥ ܕܝܢ ܕܝܘܚܢܢ ܐܫܬܠܡ. ܐܙܠ ܠܗ ܠܓܠܝܠܐ.
col 2 13 ܘܫܒܩܗ ܠܢܨܪܬ. ܘܐܬܐ ܥܡܪ ܒܟܦܪܢܚܘܡ. ܕܥܠ ܝܕ *ܝܡܐ.

ܣܛܢܐ] C E; ܐܟܠ ܩܪ̈ܨܐ S 2 ܝܘ̈ܡܝܢ] C E; + ܘܐܪ̈ܒܥܝܢ ܠܠ̈ܘܢ S Thos[256] (ܐܪ̈ܒܥܝܢ ܓܝܪ ܐܝܡ̈ܡܝܢ ܘܐܪ̈ܒܥܝܢ ܠܠ̈ܘܢ ܨܡ ܡܪܢ ܘܡܒܬܪܟܢ ܠܗ ܟܦܢ.)
3 ܗܘ ܕܡܢܣܐ] ܡܢܣܝܢܐ S ܘܐܡܪ ܠܗ] C¹ on eras
ܠܗܠܝܢ ܟܐ̈ܦܐ ܕܢܗܘܝܢ ܠܚܡܐ. S E 4 ܗܘܐ] om. S ܚܝܐ] ܢܚܐ S 5 ܩܪܢܐ]
ܟܢܦܐ S 6 ܐܪܡܐ ܢܦܫܟ ܠܬܚܬ] ܦܠ ܡܢ ܗܪܟܐ S ܟܬܝܒ] + ܗܘ S
ܥܠܝܟ] + ܕܢܛܪܘܢܟ S E ܕܥܠ] ܘܥܠ S ܕܪ̈ܥܝܗܘܢ] om. S 7 ܬܘܒ] om. S
ܠܡܪܝܐ ܐܠܗܟ. S 8 ܐܟܠ ܩܪ̈ܨܐ] ܣܛܢܐ S ܠܛܘܪܐ] ܘܐܣܩܗ ܐܣܩܗ
ܥܠ ܛܘܪܐ S E ܕܥܠܡܐ ܗܢܐ S ܘܫܘܒܚܗܝܢ] om. S 9 ܘܐܡܪ ܠܗ]
ܗܠܝܢ ܡ̈ܠܟܘܬܐ ܘܫܘܒܚܗܝܢ ܣܝܡܢ ܠܝ ܐܬܠ ܐܢܝܢ ܠܟ ܐܢ ܬܦܠ ܬܣܓܘܕ ܩܕܡܝ S
10 ܠܟ ܠܒܣܬܪܝ] ܠܒܣܬܪܟ S ܗܘ] om. S ܕܠܡܪܝܟ] ܠܡܪܝܐ S
11 ܫܒܩܗ ܐܟܠ ܩܪ̈ܨܐ] ܥܕ ܕܡ ܠܘܬܗ ܡܢܣܝܢܐ S ܘܗܐ ܡ̈ܠܐܟܐ ܩܪܒܘ]
ܘܩܪܒܘ ܡ̈ܠܐܟܐ S; ܢܚܬܘ ܡ̈ܠܐܟܐ A ܠܗ] om. A 12 ܟܕ] ܘܟܕ S ܫܡܥ]
om. S ܐܫܬܠܡ] ܐܬܬܫܠܡ S ܐܙܠ] ܥܪܩ S 13 ܘܐܬܐ ܠܗ ܠܟܦܪܢܚܘܡ S

2 to be tempted by Satan, and after forty days that he was fasting he *C S*
3 hungered. And he that tempteth drew near unto him, and said to
him: "If thou be the son of God, say that these stones become bread."
4 Jesus answered and said to him: "It is written 'Not by bread alone
liveth man, but by every utterance that goeth forth from the mouth
5 of the LORD.'" Then the Accuser took him and brought him to the
Holy City, and made him stand upon the corner of the Temple,
6 and said to him: "If thou be the son of God, cast thyself down;
for it is written 'To his angels he shall command concerning thee,
that on their arms they should bear thee up, that thou shouldest never
7 dash with thy foot against a stone.'" Again Jesus said to him: "It
8 is written 'Thou shalt not tempt thy Lord and thy God.'" Again
the Accuser took him to the hill which is exceeding high, and
9 shewed him all the kingdoms of the world and their glory, and said
to him: "These all will I give to thee, if so be that thou wilt fall
10 down and worship before me." Then Jesus said to him: "Get thee
behind me, Satan; for it is written 'Thy Lord thy God thou shalt
11 worship, and him alone shalt thou serve.'" Then the Accuser left
him for a time, §and lo, angels drew near and were serving Jesus.¶ §¶*A* 385
12 Now when Jesus heard that John was delivered up, he went
13 away to Galilee and left Nazareth and came *and* dwelt in Kaphar-

---

Satan] *C E*[42]; the Accuser *S* (διάβολος) 2 forty days] *C E*[44]; + and forty nights *S Thos* ('for our Lord fasted forty days and forty nights, and tasted nothing') 3 he that tempteth] the tempter *S* say to these stones that they become bread *S E*[44ff] 4 shall man live *S E*[46] the LORD] God *E*[46] 5 corner (*lit.* 'horn')] extremity (*lit.* 'wing') *S*; 'corner' *E*[44] 6 cast thyself down] fall from hence *S*; cast thyself from above down *E*[44] concerning thee] + that they should keep thee *S E*[44] that on] and on *S* never] not *S* 7 Again] *om. S* thy Lord and] the LORD *S* 8 the Accuser] *C*; Satan *S*; *om. E*[45] (*vid*) took him to] took him and brought *him* up *and* made him stand upon *S* (*E*[45]) of this world *S* and their glory] *om. S* 9 and said to him: "These kingdoms and their glory hast thou seen? To thee will I give them if thou wilt fall down *and* worship before me" *S* 10 Get behind, Satan *S*; 'Get thee behind, Satan' *E*[49] thy Lord] the LORD *S* 11 Then the tempter removed from him for a time *S* (*E*[49]) lo, angels drew near] angels drew near *S*; angels came down *A* 12 Jesus] he *S* delivered up] taken *S* went away] removed *S* 13 *and* dwelt in K.] to Kapharnahum *S*

C S ܒܬܚܘܡܐ ܕܙܒܘܠܘܢ ܘܕܢܦܬܠܝ. [14] ܕܢܬܡܠܐ ܡܕܡ ܕܐܬܐܡܪ ܒܝܕ
ܐܫܥܝܐ ܢܒܝܐ ܕܐܡܪ ܗܘܐ. [15] ܐܪܥܐ ܕܙܒܘܠܘܢ ܘܐܪܥܐ ܕܢܦܬܠܝ.
ܐܘܪܚܐ ܕܝܡܐ· ܒܥܒܪ̈ܘܗܝ ܕܝܘܪܕܢܢ ܢܗܪܐ. ܓܠܝܠܐ ܕܥܡ̈ܡܐ·
§A 423 [16] ܥܡܐ ܕܝܬܒ ܗܘܐ ܒܚܫܘܟܐ ܚܙܘ ܢܘܗܪܐ ܪܒܐ. § ܘܐܝܠܝܢ ܕܝܬܒܝܢ
¶A ܗܘܘ ܒܛ̈ܠܠܐ ܕܡܘܬܐ ¶. ܢܘܗܪܐ ܪܒܐ ܕܢܚ ܥܠܝܗܘܢ ·܀
[17] ܡܢ ܗܝܕܝܢ ܫܪܝ ܝܫܘܥ ܠܡܟܪܙܘ ܘܠܡܐܡܪ. ܩܪܒܬ ܠܗ̇ ܡܠܟܘܬܐ
ܕܫܡܝܐ. [18] ܘܟܕ ܡܗܠܟ ܗܘܐ ܡܪܢ ܥܠ ܝܕ ܝܡܬܐ ܕܓܠܝܠܐ.
ܚܙܐ ܠܬ̈ܪܝܢ ܐܚ̈ܝܢ. ܠܫܡܥܘܢ ܕܡܬܩܪܐ ܟܐܦܐ. ܘܠܐܢܕܪܐܘܣ
fol 5 v ܐܚܘܗܝ. ܟܕ ܪܡܝܢ ܗܘܘ ܡܨܝ̈ܕܬܗܘܢ *ܒܝܡܐ ܡܛܠ ܕܨܝ̈ܕܐ
ܗܘܘ. [19] ܐܡܪ ܠܗܘܢ ܝܫܘܥ. ܬܘ ܒܬܪܝ, ܘܐܥܒܕܟܘܢ ܨܝ̈ܕܐ
ܕܒ̈ܢܝ ܐܢܫܐ. [20] ܘܗܢܘܢ ܒܗ̇ ܒܫܥܬܐ. ܫܒܩܘ ܡܨܝ̈ܕܬܗܘܢ
ܘܐܙܠܘ ܒܬܪܗ ·܀

[21] ܘܟܕ ܥܒܪ ܡܢ ܬܡܢ. ܚܙܐ ܠܬ̈ܪܝܢ ܐܚ̈ܪܢܝܢ· ܠܝܥܩܘܒ
ܘܠܝܘܚܢܢ ܐܚܘܗܝ, ܒ̈ܢܝ ܙܒܕܝ. ܟܕ ܝܬܒܝܢ ܗܘܘ ܒܣܦܝܢܬܐ ܥܡ
ܙܒܕܝ, ܐܒܘܗܘܢ. ܘܡܬܩܢܝܢ ܡܨܝ̈ܕܬܗܘܢ. ܘܩܪܐ ܐܢܘܢ
ܝܫܘܥ. [22] ܘܗܢܘܢ ܒܗ̇ ܒܫܥܬܐ ܫܒܩܘ ܡܨܝ̈ܕܬܗܘܢ ܘܐܙܠܘ
ܒܬܪܗ. [23] ܘܗܘܐ ܡܚܕܪ ܗܘܐ ܒܟܠܗ̇ ܓܠܝܠܐ. ܘܡܠܦ ܗܘܐ

ܕܥܠ.....ܘܕܢܦܬܠܝ] ܗܝ ܕܐܝܬܝܗ ܥܠ ܓܢܒ ܝܡܐ ܒܬܚܘܡܐ ܘܒܢܦܬܠܝ S
14 ܕܬܬܡܠܐ ܡܠܬܐ ܕܐܬܐܡܪܬ ܒܐܫܥܝܐ ܢܒܝܐ ܕܐܡܪ S   15 ܕܙܒܘܠܘܢ S
ܘܒܥܒܪ̈ܘܗܝ S   16 ܗܘܐ] om. S   ܚܙܘ ܢܘܗܪܐ ܪܒܐ] ܢܘܗܪܐ ܚܙܐ S
ܘܐܝܠܝܢ ܕܝܬܒܝܢ ܗܘܘ ܒܛ̈ܠܠܐ ܕܡܘܬܐ] ܘܕܝܬܒܝܢ ܒܐܘܢܬܐ ܘܒܛܠܠ ܡܘܬܐ S;
ܘܝܬܒܝܢ ܒܐܘܢܬܐ ܘܒܛ̈ܠܠܗ ܕܡܘܬܐ A: *perh.* ܐܘܢܬܐ 'sorrow' *is a substitute for* ܐܘܢܐ 'abode'   ܪܒܐ] om. S   17. *No* § *in* S   ܫܪܝ ܗܘܐ S
ܘܠܡܐܡܪ] ܘܐܡܪ S   ܕܩܪܒܬ S   18 ܘܟܕ ܡܗܠܟ] ܘܐܝܟ ܕܥܒܪ S
ܡܪܢ] om. S   ܥܠ ܝܕ ܝܡܬܐ ܕܓܠܝܠܐ] ܥܠ ܓܢܒ ܣܦܬܗ ܕܝܡܐ S
ܠܫܡܥܘܢ.....ܘܠܐܢܕܪܐܘܣ] ܫܡܥܘܢ ܘܐܢܕܪܐܘܣ S (om. ܕܡܬܩܪܐ ܟܐܦܐ)
ܟܕ ܡܬܩܢܝܢ ܡܨܝ̈ܕܬܗܘܢ ܘܪܡܝܢ ܗܘܘ ܒܝܡܐ S   ܗܘܘ] + ܕܢܘ̈ܢܐ S
19 ܝܫܘܥ] om. S   20 ܗܢܘܢ ܕܝܢ S   ܘܐܙܠܘ] ܘܐܬܘ S   21. *No* § *in* S
ܘܟܕ.....ܚܙܐ] ܘܥܒܪ ܬܡܢ ܘܚܙܐ S   ܬܪ̈ܝܢ S   ܐܚܘܗܝ, ܒ̈ܢܝ ܙܒܕܝ] om. S
ܗܘܘ] om. S   ܝܫܘܥ] om. S   22 ܘܗܢܘܢ.....ܡܨܝ̈ܕܬܗܘܢ]
ܗܢܘܢ ܕܝܢ ܫܒܩܘ ܠܐܒܘܗܘܢ ܒܣܦܝܢܬܐ S   23 ܘܡܚܕܪ ܗܘܐ ܝܫܘܥ S

nahum, which is by the sea side in the border of Zebulun and of *C S*
14 Naphtali, that that might be fulfilled which was said through Isaiah
15 the prophet, who had said: "The land of Zebulun and the land of
Naphtali, the way of the sea, beyond the river Jordan, Galilee of
16 the peoples; the people that was sitting in darkness have seen a
great light, §and those that were sitting in the shadows of death,¶ §¶*A* 423
a great light hath risen upon them."

17 From then Jesus began to preach and to say: "The kingdom
18 of heaven hath drawn nigh." And when our Lord was walking
by the side of the lake of Galilee he saw two brothers, Simon
called Kepha and Andrew his brother, casting their nets into the
19 sea, because they were fishers. Jesus saith to them: "Come after
20 me and I will make you fishers of men." And they in the same
hour left their nets and went after him.

21 And when he removed thence he saw two other brothers, James
and John his brother, sons of Zebedee, while they were sitting in the
boat with Zebedee their father and mending their nets. And Jesus
22 called them; and they in the same hour left their nets and went
23 after him. And he was going about in all Galilee and was teaching

---

in the border... Naphtali] in Zebulun and in Naphtali *S* 14 that... which] the word...that *S* through] by *S* had] *om.* *S* 15 and beyond *S* E^{6} 16 was sitting] sit *S* have] hath *S* great] *C* $E^{6,51}$; *om.* *S* and they that sit in sorrow and in the shadow of death *S A* great] *om.* *S* 17 began] had begun *S* and to say:] and he said *S* 18 when] as *S* our Lord] he *S* walking] passing *S* by the side of the shore of the sea *S* (*om.* of Galilee) called Kepha] *om.* *S* mending their nets and casting into the sea *S* fishers] + of fish *S* 19 Jesus] He *S* 20 And they] Now they *S* went] came *S* 21 And he drew near again and saw *S* his brother, sons of Zebedee] *om.* *S* while they were] *om.* *S* Jesus] he *S* 22 and they... nets] now they left their father in the boat *S* 23 he] Jesus *S*

C S ܒܟܢܘܫܬܐ. ܘܡܟܪܙ ܗܘܐ ܤܒܪܬܐ ܕܡܠܟܘܬܐ: ܘܡܐܣܐ ܗܘܐ
col 2 ܟܠ ܬܚ̈ܘܫܝܢ *ܘܟܠ ܟܘܪ̈ܗܢܝܢ ܒܥܡܐ.[24] ܘܐܫܬܡܥ ܛܒܗ ܒܟܠܗ
ܣܘܪܝܐ. ܘܐܝܬܝܘ ܠܗ ܟܠܗܘܢ ܐܝܠܝܢ ܕܒܝܫ ܒܝܫ ܚܒܝܫܝܢ. ܘܐܝܠܝܢ
ܕܟܪ̈ܝܗܝܢ ܒܟܘܪ̈ܗܢܐ ܣ̈ܓܝܐܐ. ܘܒܬܫܢܝܩܐ ܩ̈ܫܝܐ. ܘܦܓ̈ܥܐ ܕܐܓ̈ܪܐ
ܙ̈ܢܝܢ ܗܘܘ ܒܟܠܗܘܢ. ܘܐܣܝ ܐܢܘܢ. ܘܗܘܐ ܟܠ ܚܕ ܚܕ ܡܢܗܘܢ
ܐܣܝܗ ܗܟܢ ܗܘܐ. ܘܠܟܠܗܘܢ ܡܐܣܐ ܗܘܐ.[25] ܘܐܙܠܘ ܒܬܪܗ
ܟܢ̈ܫܐ ܣ̈ܓܝܐܐ. ܡܢ ܓܠܝܠܐ ܘܡܢ ܥ̈ܣܪ ܡܕ̈ܝܢܬܐ. ܘܡܢ ܐܘܪܫܠܡ.
ܘܡܢ ܝܗܘܕ. ܘܡܢ ܥܒܪܐ ܕܝܘܪܕܢ.[1] ܟܕ ܚܙܐ ܕܝܢ ܠܟ̈ܢܫܐ. ܣܠܩ
ܝܬܒ ܠܗ ܒܛܘܪܐ. ܘܩܪܒܘ ܠܘܬܗ ܬܠܡܝ̈ܕܘܗܝ.[2] ܘܦܬܚ ܦܘܡܗ
cf A41 ܘܡܠܦ ܗܘܐ ܠܗܘܢ ܘܐܡܪ ܀
§A390, 437 fol 6 r [§3] ܛܘܒܝܗܘܢ ܠܡܣ̈ܟܢܐ *ܒܪܘܚܗܘܢ ܕܕܝܠܗܘܢ ܗܝ ܡܠܟܘܬܐ
¶A ܕܫܡܝܐ[¶]....
[5] ܛܘܒܝܗܘܢ ܠܡܟܝ̈ܟܐ ܕܗܢܘܢ ܢܐܪܬܘܢܝܗ̇ ܠܐܪܥܐ ܀
[4] ܛܘܒܝܗܘܢ ܠܐܒ̈ܝܠܐ ܕܗܢܘܢ ܢܬܒܝܐܘܢ ܀
[6] ܛܘܒܝܗܘܢ ܠܐܝܠܝܢ ܕܟܦܢܝܢ ܘܨܗܝܢ ܠܙܕܝܩܘܬܐ ܕܗܢܘܢ
ܢܣܒܥܘܢ ܀
[7] ܛܘܒܝܗܘܢ ܠܡܪ̈ܚܡܢܐ ܕܥܠܝܗܘܢ ܢܗܘܘܢ ܪ̈ܚܡܐ܂
[8] ܛܘܒܝܗܘܢ ܠܐܝܠܝܢ ܕܕܟܝܢ ܒܠܒܗܘܢ ܕܗܢܘܢ ܢܚܙܘܢܝܗܝ
ܠܐܠܗܐ ܀

S ܘܟܠ ܟܘܪ̈ܗܢܝܢ ܕܒܥܡܐ   *S* ܒܟܐܒܐ] ܬܚ̈ܘܫܝܢ   *S* ܒܟܢܘܫ̈ܬܗܘܢ
ܘܐܝܬܝܘ.....ܘܒܬܫܢܝܩܐ ܩ̈ܫܝܐ.   24 ܘܐܫܬܡܥ....ܣܘܪܝܐ] *om. S*
S ܘܩܪܒܘ ܗܘܘ ܠܗ ܦܓ̈ܥܐ ܕܒܝܫܝܢ ܗܘܘ ܒܬܫܢܝܩܐ ܩ̈ܫܝܐ ܘܒܟܘܪ̈ܗܢܐ ܣ̈ܓܝܐܐ
ܘܦܓ̈ܥܐ....ܐܓ̈ܪܐ] *om. S*   ܘܗܘܐ ܟܠ] ܘܟܠ *S*   *On ver. 24, cf Thos*[229, 230]
ܘܐܫܬܡܥ ܗܘܐ ܛܒܗ ܒܟܠ ܣܘܪܝܐ....ܘܡܝܬܝܢ ܗܘܘ ܠܗ ܟܪ̈ܝܗܐ ܕܒܝܫܝܢ ܗܘܘ
25. § *in S*   ܒܟܘܪ̈ܗܢܐ ܣ̈ܓܝܐܐ ܘܒܬܫܢܝܩܐ ܩ̈ܫܝܐ. ܘܡܫܪ̈ܝܐ...
S ܒܒܪܬܗ   *S* ܝܗܘܕܐ   *S* ܘܟܕ ܗܘܐ ܒܥܕܢܐ ܕܦܓ̈ܥܐ. ܕܡܢ] ܘܐܙܠܘ......ܡܢ
S ܣܠܩ ܠܗ ܠܛܘܪܐ ܘܟܕ ܝܬܒ ܩܪܒܘ   *S* ܦܓ̈ܥܐ +] ܠܟ̈ܢܫܐ   1 ܕܝܢ] *om. S*
S ܘܦܬܚ ܦܘܡܗ. ܘܡܠܦ ܗܘܐ ܠܗܘܢ ܟܕ ܐܡܪ] ܘܦܬܚ....ܘܐܡܪ 2   3—10 ܛܘܒܝܗܘܢ (11 ܛܘ-)]
C in red; ܛܘܒ̈ܝܗܘܢ (11 ܛܘܒ̈ܝܟܘܢ) *S*   *ver. 5 next ver. 3] C E A 41; after ver. 4 S*   5 ܢܐܪܬܘܢܝܗ̇ ܐܪܥܐ *S*   6 ܠܙܕܝܩܘܬܐ] ܠܟܐܢܘܬܐ *S*   8 ܢܚܙܘܢܝܗ *S*

in the synagogues and was preaching the gospel of the kingdom and was *C S*
24 healing all torments and all infirmities in the people. And the tale of
him was heard in all Syria; and they brought to him all those that
were ill and those that were infirm with stubborn infirmities and
with hateful torments and many that were struck with palsies and
lunatics, and he—on each one of them he was laying his hand and
25 healing them all. And there went after him great multitudes from
Galilee and from the Ten Cities and from Jerusalem and from Judæa
v 1 and from beyond Jordan. Now when he saw the multitudes he went
2 up *and* sat in the hill, and his disciples drew near unto him, and
he opened his mouth and was teaching them and saying: *cf A* 41

3 "§HAPPY is it for the poor in their spirit, that theirs is the kingdom of heaven!¶ §*A* 390, 437 ¶*A*

5 "HAPPY is it for the lowly, that they shall inherit the earth!

4 "HAPPY is it for the mourners, that they shall be comforted!

6 "HAPPY is it for them that hunger and thirst after righteousness, that they shall be satisfied!

7 "HAPPY is it for the compassionate, that upon them shall be compassion!

8 "HAPPY is it for them that are pure in their heart, that they shall see God!

---

in their synagogues *S* all torments and all infirmities] every pain and every infirmity *S* 24 And the tale....Syria] *om. S* and they brought....torments] and many were drawing near to him who were tormented with hateful torments and with stubborn infirmities *S* and many..... lunatics] *om. S* he—] *om. S* *On ver.* 24, *cf Thos* 'And the tale of him had been heard among men....and the infirm were being healed that were infirm with stubborn infirmities and with hateful torments, and the paralysed....' 25—v 2] And when there was a great multitude, which *had come* from....beyond Jordan, when he saw the great multitudes he went up to the hill; and when he sat his disciples drew near unto him, and he began to say to them *S* (*E*[62]) *ver.* 5 *next ver.* 3] *C E*[62] *A* 41; *after ver.* 4 *S*: *on the text of the Beatitudes in A* 41, *see Introd.* vol. ii. *For a justification of the renderings, see Aphraates' quotation of* Lk vi 24, *and cf also* Lk iv 36 *in S and* syr.vg 6 righteousness] uprightness *S*

C S ..ܘ..¶§9 ܛܘܒܝܗܘܢ ܠܥܒ̈ܕܝ ܫܝܢܐ ܕܗܢܘܢ ܒ̈ܢܘܗܝ ܕܐܠܗܐ ܢܬܩܪܘܢ¶..ܘ..
§¶A 275, 304 10 ܛܘܒܝܗܘܢ ܠܐܝܠܝܢ ܕܪܕܝܦܝܢ ܡܛܠ ܙܕܝܩܘܬܐ ܕܕܝܠܗܘܢ ܗܝ
ܡܠܟܘܬܐ ܕܫܡܝܐ ܀

11 ܛܘܒܝܟܘܢ ܡܐ ܕܪܕܦܝܢ ܠܟܘܢ ܒ̈ܢܝ ܐܢܫܐ ܘܡܚܣܕܝܢ ܠܟܘܢ
col 2 ܘܐܡܪܝܢ ܥܠܝܟܘܢ ܟܠ ܡܕܡ *ܕܒܝܫ ܒܕܓܠܘܬܐ ܡܛܠ ܫܡܝ.
12 ܐܢܬܘܢ ܕܝܢ ܚܕܘ ܘܪܘܙܘ ܒܗܿܘ ܝܘܡܐ. ܕܐܓܪܟܘܢ ܣܓܝ
ܒܫܡܝܐ. ܗܟܢܐ ܓܝܪ ܪܕܦܝܢ ܗܘܘ ܠܐܒ̈ܗܬܟܘܢ ܠܢܒܝ̈ܐ. ܐܝܠܝܢ
ܕܡܩܕܡܝܟܘܢ ܗܘܘ.
§¶A 457 §13 ܐܢܬܘܢ ܐܝܬܝܟܘܢ ܡܠܚܐ ܕܐܪܥܐ. ܐܢ ܕܝܢ ܡܠܚܐ ܬܦܟܗ̇¶
ܘܬܬܦܠܐ ܒܡܢܐ ܬܬܡܠܚ. ܠܡܕܡ ܠܐ ܐܙܠܐ. ܐܠܐ ܕܢܫܕܘܢܗ̇
§A 13 ܠܒܪ. ܘܢܗܘܘܢ ܕܝܫܝܢ ܠܗ̇ ܒ̈ܢܝ ܐܢܫܐ. §14 ܐܢܬܘܢ ܐܝܬܝܟܘܢ ܢܘܗܪܗ
¶A ܕܥܠܡܐ¶. ܘܠܐ ܡܫܟܚܐ ܡܕܝܢܬܐ ܕܥܠ ܛܘܪܐ ܒܢܝܐ ܕܬܬܛܫܐ.
cf A 14 15 ܘܠܐ ܐܢܫ ܡܢܗܪ ܫܪܓܐ ܘܣܐܡ ܠܗ ܬܚܝܬ ܡܘܕܝܐ. ܐܠܐ
ܣܐܡ ܠܗ ܥܠ ܡܢܪܬܐ. ܘܡܢܗܪ ܠܟܠܗܘܢ ܐܝܠܝܢ ܕܒܒܝܬܐ
§A 14 fol 6 v ܐܢܘܢ. 16 ܗܟܢܐ §ܢܢܗܪ ܢܘܗܪܟܘܢ ܩܕܡ ܒ̈ܢܝ *ܐ̈ܢܫܐ ܕܢܚܙܘܢ
¶A ܥܒܕܝܟܘܢ ܫܦܝܪ̈ܐ. ܘܢܫܒܚܘܢ ܠܐܒܘܟܘܢ ܕܒܫܡܝܐ¶܀
§A 28 §17 ܠܐ ܬܣܒܪܘܢ ܕܐܬܝܬ ܕܐܫܪܐ ܢܡܘܣܐ ܘܢܒܝ̈ܐ. ܠܐ ܐܬܝܬ

---

11 ܡܐ.....ܘܡܚܣܕܝܢ ܠܟܘܢ] ܟܕ ܢܗܘܘܢ ܚܣܕܝܢ ܠܟܘܢ ܒ̈ܢܝ ܐܢܫܐ ܘܪܕܦܝܢ ܠܟܘܢ S (ܢܗܘܘܢ may be a slip for ܗܘܘܢ) ܘܡܐ ܕܐܡܪܝܢ S ܟܠ ܡܕܡ] om. S ܒܕܓܠܘܬܐ] om. S ܫܡܝ] + ܕܝܠܝ S 12 ܣܓܝ] + ܗܘ S ܠܐܒ̈ܗܬܟܘܢ] C (sic); ܠܐܒܗܝܗܘܢ S ܐܝܠܝܢ ܕܡܩܕܡܝܟܘܢ ܗܘܘ] om. S 13. § in S: ver. 12 ends a line in C ܡܠܚܗ̇ (S) A ܐܢ ܕܝܢ] ܐܢ S; ܕܐܢ A ܬܦܟܗ̇] C (sic) A^b; see Wright's note, p. 15 ܘܬܬܦܠܐ] om. S (A) ܕܢܫܕܘܢܗ̇] ܕܬܫܬܕܐ S ܒܡܢܐ to end of ver.] ܡܠܚܐ ܒܡܠܚ ܡܬܡܠܚܐ ܘܡܬܚܠܐ A 457, but cf ܡܠܚܐ ܟܕ ܬܦܟܗ̇ (sic) ܠܒܪ ܡܫܬܕܝܐ in an allusion A 271
14. Ver. 13 ends a line in C and S, but is not clearly the end of a § in either MS
15 ܡܘܕܝܐ] ܣܐܬܐ S A 14 ܥܠ] ܠܥܠ ܡܢ S A 14 ܘܡܢܗܪ.....ܐܢܘܢ] ܘܠܟܠ ܕܐܝܬ ܒܒܝܬܐ ܡܢܗܪ. S 16 ܩܕܡ] ܠܩܕܡ S (= ܠܘܩܕܡ as often) ܫܦܝܪ̈ܐ] ܛܒ̈ܐ A 17 ܠܐ...ܕܐܬܝܬ] ܠܐ ܐܬܝܬ A ܠܡܫܪܐ S A ܢܡܘܣܐ] ܐܘܪܝܬܐ A ܠܐ ܐܬܝܬ ܕܐܫܪܐ ܐܠܐ] om. A; om. ܐܠܐ S

9 "§Happy is it for the peace-makers, that they shall be called *C S*
sons of God!¶ §¶*A* 275, 304

10 "Happy is it for them that are persecuted for righteousness' sake,
that theirs is the kingdom of heaven!

11 "Happy is it for you what *time* men persecute you and reproach
you, and say concerning you everything evil in a lie for my name's
12 sake. But ye, rejoice ye and exult in that day that your reward is
great in heaven, for so were your fathers persecuting the prophets
that were before you.

13 "§Ye are the salt of the earth; but if salt lose its savour¶ and §¶*A* 457
become foolish, wherewith shall it be salted? For nothing is it of
use but that they should throw it away, and men will trample upon
14 it. §Ye are the light of the world;¶ and the city that is built on §¶*A* 13
15 the hill cannot be concealed. And no one lighteth a lamp and setteth *cf A* 14
it under the modius, but he setteth it on the lamp-stand, and it
16 shineth for all those who are in the house. So §let your light shine §*A* 14
before men that they may see your fair deeds and glorify your Father
in heaven.¶ ¶*A*

17 "§Suppose not that I have come that I might remit the law and §*A* 28
the prophets; I have not come that I might remit them, but to fulfil

---

11 what *time*...reproach] when men are hating you and persecuting *S* and what *time* they say *S* everything] *om. S* in a lie] *om. S* my name's sake, even mine *S* 12 'Rejoice ye, and be exceeding glad; for great is your reward in heaven, and in that day rejoice' *E*[64] their fathers *S* that were before you] *om. S* 13 but if] if *S*; for if *A* and become foolish] *om. S A*: *see Notes,* vol. ii that it should be cast out *S* wherewith...salted?] the world would quickly be putrefied and corrupted *A* 457, *but comp.* 'Salt when it loses its savour is cast away' *A* 271 15 modius] bushel *S A* on] upon *S A* and to all that are in the house it giveth light *S* 16 fair] good *A* 17 Suppose not that I have come] I have not come *A E*[64] to remit *S A* law] Law *A* I have not.....remit them] *om. A E*[65]; *om.* them *S*

C S ¶A ܕܐܫܪܐ ܐܢܘܢ܆ ܐܠܐ ܠܡܫܠܡܘ ܐܢܘܢ܆¶ [18]ܐܡܝܢ ܓܝܪ ܐܡܪܢܐ

§A 30 ܠܟܘܢ܆ ܕܥܕܡܐ ܕܢܥܒܪܘܢ ܫܡܝܐ ܘܐܪܥܐ. [§]ܝܘܕ ܐܬܬܐ ܚܕܐ

ܐܘ ܦܣܩܐ ܚܕܐ ܠܐ ܬܥܒܪ ܡܢ ܢܡܘܣܐ. ܥܕܡܐ ܕܟܠ ܡܕܡ

¶A ܢܗܘܐ.¶ [19]ܟܠ ܕܢܫܪܐ ܗܟܝܠ ܚܕ ܡܢ ܦܘܩܕܢܐ ܗܠܝܢ ܙܥܘܪܐ.

ܘܢܠܦ ܗܟܢܐ ܠܒܢܝ ܐܢܫܐ. ܒܨܝܪܐ ܢܬܩܪܐ ܒܡܠܟܘܬܐ ܕܫܡܝܐ.

ܟܠ ܕܢܥܒܕ ܕܝܢ ܘܢܠܦ. ܗܢܐ ܪܒܐ ܢܬܩܪܐ ܒܡܠܟܘܬܐ ܕܫܡܝܐ.

col 2 [20]ܐܡܪܢܐ ܠܟܘܢ ܓܝܪ. ܕܐܠܐ ܬܬܝܬܪ *ܙܕܝܩܘܬܟܘܢ ܝܬܝܪ ܡܢ

ܣܦܪܐ ܘܦܪܝܫܐ. ܠܐ ܬܥܠܘܢ ܠܡܠܟܘܬܐ ܕܫܡܝܐ. [21]ܫܡܥܬܘܢ

ܕܐܬܐܡܪ ܠܩܕܡܝܐ ܕܠܐ ܬܩܛܘܠ. ܘܟܠ ܡܢ ܕܢܩܛܘܠ ܡܬܚܝܒ

ܠܕܝܢܐ. [22]ܐܢܐ ܕܝܢ ܐܡܪ ܐܢܐ ܠܟܘܢ܆ ܕܟܠ ܡܢ ܕܢܪܓܙ ܥܠ

ܐܚܘܗܝ ܐܝܩܐ ܢܗܘܐ ܚܝܒ ܠܕܝܢܐ. ܘܡܢ ܕܢܐܡܪ ܠܐܚܘܗܝ

ܪܩܐ ܢܗܘܐ ܚܝܒ ܠܟܢܘܫܬܐ. ܘܟܠ ܡܢ ܕܢܐܡܪ ܠܐܚܘܗܝ ܫܛܝܐ.

ܢܗܘܐ ܚܝܒ ܠܓܗܢܐ ܕܢܘܪܐ.

§A 37, 72 [§23]ܐܡܬܝ ܗܟܝܠ ܕܡܩܪܒ ܐܢܬ ܩܘܪܒܢܟ ܩܕܡ ܡܕܒܚܐ. ܘܬܡܢ

ܬܬܕܟܪ ܕܐܚܘܟ ܐܚܝܕ ܥܠܝܟ ܐܟܬܐ. [24]ܫܒܘܩ ܩܘܪܒܢܟ

ܬܡܢ ܩܕܡܘܗܝ ܕܡܕܒܚܐ. ܘܙܠ ܠܘܩܕܡ ܐܬܪܥܐ ܥܡ ܐܚܘܟ.

fol 7 r ¶A *ܘܗܝܕܝܢ ܬܐ ܩܪܒ ܩܘܪܒܢܟ.¶

[25]ܗܘܝܬ ܡܬܐܢܐ ܥܡ ܒܥܠܕܝܢܟ. ܥܓܠ ܥܕ ܥܡܗ ܐܢܬ

ܒܐܘܪܚܐ. ܕܠܡܐ ܒܥܠܕܝܢܟ ܢܫܠܡܟ ܠܕܝܢܐ. ܘܕܝܢܐ ܢܫܠܡܟ

---

18 ܕܡܕܡܐ S   ܐܘ ܦܣܩܐ ܚܕܐ] om. S A   ܡܢ ܐܘܪܝܬܐ ܘܢܒܝܐ ܠܐ ܬܥܒܪ A 30[4] (cf ܠܐ ܬܥܒܪ ܗܘ ܐܬܘܬܐ ܡܢ ܢܡܘܣܐ ܘܡܢ ܢܒܝܐ A 30[20])   ܡܕܡ] om. S A   19 ܟܠ] ܘܡܢ S   ܗܟܝܠ] om. S   ܚܕ S   ܘܢܠܦ 2°] + ܗܟܢܐ S   20 ܙܕܝܩܘܬܟܘܢ] so also S   ܝܬܝܪ ܡܢ ܣܦܪܐ ܘܦܪܝܫܐ] om. ܝܬܝܪ S (rest as C, sic)   21. § in S (vid); ver. 20 ends a line in C   ܕܠܐ] ܠܐ S   22 ܕܢܪܓܙ S   ܠܕܝܢܐ] ܒܕܝܢܐ S   ܘܡܢ] ܘܟܠ S   ܢܗܘܐ ܚܝܒ ult.] ܚܝܒ ܗܘ S   ܘܡܢ] ܘܟܠ ܡܢ S   ܚܝܒ ܗܘ ܒܟܢܘܫܬܐ S   23 init.] ܐܢ ܗܟܝܠ ܡܩܪܒ ܐܢܬ ܩܘܪܒܢܟ S; ܟܕ ܬܩܪܒ ܩܘܪܒܢܐ A 72, ܟܕ ܩܘܪܒܢܐ ܙܟܐ ܐܢܬ ܕܬܩܪܒ A 37   ܩܕܡ] ܥܠ S   ܩܕܡ ܡܕܒܚܐ] om. A²/₂   ܘܬܡܢ] om. A²/₂   ܕܡܕܡ....ܐܟܬܐ] ܕܐܚܘܟ ܐܚܝܕ ܥܠܝܟ ܐܟܬܐ S; ܕܥܠ ܐܚܘܟ ܐܚܝܕ ܐܝܬ ܐܟܬܐ ܡܕܡ A²/₂   24 ܬܡܢ] om. A²/₂   ܩܕܡܘܗܝ ܕ] ܥܠ S; ܩܕܡ A²/₂   ܠܘܩܕܡ] om. A²/₂   ܬܐ ܩܪܒ S A²/₂   25. No § in S

18 them.¶ For amen, I say to you Until heaven and earth shall pass C S ¶A
away §one Jôd-letter or one corner shall not pass away from the §A 30
19 law till everything come to pass.¶ Every one that shall remit there- ¶A
fore one of these little commandments, and shall teach so to men,
shall be called less in the kingdom of heaven; but every one that
shall do and teach *them*, he shall be called great in the kingdom
20 of heaven. For I say to you Except your righteousness shall
abound more than the scribes and the Pharisees, ye shall not enter
21 into the kingdom of heaven. Ye have heard that it was said to
them of old time 'Thou shalt not kill; and whosoever shall kill
22 shall be condemned in judgement.' But I say to you Whosoever
shall be wroth with his brother without cause shall be condemned to
judgement; and he that shall say to his brother 'Raca' shall be
condemned to the synagogue; and whosoever shall say to his brother
'Fool' shall be condemned to the Gehenna of fire.

23 "§Whensoever therefore thou offerest thy offering before the §A 37, 72
altar, and there thou shalt recollect that thy brother hath aught
24 against thee of enmity, leave thy offering there before the altar,
and go first be reconciled with thy brother, and then come and
offer thy offering.¶ ¶A

25 "Be agreed with thine adversary quickly while yet with him thou
art in the way; lest thine adversary deliver thee up to the judge,

---

18 or one corner] *om.* $S\ A^2/_2$: *see Introd.* vol. ii from the law] + and (from) the prophets $A^2/_2$, *with varying order* everything] all *S A* 19 Every one that] And he that *S* therefore] *om.* $S\ E^{65}$ teach *them*] teach thus *S* 20 more than] *more* than *S* (*sic*) 21 to them of old time] *om.* E^{66} 22 shall be 1°] is *S* condemned to 1° & 2°] condemned in *S*: *see Notes*, vol. ii and whosoever] and every one that *S* shall be 3° & 4°] is *S* 23 *init.*] If therefore thou offerest thy gift upon the altar *S*; when thou offerest an offering *A* 72, when an offering thou wishest to offer *A* 37 (*omitting* 'before the altar' $^2/_2$); 'when thou hast offered thy offering upon the altar' E^{65} there] *om.* $A^2/_2$ that thy brother hath against thee enmity *S*; that against thy brother thou hast aught of enmity $A^2/_2$ 24 there] *om.* $A^2/_2$ before] on *S* first] *om.* $A^2/_2\ E^{65}$

C S ܠܫܡܫܐ. ܘܬܦܠ ܒܝܬ ܐܣܝܪܐ. [26]ܘܐܡܝܢ ܐܡܪ ܐܢܐ ܠܟ. ܕܠܐ
ܬܦܘܩ ܡܢ ܬܡܢ. ܥܕܡܐ ܕܬܬܠ ܫܡܘܢܐ ܐܚܪܝܐ.܀
[27]ܫܡܥܬܘܢ ܕܐܬܐܡܪ ܠܩܕܡܝܐ ܕܠܐ ܬܓܘܪ. [28]ܐܢܐ ܕܝܢ ܐܡܪ
ܐܢܐ ܠܟܘܢ ܕܟܠ ܡܢ ܕܚܙܐ ܐܢܬܬܐ ܘܪܓܝ ܠܗ ܓܪܗ ܒܠܒܗ.
[29]ܐܢ ܕܝܢ ܥܝܢܟ ܕܝܡܝܢܐ ܡܟܫܠܐ ܠܟ ܚܨܝ ܫܕܝܗ ܡܢܟ.
ܦܩܚ ܠܟ ܓܝܪ ܕܢܐܒܕ ܗܕܡܟ ܢܐܒܕ. ܘܠܐ ܟܘܠܗ ܦܓܪܟ ܢܐܙܠ
col 2 *ܠܓܗܢܐ. [30]ܘܐܢ ܐܝܕܟ ܕܝܡܝܢܐ ܡܟܫܠܐ ܠܟ ܦܣܘܩ ܫܕܝܗ
ܡܢܟ. ܦܩܚ ܠܟ ܓܝܪ ܕܢܐܒܕ ܚܕ ܡܢ ܗܕܡܝܟ. ܘܠܐ ܟܠܗ
ܦܓܪܟ ܢܐܙܠ ܠܓܗܢܐ. [31]ܐܬܐܡܪ ܕܝܢ ܕܡܢ ܕܫܪܐ ܐܢܬܬܗ ܢܬܠ
ܠܗ ܐܓܪܬܐ ܕܕܘܠܠܐ. [32]ܐܢܐ ܕܝܢ ܐܡܪ ܐܢܐ ܠܟܘܢ ܕܡܢ
ܕܫܪܐ ܐܢܬܬܗ ܕܠܐ ܐܬܐܡܪ ܥܠܝܗ ܓܘܪܐ. ܗܘܘ ܡܓܪ ܠܗ.
ܘܡܢ ܕܢܣܒ ܫܒܘܩܬܐ ܡܓܪ ܓܐܪ.
§A499 [33]ܬܘܒ ܫܡܥܬܘܢ ܕܐܬܐܡܪ ܠܩܕܡܝܐ. §ܠܐ ܬܐܡܐ ܡܘܡܬܐ
¶A ܕܓܠܘܪܐ¶. ܐܠܐ ܬܬܠ ܠܡܪܝܐ ܡܘܡܬܟ. [34]ܐܢܐ ܕܝܢ ܐܡܪܢܐ
§¶A505 §A499–500 ܠܟܘܢ §ܕܠܘܡܝܡܘܢ ܠܐ ܬܐܡܘܢ¶. §ܠܐ ܒܫܡܝܐ ܕܟܘܪܣܝܗ ܐܝܘܢ
fol 7 v ܕܐܠܗܐ. [35]ܘܐܦ *ܠܐ ܒܐܪܥܐ ܡܛܠ ܕܟܘܒܫܐ ܗܝ ܕܬܚܬ ܪ̈ܓܠܘܗܝ.
ܘܐܦ ܠܐ ܒܐܘܪܫܠܡ ܡܛܠ ܕܡܕܝܢܬܗ ܗܝ ܕܡܠܟܐ ܪܒܐ.
[36]ܘܐܦܠܐ ܒܪܫܟ ܬܐܡܐ. ܡܛܠ ܕܠܐ ܡܫܟܚ ܐܢܬ ܠܡܥܒܕ ܒܗ
ܡܢܬܐ ܚܕܐ ܕܣܥܪܐ ܐܘܟܡܬܐ ܐܘ ܚܘܪܬܐ. [37]ܐܠܐ ܬܗܘܐ
ܡܠܬܟܘܢ ܐܝܢ ܐܝܢ ܘܠܐ ܠܐ. ܡܕܡ ܕܝܢ ܕܡܢ ܗܠܝܢ ܝܬܝܪ ܡܢ
¶A ܒܝܫܐ ܗܘ¶.܀

ܘܕܝܢܐ ܢܫܠܡܟ ܠܫܡܫܐ] *om.* S   27 ܠܩܕܡܝܐ] *om.* S   ܕܠܐ] ܠܐ S
29] *for A* 262, *see* Matt xviii 9   ܫܕܝܗ] ܫܕܝܗ S   30.] *om.* S   31. § *in* S   ܕܫܪܐ]
ܕܫܒܩ S   ܕܘܠܠܐ] ܕܕܘܠܠܐ S (= A^b116)   32 ܕܢܫܒܘܩ] ܕܫܒܘܩ S   33 ܬܘܒ] *om.* S
ܠܩܕܡܝܐ] *om.* S   ܠܐ] ܕܠܐ S A   ܡܘܡܬܐ ܫܩܪܐ S A   ܡܘܡܬܟ]
ܡܘܡܬܐ S   34 ܕܬܡܘܡܘܢ A^b   ܒܫܡܝܐ] *pr.* ܬܐܡܘܢ A   ܕܟܘܪܣܝܐ A^b
35 ܐܦ 1°] *om.* S A   ܒܐܪܥܐ] + ܬܐܡܘܢ A   ܡܛܠ 1°] *om.* S A   ܬܚܝܬ S
ܐܦ 2°] *om.* S   ܒܐܘܪܫܠܡ] + ܬܐܡܘܢ A   ܕܡܕܝܢܬܗ] ܕܟܘܪܣܗ A^b
36 ܘܠܐ ܒܪܫܟ S   ܚܕܐ] *om.* A^a   37 ܐܝܢ ܐܝܢ] *pr.* ܕ A^a   ܕܝܢ] *om.* S A

and the judge deliver thee up to the officer, and thou fall into *C S*
26 prison—and amen, I say to thee Thou wilt not go forth from
thence, till thou give the last mite.
27 "Ye have heard that it was said to them of old time 'Thou
28 shalt not commit adultery.' But I say to you Whosoever seeth a
woman and longeth for her hath committed adultery with her in
29 his heart. But if thy right eye offend thee pluck *it* out *and* throw
it from thee, for it is profitable for thee that thy one member should
30 perish, and not all thy body go to Gehenna. And if thy right hand
offend thee cut *it* off *and* throw it from thee, for it is profitable for
thee that one of thy members should perish, and not all thy body
31 go to Gehenna. It hath been said 'He that dismisseth his wife
32 shall give her a letter of divorce.' But I say to you He that
dismisseth his wife concerning whom there hath not been alleged
adultery, he causeth her to commit adultery; and he that taketh
up a divorced woman doth indeed commit adultery.
33 "Again ye have heard that it hath been said to them of old time:
'§Thou shalt not swear an oath of falsehood,¶ but shalt give to the §¶*A*499
34 LORD thy oath.' But I say to you §Ye your own selves shall §*A*505
not swear :¶—§not by the heavens, because they are the throne of ¶§*A*499–500
35 God; nor by the earth, because it is the footstool that *is* under
his feet; nor by Jerusalem, because it is the city of the great
36 King; nor *yet* by thy head shalt thou swear, because thou canst
37 not make in it one single lock black or white. But your word
shall be Yea, yea, and Nay, nay; now whatsoever is more than
these is from the Evil One.¶ ¶*A*

---

and the judge deliver thee up to the officer] *om. S* 27 to them of old time] *om. S* E^{66} 28 'whosoever looketh and lusteth hath committed adultery' E^{66} 29 *it*] it *S* 30.] *om. S* 31 dismisseth] leaveth *S* 32 taketh up] taketh *S* 33 Again] *om. S* to them of old time] *om. S* thy oath] an oath *S* 34 Ye your own selves] *see* Jn ix 34 by the heavens] *pr.* shalt thou swear *A* 35 by the earth] + shalt thou swear *A* that *is*] *om. S* by Jerusalem] + shalt thou swear *A* city] town A^b single] *om.* A^a 37 now] *om. S A*

38 ܫܡܥܬܘܢ ܕܐܬܐܡܪ ܕܥܝܢܐ ܚܠܦ ܥܝܢܐ. ܘܫܢܐ ܚܠܦ ܫܢܐ. C S
39 ܐܢܐ ܕܝܢ ܐܡܪ ܐܢܐ ܠܟܘܢ ܕܠܐ ܬܩܘܡܘܢ ܠܘܩܒܠ ܒܝܫܐ.
ܐܠܐ §ܡܢ ܕܡܚܐ ܠܟ ܥܠ ܦܟܟ ܗܦܘܟ ܠܗ ܐܚܪܢܐ. 40 ܘܡܢ §A 180
ܕܨܒܐ ܕܢܕܘܢ ܥܡܟ ܘܢܫܩܘܠ ܟܘܬܝܢܟ. *ܫܒܘܩ ܠܗ ܫܡܠ ܐܦ col 2
ܡܪܛܘܛܟ. 41 ܘܡܢ ܕܐܡܪ ܠܟ ܕܬܐܙܠ ܥܡܗ ܡܝܠ· ܙܠ ܥܡܗ
ܬܪܝܢ ܐܚܪܢܝܢ¶. 42 ܘܡܢ ܕܫܐܠ ܠܟ ܗܒ ܠܗ. ܘܡܢ ܕܨܒܐ ܕܢܐܙܦ ¶A
ܡܢܟ ܠܐ ܬܟܠܝܘܗܝ. 43 ܫܡܥܬܘܢ ܕܐܬܐܡܪ ܠܩܕܡܝܐ. ܕܪܚܡ
ܠܪܚܡܟ ܘܣܢܝ ܠܒܥܠܕܒܒܟ. 44 ܐܢܐ ܕܝܢ ܐܡܪ ܐܢܐ ܠܟܘܢ
§ܕܐܚܒܘ ܠܒܥܠܕܒܒܝܟܘܢ܆ ܘܨܠܘ ܥܠ ܐܝܠܝܢ ܕܪܕܦܝܢ ܠܟܘܢ܆¶ §¶A 34, 35
45 ܐܝܟܢܐ ܕܬܗܘܘܢ ܒ̈ܢܘܗܝ ܕܐܒܘܟܘܢ ܕܒܫܡܝܐ. ܗܘ
ܕܡܕܢܚ ܫܡܫܗ ܥܠ ܛܒܐ ܘܥܠ ܒܝܫܐ. ܘܡܚܬ ܡܛܪܗ ܥܠ
ܟܐܢܐ ܘܥܠ ܥܘܠܐ. §46 ܐܢ ܓܝܪ ܡܚܒܝܢ ܐܢܬܘܢ ܠܐܝܠܝܢ §A 35
ܕܡܚܒܝܢ ܠܟܘܢ ܡܢܘ ܐܓܪܟܘܢ܆ ܗܟܢܐ ܓܝܪ ܐܦ ܡ̈ܟܣܐ
ܥܒܕܝܢ¶. 47 ܘܐܢ ܫܐܠܝܢ *ܐܢܬܘܢ ܒܫܠܡܐ ܕܐ̈ܚܝܟܘܢ ܒܠܚܘܕ. ¶A fol 8 r
ܡܢܐ ܗܝ ܝܬܝܪܘܬܟܘܢ. ܠܐ ܗܐ ܐܦ ܚ̈ܢܦܐ ܗܟܢܐ ܥܒܕܝܢ.܀
48 ܗܘܘ ܗܟܝܠ ܓܡܝܪܐ. ܐܝܟܢܐ ܕܐܒܘܟܘܢ ܕܒܫܡܝܐ ܓܡܝܪ
ܗܘ. 1 ܐܙܕܗܪܘ ܕܠܐ ܬܥܒܕܘܢ ܡܗܝܡܢܘܬܟܘܢ ܠܥܝܢ ܒ̈ܢܝ

---

39 ܡܪܒ] *C (sic), see Introd.* vol. ii   40 ܕܢܕܘܢ ܥܡܟ] *om. A*   ܘܢܫܩܘܠ] ܘܢܣܒ *S;* ܕܢܣܒ *A* (+ ܡܢܟ *A*ᵃ)   ܫܒܘܩ] ܗܒ *A*   ܫܡܠ] *om. S A*   41.] *between vv.* 39 *and* 40 *in A*   ܘܡܢ] ܡܢ *S*   ܕܐܡܪ] ܕܡܫܚܪ *S A*   ܙܠ] ܐܙܠ *S*   ܬܪܝܢ] *pr.* ܬܘܒ *S*   42 ܠܕܫܐܠ *S*   43. § *in S*   ܠܩܕܡܝܐ] *om. S*   ܕܪܚܡ....ܘܣܢܝ] ܕܬܪܚܡ....ܘܬܣܢܐ *S*   44 ܕܐܚܒܘ] ܕܪ̈ܚܡܘ *S A*   ܠܒܥܠܕܒܒܝܟܘܢ] + ܘܒܪܟܘ ܠܡܢ ܕܠܐܛ ܠܟܘܢ *A*   ܕܪܕܦܝܢ] ܘܪܕܦܝܢ ܒܟܘܢ܆ ܕܡܬܦܠܨܝܢ *A*ᵇ (ܕܡܬܦܠܨܝܢ ܠܟܘܢ *A*ᵃ, *cf* syr. vg 2/2 ܕܕܒܪܝܢ ܠܟܘܢ ܒܩܛܝܪܐ = τῶν ἐπηρεαζόντων ὑμᾶς): Lk vi 27 *is different in* syr. vt   46 ܓܝܪ] *om. A*   ܡܚܒܝܢ ܐܢܬܘܢ] ܬܚܒܘܢ *S A*   ܠܐܝܠܝܢ] ܐܝܠܝܢ *S;* ܠܗܠܝܢ *A*   ܕܡܚܒܝܢ *A*   ܡܢܘ ܐܓܪܟܘܢ] ܡܢܐ ܗܝ ܛܝܒܘܬܟܘܢ *A* (= Lk vi 32)   ܗܟܢܐ....ܥܒܕܝܢ] ܐܦ ܡ̈ܟܣܐ ܗܟܢܐ ܥܒܕܝܢ *S;* ܐܦ ܓܝܪ ܡܚܒ ܐܝܬ ܠܗܢ ܕܡܚܒ ܠܟ. ܐܦ ܚ̈ܢܦܐ ܗܟܢܐ ܥܒܕܝܢ. ܠܗܢ ܕܡܚܒ ܠܗܘܢ ܪ̈ܚܡܝܢ ܠܗ. *A*   47.] *om. S*   48. *No* § *in S*   ܗܟܝܠ] + ܐܢܬܘܢ *S*   ܐܝܟܢܐ] *added between the lines by S**   1 ܐܙܕܗܪܘ ܕܠܐ] ܘܠܐ *S*   ܡܗܝܡܢܘܬܟܘܢ] ܙܕܩܘܬܟܘܢ *S*

38 "Ye have heard that it hath been said 'Eye for eye, and tooth *C S*
39 for tooth.' But I say to you Ye shall not stand up against the
Evil One, but §he that smiteth thee on thy cheek, offer him the §*A* 180
40 other; and he that willeth to go to law with thee and take away
41 thy coat, let him take away thy cloak also; and he that saith to thee
that thou shouldest go with him a mile, go with him two others.¶ ¶*A*
42 And he that asketh thee—give to him, and he that would borrow
43 from thee—forbid him not. Ye have heard that it hath been said
to them of old time 'Love thy neighbour and hate thine enemy.'
44 But I say to you §Be loving to your enemies, and pray for those §*A* 34, 35
45 that persecute you,¶ so that ye may become the sons of your Father ¶*A*
in heaven, he that maketh his sun to rise on the good and on the
evil, and sendeth down his rain on the upright and on the wicked.
46 §For if ye be loving to them that are loving to you what is your §*A* 35
47 reward? For so even the toll-gatherers do.¶ And if ye greet your ¶*A*
brethren only, what is your kindness? Nay, do not the pagans
do so?

48 "Become therefore perfect, as your Father in heaven is perfect.
vi 1 Beware that ye do not your gift before men, so that ye may be

---

39 ...'he that smiteth thy cheek, offer to him the other side also' $E^{65, 69, 70, 133}$ **40** go to law with thee and] *om. A* take away 1°] take *S A* (+ from thee A^a) let him take away] let him *have S*; give him *A* **41** and] *om. S* saith to thee] compelleth thee *S A* two] *pr.* again *S* **43** to them of old time] *om. S* Thou shalt love...and shalt hate *S* **44** Be loving to] Love *S A* your enemies] + bless whosoever curseth you *A* persecute] *pr.* use violence to you and A^b (accuse you and A^a) **46** For] *om. A* shall be loving *S A* them that are] him that is *A* reward] kindness *A* (= Lk vi 32) For...do] Even toll-gatherers so do *S*; for if thou art loving to him that is loving to thee, even the pagans so do—him that is loving to them they love *A* **47**.] *om. S* **48** Become] + ye *S* vi **1** *is quoted by* Ephr^{arm} *on* 1 Cor xiii 3 Beware that ye do not] And do not *S*; 'do not' *Ephr* gift] 'gifts' *Ephr*; righteousness *S*

C (S) ܣ̈ܓܝܐܐ. ܐܡܝܢܐ ܕܬܬܚܙܘܢ ܠܗܘܢ. ܕܠܐ ܐܓܪܐ ܠܝܬ ܠܟܘܢ
ܠܘܬ ܐܒܘܟܘܢ ܕܒܫܡܝܐ. [2]ܐܡܬܝ، ܗܟܝܠ ܕܥܒܕ ܐܢܬ ܙܕܩܬܐ.
ܠܐ ܬܩܪܐ ܩܪܢܐ ܩܕܡܝܟ. ܐܝܟܢܐ ܕܥܒܕܝܢ ܢܣ̈ܒܝ ܒ̈ܐܦܐ
ܒ̈ܟܢܘܫܬܐ ܘܒ̈ܫܘܩܐ. ܐܝܟܢܐ ܕܢܫܬܒܚܘܢ ܡܢ ܒ̈ܢܝ ܐܢܫܐ.
ܐܡܝܢ ܐܡܪܢܐ ܠܟܘܢ ܕܩܒܠܘ ܐܓܪܗܘܢ܂ [3]ܐܢܬ ܕܝܢ ܡܐ ܕܥܒܕ
col 2 ܐܢܬ ܙܕܩܬܐ. ܠܐ ܬܕܥ. *ܣܡܠܟ ܡܢܐ ܥܒܕܐ ܝܡܝܢܟ. [4]ܕܬܗܘܐ
ܙܕܩܬܟ ܒܟܣܝܐ. ܘܐܒܘܟ ܕܚܙܐ ܒܟܣܝܐ ܢܦܪܥܟ. [5]ܘܡܐ
ܕܡܨܠܐ ܐܢܬ. ܠܐ ܬܗܘܐ ܐܝܟ ܗܢܘܢ ܢܣ̈ܒܝ ܒ̈ܐܦܐ.
ܕܪ̈ܚܡܝܢ ܕܢܩܘܡܘܢ ܒ̈ܟܢܘܫܬܐ ܘܒܙܘ̈ܝܬܐ ܕܫ̈ܘܩܐ ܠܡܨܠܝܘ.
ܕܢܬܚܙܘܢ ܠܒ̈ܢܝ ܐܢܫܐ. ܐܡܝܢܐ ܠܟܘܢ ܕܩܒܠܘ ܐܓܪܗܘܢ܂
§A67, 68 [6]ܐܢܬ ܕܝܢ ܡܐ ܕܡܨܠܐ ܐܢܬ܂ §ܥܘܠ ܠܟ ܠܬܘܢܐ. ܘܐܚܘܕ܂
ܬܪܥܐ ܒܐ̈ܦܝܟ. ܘܨܠܐ ܠܐܒܘܟ ܒܟܣܝܐ. ܘܐܒܘܟ ܕܚܙܐ
¶A ܒܟܣܝܐ ܢܦܪܥܟ¶ ܀
[7]ܘܐܡܬܝ، ܕܡܨܠܝܢ ܐܢܬܘܢ܂ ܠܐ ܗܘܝܬܘܢ ܡܦܩܩܝܢ ܐܝܟ ܢܣ̈ܒܝ
ܒ̈ܐܦܐ. ܕܣܒܪܝܢ ܓܝܪ ܕܒܡܡܠܠܐ ܣܓܝܐܐ ܡܫܬܡܥܝܢ. [8]ܠܐ
§A68 fol 8 v ܗܟܝܠ ܬܕܡܘܢ ܠܗܘܢ܂ §ܝܕܥ ܗܘ ܓܝܪ ܐܒܘܟܘܢ܂ *ܡܢܐ
¶A §Thos ܡܬܒܥܐ ܠܟܘܢ ܥܕܠܐ ܬܫܐܠܘܢܝܗܝ.¶ [9]ܗܟܢܐ ܕܝܢ ܗܘܝܬܘܢ
313 ¶S ܡܨܠܝܢ. §ܐܒܘܢ ܕܒܫܡܝܐ ܢܬܩܕܫ ܫܡܟ. [10]ܬܐܬܐ¶ ܡܠܟܘܬܟ.

ܐܡܝܢܐ] ܐܡܝܢ S   2 ܐܡܬܝ] ܡܐ S   ܗܟܝܠ] om. S   ܐܝܟܢܐ] ܐܝܟ S   ܢܣܒܝܢ S (sic): cf Mt xxiii 13   ܘܒ̈ܫܘܩܐ] ܘܒܫܘ̈ܩܐ S: cf Lk xiv 21   ܐܡܝܢܐ] om. S   3 ܣܡܠܟ ܠܐ ܬܕܥ S   4 ܘܐܒܘܟ] ܘܐܒܐ S   ܢܦܪܥܟ] + ܒܓܠܝܐ S   5.] om. S   6 ܐܡܬܝ] ܡܐ S   ܠܟ] om. A   ܒܐ̈ܦܝܟ] om. S; cf ܘܐܚܘܕ ܬܪܥܐ....ܐܠܐ ܐܦ ܒܦܘܡܟ A 68[6]   ܘܐܒܐ ܕܒܟܣܝܐ ܚܙܐ A   ܢܦܪܥܟ] pr. ܗܘ S   7 ܘܐܡܬܝ] ܘܡܐ S   ܗܘܝܬܘܢ ܡܦܩܩܝܢ] ܬܗܘܘܢ ܐܡܪܝܢ ܒܛܠܬܐ. S (= βατταλογήσητε)   ܐܝܟ ܢܣ̈ܒܝ ܒ̈ܐܦܐ] ܐܝܟܢܐ ܕܚ̈ܢܦܐ S   ܓܝܪ] om. S   ܣܓܝܐܐ] pr. ܗܘ S   8 ܬܬܕܡܘܢ S   ܝܕܥ ܗܘ ܐܒܘܟܘܢ A   ܡܢܐ....ܬܫܐܠܘܢܝܗܝ] ܥܕ ܐܢܬܘܢ ܠܐ ܬܫܐܠܘܢܝܗܝ ܡܢܐ ܡܬܒܥܐ ܠܟܘܢ S A (ܐܢܬܘܢ om. A)   9 ܗܟܢܐ ܕܝܢ] ܗܟܢܐ ܗܟܝܠ ܐܢܬܘܢ S   ܐܒܘܢ] § in S   10 ܘܬܐܬܐ S

seen by them, else ye have no reward with your Father in heaven. *C* (*S*)
2 Whensoever therefore thou doest alms, do not blow a trumpet before
thee, as the respecters of persons do in the synagogues and in the
streets, so that they may be praised by men; amen, I say to you
3 that they have received their reward. But thou, what *time* thou
doest alms, let not thy left-hand know what thy right-hand doeth,
4 that thy alms may be in secret, and thy Father that seeth in secret
5 will repay thee. And what *time* thou prayest, be not as those
respecters of persons, that love to stand in the synagogues and
in the corners of the streets to pray, that they may be seen by
6 men: I say to you that they have received their reward. But thou,
whensoever thou prayest, §enter thou into the inner chamber, and §*A* 67, 68
shut the door in thy face and pray to thy Father in secret, and
thy Father that seeth in secret will repay thee.¶ ¶*A*

7 "And whensoever ye pray, do not be babbling as the respecters of
persons, for they hope that by much speaking they are heard.
8 Be not therefore like to them, for §your Father knoweth what is §*A* 68
9 required for you before ever ye ask it.¶ But thus be praying: ¶*A*
10 §Our Father in heaven, thy name be hallowed. Thy kingdom come.¶ §*Thos* 313 ¶*S*

---

else] *for this rendering of* ܕܠܐ *cf* Mt vi 24, ix 17, *and Introd.* vol. ii; 'but if not' *Ephr* 2 Whensoever therefore] What *time S* streets] lanes *S* (= ῥύμαις) 4 thy Father] the Father *S*: *cf* Mt x 32 *C*, xv 13 *S*, Lk ii 49 *C*, Jn vi 32 *C*, *and see Notes*, vol. ii repay thee] + in the open *S* 5.] *om. S* 6 whensoever] what *time S* in thy face] *om. S*; *cf* 'and what is the door...but thy mouth?' *A* 68 and the Father that seeth *what is* secret *A* will repay] *pr.* he *S* 7 whensoever] what *time S* babbling] saying idle *things S* (baṭṭâlâthâ, *to render* βαττταλογεῖν: *cf* syr[palest], *and* see Mt xxiii 5) as....persons] just as the pagans *S* for they] that *S* 8 knoweth before ever ye ask it what is required for you *S A* 9 But thus] Ye therefore thus *S* 10 And [thy kingdom] come *S* *Two leaves are here missing in S, to* Mt viii 3

C ܘܢܣܒܘܢ ܦܬ̈ܓܡܝܢ ܒܐܪܥܐ ܐܝܟ ܕܒܫܡܝܐ. [11]ܘܠܚܡܢ ܐܡܝܢܐ
§A37, 71 ܕܝܘܡܐ ܗܒ ܠܢ [§12]ܘܫܒܘܩ ܠܢ ܚܘ̈ܒܝܢ. ܐܝܟܢܐ ܕܐܦ ܐܢܚܢܢ
¶A ܫܒܩܢܢ ܠܚܝ̈ܒܝܢ.¶ [13]ܘܠܐ ܬܥܠܢ ܠܢܣܝܘܢܐ· ܐܠܐ ܦܨܢ ܡܢ
¶Thos ܒܝܫܐ.¶· ܡܛܠ ܕܕܝܠܟ ܗܝ ܡܠܟܘܬܐ ܘܬܫܒܘܚܬܐ· ܠܥܠܡ ܥܠܡܝܢ
ܐܡܝܢ ·ܘ·

[14]ܐܢ ܓܝܪ ܬܫܒܩܘܢ ܠܒ̈ܢܝ ܐ̈ܢܫܐ ܣ̈ܟܠܘܬܗܘܢ܆ ܐܦ ܐܒܘܟܘܢ
§A35 ܕܒܫܡܝܐ ܢܫܒܘܩ ܠܟܘܢ. [§15]ܐܢ ܕܝܢ ܐܢܬܘܢ ܠܐ ܬܫܒܩܘܢ
col 2 ܠܒ̈ܢܝ ܐ̈ܢܫܐ ܣ̈ܟܠܘܬܗܘܢ܆ ܘܐܦܠܐ ܐܒܐ ܢܫܒܘܩ *ܠܟܘܢ
¶A ܣ̈ܟܠܘܬܟܘܢ¶ ·ܘ·
§A51 [16]ܘܐܡܬܝ ܕܨܝܡܝܢ ܐܢܬܘܢ܆ ܠܐ ܬܗܘܘܢ ܐܝܟ §ܢܣ̈ܒܝ ܒܐ̈ܦܐ.
¶A ܕܡܚܒܠܝܢ ܦ̈ܪܨܘܦܝܗܘܢ܆¶ ܕܢܬܚܙܘܢ ܠܒ̈ܢܝ ܐ̈ܢܫܐ ܕܨܝܡܝܢ ܨܝܡܝܢ.
ܘܐܡܝܢ ܐܡܪܢܐ ܠܟܘܢ ܕܫܩܠܘ ܐܓܪܗܘܢ. [17]ܐܢܬ ܕܝܢ ܐܡܬܝ
ܕܨܐܡ ܐܢܬ. ܐܫܝܓ ܐ̈ܦܝܟ ܘܡܫܘܚ ܪܫܟ. [18]ܕܠܐ ܬܬܚܙܐ
ܠܒ̈ܢܝ ܐ̈ܢܫܐ ܕܨܐܡ ܐܢܬ. ܐܠܐ ܠܐܒܘܟ ܕܒܟܣܝܐ.
§A389 ܘܐܒܘܟ ܕܚܙܐ ܒܟܣܝܐ ܢܦܪܥܟ. [§19]ܠܐ ܬܣܝܡܘܢ ܠܟܘܢ ܣܝܡܬܐ
ܒܐܪܥܐ. ܐܝܟܐ ܕܣܣܐ ܡܚܒܠ· ܘܐܝܟܐ ܕܦܠܫܝܢ ܓܢ̈ܒܐ
ܘܓܢܒܝܢ. [20]ܐܠܐ ܣܝܡܘ ܠܟܘܢ ܣܝܡܬܐ ܒܫܡܝܐ. ܐܝܟܐ ܕܠܐ
ܣܣܐ ܡܚܒܠ· ܘܐܦܠܐ ܓܢ̈ܒܐ ܦܠܫܝܢ ܘܓܢܒܝܢ. [21]ܐܝܟܐ ܓܝܪ
fol 9r ¶A *ܕܣܝܡܬܟܘܢ ܬܡܢ ܢܗܘܐ ܐܦ ܠܒܟܘܢ.¶ [22]ܫܪܓܐ ܗܘ ܓܝܪ
ܕܦܓܪܐ ܥܝܢܐ ܗܝ.. ܐܢ ܥܝܢܟ ܬܗܘܐ ܦܫܝܛܐ. ܐܦ ܦܓܪܟ

ܦܬ̈ܓܡܝܢ. (*with a stop*) *Thos*[313]   11 ܘܗܒ ܠܢ ܠܚܡܐ ܐܡܝܢܐ ܕܝܘܡܐ *Thos*[313] *Jac. Serug* (*see Introd.* vol. ii)   12 ܚܘ̈ܒܝܢ] + ܘܚܛܗ̈ܝܢ *Thos*[313] *Jac*   ܐܝܟܢܐ ܕܐܦ] ܕܐܦ *A*[b] 71 *Thos*[313]; ܘܐܦ *A* 37, 71[a]   13 ܬܥܠܢ] ܬܥܠܝܢ *Jac*   *No doxology in Thos*[313]   15 ܕܝܢ] *om. A*   ܣ̈ܟܠܘܬܗܘܢ] + ܕܣ̈ܟܠܝܢ ܒܟܘܢ *A*   ܐܦ ܠܐ ܠܟܘܢ ܢܫܒܘܩ ܐܒܐ *A*   ܣ̈ܟܠܘܬܟܘܢ] *om. A*   19, 20 ܣܝܡܬܐ *A*[b]   19 ܐܝܟܐ...ܘܓܢܒܝܢ] ܐܝܟܐ ܕܦܠܫܝܢ ܓܢ̈ܒܐ ܘܓܢܒܝܢ. ܘܐܝܟܐ ܕܣܣܐ ܘܡܚܒܠ *A*   20 ܒܫܡܝܐ.] + ܣܝܡܬܐ ܕܠܐ ܚܣܝܪܐ *A* (*cf* Lk xii 33)   ܘܐܦܠܐ] ܘܠܐ *A*   ܦܠܫܝܢ ܘ] *om. A*   21 ܐܝܟܐ ܓܝܪ] ܘܐܝܟܐ *A*   ܬܡܢ ܢܗܘܐ ܐܦ ܠܒܟܘܢ *A*[b]

11 And thy wishes be *done* in earth as in heaven. And our continual *C*
12 bread of the day give us. §And forgive us our debts, so that we §*A* 37, 71
13 also may forgive our debtors.¶ And bring us not into temptation, ¶*A*
But deliver us from the Evil One.¶ Because thine is the kingdom ¶*Thos*
and the glory, For ever and ever Amen.

14 "For if ye forgive men their trespasses, your Father also in
15 heaven will forgive you; §but if ye yourselves forgive not men their §*A* 35
trespasses, neither will the Father forgive you your trespasses.¶ ¶*A*

16 "And whensoever ye fast, do not be as §the respecters of persons, §*A* 51
that make gloomy their faces,¶ that they may be seen by men that ¶*A*
they are indeed fasting—and amen, I say to you that they have
17 received their reward. But thou, whensoever thou dost fast, wash thy
18 face and anoint thy head, that thou be not seen by men that thou art
indeed fasting, but by thy Father that knoweth in secret, and the
19 Father that seeth in secret shall repay thee. §Lay not up for §*A* 389
yourselves treasure in the earth, where the moth falleth and
20 corrupteth, and where thieves break through and thieve. But lay
up for yourselves treasure in heaven, where no moth corrupteth,
21 nor thieves break through and thieve. For where your treasure
22 shall be, your heart shall be there also.¶ For the lamp of the ¶*A*
body is the eye: if thine eye be single, thy whole body also

'In earth' *separated by a stop from* 'thy wishes...' *Thos* **11** And give us the continual bread of the day *Thos Jac.Serug* (*see Introd.* vol. ii) **12** debts] + and our sins *Thos Jac* so] *om.* *A*[b]71 *Thos;* 'and we...will' *A* 37, 71[a] **13** bring us not] make us not enter *Jac* *No doxology in Thos* **15** but] *om. A* trespasses] + that they trespass against you *A* the Father *A* your trespasses] *om. A* **19, 20** treasures *A*[a] **19** where thieves break through and thieve, and where the moth falleth and corrupteth *A* **20** in the heavens] + a treasure which faileth not *A* break through and] *om. A* **21** For] And *A* there shall be your heart also *A*[b]

C ܟܠܗ ܢܗܘܐ ܢܗܝܪ. [23]ܐܢ ܕܝܢ ܥܝܢܟ ܬܗܘܐ ܒܝܫܬܐ. ܐܦ
ܦܓܪܟ ܟܠܗ ܚܫܘܟ ܗܘ. ܐܢ ܗܟܝܠ ܢܘܗܪܐ ܕܒܟ ܚܫܘܟ
ܗܘ· ܚܫܘܟܟ ܟܡܐ ܢܗܘܐ·:·
A181 [24]ܠܐ ܐܢܫ ܡܫܟܚ ܦܠܚ ܬܪ̈ܝܢ ܡܪ̈ܘܢ܆ ܕܐܠܐ ܠܚܕ ܢܣܢܐ ܘܠܐܚܪܢܐ
ܢܪܚܡ. ܐܘ ܠܚܕ ܢܝܩܪ ܘܠܐܚܪܢܐ ܢܫܘܛ. ܠܐ ܡܫܟܚܝܢ ܐܢܬܘܢ
ܠܐܠܗܐ ܠܡܦܠܚ ܘܠܡܡܘܢܐ. [25]ܡܛܠ ܗܢܐ ܐܡܪ ܐܢܐ ܠܟܘܢ.
ܕܠܐ ܬܬܝܨܦܘܢ ܠܢܦܫܟܘܢ ܡܢܐ ܬܐܟܠܘܢ܆ ܘܐܦܠܐ ܠܦܓܪ̈ܝܟܘܢ
col 2 ܡܢܐ *ܬܠܒܫܘܢ܆ ܢܦܫܐ ܓܝܪ ܝܬܝܪܐ ܗܝ ܡܢ ܬܘܪܣܝܬܐ· ܘܦܓܪܐ
Thos 194 ܡܢ ܠܒܘܫܐ· [26]ܚܙܘ ܒܦܪܚܬܐ ܕܫܡܝܐ. ܕܠܐ ܙܪܥܝܢ ܘܠܐ ܚܨܕܝܢ
ܘܠܐ ܟܢܫܝܢ. ܘܐܒܘܟܘܢ ܕܒܫܡܝܐ ܡܬܪܣܐ ܠܗܘܢ· ܠܐ
ܗܟܝܠ ܐܢܬܘܢ ܝܬܝܪ ܡܢܗܘܢ. [27]ܡܢܘ ܕܝܢ ܡܢܟܘܢ ܡܫܟܚ
ܠܡܘܣܦܘ ܥܠ ܩܘܡܬܗ ܐܡܬܐ ܚܕܐ. [28]ܘܥܠ ܠܒܘܫܐ ܝܨܦܝܢ
ܐܢܬܘܢ. ܚܙܘ ܠܫܘ̈ܫܢܐ ܕܕܒܪܐ ܐܝܟܢܐ ܡܬܪܒܝܢ. ܕܠܐ ܥܡܠܝܢ
ܘܠܐ ܥܙܠܝܢ. [29]ܘܐܡܪ ܐܢܐ ܠܟܘܢ ܕܐܦܠܐ ܫܠܝܡܘܢ ܒܟܠܗ
ܬܫܒܘܚܬܗ ܐܬܟܣܝ ܐܝܟ ܚܕܐ ܡܢܗܝܢ. [30]ܘܐܢ ܕܝܢ ܠܥܣܒܐ ܕܕܒܪܐ
ܕܝܘܡܢ ܐܝܬܘܗܝ. ܘܡܚܪ ܒܬܢܘܪܐ ܢܦܠ ܡܬܠܒܟ ܐܠܗܐ ܟܠܒܫ.
fol 9 v §¶ Thos 194 §ܒܟܡܐ ܗܟܝܠ *ܥܠܝܟܘܢ ܢܬܟܠ ܠܗ ܙܥܘܪ̈ܝ ܗܝܡܢܘܬܐ¶. [31]ܠܐ
ܗܟܝܠ ܬܬܝܨܦܘܢ ܘܬܐܡܪܘܢ܆ ܡܢܐ ܢܐܟܘܠ ܘܡܢܐ ܢܫܬܐ.
ܘܡܢܐ ܢܬܟܣܐ. [32]ܗܠܝܢ ܓܝܪ ܟܠܗܝܢ ܥܡ̈ܡܐ ܗܘ ܕܐܪܥܐ
ܒܥܝܢ ܠܗܝܢ. ܝܕܥ ܗܘ ܓܝܪ ܐܒܘܟܘܢ ܕܐܦ ܠܟܘܢ ܡܬܒܥܝܢ
ܗܠܝܢ. [33]ܐܢܬܘܢ ܕܝܢ ܒܥܘ ܠܘܩܕܡ ܡܠܟܘܬܗ ܕܐܠܗܐ ܘܙܕܝܩܘܬܗ.
§¶ Thos 194 ܘܗܠܝܢ ܟܠܗܝܢ ܢܬܬܘܣܦܢ ܠܟܘܢ. §[34]ܠܐ ܗܟܝܠ ܬܬܝܨܦܘܢ ܕܡܚܪ.
ܡܛܠ ܕܡܚܪ ܓܝܪ ܕܝܠܗ ܝܨܦ¶. ܣܦܩ ܠܗ ܠܝܘܡܐ ܒܝܫܬܗ.

---

24 ܠܐ ܓܝܪ ܡܫܟܚ ܒܪܢܫܐ ܦܠܚ ܬܪ̈ܝܢ ܡܪ̈ܘܢ A   26, 30 *Cf* Thos[194]: ܚܙܘ ܥܘܪ̈ܒܐ ܘܐܬܒܩܘ ܒܦܪܚܬܐ ܕܫܡܝܐ: ܕܠܐ ܙܪܥܝܢ ܘܠܐ ܚܨܕܝܢ: ܘܐܠܗܐ ܡܬܪܣܐ ܠܗܘܢ· [30]ܒܟܡܐ ܗܟܝܠ ܥܠܝܟܘܢ ܢܬܟܠ ܠܗ ܙܥܘܪ̈ܝ ܗܝܡܢܘܬܐ
(*The words overlined come from* Lk xii 24)

33 *Cf* A 105: ܒܥܘ ܡܠܟܘܬܗ ܘܙܕܝܩܘܬܗ. ܘܗܠܝܢ ܒܐܪܥܐ ܢܬܬܘܣܦܢ

34 ܗܟܝܠ] *om.* Thos[194]   ܕܡܚܪ ܓܝܪ] ܕܗܘ ܡܚܪ Thos[194]

23 will be light; but if thine eye be evil, thy whole body also is dark. *C*
If therefore the light in thee is dark, thy darkness—how great it
will be!
24 "No man can serve two lords; else the one he will hate and the *A* 181
other he will love, or the one he will endure and the other he will
25 despise: ye cannot serve God and mammon. Therefore I say to
you Be not anxious for your life what ye shall eat, nor for your
bodies wherewith ye shall be clothed; for the life is more than the
26 food, and the body than the clothing. Look at the birds of the *Thos* 194
heaven that they sow not nor reap nor store up, and your
Father in heaven nourisheth them; are ye not therefore more
27 than they? But which of you can add unto his stature one cubit,
28 that about clothing ye are anxious? See the lilies of the plain
29 how they grow, that they spin not nor toil—and amen, I say to
you that not even Solomon in all his glory was covered like them.
30 But if the grass of the field that to-day is, and to-morrow is plucked
up and falleth into the furnace, God doth clothe, §how much *more* §¶ *Thos* 194
31 therefore over you will he be careful, O lacking in faith?¶ Be not
therefore anxious and say 'What shall we eat and what shall we
32 drink, and wherewith shall we be covered?' For all these things
the peoples of the earth seek after, for your Father doth know
33 that for you also these things are required. But ye, seek ye first the
kingdom of God and his righteousness, and all these things shall be
34 added to you. §Be not therefore anxious for to-morrow, because to- §¶ *Thos* 194
morrow for its own is anxious.¶ Sufficient for the day is its evil.

---

24 'For no human being can serve two dominions' *A* else] *see* Mt vi 1 *and Introd.* vol. ii **26, 30** *Cf Thos*: Look at *the ravens and consider* the fowl of the heaven, that (they) neither sow nor reap, *and God* nourisheth them: [30]how much therefore... (*The italicised words come from* Lk xii 24) **33** *Cf A* 105: 'Let us seek his kingdom and his righteousness, that we may receive on earth the increase' **34** therefore] *om. Thos*

C [1]ܠܐ ܬܕܘܢܘܢ ܕܠܐ ܬܬܕܝܢܘܢ. §[2]ܒܗܘ ܓܝܪ ܕܝܢܐ ܕܕܐܢܝܢ ܐܢܬܘܢ
§¶A252 ܡܬܕܝܢܝܢ ܐܢܬܘܢ܆ ¶ ܘܒܟܝܠܬܐ ܕܟܝܠܝܢ ܐܢܬܘܢ ܡܬܟܝܠ ܠܟܘܢ܆
col 2 [3]ܡܢܐ ܕܝܢ ܓܠܐ ܕܒܥܝܢܗ *ܕܐܚܘܟ ܚܙܐ ܐܢܬ. ܘܩܪܝܬܐ ܕܐܝܬ
ܒܥܝܢܟ ܠܐ ܚܙܐ ܐܢܬ. [4]ܐܘ ܐܝܟܢܐ ܡܫܟܚ ܐܢܬ ܠܡܐܡܪ܆
ܠܐܚܘܟ. ܫܒܘܩ ܐܦܩ ܓܠܐ ܡܢ ܥܝܢܟ. ܘܗܐ ܒܥܝܢܟ ܕܝܠܟ
ܩܪܝܬܐ ܫܪܝܐ. [5]ܢܣܒ ܒܐܦܐ ܐܦܩ ܠܘܩܕܡ ܩܪܝܬܐ ܡܢ ܥܝܢܟ.
ܘܗܝܕܝܢ ܬܬܚܙܐ ܠܟ ܠܡܦܩܘ ܓܠܐ ܡܢ ܥܝܢܗ ܕܐܚܘܟ܀
[6]ܠܐ ܬܬܠܘܢ ܩܘܕܫܐ ܠܟܠܒ̈ܐ. ܘܠܐ ܬܪܡܘܢ ܡܪ̈ܓܢܝܬܐ
ܩܕܡ ܚܙܝܪ̈ܐ. ܕܠܐ ܢܕܘܫܘܢ ܐܢܝܢ ܒܪ̈ܓܠܝܗܘܢ. ܘܢܗܦܟܘܢ
§Thos223 ܢܒܙܥܘܢܟܘܢ. §[7]ܫܐܠܘ ܘܬܣܒܘܢ܆ ܘܒܥܘ ܘܬܫܟܚܘܢ܆ ܩܘܫܘ
cf A485 ¶Thos §A443 ܘܢܬܦܬܚ ܠܟܘܢ.¶ §[8]ܟܠ ܡܢ ܓܝܪ ܕܫܐܠ ܢܣܒ. ܘܡܢ ܕܒܥܐ
fol 10r ¶A ܡܫܟܚ. ܘܡܢ ܕܢܩܫ *ܡܬܦܬܚ ܠܗ.¶ [9]ܡܢܘ ܓܝܪ ܡܢܟܘܢ
ܕܢܫܐܠܝܘܗܝ ܒܪܗ ܠܚܡܐ. ܠܡܐ ܟܐܦܐ ܡܘܫܛ ܠܗ. [10]ܐܘ ܐܢ
ܢܘܢܐ ܢܫܐܠܝܘܗܝ. ܠܡܐ ܚܘܝܐ ܡܘܫܛ ܠܗ. [11]ܐܢ ܗܟܝܠ
ܐܢܬܘܢ ܕܒܝܫܐ ܐܢܬܘܢ܆ ܝܕܥܝܢ ܐܢܬܘܢ ܡܘܗܒܬܐ ܛܒ̈ܬܐ
ܠܡܬܠ ܠܒ̈ܢܝܟܘܢ܆ ܟܡܐ ܡܝܬܪܐܝܬ ܐܒܘܟܘܢ ܕܒܫܡܝܐ. ܢܬܠ
ܛܒ̈ܬܐ ܠܐܝܠܝܢ ܕܫܐܠܝܢ ܠܗ. [12]ܟܠܡܕܡ ܗܟܝܠ ܕܨܒܝܢ ܐܢܬܘܢ
ܕܢܥܒܕܘܢ ܠܟܘܢ ܒܢ̈ܝ ܐܢܫܐ. ܗܟܘܬܗܘܢ ܥܒܕܘ ܠܗܘܢ܆ ܗܢܘ
ܓܝܪ ܢܡܘܣܐ ܘܢܒ̈ܝܐ. [13]ܥܘܠܘ ܒܬܪܥܐ ܐܠܝܨܐ. ܡܛܠ ܕܦܬܝܐ
ܬܪܥܐ ܘܪܘܝܚܐ ܐܘܪܚܐ ܕܡܘܒܠܐ ܠܐܒܕܢܐ. ܘܣ̈ܓܝܐܐ ܐܢܘܢ
col 2 ܕܐܙܠܝܢ ܒܗ̇. [14]ܡܢܐ ܐܠܝܨ ܬܪܥܐ *ܘܐܠܝܨܐ ܐܘܪܚܐ ܕܡܘܒܠܐ
ܠܚܝ̈ܐ. ܘܙܥܘܪ̈ܝܢ ܐܢܘܢ ܐܝܠܝܢ ܕܡܫܟܚܝܢ ܠܗ̇܀

---

2 ܓܝܪ] *om. A*   ܡܬܕܝܢܝܢ ܐܢܬܘܢ] ܬܬܕܝܢܘܢ *A*   6. *Cf Habib* (ASD 82): ܡܬܒܥܐ ܠܝ. ܕܠܐ ܢܬܠ ܩܘܕܫܐ ܠܟܠܒ̈ܐ. ܘܠܐ ܢܪܡܐ ܡܪ̈ܓܢܝܬܐ ܩܕܡ ܚܙܝܪ̈ܐ
7 ܘܬܣܒܘܢ] ܘܢܬܝܗܒ ܠܟܘܢ *Thos*   ܘܒܥܘ] ܒܥܘ *Thos*
ܫܐܠܘ ܘܣܒܘ. ܘܒܥܘ ܘܬܫܟܚܘܢ *A* 485   8 ܓܝܪ] *om. A*   ܡܢ 2° *and* 3°] *om. A*   ܡܬܦܬܚ] ܦܬܝܚ *A*   14 *Cf* ܗܘܘ ܐܘܪܚܐ ܕܩܛܝܢܐ ܘܐܠܝܨܐ *A* 288, *and* ܢܬܠܘܢ ܩ̈ܕܫܐ ܠܐܒܘܢ. ܠܐܘܪܚܐ ܕܩܛܝܢܐ ܘܐܠܝܨܐ *A* 103; *but cf also* ܬܪܥܐ ܕܚܝ̈ܐ ܩܛܝܢܐ ܗܘ. ܘܐܘܪܚܐ ܕܫܪܪܐ ܐܠܝܨܐ ܗܝ *Addai* 9, *and* ܙܕܩ ܘܡܗܠܟܝܢ ܒܐܘܪܚܐ ܕܩܛܝܢܐ ܘܐܠܝܨܐ. ܘܥܐܠܝܢ ܒܬܪܥܐ ܐܠܝܨܐ ܕܡܠܟܘܬܐ *A* 179

vii 1, 2 Judge not, that ye be not judged. §For with what judgement C
ye judge ye are judged,¶ and with the measure that ye mete it §¶A252
3 is meted to you. Now what is the mote that in thy brother's eye
thou dost see, and the beam that is in thine eye thou dost not
4 examine? Or how canst thou say to thy brother, 'Let me put
forth the mote from thine eye,' for lo, in thine own eye a beam is
5 set? Thou respecter of persons! put forth first the beam from
thine eye, and then it will be approved for thee to put forth the
mote from thy brother's eye.

6 "Give not a holy *thing* to dogs, neither cast pearls before
swine, that they may not trample on them with their feet, and
7 return *and* rend you. §Ask, and ye shall receive; and seek, and §Thos223
8 ye shall find; knock, and it shall be opened to you.¶ §For *cf* A485 ¶Thos
whosoever asketh receiveth, and he that seeketh findeth, and he §A443
9 that knocketh—it is opened to him.¶ For which of you whose son ¶A
10 shall ask for bread, will he hand him a stone? Or if for a fish he
11 shall ask will he hand him a serpent? If therefore ye that are evil,
know how to give good gifts to your sons, how much rather your
Father in heaven *knoweth* how to give good things to those that
12 ask him. Everything therefore that ye would that men should do
to you, be ye doing to them; for this is the law and the prophets.
13 Enter by the strait gate, because wide is the gate and roomy the
way that leadeth to destruction, and many there be that go therein.
14 How strait the gate and narrow the way that leadeth unto life, and
few are they which find it!

---

2 For] *om. A* ye shall be judged *A* 6 *Cf Habib* (ASD 82): 'It is written for us that we should not give a holy *thing* to dogs, and not cast pearls before swine' 7 ye shall receive] it shall be given to you *Thos* and seek] seek *Thos* 'Ask and receive; and when ye shall seek ye shall find' *A*485 8 For] *om. A* he that 1° *and* 2°] who *A* it is opened] they open *A* 14 *Cf* 'He is the way that is narrow and strait' *A*288, *and* 'Let us prepare provender for our stopping-place, for the way that is narrow and strait' *A*103; *but cf also* 'The gate of life is narrow and the way of truth is strait' *Addai* 9, *and* 'They (the meek) journey and walk in the way that is narrow and strait, and enter by the strait gate of the kingdom' *A*179: *E*[263], *a quotation far from this context, has* 'strait is the gate'

C 15 ܛܪܘ ܢܦܫܟܘܢ ܡܢ ܢܒܝܐ ܕܫܘܩܪܐ. §ܕܐܬܝܢ ܠܘܬܟܘܢ ܒܠܒܘܫܐ

§¶ Thos 249 ܕܐܡܪ̈ܐ. ܘܡܢ ܠܓܘ ܕܐܒ̈ܐ ܐܢܘܢ ܚܛܘܦܐ.¶ 16 ܡܢ ܦܐܪ̈ܝܗܘܢ

§A 303 ܗܟܝܠ ܬܫܬܘܕܥܘܢ ܐܢܘܢ. §ܠܐ ܓܝܪ ܠܩܛܝܢ ܡܢ ܟܘܒ̈ܐ

§A 186 ܥܢܒ̈ܐ. ܐܦܠܐ ܬܐ̈ܢܐ ܡܢ ܕܪ̈ܕܪܐ. §17 ܟܠ ܐܝܠܢܐ ܛܒܐ ܦܐܪ̈ܐ

ܛܒ̈ܐ ܥܒܕ. ܘܐܝܠܢܐ ܒܝܫܐ ܦܐܪ̈ܐ ܒܝ̈ܫܐ ܥܒܕ. 18 ܠܐ ܡܫܟܚ

ܐܝܠܢܐ ܛܒܐ ܕܢܥܒܕ ܦܐܪ̈ܐ ܒܝ̈ܫܐ. ܘܐܦܠܐ ܐܝܠܢܐ ܒܝܫܐ

¶A ²/₂ ܕܢܥܒܕ ܦܐܪ̈ܐ ܛܒ̈ܐ.¶ 19 ܟܠ ܐܝܠܢܐ ܗܟܝܠ ܕܦܐܪ̈ܐ ܛܒ̈ܐ ܠܐ

ܥܒܕ. ܡܬܦܣܩ ܘܒܢܘܪܐ ܢܦܠ. 20 ܡܢ ܦܐܪ̈ܝܗܘܢ ܗܟܝܠ ܬܫܬܘܕܥܘܢ

ܐܢܘܢ ܀

fol 10 v *21 ܠܐ ܗܘܐ ܗܟܝܠ ܟܠ ܕܐܡܪ ܠܝ ܡܪܝ ܡܪܝ ܥܐܠ ܠܡܠܟܘܬܐ

ܕܫܡܝܐ. ܐܠܐ ܗܘ ܕܥܒܕ ܨܒܝܢܗ ܕܐܒܝ ܕܒܫܡܝܐ. ܗܘ ܢܥܘܠ

ܠܡܠܟܘܬ ܫܡܝܐ. 22 ܣܓܝܐܐ ܓܝܪ ܢܐܡܪܘܢ ܠܝ ܒܗܘ ܝܘܡܐ.

ܡܪܢ ܡܪܢ. ܠܐ ܒܫܡܟ ܐܟܠܢ ܘܐܫܬܝܢ. ܘܒܫܡܟ ܐܬܢܒܝܢ.

ܘܒܫܡܟ ܫܐ̈ܕܐ ܐܦܩܢ. ܘܒܫܡܟ ܚܝܠܐ ܣܓܝܐܐ ܥܒܕܢ܀

23 ܗܝܕܝܢ ܐܡܪ ܠܗܘܢ. ܕܠܐ ܡܢ ܡܬܘܡ ܝܕܥܬܟܘܢ܀ ܙܠܘ ܠܟܘܢ

ܡܢܝ ܥܒ̈ܕܝ ܥܘܠܐ ܀ ܀

24 ܟܠ ܐܢܫ ܕܫܡܥ ܡ̈ܠܝ ܗܠܝܢ ܘܥܒܕ ܠܗܝܢ. ܐܕܡܝܘܗܝ ܠܓܒܪܐ

ܚܟܝܡܐ. ܕܒܢܐ ܒܝܬܗ ܥܠ ܫܘܥܐ. 25 ܘܢܚܬ ܡܛܪܐ. ܘܐܬܘ

col 2 ܢܗܪ̈ܘܬܐ. ܘܢܫܒ ܪ̈ܘܚܐ ܘܐܬܛܪܝܘ ܒܗ ܒܒܝܬܐ ܘܠܐ *ܢܦܠ.

ܡܛܠ ܕܫ̈ܬܐܣܘܗܝ ܥܠ ܫܘܥܐ ܣܝܡܢ ܗܘܝ. 26 ܘܟܠ ܐܢܫ ܕܫܡܥ

ܡ̈ܠܝ ܗܠܝܢ ܘܠܐ ܥܒܕ ܠܗܝܢ. ܢܬܕܡܐ ܠܓܒܪܐ ܣܟܠܐ. ܕܒܢܐ

ܒܝܬܗ ܥܠ ܚܠܐ. 27 ܘܢܚܬ ܡܛܪܐ. ܘܐܬܘ ܢܗܪ̈ܘܬܐ. ܘܢܫܒ ܪ̈ܘܚܐ

ܘܐܬܛܪܝܘ ܒܗ ܒܒܝܬܐ ܗܘ ܘܢܦܠ. ܘܗܘܬ ܡܦܘܠܬܗ ܪܒܐ ܀

---

15 ܗܢܘܢ ܕܠܒܝܫܝܢ ܠܒܘܫܐ ܕܐܡܪ̈ܐ *Thos*   ܕܐܒ̈ܐ ܐܢܘܢ] ܐܝܬܝܗܘܢ ܕܐܒ̈ܐ *Thos*   16 ܓܝܪ] *om.* *A*   ܘܐܦܠܐ] ܘܠܐ *A*
17 ܟܠ] ܡܛܠ ܗ *A* 303; *om.* *A* 186   ܥܒܕ (*bis*)] ܝܗܒ (*bis*) *A* ²/₂
18 ܕܢܥܒܕ (*bis*)] ܠܡܥܒܕ (*bis*) *A* ²/₂   ܘܐܦܠܐ] ܘܠܐ *A* ²/₂
ܛܒܐ...ܒܝ̈ܫܐ...ܒܝܫܐ...ܛܒ̈ܐ] ܒܝܫܐ...ܛܒ̈ܐ...ܛܒܐ...ܒܝ̈ܫܐ *A* 186, *adding* (*from* Mt xii 33) ܡܛܠ ܕܡܢ ܦܐܪ̈ܘܗܝ ܗܘ ܡܬܝܕܥ ܐܝܠܢܐ. *For the rest of the quotation in* *A* ²/₂, *see on* Lk vi 45

15 “Keep yourselves from prophets of falsehood, §which come unto *C*
16 you in lambs' clothing, and within they are ravening wolves.¶ From §¶ *Thos* 249
their fruits therefore ye shall recognise them; §for they do not pluck §*A* 303
17 from thorns grapes, nor figs from briers. §Every good tree bringeth §*A* 186
18 forth good fruits, and the evil tree bringeth forth evil fruits. The
good tree cannot bring forth evil fruits, neither can the evil tree
19 bring forth good fruits;¶ every tree therefore that bringeth not forth ¶$A\,^{2}/_{2}$
20 good fruits is hewn down and falleth into the fire. From their
fruits therefore ye shall recognise them.

21 “Not every one therefore that shall say unto me ‘My Lord, my
Lord,’ entereth into the kingdom of heaven; but he which doeth the
will of my Father which *is* in heaven, he shall enter into the
22 kingdom of heaven. For many will say to me in that day, ‘Our
Lord, our Lord, in thy name have we not eaten and drunken, and
in thy name prophesied, and in thy name cast out devils, and in
23 thy name done many mighty works?’ Then I shall say to them
Never have I known you; go ye away from me, doers of wickedness.

24 “Every one that heareth these my words and doeth them, I will
25 liken him to a wise man, that built his house on the rock, and the
rain came down and the rivers came, and the winds blew and were
dashed against that same house and it fell not, because its foundations
26 on the rock were laid. And every one that heareth these my words
and doeth them not, shall be likened to a foolish man, that built
27 his house upon the sand, and the rain came down and the rivers
came, and the winds blew and were dashed against that same house
and it fell, and its fall was great.”

---

15 those which are clothed in lambs' clothing *Thos* (*not* E^{94}) **16** for] *om. A* **17** Every good tree] because the good tree *A* 303; the good tree *A* 186 **17** *and* **18** bring forth] *lit.* ‘make’ *C*; *lit.* ‘give’ *A* good...evil...evil...good] evil...good...good...evil *A* 186, *adding at the end of ver.* 18 (*from* Mt xii 33) ‘because from its fruits is the tree known.’ *For the rest of the quotation in* $A\,^{2}/_{2}$, *see on* Lk vi 45 *and cf* Diat^{ar} x 35—38
22 mighty works] *lit.* ‘powers’ (= δυνάμεις)

C (S) ²⁸ܘܟܕ ܫܠܡ ܝܫܘܥ ܡ̈ܠܘܗܝ ܗܠܝܢ. ܬܡܝܗܝܢ ܗܘܘ ܟܢ̈ܫܐ ܥܠ
ܝܘܠܦܢܗ. ²⁹ܕܐܝܟ ܡܫܠܛܐ ܡܠܠ ܗܘܐ ܠܗܘܢ. ܘܠܐ ܐܝܟ
ܣܦܪ̈ܝܗܘܢ ܘܦܪ̈ܝܫܐ. ¹ܘܟܕ ܢܚܬ ܡܢ ܛܘܪܐ. ܐܬܘ ܗܘܘ ܒܬܪܗ
ܟܢ̈ܫܐ ܣܓ̈ܝܐܐ. ²ܘܗܐ ܓܒܪܐ ܚܕ ܓܪܒܐ ܐܬܐ ܢܦܠ ܣܓܕ ܠܗ.
fol 11 r ܘܐܡܪ ܠܗ ܡܪܝ. ܐܢ ܨܒܐ ܐܢܬ ܡܫܟܚ. *ܐܢܬ ܠܡܕܟܝܘܬܝ.
§S ³ܘܦܫܛ §ܐܝܕܗ ܝܫܘܥ. ܘܩܪܒ ܠܗ. ܘܐܡܪ ܠܗ ܨܒܐ ܐܢܐ
ܐܬܕܟܐ. ܘܒܗ ܒܫܥܬܐ ܐܬܕܟܝ ܡܢܗ ܓܪܒܐ. ⁴ܘܐܡܪ ܠܗ
ܝܫܘܥ· ܕܠܡܐ ܠܐܢܫ ܐܡܪ ܐܢܬ. ܐܠܐ ܙܠ ܚܘܐ ܢܦܫܟ
ܠܟܗ̈ܢܐ. ܘܩܪܒ ܩܘܪܒܢܐ ܐܝܟܢܐ ܕܦܩܕ ܡܘܫܐ. ܕܬܗܘܐ ܠܗܘܢ
ܠܣܗܕܘܬܐ ܀

⁵ܟܕ ܥܠ ܕܝܢ ܠܟܦܪܢܚܘܡ. ܩܪܒ ܠܗ ܩܢܛܪܘܢܐ ܚܕ. ܘܒܥܐ
ܗܘܐ ܡܢܗ ܘܡܬܟܫܦ ܠܗ ⁶ܘܐܡܪ· ܒܪܝ, ܡܪܝ, ܘܐܪܡܝܐ ܒܒܝܬܐ
ܒܬܫܢܝܩܐ ܪܒܐ. ⁷ܐܡܪ ܠܗ ܝܫܘܥ ܐܢܐ ܐܬܐ ܘܐܣܝܘܗܝ.
⁸ܥܢܐ ܗܘ ܩܢܛܪܘܢܐ ܘܐܡܪ ܠܗ. ܡܪܝ, ܠܐ ܫܘܐ ܐܢܐ ܕܬܥܘܠ
col 2 §¶A 20 ܬܚܝܬ ܡܛܠܠܝ. *ܐܠܐ ܒܠܚܘܕ §ܐܡܪ ܒܡܠܬܐ ܘܢܬܐܣܐ ܛܠܝܝ¶.
⁹ܐܦ ܐܢܐ ܓܝܪ ܓܒܪܐ ܐܢܐ ܕܬܚܝܬ ܫܘܠܛܢܐ. ܘܐܝܬ ܠܝ
ܫܘܠܛܢܐ ܐܦ ܠܝ. ܘܐܣ̈ܛܪܛܝܘܛܐ ܐܝܬ ܬܚܝܬ ܐܝܕܝ. ܘܐܡܪ
ܐܢܐ ܠܗܢܐ ܕܙܠ ܘܐܙܠ· ܘܠܐܚܪܢܐ ܕܬܐ ܘܐܬܐ. ܘܠܥܒܕܝ
ܐܡܪ ܐܢܐ ܕܥܒܕ ܗܕܐ ܘܥܒܕ· ¹⁰ܟܕ ܫܡܥ ܕܝܢ ܝܫܘܥ ܐܬܕܡܪ.
ܘܐܡܪ ܠܐܝܠܝܢ ܕܐܬܝܢ ܒܬܪܗ. ܐܡܝܢ ܐܡܪ ܐܢܐ ܠܟܘܢ. ܕܐܦܠܐ

---

2 ܓܪܒܐ] *C**, *now washed out* 3 ܝܫܘܥ] ܡܪܢ *S* 4 ܐܡܪ ܠܗ ܡܪܢ *S*
ܙܠ] ܐܙܠ *S* ܐܝܟܢܐ] ܐܝܟ *S* 5 ܕܝܢ ܥܠ ܠܟܦܪܢܚܘܡ] *om. S*
ܩܢܛܪܘܢܐ ܚܕ] ܟܠܝܪܟܐ *S* (*so also Eus. Theoph*syr iv 2, *and see Introd.* vol. ii); ܚܕ ܡܠܟܐ *A* 20 (=Joh iv 46) ܘܡܬܟܫܦ ܠܗ] *om. S* 6 ܘܐܪܡܐ *S*
7 ܝܫܘܥ] *om. S* 8 ܩܢܛܪܘܢܐ] ܟܠܝܐܪܟܐ *S* (*sic*) ܒܠܚܘܕ] *om. S*
ܛܠܝܝ] + ܘܐܬܐܡܪ ܡܪܢ ܒܡܗܝܡܢܘܬܗ *A* 9 ܕܬܚܝܬ ܫܘܠܛܢܐ] *om. S*
ܘܐܝܬ] ܕܐܝܬ *S* ܐܦ ܠܝ] *om. S* ܘܐܣܛܪܛܝܘܛܐ *S* ܕܙܠ] ܕܐܙܠ *S*
ܕܬܐ] *pr.* ܐܡܪܢܐ *S* 10 ܝܫܘܥ] ܡܪܢ *S* ܠܐܝܠܝܢ] ܠܐܢܫܐ *S*
ܕܐܦܠܐ ܐܝܟ ܗܕܐ ܗܝܡܢܘܬܐ ܐܫܟܚܬ ܒܟܠ ܐܝܣܪܝܠ *S*

28 And when Jesus finished these his words, the multitudes were *C* (*S*)
29 astonished at his teaching, for as one authorised he was teaching
viii 1 them, and not as their scribes and the Pharisees. And when he
came down from the hill, great multitudes were coming after him.
2 And lo, a certain man, a leper, came *and* fell down *and* worshipped
him, and said to him "My Lord, if thou wilt thou canst cleanse
3 me." And Jesus stretched out §his hand and touched him, and said §*S*
to him: "I will, be thou cleansed." And in the same hour his leprosy
4 was cleansed from him. And Jesus said to him: "*Beware* lest
thou say *it* to any man, but go shew thyself to the priests, and
offer an offering as Moses commanded, that it should be for them
for witness."

5 After these things, when he entered Kapharnahum, there drew near
to him a certain centurion, and was beseeching him and entreating
6 him and saying: "My slave is paralysed and lying down in the
7 house in great torment." Jesus saith to him "I will come and
8 heal him." The centurion answered and said to him: "My Lord, I
am not worthy that thou shouldest enter under my dwelling, but only
9 §say with a word and my lad will be healed.¶ For I also am a man §¶*A* 20
under authority, and I have authority myself also, and there are
soldiers under my hand; and I say to this one 'Go,' and he goeth,
and to another 'Come,' and he cometh, and to my slave I say 'Do
10 so much,' and he doeth *it*." Now when Jesus heard he wondered,
and said to the folk coming after him: "Amen, I say to you, that

---

3 Jesus] our Lord *S* 4 And Jesus] Our Lord *S* 5 when he entered Kapharnahum] *om. S* a certain centurion] a chiliarch *S*, *cf Eus. Theoph*^{syr} iv 2 ('a Chiliarch...for to this dignity among the Romans he had attained'); a king's slave *A* 20 (= βασιλικός) and entreating him] *om. S* 7 Jesus] He *S* 8 centurion] chiliarch *S* only] *om. S* healed] + And our Lord wondered at his faith *A* 9 a man...myself also] a man that hath authority *S* Come] *pr.* I say: *S* 10 Jesus] our Lord *S* the folk] those *S* not even *aught* like this faith have I found in the House of Israel *S*; 'I have not found so great faith even in any one in Israel' E^{74}

C S ܒܐܢܫ ܒܝܬ ܐܝܣܪܝܠ ܐܫܟܚܬ ܐܝܟ ܗܕܐ ܗܝܡܢܘܬܐ. [11]ܐܡܪ
ܐܢܐ ܠܟܘܢ ܕܝܢ. ܕܣ̈ܓܝܐܐ ܢܐܬܘܢ ܡܢ ܡܕܢܚܐ ܘܡܢ ܡܥܪܒܐ.
ܘܢܣܬܡܟܘܢ ܥܡ ܐܒܪܗܡ ܘܐܝܣܚܩ ܘܝܥܩܘܒ ܒܡܠܟܘܬܐ
fol 11 v ܕܫܡܝܐ. [12]ܘܒ̈ܢܝܗ ܕܡܠܟܘܬܐ *ܢܦܩܘܢ ܠܚܫܘܟܐ ܒܪܝܐ. ܬܡܢ
ܢܗܘܐ ܒܟܝܐ ܘܚܘܪܩ ܫ̈ܢܐ. [13]ܗܝܕܝܢ ܐܡܪ ܝܫܘܥ ܠܩܢܛܪܘܢܐ ܗܘ·
ܙܠ ܐܝܟܢܐ ܕܗܝܡܢܬ ܢܗܘܐ ܠܟ. ܘܒܗ̇ ܒܫܥܬܐ ܐܬܐܣܝ ܛܠܝܗ·.·
[14]ܘܐܬܐ ܝܫܘܥ ܠܒܝܬܗ ܕܫܡܥܘܢ ܟܐܦܐ. ܘܚܙܐ ܠܚܡܬܗ
ܕܪ̈ܡܝܐ ܘܐܚܝܕܐ ܠܗ̇ ܐܫܬܐ. [15]ܘܩܪܒ ܠܐܝܕܗ̇. ܘܒܗ̇ ܒܫܥܬܐ
ܫܒܩܬܗ̇ ܐܫܬܐ. ܘܩܡܬ ܘܡܫܡܫܐ ܗܘܬ ܠܗܘܢ܀ ○○ ○○ ○○
[16]ܡܥܪ̈ܒ ܫܡܫܐ ܕܝܢ. ܩܪܒܘ ܩܕܡܘܗܝ، ܟܠܗܘܢ ܐܝܠܝܢ ܕܐܝܬ
ܗܘܐ ܠܗܘܢ ܫܐ̈ܕܐ. ܘܐܣܝ ܐܢܘܢ ܒܡܠܬܗ. ܘܐܝܠܝܢ ܕܒܝܫ
ܒܝܫ ܒܟܘܪ̈ܗܢܝܢ ܗܘܘ ܐܣܝ ܐܢܘܢ. [17]ܕܢܫܬܠܡ ܡܕܡ ܕܐܬܐܡܪ
col 2 ܒܦܘܡ *ܐܫܥܝܐ ܢܒܝܐ ܕܐܡܪ ܗܘܐ· ܕܗܘ ܢܣܒ ܟܐ̈ܒܝܢ.
ܘܢܫܩܘܠ ܟܘܪ̈ܗܢܝܢ·.·
[18]ܟܕ ܚܙܐ ܕܝܢ ܝܫܘܥ ܠܟܢܫܐ ܣܓܝܐܐ ܕܚܕܪܝܢ ܠܗ· ܦܩܕ
ܠܬܠܡ̈ܝܕܘܗܝ، ܕܢܐܙܠܘܢ ܠܥܒܪܐ ܕܠܗܠ· [19]ܘܩܪܒ ܣܦܪܐ ܚܕ
ܘܐܡܪ ܠܗ. ܡܠܦܢܐ ܐܬܐ ܒܬܪܟ ܠܐܬܪ ܕܐܙܠ ܐܢܬ. [20]ܐܡܪ
ܠܗ ܝܫܘܥ· ܠܬܥ̈ܠܐ ܢܩ̈ܒܐ ܐܝܬ ܠܗܘܢ؛ ܘܠܦܪ̈ܚܬܐ ܕܫܡܝܐ
§¶A 118 ܡܛܠܠܐ. ܠܒܪܗ ܕܝܢ ܕܐܢܫܐ §ܠܝܬ ܠܗ ܐܬܪ ܕܢܣܡܘܟ ܪܫܗ¶.
[21]ܐܚܪܢܐ ܕܝܢ ܡܢ ܬܠܡ̈ܝܕܘܗܝ، ܐܡܪ ܠܗ. ܡܪܝ، ܐܦܣ ܠܝ ܠܘܩܕܡ
§¶'Jul.' 27 ܐܙܠ ܐܩܒܘܪ ܠܐܒܝ ܘܐܬܐ. [22]ܐܡܪ ܠܗ ܝܫܘܥ. §ܫܒܘܩ ܡ̈ܝܬܐ
¶C ܩܒܪܝܢ ܡ̈ܝܬܝܗܘܢ¶ ܘܐܢܬ ܬܐ ܒܬܪܝ܀¶

---

11 ܕܝܢ] *om. S* 11, 12 ܥܡ ܐܒܪܗܡ....ܕܡܠܟܘܬܐ] *C over erasure, two extra lines being squeezed in at the foot of the page* ܘܚܘܪܩ *S (sic)* 13 ܝܫܘܥ] ܡܪܢ *S* ܠܩܢܛܪܘܢܐ] ܠܟܠܝܪܟܐ *S* ܐܬܐܣܝ] ܐܬܚܠܡ *S* 14 ܝܫܘܥ] ܡܪܢ *S* 16 ܩܕܡܘܗܝ] ܠܗ *S* ܒܡܠܬܐ *S* ܗܘܘ] *om. S* 17 ܒܦܘܡ ܐܫܥܝܐ ܢܒܝܐ] ܒܐܫܥܝܐ *S* ܟܐ̈ܒܝܢ] *C on erasure;* ܡܟ̈ܐܒܝܢ *S* ܘܢܫܩܘܠ] + ܐ· *C (to fill up the line): see Introd.* vol. ii 18 ܝܫܘܥ] ܡܪܢ *S* ܟܢܫܐ *S* ܠܬܠܡ̈ܝܕܘܗܝ] *om. S* ܕܢܐܙܠܘܢ] + ܠܗܘܢ *S* 19 ܡܠܦܢܐ] ܪܒܝ *S* 20 ܐܡܪ ܠܗ ܝܫܘܥ] ܐܡܪ ܡܪܢ *S* ܠܒܪܗ ܕܝܢ] ܘܠܒܪܗ *S* ܠܝܬ ܗܘܐ *A* ܪܫܗ *S* 21 ܠܗ. ܡܪܝ] *S illegible* 22 ܝܫܘܥ] *om. S* ܫܒܘܩܘ ܬܢ ܡ̈ܝܬܐ *Jul*

not even in any one of the House of Israel have I found *aught* *C S*
11 like this faith. But I say to you, that many shall come from
the East and from the West, and shall sit down *to meat* with
12 Abraham and Isaac and Jacob in the kingdom of heaven, and the
sons of the kingdom shall go forth into the outer darkness; there
13 shall be the weeping and the gnashing of teeth!" Then said Jesus
to that centurion: "Go, as thou hast believed it shall be unto thee;"
and in the same hour his lad was healed.

14 And Jesus came to the house of Simon Kepha, and he saw
15 his mother-in-law lying down and a fever holding her. And he
touched her hand, and in the same hour the fever left her, and she
arose and was serving them.

16 Now at sunset they brought near before him all those that had
devils and he cast them out by his word, and those that were ill
17 he healed, that that might be fulfilled which was said by the mouth
of Isaiah the prophet, who had said "He shall take our pains and
shall bear our infirmities."

18 Now when Jesus saw the great multitude that was round him,
he commanded his disciples that they should go away to the other
19 side yonder. And a certain scribe drew near and said to him:
20 "Teacher, I will come after thee wherever thou goest." Jesus saith
to him: "The foxes—they have dens, and the birds of the heaven a
dwelling; but the Son of Man, §he hath not where to rest his head."¶ §¶*A* 118
21 Now another of the disciples said to him: "My Lord, permit me first
22 to go *and* bury my father and I will come." Jesus saith to him:
"§Leave the dead to bury their dead¶ and thou come after me."¶ §¶'*Jul.*' 27 ¶*C*

---

11 But] *om. S* 12. 'They shall go forth into outer darkness' *E*[74]
13 Jesus] our Lord *S* centurion] chiliarch *S* healed] made whole *S*
14 Jesus] our Lord *S* 16 before him] to him *S* his word] a word *S*
17 the mouth of...prophet] Isaiah *S* pains] *C on erasure*; sicknesses *S*
18 Jesus] our Lord *S* his disciples] *om. S* 19 Teacher] Rabbi *S*
20 Jesus] Our Lord *S* to him] *om. S* but] and *S* hath] had *A*
(*to suit the context*) 21 to him: My Lord] *S illegible* 22 Jesus] He *S*
'Leave the sons of the dead to bury their dead' *Jul*

23|ܘܥܠܘ ܕܝܢ ܠܣܦܝܢܬܐ ܘܬܠܡܝܕܘܗܝ، ܐܬܝܢ ܗܘܘ ܒܬܪܗ S
24ܘܗܘܐ ܥܠܥܠܐ ܕܝܡܐ ܘܣܦܝܢܬܐ ܡܛܝܐ ܗܘܬ ܠܡܬܛܒܥܘ
ܒܓܠܠܐ. ܗܘ ܕܝܢ ܕܡܟ ܗܘܐ 25ܘܩܪܒܘ ܬܠܡܝܕܘܗܝ، ܘܐܥܝܪܘܗܝ،
ܘܐܡܪܝܢ ܠܗ ܡܪܢ ܐܝܢ ܡܚܠ ܕܗܐ ܐܒܕܝܢ ܐܚܢܢ 26ܐܡܪ
[ܠܗܘܢ ܚܣܝ̈ܪܝ، ܗܝܡܢܘܬܐ] ܠܡܢܐ ܕܚܠܬܝܢ ܐܢܬܘܢ ܗܝܕܝܢ
ܩܡ ܘܟܐܐ ܒܪܘܚܐ ܘܒܝܡܐ ܘܗܘܐ ܫܠܝܐ ܪܒܐ 27ܗܢܘܢ ܕܝܢ
ܐܚܝܕܐ ܬܡܝܗܝܢ ܗܘܘ ܘܐܡܪܝܢ ܡܢܘ ܗܢܐ ܕܝܡܐ ܘܪܘܚܐ
ܡܫܬܡܥܝܢ ܠܗ ܀

28ܘܟܕ ܐܬܐ ܠܐܬܪܐ ܕܓܕܪ̈ܝܐ ܦܓܥܘ ܒܗ ܬܪܝܢ ܓܒܪܝܢ ܕܐܝܬܝܗܘܢ
ܥܠܝܗܘܢ ܫܐܕܐ ܘܟܒܫܐ ܗܘܘ ܠܒܪ ܘܢܦܩܝܢ ܗܘܘ ܡܢ ܩܒܪܐ
ܕܠܐ ܐܢܫ ܡܫܟܚ ܗܘܐ. ܠܡܥܒܪ ܒܗ، ܐܘܪܚܐ 29ܘܩܥܘ ܒܩܠܐ
ܪܒܐ ܘܐܡܪܝܢ ܡܢܐ ܠܢ ܘܠܟ ܒܪܗ ܕܐܠܗܐ. ܐܬܝܬ [ܠܟܐ
ܩܕܡ ܙܒܢܐ ܕܬܫܢܩܢ. 30ܘܡܪܒܝܬܐ ܪܒܬܐ ܕܚܙܝܪ̈ܐ] ܪܥܝܐ ܗܘܬ
ܠܗܠ ܡܢܗܘܢ 31ܘܒܥܝܢ ܗܘܘ ܡܢܗ ܗܢܘܢ ܫܐܕ̈ܐ ܘܐܡܪܝܢ
ܕܐܢ ܡܦܩ ܐܢܬ ܠܢ ܫܕܪܝܢ ܠܡܪܒܝܬܐ ܗܝ، ܕܚܙܝܪ̈ܐ 32ܐܡܪ
ܠܗܘܢ ܙܠܘ. ܗܢܘܢ ܕܝܢ ܢܦܩܘ ܘܥܠܘ ܒܚܙܝܪ̈ܐ ܘܪܗܛܬ ܗܝ،
ܟܠܗ ܡܪܒܝܬܐ ܠܫܘܦܐ ܘܢܦܠܘ ܠܓܘ ܝܡܐ 33ܘܚܙܘ ܪܥܘܬܐ
ܘܥܠܘ ܠܡܕܝܢܬܐ ܘܐܫܬܥܝܘ ܟܠ ܡܕܡ ܕܗܘܐ ܘܗܠܝܢ ܕܫܐ̈ܕܐ
34ܘܢܦܩܬ ܟܠܗ ܡܕܝܢܬܐ ܠܐܘܪܥ ܕܡܪܢ ܘܟܕ ܚܙܘܗܝ، ܒܥܘ
ܡܢܗ ܕܢܫܢܐ ܡܢ ܠܘܬܗܘܢ 1[ܘܣܠܩ] ܠܣܦܝܢܬܐ ܘܥܒܪ * *
* * *2 * * * * * ܡܫܪܝܐ ܒܗ ܙܒܢܐ ܒܟܪܘܙܐ ܘܟܕ
ܚܙܐ ܡܪܢ ܗܝܡܢܘܬܗܘܢ ܐܡܪ [ܠܗܘܢ] ܡܫܪܝܐ ܠܐ [ܬܕܚܠ]
* * * * * * *3 * * * * * * * *
* * * * * * * *4 * * * * ܐܡܪ ܠܗܘܢ
ܡܢܐ [ܡܬܚܫܒܝܢ] ܐܢܬܘܢ ܒܝܫܐ ܒܠܒܟܘܢ 5ܐܝܢܐ ܦܫܝܩܐ

---

24 ܕܝܡܐ ܘܣܦܝܢܬܐ ܡܛܝܐ] ܝܡܐ ܒܡܨܥܬܐ ܘܡܛܝܐ S^ed^, *but cf* Lk viii 23 *and* ܡܫܬܥܠ ܥܡܐ *A* 42[2] 28 ܩܒܪܐ] ܩܒܘܪܐ S^ed^ 34 ܚܙܐܘܗܝ S^ed^

23 |And our Lord went up into a boat and his disciples were coming *S*
24 after him, and there was a storm [of the sea, and the boat] was
25 near to be broken in the waves. Now he was asleep; and his
disciples drew near and awoke him, and say to him: "Our Lord,
26 save our *lives*, because lo, we are perishing!" He saith [to them:
"O lacking in faith] wherefore are ye fearful?" Then he arose and
27 rebuked the wind and the sea and there was a great calm. But those
folk were astonished and say: "Who is this, that the sea and the
wind obey him?"

28 And when he came to the country of the Gadarenes there met
him two men on whom were devils; and they were evil exceedingly,
and they used to come forth from the graves, that no one could
29 pass by that way. And they cried out with a loud voice, and say:
"What have we to do with thee, Son of God? Hast thou come [hither
30 before the time to torment us?" And a great herd of swine] was
31 feeding beyond them, and those devils were beseeching him and
saying "If thou dost cast us out, send us to that herd of swine."
32 He saith to them: "Go." Now they went forth and entered into the
swine, and all that herd ran to a steep place and fell into the midst
33 of the sea. And the herdsmen fled and entered the city and declared
34 everything that he did and those things concerning the devils. And
all the city went forth to meet our Lord, and when they saw him
they besought him that he would remove from their *neighbourhood.*
ix 1, 2 [And he went up] to the boat and crossed over * * * [they brought
to him] a paralytic lying down on a bed, and when our Lord saw
their faith he said [to that] paralytic: "Be not [afraid,] * *"
3, 4 * * * * * * * * * * * he said
5 to them: "What [think] ye evil in your heart? Which is the easier,

---

23 *From this point to* x 32 *the text and translation are taken from S, as four leaves are missing from C*

ܠܡܐܡܪ ܕܡܣܝܡܝܢ ܠܟ ܚܛܗ̈ܝܟ. ܐܘ ܠܡܐܡܪ ܕܩܘܡ ܗܠܟ S
[6]ܕܬܕܥܘܢ ܕܝܢ ܕܫܠܝܛ ܗܘ ܒܪܗ ܕܐܢܫܐ ܥܠ ܐܪܥܐ ܠܡܫܒܩ
ܚܛܗ̈ܐ ܗܝܕܝܢ ܐܡܪ ܠܗܘ ܡܫܪܝܐ ܩܘܡ ܫܩܘܠ ܥܪܣܟ ܘܙܠ
ܠܒܝܬܟ [7]ܘܩܡ ܫܩܠ ܥܪܣܗ ܘܐܙܠ ܠܒܝܬܗ [8]ܘܟܕ ܚܙܘ ܟܢܫܐ
ܕܚܠܘ ܘܫܒܚܘ ܗܘܘ ܠܐܠܗܐ ܕܝܗܒ ܗܢܐ ܫܘܠܛܢܐ ܠܒ̈ܢܝ
ܐܢܫܐ ܀

[9]ܘܟܕ ܡܢ ܬܡܢ ܥܒܪ ܡܪܢ ܚܙܐ ܠܓܒܪܐ ܚܕ ܕܝܬܒ ܒܝܬ
ܡܟ̈ܣܐ ܕܫܡܗ ܡܬܝ. ܘܐܡܪ ܠܗ ܬܐ ܒܬܪܝ. ܘܩܡ ܐܙܠ ܒܬܪܗ
[10]ܘܟܕ [ܡܣܬܡܟܝܢ ܗܘܘ ܒܒܝܬܐ ܐܬܘ ܗܘܘ ܡܟ̈ܣܐ ܘܚܛ̈ܝܐ
ܣܓܝܐܐ ܐܣܬܡܟܘ ܗܘܘ ܠܘܬ] ܡܪܢ ܘܠܘܬ ܬܠܡܝܕܘ̈ܗܝ, [11]ܗܝܕܝܢ
ܟܕ ܚܙܘ ܦܪܝܫܐ ܐܡܪܝܢ ܠܬܠܡܝܕܘ̈ܗܝ, [ܠܡܢܐ ܥܡ ܡܟ̈ܣܐ ܘܚܛ̈ܝܐ]
ܐܟܠ ܪܒܟܘܢ [ܘܫܬܐ] [12]ܗܘ ܕܝܢ ܟܕ ܫܡܥ ܐܡܪ ܠܐ ܣܢܝܩܝܢ
ܚܠܝܡܐ ܠܐܣܝܐ. ܐܠܐ ܐܝܠܝܢ ܕܒܝܫ ܒܝܫ ܒܥܒܕܝܢ [13]ܐܙܠܘ ܕܝܢ
ܝܠܦܘ ܡܢܘ ܚܢܢܐ ܒܥܐ ܘܠܐ ܕܒܚܬܐ [§]ܠܐ ܓܝܪ ܐܬܝܬ ܕܐܩܪܐ §A142, 150, 455
ܠܙܕܝܩܐ ܐܠܐ ܠܚܛܝܐ ܠܬܝܒܘܬܐ[¶] [14]ܗܝܕܝܢ ܐܬܘ ܬܠܡ̈ܝܕܘܗܝ, ¶A
ܕܝܘܚܢܢ ܘܐܡܪܝܢ ܠܗ ܕܐܢܚܢܢ ܘܦܪ̈ܝܫܐ ܨܝܡܝܢ ܐܢܚܢܢ ܣܓܝܐܬ.
ܘܬܠܡܝܕܝܟ ܠܐ ܨܝܡܝܢ [15]ܐܡܪ ܠܗܘܢ ܡܪܢ ܠܐ ܡܫܟܚܝܢ
ܒܢܘ̈ܗܝ, ܕܓܢܘܢܐ ܠܡܨܡ ܟܡܐ ܕܚܬܢܐ ܥܡܗܘܢ. ܢܐܬܘܢ
ܕܝܢ ܝܘܡܬܐ ܕܢܬܥܠܐ ܡܢܗܘܢ ܚܬܢܐ ܘܗܝܕܝܢ ܢܨܘܡܘܢ ܀ ܀
[16]ܠܐ ܐܢܫ ܪܡܐ ܐܪܩܥܬܐ ܚܕܬܐ ܥܠ ܢܚܬܐ ܒܠܝܐ ܕܠܐ
ܡܠܝܘܬܗ ܕܚܕܬܐ ܡܢܬܦܐ ܡܫܠܘܬܗ ܕܒܠܝܐ ܘܗܘܐ ܨܪܝܐ
ܒܝܫ ܡܢ ܩܕܡܝܐ [17]ܘܐܦ ܠܐ ܪܡܝܢ ܚܡܪܐ ܚܕܬܐ. ܒܙܩ̈ܐ
ܒܠ̈ܝܬܐ ܕܠܐ ܚܡܪܐ ܡܨܪܐ ܠܗܝܢ ܠܙܩ̈ܐ ܘܗܘ ܚܡܪܐ ܡܬܐܫܕ.
ܘܙܩ̈ܐ ܐܒܕܝܢ. ܐܠܐ ܪܡܝܢ ܚܡܪܐ ܚܕܬܐ ܒܙܩ̈ܐ ܚܕ̈ܬܬܐ
ܘܬܪ̈ܝܗܘܢ ܡܬܢܛܪ̈ܝܢ. [18]ܟܕ ܗܘ ܕܝܢ ܡܡܠܠ ܗܘܐ ܥܡܗܘܢ.
ܘܗܐ ܪܒ ܟܢܘܫܬܗܘܢ ܚܕ ܐܬܐ ܢܦܠ ܗܘܐ ܣܓܕ ܠܗ ܘܐܡܪ

13 ܒܝܫ] *om.* A 3/3: *after* ܠܬܝܒܘܬܐ A 455 *goes on*
ܡܛܠ.... ܕܠܝܬ ܗܘܐ ܠܗܘܢ ܡܕܡ ܗܘܫܐ ܠܝܠܕܬܐ ܥܠ ܐܗܘܐ

to say 'Thy sins are forgiven thee,' or to say 'Arise *and* walk'? *S*
6 But that ye may know that the Son of Man hath authority on
earth to forgive sins—" then said he to that paralytic—" Arise, take
7 up thy bed, and go to thy house!" And he arose *and* took up his
8 bed and went to his house. And when the multitudes saw they
were afraid, and they were glorifying God who gave this authority
to men.

9 And he removed from thence. And as our Lord passed by, he
saw a certain man that was sitting at the toll-gatherers' place, whose
name was Matthew, and he said to him: "Come after me"; and he
10 arose *and* came after him. And when [they were sitting *at meat* in
the house many toll-gatherers and sinners had sat down *to meat* by]
11 our Lord and by his disciples. Then when the Pharisees see *it*, they
say to his disciples: [" Wherefore with toll-gatherers and sinners] are
12 ye eating [and drinking]?" Now he, when he heard, said: "The
13 whole have no need of a physician, but they that are ill. But go,
learn what is *meant by* 'Mercy I seek and not sacrifice,' §for I came §*A* 142,
14 not that I might call the righteous, but sinners to repentance."¶ Then 150, 455 ¶*A*
came the disciples of John, and say: "Why is it that we and the
15 Pharisees fast eagerly, and thy disciples fast not?" Our Lord saith
to them: "The sons of the bride-chamber cannot keep a *time of*
mourning as long as the bridegroom is with them; but the days
will come, that the bridegroom will be taken up from them, and
then they will fast.

16 "No man putteth a new patch on a worn-out garment, else the
fulness of the new pulleth away the weakness of the worn-out *part*,
17 and the rent becometh worse than the former one. Neither do they
put new wine into worn-out wine-skins, else the wine teareth the
wine-skins and the wine is spilt and the wine-skins perish; but they
18 put new wine into new wine-skins, and both are preserved." Now
when he was speaking with them, lo, a certain ruler of their
synagogue came *and* fell down *and* worshipped him, and said:

---

13 for] *om.* $A^{3}/_{3}$ E^{61} (*vid*): *after* 'to repentance' *A* 455 *goes on* 'Because ...there was no need to the whole ones of a physician.' *The words* 'to repentance' *are not quoted in* E^{61}

ܒܪܬܝ، ܗܫܐ ܡܝܬܬ ܐܠܐ ܣܝܡ ܐܝܕܟ ܘܬܚܐ. 19ܘܩܡ ܡܪܢ S
ܐܙܠ ܥܡܗ ܗܘ ܘܬܠܡܝܕܘܗܝ. 20ܘܗܐ ܐܢܬܬܐ ܕܕܒܐ ܗܘܐ ܕܡܗ
ܫܢܝܢ ܬܪܬܥܣܪܐ ܘܐܬܬ ܘܩܪܒܬ ܠܟܢܦܐ ܕܡܪܛܘܛܗ 21ܐܡܪܐ
ܗܘܬ ܓܝܪ ܒܢܦܫܗ ܘܒܠܒܗ. ܕܐܦ ܠܢܚܬܘܗܝ، ܘܩܪܒܐ ܐܢܐ
ܡܬܐܣܝܐ ܐܢܐ 22ܘܗܘ ܕܝܢ ܐܬܦܢܝ ܠܗ ܘܐܡܪ ܠܗ * * *
ܒܪܬܝ، ܗܝܡܢܘܬܟܝ ܐܚܝܬܟܝ ܘܡܢ ܗܝ، ܫܥܬܐ ܐܬܚܠܡܬ ܐܢܬܬܐ
ܗܝ. 23ܘܟܕ ܐܬܐ ܡܪܢ ܠܒܝܬܗ ܕܗܘ ܪܒ ܟܢܘܫܬܐ ܘܚܙܐ
ܠܙܡܪܐ ܘܠܟܢܫܐ ܗܘ ܕܡܫܬܓܫܝܢ ܗܘܘ 24ܐܡܪ ܠܗܘܢ ܫܢܘ
ܠܗܠ ܛܠܝܬܐ ܓܝܪ ܠܐ ܡܝܬܬ ܐܠܐ ܡܕܡܟܢ ܗܘ ܕܕܡܟܐ
ܗܢܘܢ ܕܝܢ ܓܚܟܝܢ ܗܘܘ ܥܠܘܗܝ. 25ܟܕ ܕܝܢ ܐܦܩܘܗܝ، ܠܟܢܫܐ
ܗܘ ܠܒܪ ܐܬܐ ܩܪܒ. ܠܐܝܕܗ ܘܒܪ ܫܥܬܗ ܩܡܬ 26ܘܢܦܩ ܛܒܐ
ܗܢܐ ܒܟܠܗ ܐܪܥܐ ܗܝ، 27ܘܟܕ ܥܒܪ ܡܪܢ ܕܟܡܘܢ، ܬܪܝܢ
ܣܡܝܐ ܘܩܥܝܢ ܒܩܠܐ ܪܡܐ ܐܬܪܚܡ ܥܠܝܢ ܒܪܗ ܕܕܘܝܕ. 28ܘܟܕ
ܐܬܐ ܠܒܝܬܐ ܩܪܒܘ ܠܗ ܣܡܝܐ ܐܡܪ ܠܗܘܢ ܡܗܝܡܢܝܢ
ܐܢܬܘܢ ܕܡܫܟܚ ܐܢܐ ܕܐܥܒܕ ܗܕܐ· ܐܡܪܝܢ ܠܗ ܐܝܢ ܡܪܢ
ܡܗܝܡܢܝܢ ܐܢܚܢܢ 29ܗܝܕܝܢ ܩܪܒ ܠܥܝܢܝܗܘܢ ܘܐܡܪ ܐܝܟܢܐ
ܕܡܗܝܡܢܝܬܘܢ ܢܗܘܐ ܠܟܘܢ 30ܘܒܗ ܒܫܥܬܐ ܐܬܦܬܚ ܥܝܢܝܗܘܢ.
ܘܟܐܐ ܒܗܘܢ ܡܪܢ ܘܐܡܪ ܠܗܘܢ ܗܐ ܚܙܘ ܕܠܡܐ ܠܐܢܫ
ܐܡܪܝܢ ܐܢܬܘܢ 31ܗܢܘܢ ܕܝܢ ܟܕ ܢܦܩܘ ܠܟܠ ܐܢܫ ܐܦܠܚܘ ܒܗ
ܒܐܪܥܐ ܗܝ، 32ܘܡܢ ܒܬܪ ܕܢܦܩܘ ܩܪܒܘ ܠܗ ܚܪܫܐ ܚܕ ܕܐܚܝܕ ܠܗ
ܫܐܕܐ 33ܘܟܕ ܢܦܩ ܡܢܗ ܫܐܕܐ ܡܠܠ ܚܪܫܐ ܗܘ. ܘܡܬܕܡܪܝܢ ܗܘܘ
ܟܢ̈ܫܐ ܘܐܡܪ̈ܝܢ ܕܠܐ ܡܡܬܘܡ ܐܬܚܙܝ، ܗܟܢܐ ܒܝܬ ܐܝܣܪܐܝܠ ܀
35ܘܡܚܕܪ ܗܘܐ ܡܪܢ ܒܡܕܝܢ̈ܬܐ ܘܒܩܘܪܝܐ ܘܡܠܦ ܗܘܐ
ܒܟܢܘܫܬܗܘܢ܇ ܘܡܟܪܙ ܗܘܐ ܣܒܪܬܐ ܕܡܠܟܘܬܐ. ܘܡܐܣܐ ܗܘܐ

---

20 ܡܪܛܘܛܗ] ܡܪܛܘܛܐ $S^{*\,vid}$ 21 ܒܢ̈ܦܫܗ] ܒܢܦܫܗ S^{ed} 27 ܘܩܥܝܢ] S (*sic*)
28 *Cf* *A* 20: ܘܟܕ ܣܡܝܐ ܩܪܒ ܠܗ ܐܡܪ ܠܗ. ܡܗܝܡܢ ܐܢܬ ܕܡܫܟܚ ܐܢܐ ܕܐܣܝܟ. ܐܡܪ ܠܗ ܗܘ ܣܡܝܐ. ܐܝܢ ܡܪܝ ܡܗܝܡܢ ܐܢܐ. ܘܡܗܝܡܢܘܬܗ ܒܥܝܢܝ ܚܙܝܬ.

"My daughter now hath died, but lay thy hand and she will live." S
19 And our Lord arose *and* went with him, he and his disciples.
20 And lo, a woman whose blood had been issuing for twelve years,
21 and she came and touched the skirt of his cloak; for she was saying
within herself "Even if his garments I should touch, I should be
22 healed." Now he turned round to her and said to her: "* * my
daughter, thy faith hath saved thee alive." And from that hour the
23 woman was made whole. And when our Lord came to the house
of the ruler of the synagogue, and he saw the singers and the
24 multitude that was making a noise, he said to them: "Remove ye
yonder, for the girl hath not died, but is indeed sleeping." Now
25 they were laughing at him. But when he had put forth that
multitude outside he came *and* touched her hand, and straightway
26, 27 she arose. And this tale went forth in all that land. And when
our Lord passed by, two blind men clave to him and cry out
28 with a loud voice: "Have compassion on us, son of David!" And
when he came to the house those blind men drew near to him.
He saith to them: "Believe ye that I can do this?" They say to him:
29 "Yea, our Lord, we believe." Then he touched their eyes, and said:
30 "As ye have believed shall it be to you." And in the same hour
their eyes were opened; and our Lord rebuked them, and said to
31 them: "Lo, see that ye say *it* not to any man." But they, when
32 they went forth, published *it* to every one in that same land. And
after they had gone forth they brought near to him a certain deaf mute
33 that was devil-ridden, and when the devil had gone forth from him
that deaf mute spake. And the multitudes were wondering and
saying: "Never has it been seen thus in the House of Israel."

35 And our Lord was walking in the cities and in the villages and
was teaching in their synagogues and was preaching the gospel of the

---

28 *Cf A* 20: And when the blind man drew near to him, he saith to him, 'Believest thou that I can heal thee?' That blind man saith to him, 'Yea, my Lord, I believe.' And his faith opened his eyes.

S ܟܘܠ ܟܐܒ ܘܟܠ ܟܘܪܗܢ܂ 36 ܟܕ ܚܙܐ ܕܝܢ ܟܢ̈ܫܐ ܐܬܪܚܡ
ܥܠܝܗܘܢ܂ ܕܠܐܝܢ ܗܘܘ ܫܒܝܪ ܐܝܟ ܥܢܐ ܕܠܝܬ ܠܗܘܢ ܪܥܝܐ
37 ܗܝܕܝܢ ܐܡܪ ܠܬܠܡܝܕܘܗܝ ܚܨܕܐ ܣܓܝ ܘܦܥܠܐ ܙܥܘܪܝܢ 38 ܒܥܘ
ܗܟܝܠ ܡܢ ܡܪܗ ܕܚܨܕܐ ܕܢܦܩ ܦܥ̈ܠܐ ܠܚܨܕܗ 1 ܘܩܪܐ ܠܬܪܬܥܣܪܬܗ
ܘܝܗܒ ܠܗܘܢ܂ ܫܘܠܛܢܐ ܠܡܦܩܘ ܪ̈ܘܚܐ ܛܢ̈ܦܬܐ ܘܠܡܐܣܝܘ
ܟܘܠ ܟܐܒ ܘܟܘܪܗܢ܂·

§Thos 172 §Sachau 311 2 ܘܗ̈ܠܝܢ ܫܡܗܐ ܕܬܠܡ̈ܝܕܘܗܝ ܬܪ̈ܥܣܪ· ܩܕܡܝܐ §§ܫܡܥܘܢ܂
ܟܐܦܐ ܘܐܢܕܪܐܘܣ ܐܚܘܗܝ ܘܝܥܩܘܒ ܘܝܘܚܢܢ ܒ̈ܢܝ ܙܒܕܝ
3 ܘܦܝܠܝܦܘܣ ܘܒܪ ܬܘܠܡܝ ܘܬܐܘܡܐ ܘܡܬܝ ܡܟܣܐ ܘܝܥܩܘܒ ܒܪ
¶Thos ܚܠܦܝ 4 ܘܫܡܥܘܢ܂ ܩܢܢܝܐ ܘܝܗܘܕܐ ܒܪ ܝܥܩܘܒ¶ ܘܝܗܘܕܐ
¶Sach ܣܟܪܝܘܛܐ ܕܗܘ ܗܘܐ ܡܫܠܡܢܐ·¶ 5 ܘܫܕܪ ܡܪܢ܂ ܗܠܝܢ ܬܪ̈ܥܣܪ
ܬܠܡ̈ܝܕܘܗܝ ܘܦܩܕ ܐܢܘܢ܂ ܘܐܡܪ ܠܗܘܢ܂ ܒܐܘܪܚܐ ܕܥܡ̈ܡܐ
ܠܐ ܬܐܙܠܘܢ܂ ܘܠܡܕܝܢܬܐ ܕܫܡܪ̈ܝܐ ܠܐ ܬܥܠܘܢ܂ 6 ܐܠܐ ܙܠܘ
ܠܟܘܢ܂ ܠܘܬ ܥܢܐ ܕܐܒܕܬ ܡܢ ܒܝܬ ܐܝܣܪܝܠ 7 ܘܗܟܐ ܕܐܙܠܝܬܘܢ܂
ܐܟܪܙܘ ܘܐܡܪܘ ܕܩܪܒܬ ܡܠܟܘܬܐ ܕܫܡܝܐ 8 ܟܪ̈ܝܗܐ ܐܣܘ ܡܝ̈ܬܐ
§A 199, 456 ܐܩܝܡܘ ܓܪ̈ܒܐ ܕܟܘ ܘܫܐ̈ܕܐ ܐܦܩܘ §ܡܓܢ ܢܣܒܬܘܢ܂ ܡܓܢ
¶A ܗܒܘ¶ 9 ܠܐ ܬܩܢܘܢ܂ ܠܟܘܢ܂ ܕܗܒܐ ܘܟܣܦܐ ܘܐܦ ܠܐ ܢܚܫܐ
ܒܟܝܣܝܟܘܢ܂ 10 ܘܠܐ ܬܪܡܠܐ ܠܐܘܪܚܐ ܘܠܐ ܬܪܬܝܢ ܟܘܬܝܢܝܢ ܘܠܐ
ܡܣܐܢܐ ܘܠܐ ܚܘܛܪܐ ܫܘܐ ܗܘ ܓܝܪ ܦܥܠܐ ܡܣܒܪܬܗ 11 ܠܐܝܢܐ
ܡܕܝܢܬܐ ܕܥܠܝܢ ܐܢܬܘܢ܂ ܫܐܠܘ ܡܢܘ ܫܘܐ ܒܗ ܘܬܡܢ ܗܘܘ
ܥܕܡܐ ܕܢܦܩܝܢ ܐܢܬܘܢ܂ 12 ܘܡܐ ܕܥܠܝܢ ܐܢܬܘܢ܂ ܠܗ ܠܒܝܬܐ ܫܐܠܘ

2—4. *For a further discussion of the list of Apostles in Thos*[172], *see Introd.* vol. ii 2 ܟܐܦܐ] *pr.* ܕܫܡܥܘܢ *cod. Sachau* 311 (*ap. Harris,* p. 101) ܘܐܢܕܪܐܘܣ *Thos Sachau* 311 ܐܚܘܗܝ] *om. Thos* ܒ̈ܢܝ ܙܒܕܝ] *om. Thos* 3 ܒܪ ܬܘܠܡܝ] *pr.* ܠܒܝܐ *Sachau* 311 4 ܕܗܘ ܗܘܐ] ܗܘ ܕܗܘܐ *Sachau* 311 5 ܕܥܡ̈ܡܐ] ܕܚܢ̈ܦܐ *A* 42 (= *Diat*)

36 kingdom, and was healing every pain and every infirmity. Now when *S*
he saw the multitudes he had compassion upon them, in that they
37 were weary *and* let loose as a flock that hath no shepherd. Then
said he to his disciples: "The harvest *is* much, and the labourers
38 few; beseech ye therefore the Lord of the harvest that he should
x 1 send forth labourers for his harvest." And he called his Twelve,
and gave them authority to cast out unclean spirits and to heal
every pain and infirmity.

2 And these *are* the names of his twelve disciples:—first §§Simon §*Thos* 172
Kepha, and Andrew his brother, and James and John the sons of §*Sachau* 311
3 Zebedee, and Philip and Bartholomew and Thomas and Matthew
4 the toll-gatherer and James the son of Halphaeus and Simon the
Cananaean and Judas the son of James,¶ and Judas Scariot who ¶*Thos*
5 himself was the betrayer.¶ And our Lord sent these his twelve ¶*Sach*
disciples and commanded them and said to them: "In the way of
the peoples ye shall not go, and into a town of the Samaritans ye
6 shall not enter, but go to the flock that hath strayed from the House
7 of Israel. And what *time* ye go, preach and say: 'The kingdom of
8 heaven hath drawn nigh.' Heal the infirm, raise the dead, cleanse
the lepers and cast out the devils; §freely ye have received, freely §*A* 199, 456
9 give.¶ Get not for yourselves gold nor silver, nor even copper in ¶*A*
10 your purses, and no wallet for the way and not two coats and no
11 shoes and no staff, for the labourer is worthy of his food. Into
whatever town ye enter, be asking who is worthy, and there
12 be until ye go forth. And what *time* ye enter the house give

---

2—4. *For a further discussion of the list of Apostles in Thos*[172], *see Introd.* vol. ii: *the lists in* Diat[ar] *and cod. Fuldensis follow* Lk vi 14—16, *but that in* Îsho'dâd (*cod. Sachau* 311) *is similar to this* 2 Kepha] *pr.* whom he named *Sachau* 311 his brother] *om. Thos* the sons of Zebedee] *om. Thos* 3 the son of Halphaeus] *pr.* Lebia *Sachau* 311 (*i. e.* 'Lebbaeus,' *or* 'Levi') 4 who himself] he which *Sachau* 311 5 the way of the peoples] the way of the pagans *A* 42 (= *Diat*): *see Introd.* vol. ii 10 no staff] *see on* Mk vi 8

S ܫܠܡܐ ܠܒܝܬܐ ܗܘ [13]ܘܐܢ ܕܫܘܐ ܒܝܬܐ ܗܘ ܫܠܡܟܘܢ
ܢܗܘܐ ܥܠܘܗܝ, ܘܐܠܐ ܫܠܡܟܘܢ ܥܠܝܟܘܢ ܢܬܘܒ [14]ܡܢ ܕܠܐ
ܡܩܒܠ ܠܟܘܢ ܘܠܐ ܫܡܥ ܡܠܝܟܘܢ ܡܐ ܕܢܦܩܝܢ ܐܢܬܘܢ ܡܢ
ܒܝܬܐ ܗܘ ܐܘ ܡܢ ܡܕܝܢܬܐ ܗܝ, ܗܦܘܟܘ ܢܦܨܘ ܚܠܐ
ܕܪ̈ܓܠܝܟܘܢ [15]ܘܐܡܝܢ ܐܡܪ ܐܢܐ ܠܟܘܢ ܕܠܐܪܥܐ ܕܣܕܘܡ
ܘܕܥܡܘܪܐ ܢܗܘܐ ܦܫܝܩ ܒܝܘܡܐ ܕܕܝܢܐ ܝܬܝܪ ܡܢ ܕܠܡܕܝܢܬܐ
ܗܝ. [16]ܗܐ ܐܢܐ ܡܫܕܪ ܐܢܐ ܠܟܘܢ ܐܝܟ ܐܡܪܐ ܒܝܢܝ ܕܐܒ̈ܐ.
ܗܘܘ ܗܟܝܠ ܚܟܝܡܝܢ ܐܝܟ ܚܘܘ̈ܬܐ ܘܬܡܝܡܝܢ ܐܝܟ ܝܘ̈ܢܐ
[17]ܐܙܕܗܪܘ ܡܢ ܒܢ̈ܝ ܐܢܫܐ ܕܡܫܠܡܝܢ ܠܟܘܢ ܠܒܝܬ ܕܝܢܐ
ܘܒܟܢܘ̈ܫܬܗܘܢ ܢܢܓܕܘܢܟܘܢ [18]ܘܩܕܡ ܡ̈ܠܟܐ ܘܗܓ̈ܡܘܢܐ
ܬܬܩܪܒܘܢ ܡܛܠ ܫܡܝ ܠܣܗܕܘܬܗܘܢ ܕܝܠܗܘܢ ܘܕܥܡ̈ܡܐ.
[19]ܡܐ ܕܡܫܠܡܝܢ ܠܟܘܢ ܠܐ ܬܐܨܦܘܢ ܐܝܟܢܐ ܬܐܡܪܘܢ
ܡܬܝܗܒ ܠܟܘܢ ܓܝܪ ܒܗ ܫܥܬܐ ܡܐ ܕܬܐܡܪܘܢ §[20]ܠܐ §A415
ܗܘܐ ܓܝܪ ܐܢܬܘܢ ܡܡܠܠܝܢ. ܐܠܐ ܪܘܚܐ ܗܝ ܕܐܒܘܟܘܢ
ܡܡܠܠܐ ܒܟܘܢ:¶ [21]ܢܫܠܡ ܓܝܪ ܐܚܐ ܠܐܚܘܗܝ ܠܡܘܬܐ ܘܐܒܐ ¶A
ܠܒܪܗ ܠܡܘܬܐ ܘܢܩܘܡܘܢ ܒܢ̈ܝܐ ܠܐܒܗܝܗܘܢ: ܘܢܡܝܬܘܢ
ܐܢܘܢ [22]ܘܬܗܘܘܢ ܣܢܝܢ ܠܟܘܢ ܒܢ̈ܝ ܐܢܫܐ ܡܛܠ ܫܡܝ ܐܢܐ
ܕܝܢ ܕܡܣܝܒܪ ܥܕܡܐ ܠܚܪܬܐ ܗܘ ܢܚܐ ·:· ·:·
[23]ܡܐ ܕܪܕܦܝܢ ܠܟܘܢ ܒܗܕܐ ܩܪܝܬܐ. ܥܪܘܩܘ ܠܟܘܢ ܡܢܗ
ܠܐܚܪܬܐ. ܘܐܢ ܒܐܚܪܬܐ ܪܕܦܝܢ ܠܟܘܢ ܥܪܘܩܘ ܠܟܘܢ
ܠܐܚܪܬܐ. ܘܐܡܝܢ ܓܝܪ ܐܡܪ ܐܢܐ ܠܟܘܢ ܕܠܐ ܬܫܠܡܘܢ
ܐܢܘܢ ܒܟܠܗܘܢ ܩܘܪ̈ܝܐ ܕܒܝܬ ܐܝܣܪܝܠ. ܥܕܡܐ ܕܐܬܐ
ܒܪܗ ܕܐܢܫܐ. [24]ܠܝܬ ܬܠܡܝܕܐ ܕܡܝܬܪ ܡܢ ܪܒܗ. [25]ܣܦܩ
ܠܗ ܠܬܠܡܝܕܐ ܕܢܗܘܐ ܐܝܟ ܪܒܗ. ܘܠܥܒܕܐ ܐܝܟ ܡܪܗ
ܘܐܢ ܠܡܪܗ ܕܒܝܬܐ ܒܥܠܙܒܘܒ ܩܪܘ ܠܒܢ̈ܝ ܒܝܬܗ ܐܟܡܐ

---

20 ܠܐ ܗܘܐ ܓܝܪ] ܡܛܠ ܕܠܐ ܗܘܐ A   ܪܘܚܐ ܗܝ ܕܐܒܘܟܘܢ] ܪܘܚܐ ܕܩܘܕܫܐ ܕܐܒܘܟܘܢ ܗܝ A (*om.* ܗܝ A^a): *cf* Lk xii 12. *For the rest of the quotation, see on* Lk xxi 12—17

13 a greeting to that house, and if it be that that house is worthy your *S*
greeting shall be upon it; and if not, your greeting upon you shall
14 return. Whosoever receiveth you not and heareth not your words,
what *time* ye go forth from that house or from that city be shaking off
15 the dust of your feet—and amen, I say to you that for the land of
Sodom and of Gomorra it shall be tolerable in the day of judgement
16 rather than for that town. Lo, I send you as lambs among wolves;
be therefore cunning as serpents and simple as doves.

17 "Beware of men, who will deliver you up to courts of justice and
18 who shall scourge you in their synagogues. And before kings and
governors ye shall stand for my name's sake and for a witness unto
19 them, even to them and the peoples. What *time* they bring you
up be not anxious what ye shall say, for it is given you in that hour
20 what ye shall say; §for not ye are speaking, but the Spirit of your §*A*415
21 Father is speaking in you.¶ For the brother will deliver up his ¶*A*
brother to death, and the father *will deliver up* his son to death,
and the sons will rise up against their fathers and will put them to
22 death. And men will be hating you for my name's sake; but he
which shall endure unto the last, he shall live.

23 "What *time* they persecute you in this town, flee ye from it to
another, and if in the other they persecute you flee ye to another;
for amen, I say to you Ye will not *even* finish all the towns of
24 the House of Israel until the Son of Man come. There is no disciple
25 that is more than his Rabbi; it is enough for the disciple that he
should be as his Rabbi and the slave as his master. And if the
master of the house they have called Beelzebub, his household how

---

16, 17] *Cf* 'Be ye then innocent as doves and wise as serpents. Beware of men..' E^{94} 20 Spirit] *pr.* Holy *A* 23] $E^{94,95}$ *has* 'Into whatsoever city ye enter, and they receive you not (Lk x 10), remove from thence into another city, and if from that they persecute you flee into another city: amen, I say to you, ye shall not be able to finish all the cities, until I come to you.'

S (C) ܢܩܪܘܢ܂ [26]ܠܐ ܗܘܝܠ ܬܕܚܠܘܢ ܡܢܗܘܢ ܠܝܬ ܓܝܪ ܡܕܡ ܕܟܣܐ
§A 13 ܕܠܐ ܢܬܓܠܐ. ܘܠܐ ܕܡܛܫܐ. ܕܠܐ ܢܬܝܕܥ. §[27]ܡܕܡ ܕܐܡܪܢܐ
¶A ܠܟܘܢ ܒܚܫܘܟܐ ܐܡܪܘܗܝ، ܐܢܬܘܢ ܒܢܘܗܪܐ.¶ ܘܡܕܡ ܕܫܡܥܬܘܢ
ܐܢܬܘܢ ܒܐܕܢܝܟܘܢ ܐܟܪܙܘ ܥܠ ܐܓܪܐ. [28]ܘܠܐ ܬܕܚܠܘܢ
ܡܢ ܐܢܫܝܢ ܕܩܛܠܝܢ ܦܓܪܐ ܘܢܦܫܐ ܠܐ ܫܠܝܛܝܢ. ܠܡܩܛܠ. ܕܚܠܘ
ܕܝܢ ܝܬܝܪܐܝܬ ܡܢ ܗܘ ܕܡܫܟܚ ܦܓܪܐ ܘܢܦܫܐ ܠܡܘܒܕܘ ܒܓܗܢܐ.
[29]ܬܪ̈ܬܝܢ ܨܦܪ̈ܝܢ ܡܙܕܒܢܢ ܒܐܣܪ ܘܚܕܐ ܡܢܗܝܢ ܠܒܪ ܡܢ ܐܒܘܟܘܢ
ܠܐ ܢܦܠܐ ܥܠ ܐܪܥܐ. [30]ܘܐ†ܦ† ܣܥܪܐ ܕܪܫܟܘܢ ܟܠܗܝܢ ܡܢܝܢ
ܐܢܝܢ [31]ܠܐ ܗܘܝܠ ܬܕܚܠܘܢ ܡܛܠ ܡܢ ܨܦܪ̈ܐ ܣܓܝܐܐ ܝܬܝܪܝܢ
§C fol 16 r ܐܢܬܘܢ | §[32]*ܟܠ ܐܢܫ ܗܘܝܠ ܕܢܘܕܐ ܒܝ ܩܕܡ ܒ̈ܢܝ ܐܢܫܐ. ܘܐܦ
ܐܢܐ ܐܘܕܐ ܒܗ ܩܕܡ ܐܒܐ ܕܒܫܡܝܐ. [33]ܘܡܢ ܕܢܟܦܘܪ ܒܝ ܩܕܡ
ܒ̈ܢܝ ܐܢܫܐ. ܐܦ ܐܢܐ ܐܟܦܘܪ ܒܗ ܩܕܡ ܐܒܝ ܕܒܫܡܝܐ.
ܘܩܕܡ ܡ̈ܠܐܟܘܗܝ. [34]ܠܐ ܐܬܝܬ ܕܐܪܡܐ ܫܝܢܐ ܒܐܪܥܐ.
ܐܠܐ ܦܠܓܘܬܐ ܕܗ̈ܘܢܐ ܘܣܝܦܐ. [35]ܐܬܝܬ ܓܝܪ ܕܐܦܠܓ ܒܪܐ
ܥܠ ܐܒܘܗܝ، ܘܒܪܬܐ ܥܠ ܐܡܗ̇. ܘܟܠܬܐ ܥܠ ܚܡܬܗ̇.
[36]ܘܒܥܠܕܒ̈ܒܘܗܝ، ܕܓܒܪܐ ܒ̈ܢܝ ܒܝܬܗ ܀
[37]ܡܢ ܕܪܚܡ ܕܝܢ ܠܐܒܘܗܝ، ܐܘ ܠܐܡܗ ܝܬܝܪ ܡܢ ܕܠܝ ܗܘ ܠܐ
ܫܘܐ ܠܝ. ܘܡܢ ܕܪܚܡ ܒܪܗ ܐܘ ܒܪܬܗ ܝܬܝܪ ܡܢ ܕܠܝ ܗܘ ܠܐ
col 2 *ܫܘܐ ܠܝ. [38]ܘܟܠ ܕܠܐ ܫܩܠ ܙܩܝܦܗ ܘܐܬܐ ܒܬܪܝ، ܠܐ ܫܘܐ ܠܝ.
[39]ܡܢ ܕܡܫܟܚ ܓܝܪ ܢܦܫܗ ܢܘܒܕܝܗ̇. ܘܡܢ ܕܢܘܒܕ ܢܦܫܗ ܡܛܠܬܝ،
ܢܫܟܚܝܗ̇. [40]ܡܢ ܕܡܩܒܠ ܠܟܘܢ ܠܝ ܗܘ ܡܩܒܠ. ܘܡܢ ܕܠܝ ܡܩܒܠ

---

27 ܐܡܪܘܗܝ A ܒܢܘܗܪܐ] ܒܢܗܝܪܐ A 30 ܘܐܦ] ܘܐܦܢ S (sic)
32 ܗܘܝܠ] om. S ܩܕܡ ܒ̈ܢܝ ܐܢܫܐ] om. S ܘܐܦ ܐܢܐ] ܐܦ S ܐܒܐ]
ܐܒܝ S 33 ܘܩܕܡ ܡ̈ܠܐܟܘܗܝ] om. S 34 ܠܐ ..... ܒܐܪܥܐ]
ܠܐ ܬܣܒܪܘܢ ܕܫܝܢܐ ܐܬܝܬ ܕܐܪܡܐ ܒܐܪܥܐ S ܐܠܐ] pr.
ܠܐ ܐܬܝܬ ܕܐܪܡܐ ܫܝܢܐ S ܦܠܓܘܬܐ ܕܗ̈ܘܢܐ ܘ] om. S 35 ܕܐܦܠܓ S
ܚܡܬܗ̇] no point over the ܗ in C* 37 ܐܘ 1°] ܘ S 38 ܙܩܝܦܗ] ܨܠܝܒܗ S
39 ܡܢ ܕܡܫܟܚ] ܟܠ ܕܡܫܟܚ S ܘܡܢ] ܘܟܠ S

26 shall they call *them*? Be not therefore afraid of them, for there is S (C)
nothing secret that shall not be revealed, nor *aught* concealed that
27 shall not be known. §That which I say to you in the darkness, say §A 13
it yourselves in the light,¶ and that which ye hear in your ears, ¶A
28 preach on the roofs. And be not afraid of them that kill the body,
but the soul they have not authority to kill; but be afraid rather
29 of him who can cast body and soul into Gehenna. Two sparrows
are sold for a farthing, and one of them apart from your Father
30 falleth not on the earth; and †even† the locks of your hair are all of
31 them numbered. Be not therefore afraid, because ye are more than
32 many sparrows. | §Every man therefore that shall confess me before §C
men, I myself also will confess him before the Father in heaven;
33 and whosoever shall deny me before men, I myself also will deny
34 him before my Father in heaven and before his angels. I have not
come to lay tranquillity in the earth, but division of minds and a
35 sword. For I have come to divide the son against his father, and
the daughter against her mother, and the bride against her mother-
36 in-law; and the enemies of a man *shall be* his household.
37 "Now he that loveth his father or his mother more than me,
he is not worthy of me; and he that loveth his son or his daughter
38 more than me, he is not worthy of me. And every one that doth
not take up his Cross and come after me is not worthy of me.
39 For he that findeth his life shall lose it, and he that shall lose his
40 life for my sake shall find it. He that receiveth you, me it is he
receiveth; and he that receiveth me, receiveth him that sent me.

---

28 have not authority] 'are not able' E^{95} **30** even] even if *S* (*sic*) **32.** *Here C begins again.* therefore] *om. S* before men] *om. S* myself] *om. S* the Father (*see on* Mt vi 4)] my Father *S* **33** and before his angels] *om. S* **34** I have not come] Suppose not that I have come *S* E^{97} but] *pr.* I have not come to lay tranquillity *S* division of minds and] *om. S* **37** or 1°] and *S* **38** Cross] *S has the word elsewhere translated* 'cross' **39** he that findeth] every one that shall find *S* he that 2°] every one that *S*

ܠܡܢ ܕܫܕܪܢܝ ܡܩܒܠ. [41]ܡܢ ܕܡܩܒܠ ܢܒܝܐ ܒܫܡ ܢܒܝܐ ܐܓܪܐ C S
ܕܢܒܝܐ ܢܣܒ. ܘܡܢ ܕܡܩܒܠ ܙܕܝܩܐ ܒܫܡ ܙܕܝܩܐ ܐܓܪܐ ܕܙܕܝܩܐ
ܢܣܒ· [42]ܘܟܠ ܡܢ ܕܢܫܩܐ ܠܚܕ ܡܢ ܗܠܝܢ ܙܥܘܪ̈ܐ ܟܣܐ ܕܩܪ̈ܝܪܐ
ܡ̈ܝܐ ܒܫܡܐ ܕܬܠܡܝܕܘܬܐ. ܐܡܝܢ ܐܡܪܢܐ ܠܟܘܢ ܕܠܐ
ܢܐܒܕ ܐܓܪܗ ܀
fol 16 v [1]ܘܗܘܐ ܟܕ ܫܠܡ ܝܫܘܥ ܠܡܦܩܕܘ ܠܬܪ̈ܥܣܪ *ܬܠܡܝܕܘܗܝ، ܥܒܪ ܠܗ
ܡܢ ܬܡܢ. ܠܡܠܦܘ ܘܠܡܟܪܙܘ ܒܡܕ̈ܝܢܬܗܘܢ.
[2]ܝܘܚܢܢ ܕܝܢ ܟܕ ܫܡܥ ܒܒܝܬ ܐܣܝܪ̈ܐ ܒܥܒ̈ܕܘܗܝ، ܕܝܫܘܥ· ܫܕܪ
ܠܬܠܡܝܕܘܗܝ، [3]ܘܐܡܪ ܠܗ. ܐܢܬ ܗܘ ܗܘ ܕܐܬܐ ܐܘ ܠܐܚܪܝܢ ܗܘ
ܡܣܟܝܢ ܐܢܚܢ. [4]ܘܥܢܐ ܝܫܘܥ ܘܐܡܪ ܠܗܘܢ. ܙܠܘ ܚܘܘ ܠܝܘܚܢܢ
ܡܕܡ ܕܚܙܝܢ ܐܢܬܘܢ ܘܡܕܡ ܕܫܡܥܝܢ ܐܢܬܘܢ· [5]ܗܐ ܣܡ̈ܝܐ
ܚܙܝܢ. ܘܚܓܝܪ̈ܐ ܡܗܠܟܝܢ. ܘܓܪ̈ܒܐ ܡܬܕܟܝܢ· ܘܚܪ̈ܫܐ
ܫܡܥܝܢ. ܘܡ̈ܝܬܐ ܡܬܚܝܝܢ. ܘܡܣ̈ܟܢܐ ܡܣܬܒܪܝܢ· [6]ܘܛܘܒܘܗܝ،
ܐܝܠܐ ܢܬܟܫܠ ܒܝ. ܀
[7]ܡܢ ܒܬܪ ܕܐܙܠܘ ܕܝܢ ܗܠܝܢ. ܫܪܝ ܗܘܐ ܝܫܘܥ ܠܡܐܡܪ ܠܟܢ̈ܫܐ
col 2 ܥܠ *ܝܘܚܢܢ· ܡܢܐ ܢܦܩܬܘܢ ܠܡܕܒܪܐ ܠܡܚܙܐ. ܩܢܝܐ ܕܡܢ
ܪܘܚܐ ܡܬܬܙܝܥ· [8]ܘܐܠܐ ܡܢܐ ܢܦܩܬܘܢ ܠܡܚܙܐ. ܓܒܪܐ
ܕܢܚ̈ܬܐ ܪ̈ܟܝܟܐ ܠܒܝܫ. ܗܐ ܐܝܠܝܢ ܕܪ̈ܟܝܟܐ ܠܒܝܫܝܢ ܒܒܝܬ ܡ̈ܠܟܐ
ܐܢܘܢ. [9]ܘܐܠܐ ܡܢܐ ܢܦܩܬܘܢ ܠܡܚܙܐ ܢܒܝܐ. ܐܝܢ ܐܡܪܢܐ

---

40 ܠܡܢ ܕܫܕܪܢܝ ܡܩܒܠ] ܡܩ' ܠܡܢ ܕܫ' S   41 ܕܡܩܒܠ 1°] + ܓܒܪ S
ܢܣܒ 1°] ܡܩܒܠ S   42 ܟܣܐ ܕܩܪ̈ܝܪܐ ܡ̈ܝܐ before ܠܚܕ....ܙܥܘܪ̈ܐ S
1 ܟܕ] pr. ܕ S (sic): cf Mt xix 1; xxvi 1; Lk i 8, 41; v 1, 17   ܝܫܘܥ] ܡܪܢ S
2. No § in S   ܕܝܫܘܥ] ܕܡܪܢ S   ܠܬܠܡܝܕܘܗܝ] C (sic, end of line); -ܘܗܝ S: cf Joh iv 8   3 ܠܐܚܪܝܢ ܗܘ] om. ܗܘ S (ܠܐܚܪܝܢ S[ed])   4 ܝܫܘܥ] S illegible
5 ܘܓܪ̈ܒܐ ܡܬܕܟܝܢ] S illegible   ܘܡܣ̈ܟܢܐ ܡܣܬܒܪܝܢ] om. S   6 ܐܝܠܐ] ܠܡܢ ܕܠܐ S   7 ܡܢ] ܘܡܢ S   ܕܐܙܠܘ ܕܝܢ] om. S   ܗܘܐ] om. S   ܝܫܘܥ] ܡܪܢ S   ܠܟܢ̈ܫܐ] ܠܟܢܫܐ S   ܩܢܝܐ] S illegible   ܕܡܢ ܪܘܚܐ] ܕܒܪܘܚܐ S   ܡܬܬܙܝܥܐ S   8 & 9 ܠܡܚܙܐ] ܠܡܚܐ S

41 He that receiveth a prophet in the name of a prophet taketh the *C S*
reward of a prophet, and he that receiveth a righteous man in the
name of a righteous man taketh the reward of a righteous man.
42 And whosoever shall give to drink to one of these little ones a cup
of cold water in the name of discipleship—amen, I say to you
that his reward shall not perish."

xi 1 And it came to pass when Jesus had finished commanding his
twelve disciples he removed from thence to teach and to preach in
their cities.

2 Now John, when he heard in prison the deeds of Jesus, de-
3 spatched his disciples and sent *word* to him: "Art thou he that
4 cometh, or for another is it *that* we are waiting?" And Jesus
answered and said to them: "Go *and* shew John that which ye
5 see and that which ye hear; for lo, the blind see and the lame walk
and the lepers are cleansed and the deaf hear and the poor are
6 sustained and the dead arise, and happy is it for him except he be
offended in me!"

7 Now after these went away Jesus had begun to say to the
multitudes concerning John: "What went ye forth to the desert
8 to see?—a reed that by the wind is shaken? But if not, what went
ye forth to see?—a man that with soft garments is clothed?
9 Lo, they that with soft *things* are clad are in kings' houses. But
if not, what went ye forth to see?—a prophet? Yea, I say to you,

---

41 He that] For he that *S* taketh 1°] receiveth *S* 42 a cup of cold water to one of these little ones *S* 1 when] *pr.* that *S* Jesus] our Lord *S* 2 Jesus] our Lord *S* 3 is it *that* we are] are we *S* 4 Jesus] *S illegible* Go...hear] 'Go and tell John not what ye have heard but what ye have seen' E^{100} 5 and the lepers are cleansed] *S illegible* and the poor are sustained] *om.* *S* E^{100} (= *k*) 6 except he be] that shall not be *S* 7 Now] And *S* went away] *om.* *S*: *cf* Mt ii 13 Jesus] our Lord *S* had begun] began *S* by the wind] in the wind *S*

C S ܠܟܘܢ ܕܝܬܝܪ ܗܘ ܡܢ ܢܒܝܐ. [10]ܗܢܘ ܕܟܬܝܒ ܥܠܘܗܝ. ܕܗܐ
ܡܫܕܪ ܐܢܐ ܡܠܐܟܝ ܩܕܡ ܦܪܨܘܦܟ. ܕܢܬܩܢ ܐܘܪܚܐ ܩܕܡܝܟ·
[11]ܐܡܝܢ ܐܡܪܢܐ ܠܟܘܢ ܕܠܐ ܩܡ ܒܝܠܕܝ ܢܫ̈ܐ ܪܒ ܡܢ ܝܘܚܢܢ
ܡܥܡܕܢܐ. ܙܥܘܪܐ ܕܝܢ ܒܡܠܟܘܬܐ ܕܫܡܝܐ ܪܒ ܗܘ ܡܢܗ. [12]ܡܢ
fol 17 r ܝܘܡ̈ܝ ܝܘܚܢܢ ܕܝܢ ܡܥܡܕܢܐ ܘܥܕܡܐ *ܠܗܫܐ. ܐܠܝܨܐ ܗܝ
ܡܠܟܘܬܐ ܕܫܡܝܐ. ܘܐܠ̈ܝܨܝܗ ܡܚܛܦܝܢ ܠܗ̇. [13]ܟܠܗܘܢ ܓܝܪ
ܢܒ̈ܝܐ ܘܐܘܪܝܬܐ ܥܕܡܐ ܠܝܘܚܢܢ ܐܬܢܒܝܘ. [14]ܘܐܢ ܨܒܝܢ
ܐܢܬܘܢ ܠܡܩܒܠܘ ܗܘܝܘ ܐܠܝܐ ܕܥܬܝܕ ܠܡܐܬܐ. [15]ܡܢ ܕܐܝܬ
ܠܗ ܐܕ̈ܢܐ ܠܡܫܡܥ ܢܫܡܥ.܀

[16]ܠܡܢ ܕܝܢ ܐܕܡܝܗ ܠܫܪܒܬܐ ܗܕܐ. ܕܡܝܐ ܠܛܠ̈ܝܐ ܕܝܬܒܝܢ
ܒܫܘܩܐ ܘܩܥܝܢ ܠܚܒܪ̈ܝܗܘܢ܆ [17]ܘܐܡܪܝܢ. ܙܡܪܢ ܠܟܘܢ ܘܠܐ
ܪܩܕܬܘܢ܆ ܘܐܠܝܢ ܠܟܘܢ ܘܠܐ ܐܪܩܕܬܘܢ܆ [18]ܐܬܐ ܓܝܪ
ܠܘܬܟܘܢ ܝܘܚܢܢ ܟܕ ܠܐ ܐܟܠ ܘܐܦܠܐ ܫܬܐ. ܘܐܡܪܝܢ
ܐܢܬܘܢ ܫܐܕܐ ܒܗ. [19]ܘܐܬܐ ܒܪܗ ܕܐܢܫܐ ܐܟܠ ܘܫܬܐ.
col 2 ܘܐܡܪܝܢ ܐܢܬܘܢ ܗܐ ܓܒܪܐ *ܐܟܘܠܐ ܘܫܬܝܐ. ܘܪܚܡܐ
ܕܡ̈ܟܣܐ ܘ̈ܕܚܛܝܐ. ܘܐܙܕܕܩܬ ܚܟܡܬܐ ܡܢ ܒ̈ܢܝܗ.܀

[20]ܗܝܕܝܢ ܫܪܝ ܗܘܐ ܝܫܘܥ ܠܡܚܣܕܘ ܡ̈ܕܝܢܬܐ. ܐܝܠܝܢ ܕܗܘܝ ܒܗܝܢ
ܚܝܠܐ ܣܓ̈ܝܐܐ ܘܠܐ ܬܒ. [21]ܘܐܡܪ ܘܝ ܠܟܝ ܟܘܪܙܝܢ ܘܝ ܠܟܝ
ܒܝܬ ܨܝܕܐ. ܕܐܠܘ ܒܨܘܪ ܘܒܨܝܕܢ ܗܘܘ ܚܝܠܐ ܕܗܘܘ ܒܟܝܢ.
ܟܒܪ ܕܝܢ ܒܣ̈ܩܐ ܘܒܩܛܡܐ ܬܒܘ. [22]ܡܛܠ ܗܢܐ ܐܡܪܢܐ ܠܟܝܢ.
ܕܠܨܘܪ ܘܠܨܝܕܢ ܢܗܘܐ ܢܝܚ ܒܝܘܡܐ ܕܕܝܢܐ ܝܬܝܪ ܡܢ ܕܠܟܝܢ.

---

9 ܕܝܬܝܪ] ܕܡܝܬܪ S   ܢܒܝܐ] *The seyâmê are not legible in S, but cf* ܡܣܗܕ ܥܠܘܗܝ ܡܪܢ ܕܪܒ ܗܘ ܡܢ ܢܒ̈ܝܐ A 123   10 ܕܟܬܝܒ ܥܠܘܗܝ] ܕܥܠܘܗܝ ܟܬܝܒ S   ܦܪܨܘܦܟ] ܐܦܝܟ S   12 ܕܝܢ] *om.* S   ܘܥܕܡܐ] *om.* ܘ S   ܡܚܛܦܝܢ] S *illegible*   13 ܘܐܘܪܝܬܐ] *om.* S: *cf* ܟܠܗ ܢܡܘܣܐ ܘܢܒܝܐ ܥܕܡܐ ܠܝܘܚܢܢ ܡܥܡܕܢܐ ܐܬܢܒܝܘ A 28 (=Lk xvi 16, *partly*)   15 ܠܡܫܡܥ] *om.* S   16 ܫܪܒܬܐ S   17 ܘܐܡܪܝܢ] *om.* S
18 ܠܘܬܟܘܢ] ܠܗ S   ܟܕ] *om.* S   ܘܐܦܠܐ] ܘܠܐ S   ܐܢܬܘܢ] *om.* S
19 ܐܢܬܘܢ] *om.* S   20 ܬܒ] ܬܒܘ S   21 ܟܘܪܙܝܢ | ܟ⌜ܘ⌝ܪ S^ed   ܒܟܝܢ] S *illegible*   22 ܘܠܨܝܕܢ S   ܢܝܚ] ܒܢܝܚ S

10 that he is more than the prophets. This is he of whom it is written *C S*
'Lo, I send my messenger before thy countenance, that he may prepare
11 a way before thee!' Amen, I say to you There hath not arisen
among them that are born of women one greater than John the
Baptist, but he that is little in the kingdom of heaven is greater
12 than he. But from the days of John the Baptist even until now
the kingdom of heaven is oppressed, and they that oppress it
13 snatch it away. For all the prophets and the Law prophesied
14 until John. And if ye wish to receive *it*, he is Elijah that is about
15 to come; he that hath ears to hear, let him hear.

16 "Now to whom shall I liken this generation? It is like unto
17 children that sit in the street and send *word* to their fellows, and
say: 'We have sung to you and ye have not danced, and we have
18 wailed to you and ye have not lamented.' For there came unto
you John neither eating nor drinking, and ye say: 'A devil in
19 him!' And there came the Son of Man eating and drinking, and
ye say: 'Lo, a man *who is* an eater and a drinker and a friend of
toll-gatherers and of sinners!' And wisdom hath been justified from
her sons."

20 Then began Jesus to reproach cities in which he shewed many
21 mighty works and they repented not. And he said: "Woe to thee,
Korazin! woe to thee, Beth Saida! for if in Tyre and in Sidon
had happened the mighty works that have happened in you, then
22 perchance in sackcloth and in ashes they had repented; therefore
I say to you that for Tyre and for Sidon it shall be easy in the

---

9 the prophets] *The plural points are not legible in S, but cf* 'Our Lord witnesseth of him that he is greater than the prophets' *A* 123 10 countenance] face *S* 12 But from] From *S* even] *om. S* snatch it away] *S illegible* 13 and the Law] *om. S*: *cf* 'All the law and the prophets prophesied until John the Baptist' *A* 28 (= Lk xvi 16, *partly*) 15 to hear] *om. S* 17 and say] *om. S* 18 unto you] to it *S* not eating and not drinking *S* ye say] they say *S* 19 ye say] they say *S* 21 and in Sidon] *om.* and *S*[ed] in you] *S illegible* 22 easy] tolerable *S*

C S [23]ܘܐܢܬ ܟܦܪܢܚܘܡ ܠܐ ܥܕܡܐ ܠܫܡܝܐ ܬܬܬܪܝܡܝܢ. ܐܠܐ ܥܕܡܐ
ܠܫܝܘܠ ܬܬܚܬܝܢ. ܕܐܠܘ ܒܣܕܘܡ ܗܘܘ ܚܝܠܐ ܐܝܠܝܢ ܕܗܘܘ ܒܟܝ.
fol 17 v ܡܩܘܝܐ *ܗܘܬ ܥܕܡܐ ܠܝܘܡܢܐ. [24]ܡܛܠ ܗܢܐ ܐܡܪܢܐ. ܕܠܐܪܥܐ
ܕܣܕܘܡ ܢܗܘܐ ܢܝܚ ܒܝܘܡܐ ܕܕܝܢܐ ܝܬܝܪ ܡܢ ܕܠܟܝ .:.

[25]ܒܗܘ ܕܝܢ ܙܒܢܐ ܥܢܐ ܝܫܘܥ ܘܐܡܪ. ܡܘܕܐ ܐܢܐ ܠܟ ܐܒܐ
ܡܪܐ ܕܫܡܝܐ ܘܕܐܪܥܐ. ܕܟܣܝܬ ܗܠܝܢ ܡܢ ܚܟܝܡܐ ܘܓܠܝܬ
§A 123, 200 ܐܢܝܢ ܠܝܠܘܕܐ. [26]ܐܝܢ ܐܒܝ ܕܗܟܢܐ ܗܘܐ ܨܒܝܢܐ ܩܕܡܝܟ. [§27]ܟܠ
¶A ܡܕܡ ܐܫܬܠܡ ܠܝ ܡܢ ܐܒܝ¶. ܘܠܐ ܐܢܫ ܝܕܥ ܠܒܪܐ ܐܠܐ ܐܢ
ܐܒܐ. ܘܐܦ ܠܐ ܠܐܒܐ ܐܠܐ ܐܢ ܒܪܐ. ܘܡܢ ܕܨܒܐ ܒܪܐ
ܕܢܓܠܐ ܠܗ .:.

§A 319 §Thos 252 [§§28]ܬܘ ܠܘܬܝ ܟܠܟܘܢ ܠܐܝܐ ܘܥܡܝܠܝ ܡܘܒܠܐ ܫܩܝܠܬܐ ܘܐܢܐ
¶Thos ܐܢܝܚܟܘܢ¶. [29]ܘܫܩܘܠܘ ܢܝܪܝ ܥܠܝܟܘܢ¶. ܘܝܠܦܘ *ܡܢܝ ܕܢܝܚ ܐܢܐ
¶A col 2 ܘܡܟܝܟ ܐܢܐ ܒܠܒܝ. ܘܬܫܟܚܘܢ ܢܝܚܐ ܠܢܦܫܬܟܘܢ. [30]ܢܝܪܝ ܓܝܪ
ܒܣܝܡ ܗܘ. ܘܡܘܒܠܝ ܩܠܝܠܐ .:.

[1]ܘܒܗܘ ܙܒܢܐ ܡܗܠܟ ܗܘܐ ܝܫܘܥ ܒܫܒܬܐ ܒܝܬ ܙܪܥܐ.
ܘܬܠܡܝܕܘܗܝ ܟܦܢܘ. ܘܫܪܝܘ ܡܠܩܛܝܢ ܫܒܠܐ ܘܦܪܟܝܢ ܒܐܝ̈ܕܝܗܘܢ
ܘܐܟܠܝܢ. [2]ܟܕ ܚܙܘ ܐܢܘܢ ܦܪܝܫܐ ܐܡܪܝܢ ܠܗ. ܡܢܐ ܥܒܕܝܢ
ܬܠܡܝܕܝܟ ܡܕܡ ܕܠܐ ܫܠܝܛ ܠܡܥܒܕ. [3]ܐܡܪ ܠܗܘܢ ܠܐ

---

23 ܘܐܢܬ ܟܦܪܢܚܘܡ (C sic)] S illegible ܠܐ...ܬܬܬܪܝܡܝܢ] * * ܕܐܬܬܪܝܡܬܝ S (rest illegible) ܐܠܐ ܥܕܡܐ and ܕܐܠܘ and ܗܘܘ] S illegible ܚܝܠܐ ܐܝܠܝܢ ܕܗܘܘ ܒܟܝ] ܘܐܬܚܙܝܘ ܕܒܟܝ ܚܝܠܐ S ܗܘܬ] ܗܘ S ܥܕܡܐ] om. S 24 ܡܛܠ ܗܢܐ] om. S ܕܠܟܝ] ܕܠܟܝ̇ S[ed] (i.e. last letter illegible) 25 ܕܝܢ] om. S 27 ܘܐܦ ܠܐ] ܘܠܐ S ܠܐܒܐ] + ܝܕܥ ܐܢܫ S ܕܨܒܐ] ܕܢܨܒܐ S 28 ܬܘ] ܐܬܘ S ܟܠܟܘܢ] om. A Thos[cod.c] ܘܥܡܠܝܢ Thos[cod.a] ܫܩܝܠܬܐ] om. S A Thos[cod.a] ܘܐܢܐ] om. Thos[cod.c] (sic) 29 ܘܫܩܘܠܘ] om. ܘ A[a] ܢܝܪܝ] ܢܝܪܝ ܕܝܠܝ A[a], ܢܝܪܐ ܕܝܠܝ A[b]: followed by ܡܛܠ ܕܢܝܪܝ ܩܠܝܠ ܗܘ ܘܒܣܝܡ 1 ܘܒܗܘ] om. ܘ S ܒܫܒܬܐ] ܒܝܘܡܐ ܕܫܒܬܐ S ܘܟܦܢܘ ܬܠܡܝܕܘܗܝ S ܘܦܪܟܝܢ ܒܐܝ̈ܕܝܗܘܢ] om. S 2 ܡܢܐ] ܠܡܢܐ S ܥܒܕܝܢ ܬܠܡܝܕܝܟ] tr. S

23 day of judgement rather than for you. And thou, Kapharnahum! *C S*
not unto heaven shalt thou be uplifted, but unto Sheol shalt thou
go down; for if in Sodom had happened the mighty works that
24 have happened in thee, it had been standing until to-day. Therefore
I say that for the land of Sodom it shall be easy in the day of
judgement rather than for thee."

25 Now at that time Jesus answered and said: "I give thanks to
thee, Father, Lord of heaven and of earth, that thou hast kept secret
these things from the wise and hast revealed them to children;
26, 27 yea, my Father, that so was the will before thee. §Everything hath §*A* 123,
been delivered unto me from my Father,¶ and no one knoweth the 200 ¶*A*
Son save the Father, neither the Father save the Son, and he to
whom the Son shall be willing to reveal *it*.

28 "§§Come unto me, all ye toilers and bearers of heavy burdens, §*A* 319
29 and I will ease you.¶ And bear my yoke upon you,¶ and learn §*Thos* 252
from me that I am easy and meek in my heart, and ye shall find ¶*Thos*
30 ease for your souls. For my yoke is gentle and my burden light." ¶*A*

xii 1 And at that time Jesus was walking on the sabbath in the
cornfields, and his disciples were hungry, and they began pulling the
2 ears *of corn* and rubbing *them* in their hands and eating. When the
Pharisees saw them, they say to him: "Why are thy disciples doing
3 that which is not lawful to do?" He saith to them: "Have ye not

---

23 And thou, Kapharnahum] *S illegible* not...uplifted] that hath been uplifted... *S* (*rest illegible*) but unto *and* for if *and* had] *S illegible* that have happened in thee] that in you were seen *S* until] unto *S* **24** Therefore] *om. S* thee] you *S*[ed] (*but the critical letter is illegible*) **25** Now at] At *S* from the wise] + 'and from the prudent' *E*[117] **27** neither the Father] + doth any one know *S*: *cf* 'no man knoweth the Father but the Son, and no man knoweth the Son but the Father' *E*[216 (not 117)] shall be] is *S* **28** all ye] *om. A Thos*[cod. c] heavy] *om. S A Thos*[cod. a] (*not E*[117]) **29** And 1°] *om. A*[a] my yoke] my yoke, even mine *A*[a], the yoke of me *A*[b]: *followed by* 'because my yoke is light and gentle' **1** And at] At *S* sabbath] sabbath-day *S* and rubbing...hands] *om. S* **2** Why] Wherefore *S*

C S ܩܪܝܬܘܢ ܡܢܐ ܥܒܕ ܕܘܝܕ܂ ܟܕ ܟܦܢ ܘܐܢܫܝܢ ܕܥܡܗ. [4]ܐܝܟܢܐ
ܥܠ ܠܒܝܬܗ ܕܐܠܗܐ. ܘܐܟܠ ܡܢ ܠܚܡ ܐ̈ܦܐ. ܕܠܐ ܠܗ ܫܠܝܛ
ܗܘܐ ܠܡܐܟܠ ܐܦܠܐ ܠܐܢܫܝܢ ܕܥܡܗ. ܐܠܐ ܐܢ ܠܟ̈ܗܢܐ
fol 18 r ܒܠܚܘܕ. [*5]ܐܘ ܠܐ ܩܪܝܬܘܢ ܒܐܘܪܝܬܐ. ܕܟ̈ܗܢܐ ܒܗܝܟܠܐ
ܗܢܘܢ ܡܚܠܝܢ ܠܗ̇ ܠܫܒܬܐ. ܘܕܠܐ ܚ̈ܛܗܝܢ ܐܢܘܢ܆ [6]ܐܡܪܢܐ
ܠܟܘܢ ܓܝܪ ܕܗܐ ܕܪܒ ܡܢ ܗܝܟܠܐ ܗܪܟܐ. [7]ܘܐܠܘ ܝܕܥܝܢ
ܗܘܝܬܘܢ ܡܢܘ ܚܢܢܐ ܨܒܐ ܐܢܐ ܘܠܐ ܕܒܚܬܐ. ܠܐ ܡܚܝܒܝܢ
ܗܘܝܬܘܢ ܠܙܟܝܐ. [8]ܡܪܗ̇ ܓܝܪ ܕܫܒܬܐ ܒܪܗ ܗܘ ܕܐܢܫܐ..
[9]ܘܟܕ ܫܢܐ ܡܢ ܬܡܢ ܘܐܬܐ ܠܟܢܘܫܬܗܘܢ܆ [10]ܘܗܘܐ ܓܒܪܐ ܚܕ܂
ܕܐܝܕܗ ܕܝܡܝܢܐ ܝܒܝܫܐ ܗܘܬ· ܘܡܫܐܠܝܢ ܗܘܘ ܠܗ ܘܐܡܪܝܢ.
ܕܐܢ ܗܘ ܕܫܠܝܛ ܒܝܘܡܐ ܕܫܒܬܐ ܠܡܐܣܝܘ. ܕܢܫܟܚܘܢ
col 2 ܢܐܟܠܘܢ ܩܪ̈ܨܘܗܝ. [11]ܐܡܪ ܠܗܘܢ. ܡܢܘ ܓܒܪܐ *ܡܢܟܘܢ ܕܐܝܬ
ܠܗ ܥܪܒܐ. ܘܢܦܠ ܒܓܘܒܐ ܒܝܘܡܐ ܕܫܒܬܐ. ܘܠܐ ܐܚܕ܂ ܡܩܝܡ
ܠܗ. [12]ܟܡܐ ܗܟܝܠ ܝܬܝܪ ܒܪ ܐܢܫܐ ܡܢ ܥܪܒܐ. ܗܟܝܠ ܫܠܝܛ
ܗܘ ܒܫܒܬܐ ܠܡܥܒܕ ܕܫܦܝܪ. [13]ܗܝܕܝܢ ܐܡܪ ܠܓܒܪܐ ܗܘ ܦܫܘܛ
ܐܝܕܟ. ܘܦܫܛ ܐܝܕܗ ܘܬܩܢܬ ܐܝܟ ܚܒܪܬܗ̇. oo oo oo
[14]ܘܟܕ ܢܦܩܘ ܦܪ̈ܝܫܐ. ܢܣܒܘ ܥܠܘܗܝ ܡܠܟܐ ܐܝܟܢܐ ܕܢܘܒܕܘܢܗ.
[15]ܝܫܘܥ ܕܝܢ ܝܕܥ ܘܫܢܐ ܠܗ ܡܢ ܬܡܢ. ܘܐܙܠܘ ܒܬܪܗ ܟܢܫܐ
ܣ̈ܓܝܐܐ. ܘܐܣܝ ܠܟܠܗܘܢ. [16]ܘܟܐܐ ܒܗܘܢ ܕܗܘܢ ܠܐܢܫ
ܠܐ ܢܓܠܘܢܝܗܝ. [17]ܕܢܬܡܠܐ ܡܕܡ ܕܐܬܐܡܪ ܒܦܘܡ ܐܫܥܝܐ

3 ܟܕ ܟܦܢ] *S illegible* 4 ܐܝܟܢܐ *to* 6 ܐܡܪܢܐ ܠܟܘܢ] *S illegible, except* ܠܗ ܫܠܝܛ *in ver.* 4 5 ܒܐܘܪܝܬܐ] ܒ *on an erasure in C* 6 ܕܪܒ] ܪܒ *S*[ed] 7 ܡܢܘ] *S illegible* 9. *No* § *in S* ܘܐܬܐ] *om.* ܘ *S* 10 ܕܐܝܕܗ] ܘܐܝܕܗ *S* ܕܐܢ ܗܘ ܕܫܠܝܛ] ܕܐܢ ܗܘ ܫܠܝܛ *S* ܒܝܘܡܐ ܕܫܒܬܐ ܠܡܐܣܝܘ] *om. S* 11 ܒܓܘܒܐ] *S illegible* 14. *Perhaps no* § *in S* ܕܢܘܒܕܘܢܗ] *om.* ܕ *S* 15 ܠܗ] *om. S* ܘܐܣܝ ܠܟܠܗܘܢ] ܘܠܟܠܗܘܢ ܐܣܝ *S* 16 ܘܟܐܐ] + ܗܘܐ *S* ܕܗܘܢ ܠܐܢܫ] ܒܗܘܢ ܕܠܐܢܫ *S* ܢܓܠܘܢܝܗܝ] ܢܐܡܪܘܢ *S* 17 ܒܦܘܡ ܐܫܥܝܐ] ܒܐܫܥܝܐ *S*

read what David did when he was hungry and they that were with C S
4 him, how he entered the house of God and ate of the Shewbread,
that for him was not lawful to eat nor for them that were with him,
5 but for the priests only? Or have ye not read in the Law that the
priests in the Temple--they profane the sabbath, and are without
6 sins? For I say to you Lo, a greater than the Temple *is* here;
7 and if ye had known what is *meant by* 'Mercy I seek and not
8 sacrifice,' ye would not have condemned the innocent. For the Lord
of the sabbath is the Son of Man."

9 And when he removed from thence and came to their synagogue,
10 and lo, a certain man whose right hand was withered, and they were
asking him and saying "If so be it were lawful on the sabbath-day
11 to heal?" that they might be able to accuse him. He saith to them:
"What man is there of you that hath a sheep and it fall into a pit on
12 the sabbath-day and doth not draw *and* take it up? How much more
therefore is a man than a sheep! Hence it is lawful on the sabbath
13 to do well." Then saith he to that man: "Stretch forth thy hand;"
and he stretched forth his hand and it was restored like its fellow.

14 And when the Pharisees went forth they took against him counsel
15 so that they might destroy him. But Jesus knew and removed from
thence, and there went after him many folk, and he healed them
16 all. And he rebuked them that they to no man should reveal him,
17 that that might be fulfilled which was said by the mouth of Isaiah

---

3 when...hungry] *S illegible* 4 how—6 I say to you] *S illegible, except* 'for him...lawful' *in ver.* 4 7 what is] *S illegible* 9 and came] he came *S*: *the text of C also can be so translated* (*cf* Lk xiii 10, 11 *S C*) 10 whose] and his *S* If so be it were] If it be *S*: *cf* Mt xviii 9, 21, *etc* on the sabbath-day to heal] *om. S* 11 into a pit] *S illegible* 14 so that] how *S* 15 he healed them all] all of them he healed *S* 16 he...reveal him] he had rebuked those same *folk* that to no man they should say *it S* 17 the mouth of] *om. S*

C S fol 18 v ܢܒܝܐ ܕܐܡܪ ܗܘܐ. [18]ܕܗܐ ܥܒܕܝ, *ܕܐܨܛܒܝܬ ܒܗ· ܘܚܒܝܒܝ
ܕܨܒܝܬ ܒܗ ܢܦܫܝ. ܪܘܚܝ ܐܣܝܡ ܥܠܘܗܝ. ܕܢܟܪܙ ܕܝܢܐ ܠܥܡ̈ܡܐ.
[19]ܠܐ ܢܨܚܐ ܘܠܐ ܢܩܥܐ. ܘܠܐ ܐܢܫ ܢܫܡܥ ܩܠܗ ܒܫܘܩܐ.
[20]ܩܢܝܐ ܪܥܝܥܐ ܠܐ ܢܬܒܪ. ܘܒܨܝܢܐ ܕܡܛܦܛܦ ܠܐ ܢܕܥܟ.
ܥܕܡܐ ܕܢܦܩ ܕܝܢܐ ܠܙܟܘܬܐ. [21]ܘܠܫܡܗ ܥܡ̈ܡܐ ܢܣܒܪܘܢ ܀
[22]ܗܝܕܝܢ ܩܪܒܘ ܩܕܡܘܗܝ, ܠܓܒܪܐ ܚܕ ܕܐܝܬ ܗܘܐ ܥܠܘܗܝ, ܫܐܕܐ.
ܘܥܘܝܪ ܘܚܪܫ. ܘܐܣܝܗ. ܘܡܠܠ ܚܪܫܐ ܗܘ ܘܚܙܐ ܘܫܡܥ·
[23]ܘܡܬܕܡܪܝܢ ܗܘܘ ܟܠܗܘܢ ܟܢ̈ܫܐ. ܘܐܡܪܝܢ ܗܘܘ ܕܕܠܡܐ ܗܢ
ܗܘ ܒܪܗ ܕܕܘܝܕ. [24]ܦܪ̈ܝܫܐ ܕܝܢ ܟܕ ܫܡܥܘ ܐܡܪܘ. ܗܢܐ ܠܐ
col 2 ܡܦܩ ܫܐ̈ܕܐ ܐܠܐ ܒܒܥܠܙܒܘܒ *ܪܫܗܘܢ ܕܕܝ̈ܘܐ. [25]ܟܕ ܚܙܐ
ܕܝܢ ܪ̈ܢܝܗܘܢ ܐܡܪ ܠܗܘܢ܂ ܟܠ ܡܠܟܘ ܕܡܬܦܠܓܐ ܥܠ ܢܦܫܗ̇
ܬܚܪܒ܂ ܘܟܠ ܒܝܬ ܘܡܕܝܢܐ ܕܡܬܦܠܓܐ ܥܠ ܢܦܫܗ ܠܐ ܢܩܘܡ.
[26]ܘܐܢ ܣܛܢܐ ܠܣܛܢܐ ܡܦܩ ܥܠ ܢܦܫܗ ܡܬܦܠܓ܂ ܐܝܟܢܐ
ܗܟܝܠ ܬܩܘܡ ܡܠܟܘܬܗ. [27]ܘܐܢ ܐܢܐ ܒܒܥܠܙܒܘܒ ܡܦܩ ܐܢܐ
ܫܐ̈ܕܐ ܡܢ ܒܢ̈ܝܟܘܢ ܒܡܢܐ ܡܦܩܝܢ ܠܗܘܢ. ܡܛܠ
ܗܢܐ ܗܢܘܢ ܢܗܘܘܢ ܠܟܘܢ ܕܝ̈ܢܐ. [28]ܐܢ ܕܝܢ ܐܢܐ ܒܪܘܚܐ
ܕܐܠܗܐ ܡܦܩ ܐܢܐ ܫܐ̈ܕܐ. ܡܛܠ ܩܪܒܬ ܥܠܝܟܘܢ ܡܠܟܘܬܗ
fol 19 r ܕܐܠܗܐ. [29]ܐܝܟܢܐ ܓܝܪ ܡܫܟܚ ܐܢܫ ܕܢܥܘܠ ܠܒܝܬܗ *ܕܚܣܝܢܐ
ܘܢܒܘܙ ܡ̈ܐܢܘܗܝ. ܐܠܐ ܐܢ ܠܘܩܕܡ ܠܗ ܠܚܣܝܢܐ ܢܐܣܘܪ.
ܘܗܝܕܝܢ ܢܒܘܙ ܒܝܬܗ· [30]ܡܢ ܕܠܐ ܗܘܐ ܥܡܝ ܠܘܩܒܠܝ ܗܘ· ܘܡܢ

---

18 ܕܗܐ] *om.* ܕ *S* ܥܒܕܝ....ܢܦܫ] *S mostly illegible: it seems to have read* ⌈ܕܒܗ⌉ ܐܨܛܒܝܬ 19 ܒܫܘܩܐ] *om. S* 21 ܘܠܫܡܗ] ܠܫ *illegible in S* ܥܡ̈ܡܐ ܢܣܒܪܘܢ] *tr. S* 22 ܩܕܡܘܗܝ] ܠܗ *S* ܕܐܝܬ....ܘܚܪܫ] *S illegible* (* * ܘܥܘܝܪ | ܗܘ * * *S*^ed) ܚܪܫܐ] *S illegible* ܘܚܙܐ] *om. S*^vid 23 ܡܬܕܡܪܝܢ ܗܘܘ ⌈ܟܢ̈ܫܐ ܟܠܗܘܢ⌉ *S*^vid ܗܘܘ 2°] *om. S* ܕܕܠܡܐ] ܕܠܡܐ *S* 24 ܫܐ̈ܕܐ ܠܐ ܡܦܩ *S* 25 ܪ̈ܢܝܗܘܢ] ܡܚܫ̈ܒܬܗܘܢ *S* ܘܟܠ ܒܝܬ] *S illegible* 25, 26 ܥܠ ܢܦܫܗ ܠܐ....ܡܦܩ] *S illegible*
26 ܐܝܟܢܐ ܗܟܝܠ] *S illegible* 27—30.] *S illegible (except* ܠܐ ܥܡܝ * * ܡܒܕܪ *in ver.* 30)

18 the prophet, who had said "Lo, my slave in whom I have been *C S*
pleased, and my beloved in whom my soul hath delighted; my spirit
will I put upon him, that he should preach judgement to the peoples.
19 He shall not cry out nor strive, neither shall any man hear his voice
20 in the street. The bruised reed shall not be broken and the lamp
that smouldereth shall not be quenched, until he send forth the
21 judgement for victory; and for his name the peoples shall hope."
22 Then they brought near before him a certain man that had a
devil upon him and was blind and deaf, and he healed him and the
23 deaf-mute spake and saw and heard. And all the multitudes were
wondering, and were saying "Can then this be the son of David?"
24 But the Pharisees, when they heard, said: "This *fellow* doth not
25 cast out devils but by Beelzebub the chief of the demons." Now
when he saw their mind he said to them: "Every kingdom that
shall be divided against itself shall be desolated, and every house
26 and city that shall be divided against itself shall not stand. And if
Satan doth cast out Satan, against himself he is divided; how
27 therefore will his kingdom stand? And if I by Beelzebub cast out
devils from your sons, your sons—by what do they cast them out?
28 Therefore they shall be for you judges. But if I by the Spirit of
God cast out devils, henceforth the kingdom of God hath drawn
29 nigh upon you. For how can anyone enter the house of the strong
man and spoil his things, except first he bind the strong man
30 himself, and then spoil his house? He that is not with me is against

---

18 my slave...delighted] *S mostly illegible* 19 in the street] *om. S* 21 for] *S illegible* shall the peoples hope *S* 22 before him] to him *S* that had....deaf] *S illegible* the deaf-mute] *S illegible* and saw] *om.* S^{vid}: *cf* 'They brought unto him a certain man possessed with a devil, deaf and dumb and blind...he healed him and caused him to hear, to speak and to see' E^{113} 23 were 2°] *om. S* 24 devils doth not cast out *S* Beelzebub] *C S* (*and* syr. vg); Beelzebul $E^{75, 160, 206}$ (= arm. vg) *and* Diat^{ar} $^2/_2$ 25 their mind] their meditation *S* and every house] *S illegible* 25, 26 against itself (2°)....cast out Satan] *S illegible* 26 how therefore] *S illegible* 27—30.] *S illegible* (*except* 'gathereth not' *and* 'scattereth' *in ver.* 30)

ܕܠܐ ܟܢܫ ܥܡܝ ܡܒܕܪܘ ܡܒܕܪ. [31]ܡܛܠܗܢܐ ܐܡܪ ܐܢܐ ܠܟܘܢ. C S
ܕܟܠ ܚܛ̈ܗܝܢ ܘܓܘܕ̈ܦܝܢ ܢܫܬܒܩܘܢ ܠܒܢ̈ܝ ܐܢܫܐ. ܟܠ ܕܥܠ
ܪܘܚܐ ܕܝܢ ܕܩܘܕܫܐ ܓܕܘܦ ܠܐ ܢܫܬܒܩ ܠܗ. [32]ܘܟܠ ܕܢܐܡܪ ܡܠܬܐ
ܥܠ ܒܪܗ ܕܐܢܫܐ ܢܫܬܒܩ ܠܗ. ܟܠ ܕܥܠ ܪܘܚܐ ܕܝܢ ܕܩܘܕܫܐ
ܓܕܦ ܠܐ ܢܫܬܒܩ ܠܗ. ܠܐ ܒܗܢܐ ܥܠܡܐ ܘܠܐ ܒܥܠܡܐ
ܕܥܬܝܕ. [33]ܐܘ ܥܒܕܘ ܐܝܠܢܐ ܛܒܐ ܘܦܐܪ̈ܘܗܝ ܛܒ̈ܝܢ. ܐܘ ܥܒܕܘ
ܐܝܠܢܐ ܒܝܫܐ *ܘܦܐܪ̈ܘܗܝ ܒܝ̈ܫܝܢ. ܡܢ ܦܐܪ̈ܘܗܝ ܕܝܢ ܡܬܝܕܥ col 2
ܐܝܠܢܐ. [34]ܝܠܕܐ ܕܐܟ̈ܕܢܐ. ܐܝܟܢܐ ܡܫܟܚܝܢ ܐܢܬܘܢ ܛ̈ܒܬܐ
ܠܡܡܠܠܘ ܕܒ̈ܝܫܐ ܐܢܬܘܢ. ܡܢ ܬܘܬܪ̈ܘܬܗ ܓܝܪ ܕܠܒܐ ܡܦܩ
ܦܘܡܐ. [35]ܘܓܒܪܐ ܛܒܐ ܡܢ ܣܝ̈ܡܬܐ ܛ̈ܒܬܐ ܕܠܒܗ ܡܦܩ
ܛ̈ܒܬܐ. ܘܓܒܪܐ ܒܝܫܐ ܡܢ ܣܝ̈ܡܬܐ ܒܝ̈ܫܬܐ ܕܠܒܗ ܒܝ̈ܫܬܐ
ܡܡܠܠ. [36]ܐܡܪܢܐ ܠܟܘܢ ܕܝܢ. §ܕܟܠ ܡܠܐ ܒܛܠܐ ܕܢܐܡܪܘܢ §A447
ܒܢ̈ܝ ܐܢܫܐ. ܢܬܠܘܢ ܥܠܝܗ ܦܬܓܡܐ ܒܝܘܡܐ ܕܕܝܢܐ. [37]ܡܢ
ܡ̈ܠܝܟ ܓܝܪ ܬܙܕܕܩ. ܘܡܢ ܡ̈ܠܝܟ ܬܬܚܝܒ¶. ¶A
[38]ܗܝܕܝܢ ܥܢܘ ܠܗ ܐܢܫܐ ܡܢ ܣܦܪ̈ܐ ܘܦܪ̈ܝܫܐ ܘܐܡܪܝܢ ܠܗ.
ܡܠܦܢܐ. ܨܒܝܢ ܐܢܚܢ *ܕܢܚܙܐ ܡܢܟ ܡܕܡ ܐܬܐ. [39]ܗܘ ܕܝܢ ܥܢܐ fol 19 v
ܘܐܡܪ ܠܗܘܢ. ܫܪܒܬܐ ܗܕܐ ܒܝܫܬܐ ܘܓܝܪܬܐ. ܐܬܐ ܒܥܝܐ
ܘܐܬܐ ܠܐ ܬܬܝܗܒ ܠܗ̇. ܐܠܐ ܐܢ ܐܬܗ ܕܝܘܢܢ ܢܒܝܐ.
[§40]ܐܝܟܢܐ ܓܝܪ ܕܗܘܐ ܝܘܢܢ ܒܟܪܣܗ ܕܢܘܢܐ ܬܠܬܐ ܝܘ̈ܡܝܢ ܘܬܠܬܐ §A222

---

31 ܟܠ] + ܡܢ S ܕܩܘܕܫܐ] om. S 33 ܥܒܕܘ 1° & 2°] ܥܒܕ S
ܕܝܢ] ܓܝܪ S[ed], *but the photograph might very well be read* ܓܝܪ: *cf* Lk xviii 25
ܡܬܝܕܥ] ܢܬܝܕܥ S 34 ܕܐܟ̈ܕܢܐ] ܕܚܘ̈ܘܬܐ S ܬܘܬܪ̈ܘܬܗ] ܬܘܬܪ̈ܐ ܗܘ
S (*sic*) 35. *For* A 303, *see on* Lk vi 45 36 ܡܠܐ ܒܛܠܬܐ S (*sic*)
ܕܢܐܡܪܘܢ] ܕܢܡܠܠܘܢ S ܢܬܠܘܢ ܥܠܝܗ ܦܬܓܡܐ] ܦܬܓܡܐ ܢܬܠܘܢ S;
ܢܬܠܘܢ ܦܬܓܡܐ A (ܡܢܗ- A[a], *sic*)
37 ܡܢ ܡ̈ܠܝܟ ܓܝܪ] ܘܬܘܒ ܬܬܚܝܒ. ܕܡܢ ܡ̈ܠܝܟ A
38 ܥܢܘ....ܘܐܡܪܝܢ ܠܗ] ܐܡܪܝܢ ܠܗ ܐܢܫܐ ܡܢ ܣܦܪ̈ܐ ܘܦܪ̈ܝܫܐ S
39 ܗܕܐ] *om.* S ܐܬܐ ܒܥܝܐ] *tr.* S ܘܐܬܐ] *om.* ܘ S ܠܗ̇] *The dot was omitted by* C* 40 ܐܝܟܢܐ ܓܝܪ] ܘܐܝܟܢܐ S; ܐܝܟ A
ܝܘܢܢ] + ܢܒܝܐ S; + ܒܪ ܡܬܝ A ܐܝܡܡ̈ܐ ܬܠܬܐ ܘܠܠܘ̈ܬܐ ܬܠܬܐ S

31 me, and he that gathereth not with me scattereth indeed. Therefore *C S*
I say to you All sins and blasphemies shall be forgiven to men,
but every one that against the Holy Spirit shall blaspheme, it shall
32 not be forgiven him. And every one that shall say a word against
the Son of Man, it shall be forgiven him; but every one that against
the Holy Spirit shall blaspheme, it shall not be forgiven him, not
33 in this world nor in the world that is to be. Either make a good
tree and *then* its fruits are good, or make an evil tree and *then* its
34 fruits are evil; but from its fruits is the tree known. Offspring of
vipers, how can ye speak good things, ye that are evil? For from
35 the superfluities of the heart doth the mouth bring forth; and the
good man from the good treasures in his heart bringeth forth good
things, and the evil man from the evil treasures in his heart evil
36 things doth speak. But I say to you §Every idle word that §*A* 447
men shall speak, they shall give for it an answer in the day of
37 judgement. For from thy words thou shalt be justified, and from
thy words thou shalt be condemned."¶ ¶*A*

38 Then drew near unto him some of the scribes and Pharisees,
and they say to him: "Teacher, we wish to see from thee some
39 sign." But he answered and said to them: "This generation evil
and adulterous—a sign it seeketh, and a sign shall not be given to
40 it, save the sign of Jonah the prophet. §For as Jonah was in the §*A* 222

---

31 every one] whosoever *S* Holy] *om. S* **33** make 1° *and* 2°] *sing. in C*; *plur. in S* but] for *S* is] shall be *S* **34** vipers] serpents *S* **35**. *For A* 303, *see on* Lk vi 45 **36** Every idle word] *S may be better translated* 'All idle words' speak] say *S* they shall give for it an answer] an answer they shall give *S*; they shall give an answer *A* (its answer A^{a}) **37** For from thy words] 'And again it is written From thy words..' *A* **38** Then drew near...say to him] Then say to him some of the scribes and Pharisees *S* **39** This generation...and a sign] A generation evil and adulterous seeketh a sign—a sign *S* (*not* E^{118}) **40** For] *C* E^{118}; and *S*; *om. A* Jonah] *C* E^{118}; + the prophet *S*; + son of Matthew *A* (*i.e.* Amittai: *cf* Jon i 1 syr. vg)

C S ܠܠܝܢ܂ ܗܟܢܐ ܐܦ ܒܪܗ ܕܐܢܫܐ ܢܗܘܐ ܒܠܒܗ ܕܐܪܥܐ¶
¶A ܬܠܬܐ ܝܘܡܝܢ ܘܬܠܬܐ ܠܠܝܢ܂ [41]ܓܒܪ̈ܐ ܒܢܝ ܢܝܢܘܐ ܢܩܘܡܘܢ
ܒܕܝܢܐ ܥܡ ܫܪܒܬܐ ܗܕܐ ܘܢܚܝܒܘܢܗ̇܂ ܕܗܢܘܢ ܬܒܘ ܒܟܪܘܙܘܬܗ
ܕܝܘܢܢ܂ ܘܗܐ ܕܝܬܝܪ ܡܢ ܝܘܢܢ ܗܪܟܐ܂ [42]ܡܠܟܬܐ ܕܬܝܡܢܐ ܬܩܘܡ
ܒܕܝܢܐ ܥܡ ܫܪܒܬܐ ܗܕܐ ܘܬܚܝܒܝܗ̇܂ ܕܐܬܬ ܡܢ ܥܒ̈ܪܝܗ̇
col 2 *ܕܐܪܥܐ ܕܬܫܡܥ ܚܟܡܬܗ ܕܫܠܝܡܘܢ܂ ܘܗܐ ܕܝܬܝܪ ܡܢ ܫܠܝܡܘܢ
ܗܪܟܐ ܀

[43]ܪܘܚܐ ܕܝܢ ܛܢܦܬܐ ܡܐ ܕܢܦܩܬ ܡܢ ܒܪ ܐܢܫܐ܂ ܐܙܠܐ
ܡܬܟܪܟܐ ܒܐ̈ܬܪܘܬܐ ܕܨ̈ܗܝܐ ܠܝܬ ܒܗܘܢ܂ ܕܬܫܟܚ ܠܗ̇ ܢܝܚܐ܂
ܘܟܕ ܕܠܐ ܐܫܟܚܬ ܠܗ̇܂ [44]ܗܝܕܝܢ ܐܡܪܐ܂ ܐܗܦܘܟ ܐܙܠ
ܠܒܝܬܝ، ܡܢ ܐܬܪ ܕܢܦܩܬ܂ ܘܐܢ ܐܬܬ ܐܫܟܚܬܗ ܕܣܪܝܩ ܘܟܢܝܫ
ܘܡܨܒܬ܂ [45]ܗܝܕܝܢ ܐܙܠܐ ܕܒܪܐ ܥܡܗ̇ ܫܒܥ ܪ̈ܘܚܝܢ ܐ̈ܚܪܢܝܢ
ܕܒܝܫܢ ܡܢܗ̇܂ ܘܥܐܠ ܘܥܡܪܢ ܒܗ܂ ܘܗܘܝܐ ܐܚܪܝܬܗ ܕܓܒܪܐ
ܗܘ ܒܝܫܐ ܡܢ ܩܕܡܝܬܗ܂ ܗܟܢܐ ܢܗܘܐ ܠܗ̇ ܠܫܪܒܬܐ ܗܕܐ
ܒܝܫܬܐ܂ ܀

fol 20 r *[46]ܥܕ ܗܘ ܡܡܠܠ ܗܘܐ ܠܟܢܫܐ܂ ܘܗܘܐ ܐܡܗ ܘܐ̈ܚܘܗܝ، ܩܝܡܝܢ
ܗܘܘ ܠܒܪ܂ ܘܒܥܝܢ ܗܘܘ ܠܡܡܠܠܘ ܥܡܗ܂ [48]ܗܘ ܕܝܢ ܥܢܐ ܘܐܡܪ
ܠܗܘ ܡܢ ܕܐܡܪ ܠܗ܂ ܡܢ ܗܝ، ܐܡܝ ܘܡܢ ܐܢܘܢ ܐ̈ܚܝ܂ [49]ܘܦܫܛ
ܐܝܕܗ ܠܘܬ ܬܠܡ̈ܝܕܘܗܝ، ܘܐܡܪ܂ ܗܐ ܐܡܝ ܘܗܐ ܐ̈ܚܝ܂ [50]ܟܠ
ܡܢ ܕܥܒܕ ܨܒܝܢܗ ܕܐܒܝ ܕܒܫܡܝܐ܂ ܗܢܘ ܗܘ ܐ̈ܚܝ
ܘܐ̈ܚܬܝ، ܘܐܡܝ ܀

ܐܦ ܒܪܗ ܕܐܢܫܐ ܢܗܘܐ] ܢܗܘܐ ܒܪܗ ܕܐܢܫܐ S; ܢܗܘܐ ܒܪܗ ܕܓܒܪܐ A (*sic! A*[a] *alone is extant at this point and in it* ܕܓܒܪܐ *has been altered by a late corrector to* ܕܐܢܫܐ, *but* ܕ..ܪܐ *is still legible underneath*) 41 ܘܢܚܝܒܘܢܗ̇] *so also* S ܒܟܪܘܙܘܬܗ S 42 ܥܒ̈ܪܝܗ̇] ܣܘܦܐ S ܫܒܚܬܐ S 43 ܛܢܦܬܐ ܕܝܢ] ܕܛܢܦܬܐ S ܠܗ̇ 2°] *om.* S 44 ܗܝܕܝܢ] *om.* S ܕܣܪܝܩ] ܕܒ ܣܪܝܩ S ܘܟܢܝܫ] ܘܡܨܒܬ S 45 ܥܡܗ̇] *om.* S ܪ̈ܘܚܝܢ ܐ̈ܚܪܢܝܢ] ܪ̈ܘܚܐ S ܕܒܝܫܢ ܡܢ̈ܗ S ܗܘ] *om.* S 46 ܗܘܐ] *om.* S ܘܗܐ] ܗܐ S ܗܘܘ 1°] *om.* S ܘܒܥܝܢ ܗܘܘ] ܘܒܥܝܢ S 48 ܠܗܘ ܡܢ] *om.* ܡܢ S ܡܢ ܗܝ] ܡܢ S ܘܡܢ] ܘܐܠܐ S 49 ܗܐ ܐܡܝ ܘܗܐ ܐ̈ܚܝ] ܗܠܝܢ ܐܢܘܢ ܐܡܝ ܘܐ̈ܚܝ S 50 ܗܢܘ ܗܘ] ܗܘܝܘ S

belly of the fish three days and three nights, so the Son of Man *C S*
also shall be in the heart of the earth¶ three days and three nights. ¶*A*
41 The men-folk of Nineve will stand up in judgement with this
generation and will make it guilty, in that they repented at the
42 preaching of Jonah, and lo, a greater than Jonah is here. The
queen of the South will stand up in judgement with this generation
and will make it guilty, in that she came from the other sides of
the earth that she might hear the wisdom of Solomon, and lo, a
greater than Solomon is here.

43 "Now the unclean spirit, what *time* it hath come forth from a
man, goeth travelling about in places where there is no water, that
it may find for itself ease; and what *time* it hath found none for
44 itself, then it saith: 'I will return *and* go to my house from where
I came forth.' And if it hath come *and* found it empty and brushed
45 and garnished, then it goeth *and* taketh with itself seven other
spirits worse than itself, and they enter and dwell therein, and the
last *state* of that man becometh worse than his first *state*. So shall
it be to this same evil generation."

46 And when he was speaking to the multitude, lo, his mother and
his brothers were standing outside, and were seeking to speak with
48 him. But he answered and said to that one which told him: "Who
49 is my mother, and who are my brothers?" And he stretched forth
his hand towards his disciples and said: "Lo, my mother; and lo,
50 my brothers! For every one which doeth the will of my Father
in heaven, this *one* is my brothers and my sisters and my mother."

---

days three and nights three *S* the Son of Man] the son of a man *A*: *the same phrase occurs in* Mk viii 38, Lk vii 34, ix 26, xxii 48, Jn xiii 31. *For the rendering, cf* Mt x 36 *and see Notes,* vol. ii also] *om. S A* **42** the other sides] the end*s* *S* **43** Now the unclean spirit] The spirit of uncleanness *S* (*not* E^{120}) for itself 2°] *om. S* **44** then] *om. S* brushed] swept *S* **45** with itself] *om. S* other] *om. S* that man] the man *S* evil] *om.* $E^{120,122}$ **46** when he was] while *S* lo] *C lit.* 'and lo' were standing] stand *S* were seeking] wish *S* **48** to that one which] him which *S* and who are] or *who* are *S* **49** Lo...my brothers] These are my mother and my brothers *S* **50** this *one* is] he is *S*

C S ¹ܘܒܗܘ ܝܘܡܐ ܢܦܩ ܝܫܘܥ ܡܢ ܒܝܬܐ. ܘܝܬܒ ܠܗ ܥܠ ܓܢܒ
ܝܡܬܐ. ²ܘܐܬܟܢܫܘ ܠܘܬܗ ܟܢܫܐ ܣܓܝܐܐ. ܘܣܠܩ ܘܝܬܒ ܠܗ
ܒܣܦܝܢܬܐ. ܘܟܠܗ ܟܢܫܐ ܩܐܡ ܗܘܐ ܥܠ ܣ̈ܦܪ ܝܡܐ. ³ܘܡܠܠ
col 2 ܥܡܗܘܢ ܣܓܝ *ܒܡܬ̈ܠܐ ܘܐܡܪ. ܗܐ ܢܦܩ ܙܪܘܥܐ ܠܡܙܪܥ.
⁴ܘܟܕ ܙܪܥ. ܐܝܬ ܕܢܦܠ ܥܠ ܝܕ ܐܘܪܚܐ ܘܐܬܬ ܦܪܚܬܐ ܕܫܡܝܐ
ܘܐܟܠܬܗ. ⁵ܐܚܪܢܐ ܕܝܢ ܢܦܠ ܥܠ ܫܘܥܐ. ܘܠܝܬ ܗܘܐ ܒܣܪܐ
ܣܓܝܐܐ. ܘܒܗ ܒܫܥܬܐ ܫܘܚܬ. ܡܛܠ ܕܠܝܬ ܒܗܘܡܐ ܕܒܣܪܐ
ܣܓܝܐܐ. ⁶ܘܟܕ ܕܢܚ ܫܡܫܐ ܕܗܘܐ ܚܡܝܡ ܫܚܢܬ. ܘܡܛܠ ܕܠܐ
ܐܥܩܪܬ ܥܩܪܐ ܒܐܪܥܐ ܝܒܫܬ. ⁷ܐܚܪܢܝܬܐ ܢܦܠܬ ܒܝܬ ܟܘ̈ܒܐ.
ܘܣܠܩܘ ܟܘ̈ܒܐ ܘܚܢܩܘܗ̇. ⁸ܘܐܚܪܢܝܬܐ ܕܝܢ ܢܦܠܬ ܒܐܪܥܐ
ܛܒܬܐ ܘܝܗܒܬ ܦ̈ܐܪܐ. ܘܥܒܕ ܘܝܗܒ. ܐܝܬ ܕܡܐܐ ܘܐܝܬ
ܕܫܬܝܢ ܘܐܝܬ ܕܬܠܬܝܢ. ⁹ܡܢ ܕܐܝܬ ܠܗ ܐܕ̈ܢܐ ܠܡܫܡܥ
ܢܫܡܥ ܀
fol 20 v *¹⁰ܘܩܪܒܘ ܬܠܡܝܕܘܗܝ ܘܐܡܪܝܢ ܠܗ. ܠܡܢܐ ܒ̈ܡܬܠܐ ܡܡܠܠ
ܐܢܬ ܥܡܗܘܢ܂ ¹¹ܘܗܘ ܥܢܐ ܘܐܡܪ ܠܗܘܢ܂ ܡܛܠ ܕܠܟܘܢ
ܗܘ ܝܗܝܒ ܠܡܕܥ ܐ̈ܪܙܐ ܕܡܠܟܘܬܐ ܕܫܡܝܐ. ܠܗܢܘܢ ܕܝܢ
ܠܐ ܝܗܝܒ ܠܗܘܢ ܠܡܕܥ. ¹²ܡܢ ܕܐܝܬ ܠܗ ܓܝܪ ܢܬܝܗܒ ܠܗ
ܘܢܬܬܘܣܦ ܠܗ. ܘܡܢ ܕܠܝܬ ܠܗ ܐܦ ܗܘ ܡܕܡ ܕܐܝܬ ܠܗ

---

1 ܘܒܗܘ] *om.* ܘ *S* ܢܦܩ]+ܗܘܐ *S* ܡܢ ܒܝܬܐ] *om.* *S* ܘܝܬܒ] *om.* ܘ *S* ܠܗ] *om.* *S* ܥܠ ܓܢܒ ܝܡܬܐ] ܥܠ ܝܕ ܝܡܬܐ *S* 3 ܘܡܠܠ] ܘܡܡܠܠ *S* ܘܐܡܪ]+ܗܘܐ *S* ܠܡܙܪܥ]+ܙܪܥܐ *S* 4 ܦܪܚܬܐ ܕܫܡܝܐ] ܥܘܦܐ ܒܢܝܐ *S*: *cf ver.* 32 ܘܐܟܠܬܗ] ܠܩܛܬܗ *S* 5 ܐܚܪܢܐ ܕܝܢ ܢܦܠ] ܘܐܝܬ ܕܢܦܠ *S* ܥܠ ܫܘܥܐ]+ܗܘܐ ܕܪܘܡܐ ܘܡܛܠ *S*^vid (*So I read the photograph: cf* Exod ii 3 syr. *For* ܕܪܘܡܐ, *S*^ed *has* ܕܪ[ܢ]ܝܐ) ܗܘܐ (*after* ܘܠܝܬ)] *om.* *S* ܘܒܗ ܒܫܥܬܐ] ܒܪ ܫܥܬܗ *S* ܫܘܚܬ] ܫܘܚ *S* ܡܛܠ ܕܠܝܬ....ܣܓܝܐܐ] *om.* *S* 6 ܫܚܢܬ] ܫܚܢ *S* ܐܥܩܪܬ] ܐܥܩܪ *S* ܒܐܪܥܐ] *om.* *S* ܝܒܫ *S* 7 ܐܚܪܢܝܬܐ ܢܦܠܬ] ܘܐܚܪܢܝܬܐ ܢܦܠ *S* ܘܣܠܩܘ] ܘܣܠܩ *S* ܘܚܢܩܘܗܝ *S* 8 ܘܐܚܪܢܝܬܐ ܕܝܢ ܢܦܠ *S* ܘܝܗܒܬ] ܘܝܗܒ *S* ܘܥܒܕ ܘܝܗܒ] *om.* *S* 9 ܠܡܫܡܥ] *om.* *S* 10 ܠܡܢܐ] ܡܛܠ ܡܢܐ ܗܘ ܕ *S* 11 ܘܗܘ] ܗܘ ܕܝܢ *S* ܕܫܡܝܐ] *om.* *S* ܠܡܕܥ 2°] *om.* *S* 12 ܕܐܝܬ ܠܗ] *om.* ܠܗ *S* (*cf* Mt xviii 9) ܘܢܬܬܘܣܦ ܠܗ] *om.* *S* ܐܦ] ܘܐܦ *S*

xiii 1 And on that day Jesus went forth from the house and sat down *C S*
2 by the side of the lake. And there were gathered unto him great
multitudes, and he went up and sat down in the boat, and all the
3 multitude was standing on the sea shore. And he spake with them
much in parables, and said: "Lo, the sower went forth to sow;
4 and when he sowed, some fell by the way-side and the birds of the
5 heaven came and ate it. Now other fell on the rock, and there was
not much earth, and in the same hour it sprouted, because there
6 was no depth of much earth; and with the shining of the sun that
was upon *the land*, it dried up, and because it had not cast a root
7 in the land it withered. Other fell among the thorns, and the
8 thorns came up with it and choked it. Now other fell in the good
land and gave fruit, and they grew up and gave some an hundred,
9 some sixty, and some thirty. Every one that hath ears to hear,
let him hear."
10 And his disciples drew near, and say to him: "Wherefore in
11 parables speakest thou with them?" And he answered and said
to them: "Because to you is given to know the mystery of the
kingdom of heaven, but to them—it is not given to them to know.
12 For he that hath, it shall be given to him and it shall be added
to him; and he that hath not, even that also which he hath shall

---

1 And on] On *S* went] had gone *S* from the house] *om. S* and sat] *and* sat *S* by the side of the lake] by the sea-side *S* 3 spake] *was* speaking *S* said] was saying *S* to sow] + seed *S* E^{124} 4 birds of the heaven] winged fowl *S* (*cf ver.* 32) ate it] plucked it up *S* 5 Now other fell] And some fell *S* on the rock] + and because it was a shallow place S^{vid}. (*For* 'a shallow place,' S^{ed} *has* 'sunrise') there was 1°] *om. S* and in the same hour] straightway *S* because...of much earth] *om. S* was 2°] *lit.* 'is' 6 upon *the land*] *lit.* 'upon it' (*fem.*): *see Notes*, vol. ii in the land] *om. S* 7 Other] And other *S* came up] sprang up *S* 8 and they grew up and gave] *om. S* 9 to hear] *om. S* (*not* $E^{72,123}$) 10 Wherefore] What is it that *S* 11 And] Now *S* of heaven] *om. S* to know 2°] *om. S* 12 hath] *S lit.* 'is' (*cf* Mt xviii 9) and it shall be added to him] *om. S* even] *om. S*

CS ܢܬܚܫܒ ܡܢܗ܂ [13]ܡܛܠ ܗܢܐ ܒܦܠ̈ܓܘܬܐ ܡܡܠܠ ܐܢܐ ܒܟܠܗܘܢ܆
ܕܒܗܘܢ ܕܚܣܝܢ ܠܐ ܫܘܝܢ܆ ܘܒܗܘܢ ܕܡܫܟܚܝܢ ܠܐ ܢܫܟܚܘܢ ܘܠܐ
ܢܫܬܠܡܘܢ܆ ܕܠܐ ܡܬܚܫܒܝܢ ܢܬܦܠܓܘܢ܆ [14]ܘܬܫܠܡ ܢܦܫܬܗ
ܕܐܢܫܐ ܢܦܫܐ ܕܐܡܪܢ ܗܘܐ. ܕܡܫܬܥܒܕ ܬܫܬܥܒܕܘܢ ܘܠܐ
col 2 ܬܫܬܠܡܘܢ܆ ܘܗܘܝܐ* ܬܫܘܘܢ ܘܠܐ ܬܫܘܘܢ܆ [15]ܐܬܒܒܘ ܠܗ ܒܪ
ܠܗܘܢ ܕܒܟܐ ܗܢܐ. ܘܐܬܪܣܝܘܢ ܐܘܦܪܘ ܕܠܐ ܢܫܟܚܘܢ܆
ܘܚ̈ܫܝܘܢ ܚܒܪܐ. ܕܠܐ ܫܘܘܢ ܚ̈ܫܝܘܢ ܘܢܫܟܚܘܢ
ܟ̈ܐܪܣܘܢ܆ ܘܢܫܬܠܡܘܢ ܒܠܗܘܢ. ܘܢܬܦܠܓܘܢ ܘܐܦܐ
ܐܢܘ܆ [16]ܕܠܗܘܢ ܕܝܢ ܬܘܒܢܘܢ ܠܚ̈ܛܝܢܘܢ ܕܣܝܡ܂ ܘܬܘܒ
ܠܐܪ̈ܣܝܘܢ ܕܢܫܬܝܢ. [17]ܐܡܝܢ ܒܪ ܐܒܪܗܡ ܠܗܘܢ܆ ܕܦ̈ܩܢܐܐ
ܢܟ̈ܠܐ ܘܙܪ̈ܘܥܐ ܐܬܬܪ̈ܥܘ ܕܢܣܘܘܢ ܡܛܠ ܕܣܝܡ ܐܢܘܢ ܘܠܐ
ܣܘ. ܘܠܡܫܬܒܕ ܡܛܠ ܕܢܫܡܥܝܢ ܐܢܘܢ ܘܠܐ ܫܡܥܘ. [18]ܐܢܘܢ
ܕܝܢ ܫܡܥܘ ܡܠܬܐ ܕܙܪܘܥܐ. [19]ܒܗܠ ܐܝܟ ܕܫܡܥܬ ܡܠܬܐ
fol 21 r ܕܡܠܟܘܬܐ ܘܠܐ ܡܣܬܟܠ. ܐܬܐ *ܒܝܫܐ ܘܚܛܦ ܠܗ ܠܙܪܥܐ ܡܢ
ܠܒܗ܂ ܗܢܐ ܗܘ ܕܐܙܕܪܥ ܥܠ ܝܕ ܐܘܪܚܐ. [20]ܘܗܘ ܕܐܙܕܪܥ
ܥܠ ܫܘܥܐ. ܗܢܐ ܗܘ ܕܫܡܥ ܡܠܬܐ. ܘܒܥܓܠܘܬܐ ܒܚܕܘܬܐ
ܡܩܒܠ ܠܗ܂ [21]ܘܡܛܠ ܕܠܝܬ ܠܗ̇ ܥܩܪܐ. ܐܠܐ ܙܒܢ ܡܩܘܐ ܒܗ.
ܡܐ ܕܗܘܐ ܕܝܢ ܐܘܠܨܢܐ ܐܘ ܪܕܘܦܝܐ ܡܛܠ ܡܠܬܐ ܒܥܓܠ
ܡܬܬܟܫܠ܂ [22]ܘܗܘ ܕܒܝܢܝ ܟܘ̈ܒܐ. ܗܢܐ ܗܘ ܕܫܡܥ ܡܠܬܐ.
ܘܪܢܝܐ ܗܘ ܕܥܠܡܐ ܗܢܐ. ܘܛܥܝܝ ܕܥܘܬܪܐ. ܘܚܢܩ ܚܢܩ
ܠܗ. ܘܕܠܐ ܦܐܪ̈ܐ ܗܘܐ. [23]ܘܗܘ ܕܒܠ ܒܐܪܥܐ ܛܒܬܐ. ܗܘ

14 ܘܬܫܠܡ] ܒܠܗܘܢ ܬܫܠܡ S   ܕܡܫܬܥܒܕ] ܥܒܕܐ S   ܘܗܘܝܐ] ܘܡܚܘܝܐ S   15 ܘܬܫܘܘܢ ܘܐܘܣܐ ܐܢܘܢ] om. S   16. § in S   ܘܬܘܒ] ܬܘܒܢܝܢ S   17 ܕܢܣܘܘܢ] ܠܡܣܘܝܐ S   ܕܣܝܡ] ܣܝܡ ܐܢܘܢ ܕܐܢܘܢ S   ܕܢܫܡܥܝܢ] ܫܡܥܝܢ ܕܐܢܘܢ S   18 ܕܝܢ] ܡܛܠ S   19 ܗܢܐ ܗܘ] ܗܘ S   20 ܗܢܐ ܗܘ] ܗܘ S   ܡܩܒܠܗ ܒܚܕܘܬܐ] om. S   ܠܗ] C (sic, no point)   21 ܘܡܛܠ] om. ܘ S   ܥܩܪܐ] + ܒܗ S   ܡܩܘܝܐ] ܡܩܘܐ S   ܪܕܘܦܝܐ S   22 ܗܢܐ ܗܘ] ܗܘ S   ܘܛܘܥܝܝ S   ܘܚܢܩ ܚܢܩ] ܘܚܢܩܝܢ ܚ̈ܢܩܝܢ S   ܦܐܪ̈ܐ] ܦܐܪ̈ܝܢ S

13 be taken from him. Therefore in parables do I speak with them, *C S*
that what they see they may not see, and what they hear they may
not hear and may not understand, that in no wise they should turn
14 round. And the prophecy of Isaiah the prophet shall be accom-
plished, who had said 'Ye shall hear indeed and shall not under-
15 stand, and a vision ye shall see and shall not see; for the heart
of this people is become gross, and their ears they have made heavy
that they should not hear, and their eyes they have closed, that
they should not see with their eyes and hear with their ears, and
understand with their heart, and turn round and I should heal
16 them.' But as for yours, happy is it for your eyes that see, and
17 happy for your ears that hear! For amen, I say to you that many
prophets and righteous men have longed that they might see that
which ye see, and they have not seen; and to hear that which ye
18 hear, and they have not heard. But ye, hear ye the similitude of
19 the sower. Every man that heareth the word of the kingdom and
understandeth not, the Evil One cometh and snatcheth away the
seed from his heart; this is that which was sown by the way-side.
20 And that which was sown on the rock, this is he which heareth the
21 word, and with joy hastily receiveth it. And because it hath no
root, a little while it remaineth in him, but what *time* there is distress
22 or persecution because of the word quickly he is offended. And
that which fell among the thorns, this is he which heareth the word,
and is with the care of this world and with the deceitfulness of
23 riches, and they choke him, and he becometh without fruit. And
that which fell in the good land, that is he which heareth the word

---

14 And...shall 1°] That...may *S* accomplished] + upon them *S* Ye shall hear indeed] A rumour ye shall hear *S* a vision ye shall see] ye shall see indeed *S* **15** and turn....heal them] *om.* *S* **16** and happy] happy is it *S* **17** righteous men] + and kings E^{155} (*cf* Lk x 24) that they might see] to see *S* **18** But ye] Ye therefore *S* **20** hastily] *om.* *S* **21** And because] Because *S* no root] + in him *S* it remaineth in him] he standeth in it *S* **22** they] these *S*

ܗܘ ܕܫܡܥ ܡܠܬܐ ܘܡܣܬܟܠ ܒܗ̇. ܘܝܗܒ ܦܐܖ̈ܐ. ܐܝܬ ܕܡܐܐ. *C S*

col 2 *ܘܐܝܬ ܕܫܬܝܢ. ܘܐܝܬ ܕܬܠܬܝܢ ܀

24 ܐܚܪܢܐ ܕܝܢ ܡܬܠܐ ܐܘܣܦ ܘܐܡܪ ܠܗܘܢ ܕܕܡܝܐ ܡܠܟܘܬܐ
ܕܫܡܝܐ ܠܓܒܪܐ ܕܙܪܥ ܙܪܥܐ ܛܒܐ ܒܩܪܝܬܗ. 25 ܘܟܕ ܕܡܟܘ
ܐܢܫܐ. ܐܬܐ ܒܥܠܕܒܒܐ ܘܙܪܥ. ܙܝܙܢܐ ܒܝܬ ܚܛܐ ܘܐܙܠ. 26 ܘܟܕ
ܡܛܐ ܥܣܒܐ ܘܥܒܕ ܦܐܖ̈ܐ. ܗܝܕܝܢ ܐܬܚܙܝܘ ܙܝܙܢܐ. 27 ܘܩܪܒܘ
ܥܒܕܘܗܝ ܕܡܪܐ ܒܝܬܐ ܘܐܡܪܝܢ ܠܗ. ܡܪܢ ܠܐ ܗܘܐ ܙܪܥܐ
ܛܒܐ ܙܪܥܬ ܒܩܪܝܬܟ. ܐܝܡܟܐ ܐܝܬ ܒܗ ܙܝܙܢܐ. 28 ܗܘ ܕܝܢ
ܐܡܪ ܠܗܘܢ. ܓܒܪܐ ܒܥܠܕܒܒܐ ܥܒܕ ܗܕܐ. ܐܡܪܝܢ ܠܗ
ܥܒܕܘܗܝ. ܐܢ ܨܒܐ ܐܢܬ ܢܐܙܠ ܢܠܩܛ ܐܢܘܢ. 29 ܐܡܪ ܠܗܘܢ
fol 21 v *ܠܐ. ܕܠܡܐ ܟܕ ܠܩܛܝܢ ܐܢܬܘܢ ܙܝܙܢܐ ܬܥܩܪܘܢ ܐܦ ܚܛܐ
ܥܡܗܘܢ. 30 ܐܠܐ ܫܒܘܩܘ ܢܪܒܝܢ ܐܟܚܕܐ ܥܕܡܐ ܠܚܨܕܐ.
ܘܒܗܘ ܙܒܢܐ ܕܚܨܕܐ ܐܡܪ ܐܢܐ ܠܚܨܘܕܐ. ܠܩܛܘ ܠܘܩܕܡ ܙܝܙܢܐ.
ܘܐܣܘܪܘ ܐܢܘܢ ܡܣܪ̈ܝܬܐ ܐܝܟ ܕܠܝܩܕܐ. ܘܚܛܐ ܟܢܫܘ ܐܝܢ
ܠܐܘܨܪ̈ܐ ܕܝܠܝ ܀

31 ܘܐܡܪ ܗܘܐ ܠܗܘܢ ܡܬܠܐ ܐܚܪܢܐ. ܕܕܡܝܐ ܡܠܟܘܬܐ
ܕܫܡܝܐ ܠܦܪܕܬܐ ܕܚܪܕܠܐ. ܕܢܣܒ ܓܒܪܐ ܘܙܪܥܗ̇ ܒܩܪܝܬܗ.
32 ܗ̇ܝ، ܕܙܥܘܪܐ ܗ̇ܝ، ܡܢ ܟܠܗܘܢ ܙܪ̈ܥܘܢܐ. ܘܡܐ ܕܪܒܬ ܪܒܐ
ܗ̇ܝ، ܡܢ ܟܠܗܘܢ ܝܪ̈ܩܘܢܐ. ܘܗܘܝܐ ܐܝܠܢܐ. ܘܐܬܝܢ ܦܪܚܬ
ܦܪܚܬܐ ܕܫܡܝܐ ܘܫܟܢܐ ܒܣܘܟܘܗ̇ ܀

col 2 *33 ܡܬܠܐ ܐܚܪܢܐ. ܕܕܡܝܐ ܡܠܟܘܬܐ ܕܫܡܝܐ ܠܚܡܝܪܐ ܕܢܣܒܬ
ܐܢܬܬܐ ܚܟܝܡܬܐ. ܘܛܡܪܬ ܒܩܡܚܐ ܥܕܡܐ ܕܗܘܐ ܟܠܗ
ܚܡܝܪ ܀

---

23 ܘܝܗܒ] ܘܗܝܕܝܢ ܝܗܒ *S* ܐܝܬ ܕܡܐܐ] *pr.* ܘܥܒܕ *S*
24 ܐܚܪܢܐ ܕܝܢ...ܠܗܘܢ] ܬܘܒ ܐܘܣܦ ܘܐܡܪ ܠܗܘܢ ܡܬܠܐ ܐܚܪܢܐ *S*
26 ܗܝܕܝܢ] *om. S* 27 ܘܩܪܒܘ] *om.* ܘ *S* ܥܒܕܘܗܝ ܕܡܪܐ ܒܝܬܐ]
ܥܒܕܘܗܝ ܠܘܬ ܡܪܗܘܢ *S* ܗܘܐ] *om. S* ܐܝܡܟܐ] *pr.* ܡܢ *S* ܐܝܬ] *om. S*
28 ܗܘ ܕܝܢ] *om. S* ܢܠܩܘܛ *S* 30 ܐܠܐ] *om. S* 31 ܘܙܪܥܗ̇] *om.* ܘ *S* 32 ܗ̇ܝ]
om. ܗܝ *S* ܕܫܡܝܐ] *om. S* 33 ܕܢܣܒܬ] ܕܢܣܒܬܗ *S* ܚܟܝܡܬܐ] *om. S*
ܘܛܡܪܬ] ܐܛܡܪܬ *S* ܒܩܡܚܐ] ܬܠܬ ܣܐܝܢ ܩܡܚܐ *S* ܚܡܝܪ] ܚܡܝܪܐ *S*

and attendeth to it, and giveth fruit, some an hundred and some C S
sixty and some thirty."
24 Now another similitude he added and said to them: "Like is
the kingdom of heaven to a man that sowed good seed in his
25 field; and when folk slept, the enemy came and sowed tares among
26 the wheat and went away. And when the green blade grew and
27 brought forth fruit, then the tares were seen. And the slaves of the
master of the house drew near and say to him: 'Our lord, was it
not good seed thou sowedst in thy field? Whence are there in it
28 tares?' Now he said to them: 'A man *that is* an enemy did this.'
His slaves say to him: 'If thou wilt, we will go *and* pluck them.'
29 He saith to them: 'Nay, lest when ye are plucking the tares, ye
30 root up also the wheat with them; but leave *them* growing up
together until the harvest, and in the time of the harvest I will
say to the reapers: Pluck first the tares and bind them *into* bundles
as for the fire, and the wheat gather into barns of mine.'"
31 And he was saying to them another similitude: "Like is the
kingdom of heaven to a grain of mustard, that a man took and
32 sowed it in his field. And it is the least of all seeds, and what
time it hath grown up, it is greater than all herbs, and becometh
a tree, and the winged fowl of the heaven come and settle in its
branches."
33 Another similitude: "Like is the kingdom of heaven to leaven,
which a wise woman took up and hid in meal until all of it was
leavened."

---

23 giveth] *pr.* then he *S* some an hundred] *pr.* and bringeth forth *S* 24 Now another...said to them] Again he added and said to them another similitude *S* 26 then] *om. S* 27 And the slaves] The slaves *S* of the master of the house] *om. S* near] + unto their lord *S* good seed] 'seeds of holiness of corn' E^{126} (*cf ver.* 37) Whence] From whence *S* there] *om. S* 28 Now he said] He saith *S* 30 of mine] *om. S* 31 of mustard] *om.* E^{127} and sowed] *and* sowed *S* 32 and (4°)....come] 'and the birds of heaven come' E^{127} of the heaven] *om. S* 33 wise] *om. S* took up] took *S* and hid] *and* concealed *S* meal] *pr.* three measures of *S*

C S [34]ܗܠܝܢ ܒܠܗܘܢ ܡܠܠ ܫܡܥܘܢ ܬ̈ܘܠܐܬܐ ܠܒܢ̈ܝܐ. ܘܕܠܐ ܦܠܐܬ̈ܐ
ܠܐ ܡܡܠܠ ܗܘܐ ܒܟܗܢ̈ܘܢ. [35]ܘܫܠܡܬ ܡܠܬܐ ܕܐܬܐܡܪܬ
ܒܢܒܝܐ ܕܐܡܪ ܗܘܐ. ܐܦܬܚ ܦܘܡܝ ܒܡ̈ܬܠܐ. ܘܐܡܠܠ
ܒܗ̈ܬܐ ܕܡܢ ܩܕܝܡ.
[36]ܗܝܕܝܢ ܢܒܥ ܠܬ̈ܠܡܝܕܐ ܘܐܬܬܐ ܠܒܝܬܐ. ܘܩܪܒܘ ܩܕܡܘܗܝ,
ܬܠܡ̈ܝܕܘܗܝ, ܘܐܡܪܝܢ ܠܗ. ܦܫܘܩ ܠܢ ܡܬܠܐ ܗܘ ܕ̈ܙܝܙܢܐ ܕܩܪܝܬܐ.
fol 22 r [37]ܗܘ ܕܝܢ ܥܢܐ ܘܐܡܪ ܠܗܘܢ܆ ܕܙܪܥ ܙܪܥܐ ܛܒܐ *ܒܪܗ ܗܘ
ܕܐܢܫܐ. [38]ܘܩܪܝܬܐ ܥܠܡܐ ܗܘ. ܗܘ ܕܝܢ ܙܪܥܐ ܛܒܐ ܗܠܝܢ
ܐܢܘܢ ܒ̈ܢܝܗ ܕܡܠܟܘܬܐ. ܘ̈ܙܝܙܢܐ ܒ̈ܢܘܗܝ, ܐܢܘܢ ܕܒܝܫܐ.
[39]ܘܒܥܠܕܒܒܐ ܗܘܘ ܒܢܫܐ. ܘܚܨܕܐ ܫܘܠܡܗ ܗܘ ܕܥܠܡܐ. ܘܚܨ̈ܘܕܐ
ܡ̈ܠܐܟܐ ܐܢܘܢ܆ [40]ܐܝܟܢܐ ܗܟܝܠ ܕܡܬܠܩܛܝܢ ܙ̈ܝܙܢܐ ܘܡܬܝܩܕܝܢ
ܒܢܘܪܐ. ܗܟܢܐ ܢܗܘܐ ܒܫܘܠܡܗ ܕܥܠܡܐ. [41]ܢܫܕܪ ܒܪܗ ܕܐܢܫܐ
ܠܡ̈ܠܐܟܘܗܝ، ܘܢܠܩܛܘܢ ܡܢ ܒܝܬ ܡܠܟܘܬܗ ܟܠܗܘܢ ܡ̈ܟܫܘܠܐ.
ܘܟܠܗܘܢ ܥ̈ܒܕܝ ܥܘܠܐ. [42]ܘܢܪܡܘܢ ܐܢܘܢ ܒܐܬܘܢܐ
ܕܢܘܪܐ. ܬܡܢ ܢܗܘܐ ܒܟܝܐ ܘܚܘܪܩ ܫ̈ܢܐ. [43]ܗܝܕܝܢ ܙ̈ܕܝܩܐ
ܢܢܗܪܘܢ ܐܝܟ ܫܡܫܐ ܒܡܠܟܘܬܗ ܕܐܒܘܗܘܢ܆ ܡܢ ܕܐܝܬ
col 2 *ܠܗ ܐ̈ܕܢܐ ܠܡܫܡܥ ܢܫܡܥ .܀
[44]ܬܘܒ ܕܡܝܐ ܡܠܟܘܬܐ ܕܫܡܝܐ ܠܣܝܡܬܐ ܕܛܫܝܐ ܒܩܪܝܬܐ. ܗܝ
ܕܐܫܟܚܗ ܓܒܪܐ ܛܫܝܗ. ܘܡܢ ܚܕܘܬܗ ܐܙܠ ܙܒܢ ܟܠ ܡܕܡ
ܕܐܝܬ ܠܗ. ܘܙܒܢܗ ܠܗ ܩܪܝܬܐ ܗܝ، .܀

34. *No* § *in S* ܬ̈ܘܠܐܬܐ ܠܒܢ̈ܝܐ] *tr. S* 35 ܘܫܠܡܬ ܡܠܬܐ] ܘܫܠܡܬ ܡܠܬܐ ܡܕܡ *S* ܕܐܬܐܡܪܬ] ܕܐܬܡܠܠ *S* ܒܟܗܢ̈ܘܢ] ܒܟܗܢ *S* (*not at the end of a line*) ܘܐܡܠܠ] ܘܐܡܪ *S* 36 ܬܠܡ̈ܝܕܘܗܝ] *om. S* 38 ܗܘ 1°] ܗܝ *S* ܗܘ ܕܝܢ ܙܪܥܐ] ܘܙܪܥܐ *S* 39 ܘܒܥܠܕܒܒܐ] ܘܒܥܠܕܒܒܐ ܗܘ *S* ܗܘ] *om. S* ܐܢܘܢ] *om. S* 41 ܠܡ̈ܠܐܟܘܗܝ] *om.* ܠ *S* ܘܢܠܩܛܘܢ] ܘܠܩܛܘܢ *S* ܡ̈ܟܫܘܠܐ] ܟܫܠܐ *S* ܥ̈ܒܕܝ ܥܘܠܐ] ܥܒܕܝ *S* 43 ܗܝܕܝܢ] *pr.* ܘ *S* ܢܢܗܪܘܢ] ܢܗܪܘܢ *S* (*sic*) ܐܝܟ ܫܡܫܐ] *om. S* ܒܡܠܟܘܬܐ *S* ܠܡܫܡܥ] ܕܢܫܡܥ *S* 44 ܕܐܫܟܚܗ ܓܒܪܐ] ܗܝ ܕܐܫܟܚܗ *S* ܘܡܢ ܚܕܘܬܗ] ܘܒܚܕܘܬܗ *S* ܟܠ ܡܕܡ] ܟܠ *S* ܘܙܒܢܗ ܠܗ ܠܩܪܝܬܐ ܗܝ *S*

34 All these *things* spake Jesus in parables to the multitudes, and C S
35 without parables he was not speaking with them; and the word
was accomplished that was said by the prophet, who had said: "I
will open my mouth in similitudes, and I will speak things secret
from of old."

36 Then he left the multitudes and came to the house, and his
disciples drew near before him, and say to him: "Explain to us
37 that similitude of the tares of the field." Now he answered and
said to them: "The sower of the good seed is the Son of Man,
38 and the field is the world, but the good seed—they are the sons of
39 the kingdom; and the tares are the sons of the Evil One, and the
sower is the Evil One, and the harvest is the conclusion of the
40 world, and the reapers are the angels. Just therefore as the tares
are plucked and burn in the fire, so shall it be in the conclusion of
41 the world: the Son of Man will send his angels, that they may choose
out from the place of the kingdom all offences and all that do
42 wickedness, and they shall cast them into the furnace of fire; there
43 shall be the weeping and the gnashing of teeth! Then the righteous
shall gleam as the sun in the kingdom of their Father. He that
hath ears to hear, let him hear.

44 "Like is the kingdom of heaven to treasure that is laid in a
field; and when a man found it he hid it, and out of his joy he
went *and* sold everything that he had, and bought himself that
field.

---

34 to the multitudes in parables *S* **35** and the word was accomplished] that it might be fulfilled *S* said 1°] spoken *S* will speak] will say *S* (= Ps lxxvii 2 syr. vg) **36** before him] *om. S* **37** good seed] 'seeds of corn of holiness' E^{174} (*cf ver.* 27) **38** but] and *S* good seed] 'seed of good *things*' E^{174} **39** the sower] the sower of them *S* is 2°] *om. S* are] *om. S* **41** that they may] and they will *S* place] *lit.* 'house' (*so also* E^{211}): *cf* Deut iii 4 syr. vg offences] *The word in S is a synonym* all that do] all doers of *S* **43** Then] And then *S* gleam] shine *S* as the sun] *om. S* to hear] that he should hear *S* **44** and when a man found it he hid it] which he that found it hid *S* out of] in *S* everything] all *S*

C S ⁴⁵ܬܘܒ. ܕܡܝܐ ܡܠܟܘܬܐ ܕܫܡܝܐ. ܠܓܒܪܐ ܬܓܪܐ ܕܒܥܐ ܗܘܐ
ܡܪ̈ܓܢܝܬܐ ܛ̈ܒܬܐ. ⁴⁶ܘܟܕ ܐܫܟܚ ܡܪܓܢܝܬܐ ܛܒܬܐ ܘܝܩܝܪܬ
ܕ̈ܡܝܐ. ܐܙܠ ܘܐܦ ܟܠ ܡܕܡ ܕܐܝܬ ܠܗ. ܘܐܬܐ ܘܙܒܢܗ̇ ܠܗ̇. .ܘ.
⁴⁷ܬܘܒ. ܕܡܝܐ ܡܠܟܘܬܐ ܕܫܡܝܐ ܠܡܨܝܕܬܐ ܪܒܬܐ ܕܢܦܠܬ
ܒܝܡܐ. ܘܡܢ ܟܠ ܓܢܣ ܟܢܫܬ. ⁴⁸ܘܟܕ ܕܝܢ ܡܠܬ ܐܣܩܘܗ̇ ܥܠ
fol 22 v ܣܦܪ ܝܡܐ. ܘܝܬܒܘ *ܓܒܘ ܢ̈ܘܢܐ ܕܛ̈ܒܝܢ ܠܡ̈ܐܢܐ. ܘܐܝܠܝܢ
cf A302 ܕܒܝܫܝܢ ܫܕܘ ܐܢܘܢ. ܠܒܪ. ⁴⁹ܗܟܢܐ ܢܗܘܐ ܒܫܘܠܡܗ ܕܥܠܡܐ.
ܢܦܩܘܢ ܡ̈ܠܐܟܐ ܘܢܦܪܫܘܢ ܠܒ̈ܝܫܐ ܡܢ ܒܝܢܬ ܙܕ̈ܝܩܐ.
⁵⁰ܘܢܪܡܘܢ ܐܢܘܢ ܒܐܬܘܢܐ ܕܢܘܪܐ. ܬܡܢ ܢܗܘܐ ܒܟܝܐ ܘܚܘܩ
ܫ̈ܢܐ. .ܘ.

⁵¹ܐܡܪ ܠܗܘܢ ܝܫܘܥ. ܠܬܠܡܝܕܘܗܝ, ܐܣܬܟܠܬܘܢ ܗܠܝܢ ܟܠܗܝܢ.
ܐܡܪܝܢ ܠܗ ܐܝܢ. ⁵²ܐܡܪ ܠܗܘܢ ܡܛܠ ܗܢܐ ܟܠ ܣܦܪܐ
ܕܡܬܬܠܡܕ ܠܡܠܟܘܬܐ ܕܫܡܝܐ. ܕܡܐ ܠܓܒܪܐ ܡܪܐ ܒܝܬܐ.
ܕܡܦܩ ܡܢ ܣܝܡܬܗ ܚܕ̈ܬܐ ܘܥܬܝܩ̈ܬܐ. .ܘ.

⁵³ܘܟܕ ܫܠܡ ܝܫܘܥ. ܡ̈ܬܠܐ ܗܠܝܢ. ܫܢܝ ܠܗ ܡܢ ܬܡܢ. ⁵⁴ܘܐܬܐ
ܠܗ ܠܡܕܝܢܬܗ. ܘܡܠܦ ܗܘܐ ܠܗܘܢ ܝܫܘܥ ܒ̈ܟܢܘܫܬܗܘܢ܆
col 2 *ܐܝܟܢܐ ܕܬܗܪܘܢ܆ ܘܗܘܘ ܐܡܪܝܢ ܐܝܟܐ ܠܗ ܠܗܢܐ
ܚܟܡܬܐ ܗܕܐ ܘܚܝܠܐ ܗܢܐ. ⁵⁵ܠܐ ܗܘܐ ܗܢܐ ܒܪ ܝܘܣܦ
ܢܓܪܐ. ܘܫܡܗ̇ ܠܐܡܗ ܡܪܝܡ. ܘܐ̈ܚܘܗܝ, ܝܥܩܘܒ ܘܝܘܣܦ
ܘܫܡܥܘܢ ܘܝܗܘܕܐ. ⁵⁶ܘܐ̈ܚܘܬܗ ܟܠܗܝܢ ܠܘܬܢ ܐܝܢ. ܐܝܟܢܐ

---

45 ܛ̈ܒܬܐ] om. S   46 ܛܒܬܐ] pr. ܚܕܐ S   ܘܐܦ] om. ܘ S   ܡܕܡ] ܡܐ S   ܘܐܬܐ] om. S   48 ܘܟܕ ܕܝܢ ܡܠܬ] ܟܕ ܡܠܝܘܗ̇ ܕܝܢ S   ܐܣܩܘܗ̇] ܢܓܕܘܗ̇ S   ܥܠ ܣܦܪ] ܠܣܦܪ S   ܘܐܝܠܝܢ ܕܒܝܫܝܢ] ܘܕܒܝܫܝܢ S: cf ܢ̈ܘܢܐ ܒ̈ܝܫܐ ܠܒܪ ܫܕܐ ܠܗܘܢ ܪ̈ܡܐ A 302   51. Apparently no § in S   ܐܡܪ....ܠܬܠܡܝܕܘܗܝ] om. S   52 ܕܡܬܬܠܡܕ S^vid   ܠܡܠܟܘܬ ܫܡܝܐ S   ܡܪܒܝܬܐ S   53. No § in S   54 ܝܫܘܥ] om. S   ܐܝܟܢܐ] ܐܝܟ S   ܘܗܘܘ ܐܡܪܝܢ] ܘܐܡܪܝܢ S   ܚܟܡܬܐ ܗܕܐ] ܠܗ ܚܟܡܬܐ ܗܕܐ S   ܗܢܐ] om. S   55 ܢܓܪܐ] om. S   56 ܐܝܢ] om. S   ܐܝܟܢܐ] pr. ܡܢ S

45 "Again, like is the kingdom of heaven to a man, a merchant, that *C S*
46 was seeking good pearls; and when he found a pearl good and of
great price, he went and sold everything that he had and came and
bought it for himself.

47 "Again, like is the kingdom of heaven to a great net that fell
48 into the sea, and of every kind it gathered. Now when it was
full they took it up on the sea shore, and sat *and* chose out the
fishes—the good *as* good, and those that were bad they threw out. *cf A* 302
49 So shall it be in the end of the world: the angels will go forth and
50 will separate the evil from among the righteous, and shall cast them
into the furnace of fire; there shall be the weeping and the gnashing
of teeth!"

51 Saith to them Jesus, to the disciples: "Have ye understood these
52 things all of them?" They say to him: "Yea." He saith to them:
"Therefore every scribe that is instructed in the kingdom of heaven
is like to a man, the master of a house, who bringeth forth from his
treasures the new and the old."

53 And when Jesus finished these similitudes, he removed from
54 thence, and came to his own city. And Jesus was teaching them
in their synagogues, so that they were astonished; and they
say: "Whence *cometh* to this one this wisdom and this power?
55 Is not this Joseph's son, the carpenter? And the name of his
mother, Mary? And his brothers James and Joseph and Simon and
56 Judas? And his sisters, all of them are with us. Whence *come*

---

45 good] *om. S* **46** a pearl] a certain pearl *S* and sold] *and* sold *S* everything that] all what *S* and came] *om. S* **47** great] *om.* E^{128} that fell] 'that is cast' E^{128} gathered] 'gathereth' E^{128} **48** when it was full] when they filled it *S* took it up on] drew it to *S* chose out the fishes—the good *as* good] (*sic*): *the Syriac does not mean* 'chose the best fishes.' *Both* E^{129} *and* arm.vg *have* (*with small variations*) 'chose the good good' those that were bad] the inferior *S*: *cf* 'the inferior fishes—the fisherman throweth them out' *A* 302 **51** Saith.... disciples] *om. S* **54** Jesus] he *S* and they say] *om.* they *S* this wisdom] *pr.* all *S* this power] *om.* this *S* **55** the carpenter] *om. S* **56** Whence] From whence *S*

C S ܠܗ ܗܠܝܢ ܟܠܗܝܢ ܠܗܢܐ. ⁵⁷ܘܡܬܟܫܠܝܢ ܗܘܘ ܒܗ. ܗܘ ܕܝܢ ܝܫܘܥ
ܐܡܪ ܠܗܘܢ܆ ܠܝܬ ܢܒܝܐ ܕܡܨܛܥܪ ܐܠܐ ܐܢ܆ ܒܡܕܝܢܬܗ
ܘܒܒܝܬܗ. ⁵⁸ܘܠܐ ܥܒܕ ܬܡܢ ܚܝ̈ܠܐ ܣܓܝ̈ܐܐ. ܡܛܠ ܚܣܝܪܘܬ
ܗܝܡܢܘܬܗܘܢ܆ ܀ ܀ ܀

¹ܒܗܘ ܕܝܢ ܙܒܢܐ ܫܡܥ ܗܪܘܕܣ ܛܛܪܪܟܐ ܫܡܥܗ ܕܝܫܘܥ.
fol 23 r ²ܘܐܡܪ ܠܥܒܕܘܗܝ. ܗܢܐ ܝܘܚܢܢ ܗܘ *ܡܥܡܕܢܐ ܗܘ ܩܡ ܡܢ ܒܝܬ
ܡܝ̈ܬܐ. ܡܛܠ ܗܢܐ ܥܒܕ ܚܝ̈ܠܐ. ³ܗܘ ܓܝܪ ܗܪܘܕܣ ܐܚܕܗ
ܗܘܐ ܠܝܘܚܢܢ ܘܐܣܪܗ. ܘܐܪܡܝܗ ܒܝܬ ܐܣܝ̈ܪܐ. ܡܛܠ ܗܪܘܕܝܐ
ܐܢܬܬ ܦܝܠܝܦܘܣ ܐܚܘܗܝ. ⁴ܐܡܪ ܗܘܐ ܠܗ ܓܝܪ ܝܘܚܢܢ. ܕܠܐ
ܫܠܝܛ ܠܟ ܕܬܗܘܐ ܠܟ ܐܢܬܬܐ. ⁵ܘܨܒܐ ܗܘܐ ܠܡܩܛܠܗ ܘܕܚܠ
ܗܘܐ ܡܢ ܥܡܐ. ܡܛܠ ܕܐܝܟ ܕܠܢܒܝܐ ܐܚܝܕܝܢ ܗܘܘ ܠܗ
ܠܝܘܚܢܢ. ܀

⁶ܘܟܕ ܗܘܐ ܒܝܬ ܝܠܕܗ ܕܗܪܘܕܣ. ܚܕܬ ܪܩܕܬ ܒܪܬܗ̇ ܕܗܪܘܕܝܐ
ܩܕܡ ܣܡ̈ܟܐ. ܘܫܦܪܬ ܠܗ ܠܗܪܘܕܣ. ⁷ܡܛܠܗܕܐ ܗܢܐ ܐܫܬܘܕܝ
ܠܗ̇ ܒܡܘܡܬܐ ܕܟܠ ܡܐ ܕܬܫܐܠܝܘܗܝ. ܢܬܠ ܠܗ̇. ⁸ܗܝ ܕܝܢ ܡܛܠ
col 2 *ܕܡܠܟܐ ܗܘܬ ܡܢ ܐܡܗ̇. ܐܡܪܬ. ܗܒ ܠܝ ܗܪܟܐ ܒܦܝܢܟܐ
ܪܫܗ ܕܝܘܚܢܢ ܡܥܡܕܢܐ. ⁹ܘܟܪܝܬ ܠܗ ܠܡܠܟܐ. ܘܡܛܠ ܡܘܡܬܐ
ܘܡܛܠ ܣ̈ܡܟܐ. ܦܩܕ ܕܢܬܝܗܒ ܠܗ̇. ¹⁰ܘܫܕܪ ܦܣܩ ܪܫܗ ܕܝܘܚܢܢ
ܒܝܬ ܐܣ̈ܝܪܐ. ¹¹ܘܐܝܬܝܘ ܪܫܗ ܕܝܘܚܢܢ ܒܦܝܢܟܐ. ܘܐܬܝܗܒ
ܠܛܠܝܬܐ. ܘܗܝ ܛܠܝܬܐ ܐܘܒܠܬܗ ܠܐܡܗ̇. ¹²ܘܩܪܒܘ ܬܠܡ̈ܝܕܘܗܝ
ܕܝܘܚܢܢ ܘܫܩܠܘ ܫܠܕܗ ܘܩܒܪܘܗܝ. ܘܐܬܘ ܘܚܘܘ ܠܝܫܘܥ. ¹³ܫܡܥ

---

57 ܗܘ ܕܝܢ ܝܫܘܥ] ܝܫܘܥ ܕܝܢ S   ܐܢ܆] om. S   1 ܒܗܘ ܕܝܢ ܙܒܢܐ] ܒܙܒܢܐ ܕܝܢ S   ܛܛܪܪܟܐ] ܪܒܥܐ ܪܒܥܝܐ S   2 ܗܢܐ ܝܘܚܢܢ ܗܘ] ܝܘܚܢܢ * * S^ed (? supply ܗܘܝܘ)   3 ܗܘ ܓܝܪ ܗܪܘܕܣ] ܗܪܘܕܣ ܓܝܪ S   ܘܐܣܪܗ] om. S   ܦܝܠܝܦܘܣ S   4 ܕܬܗܘܐ ܠܟ ܐܢܬܬܐ] ܠܡܣܒܗ̇ S   5 ܠܝܘܚܢܢ] om. S
6. Apparently no § in S   ܩܕܡ ܣܡ̈ܟܐ] om. S   ܠܗ] om. S
7 ܡܛܠܗܕܐ ܗܢܐ] ܘ S   8 ܕܡܠܟܐ] S illegible   9 ܘܟܪܝܬ ܠܗ ܠܡܠܟܐ] S illegible   ܡܘܡܬܐ and ܠܗ̇] S illegible   10 ܫܕܪ] ܫܠܚ S   ܒܝܬ] pr. ܡܢ S
11 ܠܛܠܝܬܐ] pr. ܠܗ S   ܛܠܝܬܐ] om. S   12 ܘܩܪܒܘ....ܘܫܩܠܘ] ܘܫܩܠܘ ܬܠܡ̈ܝܕܘܗܝ S   ܘܐܬܘ] S illegible   ܘܚܘܘ] om. ܘ S

57 all these things to this one? And they were offended at him. Now *C S*
Jesus said to them: "There is not a prophet who is insulted, save
58 in his city and in his house." And he did not there many mighty
works, because of the lack of their faith.

xiv 1 Now at that time Herod the Tetrarch heard the rumour of Jesus,
2 and he said to his slaves: "This is John the Baptist, he hath risen
3 from among the dead, therefore great is his power." For Herod had
seized John and bound him, and cast him into prison because of
4 Herodia the wife of Philip his brother; for John had been saying to
him "It is not lawful for thee that she should be a wife of thine."
5 And he was wishing to kill him, and was afraid of the people, because
as a prophet they were holding John.

6 And when it was the birth-day of Herod, the daughter of Herodia
entered *and* danced in the midst of the entertainment, and pleased
7 Herod; therefore he promised her with an oath that all what she
8 should ask him he would give her. Now she, because she had been
taught by her mother, said: "Give me here in a dish the head of
9 John the Baptist." And it grieved the king, but for the oath's sake
and for the sake of them that sat *at meat* he commanded that it
10 should be given to her. And he sent *and* cut off the head of John in
11 the prison, and they brought the head of John in a dish, and it was
12 given to the girl and the girl carried it away to her mother. And
the disciples of John drew near and took up his corpse and buried
13 him, and they came and shewed Jesus. Now Jesus when he heard

---

57 save] but *S* 1 at that time] at the time (*or*, in time) *S* Tetrarch] tetrarch *S* (*lit.* 'fourth head') 3 and bound him] *om. S* 4 that she should be a wife of thine] to take her *S* 5 John] him *S* 6 in the midst of the entertainment] *om. S* 7 therefore] and *S* 8 taught] *S illegible* 9 And it grieved the king] *S illegible* the oath's *and* to her] *S illegible* 10 cut off] took up *S* in] from *S* 11 and the girl] and she *S* 12 the disciples...drew near and took up] his disciples took up *S* and they came] *S illegible* and shewed] *and* shewed *S*

ܕܝܢ ܟܕ ܫܡܥ ܫܢܝ ܠܗ ܡܢ ܬܡܢ ܠܐܬܪܐ ܚܘܪܒܐ ܒܠܚܘܕܘܗܝ܆ C S
ܘܟܕ ܫܡܥܘ ܟܢ̈ܫܐ ܕܡܢ ܟܪ̈ܟܢܝܬܐ ܘܡܢ ܡܕ̈ܝܢܬܐ. ܐܙܠܘ ܠܗܘܢ
ܒܬܪܗ ܒܪܓܠ. [14]*ܘܟܕ ܚܙܐ ܟܢ̈ܫܐ ܣܓܝ̈ܐܐ. ܐܬܪܚܡ ܥܠܝܗܘܢ. fol 23 v
ܘܠܟܪ̈ܝܗܘܢ ܐܣܝ. ܀

[15]ܘܟܕ ܗܘܐ ܪܡܫܐ. ܩܪܒܘ ܬܠܡܝ̈ܕܘܗܝ ܘܐܡܪܝܢ ܠܗ. ܐܬܪܐ
ܚܘܪܒܐ ܗܘ. ܘܥܕܢܐ ܥܒܪ· ܫܪܝ ܟܢ̈ܫܐ ܗܢܘܢ ܢܐܙܠܘܢ
ܠܩܘܪ̈ܝܐ ܘܢܙܒܢܘܢ ܠܗܘܢ ܣܝܒܪܬܐ. [16]ܘܐܡܪ ܠܗܘܢ ܠܐ
ܡܬܒܥܐ ܠܗܘܢ ܠܡܐܙܠ· ܗܒܘ ܠܗܘܢ ܐܢܬܘܢ ܠܡܐܟܠ·
[17]ܐܡܪܝܢ ܠܗ ܠܝܬ ܠܢ ܬܢܢ. ܐܠܐ ܚܡܫ ܓܪ̈ܝܨܢ ܘܬܪ̈ܝܢ ܢܘܢܝܢ.
[18]ܐܡܪ ܠܗܘܢ ܐܝܬܘ ܐܢܘܢ ܠܝ. [19]ܘܦܩܕ ܠܟܢ̈ܫܐ ܠܡܣܬܡܟܘ
ܥܠ ܥܣܒܐ. ܘܢܣܒ ܗܠܝܢ ܚܡܫ ܓܪ̈ܝܨܢ ܘܬܪ̈ܝܢ ܢܘܢܝܢ. ܘܚܪ
ܒܫܡܝܐ ܘܒܪܟ. ܘܩܨܐ ܘܝܗܒ *ܠܬܠܡܝ̈ܕܘܗܝ. ܘܗܢܘܢ col 2
ܬܠܡܝ̈ܕܘܗܝ ܝܗܒܘ ܠܟܢ̈ܫܐ. [20]ܘܐܟܠܘ ܟܠܗܘܢ ܘܣܒܥܘ. ܘܫܩܠܘ
ܬܪ̈ܬܥܣܪܐ ܕܩܨ̈ܝܐ ܡܢ ܡܕܡܝܗܘܢ ܬܪܬܥܣܪ ܡܩ̈ܛܦܝܢ ܟܕ ܡܠܝܢ.
[21]ܘܗܢܘܢ ܐܢܫܐ ܕܐܟܠܘ ܗܘܝܢ ܗܘܘ ܚܡܫܐ ܐ̈ܠܦܝܢ ܓܒ̈ܪܝܢ.
ܣܛܪ ܡܢ ܢܫ̈ܐ ܘܛ̈ܠܝܐ. [22]ܘܦܩܕ ܠܬܠܡܝ̈ܕܘܗܝ ܕܢܣܩܘܢ ܒܐܠܦܐ.
ܘܢܐܙܠܘܢ ܩܕܡܘܗܝ ܠܥܒܪܐ. ܥܕ ܫܪܐ ܠܟܢ̈ܫܐ ܗܠܝܢ. [23]ܘܟܕ
ܫܪܐ ܐܢܘܢ ܣܠܩ ܠܗ ܠܛܘܪܐ ܒܠܚܘܕܘܗܝ ܠܡܨܠܝܘ. ܘܟܕ ܗܘܐ
ܪܡܫܐ ܒܠܚܘܕܘܗܝ ܗܘܐ ܬܡܢ. [24]ܘܣܦܝܢܬܐ ܦܪܝܩܐ ܗܘܬ ܡܢ

---

13 ܠܗ] *om. S*   ܚܘܪܒܐ] *S illegible*   ܒܠܚܘܕܘܗܝ] ܒܠܚܘܕܘܗ *S*
ܟܪ̈ܟܢܝܬܐ ܘܡܢ ܡܕ̈ܝܢܬܐ] *S illegible, but there is no room for* ܘܡܢ ܡܕ̈ܝܢܬܐ   ܒܬܪܗ (*ver.* 13) *to* ܠܩܘܪ̈ܝܐ (*ver.* 15)] *S illegible*   15 ܘܢܙܒܢܘܢ] ܕܢܙܒܢܘܢ *S*   ܣܝܒܪܬܐ] *S illegible*   16 ܘܐܡܪ] *om.* ܘ *S*   ܠܐ ܡܬܒܥܐ *and* ܗܒܘ ܠܗܘܢ] *S illegible*   ܠܡܐܟܠ] ܠܡܐܟܠܘ *S*   17 ܐܡܪܝܢ *and* ܠܢ ܬܢܢ ܐܠܐ] *S illegible*   ܓܪ̈ܝܨܢ (*ver.* 17) *to* ܐܡܪ (*ver.* 18)] *S illegible*   19 ܠܡܣܬܡܟܘ] ܕܢܣܬܡܟܘܢ *S*   ܥܣܒܐ] ܢܘܪܐ *S*   ܗܠܝܢ] ܠܗܠܝܢ *S*   ܘܗܢܘܢ] *om.* ܗܢܘܢ *S*   20 ܬܪ̈ܬܥܣܪܐ & ܡܕܡܝܗܘܢ & ܡܩ̈ܛܦܝܢ ܟܕ] *S illegible*   21 *to* 23 ܫܪܐ ܐܢܘܢ] *S illegible, but ver. 21 begins with* ⌈ܗ⌉ܘܘ   23 ܠܗ] *om. S*   ܗܘܐ ܬܡܢ] *S illegible*   24 ܦܪܝܩܐ] *S illegible*   ܡܢ....ܦܠܓܐܐ] *S illegible*

departed from thence to a desert place *with* them alone. And when *C S*
the multitudes from the cities and from the villages heard, they went
14 away after him on foot, and when he saw the many multitudes he had
compassion upon them, and their infirm he healed.
15 And when it was evening his disciples drew near and say to him:
"The place is desert, and the time is past; dismiss those multitudes
that they may go to the villages and buy for themselves food."
16 And he saith to them: "It is not required for them to go; give ye
17 them to eat." They say to him: "We have not here but five loaves
18, 19 and two fishes." He saith to them: "Bring them to me." And he com-
manded the multitudes to sit down *to meat* on the green grass; and
he took up these five loaves and two fishes, and looked up to heaven
and blessed, and brake bread and gave to his disciples and they, his
20 disciples, gave to the multitudes. And they all ate and were satisfied,
and they took up of the superfluity of the fragments from before
21 them twelve baskets full. And those folk that ate were five thou-
22 sand men, besides women and children. And he commanded his
disciples that they should sit in the ship and go before him to the
23 other side, until he should dismiss these multitudes. And when he
dismissed them he went up to the hill alone to pray, and when
24 it was evening he alone was there. And the boat was distant from

---

13 desert] *S illegible* *with* them alone] himself alone *S* And when *and* the cities...heard] *S illegible, but there is no room for* 'and from the villages' after him (*ver.* 13) *to* the villages (*ver.* 15)] *S illegible* 15 and buy] that they may buy *S* food] *S illegible* 16 And he] He *S* It is not required *and* give ye them] *S illegible* to eat] *S has a synonym* 17 They say *and* We..here but] *S illegible* loaves (*ver.* 17) *to* He saith (*ver.* 18)] *S illegible* 19 to sit] that they should sit *S* green grass] herbage *S* they] *om. S* 20 superfluity *&* before them *&* baskets] *S illegible* 21 *to* 23 (dismissed them)] *S illegible* 23 was there] *S illegible* 24 distant] *S illegible* from...stadia] *S illegible*

C S fol 24 r ܐܪܒܐ ܐܬܦ̈ܓܕܘܬܐ ܡܢ ܓ̈ܠܠܐ. ܘܡܫܬܢܩܝܢ ܗܘܘ ܡܢ ܓ̈ܠܠܐ*. ܡܛܠ
ܕܪܘܚܐ ܠܘܩܒܠܗܘܢ ܗܘܬ. ²⁵ܒܡܥܒܪܬܐ ܕܝܡ ܛܒܪܝܐ ܕܓܠܝܠܐ.
ܐܬܐ ܠܘܬܗܘܢ ܝܫܘܥ ܟܕ ܡܗܠܟ ܥܠ ܡ̈ܝܐ. ²⁶ܘܟܕ ܚܙܐܘܗܝ,
ܬܠܡܝܕܘܗܝ, ܕܡܗܠܟ ܥܠ ܓ̈ܠܠ ܝܡܐ ܐܬܪܗܒܘ. ܘܐܡܪܝܢ ܗܘܘ
ܕܕܡܝܐ ܗܘ. ܘܡܢ ܕܚܠܬܗܘܢ ܩܥܘ ܟܠܗ. ²⁷ܘܒܗ ܒܫܥܬܐ
ܡܠܠ ܥܡܗܘܢ: ܐܬܚܝܠܘ ܐܢܐ ܐܢܐ ܠܐ ܬܕܚܠܘܢ. ²⁸ܐܡܪ
ܠܗ ܫܡܥܘܢ ܟܐܦܐ. ܡܪܝ, ܐܢ ܐܢܬ ܗܘ ܐܦܣ ܠܝ ܐܬܐ
ܠܘܬܟ ܥܠ ܡ̈ܝܐ. ²⁹ܐܡܪ ܠܗ ܬܐ. ܘܢܚܬ ܫܡܥܘܢ ܟܐܦܐ
ܡܢ ܣܦܝܢܬܐ. ܘܡܗܠܟ ܗܘܐ ܥܠ ܡ̈ܝܐ. ܘܐܬܐ ܠܘܬ ܝܫܘܥ.
col 2 ³⁰ܘܟܕ ܚܙܐ ܪܘܚܐ* ܕܩܫܝܐ ܗܝ، ܕܚܠ ܘܫܪܝ ܠܡܛܒܥ. ܘܩܥܐ
ܒܩܠܐ ܪܒܐ ܘܐܡܪ. ܡܪܝ, ܐܚܝܢܝ. ³¹ܘܒܗ ܒܫܥܬܐ ܐܘܫܛ ܝܫܘܥ
ܐܝܕܗ ܘܐܚܕܗ. ܘܐܡܪ ܠܗ ܚܣܝܪ ܗܝܡܢܘܬܐ ܠܡܢܐ ܐܬܦܠܓܬ.
³²ܘܟܕ ܣܠܩ ܠܣܦܝܢܬܐ ܫܠܝܬ ܪܘܚܐ. ³³ܘܣܓܕܘ ܗܘܢ ܕܒܣܦܝܢܬܐ
ܣܓܕܘ ܠܗ. ܘܐܡܪܝܢ ܫܪܝܪܐܝܬ ܒܪܗ ܐܢܬ ܕܐܠܗܐ. ³⁴ܘܟܕ ܥܒܪܘ
ܠܥܒܪܐ. ܐܬܘ ܠܗܘܢ ܠܓܢܣܪ. ³⁵ܘܐܫܬܘܕܥܘܗܝ, ܓ̈ܒܪܐ ܐܬܪܐ ܗܘ.
ܘܫܕܪܘ ܠܟܠܗ ܟܦܪ ܕܠܗܘܢ: ܘܩܪܒܘ ܩܕܡܘܗܝ, ܟܠܗܘܢ ܐܝܠܝܢ

ܘܡܫܬܢܩܝܢ...ܓ̈ܠܠܐ] ܡܫܬܢܩܐ ܒܓ̈ܠܠܘܗܝ ܘܐܬܦܓܥܘ S^{vid} (* * ܘܐܬܦܓܥܘ S^{ed}): *cf* Joh vi 18 ܗܘܬ & ܡܛܠ ܕܪܘܚܐ] *S illegible* 25 ܒܡܥܒܪܬܐ & ܡܗܠܟ & ܕܓܠܝܠܐ] *S illegible* 26 ܘܟܕ...ܬܠܡܝܕܘܗܝ] ܟܕ ܚܙܘ *S* ܗܘܘ] *om. S* ܕܕܡܝܐ ܗܘ] *see Note on* Mk vi 49
27 ܘܒܗ ܒܫܥܬܐ] ܘܡܚܕܐ ܡܠܠ *S* ܐܬܚܝܠܘ] ܘܐܡܪ ܬܪܘܨܘ *S*
28 ܐܡܪ....ܟܐܦܐ] ܘܐܡܪ ܠܗ ܟܐܦܐ ܫܡܥܘܢ ܟܐܦܐ *S* ܡܪܝ] *om. S* ܠܝ] *om. S* ܐܬܐ] *pr.* ܕ *S* 29 ܐܡܪ] *pr.* ܗܘ ܕܝܢ *S* 30 ܘܟܕ] ܟܕ *S* ܕܩܫܝܐ ܗܝ] ܕܩܫܝܐ *S* 31 ܘܒܗ ܒܫܥܬܐ ܐܘܫܛ ܝܫܘܥ] ܘܡܚܕܐ ܐܘܫܛ ܝܫܘܥ *S* (*? pr.* ܘ, *as in ver.* 27: *the photograph is illegible*) ܣܦܝܪ] ܘܚܣܝܪ *S A* 21 ܠܡܢܐ] (ܘܟܕ....ܫܪܝ ܗܘܐ ܠܡܛܒܥ· ܩܥܐ ܡܪܝ ܐܚܝܢܝ ܣܦܝܪ ܗܝܡܢܘܬܐ) *S illegible* 32 ܣܠܩ] ܣܠܩܘ *S* ܫܠܝܬ] ܘܫܠܝܬ *S* 33 ܒܪܗ ܐܢܬ] ܐܢܬ ܗܘ ܒܪܗ *S* 34. § *in S, apparently* ܣܠܩ] ܣܠܩܘ *S* ܠܗܘܢ] *om. S* 35 ܘܫܕܪܘ] ܫܕܪܘ *S* (*sic*) ܠܟܠܗ ܟܦܪ ܕܠܗܘܢ] ܠܐܬܪܗܘܢ *S* ܘܩܪܒܘ ܩܕܡܘܗܝ] ܘܐܝܬܝܘ ܠܗ *S*

the land many stadia, and they were being tormented by the *C S*
25 waves because the wind was against them. But in the fourth
watch of the night Jesus came unto them walking on the water,
26 and when his disciples saw him that he *was* walking on the waves
of the sea they were troubled, and were saying "It is a devil";
27 and from their fear they gave a cry. And in the same hour
he spake with them: "Take courage; it is I, be not afraid!"
28 Saith to him Simon Kepha: "My Lord, if it be thou, permit
29 me *that* I come unto thee upon the water." He saith to him:
"Come." And Simon Kepha came down from the boat and was
30 walking on the water, and came unto Jesus. And when he saw the
wind that it was strong, he was afraid and began to sink; and he
31 called with a loud voice and said: "My Lord, save my *life*!" And
in the same hour Jesus put forth his hand and took hold of him, and
he said to him: "O lacking in faith, wherefore didst thou doubt?"
32, 33 And when he went up into the boat the wind ceased. And those in
the boat came near *and* worshipped him, and say: "Truly thou art
34 the Son of God!" And when he went up to the dry land they came
35 to Gennesar. And the people of that place recognised him, and they
sent to all their region; and they brought near before him all those

---

and they.... waves] and the lake ⌜was⌝ agitated ⌜against them⌝ *S*^{vid}; *cf* Joh vi 18 because the wind was] *S illegible* 25 watch *&* of the night *&* Jesus] *S illegible* 26 when...saw him] when they saw *S* were 2°] *om. S* a devil] *see Note on* Mk vi 49 27 And in the same hour he] And Jesus immediately *S* Take courage] and saith: Be assured *S* 28 Saith...Kepha] Simon Kepha answered and said to him *S* My Lord, if] If *S* me] *om. S* *that* I come] that I come *S* 29 He saith] Now he said *S* 30 And when] When *S* that it was strong] was mighty *S* 31 And in the same hour Jesus] Jesus immediately *S* (? *pr.* 'And' *as in ver.* 27) lacking in] little of *S A*21 ('and when..he had begun to sink, our Lord called him little of faith') wherefore] *S illegible* 32 he] they *S* ceased] abated *S*: *cf* xii 9, *and see Notes*, vol. ii 34 he] they *S* 35 and they sent] *om.* and *S* (*sic*) to all their region] to their country *S* brought near before him] brought to him *S*

C S ܕܒܝܫ ܒܝܫ ܒܒܝܕܝܢ. ³⁶ܘܒܥܝܢ ܗܘܘ ܡܢܗ ܕܢܩܪܒܘܢ ܒܠܚܘܕ
fol 24 v ܠܬܠܬܐ ܕܐܣܛܠܝܗ. *ܘܐܝܠܝܢ ܕܩܪܒܝܢ ܗܘܘ ܐܬܐܣܝܘ ܗܘܘ .:.
¹ܗܝܕܝܢ ܩܪܒܘ ܠܘܬܗ ܕܝܫܘܥ ܣ̈ܦܪܐ ܘܦ̈ܪܝܫܐ ܕܡܢ ܐܘܪܫܠܡ
ܘܐܡܪܝܢ ܠܗ. ²ܠܡܢܐ ܬܠܡ̈ܝܕܝܟ ܥܒܪܝܢ ܥܠ ܦܘܩ̈ܕܢܐ ܕܣ̈ܒܝܢ.
ܠܐ ܓܝܪ ܡܫܝܓܝܢ ܐܝ̈ܕܝܗܘܢ ܡܐ ܕܐܟܠܝܢ ܠܚܡܐ. ³ܗܘ ܕܝܢ ܥܢܐ
ܘܐܡܪ ܠܗܘܢ. ܠܡܢܐ ܐܦ ܐܢܬܘܢ ܥܒܪܝܢ ܐܢܬܘܢ ܥܠ
ܦܘܩܕܢܐ ܕܐܠܗܐ ܡܛܠ ܕܬܘܣܦܬܟܘܢ ܦܘܩ̈ܕܢܝܟܘܢ : ⁴ܐܠܗܐ ܓܝܪ
ܐܡܪ ܝܩܪ ܠܐܒܘܟ ܘܠܐܡܟ. ܘܡܢ ܕܡܨܚܐ ܠܐܒܘܗܝ ܐܘ
ܠܐܡܗ ܢܬܩܛܠ. ⁵ܐܢܬܘܢ ܕܝܢ ܐܡܪܝܢ ܐܢܬܘܢ ܐܢܫ ܠܐܒܘܗܝ
ܘܠܐܡܗ. ܩܘܪܒܢ ܬܬܗܢܐ ܡܢܝ. ⁶ܗܢܐ ܠܐ ܝܩܪ ܠܐܒܘܗܝ.
col 2 ܘܒܛܠܬܘܢ ܡܠܬܗ ܕܐܠܗܐ ܡܛܠ ܕܬܘܣܦܬܟܘܢ *ܦܘܩ̈ܕܢܝܟܘܢ :
⁷ܢܣ̈ܒܝ ܒܐܦ̈ܐ. ܫܦܝܪ ܐܬܢܒܝ ܥܠܝܟܘܢ ܐܫܥܝܐ ܢܒܝܐ ܕܐܡܪ
§A 375 ܗܘܐ. §⁸ܥܡܐ ܗܢܐ ܒܣܦܘ̈ܬܗ ܗܘ ܡܝܩܪ ܠܝ. ܘܠܒܗ ܪܚܝܩ
¶A ܡܢܝ¶. ⁹ܘܣܪܝܩܐܝܬ ܕܝܢ ܕܚܠܝܢ ܠܝ. ܘܡܠܦܝܢ ܝܘ̈ܠܦܢܐ ܕܦܘܩ̈ܕܢܐ
ܕܒܢ̈ܝܢܫܐ . .
§A 46, 306 ¹⁰ܘܩܪܐ ܠܟܢܫܐ ܘܐܡܪ ܠܗܘܢ : ܫܡܥܘ ܘܐܣܬܟܠܘ. §¹¹ܕܠܐ ܗܘܐ
ܡܕܡ ܕܥܐܠ ܠܦܘܡܐ ܡܣܝܒ ܠܗ ܠܒܪ ܐܢܫܐ. ܐܠܐ ܡܕܡ
¶A ²/₂ ܕܢܦܩ ܡܢ ܦܘܡܐ ܗܘ ܗܘ ܡܣܝܒ. ܠܗ ܠܒܪܢܫܐ¶. ¹²ܗܝܕܝܢ ܩܪܒܘ

ܒܒܝܕܝܢ] *S illegible, but adds* ܗܘܘ   36 ܒܠܚܘܕ ܠܬܠܬܐ ܕܐܣܛܠܝܗ]
ܠܟܢܦܐ ܕܡܪܛܘܛܗ ܒܠܚܘܕ *S*   ܘܐܝܠܝܢ] ܘܟܠ ܐܝܠܝܢ *S*   ܕܩܪܒܝܢ] ܕܩܪܒܘ *S*
ܐܬܐܣܝܘ] ܚܝܝܢ *S*   1 ܠܘܬܗ ܕܝܫܘܥ] ܠܗ *S*   ܡܢ ܐܘܪܫܠܡ ܣ̈ܦܪܐ ܘܦ̈ܪܝܫܐ *S*
2 ܓܝܪ] *om. S, but* ܡܫܝܓܝܢ *is illegible*   ܡܐ ܕܐܟܠܝܢ] ܘܐܟܠܝܢ *S*   3 ܘܐܡܪ]
om. ܘ *S*   ܕܬܘܣܦܬܟܘܢ] *om. S*   4 ܐܘ] ܘ *S*   ܢܬܩܛܠ] ܡܡܬ ܢܡܘܬ *S*
5 ܐܢܫ] ܡܢ ܕܐܡܪ *S*   ܩܘܪܒܢ ܬܬܗܢܐ ܡܢܝ] ܩܘܪܒܢ ܠܟ ܬܬܗܢܐ ܡܢܝ *S*
6 ܗܢܐ] *pr.* ܘ *S*   ܠܐ ܝܩܪ ܠܐܒܘܗܝ] ܠܐ ܠܐܒܘܗܝ ܘܠܐ ܠܐܡܗ ܡܝܩܪ *S*
ܕܬܘܣܦܬܟܘܢ] *om. S*   9 ܘܡܠܦܝܢ] *om.* ܘ *S*   10 ܠܟܢ̈ܫܐ *S*   11 ܕܠܐ ܗܘܐ]
om. A 46 (*pr.* ܠܐ *to* ܡܣܝܒ)   ܠܦܘܡܐ] ܠܒܪ ܐܢܫܐ A ²/₂   ܠܒܪ ܐܢܫܐ]
om. A ²/₂   ܕܢܦܩ] + ܡܢܗ A ²/₂   ܡܢ ܦܘܡܐ] ܡܢ ܦܘܡܗ A^a46; ܡܢ ܒܪܢܫܐ
A 306   ܗܘ 2°] *om. S*   ܠܒܪܢܫܐ] ܠܒܪ ܐܢܫܐ *S* (*as elsewhere*); *om.* A ²/₂

36 that were ill, and they were beseeching him that they might touch *C S*
only the fringe of his mantle, and those that had touched had been
healed.

XV 1 Then drew near unto Jesus scribes and Pharisees from Jerusalem,
2 and say unto him: "Wherefore do thy disciples transgress the com-
mandments of our ancients? for they wash not their hands what *time*
3 they eat bread." Now he answered and said to them: "Wherefore
do ye also yourselves transgress the commandment of God, because
4 ye will set up your commandments? For God said: Honour thy
father and thy mother, and he that curseth his father or his mother
5 shall be killed. But ye say each to his father and his mother: 'My
6 offering—thou shalt be profited from me!' This one hath not
honoured his father. And ye have made idle the word of God,
7 because ye will set up your commandments. Ye respecters of
8 persons, well prophesied of you Isaiah the prophet, who said: §'This §*A*375
people with their lips honoureth me, and their heart is far from me;¶ ¶*A*
9 but in vain do they fear me, and teach teachings of the command-
ments of men.'"

10 And he called the multitude and said to them: "Hear and under-
11 stand, that §not that which entereth the mouth defileth the man, but §*A*46, 306
that which cometh forth from the mouth, that defileth the man."¶ ¶$A^{2}/_{2}$

---

ill] *S illegible* 36 only...mantle] the skirt of his cloak only *S* those] *pr.* all *S* had touched] were touching *S* had been healed] were being saved alive *S* 1 unto Jesus] to him *S* from Jerusalem scribes and Pharisees *S* 2 for] *om. S, but* 'they wash' *is illegible* what...eat] and eat *S* 3 because...set up] because of *S* 4 or] and *S* shall be killed] shall die indeed *S* E^{138} 5 each] *C* E^{138}; He that shall say *S* My offering—...from me] *It is* an offering (*or*, 'Corban'), if thou shouldest be profited from me *S*; 'Come on thou, it is an offering, whatsoever thou mayest be profited from me' E^{138}: *for the rendering in C, cf* donum meum proficiet tibi *e* 6 This] And this *S* hath not...father] neither his father nor his mother honoureth *S* because...set up] because of *S* 9 and teach] teaching *S* 10 the multitudes *S* 11 that not] *om. A* 46 (+'not' *after* 'defileth') the mouth] the man $A^{2}/_{2}$ the man 1°] him $A^{2}/_{2}$ from the mouth] from the mouth itself $A^{b}46$; from his mouth itself $A^{a}46$; from the man himself *A*306 that *ult.*] *om. S* the man 2°] him $A^{2}/_{2}$

C S ܬܠܡ̈ܝܕܘܗܝ, ܘܐܡܪܝܢ ܠܗ. ܝܕܥ ܐܢܬ ܕܦܪ̈ܝܫܐ ܟܕ ܫܡܥܘ ܡܠܬܐ
§'Julian' ܗܕܐ ܐܬܟܫܠܘ. [13]ܗܘ ܕܝܢ ܥܢܐ ܘܐܡܪ ܠܗܘܢ: §ܟܠ ܢܨܒܬܐ
29 fol 25 r ¶'Jul' ܕܐܒܝ ܕܒܫܡܝܐ ܠܐ ܢܨܒܗ *ܬܬܥܩܪ.¶ [14]ܫܒܘܩܘ ܠܗܘܢ: ܥܘ̈ܝܪܐ
ܐܢܘܢ ⌈⌉ܡ̈ܕܒܪܢܐ. ܥܘܝܪܐ ܕܝܢ ܕܠܥܘܝܪܐ ܡܕܒܪ ܬܪܝܗܘܢ ܒܓܘܡܨܐ
ܢܦܠܘܢ. [15]ܥܢܐ ܫܡܥܘܢ ܟܐܦܐ ܘܐܡܪ ܠܗ. ܦܫܩ ܠܢ ܡܬܠܐ
ܗܢܐ. [16]ܐܡܪ ܠܗ ܐܦ ܠܐ ܐܢܬܘܢ ܥܕܡܐ ܠܗܫܐ ܡܣܬܟܠܝܢ
ܐܢܬܘܢ: [17]ܠܐ ܝܕܥܝܢ ܐܢܬܘܢ ܕܟܠ ܡܕܡ ܕܥܐܠ ܠܦܘܡܐ
ܠܟܪܣܐ ܗܘ ܐܙܠ. ܘܡܢ ܬܡܢ ܡܫܬܕܝܐ ܒܬܕܒܝܬܐ. [18]ܡܕܡ ܕܝܢ
ܕܢܦܩ ܡܢ ܦܘܡܐ ܡܢ ܠܒܐ ܗܘ ܢܦܩ. ܘܗܘ ܗܘ ܡܣܝܒ ܠܗ
§¶A 307 ܠܒܪܢܫܐ. [19]§ܡܢ ܠܒܐ ܗܘ ܓܝܪ ܢܦܩܝܢ ܡܚܫ̈ܒܬܐ ܒ̈ܝܫܬܐ.¶ ܕܩܛܠܐ
ܘܕܓܘܪܐ. ܘܕܙܢܝܘܬܐ. ܘܕܓܢܒܘܬܐ. ܘܣܗܕܘܬܐ ܕܫܘܩܪܐ
col 2 ܘܓܘܕܦܐ. [20]ܗܠܝܢ ܐܢܝܢ ܐܠܝܢ ܕܡܣܝܒܢ ܠܗ ܠܒܪܢܫܐ. *ܒܪ ܐܢܫ
ܕܝܢ ܢܐܟܘܠ ܠܚܡܐ ܟܕ ܠܐ ܡܫܝܓܢ ܐܝ̈ܕܘܗܝ, ܠܐ ܡܣܬܝܒ.
[21]ܘܢܦܩ ܝܫܘܥ ܡܢ ܬܡܢ. ܘܐܙܠ ܠܗ ܠܬܚܘܡܐ ܕܨܘܪ ܘܕܨܝܕܢ.
[22]ܘܗܐ ܐܢܬܬܐ ܚܕܐ ܟܢܥܢܝܬܐ ܢܦܩܬ ܡܬܚܘܡܗܘܢ ܡܢ ܬܚܘ̈ܡܐ
ܗܠܝܢ. ܘܩܥܝܐ ܗܘܬ ܘܐܡܪܐ. ܐܬܪܚܡ ܥܠܝ ܡܪܝ, ܒܪܗ ܕܕܘܝܕ.
ܒܪܬܝ, ܒܝܫܐܝܬ ܡܬܕܒܪܐ ܡܢ ܫ̈ܐܕܐ, ܫܐܕܐ. [23]ܘܗܘ ܠܐ ܝܗܒ
ܠܗ̇ ܦܬܓܡܐ. ܘܩܪܒܘ ܬܠܡ̈ܝܕܘܗܝ, ܘܒܥܝܢ ܗܘܘ ܡܢܗ ܘܐܡܪܝܢ

---

12 ܝܕܥ ܐܢܬ] ܝܕܥܬ S   13 ܠܗܘܢ] om. S   ܕܐܒܝ] ܕܐܒܐ S: see on Mt vi 4   ܬܬܥܩܪ] pr. ܟܠܗ Jul   14 ܕܡ̈ܕܒܪܢܐ] S; om. ܕ C (nunc), but a letter seems to have been washed out before ܡ   16 ܠܗܫܐ] a blank space is left in S after this word (sic)   17 Cf A 307[10]:
ܡܛܠ ܕܡܐܟܘܠܬܐ ܠܟܪܣܐ ܐܙܠܐ. ܘܡܢ ܬܡܢ ܒܬܕܒܝܬܐ ܡܫܬܕܝܐ ܠܒܪ
18 ܡܕܡ ܕܝܢ] ܘܡܕܡ S   ܕܢܦܩ....ܢܦܩ] ܕܡܢ ܠܒܐ ܢܦܩ ܡܢ ܦܘܡܐ ܗܘ ܢܦܩ S   ܗܘ ult.] om. S   19 ܡܢ....ܢܦܩܝܢ] ܗܘܝܢ ܗܘ ܒܠܒܐ A   ܘܣܗܕܘܬܐ ܕܫܘܩܪܐ] ܘܣܗܕܘܬ ܫܘܩܪܐ S (sic)   20 ܐܠܝܢ] om. S   ܡܣܬܝܒ] + ܒܪ ܐܢܫܐ S
21. *Apparently no § in S: see the Facsimile in Mrs Lewis's 'Some Pages'*
22 ܚܕܐ] om. S   ܗܠܝܢ] ܗܢܘܢ S   ܘܩܥܝܐ ܗܘܬ] ܘܩܥܬ S   ܐܬܪܚܡ] ܪܚܡ S   ܫ̈ܐܕܐ] om. S   23 ܘܗܘ] ܗܘ ܕܝܢ S   ܘܒܥܝܢ ܗܘܘ] ܘܒܥܘ S

12 Then drew near his disciples and say to him: "Knowest thou that *C S*
13 the Pharisees when they heard this word were offended?" But he
answered and said to them: §"Every plant that my Father in heaven §'*Julian*' 29
14 hath not planted shall be rooted up.¶ Let them be, they are leaders ¶'*Jul.*'
of the blind; but the blind man that leadeth the blind man with him
15 falleth in the ditch." Simon Kepha answered and said to him:
16 "Explain to us this similitude." He saith to him: "Do not even ye
17 yet understand? Do ye not know that everything which entereth the
mouth, to the belly it goeth, and from thence is thrown away in the
18 cleansing. But that which cometh forth from the mouth, from the
19 heart it cometh forth, and it is that defileth the man. §For from the §*A* 307
heart come forth evil thoughts¶ of murder and of adultery and of ¶*A*
20 fornication and of theft, and false witness and blasphemy; these are
they that defile the man. For when any one shall eat bread with
unwashen hands, he is not defiled."

21 And Jesus came forth from thence, and went away to the border
22 of Tyre and Sidon. And lo, a certain woman, a Canaanite, came forth
from those same borders, and was crying out and saith: "Have
compassion on me, my Lord, son of David! my daughter is evilly
23 entreated at the hands of a devil." And he gave her no answer.
And his disciples drew near, and were beseeching him and were

---

13 to them] *om. S* my Father] the Father *S*: *see on* Mt vi 4 rooted up] *pr.* quickly *Jul* 14 leaders of the blind] *S*; blind leaders *C* (*nunc*), *but a letter seems to have been washed out which would have made C agree with S* 17 *Cf A* 307[10]: 'Because meats to the belly go, and from thence in the cleansing are thrown away' 18 But] And *S* that which...cometh forth 2°] that which from the heart cometh forth, from the mouth it cometh forth *S* it is] *om. S* 19 from the heart come forth] in the heart arise (*lit.* 'come to be') *A E*[63] 20 he] the man *S* 22 certain] *om. S* was crying out] screamed *S*: *cf* 'The woman was crying out and was coming after and was saying, Have compassion on me' *E*[138] at the hands] *om. S* 23 And he] Now he *S E*[138] were beseeching] besought *S*

C S ܗܘܘ ܠܗ. ܫܪܝܘ ܕܗܘܐ ܡܒܝܐ ܘܐܬܬܢܐ ܒܬܪܗ̇. [24]ܗܘ ܕܝܢ ܒܒܝܐ
ܘܐܡܪ ܠܗܘܢ. ܠܐ ܐܫܬܕܪܬ ܐܠܐ ܒܬܪܗ̇ ܒܒܝܐ ܗܠܝܢ ܕܐܠܨ
ܡܢ ܒܝܬ ܐܝܣܪܐܝܠ. [25]ܗܘܝܢ ܗܝ ܡܪܒܬ ܦܓܥܬ ܠܗ ܘܐܡܪܐ.
fol 25 v *ܠܗ ܡܪܝ ܒܪܕܘܝܕ. [26]ܗܘ ܕܝܢ ܒܒܝܐ ܘܐܡܪ ܠܗ̇. ܠܐ ܘܠܐ ܠܡܣܒ
ܠܚܡܐ ܕܒܢܝܐ ܘܠܡܪܡܝܘ ܠܟܠܒܐ. [27]ܐܡܪܐ ܠܗ ܐܝܢ ܡܪܝ.
ܐܦ ܟܠܒܐ ܓܝܪ ܐܟܠܝܢ ܡܢ ܦܪ̈ܬܘܬܐ ܕܢܦܠܝܢ ܡܢ ܦܬܘܪܐ
ܕܡܪܝܗܘܢ ܘܚܝܝܢ. [28]ܘܒܗܐ ܘܐܡܪ ܠܗ̇. ܐܘ ܐܢܬܬܐ ܪܒܐ ܗܝ
ܗܝܡܢܘܬܟܝ. ܢܗܘܐ ܠܟܝ ܐܝܟ ܕܨܒܝܐ ܐܢܬܝ. ܘܐܬܬܐܣܝܬ
ܒܪܬܗ̇ ܡܢ ܗܝ ܫܥܬܐ.

[29]ܘܫܢܝ ܝܫܘܥ ܡܢ ܬܡܢ. ܘܐܬܐ ܠܗ ܥܠ ܝܕ ܝܡܬܐ ܕܓܠܝܠܐ.
ܘܣܠܩ ܝܬܒ ܠܗ ܒܛܘܪܐ. [30]ܘܩܪܒܘ ܠܗ ܟܢܫܐ ܣܓܝܐܐ. ܟܕ
ܐܝܬ ܗܘܘ ܥܡܗܘܢ ܚܓܝܪ̈ܐ ܘܣܡ̈ܝܐ ܩ̈ܫܝܪܐ ܘܦܟ̈ܝܚܐ.
ܘܣܓܝ̈ܐܐ ܕܟܐ̈ܒܐ ܐܚܪ̈ܢܐ. ܘܐܪܡܝܘ ܐܢܘܢ ܠܘܬ ܪ̈ܓܠܘܗܝ.
col 2 *ܘܐܣܝ ܐܢܘܢ. [31]ܘܐܬܕܡܪܘ ܗܘܘ ܟܢ̈ܫܐ ܗܢܘܢ. ܟܕ ܚܙܘ ܗܘܘ
ܚܪ̈ܫܐ ܕܡܡܠܠܝܢ. ܩ̈ܫܝܪܐ ܕܡܗܠܟܝܢ. ܘܣܡ̈ܝܐ ܕܚܙܝܢ. ܘܡܫܒܚܝܢ
ܗܘܘ ܠܐܠܗܐ ܕܐܝܣܪܐܝܠ. [32]ܗܘ ܕܝܢ ܝܫܘܥ ܩܪܐ ܠܬܠܡܝ̈ܕܘܗܝ
ܘܐܡܪ ܠܗܘܢ. ܡܬܪܚܡ ܐܢܐ ܥܠ ܟܢܫܐ ܗܢܐ. ܕܗܐ ܬܠܬܐ
ܝܘ̈ܡܝܢ ܩܘܝܘ ܠܘܬܝ. ܘܠܝܬ ܠܗܘܢ ܡܕܡ ܕܢܐܟܠܘܢ. ܘܕܐܫܪܐ
ܐܢܘܢ ܟܕ ܨܝܡܝܢ ܐܢܘܢ ܠܐ ܨܒܐ ܐܢܐ. ܕܠܐ ܢܥܘܦܘܢ

ܗܘܘ ܠܗ] *om. S*   24 ܒܬܪܗ̇] ܠܘܬ *S*   ܗܠܝܢ] *C S*[ed], *but the photogr. of S suggests to me* ܗܠܝܢ   ܕܐܠܨ] ܕܐܠܨܝ *S*[ed]   25 ܗܝ ܕܝܢ] ܗܘܝܢ ܗܝ *S*   ܠܗ 1°] ܠܘܬܗ *S*   26 ܘܠܡܪܡܝܘ] ܘܪܡܝܢ *S (sic)*   27 ܓܝܪ] *om. S*   ܡܢ ܦܪ̈ܬܘܬܐ ܕܢܦܠܝܢ] *om. S*   28 ܘܒܗܐ] ܗܘܝܢ ܒܒܝܐ *S*   ܠܗ̇] *om. S*   ܕܨܒܝܬܝ *S*   ܘܡܢ ܗܕܐ ܫܥܬܐ ܐܬܬܐܣܝܬ ܒܪܬܗ̇ *S*   29. *No § in S*   ܘܫܢܝ] + ܠܗ *S*   ܝܫܘܥ] *after* ܡܢ ܬܡܢ *in S*   ܝܡܬܐ] ܝܡ *S*   30 ܟܕ ܐܝܬ ܗܘܘ] ܘܐܝܬ *S*   ܘܩ̈ܫܝܪܐ] ܘܡܚܒܪ̈ܐ *S*   ܘܚܪ̈ܫܐ ܘܦܟ̈ܝܚܐ] ܘܚܪ̈ܫܐ ܘܚܓܝܪ̈ܐ *S*   ܕܟܐ̈ܒܐ] *om. S*   ܘܐܪܡܝܘ] ܘܫܕܘ *S*   ܠܘܬ] ܬܚܝܬ *S*   31 ܗܢܘܢ] *om. S*   ܟܕ ܚܙܘ ܗܘܘ] ܕܚܙܝܢ *S*   ܕܐܝܣܪܐܝܠ *S*   32. *§ in S: end of line in C*   ܗܘ ܕܝܢ ܝܫܘܥ ܩܪܐ] ܘܩܪܐ ܝܫܘܥ *S*   ܠܗܘܢ] *om. S*   ܩܘܝܘ] ܩܘܝܢ *S (sic)*   ܕܗܐ ܬܠܬܐ] ܗܐ ܓ *S*   ܟܕ ܨܝܡܝܢ ܐܢܘܢ] ܟܕ ܨܝܡܝܢ *S*

saying to him: "Dismiss her, for lo, she crieth out and cometh C S
24 after us." But he answered and said to them: "I have not been
sent save after the flock, which hath strayed from the House of
25 Israel." Then she herself drew near *and* worshipped him, and saith
26 to him: "My Lord, help me!" But he answered and said to her:
"It is not fitting to take the sons' bread and to cast *it* to the dogs."
27 She saith to him: "Yea, my Lord, for even the dogs eat of the
28 morsels that fall from the tables of their masters and live." And he
answered and said to her: "Oh woman, great is thy faith! It
shall be to thee as thou wilt." And her daughter was healed from
that hour.

29 And Jesus removed from thence, and came by the side of the lake
30 of Galilee. And he went up *and* sat in the hill, and there drew
near to him great multitudes, there being with them the lame and the
blind and the deaf and the maimed, and many with other pains, and
31 they cast them at his feet, and he healed them. And those multitudes
were wondering, when they were seeing the deaf speaking, and the
lame walking, and the blind seeing; and they were glorifying the
32 God of Israel. Now Jesus called his disciples and said to them:
"I have compassion on this multitude, for lo, three days they have
remained by me, and they have not what they may eat, and that I
should dismiss them without a meal I am not willing, that they faint

---

and were saying to him] and say *S* 24 after] unto *S* 25 Then she herself] But she *S* worshipped unto him *S* 26 and to cast] *and* cast *S* (*sic*) 27 for] *om.* *S* *E*[139] of the morsels that fall] *om.* *S*: *om.* 'that fall' *E*[139] (= Mk vii 28, *not* *S*) 28 And he] Then he *S* to her] *om.* *S* as thou wilt, and from that hour hath thy daughter been healed" *S* 29 side of the lake] lake-side *S* 30 there being] *lit.* 'when (*or*, though) there were' *C*; and there are *S* blind] blinded *S* the deaf and the maimed] the lame and the deaf *S* with other pains] others *S* cast] threw *S* (= ἔριψαν) at his feet] under his feet *S* 31 those] the *S* when they were] *om.* *S* 32 Now] And *S* to them] *om.* *S* have remained] remain *S* (*sic*) without a meal] fasting *S*

C S ܠܗܘܢ ܒܐܘܪܚܐ. [33]ܐܡܪܝܢ ܠܗ ܬܠܡܝܕܘܗܝ. ܡܢ ܐܝܡܟܐ ܠܢ
ܒܐܬܪܐ ܚܪܝܒܐ ܠܚܡܐ ܠܡܣܒܥܘ ܠܟܠܗ ܟܢܫܐ ܗܢܐ. [34]ܐܡܪ
ܠܗܘܢ ܝܫܘܥ ܟܡܐ ܠܚܡܝܢ ܐܝܬ ܠܟܘܢ. ܐܡܪܝܢ ܠܗ ܫܒܥܐ
fol 26 r ܠܚܡܝܢ. ܘܢܘܢܐ *ܙܥܘ̈ܪܐ. [35]ܘܦܩܕ ܠܟܢܫܐ ܕܢܣܬܡܟܘܢ ܥܠ
ܐܪܥܐ. [36]ܘܢܣܒ ܠܫܒܥܐ ܠܚܡܝܢ ܘ̈ܠܢܘܢܐ. ܘܒܪܟ ܘܩܨܐ ܘܝܗܒ
ܠܬܠܡܝܕܘܗܝ. ܘܬܠܡܝܕܘܗܝ ܝܗܒܘ ܠܟܢܫܐ. [37]ܘܐܟܠܘ ܟܠܗܘܢ
ܘܣܒܥܘ. ܘܫܩܠܘ ܡܢ ܦܪ̈ܬܘܬܗܘܢ ܘܬܘܪܢܐ ܕܩ̈ܘܦܐ ܡܠܐ ܫܒܥܐ
ܐܣ̈ܦܪܝܕܝܢ ܟܕ ܡܠܝܢ. [38]ܘܗܘܝܢ ܗܘܘ ܐܢܫܐ ܐܝܠܝܢ ܕܐܟܠܘ ܐܪ̈ܒܥܐ
ܐ̈ܠܦܝܢ ܓܒ̈ܪܝܢ. ܣܛܪ ܡܢ ܛ̈ܠܝܐ ܘܢ̈ܫܐ. ܀

[39]ܘܟܕ ܫܪܐ ܠܟܢܫܐ. ܣܠܩ ܝܬܒ ܠܗ ܒܣܦܝܢܬܐ. ܘܐܬܐ ܠܗ
ܠܬܚܘܡܐ ܕܡܓܕܘ ܀ [1]ܘܩܪܒܘ ܦܪ̈ܝܫܐ ܘܙܕܘ̈ܩܝܐ ܘܡܢܣܝܢ ܗܘܘ
ܠܗ. ܘܫܐܠܝܢ ܠܗ ܐܬܐ ܡܢ ܫܡܝܐ ܕܢܚܘܐ ܐܢܘܢ ܀ [2]ܗܘ ܕܝܢ
col 2 ܐܡܪ ܠܗܘܢ. [4]ܫܪܒܬܐ *ܒܝܫܬܐ ܘܓܝܪܬܐ. ܐܬܐ ܒܥܝܐ ܘܐܬܐ
ܠܐ ܬܬܝܗܒ ܠܗ̇. ܐܠܐ ܐܢ ܐܬܗ ܕܝܘܢܢ ܢܒܝܐ. ܘܫܒܩ ܐܢܘܢ
ܘܐܙܠ ܠܗ. [5]ܘܟܕ ܐܬܐ ܠܥܒܪܐ. ܐܬܘ ܬܠܡܝܕܘܗܝ ܕܢܣܒܘܢ
ܠܗܘܢ ܠܚܡܐ. [6]ܐܡܪ ܠܗܘܢ ܝܫܘܥ. ܐܙܕܗܪܘ ܡܢ ܚܡܝܪܐ
ܕܦܪ̈ܝܫܐ ܘܙܕܘ̈ܩܝܐ. [7]ܘܗܢܘܢ ܡܬܚܫܒܝܢ ܗܘܘ ܒܝܢܬܗܘܢ ܕܠܐ
ܢܣܒܘ ܠܗܘܢ ܠܚܡܐ. [8]ܝܫܘܥ ܕܝܢ ܝܕܥ. ܘܐܡܪ ܠܗܘܢ ܀ ܡܢܐ
ܡܬܚܫܒܝܢ ܐܢܬܘܢ ܒܝܢܬܟܘܢ ܚܣܝܪܝ ܗܝܡܢܘܬܐ. ܕܠܐ

---

33 ܒܐܬܪܐ....ܠܚܡܐ] ܒܚܘܪܒܐ ܠܚܡܐ S ܠܡܣܒܥܘ] ܠܟܠܗܘܢ S
34 ܠܗ] om. S ܫܒܥܐ ܠܚܡܝܢ] ܫܒܥ ܓܪ̈ܝܨܢ S ܙܥܘ̈ܪܐ] ܩܠܝܠ S
36 ܘܢܣܒ] ܘܫܩܠ S ܠܫܒܥܐ ܠܚܡܝܢ] ܠܗܠܝܢ ܫܒܥ ܓܪ̈ܝܨܢ S ܘ̈ܠܢܘܢܐ] ܘܢ̈ܘܢܐ S
ܘܒܪܟ] ܘܒܪܟ S ܝܗܒܘ] ܩܪܒܘ S 37 ܘܬܘܪܢܐ] ܬܘܬܪ̈ܐ S ܕܩ̈ܘܦܐ]
ܣ̈ܠܝܢ S ܡܠܐ] om. S ܡܦܪ̈ܕܝܢ S ܕܠܫܒܥܐ S 38 ܘܗܘܝܢ ܗܘܘ]
ܗܘܝܢ ܗܘܘ ܕܝܢ S ܐܝܠܝܢ] om. S ܓܒ̈ܪܝܢ] om. S ܛ̈ܠܝܐ ܘܢ̈ܫܐ]
ܢ̈ܫܐ ܘܛ̈ܠܝܐ S 39. *No* § *in* S ܕܡܓܕܘ S 1. § *in* S ܘܡܢܣܝܢ]
om. ܘ S^{ed}, *but the first letters of the word are marked illegible* ܗܘܘ] om. S
2 ܐܡܪ ܠܗܘܢ] ܥܢܐ ܘܐܡܪ S 5 ܐܬܐ] C (*sic*); ܐܬܘ S ܕܢܣܒܘܢ]
ܕܢܣܒܘܢ S ܠܗܘܢ] ܒܝܕܗܘܢ S 7 ܘܗܢܘܢ] ܗܢܘܢ S ܠܗܘܢ] ܒܝܕܗܘܢ S
8 ܠܗܘܢ] om. S

33 not by the way." His disciples say to him: "From whence *is it* for C S
34 us in a desert place with bread to satisfy all this multitude?" Jesus
saith to them: "How many pieces of bread are there by you?" They
35 say to him: "Seven pieces of bread and a few fishes." And he
commanded the multitudes that they should sit down *to meat* on the
36 ground. And he took up the seven pieces of bread and the fishes,
and glorified *God* and brake and gave to his disciples, and his
37 disciples gave to the multitudes. And they all ate and were satisfied,
and they took up from before them the superabundance of the frag-
38 ments full seven panniers full. And the folk which ate were four
thousand men, besides children and women.

39 And when he dismissed the multitude he went up *and* sat in the
xvi 1 boat, and went away to the border of Magedon. And there drew
near the Pharisees and the Sadducees, and were tempting him and
2 asking him for a sign from heaven that he should shew them. But
4 he said to them: "A generation evil and adulterous—a sign it seeketh
and a sign shall not be given to it, save the sign of Jonah the
5 prophet." And he left them and went away. And when he came to
the other side, his disciples forgot to carry for themselves bread.
6 Jesus saith to them: "Beware of the leaven of the Pharisees and
7 of the Sadducees." And they were thinking among themselves that
8 they had not taken for themselves bread. But Jesus knew and said
to them: "Why think ye among yourselves, O lacking in faith, in that

---

33 in a desert place with bread] with bread in a desert *S* satisfy] feed *S* 34 to him] *om. S* pieces of bread] loaves *S* a few fishes] fishes a few *S* 36 took up] took *S* the seven pieces of bread] those seven loaves *S* glorified] blessed *S* gave to 2°] set *them* for *S* (*cf* Mk vi 41) 37 superabundance] superfluity *S* fragments] pieces of bread *S* full 1° (*cf* syr. vg)] *om. S* 38 And] Now *S* which] that *S* men] *om. S* children and women] women and children *S* 39 Magedan *S* 1 were] *om. S* (*so that S reads* '⌜and⌝ they tempt him and ask..') 2 said to them] answered and said *S* 5 he came] they came *S* carry] take *S* for themselves] with them *S* 7 And they] Then they *S* for themselves] with them *S* 8 to them] *om. S*

C (S) ܫܩܠܬܘܢ ܠܟܘܢ ܠܚܡܐ. 9 ܥܕܡܐ ܠܗܫܐ ܠܐ ܡܣܬܟܠܝܢ
ܐܢܬܘܢ. ܘܠܐ ܥܗܕܝܢ ܐܢܬܘܢ ܠܚܡܫܐ ܠܚ̈ܡܝܢ. ܐܦ ܠܚܡ̈ܫܐ
fol 26 v ܐܠܦܝܢ ܕܐܟܠܘ ܡܢܗܘܢ. ܘܟܡܐ *ܩܘ̈ܦܝܢ ܫܩܠܬܘܢ ܡܢ
ܡܕܡܟܝܗܘܢ. 10 ܘܐܦ ܠܐ ܠܗܘܢ ܫܒܥܐ ܠܚ̈ܡܝܢ ܕܐܪ̈ܒܥܐ
ܐ̈ܠܦܝܢ ܐܟܠܘ ܡܢܗܘܢ. ܘܟܡܐ ܕܝܢ ܐܣܦܪ̈ܝܕܝܢ ܫܩܠܬܘܢ. 11 ܐܝܟܢܐ
ܠܐ ܡܣܬܟܠܝܢ ܐܢܬܘܢ ܕܠܐ ܗܘܐ ܥܠ ܠܚܡܐ ܐܡܪܬ ܠܟܘܢ.
ܕܐܙܕܗܪܘ ܡܢ ܚܡܝܪܐ ܕܦܪ̈ܝܫܐ ܘܕܙ̈ܕܘܩܝܐ. 12 ܗܝܕܝܢ ܐܣܬܟܠܘ
ܕܠܐ ܗܘܐ ܥܠ ܚܡܝܪܐ ܕܦܪ̈ܝܫܐ ܘܕܙ̈ܕܘܩܝܐ ܐܡܪ ܠܗܘܢ
ܕܐܙܕܗܪܘ. ܐܠܐ ܡܢ ܝܘܠܦܢܗܘܢ ܕܦܪ̈ܝܫܐ ܘܕܙ̈ܕܘܩܝܐ ·:·
13 ܘܟܕ ܐܬܐ ܕܝܢ ܝܫܘܥ ܠܐܬܪܐ ܕܩܣܪܝܐ ܕܦܝܠܝܦܘܣ. ܡܫܐܠ
ܗܘܐ ܠܬܠܡ̈ܝܕܘܗܝ ܘܐܡܪ. ܡܢܐ ܐܡܪܝܢ ܐܢܫܐ ܥܠܝ ܕܐܝܬܝ.
col 2 ܡܢܘ ܠܡ ܗܢܐ ܒܪܗ ܕܐܢܫܐ. 14 *ܐܡܪܝܢ ܠܗ ܬܠܡ̈ܝܕܘܗܝ. ܐܝܬ
ܕܐܡܪܝܢ ܕܝܘܚܢܢ ܗܘ ܡܥܡܕܢܐ. ܐܚܪ̈ܢܐ ܐܡܪܝܢ ܕܐܠܝܐ ܗܘ.
ܐܚܪ̈ܢܐ ܐܡܪܝܢ ܐܪܡܝܐ ܗܘ. ܐܚܪ̈ܢܐ ܐܡܪܝܢ ܚܕ ܡܢ ܢܒ̈ܝܐ
¶S ܗܘ. 15 ܐܡܪ ܠܗܘܢ ܘܐܢܬܘܢ¶ ܡܢܐ ܐܡܪܝܢ ܐܢܬܘܢ ܕܐܝܬܝ.
16 ܥܢܐ ܫܡܥܘܢ ܟܐܦܐ ܘܐܡܪ. ܐܢܬ ܗܘ ܡܫܝܚܐ ܒܪܗ
ܕܐܠܗܐ ܚܝܐ. 17 ܐܡܪ ܠܗ ܝܫܘܥ ܛܘܒܝܟ ܫܡܥܘܢ ܒܪܗ
ܕܝܘܢܐ. ܕܒܣܪܐ ܘܕܡܐ ܠܐ ܓܠܐ ܠܟ. ܐܠܐ ܐܒܝ ܕܒܫܡܝܐ.
18 ܐܦ ܐܢܐ ܐܡܪ ܐܢܐ ܠܟ ܕܐܢܬ ܗܘ ܟܐܦܐ. ܘܥܠ ܗܕܐ
ܟܐܦܐ ܐܒܢܝܗ ܠܥܕܬܝ. ܘܬܪ̈ܥܐ ܕܫܝܘܠ ܠܐ ܢܚܣܢܘܢܝܗ. 19 ܠܟ

ܫܩܠܬܘܢ] ܢܣܒܬܘܢ S 9 ܠܐ] *before* ܥܕܡܐ ܠܗܫܐ *in* S ܘܠܐ] *om.* ܘ S
ܐܦ ܠܚܡ̈ܫܐ] ܘ̈ܚܡܫܐ S ܡܢܗܘܢ] ܠܗܘܢ S^ed ܫܩܠܬܘܢ] ܢܣܒܬܘܢ S
10 ܘܐܦ] *om.* ܘ S ܕܐܪ̈ܒܥܐ....ܐܟܠܘ] ܘ * * ܐܪ̈ܒܥܐ....ܐܟܠܘ S:
the illegible word may be ܘܗ̈ܢܘܢ ܕܝܢ] *om.* S ܣܦܪ̈ܝܕܝܢ S ܫܩܠܬܘܢ]
ܢܣܒܬܘܢ ܡܢ ܡܕܡܟܝܗܘܢ S 11 ܕܐܙܕܗܪܘ] *om.* ܕ S 12 ܥܠ] ܡܢ S
ܕܦܪ̈ܝܫܐ ܘܕܙ̈ܕܘܩܝܐ 1°] *om.* S ܠܗܘܢ] *om.* S ܕܐܙܕܗܪܘ] ܠܡܙܕܗܪܘ S
13. *No* § *in* S ܕܝܢ] *om.* S ܠܐܬܪܐ] ܠܬܚܘܡܐ S ܐܢܫܐ ܥܠܝ] *tr.* S
ܕܐܝܬܝ] *om.* S 14 ܬܠܡ̈ܝܕܘܗܝ] *om.* S ܐܚܪ̈ܢܐ] *pr.* ܕ S ܚܕ] *pr.* ܕ S
15 ܘܐܢܬܘܢ] ܐܢܬܘܢ S 18 ܘܬܪ̈ܥܐ ܕܫܝܘܠ] ܘܡܘ̈ܟܠܐ ܕܫܝܘܠ Eus. *Theoph* iii 27, iv 11, v 40: ܡܘ̈ܟܠܐ ܕܫܝܘܠ *is also found in* Eus. *HE*^syr 417 *and* Ephr v 166E

9 ye have not carried for yourselves bread? Until now do ye not C (*S*)
understand? and do ye not recollect the five pieces of bread, *and* the
five thousand also that ate of them, and how many baskets ye took up
10 from before them? Neither also those seven pieces of bread that
11 four thousand ate of, and how many panniers ye took up? How is it
ye do not understand that not concerning bread said I to you 'Beware
12 of the leaven of the Pharisees and of the Sadducees?'" Then under-
stood they that not concerning the leaven of the Pharisees and of the
Sadducees said he to them 'Beware,' but of the teaching of the
Pharisees and of the Sadducees.

13 Now when Jesus came to the country of Caesarea of Philip, he
was asking his disciples and saying: "What say folk of me that I am?
14 'Who is this Son of Man?'" His disciples say to him: "There are
that say 'It is John the Baptist'; others say 'It is Elijah'; others
say, 'It is Jeremiah'; others say, 'It is one of the prophets.'"
15, 16 He saith to them: "And ye,¶ what say ye that I am?" Simon Kepha ¶*S*
answered and said: "Thou art the Messiah, the Son of the Living
17 God!" Jesus saith to him: "Happy is it for thee, Simon son of
Jona, to whom flesh and blood hath not revealed *it*, but my Father
18 in heaven! I also say to thee that thou art Kepha *the Stone*, and on
this stone I will build my Church, and the doors of Sheol shall not

---

carried] taken *S* 9 Until...not] Not until now do ye *S* and do] do *S* also] *om.* S^{vid} of them] those S^{ed} took up (*or*, 'carried')] took *S* 10 that four thousand ate of] ⌜and those⌝ four thousand that ate of them *S*: *the marked words are illegible* took up (*or*, 'carried')] took from before them *S* 12 concerning] of *S* of the Pharisees and of the Sadducees 1°] *om. S* to them] *om. S* 'Beware'] to beware *S* 13 Now when] When *S* country] border *S* that I am] *om. S* (*not* E^{156}): *cf* 'Who do men say of me that the Son of Man is?' E^{153}. *The text of S may be rendered* "Why say folk of me 'Who is this Son of Man?'" 14 His disciples] They *S* $E^{153, 156}$ 15 And ye] ⌜Now⌝ ye S^{vid} (*here S breaks off*) what say ye] 'whom say ye of me' E^{153} 18 Church] *see* Mt xviii 17 the doors of Sheol] the gate-bars of Sheol Eus. *Theoph* iii 27, iv 11, v 40, *and* (*in less formal quotations*) Eus. HE^{syr} 417 *and* Ephr v 166 E: 'the doors of Hades' E^{153} (= arm. vg)

C fol 27 r ܐܬܠ ܩ̈ܠܝܕܐ *ܕ̈ܬܪܥܐ ܕܡܠܟܘܬܐ ܕܫܡܝܐ. ܘܟܠ ܡܕܡ
ܕܬܐܣܘܪ ܒܐܪܥܐ ܢܗܘܐ ܐܣܝܪ ܒܫܡܝܐ. ܘܡܕܡ ܕܬܫܪܐ
ܒܐܪܥܐ ܢܗܘܐ ܫܪܐ ܒܫܡܝܐ. [20]ܗܝܕܝܢ ܟܐܐ ܒܗܘܢ ܒܬܠܡ̈ܝܕܘܗܝ،
ܕܠܐܢܫ ܠܐ ܢܐܡܪܘܢ ܥܠܘܗܝ، ܕܗܘܝܘ ܡܫܝܚܐ. ܀

[21]ܡܢ ܗܝܕܝܢ ܕܝܢ، ܗܘܐ ܝܫܘܥ ܠܡܚܘܝܘ ܐܢܘܢ ܠܬܠܡ̈ܝܕܘܗܝ.
ܕܒܥܐ ܗܘ ܕܢܐܙܠ ܠܐܘܪܫܠܡ. ܘܢܣܝܒܪ ܣܓܝ. ܘܢܚܫ ܡܢ
ܩܫ̈ܝܫܐ ܘܪ̈ܒܝ ܟܗܢܐ ܘܣ̈ܦܪܐ. ܘܢܬܩܛܠ، ܘܠܝܘܡܐ ܕܬܠܬܐ
ܢܩܘܡ. [22]ܘܩܪܒ ܫܡܥܘܢ ܟܐܦܐ ܘܐܡܪ ܚܣ ܠܟ ܡܪܝ. ܠܐ
ܬܗܘܐ ܗܕܐ. [23]ܗܘ ܕܝܢ ܝܫܘܥ ܐܬܦܢܝ ܘܐܡܪ ܠܗ ܠܫܡܥܘܢ
col 2 ܘܐܡܪ *ܠܗ· ܙܠ ܠܟ ܠܒܣܬܪ، ܣܛܢܐ ܬܘܩܠܬܐ ܐܢܬ ܠܝ. ܕܠܐ
ܡܬܪܥܐ ܐܢܬ ܕܐܠܗܐ ܐܠܐ ܕ̈ܒܢܝ ܐܢܫܐ· [24]ܗܝܕܝܢ ܐܡܪ
ܝܫܘܥ ܠܬܠܡ̈ܝܕܘܗܝ، ܡܢ ܕܨܒܐ ܕܢܐܬܐ ܒܬܪܝ، ܢܟܦܘܪ ܒܢܦܫܗ·
ܘܢܫܩܘܠ ܙܩܝܦܗ ܘܢܐܬܐ ܒܬܪܝ. [25]ܡܢ ܕܨܒܐ ܓܝܪ ܕܢܚܐ ܢܦܫܗ
ܢܘܒܕܝܗ. ܘܡܢ ܕܢܘܒܕ ܢܦܫܗ ܡܛܠܬܝ، ܢܚܝܝܗ. [26]ܡܢܐ ܓܝܪ
ܡܬܗܢܐ ܒܪܢܫܐ ܐܢ ܠܥܠܡܐ ܟܠܗ ܢܩܢܐ ܘܢܦܫܗ ܢܚܣܪ. ܐܘ
ܡܢܐ ܢܬܠ ܒܪܢܫܐ ܬܘܠܦܐ ܕܢܦܫܗ· [27]ܥܬܝܕ ܗܘ ܓܝܪ ܒܪܗ
ܕܐܢܫܐ ܕܢܐܬܐ ܒܫܘܒܚܐ ܕܐܒܘܗܝ، ܥܡ ܡܠܐܟ̈ܘܗܝ، ܘܗܝܕܝܢ
fol 27 v ܢܦܪܘܥ ܠܐܢܫ ܐܢܫ ܐܝܟ ܥܒ̈ܕܘܗܝ. [28]*ܐܡܝܢ ܐܡܪܢܐ ܠܟܘܢ
ܕܐܝܬ ܐܢܫܐ ܡܢ ܗܠܝܢ ܕܩܝܡܝܢ ܗܪܟܐ. ܕܠܐ ܢܛܥܡܘܢ
ܡܘܬܐ. ܥܕܡܐ ܕܢܚܙܘܢ ܠܒܪܗ ܕܐܢܫܐ. ܟܕ ܐܬܐ ܒܡܠܟܘܬܗ
ܘܒܫܘܒܚܗ. ○○ ○○ ○○

[1]ܒܬܪ ܫܬܐ ܝܘܡܝܢ. ܕܒܪ ܝܫܘܥ ܠܫܡܥܘܢ ܟܐܦܐ. ܘܠܝܥܩܘܒ
ܘܠܝܘܚܢܢ ܐܚܘܗܝ، ܘܐܣܩ ܐܢܘܢ ܠܛܘܪܐ ܪܡܐ ܒܠܚܘܕܝܗܘܢ.
[2]ܘܐܫܬܚܠܦ ܚܙܘܐ ܕܐ̈ܦܘܗܝ، ܠܥܝ̈ܢܝܗܘܢ. ܘܐܢܗܪ ܦܪܨܘܦܗ ܐܝܟ
ܫܡܫܐ. ܘܠܒ̈ܘܫܘܗܝ، ܚܘܪܘ ܐܝܟ ܬܠܓܐ. [3]ܘܐܬܚܙܝ، ܠܗܘܢ
ܡܘܫܐ ܘܐܠܝܐ ܟܕ ܡܡܠܠܝܢ ܥܡܗ. [4]ܐܡܪ ܫܡܥܘܢ ܟܐܦܐ
ܠܝܫܘܥ· ܫܦܝܪ ܗܘ ܠܢ ܕܗܪܟܐ ܢܗܘܐ. ܐܢ ܨܒܐ ܐܢܬ ܢܥܒܕ
col 2 ܗܪܟܐ ܬܠܬ ܡܛܠ̈ܝܢ. *ܠܟ ܚܕܐ. ܘܠܡܘܫܐ ܚܕܐ. ܘܠܐܠܝܐ

19 overpower it. To thee I will give the keys of the doors of the kingdom C
of heaven, and everything which thou shalt bind on earth shall be
bound in heaven, and that which thou shalt remit on earth shall be
20 remitted in heaven." Then he rebuked these same disciples of his,
that to no one should they say of him that he was the Messiah.

21 From then had Jesus begun to shew his disciples that he was
about to go to Jerusalem and endure much, and suffer from the
elders and the chief priests and the scribes, and they will kill him and
22 the third day he will rise. And Simon Kepha drew near and said:
23 "Be it far from thee, my Lord! This shall not be!" But Jesus
turned round and rebuked him, *even* Simon, and said to him: "Get
thee behind me, Satan, a stumbling-block art thou to me, in that thou
24 dost not consider the *things* of God, but of men." Then said Jesus to
his disciples: "He that willeth to come after me let him deny himself
25 and take up his cross and come after me. For he that willeth to save
his life shall lose it, and he that shall lose his life for my sake shall
26 find it. For what is a man profited, if he should get the whole world
and lack his life? Or what shall a man give in exchange for his
27 life? For the Son of Man is about to come in the glory of his Father
with his angels, and then he shall repay each man according to his
28 deeds. Amen, I say to you that there are some of these that stand
here, that shall not taste death until they see the Son of Man coming
in his kingdom and in his glory."

xvii 1 After six days Jesus took Simon Kepha and James and John his
2 brother and brought them up to a high hill alone. And the appear-
ance of his face was transfigured before their eyes, and his countenance
3 shone as the sun and his garments became white as the snow; and
4 there appeared to them Moses and Elijah speaking with him. Saith
Simon Kepha to Jesus: "It is well for us that we should be here; if
thou wilt, we will make here three dwellings, for thee one and for
5 Moses one and for Elijah one." And while yet he was speaking, lo, a

---

20 *Cf* 'Tell no man of me, that I am the Christ' *E*[154] 22 This shall not be!] *or*, 'May this not be!': *cf* Lk xx 16 28.] *For E*[155], *see* Mk ix 1

C [S] ܚܙܐ. ⁵ܘܟܕ ܗܘ ܡܡܠܠ. ܗܐ ܒܢܝܢܐ ܕܢܘܗܪܐ ܐܛܠܠܬ ܥܠܝܗܘܢ܆
ܘܩܠܐ ܐܫܬܡܥ ܡܢ ܒܢܝܢܐ ܗ̇ܘ، ܕܐܡܪ. ܗܢܐ ܗܘ ܒܪܝ، ܘܚܒܝܒܝ
ܕܒܗ ܨܒܝܬ. ܠܗ ܫܡܥܘ. ⁶ܘܟܕ ܫܡܥܘ ܬܠܡܝܕܘܗܝ، ܕܚܠܘ ܛܒ.
ܘܢܦܠܘ ܥܠ ܐ̈ܦܝܗܘܢ. ⁷ܘܩܪܒ ܝܫܘܥ ܘܐܩܝܡ ܐܢܘܢ ܘܐܡܪ
ܠܗܘܢ. ܠܐ ܬܕܚܠܘܢ܆ ⁸ܘܐܪܝܡܘ ܥܝ̈ܢܝܗܘܢ ܘܠܐ ܚܙܘ ܐܠܐ
ܠܝܫܘܥ ܒܠܚܘܕܘܗܝ. ⁹ܘܟܕ ܢܚܬܝܢ ܡܢ ܛܘܪܐ. ܦܩܕ ܗܘܐ ܠܗܘܢ
ܝܫܘܥ. ܘܐܡܪ ܠܗܘܢ܆ ܕܠܡܐ ܠܐܢܫ ܐܡܪܝܢ ܐܢܬܘܢ ܚܙܘܐ.
ܒܕܡܐ ܕܢܩܘܡ ܒܪܗ ܕܐܢܫܐ ܡܢ ܒܝܬ ܡ̈ܝܬܐ.܀

fol 28r *¹⁰ܘܫܐܠܘܗܝ ܗܘܘ ܠܗ ܬܠܡ̈ܝܕܘܗܝ، ܘܐܡܪܝܢ. ܠܡܢܐ ܐܡܪܝܢ
ܣ̈ܦܪܐ ܕܐܠܝܐ ܐܬܐ ܠܘܩܕܡ. ¹¹ܐܡܪ ܠܗܘܢ ܐܠܝܐ ܐܬܐ
§S ܕܢܬܩܢ ܟܠ§ܡܕܡ. ¹²ܐܡܪܢܐ ܠܟܘܢ ܕܗܐ ܕܐܠܝܐ ܐܬܐ ܘܠܐ
ܝܕܥܘܗܝ، ܐܠܐ ܥܒܕܘ ܒܗ ܟܠ ܡܐ ܕܨܒܘ. ܗܟܢܐ ܐܦ ܒܪܗ
ܕܐܢܫܐ ܥܬܝܕ ܗܘ ܕܢܣܝܒܪ ܡܢܗܘܢ܆ ¹³ܗܝܕܝܢ ܐܣܬܟܠܘ
ܬܠܡ̈ܝܕܘܗܝ، ܕܥܠ ܝܘܚܢܢ ܗܘ ܡܥܡܕܢܐ ܐܡܪ ܠܗܘܢ ܗܟܢܐ.
¹⁴ܘܟܕ ܐܬܐ ܝܫܘܥ ܠܘܬ ܟܢܫܐ. ܐܬܐ ܓܒܪܐ ܚܕ ܘܢܦܠ ܥܠ
ܒܘܪ̈ܟܘܗܝ. ܘܒܥܐ ܗܘܐ ܡܢܗ ܘܐܡܪ ܠܗ. ¹⁵ܡܪܝ، ܐܬܪܚܡ
col 2 ܥܠ. ܒܪܝ، ܒܪ ܐܓܪܐ ܐܝܬ ܠܗ. ܘܒܝܫܬܐ ܡܫܬܢܩ. ܒܙܒܢܐ *ܓܝܪ
ܙܒ̈ܢܝܢ ܒܢܘܪܐ ܢܦܠ. ܘܒܙܒܢܐ ܙܒ̈ܢܝܢ ܒܡ̈ܝܐ. ¹⁶ܘܩܪܒܬܗ ܠܬܠܡ̈ܝܕܝܟ
ܘܠܐ ܐܫܟܚܘ ܠܡܐܣܝܘܬܗ. ¹⁷ܥܢܐ ܝܫܘܥ ܘܐܡܪ ܠܗܘܢ܆ ܐܘ
ܫܪܒܬܐ ܡܗܦܟܬܐ ܘܥܩܡܬܐ. ܥܕܡܐ ܠܐܡܬܝ، ܐܗܘܐ
ܠܘܬܟܘܢ ܘܐܣܝܒܪܟܘܢ. ܐܝܬܝܘܗܝ، ܠܝ ܠܟܐ ܠܗ. ¹⁸ܘܟܐܪ ܒܗ
ܝܫܘܥ. ܘܢܦܩ ܡܢܗ ܫܐܕܐ. ܘܡܢ ܗ̇ܝ ܫܥܬܐ ܐܬܐܣܝ، ܛܠܝܐ ܗܘ.

---

12 ܕܐܠܝܐ] ܕܐܦ ܐܠܝܐ S   ܗܟܢܐ ܐܦ] ܘ S   ܕܢܣܝܒܪ] ܕܢܚܫ S
13 ܡܥܡܕܢܐ] om. S   ܗܟܢܐ] om. S   14. § in S   ܘܢܦܠ] om. ܘ S
ܘܒܥܐ ܗܘܐ ܡܢܗ] om. S   ܠܗ.] om. S   15 ܡܪܝ] om. S   ܒܪ ܐܓܪܐ]
ܪܘܚ ܦܠܓܐ S   ܐܝܬ ܠܗ] ܒܪܢܐ ܥܠܘܗܝ S   ܘܒܝܫܬܐ ܡܫܬܢܩ]
ܘܡܫܬܐܣܝܬ ܒܒܝܫ S   ܒܙܒܢܐ] pr. ܘ S   ܓܝܪ ܙܒ̈ܢܝܢ] tr. S   16 ܐܫܟܚܘ] S;
ܐܫܟܚܘ C (end of line)   17 ܠܗܘܢ] om. S   ܐܘ] ܘܐ S   ܠܟܐ]
ܠܗܪܟܐ S   18 ܘܟܐܪ] ܘܟܐܐ S   ܛܠܝܐ ܗܘ] tr. S

cloud of light overshadowed them, and a voice was heard from that C [S]
cloud, saying: "This is my son and my beloved, in whom I am
6 pleased; hear ye him!" And when his disciples heard, they were
7 afraid exceedingly and fell on their faces. And Jesus drew near and
8 raised them up, and said to them: "Be not afraid!" And they
9 lifted up their eyes, and saw no *one*, save Jesus alone. And while
they *were* coming down from the hill, Jesus was commanding them
and saying to them: "*Beware* lest to any one ye say the vision,
until the Son of Man should arise from among the dead."

10 And his disciples were asking him and saying: "Wherefore say
11 the scribes that Elijah cometh first?" He saith to them: "Elijah
12 cometh that he may prepare every§thing. But I say to you that §S
Elijah hath come, and they knew him not but did with him all
that they would; so also the Son of Man is about to endure from
13 them." Then understood his disciples that of John the Baptist he
14 said to them so. And when Jesus came unto the multitude, a
certain man came and fell on his knees, and was beseeching him and
15 saying to him: "My Lord, have compassion on me! My son—a
demon of lunacy he hath and evil*s* he endureth, for how many times
16 he falleth in the fire and how many times in the water! And I
brought him near to thy disciples, and they were not able to heal
17 him." Jesus answered and said to them: "Ah generation perverse
and without faith! until when shall I be with you and endure you?
18 Bring me thy son here." And Jesus chid him, and there came
forth from him the devil, and from that hour was that lad healed.

---

9 *Beware* lest] *cf* Mt viii 4 12 Elijah] + also *S* so also] and *S* endure] suffer *S* 13 the Baptist] *om. S* so] *om. S* 14 and fell] *and* fell *S* and was beseeching him] *om. S* to him] *om. S* 15 My Lord] *om. S* a demon ..he hath] a spirit of palsy *suddenly* visiteth him *S*: *cf* Lk xi 6 evil*s* he endureth] he is hardly treated *S* (*i.e.* 'he suffers cruelly'): *for the suggested reading of C's text as plural, see* 2 Tim ii 3, iv 5 syr. vg how many times 1°] + too *S* 17 to them] *om. S* Ah] Oh *S* here] hither S 18 chid] rebuked *S*

C S 19 ܗܝܕܝܢ ܩܪܒܘ ܠܘܬ ܝܫܘܥ ܬܠܡܝ̈ܕܘܗܝ، ܘܐܡܪܝܢ ܠܗ ܒܝܢܝܗܘܢ
ܘܠܗ. ܠܡܢܐ ܚܢܢ ܠܐ ܐܫܟܚܢ ܠܡܦܩܘܬܗ. 20 ܐܡܪ ܠܗܘܢ
ܡܛܠ ܙܥܘܪܘܬ ܗܝܡܢܘܬܟܘܢ܆ ܐܡܝܢ ܓܝܪ ܐܡܪܢܐ ܠܟܘܢ.
§A 394 fol 28 v §ܕܐܢ ܗܘ ܕܬܗܘܐ ܠܟܘܢ܆ *ܗܝܡܢܘܬܐ ܐܝܟ ܦܪܕܬܐ ܕܚܪܕܠܐ.
¶A ܬܐܡܪܘܢ ܠܛܘܪܐ ܗܢܐ ܕܢܫܢܐ ܡܢ ܗܪܟܐ ܘܢܫܢܐ¶. ܘܡܕܡ
ܠܐ ܢܚܣܢܟܘܢ܀
22 ܘܟܕ ܗܘܘ ܡܬܗܦܟܝܢ ܒܓܠܝܠܐ. ܐܡܪ ܠܗܘܢ ܝܫܘܥ. ܥܬܝܕ
ܗܘ ܕܝܢ ܒܪܗ ܕܐܢܫܐ ܕܢܫܬܠܡ ܒܐܝ̈ܕܝ، ܒܢܝ ܐܢܫܐ 23 ܘܢܩܛܠܘܢܝܗܝ.
ܘܠܝܘܡܐ ܕܬܠܬܐ ܢܩܘܡ. ܘܟܪܝܬ ܠܗܘܢ ܛܒ..
24 ܘܟܕ ܐܬܐ ܠܟܦܪܢܚܘܡ. ܐܬܘ ܗܢܘܢ ܕܓܒܝܢ ܬܪ̈ܝܢ ܕܝ̈ܢܪܝܢ
ܠܘܬ ܫܡܥܘܢ܆ ܘܐܡܪܝܢ ܠܗ ܪܒܟܘܢ ܠܐ ܝܗܒ ܬܪ̈ܝܢ ܕܝ̈ܢܪܘܗܝ،
25 ܘܐܡܪ ܫܡܥܘܢ ܐܝܢ. ܘܟܕ ܥܠܘ ܠܒܝܬܐ ܩܕܡܗ ܝܫܘܥ.
ܘܐܡܪ ܠܗ ܡܢܐ ܡܬܚܙܝܐ ܠܟ ܫܡܥܘܢ܆ ܡ̈ܠܟܝܗ ܕܐܪܥܐ ܡܢ
col 2 ܡܢ ܓܒܝܢ ܡܟܣܐ *ܘܟܣܦ ܪܫܐ. ܡܢ ܒܢ̈ܝܗܘܢ ܐܘ ܡܢ
ܢܘܟܪ̈ܝܐ. 26 ܐܡܪ ܠܗ ܫܡܥܘܢ ܡܢ ܢܘܟܪ̈ܝܐ. ܐܡܪ ܠܗ ܝܫܘܥ
ܡܕܝܢ ܒ̈ܢܝ ܚܐܪ̈ܐ ܐܢܘܢ ܒ̈ܢܝܐ. 27 ܕܠܐ ܕܝܢ ܢܟܫܠ ܐܢܘܢ܆ ܙܠ
ܠܝܡܐ ܘܐܪܡܐ ܚܟܬܐ. ܘܢܘܢܐ ܩܕܡܝܐ ܕܣܠܩ. ܗܘ ܘܦܬܚ

---

19 ܠܘܬ ܝܫܘܥ] *om.* S   ܘܐܡܪܝܢ....ܘܠܗ] ܒܝܢܝܗܘܢ ܘܠܗ. ܘܐܡܪܝܢ S
ܚܢܢ ܠܐ ܐܫܟܚܢ] ܠܐ ܐܫܟܚܢ ܐܢܚܢܢ S (*sic*): *cf* Mt xxiii 13   ܠܡܦܩܘܬܗ]
ܠܡܐܦܩܘܬܗ S   20 ܙܥܘܪܘܬ ܗܝܡܢܘܬܟܘܢ] ܕܠܝܬ ܠܟܘܢ ܗܝܡܢܘܬܐ S
ܕܐܢ ܗܘ ܕܬܗܘܐ] ܕܐܠܘ ܐܝܬ ܗܘܬ S; ܕܐܢ ܬܗܘܐ A   ܦܪܕܬܐ]
+ ܚܕܐ A   ܬܐܡܪܘܢ] ܐܡܪܬܘܢ ܕܝܢ S: *cf* Gen xliii 10, *Josh. Styl* 4[14–16]
ܕܢܫܢܐ ܡܢ ܗܪܟܐ] ܕܐܫܬܢܝܐ S A[a]; ܕܫܢܐ A[b]   ܘܢܫܢܐ] + ܡܢ ܩܕܡܝܟܘܢ A:
cf ܐܢ ܗܘܬ ܠܟܘܢ ܗܝܡܢܘܬܐ. ܐܡܪ ܠܛܘܪܐ ܢܫܢܐ ܡܢ ܩܕܡܝܟܘܢ A 21
22. *No* § *in* S   ܕܝܢ] *on an erasure in* C; *om.* S   23 ܘܠܝܘܡܐ ܕܬܠܬܐ]
ܘܡܢ ܒܬܪ ܬܠܬܐ ܝܘܡܝܢ S   24. *No* § *in* S   ܬܪ̈ܝܢ ܕܝ̈ܢܪܝܢ] ܙܘܙܐ S
ܠܘܬ ܫܡܥܘܢ] *om.* S   ܠܗ] ܠܫܡܥܘܢ S   ܬܪ̈ܝܢ 3°] *om.* S
25 ܘܐܡܪ ܫܡܥܘܢ] ܐܡܪ S   ܥܠܘ] ܥܠ S   ܠܒܝܬܐ] ܠܒܝܬܗ S
ܡܬܚܙܝܐ] ܡܬܪܓܠܐ S   26 ܫܡܥܘܢ] *om.* S   27 ܙܠ] ܐܙܠ S   ܠܝܡܐ]
om. S   ܘܐܪܡܐ] *om.* ܘ S   ܚܟܬܐ] + ܒܝܡܐ S

19 Then drew near unto Jesus his disciples and say to him between *C S*
themselves and him: "Wherefore were we ourselves not able to cast
20 it out?" He saith to them: "Because of the littleness of your faith;
for amen, I say to you §If so be that there be in you faith as a grain §*A* 394
of mustard, ye shall say to this hill that it should remove from hence
and it will remove,¶ and nothing shall overpower you." ¶*A*

22 And when they were abiding in Galilee Jesus said to them:
"Now the Son of Man is about to be delivered into the hands of men,
23 and they will kill him, and the third day he will rise." And it
grieved them exceedingly.

24 And when they came to Kapharnahum there came those that
collect the two drachmas a head unto Simon, and they say to him:
25 "Thy Rabbi—doth he not give his two drachmas?" And Simon
saith: "Yes." And when they entered the house Jesus met him
and saith to him: "What seemeth to thee, Simon? The kings of the
earth—from whom do they collect toll and head-money? from their
26 sons, or from strangers?" Simon saith to him: "From strangers."
27 Jesus saith to him: "Why then the sons are freemen; but that we
may not offend them, go to the sea and cast the hook, and the first fish

---

19 unto Jesus] *om. S* and say...themselves] by themselves, and say *S* to cast it out] to heal him *S* E^{160} 20 Because of the littleness of your faith] *C* E^{160}; Because ye have no faith *S* If so be that there be] If there had been *S*; If there be *A* a grain] one grain *A* ye shall say] *C A* E^{204}; ye would have said *S*: *cf* Gen xliii 10 that it should remove from hence] 'Be removed' *S* A^{a} $E^{204\,(vid)}$; 'Remove' A^{b} will remove] + from before you *A* E^{204}: *cf* 'If there was in you faith, even a hill would remove from before you' *A* 21 shall 2°] would *S* (*see above*) 22 Now] *on an erasure in C*; *om. S* 23 the third day] after three days *S* 24 the two...head] the drachmas *S* unto Simon] *om. S* to him] to Simon *S* two *ult.*] *om. S* 25 And Simon saith] He saith *S* they] he *S* the house] his house *S* seemeth to thee] doth it please thee *S* 26 Simon] He *S* the sons are freemen] + 'Simon said to him: Yea. Jesus said to him: Give to them thou also like the stranger' $Diat^{ar}$ xxv 6. *Cf also*: 'Go *and* give thou also as one of the strangers' E^{161} 27 to the sea] *om. S* (*not* E^{161}) and cast] *and* cast *S* the hook] + in the sea *S*; + 'there' E^{161}

C S ܦܘܡܗ. ܘܬܫܟܚܢ ܬܡܢ ܐܣܬܪܐ. ܣܒܝܗ ܘܗܒܝܗ ܚܠܦܝ
ܘܚܠܦܝܟ ܀

[1]ܘܒܗܝ ܫܥܬܐ ܩܪܒܘ ܗܘܘ ܬܠܡܝܕܘܗܝ ܕܝܫܘܥ ܘܐܡܪܝܢ ܠܗ.
ܡܢܘ ܟܝ ܢܗܘܐ ܪܒ ܒܡܠܟܘܬܐ ܕܫܡܝܐ. [2]ܘܩܪܐ ܝܫܘܥ ܠܛܠܝܐ
ܚܕ. ܘܐܩܝܡܗ ܒܝܢܬܗܘܢ [3]ܘܐܡܪ. ܐܡܝܢ ܐܡܪܢܐ ܠܟܘܢ.
§A221 §ܕܐܢ ܠܐ ܬܬܗܦܟܘܢ ܘܬܗܘܘܢ ܐܝܟ ܚܕ ܡܢ ܗܠܝܢ ܛ̈ܠܝܐ.
fol 29 r ¶A ܠܐ ܬܥܠܘܢ *ܠܡܠܟܘܬܐ ܕܫܡܝܐ.¶ [4]ܡܢ ܕܡܡܟܟ ܓܝܪ ܢܦܫܗ
ܐܝܟ ܗܢܐ ܛܠܝܐ ܗܘ ܪܒ ܒܡܠܟܘܬܐ ܕܫܡܝܐ. [5]ܘܟܠ ܕܢܩܒܠ
ܐܝܟ ܚܕ ܡܢ ܗܠܝܢ ܛ̈ܠܝܐ ܒܫܡܝ ܠܝ ܗܘ ܡܩܒܠ· [6]ܘܟܠ ܕܢܟܫܠ
ܠܚܕ ܡܢ ܗܠܝܢ ܙܥ̈ܘܪܐ ܐܠܝܢ ܕܡܗܝܡܢܝܢ ܒܝ. ܦܩܚ ܗܘܐ ܠܗ
ܕܬܗܘܐ ܬܠܝܐ ܪܚܝܐ ܕܚܡܪܐ ܒܨܘܪܗ· ܘܢܬܛܒܥ ܒܥܘ̈ܡܩܘܗܝ
ܕܝܡܐ. [7]ܘܝ ܠܗ ܠܥܠܡܐ ܡܢ ܬ̈ܘܩܠܬܐ ܕܐܬܝܢ· ܐܢܢܩܐ ܗܝ
ܓܝܪ ܕܢܐܬܝܢ ܬ̈ܘܩܠܬܐ. ܐܠܐ ܘܝ ܠܓܒܪܐ ܕܒܐܝܕܗ ܢܐܬܝܢ
ܬܘܩܠܬܐ. [8]ܐܢ ܕܝܢ ܐܝܕܟ ܐܘ ܪܓܠܟ ܡܬܩܠܐ ܠܟ ܦܣܘܩ
ܫܕܝܗ ܡܢܟ· ܦܩܚ ܠܟ ܓܝܪ ܕܬܐܬܐ ܠܚ̈ܝܐ ܟܕ ܚܓܝܪ ܐܢܬ
col 2 ܐܘ *ܟܕ ܦܫܝܚ ܐܢܬ· ܘܠܐ ܟܕ ܐܝܬ ܠܟ ܬܪ̈ܬܝܢ ܐ̈ܝܕܝܢ ܘܬܪ̈ܬܝܢ
§A262 ܪ̈ܓܠܝܢ ܬܦܠ ܒܓܗܢܐ ܕܢܘܪܐ. §[9]ܘܐܢ ܗܘ ܕܥܝܢܟ ܡܟܫܠܐ ܠܟ

ܣܒܝܗ ܘܗܒܝܗ] ܗܒ ܠܗܘܢ S   *For Thos*[312] *see Introd.* vol. ii   1. *No* § *in S*   ܘܒܗܝ] *om.* ܘ *S*   ܗܘܘ] *om. S*   ܕܝܫܘܥ] *om. S*   ܘܐܡܪܝܢ] *om.* ܘ *S*
2 ܘܩܪܐ] *om.* ܘ *S*   ܛܠܝܐ ܚܕ *S*   3 ܕܐܢ ܠܐ] ܕܐܠܐ *S A*   ܘܬܗܘܘܢ] *om.* ܘ *S*   ܚܕ ܡܢ] *om. S A*   ܗܠܝܢ] *om S*   ܠܡܠܟܘܬ ܫܡܝܐ *A*
4 ܕܡܡܟܟ] ܕܡܟܟ *S*   ܗܢܐ ܛܠܝܐ] *tr. S*   ܗܘ] + ܗܘܐ *S*   6 ܐܠܝܢ] *om. S*   ܬܠܝܐ] ܪ̈ܚܝܐ *S*   ܒܥܘܡܩܐ *S*   *For the whole verse, cf* A 151: ܟܠ ܕܡܟܫܠ ܠܚܕ ܡܢ ܗܠܝܢ ܙܥܘ̈ܪܐ. ܢܦܠ ܒܝܡܐ. ܟܕ ܪܚܝܐ ܕܚܡܪܐ ܒܨܘܪܗ
7. § *in S*: ܘܝ *begins a line in C*   ܐܢܢܩܐ ܗܝ] ܐܢܢܩܐ ܕܢܐܬܝܢ *S*   ܬܘܩܠܬܐ *ult.*] *C (sic, without seyâmê)*; *om. S*   *For the whole verse, cf* A 79: ܥܬܝܕ ܓܝܪ ܡܬܠܐ. ܕܬܐܬܐ ܬܘܩܠܬܐ ܠܥܠܡܐ. ܘܬܘܩܠܬܗܘܢ ܠܒܢ ܕܒܐܝܕܗ ܬܐܬܐ. ܘܡܫܬܥܝܐ ܬܘܩܠܬܐ ܠܥܠܡܐ. ܐܠܐ ܘܝ ܠܒܢ ܕܒܐܝܕܗ ܬܐܬܐ.
8 ܟܕ 1°] + ܐܢܬ *S** (? *washed out by a corrector*): *cf* Mk xiii 35   ܦܫܝܚ ܐܢܬ] ܫܚܝܦ *S*   ܐܘ ܬܪ̈ܬܝܢ ܪ̈ܓܠܝܢ *S*   ܬܦܠ...ܕܢܘܪܐ] ܘܬܐܙܠ ܠܢܘܪܐ ܕܠܥܠܡ *S*: *for the construction, cf* Lk xiii 10, 11, *and Notes*, vol. ii   9 ܘܐܢ ܗܘ ܕ] ܐܢ *S A*

that cometh up take and open its mouth, and thou shalt find there a *C S*
stater—take it and give it for me and for thee."
xviii 1 And on that day had the disciples of Jesus drawn near, and they
say to him: "Who then shall be greatest in the kingdom of heaven?"
2, 3 And Jesus called a certain lad and made him stand among them, and
said: "Amen, I say to you §If ye turn not yourselves and become as §*A* 221
one of these children, ye shall not enter the kingdom of heaven.¶ ¶*A*
4 For he that humbleth himself as this lad, he is greatest in the
5 kingdom of heaven. And every one that shall receive as *it were* one
6 of these children in my name, me it is he receiveth. And every one
that shall offend one of these little ones which believe in me, it were
profitable for him that an ass's millstone should be hanged about his
7 neck, and he be sunk in the depths of the sea. Woe to the world
from the offences that come! For it is necessary that offences should
8 come, but woe to the man by whose hand the offences come! But if
thy hand or thy foot offend thee, cut *it* off *and* throw it from thee;
for it is profitable for thee that thou shouldest come unto life being
lame or being mutilated, and not having two hands and two feet fall
9 into the Gehenna of fire. §And if so be that thine eye offend thee, §*A* 262

---

take it and give it] give *it* to them *S* *For Thos*[312] *see Introd.* vol. ii
1 And on that] On that *S* had—drawn] drew *S* of Jesus] *om. S*
and they say] saying *S* 2 And 1°] *om. S* 3 and become] *and* become *S*
one of] *om. S A* these] *om. S* 4 humbleth] shall humble *S*
is] shall be *S* 6 which] that *S* hanged] cast *S* *Cf A* 151:
'Every one that offendeth one of these little ones falleth into the sea having
an ass's millstone about his neck' 7 it is necessary...should come]
offences are about to come *S* the offence*s* 2°] they *S* *Cf A* 79:
'For it is written thus Good is about to be, and happy is it for him
by whose hand it shall come; and evil is about to be, but woe to him
by whose hand it shall come!' 8 lame] *pr.* if (*i.e.* 'whether') *S**,
but it was apparently washed out by a corrector: *cf* Nöld. § 374 G *anm.*
being mutilated] halt *S* and two feet] or two feet *S* fall into
the Gehenna of fire] come unto the fire eternal *S* (*lit.* 'and come...': *see
Notes*, vol. ii) 9 And if so be] If *S A*

C S ¶A ܚܨܝ ܘܫܕܝܗ ܡܢܟ¶. ܦܫܝܩ ܠܟ ܕܬܥܘܠ ܠܚܝ̈ܐ ܟܕ ܐܝܬ ܠܟ
ܥܝܢܐ ܚܕܐ. ܘܠܐ ܟܕ ܐܝܬ ܠܟ ܬܪ̈ܬܝܢ ܥܝ̈ܢܝܢ ܬܐܙܠ ܠܓܗܢܐ
§A 127 ܕܢܘܪܐ. §10 ܚܙܘ ܕܠܡܐ ܬܒܣܘܢ ܒܚܕ ܡܢ ܗܠܝܢ ܙܥܘܪ̈ܐ ܐܝܠܝܢ
ܕܡܗܝܡܢܝܢ ܒܝ. ܐܡܪܢܐ ܠܟܘܢ ܓܝܪ ܕܡ̈ܠܐܟܝܗܘܢ ܒܫܡܝܐ
¶A ܒܟܠܙܒܢ ܚܙܝܢ ܦܪܨܘܦܗ ܕܐܒܝ ܕܒܫܡܝܐ¶. 11 ܘܕܐܬܐ ܒܪܗ ܕܐܢܫܐ
ܕܢܚܐ ܗܘ ܡܕܡ ܕܐܒܕ ܗܘܐ ܀
fol 29 v 12 ܐܡܢܐ ܕܝܢ ܡܬܚܙܐ ܠܟܘܢ· ܐܢ ܢܗܘܘܢ ܠܐܢܫ *ܡܐܐ
ܥܪ̈ܒܝܢ ܘܢܛܥܐ ܚܕ ܡܢܗܘܢ؛ ܠܐ ܫܒܩ ܬܫܥܝܢ ܘܬܫܥܐ ܒܛܘܪܐ.
ܘܐܙܠ ܒܥܐ ܠܗܘ ܕܛܥܐ. 13 ܘܡܐ ܕܐܫܟܚܗ. ܐܡܝܢ ܐܡܪܢܐ
ܠܟܘܢ ܕܚܕܐ ܒܗ ܝܬܝܪ ܡܢ ܗܢܘܢ ܬܫܥܝܢ ܘܬܫܥܐ ܐܝܠܝܢ ܕܠܐ
ܛܥܘ· 14 ܗܟܢܐ ܠܐ ܨܒܐ ܐܒܘܟܘܢ ܕܒܫܡܝܐ ܕܢܐܒܕ ܚܕ ܡܢ
ܗܠܝܢ ܙܥܘܪ̈ܐ ܀
§A 298 §15 ܐܢ ܕܝܢ ܐܣܟܠ ܒܟ ܐܚܘܟ ܐܟܣܝܗܝ· ܒܝܢܝܟ ܘܠܗ ܒܠܚܘܕ.
ܐܢ ܢܫܡܥܟ ܝܬܪܬ ܐܚܘܟ. 16 ܘܐܢ ܠܐ ܢܫܡܥܟ ܕܒܪ ܥܡܟ
ܬܘܒ ܚܕ ܐܘ ܬܪ̈ܝܢ. ܕܥܠ ܦܘܡ ܬܪ̈ܝܢ ܘܬܠܬܐ ܣܗ̈ܕܝܢ ܬܩܘܡ
ܟܠ ܡܠܐ. 17 ܐܢ ܕܝܢ ܠܐ ܢܫܡܥ ܐܢܘܢ ܐܡܪ ܠܥܕܬܐ. ܘܐܢ
col 2 ܠܥܕܬܐ ܠܐ ܢܫܡܥ· ܢܗܘܐ ܚܫܝܒ *ܠܟ ܐܝܟ ܚܢܦܐ ܘܐܝܟ

ܚܨܝ] ܚܨܝܗ S   ܡܢܟ] + ܐܘ ܐܝܕܟ ܐܘ ܪܓܠܟ A (*cf ver.* 8)   ܠܟ 1°] + ܓܝܪ S   ܠܟ 3°] *so also S*   ܥܝ̈ܢܝܢ] *om. S*   ܬܐܙܠ] *pr.* ܘ *S (sic)*   **10.** § *in S*   ܚܙܘ ܕܠܡܐ] ܠܐ A   ܐܝܠܝܢ...ܒܝ] *om. S; om.* ܐܝܠܝܢ A   ܐܡܪܢܐ...ܓܝܪ] *om. A*   ܒܫܡܝܐ] *om. S*   ܦܪܨܘܦܗ] ܐܦܘܗܝ S   ܕܒܫܡܝܐ] *om. A*   *For A* 43, *see Introd.* vol. ii   **11.**] *om. S*   **12.** *No* § *in S*   ܕܝܢ] *om. S*   ܢܗܘܘܢ] ܢܗܘܐ S   ܠܐܢܫ] ܠܓܒܪܐ S   ܥܪ̈ܒܝܢ] ܥܪܒܐ S   ܘܬܛܥܐ ܚܕܐ ܡܢܗܘܢ S   ܠܐ] *pr.* ܘ S   ܘܬܫܒܩ S   ܠܗ ܕܛܥܬ S   **13** ܒܗ̇ *S*[ed] (*misprint for* ܒܗ)   ܗܢܘܢ] ܗܠܝܢ S   ܘܬܫܒܩ S   ܐܝܠܝܢ] *om. S*   ܛܥܘ S   **14** ܗܟܢܐ ܠܐ] ܠܐ ܓܝܪ A: *cf also on* Lk xv 10   ܐܟܣܝܗܝ] ܐܟܣ S; ܐܟܣܝܗ A   **15** ܐܢ *S*[ed] (*misprint*)   ܕܝܢ] *om. A*   ܐܣܟܠ] ܢܣܟܠ S   ܒܠܚܘܕ] *om. S A*   ܝܬܪܬ] ܐܬܪܬ *S* (*as* syr. vg), *but the first* ܬ *seems badly formed: cf* Mk viii 36   ܐܢ ܢܫܡܥܟ ܝܬܪܬ ܐܚܘܟ] ܘܐܢ ܬܒ ܫܒܘܩ ܠܗ A (= Lk xvii 3)   **16** ܘܐܢ] ܐܢ ܕܝܢ S   ܥܡܟ ܬܘܒ] *om. A*   ܕܥܠ ܦܘܡ] ܕܠܦܘܡ A   **17** ܐܢ...ܐܢܘܢ] ܘܐܢ ܠܗܠܝܢ ܠܐ ܢܫܡܥ A   ܠܥܕܬܐ 1° & 2°] ܠܟܢܘܫܬܐ S   ܢܗܘܐ ܚܫܝܒ] ܢܬܚܫܒ S; ܗܝܕܝܢ ܢܬܚܫܒ A

pluck *it* out *and* throw it from thee¶; it is profitable for thee that C S ¶A
thou shouldest enter life having one eye, and not having two eyes go
10 to the Gehenna of fire. §See lest ye disdain one of these little §A127
ones which believe in me; for I say to you that their angels do in
11 heaven always see the countenance of my Father in heaven,¶ and ¶A
that the Son of Man came that he might save *alive* that which
was lost.
12 "But how seemeth it to you? If any one shall have an hundred
sheep and one of them be strayed, doth he not leave the ninety and
13 nine on the hill and go seek the one that is strayed? And what *time*
he hath found it, amen, I say to you that he rejoiceth over it more
14 than *over* those ninety and nine which were not strayed. So your
Father in heaven willeth not that one of these little ones should
be lost.
15 §"But if thy brother hath trespassed against thee, reprove him §A298
between thyself and him only; if he hath heard thee, thou hast
16 inherited thy brother. And if he will not hear thee, take with thee
again one or two, that on the mouth of two and three witnesses may
17 every word stand. But if he will not hear them, say *it* to the
Church, and if the Church he will not hear, he shall be accounted

---

pluck it out *S* from thee] + or thy hand or thy foot *A* (*cf ver.* 8) it is profitable] *pr.* for *S* eyes] *om. S* go] *lit.* 'and go' *S* (*sic*): *for the construction, cf ver.* 8 **10** See lest ye] Do not *A* which] that *A* which...in me] *om. S* for...to you] *om. A* in heaven 1°] *om. S* (*not* E^{165}) countenance] face *S* in heaven 2°] *om. A* E^{165} *For A*43, *see Introd.* vol. ii **11.**] *om. S* **12** But how] How *S* any one] a man *S* an hundred sheep] a flock of one hundred *S* doth he not] and doth not *S*: *cf* Lk xii 45, 46 **13** which] that *S* **14** So] For *A*: *cf also on* Lk xv 10 your Father] my Father *S*; the Father *A* **15** But] *om. A* shall trespass *S* only] *om. S A* inherited] gained *S*: *cf* Mk viii 36 if he...brother] and if he repent, forgive him *A* (= Lk xvii 3) **16** And] But *S* with thee again] *om. A* on the mouth of] in the sight of *A* **17** But...them] And if these he will not hear *A* the Church 1° & 2°] the Synagogue *S*: *see Notes,* vol. ii he shall] *pr.* then *A*

C S

¶A ܡܟܣܐ.¶ [18]ܘܐܡܝܢ ܐܡܪܢܐ ܠܟܘܢ ܕܟܠ ܡܐ ܕܬܐܣܪܘܢ
ܒܐܪܥܐ ܢܗܘܐ ܐܣܝܪ ܒܫܡܝܐ. ܘܡܕܡ ܕܬܫܪܘܢ ܒܐܪܥܐ
ܢܗܘܐ ܫܪܐ ܒܫܡܝܐ.

[19]ܬܘܒ ܐܡܝܢ ܐܡܪܢܐ ܠܟܘܢ. ܕܐܢ ܬܪܝܢ ܡܢܟܘܢ ܢܫܬܘܘܢ
ܒܐܪܥܐ ܥܠ ܡܐ ܕܢܫܐܠܘܢ܆ ܢܗܘܐ ܠܗܘܢ ܡܢ ܠܘܬ ܐܒܝ
§A69(bis) ܕܒܫܡܝܐ. [§20]ܐܝܟܐ ܓܝܪ ܕܟܢܝܫܝܢ ܬܪܝܢ ܐܘ ܬܠܬܐ ܒܫܡܝ. ܬܡܢ
¶A ܐܢܐ ܒܡܨܥܬܗܘܢ¶ ·ܘ·

§A35 [21]ܗܝܕܝܢ ܩܪܒ ܠܘܬܗ ܫܡܥܘܢ ܟܐܦܐ ܘܐܡܪ ܠܗ. ܡܪܝ, [§]ܟܡܐ
ܙܒܢܝܢ ܐܢ ܗܘ ܕܢܣܟܠ ܒܝ ܐܚܝ ܐܫܒܘܩ ܠܗ. ܥܕܡܐ ܠܫܒܥ
¶A ܙܒܢܝܢ. [22]ܐܡܪ ܠܗ ܠܐ ܫܒܥ· ܐܠܐ ܥܠ ܫܒܥܝܢ ܫܒܥ ܫܒܥ.¶
fol 30 r [*23]ܡܛܠ ܗܢܐ ܕܡܝܐ ܡܠܟܘܬܐ ܕܫܡܝܐ ܠܓܒܪܐ ܡܠܟܐ. ܕܨܒܐ
§A37 [§]ܠܡܣܒ ܚܘܫܒܢܐ ܡܢ ܥܒܕܘܗܝ. [24]ܟܕ ܫܪܝ ܠܡܣܒ ܚܘܫܒܢܐ.
ܩܪܒ ܩܕܡܘܗܝ, ܚܕ ܡܢܗܘܢ ܕܚܝܒ ܗܘܐ ܠܗ ܪܒܘ ܟܟ̈ܪܝܢ· [25]ܘܟܕ
ܠܝܬ ܗܘܐ ܠܗ ܠܡܦܪܥ· ܦܩܕ ܕܢܙܕܒܢ ܗܘ ܘܐܢܬܬܗ ܘܒ̈ܢܘܗܝ,
ܘܟܠܡܕܡ ܕܐܝܬ ܠܗ· [26]ܘܢܦܠ ܥܒܕܐ ܗܘ ܘܣܓܕ ܠܡܪܗ.

---

18 ܕܟܠ ܡܐ] ܡܕܡ S 19 ܐܡܪ ܐܢܐ S (sic) ܕܐܢ ܬܪܝܢ ܡܢܟܘܢ] so also S ܒܐܪܥܐ] so also S^vid ܡܐ] ܒܟܠ ܨܒܘ ܡܕܡ S
20.] ܠܝܬ ܓܝܪ ܬܪܝܢ ܐܘ ܬܠܬܐ ܕܟܢܝܫܝܢ ܒܫܡܝ. ܕܠܐ ܐܢܐ ܒܡܨܥܬܗܘܢ S; ܐܬܪ ܕܬܪ̈ܝܢ ܘܬܠܬܐ ܟܢܝܫܝܢ ܒܫܡܝ. ܬܡܢ ܐܢܐ ܒܡܨܥܬܗܘܢ A 2/2 21 ܠܘܬܗ & ܠܗ] om. S ܐܢ ܗܘ ܕ] ܐܢ S A ܥܕܡܐ ܠ] om. A ܙܒܢܝܢ 2°] om. S
22 ܠܗ] + ܡܪܢ A ܠܐ ܫܒܥ] + ܒܠܚܘܕ A ܫܒܥܝܢ] + ܙܒܢܝܢ S A Cf A 298: ܐܢ ܥܠ ܫܒܥܝܢ ܙܒܢܝܢ ܫ̈ܒܥ ܫܒܥ ܢܣܟܠ ܒܟ ܡܫܡܠܝܐ ܫܒܘܩ ܠܗ ܒܚܕ ܢܦܫܐ. ܡܛܠ ܒܪܢܫܐ....ܕܒܚܕ ܢܦܫܐ ܐ̈ܬܒܒܝܐ ܘܬܫܥܝܢ ܙܒܢܝܢ ܢܣܟܠ ܒܚܒܪܗ.
23 ܠܡܣܒ] pr. ܕܫܪܝ ܠܓܒܪܐ ܕܗܘ ܬܘܬܒܐ ܗܘ ܡܪܢ A ܚܘܫܒܢܐ S
24 ܫܪܝ ܠܡܣܒ ܚܘܫܒܢܐ] om. A; om. ܚܘܫܒܢܐ S ܩܕܡܘܗܝ] ܠܗ S (not A); pr. ܥܒܕܗ A ܚܕ ܡܢܗܘܢ] om. S A ܟܟ̈ܪܝܢ] ܟܪܟܘ S
25 ܕܢܙܕܒܢܘܢ ܠܗ ܘܠܐܢܬܬܗ ܘܠܒܢܘܗܝ S ܟܠܡܕܡ] ܟܠ ܡܕܡ S 25—27.] A has: ܘܟܕ ܐܬܠܝܗ ܡܪܗ ܕܢܫܩܠ ܠܗ ܡܐ ܕܚܝܒ ܠܗ. ܘܟܕ ܠܐ ܐܫܟܚ ܠܡܦܪܥ ܚܘܒܬܗ ܠܡܪܗ. ܦܩܕ ܡܪܗ [27]ܘܫܪܝܗ. ܘܟܠ ܕܚܝܒ ܫܒܩ ܠܗ 26 ܘܢܦܠ] om. ܘ S

18 by thee as the pagan and as the toll-gatherer.¶ And amen, I say to *C S* ¶*A*
you All that ye shall bind in earth shall be bound in heaven, and
that which ye shall remit in earth shall be remitted in heaven.
19 "Again, amen, I say to you If two of you shall consent in earth
on what they shall ask, it shall be to them from my Father in
20 heaven. §For wherever two or three are gathered together in my §*A*69(*bis*)
name, there am I in their midst."¶ ¶*A*
21 Then drew near unto him Simon Kepha and said to him: "My
Lord, §how many times if so be that my brother trespass against me §*A*35
22 shall I forgive him? Until seven times?" He saith to him: "Not
seven, but for seventy sevens.¶ ¶*A*
23 "Therefore like is the kingdom of heaven to a man, a king, that
24 wished §to take a reckoning from his slaves. And when he began to §*A*37
take the reckoning there drew near before him one of them that
25 owed him ten thousand talents. And when he had not *aught* to
repay he commanded that he should be sold, he and his wife and his
26 sons, and *that* all that he had should be taken. And that slave fell

---

18 All that] That which *S* 19 If...in earth] *so also S* on what] on any matter which *S* 20.] For there are not two or three gathered together in my name, that I am not in the midst of *S*; where two and three are gathered together in my name, there am I in their midst *A* 2/2: *cf also* 'where one is, there I also am; and where two are, there will I also be' *E*[165] 21 unto him *and* to him] *om. S* if so be that] if *S A* Until] *om. A* (*not E*[163]) times 2°] *om. S* 22 He] Our Lord *A* seven] + only *A* seventy] + times *S A* (*i.e.* '70 times multiplying by 7') *Cf A* 298: 'If for seventy times multiplying by sevens a trespasser shall trespass against thee, forgive him in one day. For who is the man.... that in one day 490 times will trespass against his comrade?' 23 to take] *pr.* Our Lord hath shewn us the example of that man which began *A* 24 he began...reckoning] *om. A* the reckoning] *om. S* before him] to him *S* (*not A*); *pr.* his slave *A* one of them that] *one* that *S A* ten thousand] *pr.* for *S* 25 that they should sell him—him and his wife and his sons— *S* all that] everything which *S* 25—27.] *A has:* 'And when his lord constrained him that he should give him what he owed him, and when he could not repay his debt to his lord, his lord commanded and dismissed him, and all that he owed he forgave him' 26 And that slave] That slave *S*

C S ܘܐܡܪ ܐܓܪ ܥܠܝ ܪܘܚܟ ܘܟܠ ܡܕܡ ܦܪܥ ܐܢܐ ܠܟ. [27]ܘܐܬܪܚܡ
ܥܠܘܗܝ, ܡܪܗ ܘܫܪܝܗܝ. ܐܦ ܚܘܒܬܐ ܫܒܩ ܠܗ. [28]ܘܢܦܩ ܥܒܕܐ
ܗܘ ܘܐܫܟܚ ܠܚܕ ܡܢ ܟܢܘܬܗ. ܕܚܝܒ ܗܘܐ ܠܗ ܕܝܢܪ̈ܐ ܡܐܐ.
col 2 ܘܐܚܕܗ ܘܚܢܩ ܗܘܐ *ܠܗ. ܘܐܡܪ ܗܘܐ ܠܗ ܦܪܘܥܝܢܝ ܡܕܡ
ܕܚܝܒ ܐܢܬ ܠܝ. [29]ܘܢܦܠ ܗܘ ܟܢܘܬܗ ܘܒܥܐ ܗܘܐ ܡܢܗ ܘܐܡܪ
ܗܘܐ ܠܗ. ܐܓܪ ܥܠܝ ܪܘܚܟ ܘܐܦ ܐܢܐ ܦܪܥ ܐܢܐ. [30]ܗܘ ܕܝܢ
¶A ܠܐ ܨܒܐ ܒܡܠܬܗ. ܐܠܐ ܐܙܠ ܐܪܡܝܗ ܒܒܝܬ ܐܣܝܪ̈ܐ¶. ܥܕܡܐ
ܕܢܦܪܘܥܝܘܗܝ, ܡܕܡ ܕܚܝܒ· [31]ܟܕ ܚܙܘ ܕܝܢ ܟܢܘܬܗ ܐܝܠܝܢ ܕܗܘܘ,
ܒܪܝܬ ܠܗܘܢ ܠܒ. ܘܐܬܘ ܘܚܘܘ ܠܡܪܗܘܢ ܟܠ ܡܕܡ ܕܗܘܐ.
[32]ܗܝܕܝܢ ܩܪܝܗ, ܡܪܗ ܘܐܡܪ ܠܗ. ܥܒܕܐ ܒܝܫܐ. ܗܝ, ܟܠܗ
ܚܘܒܬܐ ܫܒܩܬ ܠܟ ܡܛܠ ܕܒܥܝܬ ܡܢܝ. [33]ܠܐ ܚܙܐ ܗܘܬ ܐܦ
fol 30 v ܐܢܬ ܕܬܚܘܢ ܠܟܢܘܬܟ ܐܝܟܢܐ ܕܐܢܐ ܚܢܬܟ. [34]ܘܪܓܙ *ܥܠܘܗܝ,
ܡܪܗ. ܘܐܫܠܡܗ ܕܢܗܘܐ ܡܬܫܢܩ. ܥܕܡܐ ܕܢܦܪܘܥ ܟܠܗ
§A 38 ܚܘܒܬܐ. §[35]ܗܟܢܐ ܢܥܒܕ ܠܟܘܢ ܐܒܐ ܕܒܫܡܝܐ. ܐܠܐ
¶A ܬܫܒܩܘܢ ܐܢܫ ܠܐܚܘܗܝ, ܡܢ ܠܒܘܬܟܘܢ¶.܀
[1]ܘܗܘܐ ܟܕ ܫܠܡ ܝܫܘܥ ܡ̈ܠܐ ܗܠܝܢ. ܥܒܪ ܠܗ ܡܢ ܓܠܝܠܐ.
ܘܐܬܐ ܠܗ ܠܬܚܘܡܐ ܕܝܗܘܕ. ܠܥܒܪܐ ܕܝܘܪܕܢ· [2]ܘܐܬܐ ܒܬܪܗ
ܟܢܫܐ ܣܓܝܐܐ. ܘܐܣܝ ܐܢܘܢ ܬܡܢ ܀

ܦܪܥ ܐܢܐ ܠܟ] ܐܦܪܥܟ S 27 ܘܐܬܪܚܡ] so also S ܡܪܗ] om. S ܐܦ] pr. ܘ S 28 ܘܢܦܩ] om. ܘ S ܗܘ ܥܒܕܐ S ܘܢܦܩ....ܘܐܫܟܚ] ܗܘ ܕܝܢ ܥܒܕܐ....ܟܕ ܢܦܩ. ܐܫܟܚ A ܠܚܕ] ܚܕ S ܗܘܐ ܠܗ] om. S; om. ܗܘܐ A ܦܪܘܥܝܢܝ] ܗܒ ܠܝ S A ܡܕܡ] ܡܐ S 29.] om. A ܗܘ] ܗܘܐ S ܘܒܥܐ] om. ܘ S ܗܘܐ ܠܗ] om. S ܐܓܪ̈ S, but the dot appears to me to have been accidental 30 ܗܘ ܕܝܢ....ܒܡܠܬܗ] ܘܠܐ ܨܒܐ ܒܡܠܬܗ ܕܟܢܘܬܗ ܕܒܥܐ ܡܢܗ A ܐܙܠ] om. S ܐܪܡܝܗ] ܘܚܒܫܗ A ܕܢܦܪܘܥ S ܡܕܡ] ܡܐ S 31 ܠܒ] om. S ܘܚܘܘ] ܐܫܬܥܝܘ S ܡܕܡ] ܡܐ S 32 ܗܝ] so also S 33 ܐܦ ܐܢܬ] om. S 34 ܟܠܗ ܚܘܒܬܐ] ܡܐ ܕܚܝܒ S (A) 35 ܗܟܢܐ] pr. ܐܫܬܠܡ ܗܘ ܠܢܫ̈ܐ ܕܢܫܢܩܘܢܝܗܝ. ܥܕܡܐ ܕܢܦܠ ܡܐ ܕܚܝܒ. ܘܐܡܪ ܠܗܘܢ. ܕ pr. A ܡܢ ܠܒܘܬܟܘܢ] ܡܢ ܠܒܟܘܢ S; om. A 1 ܟܕ] pr. ܕ S (sic): see on Mt xi 1 2 ܘܐܬܐ] ܘܐܬܘ S (foll. by ܟܢ̈ܫܐ) ܬܡܢ] om. S

down and worshipped his lord, and said: 'Be lenient with me, and *C S*
27 everything will I repay thee.' And his lord had compassion on him,
28 and dismissed him, the debt too he forgave him. And that slave
went forth and found one of his fellow-servants that had owed him
an hundred denars and he took hold of him and was strangling him,
and was saying to him: 'Repay me that which thou owest me.'
29 And that fellow-servant of his fell down and was beseeching him
and was saying to him: 'Be lenient with me, and I also will repay.'
30 Now he did not receive his supplication, but went *and* cast him into
31 prison,¶ until he should repay him that which he owed. Now when ¶*A*
his fellow-servants saw what things had happened it grieved them
exceedingly, and they went and shewed to their lord everything
32 which had happened. Then his lord called him and said to him:
'Evil slave, all that debt I forgave thee, because thou didst beseech
33 me; oughtest not thou also to have been merciful to thy fellow-
34 servant, even as I myself was merciful to thee?' And his lord was
wroth with him, and delivered him up that he might be scourged
35 until he should repay all the debt. §So will my Father in heaven do §*A* 38
to you, except ye forgive each one his brother from your hearts."¶ ¶*A*

xix 1 And it came to pass when Jesus finished these words he removed
from Galilee and came to the border of Judaea to the other side of
2 Jordan. And there came after him a great multitude, and he healed
them there.

---

will I repay thee] I will repay *S* 27 And his lord] And he *S* and the debt also *S* 28 And that slave] That slave *S*: 'Now that slave....when he went forth, found...' *A* had owed him] owed *S*; owed him *A* Repay me] Give me *S A* that which] what *S* 29.] *om A* that...fell down] the fellow-servant had fallen down *S* and was 1°] *and* was *S* was saying to him] saith *S* 30 Now he... supplication] And he did not receive the supplication of his fellow-servant that besought him *A* *and* cast him into] and shut him up in *A* that which] what *S* 31 exceedingly] *om. S* shewed] declared *S* everything which] all that *S* 33 not thou also] thou not *S* 34 all the debt] what he owed *S* 35 So] *pr.* He was delivered up to the guards that they should scourge him until he should give what he owed. And he said to them *A* from your hearts] from your heart *S*; *om. A* 1 when] *pr.* that *S* (*sic*): *see on* Mt xi 1 2 great multitudes *S* there] *om. S*

C S ³ܘܩܪܒܘ ܠܘܬܗ ܦܪ̈ܝܫܐ. ܘܡܢܣܝܢ ܗܘܘ ܠܗ ܘܐܡܪܝܢ ܗܘܘ. ܕܐܢ
ܗܘ ܕܫܠܝܛ ܠܓܒܪܐ ܕܢܫܪܐ ܐܢܬܬܗ ܥܠ ܟܠ ܥܠܐ. ⁴ܗܘ ܕܝܢ
ܥܢܐ ܘܐܡܪ ܠܗܘܢ. ܠܐ ܩܪܝܬܘܢ ܕܡܢ ܕܒܪܐ ܠܓܒܪܐ ܡܢ
col 2 ܒܪܫܝܬ ܐܦ. ܠܢܩܒܬܐ ܗܘ ܒܪܐ. *⁵ܘܐܡܪ ܕܡܛܠ ܗܢܐ ܢܫܒܘܩ
ܓܒܪܐ ܠܐܒܘܗ̈ܝ ܘܠܐܡܗ ܘܢܩܦ ܠܐܢܬܬܗ. ܘܢܗܘܘܢ ܬܪ̈ܝܗܘܢ
ܚܕ ܒܣܪ. ⁶ܗܟܝܠ ܠܐ ܗܘܘ ܬܪ̈ܝܢ. ܐܠܐ ܚܕ ܐܢܘܢ ܒܣܪ. ܡܕܡ
ܕܐܠܗܐ ܗܟܝܠ ܙܘܓ ܒܪܢܫܐ ܠܐ ܢܦܪܫ. ⁷ܐܡܪܝܢ ܠܗ ܠܡܢܐ
ܗܟܝܠ ܦܩܕ ܡܘܫܐ. ܕܡܢ ܕܒܥܐ ܕܫܪܐ ܐܢܬܬܗ ܢܬܠ ܠܗ̇
ܐܓܪܬܐ ܕܕܘܠܠܐ. ⁸ܐܡܪ ܠܗܘܢ ܡܘܫܐ ܡܛܠ ܩܫܝܘܬ ܠܒܟܘܢ
ܗܘ ܐܦܣ ܠܟܘܢ ܕܬܫܪܘܢ ܢܫ̈ܝܟܘܢ. ܡܢ ܒܪܫܝܬ ܕܝܢ ܠܐ ܗܘܐ
ܗܟܢܐ ܗܘܐ. ⁹ܐܡܪܢܐ ܠܟܘܢ ܕܝܢ ܕܡܢ ܕܫܒܩ ܐܢܬܬܗ ܕܠܐ
fol 31 r ܡܠܬܐ ܕܓܘܪܐ ܘܢܣܒ ܐܚܪܬܐ ܡܓܪ ܓܐܪ ܠܗ̇. *¹⁰ܐܡܪܝܢ ܠܗ
ܬܠܡ̈ܝܕܘܗܝ. ܐܢ ܗܟܢܐ ܐܝܬ ܥܠܬܐ ܒܝܢ ܓܒܪܐ ܠܐܢܬܬܐ.
§A 355 ܠܐ ܦܩܚ ܠܡܣܒ ܐܢܬܬܐ. ¹¹ܐܡܪ ܠܗܘܢ ܝܫܘܥ. §ܠܐ ܗܘܐ
ܟܠ ܐܢܫ ܣܦܩ ܠܗ̇ ܠܡܠܬܐ ܗܕܐ. ܐܠܐ ܐܝܠܝܢ ܕܝܗܝܒ ܠܗܘܢ
¶A ܡܢ ܠܘܬ ܐܠܗܐ¶. ¹²ܐܝܬ ܓܝܪ ܡܗ̈ܝܡܢܐ ܕܡܢ ܟܪܣܐ ܕܐܡܗܘܢ
ܗܘܘ ܡܗ̈ܝܡܢܐ. ܘܐܝܬ ܡܗ̈ܝܡܢܐ ܕܒ̈ܢܝ ܐܢܫܐ ܥܒܕܘ ܐܢܘܢ.
ܘܐܝܬ ܕܗܢܘܢ ܥܒܕܘ ܢܦܫܗܘܢ ܡܗ̈ܝܡܢܐ ܡܛܠ ܡܠܟܘܬܐ
ܕܫܡܝܐ. ܡܢ ܕܡܨܐ ܕܝܢ ܒܚܝܠܐ ܕܢܣܝܒܪ ܢܣܝܒܪ ܀
¹³ܗܝܕܝܢ ܩܪܒܘ ܠܗ ܛ̈ܠܝܐ ܕܢܣܝܡ ܐܝܕܗ ܥܠܝܗܘܢ ܘܢܨܠܐ.
col 2 ܘܟܐܐ ܒܗܘܢ ܬܠܡ̈ܝܕܘܗܝ. *¹⁴ܐܡܪ ܠܗܘܢ ܝܫܘܥ. ܫܒܘܩܘ
ܛ̈ܠܝܐ ܐܬܝܢ ܠܘܬܝ. ܘܠܐ ܬܟܠܘܢ ܐܢܘܢ ܕܢܐܬܘܢ ܠܘܬܝ.

3 ܠܘܬܗ] ܠܗ ܬܡܢ S   ܗܘܘ 2°] om. S   ܕܐܢ ܗܘ ܕ] ܕܐܢ S
4 ܡܢ ܒܪܫܝܬ] om. S   5 ܘܐܡܪ ܕ] om. S   6 ܗܟܝܠ] om. S
7 ܠܡܢܐ....ܕܘܠܠܐ] ܡܢܘ ܕܡܘܫܐ ܦܩܕ S   ܠܗ̇] S[ed] (*and in ver.* 11)
8 ܩܫܝܘܬܐ ܕܠܒܟܘܢ S   ܗܘܐ *ult.*] *om.* S   9 ܕܫܒܩ] ܕܢܫܪܐ S
ܡܠܬܐ ܕܓܘܪܐ] ܓܘܪܐ S   ܠܗ̇] *om.* S   10 ܒܝܢ] ܒܝܬ S
11 ܝܫܘܥ] *om.* S   ܠܡܠܬܐ ܗܕܐ] *om.* A   ܐܝܠܝܢ ܕܝܗܝܒ ܠܗܘܢ]
ܡܢ ܕܝܗܝܒ ܠܗ A. *For* ܕܝܗܝܒ (A^b), A^a *has* ܕܝܗܒ: *cf* Mk iv 11, Lk iv 6, 17
ܡܢ ܠܘܬ ܐܠܗܐ] *om.* S A   12 ܘܐܝܬ 1°] *om.* ܘ S   ܡܢ ܕܡܨܐ ܕܝܢ]
ܒܟܠ * * ܕܡܨܐ S: *we must supply* ܡܢ *or* ܕܝܢ   14 ܕܢܐܬܘܢ ܠܘܬܝ] *om.* S

3 And there drew near unto him the Pharisees, and they were *C S*
tempting him and were saying "*Tell us* if so be that it is lawful for
4 a man to dismiss his wife for every cause." But he answered and
said to them: "Have ye not read that He that made the male from
5 the beginning the female also made, and said 'Therefore shall the
man leave his father and his mother and shall attach himself to his
6 wife, and the two of them shall become one flesh'? Henceforth they
have become not two, but are one flesh; that which God therefore
7 hath coupled let not man separate." They say to him: "Why
therefore did Moses command that he that would dismiss his wife
8 should give her a letter of divorce?" He saith to them: "Moses—it
is because of the hardness of your heart he permitted you to dismiss
9 your wives, but from the beginning it was not so. But I say to you
He that leaveth his wife without a word of adultery, and taketh
10 another, doth indeed commit adultery against her." His disciples
say to him: "If so there is blame between man and wife it is
11 not profitable to take a wife." Jesus saith to them: "§Not every §*A*355
one is sufficient for this word, but they to whom it is given from
12 God.¶ For there are eunuchs that from their mother's womb were ¶*A*
eunuchs, and there are eunuchs that men have made, and there are
those that have made themselves eunuchs for the kingdom of heaven's
sake. But he that is capable in power to endure, let him endure."
13 Then they brought near to him children, that he should lay his
14 hand on them and pray; and his disciples rebuked them. Jesus saith
to them: "Suffer the children to come unto me and forbid them not
that they should come unto me; for they that are *such* as these,

---

3 unto him] to him there *S* were 2°] *om. S* if so be that] if *S* 4 from the beginning] *om. S* 5 and said] *om. S* 6 therefore] *om. S* 7 Why.... command] What is it that Moses commanded *S* 8 to dismiss your wives] *om.* E^{162} from the beginning] + 'of the creation' E^{162}: *cf* Mk x 6 (Gr., *not* Syrr.) 9 leaveth...taketh] shall dismiss...shall take *S* a word of] *om. S* against her] *om. S* 11 Jesus] He *S* they to whom] he to whom *A* from God] *om. S A* 12 and 1°] *om. S* But he that] Whosoever S^{vid} 14 that they...unto me] *om. S*

C S ܐܝܠܝܢ ܓܝܪ ܕܐܝܟ ܗܠܝܢ ܐܢܘܢ ܕܝܠܗܘܢ ܗܝ ܡܠܟܘܬܐ ܕܫܡܝܐ.
15 ܘܣܡ ܐܝܕܗ ܥܠܝܗܘܢ ܘܐܙܠ ܡܢ ܬܡܢ.܀
§A 392 16 ܘܩܪܒ ܠܘܬܗ ܚܕ ܘܐܡܪ ܠܗ. ܡܠܦܢܐ ܛܒܐ §ܡܢܐ ܐܥܒܕ
¶A ܕܐܪܬ ܚܝܐ ܕܠܥܠܡ¶. 17 ܐܡܪ ܠܗ ܝܫܘܥ ܡܢܐ ܡܫܐܠ ܐܢܬ ܠܝ
ܥܠ ܛܒܐ. ܚܕ ܗܘ ܓܝܪ ܛܒܐ ܐܠܗܐ. ܐܢ ܨܒܐ ܐܢܬ ܕܝܢ
§A 392 ܕܬܥܘܠ ܠܚܝܐ ܛܪ ܦܘܩܕܢܐ. 18 ܐܡܪ ܠܗ ܐܝܠܝܢ. §ܐܡܪ ܠܗ
§A 498 ܝܫܘܥ. §ܠܐ ܬܩܛܘܠ. ܘܠܐ ܬܓܘܪ. ܘܠܐ ܬܓܢܘܒ. ܘܠܐ ܬܣܗܕ
fol 31 v ܣܗܕܘܬܐ *ܕܫܘܩܪܐ. 19 ܝܩܪ ܠܐܒܘܟ ܘܠܐܡܟ. ܘܐܚܒ ܠܩܪܝܒܟ
¶A 498 ܐܝܟ ܢܦܫܟ.¶ 20 ܐܡܪ ܠܗ ܗܘ ܥܠܝܡܐ ܗܠܝܢ ܟܠܗܝܢ ܢܛܪܬ ܐܢܝܢ
ܗܐ ܡܢ ܕܛܠܐ ܐܢܐ. ܡܢܐ ܬܘܒ ܚܣܝܪܢܐ. 21 ܐܡܪ ܠܗ ܝܫܘܥ
ܐܢ ܨܒܐ ܐܢܬ ܕܬܗܘܐ ܓܡܝܪ. ܙܠ ܙܒܢ ܩܢܝܢܝܟ ܘܗܒ
ܠܡܣܟܢܐ. ܘܬܗܘܐ ܠܟ ܣܝܡܬܐ ܒܫܡܝܐ. ܘܣܒ ܨܠܝܒܟ ܘܬܐ
ܒܬܪܝ. 22 ܘܟܕ ܫܡܥ ܥܠܝܡܐ ܗܘ ܡܠܬܐ ܗܕܐ. ܐܙܠ ܟܕ ܟܪܝܐ
ܠܗ. ܡܛܠ ܕܐܝܬ ܗܘܐ ܠܗ ܩܢܝܢܐ ܣܓܝܐܐ. 23 ܝܫܘܥ ܕܝܢ ܐܡܪ

---

15 ܡܢ ܬܡܢ] *om. S*   16, 18—24. *For the full text of A* 392, *see on* Mk x 17—25   16 ܐܥܒܕ] + ܕܛܒܐ *S*   17 ܝܫܘܥ] *om. S*   ܐܠܗܐ] *om. S*   ܐܢ ܨܒܐ ܐܢܬ] ܨܒܝܬ *S*   ܕܬܥܘܠ] ܕܬܐܬܐ *S*   ܛܪ] ܛܪ *S*   18 ܠܐ ܬܩܛܘܠ] *om. A* 392   ܘܠܐ 1°] *om.* ܘ *S A* 392   ܘܠܐ ܬܓܢܘܒ] *om. S*   ܘܠܐ ܬܣܗܕ...ܕܫܘܩܪܐ] *om. A* 392   ܣܗܕܘܬ ܫܘܩܪܐ *A* 498   19 ܝܩܪ] *pr.* ܘ *A* 392   ܘܐܚܒ] ܘܬܪܚܡ *S*; ܘܪܚܡ *A* 392   ܘܐܚܒ...ܢܦܫܟ] ܘܡܕܡ ܕܥܠܝܟ ܣܢܐ ܠܚܒܪܟ ܠܐ ܬܥܒܕ *A* 498: *in Land* (Anecd. i 69) *this is given as a saying of Menander*   20 ܥܠܝܡܐ] ܓܒܪܐ *A*   ܟܠܗܝܢ] *om. A* (= Mk)   ܢܛܪܬ] ܥܒܕܬ *A* (= Mk)   ܡܢܐ ܬܘܒ ܚܣܝܪܢܐ] *om. S*; ܐܝܢܐ ܐܠܐ ܚܣܝܪ ܐܢܐ *A*   21 *init.*] *for A, see* Mk x 21   ܨܒܝܬ *S A*   ܕܬܗܘܐ ܓܡܝܪ] ܓܡܝܪܐ ܠܡܗܘܐ *A*   ܩܢܝܢܝܟ] ܟܠ ܡܕܡ ܕܐܝܬ ܠܟ *S A*   ܘܬܗܘܐ....ܒܫܡܝܐ] *om. S*   ܘܣܒ ܨܠܝܒܟ] *om. S*; ܘܫܩܘܠ ܨܠܝܒܟ *A*   ܘܬܐ *S*   22 ܘܟܕ] *om.* ܘ *S*   ܥܠܝܡܐ ܗܘ *S*   ܘܟܕ....ܟܪܝܐ ܠܗ] *for A, see* Mk x 22   ܡܛܠ....ܣܓܝܐܐ] ܡܛܠ ܕܥܬܝܪ ܗܘܐ ܒܢܟ̈ܣܐ ܛܒ *S A*   23 ܝܫܘܥ ܕܝܢ] ܟܕ ܚܙܐ ܝܫܘܥ *S*   ܝܫܘܥ....ܠܗܘܢ] ܘܐܡܪ ܝܫܘܥ *A*

15 theirs is the kingdom of heaven." And he laid his hand on them *C S*
and went from thence.
16 And a certain man drew near and said to him: "Good teacher,
17 §what shall I do that I may inherit life eternal?"¶ Jesus saith to him: §¶*A* 392
"Why dost thou ask me about the Good One? for one is good,—God.
18 Now if thou dost wish to enter life, keep the commandments." He
saith to him: "Which?" §Jesus saith to him: "§'Thou shalt not kill,' §*A* 392 §*A* 498
and 'Thou shalt not commit adultery,' and 'Thou shalt not thieve,'
19 and 'Thou shalt not bear false witness,' 'Honour thy father and thy
20 mother,' and 'Be loving to thy neighbour as thyself.'"¶ That youth ¶*A* 498
saith to him: "These all—I have kept them, lo, from when I was a
21 child! What yet lack I?" Jesus saith to him: "If thou dost wish
to become perfect, go sell thy property and give to the poor, and thou
shalt have treasure in heaven, and take thy Cross and come after
22 me." And when that youth heard this word he went away grieved,
23 because he had much property. Now Jesus said to his disciples:

---

15 from thence] *om. S* 16, 18—24. *For the full text of A* 392, *see on* Mk x 17—25 16 do] + that is good *S* *Cf* 'Good teacher' (E^{172}), 'what shall I do that I may live' (E^{168}) 17 Jesus] He *S* God] *om. S* enter life] come unto life *S* *Cf* 'There is none good but one only, God, the Father which is in heaven' E^{169} 18 Thou shalt not kill] *om. A* 392 and 1°] *om. S A* 392 and 2°...thieve] *om. S* and 3°...false witness] *om. A* 392 19 Honour] *pr.* and *A* 392 Be loving to] Thou shalt love *S*; Love *A* 392 Be loving...as thyself] That which to thee is hateful, to thy comrade thou shalt not do *A* 498: *in Land* (Anecd. i 69) *this is given as a saying of Menander* 20 youth] man *A* all] *om. A* (= Mk) kept] done *A* E^{125} (= Mk) What yet lack I?] *om. S*; But what lack I? *A* 21 *init.*] *for A, see* Mk x 21 perfect] a perfect *man A* thy property] everything which thou hast *S A*: *cf* 'all thy possessions that thou hast' E^{125} and...treasure in heaven] *om. S* and take thy Cross] *om. S*; and take up thy Cross *A* 22 And when] When *S* And... grieved] *for A, see* Mk x 22 because...property] because he was rich in wealth exceedingly *S A* 23 Now Jesus said] When Jesus saw, he said *S* Now Jesus said...I say to you] And Jesus said *A*

C S ܠܬܠܡܝܕܘܗܝ. ܐܡܝܢ ܐܡܪ ܐܢܐ ܠܟܘܢ ܕܥܛܠܐ ܗ̄ܝ، ܠܥܬܝܪܐ
ܕܢܥܘܠ ܠܡܠܟܘܬܗ ܕܐܠܗܐ. [24]ܬܘܒ ܕܝܢ ܐܡܪ ܐܢܐ ܠܟܘܢ.
col 2 ܕܦܫܝܩ ܗܘ ܠܓܡܠܐ ܕܢܥܒܪ *ܒܚܪܘܪܐ ܕܡܚܛܐ. ܐܘ ܠܥܬܝܪܐ
¶A ܠܡܠܟܘܬܐ ܕܐܠܗܐ.¶ [25]ܬܘܒ ܕܝܢ ܟܕ ܫܡܥܘ ܬܠܡܝܕܘܗܝ، ܬܡܝܗܝܢ
ܗܘܘ ܘܕܚܠܘ ܛܒ. ܘܐܡܪܝܢ ܗܘܘ ܡܢܘ ܟܝ ܡܫܟܚ ܠܡܚܐ.
[26]ܚܪ ܒܗܘܢ ܝܫܘܥ ܘܐܡܪ ܠܗܘܢ܆ ܗܕܐ ܒܝܬ ܒܢ̈ܝ ܐܢܫܐ ܠܐ
ܡܫܟܚܐ ܕܬܗܘܐ. ܐܠܗܐ ܕܝܢ ܟܠ ܡܕܡ ܡܫܟܚ ܠܡܥܒܕ.
[27]ܗܝܕܝܢ ܟܐܦܐ ܫܡܥܘܢ ܒܐܦܐ ܘܐܡܪ ܠܗ. ܗܐ ܚܢܢ ܫܒܩܢ
ܟܠ ܡܕܡ ܘܐܬܝܢ ܒܬܪܟ. ܡܢܐ ܟܝ ܢܗܘܐ ܠܢ. [28]ܐܡܪ ܠܗܘܢ
ܝܫܘܥ: ܐܡܝܢ ܐܡܪܢܐ ܠܟܘܢ ܕܐܢܬܘܢ ܕܐܬܝܬܘܢ ܒܬܪܝ،
ܒܡܘܠܕܐ ܚܕܬܐ. ܡܐ ܕܝܬܒ ܒܪܗ ܕܐܢܫܐ ܥܠ ܬܪܘܢܘܣ
§A 432 fol 32 r ܕܫܘܒܚܗ. §ܬܬܒܘܢ ܘܐܦ ܐܢܬܘܢ *ܥܠ ܬܪ̈ܥܣܪ ܟܘܪ̈ܣܘܢ܆
¶A ܘܬܕܘܢܘܢ ܠܬܪ̈ܬܥܣܪܐ ܫܒ̈ܛܝܢ ܕܒܝܬ ܐܝܣܪܝܠ.¶ [29]ܘܟܠ ܐܢܫ
ܕܫܒܩ ܒ̈ܬܐ ܘܐ̈ܚܐ. ܐܘ ܐ̈ܚܘܬܐ. ܐܘ ܐܡܗܬܐ. ܐܘ ܐܢܬܬܐ.
ܐܘ ܒ̈ܢܝܐ. ܐܘ ܩܘ̈ܪܝܐ. ܡܛܠ ܫܡܝ ܕܝܠܝ. ܢܣܒ ܚܕ ܒܡܐܐ.
ܘܒܥܠܡܐ ܕܐܬܐ ܢܐܪܬ ܚ̈ܝܐ ܕܠܥܠܡ. [30]ܣ̈ܓܝܐܐ ܕܝܢ ܩܕ̈ܡܝܐ
ܕܢܗܘܘܢ ܐ̈ܚܪܝܐ. ܘܐ̈ܚܪܝܐ ܕܢܗܘܘܢ ܩܕ̈ܡܝܐ ܀

ܕܥܛܠܐ...ܕܢܥܘܠ] ܣܘ ܡܟܢܐ ܥܛܠܐ ܠܐܝܠܝܢ ܕܬܟܝܠܝܢ ܥܠ ܢܟܣܝܗܘܢ ܕܢܥܠܘܢ A (= Mk x 23) ܠܡܠܟܘܬܐ ܕܫܡܝܐ S 24 ܬܘܒ......ܕܦܫܝܩ ܗܘ] ܘܬܘܒ ܐܡܪ. ܦܫܝܩ ܓܝܪ A (om. ܓܝܪ Aᵇ) ܠܓܡܠܐ ܕܢܥܒܪ] ܠܓܡܠܐ ܕܢܥܒܪ S; ܕܬܥܒܪ ܓܡܠܐ A (ܕܢܥܒܪ Aᵇ) ܠܥܬܝܪܐ] om. ܠ A ܠܡܠܟܘܬܗ ܕܐܠܗܐ A 25 ܬܘܒ...ܬܠܡܝܕܘܗܝ] ܘܟܕ ܫܡܥܘ ܕܝܢ ܬܠܡܝܕܐ S ܬܡܝܗܝܢ ܗܘܘ] ܘܐܬܕܡܪܘ S ܘܕܚܠܘ] *on an erasure in C; om. S* ܗܘܘ 2°] *om.* S ܡܢܘ] ܡܢ S ܠܡܚܐ] ܠܡܚܝܐ S[vid] (*cf* Mt xvii 19 S) 26 ܒܝܬ] ܡܢ S 27 ܗܐ ܚܢܢ] ܐܚܢܢ S ܠܟܠ S 28 ܠܗܘܢ] ܠܗ S ܬܪܘܢܘܣ] ܒܟܘܪܣܝܐ S: *for* A 280, *see Notes*, vol. ii ܘܐܦ ܐܢܬܘܢ] *om.* A; *om.* ܘ S ܠܬܪ̈ܬܥܣܪܐ S ܐܝܣܪܐܝܠ S 29 ܐܘ ܐ̈ܚܐ S ܐܘ ܐܢܬܬܐ] *om.* S ܕܝܠܝ] *om.* S ܚܕ ܒܡܐ̈ܐ ܢܣܒ S ܘܒܥܠܡܐ ܕܐܬܐ] ܘ S 30 ܕܝܢ] ܓܝܪ S

"Amen, I say to you It is difficult for a rich man to enter the *C S*
24 kingdom of heaven. Now again I say to you It is easier for a camel
to pass through the eye of a needle than a rich man into the kingdom
25 of heaven."¶ Now again when his disciples heard they were astonished ¶*A*
and were afraid exceedingly, and were saying: "Who then can live?"
26 Jesus looked upon them and said to them: "This among men cannot
27 be, but God everything can do." Then answered Simon Kepha and
said to him: "Lo, we have left everything and have come after thee;
28 what then shall we have?" Jesus saith to them: "Amen, I say to you
Ye that have come after me, in the new birth, what *time* the Son of
Man sitteth on the Throne of his glory, §ye shall sit yourselves also §*A* 432
upon twelve thrones and shall judge the twelve families of the
29 House of Israel.¶ And every man that hath left houses and brothers, ¶*A*
or sisters, or mother, or wife, or sons, or fields, for my sake, even
mine, shall receive an hundredfold and in the world to come shall
30 inherit life eternal. But *there are* many first that shall be last,
and last that shall be first.

It is...enter] See how difficult *it is* for them which trust in their wealth to enter *A* E^{170} (=Mk x 23) 24 Now again...easier] And again he saith: Easier peradventure *A* (*om.* peradventure A^b, *and see on* Mk x 25) for a camel to pass through] for a camel to enter *S*; that a she-camel should enter *A* (*om.* she- A^b) of heaven] of God *A* 25 Now again...heard] Now when the disciples heard *S* were astonished] wondered *S* and were afraid] *on an erasure in C*; *om. S* were saying] say *S* 26 among] from *S* 27 Lo, we] We *S* 28 to them] to him *S* Throne (θρόνος)] throne *S* (*the same word as in the latter half of the verse*): *for A* 280, *see Notes*, vol. ii yourselves also] *om. A* 29 and brothers] or brothers *S* or wife] *om. S* even mine] *om. S* an hundredfold shall receive *S* in the world to come] *om. S* 30 But] For *S*

CS [1]ܕܡܝܐ ܕܝܢ ܡܠܟܘܬܐ ܕܫܡܝܐ. ܠܓܒܪܐ ܡܪܐ ܒܝܬܐ· ܕܢܦܩ
ܒܨܦܪܐ ܠܡܐܓܪ ܦܥܠܐ ܠܟܪܡܗ. [2]ܘܫܘܝ ܥܡܗܘܢ ܥܡ ܦܥܠܐ.
ܡܢ ܕܝܢܪܐ ܚܕ ܠܦܥܠܐ ܚܕ ܒܝܘܡܐ ܚܕ. ܘܫܕܪ ܐܢܘܢ
col 2 ܠܟܪܡܗ. [3]ܘܢܦܩ ܒܬܠܬ ܫ̈ܥܝܢ. ܘܚܙܐ ܐ̈ܚܪܢܐ ܟܕ *ܩܝܡܝܢ ܒܫܘܩܐ
ܘܒܛܝܠܝܢ. [4]ܘܐܡܪ ܠܗܘܢ ܙܠܘ ܐܦ ܐܢܬܘܢ ܠܟܪܡܐ. ܘܡܕܡ
ܕܘܠܐ ܐܬܠ ܠܟܘܢ. ܘܐܙܠܘ. [5]ܘܢܦܩ ܬܘܒ ܒܫܬ ܫ̈ܥܝܢ. ܘܒܬܫܥ
ܫ̈ܥܝܢ. ܘܗܟܘܬ ܥܒܕ. [6]ܘܢܦܩ ܒܚܕܥܣܪܐ ܫ̈ܥܝܢ. ܘܐܫܟܚ ܐ̈ܚܪܢܐ
ܟܕ ܩܝܡܝܢ. ܘܐܡܪ ܠܗܘܢ ܡܢܐ ܩܝܡܝܢ ܐܢܬܘܢ ܘܒܛܝܠܝܢ
ܝܘܡܐ ܟܠܗ. [7]ܐܡܪܝܢ ܠܗ ܐܢܫ ܠܐ ܐܓܪܢ. ܐܡܪ ܠܗܘܢ
ܙܠܘ ܐܦ ܐܢܬܘܢ ܠܟܪܡܐ. ܘܡܕܡ ܕܘܠܐ ܐܬܠ ܠܟܘܢ. [8]ܘܟܕ
ܗܘܐ ܪܡܫܐ ܐܡܪ ܡܪܐ ܟܪܡܐ ܠܪܒ ܒܝܬܗ. ܩܪܝ ܠܗܘܢ
ܦܥܠܐ ܘܗܒ ܠܗܘܢ ܐܓܪܗܘܢ. ܘܫܪܐ ܡܢ ܐ̈ܚܪܝܐ ܥܕܡܐ
fol 32 v ܠܩܕ̈ܡܝܐ. [9]ܟܕ ܐܬܘ ܕܝܢ ܗܠܝܢ *ܕܒܚܕܥܣܪܐ ܫ̈ܥܝܢ ܫܩܠܘ
ܕܝܢܪܐ ܕܝܢܪܐ. [10]ܘܟܕ ܐܬܘ ܩܕ̈ܡܝܐ ܣܒܪܝܢ ܗܘܘ ܕܠܗܘܢ ܝܬܪ
ܢܬܠ· ܘܢܣܒܘ ܐܦ ܗܢܘܢ ܕܝܢܪܐ ܕܝܢܪܐ. [11]ܘܟܕ ܢܣܒܘ ܪܛܢܘ ܥܠ
ܡܪܐ ܒܝܬܐ [12]ܘܐܡܪܝܢ ܠܗ. ܗܠܝܢ ܐ̈ܚܪܝܐ ܚܕܐ ܫܥܐ ܥܒܕܘ.
ܘܐܫܘܝܬ ܐܢܘܢ ܥܡܢ ܕܫܩܠܢ ܝܘܩܪܗ ܕܝܘܡܐ ܟܠܗ ܘܫܘܒܐ.
[13]ܗܘ ܕܝܢ ܥܢܐ ܘܐܡܪ ܠܚܕ ܡܢܗܘܢ· ܪܚܡܝ ܠܐ ܬܗܘܪ. ܠܐ

---

1 ܕܝܢ] *om.* S ܡܪܒܝܬܐ S 2 ܥܡ ܦܥܠܐ] *om* S 3 ܟܕ ܩܝܡܝܢ] ܕܩܝܡܝܢ S ܘܒܛܝܠܝܢ S (*cf ver.* 6) 4 ܘܐܡܪ] *om.* ܘ S ܐܦ] *om.* ܘ S ܘܡܕܡ ܕܘܠܐ] ܘܡܐ ܕܙܕܩ S ܘܐܙܠܘ] *om.* S 5 ܫ̈ܥܝܢ 2°] *om.* S 6 ܘܐܫܟܚ] ܘܚܙܐ S ܕܩܝܡܝܢ S (*cf ver.* 3) ܘܐܡܪ] *om.* ܘ S ܐܢܬܘܢ] + ܗܪܟܐ S ܘܒܛܝܠܝܢ S (*cf ver.* 3) ܟܠܗ ܝܘܡܐ S 7 ܐܢܫ ܠܐ] *tr.* S ܠܟܪܡܐ] + ܕܝܠܝ S ܘܡܕܡ ܕܘܠܐ ܐܬܠ ܠܟܘܢ] *om.* S 8 ܗܘܐ] + ܕܝܢ S ܟܪܡܐ] *om.* S ܠܪܒܝܬܗ S ܠܗܘܢ ܦܥܠܐ] ܐܢܘܢ ܠܦܥܠܐ S ܘܫܪܐ] ܘܫܪܝ S 9 ܟܕ ܐܬܘ ܕܝܢ] ܘܟܕ ܐܬܘ S ܗܠܝܢ] ܗܢܘܢ S ܕܝܢܪ ܕܝܢܪ S 10 ܕܝܢܪ ܕܝܢܪ S 11 ܘܟܕ ܢܣܒܘ ܕܝܢ] ܟܕ ܢܣܒܘ S ܪܛܢܘ] ܪܛܢܝܢ S ܡܪܒܝܬܐ S 12 ܠܗ] *om.* S ܚܕܐ] ܗܘ ܚܕܐ S ܘܐܫܘܝܬ] *om.* ܘ S ܟܠܗ] *om.* S ܘܫܘܒܐ] ܒܫܘܒܐ S: *cf* Thos[230] 13 ܬܗܘܪ] ܡܥܘܠ ܐܢܐ ܠܟ S ܐܝܠܝܢ ܕ...ܫܩܠܘ ܝܘܩܪܗ ܕܝܘܡܐ ܟܠܗ ܒܚܘܪܐ

XX 1 "Now like is the kingdom of heaven to a man, the master of a *C S*
2 house, that went forth at dawn to hire labourers for his vineyard, and
he settled with those same labourers for one denar to one labourer
3 for one day; and he sent them to his vineyard. And he went forth
at the third hour and saw others standing in the street and idling,
4 and he said to them: 'Go ye also to the vineyard, and that which it is
5 fitting I will give you.' And they went; and he went forth again at
6 the sixth hour, and at the ninth hour, and did likewise. And he
went forth at the eleventh hour and found others standing, and he
7 said to them: 'Why are ye standing and idling all the day?' They
say to him: 'No man hath hired us.' He saith to them: 'Go ye also
8 to the vineyard and what is right I will give you.' And when it was
evening the lord of the vineyard said to his steward: 'Call those
labourers and give them their hire, and begin from the last until the
9 first.' Now when there came those of the eleventh hour they took up
10 a denar each. And when the first came they were supposing that to
11 them he would give more,—and they also took a denar each. And
when they saw they murmured against the master of the house,
12 and they say to him: 'These last--one hour have they tilled,
and thou hast made them equal with us that have borne the weight
13 of the whole day and the heat.' But he answered and said to
one of them: 'My friend, do not injure me; was it not for a

---

1 Now like] Like *S* 2 those same labourers] them *S* 4 and he said] He saith *S* that which it is fitting] what is right *S* And they went] *om. S* 5 hour 2°] *om. S* 6 found] saw *S* and he said] He saith *S* standing 2°] + here *S* (*not E*[176]) 7 vineyard] + of mine *S* and what... give you] *om. S* 8 And when] Now when *S* of the vineyard] *om. S* those] the *S* hire, and begin....first'] hire;' and he began....first *S* 9 Now] And *S* 11 And] Now *S* murmured] murmur *S* 12 to him] *om. S* These last, that one hour have tilled, thou hast made equal with us *S* whole] *om. S* and the heat] in the heat *S*: *cf Thos*[230] 'them. . that have borne the weight of the whole day at noon' 13 do not injure me] I am not injuring thee *S*

ܗܘܐ ܒܕܝܢܪܐ ܩܨܬ ܥܡܝ. ¹⁴ܣܒ ܕܝܠܟ ܘܙܠ· ܘܐܢ ܨܒܐ ܐܢܐ C S
ܕܐܬܠ ܠܗܢܐ ܐܚܪܝܐ ܐܝܟ ܕܠܟ. ¹⁵ܠܐ ܫܠܝܛ ܐܢܐ ܕܐܥܒܕ
ܒܕܝܠܝ ܡܕܡ ܕܨܒܐ ܐܢܐ. ܐܘ ܕܠܡܐ ܥܝܢܟ ܒܝܫܐ ܕܐܢܐ ܛܒ
ܐܢܐ. ¹⁶ܗܟܢܐ *ܢܗܘܘܢ ܐܚܪ̈ܝܐ ܩܕܡ̈ܝܐ. ܘܩܕܡ̈ܝܐ ܢܗܘܘܢ col 2
ܐܚܪ̈ܝܐ. ܣܓܝܐܝܢ ܐܢܘܢ ܓܝܪ ܩܪ̈ܝܐ ܘܙܥܘܪܝܢ ܓܒ̈ܝܐ ܀
¹⁷ܟܕ ܣܠܩ ܗܘܐ ܝܫܘܥ ܠܐܘܪܫܠܡ. ܕܒܪ ܗܘܐ ܥܡܗ ܠܬܪ̈ܥܣܪܬܗ
ܒܐܘܪܚܐ. ܘܐܡܪ ܠܗܘܢ ܒܠܚܘܕܝܗܘܢ܆ ¹⁸ܗܐ ܣܠܩܝܢ ܚܢܢ
ܠܐܘܪܫܠܡ. ܘܒܪܗ ܕܐܢܫܐ ܡܫܬܠܡ ܠܪ̈ܒܝ ܟܗܢܐ ܘܠܣܦܪ̈ܐ.
ܘܢܚܝܒܘܢܝܗ ܠܡܘܬܐ. ¹⁹ܘܢܫܠܡܘܢܝܗ ܠܥܡ̈ܡܐ. ܘܢܒܙܚܘܢ ܒܗ
ܘܢܢܓܕܘܢܝܗ. ܘܢܙܩܦܘܢܝܗ. ܘܠܝܘܡܐ ܕܬܠܬܐ ܢܩܘܡ ܀
²⁰ܗܝܕܝܢ ܩܪܒܬ ܠܘܬܗ ܐܡܗܘܢ ܕܒ̈ܢܝ ܙܒܕܝ، ܗܝ ܘܒܢܝܗ. ܘܢܦܠܬ
ܣܓܕܬ ܠܗ. ܘܫܐܠܐ ܗܘܬ ܠܗ ܡܕܡ. ²¹ܗܘ ܕܝܢ ܐܡܪ ܠܗ̇
ܡܢܐ *ܨܒܝܐ ܐܢܬܝ. ܐܡܪܐ ܠܗ ܡܪܝ، ܕܢܬܒܘܢ ܗܠܝܢ ܬܪ̈ܝܗܘܢ fol 33 r
ܒ̈ܢܝ ܚܕ ܡܢ ܝܡܝܢܟ ܘܚܕ ܡܢ ܣܡܠܟ ܒܡܠܟܘܬܟ ܘܒܫܘܒܚܟ.
²²ܥܢܐ ܝܫܘܥ ܘܐܡܪ ܠܗ̇. ܠܐ ܝܕܥܝܢ ܐܢܬܘܢ ܡܢܐ ܫܐܠܝܢ
ܐܢܬܘܢ܆ ܡܫܟܚܝܢ ܐܢܬܘܢ ܠܡܫܬܐ ܟܣܐ ܗܢܐ ܕܐܢܐ ܥܬܝܕ
ܠܡܫܬܐ. ܐܡܪܝܢ ܡܫܟܚܝܢ ܐܢܚܢ· ²³ܐܡܪ ܠܗܘܢ ܝܫܘܥ·
ܕܬܫܬܘܢ ܟܣܐ ܗܢܐ ܡܫܟܚܝܢ ܐܢܬܘܢ܆ ܕܬܬܥܡܕܘܢ ܕܝܢ ܚܕ ܡܢ
ܝܡܝܢܝ ܘܚܕ ܡܢ ܣܡܠܝ. ܗܕܐ ܠܐ ܗܘܬ ܕܝܠܝ ܕܐܬܠ ܠܟܘܢ܆
ܐܠܐ ܠܐܝܠܝܢ ܕܐܬܛܝܒܬ ܠܗܘܢ ܡܢ ܠܘܬ ܐܒܝ. ²⁴ܘܟܕ ܫܡܥܘ

ܒܕܝܢܪ S   ܥܡܝ] ܥܡܢ S   14 ܣܒ] ܫ̈ܩܘܠ S (one letter only illegible)
ܕܝܠܟ] ܕܝܢܪܟ S   ܘܐܢ] om. ܘ S   ܕܐܬܠ] pr. ܕܝܢ S   15 ܕܐܥܒܕ ܒܕܝܠܝ]
tr. S   ܡܕܡ] ܟܠ ܡܕܡ S   ܕܠܡܐ] om. S   16 ܢܗܘܘܢ 2°] om. S   ܓܝܪ]
om. S: for A 147, see on Mt xxii 14   17 ܗܘܐ 2°] om. S   ܥܡܗ ܒܠܚܘܕܝܗܘܢ S
18 ܚܢܢ] ܐܢܚܢ S   ܘܡܫܬܠܡ ܒܪܗ ܕܐܢܫܐ S   19 ܠܥܡ̈ܡܐ] ܠܥܡܡܐ S
20 ܠܘܬܗ] ܠܗ S.   21 ܡܢܐ ܨܒܝܐ ܐܢܬܝ] C (sic); ܨܒܝܐ ܐܢܬܝ S   ܬܪ̈ܝܗܘܢ] ܬܪܝܢ S
ܘܒܫܘܒܚܟ] om. S   22 ܠܗ̇] ܠܗܘܢ S   ܗܢܐ] om. S   23 ܕܬܬܥܡܕܘܢ....ܐܢܬܘܢ]
ܟܣܝ ܫܬܝܢ ܐܢܬܘܢ S: ܟܣܝ has been changed (? by the original scribe) into ܟܣܐ
ܚܕ] om. S   ܘܚܕ] om. ܚܕ S   ܕܝܠܝ] ܠܝ S   ܕܐܬܛܝܒܬ....ܡܢ ܠܘܬ ܐܒܝ]
ܕܡܛܝܒ ܠܗܘܢ ܐܒܝ S   24 ܘܟܕ] om. ܘ S

14 denar thou didst settle with me? Take thine own and go, and if I *C S*
15 am willing that I should give to this last as to thee, have I not
authority to do with mine own that which I will? Or perchance
16 thine eye *is* evil, that I am good?' So shall the last be first and the
first shall be last, for many are the called and few the chosen."

17 And when Jesus was going up to Jerusalem he had taken with
him his Twelve in the way, and said to them between himself and
18 them: "Lo, we go up to Jerusalem, and the Son of Man is delivered
up to the chief priests and to the scribes, and they will condemn him
19 to death, and will deliver him up to the peoples, and they will mock
at him and scourge him and crucify him, and the third day he will
rise."

20 Then drew near unto him the mother of the sons of Zebedee, she
and her sons, and she fell down *and* worshipped him, and was asking
21 him a thing. But he said to her: "What wouldest thou?" She saith
to him: "My Lord, that these my two sons may sit one on thy right
22 and one on thy left in thy kingdom and in thy glory." Jesus
answered and said to her: "Ye know not what ye are asking. Are
ye able to drink this cup that I am about to drink?" They say:
23 "We are able." Jesus saith to them: "That ye should drink this
cup ye are able; but that ye should sit one on my right and one
on my left, this is not mine that I should give *it* to you, but to those
24 for whom it hath been made ready by my Father." And when the

---

thou...with me] I settled with thee *S* 14 Take] Take up *S* thine own] thy denar *S* and if] but if *S* 15 with mine own to do *S*; in mine own house to do *E*[177] that which] what *S* perchance] *om. S* 16 shall be] *om. S* for] *om. S* 17 had taken] took *S* between themselves and him *S* 18 is delivered] will be delivered *S* 19 the peoples] the people *S* 20 unto him] to him *S* 21 and in thy glory] *om. S* 22 to her] to them *S* this cup] the cup *S* 23 That ye...ye are able] My cup ye *shall* drink *S* (*for* 'My cup' *S now has* 'The cup') one 1° *&* 2°] *om. S* mine] for me *S* for whom...my Father] for whom my Father maketh *it* ready *S* 24 And when] When *S*

C (S) ¶S ܥܣ̈ܪܐ ܪܓܙܘ ܥܠ ܗܢܘܢ ܬܪ̈ܝܢ ܐ̈ܚܝܢ.¶ [25]ܘܩܪܐ ܐܢܘܢ *ܝܫܘܥ
col 2 ܘܐܡܪ ܠܗܘܢ܆ ܝܕܥܝܢ ܐܢܬܘܢ ܕܪ̈ܫܝܗܘܢ ܕܥ̈ܡܡܐ ܡܪ̈ܝܗܘܢ
ܐܢܘܢ܆ ܘܪܘܪ̈ܒܢܝܗܘܢ ܫܠܝܛܝܢ ܐܢܘܢ ܥܠܝܗܘܢ܆ [26]ܒܝܢܬܟܘܢ
ܕܝܢ ܠܐ ܢܗܘܐ ܗܟܢܐ. ܐܠܐ ܡܢ ܕܨܒܐ ܒܟܘܢ ܕܢܗܘܐ ܪܒܐ.
ܢܗܘܐ ܠܟܘܢ ܡܫܡܫܢܐ. [27]ܘܡܢ ܕܨܒܐ ܒܟܘܢ ܕܢܗܘܐ ܩܕܡܝܐ.
ܢܗܘܐ ܠܟܘܢ ܥܒܕܐ. [28]ܐܝܟܢܐ ܕܒܪܗ ܕܐܢܫܐ ܠܐ ܐܬܐ
ܕܢܫܬܡܫ. ܐܠܐ ܕܢܫܡܫ. ܘܕܢܬܠ ܢܦܫܗ ܦܘܪܩܢܐ ܚܠܦ ܣܓ̈ܝܐܐ.
ܐܢܬܘܢ ܕܝܢ ܒܥܘ ܕܡܢ ܙܥܘܪܘܬܐ ܬܐܪܒܘܢ. ܘܠܐ ܡܢ ܪܒܘܬܐ
ܬܙܥܪܘܢ ܀

ܡܐ ܕܡܙܕܡܢܝܢ ܐܢܬܘܢ ܠܒܝܬ ܐܫܬܘܬܐ. ܠܐ ܬܗܘܘܢ
fol 33 v ܡܣܬܡܟܝܢ ܒܕܘܟܬܐ ܡܝܬܪܬܐ. ܕܠܐ ܢܐܬܐ ܡܢ *ܕܡܝܬܪ ܡܢܟ.
ܘܢܐܡܪ ܠܟ ܡܪܐ ܐܫܬܘܬܐ ܐܬܩܪܒ ܠܬܚܬ· ܘܬܬܒܗܬ ܒ̈ܝܢܝ
ܣ̈ܡܝܟܐ· ܐܢ ܕܝܢ ܬܣܬܡܟ ܒܕܘܟܬܐ ܒܨܝܪܬܐ. ܘܢܐܬܐ ܡܢ
ܕܒܨܝܪ ܡܢܟ. ܘܢܐܡܪ ܠܟ ܡܪܐ ܐܫܬܘܬܐ ܐܬܩܪܒ. ܘܐܬܥܠܐ
ܘܐܬܬܡܟ. ܘܬܗܘܐ ܠܟ ܬܫܒܘܚܬܐ ܡܝܬܪܬܐ ܒ̈ܝܢܝ
ܣ̈ܡܝܟܐ. ܀ .

[29]ܘܟܕ ܢܦܩܝܢ ܗܘܘ ܡܢ ܐܝܪܝܚܘ. ܐܬܐ ܗܘܐ ܒܬܪܗ ܟܢܫܐ
ܣܓܝܐܐ. [30]ܘܬܪܝܢ ܣ̈ܡܝܐ ܝܬܒܝܢ ܗܘܘ ܥܠ ܝܕ ܐܘܪܚܐ. ܘܟܕ
ܫܡܥܘ ܕܝܫܘܥ ܥܒܪ. ܩܥܝܢ ܗܘܘ ܘܐܡܪܝܢ. ܐܬܪܚܡ ܥܠܝܢ
ܒܪܗ ܕܕܘܝܕ. [31]ܘܟ̈ܢܫܐ ܗܢܘܢ ܟܐܝܢ ܗܘܘ ܒܗܘܢ ܕܢܫܬܩܘܢ·
ܗܢܘܢ ܕܝܢ ܐܪܝܡܘ ܩܠܗܘܢ ܘܐܡܪܝܢ. ܐܬܪܚܡ ܥܠܝܢ ܡܪܢ
col 2 *ܒܪܗ ܕܕܘܝܕ· [32]ܘܩܡ ܝܫܘܥ ܘܩܪܐ ܐܢܘܢ܆ ܘܐܡܪ ܡܢܐ ܨܒܝܢ
ܐܢܬܘܢ ܕܐܥܒܕ ܠܟܘܢ܆ [33]ܐܡܪܝܢ ܠܗ ܡܪܢ ܕܢܬܦܬܚܢ

ܪܓܙܘ] ܪܛܢܘ S   28 *fin.*] *The long interpolation here read in C could never have stood on the missing leaf of S, because the text from* xx 25 *to* xxi 20 *is more than sufficient to fill two pages of S without this passage. Probably therefore S also omitted the sentence* ܘܢܟܡܘ....ܕܢܚܘ, *added in C to the end of* xxi 9

25 Ten heard, they were wroth against those two brothers.¶ And Jesus C (S) ¶S
called them and said to them: "Ye know that the chiefs of the
peoples are their lords, and their nobles have authority over them.
26 Now among you it shall not be so, but he that would with you be
27 the great one shall be to you a servant, and he that would with you
28 be first shall be to you a slave; even as the Son of Man came not to
be served but to serve, and give his life *to be* a redemption for many.
But ye, seek ye that from littleness ye may increase, and not from
greatness become little.

"What *time* ye are bidden to a supper-party be not sitting down *to meat* in an honourable place, that there may not come one more honourable than thou, and the lord of the supper say to thee 'Bring thyself down,' and thou be confounded in the eyes of the guests. But if thou sit down *to meat* in a lesser place, and there come one less than thou, and the lord of the supper say to thee 'Bring thyself and come up and sit down *to meat*,' then thou shalt have more glory in the eyes of the guests."

29 And when they were going forth from Jericho a great multitude
30 was coming after him, and two blind men were sitting by the way-
side; and when they heard that Jesus was passing by, they were
crying out and saying: "Have compassion on us, son of David!"
31 And those multitudes were rebuking them that they should be silent,
but they lifted up their voice, and say: "Have compassion on us,
32 our Lord, son of David!" And Jesus stood and called them, and
33 said: "What would ye that I should do for you?" They say to him:

---

were wroth] murmured *S* 28 *fin.*] *The long interpolation here read in C could never have stood on the missing leaf of S, because from* xx 25 *to* xxi 20 *is more than two pages of S without this passage. Probably therefore S also omitted the sentence* 'And many went forth...that they saw', *added in C to the end of* xxi 9 then] *lit.* 'and': *cf* Lk xii 45, 46

ܥ̈ܝܢܝܢ ܘܢܚܙܝܢ. [34]ܘܐܬܪܚܡ ܥܠܝܗܘܢ܂ ܘܩܪܒ ܠܥܝܢܝܗܘܢ܂ ܘܡܢܗ̇ C
ܒܫܥܬܐ ܚܙܘ ܘܐܙܠܘ ܒܬܪܗ ܀

[1]ܘܟܕ ܩܪܒ ܠܐܘܪܫܠܡ. ܘܐܬܐ ܠܒܝܬ ܦܓܐ. ܥܠ ܓܢܒ ܛܘܪܐ
ܕܒܝܬ ܙܝܬܐ. ܗܝܕܝܢ ܫܕܪ ܝܫܘܥ ܬܪܝܢ ܡܢ ܬܠܡܝܕܘܗܝ. [2]ܘܐܡܪ
ܠܗܘܢ܂ ܙܠܘ ܠܩܪܝܬܐ ܗܕܐ ܕܠܘܩܒܠܟܘܢ܂ ܘܗܐ ܡܫܟܚܝܢ ܐܢܬܘܢ
ܥܝܠܐ ܐܣܝܪܐ ܥܡ ܐܡܗ̇. ܘܫܪܘ ܐܝܬܘ ܐܢܘܢ
ܠܝ. [3]ܘܐܢ ܐܢܫ ܢܐܡܪ ܠܟܘܢ ܡܕܡ. ܐܡܪܘ ܠܗ ܠܡܪܗܘܢ
fol 34 r ܡܬܒܥܝܢ. ܘܡܚܕܐ ܡܫܕܪ *ܠܗܘܢ܂ [4]ܗܕܐ ܕܝܢ ܕܗܘܬ. ܕܢܬܡܠܐ
ܡܕܡ ܕܐܬܐܡܪ ܡܢ ܢܒܝܐ ܕܐܡܪ ܗܘܐ. [5]ܐܡܪܘ ܠܒܪܬ
ܨܗܝܘܢ܂ ܗܐ ܡܠܟܟܝ ܐܬܐ ܠܟܝ. ܙܕܝܩ ܘܡܟܝܟ. ܘܪܟܝܒ ܥܠ
ܚܡܪܐ ܘܥܠ ܥܝܠܐ ܒܪ ܐܬܢܐ. [6]ܘܐܙܠܘ ܗܢܘܢ ܬܠܡܝܕܘܗܝ܂
ܘܥܒܕܘ ܐܝܟ ܕܦܩܕ ܐܢܘܢ ܝܫܘܥ. [7]ܘܐܝܬܝܘ ܠܚܡܪܐ ܘܠܥܝܠܐ.
ܘܣܡܘ ܗܘܘ ܡܪ̈ܛܘܛܝܗܘܢ܂ ܘܪܟܒ ܝܫܘܥ ܥܠ ܚܕ ܡܢܗܘܢ܂
[8]ܘܣܘܓܐܐ ܕܟܢܫܐ ܗܘ ܦܪܣܘ ܗܘܘ ܡܪ̈ܛܘܛܝܗܘܢ ܒܐܘܪܚܐ.
ܐܚܪ̈ܢܐ ܕܝܢ ܦܣܩܝܢ ܗܘܘ ܣ̈ܘܟܐ ܡܢ ܐ̈ܝܠܢܐ ܘܪܡܝܢ ܗܘܘ
ܒܐܘܪܚܐ. [9]ܟ̈ܢܫܐ ܕܝܢ ܕܐܙܠܝܢ ܗܘܘ ܩܕܡܘܗܝ܂ ܘܒܬܪܗ.
col 2 ܩܥܝܢ ܗܘܘ ܘܐܡܪܝܢ. ܐܘܫܥܢܐ ܠܒܪܗ ܕܕܘܝܕ. ܒܪܝܟ *ܗܘ
ܕܐܬܐ ܒܫܡܗ ܕܡܪܝܐ. ܐܘܫܥܢܐ ܒܡܪ̈ܘܡܐ. ܘܢܦܩܘ ܠܐܘܪܥܗ
ܩ̈ܠܝܬܐ. ܘܫܕܝܢ ܗܘܘ ܘܡܫܒܚܝܢ ܠܐܠܗܐ. ܥܠ ܟܠ ܡܐ
ܕܚܙܘ ܀

[10]ܘܟܕ ܥܠ ܠܐܘܪܫܠܡ. ܐܬܬܙܝܥܬ ܟܠܗ̇ ܡܕܝܢܬܐ. ܘܐܡܪܝܢ ܡܢܘ
ܗܢܐ. [11]ܐܡܪܝܢ ܠܗܘܢ ܟ̈ܢܫܐ ܗܠܝܢ. ܗܢܘ ܝܫܘܥ ܢܒܝܐ ܕܡܢ
ܢܨܪܬ ܕܓܠܝܠܐ. [12]ܘܥܠ ܝܫܘܥ ܠܗܝܟܠܐ ܕܐܠܗܐ. ܘܐܦܩ ܡܢ
ܗܝܟܠܐ ܕܐܠܗܐ ܠܟܠܗܘܢ ܙ̈ܒܘܢܐ ܘܡܙ̈ܒܢܢܐ. ܘܗܦܟ ܝܫܘܥ
ܦܬܘܪ̈ܐ ܕܡܥ̈ܪܦܢܐ. ܘܟܘܪ̈ܣܘܬܗܘܢ ܕܗܢܘܢ ܕܡܙܒܢܝܢ ܝܘ̈ܢܐ.
[13]ܘܐܡܪ ܠܗܘܢ ܟܬܝܒ ܗܘ ܕܒܝܬܝ, ܒܝܬ ܨܠܘܬܐ ܢܬܩܪܐ

---

3 ܠܡܪܗܘܢ ܡܬܒܥܝܢ] *so* Ephr IV 109 A (*with* ܕ *prefixed, sic lege*), *and see Introd.* vol. ii 9 *fin.*] *See Note to* xx 28

"Our Lord, that our eyes may be opened and we may see thee." *C*
34 And he had compassion on them, and he touched their eyes, and in
the same hour they saw and went after him.

xxi 1 And when he drew near to Jerusalem, and came to Beth Phagge
by the side of the Mount of the Olive-orchard, then sent Jesus two of
2 his disciples, and said to them: "Go to this village over against you.
Lo, ye will find a certain ass tied and her colt by her side; loose *and*
3 bring them to me. And if anyone say to you aught, say to him,
'For their Lord are they required,' and immediately he will send
4 them." Now this that came to pass *happened* that that might be
5 fulfilled which was said by the prophet, who had said: "Say to the
daughter of Zion, 'Lo, thy king cometh to thee, righteous and meek,
6 and riding on an ass and on a colt the foal of a she-ass.'" And those
7 disciples of his went and did as Jesus commanded them, and they
brought the ass and the colt, and they had spread their cloaks, and
8 Jesus rode upon them. And a number of that multitude had strewn
their cloaks in the way, but others were cutting branches from the trees
9 and were casting *them* in the way. And those multitudes that were
going before him and with him were crying out and saying: "Osanna
to the son of David! Blessed is he that cometh in the name of the
LORD! Osanna in the highest!" And many went forth to meet
him, and they were rejoicing and glorifying God for all that they
saw.

10 And when he entered Jerusalem the whole city was troubled, and
11 they say: "Who is this?" Those multitudes say to them: "This is
12 Jesus the prophet from Nazareth of Galilee." And Jesus entered
the Temple of God, and put forth from the Temple of God all the
buyers and the sellers; and Jesus overturned the tables of the
13 money-changers, and the thrones of those selling doves, and he said
to them: "It is written 'My House a House of Prayer shall be called

---

3 their Lord] *or*, 'their master': *so* Ephr IV 109 A (*sic lege*), *and see Introd.* vol. ii 9 *fin.*] *See Note to* xx 28. Diat[ar] xxxix 31—35 *gives a different combination of* Jn xii 13 *and* Lk xix 37 *with* Mt xxi 9

C [S] ܠܟܠܗܘܢ ܚܝ̈ܠܘܬܐ. ܐܢܬܘܢ ܕܝܢ ܒܒܢܝ ܟܢܘܫܬܗܘܢ، ܘܡܕܝܢ̈ܬܐ ܕܫܠܝ̈ܛܢܐ.

fol 34 v [14] ܘܐܡܪ ܠܗ *ܒܡܫܠܐ ܡܢܘ ܐܩܝܡܢܝ ܕܝܢܐ ܘܦܠܓܐ، ܥܠܝܟܘܢ. [15] ܘܐܡܪ

ܚܙܘ ܘܐܙܕܗܪܘ ܡܢ ܟܠܗ̇ ܪܥܝܢܐ ܕܥܠܝܟܘܢ ܕܠܐ ܗܘܐ ܚܝܐ ܕܒܪܢܫܐ ܒܡܕܡ ܕܐܝܬ ܠܗ.

ܕܟܠ ܡܕܡ. ܘܐܡܪ ܗܘܐ ܐܦ ܠܗܘܢ ܡܬܠܐ. ܐܝܬܘܗܝ.

ܠܗܘܢ [16] ܘܐܡܪ. ܠܐ ܐܢܫ ܐܝܬ ܗܘܐ ܥܬܝܪܐ ܐܡܪ ܗܠܝܢ. ܐܡܪ

ܠܗܘܢ ܢܦܫܝ. ܐܢܐ. ܠܐ ܡܬܒܥܝܐ ܠܝ ܕܐܬܪ ܡܢܗ ܐܘܨܪܐ ܕܥܠܠܬܐ

ܘܕܥܠܠܬܐ ܐܟܢܫ ܬܡܢ. [17] ܘܐܡܪ ܐܢܐ ܥܠܝܡܐ ܠܗ ܠܒܪ

ܡܢ ܡܬܚܫܒܐ. ܠܒܝܬ ܟܢܫܬܐ ܕܢܦܫܝ ܬܡܢ. [18] ܘܥܒܕܐ ܕܝܢ ܗܘ

ܢܦܫܝ ܠܡܬܚܫܒܘ. ܘܐܡܪ [19] ܘܐܡܪܐ ܬܬܐ ܥܕܐ ܒܐܘܪܚܐ.

ܘܐܬܐ ܠܗ̇ ܘܠܐ ܐܫܟܚ ܒܗ̇ ܡܕܡ. ܐܠܐ ܐܢܐ ܐܦܪ̈ܝܐ

ܒܠܚܘܕ. ܘܐܡܪ* ܠܗ̇ ܬܘܒ ܦ̈ܪܐ ܠܐ ܢܣܒܘܢ ܟܕ ܠܒܠܒ.

col 2 ܘܒܗ̇ ܒܥܠܬܐ ܒܥܠܬܐ ܗ̇ܝ، [20] ܘܥܒܕ ܚܘ ܬܠܝ̈ܬܐ، ܐܬܥܒܕܘ. §S

ܘܐܡܪ ܗܘܐ ܐܢܫܐ ܒܥܒܕܬܗ ܒܫܥܬ ܬܬܐ ܗܕܐ. [21] ܒܢܝܐ

ܡܫܡܥ ܘܐܡܪ ܠܗܘܢ. ܐܝܟܢ ܐܡܪܝܢܐ ܠܟܘܢ. ܕܐܢ ܬܗܘܐ

ܟܠܢ ܡܫܒܚܘܬܐ ܘܠܐ ܬܬܦܠܓܘܢ. ܠܐ ܒܠܚܘܕ ܐܝܟ ܗܕܐ

ܕܬܬܐ ܬܬܒܥܘܢ، ܐܠܐ ܐܢ ܬܬܐܡܪܘܢ ܠܦܬܓܡܐ ܗܢܐ

ܕܐܬܚܙܝ ܘܠܐ ܒܣܟܐ. ܢܦܫܐ ܠܟܘܢ ܗܢܐ. [22] ܘܟܠ ܡܕܡ

ܕܬܬܚܙܘܢ ܥܡ ܠܬܠܬܐ ܘܬܬܗܦܟܘܢ ܬܬܥܒܕܘܢ..

[23] ܘܥܒܕ ܐܬܐ ܠܡܫܠܐ. ܘܐܡܪ ܠܗ ܠܐ ܒܘ̈ܢܐ ܘܥ̈ܫܢܐ ܕܒܫܐ

fol 35 r ܘܐܡܪܝܢ *ܠܗ. ܒܐܢܫܐ ܥܘܬܪܐ ܗܘܝܢ ܒܒܪ ܐܢܫ. ܘܗܢܘܢ ܢܣܒ

ܠܝ ܥܘܬܪܢܐ ܗܢܐ. [24] ܒܢܐ ܢܣܒ ܘܐܡܪ ܠܗܘܢ. ܐܦ ܐܢܐ

ܐܫܟܠܘܢ ܡܠܬܐ ܗܕܐ ܕܬܐܡܪܘܢ ܠܝ. ܘܐܡܪ ܠܟܘܢ

ܒܐܢܫܐ ܥܘܬܪܢܐ ܒܒܢܝܐ ܗܠܝܢ [25] ܡܫܒܘܕܘܬܗ ܕܢܦܫܝܢ ܡܢ

20 ܬܠܡ̈ܝܕܘܗܝ] ܬܠܡܝܕܐ S ܗܘܘ] om. S ܗܕܐ] ܗܝ S
21 ܬܬܐ ܗܕܐ] ܬܬܐ ܗܕܐ S (sic) ܢܦܫܐ] pr. ܘ S (sic): cf Lk xi 8, xii 46
ܠܟܘܢ] om. S 22 ܡܕܡ] ܡܢ S *For the whole verse*,
cf ܐܡܪ ܕܠܝܬ ܡܕܡ ܕܬܫܐܠܘܢ ܠܐܠܗܐ ܡܢ ܠܬܠܬܝܢ ܕܠܐ ܢܬܠ ܠܟܘܢ A 487
23 ܠܗ 2°] om. S ܒܒܪ ܐܢܫ] + ܐܡܪ ܠܝ S ܘܗܢܘܢ] ܘܗܢܘ S 24 ܐܦ]
pr. ܘ S ܥܘܬܪܢ S

14 for all the peoples,' but ye have made it a den of pirates." And C [S]
there drew near to him in the Temple the blind and the deaf,
15 and he healed them. And when the scribes and the chief priests saw
the wonders that he did, and the children that were crying out in the
midst of the Temple and were saying: "Osanna to the son of David!"
16 it displeased them, and they say: "Dost thou not hear what these
are saying?" Jesus saith to them: "Yes; have ye never read 'Out
17 of the mouth of children and of infants I will make praise'?" And
he left them and went forth out from the city to Beth Ania, that he
18 might be there. Now in the morning when he was crossing over to
19 the city he hungered, and he saw a certain fig-tree in the way, and he
came unto it and did not find on it anything save leaves only, and he
said to it: "No more fruit will be on thee for ever!" And in the
20 same hour that fig-tree withered. And when §his disciples saw *it* they §S
wondered, and were saying: "How this fig-tree straightway withered!"
21 Jesus answered and said to them: "Amen, I say to you If there be
in you faith and ye doubt not, not only as this *thing* of the fig-tree
shall ye do, but if ye shall say to this hill 'Be taken up and fall
22 into the sea,' it shall be to you thus; and everything which ye shall
ask in prayer, and shall believe, ye shall receive."

23 And when he came to the Temple there drew near to him the
chief priests and the elders of the people, and they say to him:
"By what authority doest thou these things, and who gave thee this
24 authority?" Jesus answered and said to them: "I also will ask
you this word that ye shall say to me, and I will say to you by
25 what authority I do these things; the baptism of John, from

---

20 his disciples] the disciples *S* were saying] say *S* this] that *S* **21** this *thing* of the fig-tree] this fig-tree *S* it shall be] *pr.* then (*lit.* 'and') *S*: *cf* Lk xi 8, xii 46 to you] *om. S* **22** everything which] all that *S* ask] + 'of God' *E*[189] *Cf* 'He said There is nothing that ye shall ask God in your prayer that he will not give to you' *A* 487 **23** to him 2°] *om. S* these things] + say to us *S* (*cf* Lk xx 2) who] who is it *S* **24** I also] *pr.* and *S*

C S ܐܝܡܟܐ ܗܘܬ. ܡܢ ܫܡܝܐ ܐܘ ܡܢ ܒܢܝ ܐܢܫܐ. ܗܢܘܢ ܕܝܢ
ܡܬܪܥܝܢ ܗܘܘ ܒܢܦܫܗܘܢ ܘܐܡܪܝܢ ܗܘܘ. ܕܐܢ ܢܐܡܪ ܠܗ
ܕܡܢ ܫܡܝܐ ܗܝ. ܢܐܡܪ ܠܢ ܘܠܡܢܐ ܠܐ ܗܝܡܢܬܘܢ ܒܗ.
[26] ܘܐܢ ܢܐܡܪ ܕܡܢ ܒܢܝ ܐܢܫܐ ܗܝ. ܕܚܠܝܢ ܐܢܚܢ ܡܢ ܟܢܫܐ.
ܟܠܗܘܢ ܓܝܪ ܐܢܫܐ ܐܝܟ ܕܠܢܒܝܐ ܐܚܝܕܝܢ ܗܘܘ ܠܗ ܠܝܘܚܢܢ.
col 2 [27] ܘܐܡܪܝܢ ܠܗ ܠܐ ܝܕܥܝܢ ܐܢܚܢ. *ܐܡܪ ܠܗܘܢ ܝܫܘܥ. ܘܐܦ
ܠܐ ܐܢܐ ܐܡܪ ܐܢܐ ܠܟܘܢ ܒܐܝܢܐ ܫܘܠܛܢܐ ܥܒܕ ܐܢܐ
ܗܠܝܢ ܀

[28] ܐܡܟܢܐ ܕܝܢ ܡܬܚܙܝܐ ܠܟܘܢ. ܠܓܒܪܐ ܚܕ ܐܝܬ ܗܘܘ ܠܗ
ܬܪܝܢ ܒܢܝܢ. ܐܡܪ ܠܩܕܡܝܐ ܙܠ ܒܪܝ. ܝܘܡܢܐ ܥܒܕ ܥܒܕܐ
ܒܟܪܡܐ. [29] ܐܡܪ ܠܗ ܠܐ ܨܒܐ ܐܢܐ. ܐܚܪܝܬ ܕܝܢ ܬܘܬܗ
ܢܦܫܗ ܘܐܙܠ ܠܟܪܡܐ. [30] ܘܐܡܪ ܠܐܚܪܢܐ ܗܟܘܬ. ܘܗܢܐ ܘܐܡܪ
ܐܢ ܡܪܝ. ܘܠܐ ܐܙܠ. [31] ܡܢ ܡܢ ܗܠܝܢ ܬܪܝܢ ܡܬܚܙܝܐ ܠܟܘܢ ܕܥܒܕ
ܨܒܝܢܐ ܕܐܒܘܗܝ. ܐܡܪܝܢ ܠܗ ܗܘ ܩܕܡܝܐ. ܐܡܪ ܠܗܘܢ
ܝܫܘܥ. ܐܡܝܢ ܐܡܪ ܐܢܐ ܠܟܘܢ. ܕܡܟܣܐ ܘܙܢܝܬܐ ܡܩܕܡܝܢ
fol 35 v ܠܟܘܢ ܠܡܠܟܘܬܐ ܕܐܠܗܐ. [32] ܐܬܐ ܓܝܪ *ܠܘܬܟܘܢ ܝܘܚܢܢ
ܒܐܘܪܚܐ ܕܟܐܢܘܬܐ ܘܠܐ ܗܝܡܢܬܘܢܝܗܝ. ܡܟܣܐ ܕܝܢ ܘܙܢܝܬܐ
ܗܝܡܢܘ ܒܗ. ܐܢܬܘܢ ܕܝܢ ܐܦ ܠܐ ܒܬܪ ܚܙܝܬܘܢ ܬܬܘܒܘܢ
ܢܦܫܟܘܢ ܐܚܪܝܬ ܕܬܗܝܡܢܘܢܝܗܝ. ܀

[33] ܫܡܥܘ ܡܬܠܐ ܐܚܪܢܐ. ܓܒܪܐ ܚܕ ܡܪܐ ܒܝܬܐ ܐܝܬ ܗܘܐ.

---

25 ܡܬܪܥܝܢ] ܡܬܚܫܒܝܢ *S* ܗܘܘ 2°] *om. S* ܠܗ] *om. S* 26 ܐܢܫܐ 2°] *om. S* 27 ܘܐܡܪܝܢ] *pr.* ܘܥܢܘ *S* ܠܗ] ܠܝܫܘܥ *S* ܝܫܘܥ] ܗܘ ܐܦ *S* ܘܐܦ ܠܐ] ܐܦܠܐ *S* ܫܘܠܛܢ *S* 28. *Apparently no § in S* ܠܓܒܪܐ] + ܕܝܢ *S* ܙܠ] ܐܙܠ *S* ܝܘܡܢܐ] *om. S* 29 ܐܚܪܝܬ ܕܝܢ] ܘܒܐܚܪܬܐ *S* 31 ܡܢ 1°] ܡܢܘ *S* ܗܠܝܢ ܬܪܝܢ] *S illegible, but there is only room for one word* ܡܬܚܙܝܐ ܠܟܘܢ ܕ] *om. S* ܩܕܡܝܐ] ܐܚܪܢܐ *S* ܡܩܕܡܝܢ ܠܟܘܢ] ܢܩܕܡܘܢܟܘܢ *S* 32 ܗܝܡܢܬܘܢܝܗܝ] ܗܝܡܢܬܘܢ ܒܗ *S (sic)* ܗܝܡܢܘ ܒܗ] ܗܝܡܢܘܗܝ *S* ܐܦ ܠܐ] *om. S* ܬܬܘܒܘܢ] *pr.* ܒܐܚܪܬܐ *S* ܐܚܪܝܬ] *om. S* ܕܬܗܝܡܢܘܢ ܒܗ *S (sic)* 33. *Apparently no § in S* ܡܪܒܝܬܐ *S*

whence was *it*? from heaven, or from men?" Now they were con- *C S*
sidering among themselves and were saying "If we say to him that
it is from heaven, he will say to us 'And wherefore did ye not
26 believe in him?'—and if we say that it is from men, we are afraid of
the multitude," for all the folk as to a prophet were holding to John.
27 And they say to him: "We do not know." Jesus saith to them:
"And neither do I say to you by what authority I do these things.
28 "Now how seemeth it to you? A certain man, he had two sons;
he saith to the first: 'Go, my son, to-day; do work in the vineyard.'
29 He saith to him: 'I will not'; but lastly he changed his mind
30 and went to the vineyard. And he said to the other likewise,
31 and he answered and said: 'Yea, my lord'; and went not. Which
out of these twain seemeth it to you that he did the will of his
father?" They say to him: "That first one." Jesus saith to them:
"Amen, I say to you, that the toll-gatherers and the harlots go be-
32 fore you into the kingdom of God. For there came unto you John
in the way of uprightness and ye did not believe him; but the toll-
gatherers and the harlots believed in him, but ye—not even when ye
saw *it* have ye changed your mind lastly that ye should believe him!
33 "Hear another similitude. A certain man was the master of a

---

25 considering] thinking *S* were 2°] *om. S* to him] *om. S* 26 all the folk] all of them *S* 27 And they] + answered and *S* to him] to Jesus *S* Jesus] He also *S* And neither] Neither *S* 28 A certain] Now a certain *S* (*not E*[191]) to-day] *om. S* 29 but lastly] and at the last *S* 30 Yea, my lord] + 'I go' *E*[191] 31 these twain] *S illegible, but there is only room for one word*: *om.* twain *E*[191] seemeth it to you that he] *om. S E*[191] first] last *S*; 'second' *E*[191] go] shall go *S E*[191] 32 him 1°] in him *S* in him] him *S* but ye—not even.... believe him] but ye, when ye saw *it*—at the last have ye changed your mind that ye should believe in him? *S*

CS ܠܘܒ ܒܪܝܬܐ ܘܐܣܝܪܗ ܚܝܠܐ. ܘܣܦܪ ܒܗ ܡܫܝܢܘܬܐ. ܘܒܢܝܐ ܒܗ
ܡܬܒܠܐ. ܘܐܫܠܡܗ ܠܩܢܘܡܐ ܘܐܙܠ. [34]ܘܒܬܪ ܗܢܐ ܕܒܢܐ ܕܦܐܪܐ.
ܥܒܪ ܒܝܬܗܘܢ ܠܘܬ ܦܠܢܐ. ܕܢܥܒܪܘܢ ܠܗ ܦܐܪܐ. [35]ܘܐܣܒܘ
ܐܝܟܢ ܦܠܢܐ ܗܝܟܢ ܠܒܝܬܗܘܢ. ܐܬܐ ܕܢܣܒܘܢܗܘܢ. ܘܐܬܐ
ܕܢܦܩܘܢܗܘܢ. ܘܐܬܐ ܕܢܦܠܛܘܢ. [36]ܬܘܒ ܥܒܪ ܒܝܬܗܘܢ. ܣܓܝܐܐ
col 2 ܕܦܩܕܘܢ *ܡܢ ܡܕܝܢܬܐ. ܘܒܢܝܘ ܠܗܘܢ ܗܝܟܠ. [37]ܒܣܘܪܬܐ ܕܝܢ
ܥܒܪ ܠܘܬܗܘܢ ܠܒܪܗ ܘܐܡܪ. ܒܬܪ ܕܢܦܩܬܘܢ ܡܢ ܒܪ. [38]ܗܝܟܢ
ܕܝܢ ܦܠܢܐ ܒܪ ܚܘܘܗ ܠܒܪܗ. ܐܡܪܘ ܒܥܒܕܗܘܢ ܗܢܘ ܪܬܗ
ܬܘ ܢܦܠܛܘܢ. ܘܢܗܘܐ ܠܗ ܡܬܪܢܐ ܕܠܡ. [39]ܘܐܣܝܪܗܘܢ
ܘܐܦܩܗܘܢ. ܠܒܪ ܡܢ ܒܪܝܬܐ ܘܦܠܛܘܢ. [40]ܐܡܪܬ. ܗܟܝܠ ܕܐܝܬܐ
ܡܪܗ ܕܒܪܝܬܐ ܡܢܝܐ ܢܥܒܕ ܠܗܘܢ ܠܦܠܢܐ ܗܠܝܢ. [41]ܐܡܪܝܢ
ܠܗ ܕܟܕ ܒܪ ܢܟܒ ܐܝܟܢ. ܘܒܪܝܬܐ ܢܥܠܡ ܠܦܠܢܐ ܐ̈ܚܪܢܐ.
ܐܝܠܝܢ ܕܗܟܢ ܦܐܪܐ ܒܥܒܕܗܘܢ. [42]ܐܡܪ ܠܗܘܢ ܡܫܒܚ. ܠܐ
ܡܬܒܥܝܢ ܡܢܬܘܢ ܒܒܬܠܐ. ܕܐܝܟܐ ܗܝ ܕܐܦܠܝܢ ܚ̈ܝܠܐ. ܗܝ
fol 36 r *ܗܘܬ ܠܝܬܝ ܕܚܘܕܬܐ. ܡܢ ܠܘܬ ܡܪܝܐ ܗܘܬ ܗܕܐ. ܘܐܬܘܗܝ
§A484 ܬܕܒܪܬܐ ܒ̈ܝܢܝܢ. [43]ܡܛܠ ܗܢܐ ܐܡܪ ܐܢܐ ܠܟܘܢ. §ܕܬܬܝܕܥܘܢ
¶A ܒܟܘܢ ܡܠܟܘܬܐ ܕܐܠܗܐ. ܘܬܬܦܫܛ ܠܒܐ ܕܒܒܪ ܦܐܪܐ.¶
§A11 §[44]ܟܠ ܒܪ ܕܢܦܠ ܒܠ ܗܝ, ܟܐܦܐ ܢܬܬܒܪ. ܘܟܠ ܕܬܦܠ ܥܠܘܗܝ,
¶A ܬܫܚܩܝܘܗܝ.¶ [45]ܙ̈ܢܝ ܒܫ̈ܘܠܐ ܕܝܢ ܘܦܢ̈ܝܐ ܒܗ ܫܟܚܘ ܦܠܐܬܐ.

ܠܘܒ] pr. ܘ S   ܘܐܣܝܪܗ] ܘܒܢܝܐ ܠܗ S   34 ܘܒܬܪ ܗܢܐ] ܒܬܪ ܗܢܐ ܕܝܢ S
ܦܐܪܐ] pr. ܡܢ S   35 ܐܝܟܢ and ܗܝܟܢ] om. S   ܐܬܐ] pr. ܘ S
ܕܢܦܩܘܢܗܘܢ...ܕܢܦܠܛܘܢ] tr. S   36 ܣܓܝܐܐ ܒܝܬܗܘܢ] ܒܒܢܐ ܐܣܝܪܐ S
37 ܒܐܣܘܪܬܐ S   38 ܗܝܟܢ ܕܝܢ ܦܠܢܐ] ܦܠܢܐ ܕܝܢ S   ܐܡܪܘ ܒܥܒܕܗܘܢ]
ܐܡܪܝܢ S   ܪܬܗ] ܢܬܪܬܐ Sed   ܠܗ] om. S   39 ܘܐܣܝܪܘ ܐܦܩܘܗܝ S
40 ܠܗܘܢ ܠܦܠܢܐ ܗܠܝܢ] ܠܗܝܢ ܦܠܢܐ S   41 ܢܥܠܡ] ܢܬܠ S; *for* Ephr. *Lamy* i 253, *see Introd.* vol. ii   ܐܝܠܝܢ] om. S   42 ܡܬܒܥܝܢ] om. S
ܡܢܬܘܢ S   ܗܝ 1°] om. S   ܠܝܬܝ ܕܚܘܕܬܐ S   ܘܐܬܘܗܝ ܬܕܒܪܬܐ]
ܘܬܗ̇ ܗܝ S   43 ܕܬܬܝܕܥܘܢ] ܕܢܗܘܐ S Ab   ܦܐܪܐ] ܦܐܪܘܗܝ Aa; *S illegible*
44.] om. S   ܟܠ ܒܪ] ܘܟܠ A   ܢܬܬܒܪ Ab   ܕܬܦܠ] ܬܦܠ ܗܘ A
45 ܦܠܐܬܐ] ܦܠܐܬܗ S

house ; he planted a vineyard and surrounded it with a hedge and *C S*
digged in it a wine-press and built in it a tower, and he delivered
34 it over to husbandmen and went away. And when the time of fruits
drew near he sent his slaves unto the husbandmen, that they should
35 send him the fruits ; and those husbandmen took hold of his slaves,
36 one they beat and one they stoned and one they killed. Again he
sent other slaves of his more than the first, and they did to them like-
37 wise. But at the last he sent unto them his son, and said : 'Perhaps
38 they will have reverence for my son.' But those husbandmen when
they saw his son, said among themselves : 'This is his heir; come,
39 let us kill him, and the inheritance will be ours.' And they took
hold of him and put him forth out of the vineyard and killed him.
40 When therefore the lord of the vineyard shall come, what will he do
41 to those same husbandmen?" They say to him "Miserably will he
destroy them, and the vineyard he will deliver over to other husband-
42 men, who give the fruits in their season." Jesus saith to them :
"Have ye never read in Scripture 'The stone which the builders
rejected, it hath become the head of the corner ; from the LORD
43 this came to pass, and it is a wonder in our eyes'? Therefore
I say to you §The kingdom of God shall be taken away from you, §*A* 484
and shall be given to a people that bringeth forth fruits.¶ ¶*A*
44 §For every one that falleth on that stone shall be broken; and §*A* 11
45 every one whom it shall fall upon, it shall crush him."¶ Now ¶*A*
the chief priests and the Pharisees, when they heard the parable,

---

33 he planted] *pr.* and *S* surrounded it with] made for it *S* (*not* E^{192})
34 And when...near] Now when it was the time of fruits *S* the fruits] *pr.* of *S* 35 those] the *S* one 1°] *pr.* and *S* stoned...killed] *tr. S* 36 of his] *om. S* 38 those] the *S* said among themselves] say *S* his heir] the heir *S*; 'the heir of the vineyard' $E^{192, 265}$ 39 they took hold *and* put him forth *S* 40 same] *om. S* 41 them] 'those miserable men' E^{192} (= *Gr.*) deliver over] give *S; for* Ephr. *Lamy* i 253, *see Introd.* vol. ii who] that *S* 42 never (*so also* E^{193})] not *S* which] that *S* 43 bringeth forth (*lit.* 'doeth')] giveth *S* A^b fruits] its fruits A^a; *S illegible* 44.] *om. S* every one that] and he that *A* shall be] is A^b crush] 'crush and grind' E^{193} 45 the parable] his parables *S*

C S ܝܕܥܘ ܕܥܠܝܗܘܢ ܗܘ ܐܡܪ. [46]ܘܒܥܘ ܗܘܘ ܕܢܐܚܕܘܢܝܗܝ ܘܕܚܠܘ
ܡܢ ܟܢܫܐ. ܡܛܠ ܕܐܝܟ ܕܠܢܒܝܐ ܐܚܝܕܝܢ ܗܘܘ ܠܗ. ܀
[1]ܬܘܒ ܥܢܐ ܝܫܘܥ ܘܐܡܪ ܠܗܘܢ ܦ̈ܠܐܬܐ. [2]ܐܬܕܡܝܬ
ܡܠܟܘܬܐ ܕܫܡܝܐ ܠܓܒܪܐ ܡܠܟܐ. ܕܥܒܕ ܡܫܬܘܬܐ *ܠܒܪܗ. col 2
[3]ܘܫܕܪ ܠܥܒ̈ܕܘܗܝ ܕܢܩܪܘܢ ܠܗܘܢ ܕܡܙܡܢܝܢ ܠܡܫܬܘܬܐ. ܘܠܐ
ܨܒܘ ܠܡܐܬܐ ܀ ܘ
[4]ܬܘܒ ܫܕܪ ܥܒ̈ܕܐ ܐ̈ܚܪܢܐ ܘܐܡܪ. ܐܡܪܘ ܠܗܘܢ ܕܡܙܡܢܝܢ
ܗܘܘ. ܗܐ ܐܫܬܘܝܬ ܡܛܒܚܝ. ܬ̈ܘܪܝ ܦܛܡ̈ܝ ܢܟܝܣܝܢ ܐܢܘܢ.
ܘܟܠܡܕܡ ܡܛܝܒ ܗܘ ܬܘ ܠܡܫܬܘܬܐ. [5]ܗܢܘܢ ܕܝܢ ܒܣܘ.
ܘܐܢܫ ܕܐܙܠ ܠܩܪܝܬܐ. ܘܐܢܫ ܕܐܙܠ ܠܬܐܓܘܪܬܐ. [6]ܫܪ̈ܟܐ ܕܝܢ
ܕܐܫܬܚܪܘ. ܐܚܕܘ ܠܥܒ̈ܕܘܗܝ. ܘܨܥܪܘ ܐܢܘܢ ܘܩܛܠܘ. [7]ܘܪܓܙ
ܡܠܟܐ ܗܘ ܘܫܕܪ ܠܚܝܠܗ. ܘܐܘܒܕ ܐܢܘܢ ܠܩ̈ܛܘܠܐ ܗܠܝܢ.
ܘܠܡܕܝܢܬܗܘܢ ܐܘܩܕ ܒܢܘܪܐ ܀
[8]ܗܝܕܝܢ ܐܡܪ ܠܥܒ̈ܕܘܗܝ. ܡܫܬܘܬܐ ܡܛܝܒܐ ܗܝ. ܘܗܢܘܢ
fol 36 v ܕܡܙܡܢܝܢ *ܗܘܘ ܠܐ ܫܘܝܢ ܗܘܘ ܠܗ̇. [9]ܡܟܝܠ ܦܘܩܘ ܠܒܝܬ
ܐܘ̈ܪܚܬܐ. ܘܟܠ ܡܢ ܕܡܫܟܚܝܢ ܐܢܬܘܢ ܩܪܘ ܠܒܝܬ ܡܫܬܘܬܐ.
[10]ܘܢܦܩܘ ܥܒ̈ܕܐ ܗܢܘܢ ܠܒܝܬ ܐܘ̈ܪܚܬܐ. ܘܟܢܫܘ ܟܠ ܕܐܫܟܚܘ
ܒ̈ܝܫܐ ܘܛ̈ܒܐ. ܘܐܬܡܠܝ ܒܝܬ ܡܫܬܘܬܐ ܣ̈ܡܝܟܐ. [11]ܘܥܠ ܡܠܟܐ
ܕܢܚܙܐ ܣ̈ܡܝܟܐ. ܘܚܙܐ ܬܡܢ ܓܒܪܐ ܕܠܐ ܠܒܝܫ ܠܒܘܫܐ
ܕܡܫܬܘܬܐ. [12]ܐܡܪ ܠܗ ܚܒܪܝ. ܐܝܟܢܐ ܐܬܝܬ ܠܗܪܟܐ. ܕܢܚܬܐ

46 ܗܘܘ 1°] om. S ܕܢܐܚܕܘܢܝܗܝ] ܠܡܐܚܕܗ S ܡܛܠ] om. S 2 ܡܫܬܘܬܐ] For the reference to this Parable in A106, see Introd. vol. ii 3 ܠܥܒ̈ܕܘܗܝ] om. ܠ S ܕܡܙܡܢܝܢ] ܕܩܪ̈ܝܢ ܗܘܘ S 4. No § in S ܕܡܙܡܢܝܢ ܗܘܘ] ܕܩܪ̈ܝܢ S ܐܫܬܘܝܬ.....ܐܢܘܢ · ܘ] om. S ܬܘ] ܐܬܘ S ܠܡܫܬܘܬܐ] ܠܒܝܬ ܡܫܬܘ̇ S 5 ܠܩܪܝܬܗ S ܠܬܐܓܘܪܬܐ S 6 ܫܪ̈ܟܐ] pr. ܘ S ܐܢܘܢ ܘܩܛܠܘ] tr. S 7 ܡܠܟܐ ܗܘ] tr. S ܠܚܝܠܗ] ܚܝ̈ܠܘܗܝ S ܘܐܘܒܕ] ܘܐܘܒܕ ܐܢܘܢ S ܗܠܝܢ] ܗܢܘܢ S ܘܠܡܕܝܢܬܗܘܢ] om. ܠ S ܐܘܩܕܘ S 8. No § in S ܕܡܙܡܢܝܢ ܗܘܘ] ܕܩܪ̈ܝܢ S 9 ܘܟܠ ܡܢ] ܘܠܟܘܠ S ܩܪܘ] ܩܪܘܗܝ S 11 ܘܥܠ....ܘܚܙܐ] ܘܟܕ ܥܠ....ܚܙܐ S ܕܢܚܙܐ] ܠܡܚܙܐ S ܠܒܝܫ] + ܗܘܐ S ܠܒܘܫܐ] C (sic); ܠܒܘ̈ܫܐ S 12 ܚܒܪܝ] ܚܒܪ S ܐܬܝܬ] ܥܠܬ S

46 knew that against them he said *it.* And they had sought to take *C S*
hold of him, and were afraid of the people, because as to a prophet
they were holding to him.

xxii 1, 2 Again Jesus answered and said to them in parables: "The
kingdom of heaven hath become like to a man, a king, that made a
3 wedding for his son; and he sent his slaves that they should call
those bidden to the wedding, and they wished not to come.

4 "Again he sent other slaves and said: Say to those that were
bidden, 'Lo, my supper is ready and my fatted oxen are killed,
5 and everything is ready; come ye to the wedding.' But they dis-
dained *the invitation,* and one went to the field and one went to
6 merchandise, but the rest that were left behind took hold of his
7 slaves and insulted them and killed *them.* And that king was wroth
and sent his army, and it destroyed those murderers, and their
city it burned with fire.

8 "Then said he to his slaves: 'The wedding is ready and those
9 that were bidden were not worthy of it; henceforth go forth to
between the highways, and whomsoever ye find call to the wedding-
10 feast.' And those slaves went forth to between the highways, and
gathered all that they found, the bad and the good; and the wedding-
11 feast was filled with guests. And the king entered that he might see
the guests, and he saw there a man not clad in clothing for the
12 wedding. He saith to him: 'My comrade, how hast thou come

---

46 had] *om. S* because] for that *S* 2 a wedding] *For the reference to this Parable in A* 106, *see Introd.* vol. ii 3 those bidden] those that were called *S* 4 those that were bidden] those called *S* my supper...killed, and] *om. S* wedding] wedding-feast *S* 5 the field] his field *S* 6 and insulted and killed them *S* 7 army] armies *S* it 1° *&* 2°] *or,* 'he' *C*; they *S* 8 that were bidden] that *were* called *S* 9 whomsoever] every one that *S* call] + him *S* 11 the king...and he saw] when the king...he saw *S* that he might see] to see *S* not clad] *pr.* that was *S* clothing] clothes *S* 12 comrade] friend *S* come] entered *S*

C S ܕܡܫܬܘܬܐ ܠܝܬ ܠܟ. ܘܗܘ ܫܬܩ ܠܗ. [13]ܗܝܕܝܢ ܐܡܪ ܡܠܟܐ
ܠܡܫܡ̈ܫܢܐ. ܐܘܚܕܘܗܝ، ܒܐܝ̈ܕܘܗܝ، ܘܒܪ̈ܓܠܘܗܝ،. ܘܐܦܩܘܗܝ،
§A 147 ܠܚܫܘܟܐ ܒܪܝܐ. ܬܡܢ ܢܗܘܐ ܒܟܝܐ ܘܚܘܪܩ ܫ̈ܢܐ. [§14]ܣܓܝܐܐܝܢ
col 2 ¶A ܐܢܘܢ *ܓܝܪ ܩ̈ܪܝܐ ܘܙܥܘܪܝܢ ܓ̈ܒܝܐ¶. ܀

[15]ܗܝܕܝܢ ܐܙܠܘ ܦ̈ܪܝܫܐ. ܘܢܣܒܘ ܡܠܟܐ ܕܐܝܟܢܐ ܢܨܝܕܘܢܝܗܝ
ܒܡܠܬܐ. [16]ܘܫܕܪܘ ܠܘܬܗ ܬܠܡ̈ܝܕܝܗܘܢ ܥܡ ܒܢ̈ܝܐ ܕܗܪܘܕܣ
ܘܐܡܪܝܢ ܠܗ. ܡܠܦܢܐ ܝܕܥܝܢ ܚܢܢ ܕܫܪܝܪ ܐܢܬ. ܘܐܘܪܚܐ
ܕܐܠܗܐ ܒܩܘܫܬܐ ܡܠܦ ܐܢܬ. ܘܠܐ ܒܛܝܠ ܠܟ ܒܐܢܫ. ܠܐ
ܓܝܪ ܢܣܒ ܐܢܬ ܒܐܦ̈ܐ ܕܐܢܫ. [17]ܐܡܪ ܠܢ ܡܢܐ ܡܬܚܙܐ ܠܟ.
ܫܠܝܛ ܠܡܬܠ ܟܣܦ ܪܫܐ ܠܩܣܪ ܐܘ ܠܐ. [18]ܝܕܥ ܕܝܢ ܝܫܘܥ
ܒܒܝܫܘܬܗܘܢ ܘܐܡܪ ܠܗܘܢ. ܢܣ̈ܒܝ ܒܐܦ̈ܐ ܡܢܐ ܡܢܣܝܢ
ܐܢܬܘܢ ܠܝ. [19]ܚܘܐܘܢܝ ܠܕܝܢܪܐ ܕܟܣܦ ܪܫܐ. ܘܗܢܘܢ ܩܪܒܘ
fol 37 r ܠܗ ܕܝܢܪܐ. *[20]ܐܡܪ ܠܗܘܢ ܝܫܘܥ. ܕܡܢ ܨܠܡܐ ܗܢܐ ܘܟܬܒܬܐ
ܕܡܢ. [21]ܐܡܪܝܢ ܠܗ ܕܩܣܪ. ܗܝܕܝܢ ܐܡܪ ܠܗܘܢ. ܗܒܘ ܕܩܣܪ
ܠܩܣܪ. ܘܕܐܠܗܐ ܠܐܠܗܐ. [22]ܘܟܕ ܫܡܥܘ ܐܬܕܡܪܘ ܘܫܒܩܘܗܝ،
ܘܐܙܠܘ ܀

[23]ܒܗܘ ܝܘܡܐ ܩܪܒܘ ܩܕܡܘܗܝ، ܙܕܘ̈ܩܝܐ ܘܐܡܪܝܢ ܠܗ. ܕܠܝܬ
ܩܝܡܬܐ. ܘܫܐܠܘܗܝ، [24]ܘܐܡܪܝܢ ܠܗ. ܡܠܦܢܐ. ܡܘܫܐ ܐܡܪ ܠܢ.

ܘܗܘ] ܗܘ ܕܝܢ S 13 ܐܘܚܕܘܗܝ] ܐܚܘܕܘܗܝ S (sic). *Cf Thos*[315]: [2]ܠܡܫܬܘܬܐ ܐܙܕܡܢܬ [12]ܘܢܦܩܬܐ ܣܓܝܐܐ ܠܡܫܬܝ. [8]ܐܪܫܥܐ ܠܗ. [13]ܘܠܐ ܢܦܪܘܩ ܐܝ̈ܕܘܗܝ ܘܪ̈ܓܠܘܗܝ ܘܠܚܫܘܟܐ ܒܪܝܐ ܠܐ ܐܦܩܘܗ. 14 ܓܝܪ] *om.* A 15 ܢܣܒܘ S 16 ܬܠܡܝܕܘܗܝ S (*sic*) ܐܢܚܢܢ S ܘܐܘܪܚܗ S ܒܐܦ̈ܐ ܕܐܢܫ] ܒܐܦ̈ܐ ܒܪ ܐܢܫܐ S 17 ܐܡܪ ܠܢ...ܠܟ] ܐܡܪܢܐ ܕܝܢ ܡܬܚܙܝܐ ܠܟ S ܫܠܝܛ] ܘܠܐ ܠܢ S ܠܡܬܠ] ܕܢܬܠ S 18 ܝܫܘܥ] *pr.* ܡܪܢ S (*so I read the photogr.*) ܒܒܝܫܘܬܗܘܢ] ܒܒܫܘܬܗܘܢ S ܘܐܡܪ] ܐܡܪ S 19 ܚܘܐܘܢ S (*sic*) ܘܗܢܘܢ ܩܪܒܘ ܠܗ] ܘܐܩܪܒܘ ܠܗ S (*sic*) 20 ܕܡܢ] ܕܡܢܘ S 23 ܒܗܘ] *pr.* ܘ S ܩܕܡܘܗܝ] *om.* S ܕܠܝܬ] *om.* ܕ S ܩܝܡܬܐ] ܚܝܬ ܡܝ̈ܬܐ S ܘܫܐܠܘܗܝ] ܘܡܫܐܠܝܢ ܗܘܘ ܠܗ S 24 ܠܗ] *om.* S

hither, who hast no garments for the wedding?' And he was silent. *C S*
13 Then said the king to his servants: 'Take hold of him by his hands
and by his feet, and put him forth into the outer darkness; there
14 shall be the weeping and the gnashing of teeth.' §For many are §*A* 147
the called and few the chosen." ¶ ¶*A*

15 Then went the Pharisees and took counsel how they might catch
16 him with a word. And they sent unto him their disciples with
the slaves of Herod, and they say to him: "Teacher, we know that
thou art true, and the way of God in verity thou teachest, and thou
carest not for any one, for thou hast no respect of persons for
17 any one. Say to us what seemeth to thee—is it lawful to
18 give head-money to Caesar, or not?" Now Jesus knew their
thoughts and said to them: "Ye respecters of persons, why tempt
19 ye me? Shew me the coin of the head-money." And they them-
20 selves brought near to him a denar. Jesus saith to them: "This
21 image and the inscription—of whom *is it*?" They say to him:
"Caesar's." Then saith he to them: "Give what *is* Caesar's to
22 Caesar, and God's to God." And when they heard they wondered
and left him and went away.

23 On that day there drew near before him Sadducees, and
they say to him that there is no resurrection. And they
24 asked him, and say to him: "Teacher, Moses said to us,

And he] Now he *S* 13 Take hold of him] *Cf Thos*[315]: '[2]To the Wedding I have been bidden, [12]and with white garments I have been clothed; [8]may I be worthy of it, [13]and may they not fasten my hands and my feet and to the outer darkness may I not go forth' 14 For] *om. A* 15 and took] *and* took *S* 16 their disciples (*so also E*[193])] his disciples *S* (*sic*) for any one] for men *S* 17 Say...to thee] Now how doth it please thee *S* is it lawful] doth it behove us *S* to give] that we should give *S* 18 knew] *pr.* when he *S* (*sic*) thoughts] ill-will *S* and] *om. S* 19 they...near to him] they handed to him *S* 20 *is it*] is it *S* 23 On that] And on that *S* before him] *om. S* that there is] There is *S E*[193] resurrection] coming to life of the dead *S E*[193] asked] were asking *S* 24 to him] *om. S*

C S ܕܐܢ ܗܘ ܕܢܡܘܬ ܐܢܫ ܟܕ ܠܝܬ ܠܗ ܒ̈ܢܝܐ. ܬܗܘܐ ܐܢܬܬܗ
ܠܐܚܘܗܝ. ܘܢܩܝܡ ܙܪܥܐ ܠܐܚܘܗܝ. [25]ܐܝܬ ܗܘܘ ܕܝܢ ܠܘܬܢ
ܫܒܥܐ ܐܚ̈ܝܢ. ܩܕܡܝܗܘܢ ܢܣܒ ܐܢܬܬܐ ܘܡܝܬ. ܘܠܐ ܫܒܩ
col 2 ܒ̈ܢܝܐ. ܘܫܒܩܬ ܐܢܬܬܗ ܠܐܚܘܗܝ. [26]ܐܦ ܐܚܪܢܐ *ܗܟܘܬ. ܘܐܦ
ܕܬܠܬܐ. ܥܕܡܐ ܠܫܒܥܬܝܗܘܢ. [27]ܘܐܚܪܝܬ ܒܬܪ ܟܠܗܘܢ ܡܝܬܬ
§A 167 ܠܗ̇ ܗܝ ܐܢܬܬܐ. [28]§ܒܩܝܡܬܐ ܗܟܝܠ ܠܐܝܢܐ ܡܢܗܘܢ ܬܗܘܐ
ܐܢܬܬܐ. ܗܐ ܓܝܪ ܠܫܒܥܬܝܗܘܢ ܗܘܬ ܗܘܬ. [29]ܥܢܐ ܝܫܘܥ ܘܐܡܪ
ܠܗܘܢ܆ ܛܥܝܢ ܐܢܬܘܢ. ܘܠܐ ܝܕܥܝܢ ܐܢܬܘܢ ܟܬ̈ܒܐ.
(§A 429) ܐܦܠܐ ܚܝܠܗ ܕܐܠܗܐ. [30]§ܒܩܝܡܬ ܡ̈ܝܬܐ ܓܝܪ ܠܐ ܓܒܪ̈ܐ
ܢܣܒܝܢ ܢܫ̈ܐ. ܐܦ ܠܐ ܢܫ̈ܐ ܗܘܝܢ ܠܓܒܪ̈ܐ. ܐܠܐ ܐܝܟ
(¶A 429) ܡ̈ܠܐܟܐ ܐܝܠܝܢ ܕܒܫܡܝܐ¶. [31]ܘܥܠ ܩܝܡܬܐ ܕܝܢ ܕܡ̈ܝܬܐ ܠܐ
ܩܪܝܬܘܢ. ܕܐܡܝܪ ܐܠܗܐ. [32]ܕܐܢܐ ܐܢܐ ܐܠܗܗ ܕܐܒܪܗܡ.
fol 37 v (§A 420) ¶A 168 (¶A 420) ܘܐܠܗܗ ܕܐܝܣܚܩ. ܘܐܠܗܗ *ܕܝܥܩܘܒ. ܘܗܘܐ §ܐܠܗܐ ܠܐ
ܗܘܐ ܕܡ̈ܝܬܐ ܐܠܐ ܕܚܝ̈ܐ.¶ ¶.o.

[33]ܘܟܕ ܫܡܥܘ ܟܢ̈ܫܐ ܗܠܝܢ܆ ܡܬܕܡܪܝܢ ܗܘܘ ܒܝܘܠܦܢܗ. [34]ܦܪ̈ܝܫܐ
ܕܝܢ ܟܕ ܫܡܥܘ ܕܣܟܪ ܐܢܘܢ ܠܙܕܘ̈ܩܝܐ. ܐܬܟܢܫܘ ܠܘܬܗ.

ܕܐܢ ܗܘ ܕ] ܐܢ S   ܕܢܡܘܬ ܐܢܫ] ܐܢܫ ܕܡܐܬ S   ܟܕ ܠܝܬ] ܘܠܝܬ S
ܒ̈ܢܝܐ] so also S   ܘܢܩܝܡ ܙܪܥܐ ܠܐܚܘܗܝ] om. S   25 ܐܝܬ....ܐܚ̈ܝܢ]
ܘܫܒܥܐ ܐܚ̈ܝܢ ܐܝܬ ܗܘܘ S   ܩܕܡܝܗܘܢ....ܘܡܝܬ] ܘܡܝܬ ܩܕܡܝܐ S
ܘܠܐ ܫܒܩ ܒ̈ܢܝܐ] ܘܠܐ ܫܒܩ ܡܢܗ ܒܪܐ S   26 ܐܦ] pr. ܘ S
27 ܘܐܚܪܝܬ ܒܬܪ ܟܠܗܘܢ] ܒܐܚܪܝܬܐ ܕܟܠܗܘܢ S (sic)   ܠܗ̇] om. S
28 ܒܩܝܡܬܐ] ܒܩܝܡܬ ܡ̈ܝܬܐ S (sic) A: cf ver. 23   ܗܟܝܠ] om. S A
ܡܢܗܘܢ] ܡܢ ܟܠܗܘܢ ܐܝܢܐ S   ܐܢܬܬܐ] om. A   ܗܐ ܓܝܪ....ܗܘܬ]
ܗܐ ܓܝܪ ܟܠܗܘܢ ܢܣܒܘܗ S; ܕܗܢܐ ܐܢܬܬܐ ܗܘܬ ܕܟܠܗܘܢ A (inserted at the
beginning of the verse. A[a] has ܠܟܠܗܘܢ)   29 ܥܢܐ...ܠܗܘܢ]
ܗܝܕܝܢ ܐܡܪ ܠܗܘܢ ܡܪܢ A   ܛܥܝܢ] pr. ܕ A[b]   ܘܠܐ] ܕܠܐ A[a]   ܐܦܠܐ]
ܘܠܐ S A   30 ff.] *For the text of* A 167 *and* 429, *see* Lk xx 35 ff.   ܠܓܒܪ̈ܐ]
om. S   ܐܝܠܝܢ] *so also* S   31 ܘܥܠ] *om.* ܘ S A   ܕܝܢ] *so also* S   ܕܡ̈ܝܬܐ]
ܥܠ ܕܝܢ ܩܝܡܬ ܡ̈ܝܬܐ S; ܕܩܝܡܬܗܘܢ ܕܡ̈ܝܬܐ A   ܠܐ ܩܪܝܬܘܢ]+ܒܟܬܒܐ S;+ܒܟܬ̈ܒܐ A
ܐܠܗܐ]+ܠܡܘܫܐ ܡܢ ܣܢܝܐ A   32 ܕܐܢܐ ܐܢܐ] *om.* ܐܢܐ S
ܘܕܐܝܣܚܩ ܘܕܝܥܩܘܒ A   33. *No* § *in* S

that if so be that a man shall die not having sons, his wife shall *C S*
25 become his brother's and he shall raise up seed to his brother. Now
there were by us seven brothers: the first of them took a wife and
26 died and left no sons, and his wife became his brother's; the other
27 also *did* likewise, and the third also unto the seven of them, and lastly
28 after all of them that woman died. §In the resurrection therefore, §*A* 167
whose of them shall the woman be? For lo, *wife* of the seven of them
29 she became." Jesus answered and said to them: "Much do ye err, and
30 ye know not the Scriptures neither the power of God. §For in the (§*A* 429)
coming to life of the dead neither do men take women, nor do women
31 become *wives* of men, but they are as the angels of heaven.¶ Now (¶*A* 429)
concerning the resurrection of the dead, have ye not read that God
32 said 'I am the God of Abraham and the God of Isaac and the God
of Jacob'? And lo, §the God not of the dead, but of the living."¶¶ (§*A* 420) ¶*A* 168
33 And when those multitudes heard, they were wondering (¶*A* 420)
34 at his teaching. But the Pharisees, when they saw that he
had silenced the Sadducees, were gathered together unto him.

---

that if so be that] if *S* shall die] dieth *S* and he...his brother] *om.* *S* $E^{194\,(vid)}$ 25 Now...brothers] And seven brothers there were *S* the first...and died] and the first died *S* and left no sons] and he made from her no son *S* 26 the other] *pr.* and *S* 27 and lastly after all] at the last of all *S* 28 the resurrection] the coming to life of the dead *S* (*sic*) *A* $E^{194\,(vid)}$: *cf ver.* 23 *and Notes,* vol. ii therefore] *om.* *S A* (*not* E^{194}) of them] of all the brothers *S* (*not* E^{194}) the woman] she *A* E^{194} For lo,...became] For lo, all of them took her *S*; *seeing* that, lo, wife she was of all of them *A* (*inserted at the beginning of the verse. For* 'of all' A^a *has* 'to all') 29 Jesus...to them] Then said to them our Lord *A* and ye] that ye A^a neither] nor *S A* 30 ff.] *For the text of A* 167 *and* 429 (*and* E^{194}), *see* Lk xx 35 ff. men 1°] they *S* 31 of the dead] from among the dead *S*; that the dead will rise *A* that] that which *S*; *pr.* in the Scripture *A* God said] + to Moses from the Bush *A* 32 am] *om.* *S* the God 2° & 3°] *om.* *A*

35ܘܫܐܠܗ ܗܘܐ ܚܕ ܡܢܗܘܢ ܣܦܪܐ ܟܕ ܡܢܣܐ ܠܗ ܘܐܡܪ ܠܗ. C S
36ܡܠܦܢܐ ܐܝܢܐ ܦܘܩܕܢܐ ܪܒ ܘܩܕܡܝ ܒܐܘܪܝܬܐ. 37ܐܡܪ ܠܗ
ܝܫܘܥ. ܕܬܪܚܡ ܠܡܪܝܐ ܐܠܗܟ ܡܢ ܟܠܗ ܠܒܟ. ܘܡܢ ܟܠܗ ܢܦܫܟ. cf A24
ܘܡܢ ܟܠܗ ܚܝܠܟ. 38ܗܢܐ ܗܘ ܦܘܩܕܢܐ ܪܒܐ ܘܩܕܡܝܐ. 39ܘܕܬܪܝܢܗ
ܕܕܡܝܐ ܠܗ. ܕܬܪܚܡ ܠܩܪܝܒܟ ܐܝܟ ܢܦܫܟ. 40§ܒܗܠܝܢ ܬܪ̈ܬܝܢ §A24
ܦܘ̈ܩܕܢܝܢ ܬܠܝܐ ܐܘܪܝܬܐ ܘܢܒ̈ܝܐ.¶ 41ܘܟܕ ܟܢܝܫܝܢ ܦܪ̈ܝܫܐ. ܫܐܠ ¶A
ܗܘܐ *ܠܗܘܢ 42ܘܐܡܪ. ܡܢܐ ܐܡܪܝܢ ܐܢܬܘܢ ܥܠ ܡܫܝܚܐ ܒܪ col 2
ܡܢܘ. ܐܡܪܝܢ ܠܗ ܒܪ ܕܘܝܕ. 43ܐܡܪ ܠܗܘܢ ܐܝܟܢܐ ܗܟܝܠ ܕܘܝܕ
ܒܪܘܚܐ ܕܩܘܕܫܐ ܩܪܐ ܠܗ ܡܪܝ. ܐܡܪ ܓܝܪ 44ܕܐܡܪ ܡܪܝܐ
ܠܡܪܝ. ܬܒ ܠܟ ܡܢ ܝܡܝܢܝ. ܥܕܡܐ ܕܐܣܝܡ ܒܥܠܕܒܒܝܟ ܬܚܝܬ
ܪ̈ܓܠܝܟ. 45ܐܢ ܗܟܝܠ ܕܘܝܕ ܡܪܝ ܩܪܐ ܠܗ ܐܝܟܢܐ ܒܪܗ ܗܘ.
46ܘܠܐ ܐܢܫ ܐܫܟܚ ܕܢܬܠ ܠܗ ܦܬܓܡܐ. ܘܐܦܠܐ ܐܢܫ ܐܡܪܚ
ܡܢ ܗܿ ܫܥܬܐ ܠܡܫܐܠܘܬܗ ܬܘܒ.

1ܗܝܕܝܢ ܐܡܪ ܝܫܘܥ ܠܟܢܫܐ ܘܠܬܠܡ̈ܝܕܘܗܝ. 2ܥܠ ܒܘܪܣܝܐ
ܕܡܘܫܐ ܝܬܒܘ ܣ̈ܦܪܐ ܘܦ̈ܪܝܫܐ. 3ܟܠܡܕܡ ܕܐܡܪܝܢ ܠܟܘܢ
*ܗܘܝܬܘܢ ܫܡܥܝܢ ܘܥܒܕܝܢ. ܐܝܟ ܥܒ̈ܕܝܗܘܢ ܕܝܢ ܠܐ fol 38 r
ܬܥܒܕܘܢ. ܐܡܪܝܢ ܓܝܪ ܘܠܐ ܥܒܕܝܢ. 4ܘܐܣܪܝܢ ܡܘ̈ܒܠܐ
ܡ̈ܝܩܪܬܐ ܘܣܝܡܝܢ ܥܠ ܟ̈ܬܦܬܐ ܕܒ̈ܢܝ ܐܢܫܐ. ܘܗܢܘܢ ܒܨܒܥܐ
ܡܢ ܨ̈ܒܥܬܗܘܢ ܠܐ ܙܝܥܝܢ ܠܗܘܢ. 5ܟܠ ܡܕܡ ܓܝܪ ܕܥܒܕܝܢ
ܕܢܬܚܙܘܢ ܠܒ̈ܢܝ ܐܢܫܐ. ܘܡܦܬܝܢ ܒܪ̈ܘܫܐ ܕܬ̈ܦܠܝܢܗܘܢ. ܘܡܘܪܟܝܢ

35 ܘܫܐܠܗ] ܘܫܐܠ S   ܣܦܪܐ] om. S   36 ܘܩܕܡܝ] om. S   37. *The quotation in A24 is from the Syriac of* Deut vi 5, *for* ܘܡܢ ܟܠܗ ܚܝܠܟ *corresponds to* ובכל מאדך, *not to the Greek N.T.*   38 ܗܢܐ ܗܘ] ܗܢܘ S   ܘܩܕܡܝܐ] ܘܪܫܝܐ S   39 ܘܕܬܪܝܢܗ] + ܗܘ S   41 ܟܢܝܫܝܢ] + ܗܘܘ S   ܠܗܘܢ] + ܝܫܘܥ S   42 ܐܡܪܝܢ ܐܢܬܘܢ] ܡܣܬܒܪ ܠܟܘܢ S   43 ܐܝܟܢܐ ܗܟܝܠ] ܘܐܝܟܢܐ S   ܒܪܘܚܐ ܕܩܘܕܫܐ] om. S   ܡܪܝ] S *illegible*   44 ܬܒ] *pr.* ܕ S   ܕܐܣܝܡ & ܪ̈ܓܠܝܟ] S *illegible*   45 ܐܢ ܗܟܝܠ] ܘܐܢ S   ܡܪܝ] ܡܪܝܐ S: *cf* Joh xii 21 S   46 ܘܠܐ ܐܫܟܚܘ ܕܢܬܠܘܢ S   ܘܐܦܠܐ] om. ܘ S   3 ܟܠܡܕܡ] ܘܟܠ ܡܐ S   ܫܡܥܝܢ ܘ] om. S   4 ܘܗܢܘܢ] + ܕܝܢ S   ܒܨܒܥܐ ܡܢ ܨ̈ܒܥܬܗܘܢ] om. S   5 ܟܠ] ܘܟܠ S

35 And one of them, a scribe, had asked him tempting him and saying *C S*
36 to him: "Teacher, which commandment is great and first in the
37 Law?" Jesus saith to him "'Thou shalt love the LORD thy God *cf A* 24
from all thy heart and from all thy soul, and from all thy power;'
38, 39 this is the great and first commandment. And one after it that is
40 like to it *is* 'Thou shalt love thy neighbour as thyself.' §On these §*A* 24
41 two commandments hangeth the Law, and the prophets *also*."¶ And ¶*A*
42 while the Pharisees *were* gathered together he was asking them and
saying: "What say ye about the Messiah; whose son is he?" They
43 say to him: "David's son." He saith to them: "How therefore doth
44 David in the Holy Spirit call him 'my Lord'? For he said 'The
LORD said to my Lord: Sit down on my right hand, until I set thine
45 enemies under thy feet.' If therefore David call him 'my Lord,' how
46 is he his son?" And no one could give him an answer, neither did
any one dare from that hour to ask him again.

xxiii 1, 2 Then said Jesus to the multitudes and to his disciples: "On the
3 throne of Moses the scribes and the Pharisees have sat down; every-
thing that they say to you be hearing and doing, but like their deeds
4 do ye not, for they say and do not. And they bind heavy burdens
and lay *them* on the shoulders of men, and they themselves with one
5 of their fingers do not touch them. For everything that they do
is that they may seem *something* to men, and they widen the thongs

---

35 a scribe] *om. S* asked him] *om.* him *S* 36 and first] *om. S*: *cf* 'first and great' E^{194} 37. *The quotation in A* 24 *is from* Deut vi 5 38 and first] and chief *S* 41 *were*] were *S* he] Jesus *S* 42 say ye] is supposed by you *S* 43 How therefore] And how *S* in the Holy Spirit] *om. S* my Lord] *S illegible* 44 I set & thy feet] *S illegible* 45 If therefore] And if *S* my Lord] the LORD *S*: *cf* Joh xii 21 *S* 46 no one could] they could not *S* neither] nor *S* 3 everything] and all that *S* hearing and] *om. S* 4 and 3°] but *S* with one of their fingers] *om. S*

C S §A 269 ܬܟܠܬܐ ܕܡܪ̈ܛܘܛܝܗܘܢ܆ §[6]ܘܪܚܡܝܢ ܪܝܫ ܣܡ̈ܟܐ ܘܐܫ̈ܬܡܫܬܐ.
ܘܡܘ̈ܬܒܐ ܩܕ̈ܡܝܐ ܒܟ̈ܢܘܫܬܐ [7]ܘܫܠܡܐ ܒܫܘ̈ܩܐ. ܘܨܒܝܢ
¶A ܕܢܗܘܘܢ ܩܪܝܢ ܠܗܘܢ ܒ̈ܢܝ ܐܢܫܐ ܪܒܝ ܪܒܝ.¶ [8]ܐܢܬܘܢ ܕܝܢ
ܠܐ ܬܬܩܪܘܢ ܪܒܝ. ܚܕ ܗܘ ܓܝܪ ܪܒܟܘܢ ܡܫܝܚܐ. ܘܐܢܬܘܢ
col 2 ܐܚ̈ܐ ܐܢܬܘܢ. [9]ܘܐܒܐ ܠܐ ܬܩܪܘܢ* ܠܟܘܢ ܒܐܪܥܐ. ܚܕ ܗܘ
ܓܝܪ ܐܒܘܟܘܢ ܕܒܫܡܝܐ. [10]ܘܠܐ ܬܬܩܪܘܢ ܡ̈ܠܒܢܐ. ܡܛܠ
ܕܡܠܒܢܟܘܢ ܡܫܝܚܐ ܗܘ· [11]ܘܡܢ ܕܪܒܐ ܒܟܘܢ ܕܢܗܘܐ ܪܒ.
ܢܗܘܐ ܠܟܘܢ ܡܫܡܫܢܐ. [12]ܟܠ ܐܢܫ ܓܝܪ ܕܢܪܝܡ ܢܦܫܗ ܢܬܡܟܟ·
ܘܡܢ ܕܢܡܟ ܢܦܫܗ ܢܬܬܪܝܡ ·܀·
[13]ܘܝ ܠܟܘܢ ܣܦܪ̈ܐ ܘܦܪ̈ܝܫܐ ܢܣ̈ܒܝ ܒܐ̈ܦܐ. ܕܐܚܕܝܢ ܐܢܬܘܢ
ܡܠܟܘܬܐ ܕܐܠܗܐ ܩܕܡ ܒ̈ܢܝ ܐܢܫܐ. ܠܐ ܓܝܪ ܐܢܬܘܢ ܥܠܝܢ.
ܘܠܐ ܠܐܝܠܝܢ ܕܐܬܝܢ ܠܡܥܠ ܫܒܩܝܢ ܐܢܬܘܢ ·܀·
[14]ܘܝ ܠܟܘܢ ܣܦܪ̈ܐ ܘܦܪ̈ܝܫܐ ܢܣ̈ܒܝ ܒܐ̈ܦܐ. ܕܐܟܠܝܢ ܐܢܬܘܢ
fol 38 v ܒ̈ܬܐ ܕܐܪ̈ܡܠܬܐ· ܒܥܠܬܐ ܕܡܘܪܟܝܢ ܐܢܬܘܢ *ܨ̈ܠܘܬܟܘܢ܆ ܡܛܠ
ܗܢܐ ܬܩܒܠܘܢ ܕܝܢܐ ܝܬܝܪܐ ○○ ○○ ○○
§A 271 [15]ܘܝ ܠܟܘܢ ܣܦܪ̈ܐ ܘܦܪ̈ܝܫܐ ܢܣ̈ܒܝ ܒܐ̈ܦܐ. §ܕܡܬܟܪܟܝܢ ܐܢܬܘܢ

ܬܟ̈ܠܬܐ S   6 ܘܪܚܡܝܢ] ܘܝ ܠܟܘܢ ܕܪܚܡܝܢ ܐܢܬܘܢ A (cf Lk xi 43)
ܘܐܫ̈ܬܡܫܬܐ] C Aᵃ; 'ܒܐܫܬ S, 'ܒܫ̈ܬ Aᵇ   ܩܕ̈ܡܝܐ] ܩܕܡܝܐ S (sic)
ܪܝܫ....ܒܟ̈ܢܘܫܬܐ] ('ܘܐܫ̈ܬ Aᵃ) ܡܘ̈ܬܒܐ ܒܟܢܘ̈ܫܬܐ ܘܣ̈ܡܟܐ ܒܡܫܬܘ̈ܬܐ A
7 ܘܫܠܡܐ ܒܫܘ̈ܩܐ] om. A   ܘܨܒܝܢ ܕܢܗܘܘܢ] ܘܪܚܡܝܢ ܐܢܬܘܢ ܕܢܗܘܘܢ A
ܠܗܘܢ] ܠܟܘܢ A   ܒ̈ܢܝ] om. A   8 ܕܝܢ] om. S   ܓܝܪ] om. S   ܪܒܟܘܢ]
ܡܠܒܢܟܘܢ S   ܡܫܝܚܐ] om. S   ܐܚ̈ܐ ܐܢܬܘܢ] ܐܚ̈ܐ ܟܠܟܘܢ S
9. Cf ܐܒܐ ܠܐ ܬܩܪܐ (ܢܩܪܐ Aᵃ) ܠܟ ܒܐܪܥܐ. ܕܢܗܘܐ ܫܒܝܐ ܠܐܒܐ ܕܒܫܡܝܐ
A 105. With vv. 8 & 9 cf also ܪܒܐ ܒܐܪܥܐ ܠܐ ܬܬܩܪܘܢ Ephr v 491 B
10 ܘܠܐ] ܘܐܦܠܐ S   11 ܘܡܢ ܕܪܒܐ] ܘܕܪܒܐ S   12. For A 80, 189,
see Lk xiv 11   ܐܢܫ] C¹; om. S C*(vid)   ܓܝܪ ܕܢܪܝܡ] tr. S   ܘܡܢ] ܘܟܠ S
ܢܬܪܝܡ S   13 ܘܝ ܠܟܘܢ] ܕܝܢ ܘܠܟܘܢ S (sic)   ܢܣ̈ܒܝ] ܢܣܒܝܢ S: cf Mt vi 2
ܕܐܚܕܝܢ....ܕܐܠܗܐ] ܐܚܕܝܢ ܐܢܬܘܢ ܐܩܠܝܕܐ ܕܡܠܟܘܬܐ ܕܫܡܝܐ S: cf
ܐܢܬܘܢ ܐܝܟ ܐܚܝܕܝ ܐܩ̈ܠܝܕܐ A 287, and ܐܩܠܝܕܐ ܕܡܠܟ ܠܟ ܘܬܪܥܐ
ܐܚܝܕܬܘܢܝ· ܐܢܬ ܠܐ ܥܠܬ. ܘܠܕܐܬܝܢ ܠܡܥܠ ܠܐ ܫܒܩܬ ܐܢܬ A 270 f. See also
Introd. vol. ii   14.] om. S   15 ܕܡܬܟܪܟܝܢ] ܕܚܕܪܝܢ A

6 of their frontlets and lengthen the fringe of their cloaks, §and love *C S*
the chief entertainments †and† suppers and the first seats in the §*A* 269
7 synagogues and greeting in the streets, and they wish that men
8 should be calling them 'Rabbi, Rabbi.'¶ But ye yourselves, call not ¶*A*
ye *men* Rabbi; for one is your Rabbi, the Messiah, and ye yourselves
9 are brothers. And Father call not *men* for yourselves on earth, for
10 one is your Father in heaven. And be not called Teachers, because
11 your Teacher is the Messiah. And he that would among you be
12 great shall be to you a servant; for every man that shall uplift him-
self shall be humbled, and he that humbleth himself shall be uplifted.

13 "Woe to you scribes and Pharisees, respecters of persons, that ye
shut the kingdom of God before men! For ye enter not yourselves,
neither those that come to enter suffer ye.

14 "Woe to you scribes and Pharisees, respecters of persons, that
ye eat up the houses of widows in the pretext that ye are lengthening
your prayers! Therefore ye shall receive more judgement.

15 "Woe to you scribes and Pharisees, respecters of persons, §that §*A* 271
ye go about sea and land that ye may make one proselyte, and what

---

5 fringe] fringes *S* 6 and love] Woe to you, that ye love *A* (*cf* Lk xi 43) †and† suppers] *C* A^a; at suppers *S* A^b first] honourable *S* the chief... the synagogues] the seats in the synagogues and entertainments at suppers *A* (and suppers A^a) 7 and greeting in the streets] *om.* *A* and they wish] and ye love *A* men] folk *A* them] you *A* 8 But ye] Ye *S* for] *om.* *S* your Rabbi] your Teacher *S* the Messiah] *om.* *S* ye... brothers] ye are all of you brothers *S* 9. *Cf* 'A father let us not call *any one* for ourselves on earth, that we may be sons to the Father in heaven' *A* 105 (*for* 'call *any one*' A^a *has* 'get'). *With vv.* 8 *&* 9 *cf also* 'A Rabbi call not *men* on earth' Ephr v 491 B 10 And be not] Neither be *S* 12. *For* *A* 80, 189, *see* Lk xiv 11 every man] every one *S* he that] every one that *S* 13 Woe] But woe *S* that ye shut the kingdom of God] Ye hold the key of the kingdom of heaven *S* (*in Syriac the same word is used for* 'to shut' *and* 'to hold'): *cf* 'Ye are the holders of the keys' *A* 287, *and* 'The key is delivered up to thee and the door thou hast shut; thou hast not entered and them that come to enter thou sufferest not' *A* 270 f. *For* E^{211}, *see on* Lk xi 52 14.] *om.* *S* 15 go about] surround *A*

(C) S ܝܡܐ ܘܝܒܫܐ ܕܬܥܒܕܘܢ ܚܕ ܓܝܘܪܐ. ܘܡܐ ܕܗܘܐ ܥܒܕܝܢ
¶A ܐܢܬܘܢ ܠܗ ܒܪܗ ܕܓܗܢܐ¶ ܐܥܦܐ ܥܠܝܟܘܢ ..ܘ..

[16] ܘܝ ܠܟܘܢ ܢܓܘ̈ܕܐ ܣܡ̈ܝܐ. ܕܐܡܪܝܢ ܐܢܬܘܢ ܡܢ ܕܝܡܐ ܒܗܝܟܠܐ ܠܐ ܡܕܡ. ܘܡܢ ܕܝܡܐ ܒܕܗܒܐ ܕܒܗܝܟܠܐ ܚܐܒ. [17] ܣܟ̈ܠܐ ܥܘ̈ܝܪܐ ܡܢܐ ܪܒ ܕܗܒܐ ܐܘ ܗܝܟܠܐ ܕܗܘ ܡܩܕܫ ܠܗ ܠܕܗܒܐ. [18] ܘܡܢ ܕܝܡܐ [ܒܡܕܒܚܐ ܠܐ ܡܕܡ ܘܡܢ ܕܝܡܐ] ܒܩܘܪܒܢܐ ܕܥܠ ܡܕܒܚܐ ܚܐܒ. [19] ܥܘ̈ܝܪܐ ܡܢܐ ܪܒ ܩܘܪܒܢܐ ܐܘ
col 2 ܡܕܒܚܐ ܕܗܘ ܡܩܕܫ ܠܗ ܠܩܘܪܒܢܐ. [20] ܡܢ *ܕܝܡܐ ܗܟܝܠ ܒܡܕܒܚܐ ܝܡܐ ܒܗ ܘܒܟܠ ܡܐ ܕܐܝܬ ܥܠܘܗܝ. [21] ܘܡܢ ܕܝܡܐ ܒܗܝܟܠܐ ܝܡܐ ܒܗ ܘܒܡܢ ܕܥܡܪ ܒܗ. [22] ܘܡܢ ܕܝܡܐ ܒܫܡܝܐ ܝܡܐ ܒܟܘܪܣܝܗ ܕܐܠܗܐ ܘܒܡܢ ܕܝܬܒ ܥܠܘܗܝ ܀

[23] ܘܝ ܠܟܘܢ ܣܦܪ̈ܐ ܘܦܪ̈ܝܫܐ ܢܣ̈ܒܝ ܒܐ̈ܦܐ. ܕܡܥܣܪܝܢ ܐܢܬܘܢ ܢܢܥܐ ܘܫܒܬܐ ܘܟܡܘܢܐ. ܘܫܒܩܬܘܢ ܝܩܝܪ̈ܬܗ ܕܐܘܪܝܬܐ. ܕܝܢܐ ܘܚܘܒܐ ܘܗܝܡܢܘܬܐ. ܗܠܝܢ ܕܝܢ ܥܒܕܬܘܢ ܘܗܠܝܢ ܕܝܢ ܠܐ ܬܫܒܩܘܢ. [24] ܢܓܘ̈ܕܐ ܣܡ̈ܝܐ ܕܡܨܠܠܝܢ ܐܢܬܘܢ ܡܢ ܩܡܐ. ܘܒܠܥܝܢ ܐܢܬܘܢ ܓܡ̈ܠܐ.

[25] ܘܝ ܠܟܘܢ ܣܦܪ̈ܐ ܘܦܪ̈ܝܫܐ ܢܣ̈ܒܝ ܒܐ̈ܦܐ. ܕܡܕܟܝܢ ܐܢܬܘܢ
¶C ܒܪܗ ܕܟܣܐ ܘܕܦܝܢܟܐ. ܘܡܢ ܠܓܘ¶ ܡܠܝܢ ܚܛܘܦܝܐ ܘܥܠ ܛܢܦܘܬܐ. [26] ܦܪ̈ܝܫܐ ܥܘܝܪܐ ܕܟܘ ܠܘܩܕܡ ܓܘܗ ܕܟܣܐ ܘܐܦ ܒܪܗ ܕܟܐ ܗܘ :܀:

§A 307 [27] ܘܝ ܠܟܘܢ ܗܦܘܟ̈ܐ ܘܦܪ̈ܝܫܐ ܢܣ̈ܒܝ ܒܐ̈ܦܐ §ܕܕܡܝܢ ܐܢܬܘܢ ܠܩܒܪ̈ܐ ܕܡܢ ܠܒܪ ܡܫܘܦܪܝܢ. ܘܡܢ ܠܓܘ ܡܠܝܢ ܓܪ̈ܡܐ ܕܡܝ̈ܬܐ
¶A ܘܟܠܗ ܛܢܦܘܬܐ¶. [28] ܗܟܢܐ ܐܦ ܐܢܬܘܢ ܡܢ ܠܒܪ ܡܬܚܙܝܢ

ܒܪܗ ܕܓܗܢܐ A   16 ff. ܘܠܟܘܢ S   ܡܢ] pr. ܕ S   18 ⌜ܒܡܕܒܚܐ…ܕܝܡܐ⌝] supplied from S; om. C   23 ܢܢܥܐ] ܗܘܪܕܟܐ S (sic)   ܡܫܢܬܐ S   27 ܕܕܡܝܢ] ܘܕܡܝܢ A, preceded by [26] ܦܪ̈ܝܫܐ ܥܘ̈ܝܪܐ [25] ܠܒܪܐ ܒܪܗ ܕܟܣܐ ܘܕܦܝܢܟܐ ܡܫܟܚܝܢ ܐܢܬܘܢ. ܘܡܢ ܠܓܘ ܡܠܝܐ ܚܘܠܐ ܘܫܠܦܐ   ܠܩܒܪ̈ܐ] ܠܒܝܬ ܩܒܘܪܐ A   ܡܫܘܦܪܝܢ] + ܫܦܝܪܝܢ ܘܡܬܚܙܝܢ A   ܡܠܝܢ] ܡܠܝܐ A

time he hath become one ye make him a son of Gehenna¶ double as (*C*) *S*
much as yourselves! ¶*A*
16 "Woe to you blind guides, that ye say: 'He that sweareth by
the Temple, it hurteth not; and he that sweareth by the gold in the
17 Temple sinneth!' Foolish, blinded ones! Which is greater—the gold,
18 or the Temple that itself halloweth the gold? And 'He that
sweareth [by the altar, it hurteth not; and he that sweareth] by the
19 offering on the altar sinneth.' Blinded ones! Which is greater—the
20 offering, or the altar that itself halloweth the offering? He that
sweareth therefore by the altar sweareth by it and by all that is
21 upon it, and he that sweareth by the Temple sweareth by it and by
22 Him that dwelleth therein, and he that sweareth by the heavens
sweareth by the throne of God and by Him that sitteth thereon.
23 "Woe to you scribes and Pharisees, respecters of persons, that
ye tithe mint and anise and cummin, and have left the weighty
matters of the Law, judgement and mercy and faith! Now these ye
24 have done, but these have ye not left? Blind guides, in that ye
strain clear of gnats, and swallow camels!
25 "Woe to you scribes and Pharisees, respecters of persons, that
ye cleanse the outside of the cup and of the dish, and inside¶ | they ¶*C*
26 are full of extortion and all uncleanness! Blinded Pharisees! Cleanse
first the inside of the cup, and the outside also is clean.
27 "Woe to you scribes and Pharisees, respecters of persons, §that §*A*307
ye are like to graves that on the outside look white, and inside
28 they are full of the bones of the dead and all uncleanness!¶ So ye ¶*A*

---

18 'by the altar....sweareth'] *supplied from S*; *om. C* 23 mint] *S has a very rare word, said to mean* 'wild mint' Now these ye have done] *i.e.* *ταῦτα δὲ ποιῆσαι*: *see* Lk xi 42 *and Notes*, vol. ii 25 |they are full] *From this point to the end of S. Mark the text and translation are taken from S, as C is deficient* 27 that ye are like] And ye are like *A*, *preceded by* [26]'Blinded Pharisees! [25]Wherefore the outside of the cup and of the dish do ye wash, and within it is full of wickedness and extortion? graves] tombs *A* look white] + and seem fair *A* they are full] it is full *A*

ܐܢܬܘܢ ܠܒ̈ܢܝ ܐܢܫܐ ܐܝܟ ܙܕܝ̈ܩܐ ܘܡܢ ܠܓܘ ܡ̈ܠܝܢ ܥܘܠܐ S
ܘܢܟܝܘܬܐ

[29]ܘܠܟܘܢ ܣܦܪ̈ܐ ܘܦܪ̈ܝܫܐ ܢܣ̈ܒܝ ܒܐ̈ܦܐ ܕܒܢܝܢ ܐܢܬܘܢ ܩܒܪ̈ܐ
ܕܢܒ̈ܝܐ ܘܡܨܒܬܝܢ ܐܢܬܘܢ ܒܝܬ ܩܒܘܪ̈ܐ ܕܙܕܝ̈ܩܐ [30]ܘܐܡܪܝܢ
ܐܢܬܘܢ ܕܐܠܘ ܗܘܝܢ ܒܝܘܡܝ ܐܒ̈ܗܝܢ ܠܐ ܡܫܬܘܬܦܐ ܗܘܝܢ
ܠܗܘܢ ܒܕܡܐ ܕܢܒ̈ܝܐ· [31]ܡܛܠ ܡܣܗܕܝܢ ܐܢܬܘܢ ܕܒ̈ܢܝܐ ܐܢܬܘܢ
ܕܗܢܘܢ ܕܩܛܠܘ ܠܢܒ̈ܝܐ· [32]ܘܐܦ ܐܢܬܘܢ ܬܡܠܘܢ ܡܫܘܚܬܐ
ܕܐܒܗ̈ܝܟܘܢ [33]ܚܘ̈ܘܬܐ ܝܠܕܐ ܕܐܟܕ̈ܢܐ ܐܝܟܢܐ ܬܥܪܩܘܢ ܡܢ
ܕܝܢܐ ܕܓܗܢܐ [34]ܡܛܠ ܗܢܐ ܗܐ ܐܢܐ ܡܫܕܪ ܐܢܐ ܠܘܬܟܘܢ
ܢܒ̈ܝܐ ܘܚܟܝ̈ܡܐ ܘܣܦܪ̈ܐ ܡܢܗܘܢ ܬܩܛܠܘܢ ܘܬܙܩܦܘܢ
ܘܡܢܗܘܢ ܬܢܓܕܘܢ ܒܟܢܘܫܬܟܘܢ ܘܬܪܕܦܘܢ ܐܢܘܢ ܡܢ ܡܕܝܢܐ
ܠܡܕܝܢܐ. [35]ܕܢܐܬܐ ܥܠܝܟܘܢ ܕܡܐ ܟܠܗ ܙܕܝܩܐ ܕܐܬܐܫܕ
ܥܠ ܐܪܥܐ. ܡܢ ܕܡܗ ܕܗܒܝܠ ܙܕܝܩܐ ܘܥܕܡܐ ܠܕܡܗ ܕܙܟܪܝܐ
ܒܪ ܒܪܟܝܐ ܗܘ ܕܩܛܠܬܘܢ ܒܝܢ ܗܝܟܠܐ ܠܡܕܒܚܐ [36]ܐܡܝܢ
ܐܡܪ ܐܢܐ ܠܟܘܢ ܕܢܐܬܝܢ ܗܠܝܢ ܟܠܗܝܢ ܥܠ ܫܪܒܬܐ ܗܕܐ.
[37]ܐܘܪܫܠܡ ܐܘܪܫܠܡ ܕܩܛܠܬ, ܢܒ̈ܝܐ ܘܪܓܡܬ, ܠܐܝܠܝܢ ܕܫܠܝܚܝܢ
ܗܘܘ ܠܘܬܟ ܟܡܐ ܙܒܢܝܢ ܨܒܝܬ ܕܐܟܢܫ ܐܢܘܢ ܠܒ̈ܢܝܟܝ ܐܝܟ
ܬܪܢܓܘܠܬܐ ܕܟܢܫܐ ܠܦܪ̈ܘܓܝܗ ܕܬܚܝܬ ܓܦ̈ܝܗ ܘܠܐ ܨܒܝܬܘܢ
[38]ܗܐ ܫܒܝܩ ܒܝܬܟܘܢ [39]ܐܡܪ ܐܢܐ ܠܟܘܢ ܓܝܪ ܕܠܐ ܬܚܙܘܢܢܝ
ܡܢ ܗܫܐ ܥܕܡܐ ܕܬܐܡܪܘܢ ܒܪܝܟ ܗܘ ܕܐܬܐ ܒܫܡܗ
ܕܡܪܝܐ

[1]ܘܟܕ ܢܦܩ ܝܫܘܥ ܡܢ ܗܝܟܠܐ ܠܡܐܙܠ· ܘܩܪܒܘ ܬܠܡܝܕܘܗܝ،
ܡܚܘܝܢ ܠܗ ܒܢܝܢܐ ܕܗܝܟܠܐ [2]ܗܘ ܕܝܢ ܥܢܐ ܘܐܡܪ ܠܗܘܢ
ܚܙܝܢ ܐܢܬܘܢ ܗܠܝܢ ܟܠܗܝܢ ܒܟܐܦܐ ܐܡܝܢ ܐܡܪ ܐܢܐ ܠܟܘܢ
ܕܠܐ ܬܫܬܒܩ ܗܪܟܐ ܟܐܦܐ ܥܠ ܟܐܦܐ ܕܠܐ ܬܫܬܪܐ ·܀·

---

37 ܕܩܛܠܬ,] *S* (*sic*) ܠܘܬܟ....ܠܒ̈ܢܝܟܝ] *S* (*sic*) ܐܝܟ ܬܪܢܓܘܠܬܐ] *S* (*sic*) 1 ܘܩܪܒܘ...ܡܚܘܝܢ] *For the construction, cf* Matt xx 11 *S*

also on the outside appear to men as righteous, and inside are full of S
wickedness and turbulence.
29 "Woe to you scribes and Pharisees, respecters of persons, that ye
build the graves of the prophets and adorn the tombs of the righteous,
30 and say 'If we had been in the days of our fathers we would not
31 have been partakers with them in the blood of the prophets!' Hence
ye confess that ye are the sons of them that killed the prophets—
32, 33 and ye also will fill up the measure of your fathers! Serpents,
offspring of vipers! How will ye flee from the judgement of
34 Gehenna? Therefore, lo, I send unto you prophets and wise men
and scribes; some of them ye will kill and crucify, and some of them
ye will scourge in your synagogues and will persecute them from city
35 to city, that there may come upon you all the blood of the righteous
that hath been shed on the earth, from the blood of Habel the
righteous even unto the blood of Zacharia son of Barachia, him that
36 ye killed between the Temple and the altar. Amen, I say to you,
37 that all these things will come on this generation. Jerusalem,
Jerusalem, that killest the prophets and stonest them that have been
sent unto thee, how many times have I wished to gather thy sons
as the hen that gathereth her young that *are* under her wings—
38, 39 and ye would not! Lo, your house is left; for I say to you Ye
shall not see me from now, until ye say 'Blessed is he that cometh
in the name of the LORD.'"

xxiv 1 And when Jesus went forth from the Temple to go away and his
2 disciples drew near, they shew him the building of the Temple. But
he answered and said to them: "See ye all these stones? Amen, I
say to you There will not be left here a stone on a stone that will
not be thrown down."

³ܘܟܕ ܝܬܒ. ܒܛܘܪ ܙܝܬܐ ܩܪܒܘ ܬܠܡܝܕܘܗܝ, ܘܐܡܪܝܢ ܠܗ ܐܡܪ S
ܠܢ ܠܐܡܬܝ, ܢܗܘܝܢ [ܘܡܢܐ] ܗܝ, ܐܬܐ ܕܡܐܬܝܬܟ ܘܕܫܘܠܡܗ
ܕܥܠܡܐ

⁴ܥܢܐ ܝܫܘܥ ܘܐܡܪ ܠܗܘܢ ܚܙܘ ܕܠܐ ܐܢܫ ܢܛܥܝܟܘܢ ⁵ܣܓܝܐܐ
ܓܝܪ ܢܐܬܘܢ ܒܫܡܝ ܘܢܐܡܪܘܢ ܕܐܢܐ ܐܢܐ ܡܫܝܚܐ ܘܣܓܝܐܐ
ܢܛܥܘܢ ⁶ܥܬܝܕܝܢ ܐܢܬܘܢ ܕܝܢ ܠܡܫܡܥ * * ܘܫܡܥܐ
ܕܩܪܒܐ [ܚܙܘ] ܕܝܢ ܕܠܡܐ [ܬܬܕܠܚܘܢ §ܥܬܝܕܢ ܐܝܢ ܗܠܝܢ §A417
ܠܡܗܘܐ¶] ܐܠܐ ܠܐ ⌜ܥܕܟܝܠ⌝ ܫܘܠܡܐ ⁷ܢܩܘܡ ܓܝܪ ܥܡܐ ܥܠ ¶A
ܥܡܐ ܘܡܠܟܘܬܐ ܥܠ ܡܠܟܘܬܐ ܘܢܗܘܘܢ ܟܦ̈ܢܐ ܘܙܘܥܐ
ܒܐܬܪܘܢ ܐܬܪܘܢ܂ ⁸ܗܠܝܢ ܕܝܢ ܟܠܗܝܢ ܪܫܐ ܐܢܝܢ ܕܚܒܠܐ
⁹ܘܗܝܕܝܢ ܢܫܠܡܘܢܟܘܢ ܠܐܘܠܨܢܐ ܘܢܩܛܠܘܢܟܘܢ ܘܬܗܘܘܢ ܣܢܝܐ
ܠܟܘܢ ܟܠ ܐܢܫ ܡܛܠ ܫܡܝ. ¹⁰ܗܝܕܝܢ ܢܬܟܫܠܘܢ ܣܓܝܐܐ ܘܚܕ
ܠܚܕ ܢܫܠܡܘܢ ܘܢܣܢܘܢ ܚܕ ܠܚܕ. ¹¹ܘܣܓܝܐܐ ܢܒܝܐ ܕܓܠܐ
ܢܩܘܡܘܢ ܘܢܛܥܘܢ ܣܓܝܐܐ ¹²ܘܡܛܠ ܣܓܝܐܘܬ ܥܘܠܐ ܢܦܘܓ
ܚܘܒܐ ܕܣܓܝܐܐ ¹³ܐܠܐ ܡܢ ܕܢܣܝܒܪ ܥܕܡܐ ܠܚܪܬܐ ܗܘ ܢܚܐ
¹⁴†ܘܬܬܟܪܙ ܗܕܐ ܣܒܪܬܐ† ܕܡܠܟܘܬܐ ܒܟܠܗ ܥܠܡܐ ܠܣܗܕܘܬܐ
ܕ⌜ܟ⌝ܠܗܘܢ ܥܡܡܐ ܘܗܝܕܝܢ ܢܐܬܐ ܫܘܠܡܐ
¹⁵ܡܐ ܕܝܢ ܕܚܙܝܬܘܢ ܐܬܐ ܕ⌜ܛ⌝ܢ⌜ܦ⌝ܘܬܐ * * ܕܐܬܐܡܪ
ܒܝܕ ܕܢܝܐܝܠ ܢܒܝܐ ܗܘ ܕܩܪܐ ܢܣܬܟܠ ¹⁶ܗܝܕܝܢ ܐܝܠܝܢ [ܕܒܝܗܘܕ]
ܢܥܪܩܘܢ ܠܛܘܪܐ ¹⁷ܘܗܘ ܕܒܐܓܪܐ ܗܘ ܠܐ ܢܚܘܬ ܠܡܣܒ
ܡܢ ܒܝܬܗ. ¹⁸ܘܐܝܢܐ ܕܒܚܩܠܐ ܗܘ ܠܐ ܢܬܦܢܐ ܠܒܣܬܪܗ
ܠܡܣܒ ܡܐܢܘܗܝ ܀

---

6 * * ܠܡܫܡܥ] *The illegible word may be either* ܩܪܒܐ (*as* Lk xxi 9) *or* ܩܪ̈ܒܐ (*as* Mk xiii 7) ܥܬܝܕܢ...ܠܡܗܘܐ] *The illegible words are supplied from A* 9. *For the quotations in A* 415, *see on* Lk xxi 12—17
14 ܘܬܬܟܪܙ ܗܕܐ ܣܒܪܬܐ] *S*[ed]: *of these words* ܗܕܐ *is clear* 15 * * ܕ⌜ܛ⌝ܢ⌜ܦ⌝ܘܬܐ] *S*[ed]: *it would be easy to supply* ܕܚܘܪܒܐ (*or* ܚܘܪܒܢ), *but* 'Ephr' v 222 E *has* ܛܢܦܐ *only* (*sic*[ed], *omitting* ܕܚܘܪܒܐ). *Perhaps the space is really blank in S*

3 And when he sat on the Mount of Olives his disciples drew near *S*
and say to him: "Say to us when they shall be, [and what] is the
sign of thy coming and of the conclusion of the world?"
4 Jesus answered and said to them: "See that no one lead you
5 astray. For many will come in my name, and will say 'I am the
6 Messiah' and many will they lead astray. But ye are about to hear of
[wars] and rumour of wars, but [see] lest [ye be afraid; §these things §*A* 417
7 are about to be,¶] but not yet *is* the conclusion. For people will rise ¶*A*
against people and kingdom against kingdom, and there will be
8 famines and earthquakes in various countries; but all these things
9 are the beginning of travail. And then they will deliver you up to
distress and they will kill you, and every man will be hating you for
10 my name's sake. Then many will be offended and will deliver up one
11 another and will hate one another, and many prophets of falsehood
12 will arise and will lead astray many; and because of the multitude
13 of wickedness the love of many will be chilled. But he that shall
14 endure unto the last, he shall live. And †this gospel† of the kingdom
will be preached in all the world for a witness to all the peoples,
and then will come the conclusion.
15 "Now what *time* ye have seen the sign of abomination [of
desolation] that was said by Daniel the prophet—he that readeth, let
16 him understand—then they [that *are* in Judaea] let them flee to
17 the hill-*country*, and he that is on the roof let him not go down
18 to take *aught* from his house, and he which is in the field let him
not turn round behind to take his cloak.

---

6 ⌜wars⌝] *S illegible*: Lk xxi 9 *has* 'wars', Mk xiii 7 *has* 'battles' ⌜these things are about to be⌝] *These words* (*illegible in S*) *are supplied from A* 9. *For the quotations in A* 415, *see on* Lk xxi 12—17
15 the sign of abomination ⌜of desolation⌝] 'of desolation' *is illegible in S*, *and possibly was omitted*: 'Ephr' v 222 E *has* 'the unclean sign'; *E*[213] *has* 'the sign of the terror of its desolation'

S §A 37 19 ܘܝ ܕܝܢ ܠܒܛܢܬܐ ܘܠܐܝܠܝܢ ܕܡܝܢܩܢ ܒܗܘܢ ܝܘ̈ܡܬܐ. §20 ܗܘܝܬܘܢ
§A 244 ¶A 2/2 ܕܝܢ ܡܨܠܝܢ §ܕܠܐ ܬܗܘܐ ܥܪܘܩܬܟܘܢ ܒܣܬܘܐ ܘܠܐ ܒܫܒܬܐ¶
21 ܬܗܘܐ ܓܝܪ ܗܝܕܝܢ ܐܘܠܨܢܐ ܪܒܐ ܕܠܐ ܐܟܘܬܗ ܡܢ ܫܘܪܝ
ܥܠܡܐ ܥܕܡܐ ܠܗܫܐ ܘܐܦܠܐ ܬܗܘܐ 22 ܘܐܠܘ ܠܐ [ܗܘܐ]
ܟܪܝܢ ܗܘܘ ܝܘ̈ܡܬܐ ܗܠܝܢ܂ ܠܐ ܚܝܐ ܗܘܐ ܟܠ [ܒܣܪ] ܡܛܠ
ܓܒܝܐ ܕܝܢ ܢܬܟܪܘܢ܂ ܝܘ̈ܡܬܐ ܗܠܝܢ܂ 23 ܗܝܕܝܢ ܐܢ܂ ܐܢܫ ܢܐܡܪ
ܠܟܘܢ܂ ܕܗܐ ܗܪܟܐ ܗܘ ܡܫܝܚܐ ܗܐ ܬܡܢ ܗܘ ܠܐ
ܬܗܝܡܢܘܢ܂ 24 ܢܩܘܡܘܢ ܓܝܪ ܡܫܝܚܐ ܕܓܠܐ ܘܢܒ̈ܝܐ ܕܓܠܐ
ܘܢܬܠܘܢ܂ ܐܬܘܬܐ ܪܘܪܒܬܐ ܘܬܕܡܘܪܬܐ ܗܟܢܐ ܕܐܢ܂ ܡܫܟܚܐ
ܐܦ ܠܓܒܝܐ ܢܛܥܘܢ܂. 25 ܗܐ ܩܕܡܬ ܐܡܪܬ ܠܟܘܢ܂ 26 ܕܐܢ܂
ܢܐܡܪܘܢ܂ ܠܟܘܢ܂ ܗܐ ܒܡܕܒܪܐ ܗܘ. ܠܐ ܬܦܩܘܢ܂ ܐܘ ܗܐ
§ASD 25 ܒܬܘܢܐ ܗܘ ܠܐ ܬܗܝܡܢܘܢ܂ §27 ܐܝܟܢܐ ܕܒܪܩܐ ܓܝܪ ܢܦܩ ܡܢ
ܡܕܢܚܐ ܘܡܬܚܙܐ ܥܕܡܐ ܠܡܥܪܒܐ ܗܟܢܐ ܬܗܘܐ ܡܐܬܝܬܗ
¶ASD ܕܒܪܗ ܕܐܢܫܐ¶ 28 ܐܝܟܐ ܕܦܓܪܐ ܬܡܢ ܢܬܟܢܫܘܢ܂ ܢܫܪ̈ܐ ܀
29 ܡܚܕܐ ܕܝܢ ܡܢ ܒܬܪ ܐܘܠܨܢܐ ܕܗܢܘܢ܂ ܝܘ̈ܡܬܐ ܢܚܫܘܟ ܫܡܫܐ
ܘܣܗܪܗ ܕܣܗܪܐ ܠܐ ܢܢܗܪ ܘܢܦܠܘܢ܂ ܟܘܟܒܐ ܡܢ ܫܡܝܐ
ܘܢܙܘܥܘܢ܂ ܚܝܠܘܬܐ ܕܫܡܝܐ 30 ܘܗܝܕܝܢ ܬܬܚܙܐ ܢܝܫܗ ܕܒܪܗ
ܕܐܢܫܐ ܒܫܡܝܐ ܘܢܚܙܘܢ܂ ܠܒܪܗ ܕܐܢܫܐ ܕܐܬܐ ܥܠ ܥܢ̈ܢܝ
ܫܡܝܐ ܥܡ ܚܝܠܐ ܪܒܐ ܘܫܘܒܚܐ 31 ܘܢܫܕܪ ܡܠܐܟܘܗܝ, ܥܡ
ܩܪܢܐ ܪܒܬܐ ܘܢܟܢܫ ܠܓܒ̈ܝܘܗܝ, ܡܢ ܐܪ̈ܒܥ ܪ̈ܘܚܐ ܡܢ ܥܒܪܐ
ܕܫܡܝܐ ܥܕܡܐ ܠܥܒܪܐ 32 ܡܢ ܬܬܐ ܕܝܢ ܝܠܦܘ ܦܠܐܬܐ ܕܡܬܐ
ܕܪܟܒܘ ܫܘ̈ܟܝܗ ܘܦܪܥܘ ܛܪ̈ܦܝܗ ܝܕܥܝܢ ܐܢܬܘܢ܂ ܕܩܪܝܒ ܗܘ
ܩܝܛܐ 33 ܗܟܢܐ ܐܦ ܐܢܬܘܢ܂ ܡܐ ܕܚܙܝܬܘܢ܂ ܗܠܝܢ ܟܠܗܝܢ
ܝܕܥܝܢ ܐܢܬܘܢ܂ ܕܩܪܒܬ ܠܬܪܥܐ 34 ܐܡܝܢ ܐܡܪܢܐ ܠܟܘܢ܂ ܕܠܐ
§A 266 ܬܥܒܪ ܫܪܒܬܐ ܗܕܐ ܥܕܡܐ ܕܗܠܝܢ ܟܠܗܝܢ ܢܗܘܝܢ §35 ܫܡܝܐ
¶A ܘܐܪܥܐ ܢܥܒܪܘܢ܂ ܘܡܠܝ ܠܐ ܢܥܒܪܢ܂¶ ܀

---

20 ܗܘܝܬܘܢ ܕܝܢ ܡܨܠܝܢ] ܨܠܘ A 37   ܘܠܐ ܒܫܒܬܐ] ܘܒܫܒܬܐ A 2/2
27 ܐܝܟܢܐ....ܢܦܩ] ܐܝܟ ܒܪܩܐ ܕܢܦܩ ASD   32 ܕܪܟܒܘ] *see* Mk xiii 28

19 "Now woe to them with child, and to them that are giving suck *S*
20 in those days! §But be praying §that your flight may not be in the §*A* 37
21 winter nor on the sabbath.¶ For there will be then great distress, §*A* 244 ¶*A* 2/2
the like of which *hath* not *been* from the *first* habitation of the world
22 until to-day, neither shall be. And if it had not [been *that*] those
days were short no [flesh] would live, but because of the chosen ones
23 those days will be shortened. Then if any one shall say to you 'Lo,
24 here is the Messiah'—'Lo, there he is'—do not believe. For there
will arise lying Messiahs and lying prophets and they will give great
signs and wonders, so that if possible even the chosen ones they will
25, 26 lead astray. Lo, I beforehand have said to you, that if they shall say
to you 'Lo, he is in the desert' do not go forth, or 'Lo, he is in the
27 inner chamber' do not believe; §for as the lightning lighteneth from §ASD 25
the east and is seen unto the west, so will be the coming of the Son
28 of Man.¶ Where the body *is*, there will be gathered the vultures. ¶ASD
29 "Now immediately after the distress of those days the sun will be
darkened and the light of the moon will not shine, and the stars will
30 fall from heaven and the powers of heaven will tremble, and then
will be seen the signal of the Son of Man in heaven, and ye will
see the Son of Man coming on the clouds of heaven with great
31 power and glory. And he will send his angels with a great trumpet
and will gather his chosen from the four winds from across the
32 heaven unto the other side. Now from the fig-tree learn a parable,
that what *time* its branches have become tender and its leaves are
33 put forth ye know that the summer is near; so ye also, what *time* ye
have seen all these things, ye know that it hath drawn nigh to the
34 door. Amen, I say to you that this generation will not pass away
35 until all these things be. §Heaven and earth will pass away, and my §*A* 266
words will not pass away.¶ ¶*A*

---

20 But be praying] Pray *A* 37 nor] and *A* 2/2 22. *For* E^{215}, *see on* Mk xiii 20 27 for] *om.* ASD lighteneth] *pr.* that ASD (*so also* $E^{211 \text{ vid}}$)

³⁶ܥܠ ܝܘܡܐ ܕܝܢ ܘܥܠ ܫܥܬܐ ܗܿ ܐܢܫ ܠܐ ܝܕܥ ܘܐܦܠܐ S
ܡܠܐܟܐ ܫܡܝܢܐ ܐܠܐ ܐܒܐ ܒܠܚܘܕ. ³⁷ܐܝܟ ܕܗܘܐ ܓܝܪ ܒܝܘܡܝ
ܢܘܚ ܗܟܢܐ ܬܗܘܐ ܡܐܬܝܬܗ ܕܒܪܗ ܕܐܢܫܐ. ³⁸ܐܝܟܢܐ ܓܝܪ
ܕܗܘܘ ܩܕܡ ܛܘܦܢܐ ܐܟܠܝܢ ܗܘܘ ܘܫܬܝܢ ܘܡܟܪܝܢ ܘܡܡܟܪ̈ܝܢ
ܒܝܘܡܐ ܕܥܠ ܢܘܚ ܠܩܒܘܬܐ. ³⁹ܘܠܐ ܝܕܥܘ ܒܝܘܡܐ ܕܐܬܐ
ܛܘܦܢܐ ܘܫܩܠ ܠܟܠܗܘܢ. ܗܟܢܐ ܬܗܘܐ ܡܐܬܝܬܗ ܕܒܪܗ
ܕܐܢܫܐ. ⁴⁰ܗܝܕܝܢ ܬܪܝܢ ܢܗܘܘܢ ܒܚܩܠܐ ܚܕ ܢܬܕܒܪ ܘܚܕ ܢܫܬܒܩ
⁴¹ܘܬܪܬܝܢ ܢܗܘܝܢ ܛܚܢܢ ܒܪܚܝܐ ܚܕܐ ܡܬܕܒܪܐ ܘܚܕܐ ܡܫܬܒܩܐ
⁴²ܗܘܘ ܥܝܪܝܢ ܕܠܐ ܝܕܥܝܢ ܐܢܬܘܢ ܒܐܝܕܐ ܫܥܬܐ ܐܬܐ ܡܪܟܘܢ
⁴³[ܘ]ܗܕܐ [ܗܘܝܬܘܢ] ܝܕܥܝܢ ܕܐܠܘ ܝܕܥ ܗܘܐ ܡܪܐ ܒܝܬܐ
ܒܐܝܕܐ ܡܛܪܬܐ ܐܬܐ ܗܘܐ ܓܢܒܐ ܡܬܬܥܝܪ ܗܘܐ ܘܠܐ
ܫܒܩ ܗܘܐ ܕܢܬܦܠܫ ܒܝܬܗ. ⁴⁴ܡܛܠ ܗܢܐ ܐܦ ܐܢܬܘܢ ܗܘܝܬܘܢ
ܡܛܝܒܝܢ ܕܒܫܥܬܐ ܕܠܐ ܣܒܪܝܢ ܐܢܬܘܢ ܐܬܐ ܒܪܗ ܕܐܢܫܐ
⁴⁵[ܡܢܘ ܟܝ] ܐܝܬܘܗܝ, ܐܝܢܐ [ܥܒܕܐ] ܡܗܝܡܢܐ ܘ[ܚܟܝܡܐ]
ܕܐܘܩܡܗ ܡܪܗ ܥܠ ܒܢܝ ܒܝܬܗ. ܕܢܬܠ ܠܗܘܢ ܦܪܢܣܐ ܒܥܕܢܗ.
⁴⁶ܛܘܒܘܗܝ, ܠܥܒܕܐ ܗܘ ܕܐܬܐ ܢܐܬܐ ܡܪܗ ܢܫܟܚܝܘܗܝ, ܕܥܒܕ
ܗܟܢܐ. ⁴⁷ܐܡܝܢ ܐܡܪܢܐ ܠܟܘܢ ܕܢܫܠܛܝܘܗܝ, ܥܠ ܟܠ ܡܐ
ܕܐܝܬ ܠܗ. ⁴⁸ܐܢ ܕܝܢ ܢܐܡܪ ܥܒܕܐ ܒܝܫܐ ܒܠܒܗ ܕܡܘܚܪ,
ܡܪܝ ܠܡܐܬܐ ⁴⁹ܘܢܫܪܐ ܠܡܡܚܐ ܠܟܢܘܬܗ ܘܢܗܘܐ ܐܟܠ ܘܫܬܐ
ܥܡ ܪܘܝܐ ⁵⁰ܢܐܬܐ ܡܪܗ ܕܥܒܕܐ ܗܘ ܒܝܘܡܐ ܕܠܐ ܣܒܪ
ܘܒܫܥܬܐ ܕܠܐ ܝܕܥ ⁵¹ܘܢܦܠܓܝܘܗܝ, ܘܢܣܝܡ ܡܢܬܗ ܥܡ ܢܣܒ̈ܝ
ܒܐܦ̈ܐ ܬܡܢ ܢܗܘܐ ܒܟܝܐ ܘܚܘܪܩ ܫܢܐ ܀
¹ܗܝܕܝܢ ܬܬܕܡܐ ܡܠܟܘܬܐ ܕܫܡܝܐ ܠܥܣܪ̈ ܒܬܘܠܢ ܕܫܩܠ
ܠܡܦ̈ܢܝܗܝܢ ܘܢܦܩ ܠܐܘܪܥ ܚܬܢܐ ܘܟܠܬܐ. ²ܚܡܫ ܕܝܢ ܡܢܗܝܢ
ܚܟܝܡܢ ܗܘܝ, ܘܚܡܫ ܣܟܠܢ. ³ܘܗܢܝܢ ܣܟܠܬܐ ܢܣܒ ܠܡܦ̈ܢܝܗܝܢ ܘܠܐ

39 ܕܒܪܗ ܕܐܢܫܐ] *S (sic): the right-hand stroke of* ܗ *is visible in the photograph* 43 ܘ[ܗ]ܕܐ ܗܘܝܬܘܢ ܝܕܥܝܢ] *This occupies one line of S, and nothing is lost at the end.* S^{ed} *has* ܗܕܐ ܕܝܢ ܝܕܥܝܢ * * *

36 "Now of the day and of that hour no one knoweth, not even the S
37 angels of heaven, but the Father only. For as it was in the days of
38 Noah, so will be the coming of the Son of Man. For just as before
the Flood they were eating and drinking and betrothing and being
39 betrothed until Noah entered the ark, and they knew not until the
Flood came and took them all away, so will be the coming of the Son
40 of Man. Then two *men* will be in the hill, one will be taken and one
41 will be left; and two *women* will be grinding at the mill, one *to be*
taken and one left.

42 "Be watchful, for that ye know not at which hour cometh your
43 Lord. [And] this know, that if the master of the house were to know
at which watch the thief would be coming, he would be watching and
44 would not suffer that his house should be broken through. There-
fore ye also be ready, for that in an hour that ye expect not will
45 come the Son of Man. [Who then] is that [slave,] faithful and [wise],
which his lord hath set up over his fellow-servants, that he may
46 give them the ration *of food* in its time? Happy is it for that slave,
47 whom if his lord come he shall find doing so. Amen, I say to you
48 that he will give him authority over all that he hath. But if the
49 evil slave say in his heart 'My lord delayeth to come,' and he
begin to beat his fellow-servants, and be eating and drinking with
50 the drunkards, the lord of that slave will come in a day that he doth
51 not expect and in an hour that he doth not know, and will divide
him and set his portion with the respecters of persons, and there
shall be the weeping and the gnashing of teeth!

xxv 1 "Then will the kingdom of heaven be likened to ten virgins that
took their torches and went forth to meet the bridegroom and the
2, 3 bride. Now five of them were foolish and five wise; and the foolish

---

43 ⌜And⌝ this know] *S partly illegible* **45** that ⌜slave,⌝ faithful and ⌜wise⌝] *S partly illegible*: 'the overseer, the faithful servant, good and wise' E^{218} (*cf* Lk xii 42) **51** weeping] 'weeping of eyes' E^{218} **2** foolish... wise] *so also* E^{218} (*and* arm. vg)

ܢܣܒ ܒܟܗܘܢ ܡܫܝܚܐ [4]ܫܒܝܚܘܬܐ ܕܝܢ ܢܣܒ ܡܫܝܚܐ ܒܡܐܡܢܐ ܒܡ S
ܠܡܥܒܕܝܗܘܢ. [5]ܟܕ ܐܡܪ ܕܝܢ ܫܠܝܚܐ ܠܗ ܒܩܠܗܘܢ ܘܕܡܟܝܢ. [6]ܒܦܠܓܐ
ܕܝܢ ܕܠܠܝܐ ܗܘܐ ܥܠܗ ܗܐ ܫܠܝܚܐ ܐܬܐ ܦܘܩܐ ܠܐܘܪܚܗ
[7]ܗܝܕܝܢ ܡܢ ܟܠܗܘܢ ܩ̈ܘܠܬܐ ܗܠܝܢ ܘܬܘܒ ܠܡܥܒܕ̈ܝܗܘܢ [8]ܐܡܪ̈ܝܢ
ܗܠܝܢ ⌜ܩ̈ܠܬܐ⌝ ܠܗܠܝܢ ܫܒܝܚ̈ܬܐ ܗܟܝܢ ܠܝ ܡܢ ܡܫܝܚܝܢ ܕܗܘܐ
ܕܒܝܢ ܠܗܘܢ ܠܡܥܒܕܝܢ [9]ܐܡܪ̈ܝܢ ܠܗܘܢ ܗ̈ܠܝܢ ܫܒܝܚ̈ܬܐ ܕܠܡܐ
ܠܐ ܢܥܒܕ ܠܝ ܘܠܒ̈ܢܝ. ܐܠܐ ܐܠܝܢ ܠܗܬ ܐܝܠܝܢ ܕܡܒܪܟܝܢ ܘܒܢܝܢ
ܠܒ̈ܢܝ. [10]ܘܟܕ ܐܙܠ ܠܡܒܥܐ ܐܬܐ ܫܠܝܚܐ ܘܗܘܝܢ ܕܡܠܝܟܝܢ ܗܘܘ، ܟܠ
ܒܝܘܡ ܠܒܝܬ ܡܫܬܘܬܐ. ܘܐܬܐ ܠܗ ܬܪܥܐ [11]ܒܐܚܪܝܬܐ ܕܝܢ
ܐܬܝ، ܗ̈ܢܝܢ ܒܬܘ̈ܠܬܐ ܘܐܡܪ̈ܝܢ ܡܪܢ ܦܬܚ ܠܢ. [12]ܗܘ ܕܝܢ
ܥܢܐ ܘܐܡܪ ܐܡܝܢ ܐܡܪܢܐ ܠܟ̈ܝܢ ܕܠܐ ܝܕܥܢܐ ܠ̈ܟܝܢ [13]ܐܬܒܥܪܘ
ܗܒܝܠ ܕܠܐ ܐܢܬܘܢ ܝܕܥܬܘܢ ܠܗ ܠܝܘܡܐ ܘܠܐ ܠܫܥܬܐ
[14]⌜ܐܬܒܢܐ⌝ ܓܒܪ ܕܥܒܪܐ ⌜ܕܐܙܠ⌝ ܘܩܪܐ ܠܥܒܕܘܗܝ، ܘܐܫܠܡ ܠܗܘܢ
ܩܢܝܢܗ [15]ܐܝܬ ܕܝܗܒ ܠܗ ܚܡܫ ⌜ܟܟܪ̈ܝܢ⌝ ܘܐܝܬ ܕܬܪ̈ܬܝܢ ܘܐܝܬ
ܕܚܕܐ * * [16]* * * * * * [17]ܘܗܒܘܬ [ܐܦ] ܗܘ
ܕܬܪ̈ܬܝܢ * * * ܓܪ ܒܬܪ̈ܬܝܢ * * [18]ܗܘ ܕܝܢ ⌜ܕܢܣܒ⌝ ܚܕܐ
ܐܙܠ [ܚܦܪ] ܒܐܪܥܐ ܘܛܡܪ ܟܣܦܐ ܕܡܪܗ [19]ܒܬܪ ܕܝܢ ܙܒܢܐ
ܣܓܝܐܐ ܐܬܐ [ܡܪܗܘܢ] ܕܗܢܘܢ ܥܒܕ̈ܐ ܘܢܣܒ ܡܢܗܘܢ
ܚܘܫܒܢܐ [20]ܘܩܪܒ ܗܘ ܕܢܣܒ ܚܡܫ ⌜ܟܟܪ̈ܝܢ⌝ ܘܩܪܒ ܚܡܫ ܐܚܪ̈ܢܝܢ
ܘܐܡܪ ܡܪܝ، ܚܡܫ ⌜ܟܟܪ̈ܝܢ⌝ ܝܗܒܬ ܠܝ ܗܐ * * * * * *

[21–25] *[One column here illegible]*

* * * * * * * * * * * * * * *

ܗܐ ⌜ܡܒܠ⌝ ⌜ܕܝܠܟ⌝ [26]ܥܢܐ ܡܪܗ ܘܐܡܪ ܠܗ ܥܒܕܐ ܒܝܫܐ
[ܘܚܒܢܢܐ] ܝܕܥ ܗܘܝܬ ⌜ܠܝ⌝ ܕܩܫܝܐ ܐܢܐ [ܐܬܪ ܕܠܐ ܙܪܥܬ]
ܘܡܟܢܫ ⌜ܐܢܐ⌝ [ܐܬܪ ܕܠܐ] ܒܕܪܬ *[27] * * ܕܝܢ * * *

15, 20 *bis*. ⌜ܟܟܪ̈ܝܢ⌝] *The word is illegible in all three places: it is said to look more like* ܕܪ̈ܟܝܢ (? = ܕܪ̈ܟܡܘܢܝܢ). *There is no mention of* 'Talents' *in Thos*[314], *but cf* ܕܝܗܒ ܡܪܢ ܘܟܟܪܗ ܚܡܫ ܟ̈ܟܪܝܢ *A* 433 17 ܓܒܪ*] ܓܒܪ S[ed]

4 ones took their torches and took with them no oil, but the wise took *S*
5 oil in the vessels with their torches. Now when the bridegroom
6 delayed they all slumbered and slept, but in the middle of the night
there was a cry: 'Lo, the bridegroom cometh; go forth to meet
7 him!' Then arose all those virgins and trimmed their torches.
8 The foolish ones say to the wise ones: 'Give us of your oil, for lo,
9 our torches are going out!' The wise ones say to them: '*Nay*, lest
it suffice not for us and for you; but go unto them that sell, and buy
10 for yourselves.' And while they *were* going to buy the bridegroom
came, and they that were ready entered with him to the wedding-
11 feast, and the door was shut. Now at the last came those virgins and
12 say: 'Our Lord, open to us!' But he answered and said: 'Amen, I
13 say to you I know you not.' Watch therefore, for that ye know not
14 the day nor the hour. For as a man that set off *on a journey* and
15 called his slaves and delivered to them his property, there was one to
whom he gave five [talents], and one with two, and one with one
16, 17 * * * * * * and similarly [also] he with the two
18 [talents] * * [traded] with the two * * But he
that received one went [*and* digged] in the earth and hid the silver of
19 his master. Now after a long time came [the lord] of those slaves
20 and took of them a reckoning. And he drew near which received five
[talents] and offered five others and said: 'My lord, five [talents] thou
21–25 gavest me, lo, * * * * * * * * * *
* * * * * * * * * * * * *
26 lo, accept thine own.' His lord answered and said to him: 'Evil
slave [and lazy], thou knewest me that I reap [where I have not
27 sown] and gather [where I have not] scattered. But * * *

15, 20 *bis.* ⌜talents⌝] *The word is illegible in all three places: it is said to look like a word which may mean* 'Darics.' *There is no mention of* 'Talents' *in Thos*[314], *but cf* 'He that made his Pound and his Talent five portions...' *A* 433

ܥܠ * * * ܕܝܢ * * * * * * * * * * S

[28–31] [*More than half a column here illegible*]

* * * * * * * * * * * * * *

[32]ܘܐܬܦܢܝ⌈ ⌉ ܡܣܥܘܕܝܗܝ, ܠܟܠܗܘܢ ܒܥܡܡܐ ܘܦܩܘܪ ܐܢܘܢ ܚܝ ܡܢ

ܚܝ ܐܢܬ ⌈ ⌉ ܕܒܝܫܐ ⌈ ⌉ ܚܕܐ ܡܢ ܠܒܝܫܐ [33]ܘܐܡܪ [ܒܪܢܫܐ]

ܡܢ ܡܚܒܘܫܝܐ ܘܠܒܝܬܐ ܡܢ ܩܛܠܐ [34]ܫܡܥܘܢ ܐܡܪ ܐܢܐ ⌈ܟܠ⌉ܒ⌈ܐ⌉ ܠܡܘܬ

§A 380 f. §A 74 ܕܡܢ ܡܚܒܘܫ ܬܘ§ ܒܪܬܡܗ, ܕܐܟܝ ܬܪܬܘ * * * ܗܘܬ

* * * * * * * * * * * [35]* * *

ܐܡܣܟܝܢܐ ܗܘܝܬ ܘܡܣܬܒܪܬܘܢ [36]ܒܪܓܠܐ ܗܘܝܬ ܘܐܬܚܠܦܬܘܢ

¶A 74 * * ܠܗ * * * [37]ܠܘܬ, * * ¶* * * * *

ܐܘ ܒܪܝ ܐܡܪܬ, ܚܫܒܢ * * ܐܢܬ * * * * *

31. *Cf A* 289 (ܬܪܬܝܢ *A*ª) ܬܪܬܡܫ ܥܠ ܬܪܥܝܢ ܕܢܫܝܐ ܕܬܠܡܝܕܐ ܕܥܡܝ ܘܗܘܘ ܒܪܐ ܬܪܥܣܪ ܫܒܛܐ. ܘܗܘܘ ܕܢܬܪܥ ܠܟܠܗܘܢ ܘܡܫܪ ܠܫܒܛܐ. *Cf also* Mt xix 28

32 ff. *The text of S is here so imperfect that I give the quotations and allusions in A below in full.*

A 74

(32, 33) ܒܟ ܒܥܐ ܘܐܬܩܢ

ܡܢ ܚܒܘܫܝܐ ܘܡܢ ܩܛܠܐ.

34ª ܫܡܥܘܢ ܐܡܪ ܠܟ ܕܡܢ ܚܒܘܫܝܐ.

35ª ܕܟܕ ܫܕܪܬܟܘܢ ܠܐ ܠܡܐܟܠ.

ܘܐܦ ܗܘܐ ܗܘܝܬ ܘܐܬܡܣܟܢܬܘܢ.

36ᵇ ܘܐܬܚܪܬ ܘܚܪܬܘܢ.

35ᵇ ܘܐܬܒܪܐ ܗܘܝܬ ܘܒܣܒܪܬܘܢ.

A 380, 381

(32, 33) ܒܟ ܒܥܐ ܘܐܬܩܢ

ܡܢ ܚܒܘܫܝܐ ܘܡܢ ܩܛܠܐ...

34 ܐܡܪ ܠܗ ܠܫܡܥܘܢ ܚܒܘܫܝܐ.

ܬܘ ܒܪܬܡܗܝ ܕܐܟܝ. ܬܪܬܘ (ܘܬܪܬܘ *A*ª)

ܡܠܟܘܬܐ ܕܐܒܘܗܝ ܗܘܬ ܠܗܘܢ

ܡܢ ܒܪܝܬܐ.

35ª ܡܛܠ ܕܫܕܪܬ ܘܫܡܥܬܘܢ ܠܝ ܠܡܐܟܠ.

ܘܐܦ ܗܘܐ ܗܘܝܬ ܘܐܬܡܣܟܢܬܘܢ.

36ª ܘܒܪܓܠ ܗܘܝܬ ܘܐܬܚܠܦܬܘܢ.

35ᵇ ܘܐܡܣܟܝܢܐ ܗܘܝܬ ܘܡܣܬܒܪܬܘܢ.

36ᵇ ܘܐܬܚܪܬ ܘܚܪܬܘܢ.

ܘܗܘܬ ܐܚܪܝܐ ܗܘܝܬ ܘܐܬܚܬܘܢ ܠܘܬܝ.

37–39 ܗܘܝܬ ܗܘܘ ܕܢܫܩܘܢ..... ܒܗ ܘܐܬܚܪܝܢ ܠܗ.

ܐܬܚܘܝ ܚܫܝܒ ܒܪܝ. (ܒܪܝ ܐ' ܚ' *A*ª)

ܒܛܘܪܐ ܕܙܝܬܐ ܘܡܢܐ ܠܝ ܗܘܐ.

28–31 * * * * * * * * * * * * * S
* * * * * * * * * * * * *

32 and there will be gathered before him all the peoples, and he will
separate them one from another as the shepherd that separateth
33 the sheep from the goats, and he will make [the sheep] stand on
34 his right and the goats on his left. Then will the King say to
those on his right: §'Come, ye blessed of my Father, inherit [the §A 380 f.
35 kingdom that] was [for you prepared] * * * * * §A 74
* * * * * * * * * * * * *

36 I was a stranger and ye gathered me, I was a naked man and ye
clothed me, [I was an infirm man and ye visited me,¶ I was in prison ¶A 74
37 and ye came] unto me.' [Then will the righteous say] to him: 'Oh,
our Lord! when saw we thee [that] thou [wast hungry and gave thee

---

31. *Cf* A 289: 'He is the Judge of the dead and of the living, that sitteth on the Throne and judgeth the Tribes, and he it is that giveth inheritance in the kingdom and sendeth to torment': *cf also* Mt xix 28

32 ff. *The text of S is here so imperfect that I give the quotations and allusions in A below in full.*

A 380, 381	*A* 74
(32, 33) When he separated and made *them* stand on his right and on his left	(32, 33) When he separated and made *them* stand on his right and on his left,
34 For he said to them on his right:	34[a] thus he said to them on his right
'Come, ye blessed of my Father, inherit ('and inherit' *A*[a])	
the kingdom that hath been prepared for you from the beginning;	
35[a] because I was an hungred and ye gave me to eat,	35[a] 'I was an hungred and ye gave me to eat,
and I was thirsty and ye gave me to drink,	and I was thirsty and ye gave me drink,
36[a] and I was naked and ye clothed me,	
35[b] and I was a stranger and ye gathered me,	36[b] and I was infirm and ye visited me,
36[b] and I was infirm and ye visited me,	35[b] and I was a stranger and ye gathered me.'
and I was in prison and ye came unto me.'	
37–39 Then those righteous...answered and say to him:	
'When saw we thee, our Lord,	
in this need, and did to thee thus?'	

S ܨܗܝܬ ܘܐܫܩܝܢܟ 38 ܘܐܡܬܝ, ܚܙܝܢܟ ܕܐܟܣܢܝܐ ܗܘܝܬ ܘܟܢܫܢܟ.
A381 (cont.) ܐܘ ܥܪܛܠܝܐ ܗܘܝܬ ܘܐܠܒܫܢܟ 39 ܐܘ ܐܡܬܝ, ܚܙܝܢܟ ܟܕ ܟܪܝܗ
ܐܘ ܒܝܬ ܐܣܝܪ̈ܐ ܗܘܝܬ ܘܐܬܝܢ ܠܘܬܟ 40 ܘܥܢܐ ܘܐܡܪ ܠܗܘܢ
cf A389 ܐܡܝܢ ܐܡܪܢܐ ܠܟܘܢ [ܕܡܕܡ] ܕܥܒܕܬܘܢ ܠܚܕ ܡܢ ܗܠܝܢ
ܐܚܝ ܙܥܘܪ̈ܐ, ܠܝ ܗܘ ܥܒܕܬܘܢ 41 ܗܝܕܝܢ ܢܐܡܪ ܠܗܢܘܢ ܕܡܢ
ܣܡܠܗ ܙܠܘ ܠܟܘܢ ܡܢܝ ܠܝܛܐ ܠܢܘܪܐ ܕܠܥܠܡ ܗܝ, ܕܡܛܝܒܐ
ܠܐܟܠ ܩܪ̈ܨܐ ܘܠܡܠܐܟܘܗܝ, 42 ܟܦܢܬ ܓܝܪ ܘܠܐ ܝܗܒܬܘܢ ܠܝ
ܠܡܐܟܠ ܨܗܝܐ ܗܘܝܬ ܘܠܐ ܐܫܩܝܬܘܢܢܝ 43 ܘܥܪܛܠܝܐ ܗܘܝܬ ܘܠܐ
[ܐܠܒܫܬܘܢܢܝ] ܟܪܝܗܐ ܗܘܝܬ ܘܒܝܬ ܐܣܝܪ̈ܐ ܗܘܝܬ ܘܠܐ
ܣܥܪܬܘܢܢܝ 44 ܗܝܕܝܢ ܢܥܢܘܢ ܐܦ ܗܢܘܢ ܘܢܐܡܪܘܢ ܡܪܢ ܐܡܬܝ,
ܚܙܝܢܟ ܟܕ ܟܦܢ ܐܢܬ ܐܘ ܟܕ ܨܗܐ ܐܢܬ ܐܘ ܟܕ ܐܟܣܢܝܐ ܐܢܬ
ܐܘ ܥܪܛܠܝ ܐܘ ܟܪܝܗ ܐܘ ܒܝܬ ܐܣܝܪ̈ܐ ܐܢܬ ܘܠܐ ܫܡܫܢܟ
45 ܗܝܕܝܢ ܢܥܢܐ ܘܢܐܡܪ ܠܗܘܢ ܐܡܝܢ ܐܡܪܢܐ ܠܟܘܢ ܕܗܘ
ܕܠܚܕ ܡܢ ܗܠܝܢ ܙܥܘܪ̈ܐ ܠܐ ܥܒܕܬܘܢ ܐܦ ܠܝ ܠܐ ܥܒܕܬܘܢ
¶A381 46 ܘܢܐܙܠܘܢ ܗܠܝܢ ܠܬܫܢܝܩܐ ܕܠܥܠܡ ܘܙܕܝܩ̈ܐ ܠܚ̈ܝܐ ܕܠܥܠܡ¶

A 389

40 ܗܘ ܕܠܗܠܝܢ ܥܒܕܬܘܢ
ܠܝ ܕܝܠܝ ܥܒܕܬܘܢ

A 381 (cont.)

40 ܗܝܕܝܢ ܐܡܪ ܠܗܘܢ
ܕܡܕܡ ܕܥܒܕܬܘܢ ܠܚܕ ܡܢ ܗܠܝܢ
ܐܚ̈ܝ ܕܩܛ̈ܝܢܐ (A^{a} ܙܥܘܪ̈ܐ)
ܠܝ ܗܘ ܕܝܠܝ ܥܒܕܬܘܢ
41 ܘܐܬܦܢܝ ܠܘܬ ܗܢܘܢ ܕܡܢ ܣܡܠܗ ܘܐܡܪ ܠܗܘܢ.
ܙܠܘ ܠܟܘܢ ܡܢܝ ܠܝܛܐ (om. ܡܢܝ A^{a})
ܠܢܘܪܐ ܗܝ ܕܡܛܝܒܐ ܠܣܛܢܐ ܘܠܡܠܐܟܘ̈ܗܝ
(42, 43) ܟܠܗ ܕܫܠܡ ܠܐ ܥܒܕܬܘܢ ܠܝ.
44 ܗܝܕܝܢ ܘܐܦ ܗܢܘܢ ܕܡܢ ܣܡܠܗ ܥܢܘ ܘܐܡܪܘ ܠܗ.
ܕܐܡܬܝ ܡܪܢ ܚܙܝܢܟ ܒܚܕܐ ܡܢ ܗܠܝܢ ܘܠܐ ܫܡܫܢܟ.
45 ܐܡܪ ܠܗܘܢ.
ܗܘ ܕܠܐ ܥܒܕܬܘܢ ܠܗܠܝܢ ܩܛܝܢܐ. ܐܦܠܐ ܠܝ ܕܝܠܝ ܥܒܕܬܘܢ.
(46) ܘܙܕܝܩܐ ܕܫܡܫܘ ܠܡܫܝܚܐ ܒܩܛܝܢܐ. ܐܙܠܘ ܠܚ̈ܝܐ ܕܠܥܠܡ.
ܘܥܘ̈ܠܐ ܐܙܠܘ ܠܢܘܪܐ ܘܫܘܢܩܐ.

38 to eat, or] wast thirsty and gave thee to drink? And when did we S
see thee that thou wast a stranger and gathered thee, or wast a naked A381 (*cont.*)
39 man and clothed thee? Or when did we see thee infirm or in prison
40 and came unto thee?' And he answered and said to them: 'Amen,
I say to you [What] ye have done to one of these my brothers, my *cf* A389
41 little ones, to me it is ye have done *it*.' Then will he say to those
on his left: 'Go away from me, ye cursed, to the fire eternal which is
42 prepared for the Accuser and for his angels. For I was hungry and
ye did not give me to eat, I was thirsty and ye gave me not to
43 drink, and I was a naked man and ye did not [clothe me], I was an
44 infirm man and I was in prison and ye did not [visit] me.' Then
will they also answer and will say: 'Our Lord, when did we see
thee hungry, or thirsty, or a stranger, or naked, or infirm, or in
45 prison, and did not serve thee?' Then will he answer and will say to
them: 'Amen, I say to you That which to one of these little ones
46 ye did not, to me also ye did *it* not.' And these will go to torment
eternal, and the righteous to life eternal."¶ ¶A381

A 381 (*cont.*)

40 Then he said to them
'That which ye did to one of these
my brothers, *even* the smallest ones
('the little ones' A^a)
to me it is, even me, ye did *it*'

41 And he turned round unto those on his left and said to them:
'Go away from me, ye cursed, (*om.* 'from me' A^a)
to the fire which is prepared for the Evil One and his angels,

(**42**, **43**) because these things ye did not to me.'

44 Then those also on his left answered and said to him
'When, our Lord, saw we thee in one of these *things* and did not serve thee?'

45 He saith to them:
'What ye did not to these needy ones neither to me, even me, ye did.'

(**46**) And the righteous that served the Messiah in the needy ones went to life eternal,
and the wicked went to fire and darkness.

A 389

40 'What to these ye did
to me, even me, ye did *it*'

41. *Cf also*: 'Depart from me, ye cursed of my Father, into the everlasting fire, which is kept for Satan and his angels' E^{75} *and* 'Depart... fire, because I know you not' E^{216}

¹ܘܗܘܐ ܒܗ̇ ܥܠܡ ܫ̈ܡܥܘܗܝ [ܗܠܝܢ ܐܡܪ] ܠܬܠܡܝܕܘܗܝ ²ܝܘܚܢܢ S
ܐܝܬܘܗܝ ܕܩ⌈ܡ⌉ [ܒܬܪ] ܬܘܒ ܡܢ ܡ̈ܝܬܐ [ܗܘܐ] ܚܝܠܐ ܘܒܪܗ
[ܕܐܢܫܐ] ܡܫܬܠܡ [ܕܝܘܚܢܢ] ³ܗܪܘܕܣ ܐܬܚܒܫܘ ܙܢܝ [ܒܗ̇ ܫ̈ܢܝܐ ܘܐܣܝܪܐ]
ܘܡܚܫܐ [ܕܒܝܬܐ] ܠܝܘܚܢܢ ܕܪܒ ܒܗܢܐ ⁴ܘܡܬܚܫܒܝܢ ܗܘܘ ܕܢܩܛܠܐ
[ܠܝܘܚܢܢ] ܠܫܘܒ ܘܠܦܝܠܝܦܘܣ ⁵ܐܡܪܝܢ [ܗܘܘ ܕܝܢ] ܘܠܐ
[ܒܡܕܝܢܬܐ ܕܠܐ] ܢܗܘܐ [ܪܘܒܐ] ܒܥܡܐ ⁶ܘܟܕ ܗܘܐ ܝܘܡ
ܒܝܬ ܚܝܐ ܒܝܘܡܗ ܕܝܠܕܗ ܠܗܪܘܕܐ ⁷ܪܩܕܬ ܐܢܬܬܐ ܚܕܐ
ܘܐܝܬ ܗ⌈ܘ⌉ܬ ܠܗ ܥܠܝܡܬܐ ܕܫܦܝܪܐ ܕܫܡܥܬܐ ܕܩܕ̈ܡܝ ܕܡ⌈ܠ⌉ܟܘܬܗ
ܘܐܫܬܦܪܬ ܒܗ ܥܠ ܪܗܛ ܕܫܒܩ ܒܗ ܡ⌈ܠܟܐ⌉ ⁸ܚܝܘ ܕܝܢ ܬܠܡܝܕܘܗܝ
ܘܐܡܪܘ ܠܡܠܟܐ ܐܝܟܢܐ ܗܢܐ ⁹ܡܫܟܚ ܗܘܐ ܟܕ ܗܕ⌈ܐ⌉ ܕܚܙܝܢ
ܒܥܠܡ ܘܬܘܗܒ [ܠܡܫܡܥܢܐ] ¹⁰ܫܩܠ ܕܝܢ ܚܕ ܘܐܡܪ ܠܗܘܢ
ܗ⌈ܢܐ⌉ ܡܠܟܝܢ† ܠܗ ܠܐܝܬܘܬܐ ܒܥܕܐ ܫܦܝܪܐ ܠܓܒܐ ܒܒܝܬ
ܠܘܬ, ¹¹ܐܬܘܗܝ ܡ⌈ܫ⌉ܡܫܢܐ ܟܕ ܒܠܝܢ ܠܘܬܗܘܢ [ܐܝܟ
ܐܢܐ ܕܝܢ] ܠܐ ܒܠܝܢ ܠܘܬܗܘܢ ܐܢܐ ¹²ܗܕܐ ܕܝܢ ܕܐܬܪܡܝܬ
ܡܫܝܚܐ ܗܢܐ ܥܠ ܦ⌈ܬ⌉ܪ, ܐܝܟ ܕܠܡܒܪܬܐ ܒܒܝܬ ¹³ܐܡܪܝܢ ܐܡܪܝܢܐ
ܠܗܘܢ ܕܐܝܟܢܐ ܕܬܬܒܪ ܫܒܝܬ, ܗܕܐ ܒܟܠܗ ܥܠܡܐ ܬܬܡܠܠ
ܐܦ ܡܕܡ ܕܒܝܬ [ܐܝܬܘܬܐ] ܗܕܐ ܠܕܘܟܪܢܗ ○ ○ ○
¹⁴ܗܝܕܝܢ ܐܙܠ ܚܕ ܡܢ ܬܪܥܣܪ ܕܡܬܩܪܐ ⌈ܝܗܘܕܐ⌉ ܐܣܟܪܝܘܛܐ ܠܘܬ
ܪ̈ܒܝ ⌈ܟ⌉ܗܢܐ ¹⁵ܘܐܡܪ ܠܗܘܢ ܡܢܐ ܐܝܬܘܗܝ ⌈ܨܒܝܢ⌉ ܐܢܬܘܢ
ܠܡܬܠ ܘܐܢܐ ܡܫܠܡ ܠܗ ܠܟܘܢ ܘܐܩܝܡܘ ܠܗ ܬܠܬܝܢ ܕܟܣܦܐ
¹⁶ܘܡܢ ܗܝܕܝܢ ܒܥܐ ܗܘܐ ܠܗ ܦܠܚܐ ܕܢܫܠܡܝܘܗܝ, ¹⁷ܒܝܘܡܐ ܕܝܢ
ܩܕܡܝܐ ܕܦܛܝܪܐ ܩܪܒܘ ܬ⌈ܠ⌉ܡ⌈ܝ⌉ܕܘܗܝ, ܕܢܫܐܠ ܘܐܡܪܝܢ ܠܗ ܐܝܟܐ
ܨܒܐ ܐܢܬ ܕܢܛܝܒ ⌈ܠܟ⌉ ܕܬܐܟܘܠ ܦܨܚܐ. ¹⁸ܐܡܪ ܠܗܘܢ ܙܠܘ
ܠܡܕܝܢܬܐ ܠܘܬ ܦܠܢ ܘܐܡܪܘ ܠܗ ܪܒܢ ܐܡܪ ܙܒܢܝ ܩܪܒ ܗܘ

1 ܒܗ] ܒܗ̇ ⌈ܗ̇⌉ܕܐ *S^ed^*: *cf* Mt xi 1, Lk i 8 *etc.* 4 ܘܢܦܠܛܘܢܝܗ] ܘܢܦܠܛܘܢܝܗܝ *S^ed^* (*photograph illegible*) 5 ܘܠܐ] *S* (*sic*) 10 ܡܠܟܝܢ] *S*: *it ought to have been followed by* ܐܢܬܘܢ, *as in* syr. vg ܠܓܒܐ] *S^ed^*: *photograph illegible*
13 ܬܬܡܠܠ] *S*: *it should have been* ܬܬܡܠܠ, *as in* syr. vg

xxvi 1 And it came to pass when he finished [these] his words S
2 [he said] to his disciples: "Ye know that [after] two days [it
is] the Passover, and the Son [of Man] is delivered up [to be
3 crucified]." Then were gathered together the chief [priests and the
scribes] and the elders [of the people] to the court of the chief
4 priest, and they were thinking that with guile [they should take hold
5 of] Jesus and kill him, [but they were] saying "And not [on the
6 Feast, that] there be [not an uproar] among the people." And when
7 Jesus was in Beth Ania in the house of Simon the leper there drew
near a certain woman; and she had a vase of oil of perfume, the price
of which is dear, and she poured it on the head of Jesus as he sat *at*
8 *meat.* Now his disciples saw, and said: "Wherefore *is* this waste?
9 For this could have been sold for much and given [to the poor]."
10 Now Jesus knew and said to them: "Why weary †they† the woman?
11 A deed fair *and* good hath she done unto me. For there are the
poor—at all times [they are] by you; [but I,] not at all times am
12 I by you. Now this—that she hath cast this oil on my body—as if
13 for my burial she hath done *it.* Amen, I say to you Wheresoever
this my gospel shall be preached in all the world it will be spoken,
even that which this [woman] hath done, for her memory."

14 Then went one of the Twelve, called Judas Scariot, unto the
15 chief priests, and said to them: "What are ye willing to give, and I
will deliver him up to you?" And they settled for him thirty *pieces*
16 of silver; and from then he was seeking for himself an opportunity
17 that he should deliver him up. Now on the first day of the Unleavened Bread the disciples of Jesus came near, and they say to
him: "Where wilt thou that we make ready for thee that thou
18 mayest eat the Passover?" He saith to them: "Go to the city unto
such an one, and say to him: "Our Rabbi saith, 'My time is near;

---

5 And not] *S* (*sic*) 10 weary †they†] *S*; *the pronoun which would have turned the text into* 'weary ye' *is omitted, probably by accident*

ܠܘܬܟ ܥܒܕܢܐ ܦܨܚܐ ܥܡ ܬܠܡܝܕܝ܂ ¹⁹ܘܥܒܕܘ ܬܠܡܝܕܘܗܝ, S
ܐܝܟܢܐ ܕܦܩܕ ܐܢܘܢ ܝܫܘܥ ܘܛܝܒܘ ܦܨܚܐ ²⁰ܘܟܕ ܗܘܐ ܪܡܫܐ
ܣܡܝܟ ܗܘܐ ܠܘܬ ܬܪܬܥܣܪܬܗ ²¹ܘܟܕ ܗܢܘܢ ܠܚܡܝܢ. ܐܡܪ
ܠܗܘܢ ܐܡܝܢ ܐܡܪܢܐ ܠܟܘܢ ܕܚܕ ܡܢܟܘܢ ܢܫܠܡܢܝ ²²ܘܟܪܝܬ
ܠܗܘܢ ܛܒ ܘܫܪܝܘ ܠܡܐܡܪ ܚܕ ܚܕ ܡܢܗܘܢ ܕܠܡܐ ܐܢܐ
ܗܘ ܡܪܝ܇ ²³ܐܡܪ ܠܗܘܢ ܗܘ ܕܡܥܡܕ ܐܝܕܗ ܥܡܝ ܒܠܓܬܐ
ܗܘ ܢܫܠܡܢܝ. ²⁴ܘܒܪܗ ܕܐܢܫܐ ܐܙܠ ܐܝܟܢܐ ܕܟܬܝܒ ܥܠܘܗܝ, ܘ
ܘܝ ܠܗܘ ܓܒܪܐ ܕܒܐܝܕܗ ܡܫܬܠܡ ܐܢܐ. ܦܩܚ ܗܘܐ ܠܗ
ܐܠܘ ܠܐ ܐܬܝܠܕ. ²⁵ܘܥܢܐ ܝܗܘܕܐ ܡܫܠܡܢܐ ܘܐܡܪ ܕܠܡܐ
ܐܢܐ ܗܘ ܪܒܝ. ܐܡܪ ܠܗ. ܐܢܬ ܐܡܪܬ ²⁶ܘܟܕ ܗܢܘܢ ܠܚܡܝܢ
§ܢܣܒ ܝܫܘܥ ܠܚܡܐ ܘܒܪܟ ܥܠܘܗܝ, ܘܩܨܐ ܘܝܗܒ ܠܬܠܡܝܕܘܗܝ, §A 221
ܘܐܡܪ ܣܒܘ ܐܟܘܠܘ ܗܢܘ ܦܓܪܝ, ²⁷ܘܢܣܒ ܟܣܐ ܘܐܘܕܝ, ܥܠܘܗܝ,
ܘܝܗܒ. ܠܗܘܢ ܘܐܡܪ ܣܒܘ ܐܫܬܘ ܡܢܗ ܟܠܟܘܢ ²⁸ܗܢܘ
ܕܡܝ ܕܝܠܝ ܕܝܬܩܐ ܚܕܬܐ ܕܡܬܐܫܕ ܚܠܦ ܣܓܝܐܐ ܠܫܘܒܩܢܐ ܕܚܛܗܐ¶ ¶A
²⁹ܐܡܪܢܐ ܠܟܘܢ ܕܠܐ ܐܫܬܐ ܡܢ ܗܫܐ ܡܢ ܦܐܪܐ
ܕܓܦܬܐ ܥܕܡܐ ܠܝܘܡܐ ܕܐܫܬܝܘܗܝ, ܥܡܟܘܢ ܚܕܬܐ
ܒܡܠܟܘܬܗ ܕܐܒܝ ³⁰ܘܟܕ ܫܒܚܘ. ܐܙܠܘ ܠܛܘܪܐ ܕܙܝܬܐ ³¹ܗܝܕܝܢ
ܐܡܪ ܠܗܘܢ ܝܫܘܥ ܟܠܟܘܢ ܬܬܟܫܠܘܢ ܒܝ ܒܗܢܐ ܠܠܝܐ
ܟܬܝܒ ܗܘ ܓܝܪ ܕܐܡܚܐ ܠܪܥܝܐ ܘܢܬܒܕܪܘܢ ܐܡܪܐ ܕܥܢܗ.
³²ܘܒܬܪ ܕܩܡܬ ܡܩܕܡܢܐ ܠܟܘܢ ܠܓܠܝܠܐ ܀

³³ܥܢܐ ܫܡܥܘܢ ܟܐܦܐ ܘܐܡܪ ܐܢ ܟܠܟܘܢ ܬܬܟܫܠܘܢ ܒܟ
ܐܢܐ ܠܥܠܡ ܠܐ ܡܬܟܫܠܢܐ ܒܟ ³⁴ܐܡܪ ܠܗ ܝܫܘܥ ܐܡܝܢ

---

24 ܡܫܬܠܡ] *pr.* ܕ S^{ed} 26 ܢܣܒ] *pr.* ܒܬܪ ܕܢܦܩ ܝܗܘܕܐ ܡܢ ܠܘܬܗܘܢ *A* (*cf* Joh xiii 30) ܝܫܘܥ] *om. A* ܥܠܘܗܝ ܘܩܨܐ] *om. A* ܘܐܡܪ] + ܠܗܘܢ *A* ܣܒܘ....ܦܓܪܝ] ܕܗܢܘ ܦܓܪܝ. ܣܒܘ ܐܟܘܠܘ ܡܢܗ ܟܠܟܘܢ *A* 27.] *A has* ܘܐܦ ܥܠ ܚܡܪܐ ܗܟܢܐ ܒܪܟ ܘܐܡܪ ܠܗܘܢ 28 ܕܝܬܩܐ] *S* A^a; *pr.* ܕ A^{ed} (*hiat* A^b) ܕܝܠܝ ܩܝܡܐ ܡܬܐܡܪ *A* ܕܚܛܗܐ] + ܗܟܢܐ ܠܡ ܗܘܝܬܘܢ ܥܒܕܝܢ ܠܥܘܗܕܢܝ ܐܡܬܝ ܕܡܬܟܢܫܝܢ ܐܢܬܘܢ *A* (= 1 Cor xi 25, 20)

19 at thy *house* I do the Passover with my disciples.'" And his *S*
disciples did as Jesus commanded them and made ready the Pass-
20 over. And when it was evening he was sitting *at meat* by his
21 Twelve; and while they *were* eating he said to them: "Amen, I
22 say to you One of you will betray me." And it grieved them
exceedingly, and they began to say each one of them: "Can it
23 be I, my Lord?" He saith to them: "He which putteth forth
24 his hand with me in the bowl, he will betray me. And the Son of
Man goeth as is written of him, but woe to that man by whose hand
I am betrayed; it were profitable for him if he had not been
25 born!" And Judas the betrayer answered and said: "Can it be I,
26 Rabbi?" He saith to him: "Thou hast said *it*." And while they
were eating §Jesus took bread and blessed *God* over it, and brake §*A* 221
and gave to his disciples, and said: "Take, eat; this is my body."
27 And he took a cup and gave thanks over it, and gave to them and
28 said: "Take, drink of it all of you; this is my blood, the new
29 covenant, that is shed for many to forgiveness of sins.¶ For I say ¶*A*
to you that I shall not drink from now of the fruit of the vine, until
the day that I shall drink it with you new in the kingdom of my
30 Father." And when they had glorified *God* they went to the Mount
31 of Olives. Then said Jesus to them: "All of you will be offended
in me in this night, for it is written 'I will smite the shepherd
32 and the lambs of his flock will be scattered.' And what *time* I have
arisen, I go before you to Galilee."
33 Simon Kepha answered and said: "If all of them shall be
34 offended in thee, I for ever will not be offended in thee." Jesus

---

26 Jesus took] *pr.* After Judas went forth from them *A* (*cf* Joh xiii 30) Jesus] he *A* over it and brake] *om. A* said] + to them *A* Take... body] This is my body; take, eat of it all of you *A* 27.] *A has* 'And also over the wine thus he blessed *God* and said to them' 28 the new covenant] *S* A^{a}; *pr.* 'of' A^{ed} that for many is shed *A* of sins] + so, quoth he, be ye doing for my memory whenever ye be gathered together *A* (= 1 Cor xi 25, 20) 29. *For* E^{222}, *see* Lk xxii 18

ܐܡܝܢܐ ܠܟ ܕܒܗܢܐ ܠܠܝܐ ܒܥܕܠܐ ܢܩܪܐ ܬܪܢܓܠܐ ܬܠܬ ܙܒܢܝܢ S
ܬܟܦܘܪ ܒܝ. [35]ܐܡܪ ܠܗ ܫܡܥܘܢ ܟܐܦܐ ܐܢ ܢܗܘܐ ܠܝ
ܠܡܡܬ ܥܡܟ ܠܐ ܐܟܦܘܪ ܒܟ ܘܐܦ ܟܠܗܘܢ ܬܠܡܝܕܐ ܗܟܢܐ
ܐܡܪܘ [36]ܗܝܕܝܢ ܐܬܐ ܥܡܗܘܢ ܝܫܘܥ ܠܐܬܪܐ ܕܡܬܩܪܐ
ܓܕܣܡܢ ܐܡܪ ܠܬܠܡܝܕܘܗܝ ܬܒܘ ܗܪܟܐ ܥܕ ܐܙܠ ܐܨܠܐ
[37]ܘܕܒܪ ܠܟܐܦܐ ܘܠܬܪܝܗܘܢ ܒܢܝ ܙܒܕܝ، ܘܫܪܝ ܗܘܐ ܠܡܬܟܡܪܘ
ܘܠܡܬܥܩܘ. [38]ܗܝܕܝܢ ܐܡܪ ܠܗܘܢ ܗܐ ܟܪܝܐ ܗܝ ܠܗ ܠܢܦܫܝ
ܥܕܡܐ ܠܡܘܬܐ ܩܘܘ ܗܪܟܐ ܘܐܬܬܥܝܪܘ ܥܡܝ [39]ܘܥܒܪ ܡܢܗܘܢ
ܩܠܝܠ ܢܦܠ ܥܠ ܐܦܘܗܝ ܘܡܨܠܐ ܗܘܐ ܘܐܡܪ ܗܘܐ §ܐܒܝ §A459
ܐܢ ܡܫܟܚ ܕܢܥܒܪ ܡܢܝ ܟܣܐ ܗܢܐ¶ ܒܪܡ ܠܐ ܨܒܝܢܝ ܕܝܠܝ ¶A
ܢܗܘܐ ܐܠܐ ܐܢ ܕܝܠܟ. [40]ܘܐܬܐ ܠܘܬ ܬܠܡܝܕܘܗܝ ܘܐܫܟܚ
ܐܢܘܢ ܟܕ ܕܡܟܝܢ ܘܐܡܪ ܠܟܐܦܐ ܗܟܢܐ ܐܦܠܐ ܚܕܐ ܫܥܐ
ܐܫܟܚܬܘܢ ܠܡܬܥܪ ܥܡܝ [41]ܐܬܬܥܝܪܘ ܘ§ܨܠܘ ܕܠܐ ܬܥܠܘܢ §A487
ܠܢܣܝܘܢܐ¶ ܪܘܚܐ ܨܒܝܐ ܐܠܐ ܦܓܪܐ ܟܪܝܗ [42]ܬܘܒ ܕܬܪܬܝܢ ܙܒܢܝܢ ¶A
ܐܙܠ ܠܡܨܠܝܘ ܐܡܪ ܐܒܝ ܐܢ ܠܐ ܡܫܟܚ ܟܣܐ ܗܢܐ ܕܢܥܒܪ
ܐܠܐ ܐܢ ܐܫܬܝܬܗ ܢܗܘܐ ܨܒܝܢܟ. [43]ܘܐܬܐ ܬܘܒ ܘܐܫܟܚ
ܐܢܘܢ ܟܕ ܕܡܟܝܢ ܡܛܠ ܕܥܝܢܝܗܘܢ ܒܥܬܐ ܗܘܝ ܗܘܝ.
[44]ܘܫܒܩ ܐܢܘܢ ܘܐܙܠ ܠܡܨܠܝܘ ܕܬܠܬ ܙܒܢܝܢ ܘܬܘܒ ܗܟܘܬ
ܐܡܪ. [45]ܗܝܕܝܢ ܐܬܐ ܠܘܬ ܬܠܡܝܕܘܗܝ ܘܐܡܪ ܠܗܘܢ ܕܡܟܘ
ܡܟܝܠ ܘܐܬܢܝܚܘ ܗܐ ܩܪܒܬ ܫܥܬܐ ܘܒܪܗ ܕܐܢܫܐ ܡܫܬܠܡ
ܒܐܝܕܝܗܘܢ ܕܚܛܝܐ. [46]ܩܘܡܘ ܢܐܙܠ ܡܟܐ ܩܪܒ ܠܗ ܗܘ
ܕܡܫܠܡ ܠܝ ⁘ ⁘

[47]ܟܕ ܗܘ ܡܡܠܠ ܗܘܐ ܝܗܘܕܐ ܚܕ ܡܢ ܬܪܥܣܪܬܐ ܐܬܐ ܘܥܡܗ
ܟܢܫܐ ܣܓܝܐܐ ܒܣܝܦܐ ܘܚܘܛܪܐ ܡܢ ܠܘܬ ܪ̈ܒܝ ܟܗ̈ܢܐ ܘܩܫܝܫܐ
ܕܥܡܐ. [48]ܝܗܘܕܐ ܕܝܢ ܡܫܠܡܢܐ ܝܗܒ ܠܗܘܢ ܐܬܐ ܘܐܡܪ
ܕܠܗܘ ܐܢܐ ܕܢܫܩܢܐ ܠܗ ܗܘ ܐܚܘܕܘ [49]ܘܩܪܒ ܠܘܬ ܝܫܘܥ

---

34 ܒܥܕܠܐ] *S* (*sic*): *see* Mt i 18　　36 ܓܕܣܡܢ] *S* (*sic*): *cf* Lk xx 29
39 ܐܒܝ....ܐܢ] ܐܢ ܡܫܟܚܐ ܢܥܒܪܝܢ *A*: *see* Lk xxii 42

saith to him: "Amen, I say to thee In this night, before ever the S
35 cock crow, three times thou wilt deny me." Simon Kepha saith to
him: "If it shall be for me to die with thee, I will not deny thee."
36 And the disciples all of them also so said. Then came Jesus with
them to the place called Gysmani. He saith to his disciples: "Sit
37 here, while I go *and* pray." And he took Simon and the two sons of
38 Zebedee, and he had begun to be gloomy and to be anxious. Then
saith he to them: "Lo, it doth grieve my soul even unto death; re-
39 main here and watch with me." And he removed from them a little,
and fell on his face and was praying, and he was saying: "§My Father, §*A*459
that if it can be that this cup should pass from me¶—nevertheless not ¶*A*
40 my will, mine, be *done*, but thine!" And he came unto his disciples
and found them sleeping, and he said to Simon: "So not even one
41 hour have ye been able to watch with me? Watch and §pray that ye §*A*487
enter not into temptation;¶ the spirit is willing, but the body is ¶*A*
42 infirm." Again for the second time he went to pray, *and* saith:
"My Father, if this cup cannot pass but if I drink it, thy will be
43 *done*!" And he came again and found them sleeping, because their
44 eyes with sleep were heavy; and he left them and went to pray for
45 the third time, and again thus he said. Then came he unto his
disciples, and said to them: "Sleep then and take your ease; for lo,
the hour is nigh, and the Son of Man is betrayed into the hands
46 of the sinners. Arise, let us go hence; he that betrayeth me hath
arrived."

47 While yet he was speaking, lo, Judas, one of the Twelve, came,
and with him a great multitude with swords and staves from the
48 chief priests and the elders of the people. Now Judas the betrayer
gave them a sign and said "That one which I kiss, him take hold

---

39 that if...from me] if it can be, let this cup pass me *A*: *see* Lk xxii 42
41 willing] 'willing and ready' E^{231} 47 lo] *lit.* 'and lo': *see Notes*, vol. ii

ܘܢܫܩܗ ܘܐܡܪ ܠܗ ܫܠܡ ܪܒܝ. [50]ܝܫܘܥ ܕܝܢ ܐܡܪ ܠܗ ܥܠ ܡܢܐ S
⸢ܐ⸣ܬܝܬ ܚܒܪܝ، ܗܝܕܝܢ ܩܪܒܘ ܘܐܪܡܝܘ ܥܠܘܗܝ، ܐܝܕܝܐ ܘܐܚܕܘܗܝ،
ܠܝܫܘܥ. [51]ܘܗܐ ܚܕ ܡܢ ܬܠܡܝܕܘܗܝ، ܕܝܫܘܥ ܐܘܫܛ ܐܝܕܗ ܘܫܡܛ
ܣܝܦܐ ܘܡܚܝܗ، ܠܥܒܕܗ ܕܪܒ ܟܗ̈ܢܐ ܘܫܩܠܗ ܐܕܢܗ. [52]ܗܝܕܝܢ
§¶Thos 256 §ܐܡܪ ܠܗ ܝܫܘܥ ܐܗܦܟ ܣܝܦܐ ܠܕܘܟܬܗ¶ ܟܠܗܘܢ ܓܝܪ
§Thos ܐܝܠܝܢ ܕܢܣܒܘ ܣܝܦܐ ܒܣܝܦܐ ܢܐܒܕܘܢ. [53]§ܐܘ ܣܒܪ ܐܢܬ ܕܠܐ
ܡܫܟܚ ܐܢܐ ܕܐܒܥܐ ܡܢ ܐܒܝ ܘܢܩܝܡ ܠܝ ܝܬܝܪ ܡܢ ܬܪܬܥܣܪܐ
¶Thos ܠܓ̈ܝܘܢܝܢ ܕܡܠܐܟܐ¶ [54]ܐܠܐ ܐܝܟܢܐ ܢܬܡܠܘܢ ܟܬܒܐ ܕܗܟܢܐ
ܘܠܐ ܠܡܗܘܐ. [55]ܒܗ، ܒܫܥܬܐ ܐܡܪ ܝܫܘܥ ܠܟܢܫܐ ܐܝܟ ܕܥܠ
ܓܝܣܐ ܢܦܩܬܘܢ ܥܠܝ ܒܣܝ̈ܦܐ ܘܒܚܘܛܪ̈ܐ ܠܡܐܚܕܢܝ ܟܠܝܘܡ
ܒܗܝܟܠܐ ܝܬܒ ܗܘܝܬ ܘܡܠܦ ܗܘܝܬ ܘܠܐ ܐܚܕܬܘܢܝ. [56]ܗܠܝܢ
ܕܝܢ ܟܠܗܝܢ ܕܗܘܝ، ܕܢܬܡܠܘܢ ܟܬܒܐ ܕܢܒ̈ܝܐ ܀

ܗܝܕܝܢ ܫܒܩܘܗܝ، ܬܠܡܝܕܘܗܝ، ܟܠܗܘܢ ܘܥܪܩܘ. [57]ܘܐܚܕܘܗܝ، ܗܢܘܢ
ܘܐܘܒܠܘܗܝ، ܠܘܬ ܩܝܦܐ ܪܒ ܟܗܢܐ ܐܬܪ ܕܟܢܝܫܝܢ ܣܦܪ̈ܐ
ܘܩܫܝܫܐ ܕܥܡܐ. [58]ܫܡܥܘܢ ܕܝܢ ܐܙܠ ܗܘܐ ܒܬܪܗ ܡܢ ܪܘܚܩܐ
ܥܕܡܐ ܠܕܪܬܗ ܕܪܒ ܟܗܢܐ ܘܥܠ ܠܓܘ ܘ⸢ܝܬ⸣ܒ ܗܘܐ ܥܡ
ܕܚܫܐ ܕܢܚܙܐ ܚܪܬܐ. [59]ܘ⸢ܟ⸣ܠܗ ܟܢܘܫܬܐ ܒܥܝܢ ܗܘܘ [ܥܠܘܗܝ، ܥܠ]
ܢܣܒ ܣܗܕܐ ܐܝܟ ܕܢܡܝܬܘܢܝܗܝ، [60]ܘܠܐ ܐܫܟܚܘ ܘܐܬܘ
ܣܗ̈ܕܐ ܣܓܝ̈ܐܐ، ܫܩܘܪ̈ܐ ܘܠܐ ܐܫܟܚܘ ܠܒ * * ܫ * * ܬܐ
ܒܐܚܪܬܐ ܘܐܬܘ ܬܪܝܢ ܐܚܪܢܝܢ ܣܗܕܐ ܕܫܩܪܐ [61]ܘܐܡܪܝܢ ܗܢܐ
ܐܡܪ ܕܡܫܟܚܢܐ ܕܐܣܬܪܝܘܗܝ، ܠܗܝܟܠܐ ܗܢܐ ܘܠܬܠܬܐ ܝܘܡܝܢ
ܐܒܢܝܘܗܝ، [62]ܘܩܡ ܪܒ ܟܗ̈ܢܐ ܘܐܡܪ ܠܗ ܠܐ ܡܦܢܐ ܐܢܬ ܦܬܓܡܐ

50 ܐܬܝܬ] ܕܐܬܝܬ S^{ed}: ἐφ' ὃ πάρει *is read as a question (against* syr.vg) *in* E^{235} *and* Diat[ar] xlviii 26 52 ܐܡܪ....ܠܕܘܟܬܗ] *Thos*[256] ܐܡܪ ܓܝܪ ܡܪܢ ܠܫܡܥܘܢ ܟܐܦܐ. ܐܗܦܟ ܣܝܦܟ ܠܕܘܟܬܗ
53.] *Thos*[256] ܐ̄ ܓܒ̈ܐ ܐܢܐ ܐܢܐ ܕܐܫܐܠ ܚܝܠܐ ܡܢ ܐܒܝ. ܡܛܒ ܠܝ....ܕܡܠܐ̈ܟܐ (*cont. from ver.* 52): *cf* ܐܡܪ ܠܫܡܥܘܢ ܬܠܡܝܕܗ. ܕܠܡܢܐ ܣܒܪ ܐܢܬ. ܕܐ ܐ̄ *A* 385 ܓܒ̈ܐ ܐܢܐ ܡܢ ܐܒܝ ܚܝܠܐ ܕܡܠܐ̈ܟܐ ܥܣܪܝܢ ܠܐ ܡܛܒ ܠܝ.
60 ܠܒ * * ܫ * * ܬܐ] *the photograph suggests to me* ܠܒ⸢ܣܘܗܘ⸣ ܫ⸢ܪܝ⸣ܪܬܐ

49 of." And he drew near unto Jesus and kissed him and said to him: *S*
50 "Hail, Rabbi!" But Jesus said to him: "For what †hast thou†
come, my comrade?" Then they drew near and laid hands upon
51 him, and took hold of Jesus. And lo, one of the disciples of Jesus
put forth his hand and drew a sword, and smote the chief priest's
52 lad and took off his ear. Then §Jesus said to him: "Put back the §¶*Thos*
sword into its place,¶ for all they that take up the sword by the sword 256
53 will perish. §Or dost thou suppose that I cannot beseech my Father, §*Thos*
54 and he would give me more than twelve legions of angels?¶ But how ¶*Thos*
55 would the Scriptures be fulfilled, that so it ought to be?" In that
hour said Jesus to the multitudes: "As against a robber have ye
come forth against me with swords and with staves to take hold
of me! Daily in the Temple I was sitting and teaching, and ye did
56 not take hold of me. Now all these things that have come to pass
are that the Scriptures of the Prophets might be fulfilled."

57 Then his disciples all of them left him and fled. And those *others*
took hold of him and carried him along unto Caiapha the chief
priest, where *were* gathered the Scribes and the elders of the people.
58 Now Simon was going after him from afar even unto the court of the
chief priest, and he entered into the midst and was sitting with the
59 attendants that he might see the last. And all the synagogue were
seeking [against him, even] Jesus, witnesses, so that they might put
60 him to death, and found *them* not. And there came many witnesses
of falsehood, and they did not find *how* to * *. At the last came two
61 others, witnesses of falsehood, and they say: "This *man* said 'I am
62 able to pull down this Temple, and in three days to build it.'" And
the chief priest arose and said to him: "Givest thou no answer?

---

50 †hast thou†] thou hast S^{ed}, *but cf* 'Now wherefore art thou come, friend?' E^{235} *and* 'Is it for this thou hast come, my friend?' $Diat^{ar}$ xlviii 26
52 Jesus.... its place] 'For our Lord said to Simon the apostle: Put back thy sword behind' $Thos^{256}$: *cf* 'Put up again thy sword into its place' $E^{186, 232, 236}$
53.] 'If I will to ask an army (*lit.* 'power') of my Father, he would give me more than twelve legions of angels' $Thos^{256}$: *cf* He said to Simon his disciple 'Dost thou suppose that if I beseech my Father for an army of angels of heaven he would not give *it* to me?' *A* 385 60.] *See Notes*, vol. ii

S ܡܢܐ ܗܠܝܢ ܡܣܗܕܝܢ ܥܠܝܟ܂ [63]ܝܫܘܥ ܕܝܢ ܫܬܝܩ ܗܘܐ ܥܢܐ
ܪܒ ܟܘ̈ܡܪܐ ܘܐܡܪ ܠܗ ܡܘܡܐ ܠܟ ܒܐܠܗܐ ܚܝܐ. ܕܬܐܡܪ
ܠܢ ܐܢ ܐܢܬ ܗܘ ܡܫܝܚܐ ܒܪܗ ܕܐܠܗܐ· [64]ܐܡܪ ܠܗ ܐܢܬ
ܐܡܪܬ ܐܡܪ ܐܢܐ ܠܟܘܢ ܕܡܢ ܗܫܐ ܬܚܙܘܢܝܗܝ ܠܒܪܗ
ܕܐܢܫܐ ܕܝܬܒ ܡܢ ܝܡܝܢܐ ⌜ܕܚܝܠܐ⌝ ܘܐܬܐ ܥܠ ܥܢ̈ܢܝ ܫܡܝܐ
[65]ܗܝܕܝܢ ܪܒ ܟܘܡܪܐ ⌜ܨܪ⌝ ⌜ܡܐܢܘܗܝ⌝ ܘܐܡܪ ܓܕܦ ܗܢܐ ܬܘܒ
ܡܬܒܥܝܐ ܠܢ ܣܗ̈ܕܐ ܗܐ ܫܡܥܬܘܢ ܡܢ ܦܘܡܗ ܓܘܕܦܐ [66]ܡܢܐ
* * ܨܒܝܢ ܐܢܬܘܢ ܒܗ [ܥܠܘܗܝ] ܘܐܡܪܘ ⌜ܕܚܝܒ⌝ ⌜ܗ⌝ܘ
ܠܡܘܬܐ [67]ܗܝܕܝܢ ⌜ܪܩܘ⌝ ⌜ܠܗ⌝ ܘܪܩܘ ⌜ܒܐ⌝ܦܘܗܝ, ܘܡܩܦܚܝܢ ܗܘܘ ܠܗ
[ܘܡܟܬܫܝܢ ܒܗ] ܐܚܪ̈ܢܐ ܕܝܢ ܡܩ̈ܦܚܝܢ ܗܘܘ ܦܟ̈ܘܗܝ, [68]ܘܐܡܪ̈ܝܢ
ܐܬܢܒܐ ܠܢ ܡܫܝܚܐ ܡܢܘ ܡܚܝܟ.

[69]ܫܡܥܘܢ ܕܝܢ ܝܬܒ ܗܘܐ ܠܒܪ ܒܕܪܬܐ ܘܩܪܒܬ ܥܠܝܡܬܐ ܚܕܐ
ܘܐܡܪܐ ܠܗ ܘܐܦ ܐܢܬ ܥܡ ܝܫܘܥ ܗܘܝܬ ܓܠܝܠܝܐ· [70]ܗܘ ܕܝܢ
ܟܦܪ ܠܥܝܢ ܟܠܗܘܢ ܘܐܡܪ ܠܐ ܝܕܥܢܐ ܡܢܐ ܐܡܪܬܝ, ܘܐܦ
ܠܐ ܣܟܠܢܐ [71]ܘܟܕ ܢܦܩ ܠܬܪܥܐ ܕܕܪܬܐ ܚܙܬܗ ܐܚܪܬܐ
ܘܐܡܪܐ ܠܗܘܢ ܗܢܐ ܥܡ ܝܫܘܥ ܗܘܐ ܢܨܪܝܐ [72]ܘܬܘܒ ܟܦܪ
ܘܝܡܐ ܕܠܐ ܝܕܥܢܐ ܠܗ ܠܓܒܪܐ ܗܢܐ. [73]ܘܡܢ ܒܬܪ ܩܠܝܠ ܩܪܒܘ
ܗܢܘܢ ܕܩܝܡܝܢ. ܘܐܡܪܘ ܠܫܡܥܘܢ ܫܪܝܪܐܝܬ ܡܢܗܘܢ ܐܢܬ ܕܐܦ
ܡܡܠܠܟ ܓܠܐ ܕܐܝܟܐ ܗܘ [74]ܗܝܕܝܢ ܫܪܝ ܠܡܚܪܡܘ ܘܠܡܐܡܐ
ܕܠܐ ܝܕܥܢܐ ܠܗ ܠܓܒܪܐ ܗܢܐ· ܘܒܗ ܒܫܥܬܐ ܩܪܐ ܬܪܢܓܠܐ.
[75]ܘܐܬܕܟܪ ܫܡܥܘܢ ܡܠܬܗ ܕܝܫܘܥ ܕܐܡܪ ܗܘܐ ܠܗ ܕܥܕܠܐ
ܢܩܪܐ ܬܪܢܓܠܐ ܬܠܬ ܙܒ̈ܢܝܢ ܬܟܦܘܪ ܒܝ. ܘܟܕ ܢܦܩ ܠܒܪ ܒܟܐ
ܡܪܝܪܐܝܬ.

[1]ܘܟܕ ܨܦܪܬ. ܫܩܠܘ ܡܠܟܐ ܟܠܗܘܢ ܪ̈ܒܝ ܟܘ̈ܡܪܐ ܘܩܫ̈ܝܫܐ ܕܥܡܐ
ܥܠ ܝܫܘܥ ܕܢܡܝܬܘܢܝܗܝ. [2]ܘܐܣܪܘܗܝ, ܘܐܘܒܠܘܗܝ, ܘܐܫܠܡܘܗܝ,
ܠܦܝܠܛܘܣ ܗܓܡܘܢܐ ·܀·

66 * * ܡܢܐ] *The illegible word may have been* ܕܝܢ   67 ⌜ܪܩܘ⌝ ⌜ܠܗ⌝] ⌜ܡܚܠܘܗܝ S^{ed}: *cf* Diat^{ar} xlix 40   69 ܓܠܝܠܝܐ] *S (sic)*: *cf* Mk xiv 70, Lk xxii 59
74.] *Cf* ܘܐܚܪܡ ܘܝܡܐ ܕܠܐ ܝܕܥܢܐ ܠܗ *A* 143

63 What are these bearing witness against thee?" Now Jesus was silent. *S*
The chief priest answered and said to him: "I adjure thee by the
Living God, that thou say to us if thou art the Messiah, the
64 Son of God!" He saith to him: "Thou hast said *it*. I say to you
From now ye will see the Son of Man sitting on the right *hand* of
65 Power and coming on the clouds of heaven." Then the chief priest
rent his things and said: "He hath blasphemed; why yet is there
required for us witnesses? Lo, ye have heard from his mouth the
66 blasphemy. What * will ye?" They answered [all of them] and said
67 "He is guilty of death." Then [they drew near] to [him] and spat in
his face and were buffeting him [and mocking at him], but others
68 were slapping his cheeks and saying: "Prophesy to us, Messiah, who
is it hath smitten thee?"

69 Now Simon was sitting outside in the court, and a certain maid
drew near and saith to him: "And thou also wast with Jesus the
70 Galilean." But he denied in the sight of all and said: "I know not
71 what thou sayest, neither am I acquainted." And when he went forth
to the door of the court another saw him, and she saith to them:
72 "This one was with Jesus the Nazarene." And again he denied and
73 sware "I know him not, this man." And after a little those
standing *by* drew near, and they said to Simon: "Truly thou art of
74 them, for thy speech also is like." Then he began to asseverate and
to swear "I know him not, this man"; and in the same hour the
75 cock crew. And Simon remembered the word of Jesus, that he had
said to him "Before ever the cock crow, three times thou wilt deny
me"; and when he went forth outside he wept bitterly.

xxvii 1 And when *day* dawned all the chief priests and the elders of the
people took counsel against Jesus that they should put him to death;
2 and they bound him and carried him along and delivered him up to
Pilate the governor.

---

64. *Cf* 'Hereafter shall ye see the Son of Man coming with bright clouds with the angels of heaven' E^{237} **66** what *] *Perhaps the reading of S corresponded to* 'But what' **67** ⌜drew near to him⌝] 'received him' S^{ed}, *but cf* 'Then some of them drew near and spat in his face' Diat^{ar} xlix 40
74.] *Cf* 'And he asseverated and sware I know him not' *A* 143

³ܗܝܕܝܢ ܟܕ ܚܙܐ ܝܗܘܕܐ ܡܫܠܡܢܐ ܕܐܬܚܝܒ ܐܬܬܘܝ، ܘܐܗܦܟ S
ܗܠܝܢ ܬ̈ܠܬܝܢ ܕܟܣܦܐ ܠܪ̈ܒܝ ܟܗܢܐ ܘܠܩܫ̈ܝܫܐ ⁴ܘܐܡܪ ܚܛܝܬ
ܕܐܫܠܡܬ ܕܡܐ ܕܙܕܝܩܐ ܐܡܪ̈ܝܢ ܠܗ ܠܢ ܡܢܐ ܠܢ ܐܢܬ ܬܕܥ·
⁵ܗܘ ܕܝܢ ܫܕܝܗܝ، ܟܣܦܐ ܒܗܝܟܠܐ ܘܫܢܝ ܘܐܙܠ ܬܠܐ ܠܗ
ܘܐܬܚܢܩ· ⁶ܪ̈ܒܝ ܟܗܢܐ ܕܝܢ ܫܩܠܘܗܝ، ܠܟܣܦܐ ܘܐܡܪ̈ܝܢ ܠܐ
ܫܠܝܛ ܠܡܪܡܝܘܬܗ ܒܝܬ ܩܘܪܒܢܐ ܡܛܠ ܕܕ̈ܡܝܐ ܐܢܘܢ ܕܕܡ̈ܐ
⁷ܘܢܣܒܘ ܡܠܟܐ. ܘܙܒܢܘ ܒܗ ܩܘܪܝܬ ܦܚܪܐ ܕܒܝܬ ܩܒܘܪܐ
ܕܐܟܣܢܝܐ. ⁸ܡܛܠ ܗܢܐ ܐܬܩܪܝܬ ܗ̇ܝ، ܩܘܪܝܬ ܕܡ ܒܕܡܐ
ܠܝܘܡܢܐ. ⁹ܗܝܕܝܢ ܐܬܡܠܝ ܡܕܡ ܕܐܬܐܡܪ ܒܢܒܝܐ ܕܐܡܪ ܗܘܐ
ܕܢܣܒܬ ܬ̈ܠܬܝܢ ܕܟܣܦܐ ܕܛܝܡܗ، ܕܝܩܝܪܐ ܕܝܩܪܘܬ ܡܢ ܒܢ̈ܝܗܘܢ
ܕܐܝܣܪܐܝܠ ¹⁰ܘܝܗܒܬ ܐ̈ܢܝܢ ܠܩܘܪܝܬ ܦܚܪܐ ܐܝܟ ܕܦܩܕ ܠܝ
ܡܪܝܐ ܀

¹¹ܝܫܘܥ ܕܝܢ ܩܡ ܩܕܡ ܗܓܡܘܢܐ ܘܫܐܠܗ ܘܐܡܪ ܠܗ ܐܢܬ ܗܘ
ܡܠܟܐ ܕܝܗܘ̈ܕܝܐ. ܐܡܪ ܠܗ ܝܫܘܥ ܐܢܬ ܐܡܪܬ. ¹²ܘܟܕ ܐܟܠܝܢ
ܗܘܘ ܩܪ̈ܨܘܗܝ، ܪ̈ܒܝ ܟܗܢܐ ܘܩܫ̈ܝܫܐ ܗܘ ܡܕܡ ܦܬܓܡ ܠܐ
ܝܗܒ ܗܘܐ ܠܗܘܢ. ¹³ܗܝܕܝܢ ܐܡܪ ܠܗ ܦܝܠܛܘܣ ܠܐ ܫܡܥ
ܐܢܬ ܟܡܐ ܣܗܕܝܢ ܡܣܗ̈ܕܝܢ ܥܠܝܟ. ¹⁴ܗܘ ܕܝܢ ܦܬܓܡ ܠܐ
ܝܗܒ ܠܗ ܘܛܒ ܡܬܕܡܪ ܗܘܐ ܗܓܡܘܢܐ. ¹⁵ܒܟܠ ܒܥܐܕܐ ܕܝܢ
ܡܥܕ ܗܘܐ ܗܓܡܘܢܐ ܕܢܫܪܐ ܠܥܡܐ ܐܣܝܪܐ ܚܕ ܐܝܢܐ
ܕܗܘܢ ܨܒܝܢ ܗܘܘ. ¹⁶ܘܐܣܝܪ ܗܘܐ ܠܗܘܢ ܓܒܪܐ ܚܕ ܝܕܝܥܐ
ܕܫܡܗ ܗܘܐ ܝܫܘܥ ܒܪ ܐܒܐ. ܐܣܝܪܐ ܗܘܐ ܒܝܬ ܐܣܝܪ̈ܐ
ܡܛܠ ܒܝ̈ܫܬܐ ܕܥܒܕ ܗܘܐ ܘܩܛܠ ܗܘܐ ܩܛܠܐ. ¹⁷ܘܟܕ ܟܢܝܫܝܢ
ܟܠܗܘܢ ܝܗܘܕܝܐ ܐܡܪ ܠܗܘܢ ܦܝܠܛܘܣ. ܠܡܢ ܨܒܝܢ ܐܢܬܘܢ
ܕܐܫܪܐ ܠܟܘܢ؛ ܠܝܫܘܥ ܒܪ ܐܒܐ ܐܘ ܠܝܫܘܥ ܕܡܬܩܪܐ ܡܫܝܚܐ.
¹⁸ܝܕܥ ܗܘܐ ܓܝܪ ܕܡܛܠ ܚܣܡܐ ܗܘ ܐܫܠܡܘܗܝ، ܠܗ. ¹⁹ܘܟܕ ܗܘ
ܝܬܒ ܥܠ ܒܝܡ. ܫܠܚܐ ܠܗ ܐܢܬܬܗ. ܘܐܡܪܐ ܠܗ ܠܐ ܠܟ
ܘܠܗܘ ܙܕܝܩܐ. ܣܓܝ ܓܝܪ ܚܫܬ ܝܘܡܢܐ ܒܚܠܡܝ ܡܛܠܬܗ ܀
²⁰ܪ̈ܒܝ ܟܗܢܐ ܕܝܢ ܘܩܫܝܫܐ ܐܦܝܣܘ ܠܥܡܐ ܕܢܫܐܠܘܢ ܠܒܪ ܐܒܐ.

3 Then when Judas the betrayer saw that he was condemned he *S*
changed his mind and returned those thirty *pieces* of silver to the chief
4 priests and to the elders, and said: "I have sinned that I betrayed
the blood of the righteous!" They say to him: "What *is it* to us?
5 Thou wilt know." But he threw the silver into the Temple and
6 departed and he went *and* hanged himself and was strangled. Now
the chief priests took up the silver, and say: "It is not lawful to put
7 it into the offertory, because it is the price of blood." And they took
counsel and bought of it the Potter's Field, *the field* of the tombs of
8 the strangers. Therefore that hath been called Field of Blood unto
9 this day. Then was fulfilled that which was said by the prophet, who
had said "I took the thirty *pieces* of silver, the price of the dear
10 one that I held more dear than the sons of Israel, and I gave them
for the Potter's Field, as the LORD commanded me."
11 Now Jesus stood before the governor, and he asked him and said
to him: "Art thou the king of the Jews?" Jesus saith to him:
12 "Thou hast said *it*." And while the chief priests and the Pharisees
13 were accusing him he was giving not any answer to them. Then
said Pilate to him: "Hearest thou not how many witnesses are
14 bearing witness against thee?" But he gave no answer to him, and
15 exceedingly was the governor wondering. Now at every Feast the
governor was wont that he should be releasing to the people one
16 prisoner, whichever they were wishing *for*; and there had been
imprisoned by them one well-known man whose name was Jesus
Bar Abba; he was lying in prison because of evil *deeds* that he
17 had done, and he had committed murder. And while all the Jews
were gathered together Pilate saith to them: "Whom will ye that
I release to you—Jesus Bar Abba, or Jesus called the Messiah?"
18 For he knew that it was because of envy they delivered him up to
19 him. And while he *was* sitting at the tribunal, his wife sendeth *word*
to him and saith to him: "Have thou naught *to do* with that
righteous one! For much have I suffered this day in my dream
because of him."
20 Now the chief priests and the elders persuaded the people that

---

4 blood of the righteous] 'righteous blood' *E*[239] 5 hanged himself and was strangled] *cf* 'hanged himself and died' *E*[240] 9 more dear than] *cf* Nöld. § 249 E 16, 17 Jesus Bar Abba] *See Notes*, vol. ii

ܘܢܩܒܘܢ ܠܢܫ̈ܐ. ²¹ܥܡܗܐ ܡܫܠܡܢܐ ܘܐܡܪ ܠܗܘܢ ܠܗܝܢ ܢܦܫܝܢ S
ܐܢܬܘܢ ܕܐܢܫܐ ܠܒܘܢ ܐܡܪܝܢ ܠܗ ܠܒܪ ܐܢܫܐ ²²ܐܡܪ ܠܗܘܢ
ܦܠܓܘܣ ܘܡܠܟܐ ܐܚܪܢ ܠܢܫ̈ܐ ܕܡܬܝܪܐ ܡܫܡܫܢܐ ܐܡܪܝܢ
ܟܠܗܘܢ ܢܫ̈ܘܢ ²³ܐܡܪ ܠܗܘܢ ܡܠܟܐ ܠܒܪ ܕܟܢ ܟܢܫ ܠܗ
ܗܘܝܢ ܡܬܪܐܫ ܡܢܝܢ ܗܘܘ ܘܐܡܪܝܢ ܢܫ̈ܘܢ ²⁴ܟܕ ܚܙܐ ܕܝܢ
ܦܠܓܘܣ ܕܟܕܡ ܠܐ ܡܘܬܪ ܠܗ ܐܠܐ ܒܒܝܬܐ * * ܘܪܒܐ
ܡܫܒܐ ܫܒܐ ܢܣܒ ܡܠܟܐ ܘܐܫܬܘܝ ܐܢܫܘܗܝ, ܠܒܝܢ ܟܠܗ ܒܢܫܐ
ܘܐܡܪ ܐܦ ܐܢܐ ܡܢ ܕܡܠܟܐ ܗܢܐ ܐܢܬܘܢ ܡܢܝܢ ²⁵ܘܡܠܟܐ
ܟܘܠܗ ܒܡܟܐ ܘܐܡܪܘ ܕܡܠܗ ܕܗܢܐ ܟܠܝܢ ܘܟܠ ܒܢ̈ܝܢ ²⁶ܗܢܝܢ
ܫܪܐ ܠܗܘܢ ܠܒܪ ܐܢܫܐ ܘܢܩܦ ܒܦܪܓܠܐ ܠܢܫ̈ܐ ܘܐܫܠܡܗ
ܠܗܘܢ ܕܢܬܘܦ ²⁷ܗܢܝܢ ܐܦܛܪܦܘܦܐ ܕܡܠܟܘܬܐ ܐܟܠܘܗܝ,
ܠܢܫ̈ܐ ܠܦܪܓܠܝܢ. ܘܒܢܫܐ ܟܠܘܗܝ, ܒܢܫܐ ²⁸ܘܐܠܒܫܘܗܝ, ܢܫ̈ܬܐ.
ܕܐܣܪܬܐ ܘܐܬܪܓܘܢܐ ²⁹ܘܓܕܠܘ ܟܠܠܐ ܕܒܫ̈ܡܐ ܘܥܡܘ ܒܪܫܗ
ܘܐܘܣܕܘ ܡܢܗ ܒܡܟܣܗ ܘܒܪܟܘ ܒܠ ܒܘܪܟܝܗܘܢ ܡܕܡܘܗܝ,
ܘܡܒܐܣܝܢ ܗܘܘ ܒܗ. ܘܐܡܪܝܢ ܥܠܡ ܠܝ ܡܠܟܐ ܕܗܘܕܝܐ.
³⁰ܘܪ̈ܘܒ ܒܐܦ̈ܘܗܝ, ܘܫܡܠܘ ܡܢܗ ܘܡܫܝܢ ܗܘܘ ܠܗ ܒܠ ܪܫܗ ³¹ܘܟܕ
ܒܝܘܡ ܒܗ ܐܫܠܡܘܗܝ, ܢܫ̈ܬܐ ܗܝܢ ܕܠܒܫ ܗܘܐ ܘܐܠܒܫܘܗܝ,
ܢܫ̈ܬܗ, ܘܕܒܪܘܗܝ, ܘܐܙܠܘ ܠܒܝܬܗܘܢ. ³²ܘܟܕ ܢܦܩܝܢ ܕܝܢ ܐܫܟܚܘ
ܓܒܪܐ ܡܪܝܡܐ ܕܢܫ̈ܡܗ ܫܡܥܘ ܘܫܡܪܘܗܝ, ܕܢܫܩܘܠ ܪܘܒܗ.
³³ܘܐܬܐ ܠܐܬܪܐ ܕܡܠܟܘܬܐ ܓܠܓܠܬܐ ³⁴ܘܢܣܒܘ ܠܗ ܠܡܫܬܝܐ
ܫܡܪܐ ܟܕ ܚܠܝܦ ܒܡܪ̈ܙܬܐ ܘܓܒܗܝܢ ܘܠܐ ܢܒܥܐ ܠܡܫܬܘܬܗ ³⁵ܘܟܕ
ܘܡܒܗ, ܦܠܓܗ ܠܒܘܢ̈ܘܗܝ, ܘܫܩܘ ܟܠܗܘܢ ³⁶ܘܬܒܝܢ ܗܘܘ ܘܢܦܪܝܢ
ܬܒܢ ³⁷ܘܟܕ ܗܢܘܢ ܬܒܝܢ. ܒܬܒܘ ܫܟܠܘܬܐ ܫܡܥܘ ܒܠ ܪܫܗ
ܢܫܒ ܡܠܟܐ ܕܗܘ̈ܕܝܐ ·܀·܀

³⁸ܗܢܝܢ ܐܘܕܘܥܘ ܒܫܡܗ ܬܪܝܢ ܒܒ̈ܪ, ܒܢܩ̈ܝܬܐ ܚܕ ܡܢ ܡܢܝܢܗ ܘܚܕ
ܡܢ ܫܡܠܗ ³⁹ܘܗܢܘܢ ܕܒܒܪܝܢ ܗܘܘ ܡܓܕܦܝܢ ܗܘܘ ܟܠܘܗܝ,
ܘܡܢܝܢ ܒܪ̈ܢܫܗܘܢ ⁴⁰ܘܐܡܪ̈ܝܢ ܫܦܝܪ ܗܟܠܐ ܘܡܢܐ ܠܗ ܠܬܠܬܐ

24 * * ܒܒܝܬܐ] *The illegible word may have been* ܕܝܢ

21 they should ask for Bar Abba and destroy Jesus. The governor S
answered and said to them: "Whom wish ye that I should release
22 to you?" They say to him: "Bar Abba." Pilate saith to them:
"And what shall I do to Jesus called the Messiah?" They say
23 all of them: "Let him be crucified." He saith to them: "*Why?*
For what evil hath been done by him?" Then the more were they
24 crying out and saying: "Let him be crucified." Now when Pilate
saw that nothing it gained him, but how much [more] the uproar
indeed increased, he took water and washed his hands in the sight of
all the multitude, and saith: "I am innocent of this blood; ye know
25 *it.*" And all the people answered and they said: "The blood of this
26 one *be* on us and on our sons!" Then he released to them Bar Abba,
and scourged with a whip Jesus, and delivered him up to them
27 that he should be crucified. Then the soldiers of the governor
brought in Jesus to the Praetorium, and they gathered against him
28 a multitude, and they clothed him in garments of scarlet and of
29 purple, and plaited a crown of thorns and set *it* on his head, and
made *him* hold a reed in his right *hand*, and they knelt on their
knees before him, and were mocking at him and saying: "Hail to
30 thee, king of the Jews!" And they spat in his face and took up the
31 reed and were smiting him upon his head. And when they *had*
mocked at him they stripped him of those garments that he was
clothed *with*, and clothed him in his garments and led him away
32 and went to crucify him. Now while going forth they found a
man, a Cyrenian whose name *was* Simon, and they compelled him
33 that he should take up his cross. And they came to the place
34 called Gagultha; and they gave him to drink wine mixed with
35 myrrh, and he tasted it and would not drink it. And when they
36 crucified him they divided his clothes and drew lots for them; and
37 they were sitting and keeping *watch* there. And while they were
sitting they wrote the trespass *and* set *it* over his head: "Jesus, the
King of the Jews."

38 Then were crucified with him two evil-doers, one on his right
39 and one on his left. And those that were passing by were blaspheming
40 against him and wagging their heads and saying: "Puller down of

---

24 how much ⌜more⌝] *or*, 'how much ⌜indeed⌝' 34 wine mixed with myrrh] 'And they gave him to drink vinegar and gall' E^{245} 37 Jesus, the King of the Jews] 'This is the Christ, the King of the Jews' E^{243}

ܘܩܒ̈ܠܝܢ ܐܢ ܒܪܗ ܐܝܬ ܕܐܠܗܐ ܐܝܟܢ ܢܦܩ ܘܗܘܬ ܡܢ ܙܘܓܐ. S
[41]ܘܐܦ ܙ̈ܘ ܒܗ̈ܢܐ ܐܝܟ ܦܘ̈ܪܐ ܘܦܪ̈ܫܐ ܡܚܒܫܝܢ ܗܘܘ ܒܗ
ܘܡܫܘܕܝܢ ܗܘܘ ܠܗ [42]ܘܐܡ̈ܪܝܢ ܕܠܐܘܪ̈ܚܐ ܕܚܝܐ. ܢܦܫܗ ܠܐ
ܡܫܡܫ. ܗܘܐ ܠܚܘܫܒܐ ܐܢ ܡܠܟܐ ܗܘ ܕܐܬܦܪܣ ܠܘܬ ܗܫܐ
ܡܢ ܙܘܓܐ ܘܢܫܡܬܝܢ ܒܗ [43]ܘܗܘ ܬܒܥܠ ܗܘܐ ܒܠ ܐܠܗܐ
ܢܠܦܘܗܝ, ܗܫܐ ܐܢ ܝܐܐ ܒܗ ܐܡܪ ܠܢ ܕܒܪܗ ܐܝܬ
ܕܐܠܗܐ. [44]ܘܐܦ ܗܢܘܢ ܒܢ̈ܝ, ܒܝܫܬܐ ܕܐܙܕܘܓܘ ܒܗܘܢ ܐܝܟ
ܙܘܓܐ ܡܫܘܕܝܢ ܗܘܘ ܠܗ. [45]ܘܡܢ ܫܢܬ ܫܚܝܢ ܗܘܐ ܫܘܒܚܐ ܒܠ
ܒܗܠܝܢ ܐܪܒܥܐ ܒܙܘܓܐ ܠܒ̈ܢܝܐ ܬܒ̈ܥ. [46]ܘܡܬܒ̈ܥ ܬ̈ܒܥܝܢ ܠܒܥܐ
ܫܘܒ ܒܗܠܝܢ ܙܘܓܐ ܘܐܡܪ ܐܠ ܐܠ ܠܚܝܐ ܫܒܘܬܐ ܀
[47]ܘܐܢܫܐ ܗܢܘܢ ܕܢܒܥܝܢ ܗܘܘ ܬܡܢ ܒܙ ܫܒܥܘ ܐܡܪܝܢ ܗܢܐ
ܠܐܠܗܐ ܡܪܐ. [48]ܘܒܗ ܒܫܒܥܬܐ ܪܗܛ ܚܙ ܡܒܗܘܢ ܘܢܫܒ
ܗܘܟܢܐ ܘܢܓܒܗ ܒܫܠܐ ܘܗܦܪ ܒܡܢܝܐ ܘܐܘܫܦ ܠܗ ܠܡܫܬܝܐ.
[49]ܐܚܪܢܐ ܕܝܢ ܐܡܪܝܢ ܫܒܥܘ ܚܝܐ ܐܢ ܐܬܬܐ ܐܠܗܐ ܘܡܚܝܐ
ܠܗ [50]ܫܘܒ ܕܝܢ ܡܢܐ ܒܗܠܝܢ ܙܘܓܐ ܘܗܠܘܬ ܪܘܚܗ [51]ܘܒܗ ܒܫܒܥܬܐ
ܐܝܟܢܝ, ܫ̈ܒܥ ܬܪܥܐ ܕܒܗܬ ܡܕܒܚܐ ܡܢ ܕܒܠ ܪܚ· ܘܐܬܪܥܒܬ
ܐܪܒܥܐ ܘܐܝܟܢܝ, ܒܐܦ̈ܐ. [52]ܘܐܬܦܬܚܘ ܒܗܬ ܡܒܘܪ̈ܐ. ܘܦ̈ܓܠܐ
ܦܓ̈ܪܐ ܕܙܕܘܩܐ ܐܝܠܝܢ ܕܒܒܝܢ ܡܒܐ [53]ܘܢܦܩܘ ܡܢ ܒܗܬ ܡܒܘܪ̈ܐ
ܡܢ ܒܬܪ ܡܢܬܗ ܐܬܘ ܠܡܕܝܢܬ ܡܕܒܚܐ ܘܐܬܚܙܝܘ ܠܦ̈ܓܠܐ ܀
[54]ܡܠܦ̈ܢܐ ܕܝܢ ܘܐܝܠܝܢ ܕܠܦܪܝܢ ܗܘܘ ܒܗܡ ܠܫܘܒ ܒܙ ܫܢܘ
ܙܘܓܐ ܘܐܝܠܝܢ ܕܗܘ, ܕܫܠܘ ܠܒ. ܘܐܡܪܝܢ ܫܪܪܐܝܬ ܗܢܐ
ܒܪܗ ܗܘ ܕܐܠܗܐ ܀ ܀ ܀
[55]ܘܐܝܬ ܗܘ̈ܘ, ܬܡܢ ܢܒ̈ܝܐ ܦܠܣܦ̈ܘܬܐ ܘܡܢ ܪܘܡܐ ܚܝܢ ܗܘܘ,
ܐܝܠܝܢ ܕܐܬܝܢ ܗܘܘ, ܒܬܪ ܫܘܒ ܡܢ ܓܠܝܠܐ ܘܡܫܟ̈ܚܝܢ ܗܘܘ,
ܠܗ [56]ܡܒܝܢ ܡܓܒܠܬܐ ܘܡܒܝܢ ܒܬܪ ܡܢܘܒ. ܘܐܡܪܗ ܕܢܘܦ

50 ܘܗܠܘܬ ܪܘܚܗ] *Cf* ASD 84, *and see Notes*, vol. ii

the Temple and builder of it in three days, if thou art the Son of *S*
41 God save thyself alive and come down from the cross!" And the
chief priests also, like the Scribes and the Pharisees, were mocking
42 at him and were reproaching him and saying "He that saveth others
alive, himself could he not save alive? If he is the King of Israel, let
43 him come down now from the cross and we shall believe in him. He
hath trusted in God,—let him deliver him now if he is pleased with
44 him; for he said 'I am the son of God.'" And those evil-doers also
45 that were crucified with him like the rest were reproaching him. And
from the sixth hour there was darkness on all the land unto the
46 ninth hour, and at the ninth hour Jesus exclaimed with a mighty
voice and said: "Eli, Eli, wherefore hast thou left me?"

47 And those folk that were standing there, when they heard *it*, say:
48 "This *man* for Elijah hath called!" And in the same hour one of
them ran and took a sponge and dipped it in vinegar and stuck *it* on
49 a reed and handed *it* for him to drink. But others say: "Let be;
50 we shall see if Elijah cometh and saveth him alive." Now Jesus
51 cried out with a loud voice, and his spirit went up. And in the
same hour was rent the veil of the Sanctuary from the very top, and
52 the earth quaked and the stones were rent and the tombs were
opened, and many bodies of the righteous which were asleep arose
53 and went forth from the tombs after his resurrection *and* came to
the Holy City and appeared to many.

54 Now the centurion and they that were keeping *watch* with him
upon Jesus, when they saw the earthquake and the things that came
to pass, feared exceedingly, and say: "Truly this is the Son of God!"

55 And there were there many women, and from afar they were
seeing, which were coming after Jesus from Galilee and were serving
56 him—Mary Magdalene, and Mary daughter of James and mother of

---

46 Eli, Eli] *Quoted twice* E^{247}. *In the first quotation the Armenian has* 'God, my God'; *in the second the better* MS *has* 'Eli, Eli,' *but the other has* 'El, El,' *as in* syr.vg 49. *There is no Syriac evidence for the insertion here of words corresponding to* Joh xix 34. *The spear-piercing is mentioned in* E^{259} *after* Mt xxvii 55 50 and his spirit went up] *cf* ASD 84

ܘܐܡܗܘܢ ܕܢܫ̈ܐ ܘܒܢ̈ܝ. [57]ܘܟܕ ܗܘܐ ܙܒܢܐ ܣܓܝ ܠܡܪܝܐ ܚܙ S
ܒܬܪܐ ܗܝ ܙܒܢܐ ܘܫܡܥܗ ܝܫܘܥ ܘܐܡܪ ܗܘ ܬܠܡܝܕܐ ܗܘܐ
ܕܫܡܥ [58]ܗܢܐ ܡܪܢ ܠܦܝܠܝܦܘܣ ܘܐܡܪ ܦܪܘܩܗ ܕܫܡܥ ܘܩܡ
ܦܝܠܝܦܘܣ ܕܢܬܚܙܐ ܠܗ. [59]ܘܟܕ ܫܐܠ ܝܘܣܦ ܦܪܘܩܐ ܪܒܗ ܒܚܕܬܐ
ܚܙܬܐ [60]ܘܫܡܥܗ ܒܝܬ ܡܥܘܪܐ ܚܙܬܐ ܕܐܠܗ ܢܗܝܪܐ ܕܢܗܪ ܗܘܐ
ܠܗ ܒܫܒܥܐ ܘܐܪܒܥ ܒܐܦܐ ܚܙܐ ܙܒܢܐ ܥܠ ܬܪܥܐ ܕܒܝܬ
ܡܥܘܪܐ ܘܐܙܠ ܀ ܀

[61]ܘܐܝܬ ܗܘ̇ ܬܡܢ ܡܢܝܢ ܡܫܠܡܢܘܬܐ ܘܡܢܝܢ ܐܚܪܢܐ ܬܠܬܝܢ
ܗܘ̇ ܠܡܥܠܗ ܕܒܝܬ ܡܥܘܪܐ. [62]ܠܝܘܡܐ ܕܝܢ ܐܚܪܢܐ ܕܒܬܪ
ܥܪܘܒܬܐ ܐܬܟܢܫܘ ܬ̈ܪܝ ܒܢ̈ܝܐ ܘܦܬ̈ܝܫܐ ܠܘܬ ܦܝܠܝܦܘܣ [63]ܘܐܡܪܝܢ
ܠܗ ܡܪܢ ܐܬܩܪܝܢ ܕܗܘ ܡܫܝܚܐ ܐܡܪ ܗܘܐ ܟܕ ܗܘ ܚܝ
ܕܒܬܪ ܬܠܬܐ ܝܘܡܝܢ ܩܐܡ ܐܢܐ. [64]ܐܠܐ §ܦܩܕ ܡܙܕܗܪܝܢ ܒܡܥܪܬܐ¶ §¶A411
ܥܕܡܐ ܠܬܠܬܐ ܝܘܡܝܢ. ܕܠܐ ܢܐܬܘܢ ܬܠܡܝܕܘܗܝ ܒܠܠܝܐ
ܘܢܓܢܒܘܢܗ ܘܢܐܡܪܘܢ ܠܥܡܐ ܕܩܡ ܠܗ ܡܢ ܒܝܬ ܡܝ̈ܬܐ ܘܬܗܘܐ
ܛܥܝܐ ܦܠܚܝ ܐܚܪܝܬܐ ܡܢ ܩܕܡܝܬܐ ܀

[65]ܐܡܪ ܠܗܘܢ ܦܝܠܝܦܘܣ ܐܝܬ ܠܟܘܢ ܡܣܦܩܘܬ, ܕܠܘ ܐܙܕܗܪܘ
ܒܗ ܒܡܥܪܐ ܐܝܟ ܕܐܡܪܝܢ ܐܢܬܘܢ. [66]ܐܠܘ ܐܙܕܗܪܘ ܒܡܥܪܗ
ܘܢܛܪܘܗ ܒܐܦܐ ܗܘ, ܟܕ ܡܣܦܩܘܬܐ [1]ܒܪܡܫܐ ܕܝܢ ܒܫܒܬܐ
ܕܝܠܗ ܚܙ ܒܫܒܥܐ ܐܬܬ ܡܢܝܢ ܡܫܠܡܢܘܬܐ ܘܡܢܝܢ ܐܚܪܢܐ
ܕܫܡܝܢ ܡܥܪܐ [2]ܘܗܐ ܗܘܐ ܙܘܥܐ ܪܒܐ ܡܛܠ ܕܡܠܐܟܗ
ܕܡܪܝܐ ܢܚܬ ܡܢ ܫܡܝܐ. ܘܓܠܠ ܠܟܐܦܐ ܘܝܬܒ ܠܥܠ ܡܢܗ
[3]ܘܕܡܘܬܐ ܗܘܐ ܚܙܘܗ ܠܒܪܩܐ ܘܠܒܘܫܗ ܐܝܟ ܬܠܓܐ [4]ܘܡܢ
ܕܚܠܬܗ ܐܬܬܙܝܥܘ ܗܢܘܢ ܕܢܛܪܝܢ ܗܘܘ ܐܝܟ ܡܝ̈ܬܐ [5]ܥܢܐ

64 ܦܩܘܕ A   ܘܢܓܢܒܘܢܗ] S (*sic*), *for* ܘܢܓܢܒܘܢܗ

57 Joseph, and the mother of the sons of Zebedee. And when it was S
evening there drew near a certain rich man from Ramtha, and his
58 name *was* Joseph and he also was a disciple of Jesus,—this *man*
drew near to Pilate and asked for the body of Jesus, and Pilate
59 commanded that it should be given to him. And when Joseph took
60 the body he wrapped it in a new linen cloth and laid it in a new
tomb of his, a hewn *one* that had been hewn for him in the rock,
and he laid one great stone against the door of the tomb and
went away.

61 And there were there Mary Magdalene and the other Mary, *and*
62 they were sitting opposite the tomb. Now the next day after the
Friday the chief priests and the Pharisees were gathered together
63 unto Pilate, and they say to him: "Our Lord, we have remembered
that that deceiver was saying when he *was* alive 'After three days
64 I arise'; but §command them to take heed to the grave¶ until three §¶*A*411
days *are past*, that his disciples may not come in the night and steal
him away, and say to the people that he hath risen from among
the dead, and the last error be worse than the first."

65 Pilate saith to them: "Ye have a guard; go, take heed to the
66 grave as ye know *how*." They went *and* took heed to his grave and
xxviii 1 they sealed that stone with the guard. Now in the evening on the
sabbath that *was* dawning into the first *day* of the week came Mary
2 Magdalene and the other Mary, that they might see the grave. And
lo, there was a great earthquake, because the angel of the LORD came
down from heaven, and he rolled *away* the stone and sat upon it;
3 and his appearance was like to lightning and his clothing as the
4 snow, and for fear of him trembled those that were keeping *watch*
5 as the dead. The angel answered and said to the women: "Ye

ܡܠܐܟܐ ܘܐܡܪ ܠܢܫܐ ܐܢܬܝܢ ܠܐ ܬܕܚܠܢ ܝܕܥܢܐ ܓܝܪ ܕܠܝܫܘܥ S
ܗܘ ܕܐܙܕܩܦ ܒܥܝܢ ܐܢܬܝܢ [6]ܠܐ ܗܘܐ ܗܪܟܐ ܗܘ ܩܡ ܠܗ ܐܝܟܢܐ
ܕܐܡܪ ܠܟܝܢ ܬܘ ܚܙܝܢ ܕܘܟܬܐ ܗܝ ܕܣܝܡ ܗܘܐ ܒܗ. [7]ܐܙܠܝܢ
ܒܥܓܠ ܘܐܡܪܝܢ ܠܬܠܡܝܕܘܗܝ ܕܩܡ ܘܗܐ ܡܩܕܡ ܠܟܘܢ ܠܓܠܝܠܐ
ܬܡܢ * * * * * * * * * * * * *

[*The leaf of S which contained* Matt xxviii 7—Mk i 12 *is missing.*]

---

18. *At the end of this verse, after* ܐܬܝܗܒ ܠܝ ܟܠ ܫܘܠܛܢ ܒܫܡܝܐ ܘܒܐܪܥܐ, syr. vg *adds* ܘܐܝܟܢܐ ܕܫܕܪܢܝ ܐܒܝ ܐܦ ܐܢܐ ܡܫܕܪ ܐܢܐ ܠܟܘܢ (*from* Joh xx 21). *As no Greek* MS *has this addition it was probably taken over by* syr. vg *from the Old Syriac version. The Diatessaron had a different arrangement*

19. *Cf* ܥܒܪܘ ܬܠܡܕܘ (ܐܒܪܘ A[a]) ܠܟܠܗܘܢ ܥܡ̈ܡܐ. ܘܢܗܡܢܘܢ ܒܝ A 12

20. *Cf* ܥܡܟܘܢ ܐܢܐ ܥܕܡܐ ܠܫܘܠܡܗ ܕܥܠܡܐ A 484 *and*
ܥܡܟܘܢ ܐܢܐ ܥܕܡܐ ܕܢܫܠܡ ܥܠܡܐ A 120 ASD 32

NOTE

The invocation of the Trinity at Baptism is attested by the Acts of Thomas (pp. 193, 301, 324), *by the Doctrine of Addai* (pp. 20, 30, 34), *and by Aphraates* (p. 496). *The most striking formula is that in the Acts of Thomas* 324, *as preserved in the* 6*th century palimpsest fragments at Sinai* (*Studia Sinaitica* ix 34), *viz:*

ܐܫܛ ܐܢܘܢ ܠܒܢܝܐ ܘܐܡܪ ܠܗܘܢ
ܒܫܡ ܐܒܐ ܘܒܪܐ ܘܪܘܚܐ ܩܕܝܫܬܐ
ܒܫܡܟ ܡܐܡܪܐ ܫܒܝܚܐ

But there is nothing to shew that these passages are not based on Liturgical rather than direct Biblical authority, except the Doctrine of Addai 20, *which says:*

ܗܟܢܐ ܐܬܦܩܕܢ ܡܢܗ. ܕܢܥܡܕ ܘܢܫܡܫ ܠܐܝܠܝܢ ܕܡܗܝܡܢܝܢ.
ܒܫܡ ܐܒܐ ܘܒܪܐ ܘܪܘܚܐ ܕܩܘܕܫܐ.

women, do not ye fear; for I know that Jesus, him that was S
6 crucified, are ye seeking. He is not here; he hath risen as
7 he said to you: come, see the place that he was laid in! Go
quickly, and say to his disciples that he hath risen, and lo, he goeth
before you to Galilee, there * * * * * * * *

[*The leaf of S which contained* Matt xxviii 7—Mk i 12 *is missing.*]

---

18. *At the end of this verse, after* 'All authority hath been given to me in heaven and in earth,' syr.vg *adds* (*from* Joh xx 21) 'and as my Father hath sent me I also send you.' *As no Greek* MS *has this addition it was probably taken over by* syr.vg *from the Old Syriac version. The Diatessaron had a different arrangement.* 19. *Cf* 'Go forth *and* make disciples of (preach to *A*[a]) all the peoples, and they shall believe in me' *A* 12 20. *Cf* 'With you am I until the conclusion of the world' *A* 484, *and* 'With you am I until the world is finished' *A* 120 ASD 32

NOTE

The invocation of the Trinity at Baptism is attested by the Acts of Thomas (pp. 193, 301, 324), *by the Doctrine of Addai* (pp. 20, 30, 34), *and by Aphraates* (p. 496). *The most striking formula is that in the Acts of Thomas* 324, *as preserved in the 6th century palimpsest fragments at Sinai* (*Studia Sinaitica* ix 34), *viz*: "He (Thomas) made them go down to the water and said to them 'In the Name of Father and Son and holy Spirit—in thy Name, Heavenly Speech.'" *A phrase almost identical with that translated* 'Heavenly Speech' *occurs again in these Acts*, p. 250.

But there is nothing to shew that these passages are not based on Liturgical rather than direct Biblical authority, except the Doctrine of Addai 20, *which says:* "Thus were we commanded by Him, that we should baptize and absolve them that believe in the name of the Father and the Son and the Holy Spirit."

[ܐܘܢܓܠܝܘܢ ܕܡܪܩܘܣ]

S * * * * * * * * * * * * * *

12ܐܦܩܬܗ ܪܘܚܐ ܠܡܕܒܪܐ. 13ܘܗܘܐ ܬܡܢ ܝܘܡ̈ܬܐ ܐܪ̈ܒܥܝܢ ܟܕ
ܡܬܢܣܐ ܡܢ ܣܛܢܐ ܘܗܘܐ ܥܡ ܚܝ̈ܘܬܐ ܘܡܠܐ̈ܟܐ ܡܫܡܫܝܢ
ܗܘܘ ܠܗ ·o·o·o·o·o·
14ܘܒܬܪ ܕܐܫܬܠܡ ܝܘܚܢܢ ܐܬܐ ܝܫܘܥ ܠܓܠܝܠܐ. ܘܡܟܪܙ ܗܘܐ
ܣܒܪܬܐ ܕܐܠܗܐ 15ܕܫܠܡ ܙܒܢܐ ܘܡܛܬ ܡܠܟܘܬܐ ܕܐܠܗܐ
ܬܘܒܘ ܘܗܝܡܢܘ ܒܣܒܪܬܗ. 16ܘܟܕ ܡܗܠܟ ܗܘܐ ܥܠ ܓܢܒ
ܝܡܬܐ ܕܓܠܝܠܐ. ܚܙܐ ܠܫܡܥܘܢ ܘܠܐܢܕܪܘܣ ܐܚܘܗܝ, ܟܕ ܪ̈ܡܝܢ
ܡܨܝܕܬܗܘܢ ܒܝܡܐ. ܡܛܠ ܕܨ̈ܝܕܐ ܗܘܘ. 17ܘܐܡܪ ܠܗܘܢ
ܝܫܘܥ ܬܘ ܒܬܪܝ, ܘܐܥܒܕܟܘܢ ܨ̈ܝܕܐ ܕܒܢ̈ܝ ܐܢܫܐ. 18ܘܒܗ
ܒܫܥܬܐ ܫܒܩܘ ܡܨܝ̈ܕܬܗܘܢ ܘܐܙܠܘ ܒܬܪܗ. 19ܘܟܕ ܗܠܟ ܬܘܒ
ܩܠܝܠ ܚܙܐ ܠܝܥܩܘܒ ܒܪ ܙܒܕܝ, ܘܠܝܘܚܢܢ ܐܚܘܗܝ, ܐܦ ܠܗܘܢ
ܟܕ ܝܬܒܝܢ ܒܣܦܝܢܬܐ ܘܡܬܩܢܝܢ ܡܨܝ̈ܕܬܗܘܢ܆ 20ܘܒܗ ܒܫܥܬܐ.
ܩܪܐ ܐܢܘܢ. ܘܫܒܩܘ ܠܙܒܕܝ, ܐܒܘܗܘܢ ܥܡ ܐ̈ܓܝܪܐ ܒܣܦܝܢܬܐ
ܘܐܙܠܘ ܒܬܪܗ ܀ ܀
21ܘܥܠ ܗܘܐ ܒܫܒܬܐ ܒܟܢܘܫܬܐ 22ܘܬܡܗܝܢ ܗܘܘ ܒܝܘܠܦܢܗ
ܐܝܟ ܡܫܠܛܐ ܓܝܪ ܡܠܦ ܗܘܐ ܘܠܐ ܐܝܟ ܣܦܪ̈ܝܗܘܢ. 23ܘܐܝܬ
ܗܘܐ ܒܗ ܒܟܢܘܫܬܗܘܢ ܓܒܪܐ ܕܐܝܬ ܗܘܬ ܒܗ ܪܘܚܐ
ܛܢܦܬܐ ܘܩܥܐ ܗܘܐ 24ܘܐܡܪ ܡܢܐ ܠܢ ܘܠܟ ܝܫܘܥ ܢܨܪܝܐ
ܐܬܝܬ ܠܡܘܒܕܘܬܢ. ܝܕܥܢܐ ܠܟ ܡܢ ܐܢܬ ܕܩܕܝܫܗ ܐܢܬ
ܕܐܠܗܐ. 25ܘܟܐܐ ܒܗ ܝܫܘܥ ܘܐܡܪ ܠܗ ܣܟܘܪ ܦܘܡܟ ܘܦܘܩ
ܡܢܗ 26ܘܫܕܬܗ ܪܘܚܐ ܗܝ, ܛܢܦܬܐ ܘܩܥܬ ܒܩܠܐ ܪܒܐ
ܢܦܩܬ ܡܢܗ 27ܘܬܡܗܐ ܐܚܕ ܗܘܐ ܠܟܠܗܘܢ ܘܐܡܪܝܢ ܗܘܘ

[EVANGEL OF MARK]

* * * * * * * * * * * * * S

i 12, 13 the Spirit sent him forth into the wilderness ; and he was there forty
days being tempted by Satan, and he was with the beasts, and angels
were serving him.

14 And after that John was delivered up Jesus came to Galilee, and
15 he was preaching the gospel of God, *saying* "The time is ac-
complished and the kingdom of God hath arrived ; repent ye, and
16 believe in his gospel." And while he was walking by the side of the
lake of Galilee, he saw Simon and Andrew his brother casting their
17 nets into the sea, because they were fishers. And Jesus said to
18 them : "Come after me, and I will make you fishers of men"; and in
19 the same hour they left their nets and went after him. And when
he walked on again a little he saw James the son of Zebedee and
John his brother also sitting in the boat and mending their nets ;
20 and in the same hour he called them, and they left Zebedee their
father with the hired men in the boat and went after him.

21, 22 And he was teaching on the sabbath in the synagogue, and they
were astonished at his teaching, for as one authorised he was teaching
23 and not as ~~their~~ scribes. And there was in that same synagogue
of theirs a man in whom there was an unclean spirit, and he was
24 crying out and saying : "What have we to do with thee, Jesus the
Nazarene? Hast thou come to destroy us? I know thee who thou
25 art, that thou art the Holy One of God!" And Jesus rebuked him
26 and said to him : "Shut thy mouth and go forth from him." And
that unclean spirit threw him down, and when it *had* cried out with a
27 mighty voice it went forth from him. And astonishment was taking

ܚܙ. ܠܡܢ. ܡܢܐ ܗܘ ܗܢܐ ܘܡܠܦܢܐ ܚܕܬܐ ܕܐܝܬ ܠܗ ܫܘܠܛܢܐ S
ܘܦܩܕ ܠܪ̈ܘܚܐ ܛܢܦܬܐ ܘܡܫܬܡܥܢ ܠܗ. 28ܘܢܦܩ ܗܘܐ ܛܒܗ
ܒܟܠܗ ܥܒܪ ܕܓܠܝܠܐ. ܘܣܓܝܐܐ ܐܙܠܝܢ ܗܘܘ ܒܬܪܗ. 29ܘܢܦܩ
ܡܢ ܟܢܘܫܬܐ ܘܐܬܘ ܠܒܝܬܗ ܕܫܡܥܘܢ ܟܐܦܐ ܘܕܐܕܪܐܘܣ
ܘܝܥܩܘܒ ܘܝܘܚܢܢ ܥܡܗ ܗܘܘ 30ܘܚܡܬܗ ܕܫܡܥܘܢ ܟܪܝܗܐ
ܗܘܬ ܒܐܫܬܐ. ܘܐܡܪܘ ܠܗ ܥܠܝܗ. 31ܘܩܪܒ ܘܐܚܕܗ ܘܐܩܝܡܗ.
ܘܒܗ ܒܫܥܬܐ ܫܒܩܬܗ ܐܫܬܐ ܘܩܡܬ ܘܡܫܡܫܐ ܗܘܬ ܠܗܘܢ
32ܡܥܪ̈ܒ ܫܡܫܐ ܕܝܢ ܡܥܠܝܢ ܗܘܘ ܠܟܠܗܘܢ ܐܝܠܝܢ ܕܒܝܫ ܒܝܫ
ܒܝܫܝܢ ܗܘܘ ܒܟܘܪ̈ܗܢܐ ܡܫ̈ܢܐ. 33ܘܡܕܝܢܬܐ ܟܠܗ ܟܢܝܫܐ ܗܘܬ
ܥܠ ܬܪܥܗ. 34ܘܐܣܝ ܗܘܐ ܠܣܓ̈ܝܐܐ ܘܡܦܩ ܗܘܐ ܫ̈ܐܕܐ
ܣܓ̈ܝܐܐ ܘܠܐ ܡܫܒܩ ܗܘܐ ܠܗܘܢ ܠܡܡܠܠܘ ܡܛܠ ܕܝܕܥܝܢ
ܗܘܘ ܠܗ ܀
35ܘܒܨܦܪܐ ܪܒܐ ܢܦܩ ܐܙܠ ܠܐܬܪܐ ܚܘܪܒܐ ܘܬܡܢ ܡܨܠܐ ܗܘܐ.
36ܘܒܥܝܢ ܗܘܘ ܠܗ ܫܡܥܘܢ ܘܗܢܘܢ ܕܥܡܗ. 37ܘܟܕ ܐܫܟܚܘܗ,
ܐܡܪܝܢ ܠܗ ܐܢܫܐ ܣܓ̈ܝܐܐ ܒܥܝܢ ܗܘܘ ܠܟ. 38ܐܡܪ ܠܗܘܢ
ܗܠܟܘ ܢܐܙܠ ܠܩܘ̈ܪܝܐ ܘܠܡܕ̈ܝܢܬܐ ܕܩܪܝܒܢ. ܘܐܦ ܬܡܢ ܐܟܪܘܙ.
ܠܗܕܐ ܗܘ ܓܝܪ ܐܬܝܬ. 39ܘܡܟܪܙ ܗܘܐ ܒܟܠܗܘܢ ܒܟܢܘܫܬܐ
ܕܓܠܝܠܐ ܘܡܦܩ ܗܘܐ ܫ̈ܐܕܐ. 40ܘܐܬܐ ܠܘܬܗ. ܓܒܪܐ ܚܕ
ܘܒܥܐ ܗܘܐ ܡܢܗ ܘܢܦܠ ܥܠ ܪ̈ܓܠܘܗ, ܘܐܡܪ ܠܗ ܕܐܢ ܨܒܐ
ܐܢܬ ܡܫܟܚ ܐܢܬ ܠܡܕܟܝܘܬܝ. 41ܗܘ ܕܝܢ ܝܫܘܥ ܐܬܪܚܡ ܥܠܘܗ.,
ܘܦܫܛ ܐܝܕܗ ܘܩܪܒ ܠܗ. ܘܐܡܪ ܠܗ ܨܒܝܢܐ ܐܬܕܟܐ. 42ܘܒܗ
ܒܫܥܬܐ ܐܬܕܟܝ. 43ܘܟܐܐ ܒܗ 44ܘܐܡܪ ܚܙܝ ܕܠܡܐ * * *

[*The leaf of S which contained* Mk i 44—ii 21 *is missing.*]

21ܪܘܩܥܬܐ ܚܕܬܐ ⌜ܥܠ⌝ ⌜ܡܐܢܐ⌝ ܒܠܝܐ ܕܠܐ ⌜ܡ⌝⌜ܠܝܠܘܬܗ ܕܚ⌝ܕܬܐ
ܡܫܬܩܠܐ ܡ⌜ܚܝ⌝ܠܘܬܗ ܕܒܠܝܐ ܘܗܘܐ ܨܪܝܐ ܒܝܫ ܡܢ ܩܕܡܝܐ
22ܘܠܐ ܐܢܫ ܪܡܐ ܚܡܪܐ ܚܕܬܐ ܒܙܩܐ ܒܠܝܬܐ ܕܠܐ ܚܡܪܐ

---

29 ܘܕܐܕܪܐܘܣ] *S* (*sic*), *for* ܘܕܐܢܕܪܐܘܣ

hold of them all, and they were saying one to another: "What is this S
new teaching, that he hath authority and commandeth the unclean
28 spirits, and they obey him?" And the tale of him was going forth
29 in all the region of Galilee, and many were going after him. And
he went forth from the synagogue and they came to the house of
Simon Kepha and of Andrew, and James and John were with him.
30 And the mother-in-law of Simon was infirm with fever, and they said
31 to him about her. And he drew near and took hold of her and
raised her up, and in the same hour the fever left her, and she arose
32 and was serving them. Now at the setting of the sun they were
33 bringing all them that were ill with hard infirmities, and the city
34 was all gathered together at his door and he had healed many, and
was casting out many devils and was not suffering them to speak,
because they knew him.

35 And at the early dawn he came forth *and* went to a desert place,
36 and there he was praying. And Simon and those with him were
37 seeking him, and when they found him they say to him: "Many folk
38 were seeking thee." He saith to them: "Come away, let us go to the
villages and to the cities that are near, and there also will I preach,
39 for it is to this *end* I have come." And he was preaching in all the
40 synagogues of Galilee and was casting out devils. And there came
unto him a certain leper and he was beseeching him, and he fell at
his feet and said to him "If thou wilt, thou canst cleanse me."
41 Now Jesus had compassion on him and stretched forth his hand and
42 touched him, and said to him: "I will, be thou cleansed." And in
43, 44 the same hour he was cleansed. And he rebuked him and said:
"See lest * * * * * * * * * * * *

[*The leaf of S which contained* Mk i 44—ii 21 *is missing.*]

ii 21 a new patch on a worn out thing, else the fulness of the new pulleth
away the weakness of the worn out *part*, and the rent becometh
22 worse than the former one. And no man doth put new wine into
worn out wine-skins, else the wine teareth the wine-skins, and the

---

41 had compassion on him] being angry $E^{143ff.}$ ii **14**. 'He chose James the toll-gatherer' E^{58}

ܡܙܪܐ ܠܗܝܢ ܠܙ̈ܩܐ. ܘܗܘ ܚܡܪܐ ܡܬܐܫܕ ܘܙ̈ܩܐ ܐܒܕܝܢ S
ܐܠܐ ܪܡܝܢ ܚܡܪܐ ܚܕܬܐ ܒܙ̈ܩܐ ܚܕ̈ܬܬܐ.
[23]ܘܗܘܐ ܒܝܘܡܐ ܕܫܒܬܐ ܡܗܠܟ ܗܘܐ ܒܝܬ ܙ̈ܪܥܐ ܘܐܟܠܝܢ
ܗܘܘ ܬܠܡܝ̈ܕܘܗܝ܆ ܫܒܠܐ. [24]ܐܡܪܝܢ ܠܗ ܦܪ̈ܝܫܐ ܠܡܢܐ ܬܠܡܝ̈ܕܝܟ
ܥܒܕܝܢ ܒܫܒܬܐ ܡܕܡ ܕܠܐ ܫܠܝܛ. [25]ܐܡܪ ܠܗܘܢ [ܠܐ] ܡܡܬܘܡ
ܩܪܝܬܘܢ ܡܢܐ ܕܥܒܕ [ܕܘܝܕ] * * * * * * * *
[26]ܐܝܟܢܐ ܥܠ ܠܒܝܬܗ ܕܐܠܗܐ ܘܠܚܡܐ ܕܩܘܕܫ ܐܟܠ ܡܕܡ ܕܠܐ
ܫܠܝܛ ܗܘܐ ܠܡܐܟܠ ܐܠܐ ܐܢ ܠܟܗܢܐ ܘܝܗܒ ܐܦ ܠܗܘܢ
ܕܥܡܗ ܗܘܘ. [27]ܘܐܡܪ ܗܘܐ ܠܗܘܢ ܕܫܒܬܐ ܡܛܠ ܒܪ ܐܢܫܐ
ܐܬܒܪܝܬ. [28]ܡܛܠ ܗܢܐ ܡܪܗ ܕܫܒܬܐ ܒܪܗ ܗܘ ܕܐܢܫܐ ○ ○ ○
[1]ܘܥܠ ܬܘܒ ܠܟܢܘܫܬܐ ܘܐܝܬ ܗܘܐ ܬܡܢ ܓܒܪܐ ܕܝܒܝܫܐ ܗܘܬ
ܐܝܕܗ. [2]ܘܢܛܪܝܢ ܗܘܘ ܠܗ ܕܐܢ ܡܐܣܐ ܠܗ ܒܫܒܬܐ ܕܢܐܟܠܘܢ
ܩܪ̈ܨܘܗܝ. [3]ܐܡܪ ܠܗ ܠܓܒܪܐ ܕܝܒܝܫܐ ܐܝܕܗ ܩܘܡ ܒܡܨܥܬܐ
[4]ܐܡܪ ܕܝܢ ܐܦ ܠܗܘܢ * * * * * * * * ܢܦܫܐ
* * ܠܡܚܝܘ ܐܘ * * * * * * * *[5] * * * *
ܟܪܐ ܠܗ ܥܠ ܩܫܝܘܬ ܠܒܗܘܢ܆ ܘܐܡܪ ܠܗ ܠܓܒܪܐ ܦܫܘܛ
ܐܝܕܟ ܘܦܫܛ ܘܬܬܩܢܬ ܐܝܟ ܚܒܪܬܗ. [6]ܘܟܕ ܥܒܕܗ ܢܦܩܘ ܦܪ̈ܝܫܐ
ܥܡ ܕܒܝܬ ܗܪܘܕܣ ܘܐܬܡܠܟܘ ܕܢܘܒܕܘܢܝܗܝ. [7]ܘܝܫܘܥ ܐܙܠ ܠܗ ܥܡ
ܬܠܡܝ̈ܕܘܗܝ܆ ܠܝܡܐ ܘܟܢ̈ܫܐ ܣ̈ܓܝܐܐ ܕܡܢ ܓܠܝܠܐ ܘܡܢ ܝܗܘܕ
[8]ܘܡܢ ܐܘܪܫܠܡ ܘܡܢ ܥܒܪܐ ܕܝܘܪܕܢܢ ܘܡܢ ܨܘܪ ܘܡܢ ܨܝܕܢ
ܕܫܡܥܝܢ ܗܘܘ ܟܠܡܕܡ ܕܥܒܕ ܐܬܘ ܠܘܬܗ. [9]ܘܐܡܪ ܗܘܐ
ܠܬܠܡܝ̈ܕܘܗܝ܆ ܕܢܩܪܒܘܢ ܠܗ ܣܦܝܢܬܐ ܡܛܠ ܟܢܫܐ ܕܠܐ ܢܚܒܨܘܢܝܗܝ.
[10]ܣܓܝܐܐ ܓܝܪ ܡܐܣܐ ܗܘܐ. ܘܣ̈ܓܝܐܐ ܚܛܝܢ ܗܘܘ ܕܢܩܪܒܘܢ
ܠܗ [11]ܘܐܝܠܝܢ ܕܐܝܬ ܗܘܘ ܒܠܗܘܢ ܡܟܐܘܒܘܬܐ ܕܟܘܪ̈ܗܢܐ ܠܦܓܥܬܐ
ܢܦܠܝܢ ܗܘܘ ܥܠܘܗܝ܆ ܘܩܥܝܢ ܗܘܘ ܘܐܡܪܝܢ ܐܢܬ ܗܘ ܒܪܗ
ܕܐܠܗܐ [12]ܘܗܘ ܣܓܝ ܟܐܐ ܗܘܐ ܒܗܘܢ ܕܠܐ ܢܓܠܘܢܝܗܝ ܀

10 ܕܢܩܪܒܘܢ] *or,* ܕܢܬܩܪܒܘܢ; *only the last two letters are legible*
11 ܐܝܬ ܗܘܘ...ܡܟܐܘܒܘܬܐ] *S (sic): cf* Lk x 34

wine is spilt and the wine-skins perish. But they put new wine in S
new wine-skins."
23 And it came to pass on the sabbath-day he was walking among
24 the cornfields, and his disciples were eating the ears *of corn.* The
Pharisees say to him: "Wherefore do thy disciples on the sabbath
25 that which is not lawful?" He saith to them: "Have ye never read
26 what [David] did * * * *, how he entered the house of
God and the bread that was set *before God* he ate, that which was
not lawful to eat save for the priests, and he gave to them also that
27 were with him?" And he was saying to them "The sabbath
28 because of man was created, therefore the Lord of the sabbath is the
Son of Man."
iii 1 And he entered again into the synagogue, and there was there a
2 man whose hand was withered; and they were watching him, whether
3 he would heal him on the sabbath, that they might accuse him. He
saith to that man whose hand *was* withered: "Stand up in the midst."
4 Now he saith to them also * * * * * * * * a life
5 * * to save or * * * * * * * * * * * *
grieved at the deadness of their heart, and he said to that man:
"Stretch forth thy hand"; and he stretched *it* forth and it was
6 restored like its fellow. And straightway the Pharisees with the
Herodians went forth and took counsel that they might destroy him.
7 And Jesus went away with his disciples to the sea, and great
8 multitudes from Galilee and from Judaea and from Jerusalem and
from the other side of the Jordan and from Tyre and from Sidon
9 that were hearing everything that he did, came unto him. And he
had said to his disciples that they should bring near to him a boat
because of the multitudes, that they should not press upon him.
10 For many was he healing, and many were pressed together [that they
11 might touch] him. And those on whom were plagues of unclean
spirits were falling before him and were crying out and saying:
12 "Thou art the Son of God!" And much was he rebuking them that
they should not recognise him.

---

27 was created] 'was made' (*i.e.* ἐγένετο) $E^{62, 148}$

13 ܘܣܠܩ ܠܛܘܪܐ. ܘܩܪܐ ܗܘܐ ܠܐܝܠܝܢ ܕܨܒܐ ܘܐܙܠܘ ܠܘܬܗ. S
14 ܘܓܒܐ ܡܢܗܘܢ ܬܪ̈ܥܣܪ ܕܢܗܘܘܢ ܠܘܬܗ ܕܢܗܘܐ ܡܫܕܪ
ܠܗܘܢ ܡܟܪܙ 15 ܘܕܢܗܘܘܢ ܫܠܝܛܝܢ ܕܢܐܣܘܢ ܟܪ̈ܝܗܐ ܘܢܦܩܘܢ
ܫܐܕ̈ܐ 16 ܘܩܪܐ ܠܫܡܥܘܢ ܟܐܦܐ 17 ܘܠܝܥܩܘܒ ܒܪ ܙܒܕܝ، ܘܠܝܘܚܢܢ
ܐܚܘܗܝ، ܩܪܐ ܐܢܘܢ ܒܢܝ ܪ̈ܓܫܝ 18 ܘܠܐܢܕܪܐܘܣ ܘܠܦܝܠܝܦܘܣ ܘܠܒܪ
ܬܘܠܡܝ ܘܠܡܬܝ، ܘܠܬܐܘܡܐ ܘܠܝܥܩܘܒ ܒܪ ܚܠܦܝ، ܘܠܬܕܝ، ܘܠܫܡܥܘܢ
⌜ܩ⌝ܢܢܝܐ 19 ܘܠܝܗܘܕܐ ܣܟܪܝܘܛܐ ܡܫܠܡܢܐ

ܘܐܬܐ ܗܘܐ ܠܒܝܬܐ 20 ܘܐܬܐ ܠܘܬܗ ܬܘܒ ܟܢܫܐ ܣܓܝܐ ܐܟܚܕܐ
ܕܐܦܠܐ ܠܠܚܡܐ ܡܫܟܚܝܢ ܗܘܘ ܠܡܐܟܠ 21 ܘܟܕ ܫܡܥܘ ܐܚܘܗܝ،
ܢܦܩܘ ܗܘܘ ܠܡܐܚܕܗ ܐܡܪܝܢ ܗܘܘ ܓܝܪ ܕܡܢ ܗܘܢܗ ܢܦܩ
22 ܘܣܦܪܐ ܐܝܠܝܢ [ܕܡܢ] ܐܘܪܫܠܡ ܢܚ⌜ܬ⌝ܘ ܐܡܪܝܢ ܗܘܘ ܕܒܥܠܙܒܘܒ
ܐܝܬ ܒܗ ܘܒ⌜ܪ⌝ܝܫܐ ܕܫܐܕ̈ܐ ܡ⌜ܦܩ⌝ [ܗܘܐ] ܫܐܕ̈ܐ
23 ܘܡܠܠ [ܥܡܗܘܢ ܝܫܘܥ] ܒܡܬܠܐ ܘܐܡܪ ܠܗ ܐܝܟܢܐ ܡܫܟܚ ܣܛܢܐ
ܠܣܛܢܐ ܠܡܦܩܘ 24 ܘܐܢ ܡܠܟܘܬܐ ܥܠ ܢܦܫܗ ܬܬܦܠܓ ܠܐ
ܡܫܟܚܐ ܠܡܩܡ ܡܠܟܘܬܐ ܗܝ، 25 ܘܐܢ ܒܝܬܐ ܥܠ ܢܦܫܗ ܢܬܦܠܓ
ܠܐ ܡܫܟܚ ܒܝܬܐ ܗܘ ܠܡܩܡ 26 ܘܐܢ ܣܛܢܐ ܥܠ ܢܦܫܗ ܐܬܦܠܓ
ܠܐ ܡܫܟܚ ܠܡܩܡ ܐܠܐ ܫܘܠܡܗ ܗܘ 27 ܠܐ ܐܢܫ ܡܫܟܚ
ܠܡܥܠ ܠܒܝܬܗ ܕܚܣܝܢܐ ܘܢ⌜ܒܘ⌝ܙ ܡܐܢܘܗܝ، ܐܠܐ ܐ⌜ܢ⌝
ܠܘܩܕܡ ܠܚܣܝܢܐ ܢܐܣܘܪ ܘܗܝܕܝܢ [ܢܒܘܙ] ܡܐܢܘܗܝ، 28 * *
ܐܡܝܢ ܐܡܪܢܐ ܠܟܘܢ ܕܟܠ ܚ⌜ܛ⌝ܗܐ ܕܡܓܕܦܝܢ ܢܫܬܒܩܘܢ
ܠܒܢܝ ܐܢܫܐ 29 ܟܘܠ [ܕܡܢ] ܕܡܓܕܦ [ܥܠ] ܪܘܚܐ ܕܩܘܕܫܐ
ܠܐ * * * * ܫܒܩܐ ܠܥܠܡ 30 ܕܐܡܪܝܢ ܗܘܘ ܕܪܘܚܐ ܛܢܦܬܐ
ܐܝܬ ܒܗ .܀.

14 ܘܓܒܐ] *There seems to have been an alteration of the* ܓ *in S*
28 ܕܡܓܕܦܝܢ & 29 ܕܡܓܕܦ | [ܕܡܢ] *so I read the photograph of S*
29 ܠܐ . . . ܫܒܩܐ ܠܥܠܡ] *The full restoration is exactly one line too long, i.e.* ܠܐ ܢܫܬܒܩ ܠܗ ܠܥܠܡ ܐܠܐ ܚܝܒ ܗܘ ܫܒܩܐ ܠܥܠܡ : *cf* Joh viii 47ᵇ

13 And he went up into the hill, and he had called whom he would, *S*
14 and they went unto him. And he chose from them twelve to be by
15 him, that he might be sending them preaching, and that they might
16 be authorised to heal the infirm and cast out devils. And he called
17 Simon, Kepha ; and James the son of Zebedee and John his brother,
18 he called them 'Bĕnai-Ragsh'; and Andrew, and Philip, and Bar-
tholomew, and Matthew, and Thomas, and James the son of Halphaeus,
19 and Thaddaeus, and Simon the Cananaean, and Judas Scariot the
betrayer.

20 And he had come to the house, and the multitude came again
21 unto him, so that not even bread could they eat. And when his
brothers heard they had gone forth to take hold of him, for they
22 were saying "He hath gone out of his mind." And the scribes
which [from] Jerusalem came down were saying: "Beelzebub is in
him, and by the chief of the devils doth [this *fellow* cast out] devils."
23 And [Jesus] spoke [with them] in similitudes and said: "Satan
24 cannot cast out Satan. And if a kingdom against itself be divided,
25 that kingdom cannot stand ; and if a house against itself be divided,
26 that house cannot stand. And if Satan against himself hath been
27 divided, he cannot stand but it is the conclusion of him. No one can
enter the house of the strong man and seize his things, except
first he bind the strong man and then [he will seize] his things.
28 [Amen,] amen, I say to you All sins that they blaspheme shall
29 be forgiven to men, [but] every one that blasphemeth [against]
the Holy Spirit [shall] not [be forgiven * * *] sins for ever."
30 For that they were saying "An unclean spirit is in him."

---

17 Bĕnai-Ragsh] *or*, 'Sons of Ragshŷ,' *the final* y *being unsounded. The same transliteration is retained in* syr. vg. Arm. vg *has* 'Banereges'
29 not ⌜be forgiven⌝ * * * sins for ever] *The full restoration would be* 'not ⌜be forgiven for ever but is guilty of⌝ sins for ever', *but this is exactly one line too long* (*cf* Joh viii 47b); 'shall be guilty of the eternal sin' E^{112}. *In the word for* 'sin' *the difference in writing between the sing. and the plur. does not only depend on the presence or absence of diacritic points* (*cf* Joh ix 41), *according to the usage of this version.*

S * * * * ܫܕܪܘ [ܠܒܪ] ܩܝܡܝܢ [ܘܐܚܘܗܝ،] ܐܡܗ [ܐܬܘ] ܘܟܕ[31]

[32]ܝܬܒ ܗܘܐ * * * * ܘܟܕ ܐܡܪܝܢ ܗܘܐ ܐܡܟ ܘܐܚܝܟ

[ܩܝܡܝܢ] ܠܒܪ ܘܒܥܝܢ ܠܟ [33]ܐܡܪ ܠܗܘܢ ܡܢ ܐܡܝ ܐܘ ܐܚܝ

[34]ܘܚܪ ܒܐܝܠܝܢ ܕܝܬܒܝܢ ܠܘܬܗ ܘܐܡܪ ܗܐ ܐܡܝ ܘܗܐ ܐܚܝ [35]ܟܠ

ܐܢܫ ܓܝܪ ܕܥܒܕ ܨܒܝܢܗ ܕܐܠܗܐ ܗܘ ܐܚܝ ܘܚܬܝ، ܘܐܡܝ [1]ܘܬܘܒ

ܫܪܝ، ܗܘܐ ܡܠܦ ܥܠ ܝܡܬܐ ܘܐܬܟܢܫ ܗܘܐ ܠܘܬܗ ܟܢܫܐ

ܣܓܝܐܐ ܗܘܘ [ܘܣܠܩ] ܝܬܒ ܠܗ ܒܣܦܝܢܬܐ ܒܝܡܬܐ ܘܟܠܗ

ܟܢܫܐ ܩܐܡ ܗܘܐ ܥܠ ܣܦܬܐ [2]ܘܡܠܦ ܗܘܐ ܠܗܘܢ ܣܓܝ

ܒܡܬܠܐ ܘܟܕ ܡܠܦ ܗܘܐ ܠܗܘܢ [ܐܡܪ] [3]ܫܡܥܘ ܗܐ ܢܦܩ

ܙܪܘܥܐ ܠܡܙܪܥ [4]ܘܟܕ ܙܪܥ ܐܝܬ ܕܢܦܠ ܥܠ ܝܕ ܐܘܪܚܐ ܘܐܬܬ

ܦܪܚܬܐ ܘܐܟܠܬܗ [5]ܘܐܝܬ ܕܢܦܠ ܥܠ ܫܘܥܐ ܘܟܐܦܐ ܘܡܛܠ

ܕܠܝܬ ܗܘܐ ܥܘܡܩܐ ܕܐܪܥܐ ܬܚܝܬ ܒܥܩܪܘܗܝ [6]* *

*ܫܡܫܐ ܕܗܘܐ ܠܗܘܢ ܘܝܒܫ [7]ܘܐܝܬ ܕܢܦܠ ܒܝܬ ܟܘܒܐ

ܘܣܠܩܘ ܟܘܒܗ ܘܚܢܩܘܗܝ، ܘܦܐܪܐ ܠܐ ܝܗܒ [8]ܘܐܝܬ ܕܢܦܠ

ܥܠ ܐܪܥܐ ܛܒܬܐ. ܘܝܗܒ ܦܐܪܐ [ܘܪܒܐ] ܘܝܗܒ ܒܬܠܬܝܢ ܘܒܫܬܝܢ

ܘܒܡܐܐ [9]ܘܐܡܪ ܗܘܐ ܕܡܢ ܕܐܝܬ ܠܗ ܐܕܢܐ ܕܢܫܡܥ ܢܫܡܥ.

[10]ܘܟܕ ܗܘܐ [ܒܠܚܘܕܘܗܝ،] ܫܐܠܘܗܝ، ܬܠܡܝܕܘܗܝ، ܥܠ ܡܬܠܐ

ܗܢܘܢ [11]ܘܐܡܪ ܗܘܐ ܠܗܘܢ ܕܠܟܘܢ ܗܘ ܝܗܒ ܐܪܙܐ

ܕܡܠܟܘܬܗ ܕܐܠܗܐ ܠܗܘܢ ܕܝܢ ܕܒܪܐ ܟܘܠ ܡܕܡ ܒܡ̈ܬܠܐ

ܗܘܐ [12]ܕܟܕ ܚܙܝܢ ܠܐ ܢܚܙܘܢ ܘܟܕ ܫܡܥܝܢ ܡܫܡܥܝܢ ܠܐ

ܢܣܬܟܠܘܢ ܕܠܡܐ ܢܬܘܒܘܢ ܘܢܫܬܒܩܘܢ ܠܗܘܢ ܚܛܗܝܗܘܢ

[13]ܘܐܡܪ ܠܗܘܢ ܠܐ ܝܕܥܝܢ ܐܢܬܘܢ ܠܗ ܡܬܠܐ ܗܢܐ ܘܐܝܟܢܐ

ܟܠܗܘܢ ܡܬܠܐ ܕܬܕܥܘܢ [14]ܙܪܘܥܐ ܡܠܬܐ ܙܪܥ [15]ܗܢܘܢ ܕܝܢ

ܕܥܠ ܝܕ ܐܘܪܚܐ ܗܢܘܢ ܐܝܢܘܢ ܕܫܡܥܝܢ ܡܠܬܐ ܘܡܚܕܐ ܕܫܡܥܘܗ

ܐܬܐ ܣܛܢܐ ܘܫܩܠ ܠܗ ܠܡܠܬܐ ܕܙܪܝܥܐ ܒܠܒܗܘܢ [16]ܘܗܢܘܢ

ܕܥܠ ܫܘܥܐ ܗܢܘܢ ܐܝܢܘܢ ܕܟܕ ܫܡܥܝܢ ܡܠܬܐ ܒܚܕܘܬܐ

5, 6] *S* (*sic*)   7 ܘܣܠܩܘ ܟܘܒܗ] *S* (*sic*)   11 ܝܗܒ] *S* (*sic*): *cf* Mt xix 11, Lk iv 6, 17. *The same spelling is also found in* A^{a} 114, *and in* Dan vii 14
12 ܠܐ | ܡܫܡܥܝܢ] *so I read the photograph:* ܘܠܐ | ܢܫܡܥܘܢ S^{ed}

31 [And when] his mother [and his brothers came] standing [outside] *S*
32 they sent * * he was sitting * * ; and when they say:
"Lo, thy mother and thy brothers [are standing] outside and seeking
33 for thee," he saith to them: "Who is my mother, or my brothers?"
34 And he looked on them that *were* sitting by him, and said: "Lo,
35 my mother! and lo, my brothers! For every man that doeth the
iv 1 will of God, he is my brother and my sister and my mother." Again
he had begun teaching by the lake, and there had gathered
together unto him a great multitude; and he [went up *and*] sat in
the boat in the lake, and all the multitude was standing by the lake,
2 and he was teaching them much in similitudes. And while he was
3 teaching them [he said]: "Hear ye; lo, the sower went forth to sow.
4 And when he sowed, some fell by the way-side and the birds came
5 and ate it. And some fell on the rock and it sprang up; and because
6 there was no depth of land under their roots, * * *
7 the sun that was upon them, and it withered. And some fell
among thorns, and the thorns came up with it and choked it, and
8 fruit it did not give. And some fell on good land and gave fruit
[and grew up] and gave thirty-fold and sixty-fold and an hundred-
9 fold." And he was saying "He that hath ears to hear, let him
hear."

10 And when he was [alone], his disciples asked him about those
11 similitudes. And he was saying to them "To you is given the
mystery of the kingdom of God, but to those outside everything in
12 similitudes cometh to pass, that though seeing they may not see,
and though hearing they may hearing not understand, lest they
13 repent and their sins be forgiven them." And he saith to them:
"Ye know it not, this similitude? And how *will it be with* all
14 the similitudes that ye will know? The sower—the word he
15 soweth. Now those by the way-side, those are they that hear the
word, and what *time* they have heard Satan cometh and taketh
16 away the word that is sown in their heart. And those on the
rock, those are they that what *time* they hear the word with joy

ܡܩܒܠܝܢ ܠܗ ¹⁷ܘܠܝܬ ܠܗܘܢ ܒܗ ܥܩܪܐ ܐܠܐ ܥܠ ܙܒܢ ⌜ܐܢܘܢ⌝ S
ܘܡܐ ܕܗܘܐ ܐܘܠܨܢܐ ܐܘ ܪܕܘܦܝܐ ܥܠ ܡ⌜ܠ⌝ܬܐ * * * * *

[*The leaf of S which contained* Mk iv 18—41 *is missing.*]

⁴¹ܡܫܬܡܥܝܢ ܠܗ ○ ○ ○

¹ܘܐܬܬ ܠܥܒܪܐ ܠܐܬܪܐ ܕܓܪܓܣܝܐ. ²ܘܟܕ ܢܦܩ ܡܢ
ܣܦܝܢܬܐ ܦܓܥ ܒܗ ܓܒܪܐ ܚܕ ܕܐܝܬ ܗܘܬ ܒܗ ܪܘܚܐ ܛܢܦܬܐ.
³ܕܒܩܒܪ̈ܐ ܗܘܬ ܒܝܬ ܡܥܡܪܗ ܘܠܐ ܡܫܟܚ ܗܘܐ ܐܢܫ ܒܫܫܠܬܐ
ܠܡܐܣܪܗ ⁴ܡܛܠ ܕܙܒܢ ܣܓܝܐܢ ܘܫܫܠܬܐ ܡܬܒܪ ܗܘܐ ܘܢܦܩ
ܘܠܐ ܐܢܫ ܡܫܟܚ ܗܘܐ ܠܡܟܒܫܗ ⁵ܘܒܟܠܝܘܡ ܒܠܠܝܐ ܘܒܐܝܡܡܐ
ܒܝܬ ܩܒܘܪ̈ܐ ܘܒܛܘܪ̈ܐ ܩܥܐ ܗܘܐ ܘܡܚܒܠ ܗܘܐ ܢܦܫܗ
ܒܟܐܦܐ. ⁶ܘܟܕ ܚܙܐ ܠܝܫܘܥ ܡܢ ܪܘܚܩܐ ܪܗܛ ܣܓܕ ܠܗ
⁷ܘܩܥܐ ܒܩܠܐ ܪܡܐ ܘܐܡܪ ܡܢܐ ܠܝ ܘܠܟ ܝܫܘܥ ܒܪܗ ܕܐܠܗܐ
ܪܡܐ. ܡܘܡܐ ܐܢܐ ܠܟ ܒܐܠܗܐ ܕܠܐ ܬܫܢܩܢܝ ܒܝ. ⁸ܐܡܪ ܗܘܐ
ܠܗ ܓܝܪ ܕܦܘܩ ܪܘܚܐ ܛܢܦܬܐ ܡܢ ܓܒܪܐ. ⁹ܘܡܫܐܠ ܗܘܐ ܠܗ
ܕܐ⌜ܝ⌝ܢܐ ܫܡܟ ܘܐܡܪ ܠܗ ܠܓܝܘܢ ܫܡܢ ܡܛܠ †ܕܗܠܓܝܘܢܐ† ܐܢܚܢ
¹⁰ܘܒܥܝܢ ܗܘܘ ܡܢܗ ܗܢܘܢ ܫܐܕ̈ܐ ܕܠܐ ܢܦܩ ܐܢܘܢ ܠܒܪ ܡܢ
ܐܬܪܐ ¹¹ܘܐܝܬ ܗܘܬ ܕܝܢ ܬܡܢ ܠܘܬ ܛܘܪ̈ܐ ܒܩܪܐ ܪܒܬܐ
ܕܚܙܝܪ̈ܐ ܕܪܥܝܐ ܗܘܬ ¹²ܘܒܥܝܢ ܗܘܘ ܡܢܗ ܗܢܘܢ ܫܐܕ̈ܐ ܕܫܕܪܝܢ
ܠܗܘܢ ܚܙܝܪ̈ܐ ܘܢܥܘܠ ܒܗܘܢ܆ ¹³ܘܐܦܣ ܠܗܘܢ ܘܟܕ ܢܦܩ
ܪ̈ܘܚܐ ܛܢܦܬܐ ܥܠ ܒܚܙܝܪ̈ܐ ܘܪܗܛܬ ܗܝ ܒܩܪܐ ܘܢܦܠܬ
ܒܝܡܐ ܡܢܝܢܐ ܐܝܟ ܬܪ̈ܝܢ ܐܠܦܝܢ ܘܐܬܚܢܩܘ ܒܡܝܐ ¹⁴ܘܗܢܘܢ
ܕܪܥܝܢ ܗܘܘ ܠܗܘܢ܆ ܥܪܩܘ ܘܐܡܪܘ ܒܡܕ̈ܝܢܬܐ ܘܐܦ ܒܩܘܪܝܐ
ܘܢܦܩܘ ܠܡܚܙܐ ܡܢܐ ܕܗܘܐ ¹⁵ܘܐܬܘ ܠܘܬ ܝܫܘܥ ܘܚܙܘܗܝ،
ܠܗܘ ܕܐܚܝܕ ܗܘܐ ⌜ܠܓܝܘܢ⌝ ܫܐܕܐ ܟܕ [ܝܬܒ] ܘܠܒܝܫ ܘܡܬܢܟܦ
ܘܕܚܠܘ ¹⁶ܘܐܫܬܥܝܘ ܠܗܘܢ ܗܢܘܢ ܕܚܙܘ ܕܐܝܟܢܐ ܗܘܐ ܠܗܘ

17 ܒܗ] *S (sic)*: *cf* Mt xiii 21 v 8 ܕܦܘܩ] *S (sic)* 9 ܕܗܠܓܝܘܢܐ] *om.* ܕ *S (sic)* 13 ܢܦܩ.....ܥܠ] *S (sic)*: *see Appendix* III

17 receive it, and they have in it no root, but are for a time and what *S*
time there is distress or persecution for the word * * * *

[*The leaf of S which contained* Mk iv 18—41 *is missing.*]

41 obey him?"

v 1 And he came to the other side of the sea to the land of the
2 Gergesenes. And when he came up from the boat there met him a
3 certain man in whom was an unclean spirit that was dwelling in the
4 tombs, and no man was able with chains to bind him, because often
the fetters and chains he used to break and go forth, and no man
5 was able to chastise him. And at all times by night and day in the
tombs and in the hills he was crying out and was wounding himself
6 with stones. And when he saw Jesus from afar he ran *and* worshipped
7 him and cried out with a mighty voice and said: "What have I to do
with thee, Jesus, Son of the Most High God? I adjure thee by God
8 that thou torture me not." For he was saying to him "Go forth,
9 *thou* unclean spirit, from the man." And he was asking him "What
is thy name?" And he saith to him: "Legion is our name, because
10 we are many." And those devils were beseeching him that he would
11 not send them forth out of the country. Now there was there by the
12 hills a great herd of swine that was feeding, and those devils were
beseeching him "Send us into those swine and we will enter into
13 them." And he permitted them; and when those unclean spirits
went forth, they entered into the swine, and the herd ran and fell
into the midst of the sea, about two thousand, and were choked in
14 the sea. And they that were tending them fled and said *the news* in
the cities and in the villages also, and they went forth to see what was
15 come to pass. And they came unto Jesus, and saw him from whom
he had cast out the devil [sitting] and clad and modest, and they were
16 afraid. And those that saw declared to them how it befel him [in

---

17 in it] *S* (*sic*) v 10 *Cf* 'And the devils began to beseech him, that he would not drive them out of that place...' E^{75}: *see also* Lk viii 31

ܕܗܘܐ ܒܗ [ܫܐܕܐ] ܘܐܦ ܥܠ ܚܙܝܪܐ. ¹⁷ܘܫܪܝܘ ܗܘܘ ܒܥܝܢ S
ܡܢܗ ܕܢܐܙܠ ܠܗ ܡܢ ܬܚܘܡܗܘܢ. [18][ܘܟܕ ܣܠܩ] ܬܠܡܝܕܘܗܝ
ܒܣܦܝܢܬܐ ܒܥܐ ܗܘܐ ܡܢܗ ܗܘ ܕܫܐܕܗ ܕܠܘܬܗ ܢܗܘܐ.
[19]ܘܠܐ ܫܒܩܗ ܐܠܐ ܐܡܪ ܠܗ ܙܠ ܠܒܝܬܟ ܠܘܬ ܐܢ̈ܫܝܟ ܘܚܘܐ
ܐܢܘܢ ܡܕܡ ܕܥܒܕ ܠܟ ܡܪܝܐ ܘܐܬܪܚܡ ܥܠܝܟ. [20]ܘܐܙܠ ܘܫܪܝ
ܠܡܟܪܙܘ ܒܥܣܪܬ ܡܕܝܢ̈ܬܐ ܡܕܡ ܕܥܒܕ ܠܗ ܝܫܘܥ ܘܟܠܗܘܢ
ܬܡܝܗܝܢ ܗܘܘ.
[21]ܘܟܕ ܥܒܪ ܝܫܘܥ ܠܗܘ ܥܒܪܐ ܟܢܫ ܥܠܘܗܝ, ܟܢܫܐ ܣܓܝܐܐ ܥܠ
ܝܕ ܝܡܐ. [22]ܘܐܬܐ ܚܕ ܡܢ ܪ̈ܒܝ ܟܢܘܫܬܐ ܕܫܡܗ ܗܘܐ ܝܘܐܪܫ
ܟܕ ܚܙܝܗ, ܢܦܠ ܥܠ ܪ̈ܓܠܘܗܝ, [23]ܘܒܥܐ ܗܘܐ ܡܢܗ. ܘܐܡܪ ܠܗ.
ܒܪܬܝ, ܒܚܪ̈ܬܐ ܗܝ ܬܐ ܣܝܡ ܥܠܝܗ ܐܝܕܟ. ܘܬܚܐ. [24]ܘܐܙܠ
ܥܡܗ. ܘܐܬܐ ܗܘܐ ܒܬܪܗ ܟܢܫܐ ܣܓܝܐܐ. ܘܚܒܨܝܢ ܗܘܘ ܠܗ
[25]ܘܐܢܬܬܐ ܚܕܐ ܐܝܬ ܗܘܬ ܕܪܕܐ ܗܘܐ ܕܡܗ ܫܢ̈ܝܢ ܬܪܬܥܣܪܐ
[26]ܘܣܓܝ ܣܒܪܬ ܡܢ ܐܣܘܬܐ ܣܓܝ̈ܐܐ ܘܐܘܒܕܬ ܟܠ ܡܕܡ ܕܐܝܬ
ܗܘܐ ܠܗ ܘܡܕܡ * * * * * * * * * * * *

[*The leaf of S which contained* Mk v 26—vi 5 *is missing.*]

[5]ܬܡܢ ܚܕ ܡܢ ܚܝܠܐ. ܐܠܐ ܥܠ ܟܪ̈ܝܗܐ ܩܠܝܠ ܣܐܡ ܐܝܕ̈ܘܗܝ,
ܘܐܬܐܣܝܘ. [6]ܘܡܬܕܡܪ ܗܘܐ ܒܚܣܝܪܘܬ ܗܝܡܢܘܬܗܘܢ. ○:○
ܘܡܬܟܪܟ ܗܘܐ ܒܩܘܪܝܐ ܘܡܠܦ. [7]ܘܩܪܐ ܗܘܐ ܠܬܪܥܣܪ
ܬܠܡܝܕܘܗܝ, ܘܫܕܪ ܐܢܘܢ ܬܪܝܢ ܬܪܝܢ ܘܝܗܒ ܗܘܐ ܠܗܘܢ
ܫܘܠܛܢܐ ܥܠ ܪܘܚܐ ܛܢ̈ܦܬܐ. [8]ܘܦܩܕ ܗܘܐ ܐܢܘܢ ܕܠܐ
ܢܫܩܠܘܢ ܡܕܡ ܠܐܘܪܚܐ ܐܠܐ ܐܢ ܫܒܛܐ ܒܠܚܘܕ. ܠܐ
ܬܪܡܠܐ ܘܠܐ ܠܚܡܐ ܘܠܐ ܢܚܫܐ ܒܚܨ̈ܝܗܘܢ. [9]ܘܣܢܕܠܐ ܗܘܘ
ܣܐܢܝܢ. ܘܠܐ ܢܠܒܫܘܢ ܬܪܬܝܢ ܟܬܘܢܝܢ. [10]ܠܐܝܢܐ ܒܝܬܐ ܕܥܠܝܢ
ܐܢܬܘܢ ܠܗ. ܬܡܢ ܗܘܘ ܥܕܡܐ ܕܢܦܩܝܢ ܐܢܬܘܢ ܡܢ ܬܡܢ
[11]ܘܟܠ ܕܠܐ ܢܩܒܠܘܢ ܘܠܐ ܢܫܡܥܘܢܟܘܢ ܡܟܐ ܕܢܦܩܝܢ ܐܢܬܘܢ
ܡܢ ܬܡܢ ܦܨܘ ܚܠܐ ܕܪ̈ܓܠܝܟܘܢ ܠܣܗܕܘܬܗܘܢ.

---

18 ܗܘ ܕܫܐܕܗ] *S* (*sic*)

17 whom was the devil] and also about the swine. And they had begun *S*
18 beseeching him that he would go away from their border. [And
when] his disciples [went up] into the boat the man with the devil
19 was beseeching him that he might be with him, and he suffered him
not, but said to him: "Go to thy house unto thy kinsfolk, and shew
them that which the LORD hath done for thee and *how* he hath had
20 compassion upon thee." And he went and began to preach in the
Ten Cities what Jesus did for him, and all were astonished.

21 And when Jesus crossed over to that other side a great multitude
22 gathered together unto him by the side of the sea. And there came
one of the chiefs of the synagogue whose name was Ioârâsh, *and*
23 when he saw him he fell at his feet and was beseeching him, and
saith to him: "My daughter is very ill; come lay on her thy hand,
24 and she will live." And he went with him; and there was coming
25 after him a great multitude, and they were pressing upon him. And
26 a certain woman there was, whose blood was issuing twelve years, and
much she suffered from many physicians, and spent everything that
she had and [was no]thing * * * * * * * * *

[*The leaf of S which contained* Mk v 26—vi 5 *is missing.*]

vi 5 there one of the mighty works, but on a few infirm *folk* he layeth his
6 hands and they were healed. And he was wondering at the lack of
their faith.

7 And he was going about in the villages and teaching. And he had
called his twelve disciples, and sent them two by two, and had given
8 them authority over the unclean spirits. And he had commanded
them that they should take nothing for the way but a stick only,—
9 "no wallet and no bread and no copper in your purses, and sandals
be ye shod with,"—and *that* they should not be clothed with two coats.
10 "Whatsoever house ye enter into, there be until ye go forth from
11 thence; and every one that shall not receive you nor hear you—what
time ye go forth from thence, shake off the dust of your feet for a
testimony of them."

---

18 the man with the devil] *lit.* 'he of his devil' (*sic*): *cf* Nöld. § 224* vi **5** mighty works] *lit.* 'powers' (*as in the Greek*) **8** but a stick only] *cf the Syriac text of* Mt x 10, Lk ix 3, *and of* Mk xiv 43; *also* 'Possess....a stick....no staff' E^{91} *and* Diat^{ar} xii 49: *see Introd.* vol. ii

[12]ܘܢܦܩܘ ܗܘܘ ܡܟܪ̈ܙܝܢ ܕܢܬܘܒܘܢ [13]ܘܫܐ̈ܕܐ ܣܓܝ̈ܐܐ ܡܦܩܝܢ ܗܘܘ S
ܘܡܫܚܝܢ ܗܘܘ ܒܡܫܚܐ ܠܣܓܝ̈ܐܐ ܘܡܐܣܝܢ ܗܘܘ ܠܟܪ̈ܝܗܐ
[14]ܘܫܡܥ ܗܪܘܕܘܣ ܡܠܟܐ ܐܬܝܕܥ ܗܘܐ ܠܗ ܓܝܪ ܫܡܗ ܛܒ
ܘܐܡܪ ܕܝܘܚܢܢ ܗܘ ܡܥܡܕܢܐ ܩܡ ܡܢ ܒܝܬ ܡܝ̈ܬܐ ܘܡܛܠ ܗܢܐ
ܥܒܕ ܚܝ̈ܠܐ [15]ܐܚܪ̈ܢܐ ܕܝܢ ܐܡܪܘ ܕܐܠܝܐ ܗܘ ܐܚܪ̈ܢܐ ܕܝܢ
ܐܡܪܝܢ ܕܢܒܝܐ ܗܘ ܐܝܟ ܚܕ ܡܢ ܢܒܝ̈ܐ [16]ܟܕ ܫܡܥ ܕܝܢ ܗܪܘܕܘܣ
ܐܡܪ ܗܢܐ ܝܘܚܢܢ ܗܘ ܕܦܣܩܬ ܪܫܗ ܩܡ [17]ܗܘ ܓܝܪ ܗܪܘܕܘܣ
ܫܕܪ ܐܚܕܗ ܠܝܘܚܢܢ ܘܐܣܪܗ ܒܒܝܬ ܐܣܝܪ̈ܐ ܡܛܠ ܗܪܘܕܝܐ ܐܢܬܬ
ܦܝܠܝܦܘܣ ܐܚܘܗܝ، ܕܢܣܒܗ ܗܘܐ. [18]ܐܡܪ† ܗܘܐ ܠܗ ܓܝܪ
ܝܘܚܢܢ ܠܗܪܘܕܘܣ ܕܠܐ ܫܠܝܛ ܠܟ ܠܡܣܒ ܐܢܬܬ ܐܚܘܟ. [19]ܗܝ ܕܝܢ
ܗܪܘܕܝܐ ܠܒܝܫܐ ܗܘܬ ܠܗ ܘܨܒܝܐ ܗܘܬ ܠܡܩܛܠܗ ܘܠܐ
ܡܫܟܚܐ ܗܘܬ [20]ܗܘ ܓܝܪ ܗܪܘܕܘܣ ܕܚܠ ܗܘܐ ܡܢܗ ܡܢ ܝܘܚܢܢ.
ܕܝܕܥ ܗܘܐ ܕܙܕܝܩܐ ܘܩܕܝܫܐ. ܘܢܛܪ ܗܘܐ ܠܗ ܘܣܓܝܐܬܐ
ܕܫܡܥ ܗܘܐ ܡܢܗ ܥܒܕ ܗܘܐ ܘܒܣܝܡܐܝܬ ܫܡܥ ⸢ܗܘܐ⸣ ܠܗ
[21]ܘܓܕܫ ܒܝܘܡܐ ܕܒܝܬ ܝܠܕܗ ܕܗܪܘܕܘܣ ܥܒܕ ܗܘܐ ܐܚܫܡܝܬܐ
ܠܪ̈ܘܪܒܢܘܗܝ، ܘܠܟܠܝܪ̈ܟܘܗܝ، ܘܠܪ̈ܫܐ ܕܓܠܝܠܐ. [22]ܘܥܠܬ ܒܪܬܗ
ܕܗܪܘܕܝܐ ܘܪܩܕܬ ܠܗ ܠܗܪܘܕܘܣ ܘܠܐܝܠܝܢ ܕܣܡܝܟܝܢ ܥܡܗ
ܘܐܡܪ ܠܗ ܡܠܟܐ ܠܛܠܝܬܐ ܫܐܠ ܡܢܝ ܘܐܬܠ ܠܟܝ [23]ܘܝܡܐ
ܠܦܠܓܐ ܕܡܠܟܘܬܝ، ܘܝܡܐ ܠܗ ܒܡܘܡܬܐ [24]ܘܢܦܩܬ ܗܝ، ܛܠܝܬܐ
ܐܬܡܠܟܬ ܒܐܡܗ ܡܢܐ ܐܫܐܠܝܘܗܝ، ܐܡܪܐ ܠܗ ܪܫܗ ܕܝܘܚܢܢ
ܡܥܡܕܢܐ. [25]ܘܥܠܬ ܒܥܓܠ ܠܘܬ ܡܠܟܐ. ܘܐܡܪܐ ܠܗ ܨܒܝܐ
ܐܢܐ ܕܬܬܠ ܠܝ ܒܗܕܐ ܫܥܬܐ ܪܫܗ ܕܝܘܚܢܢ ܡܥܡܕܢܐ ܒܦܝܢܟܐ.
[26]ܘܟܪܝܬ ܠܗ ܛܒ ܠܡܠܟܐ. ܘܡܛܠ ܡܘܡܬܐ ܘܡܛܠ ܣܡܝܟܐ
ܠܐ ܐܨܒܝ ܕܢܦܓܘܗ. [27]ܘܫܕܪ ܐܣܦܘܩܠܛܪܐ ܕܢܦܣܘܩ ܢܝܬܐ ܪܫܗ
ܘܐܙܠ ܦܣܩ ܪܫܗ ܒܝܬ ܐܣܝܪ̈ܐ [28]ܘܐܝܬܝܘܗܝ، ܒܦܝܢܟܐ ܘܝܗܒܗ
ܠܗ ܠܛܠܝܬܐ ܗܝ، ܛܠܝܬܐ ܐܘܒܠܬܗ ܠܐܡܗ. [29]ܘܟܕ ܫܡܥܘ
ܬܠܡܝܕܘܗܝ، ܐܬܘ ܫܩܠܘ ܫܠܕܗ ܘܩܒܪܘܗܝ ܒܒܝܬ ܩܒܘܪܐ. [30]ܘܐܬܘ
ܫܠܝ̈ܚܐ ܠܘܬ ܝܫܘܥ. ܘܐܫܬܥܝܘ ܠܗ ܟܠ ܕܥܒܕ ܘܐܠܦ

18 ܐܡܪ|ܐܡܪܐ *S (sic, bis)* 30 ܕܥܒܕ ܘܐܠܦ] *S, in error for* ܕܥܒܕܘ ܘܐܠܦܘ

12, 13 And they had gone forth preaching that *men* should repent, and *S*
many devils were they casting out, and were anointing with oil many,
14 and were healing the infirm. And Herod the king heard, for his fame
had become known to him well, and he said: "It is John the Baptist;
he hath risen from among the dead, therefore great is his power."
15 But others said "It is Elijah"; but others say "It is a prophet
16 like one of the prophets." But when Herod heard, he said: "This
17 John, he whose head I cut off, hath risen." For Herod sent *and*
laid hold of John and bound him in prison because of Herodia the
18 wife of Philip his brother, in that he had taken her. For John was
saying to Herod "It is not lawful for thee to take thy brother's
19 wife." Then Herodia was threatening him and was wishing to kill
20 him, and could not. For Herod was afraid of that same John, for he
knew *him* for a righteous man and a holy, and was protecting him,
and many things that he used to hear from him he did, and gladly
21 used to hear him. And it chanced on the day of Herod's birth-
day *that* he had made a supper for his nobles and for his chiliarchs
22 and for the chiefs of Galilee, and the daughter of Herodia came
in and danced, and she pleased Herod and those sitting *at meat*
with him. And the king said to the girl: "Ask of me, and I will give
23 to thee unto the half of my kingdom." And he sware to her with
24 an oath. And the girl went out, *and* took counsel with her mother,
saying: "What shall I ask?" She saith to her: "The head of John
25 the Baptist." And she came in at once unto the king, and saith to
him: "I will that thou give me this very hour the head of John the
26 Baptist in a dish." And it much grieved the king, and *yet* for the
oath's sake and for the sake of them that sat *at meat* he could not
27 turn back. And he sent a soldier of his guard to cut off *and* bring his
28 head. And he went *and* cut off his head in the prison and brought
it in a dish, and he gave it to the girl and the girl carried it away to
29 her mother. And when his disciples heard, they came *and* took up
30 his corpse, and laid it in a tomb. And the apostles came unto Jesus
and declared to him all that †he† did and taught.

---

22 the daughter of Herodia] *so also* E^{132} 30 †he† did and taught] *probably a mere error of S for* 'they did and taught', *the pronunciation being the same in Syriac*

[31] ܘܐܡܪ ܠܗܘܢ ܬܘ ܢܐܙܠ ܠܡܕܒܪܐ ܒܠܚܘܕܝܢ ܘܐܬܢܝܚܘ ܩܠܝܠ S
ܣ̈ܓܝܐܐ ܐܝܠܝܢ ܗܘܘ ܘܐܬܝܢ ܠܘܬܗ. ܘܠܐ ܗܘܐ ܠܗܘܢ ܐܬܪܐ
ܐܦܠܐ ܠܠܚܡܐ ܠܡܐܟܠ [32] ܘܐܙܠܘ ܠܐܬܪܐ ܚܘܪܒܐ ܒܣܦܝܢܬܐ
ܒܠܚܘܕܝܗܘܢ [33] ܘܚܙܘ ܐܢܘܢ ܣ̈ܓܝܐܐ ܘܐܫܬܘܕܥܘ ܐܢܘܢ
ܘܐܙܠܘ ܒܝܒܫܐ ܠܬܡܢ. ܡܢ ܟܠܗܝܢ ܡܕ̈ܝܢܬܐ ܘܟܕ ܐܬܘ [34] ܘܚܙܐ
ܟܢܫܐ ܣ̈ܓܝܐܐ ܐܬܪܚܡ ܥܠܝܗܘܢ ܕܕܡܝܢ ܗܘܘ ܠܥ̈ܢܐ ܕܠܝܬ
ܠܗܘܢ ܪܥܝܐ. ܘܫܪܝ, ܗܘܐ ܠܡܠܦܘ ܐܢܘܢ܂ [35] ܘܟܕ ܫܪܝ, ܪ̈ܡܫܐ
ܠܡܗܘܐ ܩܪܒܘ ܬܠܡܝ̈ܕܘܗܝ, ܘܐܡܪܝܢ ܠܗ ܐܬܪܐ ܚܘܪܒܐ ܗܘ
ܘܥܕܢܐ ܥܒܪ [36] ܫܪܝ, ܐܢܘܢ ܐܢܫܐ ܗܢܘܢ ܢܐܙܠܘܢ ܠܩܘܪ̈ܝܐ
ܗܠܝܢ ܕܣܕܪܝܢ ܘܢܙܒܢܘܢ ܠܗܘܢ ܡܐ ܕܠܡܐܟܠ܂ [37] ܐܡܪ ܠܗܘܢ
ܗܒܘ ܠܗܘܢ ܐܢܬܘܢ ܠܡܐܟܠ܂ ܐܡܪܝܢ ܠܗ ܢܐܙܠ ܢܙܒܢ
ܒܡܐ̈ܬܝܢ ܕܝܢܪ̈ܝܢ ܠܚܡܐ ܢܬܠ ܠܗܘܢ ܠܡܐܟܠ [38] ܐܡܪ ܠܗܘܢ ܙܠܘ
ܚܙܘ ܟܡܐ ܠܚܡܝܢ ܐܝܬ ܠܟܘܢ ܐܡܪܝܢ ܠܗ ܚܡܫ ܠܚܡܝܢ ܘܬܪܝܢ
ܢܘܢܝܢ [39] ܘܦܩܕ ܠܗܘܢ ܕܢܣܬܡܟܘܢ ܟܠܗܘܢ ܥܠ ܥܣܒܐ.
[40] ܘܐܣܬܡܟܘ ܣܕ̈ܪܝܢ ܣܕ̈ܪܝܢ܂ ܕܡܐܐ ܡܐ̈ܐ ܘܚܡܫܝܢ܂ [41] ܘܢܣܒ
ܗܘ ܠܗܢܘܢ ܚܡ̈ܫܐ ܠܚܡܝܢ ܘܬܪܝܢ ܢܘܢܝܢ ܘܚܪ ܒܫܡܝܐ ܘܒܪܟ
ܘܩܨܐ ܠܚܡܐ ܘܝܗܒ ܠܬܠܡܝ̈ܕܘܗܝ, ܕܢܣܝܡܘܢ ܠܗܘܢ ܘܗܢܘܢ
ܬܪܝܢ ܢܘܢܝܢ ܦܠܓܗ ܐܢܘܢ ܠܟܠܗܘܢ [42] ܘܐܟܠܘ ܟܠܗܘܢ ܘܣܒܥܘ
[43] ܘܫܩܠܘ ܡ̈ܢ ܡܪ̈ܣܝܣܗܘܢ ܩܨܝܐ ܬܪ̈ܬܥܣܪ ܩܘܦܝܢ ܟܕ ܡܠܝܢ
ܡܢ ܢܘܢܐ ܕܗܠܝܢ ܣܚ̈ܕܐ ܚܐܣ ܘܕܗܘܢ ܬܪܝܢ ܢܘܢܝܢ [44] ܗܘܘ
ܗܘܘ ܕܝܢ ܗܢܘܢ ܕܐܟܠܘ ܡܢܗܘܢ ܚܡܫܐ ܐܠܦܝܢ ܓܒܪܝܢ ܀:܀
[45] ܘܡܢ ܚܕܐ ܟܦܪ ܠܬܠܡܝ̈ܕܘܗܝ, ܕܢܣܩܘܢ ܠܣܦܝܢܬܐ ܕܢܐܙܠܘܢ
ܡܩܕܡܘܗܝ, ܠܒܝܬ ܨܝܕܐ ܥܕ ܫܪܐ ܗܘܐ ܠܗܘܢ ܟܢܫܐ [46] ܘܟܕ ܫܪܐ
ܐܢܘܢ ܐܙܠ ܗܘܐ ܠܛܘܪܐ ܠܡܨܠܝܘ. [47] ܟܕ ܗܘܐ ܕܝܢ ܪܡܫܐ
ܘܣܦܝܢܬܐ ܒܓܘ ܗܘܬ ܕܝܡܐ ܘܗܘ ܒܠܚܘܕܘܗܝ, ܗܘܐ ܥܠ
ܐܪܥܐ [48] ܘܚܙܐ ܐܢܘܢ ܕܡܫܬܢܩܝܢ. ܡܢ ܕܢܠܬܐ ܕܓܠ̈ܠܐ
ܡܛܠ ܕܪܘܚܐ ܠܩܘܒܠܗܘܢ ܗܘܬ܂ ܐܬܐ ܠܘܬܗܘܢ ܟܕ ܡܗܠܟ
ܥܠ ܡ̈ܝܐ. ܘܨܒܐ ܗܘܐ ܕܢܥܒܪ ܐܢܘܢ [49] ܟܕ ܚܙܘܗܝ, ܥܠ

36 ܕܣܕ̈ܪܝܢ S (sic)

31 And he said to them: "Come, let us go to the wilderness ourselves S
alone, and take your ease a little." Many were going and coming
32 unto him, and they had no place even bread to eat. And they went
33 to a desert place in the boat themselves alone. And many saw them
and recognised them, and went by land after him from all the cities.
34 And when they came and he saw a great multitude he had com-
passion upon them in that they were like to sheep which have no
35 shepherd, and he had begun to teach them. And when it began to
be evening his disciples drew near and say to him: "The place is
36 desert and the time is past; dismiss those folk *that* they may go to
these villages that are round us and buy for themselves somewhat to
37 eat." He saith to them: "Give ye them to eat." They say to him:
"Shall we go *and* buy for a hundred denars bread, *and* bring to
38 them as they eat?" He saith to them: "Go, see how many pieces of
bread there are with you." They say to him: "Five pieces of bread
39 and two fishes." And he commanded them that they should all sit
40 *at meat* on the green grass, and they sat down *to meat* companies by
41 companies of hundreds by hundreds and *by* fifty; and he took those
five pieces of bread and the two fishes. And he looked up to heaven
and blessed and brake the bread, and gave to his disciples that they
should set *it* for them, and those two fishes they divided to all.
42, 43 And they all ate and were satisfied, and they took up from before
them the fragments, twelve baskets full of the superabundance of
44 these five loaves and of those two fishes. Now those that ate of them
were five thousand men.

45 And immediately he commanded his disciples that they should go
up into the boat, that they should go before him to Beth Saida while
46 yet he was dismissing that multitude. And when he dismissed them,
47 he had gone to the hill to pray. Now when it was evening and the
48 boat was in the midst of the lake and he alone was on the land, and
when he saw them tormented from fear of the waves because the
wind was against them, he came unto them walking on the water and
49 was wishing that he should pass them. When they saw him on the

ܬ̈ܢܢܐ ܕܡܗܠܟ ܣܒܪܘ ܕܕܝܘܐ ܗܘ. [50]ܘܟܕ ܚܙܐܘܗܝ، ܟܠܗܘܢ *S*
ܢܗܒܘ ܥܠܝܗ. ܘܗܘ ܒܫܥܬܐ ܡܠܠ ܥܡܗܘܢ ܘܐܡܪ ܠܗܘܢ
ܬܬܩܦܘ ܐܢܐ ܐܢܐ. ܠܐ ܬܕܚܠܘܢ· [51]ܘܣܠܩ ܠܘܬܗܘܢ ܠܣܦܝܢܬܐ
ܘܫܠܝܬ ܪܘܚܐ ܘܡܬܕܡܪܝܢ ܗܘܘ ܒܝܢܬܗܘܢ. [52]ܠܐ ܓܝܪ ܐܣܬܟܠܘ
ܗܘܘ ܡܢ ܠܚܡܐ. ܡܛܠ ܕܠܒܗܘܢ ܥܒܝܪ ܗܘܐ. [53]ܘܟܕ ܥܒܪܘ
ܣܠܩܘ ܠܐܪܥܐ ܕܓܢܣܪ [54]ܘܟܕ ⌜ܢܦܩܘ⌝ ܡܢ ܣܦܝܢܬܐ ܒܗ ܒܫܥܬܐ
ܗ، ܕܐܫܬܘܕܥܘܗܝ، [55]ܪܗܛܘ ܠܟܠܗ ܥܒܪ. ܘܐܝܬܝܘ ܠܟܠܗܝܢ ܕܒܝܫ
ܒܝܫ ܒܝܫܝܢ ܟܕ ܥܒܝܪ ܠܗܘܢ ܒܟܪܝܗܘܬܐ. [56]ܘܐܬܪ ܕܥܐܠ ܗܘܐ
ܥܡܗ ܠܩܪܝܬܐ ܐܘ ܠܡܕܝܢܬܐ ܐܘ ܠܐܓܘܪ̈ܣܐ ܒܫܘ̈ܩܐ ܣܝܡܝܢ
ܗܘܘ ܒܪ̈ܝܗܬܐ ܕܟܪ̈ܝܗܐ ܘܒܥܝܢ ܗܘܘ ܡܢܗ. ܕܐܦ ܠܟܢܦܐ
ܕܡܪ̈ܛܘܛܗ ܢܬܩܪܒܘܢ· ܘܟܠ ܕܡܬܩܪܒܝܢ ܗܘܘ ܚܝܝܢ ܗܘܘ
[1]ܘܐܬܟܢܫܘ ܠܘܬܗ ܦܪ̈ܝܫܐ ܘܣܦܪ̈ܐ ܕܐܬܘ ܡܢ ܐܘܪܫܠܡ. [2]ܘܚܙܘ
ܠܬܠܡܝܕܘܗܝ، ܕܟܕ ܐܟܠܝܢ ܠܚܡܐ. ܟܕ ܠܐ ܡܫܝܓܢ ܐܝܕܝܗܘܢ܆
[3]ܡܛܠ ܕܟܠܗܘܢ ܝܗܘܕ̈ܝܐ ܘܦܪ̈ܝܫܐ ܐܠܐ ܡܫܝܓܝܢ ܐܝܕܝܗܘܢ
ܠܐ ܐܟܠܝܢ ܠܚܡܐ. ܕܐܚܝܕܝܢ ܡܫܠܡܢܘܬܐ ܕܩܫ̈ܝܫܐ. [4]ܘܡܢ ܫܘܩܐ
ܐܠܐ ܡܥܡܕܝܢ ܠܐ ܐܟܠܝܢ ܘܣܓܝ̈ܐܬܐ ܐܚܪ̈ܢܝܢ ܕܩܒܠܘ ܢܛܪܝܢ ܗܘܘ.
ܘܒܥܡܕܘܬܐ ܕܟܣ̈ܐ ܘܩܣ̈ܛܐ. [5]ܘܫܐܠܘ ܗܠܝܢ ܫܐܠܘܗܝ، ܦܪ̈ܝܫܐ
ܘܣܦܪ̈ܐ ܘܐܡܪ̈ܝܢ ܠܗ ܕܠܡܢܐ ܬܠܡܝܕܝܟ ܠܐ ܢܛܪܝܢ ܦܘܩܕܢܐ
ܕܩܫ̈ܝܫܐ ܠܐ ܓܝܪ ܡܫܝܓܝܢ ܐܝܕܝܗܘܢ ܘܐܟܠܝܢ ܠܚܡܐ. [6]ܐܡܪ
ܠܗܘܢ ܝܫܘܥ ܫܦܝܪ ܐܬܢܒܝ ܥܠܝܟܘܢ ܐܫܥܝܐ ܢܒܝܐ ܐܝܟܢܐ
ܕܟܬܝܒ ܕܐܡܪ ܗܘܐ ܕܥܡܐ ܗܢܐ ܒܣ⌜ܦܘ̈ܬܗ⌝ ܡܝܩܪ ܠܝ.
ܠܒܗ ܕܝܢ ܪܚܝܩ ܡܢܝ. [7]ܘܣܪܝܩܐܝܬ ܕܝܢ ܕܚܠܝܢ ܠܝ. ܕܡܠܦܝܢ ܝܘܠܦܢܐ
ܕܦܘ̈ܩܕܢܐ ܕܒܢܝ̈ ܐܢܫܐ. [9]ܫܦܝܪ ܒܛܠܝܢ ܐܢܬܘܢ ܕܫܒܩܝܢ ܐܢܬܘܢ
ܦܘܩܕܢܐ ܕܐܠܗܐ ܕܬܩܝܡܘܢ ܦܘܩܕܢܝܟܘܢ. [10]ܡܘܫܐ ܓܝܪ
ܐܡܪ ܕܝܩܪ ܐܒܘܟ ܘܐܡܟ ܘܡܢ ܕܡܨܛܐ ܠܐܒܘܗܝ، ܘܠܐܡܗ

---

49 ܗܘ ܕܕܝܘܐ] *so also* Mt xiv 26 *S C and* Ephr[loc], *for Barsalibi on* Mt *says:* ܕܝܘܐ ܗܘ ܕܠܐ ܕܢܘܫܐ ܡܢܐ ܐܦܪܝܡ. ܐܡܒܪܘ ܡܢ ܕܕܝܘܐ ܐܝܬܘܗܝ (B.M. *Add.* 7184, *fol.* 91)   56 ܒܫܘ̈ܩܐ] *S* (*sic*)   ܕܡܪ̈ܛܘܛܗ *S* (*sic*)

50 water *and* walking they supposed it was a devil, and when they all *S*
saw him they gave a cry. And in the same hour he spake with them,
51 and said to them: "Be assured; it is I, be not afraid." And he
went up unto them to the boat, and the wind ceased. And they
52 were wondering among themselves, for they had not perceived from
53 the bread, because their heart was blind. And when they crossed
54 over they went up to the land of Gennesar. And when he went up
55 from the boat, in that same hour that they perceived him they sent
to all the district, and brought those that were ill, carrying them in
56 beds. And wheresoever Jesus was entering, into cities or villages or
farmsteads, in the streets they were laying the beds of the infirm,
and they were beseeching him even if the skirt of his cloak they
vii 1 might touch; and all that were touching lived. And there were
gathered together unto him Pharisees and scribes that came from
2 Jerusalem, and they saw his disciples eating bread with unwashen
3 hands. Because all the Jews and the Pharisees, except they wash their
4 hands, do not eat bread, who hold the tradition of the elders; and
from the street, except they baptize themselves, they eat not, and
many things which they received they used to keep, and baptisms of
5 cups and pots. And after these things the scribes and Pharisees asked
him, and say to him "Wherefore do thy disciples not keep the com-
mandment of our ancients? for they wash not their hands and eat
6 bread." Jesus saith to them: "Well did Isaiah the prophet prophesy
of you, as it is written that he had said 'This people with its lips
7 honoureth me, but in its heart it is far from me; but in vain do they
9 fear me, that teach a teaching of commandments of men.' Well
do ye, in that ye leave the commandment of God that ye may
10 set up your commandments. For Moses said 'Honour thy father
and thy mother, and he that curseth his father and his mother

---

49 it was a devil] *so also* Mt xiv 26 *SC and* Ephr[loc], *as is clear from Barsalibi on* Mt xiv 26, *who says*: "'It was a false vision' (*so* syr.vg *in both places for* φάντασμά ἐστιν). From Holy St Ephraim:—'For they supposed that it was a devil.'" *Mösinger* 135 *has*: 'ipsi autem opinabantur spectrum esse.' *See Notes*, vol. ii 4 and from the street] *so also* syr.vg (= καὶ ἀπ' ἀγορᾶς); 'and what has been bought from the street' *Diat*[ar] xx 20; 'and what is from the street' aeth.vg

ܡܚܬ ܢܚܘܬ [11]ܐܢܬܘܢ ܕܡܢ ܐܡܪܝܢ ܐܢܬܘܢ ܕܐܢ ܢܐܡܪ S
ܠܐܒܘܗܝ، ܘܠܐܡܗ ܡܘܩܪܝܢ ܕܬܬܗܢܐ ܡܢܗ. [12]ܘܠܐ ܫܡܥܝܢ ܐܢܬܘܢ
ܠܗ ܕܢܝܩܪ ܠܐܒܘܗܝ، ܐܘ ܠܐܡܗ. [13]ܘܡܫܡܠܝܢ ܐܢܬܘܢ ܡܠܬܐ
ܕܐܠܗܐ ܡܛܠ ܦܘܩܕܢܟܘܢ ۰۰

ܘܫܐܠܬܐ ܐܝܟ ܗܠܝܢ ܒܥܕܢ ܐܢܬܘܢ܆ [14]ܘܩܪܐ ܠܟܘܠܗ ܟܢܫܐ
ܘܐܡܪ ܠܗܘܢ ܫܡܥܘ ܟܘܠܟܘܢ ܘܐܣܬܟܠܘ. [15]ܠܝܬ ܡܕܡ
ܕܠܒܪ ܡܢ ܒܪ ܐܢܫܐ ܘܥܐܠ ܠܗ ܘܡܫܟܚ ܠܡܣܝܒܘܬܗ ܐܠܐ
ܡܕܡ ܕܢܦܩ ܡܢ ܒܪ ܐܢܫܐ ܗܘ ܗܘ ܡܣܝܒ ܠܗ ܠܒܪ ܐܢܫܐ.
[16]ܡܢ ܕܐܝܬ ܠܗ ܐܕܢܐ ܕܢܫܡܥ ܢܫܡܥ ·܀·܀·

[17]ܘܟܕ ܥܐܠ ܗܘܐ ܠܒܝܬܐ ܡܢ ܟܢܫܐ. ܫܐܠܘܗܝ، ܗܘܘ ܬܠܡܝܕܘܗܝ،
ܥܠ ܡܬܠܐ. [18]ܗܘ ܕܝܢ ܐܡܪ ܠܗܘܢ܆ ܗܟܢܐ ܐܦ ܐܢܬܘܢ
ܣܟܠܝܢ ܐܢܬܘܢ ܠܐ ܡܣܬܟܠܝܢ ܐܢܬܘܢ ܡܕܡ ܕܠܐ ܗܘܐ ܟܘܠ
ܡܕܡ ܕܥܐܠ ܠܒܪ ܐܢܫܐ ܡܣܝܒ ܠܗ [19]ܡܛܠ ܕܠܐ ܗܘܐ ܓܝܪ
ܠܠܒܐ ܥܐܠ ܐܠܐ ܠܟܪܣܐ ܘܡܫܬܕܐ ܠܒܪ ܘܡܬܕܟܝܐ. ܟܘܠܗ
ܡܐܟܘܠܐ. [20]ܐܠܐ ܡܕܡ ܕܢܦܩ ܡܢ ܒܪ ܐܢܫܐ ܗܘ ܗܘ ܡܣܝܒ
ܠܗ ܠܒܪ ܐܢܫܐ [21]ܡܢ ܠܒܐ ܗܘ ܓܝܪ ܢܦܩܝܢ ܡܚܫܒܬܐ ܒܝܫܬܐ.
ܕܒܢܝ ܐܢܫܐ ܓܘܪܐ ܙܢܘܬܐ ܩܛܠܐ [22]ܓܢܒܘܬܐ. †ܥܠܘܒܘܬܐ
ܒܝܫܬܐ† ܢܟܠܐ ܨܝܢܘܬܐ ܥܝܢܐ ܒܝܫܬܐ ܓܘܕܦܐ ܫܒܗܪܘܬܐ
ܫܛܝܘܬܐ. [23]ܟܘܠܗܝܢ ܒܝܫܬܐ. ܡܢ ܠܓܘ ܢܦܩܢ ܘܡܣܝܒܢ ܠܗ ܠܒܪ
ܐܢܫܐ. [24]ܘܩܡ ܘܐܙܠ ܠܗ ܠܬܚܘܡܐ ܕܨܘܪ ܘܟܕ ܥܠ ܠܒܝܬܐ.
ܠܐ ܨܒܐ ܗܘܐ ܕܐܢܫ ܢܕܥ ܒܗ ܘܠܐ ܡܫܟܚ ܗܘܐ ܠܡܬܛܫܝܘ.
[25]ܘܟܕ ܫܡܥܬ ܐܢܬܬܐ ܕܐܝܬ ܗܘܬ ܠܒܪܬܗ ܪܘܚܐ ܛܢܦܬܐ ܐܬܬ
ܢܦܠܬ ܩܕܡܘܗܝ. [26]ܗܝ، ܐܢܬܬܐ ܐܪܡܠܬܐ ܗܘܬ ܡܢ ܬܚܘܡܐ
ܕܨܘܪ ܕܦܢܝܩܐ ܘܒܥܝܐ ܗܘܬ ܡܢܗ ܕܢܦܩ ܪܘܚܐ ܡܢ ܒܪܬܗ
[27]ܐܡܪ ܠܗ ܝܫܘܥ ܫܒܘܩܝ ܠܘܩܕܡ ܢܣܒܥܘܢ ܒܢܝܐ ܠܐ ܫܦܝܪ
ܠܡܣܒ ܠܚܡܐ ܕܒܢܝܐ ܘܠܡܪܡܝܘ ܠܟܠܒܐ. [28]ܐܡܪܐ ܠܗ ܗܝ،
ܐܢܬܬܐ ܡܪܝ، ܐܦ ܟܠܒܐ ܐܟܠܝܢ ܡܢ ܦܪ̈ܬܘܬܐ ܕܢܦܠ̈ܝܢ ܡܢ

---

19 ܘܡܬܕܟܝܐ. ܟܘܠܗ ܡܐܟܘܠܐ.] S (sic) 22 ܥܠܘܒܘܬܐ ܒܝܫܬܐ S

26 ܐܪܡܠܬܐ] S (*sic*), *for* ܐܪܡܝܬܐ: *cf Wellhausen in* GGN 1895, p. 12

28 *Cf* ܕܬܘܣܦܬ ܐܝܟ ܡܢ ܦܪ̈ܬܘܬܐ ܕܡܢ ܦܬܘܪ ܒܢܝܐ ܢܦܠܝܢ ܗܘܘ Ephr. *Lamy* i 163

11 shall indeed die.' But ye say that if he shall say to his father and his *S*
12 mother '*It is* an offering what thou shalt be profited from me—' and
13 ye suffer him not to honour his father or his mother! And ye reject
the word of God because of your commandments.
14 "And many things like these ye do." And he called all the
multitude and said to them: "Hear all of you and be persuaded!
15 There is nothing which *being* outside a man and entering into him
can defile him, but that which goeth forth from a man, that it is
16 defileth the man. He that hath ears to hear, let him hear."
17 And when he was entering the house from the multitude his
18 disciples had asked him about the similitude. But he said to them:
"So even ye are stubborn? Do ye not perceive at all, that not
19 anything that entereth the man defileth him? Because not the heart
doth it enter but the belly, and it is thrown away and cleansed—
20 †*even* all meat.† But that which cometh forth from a man, that it is
21 defileth the man. For from the heart come forth the evil thoughts of
22 men; adultery, fornication, murder, theft, covetousness, ill-will, guile,
23 lasciviousness, an evil eye, blasphemy, pride, folly,—all of them evil,
24 —from within come forth and defile the man." And he arose and
went away to the border of Tyre; and when he entered a house he was
not wishing that any one should know of him, and he could not be
25 concealed. And when a woman whose daughter had an unclean spirit
26 heard, she came *and* fell down before him. The woman was a †widow†
from the border of Tyre of Phoenicia, and she was beseeching him that
27 he would cast out the spirit from her daughter. Jesus saith to her:
"Suffer first the sons to be satisfied. It is not well to take the
28 sons' bread and to cast *it* to the dogs." The woman saith to him:
"My Lord, even the dogs eat of the morsels that drop down from

---

15 can] *for the rendering, cf* Lk xiii 10, 11 19.] *see Notes*, vol. ii
26 a widow] *S* (*sic*), *but the shortening of one stroke would give the word for* 'a Gentile' 28 *Cf* 'That thou mayest satisfy them from the morsels that from the sons' table were falling' Ephr.*Lamy* i 163; 'the table of the sons' *is found also in* E^{138} (cod. B), *and in* arm.vg

ܒܬܘܪܐ ܕܒܢܝܐ. [29]ܐܡܪ ܠܗ ܡܛܠ ܗܕܐ ܡܠܬܐ ܐܙܠܝ ܗܐ ܢܦܩ S
ܫܐܕܐ ܡܢ ܒܪܬܟܝ. [30]ܘܟܕ ܐܙܠܬ ܠܒܝܬܗ ܐܫܟܚܬܗ ܠܒܪܬܗ
ܘܢܦܝܩ ܡܢܗ ܫܐܕܐ ܘܪܡܝܐ ܒܥܪܣܐ. [31]ܘܬܘܒ ܟܕ ܢܦܩ ܡܢ ܬܚܘܡܐ
ܕܨܘܪ ܘܨܝܕ̈ܢ ܐܬܐ ܠܝܡܬܐ ܕܓܠܝܠܐ ܒܝܢܬ ܬܚܘܡܐ ܕܥܣܪܬ
ܡܕ̈ܝܢܬܐ [32]ܘܐܝܬܝܘ ܠܗ ܚܪܫܐ ܚܕ ܦܐܡܐ ܘܒܥܝܢ ܗܘܘ ܡܢܗ
ܕܢܣܝܡ ܥܠܘܗܝ ܐܝܕܗ. [33]ܘܢܓܕܗ ܡܢ ܟܢܫܐ ܘܫܕܐ ܨܒܥܬܗ ܘܪܩ
ܒܐܕ̈ܢܘܗܝ، ܘܩܪܒ ܠܠܫܢܗ [34]ܘܚܪ ܒܫܡܝܐ ܘܐܬܬܢܚ ܘܐܡܪ ܠܗ
ܐܬܦܬܚ [35]ܘܒܗ ܒܫܥܬܐ ܐܬܦܬܚ ܐܕ̈ܢܘܗܝ، ܘܐܫܬܪܝ، ܐܣܘܪܐ
ܕܠܫܢܗ ܘܡܠܠ ܗܘܐ ܦܫܝܛܐܝܬ. [36]ܘܦܩܕ ܐܢܘܢ ܕܠܐܢܫ ܠܐ
ܢܐܡܪܘܢ. ܘܟܡܐ ܕܗܘ ܡܦܩܕ ܗܘܐ ܠܗܘܢ ܗܢܘܢ ܝܬܝܪܐܝܬ
ܡܟܪ̈ܙܝܢ ܗܘܘ ܠܗ [37]ܘܝܬܝܪ ܡܬܕܡܪܝܢ ܗܘܘ ܘܐܡܪ̈ܝܢ ܕܟܠܡܕܡ
ܫܦܝܪ ܥܒܕ ܘܠܚܪ̈ܫܐ ܥܒܕ ܕܢܫܡܥܘܢ ܘܢܡܠܠܘܢ [1]ܘܒܗܘܢ ܕܝܢ
ܒܝܘܡܬܐ ܗܢܘܢ ܬܘܒ ܟܕ ܟܢܫܐ ܣܓܝܐܐ ܐܝܬ ܗܘܐ ܘܠܐ
ܐܝܬ ܗܘܐ ܠܗܘܢ ܡܐ ܕܢܐܟܠܘܢ ܩܪܐ ܠܬܠܡܝܕ̈ܘܗܝ، ܘܐܡܪ
ܠܗܘܢ [2]ܡܬܪܚܡ ܐܢܐ ܥܠ ܟܢܫܐ ܗܢܐ ܕܗܐ ܬܠܬܐ ܝܘܡܝܢ
ܩܘܝܘ ܠܘܬܝ، ܘܠܝܬ ܠܗܘܢ ܡܕܡ ܕܢܐܟܠܘܢ [3]ܘܐܢ ܗܘ ܕܫܪܐ ܐܢܐ
ܐܢܘܢ ܟܕ ܨܝܡܝܢ ܠܒ̈ܬܝܗܘܢ ܢܫܬܪܘܢ ܒܐܘܪܚܐ ܘܐܢܫܐ
ܡܢܗܘܢ ܡܢ ܪܘܚܩ ܐܬܘ. [4]ܐܡܪܝܢ ܠܗ ܬܠܡܝܕ̈ܘܗܝ، ܐܝܡܟܐ
ܡܫܟܚ ܐܢܫ ܗܪܟܐ ܕܢܣܒܥ ܐܢܘܢ ܠܚܡܐ ܒܚܘܪܒܐ [5]ܘܫܐܠ
ܐܢܘܢ ܘܐܡܪ ܠܗܘܢ ܟܡܐ ܠܚܡܝܢ ܐܝܬ ܠܟܘܢ ܐܡܪܝܢ ܠܗ
ܫܒܥܐ [6]ܘܦܩܕ ܠܟܢܫܐ ܕܢܣܬܡܟܘܢ ܥܠ ܐܪܥܐ ܘܢܣܒ ܗܢܘܢ
ܫܒܥܐ ܠܚܡܝܢ ܘܒܪܟ ܘܩܨܐ ܘܝܗܒ ܠܬܠܡܝܕ̈ܘܗܝ، ܕܢܣܝܡܘܢ
ܩܕܡܝܗܘܢ ܘܣܡܘ ܩܕܡ ܟܢܫܐ [7]ܘܐܝܬ ܗܘܘ ܢܘܢܐ ܩܠܝܠ ܘܐܦ
ܥܠܝܗܘܢ ܟܕ ܒܪܟ ܐܡܪ ܕܢܣܝܡܘܢ ܩܕܡܝܗܘܢ [8]ܘܐܟܠܘ
ܘܣܒܥܘ ܘܫܩܠܘ ܝܬܝܪܘܬܐ ܕܩܨܝܐ ܫܒܥܐ ܣܦܪܝܕܝܢ [9]ܗܘܝܢ ܗܘܘ

30 ܘܢܦܝܩ] ܘܢܦܩ S^{ed} 31 ܟܕ] S (*sic*) ܕܥܣܪܬ S, *for* ܕܥܣܪ̈ܬ

33 *Cf* ܢܗܡ ܠܟ ܡܢ ܦܘܡܗ ܘܪܘܩ ܒܐܨܒ̈ܥܬܗ ܕܐܣܝܘܗܝ ܚܪܫܐ ܘܗܘ Ephr. *Lamy* i 171: *see Introd.* vol. ii 35 ܐܬܦܬܚ] ܐܬܦܬܚ S^{ed}: *see Appendix* III

29 the sons' tables." He saith to her: "Because of this saying go; lo, the *S*
30 devil hath gone forth from thy daughter!" And when she went to her
house she found her daughter, and the devil was gone forth from her
31 and she was lying in the bed. And again [when] he went forth from
the border of Tyre [and] Sidon he came to the lake of Galilee between
32 the border of the Ten Cities. And they brought to him a certain
inarticulate deaf-mute, and they were beseeching him that he would
33 lay on him his hand. And he drew him from the multitude, and he
34 put his fingers and spat in his ears and touched his tongue and looked
35 up to heaven and groaned and said to him: "Be opened!" And in
the same hour his ears were opened and the bond of his tongue was
36 loosed and he had spoken easily. And he commanded them that to
no one they should say *it*; and the more that he was commanding
37 them, they the rather were preaching him. And all the more were
they wondering and saying "Everything he doeth well, and the
viii 1 deaf-mutes he maketh that they hear and speak!" Now in those
same days again, when there was a great multitude and they had not
what they should eat, he called his disciples and said to them:
2 "I have compassion on this multitude, for lo, three days they have
3 remained by me and there is not what they may eat, and if so be
that I should dismiss *them* fasting to their houses they would be
4 fainting on the way; and some of them from far have come." His
disciples say to him: "Whence canst thou here satisfy them with
5 bread in the desert?" And he asked them and saith to them:
"How many pieces of bread have ye?" They say to him: "Seven."
6 And he commanded the multitude that they should sit down *to meat*
on the ground. And he took those seven pieces of bread and blessed
and brake and gave to his disciples that they should set before them,
7 and they set *them* before the multitude. And there were a few
fishes; and upon them also having blessed, he said that they should
8 set *them* before them. And they ate and were satisfied, and they
9 took up the superabundance of the fragments seven panniers. The

---

33 *Cf* 'He spat' (it saith) 'on his fingers, and put *it* in the ears of that deaf-mute' Ephr.*Lamy* i 171: *so also* Diat^{ar} xxi 3

ܐܢܫܐ ܕܐܟܠܘ ܐܝܟ ܐܪܒܥܐ ܐܠܦܝܢ. ܘܫܪܐ ܐܢܘܢ. ¹⁰ܘܣܠܩ S
ܝܬܒ ܠܗ ܒܣܦܝܢܬܐ ܥܡ ܬܠܡܝܕܘܗܝ، ܘܐܬܐ ܠܗܘܢ ܠܛܘܪܐ
ܕܡܓܕܢ. ¹¹ܘܢܦܩܘ ܦܪ̈ܝܫܐ ܘܫܪܝܘ ܒܥܝܢ ܡܢܗ ܘܫܐܠܝܢ ܠܗ ܐܬܐ
ܡܢ ܫܡܝܐ ܟܕ ܡܢܣܝܢ ܠܗ. ¹²ܘܐܬܬܢܚ ܒܪܘܚܐ ܘܐܡܪ ܡܢܐ
ܒܥܝܐ ܐܬܐ ܫܪܒܬܐ ܗܕܐ. ܐܡܝܢ ܐܡܪܢܐ ܠܟܘܢ ܕܠܐ
ܬܬܝܗܒ ܠܗ ܐܬܐ ܠܫܪܒܬܐ ܗܕܐ. ¹³ܘܫܒܩ ܐܢܘܢ ܬܘܒ ܘܣܠܩ
ܒܣܦܝܢܬܐ. ܘܐܙܠ ܠܗܘ ܥܒܪܐ ܕܝܡܬܐ. ¹⁴ܘܛܥܘ ܕܢܣܒܘܢ
ܥܡܗܘܢ ܠܚܡܐ ܚܕܐ ܓܪܝܨܬܐ ܠܝܬ ܗܘܬ ܥܡܗܘܢ
ܒܣܦܝܢܬܐ. ¹⁵ܘܦܩܕ ܐܢܘܢ ܘܐܡܪ ܠܗܘܢ ܐܙܕܗܪܘ ܡܢ ܚܡܝܪܐ
ܕܦܪ̈ܝܫܐ ܘܡܢ ܚܡܝܪܗ ܕܗܪܘܕܣ. ¹⁶ܘܡܬܚܫܒܝܢ ܗܘܘ ܚܕ ܥܡ ܚܕ
ܘܐܡܪܝܢ ܕܠܝܬ ܠܚܡܐ. ¹⁷ܝܕܥ ܕܝܢ ܝܫܘܥ ܘܐܡܪ ܠܗܘܢ ܡܢܐ
ܡܬܚܫܒܝܢ ܐܢܬܘܢ ܕܠܚܡܐ ܠܝܬ ܠܟܘܢ. ܠܐ ܒܕܡܐ ܠܗܫܐ
ܝܕܥܝܢ ܐܢܬܘܢ ܘܠܐ ܡܣܬܟܠܝܢ ܐܢܬܘܢ ܒܕܡܐ ܠܗܫܐ ܡܒܘܪ
ܠܒܟܘܢ. ¹⁸ܘܥܝܢܐ ܐܝܬ ܠܟܘܢ ܘܠܐ ܚܙܝܢ ܐܢܬܘܢ ܘܐܕܢܐ
ܐܝܬ ܠܟܘܢ ܘܠܐ ܫܡܥܝܢ ܐܢܬܘܢ ܘܠܐ ܒܗܕܝܢ ܐܢܬܘܢ
¹⁹ܗܘܢ ܫܒܥܐ ܠܚܡܝܢ ܕܩܨܝܬ ܠܐܠܦܝܢ ܐܟܠܘ ܡܢܗܘܢ ܘܟܡܐ
ܩܘܦܝܢ ܕܩܨܝܐ ܟܕ ܡܠܝܢ [ܫܩܠܬܘܢ] ܐܡܪܝܢ ܠܗ ܬܪܥܣܪ
²⁰ܐܡܪ ܠܗܘܢ ܘܟܕ ܫܒܥܐ ܠܐܪܒܥܐ ܐܠܦܝܢ ܟܡܐ ܐܣܦܪܝܕܝܢ
ܕܩܨܝܐ ܫܩܠܬܘܢ ܐܡܪܝܢ [ܠܗ] ܫܒܥܐ ²¹ܐܡܪ ܠܗܘܢ ܠܐ
ܒܕܡܐ ܠܗܫܐ ܡܣܬܟܠܝܢ ܐܢܬܘܢ

²²ܘܐܬܐ ܠܒܝܬ ܨܝܕܐ ܘܐܝܬܝܘ ܠܗ ܣܡܝܐ ܘܒܥܝܢ ܗܘܘ ܡܢܗ
ܕܢܩܪܘܒ ܠܗ ²³†ܘܐܚܕܗ† ܒܐܝܕܗ ܕܣܡܝܐ ܘܐܦܩܗ ܠܒܪ ܡܢ ܩܪܝܬܐ
ܘܪܩ ܒܥܝܢܘܗܝ، ܘܣܡ ܐܝܕܗ ܘܫܐܠܗ ܘܐܡܪ ܠܗ ܡܢܐ [ܐܢ]ܬ
†ܬܚܙܐ† ²⁴[ܘܐܡܪ ܚܙ]ܝܬ ܠܒܢܝ ܐܢܫܐ ܐܝܟ ܐܝܠܢܐ ܕܡܗܠܟܝܢ
²⁵ܘܬܘܒ ܣܡ ܐܝܕܗ ܥܠ ܥܝܢܘܗܝ، [ܘܚܙ]ܐ ܘܬܩܢ ܘܚܙܐ ܗܘܐ ܟܠ

18] *Cf Thos*[252]
ܐܡܪ ܗܘܐ ܠܢ ܡܪܢ ܠܫܡܥܘܢ ܒܢܝܐ ܕܐܬܘ ܗܘܘ ܠܘܬܗ. ܕܐܕ̈ܢܐ ܐܝܬ
ܠܟܘܢ ܘܠܐ ܫܡܥܝܢ ܐܢܬܘܢ ܘܥܝܢܐ ܐܝܬ ܠܟܘܢ ܘܠܐ ܚܙܝܢ ܐܢܬܘܢ.

23 ܘܐܚܕܗ] *S (sic)* 25 ܘܚܙܐ] *only the final* ܐ *is legible in S;* ܕܡܫܟܚܐ *is suggested by Mrs Lewis* (*Expositor,* Aug. 1897, p. 114), *but cf cod. Bobiensis* (*k*) *and* arm.vg aeth.vg

folk that ate were about four thousand; and he dismissed them. S
10 And he went up *and* sat in the boat with his disciples, and they came
11 to the hill of Magadan. And the Pharisees came forth and began
beseeching him and asking him for a sign from heaven, tempting
12 him. He was excited in spirit and said: "Why doth this generation
seek a sign? Amen, I say to you that a sign shall not be given
13 to this generation." And he left them again and sat in the boat, and
14 went to the other side of the lake. And they forgot to take with
them *any* bread, for not one loaf was there with them in the boat.
15 And he commanded them and said to them: "Beware of the leaven
16 of the Pharisees and of the leaven of Herod." And they were
17 thinking one with another and saying "There is no bread." Now
Jesus knew and said to them: "Why think ye that ye have no
bread? Not until now do ye know nor understand? Until now is
18 your heart blinded, and eyes have ye and see not, and ears have ye
19 and hear not? And do ye not recollect those five pieces of bread
that five thousand ate of, and how many baskets of fragments full
20 [took ye up?]" They say to him: "Twelve." He saith to them:
"And when *there were* seven for four thousand how many panniers of
21 fragments took ye up?" They say [to him]: "Seven." He saith to
them: "Not until now do ye understand?"

22 And he came to Beth Saida; and they brought to him a blind
23 man, and they were beseeching him that he would touch him. And
he took hold† of the hand of the blind man and brought him forth
out of the village, and he spat in his eyes and laid his hand and asked
24 him and saith to him: "What †wilt† thou see?" [And he saith:]
25 "I have [seen] men as trees walking." And again he laid his hand
on his eyes, [and he saw] and was restored and was seeing everything

---

18] *Cf Thos*[252]: 'For our Lord said to those multitudes that were coming unto him Ears have ye and hear not, and eyes have ye and see not?'
23 wilt thou see] *see Notes*, vol. ii 25 ⌜and he saw⌝] *It would be equally possible to supply* 'of the blind man' *instead of* 'and he saw', *but the latter is read in the O. Latin* (*k*), *the Armenian and the Ethiopic*

ܡܕܡ ܢܗܝܪܐܝܬ ²⁶ܘܫܕܪܗ ܠܒܝܬܗ ܘܐܡܪ ܠܗ ܕܐܦܠܐ ܠܩܪܝܬܐ *S*
ܬܥܘܠ ܀

²⁷ܘܢܦܩ ܝܫܘܥ ܘܬܠܡܝܕܘܗܝ ܠܩܘܪܝܐ ܕܩܣܪܝܐ ܕܦܝܠܝܦܘܣ
ܘܫܐܠ ܗܘܐ ܠܗܘܢ ܠܬܠܡܝܕܘܗܝ ܒܐܘܪܚܐ ܘܐܡܪ ܠܗܘܢ
ܕܡܢܐ ܐܡܪܝܢ ܐܢܫܐ ܥܠܝ ܕܐܝܬܝ. ²⁸ܐܡܪܝܢ ܠܗ ܐܝܬ ܕܐܡܪܝܢ
ܕܝܘܚܢܢ ܗܘ ܡܥܡܕܢܐ. ܘܐܚܪܢܐ ܐܡܪܝܢ ܕܐܠܝܐ. ܘܐܚܪܢܐ
ܕܚܕ ܡܢ ܢܒܝܐ. ²⁹ܐܡܪ ܠܗܘܢ ܘܐܢܬܘܢ ܡܢܐ ܐܡܪܝܢ ܐܢܬܘܢ
ܕܐܝܬܝ. ܐܡ⌜ܪ ܠ⌝ܗ ܟܐܦܐ ܐܢܬ ܗܘ ܡܫܝܚܐ ³⁰ܘܟܐܐ ܒܗܘܢ
ܕܠܐܢܫ ܠܐ ܢܐܡܪܘܢ ܥܠܘܗܝ. ³¹ܘܫܪܝ ܗܘܐ ܠܡܠܦܘ ܐܢܘܢ
ܕܥܬܝܕ ܗܘ ܒܪܗ ܕܐܢܫܐ ܕܢܚܫ ܣܓܝ. ܘܕܢܣܬܠܐ ܡܢ ܩܫ̈ܝܫܐ
ܘܡܢ ܪ̈ܒܝ ܟܗܢܐ ܘܡܢ ܣܦܪ̈ܐ ܘܢܩܛܠܘ⌜ܢܝܗ⌝ ܘܠܝܘܡܐ ܕܬܠܬܐ
ܢܩܘܡ ³²ܘܡܒܣܒ⌜ܪ⌝ܐ ܡܠܬܐ ܢܡܠܠ ܥܡܗܘܢ ܕܝܢ ܟܐܦܐ ܐܝܟ
ܕܚܐܣ ܥܠܘܗܝ، ܐܡܪ ܠܗ ܕܚܘܣ ܠܟ. ³³ܘܟܕ ܐܬܗܦܟ ܚܪ
ܒܬܠܡܝܕܘܗܝ. ܘܟܐܐ ܒܟܐܦܐ ܘܐܡܪ ܠܗ ܙܠ ܠܒܣܬܪܝ، ܣܛܢܐ ܕܠܐ
ܪܢܐ ܐܢܬ ܕܐܠܗܐ. ܐܠܐ ܕܒ̈ܢܝ ܐܢܫܐ ܀ ܀ ܀

³⁴ܘܩܪܐ ܠܟܢܫܐ ܥܡ ܬܠܡܝܕܘܗܝ، ܘܐܡܪ ܠܗܘܢ ܡܢ ܕܨܒܐ
ܕܢܐܬܐ ܒܬܪܝ، ܢܟܦܘܪ ܒܢܦܫܗ ܘܢܫܩܘܠ ܙܩܝܦܗ ܘܢܐܬܐ. ³⁵ܟܠ
ܓܝܪ ܕܨܒܐ ܕܢܚܐ ܢܦܫܗ ܢܘܒܕܝܗ. ܘܟܠ ܕܢܘܒܕ ܢܦܫܗ ܡܛܠ
ܣܒܪܬܝ، ܢܚܝܗ. ³⁶ܡܢܐ ܓܝܪ ܢܬܗܢܐ ⌜ܒ⌝ܪ ܐܢܫܐ ܐܢ ܗܘ
ܕܠܥܠܡܐ ܟܘܠܗ ܢܐܪܬ ܘܢܦܫܗ ܢܚܣܪ. ³⁷ܘܡܢܐ ܢܬܠ ܒܪ ܐܢܫܐ
ܬܘܚܠܦܐ ܕܢܦܫܗ. ³⁸ܟܠ ܕܢܒܗܬ ܒܝ ܓܝܪ ܘܒܡ̈ܠܝ ܒ̈ܢܝ ܫܪܒܬܐ
⌜ܗ⌝ܕܐ ܚܛܝܬܐ ܘܓܝܪܬܐ. ܐܦ ܒܪܗ ܕܓܒܪܐ ܢܒܗܬ ܒܗ ܗܘ ܡܐ
ܕܐܬܐ ܒܫܘܒܚܗ ܕܐܒܘܗܝ، ܘܡܠܐܟ̈ܐ ܩܕ̈ܝܫܐ ¹ܐܡܪ ܗܘܐ
ܠܗܘܢ ܐܡܝܢ ܐܡܪܢܐ ܠܟܘܢ ܕܐܝܬ ܬܢܢ ܐܢܫܐ ܡܢ ܗܠܝܢ
ܕܩܝܡܝܢ ܕܠܐ ܢܛܥܡܘܢ ܡܘܬܐ ܥܕܡܐ ܕܢܚܙܘܢ ܡܠܟܘܬܗ
ܕܐܠܗܐ ܕܐܬܝܐ ܒܚܝܠܐ ²ܘܡܢ ܒܬܪ ܫܬܐ ܝܘܡܝܢ ܕܒܪ ܝܫܘܥ
ܠܟܐܦܐ ܘܠܝܥܩܘܒ ܘܠܝܘܚܢܢ. ܘܐ⌜ܣܩ⌝ ܐܢܘܢ ܠܛܘܪܐ ܪܡܐ

---

38 ܒܪܗ ܕܓܒܪܐ] *see* Mt xii 40   2 ܫܬܐ] ܫܬ *S* (*cf* Joh i 39)

26 clearly. And he sent him to his house and said to him "Not even S
into the village shalt thou enter."
27 And Jesus went forth, and his disciples, to the villages of Caesarea
of Philip, and he was asking his disciples in the way, and saith to
28 them "What say folk of me that I am?" They say to him "There
are that say 'It is John the Baptist,' and others say 'Elijah,' and
29 others 'One of the prophets.'" He saith to them: "And ye, what
say ye that I am?" Kepha saith to him: "Thou art the Messiah."
30 And he rebuked them, that to no man should they say *it* of him.
31 And he had begun to teach them, *saying* "The Son of Man is about
to suffer much, and be rejected by the elders and by the chief priests
and by the scribes, and they will kill him, and the third day he will
32 rise and openly speak the word." Now Simon Kepha, as if pitying
33 him said to him "Be it far from thee!" And when he *had* turned
himself he looked on his disciples, and rebuked Kepha and said:
"Get thee behind me, Satan, for that thou dost not give thought to
the *things* of God, but of men."
34 And he called the multitude with his disciples and said to them:
"He that willeth to come after me, let him deny himself and take up
35 his cross and come. For every one that willeth to save his life shall
lose it, and every one that shall lose his life because of my gospel shall
36 save it. For what shall a man be profited, if so be that he should
37 inherit the whole world and lack his life? And what shall a man
38 give in exchange for his life? For every one that shall be ashamed
of me and of my words among the sons of this adulterous and sinful
generation, the son of a man also shall be ashamed of him what *time*
ix 1 he cometh in the glory of his Father, and the holy angels." He had
said to them: "Amen, I say to you that there are here some of
these that stand *by*, that shall not taste death until they see the
2 kingdom of God that cometh in power." And after six days Jesus
took Kepha and James and John and brought them up to a high hill

---

31, 32 will rise [32]and openly speak the word] 'will rise and say a saying openly' Diat^{ar} xxiii 42 (*sic*): *cf* 'resurgere et cum fiducia sermonem loqui' *k* 32 as if pitying him] 'as if suffering for him' Diat^{ar} xxiii 42 (*thus reading* ḥâ'esh *for* ḥâ'es) 38 the son of a man] *see on* Mt xii 40, Lk xxii 48 1 that stand *by*] *or*, 'that exist *in this world*' (*cf* 1 Cor iii 22 syr. vg): 'that now stand here with me' *E*^{155} Diat^{ar} xxiv 1 (cod. B)

S ܒܠܚܘܕܝܗܘܢ ܘܐܫܬܚܠܦ ܩܕܡܝܗܘܢ ܘܡܨܡܚ ܗܘܐ [3]ܘܠܒܘܫܗ
ܡܚܘܪ ܗܘܐ ܐܝܟ ܬܠܓܐ [4]ܘܐܬܚܙܝܘ ܠܗܘܢ ܡܘܫܐ ܘܐܠܝܐ
ܟܕ ܡܡܠܠܝܢ ܥܡܗ. [5]ܥܢܐ ܟܐܦܐ ܘܐܡܪ ܠܝܫܘܥ. ܪܒܝ ܫܦܝܪ
ܗܘܐ ܕܗܪܟܐ ܢܗܘܐ. ܘܢܥܒܕ ܬܠܬ ܡܛܠܠܢ ܠܟ ܚܕܐ ܘܠܡܘܫܐ
ܚܕܐ ܘܠܐܠܝܐ ܚܕܐ. [6]ܘܠܐ ܝܕܥ ܗܘܐ ܡܢܐ ܐܡܪ ܗܘܐ
ܡܛܠ ܕܕܚܠܬܐ ܢܦܠܬ ܗܘܬ ܥܠܝܗܘܢ. [7]ܘܥܢܢܐ ܡܛܠܠܐ ܗܘܬ
ܥܠܝܗܘܢ، ܘܩܠܐ ܐܬܐ ܡܢ ܥܢܢܐ ܗܢܐ ܗܘ ܒܪܝ، ܕܚܒܝܒ ܠܗ
ܫܡܥܘ. [8]ܘܡܢ ܫܠܝܐ ܬܘܒ ܟܕ ܚܪܘ ܬܠܡܝܕܘܗܝ، ܐܢܫ ܠܐ ܐܬܚܙܝ،
ܠܗܘܢ ܐܠܐ ܐܢ ܝܫܘܥ ܒܠܚܘܕܘܗܝ، [9]ܟܕ ܢܚܬܝܢ ܡܢ ܛܘܪܐ.
ܦܩܕ ܗܘܐ ܠܗܘܢ ܕܠܐܢܫ ܠܐ ܢܐܡܪܘܢ ܡܕܡ ܕܚܙܘ ܐܠܐ
ܡܐ ܕܩܡ ܒܪܗ ܕܐܢܫܐ ܡܢ ܒܝܬ ܡܝܬܐ [10]ܘܡܠܬܐ ܐܚܕܘ ܒܗ
ܠܢܦܫܗܘܢ ܡܬܪܥܝܢ ܗܘܘ ܘܐܡܪ̈ܝܢ ܕܡܢܐ ܗܝ، ܗܕܐ ܡܠܬܐ ܗܕܐ
ܕܐܡܪ ܕܒܪܗ ܕܩܡ ܡܢ ܒܝܬ ܡܝ̈ܬܐ ܀

[11]ܘܡܫܐܠܝܢ ܗܘܘ ܠܗ ܘܐܡܪ̈ܝܢ. ܕܐܡ̈ܪܝܢ ܣܦܪ̈ܐ ܕܐܠܝܐ ܗܘ
ܐܬܐ ܠܡܬܩܢ [12]ܥܢܐ ܘܐܡܪ ܠܗܘܢ ܐܠܝܐ ܐܬܐ ܠܡܬܩܢ ܕܟܠ
ܡܕܡ ܢܩܡ. ܘܐܝܟܢܐ ܟܬܝܒ ܥܠ ܒܪܗ ܕܐܢܫܐ ܠܐ ܕܣܓܝ ܢܚܫ
ܘܢܬܒܣܐ. [13]ܐܠܐ ܐܡܪ ܐܢܐ ܠܟܘܢ ܕܐܠܝܐ ܐܬܐ ܘܥܒܕܘ ܒܗ
ܟܠ ܡܐ ܕܨܒܘ ܐܝܟܢܐ ܕܟܬܝܒ ܥܠܘܗܝ، [14]ܟܕ ܐܬܐ ܠܘܬ
ܬܠܡܝܕܘܗܝ، ܚܙܘ ܠܘܬܗܘܢ ܟܢܫܐ ܣܓܝܐܐ ܘܣܦܪ̈ܐ ܟܕ ܒܥܝܢ
ܥܡܗܘܢ [15]ܘܗܘ ܟܡܠܬܐ ܟܕ ܚܙܘܗܝ، ܬܗܘ ܘܪܗܛܘ ܫܐܠܘ
ܒܫܠܡܗ [16]ܘܡܫܐܠ ܗܘܐ ܠܗܘܢ ܕܡܢܐ ܒܥܝܢ ܐܢܬܘܢ ܥܡܗܘܢ
[17]ܘܥܢܐ ܚܕ ܡܢ ܟܢܫܐ ܘܐܡܪ ܡܠܦܢܐ ܐܝܬܝܬ ܠܘܬܟ ܒܪܝ، ܕܐܝܬ
ܠܗ ܪܘܚܐ [18]ܘܐܝܟ̈ܐ ܕܡܕܪܟܐ ܠܗ ܪܡܝܐ [ܠܗ] ܘܡܪܥܬ ܘܡܚܪܩ
ܫܢܘܗܝ، ܘܝܒܫ ܘܐܡܪ̈ܬ ܠܬܠܡܝܕ̈ܝܟ ܕܢܦܩܘܢܝܗ، ܘܠܐ ܐܫܟܚܘ
[19]ܥܢܐ ܝܫܘܥ ܘܐܡ̣ܪ ܠܗܘܢ ܐܘ ܫܪܒܬܐ ܕܠܐ ܗܝܡܢܘܬܐ
ܥܕܡܐ ܠܐܡܬܝ، ܐܗܘܐ ܠܘܬܟܘܢ ܘܐܣܝܒܪܟܘܢ܆ ܐܝܬܝܘܗܝ، ܠܝ
ܠܒܪܟ [20]ܘܐܝܬܝܘܗܝ ܠܘܬܗ ܘܟܕ ܚܙܝܗ، ܐܪܥܠܬܗ ܪܘܚܐ ܒܗ

2 ܘܐܫܬܚܠܦ] ܘܐܬܚܠܦ S^{ed} (mea culpa): *photograph illegible*

alone, and he was transfigured before them, and he became gleaming *S*
3, 4 and his clothing became whitened as the snow; and there appeared
5 to them Moses and Elijah speaking with him. Kepha answered
and said to Jesus: "Rabbi, it was well that we should be here; and
we will make three dwellings, for thee one and for Moses one and for
6 Elijah one." And he knew not what he was saying, because fear had
7 fallen upon him. And a cloud was overshadowing him, and a voice
came from the cloud: "This is my son beloved; hear ye him!"
8 And suddenly again when his disciples saw, no one appeared to them
9 save Jesus alone. While they *were* coming down from the hill he
was commanding them, that to no one they should say aught that
they had seen, save what *time* the Son of Man hath risen from among
10 the dead. And the word they took hold of as with themselves they
were meditating and saying "What is then this word that he saith
'What *time* he hath risen from among the dead'?"

11 And they were asking him, and saying "The scribes say that
12 Elijah cometh first." He answered and said to them: "Elijah cometh
first that he may restore everything. And how is it written of the
Son of Man? is it not that he should suffer much and be crucified?
13 But I say to you that Elijah hath come, and they did with him all
14 that they would, as it is written of him." When he came unto his
disciples they saw by them a great multitude and scribes seeking *a*
15 *dispute* with them. And in the same hour when they saw him they
16 were amazed, and ran *and* greeted him. And he was asking them
17 "What seek ye with them?" And one out of the multitude answered
and said: "Teacher, I have brought unto thee my son, who hath a
18 spirit, and wheresoever it overtaketh him it casteth [him] down and
he foameth and gnasheth his teeth and pineth away; and I said to
19 thy disciples that they should cast it out, and they could not." Jesus
answered and said to them: "Ah faithless generation! until when
20 shall I be with you and endure you? Bring me thy son." And he
brought him unto him, and when he saw him the spirit cast him

---

10 as] *or*, 'though' **15** ran *and* greeted] *cf* Diat[ar] xxiv **26**: 'and the folk when they saw Jesus were amazed (*leg.* حاروا *instead of* جاروا), and in the midst of their joy ran and greeted him.' *This seems to imply a conflation of the readings* προσχαίροντες *and* προστρέχοντες

S ܒܫܥܬܐ ܘܢܦܠ ܥܠ ܐܪܥܐ ܘܡܬܟܒܟܒ ܗܘܐ ܟܕ ܡܪܒܥ. [21]ܘܫܐܠ
ܗܘܐ ܝܫܘܥ ܠܐܒܘܗܝ܆ ܕܟܡܐ ܠܗ ܙܒܢܐ ܗ̇ܘܐ ܡܢ ܕܗܕܐ
ܗܘܐ ܐܡܪ ܠܗ ܗܐ ܡܢ ܛܠܝܘܬܗ. [22]ܘܣܓܝ ܒܢܘܪܐ ܐܪܡܝܬܗ
ܘܒܡ̈ܝܐ ܕܬܘܒܕܝܘܗܝ܆ ܐܠܐ ܒܡܐ ܕܡܫܟܚ ܐܢܬ ܡܪܝ܆ ܥܕܪܢܝ
ܘܐܬܪܚܡ ܥܠܝ. [23]ܐܡܪ ܠܗ ܝܫܘܥ ܐܢ ܡܗܝܡܢ ܐܢܬ ܠܟܠܡܕܡ
ܡܫܟܚ ܠܡܗܘܐ ܠܟ. [24]ܘܗܘ ܒܫܥܬܐ ܩܥܐ ܐܒܘܗܝ܆ ܕܛܠܝܐ
ܘܐܡܪ ܡܗܝܡܢܐ ܡܪܝ܆ ܥܕܪ ܠܚܣܝܪܘܬܝ. [25]ܟܕ ܚܙܐ ܝܫܘܥ
ܕܪܗܛܝܢ ܐܢܫܐ ܕܐܬܝܢ ܟܐܐ ܒܗ܆ ܪܘܚܐ ܘܐܡܪ ܠܗ ܠܟܝ
ܦܓܝܡܐ ܪܘܚܐ ܚܪܫܬܐ ܕܠܐ ܡܡܠܠܐ ܦܘܩ ܡܢܗ ܘܬܘܒ ܠܐ
ܬܥܘܠ ܠܗ. [26]ܘܩܥܐ ܘܚܢܩܗ ܣܓܝ ܘܢܦܩ ܡܢܗ ܘܗܘܐ ܐܝܟ
ܡܝܬܐ ܘܣܒܪܘ ܣܓܝܐܐ ܕܡܝܬ ܠܗ. [27]ܗܘ ܕܝܢ ܝܫܘܥ ܐܚܕܗ
ܒܐܝܕܗ ܘܐܩܝܡܗ ܘܐܫܠܡܗ ܠܐܒܘܗܝ. [28]ܘܟܕ ܥܠ ܠܒܝܬܐ
ܫܐܠܘܗܝ ܬܠܡܝܕܘܗܝ ܒܝܢܝܗܘܢ ܘܠܗ ܕܠܡܢܐ ܠܐ ܡܫܟܚܝܢ
ܐܢܚܢ ܠܡܦܩܘܬܗ. [29]ܐܡܪ ܠܗܘܢ ܗܢܐ ܓܢܣܐ ܒܡܕܡ ܠܐ
ܢܦܩ ܐܠܐ ܒܨܘܡܐ ܘܒܨܠܘܬܐ ܀

[30]ܘܟܕ ܢܦܩܘ ܡܢ ܬܡܢ ܪܕܝܢ ܗܘܘ ܒܓܠܝܠܐ ܘܠܐ ܨܒܐ ܗܘܐ
ܕܐܢܫ ܢܕܥ ܒܗ. [31]ܘܡܠܦ ܗܘܐ ܠܗܘܢ ܠܬܠܡܝܕܘܗܝ܆ ܘܐܡܪ
ܠܗܘܢ ܕܒܪܗ ܕܐܢܫܐ ܡܫܬܠܡ ܒܐܝܕܝ܆ ܒܢ̈ܝ ܐܢܫܐ ܘܢܩܛܠܘܢܝܗܝ܆
ܘܡܐ ܕܢܩܛܠܘܗܝ܆ ܒܝܘܡܐ ܕܬܠܬܐ ܢܩܘܡ. [32]ܘܗܢܘܢ ܠܐ
ܡܣܬܟܠܝܢ ܗܘܘ ܡܕܡ ܕܐܡܪ ܠܗܘܢ܂ ܘܕܚܠܝܢ ܗܘܘ ܕܢܫܐܠܘܢܝܗܝ܂
[33]ܘܐܬܐ ܠܟܦܪܢܚܘܡ. ܘܟܕ ܥܠ ܠܒܝܬܗ ܡܫܐܠ ܗܘܐ ܠܗܘܢ
ܕܡܢܐ ܡܡܠܠܝܢ ܗܘܝܬܘܢ ܚܕ ܥܡ ܚܕ ܒܐܘܪܚܐ. [34]ܘܗܢܘܢ
ܫܬܝܩܝܢ ܗܘܘ ܗܠܝܢ ܓܒܪ ܡܬܚܫܒܝܢ ܗܘܘ ܕܡܢܘ ܢܗܘܐ ܪܒ
[35]ܘܝܬܒ ܘܩܪܐ ܠܬܪܥܣܪܬܗ ܘܐܡܪ ܠܗܘܢ ܡܢ ܕܨܒܐ ܕܢܗܘܐ
ܩܕܡܝܐ ܢܗܘܐ ܐܚܪܝܐ ܕܟܠ ܐܢܫ ܘܡܫܡܫܢܐ ܕܟܠ ܐܢܫ. [36]ܘܢܣܒ

23, 24] *Cf A* 20 ܠܘ̇ ܕܒܪܗ ܒܪܝܗ ܗܘܐ ܐܡܪ ܠܗ. ܗܝܡܢ ܘܚܝܐ ܒܪܟ. [24]ܐܡܪ ܠܗ ܡܗܝܡܢ ܐܢܐ ܡܪܝ. ܥܕܪ ܠܡܚܝܠܘܬܝ ܕܗܝܡܢܘܬܐ. ܘܡܗܝܡܢܘܬܗ ܐܬܚܠܡ ܛܠܝܗ.

28 ܕܠܡܢܐ] *S* (*sic*)

down in the same hour, and he fell on the earth and wallowed S
21 foaming. And Jesus had asked his father "How long a time *was it*,
22 lo, since so he was?" He saith to him: "Lo, from his boyhood, and
often in the fire it hath cast him and in the water that it might
destroy him; but as much as thou canst, my Lord, help me and
23 have compassion upon me!" Jesus saith to him: "If thou believest,
24 everything can come to pass to thee." And in the same hour the
father of the lad cried out and said: "I believe, my Lord; help my
25 lack!" When Jesus saw that some were running that were coming
near, he rebuked that spirit and said to it: "Thee I command, deaf
spirit that speakest not, go forth from him and no more enter into
26 him." And he cried out and convulsed him much and went forth
from him, and he became as one dead; and many supposed that he
27 had died. But Jesus took him by his hand and raised him up and
28 delivered him to his father. And when he entered the house his
disciples asked him between themselves and him "Wherefore
29 cannot we cast it out?" He saith to them: "This kind by nothing
goeth forth save by fasting and by prayer."

30 And when they went forth from thence they were journeying
through Galilee, and he was not willing that any one should be
31 aware of him. And he was teaching his disciples and saying to them
"The Son of Man is delivered into the hands of men, and they will
kill him; and what *time* they have killed him, on the third day he
32 will rise." And they were not recognising aught that he said to
33 them and were afraid to ask him. And he came to Kapharnahum,
and when he entered his house he was asking them "What were ye
34 speaking one with another in the way?" And they were silent, for
35 these *men* were thinking who should be greatest. And he sat and
called his Twelve, and said to them: "He that willeth to be first
36 shall be last of every one and servant of every one." And he had

---

23, 24] *Cf A* 20 'To him whose son was infirm he said: Believe, and thy son will live. [24]He saith to him: I believe, my Lord; help my little faith! And by his faith his boy was made whole.' *Cf also* 'He saith to the man: "He that believeth—all things are possible to him;" and he saith to them (the disciples): "Because of your little faith"' *E*[160] 25 'I say to thee, unclean spirit, deaf and dumb, go out *and* depart from him, and enter no more into him' *E*[160f.]

ܗܘܐ ܛܠܝܐ ܚܕ ܘܐܘܩܡܗ ܒܡܨܥܬܗܘܢ܆ ܘܓܦܗ ܘܐܡܪ ܠܗܘܢ S
[37]ܕܟܠ ܕܢܩܒܠ ܐܝܟ ܛܠܝܐ ܗܢܐ ܒܫܡܝ ܠܝ ܗܘ ܡܩܒܠ † ܠܐ
ܗܘܐ ܠܝ ܡܩܒܠ. ܐܠܐ ܠܡܢ ܕܫܕܪܢܝ. [38]ܥܢܐ ܝܘܚܢܢ ܘܐܡܪ ܠܗ
ܪܒܢ ܚܙܝܢ ܚܕ ܕܡܦܩ ܫܐܕ̈ܐ ܒܫܡܟ ܘܟܠܝܢܝܗܝ، ܥܠ ܕܠܐ ܐܬܐ
ܒܬܪܢ܆ [39]ܗܘ ܕܝܢ ܐܡܪ ܠܗܘܢ܆ ܠܐ ܬܟܠܘܢܝܗܝ، ܠܝܬ ܓܝܪ ܐܢܫ
ܕܥܒܕ ܚܝܠܐ ܒܫܡܝ ܘܡܫܟܚ ܕܢܐܡܪ ܥܠܝ ܕܒܝܫ [40]ܡܢ ܕܠܐ ܗܘܐ
ܓܝܪ ܠܘܩܒܠܢ ܚܠܦܝܢ ܗܘ [41]ܟܠ ܕܢܫܩܝܟܘܢ܆ ܓܝܪ ܟܣܐ ܕܡܝ̈ܐ
ܒܫܡܐ ܕܕܡܫܝܚܐ ܐܢܬܘܢ܆ ܐܡܝܢ ܐܡܪ ܐܢܐ ܠܟܘܢ܆ ܕܠܐ
ܐܘܒܕ ܐܓܪܗ [42]ܘܟܠ ܕܢܟܫܠ ܠܚܕ ܡܢ ܗܠܝܢ ⌜ܙܥܘ̈ܪܐ⌝ ܕܡܗܝܡܢܝܢ
ܒܝ ܦܩܚ ܗܘܐ ܠܗ ܐܠܘ ܪܚܝܐ ܕܚܡܪܐ ܒܨܘܪܗ
ܘܡܬܛܒܥ ܒܝܡܐ [43]ܘܐܢ ܐܝܕܟ ܗܝ ܡܟܫܠܐ ܠܟ ܦܣܘܩܝܗ
ܡܛܠ ܦܩܚ ܠܟ ܓܝܪ ܕܟܕ ܐܝܬ ܠܟ ܚܕܐ ܐܝܕܐ ܬܥܘܠ ܠܚܝܐ
ܘܠܐ ܟܕ ܐܝܬ ܠܟ ܬܪ̈ܬܝܢ ܐܝܕܝܢ ܬܐܙܠ ܠܓܗܢܐ ܕܠܐ ܕܥܟܐ
[45]ܘܐܢ ܪܓܠܟ ܡܟܫܠܐ ܠܟ ܦܣܘܩ ܫܕܝܗ ܡܛܠ ܦܩܚ ܠܟ ܓܝܪ
ܕܟܕ ܚܓܝܣ ܐܢܬ ܬܥܘܠ ܠܚܝܐ ܘܠܐ ܟܕ ܐܝܬ ܠܟ ܬܪ̈ܬܝܢ
ܪ̈ܓܠܝܢ ܬܐܙܠ ܠܓܗܢܐ [47]ܘܐܢ ܥܝܢܟ ܡܟܫܠܐ ܠܟ ܚܨܝܗ ܡܛܠ
ܦܩܚ ܠܟ ܓܝܪ ܕܟܕ ܚܕܐ ܗܝ ܠܟ ܥܝܢܐ. ܬܥܘܠ ܠܡܠܟܘܬܐ
ܕܐܠܗܐ. ܘܠܐ ܟܕ ܐܝܬ ܠܟ ܬܪ̈ܬܝܢ ܥܝܢܝܢ ܬܐܙܠ ܠܓܗܢܐ
[48]ܐܬܪ ܕܠܐ ܬܘܠܥܬܗܘܢ ܡܝܬܐ ܘܠܐ ܢܘܪܗܘܢ ܕܥܟܐ [49]ܟܠ
ܐܢܫ ܓܝܪ ܒܢܘܪܐ ܢܬܡܠܚ. [50]ܛܒܐ ܗܝ ܡܠܚܐ ܐܢ ܕܝܢ ܡܠܚܐ
ܠܐ ܬܦܟܪ ܒܡܢܐ ܢܬܒܣܡ ܬܗܘܐ ܠܟܘܢ ܡܠܚܐ ܘܐܫܬܝܢܘ
ܚܕ ܥܡ ܚܕ. [1]ܘܩܡ ܡܢ ܬܡܢ ܘܐܬܐ ܠܬܚܘܡܐ ܕܝܗܘܕ ܠܥܒܪܐ
ܕܝܘܪܕܢ ܘܐܙܠ ܬܘܒ ܠܘܬܗ ܟܢܫܐ ܘܐܝܟ ܕܡܥܕ ܗܘܐ ܡܥܕܐ
ܘܡܠܦ ܗܘܐ ܠܗܘܢ܆ [2]ܘܫܐܠܝܢ ܗܘܘ ܠܗ ܟܕ ܡܢܣܝܢ ܠܗ ܕܐܢ
ܫܠܝܛ ܠܓܒܪܐ ܕܢܫܒܘܩ ܐܢܬܬܗ [3]ܘܥܢܐ ܘܐܡܪ ܠܗܘܢ ܡܘܫܐ
⌜ܡܢܐ ܦܩܕܟܘܢ܀ [4]ܐܡܪܝܢ ܠܗ ܡܘܫܐ ܐܦܣ ܠܢ ܕܢܟܬܘܒ ܟܬܒܐ
ܕܫܘܒܩܢܐ ܘܢܫܒܘܩ ܠܗ ܘܢܫܪܝܗ. [5]ܥܢܐ ܝܫܘܥ ܘܐܡܪ ܠܗܘܢ

45 & 47 ܬܐܙܠ] *S (sic), but the* ܬ *is rather lengthened out in ver.* 45

taken a certain lad and made him stand among them, and he looked S
37 at him and said to them "Every one that shall receive as *it were*
this lad in my name, me it is he receiveth [†] not me he receiveth,
38 but him that sent me." John answered and said to him: "Rabban,
we saw one casting out devils in thy name, and we forbad him on *the*
39 *ground* that he cometh not after us." But he saith to them: "Forbid
him not, for there is no one that doeth aught in my name and can
40 say against me what *is* evil; for he that is not against us is with us.
41 For every one that shall give you to drink a cup of water in the
name that ye are the Messiah's—amen, I say to you that he hath
42 not lost his reward. And every one that shall offend one of these
little ones that believe in me, it were profitable for him if an ass's
millstone were to be laid about his neck and he were sunk in the sea.
43 And if thy hand therefore offend thee, cut it off from thee; for it
is profitable for thee that having one hand thou shouldest enter
life, and not having two hands go to the fire that is not quenched.
45 And if thy foot offend thee, cut *it* off *and* throw it from thee; for it
is profitable for thee that being halt thou shouldest enter life, and
47 not having two feet go to Gehenna. If thine eye offend thee pluck
it out from thee; for it is profitable for thee that having one eye
thou shouldest enter the kingdom of God, and not having two eyes
48 go to Gehenna, where neither their worm dieth nor is their fire
49, 50 quenched. For every one with fire shall be salted. Excellent is salt;
but if the salt be not right, wherewith shall one season it? Have
X 1 for yourselves salt, and be at peace one with another." And he
arose from thence, and came to the border of Judaea to the other
side of the Jordan, and there went again unto him a multitude, and
2 as he was accustomed he was healing and teaching them. And they
were asking him, tempting him, if it be lawful for a man that he
3 should leave his wife? And he answered and said to them: "Moses
4 —what hath he commanded you?" They say to him: "Moses permitted us that we should write a bill of remission and give *it* her and
5 dismiss her." Jesus answered and said to them: "Moses because

ܡܘܫܐ ܡܛܠ ܩܫܝܘܬ ܠܒܟܘܢ ܟܬܒ ܠܟܘܢ ܦܘܩܕܢܐ ܗܢܐ [6]ܡܢ *S*
ܒܪܝܬ ܕܝܢ ܕܒܪܐ ܘܥܒܕܬܐ ܥܒܕ ܐܢܘܢ ܐܠܗܐ [7]ܡܛܠ ܗܢܐ
ܢܫܒܘܩ ܓܒܪܐ ܠܐܒܘܗܝ ܘܠܐܡܗ [8]ܘܢܗܘܘܢ ܬܪܝܗܘܢ ܚܕ
ܒܣܪ. ܡܛܠ ܠܐ ܗܘܘ ܬܪܝܢ ܐܠܐ ܚܕ ܐܢܘܢ ܒܣܪ. [9]ܡܕܡ
ܕܐܠܗܐ ܙܘܓ ܒܪ ܐܢܫ ܠܐ ܢܦܪܘܫ. [10]ܟܕ ܥܠ ܠܒܝܬܐ
ܬܘܒ ܫܐܠܘܗܝ ܬܠܡܝܕܘܗܝ ܥܠ ܗܕܐ. [11]ܐܡܪ ܠܗܘܢ ܐܝܢܐ
ܐܢܬܬܐ ܕܫܒܩܐ ܒܥܠܗ ܘܗܘܝܐ ܠܐܚܪܢܐ ܓܝܪ ܓܒܪܐ. [12]ܘܐܝܢܐ
ܓܒܪܐ ܕܫܒܩ ܐܢܬܬܗ ܘܢܣܒ ܐܚܪܬܐ ܓܝܪ ܠܓܒܪ :o:

[13]ܘܩܪܒܘ ܠܗ ܛܠܝܐ ܕܢܣܝܡ ܐܝܕܗ ܥܠܝܗܘܢ. ܘܟܐܘ ܒܗܘܢ
ܬܠܡܝܕܘܗܝ ܒܗܘܢ ܕܡܩܪܒܝܢ ܗܘܘ ܠܗܘܢ. [14]ܟܕ ܚܙܐ ܝܫܘܥ
ܐܬܟܐܫ ܠܗ ܘܟܐܐ ܒܗܘܢ ܘܐܡܪ ܠܗܘܢ ܫܒܘܩܘ ܛܠܝܐ
ܐܬܝܢ ܠܘܬܝ, ܘܠܐ ܬܟܠܘܢ ܐܢܘܢ ܕܐܝܠܝܢ ܓܝܪ ܕܐܟܘܬܗܘܢ ܗܠܝܢ
ܐܢܘܢ ܕܝܠܗܘܢ ܗܝ ܡܠܟܘܬܐ ܕܐܠܗܐ. [15]ܐܡܝܢ ܐܡܪܢܐ
ܠܟܘܢ ܕܟܠ ܕܠܐ ܢܩܒܠ ܡܠܟܘܬܐ ܕܐܠܗܐ ܐܝܟ ܛܠܝܐ ܠܐ
ܢܥܘܠ ܠܗ. [16]ܘܩܪܐ ܐܢܘܢ ܘܣܡ ܐܝܕܗ ܥܠܝܗܘܢ ܘܡܒܪܟ ܗܘܐ
ܠܗܘܢ ·܀·܀·

[17]ܟܕ ܪܕܐ ܒܐܘܪܚܐ ܪܗܛ ܚܕ ܢܦܠ ܥܠ ܒܘܪܟܘܗܝ, ܘܐܡܪ ܠܗ
§A392 ܡܠܦܢܐ ܛܒܐ [§]ܡܢܐ ܐܥܒܕ ܕܐܪܬ ܚܝܐ ܕܠܥܠܡ. [18]ܐܡܪ ܠܗ
¶A ܝܫܘܥ[¶] ܡܢܐ ܩܪܐ ܐܢܬ ܠܝ ܛܒܐ ܠܝܬ ܛܒܐ ܐܠܐ ܐܢ ܚܕ
§A ܐܠܗܐ [19]ܦܘܩܕܢܐ ܕܝܢ ܝܕܥ ܐܢܬ. ܠܐ ܬܩܛܘܠ [§]ܠܐ ܬܓܘܪ ܠܐ
ܬܓܢܘܒ ܠܐ ܬܣܗܕ ܣܗܕܘܬܐ ܕܟܕܒܘܬܐ ܝܩܪ ܠܐܒܘܟ ܘܠܐܡܟ
[20]ܗܢܐ ܘܐܡܪ ܠܗ ܡܠܦܢܐ ܗܠܝܢ ܥܒܕܬ ܐܢܝܢ ܗܐ ܡܢ ܕܛܠܝܐ
ܐܢܐ. [21]ܘܝܫܘܥ ܚܪ ܒܗ ܡܚܒܒܐܝܬ ܘܐܡܪ ܠܗ ܚܕܐ ܚܣܝܪܐ ܠܟ

---

18 ܝܫܘܥ] ܡܪܢ *A* 21 ܘܝܫܘܥ] *S*^vid (*sic*); ܗܘ ܕܝܢ *A* ܡܚܒܒܐܝܬ] *S* (*sic*); *pr.* ܝܫܘܥ *A*

19—23, 25 *appear in A* 392 *thus*:—

Mk x 19b, Mt xix 18b, 19 ܠܐ ܬܓܘܪ ܘܠܐ ܬܓܢܘܒ. ܘܝܩܪ ܠܐܒܘܟ ܘܠܐܡܟ Mt xix 19 ܘܪܚܡ
ܠܩܪܝܒܟ ܐܝܟ ܢܦܫܟ. [20]ܐܡܪ ܠܗ ܗܘ ܓܒܪܐ Mk x 20b ܗܠܝܢ ܥܒܕܬ ܐܢܝܢ ܗܐ
ܡܢ ܕܛܠܝܐ ܐܢܐ. Mt xix 20b ܐܠܐ ܡܢܐ ܚܣܝܪ ܐܢܐ. [21]Mk x 21 ܗܘ ܕܝܢ ܚܪ ܒܗ ܝܫܘܥ
ܡܚܒܒܐܝܬ ܘܐܡܪ ܠܗ. ܚܕܐ ܚܣܝܪܐ ܠܟ. Mt xix 21 ܐܢ ܨܒܐ ܐܢܬ ܓܡܝܪܐ

6 of the hardness of your heart permitted you this commandment, but *S*
7 from the beginning male and female God made them. Therefore
8 shall a man leave his father and his mother, and the two of them
shall become one flesh. Then they have become not two, but are
9 one flesh; that which God therefore hath coupled let not man
10 separate." When he entered the house again his disciples asked
11 him about this. He saith to them: "That woman which leaveth
her husband and becometh *the wife* of another doth indeed commit
12 adultery, and that man which leaveth his wife and taketh another
doth indeed commit adultery."

13 And they brought near to him children, that he should lay his
hand upon them; and his disciples rebuked those that were bringing
14 them near. When Jesus saw, it displeased him, and he rebuked
them and said to them: "Suffer the children to come unto me, and
forbid them not; for they that are *such* as these, theirs is the
15 kingdom of God. Amen, I say to you Every one that shall not
16 receive the kingdom of God as a child shall not enter it." And he
called them and laid his hands upon them and was blessing them.

17 While journeying in the way, a certain one ran *and* fell on his
knees and said to him: "Good teacher, §what shall I do that I may §*A*392
18 inherit life eternal?" Jesus saith to him:¶ "Why callest thou me ¶*A*
19 Good? There is none good save one,—God. Now the commandments
thou knowest, 'Thou shalt not kill,' §'Thou shalt not commit adultery,' §*A*
'Thou shalt not thieve,' 'Thou shalt not bear false witness,' 'Honour
20 thy father and thy mother.'" He answered and said to him:
"Teacher, these—I have done them, lo, from when I was a child."
21 [And Jesus] looked on him lovingly and said to him: "One thing is

---

18 Jesus] Our Lord *A* 21 And Jesus looked] S^{vid} (*sic*); Then did Jesus look *A* lovingly] *S* (*sic*) *A* $E^{171, 172, 173}$ 19—23, 25 *appear in A* 392 *thus*:—[Mk x 19b / Mt xix 18b, 19] Thou shalt not commit adultery and Thou shalt not thieve and Honour thy father and thy mother [Mt xix 19] *and Love thy neighbour as thyself.* [20] *That man saith to him* [Mk x 20b] These—I have done them, lo, from when I was a child, [Mt xix 20b] *but what do I lack?* [Mk x 21] Then Jesus looked upon him lovingly and said to him: One thing is lacking to thee;

ܙܠ ܙܒܢ ܟܠ ܡܕܡ ܕܐܝܬ ܠܟ ܘܗܒ ܠܡܣܟܢܐ ܘܬܗܘܐ ܠܟ *S*
ܣܝܡܬܐ ܒܫܡܝܐ ܘܫܩܘܠ ܙܩܝܦܟ ܘܬܐ ܒܬܪܝ. [22]ܘܟܡܪܬ ܠܗ
ܥܠ ܗܕܐ ܡܠܬܐ. ܘܐܙܠ ܟܕ ܟܪܝܐ ܠܗ ܡܛܠ ܕܢܟܣܐ ܣܓܝܐܐ
ܐܝܬ ܗܘܘ ܠܗ. [23]ܘܚܪ ܝܫܘܥ ܒܬܠܡܝܕܘܗܝ، ܘܐܡܪ ܟܡܐ ܥܛܠܐ
ܠܐܝܠܝܢ ܕܬܟܝܠܝܢ ܥܠ ܢܟܣܝܗܘܢ ܕܢܥܠܘܢ ܠܡܠܟܘܬܗ ܕܐܠܗܐ.¶ ¶*A*
[24]ܘܬܠܡܝܕܘܗܝ، ܡܬܕܡܪܝܢ ܗܘܘ ܥܠ ܡܠܘܗܝ، ܬܘܒ ܥܢܐ ܝܫܘܥ
ܘܐܡܪ ܠܗܘܢ ܒܢܝ ܟܡܐ ܥܛܠܐ ܠܐܝܠܝܢ ܕܬܟܝܠܝܢ ܥܠ ܢܟܣܝܗܘܢ
ܕܢܥܠܘܢ ܠܡܠܟܘܬܗ ܕܐܠܗܐ. [25]§ܦܫܝܩ ܗܘ ܓܝܪ ܠܓܡܠܐ ܠܡܥܠ §*A*
ܒܚܪܘܪܐ ܕܡܚܛܐ ܐܘ ܠܥܬܝܪܐ ܠܡܠܟܘܬܐ ܕܫܡܝܐ¶ [26]ܗܢܘܢ ¶*A*
ܕܝܢ ܬܘܪܐܝܬ ܡܬܕܡܪܝܢ ܗܘܘ ܒܢܦܫܗܘܢ ܡܢܘ ܟܝ ܡܫܟܚ
ܠܡܚܐ. [27]ܚܪ ܒܗܘܢ ܝܫܘܥ ܘܐܡܪ ܠܗܘܢ ܗܕܐ ܠܘܬ ܒܢܝ
ܐܢܫܐ ܠܐ ܡܫܟܚܐ ܐܠܐ ܡܢ ܠܘܬ ܐܠܗܐ. ܠܘܬ ܐܠܗܐ ܕܝܢ
ܟܘܠ ܡܕܡ ܡܫܟܚ. [28]ܐܡܪ ܠܗ ܟܐܦܐ ܗܐ ܐܚܢܢ ܫܒܩܢ
ܟܠܡܕܡ ܘܐܬܝܢ ܒܬܪܟ. [29]ܥܢܐ ܝܫܘܥ ܘܐܡܪ ܐܡܝܢ ܐܡܪܢܐ
ܠܟܘܢ ܕܟܠ ܐܢܫ ܕܢܫܒܘܩ ܒܝܬܐ ܐܘ ܐܚ̈ܐ ܐܘ ܐܚܘܬܐ ܐܘ
ܐܡܐ ܐܘ ܐܒܐ ܐܘ ܒܢܝܐ ܐܘ ܩܘܪ̈ܝܐ ܡܛܠܬܝ، ܘܡܛܠ
ܣܒܪܬܝ، [30]ܐܠܐ ܢܩܒܠ ܚܕ ܒܡܐܐ ܒܙܒܢܐ ܗܢܐ ܒܬܐ ܘܐܚ̈ܐ
ܘܐܚܘܬܐ ܘܐܡܗܬܐ ܘܒܢܝܐ ܘܩܘܪܝܐ ܥܡ ܪܕܘܦܝܐ ܘܒܥܠܡܐ
ܕܐܬܐ ܢܐܪܬ ܚܝܐ ܕܠܥܠܡ. [31]ܣܓܝܐܐ ܓܝܪ ܩܕܡܝܐ ܕܢܗܘܘܢ
ܐܚܪܝܐ ܘܐܚܪܝܐ ܕܢܗܘܘܢ ܩܕܡ̈ܝܐ ܀

ܠܡܣܟܢܐ. Mk x 21b Mt xix 21 ܙܠ ܙܒܢ ܟܠ ܡܕܡ ܕܐܝܬ ܠܟ ܘܗܒ ܠܡܣ̈ܟܢܐ. Mk x 21c ܘܫܩܘܠ
ܙܩܝܦܟ ܘܬܐ ܒܬܪܝ. ܘܗܘ ܟܪܝܐ ܒܗ ܥܒܕ Mk x 22 ܟܪܝܬ ܠܗ ܥܠ. ܘܐܙܠ
ܠܒܝܬܗ ܒܗ ܩܝܡܐ· Mt xix 22b ܡܛܠ ܕܩܢܝܢܐ ܣܓܝܐܐ ܒܢܟܣܐ ܠܗ. ܘܐܡܪ ܝܫܘܥ
Mk x 23 ܚܙܘ ܟܡܐ ܥܛܠܐ ܠܐܝܠܝܢ ܕܬܟܝܠܝܢ ܥܠ ܢܟܣܝܗܘܢ ܕܢܥܠܘܢ ܠܡܠܟܘܬ
(Mt) ܥܬܝܪܐ. ܘܬܘܒ ܐܡܪ. Mk x 25 ܦܫܝܩ ܓܝܪ ܕܬܥܘܠ ܓܡܠܐ ܒܚܪܘܪܐ
ܕܡܚܛܐ ܐܘ ܥܬܝܪܐ ܠܡܠܟܘܬܗ ܕܐܠܗܐ. (*A*[b] ܦܫܝܩ ܕܢܥܘܠ ܓܡܠܐ)

lacking to thee; go, sell everything that thou hast and give to the *S*
poor, and thou shalt have treasure in heaven, and take up thy cross
22 and come after me." And it pained him at this word and he went
23 away grieved, because he had much wealth. And Jesus looked upon
his disciples and said: "How difficult for them which trust in their
24 wealth to enter the kingdom of God!" ¶ And his disciples were ¶*A*
wondering at his words. Again Jesus answered and said to them:
"My sons, how difficult for them which trust in their wealth to enter
25 the kingdom of God!" § For it is easier for a camel to enter through §*A*
the eye of a needle than a rich man into the kingdom of heaven." ¶ ¶*A*
26 Now they were the more wondering in themselves *saying:* "Who
27 then can live?" Jesus looked upon them, and said to them: "This
with men is not possible save from God; but with God everything
28 is possible." Kepha saith to him: "Lo, we have left everything, and
29 have come after thee." Jesus answered and said: "Amen, I say to
you Every man that shall leave house or brothers or sisters or
mother or father or sons or fields for my sake and for my gospel's—
30 but he shall receive an hundredfold in this time, houses and brothers
and sisters and mother and sons and fields, with persecution, and in
31 the world to come he shall inherit life eternal. For *there are* many
first that shall be last, and last that shall be first."

[Mt xix 21] *if thou dost wish to become a perfect man,* [Mk x 21b Mt xix 21] go, sell everything that thou hast and give to the poor, [Mk x 21c] and take up thy Cross and come after me. *And that man, when he heard,* [Mk x 22] it grieved him much and he went to his house sorry, [Mt xix 22b] *because he was rich in wealth exceedingly. And Jesus said* [Mk x 23] See, how difficult for them which trust in their wealth to enter the kingdom of *heaven*! *And again he said* [Mk x 25] Easier peradventure for a she-camel to enter through the eye of a needle than a rich man into the kingdom of God.

(*A*[b] *omits* 'peradventure' *and reads* 'camel' *instead of* 'she-camel': *the word translated* 'peradventure' *is literally* 'quickly,' *i.e.* τάχα)

[32]ܘܟܕ ܣܠܩܝܢ ܗܘܘ ܒܐܘܪܚܐ ܠܐܘܪܫܠܡ. ܘܗܘ ܝܫܘܥ ܐܙܠ ܗܘܐ S
ܩܕܡܝܗܘܢ ܘܡܬܕܡܪܝܢ ܗܘܘ ܐܝܠܝܢ ܕܒܬܪܗ ܗܘܘ ܟܕ ܕܚܠܝܢ ܘܩܪܒ
ܠܬܪܥܣܪܬܗ ܘܫܪܝ, ܗܘܐ ܕܢܐܡܪ ܠܗܘܢ ܡܕܡ ܕܥܬܝܕ ܠܗ.
[33]ܕܗܐ ܣܠܩܝܢ ܐܢܚܢ ܠܐܘܪܫܠܡ ܘܒܪܗ ܕܐܢܫܐ ܡܫܬܠܡ ܠܪ̈ܒܝ
ܟܗܢܐ ܘܠܣܦܪ̈ܐ ܘܢܚܝܒܘܢܝܗ ܠܡܘܬܐ. ܘܢܫܠܡܘܢܝܗ ܠܥܡܡܐ
[34]ܘܢܬܒܙܚܘܢ ܒܗ ܘܢܢܓܕܘܢܝܗ ܘܢܪܩܘܢ ܒܐܦܘܗܝ, ܘܢܙܩܦܘܢܝܗ,
ܘܒܝܘܡܐ ܕܬܠܬܐ ܢܩܘܡ ○
[35]ܘܩܪܒܘ ܠܘܬܗ ܝܥܩܘܒ ܘܝܘܚܢܢ ܒܢܝ ܙܒܕܝ, ܘܐܡܪܝܢ ܠܗ ܪܒܢ
ܨܒܝܢ ܐܢܚܢ ܕܟܠ ܕܢܫܐܠܟ ܬܥܒܕ ܠܢ [36]ܐܡܪ ܠܗܘܢ ܡܢܐ
ܨܒܝܢ ܐܢܬܘܢ ܕܐܥܒܕ ܠܟܘܢ [37]ܐܡܪܝܢ ܠܗ ܗܒ ܠܢ ܢܬܒ ܡܢ
ܝܡܝܢܟ ܘܡܢ ܣܡܠܟ ܒܫܘܒܚܟ. [38]ܗܢܐ ܝܫܘܥ ܘܐܡܪ ܠܗܘܢ
ܠܐ ܝܕܥܝܢ ܐܢܬܘܢ ܡܢܐ ܫܐܠܝܢ ܐܢܬܘܢ ܡܫܟܚܝܢ ܐܢܬܘܢ
ܬܫܬܘܢ ܟܣܐ ܕܐܢܐ ܫܬܐ. ܐܘ ܡܥܡܘܕܝܘܬܐ ܥܡܕܝܢ
ܐܢܬܘܢ [39]ܐܡܪܝܢ ܠܗ ܡܫܟܚܝܢ ܐܢܚܢ ܐܡܪ ܠܗܘܢ ܝܫܘܥ
ܕܬܫܬܘܢ ܟܣܐ ܕܫܬܐ ܐܢܐ ܡܫܟܚܝܢ ܐܢܬܘܢ ܘܕܬܥܡܕܘܢ
ܡܥܡܘܕܝܘܬܐ ܕܥܡܕ ܐܢܐ ܡܫܟܚܝܢ ܐܢܬܘܢ : [40]ܕܬܬܒܘܢ ܕܝܢ
ܡܢ ܝܡܝܢܝ ܐܘ ܡܢ ܣܡܠܝ ܗܕܐ ܠܐ ܗܘܬ ܕܝܠܝ ܠܡܬܠ ܠܐܚܪܢ
ܕܡ ܡܛܝܒܐ [41]ܘܟܕ ܫܡܥܘ ܥܣܪܐ ܫܪܝܘ ܪ̈ܛܢܝܢ ܥܠ ܝܥܩܘܒ ܘܥܠ
ܝܘܚܢܢ [42]ܘܩܪܐ ܐܢܘܢ ܘܐܡܪ ܠܗܘܢ. ܝܕܥܝܢ ܐܢܬܘܢ ܕܪ̈ܫܝܗܘܢ
ܕܥܡ̈ܡܐ ܡܪ̈ܝܗܘܢ ܐܢܘܢ [43]ܠܐ ܗܟܢܐ ܢܗܘܐ ܒܝܢ̈ܬܟܘܢ
ܐܠܐ ܡܢ ܕܨܒܐ ܒܟܘܢ ܕܢܗܘܐ ܪܒܐ ܢܗܘܐ ܠܟܘܢ ܡܫܡܫܢܐ
[44]ܘܐܝܢܐ ܡܢܟܘܢ ܕܨܒܐ ܕܢܗܘܐ ܩܕܡܝܐ ܢܗܘܐ ܥܒܕܐ ܕܟܠ
ܐܢܫ. [45]ܐܝܟܢܐ ܕܒܪܗ ܕܐܢܫܐ ܠܐ ܐܬܐ ܕܢܫܬܡܫ ܐܠܐ ܕܢܫܡܫ
ܘܕܢܬܠ ܢܦܫܗ ܦܘܪܩܢܐ ܚܠܦ ܣܓ̈ܝܐܐ ܀

35 ܬܥܒܕ] *S (sic)* 40 ܠܐܚܪܢ] *S (sic), much squeezed up at the end of a line. The word is probably meant for* ܠܐܚܪ̈ܢܝܢ *or* ܠܐܚܪ̈ܢܐ *(i.e. ἄλλοις), since the abs. sing. in S is elsewhere always spelt* ܐܚܪܢ *not* ܐܚܪܢ*, with the somewhat doubtful exception of* Lk vii 20

32 And while they were going up in the way to Jerusalem, and *S*
Jesus himself was going before them, they that were with him were
wondering, being afraid. And he took his Twelve and had begun to
33 say to them that which was about to *befal* him, *saying* "Lo, we go
up to Jerusalem, and the Son of Man is to be delivered up to
the chief priests and to the scribes, and they will condemn him to
34 death, and will deliver him up to the peoples, and they will make
sport of him and scourge him and spit in his face and kill him, and
on the third day he will rise."

35 And there drew near unto him James and John the sons of
Zebedee, and they say to him: "Rabbi, we would that all that we
36 shall ask thee thou wilt do for us." He saith to them: "What would
37 ye that I should do for you?" They say to him: "Give us to sit on
38 thy right and on thy left in thy glory." Jesus answered and said
to them: "Ye know not what ye are asking. Are ye able to drink
39 the cup that I drink, or with the baptism are ye baptized?" They
say to him: "We are able." Jesus saith to them: "That ye should
drink the cup that I drink ye are able, and that ye should be
baptized with the baptism wherewith I am baptized ye are able;
40 but that ye should sit on my right or on my left, this is not mine
41 to give, but for †others† it is made ready." And when the Ten
heard, they began murmuring against James and against John.
42 And he called them and said to them: "Ye know that the chiefs
43 of the peoples are their lords. Not so shall it be among you, but
he that would with you be the great one shall be to you a servant,
44 and he of you which would be first shall be the slave of every one;
45 even as the Son of Man came not to be served but to serve, and
to give his life *to be* a redemption for many."

---

36 He saith....do for you?] 'He saith to them: I will do *it* for you' *E*[178] 40 but for others] *The word corresponding to* 'other' *is never found elsewhere so spelt in S; it seems to be meant for the plural. The word for* 'but' *corresponds to* δέ, *not* ἀλλά

46 ܘܐܬܐ ܠܐܝܪܝܚܘ ܘܟܕ ܢܦܩ ܡܢ ܐܝܪܝܚܘ ܗܘ ܘܬܠܡ̈ܝܕܘܗܝ، S
ܘܟܢܫܐ ܣܓܝܐܐ. ܘܦܠܛܝ ܒܪ ܛܝܡܝ ܣܡܝܐ ܝܬܒ ܗܘܐ ܥܠ
ܐܘܪܚܐ ܘܚܕܪ 47 ܘܟܕ ܫܡܥ ܕܝܫܘܥ ܗܘ ܢܨܪܝܐ. ܫܪܝ ܠܡܩܥܐ
ܘܠܡܐܡܪ ܒܪܗ ܕܕܘܝܕ ܐܬܪܚܡ ܥܠܝ 48 ܘܟܐܘ ܒܗ ܣ̈ܓܝܐܐ
ܕܢܫܬܘܩ ܘܬܘܒ ܐܘܣܦ ܘܩܥܐ ܒܪܗ ܕܕܘܝܕ ܐܬܪܚܡ ܥܠܝ 49 ܘܩܡ
ܝܫܘܥ ܘܐܡܪ ܕܢܩܪܘܢܝܗܝ ܘܩܪܘܗܝ، ܠܣܡܝܐ ܘܐܡܪ̈ܝܢ ܠܗ ܠܐ
ܬܕܚܠ ܩܘܡ ܩܪܐ ܠܟ 50 ܘܩܡ ܫܕܐ ܡܐܢ̈ܘܗܝ، ܘܐܬܐ ܠܘܬ
ܝܫܘܥ 51 ܥܢܐ ܝܫܘܥ ܘܐܡܪ ܠܗ ܡܢܐ ܨܒܐ ܐܢܬ ܐܥܒܕ ܠܟ
ܐܡܪ ܠܗ ܣܡܝܐ ܪܒܘܠܝ ܕܐܚܙܐ 52 ܐܡܪ ܠܗ ܙܠ ܗܝܡܢܘܬܟ
ܐܚܝܬܟ ܘܒܗ ܒܫܥܬܐ ܐܬܦܬܚ ܥܝܢ̈ܘܗܝ، ܘܐܬܐ ܗܘܐ ܒܬܪܗ
ܒܐܘܪܚܐ 1 ܘܟܕ ܩܪܒܘ ܠܐܘܪܫܠܡ ܠܒܝܬ ܦܐܓܐ ܠܒܝܬ ܥܢܝܐ ܠܘܬ
ܠܛܘܪ ܕܙܝ̈ܬܐ ܫܕܪ ܬܪܝܢ ܡܢ ܬܠܡܝܕܘܗܝ، 2 ܘܐܡܪ ܙܠܘ ܠܩܪܝܬܐ ܗܝ
ܕܠܩܘܒܠܟܘܢ؛ ܘܒܗ ܒܫܥܬܐ ܗܟܐ ܕܥܠܝܢ ܐܢܬܘܢ ܠܗ ܬܫܟܚܘܢ
ܥܝܠܐ ܟܕ ܐܣܝܪ ܕܐܢܫ ܡܢ ܒܢܝ ܐܢܫܐ ܠܐ ܪܟܒܗ. ܫܪܘ
†ܘܐܝܬܘܗܝ،† 3 ܘܐܢ ܐܢܫ ܢܐܡܪ ܠܟܘܢ ܡܕܡ ܐܡܪܘ ܠܗ
ܕܠܡܪܗ ܡܬܒܥܐ ܘܡܚܕܐ ܡܫܕܪ ܠܗ ܠܟܐ. 4 ܘܐܙܠܘ ܘܐܫܟܚܘ
ܥܝܠܐ ܟܕ ܐܣܝܪ ܥܠ ܬܪܥܐ ܕܕܪܬܐ ܒܫܘܩܐ ܘܟܕ ܫܪܝܢ ܠܗ
5 ܐܡܪ̈ܝܢ ܡܢ ܐܢܫܐ ܕܩܝܡܝܢ ܬܡܢ ܡܢܐ ܥܒܕܝܢ ܐܢܬܘܢ ܘܫܪ̈ܝܢ
ܐܢܬܘܢ ܥܝܠܐ 6 ܘܗܢܘܢ ܐܡܪܘ ܠܗܘܢ ܐܝܟܢܐ ܕܐܡܪ ܠܗܘܢ
ܝܫܘܥ 7 ܘܐܝܬܝܘܗܝ، ܠܥܝܠܐ ܠܘܬ ܝܫܘܥ ܘܐܪܡܝܘ ܡܪ̈ܛܘܛܝܗܘܢ
ܘܐܪܟܒ ܥܠܘܗܝ، 8 ܘܣܓܝܐܐ ܡܫܘܝܢ ܗܘܘ ܡܪ̈ܛܘܛܝܗܘܢ ܒܐܘܪܚܐ
9 ܘܐܝܠܝܢ ܕܐܙܠܝܢ ܗܘܘ ܩܕܡܘܗܝ، ܘܕܐܬܝܢ ܒܬܪܗ ܩܥܝܢ ܗܘܘ
ܘܐܡܪ̈ܝܢ ܐܘܫܥܢܐ ܒܪܝܟ ܗܘ ܕܐܬܐ ܒܫܡܗ ܕܡܪܝܐ 10 ܒܪܝܟܐ
ܗܝ، ܡܠܟܘܬܐ ܕܐܬܝܐ ܕܐܒܘܢ ܕܘܝܕ ܫܠܡܐ ܒܡܪܘܡܐ 11 ܘܥܠ
ܠܐܘܪܫܠܡ ܘܥܠ ܠܗܝܟܠܐ ܘܚܙܐ ܟܠ ܡܕܡ. ܟܕ ܗܘܐ ܕܝܢ
ܪܡܫܐ ܢܦܩ ܗܘܐ ܠܒܝܬ ܥܢܝܐ ܥܡ ܬܪ̈ܥܣܪ. ∴

2 ܕܠܩܘܒܠܟܘܢ] S (*sic*)   ܘܐܝܬܘܗܝ] ܘܐܝܬܝܘܗܝ S (*sic*)
3 ܕܠܡܪܗ] S (*sic*): *see Journ. of Theol. Stud.* i 569 ff.

46 And he came to Jericho, and when he went forth from Jericho, *S*
he and his disciples and a great multitude, Timaeus Bar Timaeus
47 the blind man was sitting by the way and begging. And when he
heard that it was Jesus the Nazarene, he began to cry out and to
48 say: "Son of David, have compassion on me!" And many rebuked
him that he should be silent, and again he went on crying out:
49 "Son of David, have compassion on me!" And Jesus stood and
said that they should bring him near, and he called the blind man,
50 and they say to him: "Fear not; stand up, he calleth thee." And
51 he stood *and* took up his things, and came unto Jesus. Jesus
answered and said to him: "What wouldest thou I should do for
52 thee?" The blind man saith to him: "Rabbûlî, that I may see." He
saith to him: "Go, thy faith hath saved thee alive." And in the same
hour his eyes were opened, and he was coming after him in the way.
xi 1 And when they drew near to Jerusalem, to Beth Phagge to Beth
2 Ania by the Mount of Olives, he sent two of his disciples and saith:
"Go to that village over against you, and in the same hour what *time*
ye are entering it ye will find a colt tied that no human being hath
3 ridden upon; loose and bring it. And if anyone say to you aught,
say to him that for its Lord it is required, and immediately he will
4 send it here." And they went and they found the colt tied at the
5 door of the court in the street. And while loosing it some of the
folk standing there say: "What are ye doing and loosing the colt?"
6, 7 And those *disciples* said to them as Jesus said to them, and they
brought the colt unto Jesus and they cast *on it* their cloaks and he
8 rode upon it, and many were spreading their cloaks in the way.
9 And they that were going before him and that were coming after
him were crying out, and saying: "Osanna! Blessed is he that
10 cometh in the name of the LORD; blessed is the kingdom that
cometh, *the kingdom* of our father David! Peace in the highest!"
11 And they entered Jerusalem; and he entered the Temple and saw
everything, but when it was evening he had gone forth to Beth Ania
with the Twelve.

---

46 Timaeus Bar Timaeus] *or*, 'Timaeus the son of Timaeus'; *in* E^{181} *one* MS *has* 'Bartimaeus, the son of Timaeus,' *and the other has* 'Timaeus, the son of Bartimaeus' 50 took up] 'cast away' E^{181} 51 Rabbûlî] *cf* Joh xx 16 1 to Beth Ania] *or*, 'belonging to Beth Ania' 3 its Lord (*or*, 'its master')] *S* (*sic*): *see Journ. of Theol. Stud.* i 569 ff.

S 12ܘܠܝܘܡܐ ܐܚܪܢܐ ܟܕ ܢܦܩ ܡܢ ܒܝܬ ܥܢܝܐ ܟܦܢ 13ܘܚܙܐ ⌜ܬܬܐ⌝
ܡܢ ܪܘܚܩܐ ܕܝܢ ⌜ܐܝܬ⌝ ܒܗ̇ ܛܪ̈ܦܐ. ܘܐܬܐ ܠܘܬܗ̇ ܕܠܡܐ
ܢܫܟܚ ܒܗ̇ ܡܕܡ ܘܐܬܐ ܘܠܐ ܐܫܟܚ ܐܠܐ ܐܢ ܛܪ̈ܦܐ ܠܐ
ܗܘܐ ܗܘܐ ܙܒܢܐ ܕܬܐܢ̈ܐ 14ܥܢܐ ܘܐܡܪ ܠܗ̇ ܡܟܝܠ ܘܠܥܠܡ ܐܢܫ
ܡܢ ܦܐܪ̈ܝܟܝ ܠܐ ܢܐܟܘܠ ܘܫܡܥܘ ܗܘܘ ܬܠܡܝܕܘܗܝ, 15ܘܟܕ ܐܬܐ
⌜ܠ⌝ܐܘܪܫܠܡ ܘܥܠ ܗܘܐ ܠܗܝܟܠܐ ܕܐܠܗܐ ܘܫܪܝ, ܕܢܦܩ ܠܐܝܠܝܢ
ܕܙܒܢܝܢ ܘܡܙܒܢܝܢ ܒܗܝܟܠܐ ܘܦܬܘܪ̈ܐ ܕܡܥܪ̈ܦܢܐ ܘܦܬܘܪ̈ܐ ܕܐܝܠܝܢ
ܕܡܙܒܢܝܢ ܝܘܢ̈ܐ 16ܘܠܐ ܫܒܩ ܗܘܐ ܠܐܢܫ ܕܢܥܒܪ ܡܐܢܐ ܒܓܘ
ܗܝܟܠܐ 17ܘܡܠܦ ܘܐܡܪ ܠܐ ܗܘܐ ܗܟܢܐ ܟܬܝܒ. ܕܒܝܬܝ, ܒܝܬ
ܨܠܘܬܐ ܡܬܩܪܐ ܠܟܠܗܘܢ ܥܡܡ̈ܐ ܐܢܬܘܢ ܕܝܢ ܥܒܕܬܘܢܝܗܝ,
ܡܥܪܬܐ ܕܓܝܣܐ 18ܘܫܡܥܘ ܗܘܘ ܪ̈ܒܝ ܟܗܢܐ ܘܣܦܪ̈ܐ ܘܒܥܝܢ
ܗܘܘ ܕܐܝܟܢܐ ܢܘܒܕܘܢܝܗܝ ܕܚܠܝܢ ܗܘܘ ܓܝܪ ܡܢܗ ܟܠܗ ܥܡܐ
ܓܝܪ ܬܡܝܗܘ ܒܝܘܠܦܢܗ 19ܘܡܐ ܕܗܘܐ ܗܘܐ ܪܡܫܐ ܢܦܩ ܗܘܐ
ܠܗ ܠܒܪ ܡܢ ܡܕܝܢܬܐ 20ܘܟܕ ܥܒܪܝܢ ܗܘܘ ܒܨܦܪܐ ܚܙܘ ܠܬܬܐ
ܗܝ, ܟܕ ܝܒܝܫܐ ܡܢ ܥܩܪܗ 21ܘܟܕ ܐܬܕܟܪ ܟܐܦܐ ܐܡܪ ܠܗ ܪܒܝ
ܬܬܐ ܗܝ, ܕܠܛܬ ܝܒܫܬ 22ܥܢܐ ܝܫܘܥ ܘܐܡܪ ܠܗܘܢ ܐܢ
ܐܝܬ ܒܟܘܢ ܗܝܡܢܘܬܐ ܗܝ, ⌜ܕ⌝ܐܠܗܐ 23ܐܡܝܢ ܐܡܪܢܐ ܠܟܘܢ
ܕܐܢ ܬܐܡܪܘܢ ܠܛܘܪܐ ܗܢܐ ܕܐܫܬܩܠ ܘܦܠ ܒܝܡܐ ܘܠܐ
ܢܬܦܠܓ ܒܠܒܗ ܐܠܐ ܢܗܝܡܢ ܕܡܕܡ ܕܐܡܪ ܕܗܘܐ ܢܗܘܐ
24ܡܛܠ ܗܢܐ ܐܡܪ ܐܢܐ ܠܟܘܢ ܕܟܠ ܡܕܡ ܕܡܨܠܝܢ ܐܢܬܘܢ
ܘܡܗܝܡܢܝܢ ܐܢܬܘܢ ܕܢܣܒܝܢ ܐܢܬܘܢ ܢܗܘܐ ܠܟܘܢ 25ܘܡܐ
ܕܩܝܡܝܢ ܐܢܬܘܢ ܘܡܨܠܝܢ. ܗܘܝܬܘܢ ܫܒܩܝܢ ܡܕܡ ܕܐܝܬ ܠܟܘܢ
ܥܠ ܐܢܫ ܕܐܦ ܐܒܘܟܘܢ ܕܒܫܡܝܐ ܢܫܒܘܩ ܠܟܘܢ ܣܟܠܘܬܟܘܢ ⁘
27ܘܐܬܘ ܗܘܘ ܬܘܒ ܠܐܘܪܫܠܡ ܘܡܗܠܟ ܗܘܐ ܒܗܝܟܠܐ ܘܐܬܘ
ܠܘܬܗ ܪ̈ܒܝ ܟܗܢܐ ܘܣܦܪ̈ܐ ܘܩܫܝ̈ܫܐ. 28ܘܐܡܪܝܢ ܠܗ ܒܐܝܢܐ
ܫܘܠܛܢܐ ܗܠܝܢ ܥܒܕ ܐܢܬ ܘܡܢܘ ܝܗܒ ܠܟ ܫܘܠܛܢܐ ܗܢܐ.
29ܥܢܐ ܝܫܘܥ ܘܐܡܪ ܠܗܘܢ ܐܦ ܐܢܐ ܐܫܐܠܟܘܢ ܡܠܬܐ

13 ⌜ܬܬܐ⌝] S^ed adds ⌜ܚܕܐ⌝, *but there is no room for it* 20 ܥܒܪܝܢ] S (*sic*)
22 ܗܝ] *This word is not visible in the photograph* 23 ܕܗܘܐ] S (*sic*)

12 And the next day, when he went forth from Beth Ania, he S
13 hungered. And he saw a fig-tree from afar having on it leaves,
and he came unto it, if haply he might find on it something,
and he came and found not *anything* save leaves; it had not
14 been the time of figs. He answered and said to it: "Henceforth
and for ever no one of thy fruits shall eat!" And his disciples had
15 heard. And when he came to Jerusalem and had entered the
Temple of God, he began to put forth them that buy and sell in
the Temple and the tables of the moneychangers and the tables of
16 them that sell doves; and he was not suffering any one to cause
17 vessels to pass through within the Temple, and *he was* teaching and
saying: "Is it not so written 'My House a House of Prayer is
called for all the peoples,' but ye have made it a den of thieves."
18 And the chief priests and scribes had heard, and they were seeking
how they might destroy him; for they were afraid of him, for all
19 the people were astonished at his teaching. And what *time* it had
20 become evening he had gone forth out of the city; and when they
were crossing over in the morning they saw that fig-tree withered
21 from its root, and when Kepha remembered he said to him: "Rabbi,
22 that fig-tree which thou cursedst hath withered!" Jesus answered
23 and said to them: "If there be in you faith †in† God, amen, I say
to you that if ye shall say to this hill 'Be taken up and fall into the
sea,'—and *if* he shall not doubt in his mind but shall believe that that
24 which he hath said cometh to pass will come to pass,—therefore I say
to you Everything that ye pray *for* and believe that ye will receive,
25 it shall be to you. And what *time* ye stand and pray, be forgiving
that which ye have against any, that your Father also in heaven may
forgive you your sins."

27 And they had come again to Jerusalem and he was walking in
the Temple, and there came unto him the chief priests and scribes
28 and elders and they say to him: "By what authority doest thou
29 these things? and who gave thee this authority?" Jesus answered
and said to them: "I also will ask you one word that ye shall say

ܚܕܐ ܕܬܐܡܪܘܢ ܠܝ. ܘܐܡܪܢܐ ܠܟܘܢ ܒܐܝܢܐ ܫܘܠܛܢܐ S
ܥܒܕܢܐ ܗܠܝܢ [30] ܡܥܡܘܕܝܬܗ ܕܝܘܚܢܢ ܡܢ ܫܡܝܐ ܗܝ، ܐܘ ܡܢ
ܒ̈ܢܝ ܐܢܫܐ ܐܡܪܘ ܠܝ. [31] ܘܐܬܚܫܒܘ ܘܐܡܪܝܢ ܕܐܢ ܢܐܡܪ ܕܡܢ
ܫܡܝܐ ܢܐܡܪ ܠܢ ܐܝܟܢܐ ܠܐ ܗܝܡܢܬܘܢ ܒܗ [32] ܘܐܢ ܢܐܡܪ
ܕܡܢ ܒ̈ܢܝ ܐܢܫܐ ܗܝ، ܕܚܠܝܢ ܗܘܘ ܡܢ ܥܡܐ ܟܠܗܘܢ ܓܝܪ
ܐܚܝܕܝܢ ܗܘܘ ܠܗ ܠܝܘܚܢܢ ܡܛܠ ܕܢܒܝܐ ܗܘܐ. [33] ܐܡܪܝܢ ܠܗ ܠܐ
ܝܕܥܝܢ ܐܢܚܢܢ ܝܫܘܥ ܕܝܢ ܘܐܡܪ ܠܗܘܢ ܐܦܠܐ ܐܢܐ ܐܡܪܢܐ
ܠܟܘܢ ܒܐܝܢܐ ܫܘܠܛܢܐ ܥܒܕ ܐܢܐ ܗܠܝܢ [1] ܘܫܪܝ ܗܘܐ ܕܢܡܠܠ
ܒܡܬ̈ܠܐ ܓܒܪܐ ܢܨܒ ܟܪܡܐ ܘܐܚܕܪܗ ܣܝܓܐ ܘܚܦܪ ܒܗ
ܡܥܨܪܬܐ ܘܒܢܐ ܒܗ ܡܓܕܠܐ ܘܐܘܚܕܗ ܠܦܠܚ̈ܐ ܘܥܒܪ. [2] ܘܫܕܪ
ܒܙܒܢܐ ܕܦܐܪܐ ܠܘܬ ܦܠܚ̈ܐ ܠܥܒܕܗ ܕܢܣܒܘܢ ܠܗ ܡܢ ܦܐܪܐ
ܕܟܪܡܗ [3] ܘܗܢܘܢ ܐܚܕܘܗܝ، ܘܡܚܘܗܝ، ܘܫܕܪܘܗܝ، ܟܕ ܣܪܝܩ.
[5] ܘܬܘܒ ܫܕܪ ܠܘܬܗܘܢ ܠܥܒܕܐ ܐܚܪܢܐ ܘܐܦ ܠܗ ܩܛܠܘܗܝ،
ܘܣܓܝܐܐ ܐܚܪ̈ܢܐ ܡܢܗܘܢ ܡܚܘ ܘܡܢܗܘܢ ܩܛܠܘ. [6] ܚܕ ܒܪܐ
ܚܒܝܒܐ ܐܝܬ ܗܘܐ ܠܗ ܫܕܪ ܠܘܬܗܘܢ ܘܐܡܪ ܒܪܝ ܢܒܗܬܘܢ
ܡܢ ܒܪܝ. [7] ܗܢܘܢ ܕܝܢ ܦܠܚ̈ܐ ܐܡܪܘ ܒܢܦܫܗܘܢ ܕܗܢܘ ܒܪܗ
ܝܪܬܗ ܗܘ ܬܘ ܢܩܛܠܝܘܗܝ، ܘܢܗܘܐ ܠܢ ܝܘܪܬܢܐ ܕܝܠܗ. [8] ܘܐܚܕܘ
ܩܛܠܘܗܝ، ܘܐܦܩܘܗܝ، ܠܒܪ ܡܢ ܟܪܡܐ. [9] ܡܢܐ ܕܐܬܐ ܡܪܗ
ܕܟܪܡܐ ܡܢܐ ܢܥܒܕ ܢܘܒܕ ܐܢܘ ܠܦܠܚ̈ܐ ܘܢܫܠܡܝܘܗܝ، ܠܟܪܡܗ
ܠܐܚܪ̈ܢܐ. [10] ܘܐܦܠܐ ܗܕܐ ܟܬܒܐ ܩܪܝܬܘܢ ܕܟܐܦܐ ܕܐܣܠܝܘ
ܒ̈ܢܝܐ ܗܝ، ܗܘܬ ܠܪܫܐ ܕܙܘܝܬܐ [11] ܡܢ ܠܘܬ ܡܪܝܐ ܗܘܬ ܗܕܐ
ܘܬܕܡܪܬܐ ܐܝܬܝܗ ܒܥܝ̈ܢܝܢ. [12] ܘܒܥܝܢ ܗܘܘ ܠܡܐܚܕܗ. ܘܕܚܠܘ
ܡܢ ܥܡܐ. ܐܣܬܟܠܘ ܗܘܘ ܓܝܪ ܕܥܠܝܗܘܢ ܗܘ ܐܡܪ ܡܬܠܐ
ܗܢܐ ܘܫܒܩܘܗܝ، ܘܐܙܠܘ. [13] ܘܫܕܪܘ ܠܘܬܗ ܐܢܫܐ ܡܢ ܦܪ̈ܝܫܐ
ܘܡܢ ܕܒܝܬ ܗܪܘܕܣ ܕܢܐܚܕܘܢܝܗܝ ܒܡܠܬܐ [14] ܘܫܪܝܘ ܕܢܐܡܪܘܢ
ܠܗ ܒܢܟܠܐ. ܡܠܦܢܐ ܝܕܥܝܢ ܐܢܚܢ ܕܫܪܝܪ ܐܢܬ ܘܠܐ ܒܛܝܠ ܠܟ
ܒܐܢܫ ܠܐ ܓܝܪ ܢܣܒ ܐܢܬ ܒܐܦ̈ܐ ܕܐܢܫ ܐܠܐ ܐܘܪܚܐ

---

1 ܡܬ̈ܠܐ *S*: *cf* Lk xvii 23

to me, and I will say to you by what authority I do these things; S
30 the baptism of John, from heaven is it or from men?—say to me."
31 And they considered and said "If we say 'From heaven,' he will
32 say to us 'How is it ye did not believe in him?' And if we say
that it is from men—" they were afraid of the people, for all of
33 them were holding to John, because he was a prophet. They say
to him: "We do not know." Jesus answered and said to them:
xii 1 "Neither do I say to you by what authority I do these things." And
he had begun to speak in similitudes: "A man planted a vineyard
and surrounded it with a hedge and digged in it a wine-press and
2 built in it a tower and let it out to husbandmen and departed. And
he sent in the time of fruits unto the husbandmen his slave, that
3 they might send him of the fruits of his vineyard. And they took
5 hold of him and beat him and sent him away empty. And again he
sent unto them another slave, and him also they killed, and many
6 others—some of them they beat and some of them they killed. One
beloved son had he; he sent *him* unto them, and said: 'Perhaps
7 they will have reverence for my son.' But those husbandmen said
in themselves 'This is his son, his heir; come, let us kill him, and
8 the inheritance will be ours.' And they took hold *and* killed him
9 and put him forth out of the vineyard. What *time* the lord of the
vineyard cometh, what will he do? He will destroy the husbandmen
10 and will give the vineyard to others. And not even this Scripture
have ye read 'The stone that the builders rejected, it hath become
11 the head of the corner; from the LORD this came to pass, and a
12 wonder it is in our eyes.'" And they were seeking to take hold
of him, and they were afraid of the people, for they had perceived
that against them he said this similitude; and they left him and
13 went away. And they sent unto him folk from the Pharisees and
from the Herodians that they might take hold of him with a word.
14 And they began to say to him with guile: "Teacher, we know that
thou art true and carest not for any one, for thou hast no respect
of persons for any one, but the way of God in truth thou teachest—

ܕܐܠܗܐ ܒܫܪܪܐ ܡܠܦ ܐܢܬ ܫܠܝܛ ܠܡܬܠ ܟܣܦܐ ܕܪ̈ܫܐ ܠܩܣܪ S
ܐܘ ܠܐ ܢܬܠ [15]ܘܗܘ ܝܕܥ ܗܘܐ ܢܟܠܗܘܢ ܐܡܪ ܠܗܘܢ ܡܢܐ
ܡܢܣܝܢ ܐܢܬܘܢ ܠܝ ܐܝܬܘ ܠܝ ܕܝܢܪܐ ܐܚܙܘܢܝ، [16]ܘܐܝܬܝܘ ܠܗ.
ܐܡܪ ܠܗܘܢ ܕܡܢ ܗܘ ܨܠܡܐ ܗܢܐ. ܘܟܬܒܬܐ ܐܡܪ̈ܝܢ ܠܗ
ܕܩܣܪ [17]ܥܢܐ ܝܫܘܥ ܘܐܡܪ ܠܗܘܢ ܗܒܘ ܕܩܣܪ ܠܩܣܪ ܘܕܐܠܗܐ
ܠܐܠܗܐ ܘܬܡܗܘ ܗܘܘ ܒܗ.
[18]ܘܐܬܘ ܠܘܬܗ ܙܕܘܩܝܐ ܗܢܘܢ ܕܐܡܪ̈ܝܢ ܗܘܘ ܕܠܝܬ ܩܝܡܬܐ
ܘܫܐܠܝܢ ܗܘܘ ܠܗ ܘܐܡܪ̈ܝܢ [19]ܡܠܦܢܐ ܡܘܫܐ ܟܬܒ ܠܢ ܕܡܢ
ܕܡܝܬ ܐܚܘܗܝ، ܕܓܒܪܐ ܘܐܝܬ ܠܗ ܐܢܬܬܐ ܘܠܐ ܒܪܐ ܫܒܩ * * * *
ܢܣܒ * * * ܕܢܩܝܡ ܙܪܥܐ ⌜ܠܐܚܘܗܝ،⌝ [20]ܫܒܥܐ ܐܚܝܢ ܐܝܬ ܗܘܘ
ܘܩܕܡܝܐ ⌜ܢܣܒ⌝ ܐܢܬܬܐ ܘܡܝܬ ܘܠܐ ܫܒܩ * * *[21] * * * *
* * * * * * [22]ܘܗܘܬ ܠܫܒܥܬܝܗܘܢ ܘܠܐ ܫܒܩܘ ܙܪܥܐ
ܐܚܪܝܬ ܟܠܗܘܢ ܡܝܬܬ ⌜ܐܦ⌝ ܗܝ، ܐܢܬܬܐ [23]ܒܩܝܡܬܐ ܗܟܝܠ ܡܢܐ
ܕܡܢܗܘ ܕܡܢ ܡܢܗܘܢ ܬܗܘܐ ܐܢܬܬܐ ܗܘܐ ܓܝܪ ܫܒܥܬܝܗܘܢ
ܢܣܒܘܗ [24]ܥܢܐ ܝܫܘܥ ܘܐܡܪ ܠܗܘܢ ܡܛܠ ܗܢܐ ܗܘ ܛܥܝܢ
ܐܢܬܘܢ ܕܠܐ ܝܕܥܝܢ ܐܢܬܘܢ ܟܬܒܐ ⌜ܐܦ⌝ ܠܐ ܚܝܠܗ ܕܐܠܗܐ
[25]ܡܛܠ ܕܩܡܘ ܓܝܪ ܡܢ ܒܝܬ ܡ̈ܝܬܐ ܠܐ ܢܫܐ ܢܣܒܘܢ ܘܐܦܠܐ
ܢܫܐ ܗܘܝܢ ܠܓܒܪܐ ܐܠܐ ⌜ܐܝܟ⌝ ⌜ܡ̈ܠܐܟܐ⌝ ܕܒܫܡܝܐ ܐܝܬܝܗܘܢ
[26]ܥܠ ܡ̈ܝܬܐ ܕܝܢ ܕܡܬܩܝܡܝܢ ܠܐ ܩܪܝܬܘܢ [ܒܟܬܒܐ ܕܡܘܫܐ
ܐܝܟܢܐ] ܐܠܗܐ ܐܡܪ [ܡܢ ܣܢܝܐ] ܐܢܐ [ܐܢܐ] ܐܠܗܗ ܕܐܒܪܗܡ
ܘܐܠܗܗ ܕܐܝܣܚܩ ܘܐܠܗܗ ܕܝܥܩܘܒ [27]ܘܗܐ ܐܠܗܐ ܠܐ [ܗܘܐ]
ܕܡ̈ܝܬܐ ܐܠܐ ܕܚܝܐ ܐܢܬܘܢ ܕܝܢ ܣܓܝ ܛܥܝܢ ܐܢܬܘܢ [28]ܘܩܪܒ
⌜ܥܡܗ⌝ ܚܕ ܡܢ ܣܦܪܐ ܕܫܡܥ ܐܢܘܢ ⌜ܠܗܘܢ⌝ ܡܬܚܪܝܢ ܠܗܘܢ
ܕܚܙܝܢ ⌜ܗܘܘ⌝ ܒܥܕܗ ܫܐܠܗ ܐܝܢܐ ܗܘ ܦܘܩܕܢܐ ܩܕܡܝܐ [29]ܥܢܐ
ܝܫܘܥ ܘܐܡܪ ܩܕܡܝ ܡܢ ܟܠܗܘܢ ⌜ܫܡܥ⌝ ܐܝܣܪܝܠ * ܡܪܝܐ
ܐܠܗܢ ܚܕ ܗܘ [30]ܘܬܪܚܡ ܠܡܪܝܐ ܐܠܗܟ ܡܢ ܟܠܗ ܠܒܟ ܘܡܢ

23 ܕܡܢܗܘ] *S* (*sic*) ܕܡܢ] *S* (*sic*) ܗܘܐ ܓܝܪ] *S* (*sic*) 24 ܗܢܐ] *S* (*sic*)
⌜ܐܦ⌝ ܠܐ] *S* (*sic*) 25 ܢܫܐ....ܢܫܐ] *S* (*sic*) 26 ܕܐܝܣܚܩ] *S* (*sic*)
29 ܕܚܙܝܢ] *S* (*sic*) ܐܝܣܪܝܠ * ܡܪܝܐ] S^{ed}, *but cf* lat^{vt}

is it lawful to give money for heads to Caesar, or shall we not give?" S
15 And he, he had known their guile *and* saith to them: "Why tempt
16 ye me? Bring me a denar *that* I may see it." And they brought *it*
to him. He saith to them: "Whose is this image, and the inscrip-
17 tion?" They say to him: "Caesar's." Jesus answered and said to
them: "Give what *is* Caesar's to Caesar, and God's to God." And
they had been astonished at him.

18 And there came unto him Sadducees, they that were saying that
there is no resurrection, and they were asking him and saying:
19 "Teacher, Moses wrote for us that what *time* a man's brother hath
died, and he hath a wife and hath not left * * * he shall
take [his brother's wife] that he may raise up seed to his brother.
20 Seven brothers there were, and the first took a wife and died and
21, 22 left no * * * * * * * * * * and she became *wife* of
the seven of them, and they left no seed; last of all died that
23 woman also. In the resurrection, therefore, what *time* they have
risen, whose of them shall the woman be? For lo, the seven of them
24 took her." Jesus answered and said to them: "Because of this it
is ye err—that ye know not the Scriptures nor the power of God.
25 For what *time* they have risen from among the dead they will not
take women, nor do women become *wives* of men, but as the angels
26 in heaven are they. Now concerning the dead that they rise, have
ye not read [in the book of Moses how] God said [from the Bush] 'I
[am] the God of Abraham and the God of Isaac and the God of
27 Jacob'? And lo, the God not of the dead, but of the living. But
28 ye, much do ye err." And when one of the scribes heard that well
he returned answer to those that were seeking *a dispute* with him,
29 he asked him: "Which is the first commandment?" Jesus answered
and said: "First of all of them *is* 'Hear, O Israel, * the LORD our
30 God is one,' and 'Thou shalt love the LORD thy God from all thy

---

29 Israel * the LORD] *The unread space in S between these words is probably blank, so that nothing is lost.* $E^{152,169}$ *has twice over* 'Hear, O Israel, the Lord thy God is one Lord,' *but out of this context.*

ܟܠܗ ܢܦܫܟ ܘܡܢ ܟܘܠܗ ⌜ܬܪܥܝܬܟ⌝ ܘܡܢ ܟܘܠܗ ܚܝܠܟ. ܗܢܘ S
ܦܘܩܕܢܐ ܩܕܡܝܐ [31]ܘܕܬܪ̈ܝܢ ܕܕܡܐ ܠܗ. ܕܬܪܚܡ ܠܩܪܝܒܟ ܐܝܟ
ܢܦܫܟ. ܦܘܩܕܢܐ ܐܚܪܢܐ ܕܪܒ ܡܢ ܗܠܝܢ ܠܝܬ. [32]ܐܡܪ ܠܗ ܗܘ
ܣܦܪܐ ܪܒܝ ܫܦܝܪ ܒܫܪܪܐ ܐܡܪܬ ܕܚܕ ܗܘ ܐܠܗܐ. ܘܠܝܬ ܐܚܪ̈ܢ
ܠܒܪ ܡܢܗ [33]ܕܢܫܬܡܥܘܢ, ܐܝܟ ܡܢ ܟܘܠܗ ܠܒܗ. ܘܡܢ ܟܘܠܗ
ܢܦܫܗ ܘܡܢ ܟܠܗ ܚܝܠܗ ܘܕܢܪܚܡ ܠܩܪܝܒܗ ܐܝܟ ܢܦܫܗ ܡܝܬܪ
ܗܘ ܡܢ ܟܘܠܗܘܢ ܝܩ̈ܕܐ ܘܕܒܚ̈ܐ. [34]ܝܫܘܥ ܟܕ ܚܙܐ ܕܫܦܝܪ
ܐܬܝܒܗ ܦܬܓܡܐ ܒܝܢܐ ܘܐܡܪ ܠܗ ܠܐ ܗܘܝܬ ܪܚܝܩ ܡܢ
ܡܠܟܘܬܐ ܕܐܠܗܐ ܘܐܢܫ †ܘܬܘܒ.† ܠܐ ܐܡܪܚ ܠܡܫܐܠܘܬܗ ○
[35]ܐܡܪ ܝܫܘܥ ܟܕ ܡܠܦ ܒܗܝܟܠܐ ܐܝܟܢܐ ܐܡܪܝܢ ܣܦܪ̈ܐ
ܕܡܫܝܚܐ ܒܪܗ ܗܘ ܕܕܘܝܕ. [36]ܘܗܘ ܕܘܝܕ ܐܡܪ ܒܪܘܚܐ ܕܩܘܕܫܐ
ܕܐܡܪ ܡܪܝܐ ܠܡܪܝ, ܕܬܒ ܡܢ ܝܡܝܢܝ ܥܕܡܐ ܕܐܣܝܡ ܒܥܠܕܒܒܝܟ
ܬܚܝܬ ܪ̈ܓܠܝܟ. [37]ܘܐܢ ܕܘܝܕ ܡܪܝ ܩܪܐ ܠܗ ܐܝܟܢܐ ܒܪܗ
ܗܘܐ ܘܟܠܗ ܥܡܐ ܒܣܝܡܐܝܬ ܫܡܥ ܗܘܐ ܠܗ [38]ܘܐܡܪ ܗܘܐ
ܟܕ ܡܠܦ ܙܗܪܘ ܢܦܫܟܘܢ ܡܢ ܣܦܪ̈ܐ ܕܨܒܝܢ ܕܢܗܠܟܘܢ ܒܐܣܛܠܐ
ܘܪܚܡܝܢ ܫܠܡܐ ܒܫܘܩ̈ܐ [39]ܘܪܫ ܡܘܬܒܐ ܒܟܢܘܫ̈ܬܐ ܘܪܫ ܣܡܟܐ
ܒܐܚܫܡܝܬܐ [40]ܘܐܟܠܝܢ ܒ̈ܬܐ ܕܐܪ̈ܡܠܬܐ ܒܥܠܬܐ ܕܡܘܪܟܝܢ
ܨܠܘܬܗܘܢ ܘܗܢܘܢ ܢܩܒܠܘܢ ܕܝܢܐ ܝܬܝܪܐ ○ ○
[41]ܘܟܕ ܩܐܡ ܗܘܐ ܝܫܘܥ ܠܩܒܠ ܒܝܬ ܓܙܐ ܚܙܐ ܗܘܐ ܠܟܢܫܐ
ܕܪܡܝܢ ܒܘܙܦܢܐ ܒܝܬ ܓܙܐ ܘܩ̈ܠܝܢܐ ܡܢ ܒܝܬܪ̈ܐ ܕܪܡܝܢ ܗܘܘ
ܗܟܢ [42]ܘܐܬܬ ܐܪܡܠܬܐ ܚܕܐ ܡܣܟܢܬܐ ܐܪܡܝܬ ܬܪ̈ܝܢ ܫܡܘܢܝܢ
ܕܐܝܬܝܗܘܢ ܪܘܒܥܐ [43]ܘܩܪܐ ܝܫܘܥ ܠܬܠܡܝܕܘܗܝ, ܘܐܡܪ ܠܗܘܢ
ܐܡܝܢ ܐܡܪܢܐ ܠܟܘܢ ܕܗܕܐ ܐܪܡܠܬܐ ܡܣܟܢܬܐ ܐܪܡܝܬ ܝܬܝܪ
ܡܢ ܟܘܠ ܐܢܫ ܒܝܬ ܓܙܐ [44]ܟܠ ܐܢܫ ܓܝܪ ܡܢ ܡܕܡ ܕܝܬܝܪ ܗܘܐ

---

32 ܐܚܪ̈ܢ] S (*sic*) 33 ܡܝܬܪ ܗܘ] S (*sic*) 34 ܘܐܢܫ|ܘܬܘܒ] S (*sic*), *for* ܘܐܢܫ ܬܘܒ 42 ܬܪ̈ܝܢ ܫܡܘܢܝܢ ܕܐܝܬܝܗܘܢ ܪܘܒܥܐ] S (*sic*): syr.vg *has* ܬܪ̈ܝܢ ܡܢܝܢ ܕܐܝܬܝܗܘܢ ܫܡܘ̈ܢܐ, *for which cf* Ephr.*Nis* xlvi 36 ܠܡܢܝܢ ܘܫܡܘܢܝܢ ܐܘܪܘܗ ܕܐܪܡܠܬܐ. *See Introd.* vol. ii

heart and from all thy soul and from all thy understanding and from *S*
31 all thy power.' This is the first commandment. And a second that
is like to it *is* 'Thou shalt be loving to thy neighbour as thyself.'
32 Another commandment greater than these there is not." That scribe
saith to him: "Rabbi, well in truth hast thou said that God is one
33 and there is no other apart from him; that a man should love
him from all his heart and from all his soul and from all his power
and that he should love his neighbour as himself is better than all
34 burnt-offerings and sacrifices." Jesus, when he saw that well he
returned answer, answered and said to him: "Thou art not far from
the kingdom of God." And no one †again dared ask him.

35 Saith Jesus while teaching in the Temple: "How say the scribes
36 that the Messiah is the son of David? And David himself hath said
in the Holy Spirit 'The LORD said to my Lord, Sit on my right
37 hand, until I set thine enemies under thy feet.' And if David call
him 'our Lord,' how was he his son?" And all the multitude gladly
38 was hearing him. And he was saying while teaching: "Keep your-
selves from the scribes that wish to walk in porches, and love
39 greeting in the streets and the chief seats in the synagogues and
40 the chief entertainments at suppers, and eat up the houses of widows
in the pretext that they are lengthening their prayers—and they
themselves shall receive the more judgement."

41 And when Jesus was standing over against the treasury he was
seeing the many that *were* casting in money into the treasury, and
42 many of the rich that were casting in much. And a certain poor
43 widow came *and* cast in two mites, which are a quarter. Jesus
called his disciples and said to them: "Yea, I say to you that this
44 poor widow hath cast in more than any one into the treasury; for
every one of that which was abundant to him hath cast in, but this

---

34 And no one †again] And no one and again *S* (*sic*) 42 two mites, which are a quarter] syr.vg *has* 'two pounds, which are a farthing,' *for which cf* Ephr.*Nis* xlvi 36 'The pound and the farthing of the widow He increased' (*see Introd.* vol. ii). *The word translated* 'pound' *is that used in* Lk xix 13 ff.

ܠܗ ܐܪܡܝ. ܗܕܐ ܕܝܢ ܟܠ ܡܕܡ ܕܩܢܝܐ ܗܘܬ ܐܪܡܝܬܗ. [1]ܘܟܕ S
ܢܦܩ ܗܘܐ ܝܫܘܥ ܡܢ ܗܝܟܠܐ ܐܡܪ ܠܗ ܚܕ ܡܢ ܬܠܡܝܕܘܗܝ، ܪܒܝ
ܗܐ ܚܙܝ، ܟܐܦܐ ܘܒܢܝܢܐ ܪ̈ܒܐ [2]ܐܡܪ ܠܗ ܝܫܘܥ ܚܙܝ، ܗܢܐ ܒܢܝܢܐ
ܠܐ ܬܫܬܒܩ ܗܪܟܐ ܟܐܦܐ ܥܠ ܟܐܦܐ ܕܠܐ ܬܫܬܪܐ ܀
[3]ܘܟܕ ܝܬܒ ܒܛܘܪ ܙܝܬܐ ܠܘܩܒܠ ܗܝܟܠܐ ܫܐܠܘܗܝ، ܟܐܦܐ ܘܝܥܩܘܒ
ܘܝܘܚܢܢ ܘܐܢܕܪܐܘܣ ܒܠܚܘܕܝܗܘܢ [4]ܐܡܪ ܠܢ ܐܡܬܝ، ܗܠܝܢ ܢܗܘܝܢ
ܘܡܢܐ ܐܬܐ ܕܗܘ ܗܠܝܢ ܡܫܬܠܡܢ [5]ܐܡܪ ܠܗܘܢ ܝܫܘܥ ܚܙܘ
ܠܡܐ ܐܢܫ ܢܛܥܝܟܘܢ [6]ܣܓܝܐܐ ܓܝܪ ܢܐܬܘܢ ܒܫܡܝ ܘܢܐܡܪܘܢ
ܕܐܢܐ ܐܢܐ ܘܣܓܝܐܐ ܢܛܥܘܢ܂ [7]ܡܐ ܕܫܡܥܬܘܢ ܕܝܢ ܩܪ̈ܒܐ
ܘܫܡܥܐ ܕܩܪ̈ܒܐ ܠܐ ܬܬܕܘܠܘܢ ܚܙܝܐ ܗܘ ܓܝܪ ܕܢܗܘܐ ܐܠܐ
ܠܐ ܒܙܒܢܐ ܠܗܫܐ ܫܘܠܡܐ [8]ܢܩܘܡ ܓܝܪ ܥܡܐ ܥܠ ܥܡܐ
ܘܡܠܟܘܬܐ ܥܠ ܡܠܟܘܬܐ. ܘܢܗܘܘܢ ܙܘ̈ܥܐ ܒܕܘܟܐ ܕܘܟܐ
ܟܦܢܐ ܘܫܓܘܫܝܐ ܪܫܐ ܐܝܟ ܕܚܒܠܬܐ [9]ܘܢܫܠܡܘܢܟܘܢ ܠܕܝܢܐ
ܘܠܒܝܬ ܟܢܘܫܬܐ ܘܩܕܡ ܡܠ̈ܟܐ ܬܩܘܡܘܢ ܘܬܬܢܓܕܘܢ ܘܩܕܡ
ܗܓܡܘܢܐ ܡܛܠܬܝ، ܠܣܗܕܘܬܐ ܠܗܘܢ [10]ܘܠܟܠܗܘܢ ܥܡ̈ܡܐ
ܠܘܩܕܡ ܓܝܪ ܬܬܟܪܙ ܣܒܪܬܐ ܗܕܐ [11]ܡܐ ܕܡܩܪܒܝܢ ܕܝܢ ܠܟܘܢ
ܕܢܫܠܡܘܢܟܘܢ ܠܐ ܬܪܢܘܢ ܡܢܐ ܬܐܡܪܘܢ ܐܠܐ ܡܕܡ
ܕܡܬܝܗܒ ܠܟܘܢ ܒܗ، ܒܫܥܬܐ ܗܘ ܡܠܠܘ. ܠܐ ܗܘܐ ܓܝܪ
ܐܢܬܘܢ ܡܡܠܠܝܢ ܐܠܐ ܪܘܚܐ ܩܕܝܫܬܐ. [12]ܢܫܠܡ ܓܝܪ ܐܢܫܐ
ܠܐܚܘܗܝ، ܠܡܘܬܐ ܘܐܒܐ ܠܒܪܗ ܘܢܩܘܡܘܢ ܒ̈ܢܝܐ ܥܠ ܐܒܗܬܐ
ܘܢܡܝܬܘܢ ܐܢܘܢ [13]ܘܬܗܘܘܢ ܣܢܝܐ ܠܟܘܢ ܥܠ ܐܢܫ ܡܛܠ ܫܡܝ
ܟܠ ܕܢܣܝܒܪ ܒܕܘܟܐ ܠܚܪܬܐ ܗܘ ܢܚܐ [14]ܡܐ ܕܚܙܝܬܘܢ ܐܬܐ
ܕܛܢܦܘܬܐ ܕܚܘܪܒܐ ܕܩܐܡ ܐܬܪ ܕܠܐ ܐܢܢܩܝ ܗܘ ܕܩܪܐ
ܢܣܬܟܠ ܗܝܕܝܢ ܗܢܘܢ ܕܒܝܗܘܕ ܢܥܪܩܘܢ ܠܛܘܪܐ [15]ܘܡܢ
ܕܒܐܓܪܐ ܗܘ ܠܐ ܢܚܘܬ ܠܒܝܬܐ ܘܠܐ ܢܥܘܠ ܕܢܫܩܘܠ ܡܕܡ
ܡܢ ܒܝܬܗ [16]ܘܡܢ ܕܒܚܩܠܐ ܗܘ ܠܐ ܢܬܗܦܟ ܠܒܣܬܪܗ ܕܢܫܩܘܠ
ܠܒܘܫܗ ܀

---

11 ܠܐ ܬܪܢܘܢ ܡܢܐ ܬܐܡܪܘܢ] *Cf* ܠܐ ܬܬܪܢܘܢ ܡܢ ܩܕܡ ܕܡܢܐ ܡܢܐ ܬܡܠܠܘܢ A 415 (*for the rest of this quotation, see on* Mt x 20, Lk xxi 12—17)
15 ܘܠܐ] *S* (*sic*)

xiii 1 *woman* everything that she was possessing cast in." And when Jesus *S*
was going forth from the Temple one of his disciples saith to him:
2 "Rabbi, lo, see the stones and the great building!" Jesus saith to
him: "See this building—there will not be left here a stone on a
stone that will not be thrown down."

3 And when he sat on the Mount of Olives over against the Temple,
Kepha and James and John and Andrew themselves alone asked
4 him: "Say to us when these things shall be, and what the sign with
5 which these things are accomplished?" Jesus saith to them: "See
6 lest any lead you astray. For many will come in my name, and will
7 say 'I am he,' and many will they lead astray. Now what *time* ye
have heard of battles and tales of battles, be not afraid; for that
8 is about to be, but not as yet *is* the last. For people will rise
against people and kingdom against kingdom, and there will be
earthquakes in various places; famines and tumults are the be-
9 ginning of travail. And they will deliver you up to the peoples
and to the Synagogues, and before kings ye shall stand and ye shall
be scourged before governors for my sake, for a witness to them
10 and to all the peoples; for firstly this gospel shall be preached.
11 Now what *time* they bring you up that they may deliver you over, do
not give thought to what ye shall say, but that which is given to you
in that hour—that speak ye; for not ye are speaking but a holy
12 Spirit. For the brother will deliver up his brother to death and the
father his son, and the sons will rise up against the fathers and will
13 put them to death, and every man will be hating you for my name's
sake. Every one that shall endure unto the last, he shall live.
14 What *time* ye have seen the sign of abomination of desolation
standing where it is not necessary—he that readeth, let him under-
stand—then they that *are* in Judaea let them flee to the hill-*country*,
15 and he that is on the roof let him not go down to the house nor
16 enter that he may take away aught from his house, and he that
is in the field let him not turn behind that he may take away his
clothing.

---

11 do not give thought.....say] *Cf* 'do not cogitate before the time what ye shall speak' *A* 415 (*for the rest of this quotation, see on* Mt x 20, Lk xxi 12—17) a holy Spirit] *cf* Lk ii 25, 26, Jn xx 22

[17]ܘܝ ܕܝܢ ܠܒܛܢܬܐ ܘܠܐܝܠܝܢ ܕܡܝܢܩܢ ܒܗܘܢ ܝܘܡܬܐ. [18]ܨܠܘ ܕܝܢ S
ܕܠܐ ܢܗܘܐ ܒܣܬܘܐ [19]ܢܗܘܐ ܓܝܪ ܐܘܠܨܢܐ ܒܝܘܡܬܐ ܗܢܘܢ
ܕܠܐ ܗܘܐ ܐܟܘܬܗ ܡܢ ܫܘܪܝܐ ܕܒܪܐ ܐܠܗܐ ܠܥܠܡܐ
ܘܥܕܡܐ ܠܫܘܠܡܐ ܘܬܘܒ ܠܐ ܢܗܘܐ [20]ܘܐܠܘ ܠܐ ܟܪܝܢ ܗܘܘ
ܝܘܡܬܐ ܗܢܘܢ ܠܐ ܚܝܐ ܗܘܐ ܟܠ ܒܣܪ. ܐܠܐ ܡܛܠ ܓܒܝܐ
ܕܓܒܐ ܓܒܝܢ ܝܘܡܬܐ. [21]ܘܗܝܕܝܢ ܐܢ ܐܢܫ ܢܐܡܪ ܠܟܘܢ ܕܗܐ
ܗܪܟܐ ܗܘ ܡܫܝܚܐ ܗܐ ܗܪܬܡ ܠܐ ܬܗܝܡܢܘܢ [22]ܡܛܠ
ܕܢܩܘܡܘܢ ܓܝܪ ܡܫܝܚܐ ܕܓܠܐ ܘܢܒܝܐ ܕܕܓܠܘܬܐ ܘܢܬܠܘܢ
ܐܬܘܬܐ ܘܬܕܡܪ̈ܬܐ ܗܘܝܐ ܕܐܢ ܡܫܟܚܝܢ ܢܛܥܘܢ ܐܦ
ܠܓܒܝܐ. [23]ܐܢܬܘܢ ܕܝܢ ܚܙܘ ܗܐ ܩܕܡܬ ܐܡܪܬ ܠܟܘܢ ܟܠܡܕܡ
[24]ܐܠܐ ܗܢܘܢ ܒܗܘܢ ܝܘܡܬܐ ܒܬܪ ܐܘܠܨܢܐ ܗܘ ܢܚܫܟ
ܫܡܫܐ ܘܣܗܪܐ ܢܘܗܪܗ ܠܐ ܢܚܘܐ [25]ܘܢܦܠܘܢ ܟܘܟܒܐ ܡܢ
ܫܡܝܐ ܘܢܘܚܒܘܢ ܚܝܠܘܬܗ ܕܫܡܝܐ [26]ܘܗܝܕܝܢ ܢܚܙܘܢ ܠܒܪܗ
ܕܐܢܫܐ ܟܕ ܐܬܐ ܥܠ ܥܢܢܐ ܥܡ ܚܝܠܐ ܪܒܐ ܘܥܡ ܫܘܒܚܐ
[27]ܘܗܝܕܝܢ ܢܫܕܪ ܡܠܐܟܘܗܝ, ܘܢܟܢܫ ܠܓܒܘܗܝ, ܡܢ ܐܪܒܥܬܗܘܢ
ܪܘܚܐ ܡܢ ܪ̈ܫܐ ܕܐܪܥܐ ܥܕܡܐ ܠܪܫܗ ܕܫܡܝܐ [28]ܡܢ ܬܬܐ
ܕܝܢ ܝܠܦܘ ܦܠܐܬܐ ܕܡܐ ܕܪ̈ܟܒ ܣܘܟܝܗ ܘܦܪܥܘ ܛܪܦܝܗ ܝܕܥܝܢ
ܐܢܬܘܢ ܕܩܪܝܒ ܩܝܛܐ [29]ܗܟܢܐ ܐܦ ܐܢܬܘܢ ܡܐ ܕܚܙܝܬܘܢ
ܗܠܝܢ ܕܗܘܝܢ ܕܗܘ ܕܩܪܝܒ ܠܬܪܥܐ [30]ܐܡܝܢ ܐܡܪܢܐ ܠܟܘܢ
ܕܠܐ ܬܥܒܪ ܫܪܒܬܐ ܗܕܐ ܥܕܡܐ ܕܗܠܝܢ ܟܠܗܝܢ ܢܗܘܝܢ
[31]ܫܡܝܐ ܘܐܪܥܐ ܢܥܒܪܘܢ ܘܡܠܝ ܠܐ ܢܥܒܪܢ [32]ܥܠ ܝܘܡܐ
ܗܘ ܕܝܢ ܘܥܠ ܫܥܬܐ ܗܝ, ܐܢܫ ܠܐ ܝܕܥ ܘܐܦܠܐ ܡܠ̈ܐܟܐ
ܕܒܫܡܝܐ ܘܐܦ ܠܐ ܒܪܐ ܐܠܐ ܐܢ ܐܒܐ [33]ܗܘܝܬܘܢ ܕܝܢ
ܥܝܪܝܢ ܘܡܨܠܝܢ ܠܐ ܓܝܪ ܝܕܥܝܢ ܐܢܬܘܢ ܠܗ ܠܙܒܢܐ [34]ܐܝܟܢܐ
ܓܒܪܐ ܕܐܙܠ ܘܫܒܩ ܒܝܬܗ ܘܝܗܒ ܠܥܒܕܘܗܝ, ܡܫܠܡ
ܠܐܢܫ ܐܢܫ ܒܒܝܬܗ ܘܦܩܕ ܠܬܪܥܐ ܕܢܗܘܐ ܥܝܪ [35]ܗܘܝܬܘܢ
ܗܟܝܠ ܥܝܪܝܢ ܠܐ ܓܝܪ ܝܕܥܝܢ ܐܢܬܘܢ ܐܡܬܝ, ܐܬܐ ܡܪܗ

---

25 ܘܢܘܚܒܘܢ] *S* (*sic*)   28 ܕܪ̈ܟܒ] *S* (*sic*): *cf* Mt xxiv 32, *and see Appendix* III

17 Now woe to them with child, and to them that are giving suck in S
18, 19 those days! But pray that it may not be in the winter. For there
will be distress in those days, the like of which hath not been from
the day that God created the world even unto to-day, neither again
20 shall be. And if those days had not been short no flesh would
live, but because of the chosen ones whom he hath chosen the
21 days are short. And then if any one shall say to you 'Lo, here
22 is the Messiah,' 'Lo, there,'—do not believe him; because there
will arise lying Messiahs and prophets of untruth and they will
give signs and wonders, so that if possible they will lead astray
23 even the chosen ones. Now yourselves, see,—lo, I beforehand have
24 said to you everything. But in those same days after that distress
the sun will be darkened and the moon her light will not shew,
25 and the stars will fall from heaven and the powers of heaven will
26 tremble, and then they will see the Son of Man coming on the
27 clouds with great power and with glory. And then he will send
his angels and will gather together his chosen ones from the four
winds, from the uttermost part of the earth unto the uttermost part
28 of the heaven. Now from the fig-tree learn a parable, that what
time its branches have become tender and its leaves are put forth
29 ye know that the summer *is* near; so ye also, what *time* ye have
seen these things that are coming to pass, know ye that it hath
30 drawn nigh to the door. Amen, I say to you that this generation
31 will not pass away until all these things be. Heaven and earth
32 will pass away, and my words will not pass away. Now of that
day and of that hour no one knoweth, not even the angels in heaven
33 nor the Son, but the Father. Now be ye watchful and praying,
34 for ye know not the time. For just as a man that departed and
left his house and gave to his slaves his property, to each man his
work, and commanded the doorkeeper that he should be watchful—
35 be ye therefore watchful, for ye know not when the master of the

---

20 And if those days....short] 'And except God (*one* MS *om.*) had shortened those days' E^{215}. *Thus S is harmonised to* Mt xxiv 22 *against E* 28 what *time*....put forth] *Cf* 'when the branches become tender, and the leaf springs forth and buds' $E^{186, 187}$ 33] *so also* E^{216}

ܕܐܬܐ ܠܐ ܐܢ ܒܪܡܫܐ ܘܠܐ ܐܢ ܒܦܠܓܗ ܕܠܠܝܐ ܘܠܐ ܐܢ *S*
ܒܩܪܝܬܐ ܘܠܐ ܐܢ ܒܨܦܪܐ [36]ܘܠܡܐ ܢܐܬܐ ܡܢ ܫܠܝܐ
ܢܫܟܚܟܘܢ ܟܕ ܕܡܟܝܢ ܐܢܬܘܢ܂ [37]ܘܡܕܡ ܕܠܟܘܢ ܗܘ ܐܡܪܢܐ
ܠܟܠܟܘܢ ܗܘ ܐܡܪܢܐ ܗܘܝܬܘܢ ܥܝܪܝܢ ܀

[1]ܡܢ ܩܕܡ ܬܪܝܢ ܝܘܡܝܢ ܕܗܘܐ ܗܘܐ ܦܛܝܪܐ ܕܦܨܚܐ ܒܥܝܢ
ܗܘܘ ܪܒܝ ܟܗܢܐ ܘܣܦܪܐ ܐܝܟܢܐ ܒܢܟܠܐ ܢܐܚܕܘܢܝܗ ܘܢܩܛܠܘܢܝܗ.
[2]ܐܡܪܝܢ ܗܘܘ ܓܝܪ ܕܠܐ ܒܥܕܥܕܐ ܕܠܐ ܢܗܘܐ ܪܘܒܐ ܕܥܡܐ.
[3]ܘܟܕ ܗܘܐ ܒܒܝܬ ܥܢܝܐ ܒܒܝܬܗ ܕܫܡܥܘܢ ܓܪܒܐ ܟܕ ܣܡܝܟ
ܐܬܬ ܐܢܬܬܐ ܚܕܐ ܟܕ ܫܩܝܠܐ ܫܛܝܦܬܐ ܕܒܣܡܐ ܢܪܕܝܢ
ܦܝܣܛܝܩܘܢ ܣܓܝ ܕܝܩܝܪ ܕܡܘܗܝ، ܘܬܒܪܬܗ ܘܐܫܦܟܬܗ ܥܠ
ܪܫܗ [4]ܘܐܝܬ ܗܘܘ ܐܢܫܐ ܕܐܬܟܐܒ ⌜⌝ ܠܗܘܢ ⌜ܒܢܦܫܗܘܢ⌝
ܘܐܡܪܝܢ ܕܠܡܢ⌜⌝ܐ [ܐܒܕܢܐ] ܗܢܐ [5]ܡܫܟܚ ⌜ܗܘܐ⌝ ܓܝܪ ܕܢܙܕܒܢ
ܒܬܠܬܡܐܐ ܕܝܢܪܝܢ ܘܠܡܬܝܗܒܘ ܠܡܣܟܢܐ ܘܡܬܪܓܢܝܢ ܗܘܘ
ܒܢܝ⌜⌝ܬܗܘܢ ܥܠܝܗ [6]ܝܫܘܥ ܕܝܢ ܐܡܪ ܠܗܘܢ ܫܒܩܘܗ ܠܗ ܡܢܐ
ܡܗܪܝܢ ܐܢܬܘܢ ܠܗ. ܥܒܕܐ ܓܝܪ ܫܦܝܪܐ ܥܒܕܬ ܠܘܬܝ, [7]ܒܟܠ
ܙܒܢ ܓܝܪ ܡܣܟܢܐ ܠܘܬܟܘܢ ܐܢܘܢ܆ ܘܐܡܬܝ ܕܨܒܝܢ ܐܢܬܘܢ
ܡܫܟܚܝܢ ܐܢܬܘܢ ܕܬܥܒܕܘܢ ܠܗܘܢ ܐܢܐ ܕܝܢ ܒܟܠܙܒܢ ܠܐ
ܗܘܝܬ ܠܘܬܟܘܢ [8]ܗܕܐ ܓܝܪ ܡܕܡ ܕܥܒܕܬ ܐܝܟ ܕܠܡܩܒܪܢܝ
ܗܐ ܥܒܕܬ ܘܩܕܡܬ ܒܣܡܬ ܦܓܪܝ [9]ܐܡܝܢ ܐܡܪܢܐ ܠܟܘܢ
ܕܟ⌜⌝ܪ ܕܬܬܟܪܙ ܣܒܪܬܝ. ܒܟܠܗ ܥܠܡܐ ܢܗܘܐ ܠܗ ܕܘܟܪܢܐ
ܕܗܕܐ ܡܕܡ ܕܥܒܕܬ ܀

[10]ܘܝܗܘܕܐ ܣܟܪܝܘܛܐ ܚܕ ܡܢ ܬܪܥܣܪ ⌜ܐܙܠ⌝ ܠܘܬ ܪ̈ܒܝ ܟܗܢܐ
ܐܝܟ ܕܢܫܠܡܝܘܗܝ, [11]ܘܗܢܘܢ ܟܕ ܫܡܥܘ ܚܕܝܘ ܘܐܫܬܘܕܝܘ ܕܢܬܠܘܢ
ܠܗ ܟܣܦܐ ܘܒܥܐ ܗܘܐ ܦܠܐ ܐܝܟ ܕܢܫܠܡܝܘܗܝ. [12]ܒܝܘܡܐ
ܩܕܡܝܐ ܕܦܛܝܪܐ ܟܕ ܡܬܢܟܣ ܗܘܐ ܦܨܚܐ ܐܡܪܘ ܠܗ ܬܠܡܝܕܘܗܝ,

36 ܘܠܡܐ] *S* (*sic*) 4 ܕܠܡܢ⌜⌝ܐ] ܕܠܡܢܐ S^{ed} 5 ܒܢܝܬܗܘܢ] *S*, *the end of* ܒ *coming almost over the* ܝ; ܒܢܝ̈ܬܗܘܢ S^{ed}: *cf* Joh xi 38 9 ܕܟܪ] *so* $Merx^{loc}$; ܕܟܕ S^{ed}: *cf ver.* 14 *and* Mt ii 9 ܣܒܪܬܝ.] *S* (*sic*) 12 ܡܬܢܟܣ] *S* (*sic*): *the* ܒ *is clear, and cf* Lk xxii 7

house cometh, not if *it be* in the evening-time, nor if in the S
36 mid-night, nor if in the twilight, nor if in the dawn,—and shall he
37 come suddenly *and* find you sleeping? And that which to you
I say, to all of you I say—be ye watchful!"

xiv 1 Two days before it was the Unleavened Bread of Pasek the chief
priests and scribes were seeking how with guile they should take
2 hold of him and kill him, for they were saying "Not on the Feast,
3 that there be not an uproar of the people." And when he was in
Beth Ania in the house of Simon the leper, while sitting *at meat*,
there came a certain woman carrying a vase of perfume, nard of
good pistic, the price of which was great, and she brake it and
4 poured it on his head. And there were some whom it displeased
5 in their soul and they say "Wherefore *is* this [waste]? For it
could have been sold for three hundred denars and be given to the
poor." And they were murmuring among themselves against her.
6 Now Jesus said to them: "Suffer her; why injure ye her? for a
7 fair deed hath she done unto me. For at all times the poor are
by you, and whensoever ye will ye can do for them; but I, at all
8 times I am not by you. For this which she hath done, as if for
my burial, lo, she hath done *it* and beforehand hath perfumed my
9 bodily frame. Amen, I say to you Wherever my gospel shall be
announced, in all the world there will be for her the memory of this
which she hath done."

10 And Judas Scariot, one of the Twelve, went unto the chief priests
11 so that he might deliver him up. And they, when they heard,
rejoiced and promised that they would give him silver; and he was
12 seeking an opportunity so that he might deliver him up. On the first
day of the Unleavened Bread, when the Passover was slaughtered

5 among themselves] *S*: *so I read the photograph* 12 slaughtered] *S* (*sic*): *cf* Lk xxii 7

ܐܝܟܐ ܨܒܐ ܐܢܬ ܕܢܐܙܠ ܢܛܝܒ ܕܬܐܟܠ ܦܨܚܐ [13]ܘܫܕܪ ܬܪܝܢ S
ܡܢ ܬܠܡܝܕܘܗܝ، ܘܐܡܪ ܠܗܘܢ ܙܠܘ ܠܡܕܝܢܬܐ ܗܐ ܦܓܥ ܒܟܘܢ
ܓܒܪܐ ܚܕ ܕܫܩܝܠ ܡܐܢܐ ܕܡܝܐ. ܙܠܘ ܒܬܪܗ [14]ܠܒܪ ܕܥܐܠ
ܘܐܡܪܘ ܠܡܪܐ ܒܝܬܐ. ܪ̈ܒܢ ܐܡܪ ܕܟܕ ܡܛܠܐ ܠܗ ܐܝܟܐ ܗܘ ܗܘ
ܒܝܬ ܡܫܪܝ، ܐܝܟܐ ܕܐܟ̈ܠܗ ܦܨܚܐ ܥܡ ܬܠܡܝܕ̈ܝ، [15]ܘܗܘܐ
ܡܚܘܐ ܠܟܘܢ ܥܠܝܬܐ ܚܕܐ ܪܒܬܐ ܟܕ ܡܫܘܝܐ ܘܡܬܩܢܐ ܬܡܢ
ܛܝܒܘ ܠܢ [16]ܐܙܠܘ ܬܠܡܝܕܘܗܝ، ܐܝܟܢܐ [ܕܐܡܪ] ܠܗܘܢ ܘܐܬܘ
ܠܡܕܝܢܬܐ ܘܐܫܟܚܘ ܐܝܟܢܐ ܕܐܡܪ ܠܗܘܢ܆ ܘܛܝܒܘ ܠܦܨܚܐ [17]ܘܟܕ
ܗܘܐ ܪܡܫܐ ܐܬܐ ܥܡ ܬܪ̈ܥܣܪܬܗ. [18]ܘܟܕ ܣܡܝܟܝܢ ܘܐܟܠܝܢ
ܐܡܪ ܠܗܘܢ ܝܫܘܥ. ܐܡܝܢ ܐܡܝܢ ܐܡܪܢܐ ܠܟܘܢ܆ ܕܚܕ
ܡܢܟܘܢ ܕܐܟܠ ܥܡܝ ܗܘ ܢܫܠܡܢܝ [19]ܗܢܘܢ ܕܝܢ ܫܪܝܘ ܕܬܬܟܪ
ܠܗܘܢ. ܘܐܡܪܝܢ ܗܘܘ ܠܗ ܚܕ ܚܕ ܡܢܗܘܢ܆ ܕܠܡܐ ܐܢܐ
[20]ܗܘ ܕܝܢ ܐܡܪ ܠܗܘܢ܆ ܚܕ ܡܢ ܬܪ̈ܥܣܪ ܕܐܘܥܠ ܐܝܕܗ ܥܡܝ
ܒܠܓܬܐ [21]ܘܒܪܗ ܕܐܢܫܐ ܐܙܠ ܐܝܟܢܐ ܕܟܬܝܒ ܥܠܘܗܝ، ܘܝ ܕܝܢ
ܠܓܒܪܐ ܗܘ ܕܒܐܝܕܗ ܡܫܬܠܡ ܒܪܗ ܕܐܢܫܐ ܦܩܚ ܗܘܐ ܠܗ
ܐܠܘ ܠܐ ܐܬܝܠܕ. ○○

[22]ܘܟܕ ܐܟܠܝܢ ܠܚܡܐ ܒܪܟ ܘܩܨܐ ܘܝܗܒ ܠܬܠܡܝܕܘܗܝ، ܘܐܡܪ
ܠܗܘܢ ܣܒܘ ܗܢܐ ܦܓܪܝ، [23]ܘܢܣܒ ܟܣܐ ܘܒܪܟ ܘܝܗܒ ܠܗܘܢ
ܘܫܬܝܘ ܡܢܗ. [24]ܘܐܡܪ ܠܗܘܢ ܗܢܐ ܕܡܝ ܕܕܝܬܩܐ ܚܕܬܐ ܕܚܠܦ
ܣܓܝܐܐ ܡܬܐܫܕ. [25]ܐܡܝܢ ܐܡܪ ܐܢܐ ܠܟܘܢ ܕܬܘܒ ܠܐ ܐܫܬܐ
ܡܢ ܝܠܕܐ ܕܓܦܬܐ ܥܕܡܐ ܠܗܘ ܝܘܡܐ ܕܒܗ ܐܫܬܝܘܗܝ، ܥܡܟܘܢ
ܚܕܬܐܝܬ ܒܡܠܟܘܬܗ ܕܐܠܗܐ. [26]ܘܫܒܚܘ ܗܘܘ ܘܢܦܩܘ ܠܛܘܪ ܙܝܬܐ.
[27]ܐܡܪ ܠܗܘܢ ܝܫܘܥ. ܕܟܠܟܘܢ ܬܬܟܫܠܘܢ ܒܝ ܟܬܝܒ ܗܘ ܓܝܪ
ܕܐܡܚܐ ܠܪܥܝܐ ܘܢܬܒܕܪܘܢ ܐܡܪ̈ܐ. [28]ܘܡܐ ܕܩܡܬ ܡܩܕܡܢܐ
ܠܟܘܢ ܠܓܠܝܠܐ [29]ܥܢܐ ܟܐܦܐ ܘܐܡܪ ܠܗ. ܐܢ ܟܠܗܘܢ

13 ܒܟܘܢ] *S* (*sic*)   14 ܪ̈ܒܢ] * ܪܒ *S*^ed   ܡܫܪܝ] *S* (*sic*): *there is no room for* ܡܫܪܝܐ   ܐܝܟܐ ܕܐܟ̈ܠܗ] *S* (*sic*)   19 ܕܬܬܟܪ] *S* (*sic*)   22 ܘܝܗܒ] *S* (*sic*)
24 ܕܕܝܬܩܐ] *S* (*sic*); ܕܝܬܩܐ *S* (Mt) *and* *S* (Lk): *cf* *A*221 *at* Lk xxii 20

his disciples said to him: "Where wilt thou that we go *and* S
13 make ready that thou eat the Passover?" And he sent two of his
disciples, and said to them: "Go to the town; lo, there will meet
14 you a certain man carrying a vessel of water. Go after him to
wherever he entereth, and say to the master of the house: [Our]
Rabbi saith, 'My time hath arrived; where is my guest-chamber
15 where I may eat the Passover with my disciples?" And lo, he
will shew you a certain large upper-room furnished and made ready;
16 there prepare for us. His disciples went as [he said] to them and
came to the town and found as he said to them; and they made
17 ready the Passover. And when it was evening he came with his
18 Twelve, and while they were sitting *at meat* and eating Jesus said
to them: "Amen, amen, I say to you One of you that eateth with
19 me, he will betray me." Now they began to be grieved and were
20 saying to him each one of them "Is it I?" But he said to them:
"One of the Twelve, that hath put forth his hand with me in the
21 bowl. And the Son of Man goeth as is written of him, but woe to
that man by whose hand the Son of Man is betrayed; it were
profitable for him if he had not been born!"

22 And while they were eating bread he blessed, and brake and
gave to his disciples, and said to them: "Take, this *is* my body."
23 And he took a cup and blessed, and gave to them and they drank
24 from it. And he said to them: "This *is* my blood of the new
25 covenant, that for many is shed. Amen, I say to you that no
more shall I drink of the offspring of the vine, until that day in
26 which I shall drink it with you newly in the kingdom of God." And
27 they had glorified *God* and went out to the Mount of Olives. Jesus
saith to them "All of you will be offended in me, for it is written
28 'I will smite the shepherd and the lambs will be scattered.' And
29 what *time* I have arisen, I go before you to Galilee." Kepha
answered and said to him: "If all of them shall be offended, I not."

---

19 to be grieved] *lit.* 'that it should grieve them' 24 of the... covenant] *S* (*sic*); *om.* 'of' *S* (Mt) *and S* (Lk): *cf* Lk xxii 20 25 offspring] *so also* E^{222}: *see on* Lk xxii 18

ܢܬܟܫܠܘܢ ܐܢܐ ܠܐ ‎30ܐܡܪ ܠܗ ܝܫܘܥ. ܐܡܝܢ ܐܡܝܢ ܐܡܪܢܐ S
ܠܟ ܕܐܢܬ ܝܘܡܢܐ ܒܠܠܝܐ ܗܢܐ ܥܕܠܐ ܢܩܪܐ ܬܪܢܓܠܐ ܬܪܬܝܢ
ܙܒܢܝܢ ܬܠܬ ܙܒܢܝܢ ܬܟܦܘܪ ܒܝ. ‎31ܘܫܡܥܘܢ ܡܢ ܝܬܝܪ ܐܡܪ
ܕܐܢ ܢܗܘܐ ܠܝ ܕܐܡܘܬ ܥܡܟ ܠܐ ܐܟܦܘܪ ܒܟ ܘܗܟܢܐ ܐܦ.
ܟܠܗܘܢ ܐܡܪܘ ‎32ܘܐܬܘ ܠܕܘܟܬܐ ܐܝܕܐ ܕܡܬܩܪܝܐ ܓܕܣܡܢܐ
ܘܐܡܪ ܠܬܠܡܝܕܘܗܝ, ܬܒܘ ܗܪܟܐ ܥܕ ܡܨܠܐ ܐܢܐ ‎33ܘܕܒܪ ܠ⸢ܟܐܦܐ⸣
ܘܠܝܥܩܘܒ ܘܠܝܘܚܢܢ ܥܡܗ, ܘܫܪܝ ܠܡܬܡܗܘ ܘܠܡܬܬܥܝܩܘ. ‎34ܘܐܡܪ
ܠܗܘܢ ܟܪܝܐ ܗܝ, ܠܗ ܠܢܦܫܝ ܥܕܡܐ ܠܡܘܬܐ ‎35ܘܩܕܡ ܩܠܝܠ
ܘܢܦܠ ܥܠ ܐܦܘܗܝ., ܥܠ ܐܪܥܐ ܘܡܨܠܐ ܗܘܐ ܕܐܢ ܡܫܟܚܐ
ܕܬܥܒܪ ܡܢܗ ܫܥܬܐ. ‎36ܘܐܡܪ ܐܒܝ ܟܠ ܡܕܡ ܒܐܝ̈ܕܝܟ ܡܦܠܐ
ܐܥܒܪ ܡܢܝ ܟܣܐ ܗܢܐ ܐܠܐ ܠܐ ܨܒܝܢ ܕܝܠܝ ܢܗܘܐ ܐܠܐ
ܕܝܠܟ ‎37ܘܐܬܐ ܘܐܫܟܚ ܐܢܘܢ ܕܕܡܟܝܢ ܘܐܡܪ ܠܟܐܦܐ ܫܡܥܘܢ
ܕܡܟܬ ܠܟ ܐܫܟܚܬ ܚܕܐ ܫܥܐ ܕܬܬܬܥܝܪ. ‎38ܐܬܬܥܝܪܘ ܘܨܠܘ
ܕܠܐ ܬܥܠܘܢ ܠܢܣܝܘܢܐ ܪܘܚܐ ܨܒܝܐ ܐܠܐ ܦܓܪܐ ܟܪܝܗ.
‎39ܘܐܙܠ ܬܘܒ ܨܠܝ ܘܗܝ, ܗܝ, ܡܠܬܐ ܐܡܪ ‎40ܘܐܬܐ ܘܐܫܟܚ
ܐܢܘܢ ܬܘܒ ܟܕ ܕܡܟܝܢ ܗܘܘ, ܓܝܪ ܥܝܢܝܗܘܢ ܝܩܝܪܢ
ܘܠܐ ܝܕܥܝܢ ܗܘܘ ܡܢܐ ܢܐܡܪܘܢ ܠܗ. ‎41ܘܐܬܐ ܕܬܠܬ ܙܒܢܝܢ
ܘܐܡܪ ܠܗܘܢ ܕܡܟܘ ܘܐܬܬܢܝܚܘ. ܐܬܬ ܫܥܬܐ ܡܛܬ ܫܥܬܐ
ܗܐ ܡܫܬܠܡ ܒܪܗ ܕܐܢܫܐ ܠܐܝܕܝܗܘܢ ܕܚ̈ܛܝܐ ‎42ܩܘܡܘ ܢܐܙܠ
ܗܐ ܡܛܐ ܗܘ ܕܡܫܠܡ ܠܝ ‎43ܘܟܕ ܗܘ ܡܡܠܠ ܐܬܐ ܝܗܘܕܐ ܚܕ
ܡܢ ܬܪܥܣܪ ܘܥܡܗ ܟܢܫܐ ܣܓܝܐܐ. ܟܕ ܫܩܝܠܝܢ ܣܦܣܪ̈ܐ
ܘܩܝ̈ܣܐ ܡܢ ܠܘܬ ܪܒܝ ܟܗܢܐ ܘܣܦ̈ܪܐ ‎44ܘܝܗܒ ܠܗܘܢ
ܐܬܐ ܗܘ ܕܡܫܠܡ ܠܗ ܕܐܡܪ ܠܗܘܢ ܗܘ ܕܢܫܩܢܐ ܠܗ ܗܘܝܘ
ܐܚܘܕܘܗܝ, ܘܙܗܝܪܐܝܬ ܘܐܘܒܠܘܗܝ, ‎45ܘܡܚܕܐ ܐܬܐ ܠܘܬܗ ܘܐܡܪ
ܠܗ ܪܒܝ ܘܢܫܩܗ ‎46ܘܗܢܘܢ ܐܪܡܝܘ ܥܠܘܗܝ, ܐܝܕ̈ܝܐ ܘܐܚܕܘܗܝ,
‎47ܘܚܕ ܡܢ ܐܝܠܝܢ ܕܩܝܡܝܢ ܫܡܛ ܣܦܣܪܐ ܘܡܚܝܗ ܠܥܒܕܐ ܕܪܒ
ܟܗܢܐ ܘܢܣܒܗ ܐܕܢܗ ‎48ܥܢܐ ܝܫܘܥ ܘܐܡܪ ܠܗܘܢ ܐܝܟ ܕܥܠ
ܓܝܣܐ ܢܦܩܬܘܢ ܒܣܦܣܪܐ ܘܒܩܝ̈ܣܐ ܕܬܐܚܕܘܢܢܝ ‎49ܟܠܝܘܡ

30 Jesus saith to him: "Amen, amen, I say to thee Thou to-day in S
this night, before ever the cock crow twice, three times thou wilt
31 deny me." And Simon all the more said "If it shall be for me
that I should die with thee, I will not deny thee." And so all of
32 them also said. And they came to the place which is called
Gedsemane, and he said to his disciples: "Sit here, while I pray."
33 And he took Kepha and James and John, and he began to be
34 gloomy and to be in trouble. And he said to them: "It doth
35 grieve my soul even unto death." And he departed a little, and he fell
on his face on the earth and was praying if it could be that the hour
36 should pass from him. And he said: "My Father, everything is in
thy power; cause this cup to pass from me—but not my will, mine,
37 be *done*, but thine!" And he came and found them sleeping, and
he said to Kepha: "Simon, thou hast slept; hast thou not been
38 able one hour to watch? Watch and pray that ye enter not into
39 temptation; the spirit is willing, but the body is infirm." And he
40 went again *and* prayed, and the same word he said. And he came
and found them again asleep, for their eyes were laden with sleep,
41 and they knew not what they should say to him. And he came for
the third time and said to them: "Sleep and take your ease; the
hour hath come, the end hath arrived—lo, betrayed is the Son of
42 Man into the hands of the sinners! Arise, let us go; lo, he that
43 betrayeth me hath drawn near." And while yet he *was* speaking
Judas, one of the Twelve, came, and with him a great multitude
carrying scimitars and staves from the chief priests and scribes and
44 elders. And he gave them a sign, he which *was* betraying him, in
that he said to them: "He which I kiss, he it is; take hold of him
45 warily and carry him along." And immediately he came unto him
46 and said to him: "Rabbi!" and kissed him. And they laid hands
47 upon him, and took hold of him. And one of those standing
by drew a sword and smote the chief priest's slave and took *off*
48 his ear. Jesus answered and said to them: "As against a robber
have ye come forth with swords and with staves that ye might
49 take hold of me! Daily with you *am* I in the Temple—while

---

36 My Father] 'Father' E^{229} 38 willing] 'willing and ready' E^{231}

S ܠܬܠܬܝܢ ܐܢܐ ܒܡܕܒܪܐ. ܟܕ ܡܠܟ ܐܢܐ ܠܐ ܐܚܙܝܬ ܗܘܝܬܘܢ
ܠܝ. ܐܠܐ ܡܛܠ ܕܢܫܠܡܘܢ ܒܬܒܐ ܘ[50]ܢܒܥܘܢܗ، ܗܘܘ ܒܥܠܡܘܢ
ܬܠܡܝܕܘܗܝ، ܘܒܪܘܢ ܘ[51]ܒܠܝܠܝܐ ܚܕ ܐܬܐ ܗܘܐ ܒܬܪܗ ܘܒܠܥ
ܗܘܐ ܫܘܒܩܐ ܘܐܙܠ ܐܢܫܐ ܫܠܝܐ ܘܐܚܝܕܘܗܝ، [52]ܘܗܘܘ ܥܒܕ
ܢܬܐ ܒܐܚܝܕܘܗܝ ܘܒܪܘ ܡܚܝܘܗܝ ܒܪܓܠ [53]ܘܐܘܒܠܘܗܝ، ܠܥܘܒ
ܠܘܬ ܐ̈ܒܐ ܒܗܢܐ ܘܐܬܝܢ ܗܘܘ ܒܗܝܢ ܒܥܠܡܘܢ ܐ̈ܒܐ ܒܗܢܐ
ܘܥܢܝܐ ܘܫܦܪܐ ܘ[54]ܒܐܝܟܐ ܐܬܐ ܗܘܐ ܡܢ ܪܘܚܩܐ ܒܬܪܗ
ܕܥܡܐ ܠܒܝܬܗ ܕܝܢ ܒܗܢܐ ܘܐܬܒ ܗܘܐ ܠܘܬ ܕܝ̈ܢܐ ܘܥܢܝ
ܗܘܐ [55]ܐ̈ܒܐ ܒܗܢܐ ܕܝܢ ܘܒܥܠܡܗ ܒܢܫܐ ܒܒܝܢ ܗܘܘ ܠܟ ܥܘܒ
ܡܗܕܘܬܐ ܕܢܫܬܠܝܢܗ، ܘܠܐ ܡܕܒܝܢ ܗܘܘ [56]ܘܣܓܝܐܐ ܡܥܡܕܝܢ
ܗܘܘ ܟܠܗ، ܡܗ̈ܕܘܬܐ ܕܟܠܬܐ ܘܠܐ ܥܒܝܢ ܗܘ، ܡܗܕܘܬܗܘܢ
[57]ܐܢܫܝܢ ܕܝܢ ܡܢܗ ܒܠܘܗ، ܘܐܡܪܝ̈ܢ [58]ܕܐܢܫܝܢ ܥܡܪܝܢܗ،. ܕܐܡܪ
ܕܐܢܐ ܐܫܬܪܝܗ، ܠܗܡܠܐ ܕܒܒܝܢ ܐܢܫܐ ܘܠܬܠܬܐ ܝܘܡܝܢ
ܒܕܝܢܐ ܐܚܪܢܐ ܕܠܐ ܒܒܢ ܐܢܫܐ [59]ܘܐܟܠܐ ܗܒܢܐ ܥܒܝܢ ܗܘ،
ܡܗܕܘܬܗܘܢ [60]ܘܒܥܕ ܕܝܢ ܒܗܢܐ ܒܡܟܝܟܘܬܐ ܘܫܐܠܗ ܠܥܘܒ
ܘܐܡܪ ܠܗ ܠܐ ܡܒܥܐ ܐܢܬ ܦܬܟܪܐ ܡܢܐ ܡܥܡܕܝܢ ܒܠܝܢ
[61]ܘܗܘ ܕܝܢ ܥܬܝܕ ܗܘܐ ܘܡܕܡ ܠܐ ܐܬܒ. ܘܬܘܒ ܫܐܠܗ
ܕܝܢ ܒܗܢܐ ܕܬܪ̈ܬܝܢ ܕܝܢܐ ܘܐܡܪ ܠܗ ܐܢܬ ܗܘ ܡܥܢܝܐ ܒܪܗ
ܕܡܒܪܟܐ [62]ܒܝܢܐ ܥܘܒ ܘܐܡܪ ܠܗ ܐܢܐ ܐܢܐ ܘܡܛܠ ܬܫܘܝܗ
ܠܒܪܗ ܕܐܢܫܐ ܕܐܬܒ ܡܢ ܥܡܝܢܐ ܕܢܠܐ ܘܒܕ ܐܬܐ ܟܠ
ܒܢܝܐ ܕܥܡܝܐ. [63]ܘܐܒ ܒܗܢܐ ܗܘܝܢ ܟܪ، ܠܒܥܘܬܗ. ܘܐܡܪ
ܡܢܐ ܡܛܠ ܡܬܒܥܐ ܠܒܗ̈ ܗܘܗܝܢ [64]ܗܐ ܒܝܪ ܒܥܠܡܘܢ
ܥܡܒܬܘܢ ܒܗܘܗܝ ܡܢܐ ܡܬܢܚܐ ܠܒܗ̈ ܘܒܥܠܡܘܢ ܕܚܝܝܢ
ܗܘܘ ܠܗ ܕܢܝܒ ܗܘ ܠܡܒܥܬܐ [65]ܘܫܪܘܗ ܡܢܝܘܗܝ ܠܡܪܗ ܒܗ
ܘܠܡܒܥܝܘ ܘܐܡܪ̈ܝܢ ܐܬܒܢܐ ܠܝ ܗܟܢܐ ܘܕܝܢܐ ܡܢܝܢ ܗܘܘ ܠܗ

---

54 ܒܬܪܗ] *S (sic)*   56 ܘܣܓܝܐܐ] *om.* ܘ *S^ed*   62 ܕܐܬܒ] *S (sic)*

teaching ye were not laying hold of me—but because the Scriptures S
50 should be accomplished." And all his disciples had left him and
51 fled. And a certain youth was coming after him, and he was dressed
52 in a cloth, and there went many folk and took hold of him; and he
53 left the garment in their hands and fled from them naked. And
they carried Jesus along unto the chief priests, and they were
54 bringing with him all the chief priests and elders and scribes. And
Kepha was coming from afar after him as far as the house of the
chief priest, and was sitting by the guards and was warming himself.
55 Now the chief priests and all the multitude were seeking against
Jesus witness that they might kill him, and were not finding *any*;
56 and many were witnessing against him lying witness, and their witness
57, 58 did not agree. Now some rose up against him and say "We
ourselves have heard him that he said 'I will pull down the Temple
made with hands, and in three days I *will* make another not made
59, 60 with hands.'" And not even so did their witness agree. And the
chief priest rose in the midst and asked Jesus, and said to him:
"Dost thou offer no answer? What are these bearing witness
61 against thee?" Now he himself was silent, and not any *answer*
did he return. And again the chief priest asked him the second
time and said to him: "Art thou the Messiah, the Son of the
62 Blessed?" Jesus answered and said to him: "I am *he*, and hence-
forth ye will see the Son of Man sitting on the right *hand* of Power
63 and coming on the clouds of heaven." And the chief priest then
rent his clothing and said: "Why henceforth is there required for you
64 our witnesses? For lo, all of you have heard his blasphemy. What
seemeth it to you?" And all of them were judging him guilty of
65 death. And some of them began to spit at him and to buffet *him*,
and say: "Prophesy to us now." And the guards were smiting him

---

62, 63] *see on* Mt xxvi 64 63 our witnesses] *S*[ed] (*sic*)

S ܥܠ ܦܟܘܗܝ܂ [66]ܘܟܕ [ܗܘܐ] ܟܐܦܐ ܒܕܪܬܐ ܕܪܒ ܟܗ̈ܢܐ ܚܙܬܗ
[67]ܟܕ ܫܚܢ ܥܠܝܡܬܐ ܚܕܐ ܕܪܒ ܟܗܢܐ ܘܐܡܪܐ ܠܗ ܘܐܦ ܐܢܬ
ܥܡ ܝܫܘܥ ܗܘܝܬ ܢܨܪܝܐ. [68]ܗܘ ܕܝܢ ܟܦܪ ܘܐܡܪ ܠܐ ܝܕܥܢܐ
ܘܠܐ ܚܟܡ ܐܢܐ ܡܢܐ ܐܡܪܬܝ܂ ܘܢܦܩ ܠܕܪܬܐ ܒܪܝܬܐ [69]ܘܬܘܒ
ܚܙܬܗ ܥܠܝܡܬܐ ܘܫܪܝܬ ܠܡܐܡܪ ܠܗܘܢ ܕܩܝܡܝܢ ܘܐܦ ܗܢܐ
ܡܢܗܘܢ ܗܘ. [70]ܗܘ ܕܝܢ ܬܘܒ ܟܦܪ. ܘܬܘܒ ܒܬܪ ܩܠܝܠ ܗܢܘܢ
ܕܩܝܡܝܢ ܐܡܪܘ ܠܟܐܦܐ. ܫܪܝܪܐܝܬ ܡܢܗܘܢ ܐܢܬ. ܡܛܠ
§¶A I 43 ܕܓܠܝܠܝܐ ܐܢܬ [§71]ܘܡܚܪܡ ܗܘܐ ܘܝܡܐ ܕܠܐ ܝܕܥܢܐ ܠܗ¶ ܠܓܒܪܐ
ܗܢܐ ܕܐܡܪܝܢ ܐܢܬܘܢ܂ [72]ܘܩܪܐ ܬܪܢܓܠܐ ܕܬܪ̈ܬܝܢ ܙܒܢܝܢ ܘܥܗܕ
ܟܐܦܐ ܡܠܬܐ ܕܐܡܪ ܗܘܐ ܠܗ ܝܫܘܥ [ܕܥܕ] ܠܐ ܢܩܪܐ
ܬܪܢܓܠܐ ܬܪ̈ܬܝܢ ܬܠܬ ܙܒ̈ܢܝܢ ܬܟܦܘܪ ܒܝ ܘܫܪܝ ܗܘܐ
ܕܢܒܟܐ ○

[1]ܘܒܨܦܪܐ ܢܣܒܘ ܡܠܟܐ ܪ̈ܒܝ ܟܗ̈ܢܐ ܘܩܫ̈ܝܫܐ ܘܣܦܪ̈ܐ ܘܟܠܗ
ܟܢܫܐ ܘܐܣܪܘܗܝ܂ ܠܝܫܘܥ ܘܐܘܒܠܘܗܝ܂ ܘܐܫܠܡܘܗܝ܂ ܠܦܝܠܛܘܣ
[2]ܘܫܐܠܗ ܦܝܠܛܘܣ ܐܢܬ ܗܘ ܡܠܟܗܘܢ ܕܝܗܘܕܝܐ ܥܢܐ ܘܐܡܪ
ܠܗ ܐܢܬ ܐܡܪܬ. [3]ܘܐܟܠܝܢ ܗܘܘ ܪ̈ܒܝ ܟܗ̈ܢܐ ܩܪ̈ܨܘܗܝ܂ ܣܓܝܐܐ
ܘܗܘ ܦܬܓܡܐ ܠܐ ܝܗܒ ܗܘܐ ܠܗܘܢ. [4]ܘܬܘܒ ܐܡܪ ܠܗ
ܦܝܠܛܘܣ ܠܐ ܡܦܢܬ. ܐܢܬ ܠܗܘܢ ܦܬܓܡܐ ܠܐ ܚܙܝܬ ܟܡܐ
ܡܣܗܕܝܢ ܥܠܝܟ [5][ܗܘ ܕܝܢ ܝܫܘܥ] ܡܕܡ ܦܬܓܡܐ ܠܐ ܝܗܒ
[ܐܝܟܢܐ ܕܢܬܕܡܪ] ܗܘܐ ܦܝܠܛܘܣ
[6][ܒܟܠ ܥܐܕܐ ܕܝܢ] ܫܪܐ ܗܘܐ ܠܗܘܢ ܐܣܝܪܐ ܚܕ ܐܝܢܐ ܕܫܐܠܝܢ
[ܗܘܘ ܡܢܗ] [7]ܘܐܣܝܪ ܗܘܐ ܓܒܪܐ ܚܕ ܒܫܡܐ ܕܡܬܩܪܐ ܒܪ
ܐܒܐ ܘܐܝܬ ܗܘܐ ܓܒܪܐ ܕܥܒܕ ܒܫܬܐ ܘܩܛܠ ܩܛܠܐ [8]ܘܓܥܐ
ܟܢܫܐ ܘܫܪܝ܂ ܠܡܫܐܠ ܕܢܥܒܕ ܠܗܘܢ [9]ܥܢܐ ܦܝܠܛܘܣ ܘܐܡܪ ܠܗܘܢ܆

70 ܕܓܠܝܠܝܐ] *S (sic)*: *cf* Mt xxvi 69   71 ܘܡܚܪܡ ܗܘܐ] ܘܐܚܪܡ *A*
7 ܘܐܣܝܪ] ܘܐܣܝܪܐ *S*[ed]   8 ܘܓܥܐ] *S (sic)*: ܓܥܐ *corresponds to* ἀναβοᾶν, *as in* Mt xxvii 46

66 on his cheeks. And when Kepha [was] in the court of the chief *S*
67 priest a certain maid of the chief priest saw him warming himself,
and she saith to him: "And thou also wast with Jesus the
68 Nazarene." But he denied and said: "I know *him* not, and I
am not acquainted with what thou sayest." And he went forth to
69 the outer court and again the maid saw him, and she began to say
70 to those standing *by*: "And this *one* also is of them." But he again
denied. And again after a little those standing *by* said to Kepha:
71 "Truly thou art of them, because thou art a Galilaean." §And he was §*A* 143
asseverating and sware "I know him not,¶ this man that ye say." ¶*A*
72 And the cock crew the second time, and Kepha recollected the word
that Jesus had said to him ["Before] ever the cock crow twice, three
times thou wilt deny me." And he had begun to weep.

XV 1 And in the morning the chief priests and elders and scribes and
all the people took counsel, and they bound Jesus and carried him
2 along and delivered him up to Pilate. And Pilate asked him:
"Art thou the king of the Jews?" He answered and said to him:
3 "Thou hast said *it*." And the chief priests were accusing him much,
4 and he no answer was giving them. And again Pilate saith to him:
"Dost thou return them no answer? Seest thou not how many are
5 bearing witness against thee?" [Now Jesus] gave not any answer,
[so that] Pilate was [wondering.]

6 [Now at every Feast] he was releasing to them one prisoner,
7 whichever they [were] asking [of him]; and there was imprisoned a
man, an evil-doer called Bar Abba, and he had been a man that did
8 evil deeds and committed murders. And the people exclaimed and
9 began to ask that he should do *something* for them. Pilate answered

---

71 was asseverating] asseverated *A* 8 exclaimed] *S* (*sic*), *i.e.* ἀναβοήσας

ܨܒܝܢ ܐܢܬܘܢ ܕܐܫܪܐ ܠܟܘܢ ܠܡܠܟܗܘܢ ܕܝܗܘ̈ܕܝܐ ¹⁰ܝܕܥ ܗܘܐ S
ܓܝܪ ܦܝܠܛܘܣ ܕܡܢ ܚܣܡܐ ܐܫܠܡܘܗܝ ¹¹ܘܪ̈ܒܝ ܟܗܢܐ ܐܦ⸢ܝ⸣ܣܘ
ܠܟܢܫܐ ܕܠܒܪ ܐܒܐ ܢܫܐܠ ܕܢܫܪܐ ܠܗܘܢ ¹²ܥܢܐ ܬܘܒ ܦܝܠܛܘܣ
ܘܐܡܪ ܠܗܘܢ ܡܢܐ ܗܟܝܠ ܨܒܝܢ ܐܢܬܘܢ [ܐܥܒܕ ܠܗ
ܠܡܠܟܗܘܢ ܕܝܗܘ̈ܕܝܐ ¹³ܘܗܢܘܢ ܬܘܒ ܩܥܝܢ ܗܘܘ ܘܐܡܪܝܢ]
¹⁴ܗܘ ܕܝܢ ܦܝܠܛܘܣ ܐܡܪ [ܠܗܘܢ ܡܢܐ ܓܝܪ ܕܒܝܫ ܥܒܕ ܠܗ]
ܘܗܢܘܢ ܝܬܝܪܐܝܬ ܩܥܝܢ ܗܘܘ ܘܐܡܪܝܢ ¹⁵ܦܝܠܛܘܣ ܕܝܢ ܨܒܐ
⸢ܗ⸣ܘܐ ܕܢܥܒܕ ܨܒܝܢܐ ܕܟܢܫܐ ܘܫܪܐ ܠܗܘܢ ܠܒܪ ܐܒܐ ܘܐܫܠܡ
ܠܗܘܢ ܠܝܫܘܥ ܟܕ ܡܢܓܕ ܕܢܙܕܩܦ. ¹⁶ܘܐܣܛܪ̈ܛܝܘܛܐ ܐܘܒ⸢ܠ⸣ܘܗܝ
ܠ⸢ܓ⸣ܘ ܕܪܬܐ ܕܐܝܬܝܗ ܦܪܛܘܪܝܢ ܘܩܪܘ ܠܟܠܗ ܐܣܦܝܪ ¹⁷ܘܐܠܒܫܘܗܝ
ܐܪܓܘܢܐ ܘܓܕܠܘ ܟܠܝܠܐ ܕܟܘ̈ܒܐ ܘܣܡܘ ܠܗ ¹⁸ܘܫܪܝܘ ܠܡܫܐܠ
ܒܫܠܡܗ ܫܠܡ ܡܠܟܗܘܢ ܕܝܗܘ̈ܕܝܐ ¹⁹ܘܡܚܝܢ ܗܘܘ ܠܗ ܥܠ ܪܫܗ
ܒܩܢܝܐ ܘܪܩܝܢ ܗܘܘ ܒܐܦ̈ܘܗܝ. ܘܢܦܠܘ ܥܠ ܒܘ̈ܪܟܝܗܘܢ ܘܣܓܕܝܢ
ܗܘܘ ܠܗ. ²⁰ܘܟܕ ܒܙܚܘ. ܐܫܠܚܘܗܝ ܐܪ̈ܓܘܢܗܝ ܘܐܠܒܫܘܗܝ
ܢܚܬܘܗܝ ܕܢܦܫܗ, ܘܐܦܩܘܗܝ ܕܢܙܩܦܘܢܗ. ²¹ܘܫܚܪܘ ܠܫܡܥܘܢ
ܓܒܪܐ ܩܘܪܝܢܝܐ ܕܐܬܐ ܗܘܐ ܡܢ ܩܪܝܬܐ ܐܒܘܗܝ ܕܐܠܟܣܢܕܪܘܣ
ܘܕܪܘܦܘܣ ܕܢܫܩܘܠ ܙܩܝܦܗ. ²²ܘܐܝܬܝܘܗܝ ܠܕܘܟܬܐ ܕܡܬܩܪܝܐ
ܓܓܘܠܬܐ ܕܡܬܬܪܓܡܐ ܩܪܩܦܬܐ ²³ܘܝܗܒܘ ܠܗ ܚܡܪܐ ܕܡܙܝܓ
ܒܡܘܪܐ. ܘܗܘ ܠܐ ܢܣܒ. ²⁴ܘܙܩܦܘܗܝ ܘܦܠܓܘ ܢܚܬܘܗܝ
ܒܝܢܬܗܘܢ. ܘܐܪܡܝܘ ܥܠܝܗܘܢ ܦ̈ܣܐ. ²⁵ܘܐܝܬܝܗܝܢ ܗܘܝ ܕܝܢ
ܫܥ̈ܐ ܬܠܬ ܘܙܩܦܘܗܝ ²⁶ܘܟܬܝܒܬܐ ܗܘܬ ܥܠܬܗ ܗܢܐ ܡܠܟܗܘܢ
ܕܝܗܘ̈ܕܝܐ. ²⁷ܘܙ̈ܩܝܦܝܢ ܗܘܘ ܥܡܗ ܬܪ̈ܝܢ ܓܝ̈ܣܐ ܚܕ ܡܢ ܝܡܝܢܗ
ܘܚܕ ܡܢ ܣܡܠܗ. ²⁹ܘܡ⸢ܓܕ⸣ܦܝܢ ܗܘܘ ܥܠܘܗܝ ܘܡܢܝܕܝܢ ܪ̈ܫܝܗܘܢ
ܘܐܡܪܝܢ. ܐܘ̈ ܣܬܪ ܗܝܟܠܐ ܘܒܢܐ ܠܗ ܠܬܠܬ̈ܐ ܝܘܡܝܢ.

---

11 ܐܦ⸢ܝ⸣ܣܘ] ܐܦܣܘ *S*^ed (mea culpa): *cf* Mt xxvii 20 13, 14 *For the restoration, cf especially* arm^loc 16 ܠܓܘ ܕܪܬܐ] ܠܓܘ ܕܕܪܬܐ *S*^ed
23 ܒܡܘܪܐ] *S* (*sic*)

and said to them: "Do ye wish that I release to you the king of the S
10, 11 Jews?" For Pilate knew that from envy they delivered him up. And
the chief priests persuaded the people that for Bar Abba they should
12 ask, that he should release *him* to them. Pilate answered again and
said to them: "What therefore do ye wish [that I do to the king of
13, 14 the Jews?" And they again were crying out: "Crucify him!"] Now
Pilate said [to them: "*Why?* For what evil hath been done by
15 him?"] And they the more were crying out: "Crucify him!" Now
Pilate was wishing to do the will of the multitude, and he released to
them Bar Abba and delivered up to them Jesus when scourged, that
16 he might be crucified. And the soldiers carried him along within the
17 court, which is the Praetorium, and called all the cohort; and they
clothed him in purple and plaited a crown of thorns and set *it* for
18 him and began to greet him, *saying*: "Hail, king of the Jews!"
19 And they were smiting him upon his head with a reed and were
spitting in his face, and they fell on their knees and were worshipping
20 him. And when they *had* mocked they stripped him of his purple
and clothed him in his own garments, and brought him forth that
21 they might crucify him. And they compelled Simon, a Cyrenian, who
was coming from the field, the father of Alexander and of Rufus, that
22 he should take up his cross. And they brought him to the place
23 called Gugaltha, which is interpreted 'Skull'; and they gave him
24 wine perfumed with perfume, and he took *it* not. And they crucified
him and divided his garments among them and cast for them lots.
25, 26 Now it was the third hour, and they crucified him; and his trespass
27 was written: "This *is* the king of the Jews." And there were
crucified with him two robbers, one on his right and one on his
29 left. And they were blaspheming against him and wagging their
heads and saying: "Oh! Destroyer of the Temple and builder of it

[30]ܦܨܐ ܢܦܫܟ ܘܚܘܬ ܡܢ ܙܩܝܦܐ. [31]ܘܗܟܘܬ ܐܦ ܪ̈ܒܝ ܟܗ̈ܢܐ ܒܗ. S
ܡܒܙܚ̈ܝܢ ܚܕ. ܥܡ ܚܕ. ܘܣܦܪ̈ܐ ܐܡܪ̈ܝܢ ܠܐܚܪ̈ܢܐ ܐܚܝ ܢܦܫܗ
ܠܐ ܐܫܟܚ ܠܡܚܝܘ. [32]ܡܫܝܚܐ ܡܠܟܗ ܕܐܝܣܪܐܝܠ. ܢܚܘܬ ܡܢ
ܙܩܝܦܐ ܕܢܚܙܐ ܘܢܗܝܡܢ ܘܐܦ ܗܢܘܢ ܕܐܙܕܩܦܘ ܗܘܘ ܥܡܗ
ܡܚܣܕܝܢ ܗܘܘ ܠܗ. ܀

[33]ܘܟܕ ܗܘܝ ܫܬ ܫ̈ܥܝܢ ܗܘܐ ܚܫܘܟܐ ܒܟܠܗ ܐܪܥܐ ܥܕܡܐ ܠܬܫ̈ܥ ܫ̈ܥܝܢ
[34]ܘܒܬܫ̈ܥ ܫ̈ܥܝܢ ܩܪܐ ܒܩܠܐ ܪܡܐ ܐܠܗܝ، ܐܠܗܝ، ܠܡܢܐ ܫܒܩܬܢܝ.
[35]ܘܐܢܫܐ ܡܢ ܗܢܘܢ ܕܩܝܡܝܢ ܬܡܢ. ܘܐܡܪ̈ܝܢ ܕܠܐܠܝܐ ܩܪܐ.
[36]ܘܪܗܛ ܚܕ. ܡܠܐ ܐܣܦܘܓܐ ܚܠܐ ܘܣܡ ܒܩܢܝܐ ܘܐܫܩܝܗ·
ܘܐܡܪ̈ܝܢ ܫܒܘܩܘ ܢܚܙܐ ܐܢ ܐܬܐ ܐܠܝܐ ܡܚܬ ܠܗ. [37]ܘܗܘ
ܝܫܘܥ ܕܝܢ ܩܥܐ ܒܩܠܐ ܪܡܐ ܫܠܡ. ܀

[38]ܘܐܦܝ̈ܗ، ܨܛܪܝ ܬܪܥܐ ܕܗܝܟܠܐ ܠܬܪ̈ܝܢ ܡܢ ܠܥܠ ܘܥܕܡܐ ܠܬܚܬ.
[39]ܟܕ ܚܙܐ ܕܝܢ ܩܢܛܪܘܢܐ ܗܘ ܕܩܐܡ ܗܘܐ ܠܘܬܗ. ܘܟܕ ܩܥܐ
ܫܠܡ. ܐܡܪ ܗܢܐ ܫܪܝܪܐܝܬ ܒܪܗ ܗܘ ܕܐܠܗܐ. [40]ܘܐܝܬ ܗܘ̈ܝ
ܢܫ̈ܐ ܕܚܙܝܢ ܡܢ ܪܘܚܩܐ ܕܐܝܢ ܡܪܝܡ ܡܓܕܠܝܬܐ ܘܡܪܝܡ ܒܪܬ
ܝܥܩܘܒ ܙܥܘܪܐ ܐܡܗ ܕܝܘܣܦ ܘܫܠܘܡ [41]ܗܢܝܢ ܕܐܬܝ، ܒܬܪܗ ܡܢ
ܓܠܝܠܐ ܘܐܚܪ̈ܢܝܬܐ ܣܓܝ̈ܐܬܐ ܕܡܫܡ̈ܫܢ ܗܘ̈ܝ، ܠܗ ܕܣܠܩ ܗܘ̈ܝ،
ܥܡܗ ܠܐܘܪܫܠܡ. [42]ܘܗܘܐ ܒܥܪܘܒܬܐ. [43]ܘܐܬܐ ܗܘܐ ܝܘܣܦ ܡܢ
ܪܡܬܐ ܒܪܢܫܐ ܡܝܩܪܐ ܒܡܠܟܘܬܐ ܘܐܦ ܗܘ ܡܣܟܐ ܗܘܐ
ܠܡܠܟܘܬܐ ܕܫܡܝܐ. ܘܐܡܪܚ ܘܥܠ ܠܘܬ ܦܝܠܛܘܣ ܘܫܐܠ ܫܠܕܗ
ܕܝܫܘܥ. [44]ܘܬܡܗ ܗܘܐ ܦܝܠܛܘܣ ܕܡܝܬ ܡܢ ܟܕܘ ܘܫܕܪ ܩܪܐ
ܠܩܢܛܪܘܢܐ ܘܫܐܠܗ ܕܐܢ ܡܝܬ [45]ܘܟܕ ܝܠܦ ܡܢ ܩܢܛܪܘܢܐ ܝܗܒ

40 ܕܚܙܝܢ] ܕܚܙܝܢ S

30 in three days, save thyself alive and come down from the cross!" S
31 And again the chief priests also, laughing one with another, with the
scribes, say: "Others he saved alive, himself he could not save alive;
32 the Messiah, the king of Israel—let him come down from the cross,
that we may see and believe!" And those also that were crucified
with him were reproaching him.

33 And when it was the sixth hour there was darkness unto the
34 ninth hour, and at the ninth hour he called with a mighty voice:
35 "My God, my God, wherefore hast thou left me?" And some folk of
those standing *by* heard and say "For Elijah he hath called!"
36 And one ran *and* filled a sponge with vinegar and set *it* on a reed
and gave him to drink. And they say: "Let be; we shall see if
37 Elijah cometh *and* taketh him down." And he, Jesus, crying out
with a mighty voice expired.

38 And the veil of the Temple was rent in twain from the top unto the
39 bottom. Now when the centurion who was standing by him saw, and
when crying out he *had* expired, he said: "This truly is the Son of
40 God!" And there were women standing from afar that *were* seeing—
Mary Magdalene, and Mary daughter of James the Little, the mother
41 of Joseph, and Salome,—those that came with him from Galilee, and
many others that were serving him, that had come up with him to
42, 43 Jerusalem. And it was on the sabbath, and there had come Joseph
from Ramtha, an honourable man, a counsellor, and he also was
looking for the kingdom of heaven; and he dared and went in unto
44 Pilate and asked for the corpse of Jesus. And Pilate was astonished
that he was dead already, and he sent *and* called the centurion and
45 asked him if he were dead. And when he learned from the centurion

ܫܠܡܗ ܠܝܘܣܦ ⁴⁶ܘܗܘ ܙܒܢ ܟܬܢܐ ܘܐܚܬܗ، ܟܪܟܗ ܒܣܕܘܢܐ ܘܣܡܗ S
ܒܝܬ ܩܒܘܪܐ ܕܢܩܝܪ ܗܘܐ ܠܗ ܒܟܐܦܐ ܘܥܓܠ ܟܐܦܐ ܐܘܪܒ
ܥܠ ܬܪܥܗ ܕܒܝܬ ܩܒܘܪܐ. ⁴⁷ܡܪܝܡ ܕܝܢ ܡܓܕܠܝܬܐ ܘܡܪܝܡ ܒܪܬ
ܝܥܩܘܒ ܚܙܝ، ܗܘܝ، ܐܝܟܐ ܕܐܬܬܣܝܡ. ¹ܘܟܕ ܥܒܪܬ ܫܒܬܐ. ܙܒܢ
ܒܣܡܐ ܘܗܪ̈ܘܡܐ. ܡܪܝܡ ܡܓܕܠܝܬܐ. ܘܡܪܝܡ ܒܪܬ ܝܥܩܘܒ
ܘܫܠܘܡ. ܕܢܐܬܝܢ ܢܡܫܚܢܝܗܝ، ²ܘܒܨܦܪܐ ܒܚܕܒܫܒܐ ܐܬܝ، ܠܒܝܬ
ܩܒܘܪܐ ܟܕ ܕܢܚ ܫܡܫܐ. ³ܘܐܡܪ̈ܢ ܗܘܝ، ܒܢܦܫܗܝܢ ܡܢ ܕܝܢ
ܢܥܓܠ ܠܢ ܟܐܦܐ ܕܒܝܬ ܩܒܘܪܐ. ⁴ܡܛܠ ܕܪܒܐ ܗܘܬ ܛܒ. ܘܐܬܝ،
ܘܚܙܝ، ܕܡܬܥܓܠܐ ܗܘܬ ܗܝ، ܟܐܦܐ ⁵ܘܥܠ ܠܒܝܬ ܩܒܘܪܐ ܘܚܙܝ،
ܥܠܝܡܐ ܕܝܬܒ ܡܢ ܝܡܝܢܗܘܢ ܘܥܛܝܦ ܐܣܛܠܐ ܚܘܪܬܐ. ܘܕܚܠ
⁶ܘܐܡܪ ܠܗܝܢ ܠܐ ܬܕܚܠܢ ܠܝܫܘܥ ܗܘ ܢܨܪܝܐ ܒܥܝܢ ܐܢܬܝܢ. ܗܘ
ܕܙܩܝܦ ܗܘܐ. ܩܡ ܠܗ ܘܠܐ ܗܘܐ ܬܢܢ ܗܐ ܕܘܟܬܗ ܐܬܪ
ܕܣܝܡ ܗܘܐ. ⁷ܐܠܐ ܙ̈ܠܢ ܐܡܪ̈ܝܢ ܠܬܠܡܝܕܘܗܝ، ܘܠܟܐܦܐ ܕܗܐ
ܡܩܕܡ ܠܗܘܢ ܠܓܠܝܠܐ ܬܡܢ ܬܚܙܘܢܗ ܐܝܟܢܐ ܕܐܡܪ ܠܗܘܢ
⁸ܘܟܕ ܫܡܥ ܢܦܩ[.] ܘܐܙܠ ܘܠܐܢܫ ܡܕܡ ܠܐ ܐܡܪ ܡܛܠ ܕܕܚܠ
ܗܘ، ○ ○ ○ ○ ○ ○ ○

ܫܠܡ ܐܘܢܓܠܝܘܢ
ܕܡܪܩܘܣ.

·○·○·○·○·○·○·○·○·○·

ܐܘܢܓܠܝܘܢ ܕܠܘܩܐ.

In Mk xvi 1—8 S^{B} *denotes the readings of my transcript, made at Sinai in* 1893.

2 ܐܬܝ] S^{B}; ܐܬܝܢ S^{ed} 4 ܘܐܬܝ] S^{B}; ܘܐܙܠ S^{ed}: *see Appendix* III
5 ܘܥܠ] S^{B}; ܘܥܠ S^{ed} ܘܕܚܠ] S^{B}; ܘܕܚܠ S^{ed} 7 ܙ̈ܠܢ ܐܡܪ̈ܝܢ] S^{B}; ܐܙܠ ܐܡܪܝ S^{ed} ܬܚܙܘܢܗ] S^{B}; ܚܙܘܢܗ S^{ed} 8 ܫܡܥ] S^{B}; ܫܡܥܢ S^{ed}
ܢܦܩ[.] ܢܦܩ S^{B}; ܢܦܩܝ S^{ed} ܕܕܚܠ] S^{B}; ܕܕܚܠܝ S^{ed}: *cf* Mk ix 6

46 he gave his corpse to Joseph. And he bought a cloth and brought S
and wrapped it in the cloth and laid it in a tomb that was hewn for
him in the rock, and he rolled a stone *and* put *it* against the door of
47 the tomb. Now Mary Magdalene and Mary the daughter of James
xvi 1 had seen where he was laid. And when the sabbath was past they
bought oil and spices—Mary Magdalene, and Mary the daughter of
2 James, and Salome—that they might come *and* anoint him. And at
the dawn on the first *day* of the week they came to the tomb when
3 the sun was up. And they were saying in themselves: "Now who
4 hath rolled *away* for us the stone of the tomb? Because it was great
exceedingly." And they came, and they saw that the stone was rolled
5 *away*, and they entered the tomb and saw a youth sitting on their
6 right *hand* and dressed in a white robe, and they were afraid. And
he saith to them: "Fear not; Jesus the Nazarene ye seek, him that
was crucified. He hath risen and is not here; lo, his place where he
7 had been laid! But go, say to his disciples and to Kepha 'Lo, he
goeth before you to Galilee: there shall ye see him, as he said to
8 you.'" And when they heard they came forth, and they went away
and to no one aught said they, because they had been afraid.

[*Subscription in S*]

HERE ENDETH THE EVANGEL OF MARK.

EVANGEL OF LUKE.

---

2 they came] S^{B}; they come S^{ed} 4 And they came] S^{B}; And they went S^{ed}: *see Appendix* III 7 ye see] S^{B}; they see S^{ed} 8 had been afraid] S^{B}; were afraid (*or*, were fearing) S^{ed}

[The following fragment is all that survives of S. Mark in C.]

C * * * * * * * * * * * * * * * * *

fol 39 r
17 ܕܗܝܡܢܝܢ ܒܝ. ܗܠܝܢ ܒܫܡܝ ܫ̈ܐܕܐ ܢܦܩܘܢ܂ ܒܠܫܢܐ ܚܕܬܐ
ܢܡܠܠܘܢ܆ 18 ܚ̈ܘܘܬܐ ܢܫܩܠܘܢ ܒܐ̈ܝܕܝܗܘܢ܆ ܘܐܢ ܡܕܡ ܗܘܐ
ܕܡܡܝܬܐ ܢܫܬܘܢ ܠܐ ܢܗܪܐ ܐܢܘܢ܆ ܥܠ ܟܪ̈ܝܗܐ ܢܣܝܡܘܢ
ܐ̈ܝܕܝܗܘܢ ܘܢܬܚܠܡܘܢ ܀
19 ܡܪܢ ܕܝܢ ܝܫܘܥ ܡܢ ܒܬܪ ܕܦܩܕ ܠܬܠܡ̈ܝܕܘܗܝ܇ ܐܬܥܠܝ ܠܫܡܝܐ.
ܘܝܬܒ ܡܢ ܝܡܝܢܐ ܕܐܠܗܐ. 20 ܗܢܘܢ ܕܝܢ ܢܦܩܘ ܘܐܟܪܙܘ ܒܟܠ
ܕܘܟܐ. ܟܕ ܡܪܢܐ ܒܥܕܪܗܘܢ ܒܟܠ܂ ܘܡܠܬܗܘܢ ܡܫܪܪ ܗܘܐ
ܒܐ̈ܬܘܬܐ ܕܥܒܕܝܢ ܗܘܘ. ܀

ܫܠܡ. ܐܘܢܓܠܝܘܢ܆

✤ ܕܡܪܩܘܣ ✤

·o·o·o·o·o·o·o·o·o·o·

col 2
*ܐܘܢܓܠܝܘܢ. ܕܠܘܩܣ.

[xvi 9—20]

15 *Cf Addai* 8: ܐܬܦܫܛܬ ܕܝܢ ܟܪܘܙܘܬܗ ܒܟܠܗ ܒܪܝܬܐ 16 *Cf A*21: ܘܟܕ ܡܦܩ ܬܘܒ ܡܪܢ ܐܪܙܐ ܕܡܥܡܘܕܝܘܬܐ ܠܫ̈ܠܝܚܘܗܝ. ܗܟܢܐ ܐܡܪ ܠܗܘܢ. ܕܟܠ ܕܡܗܝܡܢ ܘܡܥܡܕ (MS ܘܡܥܡܪ) ܚܝܐ. ܘܟܠ ܕܠܐ ܡܗܝܡܢ ܡܬܕܝܢ.

17, 18.] *A*21:
17 ܗܕܐ ܐܬܐ ܬܗܘܐ ܠܐܝܠܝܢ ܕܡܗܝܡܢܝܢ. ܕܒܠܫܢܐ ܚ̈ܕܬܐ ܢܡܠܠܘܢ. ܘܫ̈ܐܕܐ ܢܦܩܘܢ ܒܫܡܝ. 18b ܘܐ̈ܝܕܝܗܘܢ ܢܣܝܡܘܢ ܥܠ ܟܪ̈ܝܗܐ ܘܡܬܚܠܡܝܢ.

19 *Cf A*406, 409 ܘܣܠܩ ܗܦܟ ܠܫܡܝܐ ܘܝܬܒ ܡܢ ܝܡܝܢܐ ܕܐܒܘܗܝ. (*A*409 *has* ܘܐܬܪܘܡ *for* ܘܣܠܩ, *and omits* ܠܫܡܝܐ)

[*The following fragment is all that survives of S. Mark in C.*]

* * * * * * * * * * * * * *C*

[xvi] 17 that believe in me: these in my name demons shall cast out, with a
18 new tongue they shall speak, serpents they shall take up in their
hands, and if any poison of death they shall drink it shall not hurt
them; on the infirm they shall lay their hands and they shall be
made whole."

19 Now our Lord Jesus, after he commanded his disciples, was taken
20 up to heaven, and he sat on the right *hand* of God. But they went
forth and preached in every place, the LORD being with them in all,
and their word he was confirming by the signs that they were doing.

[*Subscription in C*]

HERE ENDETH THE EVANGEL OF MARK.

EVANGEL OF JOHN.

[xvi 9—20]

15 *Cf Addai* 8: 'We have been commanded to preach his gospel in all the creation.' 16 *Cf A* 21: 'And when again our Lord gave the mystery of Baptism to his apostles, thus he said to them "He that believeth and is baptized shall live, and he that believeth not is judged."' 17, 18.] *A* 21 *has*: '[17]This shall be the sign for them which believe—that with new tongues they shall speak, and devils they shall be casting out, [18b]and their hands they shall be laying on the infirm and they are made whole.' 19 *Cf A* 406, 409: 'And Jesus went up to heaven and sat on the right *hand* of his Father' (*A* 409 *has* 'Our Saviour' *for* 'Jesus,' *and omits* 'to heaven')

ܐܘܢܓܠܝܘܢ ܕܠܘܩܐ

[1]ܡܛܠ ܕܣܓܝܐܐ ܨܒܘ ܠܡܟܬܒ ܘܠܡܫܬܥܝܘ ܥܠ ܨ̈ܒܘܬܐ ܐܝܠܝܢ S
ܕܒܢ ܡܫܬ̈ܪܪܢ. [2]ܐܝܟܢܐ ܕܐܫܠܡܘ ܠܢ ܗܢܘܢ̇ ܕܡܢ ܩܕܝܡ ܗܘܘ
ܚ̈ܙܝܐ ܘܡܫܡܫܢܐ ܕܡܠܬܐ. [3]ܐܬܚܙܝ، ܠܝ ܐܦ ܠܝ ܕܒܚܦܝܛܘܬ ܐܝܟ
ܟܠܗܝܢ ܡܢ ܪ̈ܫ. ܒܛܟܣܐܝܬ ܚܕܐ ܚܕܐ ܡܟܝܢ ܠܡܟܬܒ ܠܟ
ܢܨܝܚܐ ܬܐܘܦܝܠܐ [4]ܕܬܕܥ ܫܪܪܐ ܕܡ̈ܠܐ ܕܐܬܬܠܡܕܬ ܠܗܝܢ ܀
[5]ܗܘܐ ܒܝܘܡܬܗ ܕܗܪܘܕܣ ܡܠܟܐ ܕܝܗܘܕ ܟܗܢܐ ܚܕ ܕܫܡܗ
ܗܘܐ ܙܟܪܝܐ ܡܢ ܦܠܓܘܬܐ ܕܒܝܬ ܐܒܝܐ. ܘܐܢܬܬܗ ܡܢ ܒܢܬܗ
ܗܘܬ ܕܐܗܪܘܢ ܫܡܗ ܗܘܐ ܐܠܝܫܒܥ. [6]ܬܪ̈ܝܗܘܢ ܕܝܢ ܙܕܝܩܝܢ
ܗܘܘ ܩܕܡ ܐܠܗܐ. ܘܡܗ̈ܠܟܝܢ ܗܘܘ ܒܟܠܗܘܢ ܦܘܩܕܢܘܗܝ,
ܘܒܟܐܢܘܬܗ ܕܡܪܝܐ. ܘܕܠܐ ܥܕܠ ܗܘܘ ܒܟܠܗ ܒܡܥܒܕܘܗ̇. [7]ܒܪܐ
ܕܝܢ ܠܝܬ ܗܘܐ ܠܗܘܢ̇ ܡܛܠ ܕܐܠܝܫܒܥ ܥܩܪܬܐ ܗܘܬ. ܘܬܪ̈ܝܗܘܢ
ܩܫܝܐ, ܡܣܒܝܬܐ ܗܘܘ ܀ ܀ ܀
[8]ܗܘܐ ܗܘܐ ܕܝܢ ܟܕ ܡܟܗܢ ܗܘܐ ܒܛܟܣܐ ܕܚܘ̈ܒܢܐ ܩܕܡ
ܐܠܗܐ [9]ܒܥܝܕܐ ܕܬܫܡܫܬܐ ܕܟܗܢܐ. ܡܛܝܗ, ܗܘܐ ܠܡܥܠ
ܒܩܘ̈ܕܫܐ. ܘܥܕ ܥܠ ܠܗܝܟܠܐ. [10]ܘܟܢܫܐ ܕܥܡܐ ܩܐܡ ܗܘܐ
ܘܡܨܠܐ ܒܙܒܢܐ ܕܒܣ̈ܡܐ. [11]ܘܐܬܚܙܝ، ܠܗ ܠܙܟܪܝܐ ܡܠܐܟܐ
ܕܡܪܝܐ ܟܕ ܩܐܡ ܡܢ ܝܡܝܢܐ ܕܡܕܒܚܐ ܕܒܣܡܐ. [12]ܘܐܫܬܓܫ
ܘܙܟ ܟܕ ܚܙܝܗ، ܠܡܠܐܟܐ. ܘܕܚܠܬܐ ܢܦܠܬ ܥܠܘܗܝ، [13]ܐܡܪ ܠܗ
§A57 ܡܠܐܟܐ. ܠܐ ܬܕܚܠ ܙܟܪܝܐ. ܗܐ ܓܝܪ §ܫܡܥ ܐܠܗܐ ܒܩܠ
¶A ܨܠܘܬܟ.¶ ܘܐܢܬܬܟ ܐܠܝܫܒܥ ܬܐܠܕ ܠܟ ܒܪܐ. ܘܬܩܪܐ ܫܡܗ
ܝܘܚܢܢ. [14]ܘܬܗܘܐ ܠܟ ܚܕܘܬܐ ܘܫܘܒܗܪܐ ܘܣ̈ܓܝܐܐ ܢܚܕܘܢ

13 ܫܡܥ.....ܨܠܘܬܟ] ܐܫܬܡܥܬ ܨܠܘܬܟ ܩܕܡ ܐܠܗܐ A

EVANGEL OF LUKE

i 1 Because many have wished to write and to declare concerning *S*
2 those matters which among us have been completed, as they who
from of old were eyewitnesses and servants of the word have
3 delivered to us, it hath seemed *good* to me, even me, who have
investigated them all from the beginning, carefully one by one to
4 write *them* to thee, illustrious Theophilus, that thou mayest know
the truth of the words which thou hast been taught.

5 There was in the days of Herod the king of Judaea a certain
priest whose name was Zacharia of the division of Beth Abiam, and
his wife was of the daughters of Aaron—her name was Elisabeth.
6 Now both of them were righteous before God and were walking in
all his commandments and in the uprightness of the LORD, and were
7 blameless in all their way of life. But no son had they, because
Elisabeth was barren and both of them were advanced in days.

8 Now it had come to pass when he was serving in the order of the
9 priests before God, *that* in the custom of the service of priests it had
arrived to him to bring in incense; and when he entered the Temple
10 a number of the people were standing and praying at the season of
11 the incense. And there appeared to him, *even* Zacharia, an angel of
12 the LORD standing on the right *hand* of the altar of incense; and he
was agitated and trembled when he saw the angel, and fear fell upon
13 him. The angel saith to him: "Fear not, Zacharia; for lo, §God hath §*A* 57
hearkened to the voice of thy prayer,¶ and thy wife Elisabeth shall bear ¶*A*
14 thee a son, and thou shalt call his name John. And thou shalt have

---

6 way of life] *or*, 'habitation.' *So also* E^7 ('They were blameless in all their habitation'): *cf* Lk ii 37 13 God.....thy prayer] thy prayer hath been heard before God *A* $E^{8,12,14}$

S ܒܡܘܠܕܗ. [15]ܡܛܠ ܕܢܗܘܐ ܪܒ ܩܕܡ ܡܪܝܐ ܘܚܡܪܐ ܘܫܟܪܐ
ܠܐ ܢܫܬܐ. ܘܪܘܚܐ ܕܩܘܕܫܐ ܢܬܡܠܐ ܟܕ ܗܘ ܒܟܪܣܗ ܕܐܡܗ.
[16]ܘܣܓܝܐܐ ܡܢ * * * * * * * * * * *

[*The leaf of S which contained* Lk i 16—38 *is missing.*]

[38]ܡܠܐܟܐ ܡܢ ܠܘܬܗ [39]ܘܩܡܬ ܡܪܝܡ ܒܗܘܢ ܒܝܘܡܬܐ ܗܢܘܢ
ܘܐܙܠܬ ܒܛܠܝܠܘܬܐ ܠܛܘܪܐ ܠܡܕܝܢܬܐ ܕܝܗܘܕ. [40]ܘܥܠܬ ܠܒܝܬܗ
ܕܙܟܪܝܐ ܘܫܐܠܬ ܒܫܠܡܗ ܕܐܠܝܫܒܥ. [41]ܘܗܘܐ ܟܕ ܫܡܥܬ ܐܠܝܫܒܥ
ܫܠܡܗ ܕܡܪܝܡ ܕܨ ܥܘܠܐ ܒܟܪܣܗ ܘܐܬܡܠܝܬ ܐܠܝܫܒܥ. ܒܪܘܚܐ
ܕܩܘܕܫܐ [42]ܘܒܩܠܐ ܪܡܐ ܩܥܬ ܘܐܡܪܬ ܠܡܪܝܡ ܐܢܬܝ ܗܝ
ܒܪܝܟܬ ܒܢ̈ܫܐ ܘܡܒܪܟ ܗܘ ܦܐܪܐ ܕܒܟܪܣܟܝ. [43]ܘܡܢܘ ܚܒܒ ܠܝ
ܗܕܐ ܕܐܡܗ ܕܡܪܝ ܬܐܬܐ ܠܘܬܝ. [44]ܗܐ ܓܝܪ ܟܕ ܢܦܠ ܩܠܐ
ܕܫܠܡܟܝ ܒܐܕܢܝ ܒܚܕܘܬܐ ܪܒܬܐ ܕܨ ܥܘܠܐ ܒܟܪܣܝ. [45]ܘܛܘܒܝܗ
ܠܐܝܕܐ ܕܬܗܝܡܢ ܕܗܘܐ ܫܘܠܡܐ ܠܐܝܠܝܢ ܕܐܬܡܠܠ ܥܡܗ ܡܢ
ܠܘܬ ܡܪܝܐ. [46]ܐܡܪܐ ܡܪܝܡ ܡܘܪܒܐ ܢܦܫܝ ܠܡܪܝܐ [47]ܘܚܕܝܬ
ܪܘܚܝ ܒܐܠܗܐ ܡܚܝܢܐ [48]ܕܚܪ ܒܡܟܝܟܘܬܗ ܕܐܡܬܗ ܡܢ ܗܫܐ
ܓܝܪ ܛܘܒܐ ܢܗܘ̈ܝܢ ܝܗܒܢ ܠܝ ܟܠܗ̈ܝܢ ܫܪ̈ܒܬܐ [49]ܕܥܒܕ ܠܘܬܝ
ܪܘܪܒܬܐ. ܗܘ ܐܝܢܐ ܕܚܝܠܬܢ ܘܩܕܝܫ ܫܡܗ. [50]ܘܚܢܢܗ ܠܕܪ ܕܪܐ
ܘܥܠ ܫܪ̈ܒܬܐ ܠܕܕܚܠܝܢ ܠܗ [51]ܘܥܒܕ ܐܘܚܕܢܐ ܒܕܪܥܗ ܘܒܕܪ
ܬܪ̈ܥܝܬܐ ܕܠܒܘܬܐ ܕܫܒ̈ܪܐ [52]ܘܐܢܚܬ ܬܩܝܦܐ ܡܢ ܟܘܪܣܘܬܗܘܢ
ܘܐܪܝܡ ܡܟܝܟܐ [53]ܘܡܠܐ ܟܦܢܐ ܡܢ ܛܒܬܗ ܘܫܦܩ ܥܬܝܪ̈ܐ ܟܕ
ܣ̈ܦܝܩܝܢ [54]ܘܐܬܟܠܠ ܠܗ ܥܠ ܐܝܣܪܝܠ ܥܒܕܗ. ܘܐܬܕܟܪ ܚܢܢܗ
[55]ܐܝܟܢܐ ܕܡܠܠ ܥܡ ܐܒܗܝܢ ܥܡ ܐܒܪܗܡ ܘܥܡ ܙܪܥܗ ܠܥܠܡ.
[56]ܘܩܘܝܬ ܕܝܢ ܡܪܝܡ ܠܘܬ ܐܠܝܫܒܥ. ܐܝܟ ܝܪ̈ܚܐ ܬܠܬܐ ܘܗܦܟܬ
ܠܒܝܬܗ ܀

---

28 *Cf A* 180: ܟܕ ܦܪܣܗ ܓܝܪ ܓܒܪܝܐܝܠ... ܐܡܪ ܠܗ. ܫܠܡ ܠܟܝ ܒܪܝܟܬ ܒܢ̈ܫܐ

30 *A* 57 ܐܫܟܚܬܝ (A^a ܗܐ ܐܫܟܚܬܝ) ܛܝܒܘܬܐ ܩܕܡ ܐܠܗܐ

46, 48 *Cf A* 180 ܘܫܒܚܬ ܘܐܘܕܝܬ (A^a ܘܐܘܕܝܬ) ܠܡܪܝܐ. ܐܝܟܐ ܕܒܡܟܝܟܘܬܗ ܕܐܡܬܗ

53 ܘܫܦܩ] *S* (*sic*): *probably a corruption of* ܘܫܒܩ, *as* syr[palest]

15 joy and boasting, and many shall rejoice in his birth; because he S
shall be great before the Lord, and wine and strong drink he shall
not drink, and with the Holy Spirit he shall be filled while yet he is
16 in the womb of his mother, and many of * * * * *

[*The leaf of S which contained* Lk i 16—38 *is missing.*]

38, 39 the angel from her. And Mary arose in those same days and went
40 up with care to the hill-*country* to a town of Judaea. And she
41 entered the house of Zacharia and greeted Elisabeth, and it came to
pass when Elisabeth heard the greeting of Mary the babe leaped in
42 her womb. And Elisabeth was filled with the Holy Spirit and with
a loud voice she cried out and said to Mary: "Thou art the blessed
43 among women, and blessed is the fruit in thy womb! What is it
hath done me this, that the mother of my Lord should come unto
44 me? For lo, when the voice of thy greeting fell in my ears, with
45 great joy leaped the babe in my womb! And happy is it for her
which shall believe that there cometh to pass a fulfilment for those
46 things that were spoken with her from the Lord." Saith Mary:
47 "My soul doth magnify the Lord and my spirit hath rejoiced in God
48 the Life-giver, in that he hath looked upon the lowliness of his hand-
49 maiden; for from now all generations will be calling me happy, in
50 that he hath done unto me great things—he, whose Name of mercy
is glorified and holy unto the age and on the stock of them that fear
51 him. And he hath made a dominion with his arm and scattered the
52 understanding of the hearts of the proud. And he hath brought
53 down the mighty from their thrones and lifted up the lowly, and he
hath filled the poor from his goodness and †despised† the rich
54 empty. And he hath cared for Israel his son, and hath remembered
55 his mercy; as he spake with our fathers, with Abraham and with
56 his seed for ever." Now Mary remained by Elisabeth about three
months and returned to her house.

---

14 boasting] 'gladness' E^7 28 *Cf* *A* 180: 'For when Gabriel announced to her *the good tidings*.... he said to her: Hail to thee, blessed among women!'. *So also in* E^{49} *there is no trace of the other clauses.* 30 'Thou hast found grace before God' (A^a *pr.* 'Lo') *A* 57 46, 48 *Cf* 'And she glorified and magnified (and thanked A^a) the Lord, in that he was pleased with the lowliness of his handmaiden' *A* 180 53 despised] *S* (*sic*): *probably a mistake for* 'sent away'

[57]ܘܟܕ ܫܠܡ ܙܒܢܐ ܕܡܘܠܕܗ ܕܐܠܝܫܒܥ ܝܠܕܬ ܒܪܐ [58]ܘܫܡܥܘ S
ܫܒܒܝܗ ܘܒܢܝ ܛܘܗܡܗ ܕܐܘܣܦ ܡܪܝܐ ܚܢܢܗ ܠܘܬܗ. ܘܚܕܝܢ
ܗܘܘ ܠܗ. [59]ܘܗܘܐ ܠܝܘܡܐ ܕܬܡܢܝܐ ܐܬܘ ܠܡܓܙܪܗ ܕܛܠܝܐ.
ܘܩܪܝܢ ܗܘܘ ܠܗ ܒܫܡܐ ܕܐܒܘܗܝ ܙܟܪܝܐ. [60]ܘܐܡܪܬ ܐܡܗ ܕܠܐ
ܗܟܢܐ ܐܠܐ ܢܬܩܪܐ ܝܘܚܢܢ. [61]ܘܐܡܪ̈ܝܢ ܠܗ ܠܝܬ ܐܢܫ ܒܫܪܒܬܟܝ
ܕܡܬܩܪܐ ܒܫܡܐ ܗܢܐ ܝܘܚܢܢ. [62]ܘܐܡܪܘ ܗܘܘ ܐܦ ܠܐܒܘܗܝ
ܕܐܝܟܢܐ ܨܒܐ ܕܢܬܩܪܐ. [63]ܘܫܐܠ ܦܢܩܝܬܐ ܘܟܬܒ ܒܗ ܕܝܘܚܢܢ
ܗܘ ܫܡܗ. [64]ܘܒܗ ܒܫܥܬܐ ܐܫܬܪܝ ܐܣܘܪܐ ܕܠܫܢܗ. ܘܒܪܟ
ܠܐܠܗܐ [(63)]ܘܐܬܕܡܪܘ ܟܠܗܘܢ : [65]ܘܗܘܬ ܕܚܠܬܐ ܥܠ ܟܠܗܘܢ
ܫܒܒܝܗܘܢ ܘܒܟܠܗ ܛܘܪܐ ܕܝܗܘܕ ܗܠܝܢ ܡܬܡܠܠ ܗܘܝ. [66]ܘܫܡܥܝܢ
ܗܘܘ ܟܠܗܘܢ ܘܐܡܪܝܢ ܗܘܘ ܡܢܐ ܢܗܘܐ ܛܠܝܐ ܗܢܐ ܕܐܝܕܗ
ܕܡܪܝܐ ܥܡܗ. [67]ܘܐܬܡܠܝ ܙܟܪܝܐ ܐܒܘܗܝ ܒܪܘܚܐ ܕܩܘܕܫܐ
ܘܐܬܢܒܝ ܘܐܡܪ [68]ܡܒܪܟ ܗܘ ܐܠܗܐ ܕܐܝܣܪܐܝܠ ܕܣܥܪ ܠܥܡܗ.
ܘܥܒܕ ܠܗ ܦܘܪܩܢܐ. [69]ܘܐܩܝܡ ܠܢ ܩܪܢܐ ܕܚ̈ܝܐ ܒܒܝܬܗ ܕܕܘܝܕ
ܥܒܕܗ [70]ܐܝܟܢܐ ܕܐܡܪ ܒܦܘܡܐ ܕܢܒܝ̈ܘܗܝ ܩܕܝ̈ܫܐ ܕܡܢ ܥܠܡ.
[71]ܘܐܚܝܢ ܠܚ̈ܝܐ ܡܢ ܐܝܕܐ ܕܒܥܠܕܒܒܝܢ. ܘܕܟܠ ܕܣܢܝܢ ܠܢ. [72]ܕܢܥܒܕ
ܚܢܢܐ ܥܡ ܐܒܗܝܢ ܘܐܬܕܟܪ ܠܕܝܬܩܘܗܝ ܩܕܝܫܬܐ [73]ܡܘܡܬܐ
ܕܝܡܐ ܠܐܒܪܗܡ ܐܒܘܢ [74]ܕܢܬܠ ܠܢ ܕܕܠܐ ܕܚܠܐ ܢܬܦܪܩ ܡܢ
ܐܝܕܐ ܕܒܥܠܕ̈ܒܒܝܢ ܕܢܦܠܘܚ ܩܕܡܘܗܝ [75]ܒܟܐܝܢܘܬܐ ܘܒܙܕܝܩܘܬܐ
ܟܠܗܘܢ ܝܘܡܬܐ ܕܚ̈ܝܝܢ. [76]ܘܐܢܬ ܛܠܝܐ ܢܒܝܗ ܕܥܠܝܐ ܬܬܩܪܐ
ܬܐܙܠ ܓܝܪ ܩܕܡ ܦܪ̈ܨܘܦܗ ܕܡܪܝܐ ܠܡܛܝܒܘ ܐܘܪܚܬܗ [77]ܕܢܬܠ ܡܕܥܐ
ܕܚܝܐ ܠܥܡܗ ܒܫܘܒܩܢܐ ܕܚܛܗ̈ܝܗܘܢ [78]ܡܛܠ ܚܢܢܐ ܕܪ̈ܚܡܘܗܝ
ܕܐܠܗܢ ܕܒܗܘܢ ܢܣܥܪܢ ܡܕܢܚܐ ܡܢ ܪܘܡܐ. [79]ܬܢܗܪ
ܠܐܝܠܝܢ ܕܒܚܫܘܟܐ ܘܒܛ̈ܠܠܝܗܘܢ ܕܡܘܬܐ ܝܬܒܝܢ ܕܢܬܪܘܨ ܪ̈ܓܠܝܢ
ܒܐܘܪܚܐ ܕܫܠܡܐ. [80]ܛܠܝܐ ܕܝܢ ܪܒܐ ܗܘܐ ܘܡܬܚܝܠ ܒܪܘܚܐ
ܘܒܡܕܒܪ̈ܐ ܐܝܬ [ܗܘܐ] ܥܕܡܐ ܠܝܘܡܐ ܕܬܚܘܝܬܗ ܕܠܘܬ
ܐܝܣܪܐܝܠ ܀

78 ܢܣܥܪܢ ܡܕܢܚܐ] *S (sic)* 79 ܬܢܗܪ] *The* ܪ *appears to be undotted in S*

57 And when the time of Elisabeth's child-bearing was accomplished S
58 she bare a son, and her neighbours and the members of her family
heard that the Lord *had* multiplied his mercy unto her, and they
59 were rejoicing for her. And it was the eighth day *when* they came
to circumcise the lad, and they were calling him by the name of his
60 father Zacharia. And his mother said "Not so, but he shall be
61 called John." And they say to her: "There is no one in thy stock
62 that is called by this name 'John.'" And they had said to his
63 father also how he wished that he should be called; and he asked
64 for a writing-tablet and wrote on it "John is his name," and in the
same hour was unloosed the band of his tongue. And he blessed
(63), 65 God, and all of them were astonished. And fear came on all their cf. D
neighbours, and in all the hill-*country* of Judaea these things were
66 being spoken, and they were laying *them* up in their heart and were
saying: "What will this lad become, whom the hand of the Lord is
67 with?" And Zacharia his father was filled with the Holy Spirit and he
68 prophesied and said: "Blessed is the God of Israel that hath visited cf. Vg am
69 his people and made for it a redemption, and raised up for us a horn of
70 life in the house of David his slave, as he said by the mouth of his holy
71 prophets from eternity; and he hath snatched us away to life from the
72 hand of our enemies and of all that hate us, that he might do mercy
73 with our fathers. And he hath remembered his holy covenants, the
74 oaths that he sware to Abraham our father, that he would give to us
that without fear we should be redeemed from the hand of our
75 enemies, that we might serve before him in uprightness and in
76 righteousness all the days of our life. And thou, lad, the prophet
of the Highest shalt thou be called; thou shalt go before the
77 countenance of the Lord, to make ready his ways that he may give
the knowledge of life to his people by the forgiveness of their sins,
78 because of the mercy of the compassion of our God, wherewith he
79 will visit us *as* the sunrise from on high; thou shalt shine to them
that in darkness and in the shadows of death are sitting, that we
80 may direct our feet in the way of peace." Now the lad was growing
up and waxing strong in spirit, and in the wilderness he was until
the day of the shewing of him unto Israel.

---

76 thou shalt go] *so also* E^{7}, *without connecting particle* 78 sunrise] 'sun' E^{20} (*not* E^{30}) 79 thou shalt shine] *or*, 'it will shine' we] *or*, 'he'

S [1]ܘܗܘܐ ܒܝܘ̈ܡܬܐ ܗܠܝܢ ܦܩܕ ܗܘܐ ܐܓܘܣܛܘܣ ܩܣܪ
ܕܝܬܟܬܒܘܢ ܟܘܠܗ ܐܪܥܐ.[2] ܗܕܐ ܕܝܢ ܡܟܬܒܘܬܐ ܩܕܡܝܬܐ
ܗܘܬ ܒܝ̈ܡܝ ܩܘܪܝܢܘܣ ܗܓܡܘܢܐ ܕܣܘܪܝܐ[3] ܟܘܠ ܐܢܫ ܕܝܢ [ܐܙܠ
ܗܘܐ] ܠܡ⌜ܬܟܬ⌝ܒܘ ܐܦ ܡܢ ܡܕܝܢܬ * * ܐܙܠ ܗܘܐ ܠܐܬܪܗ
ܕܬܡܢ ܢܬܟܬܒ [4a]ܘܐܦ ܝܘܣܦ ⌜ܣ⌝ܠܩ ܗܘܐ ܡܢ ܢܨܪܬ ܡܕܝܢܬܐ
ܕܓܠܝܠܐ ܠܝܗܘܕ ܠܡܕܝܢܬܗ ܕܕܘܝܕ ܕܡܬܩܪܝܐ ܒܝܬ ܠܚܡ[5] ܗܘ
ܘܡܪܝܡ ܐܝܬܬܗ ܟܕ ܒܛܢܐ ܕܬܡܢ ܢܬܟܬܒܘܢ[4b]ܡܛܠ ܕܬܪ̈ܝܗܘܢ
ܡܢ ܒܝܬܗ ܗܘܘ ܕܕܘܝܕ.[6] ܘܟܕ ܬܡܢ ܐܢܘܢ ܐܫܬܠܡܘ ܝܘ̈ܡܬܗ
ܠܡܐܠܕ.[7] ܘܝܠܕܬܗ ܠܒܪܗ ܒܘܟܪܐ. ܘܟܪܟܬܗ ܒܥܙܪܘܪܐ ܘܐܪܒܥܬܗ
ܒܐܘܪܝܐ ܡܛܠ ܕܠܝܬ ܗܘܬ ܠܗܘܢ ܕܘܟܬܐ[8] ܪܥܘܬܐ ܕܝܢ ܐܝܬ
ܗܘܘ ܬܡܢ ܒܗ ܒܐܬܪܐ [ܘܟܕ] ܪܥܝܢ ܗܘܘ ܘܢܛܪܝܢ ܡܛܪܬܐ ܥܠ
ܢܘܩܬܗܘܢ[9] ܐܬܚܙܝܘ ܠܗܘܢ ܡܠܐ⌜ܟܐ⌝ [ܕܡܪܝܐ] ܟܕ ܩܐܡ *
ܘܬܫܒܘܚܬܗ ܕܡܪܝܐ ܢܗ⌜ܪ⌝ܐ ܗܘܬ ܥܠܝܗܘܢ ܘܚܫܘ ܕܚܠܘ
ܕܚܠܬܐ ܪܒܬܐ[10] ܐܡܪ ܠܗܘܢ ܡܠܐܟܐ ܠܐ ܬܕܚܠ⌜ܘܢ⌝ ܡܛܠ
ܕܗܐ ܡܣܒܪܐ ܠܟܘܢ ܚܕܘܬܐ ܪܒܬܐ ܕܬܗܘܐ ܠܟܠܗ ܥܡܐ
[11]ܕܐܬܝܠܕ ⌜ܠܟܘܢ⌝ ܝܘܡܢܐ ܦܪܘܩܐ ܕܐܝܬܘܗܝ، ܡܪܝܐ ܡܫܝܚܐ
ܒܡܕܝܢܬܗ ܕܕܘܝܕ.[12] [ܗܐ ܗܕܐ] ܠܟܘܢ ܐܬܐ ܡܫܟܚܝܢ ܐܢܬܘܢ
ܠܛܠܝܐ ܟܕ ܟܪܝܟ ܒܥܙܪ̈ܘܪܐ ܘܫܟܝܒ ܒܐܘܪܝܐ[13]ܘܡܢ ܫܠܝܐ
ܐܬܚܙܝܘ ܠܘܬܗ ܚ⌜ܝܠ⌝ܐ ܘܡܠܐ⌜ܟܐ⌝ [ܕܫܡܝܐ] ܘܠܐܠܗܐ ܡܫܒܚܝܢ
§A 180, 385 ܠܐܠܗܐ ܘܐܡܪ̈ܝܢ.[§14] ܫܘܒܚܐ ܠܐܠܗܐ ܒܡܪ̈ܘܡܐ ܘܫܠܡܐ
¶A ܒܐܪܥܐ ܘܐܪܥܘܬܐ ܠܒܢ̈ܝ ܐܢܫܐ[¶] ○ ○

---

2 ܒܝ̈ܘܡ] *S* (*sic*) 3 * * ܡܕܝܢܬ] *S*[ed]: *photograph illegible* 4[b] *Cf A* 472 ܐܝܟ ܕܟܬܝܒ. ܕܝܘܣܦ ܘܡܪܝܡ ܡܟܪܝܬܗ. ܬܪ̈ܝܗܘܢ ܡܢ ܒܝܬܗ (ܗܘܘ + *A*[a]) ܕܕܘܝܕ
8 ⌜ܘܟܕ⌝ ܪܥܝܢ] ܕ⌜ܪ⌝ܥܝܢ *S*[ed] 9 * | ܟܕ ܩܐܡ] *There seems hardly room at the beginning of the next line after* ܩܐܡ *to supply* ܥܠܝܗܘܢ 10 ܠܟܠܗ ܥܡܐ] *S* (= syr. vg): *cf* Mt i 21 *and Dalman's* Worte Jesu 144 11 ܡܪܝܐ] *S* (= syr.vg *and* ASD 44[ad fin.]) 12 ⌜ܗܐ ܗܕܐ⌝] ܗܐ ܘܗܢܐ *S*[ed]; *possibly the scribe wrote* ܗܘ ܗܢܐ *and took* ܐܬܐ *for a verb*
14 ܫܘܒܚܐ......ܒܐܪܥܐ] ܫܠܡܐ ܒܡܪ̈ܘܡܐ ܘܬܫܒܘܚܬܐ ܒܐܪܥܐ. *A* 180; ܬܫܒܘܚܬܐ ܠܐܠܗܐ ܒܡܪ̈ܘܡܐ. *A* 385 ܘܐܪܥܘܬܐ] *S* (*sic*, *cf* ܘܐܪܟܒ Mk xi 7); ܘܣܒܪܐ ܛܒܐ $A^2/_2$

ii 1 And it came to pass in those days Augustus Caesar had commanded *S*
2 all the earth that they should be enrolled. Now this was the first
3 enrolment in the years of Quirinus, governor of Syria. Now every
one [was going] to be [enrolled], even from [his] city was *each one*
4a going to his place that there he might be enrolled. And Joseph also
had gone up from Nazareth a city of Galilee to Judaea, to the city of
5 David that is called Beth Lehem, he and Mary his wife *who was*
4b great with child, that there they might be enrolled, because both of
6 them were of the House of David. And when they were there her
7 days were fulfilled to bear, and she bare her first-born son; and she
wrapped him in swaddling-clothes and put him in a manger, because
8 there was no room for them. Now there were shepherds there in that
same place [and while] they were watching and keeping guard over
9 their ewes, there appeared to them an angel [of the LORD] standing
[by them] and the glory of the LORD was shining upon them, and they
10 feared with a great fear. The angel saith to them: "Fear ye not;
because lo, I announce to you a great joy that shall be for all the
11 world—that there hath been born for you to-day a Life-giver, who is
12 the LORD, the Messiah, in the city of David. †Lo, this† *is* for you
the sign: ye will find the lad wrapped in swaddling-clothes and laid
13 in a manger." And suddenly there appeared by him a host, and the
14 many angels [of heaven] glorify God and say: §"Glory to God in the §*A* 180,
highest, and peace in earth, and favour to the sons of men."¶ ¶*A* 385

---

2 the years of] *S* (*sic*) 4b because both......of David] *Cf* '*as it is written* Joseph and Mary his betrothed, both of them were of the House of David' *A* 472: *so also* E^{16} *and* Ephr.*arm* (*on* 2 Tim ii 8) 10 all the world] *S* (= syr.vg): *cf* Mt i 21 11 the LORD, the Messiah] *S* (= syr.vg); the LORD's Messiah E^{27} *and* syr[palest] 12 †Lo, this†] Lo, and he S^{ed}. *Perhaps the scribe meant the text to mean:*—'...the Messiah, in the city of David: He Himself to you hath come. Ye will find....' 14 Glory....earth] Peace in heaven and glory in earth *A* 180; Glory to God in heaven *A* 385 favour] good hope $A^{2}/_{2}$ E^{27} (*as* syr.vg)

S [15]ܗܡ ܒܬܪ ܕܐܙܠܘ ܡܢ ܠܘܬܗܘܢ ܡܠܐܟܐ ܗܢܘܢ ܠܫܡܝܐ
ܐܡܪܝܢ ܗܘܘ ܪܥܘܬܐ ܚܕ ܠܚܕ ܬܘ ܢܙܠ ܠܒܝܬ ܠܚܡ ܘܢܚܙܐ
ܗܢܐ ܡܠܐ ܕܗܘܐ ܐܝܟܢܐ ܕܡܠܐܟܐ ܚܘܝܢ [16]ܘܐܙܠܘ ܡܣܪܗܒܐܝܬ
ܘܐܫܟܚܘ ܠܝܘܣܦ ܘܠܡܪܝܡ ܘܠܛܠܝܐ ܟܕ ܣܝܡ ܒܐܘܪܝܐ
[17]ܘܐܫܬܥܝܘ ܡܕܡ ܕܐܬܡܠܠ ܥܡܗܘܢ ܥܠܘܗܝ، ܥܠ ܛܠܝܐ [18]ܟܠ
ܐܝܢܐ ܕܝܢ ܕܫܡܥ ܗܘܐ ܡܢ ܪ̈ܥܘܬܐ ܟܕ ܡܫܬܥܝܢ ܗܘܘ ܥܠ
ܐܠܝܢ ܕܚܙܘ ܘܫܡܥܘ ܬܡܝܗܝܢ ܗܘܘ ܘܡܬܕܡܪܝܢ [19]ܡܪܝܡ ܕܝܢ
ܟܠ ܡܕܡ ܚܫܒܐ ܗܘܬ ܒܠܒܗ ܘܡܚܫܒܐ ܗܘܬ ܒܪܥܝܢܗ
[20]ܘܗܦܟܘ ܪ̈ܥܘܬܐ ܗܢܘܢ ܟܕ ܡܫܒܚܝܢ ܠܐܠܗܐ ܘܡܗܠܠܝܢ ܥܠ
ܐܠܝܢ ܕܚܙܘ ܘܫܡܥܘ ܐܝܟܢܐ ܕܐܬܐܡܪ ܠܗܘܢ ܀

[21]ܘܟܕ ܡܠܘ ܬܡܢܝܐ ܝܘ̈ܡܝܢ ܐܬܓܙܪ ܛܠܝܐ ܘܐܬܩܪܝ، ܫܡܗ ܝܫܘܥ
ܐܝܟܢܐ ܕܐܬܐܡܪ ܡܢ ܡܠܐܟܐ ܡܢ ܩܕܡ ܕܢܬܒܛܢ ܒܟܪܣܐ
[22]ܘܟܕ ܡܠܘ ܝܘ̈ܡܬܐ ܕܬܕܟܝܬܗ ܐܝܟܢܐ ܕܟܬܝܒ ܒܢܡܘܣܐ ܕܡܘܫܐ
ܗܕܝܢ ܐܣܩܘܗܝ، ܠܐܘܪܫܠܡ ܕܢܩܝܡܘܢܝܗ ܩܕܡ ܡܪܝܐ [23]ܐܝܟܢܐ
ܕܟܬܝܒ ܒܢܡܘܣܐ ܕܡܪܝܐ ܕܟܠ ܒܘܟܪܐ ܦܬܚ ܡܪܚܡܐ ܩܕܝܫܗ
ܕܡܪܝܐ ܢܬܩܪܐ [24]ܘܕܢܬܠ ܕܒܚܬܐ ܐܝܟܢܐ ܕܟܬܝܒ ܒܢܡܘܣܐ
ܕܡܪܝܐ ܙܘܓܐ ܕܫ̈ܦܢܝܢܐ ܐܘ ܬܪܝܢ ܦܪ̈ܘܓܐ ܕܝܘܢܐ ܀

[25]ܓܒܪܐ ܕܝܢ ܚܕ ܐܝܬ ܗܘܐ ܒܐܘܪܫܠܡ ܫܡܗ ܗܘܐ ܫܡܥܘܢ
ܗܢ ܗܘܐ ܘܙܕܝܩ ܘܡܩܒܠ ܗܘܐ ܒܒܘܝܐܐ ܕܐܝܣܪܝܠ ܘܪܘܚܐ
ܩܕܝܫܬܐ ܐܝܬ ܗܘܬ ܥܠܘܗܝ، [26]ܘܐܡܝܪ ܗܘܐ ܠܗ ܡܢ ܗܝ، ܪܘܚܐ
ܩܕܝܫܬܐ ܕܡܘܬܐ ܠܐ ܢܚܙܐ ܥܕܡܐ ܕܢܚܙܐ ܠܡܫܝܚܗ ܕܡܪܝܐ
[27]ܘܐܬܐ ܒܪܘܚܐ ܠܗܝܟܠܐ ܘܟܕ ܡܥܠܝܢ ܠܗ ܐܒܗܘܗܝ، ܠܝܫܘܥ
ܛܠܝܐ ܕܢܥܒܕܘܢ ܠܗ ܐܝܟܢܐ ܕܦܩܝܕ ܒܐܘܪܝܬܐ [28]ܗܘ ܫܡܥܘܢ
ܡܩܒܠܗ ܥܠ ܕܪܥܘܗܝ، ܘܒܪܟ ܠܐܠܗܐ ܘܐܡܪ [29]ܡܟܝܠ ܫܪܐ
ܐܢܬ ܠܗ ܡܪܝ، ܒܫܠܡܐ ܠܥܒܕܟ ܐܝܟܢܐ ܕܐܡܪܬ [30]ܕܗܐ ܚܙ̈ܝ،
ܥܝ̈ܢܝ ܚܢܢܟ [31]ܗܘ ܕܛܝܒܬ ܩܕܡ ܦܪܨܘܦܐ ܕܟܠܗܘܢ ܥܡܡܐ

15 ܬܘ ܢܙܠ] *emended from* syr^palest (*for this spelling of* ܢܐܙܠ *see* Lk ix 51); * * ܬܘ ܢܬ S^ed 30 ܚܢܢܟ] S (*sic*): *the first nûn was certainly visible in 1893*

15 After those angels went away from them to heaven the shepherds *S*
were saying one to the other: "Come, let us [go] to Beth Lehem and
16 see this which hath come to pass, as the angel hath shewed us." And
they went hastily and found Joseph and Mary, and the babe laid in a
17 manger, and they declared that which was spoken with them about
18 that same lad. Now every one that was hearing from the shepherds
when they were declaring about the things that they saw and heard
19 were (*sic*) astonished and wondering, but Mary everything was laying
20 in her heart and was comparing *them* in her mind. And those
shepherds returned glorifying God and speaking about the things
that they saw and heard, as was said to them.

21 And when eight days were fulfilled the lad was circumcised, and
his name was called Jesus, as was said by the angel before he was
22 conceived in the womb; and the days of his cleansing were finished,
as it is written in the law of Moses. Then they took him up to
23 Jerusalem, that they might make him stand before the LORD, as is
written in the law of the LORD "Every first-born *male* opening the
24 matrix, the Holy one of the LORD he shall be called," and that he
might give the sacrifice, as is written in the law of the LORD: "A
pair of turtle-doves, or two young doves."

25 Now there was a certain man in Jerusalem—his name was Simon
—upright he was and righteous, and he was receiving the supplication
26 of Israel and a holy Spirit there was upon him; and it had been said
to him by that holy Spirit, that death he should not see until he
27 should see the LORD's Messiah. And he came in the Spirit to the
Temple, and when his parents were bringing him in, *even* the lad
28 Jesus, that they might do for him as is commanded in the Law, he—
29 Simon—received him in his arms and blessed God and said: "Hence-
forth thou dost dismiss him, my Lord, in peace—*even* thy servant, as
30, 31 thou hast said. For lo, mine eyes have seen thy mercy which thou

25, 26 a holy Spirit] *cf* Mk xiii 11, Joh xx 22 26 the LORD's Messiah] 'the Lord Christ' E^{226} (*quoted away from the context*) 30 thy mercy] *S* (*sic*) E^{28} *and* syr.vg

[32]ܢܘܗܪܐ ܠܓܠܝܢܐ ܕܥܡ̈ܡܐ. ܘܫܘܒܚܐ ܕܥܡܟ ܐܝܣܪܝܠ. [33]ܐܒܘܗܝ، S
ܕܝܢ ܘܐܡܗ ܬܡܝܗܝܢ ܗܘܘ ܥܠ ܐܝܠܝܢ ܕܡܬܡܠܠܢ ܥܠܘܗܝ. [34]ܘܒܪܟ
ܐܢܘܢ ܫܡܥܘܢ ܘܐܡܪ ܠܡܪܝܡ ܐܡܗ. ܗܐ ܗܢܐ ܣܝܡ
ܒܐܝܣܪܝܠ ܠܡܦܘܠܬܐ ܘܠܩܝܡܬܐ ܕܣ̈ܓܝܐܐ ܘܠܐܬܐ ܕܚܪܝܢܐ
ܕܡܬܡܠܠܐ. [35]ܘܠܢܦܫܟܝ ܕܝܠܟܝ ܬܥܒܪܝܘܗܝ ܪܘܡܚܐ ܕܢܬܓܠܝܢ ܡܚܫ̈ܒܬܐ
ܡܢ ܠܒܘ̈ܬܐ ܕܣ̈ܓܝܐܐ. [36]ܘܐܦ ܚܢܐ ܢܒܝܬܐ ܒܪܬܗ ܕܦܢܘܐܝܠ
ܡܢ ܫܒܛܐ ܕܐܫܝܪ ܘܐܦ ܗܝ، ܩܫܝܫܐܬ ܒܝܘ̈ܡܬܐ ܗܘܬ ܘܫܒܥܐ
ܫܢܝܢ ܥܡ ܒܥܠܗ. ܥܡ ܓܒܪܐ ܗܘܬ ܡܢ ܒܬܪ ܒܬܘܠܘܬܗ [37]ܘܐܪܡܠܐ
ܕܝܢ ܕܒܡܪܘܗ ܒܐܪܡܠܘܬܐ ܗܘܬ ܫܢܝܢ ܬܡܢܝܢ ܘܐܪ̈ܒܥ.
ܗܝ، ܗܕܐ ܡܢ ܗܝܟܠܐ ܠܐ ܢܦܩܐ ܗܘܬ. ܘܒܨܘܡܐ ܘܒܨܠܘܬܐ
ܘܒܒܥܘܬܐ ܒܐܝܡܡܐ ܘܒܠܠܝܐ ܦܠܚܐ ܗܘܬ [38]ܘܐܦ ܗܝ، ܩܡܬ
ܒܗ ܒܫܥܬܐ ܘܐܘܕܝܬ ܠܡܪܝܐ. ܘܡܡܠܠܐ ܗܘܬ ܥܠܘܗܝ، †ܥܡ†
ܟܘܠ ܐܢܫ ܕܡܣܟܐ ܗܘܐ ܠܦܘܪܩܢܗ ܕܐܘܪܫܠܡ. [39]ܝܘܣܦ ܕܝܢ
ܘܡܪܝܡ ܟܕ ܫܠܡܘ ܒܡܫܠܡܐ ܟܠ ܒܢܡܘܣܐ ܟܘܠ ܡܕܡ ܕܟܬܝܒ
ܒܐܘܪܝܬܐ ܗܦܟܘ ܠܓܠܝܠܐ ܠܢܨܪܬ ܡܕܝܢܬܗܘܢ ° ° °
[40]ܛܠܝܐ ܕܝܢ ܪܒܐ ܗܘܐ ܘܡܬܚܝܠ ܘܡܬܡܠܐ ܚܟܡܬܐ ܘܛܝܒܘܬܐ
ܕܐܠܗܐ ܐܝܬ ܗܘܬ ܥܠܘܗܝ، [41]ܘܐܒܗܘܗܝ، ܒܟܠ ܫܢܐ ܐܙܠܝܢ ܗܘܘ
ܠܐܘܪܫܠܡ ܒܥܐܕܐ ܕܦܛܝ̈ܪܐ ܕܦܨܚܐ. [42]ܘܟܕ ܗܘܐ ܒܪ ܫܢܝܢ
ܬܪܬܥܣܪܐ ܣܠܩܘ ܐܝܟ ܥܝܕܐ ܕܥܝܕܝܢ ܗܘܘ ܠܥܐܕܐ. [43]ܘܟܕ ܫܠܡܘ
⌜ܝܘ̈ܡܬܐ⌝ ⌜ܕܥܐܕܐ⌝ ⌜ܗܦܟܘ⌝ ܠܗܘܢ ܘܫܒܩܘ ܛܠܝܐ ܦܫ ܠܗ
⌜ܚܢܝܢܘ⌝ ܒܐܘܪܫܠܡ ܘܐܒܗܘܗܝ، ܠܐ ܝܕܥܘ [44]ܣܒܪܝܢ ܗܘܘ ܓܝܪ
ܕܥܡ ܠܘܝܬܗܘܢ ܢܗܘܐ ܘܟܕ [ܐܬܘ ܡܪܕܐ] ܕܝܘܡ ܚܕ ܒܥܘܗܝ ܒܝܢ
ܗܘܘ ܠܗ ܠܝܫܘܥ ܠܘܬ ܒܢܝ ܠܘܝܬܗܘܢ ܘܠܘܬ ⌜ܐܚܝܢܘܬܗܘܢ⌝

35 *Cf* Ishô'dâd (*Harris*, p. 34): ܡܪܝ ܐܦܪܝܡ. ܒܥܒܕܐ ܠܟ ܬܥܒܪܝܘܗܝ ܪܘܡܚܐ. ܕܢܬܓܠܘܢ ܡܢ ܠܒܘ̈ܬܐ ܕܣ̈ܓܝܐܐ ܡܚܫ̈ܒܬܐ ܗܢܘܢ ܕܐܬܟܣܝܘ. (ܕܣ̈ܓܝܐܐ *cod.*)
36 ܘܡܢܗܝܢ] ܥܡ ܒܬܪܐ ܗܘܬ ܗܘܬ ܡܩ̈ܕܡ ܠܟ ܥܡܟܐ Ephr. *Lamy* iii 813
38 ܥܡ] ܥܠ *S* (*sic*)   ܕܡܣܟܝܢ ܗܘܐ] *S* (*sic*)   43 ⌜ܚܢܝܢܘ⌝] ⌜ܒܡܘܬܪܗܘܢ⌝ *S*[ed], *but there hardly seems space enough*   44 ܕܝܢ] *S* (*sic*)   ܒܥܝܢ ܗܘܘ] *S* (*sic*)

32 hast made ready before the countenance of all the peoples,—a light S
33 for revelation of the peoples, and a glory of thy people Israel." Now
his father and his mother were astonished at the things that were
34 being spoken about him. And Simon blessed them and said to Mary
his mother: "Lo, this *child* is set in Israel for the fall and for the
35 rising of many, and for a sign of contention that is spoken of; and
thine own soul thou shalt cause a spear to pass through, that the
36 thoughts may be revealed from the hearts of many." And Hanna
also, a prophetess, the daughter of Phanuel of the tribe of Asher—
and she also was advanced in days, and seven days only with a
37 husband she was after her virginity, but the rest of her way of
life in widowhood was eighty and four years,—this person from
the Temple used not to go forth, and with fasting and with prayer
38 and with supplication by day and by night used to serve *God*—and
she also stood up in the same hour and gave thanks to the LORD, and
she was speaking about him †with† every one that was announcing a
39 redemption of Jerusalem. Now Joseph and Mary, when they finished
in the Temple concerning the first-born everything that is written in
the Law, returned to Galilee to Nazareth their city.

40 Now the lad was growing up and waxing strong and being filled
41 with wisdom, and the grace of God was upon him. And his kinsfolk
every year were going to Jerusalem at the Feast of unleavened bread,
42 of Pasek; and when he was twelve years old they went up, as they
43 were accustomed, to the Feast. And when the days of the Feast
were finished they returned, and the lad Jesus stayed from them in
44 Jerusalem. And his kinsfolk knew *it* not, for they were supposing
that with their company he went forth, and when [they had come a
journey] of one day they were seeking him, *even* Jesus, among their

35 *Cf* Ishô'dâd (*Harris*, p. 34): 'S. Ephraim. Through thy soul (saith he) thou shalt cause a spear to pass, that there may be revealed from the hearts many minds—those who doubted.' $E^{28f.}$ *has three times* 'Thou shalt cause a sword to pass,' *as in the text here* (J. Armitage Robinson *in the* 'Guardian' *for Dec* 18, 1895) 36 days] 'Seven days she had been with a husband' Ephr. *Lamy* iii 813 38 †with†] 'about' *S* (*sic*) that..... Jerusalem] *or*, 'that a redemption of Jerusalem was being announced' 43 from them] after them S^{ed}

S [C] ܘܠܘܬ ܡܢ ܕܝܕܥ ܠܗܘܢ [45]ܘܟܕ ܠܐ ܐܫܟܚܘܗܝ ܗܦܟܘ ܠܗܘܢ
ܠܐܘܪܫܠܡ ܘܬܡܢ ܒܥܝܢ ܗܘܘ ܠܗ. [46]ܘܡܢ ܒܬܪ ܬܠܬܐ ܝܘܡܝܢ
ܐܫܟܚܘܗܝ ܒܗܝܟܠܐ ܟܕ ܝܬܒ ܡܨܥܬ ܡܠܦܢܐ ܘܫܡܥ ܗܘܐ
ܠܗܘܢ ܘܡܫܐܠ ܗܘܐ ܠܗܘܢ [47]ܘܬܡܝܗܝܢ ܗܘܘ ܟܠܗܘܢ ܐܝܠܝܢ
ܕܫܡܥܝܢ ܗܘܘ ܠܗ. ܘܡܬܕܡܪܝܢ ܗܘܘ ܒܚܟܡܬܗ ܘܒܦܬܓܡܘܗܝ.
[48]ܘܟܕ ܐܫܟܚܘܗܝ ܐܒܘܗܝ ܬܡܗܘ. ܘܐܡܪܐ ܠܗ ܐܡܗ ܒܪܝ
§C fol 53 r ܠܡܢܐ §*ܥܒܕܬ ܠܢ ܗܟܢܐ. ܕܗܐ ܐܚܝܢ ܒܟܪܝܘܬܐ ܘܒܛܘܪܦܐ
ܦܠܐܐ ܒܥܝܢ ܗܘܝܢ ܠܟ. [49]ܐܡܪ ܠܗܘܢ ܡܢܐ ܒܥܝܢ ܐܢܬܘܢ
ܠܝ. ܠܐ ܝܕܥܝܢ ܐܢܬܘܢ ܕܒܝܬ ܐܒܐ ܘܠܐ ܠܝ ܕܐܗܘܐ. [50]ܗܢܘܢ
ܕܝܢ ܠܐ ܐܣܬܟܠܘܗ ܠܡܠܬܐ ܕܐܡܪ ܠܗܘܢ܆ [51]ܘܢܚܬ ܥܡܗܘܢ
ܘܐܬܐ ܠܢܨܪܬ܂ ܘܡܫܬܥܒܕ ܗܘܐ ܠܗܘܢ܆ ܐܡܗ ܕܝܢ ܟܠܗܝܢ
ܗܠܝܢ ܡ̈ܠܐ ܢܛܪܐ ܗܘܬ ܒܠܒܝܗ. [52]ܝܫܘܥ ܕܝܢ ܪܒܐ ܗܘܐ
ܒܩܘܡܬܗ. ܘܣܓܐ ܒܚܟܡܬܗ ܘܒܛܝܒܘܬܗ܂ ܠܘܬ ܐܠܗܐ ܘܠܘܬ
ܒ̈ܢܝ ܐܢܫܐ ܀

[1]ܒܫܢܬ ܚܡܫܥܣܪܐ ܕܝܢ. ܒܡܕܒܪܢܘܬܐ ܕܛܒܪܝܘܣ ܩܣܪ.
ܒܗܓܡܘܢܘܬܐ ܕܦܝܠܛܘܣ ܒܝܗܘܕ. ܟܕ ܪܫܐ ܐܪܒܥܝܐ
col 2 *ܗܪܘܕܣ ܕܓܠܝܠܐ. ܘܦܝܠܝܦܘܣ ܐܚܘܗܝ ܪܫܐ ܐܪܒܥܝܐ ܕܐܬܪܐ
ܕܐܝܛܘܪܝܐ. ܘܒܟܘܪ ܕܛܪܟܘܢܐ. ܘܠܘܣܢܝܐ ܪܫܐ ܐܪܒܥܝܐ ܕܐܬܪܐ
ܕܐܒܝܠܢܐ. [2]ܒܪܒܢܘܬ ܟܗܢܘܬܐ ܕܚܢܢ ܘܕܩܝܦܐ. ܗܘܬ ܡܠܬܐ
ܕܐܠܗܐ ܥܠ ܝܘܚܢܢ ܒܪ ܙܟܪܝܐ. [3]ܘܡܟܪܙ ܗܘܐ ܡܥܡܘܕܝܬܐ ܘܒܟܠܗ
ܐܬܪܐ ܕܚܕܪ ܝܘܪܕܢ. ܡܥܡܘܕܝܬܐ ܕܬܝܒܘܬܐ ܠܫܘܒܩܢܐ
ܕܚ̈ܛܗܐ. [4]ܐܝܟ ܕܟܬܝܒ ܒܟܬܒܘܗܝ ܕܐܫܥܝܐ ܢܒܝܐ. ܩܠܐ
ܕܩܪܐ ܒܡܕܒܪܐ. ܦܢܘ ܐܘܪܚܐ ܠܡܪܝܐ. ܘܬܪܘܨܘ ܒܦܩܥܬܐ

---

45 ܘܟܕ ܠܐ] S (*sic*)   48 ܐܚܝܢ] ܐܒܘܟ ܘܐܢܐ S   ܒܟܪܝܘܬܐ ܘ] *om.* S
49 ܐܢܬܘܢ] ܗܘܝܬܘܢ S (*in both places*)   ܐܒܐ] ܐܒܝ S   ܘܠܐ] + ܗܘܐ S
51 ܟܠܗܝܢ S (*as often*)   ܗܠܝܢ] *om.* S   ܒܠܒܝܗ] C (*sic*); *om.* S   52 ܘܣܓܐ] + ܗܘܐ S   ܘܒܛܝܒܘܬܗ] *so also* S   1 ܕܛܒܪܝܘܣ] S *illegible*   ܒܗܓܡܘܢܘܬܐ] S vid (*sic*): *the* ܗ *in* C *has disappeared in a hole*   ܒܝܗܘܕ] *so also* S*(vid); ܒܝܗܘܕܐ S1 (& ed)   ܐܪܒܥܐ S (*in each place*)   ܪܫܐ 2° & 3°] ܪܝܫܐ Sed
ܒܛܪܟܘܢܐ S   ܕܐܒܝܠܝܢܐ Sed   4 ܒܟܬܒܘܬܐ S   ܦܢܘ] ܦܢܘ S   ܘܬܪܨܘ S

company and among their kindred and among whosoever knew them. *S* [*C*]
45 And when they found him not, they returned to Jerusalem and there
46 they were seeking him. And after three days they found him in the
Temple sitting amidst the teachers, and he was hearing them and
47 was asking them *questions.* And all of them that were hearing him
were astonished, and were wondering at his wisdom and at his
48 answers. And when his kinsfolk found him they were astonished;
and his mother saith to him: "My son, wherefore | §hast thou done §*C*
to us thus? For lo, we in trouble and in much perturbation have
49 been seeking thee." He saith to them: "Why are ye seeking me?
Know ye not that at the Father's House it behoves me to be?"
50, 51 Now they did not recognise the word that he said to them. And he
went down with them and came to Nazareth, and was subject to
them, but his mother all these words was keeping in †her† mind.
52 Now Jesus was growing up in his stature, and increasing in his
wisdom and in his grace with God and with men.

iii 1 Now in the fifteenth year, in the reign of Tiberius Caesar, in the
governorship of Pontius Pilate in Judaea, Herod being tetrarch in
Galilee, and Philip his brother tetrarch in the country of Ituraea and
in the district of Trachonitis, and Lysanias tetrarch in the country of
2 the Habilenes, in the high priesthood of Hanan and of Caiapha,—came
3 the word of God upon John the son of Zacharia, and he was preaching
in the wilderness and in all the country around Jordan the baptism
4 of repentance for remission of sins; as is written in the prophecy of
Isaiah the prophet: "A voice that calleth in the wilderness, 'Clear

---

48 we] thy father and I *S*; I and thy father $E^{24,40}$ in trouble and] *om. S* (*not* $E^{24,40}$) **49** are ye....Know ye] were ye....Knew ye *S* the Father's (*see on* Matt vi 4)] my Father's *S* behoves] behoved *S* **51** these words] the words *S* in †her† mind] *om. S*; *by the omission of a point C reads* 'in his mind' **52** increasing] *pr.* was *S* **1** Tiberius] *S illegible*; *C has* 'Tiberinus' Judaea] *so also* $S^{*(vid)}$; Judah $S^{1(\&\ ed)}$ of Trachonitis] in Trachonitis *S* the Habilenes] Habilene S^{ed}, *but with the plural sign* **4** Clear ye] Make ye ready *S*

C S ܫ̈ܒܝܠܐ ܠܐܠܗܢ܀ ⁵ܟܠܗܘܢ ܢܚ̈ܠܐ ܢܬܡܠܘܢ܂ ܘܟܠܗܘܢ ܛܘܪ̈ܐ
§A 330 ܘܪ̈ܡܬܐ ܢܬܡܟܟܘܢ܀ §ܘܢܗܘܐ ܚܘܪܒܐ ܠܦܫܝܩܐ. ܘܐܬܪܐ ܥܣܩܐ
fol 53 v *ܠܦܫܝܛܬܐ. ⁶ܘܢܬܓܠܐ ܐܝܩܪܗ ܕܡܪܝܐ. ܘܢܚܙܘܢܗ ܐܢܫ̈ܐ ܟܠ
¶A ܒܣܪ.¶ ܡܛܠ ܕܦܘܡܗ ܕܡܪܝܐ ܡܠܠ. ܀

⁷ܘܐܡܪ ܗܘܐ ܠܟܢ̈ܫܐ ܐܝܠܝܢ ܕܐܬܝܢ ܗܘܘ ܠܘܬܗ. ܝܠܕܐ ܕܐ̈ܟܕܢܐ
ܡܢܘ ܚܘܝܟܘܢ ܠܡܥܪܩ ܡܢ ܪܘܓܙܐ ܕܐܬܐ. ⁸ܥܒܕܘ ܗܟܝܠ
ܦܐܪ̈ܐ ܕܫܘܝܢ ܠܬܝܒܘܬܐ. ܘܠܐ ܬܫܪܘܢ ܠܡܐܡܪ ܕܐܒܐ ܐܝܬ
ܠܢ ܐܒܪܗܡ. ܐܡܪܢܐ ܠܟܘܢ ܓܝܪ ܕܡܫܟܚ ܐܠܗܐ ܕܡܢ ܗܠܝܢ
ܟܐ̈ܦܐ ܠܡܩܡܘ ܒ̈ܢܝܐ ܠܐܒܪܗܡ. ⁹ܘܗܐ ܡܛܠ ܠܗ ܢܪܓܐ ܠܘܬ
ܥܩܪܘܗܝ ܕܐ̈ܝܠܢܐ. ܟܘܠ ܐܝܠܢܐ ܕܝܢ ܕܦܐܪ̈ܐ ܛܒ̈ܐ ܠܐ ܥܒܕ
ܡܬܦܣܩ ܘܒܢܘܪܐ ܢܦܠ. ܀

col 2 ¹⁰ܘܡܫܐܠܝܢ ܗܘܘ ܠܗ *ܟܢ̈ܫܐ. ܡܢܐ ܢܥܒܕ ܘܢܚܐ. ¹¹ܐܡܪ ܠܗܘܢ
ܡܢ ܕܐܝܬ ܠܗ ܬܪ̈ܬܝܢ ܟܘ̈ܬܝܢܝܢ ܢܬܠ ܚܕܐ ܡܢܗܝܢ ܠܡܢ ܕܠܝܬ
ܠܗ. ܘܡܢ ܕܐܝܬ ܠܗ ܬܘܪܣܝܬܐ ܗܟܢܐ ܢܥܒܕ. ¹²ܘܐܬܘ ܐܦ
ܡ̈ܟܣܐ ܠܡܥܡܕ. ܐܡܪܝܢ ܠܗ ܡܢܐ ܢܥܒܕ. ¹³ܐܡܪ ܠܗܘܢ ܠܐ
ܬܓܒܘܢ ܡܕܡ ܝܬܝܪ ܥܠ ܡܕܡ ܕܦܩܝܕ ܠܟܘܢ܀ ¹⁴ܘܫܐܠܘܗܝ
ܗܘܘ ܐܦ ܐ̈ܣܛܪܛܝܘܛܐ ܘܐܡܪܝܢ ܠܗ. ܡܢܐ ܢܥܒܕ ܐܦ ܚܢܢ.
ܐܡܪ ܠܗܘܢ ܠܐܢܫ ܠܐ ܬܬܥܫܩܘܢ܀ ܘܠܐܢܫ ܠܐ ܬܬܛܠܡܘܢ܀
ܣܦܩ ܠܟܘܢ ܐ̈ܦܘܣܢܝܘܬܟܘܢ܀ ¹⁵ܘܐܢܫܐ ܕܡܣܟܝܢ ܗܘܘ ܠܗ
ܡܬܪܢܝܢ ܗܘܘ ܒܠܒܗܘܢ ܘܐܡܪܝܢ ܠܡܢܐ ܠܐ ܗܘܝܘ ܡܫܝܚܐ[·]

5 ܘܟܠܗܘܢ] om. S   ܘܢܗܘܐ] ܢܗܘܐ ܕܒܟܐܬܬܗ ܕܟܬܝܒ ܐܝܟ A
6 ܘܢܚܙܘܢܗ] ܘܢܚܙܘܢܝܗ̇ S; ܘܢܚܙܐ ܟܠ ܒܣܪ ܚܝ̈ܘܗܝ ܕܐܠܗܐ A (om. rel.)
(syr.vg has ܚ̈ܝܐ ܕܐܠܗܐ)   ܡܛܠ....ܡܠܠ.] om. S A   7 ܠܘܬܗ] ܠܗ ܠܡܥܡܕ S
ܕܐܬܐ] ܕܥܬܝܕ S   8. For A 63, 331, see Matt iii 9   ܕܐܒܐ ܐܝܬ ܠܢ]
ܐܝܬ ܠܢ ܐܒܐ S   ܠܡܩܡܘ] ܢܩܝܡ S   9 ܘܗܐ...ܕܡܢ] ܘܟܠ...ܗܟܝܠ S
ܕܦܐܪ̈ܐ......ܥܒܕ] ܕܠܐ ܥܒܕ ܦܐܪ̈ܐ ܛܒ̈ܐ S (sic)   10. No fresh § in S
ܘܢܚܐ] om. S   11 ܡܢܗܝܢ] om. S   ܕܠܝܬ ܠܗ] + "ܘ" C (to end the line)
12 ܘܐܡܪܝܢ S   13 ܬܓܒܘܢ] ܬܓܒܘܢ S (sic)   14 ܣܛܪ̈ܛܝܘܛܐ S
ܠܗ] om. S   ܘܐܡܪܝܢ] om. ܘ S   ܣܦܩ ܠܟܘܢ] C (sic) S^vid, but there is a blurred space in S between the words   15 ܒܠܒܗܘܢ] + ܥܠ ܝܘܚܢܢ S
ܠܡܢܐ] ܕܠܡܢܐ S   ܠܐ] after ܗܘܝܘ in S   *C is slightly torn here, but legible.*

ye a way for the LORD, and direct in the plain paths for our God.' C S
5 All the valleys shall be filled and all the hills and heights shall
become low, §and the rough shall become a level and the broken §A330
6 country a plain. And the honour of the LORD shall be revealed and
all flesh shall see it together,¶ because the mouth of the LORD hath ¶A
spoken."

7 And he was saying to the multitudes that were coming unto him:
"Offspring of vipers, who is it hath shewed you to flee from the wrath
8 that is coming? Bring forth therefore fruits meet for repentance;
and do not begin to say 'For a father we have Abraham,' for I
say to you that God is able from these stones to raise up sons to
9 Abraham. And lo, the axe hath arrived at the root of the trees;
but every tree that bringeth not forth good fruits is hewn down and
falleth in the fire."

10 And the multitudes were asking him: "What shall we do, and
11 live?" He saith to them: "He that hath two coats, let him give one
of them to him that hath not; and he that hath food, let him do
12 likewise." And there came toll-gatherers also to be baptized. They
13 say to him: "What shall we do?" He saith to them: "Do not
14 exact any more above that which is appointed to you." And soldiers
also had asked him and they say to him: "What shall we do, even
we?" He saith to them: "Do not oppress any one, and do not use
15 violence to any one; sufficient for you are your allowances." And
the folk that were hearing him were meditating in themselves and

---

5 and all] *om.* *S* and the rough] 'As it is written that at his coming the rough...' *A* 6 shall see it together] shall see the life of God *A* because....spoken] *om.* *S A* 7 unto him] to him to be baptized *S* coming 2°] about *to be S* 8. *For A* 63, 331, *see* Matt iii 9 We have for a father *S* 9 arrived] *see* Matt iii 10 but every tree] and every tree therefore *S* 10 and live] *om.* *S* 11 of them] *om.* *S* 12 They say] and they say *S* 13 exact] thieve *S* (*sic*) 14 to him] *om.* *S* and do not] *om.* and *S* 15 in themselves] + about John *S*

(C) S ¶C ¹⁶ܐܡܪ ܠܗܘܢ ܐܢܐ ܗܐ ܡܥܡܕܢܐ ܠܟܘܢ ܒܡ̈ܝܐ¶|. ܐܬܐ ܕܝܢ
[ܒܬܪܝ], ܕܚܝܠ ܚܝܠܬܢ· ܗܘ ܕܠܐ ܫܘܐ ܐܢܐ ܕܐܫܪܐ ܥܪ̈ܩܐ
ܕܡܣܢܘܗܝ. ܗܘ ܢܥܡܕܟܘܢ ܒܢܘܪܐ ܘܒܪܘܚܐ ܕܩܘܕܫܐ ¹⁷ܗܘ
ܕܐܝܬ ܪܦܫܐ ܒܐܝܕܗ ܘܡܕܟܐ ܐܕܪܗ ⌜ܘܟܢ⌝ܫ ܚܛܐ ܠܐܘܨܪܗ·
ܘܬܒܢܐ ܢܘܩܕ ܒܢܘܪܐ ܕܠܐ ܕܥܟܐ ¹⁸ܐܦ ܐܚܪ̈ܢܝܬܐ ܣܓܝ̈ܐܬܐ.
ܟܕ ܡܬܟܫܦ ܗܘܐ ܡܣܒܪ ܠܥܡܐ ¹⁹ܗܪܘܕܣ ܕܝܢ ܛܛܪܪܟܐ ܡܛܠ
ܕܡܟܣ ܗܘܐ ܠܗ ⌜ܝܘ⌝ܚܢܢ ܡܛܠ ܗܪܘܕܝܐ ܐܢܬܬܗ ܕܐܚܘܗܝ,
ܕܗ⌜ܪ⌝ܘܕܣ. ܘܥܠ ܟܠܗܝܢ ܒܝ̈ܫܬܐ ܐܝܠܝܢ ܕܥܒܕ ܗܘܐ ²⁰ܐܘܣܦ
ܗܘܐ· ܗܪܘܕܣ ܐܦ ܗܕܐ ܥܠ ܟܠܗܝܢ. ܘܚܒܫܗ ܠܝܘܚܢܢ ܒܒܝܬ
ܐܣܝܪ̈ܐ ○ ○ ·○·

²¹ܘܟܕ ܥܡܕ ܗܘܐ ܟܠܗ ܥܡܐ ܐܦ ܝܫܘܥ ܥܡܕ ܘܟܕ ܡܨܠܐ
ܗܘܐ ܐܬܦܬܚܘ ܫܡܝܐ ²²ܘܢܚܬܬ ܥܠܘܗܝ, ܪܘܚܐ ܕܩܘܕܫܐ
ܒܕܡܘܬ ܓܘܫܡܐ ܕܝܘܢܐ ܘܩܠܐ ܐܫܬܡܥ ܡܢ ܫܡܝܐ ܐܢܬ ܗܘ
ܒܪܝ, ܘܚܒܝܒܝ ܕܒܟ ܐܨܛܒܝܬ ○

²³ܝܫܘܥ ܕܝܢ ⌜ܟܕ⌝ ܗܘ ܐܝܟ ⌜ܒܪ⌝ ܫܢܝ̈ܢ ܬܠܬܝܢ [ܗܘܐ] ⌜ܡ⌝ܣܬ⌜ܒ⌝ܪ ܕܒܪܗ
ܗܘ ܕܝܘܣܦ ܒܪ ܗܠܝ ²⁴ܒܪ ܡܛܬܬ ܒܪ * * ܒܪ ܝܢܐ ܒܪ
* * ²⁵ܒܪ ܡܛܬܝܐ ܒܪ ܥܡ⌜ܘ⌝ܨ ܒܪ ܢܚܘܡ ܒܪ ܚܣܠܝ ܒܪ
ܢ * * ²⁶ܒܪ * * * ܡܛܛ ܒܪ ܫܡܥܝ ܒܪ ܝܘܣܦ ܒܪ ܝܗܘܕܐ
²⁷ܒܪ ܝܘܚܢ ܒܪ ܪܝܣܐ ܒܪ ܙܪܘܒܒܠ ܒܪ ܫܠܬܐܝܠ ܒܪ ܢܪܝ, ²⁸ܒܪ
ܡܠܟܝ ܒܪ ܐܕܝ, ܒܪ ܩܘܣܡ ܒܪ ܐܠܡܘܕܡ ܒܪ ܥܝܪ ²⁹ܒܪ ܝܫܘܥ ܒܪ
ܐܠܝܥܙܪ ܒܪ ܝܘܪܡ ܒܪ ܡܛܬܬ ܒܪ ܠܘܝ, ³⁰ܒܪ ܫܡܥܘܢ ܒܪ ܝܗܘܕܐ
ܒܪ ܝܘܣܦ. ܒܪ ܝܘܢܡ ܒܪ ܐܠܝܩܝܡ ³¹ܒܪ ܡܠܝܐ ܒܪ ܡܢܢ ܒܪ
ܡܛܬܐ ܒܪ ܢܬܢ ܒܪ ܕܘܝܕ ³²ܒܪ ܐܝܫܝ ܒܪ ܥܘܒܝܕ ܒܪ ܒܥܙ ܒܪ
ܫܠܐ ܒܪ ܢܚܫܘܢ ³³ܒܪ ⌜ܐܕ⌝ܡܝ ܒܪ [ܐܪܢܝ] ܒܪ ܚܨܪܘܢ ܒܪ ܦܪܨ ܒܪ

---

16 ܐܡܪ ܠܗܘܢ] *pr.* ܥܢܐ ܠܟܠ ܐܢܫ ܘ *S* ⌜ܒܬܪܝ⌝] *only the suffix is legible in S: cf* syr.vg 23 *Cf* ܝܫܘܥ ܐܝܟ ܒܪ ܫܢܝ̈ܢ ܬܠܬܝܢ ܐܬܐ ܠܝܘܪܕܢܢ ܕܢܥܡܕ *A*405: *see* Matt iii 13 ܗܘܐ ܡܣܬܒܪ ܕܒܪܗ] *so I now read the photograph: S*[ed] *had* ܐܝܟ ܕܡܬܒܪܐ ܒܪܗ 33 ܐܕܡܝ ܒܪ ܐܪܢܝ ܒܪ] *added in S between the lines* (*cf* Lk iii 1, Joh xiii 16)

16 saying: "Can then he be the Messiah?" He saith to them: "I, lo, (*C*) *S*
I baptize you with water,¶ | but there cometh [after] me he that is ¶*C*
mightier than I, the thong of whose shoes I am not worthy to
17 unloose; he shall baptize you with fire and with the Holy Spirit,—he
who holdeth a fan in his hand and cleanseth his threshing-floor, and
gathereth the wheat into his barn, and the chaff he burneth with fire
18 unquenchable." Many other things also while entreating he was
19 announcing to the people. Now Herod the Tetrarch, because John
was reproving him because of Herodia the wife of Herod's brother
20 and for all the evil things that he was doing,—Herod had added this
also above all of them and shut up John in prison.

21 And when all the people were being baptized Jesus also was
22 baptized; and when he was praying the heavens were opened and
the Holy Spirit came down upon him in the likeness of the bodily
frame of a dove, and a voice was heard from heaven: "Thou art my
Son and my beloved in whom I have been pleased."

23 Now Jesus, being about thirty years old, [was] supposed to be the
24 son of Joseph, son of Heli, son of Matthath, son of * *, son of
25 Janna, son of * *, son of Mathatha, son of Amoz, son of Nahum,
26 son of Hesli, son of N * *, son of * *, * * Mattat, son of
27 Shemei, son of Joseph, son of Judah, son of John, son of †Kesha†,
28 son of Zorobabel, son of Shealtiel, son of Neri, son of Melchi, son of
29 Addi, son of Cosam, son of Eldom, son of Er, son of Jesus, son of
30 Eliezer, son of Joram, son of Mathiath, son of Levi, son of Simeon,
31 son of Judah, son of Joseph, son of Jonam, son of Eliacim, son of
Melia, son of Menan, son of Mattatha, son of Nathan, son of David,
32 son of Jesse, son of Jobel, son of Bosh, son of Shala, son of Nahshon,
33 son of A[dam], son of [Arni], son of Hezron, son of Perez, son of

---

16 He saith] He answered to every one and said *S* ⌜after⌝] *S illegible*
22. *There is no Syriac evidence known for the introduction here of* Ps ii 7
23 *Cf* 'Jesus about thirty years old came to Jordan that he might be baptized' *A* 405: *see* Matt iii 13 ⌜was⌝ supposed to be] *the reading of S here is practically certain* 33 A⌜dam⌝ son of ⌜Arni⌝ son of] *added in S between the lines* (*cf* Lk iii 1, Joh xiii 16)

ܕܝܗܘܕܐ ³⁴ܒܪ ܝܥܩܘܒ ܒܪ ܐܝܣܚܩ ܒܪ ܐܒܪܗܡ ܒܪ ܬܪܚ ܒܪ S
ܢܚܘܪ ³⁵ܒܪ ܣܪܘܓ ܒܪ ܐܪܥܘ ܒܪ ܦܠܓ ܒܪ ܥܒܪ ܒܪ ܫܠܚ ³⁶ܒܪ
ܩܝܢܢ ܒܪ ⌜ܐܪܦܟܫܕ⌝ ܒܪ ܫܝܡ ܒܪ ܢܘܚ ܒܪ ܠܡܟ ³⁷ܒܪ ܡܬܘܫܠܚ
ܒܪ ܚܢܘܟ ܒܪ ܝܪܕ ܒܪ ܡܗܠܠܐܝܠ ܒܪ ܩܝܢܢ ³⁸ܒܪ ܐܢܘܫ ܒܪ
ܫܝܬ ܒܪ ܐܕܡ ܒܪ ܐܠܗܐ ○ ○ ○

¹ܝܫܘܥ ܕܝܢ ܟܕ ܡܠܐ ܒܪܘܚܐ ܕܩܘܕܫܐ ܗܦܟ ܡܢ ܝܘܪܕܢ
ܘܕܒܪܬܗ ܪܘܚܐ ܕܩܘܕܫܐ ܘܐܦܩܬܗ ܠܡܕܒܪܐ ²ܕܢܬܢܣܐ ܡܢ
ܣܛܢܐ. ܘܗܘܐ ܬܡܢ ܝܘܡ̈ܬܐ ܐܪ̈ܒܥܝܢ ܘܡܢ ܒܬܪ ܐܪ̈ܒܥܝܢ ܝܘܡܬܐ
ܕܨܐܡ ܗܘܐ ܟܦܢ. ³ܘܐܡܪ ܠܗ ܐܟܠ ܩܪܨܐ ܐܢ ܒܪܗ ܐܢܬ
ܕܐܠܗܐ. ܐܡܪ ܠܗܕܐ ܟܐܦܐ ܕܬܗܘܐ ܠܚܡܐ. ⁴ܐܡܪ ܠܗ
ܝܫܘܥ ܟܬܝܒ ܗܘ ܕܠܐ ܒܠܚܡܐ ܒܠܚܘܕ ܚܝܐ ܒܪ ܐܢܫܐ.
⁵ܘܕܒܪ ܐܣܩܗ ܣܛܢܐ. ܘܚܘܝܗ ܟܠ̈ܗܝܢ ܡܠܟܘܬܐ ܕܐܪܥܐ ܕܬܒܝܠ
ܒܪܓܥܐ. ⁶ܘܐܡܪ ܠܗ ܗܠܝܢ ܟܠܗܝܢ ܡܠܟܘܬܐ ܘܫܘܒܚܗܝܢ ܕܠܝ
ܡܫܠܡܢ ܠܝ ܝܗܒ ܐܢܐ ܫܘܠܛܢܐ ܗܢܐ ܟܠܗ ܘܫܘܒܚܐ ܡܛܠ
ܕܠܝ ܝܗܒ ܘܠܡܢ ܕܨܒܐ ܝܗܒ ܐܢܐ ܠܗ. ⁷ܐܢܬ ܐܢ ܬܣܓܘܕ
ܩܕܡ ܠܝ ܢܗܘܐ ܟܠܗ· ⁸ܥܢܐ ܝܫܘܥ ܘܐܡܪ ܠܗ ܟܬܝܒ
ܠܡܣܓܕ ܠܡܪܝܐ ܐܠܗܟ ܘܠܗ ܒܠܚܘܕܘܗܝ ܬܦܠܘܚ. ⁹ܘܐܝܬܝܗ
ܠܐܘܪܫܠܡ ܘܐܩܝܡܗ ܥܠ ܩܪܢܐ ܕܗܝܟܠܐ ܘܐܡܪ ܠܗ ܐܢ
ܒܪܗ ܐܢܬ ܕܐܠܗܐ ܐܪܡܐ ܢܦܫܟ ܡܢ ܗܪܟܐ ¹⁰ܟܬܝܒ ܗܘ
ܓܝܪ ܕܠܡ̈ܠܐܟܘܗܝ ܢܦܩܕ ܥܠܝܟ ܕܢܛܪܘܢܟ ¹¹ܘܥܠ ܐܝܕ̈ܝܗܘܢ
ܢܫܩܠܘܢܟ ܕܠܐ ܬܬܩܠ ܒܟܐܦܐ. ¹²ܥܢܐ ܝܫܘܥ ܘܐܡܪ ܠܗ ܠܐ
ܬܢܣܐ ܠܡܪܝܐ ܐܠܗܟ· ¹³ܘܟܕ ܫܠܡ ܣܛܢܐ ܢܣܝܘܢܘܗܝ. ܦܪܩ ܡܢ
ܠܘܬܗ ܥܕ ܙܒܢܐ

34—38 *The names from* Adam *to* Terah *are given in A* 473, *but the rest of the genealogy in A follows* Matt i 2—16   36 ܒܪ ܩܝܢܢ] *om. A* 473   ⌜ܐܪܦܟܫܕ⌝] *A* 473 *and* syr.vg; ܐܪ* *S* (*rest illegible*)   37 ܝܪܕ] *S*[vid]; ܝܪܕ *A* 473

1, 2 *Cf A* 129 ܘܗܝܕܝܢ ܐܦܩܬܗ ܪܘܚܐ ܕܢܬܢܣܐ ܡܢ ܣܛܢܐ   2 *Cf Thos*[256] ܐܪ̈ܒܥܝܢ ܝܘܡܝܢ ܘܐܪ̈ܒܥܝܢ ܠܠܝ̈ܢ ܨܡ ܡܢ ܟܠ. ܘܡܒܬܪ ܟܢ ܟܦܢ. *See also* Matt iv 1, 2   6 ܕܠܝ ܝܗܒ] *S* (*sic*): *cf ver.* 17 *and* Mk iv 11

34 Judah, son of Jacob, son of Isaac, son of Abraham, son of Terah, son S
35 of Nahor, son of Serug, son of Reu, son of Peleg, son of Eber, son of
36 Shelah, son of Elam, son of Ar[phaxar], son of Shem, son of Noah,
37 son of Lamech, son of Methuselah, son of Henoch, son of Jared, son
38 of Mahalaleel, son of Cainan, son of Enos, son of Seth, son of Adam,
son of God.

iv 1 Now Jesus, being filled with the Holy Spirit returned from the
Jordan; and the Holy Spirit took him and sent him forth into the
2 wilderness, that he might be tempted by Satan. And he was there
forty days; and after forty days that he was fasting he hungered.
3 And the Accuser said to him: "If thou be the son of God, say to this
4 stone that it become bread." Jesus saith to him: "It is written
5 'Not by bread alone liveth man.'" And Satan took *and* brought him
6 up and shewed him all the kingdoms of the earth in a little time, and
said to him: "All these kingdoms and their glory that to me are
delivered—to thee I give all this authority and glory, because to me it
7 is given and to whom I will do I give it; thou, if thou wilt worship
8 before me, for thee shall it all be." Jesus answered and said to
him: "It is written to worship the LORD thy God, and him alone
9 shalt thou serve." And he brought him to Jerusalem, and made him
stand upon the corner of the Temple, and said to him: "If thou be
10 the son of God, cast thyself from hence; for it is written 'To his
angels he shall command concerning thee that they should keep thee
11 and on their hands should bear thee up, that thou shouldest not dash
12 against a stone.'" Jesus answered and said to him: "Thou shalt not
13 tempt the LORD thy God." And when Satan finished his temptations
he departed from him for a time.

34—38 *The names from* Adam *to* Terah *are given in A* 473, *but the rest of the genealogy in A follows* Matt i 2—16 36 son of Elam] *om. A* 473 Ar⌜phaxar⌝] *A* 473 *and* syr.vg; *only* Ar.... *is legible in S* 1, 2 *Cf A* 129: 'And then the Spirit sent him forth that he might be tempted by Satan. *E*[42] *has*: 'Immediately the Holy Spirit took *and* led him out into a desert, to be tempted by Satan' 2 *Cf Thos*[256]: 'For forty days and forty nights did our Lord fast, and nothing did he taste.' *E*[44] *has* 'And after forty days that he fasted, he hungered.' *See also* Matt iv 1, 2 6 *Cf* 'The kingdoms and their glory will I give thee' *E*[47], 'Mine are all the kingdoms' *E*[45], 'Thou shalt fall on thy face and humbly worship me' *E*[45]; *cf also* 'All these kingdoms and their glory will I give thee, if thou shalt fall on thy face and humbly worship me' Ephr. *arm* (*on* 1 Cor xv 28)

14ܘܗܦܟ ܝܫܘܥ ܒܚܝܠܐ ܕܪܘܚܐ ܠܓܠܝܠܐ ܘܢܦܩ ܥܠܘܗܝ، ܛܒܐ S
ܒܟܠܗ ܗܘ ܐܬܪܐ. 15ܘܗܘ ܡܠܦ ܗܘܐ ܠܗܘܢ ܒܟܢܘ̈ܫܬܗܘܢ
ܘܡܫܬܒܚ ܗܘܐ ܡܢ ܟܠ ܐܢܫ. 16ܘܐܬܐ ܠܢܨܪܬ ܐܬܪ ܕܐܬܪܒܝ
ܗܘܐ ܘܥܠ ܠܟܢܘܫܬܐ ܒܝܘܡܐ ܕܫܒܬܐ ܐܝܟ ܕܡܥܕ ܗܘܐ
17ܘܝܗܒ ܠܗ ܟܬܒܐ ܕܐܫܥܝܐ ܢܒܝܐ ܘܗܦܟ ܠܣܦܪܐ ܟܕ ܦܬܚ
ܟܬܒܐ ܐܫܟܚ ܕܟܬܝܒ 18ܪܘܚܐ ܕܡܪܝܐ ܥܠܝ ܕܡܛܠܬܗ
ܡܫܚܢܝ ܠܡܣܒܪܘ ܠܡܣܟ̈ܢܐ ܘܫܠܚܢܝ ܠܡܟܪܙܘ ܠܫ̈ܒܝܐ ܫܘܒܩܢܐ
ܘܠܥܘ̈ܝܪܐ ܚܙܝܐ ܘܐܫܪܪ ܠܬ̈ܒܝܪܐ ܒܫܘܒܩܢܐ 19ܘܠܡܟܪܙܘ ܫܢܬܐ
ܕܡܪܝܐ ܡܩܒܠܬܐ. 20ܘܟܪܟ ܣܦܪܐ ܘܝܗܒܗ ܠܡܫܡܫܢܐ ܘܝܬܒ
ܘܟܠܗܘܢ ܒܗ ܚܝܪܝܢ ܗܘܘ 21ܘܫܪܝ، ܠܡܐܡܪ ܠܗܘܢ. ܕܝܘܡܢܐ
ܐܫܬܠܡ ܟܬܒܐ ܗܢܐ ܒܐܕܢ̈ܝܟܘܢ 22ܘܣܗܕܝܢ ܗܘܘ ܠܗ ܟܠܗܘܢ
ܘܡܬܕܡܪܝܢ ܗܘܘ ܒܡܠܐ ܦܐܝ̈ܬܐ ܕܢܦܩܢ ܗܘܝ، ܡܢ ܦܘܡܗ.
ܘܐܡܪܝܢ ܗܘܘ ܗܢܐ ܠܐ ܗܘܐ ܒܪܗ ܕܝܘܣܦ 23ܐܡܪ ܠܗܘܢ
ܒܪ ܬܐܡܪܘܢ ܠܝ ܡܬܠܐ ܗܢܐ ܐܣܝܐ ܐܣܐ ܢܦܫܟ ܘܐܝܠܝܢ
ܕܫܡܥܢܢ ܕܥܒܕܬ ܒܟܦܪܢܚܘܡ ܬܐܡܪܘܢ ܠܝ ܥܒܕ ܐܦ ܗܪܟܐ
ܒܡܕܝܢܬܟ 24ܐܡܪ ܠܗܘܢ ܐܡܝܢ ܐܡܪܢܐ ܠܟܘܢ ܕܠܝܬ ܢܒܝܐ
ܕܡܬܩܒܠ ܒܡܕܝܢܬܗ· 25ܫܪܪܐ ܐܡܪܢܐ ܠܟܘܢ ܕܣܓܝ̈ܐ ܐܪ̈ܡܠܬܐ
ܐܝܬ ܗܘܝ، ܒܝܬ ܐܝܣܪܐܝܠ ܒܝܘܡܝ ܐܠܝܐ ܢܒܝܐ ܟܕ ܐܬܚܕܘ
ܫܡܝܐ ܫܢܝ̈ܢ ܬܠܬ ܘܝܪ̈ܚܐ ܫܬܐ ܟܕ ܗܘܐ ܟܦܢܐ ܪܒܐ ܒܟܠܗ
ܐܪܥܐ 26ܘܠܘܬ ܚܕܐ ܡܢܗܝܢ ܠܐ ܐܫܬܕܪ ܐܠܝܐ ܐܠܐ ܠܨܪܦܬ
ܕܨܝܕܢ ܠܘܬ ܐܢܬܬܐ ܐܪܡܠܬܐ 27ܘܣܓܝ̈ ܓܪ̈ܒܐ ܐܝܬ ܗܘܘ ܒܝܬ
ܐܝܣܪܐܝܠ ܒܝܘܡܘܗܝ، ܕܐܠܝܫܥ ܢܒܝܐ ܘܚܕ ⌜ܡܢ⌝⌜ܗܘܢ⌝ ܠܐ ⌜ܐܬܕ⌝ܟܝ
ܐܠܐ ܐܢܥܡܢ 28ܘ⌜ܟܕ⌝ ܫܡܥܘ ܗܠܝܢ ܕܒܟܢܘܫܬܐ ܐܬܡܠܝܘ ܚܡܬܐ
29ܘܐܦܩܘܗܝ، ܠܒܪ ܡܢ ܡܕܝܢܬܐ ܘܐܝܬܝܘܗܝ، ܥܕܡܐ ܠܦܪܘܣ ܛܘܪܐ

---

17 ܘܝܗܒ] *S* (*sic*), *cf* Mt xix 11, Mk iv 11 : *the same passive form is found in* *A*ᵃ114, 355 18 ܘܐܫܪܪ] *S* (*sic*). Syr.vg *has* ܘܠܡܫܪܪܘ: *see Notes*, vol. ii 28 ⌜ܘܟܕ⌝] *S*ᵛⁱᵈ (*sic*): *the* ܕ *is clear* 29 ܥܕܡܐ ܠܦܪܘܣ] *S*, *i.e.* ἕως ὀφρύος (*cf Wellhausen* GGA 1895, p. 4); *possibly* ܦܪܘܣ *was taken to mean* Φᾶρος, *spelt elsewhere* ܦܐܪܘܣ *and* ܦܪܘܢ

14 And Jesus returned in the power of the Spirit to Galilee, and *S*
15 there went forth concerning him a tale in all that country; and he
was teaching them in their synagogues, and was glorified of every
16 one. And he came to Nazareth where he had been brought up, and
17 entered the synagogue on the sabbath-day as he was wont. And
there was given him the book of Isaiah the prophet, and he stood up
to read. When he opened the book he found the place that is
18 written: "The Spirit of the LORD *is* upon thee, because of which he
hath anointed thee to announce *the gospel* to the poor; and he hath
despatched me to preach to the captives forgiveness, and to the blind
19 sight, and I will strengthen the broken with forgiveness; and to
20 preach the acceptable year of the LORD." And he rolled up the
volume and gave it to the servant and sat down, and all of them on
21 him were looking. And he began to say to them: "To-day hath this
22 book been accomplished in your ears." And they were all bearing
him witness and were wondering at the gracious words that were
coming forth from his mouth, and they were saying: "This one—is
23 not he the son of Joseph?" He saith to them: "Perchance ye will
say to me this similitude 'Physician, heal thyself'; and the things
that ye have heard that I have done in Kapharnahum—ye will say
24 to me, 'do *them* here also in thy city.'" He saith to them: "Amen,
25 I say to you There is no prophet that is received in his city. The
truth I say to you Many widows there were in the House of Israel
in the days of Elijah the prophet, when the heavens were shut up
three years and six months, when a great famine was in all the land,
26 and unto none of them was Elijah sent but to Zarephath of Sidon
27 unto a widow woman; and many lepers there were in the House
of Israel in the days of Elisha the prophet, and none of them was
28 cleansed but a Gentile." [And] when they that were in the synagogue
29 heard these things they were filled with fury, and they put him forth
out of the city and brought him even unto the Pharos (?) the hill

---

18 and I will strengthen] *S* (*sic*): syr.vg *has* 'and to strengthen,' *i.e. another part of the same verb* 28 when] *S* (*sic*) 29 even unto the Pharos, the hill] *S* (*see the Syriac Note*); 'to the side of the hill' E^{129}

ܗܘ ܕܡܬܚܫܒܬܗܘܢ ܒܢܦܫܐ ܗܘܬ ܥܠܘܗܝ ܐܝܟ ܕܢܬܠܘܢܝܗܝ. [30]ܘܗܘ S
ܐܦ ܒܝܢܬܗܘܢ ܥܒܪ ܗܘܐ [31]ܘܢܚܬ ܠܟܦܪܢܚܘܡ ܡܕܝܢܬܐ
ܕܓܠܝܠܐ ܘܡܠܦ ܗܘܐ ܠܗܘܢ ܒܫܒ̈ܐ. [32]ܘܬܡܗܝܢ ܗܘܘ ܒܝܘܠܦܢܗ.
ܕܡܫܠܛܐ ܗܘܬ ܡܠܬܗ. [33]ܘܐܝܬ ܗܘܐ ܒܗ ܒܟܢܘܫܬܗܘܢ ܓܒܪܐ
ܕܐܝܬ ܒܗ ܪܘܚܐ ܕܫܐܕܐ ܛܢܦܐ ܘܩܥܐ ܒܩܠܐ ܪܒܐ [34]ܡܢܐ
ܠܢ ܘܠܟ ܝܫܘܥ ܢܨܪܝܐ ܐܬܝܬ ܠܡܘܒܕܘܬܢ. ܝܕܥ ܐܢܐ ܠܟ ܡܢ
ܐܢܬ ܩܕܝܫܗ ܕܐܠܗܐ. [35]ܘܟܐܐ [ܒܗ] ܝܫܘܥ. ܘܐܡܪ ܠܗ ܣܟܘܪ
ܦܘܡܟ ܘܦܘܩ ܡܢܗ ܘܫܕܝܗܝ ܫܐܕܐ ܠܡܨܥܬܐ ܘܢܦܩ ܡܢܗ ܟܕ
ܡܕܡ ܠܐ ܐܗܪܗ. [36]ܘܬܡܗܐ ܐܚܕ ܗܘܐ ܠܟܠܗܘܢ ܘܡܡܠܠܝܢ
ܗܘܘ ܚܕ ܥܡ ܚܕ ܘܐܡܪܝܢ ܐܝܕܐ ܗܝ ܕ ܡܠܬܐ ܗܕܐ ܕܒܫܘܠܛܢܐ
ܘܒܚܝܠܐ ܦܩܕܐ ܠܪ̈ܘܚܐ ܗܠܝܢ ܛܢܦܬܐ ܘܢܦܩܢ [37]ܘܢܦܩ ܗܘܐ
ܥܠܘܗܝ ܛܒܐ ܒܟܠܗ ܐܬܪܐ ܕܚܕܪܝܗܘܢ. [38]ܘܟܕ ܢܦܩ ܡܢ
ܟܢܘܫܬܐ ܥܠ ܠܒܝܬܐ ܕܫܡܥܘܢ ܘܚܡܬܗ ܕܫܡܥܘܢ ܐܚܝܕܐ
ܗܘܬ ܠܗ ܐܫܬܐ ܪܒܬܐ [39]ܘܟܐܐ ܒܐܫܬܗ ܘܫܒܩܬܗ ܘܒܪ
ܫܥܬܗ ܡܚܕܐ ܘܡܫܡܫܐ ܗܘܬ ܠܗܘܢ [40]ܡܥܪܒ ܫܡܫܐ ܕܝܢ
ܒܠܗܘܢ ܐܝܠܝܢ ܕܐܝܬ ܗܘܘ ܠܗܘܢ ܕܟܪܝܗܝܢ ܒܟܘܪ̈ܗܢܐ ܡܫ̈ܚܠܦܐ
ܐܝܬܝܘ ܐܢܘܢ ܠܘܬܗ ܘܟܠ ܚܕ ܚܕ ܡܢܗܘܢ ܐܝܕܗ ܣܐܡ
ܗܘܐ ܘܠܟܠܗܘܢ ܡܐܣܐ ܗܘܐ. [41]ܘܢܦܩܝܢ ܗܘܘ ܫܐ̈ܕܐ ܡܢ
ܣܓܝܐܐ ܟܕ ܡܩܥܝܢ ܘܐܡܪܝܢ ܐܢܬ ܗܘ ܒܪܗ ܕܐܠܗܐ ܘܟܐܐ
ܗܘܐ ܒܗܘܢ ܘܠܐ ܫܒܩ ܗܘܐ ܠܗܘܢ ܕܢܐܡܪܘܢ ܡܛܠ
ܕܝܕܥܝܢ ܗܘܘ ܠܗ ܕܗܘܝܘ ܡܫܝܚܐ ܀
[42]ܘܠܦܪܗ ܕܨܦܪܐ ܢܦܩ ܗܘܐ ܘܐܙܠ ܠܗ ܠܐܬܪܐ ܚܘܪܒܐ
ܘܟܢܫܐ ܣܓܝܐܐ ܒܥܝܢ ܗܘܘ ܠܗ ܘܐܬܘ ܠܘܬܗ ܘܐܚܕܘ ܠܗ
ܕܠܐ ܢܐܙܠ ܠܗ ܡܢ ܠܘܬܗܘܢ. [43]ܗܘ ܕܝܢ ܐܡܪ ܠܗܘܢ ܕܐܦ
ܠܡܕܝܢܬܐ ܐܚܪܢܝܬܐ ܘܠܐ ܠܝ ܕܐܣܒܪ ܡܠܟܘܬܗ ܕܐܠܗܐ
[44]ܘܡܟܪܙ ܗܘܐ ܒܟܢܘܫܬܐ ܕܝܗܘܕ †[1] * * ܒܥܝܢܐ * * † ܗܘܐ

---

35 ܦܘܡܟ] S (*sic*)   36 ܐܚܕ] ܐܚܕ S^{ed}: *cf* Mk i 27   40 ܒܠܗܘܢ] S (*sic*)
1 * * ܒܥܝܢܐ * *] *The reading of S is here very uncertain: see Notes*, vol. ii

30 that their city was built on, so that they might hang him. And he *S*
31 even through them was passing, and he came down to Kapharnahum,
32 a city of Galilee; and he was teaching them on the sabbaths, and
they were astonished at his teaching, in that authoritative was his
33 word. And there was in that same synagogue of theirs a man in
whom was the spirit of an unclean devil, and he screamed with a loud
34 voice: "What have we to do with thee, Jesus the Nazarene? Hast
thou come to destroy us? I know thee who thou art, the Holy One
35 of God!" [And] Jesus [rebuked him] and said to him: "Shut thy
mouth, go forth from him." And the devil threw him down into the
36 midst and went forth from him, not at all having hurt him. And
astonishment was taking hold of them all, and they were speaking
one with another and saying: "What is then this word, that with
authority and with power commandeth these unclean spirits and they
37 go forth?" And there was going forth concerning him a tale in all the
38 country round about them. And when he arose from the synagogue
he entered the house of Simon, and the mother-in-law of Simon—a
39 great fever was holding her. And he rebuked her fever and it left her,
40 and straightway she arose and was serving them. Now at the setting
of the sun all they that had them that were infirm with stubborn
infirmities brought them unto him, and on each one of them his hand
41 he was laying, and all of them was he healing. And the devils were
going forth from many, screaming and saying: "Thou art the Son of
God!" And he was rebuking them and was not suffering them to
say *it*, because they knew him that he was the Messiah.

42 And with the morrow of the day he had come forth and he went
away to a desert place, and many multitudes were seeking him and
they came unto him and they took hold of him that he should not go
43 away from them. But he said to them "To other cities also it
behoves me that I announce the kingdom of God."

44, V 1 And he was preaching in the synagogues of Judaea. †* * the

---

so that they might hang him] *S*; 'and they cast him down' *E*[129]: *see Notes*, vol. ii 1. *In the first clause of this verse the reading of S is very uncertain: see Notes*, vol. ii

ܕܢܫܡܥ ܡܢܗ ܡܠܬܗ ܕܐܠܗܐ ܘܗܘ ܩܐܡ ܗܘܐ ܥܠ ܝܕ ܝܡܬܐ S
ܕܓܢܣܪ [2]ܘܚܙܐ ܬܪܬܝܢ ܣܦܝܢܐ ܕܩܝܡܢ ܥܠ ܓܢܒ ܝܡܬܐ ܘܨܝܕܝܗ
ܕܣܠܩܘ ܡܢܗ̈ܝܢ ܘܡܫܝܓܝܢ ܗܘܘ ܡܨܝܕܬܗܘܢ [3]ܘܚܕܐ ܡܢܗܝܢ
ܕܫܡܥܘܢ ܗܘܬ ܘܣܠܩ ܝܬܒ ܒܗ ܘܐܡܪ ܕܢܕܒܪܘܢܗ ܡܢ
ܝܒܫܐ ܩܠܝܠ ܠܡ̈ܝܐ ܘܝܬܒ. ܗܘܐ ܘܡܠܦ ܡܢ ܣܦܝܢܬܐ ܠܟܢܫܐ [4]ܘܟܕ
ܫܠܝ ܡܢ ܡܡܠܠܗ ܥܢܐ ܘܐܡܪ ܠܫܡܥܘܢ ܕܒܪܘ ܠܥܘܡܩܐ ܘܐܪܡܘ
ܡܨܝܕܬܟܘܢ ܠܨܝܕܐ. [5]ܥܢܐ ܫܡܥܘܢ ܘܐܡܪ ܠܗ ܪܒܝ ܠܠܝܐ
ܟܠܗ ܠܐܝܢ ܘܡܕܡ ܠܐ ܐܚܕܢ. ܗܫܐ ܕܝܢ ܥܠ ܡܠܬܟ ܢܕܒܪ
ܡܨܝܕܬܐ [6]ܘܟܕ ܥܒܕܘ ܡܨܝܕ̈ܬܗܘܢ ܚܒܫܘ ܢܘܢ̈ܐ ܣܓ̈ܝܐܐ
ܘܡܨܛܪ̈ܝܢ ܗܘܘ ܡܨܝܕ̈ܬܗܘܢ. [7]ܘܐܪܡܙܘ ܠܫܘܬ̈ܦܝܗܘܢ· ܕܒܣܦܝܢܐ
ܐܚܪ̈ܝܬܐ ܕܢܐܬܘܢ ܢܥܕܪܘܢ ܐܢܘܢ܆ ܘܟܕ ܐܬܘ ܐܣܩܘ ܢܘܢܐ
ܘܡܠܘ ܣܦܝܢܐ ܬܪ̈ܬܝܗܝܢ ܘܩܪ̈ܝܒܢ ܗܘܘ، ܡܢ ܡܛܒܥܢ ܠܡܛܒܥ
[8]ܘܟܕ ܚܙܐ ܫܡܥܘܢ ܢܦܠ ܥܠ ܐܦ̈ܘܗܝ، ܩܕܡ ܪ̈ܓܠܘܗܝ، ܕܝܫܘܥ
ܘܐܡܪ ܠܗ ܡܪܝ، ܦܘܩ ܠܟ ܡܢܝ ܡܛܠ ܕܓܒܪܐ ܐܢܐ ܚܛܝܐ
[9]ܬܗܡܐ ܓܝܪ ܐܚܕܗ ܘܠܟܠܗܘܢ ܕܥܡܗ ܡܢ ܨܝܕܐ ܗܘ ܕܢܘ̈ܢܐ
ܕܐܚܕܘ [10]ܘܗܟܢܐ ܐܦ ܝܥܩܘܒ ܘܝܘܚܢܢ ܒ̈ܢܝ ܙܒܕܝ، ܡܛܠ
ܕܫܘܬ̈ܦܘܗܝ، ܗܘܘ ܕܫܡܥܘܢ܆ ܘܐܡܪ ܝܫܘܥ ܠܫܡܥܘܢ
ܠܐ ܬܕܚܠ ܡܢ ܗܫܐ ܒ̈ܢܝ ܐܢܫܐ ܬܗܘܐ ܨܐܕ ܠܚ̈ܝܐ.
[11]ܘܩܪܒܘ ܐܢܝܢ ܣܦܝܢ̈ܬܐ ܠܐܪܥܐ ܘܫܒܩܘ ܟܘܠ ܡܕܡ ܘܐܬܘ
ܒܬܪܗ ○ ○ ○ ○ ○

[12]ܘܟܕ ܗܘܐ ܒܚܕܐ ܡܢ ܡܕ̈ܝܢܬܐ ܐܬܐ ܓܒܪܐ ܚܕ ܕܡܠܐ
ܓܪܒܐ. ܚܙܐ ܠܝܫܘܥ ܘܢܦܠ ܥܠ ܐܦ̈ܘܗܝ، ܘܒܥܐ ܗܘܐ ܡܢܗ
ܘܐܡܪ ܠܗ ܡܪܝ، ܐܢ ܨܒܐ ܐܢܬ ܡܫܟܚ ܐܢܬ ܠܡܕܟܝܘܬܢܝ.
[13]ܘܐܘܫܛ ܐܝܕܗ ܩܪܒ ܠܗ ܘܐܡܪ ܠܗ. ܨܒܐ ܐܢܐ ܐܬܕܟܐ. ܘܒܪ
ܫܥܬܗ ܦܪܩ ܡܢܗ ܓܪܒܗ. [14]ܘܦܩܕܗ ܝܫܘܥ ܕܠܐܢܫ ܠܐ ܢܐܡܪ
ܐܠܐ ܙܠ ܚܘܐ ܢܦܫܟ ܠܟܗܢܐ ܘܩܪܒ ܥܠ ܬܕܟܝܬܟ ܐܝܟܢܐ
ܕܦܩܕ ܡܘܫܐ ܕܬܗܘܐ ܠܗܘܢ ܠܣܗܕܘܬܐ. [15]ܘܢܦܩ ܗܘܐ ܥܠܘܗܝ،
ܛܒܐ ܘܡܬܟܢܫܝܢ ܗܘܐ ܟܢܫܐ ܣܓܝܐܐ ܠܡܫܡܥ ܡܢܗ

multitude was * *† that it might hear from him the word of God, S
2 and he was standing by the edge of the Lake of Gennesar. And he
saw two boats that were standing by the side of the lake and the
fishermen thereof that *had* gone up from them and were washing their
3 nets. And one of them was Simon's, and Jesus went up *and* sat in it
and said that they should put it out from the dry land a little into
the water. And he was sitting and teaching the multitude from the
4 boat. And when he ceased from his speaking he answered and said
to Simon: "Put out into the deep *water* and cast your nets for a
5 catch." Simon answered and said to him: "Rabbi, the whole night
we have toiled and nothing have we found; but now at thy word we
6 will put out the net." And when they cast their nets they inclosed
7 many fishes and their nets were being rent. And they beckoned to
their comrades in the other boats that they should come *and* help
them; and when they came they took up the fishes and filled both of
8 the boats, and they were near from their weight to sink. And when
Simon saw he fell on his face before the feet of Jesus and said to him:
"My Lord, depart away from me, because I am a man, a sinner!"
9 For astonishment took hold of him and of all them that were with
10 him at that catch of fishes which they took,—and likewise James also
and John, the sons of Zebedee, because they were partners of Simon.
And Jesus saith to Simon: "Fear not, from now men shalt thou be
11 catching unto life!" And they brought the boats near to the land
and left everything and came after him.

12 And when he was in one of the cities there came a certain man
that was full of leprosy; he saw Jesus and fell on his face and was
beseeching him and saying to him: "My Lord, if thou wilt, thou
13 canst cleanse me." And he put forth his hand *and* touched him, and
said to him: "I will, be thou cleansed." And straightway his leprosy
14 departed away from him. And Jesus warned him that to no one
should he say *it*, "but go, shew thyself to the priests, and offer for
thy cleansing as Moses commanded that it should be for them for
15 a witness." And there was going forth concerning him a tale *all* the
more, and a great multitude was being gathered together to hear

S ܘܠܡܬܐܣܝܘ ܡܢ ܟܘܪ̈ܗܢܝܗܘܢ. 16ܘܗܘ ܡܬܛܫܐ ܗܘܐ ܠܡܕܒܪܐ
ܘܡܨܠܐ ܗܘܐ ° ° °

17ܘܗܘܐ ܒܚܕ ܡܢ ܝܘܡܬܐ ܟܕ ܡܠܦ ܗܘܐ ܝܬܒܝܢ ܗܘܘ ܦܪܝܫܐ
ܘܡܠܦܝ ܢܡܘܣܐ. ܘܕܐܬܘ ܡܢ ܟܠ ܩܪܝܐ ܕܓܠܝܠܐ ܕܝܗܘܕ
ܘܕܐܘܪܫܠܡ ܘܚܝܠܐ ܗܘܐ ܒܝܫܘܥ ܕܗܘܐ ܡܐܣܐ 18ܘܗܐ ܐܢܫܐ
ܐܝܬܝܘ ܓܒܪܐ ܚܕ ܡܫܪܝܐ ܒܥܪܣܐ ܘܒܥܝܢ ܗܘܘ ܕܐܝܟܢܐ
ܢܥܠܘܢܝܗ ܘܢܣܝܡܘܢܝܗ ܩܕܡܘܗܝ, 19ܘܠܐ ܐܫܟܚܘ ܕܢܥܠܘܢܝܗ, ܡܛܠ
ܟܢܫܐ ܘܣܠܩܘ ܠܗܘܢ ܠܐܓܪܐ ܘܫܒܩܘܗܝ, ܥܡ ܥܪܣܗ ܠܡܨܥܬܐ
ܩܕܡܘܗܝ, ܕܝܫܘܥ. 20ܘܟܕ ܚܙܐ ܗܝܡܢܘܬܗܘܢ ܐܡܪ ܠܡܫܪܝܐ
ܒܪܝ ܫܒܝܩܝܢ ܠܟ ܚܛܗܝܟ. 21ܘܫܪܝܘ [ܣܦܪܐ] ܘܦܪܝܫܐ ܡܬܚܫܒܝܢ
ܗܘܘ ܘܐܡܪܝܢ ܡܢܘ ܗܢܐ ܕܡܡܠܠ ܓܘܕܦܐ ܡܢܘ ܡܫܟܚ
ܠܡܫܒܩ ܚܛܗܐ ܐܠܐ ܐܢ ܐܠܗܐ ܒܠܚܘܕ. 22ܝܕܥ ܕܝܢ ܒܗ
ܚܕ ܡܚܫܒܬܗܘܢ ܥܢܐ ܘܐܡܪ ܠܗܘܢ ܡܢܐ ܡܬܚܫܒܝܢ
ܐܢܬܘܢ ܒܠܒ̈ܘܬܟܘܢ. 23ܐܝܢܐ ܦܫܝܩܐ ܠܡܐܡܪ ܕܫܒܝܩܝܢ ܠܟ
ܚܛܗܝܟ ܐܘ ܠܡܐܡܪ ܕܩܘܡ ܗܠܟ. 24ܕܬܕܥܘܢ ܕܝܢ ܐܢܬܘܢ
ܕܫܠܝܛ ܗܘ ܒܪܗ ܕܐܢܫܐ ܕܢܫܒܘܩ ܚܛܗܐ ܒܐܪܥܐ ܐܡܪ
ܠܡܫܪܝܐ ܠܟ ܐܡܪ ܐܢܐ ܩܘܡ ܫܩܘܠ ܥܪܣܟ ܘܐܙܠ ܠܒܝܬܟ
25ܘܒܗ ܒܫܥܬܐ ܩܡ ܩܕܡܝܗܘܢ, ܘܫܩܠ ܡܕܡ ܕܪ̈ܡܐ ܗܘܐ
ܒܠܒܗ, ܘܐܙܠ ܠܒܝܬܗ ܟܕ ܡܫܒܚ ܠܐܠܗܐ. 26[ܘܬܗܪܐ ܐܚܕ]
ܐܢܘܢ ܠܟܠܗܘܢ [ܘܡܫܒܚܝܢ] ܗܘܘ [ܠܐܠܗܐ] ܘܐܡܪܝܢ ܕܚܙܝܢ
ܬܕܡܪ̈ܬܐ ܘܪ̈ܒܬܐ ܝܘܡܢܐ

27ܒܬܪ ܗܠܝܢ ܢܦܩ ܝܫܘܥ ܘܚܙܐ [ܡܟܣܐ] ܕܝܬܒ ܒܝܬ ܡܟܣܐ
ܕܫܡܗ ܠܘܝ, ܘܐܡܪ ܠܗ ܬܐ ܒܬܪܝ, 28ܘܫܒܩ ܟܠ ܡܕܡ ܘܐܙܠ

---

17 ܘܕܐܬܘ] *S: the first three letters are certain* ܕܝܗܘܕ ܘܕܐܘܪܫܠܡ] *S (sic)* ܘܚܝܠܐ ܗܘܐ ܒܝܫܘܥ] *S (sic): the* ܗ *is clear* 18 ܘܗܐ | ܐܢܫܐ] *S (sic)* ܡܫܪܝܐ ܒܥܪܣܐ] *S*vid ܕܐܝܟܢܐ | ܢܥܠܘܢܝܗ] *S (sic)*
22 ܒܠܒ̈ܘܬܟܘܢ *S*ed *(this plural form occurs in* Lk xxi 14, *not elsewhere): the photograph looks like* ܒܠܒܘ//////////, *i.e.* ܒܠܒܘܬܟܘܢ 25 ܘܒܗ ܒܫܥܬܐ ܩܡ] *S (sic)*

16 from him and to be healed from their infirmities. And he was S
removing to the open country and was praying.
17 And it came to pass on one of the days when he was
teaching, there were sitting Pharisees and teachers of the law, and
they that came from every village of Galilee, of Judaea and of
Jerusalem, and the power was in Jesus that he should be healing.
18 And lo, folk brought a certain man, a paralytic on a bed, and they
were seeking how they might bring him in that they might set him
19 before him; and they could not bring him in because of the people.
And they went up to the roof and lowered him with his bed into the
20 midst before Jesus. And when he saw their faith he said to the
21 paralytic: "Man, thy sins are forgiven thee!" And [the scribes] and
the Pharisees began thinking and saying: "Who is this that speaketh
22 blasphemy? Who is it can forgive sins save God alone?" Now
Jesus when he knew their thoughts answered and said to them:
23 "Why are ye thinking in your heart? Which is the easier, to say
24 'Thy sins are forgiven thee,' or to say 'Arise *and* walk'? But
that ye may know yourselves that the Son of Man hath authority
that he should forgive sins on earth"—he saith to the paralytic—"To
25 thee I say, Arise, take up thy bed and go to thy house." And in
the same hour he arose before them and took up that which he was
26 lying on, and went to his house, glorifying God. [And astonish-
ment took hold of] them [all, and they] were [glorifying God] and
saying "We have seen wonders and great things to-day."
27 After these things Jesus went forth and saw [a toll-gatherer]
sitting at the toll-gatherers' place whose name *was* Levi, and he
28 saith to him: "Come after me." And he left everything and went

---

17 of Judaea (*without* 'and' *prefixed*)] *S* (*sic*) the power was in Jesus] *S* (*sic*) 22 heart] hearts S^{ed}, *but cf* Matt ix 4

S * * * * * * * * * * * * * *

[*The leaf of S which contained* Lk v 28—vi 11 *is missing.*]

¹²ܘܒܗܘܢ ܒܗܘܢ ܝܘܡܬܐ ܢܦܩ ܗܘܐ ܠܛܘܪܐ ܠܡܨܠܝܘ ܘܬܡܢ
ܡܓܢܗ ܗܘܐ ܠܠܝܐ ܟܘܠܗ ܒܨܠܘܬܗ ܕܐܠܗܐ ¹³ܘܟܕ ܢܓܗ ܩܪܐ
ܠܬܠܡܝܕܘܗܝ ܘܓܒܐ ܡܢܗܘܢ ܬܪܥܣܪ ܗܢܘܢ ܕܫܠܝܚܐ ܫܡ
ܐܢܘܢ ¹⁴ܫܡܥܘܢ ܗܘ ܕܟܐܦܐ ܫܡ ܠܗ ܘܐܢܕܪܐܘܣ ܐܚܘܗܝ
ܘܝܥܩܘܒ ܘܝܘܚܢ ܒܢܝ ܙܒܕܝ ܘܦܝܠܝܦܘܣ ܘܒܪ ܬܘܠܡܝ ¹⁵ܘܡܬܝ
ܘܬܐܘܡܐ ܘܝܥܩܘܒ ܒܪ ܚܠܦܝ ܘܫܡܥܘܢ ܕܡܬܩܪܐ ⌜ܛܢܢܐ⌝
¹⁶ܘܝܗܘܕܐ ܒܪ ܝܥܩܘܒ ܘܝܗܘܕܐ ܣܟܪܝܘܛܐ ܗܘ ܕܗܘܐ ܗܘܐ
ܡܫܠܡܢܐ ¹⁷ܘܢܚܬ ܥܡܗܘܢ ܠܦܩܥܬܐ ܘܩܡ ܗܘ ܘܟܢܫܐ
ܕܬܠܡܝܕܘܗܝ ܘܣܓܝܐܐ ܕܟܢܫܐ ܕܥܡܐ ܕܐܬܘ ܡܢ ܟܘܠܗ ܝܗܘܕ
ܘܡܢ ܐܘܪܫܠܡ ܘܡܢ ܦܢܝܬ ܘܡܢ ܨܘܪ ܘܡܢ ܨܝܕܢ ܕܐܬܘ
ܕܢܫܡܥܘܢܗ ܘܢܬܐܣܘܢ ܡܢ ܟܠܗܘܢ ܟܘܪܗܢܝܗܘܢ ¹⁸ܘܡܬܐܢܣܝܢ
ܗܘܘ ܡܢ ܪܘܚܐ ܛܢܦܬܐ ܘܡܬܐܣܝܢ ܗܘܘ ¹⁹ܟܘܠܗ ܒܥܐ ܗܘܐ
ܠܡܬܩܪܒܘ ܠܗ ܚܝܠܐ ܓܝܪ ܢܦܩ ܗܘܐ ܡܢܗ ܘܠܟܠܗܘܢ ܡܐܣܐ
ܗܘܐ ²⁰ܘܗܘ ܐܪܝܡ ܥܝܢܘܗܝ ܥܠ ܬܠܡܝܕܘܗܝ ܘܐܡܪ
ܛܘܒܝܗܘܢ ܠܡܣܟܢܐ §ܕܕܠܗܘܢ ܗܝ ܡܠܟܘܬܐ ܕܫܡܝܐ¶ ܀ ܀ §¶*A* 390
²¹ܛܘܒܝܗܘܢ ܠܕܟܦܢܝܢ ܗܫܐ ܕܢܣܒܥܘܢ ܀
ܛܘܒܝܗܘܢ ܠܕܒܟܝܢ ܗܫܐ ܕܢܓܚܟܘܢ ܀
²²ܛܘܒܝܟܘܢ ܡܐ ܕܣܢܝܢ ܠܟܘܢ ܒܢܝ ܐܢܫܐ. ܘܡܦܪܫܝܢ ܠܟܘܢ.
ܘܡܚܣܕܝܢ ܘܡܦܩܝܢ ܥܠܝܟܘܢ ܫܡܐ ܕܒܝܫ ܡܛܠ ܒܪܗ ܕܐܢܫܐ
²³ܐܬܚܕܘ ܕܝܢ ܚܕܘ ܒܗ̇، ܫܒܬܐ [ܘܪܘܙܘ] ܘܕܘܨܘ ܕܐܓܪܟܘܢ
⌜ܣܓܝ⌝ ܒܫܡܝܐ ܗܟܢܐ ܓܝܪ ܥܒܕܝܢ ܗܘܘ ܐܒܗܬܗܘܢ ܠܢܒܝܐ ·܀·

---

32. *See on* Matt ix 12, 13

14—16. *For the List of the Apostles in Thos*[172], *see on* Matt x 2—4

18 ܘܡܬܐܢܣܝܢ] *S (sic): what is wanted is* ܘܕܡܬܐܢܣܝܢ   20. *A* 390 *has* ܘܥܠ ܡܣܟܢܐ ܐܡܪ. ܕܕܠܗܘܢ ܗܝ ܡܠܟܘܬܐ ܕܫܡܝܐ *on the same page as a full quotation of* Matt v 3   23 ܐܬܚܕܘ ܕܝܢ] *S (sic)*

* * * * * * * * * * * * * S

[*The leaf of S which contained* Lk v 28—vi 11 *is missing.*]

vi 12 And in those same days he had gone forth to the hill to pray, and
there he was spending the whole night until dawn in prayer to God;
13 and when *day* dawned he called his disciples and chose from them the
14 Twelve whom he named Apostles:—Simon whom he named Kepha,
and Andrew his brother, and James and John the sons of Zebedee,
15 and Philip and Bartholomew and Matthew and Thomas and James
16 the son of Halphaeus and Simon called Zealot and Judas the son
17 of James, and Judas Scariot, he who was the betrayer. And he
went down with them to a plain and stood up, he and a multitude of
his disciples and a number of the multitude of the people that came
from all Judaea and from Jerusalem and from the Littoral and from
Tyre and from Sidon, that came that they might hear him and be
18 healed from all their infirmities, and were distressed by unclean
19 spirits that they might be healed—each one of them was wishing to
touch him, for power was going forth from him and all of them he
20 was healing. And he himself lifted up his eyes on his disciples and
said

"Happy is it for the poor, §that theirs is the kingdom of heaven! ¶ §¶*A*390

21 "Happy is it for them that hunger now, that they shall be satisfied!

"Happy is it for them that weep now, that they shall laugh!

22 "Happy is it for you, what *time* men hate you and separate you
and reproach *you*, and put forth concerning you a name that is evil,
23 because of the Son of Man. Now ye, rejoice ye in that hour [and
exult] and leap *for joy* that your reward is great in heaven, for so
were their fathers doing to the prophets.

---

32. *See on* Matt ix 12, 13

14—16. *For the List of the Apostles in Thos*[172], *see on* Matt x 2—4 18 and were distressed] *S* (*sic*) 19 power] 'much power' *E*[83] (*and* arm.vg)

20. *A* 390, *on the same page as a full quotation of* Matt v 3, *has*: 'And of the poor he said that theirs is the kingdom of heaven' that theirs] *or*, 'whose' 21 that they] *or*, 'who' (*in each place*)

²⁴ܒܪܡ §ܘܝ ܠܟܘܢ ܥܬܝܪܐ ܕܩܒܠܬܘܢ ܒܒܘܬܟܘܢ¶ S §¶A 390
²⁵ᵇܘܝ ܠܓܚܘܟܝܢ ܗܫܐ ܕܬܒܟܘܢ ܘܬܬܐܒܠܘܢ
²⁶ܘܝ ܠܟܘܢ ܟܕ ܢܗܘܘܢ ܐܡܪܝܢ ܥܠܝܟܘܢ ܟܠ ܐܢܫܐ ܕܫܦܝܪ.
ܗܟܢܐ ܓܝܪ ܥܒܕܝܢ ܗܘܘ ܠܢܒܝܐ ܕܕܓܠܘܬܐ ²⁷ܠܟܘܢ ܕܝܢ
ܐܡܪܢܐ ܕܫܡܥܝܢ ܐܢܬܘܢ ܠܒܥܠܕܒܒܝܟܘܢ ܘܥܒܕܘ ܕܫܦܝܪ ܠܐܝܠܝܢ
ܕܣܢܝܢ ܠܟܘܢ ²⁸ܒܪܟܘ ܠܐܝܠܝܢ ܕܠܝܛܝܢ ܠܟܘܢ܂ ܘܨܠܘ ܥܠ
ܐܝܠܝܢ ܕܒܥܛܝܢ ܠܟܘܢ ²⁹ܘܠܡܢ ܕܡܚܐ ܠܟ ܥܠ ܦܟܟ ܩܪܒ
ܠܗ ܐܚܪܢܐ ܘܡܢ ܕܫܩܠ ܡܪܛܘܛܟ ܐܦ ܟܘܬܝܢܟ ܠܐ ܬܟܠܝܘܗܝ
³⁰ܘܠܡܢ ܕܫܐܠ ܠܟ ܗܒ ܠܗ ܘܠܡܢ ܕܨܒܐ ܕܢܫܩܘܠ ܕܝܠܟ
ܠܐ ܬܬܒܥܘܗ ³¹ܘܐܝܟܢܐ ܕܨܒܝܢ ܐܢܬܘܢ ܕܢܥܒܕܘܢ ܠܟܘܢ
ܟ̈ܠ ܐܢܫܐ ⌜ܕܫܦܝܪ⌝ ܗܟܢܐ ܥܒܕܘ ܠܗܘܢ ³²ܘܐܢ ܡܚܒܝܢ ܐܢܬܘܢ
ܠܐܝܠܝܢ ܕܡܚܒܝܢ ܠܟܘܢ ܡܢܐ ܗܝ ܛܝܒܘܬܟܘܢ §³³ܘܐܦ A 35
ܥܒܕܝܢ ܐܢܬܘܢ ܕܛܒ ܠܟܠ ⌜ܡ̈ܢ⌝ ܕܥܒܕ ܢܛܒܘܢ ܕܛܒ ⌜ܡܢܐ⌝ ܗܝ
ܛܝܒܘܬܟܘܢ ܐܦ ܚܛܝܐ ܗܟܢܐ ܥܒܕܝܢ¶ ³⁴ܘܐܦ ܡܘܙܦܝܢ ¶A
ܐܢܬܘܢ ܠܡܢ ܕܡܣܒܝܢ ܐܢܬܘܢ ܕܬܬܦܪܥܘܢ ܡܢܗ ܡܢܐ ܗܝ
ܛܝܒܘܬܟܘܢ ⌜ܗܐ⌝ ܓܝܪ ܐܦ ܚܛܝܐ ܠܚܛܝܐ ܡܘܙܦܝܢ ܕܢܬܦܪܥܘܢ
³⁵ܒܪܡ ܕܝܢ ܐܚܒܘ ܠܒܥܠܕܒܒܝܟܘܢ ܘܐܛܐܒܘ ܠܗܘܢ ܘܐܘܙܦܘ.
ܘܠܐ ܬܦܣܩܘܢ ܣܒܪܐ ܕܐܢܫ ܕܢܗܘܐ ܐܓܪܟܘܢ ܣܓܝ
ܒܫܡܝܐ ܘܬܗܘܘܢ ܒܢܘܗܝ ܕܪܡܐ ܗܘ ܕܗܘ ܒܣܝܡ ܥܠ ܒܝ̈ܫܐ
ܘܥܠ ܟܦܘܪ̈ܐ ܛܝܒܘܬܐ ³⁶ܗܘܘ ܡܪܚܡܢܝܢ ܐܝܟܢܐ ܕܐܒܘܟܘܢ

---

24 ܒܒܘܬܟܘܢ] *S (sic) A (very expressly)* 27, 28. *For A* 34, *see on* Matt v 44 30. *Cf A* 270: ܐܝܟܢܐ ܬܠܒܢ ܕܐܝܟ ܥܫܩ ܐܢܫ ܕܝܠܟ ܠܐ ܬܬܒܥ 32. *For A* 35, *see on* Matt v 46 33 ܘܐܦ] ܕܐܦ. ܡܚܣܢ ܐܡܪ ܬܘܒ *A* ܠܟܠ ⌜ܡ̈ܢ⌝ ܕܥܒܕ] *S (sic)*; ܠܡܢ ܕܥܒܕ *A* ܢܛܒܘܢ] *S (sic)*; ܢܐܛܒܘܢ *A*ᵇ (ܠܟܘܢ *A*ᵃ) ܕܛܒ 2°] *S (sic)*; ܕܫܦܝܪ *A* ܐܦ] *pr.* ܗܕܐ *A* ܚܛܝܐ] ܡܟ̈ܣܐ ܘܚܛܝܐ *A* 34 ⌜ܗܐ⌝] *S (sic)* 35. *Cf A* 35 (*in continuation*): ܐܠܐ ܠܡ ܐܢܬܘܢ. ܡܛܠ ܕܐܬܬܩܪܝܬܘܢ ܒ̈ܢܝܐ ܠܐܠܗܐ ܚܝܐ ܕܒܫܡܝܐ. ܠܗ ܗܘܝܬܘܢ ܡܬܕܡܝܢ. ܕܡܢܝܚ ܐܦ ܥܠ ܒܝ̈ܫܐ ܛܝܒܘܬܐ. (*om.* ܚܝܐ *A*ᵇ)

24 "Nevertheless §woe to you, rich, that ye have received your *S*
supplication ! ¶ §¶*A* 390
25[b] "Woe to *you* that laugh now, that ye shall weep and mourn !
26 "Woe to you when men shall be saying concerning you what is well,
27 for so were they doing to the prophets of lying. Now to you I say that
hear: Be loving to your enemies and do what is well to them that
28 hate you, bless them that curse you and pray for them that oppress
29 you. And him that smiteth thee on thy cheek, offer him the other ;
and he that taketh away thy cloak or thy coat,—forbid him not.
30 And him that asketh thee, give to him ; and him that would take
31 away *what is* thine, require it not *back*. And as ye would that men
32 should do to you what is well, so do to them. And if ye are loving
33 to them that are loving to you, what is your kindness ? §And if ye do §*A* 35
what is good to every one that doeth by you what is good, what is
34 your kindness ? Even the sinners so do.¶ And if ye lend to him ¶*A*
that ye hope to be repaid by, what is your kindness ? For lo,
35 even sinners to sinners lend that they may be repaid. But never-
theless be loving to your enemies and be good to them and lend, and
do not give up hope of any one, that your reward may become great
in heaven and ye may become the sons of the Most High, he who is
36 gentle with the evil and with the ungrateful for kindness. Be

---

24 supplication] *S* (*sic*) *A* (*very expressly*) 24, 25 that ye] *or*, 'who' (*in each place*) 27, 28. *For A* 34, *see on* Matt v 44 30. Cf *A* 270: 'How wilt thou teach me "If any one take *what is* thine, do not require *back*"?' 32. *For A* 35, *see on* Matt v 46 33 And if] Again our Life-giver said If *A* every one that] him that *A* by you] *S* (*sic*) A^b; to you A^a good 2°] well *A* Even] for lo, even *A* the sinners] *pr.* the toll-gatherers and *A* 35 *Cf A* 35 (*in continuation*): 'But (quoth he) ye, because ye have been called sons to the Living God in heaven, to him become likened, who hath compassion even on the ungrateful for kindness.' [*om.* Living A^b]

ܡܪܚܡܢܐ ܗܘ. ³⁷ܠܐ ܬܕܘܢܘܢ ܘܠܐ ܬܬܕܝܢܘܢ. ܠܐ ܬܚܝܒܘܢ S
§¶A 35 ܘܠܐ ܬܬܚܝܒܘܢ: ܫܪܘ§ ܘܬܫܬܪܘܢ. ³⁸ܗܒܘ ܘܡܬܝܗܒ ܠܟܘܢ¶
ܒܟܝܠܬܐ ܛܒܬܐ ܘܡܫܦܥܬܐ ܢܪܡܘܢ ܒܥܘܒܟܘܢ. ܒܗ̇ ܒܟܝܠܬܐ
ܕܟܝܠܝܢ ܐܢܬܘܢ ܡܬܟܝܠ ܠܟܘܢ. ³⁹ܘܐܡܪ ܗܘܐ ܠܗܘܢ ܡܬܠܐ
ܗܢܐ ܠܡܐ ܡܫܟܚ ܣܡܝܐ ܠܣܡܝܐ ܠܡܕܒܪܘ ܘܠܐ ܬܪܝܗܘܢ
ܒܓܘܡܨܐ ܢܦܠܝܢ. ⁴⁰ܠܝܬ ܬܠܡܝܕܐ ܕܝܬܝܪ ܐܝܟ ܪܒܗ ܒܫܡܠܝܘܬܐ
⁴¹ܡܢܐ ܕܝܢ ܓܠܐ ܕܒܥܝܢܗ ܕܐܚܘܟ ܚܙܐ ܐܢܬ ܘܩܪܝܬܐ ܕܒܥܝܢܟ
ܠܐ ܡܬܚܙܝܐ ܠܟ. ⁴²ܐܝܟܢܐ ܡܫܟܚ ܐܢܬ ܠܡܐܡܪ ܠܐܚܘܟ
ܐܚܝ ܫܒܘܩ ܐܦܩ ܓܠܐ ܡܢ ܥܝܢܟ ܘܗܐ ܒܥܝܢܟ ܕܝܠܟ ܩܪܝܬܐ
ܩܝܡܐ ܢܣܒ ܒܐܦܐ. ܐܦܩ ܠܘܩܕܡ ܩܪܝܬܐ ܡܢ ܥܝܢܟ ܘܗܝܕܝܢ
ܬܬܚܙܐ ܠܟ ܠܡܦܩܘ ܓܠܐ ܡܢ ܥܝܢܗ ܕܐܚܘܟ. ⁴³ܠܐ ܓܝܪ ܐܝܬ
ܐܝܠܢܐ ܛܒܐ ܕܥܒܕ ܦܐܪܐ ܒܝܫܐ ܐܦܠܐ ܐܝܠܢܐ ܒܝܫܐ ܕܥܒܕ
ܦܐܪܐ ܛܒܐ ⁴⁴ܟܠ ܐܝܠܢ ܡܢ ܦܐܪܘܗܝ ܡܬܝܕܥ ܠܐ
ܠܩܛܝܢ ܡܢ ܟܘܒ̈ܐ ܬܐܢܐ ܘܐܦܠܐ ܡܢ ܣܢܝܐ ܥܢܒܐ
§A 303, 186 f. §⁴⁵ܓܒܪܐ ܛܒܐ ܡܢ ܣܝܡܬܐ ܛܒܬܐ ܕܠܒܗ. ܡܦܩ ⌜ܛܒܬܐ⌝
ܘܓܒܪܐ ܒܝܫܐ ܡܢ ܣܝܡܬܐ ܒܝܫܬܐ ܕܠܒܗ ܡܦܩ ܒܝܫܬܐ ܡܢ
¶A²/₂ ܬܘܬܪ̈ܐ. ܠܒܐ ܓܝܪ ܡܡܠܠ ܦܘܡܐ.¶ ⁴⁶ܡܢܐ ܕܝܢ ܩܪܝܢ ܐܢܬܘܢ
ܠܝ ܡܪܝ ܡܪܝ، ܘܡܕܡ ⌜ܕܐܡܪܢܐ⌝ ܠܟܘܢ ܠܐ ܥܒܕܝܢ ܐܢܬܘܢ:

---

37 ܫܪܘ] ܘܫܪܘ ܠܟܘܢ: ܘܢܫܬܒܩܘܢ ܕܫܒܩܘܢ ܡܢܟܘܢ. ܐܡܪ ܬܘܒ A 35 (*in continuation*)   38 ܗܒܘ] ܘܗܒܘ A   ܘܢܬܝܗܒ A   43—45. *The long quotation in* A 303, 187 (*combining* Matt vii 16—18 *with* Lk vi 45), *is from the Diatessaron* (Diat[ar] x 35—38). *For the variants to vv.* 43, 44, *see notes to* Matt vii 16—18   44 ܠܐ ܠܩܛܝܢ ܡܢ ܟܘܒ̈ܐ] S (*sic*): ܡܢ *appears in the photograph to have been added later above the line*   45 ܓܒܪܐ ܛܒܐ] ܒܪܢܫܐ ܛܒܐ A^{b} 303. *In* A 303 *this immediately follows* Matt vii 18; A 186 *inserts* Matt xii 33 (= Lk vi 44) *between* Matt vii 18 *and* Lk vi 45 *thus*:

ܡܛܠ ܕܡܢ ܦܐܪܘܗܝ ܗܘ ܡܬܝܕܥ ܐܝܠܢܐ. ܗܟܢܐ ܓܒܪܐ ܛܒܐ...

ܕܠܒܗ 1°] ܕܐܝܬ ܒܠܒܗ A 187   ܡܦܩ 1°] + ܘܡܡܠܠ A²/₂   ܡܢ...ܕܠܒܗ 2°]
ܡܢ ܬܘܬܪ̈ܐ ܠܒܗ A 303; ܡܢ ܣܝܡܬܐ ܒܝܫܬܐ ܕܐܝܬ ܒܠܒܗ A 187   ܡܦܩ 2°]
+ ܘܡܡܠܠ A²/₂   ܡܢ ܬܘܬܪ̈ܐ ܠܒܐ ܓܝܪ] ܗܘ ܠ' ܬ' ܕܡܢ ܟܠ A²/₂
ܡܡܠܠ ܦܘܡܐ] ܡܡܠܠܝܢ ܣܦܘ̈ܬܐ A²/₂

37 compassionate, as your Father is compassionate. Judge not, that ye *S*
be not judged; condemn not, that ye be not condemned; §remit §*A*35
38 and ye shall be remitted, give and it is given to you,¶—in good ¶*A*
measure and overflowing shall they cast in your bosoms. With that
39 measure which ye mete it is meted to you." And he was saying
to them this similitude: "Can the blind man lead the blind man
40 and not both of them fall into the ditch? There is no disciple†
41 that is perfect as his Rabbi in teaching. Now why the mote in
thy brother's eye dost thou see, and the beam in thine eye doth
42 not appear to thee? How canst thou say to thy brother 'My
brother, let me put forth the mote from thine eye,' and lo, in thine
own eye a beam is set? Thou respecter of persons! put forth first
the beam from thine eye, and then it will appear to thee *how* to put
43 forth the mote from thy brother's eye. For there is no good tree
that bringeth forth evil fruits, nor an evil tree that bringeth forth
44 good fruits. Every tree from its fruits is known; they do not pick
45 from thorns figs, nor from bushes do they gather in grapes. §The §*A*303, 186 f.
good man from the good treasures in his heart bringeth forth
good things, and the evil man from the evil treasures in his heart
bringeth forth evil things, for from the superfluities of the heart
46 speaketh the mouth.¶ Now why call ye me 'My Lord, my Lord,' and ¶$A^2/_2$

---

37 remit] *A* 35 (*in continuation*): 'Again our Saviour said "Forgive, and it shall be forgiven to you, and remit..."' 38 give] *pr.* and *A* is given] shall be given *A* 43—45. *The long quotation in A* 303, 187 (*combining* Matt vii 16—18 *with* Lk vi 45), *is from the Diatessaron* ($Diat^{ar}$ x 35—38). *For the variants to vv.* 43, 44, *see notes to* Matt vii 16—18 45 The good man] The good slave A^b303. *In A 303 this immediately follows* Matt vii 18, *as in* $Diat^{ar}$ x 37, 38; *A* 186 *inserts* Matt xii 33 (=Lk vi 44) *between* Matt vii 18 *and* Lk vi 45, *thus*: 'because it is from its fruits the tree is known; so the good man...' in his heart 1°] *pr.* that is *A* 187 bringeth forth 1°] + and speaketh $A^2/_2$ from...in his heart 2°] from the superfluities of his heart *A* 303; from the evil treasures that are in his heart *A* 187 bringeth forth 2°] + and speaketh $A^2/_2$ for from] because from $A^2/_2$ speaketh the mouth] speak the lips $A^2/_2$

⁴⁷ܟܠ ܐܢܫ ܓܒܪ ܕܐܬܐ ܠܘܬܝ، ܘܫܡܥ ܡܠܝ ܘܥܒܕ ܠܗܝܢ S
ܐܚܘܝܟܘܢ ܠܡܢܐ ܕܡܐ. ⁴⁸ܠܓܒܪܐ ܕܒܢܐ ܒܝܬܐ. ܘܚܦܪ ܘܥܡܩ.
ܘܣܡ ܫܬܐܣܬܐ ܥܠ ܫܘܥܐ ܘܟܕ ܗܘܘ ܡܠܐܐ ܘܡܠܐ ܢܗܪܐ
ܐܬܛܪܝܘ ܒܗ ܒܒܝܬܐ ܗܘ ܘܠܐ ܐܫܟܚܘ ܕܢܙܝܥܘܢܗ ⁴⁹ܘܗܘ
ܕܫܡܥ ܘܠܐ ܥܒܕ ܕܡܐ ܠܓܒܪܐ ܕܒܢܐ ܒܝܬܗ ܥܠ ܐܪܥܐ
ܕܠܐ ܫܬ ܐܣܬܐ ܘܐܬܛܪܝ، ܒܗ ܢܗܪܐ ܘܒܪܫܥܬܗ ܐܬܪܡܝܗ ܘܗܘܬ
ܡܦܘܠܬܐ ܕܒܝܬܐ ܗܘ ܪܒܐ ܀

¹ܘܟܕ ܐܫܠܡ ܡ̈ܠܐ ܟܠܗܝܢ ܠܡܫܡܥܬܗ ܕܥܡܐ. ܥܠ ܠܟܦܪܢܚܘܡ
²ܘܥܒܕܗ ܕܩܢܛܪܘܢܐ ܚܕ ܒܝܫ ܗܘܐ ܒܝܫ. ܘܡܝܩܪ ܗܘܐ
ܥܠ ܡܪܗ. ܘܡܛܐ ܗܘܐ ܠܡܡܬ ³ܘܫܡܥ ܥܠ ܝܫܘܥ ܘܫܕܪ
ܠܘܬܗ ܩܫܝ̈ܫܐ ܕܝܗܘܕܝܐ ܘܒܥܐ ܗܘܐ ܡܢܗ ܕܢܐܬܐ ܢܚܝܐ
ܠܥܒܕܗ ⁴ܘܐܬܘ ܠܘܬ ܝܫܘܥ ܘܒܥܝܢ ܗܘܘ ܡܢܗ ܒܝܨܝܢܐܝܬ.
ܘܐܡܪܝܢ ܫܘܐ ܗܘ ܕܬܥܒܕ ܠܗ ܗܕܐ. ⁵ܪܚܡ ܗܘ ܓܝܪ ܥܡܢ
ܘܐܦ ܒܝܬ ܟܢܘܫܬܐ ܗܘ ܒܢܐ ܠܢ. ⁶ܘܐܙܠ ܗܘܐ ܥܡܗܘܢ
ܝܫܘܥ ܘܟܕ ܩܪܒ ܕܝܢ ܩܠܝܠ ܡܢ ܒܝܬܐ ܗܘ ܫܕܪ ܠܘܬܗ ܩܢܛܪܘܢܐ
ܗܘ ܠܪ̈ܚܡܘܗܝ، ܘܫܠܚ ܠܗ ܡܪܝ، ܠܐ ܬܬܥܡܠ ܠܐ ܓܝܪ ܫܘܐ
ܐܢܐ ܕܬܥܘܠ ܬܚܝܬ ܡܛܠܠܝ. ⁷ܐܠܐ ܐܡܪ ܒܡܠܬܐ ܘܢܬܐܣܐ
ܛܠܝܐ. ⁸ܐܦ ܐܢܐ ܓܝܪ ܓܒܪܐ ܐܢܐ ܕܡܫܥܒܕܢܐ ܬܚܝܬ ܫܘܠܛܢܐ
ܘܐܝܬ ܬܚܝܬ ܐܝܕܝ، ܦܠܓܘܣܐ ܘܐܡܪ ܐܢܐ ܠܗܢܐ ܕܐܙܠ ܘܐܙܠ.
ܘܠܐܚܪܢܐ ܕܬܐ ܘܐܬܐ. ܘܠܥܒܕܝ، ܕܥܒܕ ܗܕܐ ܘܥܒܕ. ⁹ܘܟܕ
ܫܡܥ ܝܫܘܥ ܐܬܕܡܪ ܒܗ ܘܐܬܦܢܝ ܘܐܡܪ ܠܟܢܫܐ ܗܘ ܕܐܬܐ
ܒܬܪܗ ܐܡܪ ܐܢܐ ܠܟܘܢ ܕܐܦܠܐ ܒܝܬ ܐܝܣܪܐܝܠ ܐܫܟܚܬ
ܐܟܢ ܗܕܐ ܗܝܡܢܘܬܐ ¹⁰ܘܗܦܟܘ ܗܢܘܢ ܕܐܫܬܕܪܘ ܘܐܫܟܚܘ
ܠܥܒܕܐ ܗܘ ܟܕ ܚܠܝܡ ¹¹ܘܡܢ ܒܬܪܗ ܐܙܠ ܠܡܕܝܢܬܐ ܕܫܡܗ̇
ܢܐܝܢ ܘܬܠܡܝܕܘܗܝ، ܐܙܠܝܢ ܗܘܘ ܥܡܗ ܘܟܢܫܐ ܣܓܝܐܐ ¹²ܘܩܪܒ
ܠܬܪܥܐ ܕܡܕܝܢܬܐ [ܘܚܙܐ ܟܕ ܡܠܘܐ]ܝ [ܡܝܬܐ ܕܝܚܝܕܝܐ] ܗܘܐ
ܠܐܡܗ. ܘܗܝ، ܐܪܡܠܬܐ ܗܘܬ. ܘܐܝܬ ܗܘܐ ܥܡܗ ܟܢܫܐ ܣܓܝܐܐ

49 ܫܬ ܐܣܬܐ] S (*sic*)   7 ܐܡܪ...ܛܠܝܐ] *For* A 20, *see* Matt viii 8

47 that which I say to you ye do not? For every one that cometh unto S
me and heareth my words and doeth them, I will shew you what he
48 is like :—to a man that built a house and digged and went deep and
laid the foundation on the rock ; and when the floods were *out* and
the river was full they were dashed against that same house, and they
49 were not able to shake it. And he who heareth and doeth not is like
to a man that built his house on land without a foundation, and the
river was dashed against it, and straightway cast it *down*, and the
fall of that house was great."

vii 1 And when all the words were fulfilled in the hearing of the
2 people he entered Kapharnahum. And the slave of a certain
centurion was ill, and he was dear to his lord ; and he was near to
3 die. And he heard of Jesus and sent unto him elders of the Jews,
and was beseeching him that he should come *and* save his slave alive.
4 And they came unto Jesus and were beseeching him carefully and
5 saying : "He is worthy that thou shouldest do for him this, for he
6 loveth our people and a synagogue also he hath built for us." And
Jesus was going with them. Now when he was near, a little *way*
from the house, lo, that centurion despatched unto him his friends and
sent *word* to him : "My Lord, do not trouble, for I am not worthy
7 that thou shouldest enter under my dwelling ; but say with a word
8 and my lad will be healed. For I also am a man that am subject
under authority, and there are under my hand soldiers ; and I say to
this one 'Go,' and he goeth, and to another 'Come,' and he cometh,
9 and to my slave 'Do this,' and he doeth *it*." And when Jesus
heard he wondered at him, and he turned round and said to that
multitude that *was* coming after him : "I say to you, that not even
10 in the House of Israel have I found *aught* like this faith." And they
11 that were sent returned and found that slave whole. And afterwards
they went to a city whose name *was* Nain, and his disciples were
12 going with him and a great multitude. He drew near to the gate of
the city, [and saw *folk* accompanying a dead man, who] was [the only
son] of his mother, and she was a widow. And there was with her a

6 despatched...sent *word*] *cf* Matt xi 2 7 say...be healed] *For* *A* 20, *see* Matt viii 8

ܘܟܢܫܐ ܡܢ ܒ̈ܢܝ ܡܕܝܢܬܐ [13]ܘܚܙܗ ܝܫܘܥ ܘܐܬܪܚܡ ܥܠܝܗ ܘܐܡܪ S
ܠܗ ܠܐ ܬܒܟܝܢ [14]ܘܗܘ ܐܙܠ ܘܩܪܒ. ܠܐ⌜ܪ⌝ܘܢܐ ܘܗܢܘܢ ܕܫܩܝܠܝܢ
ܗܘܘ ܩܡܘ ܐܡܪ ܥܠܝܡܐ ܠܟ ܐܡܪܢܐ ܩܘܡ [15]ܘܐܬܬܩܝܡ ܗܘ
ܡܝܬܐ ܘܝܬܒ ܘܫܪܝ ܠܡܡܠܠܘ ܘܝܗܒܗ ܠܐܡܗ [16]ܘܐܚܕܬ ܐܢܘܢ
ܕܚܠܬܐ ܠܟܠܗܘܢ ܘܫܒܚܘ ܠܐܠܗܐ ܘܐܡܪܝܢ ܕܢܒܝܐ ܪܒܐ ܩܡ
ܒܢ ܘܣܥܪ ܐܠܗܐ ܠܥܡܗ [17]ܘܢܦܩܬ ܥܠܘܗܝ ܗܕܐ ܒܟܠܗ ܐܪܥܐ
ܕܝܗܘܕ ܘܒܟܠܗ ܐܬܪܐ ܕܚܕܪܝܗܘܢ

[18]ܘܐܫܬܥܝܘ ܠ[ܝܘܚܢܢ ܬܠܡܝܕܘܗܝ ܗܠܝܢ ܟܠܗܝܢ] [19]ܘܩܪܐ ܝܘܚܢܢ ܠܬܪܝܢ
ܡܢ ܬܠܡܝ̈ܕܘܗܝ ܘܫܕܪ ܠܘܬ ܝܫܘܥ ܘܐܡܪ ܐܢܬ ܗܘ ܕܐܬܐ ܐܘ
ܠܐܚܪܢ ܗܘ ܡܣܟܝܢ ܐܢܚܢ· [20]ܘܐܬܘ ܠܘܬܗ ܘܐܡܪܝܢ ܠܗ ܝܘܚܢܢ
ܡܥܡܕܢܐ ܫܕܪܢ ܠܘܬܟ ܘܐܡܪ ܐܢܬ ܗܘ ܕܐܬܐ ܐܘ ܠܐܚܪܢ
ܡܣܟܝܢ ܐ⌜ܢ⌝ܚܢ [21]ܘܒܗ ܒܫܥܬܐ [ܘܟܐܒܐ] ܐܣܐ ܡܢ ܟܘܪܗܢܐ ܘܡܢ
ܡܚܘܬܐ ܘܡܢ ܪܘܚܐ ܒܝܫܬܐ ܘܠܣ̈ܓܝܐܐ ܣܡ̈ܝܐ ܝܗܒ ܗܘܐ ܕܢܚܙܘܢ
[22]ܘܥܢܐ ܘܐܡܪ ܠܗܘܢ ܐܙܠܘ ܘܐܡܪܘ ܠܝܘܚܢܢ ܟܠܡܕܡ ܕܚܙܝܬܘܢ
ܘܡܕܡ ܕܫܡܥܬܘܢ ܕܣܡ̈ܝܐ ܚܙܝܢ ܘܚ̈ܓܝܪܐ ܡܗܠܟܝܢ ܘܓܪ̈ܒܐ
ܡܬܕܟܝܢ ܘܚܪ̈ܫܐ [ܫܡܥܝܢ] ܘܡܣ⌜ܟ̈⌝ܢܐ [* * *] ܘܡ⌜ܝ̈⌝ܬܐ [ܡܬܚܝܢ
[23]ܘܛܘܒܘܗܝ] ܠܡܢ ܕܠܐ ܢܬܟܫܠ ܒܝ [24]ܘܟܕ ܐܙܠܘ ܬܠܡܝܕܘܗܝ
ܕܝܘܚܢܢ ܫܪܝ ܠܡܐܡܪ ܠܟܢܫܐ ܥܠ ܝܘܚܢܢ ܡܢܐ ܢܦܩܬܘܢ
ܠܡܚܙܐ ܩܢܝܐ ܕܡܢ ܪܘܚܐ ܡܬܬܙܝܥ [25]ܘܐܠܐ ܡܢܐ ܢܦܩܬܘܢ
ܠܡܚܙܐ ܓܒܪܐ ܕܢܚܬܐ ܪܟܝܟܐ ܠܒܝܫ ܗܐ ܗܢܘܢ ܕܒܠܒܘ̈ܫܐ
ܡܫܒܚܐ ܘܡܦܢܩܐ ܐܝܬܝܗܘܢ ܒܒܝܬ ܡ̈ܠܟܐ ܐܢܘܢ· [26]ܘܐܠܐ

---

14 ܠܐ⌜ܪ⌝ܘܢܐ] ܠܐ..ܐ *S* (*sic*), *rest illegible. We must supply* ܠܐ⌜ܪ⌝ܘܢܐ (*not* ܠܐܪܘܢܐ), *with* syr^palest (ܠܪܘܢܐ, *cf* إِرَانٌ). ܐܪܘܢܐ *in Syriac is a loan-word from the Hebrew and means 'The Ark of the Covenant'* 14, 15 ܐܡܪ....ܘܐܬܬܩܝܡ] *Cf A* 165: ܠܒܪܗ ܒܪ ܕܐܪܡܠܬܐ. ܟܕ ܐܚܝܗ. ܥܠܝܡܐ ܬܘܒ ܩܘܡ. ܟܕ ܐܡܪ: ܠܗ. ܥܠܝܡܐ ܥܠܝܡܐ ܩܘܡ. ܘܚܝܐ ܘܩܡ (*cf also* Lk viii 54, 55). *Cf also* Ephr. *Nisib.* xxxix 179f: ܩܥܐ ܗܘ ܩܪܐ ܠܡܝܬܐ. ܥܠܝܡܐ ܥܠܝܡܐ. 20 ܠܐܚܪܢ (*as ver.* 19)] *S* (*sic*)   ܐ⌜ܢ⌝ܚܢ] ܚܢ S^{ed} 22. *The missing word corresponding to* εὐαγγελίζονται *should be* ܡܬܣܒܪܝܢ, *but cf* Matt xi 5 *C*

13 great multitude from the men of the city. Jesus saw her and had S
14 compassion on her and said to her: "Weep not." And he himself
went and touched the bier, and they that were carrying *it* stood *still*.
15 Saith he: "Youth, to thee I say Arise!" And the dead lifted
himself up and sat and began to speak, and he gave him to his
16 mother. And fear took hold of them all, and they glorified God and
say "A great prophet hath arisen among us, and God hath visited
17 his people." And this went forth concerning him in all the land of
Judaea and in all the country round about them.

18, 19 And [his disciples] declared to [John all these things]. And John
called two of his disciples and sent unto Jesus and said: "Art thou
20 he that cometh, or for another is it *that* we are waiting?" And they
came unto him and say to him: "John the Baptist sent us unto thee
and saith: 'Art thou he that cometh, or for another is it *that* we are
21 waiting?'" And in the same hour [many] he healed of infirmities
and of plagues and of evil spirits, and to many blind he was giving
22 that they should see. And he answered and said to them: "Go and
say to John everything which ye have seen and which ye have
heard—that the blind see and the lame walk and the lepers are
cleansed and the deaf [hear and] the poor [are * * and] the
23 dead [arise. And happy is it] for him that shall not be offended in
24 me." And when the disciples of John went he began to say to the
multitudes concerning John: "What went ye forth to see?—a reed
25 that by the wind is shaken? But if not, what went ye forth to see?
—a man that with soft garments is clad? Lo, those that are in
26 glorious and sumptuous clothing are in kings' houses. But if not,

---

14 the bier] *S partly illegible. The true spelling of the rare word to be supplied is to be inferred from the word here used in* syr[palest] ('ĕrânâ, *not* 'arônâ)
14, 15 Saith he...lifted himself up] *Cf A* 165: 'For the son of the widow—when he saved him alive, he called him twice, saying to him "Youth, youth, arise!" And he lived and arose' (*cf also* Lk viii 54, 55). *Cf also* Ephr. *Nisib.* xxxix 179f: 'But Jesus called to the dead, *saying* "Youth, youth"'
22 the poor are * * *] *The missing word should be* 'announced the good tidings' (*as in* Lk xvi 16), *but cf* Matt xi 5 *C*

S [C] ܡܢܐ ܢܦܩܬܘܢ ܠܡܚܙܐ ܢܒܝܐ ܐܝܢ· ܐܡܪܢܐ ܠܟܘܢ ܕܝܬܝܪ
ܗܘ ܡܢ ܢܒܝܐ. [27]ܗܢܘ ܕܥܠܘܗܝ ܟܬܝܒ ܕܗܐ ܡܫܕܪܢܐ ܡܠܐܟܝ
ܩܕܡ ܦܪ̈ܨܘܦܝܟ ܘܢܬܩܢ ܐܘܪܚܐ ܩܕܡܝܟ. [28]ܐܡܪܢܐ ܠܟܘܢ ܕܠܐ
ܩܡ ܒܝܠ̈ܕܝ ܢܫ̈ܐ ܢܒܝܐ ܕܪܒ ܡܢ ܝܘܚܢܢ [ܡܥܡܕܢܐ ܙܥܘܪܐ ܕܝܢ
ܒܡܠܟܘܬܐ] ܕܐܠܗܐ ܪܒ ܗܘ ܡܢܗ. [29]ܘܟܠܗ ܥܡܐ ܘܡܟܣܐ
ܕܫܡܥܘ ܙܕܩܘ ܢܦܫܗܘܢ ܠܐܠܗܐ ܕܥܡܕܘ ܒܡܥܡܘܕܝܬܗ ܕܝܘܚܢܢ
[30]ܦܪ̈ܝܫܐ ܕܝܢ ܘܣܦܪ̈ܐ ܛܠܡܘ ܒܢܦܫܗܘܢ ܨܒܝܢܐ ܕܐܠܗܐ ܕܠܐ
ܐܬܥܡܕܘ ܡܢܗ. [31]ܠܡܢ ܗܟܝܠ ܐܕܡܐ ܐܢܘܢ ܐܢܫܐ ܕܫܪܒܬܐ
ܗܕܐ ܘܠܡܢܐ ܕܡܝܢ. [32]ܕܡܝܢ ܠܛܠܝ̈ܐ ܕܝܬܒܝܢ ܒܫܘܩܐ ܘܩܥܝܢ
ܠܚܒܪ̈ܝܗܘܢ ܘܐܡܪܝܢ ܠܗܘܢ ܘܠܐ ܪܩܕܬܘܢ ܘܐܠܝܢ ܠܟܘܢ ܘܠܐ
§C fol 54 r ܒܟܝܬܘܢ. [33]ܐܬܐ ܓܝܪ ܠܘܬܟܘܢ. ܝܘܚܢܢ ܡܥܡܕܢܐ ܠܐ | §*ܐܟܠ
ܘܠܐ ܫܬܐ. ܐܡܪܝܢ ܐܝܬܘܗܝ ܫܐܕܐ ܒܗ. [34]ܘܐܬܐ ܒܪܗ
ܕܓܒܪܐ ܐܟܠ ܘܫܬܐ. ܐܡܪܝܢ ܐܝܬܘܗܝ ܗܐ ܓܒܪܐ ܐܟܘܠܐ
ܘܪܘܝܐ. ܘܪܚܡܐ ܕܡܟܣܐ ܘܕܚ̈ܛܝܐ. [35]ܘܐܙܕܕܩܬ ܚܟܡܬܐ ܡܢ
ܒ̈ܢܝܗ ··

[36]ܘܐܬܐ ܦܪܝܫܐ ܚܕ ܒܥܐ ܡܢܗ ܕܢܠܥܣ ܠܘܬܗ. ܘܥܠ ܠܒܝܬܗ
ܕܦܪܝܫܐ ܗܘ. ܘܟܕ ܐܣܬܡܟ· [37]ܐܢܬܬܐ ܚܕܐ ܚܛܝܬܐ ܐܝܬ ܗܘܬ
ܒܗ̇ ܡܕܝܢܬܐ. ܟܕ ܝܕܥܬ ܕܒܒܝܬܗ ܕܗܘ ܦܪܝܫܐ ܣܡܝܟ. ܢܣܒܬ
ܫܛܝܦܬܐ ܕܡܫܚܐ ܕܒܣܡܐ. [38]ܘܩܡܬ ܡܢ ܒܣܬܪܗ ܠܘܬ ܪ̈ܓܠܘܗܝ
col 2 ܘܒܟܝܐ ܗܘܬ. ܘܒܕ̈ܡܥܝܗ̇ ܪ̈ܓܠܘܗܝ ܨܒܥܬ. *ܘܒܣܥܪܐ ܕܪܫܗ̇
ܡܫܘܐ ܗܘܬ ܠܗܝܢ. ܘܡܢܫܩܐ ܗܘܬ ܪ̈ܓܠܘܗܝ. ܘܡܫܚܐ ܗܘܬ
ܡܢ ܗܘ ܡܫܚܐ. [39]ܟܕ ܚܙܐ ܕܝܢ ܦܪܝܫܐ ܗܘ ܕܩܪܝܗ، ܐܬܚܫܒ
ܒܢܦܫܗ ܘܐܡܪ. ܗܢܐ ܐܠܘ ܢܒܝܐ ܗܘܐ ܝܕܥ ܗܘܐ ܡܢ ܗܝ.
ܐܘ ܡܢܐ ܓܢܣܗ̇ ܕܐܢܬܬܐ ܗܝ، ܚܛܝܬܐ ܕܩܪܒܬ ܠܗ. [40]ܐܡܪ ܠܗ
ܝܫܘܥ. ܫܡܥܘܢ· ܐܝܬ ܠܝ ܡܕܡ ܕܐܡܪ ܠܟ. ܐܡܪ ܠܗ ܐܡܪ

---

33 ܫܐܕܐ] + ܐܝܬ S   35 ܒ̈ܢܝܗ] *pr.* ܟܠܗܘܢ S   36 ܠܘܬܗ] ܥܡܗ S
ܘܥܠ] ܥܠ S   37 ܟܕ] ܘܟܕ S   38 ܘܒܣܥܪ̈ܐ S (*and in ver.* 44)   39 ܗܘ ܦܪܝܫܐ S
ܡܢ ܗܝ] ܡܢܘ S   ܐܘ ܡܢܐ] ܘܡܢܐ S

what went ye forth to see?—a prophet? Yea, I say to you, one that is S [C]
27 more than the prophets. This is he of whom it is written 'Lo, I send
my messenger before thy countenance, and he shall prepare a way
28 before thee.' I say to you There hath not arisen among them that
are born of women a prophet greater than John [the Baptist, but he
29 that is little in the kingdom of] God is greater than he. And all
the people and the toll-gatherers that heard justified themselves to
30 God in that they were baptized with the baptism of John; but the
scribes and the Pharisees defrauded in themselves the will of God in
31 that they did not receive baptism from him. To whom therefore shall
32 I liken the folk of this generation, and to what are they like? They
are like to children that sit in the street and send *word* to their
fellows: 'We have sung to you and ye have not danced, and we have
33 wailed to you and ye have not wept.' For there came unto you John
the Baptist not | §eating nor drinking; ye say: 'A devil in him.' §C
34 And there came the son of a man eating and drinking; ye say: 'Lo,
a man *who is* an eater and a drunkard and a friend of toll-gatherers
35 and of sinners!' And wisdom hath been justified from her sons."
36 And there came a certain Pharisee beseeching him that he would
dine at his *house*. And he entered the house of that Pharisee; and
37 when he sat down *to meat*, there was a certain woman, a sinner, in
that city,—when she knew that in the house of that Pharisee he was
38 sitting *at meat*, she took a vase of oil of sweet smell and stood up
behind him at his feet and was weeping, and with her tears his feet
she moistened and with the hair of her head she was wiping them,
and she was kissing his feet and was anointing *them* with that oil.
39 Now when that Pharisee who had bidden him saw *it* he thought in
himself and said: "This *man*, if he were a prophet, would know who
she is, or what the tale *is* of that woman, the sinner, that hath
40 touched him." Jesus saith to him: "Simon, I have something that I

33 in] *pr.* is *S* 34 the son of a man] *see on* Matt xii 40, Lk xxii 48 35 her sons] *pr.* all *S* 36 at his *house*] with him *S* and when] *om.* and *S* 37 when] *pr.* and *S* 39 or] and *S* *For the whole verse, cf E*[113]: 'This man, if he were a prophet, how knew he not of what manner of works this woman is, that is, that she is a sinner?'

C S ܪܒܝ. 41ܐܡܪ ܠܗ ܫܡܥܘܢ· ܬܪ̈ܝܢ ܚܝܒܝܢ ܐܝܬ ܗܘܘ ܠܚܕ ܡܪܐ
ܚܘܒܐ. ܚܕ ܚܝܒ ܗܘܐ ܠܗ ܕ̈ܝܢܪܐ ܚܡܫܡܐܐ. ܘܚܕ ܕ̈ܝܢܪܐ
ܚܡ̈ܫܝܢ. 42ܘܟܕ ܠܐ ܐܝܬ ܗܘܐ ܠܗܘܢ ܠܡܦܪܥ ܠܬܪ̈ܝܗܘܢ ܫܒܩ.
fol 54 v ܐܝܢܐ ܡܢܗܘܢ ܢܚܒܝܘܗܝ، *ܝܬܝܪܐܝܬ. 43ܐܡܪ ܠܗ ܫܡܥܘܢ.
ܣܒܪ ܐܢܐ ܕܗܘ ܕܝܬܝܪ ܐܫܬܒܩ ܠܗ. ܐܡܪ ܠܗ ܝܫܘܥ. ܫܦܝܪ
ܕܢܬ· 44ܘܐܬܦܢܝ ܠܘܬ ܐܢܬܬܐ ܘܐܡܪ ܠܫܡܥܘܢ܂ ܚܙܐ ܐܢܬ
ܐܢܬܬܐ ܗܕܐ. ܠܒܝܬܟ ܥܠܬ. ܡ̈ܝܐ ܠܪ̈ܓܠܝ ܠܐ ܝܗܒܬ ܠܝ. ܗܝ،
ܕܝܢ ܒܕ̈ܡܥܝܗ ܪ̈ܓܠܝ ܨܒܥܬ. ܘܒܣܥܪܐ ܕܪܫܗ̇ ܫܘܝܬ ܐܢܝܢ. 45ܐܢܬ
ܠܐ ܢܫܩܬܢܝ. ܗܝ، ܕܝܢ ܡܢ ܕܥܠܬ ܠܐ ܫܠܝܬ ܪ̈ܓܠܝ ܠܡܢܫܩܘ.
46ܐܢܬ ܠܐ ܡܫܚܬܢܝ. ܗܝ، ܕܝܢ ܒܡܫܚܐ ܕܒܣܡܐ ܡܫܚܬ ܪ̈ܓܠܝ.
47ܡܛܠ ܗܢܐ ܐܡܪܢܐ ܠܟ ܫܒܝܩܝܢ ܠܗ̇ ܚܛ̈ܗܝܗ ܣܓܝ̈ܐܐ. ܡܛܠ
ܕܣܓܝ ܐܚܒܬ. ܡܢ ܕܩܠܝܠ ܓܝܪ ܐܫܬܒܩ ܠܗ. ܩܠܝܠ ܗܘ ܡܚܒ.
col 2 48ܐܡܪ ܠܗ̇ ܠܗܝ، ܐܢܬܬܐ. ܕܫܒܝܩܝܢ *ܠܟܝ ܚܛ̈ܗܝܟܝ. 49ܘܫܪܝܘ ܗܢܘܢ
ܕܡܣܬܡܟܝܢ ܐܡܪܝܢ ܒܢܦܫܗܘܢ· ܡܢܘ ܗܢܐ ܕܐܦ ܚܛ̈ܗܐ ܫܒܩ.
50ܘܐܡܪ ܠܐܢܬܬܐ ܗܝ، ܗܝܡܢܘܬܟܝ ܐܚܝܬܟܝ ܙܠܝ ܒܫܠܡܐ. ·:·
1ܘܡܢ ܒܬܪ ܗܠܝܢ. ܡܬܟܪܟ ܗܘܐ ܒܩܘܪ̈ܝܐ ܘܒܡܕ̈ܝܢܬܐ. ܘܡܣܒܪ
ܡܠܟܘܬܗ ܕܐܠܗܐ. ܐܦ ܬܪ̈ܥܣܪܬܗ ܥܡܗ. 2ܘܢܫ̈ܐ ܗܠܝܢ
ܕܐܬܐܣܝ، ܗܘܝ، ܡܢ ܪ̈ܘܚܐ ܒܝܫܬܐ. ܘܡܢ ܟܘ̈ܪܗܢܐ. ܡܪܝܡ
ܕܡܬܩܪܝܐ ܡܓܕܠܝܬܐ. ܗܝ، ܕܫܒܥܐ ܫܐ̈ܕܝܢ ܐܦܩ ܗܘܐ ܡܢܗ̇.
3ܘܝܘܚܢ ܐܢܬܬ ܟܘܙܐ ܐܦܛܪܘܦܗ ܕܗܪܘܕܣ. ܘܫܘܫܢ. ܘܐ̈ܚܪܢܝܬܐ
ܣܓܝ̈ܐܬܐ ܕܡܫܡܫܢ ܗܘܝ، ܠܗܘܢ ܡܢ ܡܕܡ ܕܐܝܬ ܗܘܐ ܠܗܝܢ.·:·

---

40 ܪܒܝ] ܪܒܝ S   41 ܠܚܕ ܡܪܐ ܚܘܒܐ] ܠܡܪܐ ܡܘܙܦܢܐ S and Ephr. Lamy ii, p. xxii   ܚܡ̈ܫܝܢ....ܚܡܫܡܐܐ S   42 ܘܟܕ ܠܐ ܐܝܬ] ܘܟܕ ܠܝܬ S   43 ܕܝܬܝܪ....ܠܗ.] ܕܐܫܬܒܩ ܠܗ ܣܓܝ. S   44 ܚܙܐ ܐܢܬ] ܚܙܬ S (sic)   ܗܝ] ܗܕܐ S   ܪ̈ܓܠܝ ܨܒܥܬ] ܨܒܥܬ ܐܢܝܢ S   46 ܪ̈ܓܠܝ ܡܫܚܬ S   47 ܠܟ] om. S   ܐܫܬܒܩ] ܡܫܬܒܩ S   ܗܘ] om. S   48 ܐܡܪ ܠܗ̇ ܠܗܝ ܐܢܬܬܐ] ܘܐܡܪ ܠܗ̇ S
1 ܘܒܡܕ̈ܝܢܬܐ] + ܘܬܪ̈ܥܣܪܬܗ ܥܡܗ S (om. ܐܦ...ܥܡܗ at end of ver.)
2 ܐܦܩ ܗܘܐ] ܢܦܩܘ ܗܘܘ S   3 ܡܢ ܡܕܡ ܕܐܝܬ ܗܘܐ ܠܗܝܢ] ܡܢ ܩܢܝ̈ܢܗܝܢ S

41 would say to thee." He saith to him: "Say *it*, Rabbi." Jesus saith C S
to him: "Two debtors there were to a certain creditor; one was
42 indebted to him five hundred denars and one fifty denars, and when
they had not *aught* to repay he forgave them both. Which of them
43 will be loving to him the more?" Simon saith to him: "I suppose
him whom more was forgiven to." Jesus saith to him: "Well hast
44 thou judged." And he turned round unto the woman and said to
Simon: "Seest thou this woman? Thy house I entered—water for
my feet thou gavest me not, but she with her tears my feet hath
45 moistened and with the hair of her head hath wiped them. Thou
didst not kiss me, but she since I entered hath not ceased my feet to
46 kiss. Thou didst not anoint me, but she with oil of sweet smell hath
47 anointed my feet. Therefore I say to thee: Her many sins are
forgiven her, because much she hath been loving. For he that little
48 hath been forgiven to, little is he loving." Saith he to her, to that
49 woman, "Thy sins are forgiven thee." And they that were sitting
at meat began saying in themselves: "Who is this that forgiveth
50 sins also?" And he saith to that woman: "Thy faith hath saved thee
alive; go in peace."

viii 1 And after these things he was going about in the villages and in
the cities and announcing the kingdom of God, his Twelve also with
2 him, and these women that had been healed from evil spirits and from
infirmities—Mary called Magdalene from whom seven devils he had
3 cast out, and Johan wife of Kuza the agent of Herod, and Susan,
and many others that were serving them from that which they had.

---

40 Rabbi] Rabban *S* 41 a certain creditor] a man, a money-lender *S* *E*[114] *and* Ephr. *Lamy* ii, p. xxii five hundred....fifty] *tr.* *S* (*not* *E*[114]) 43 whom...forgiven to] to whom was forgiven much *S* 44 Seest thou] *the reading of S seems to be a mistake for* 'hast thou seen' but she] but this *woman* *S* my feet hath moistened] hath moistened them *S* 46 my feet hath anointed *S* 47 to thee] *om.* *S* hath been 2°] is *S* he 2°] *om.* *S* 48 Saith.....woman] And he saith to her *S* 1 cities] + and his Twelve with him *S* (*om.* his Twelve also with him *at end of ver.*) 2 he had cast out] *so also* *E*[120]; had gone forth *S* 3 that which they had] their properties *S*

C S fol 55 r *[4]ܘܟܕ ܐܬܟܢܫ ܟܢܫܐ ܣܓܝܐܐ. ܘܐܝܠܝܢ ܕܡܢ ܡܕܝܢܬܐ ܐܬܝܢ ܗܘܘ
ܠܘܬܗ. ܐܡܪ ܠܗܘܢ ܒܡܬܠܐ. [5]ܗܐ ܢܦܩ ܙܪܘܥܐ ܠܡܙܪܥ.
ܘܟܕ ܙܪܥ. ܐܝܬ ܕܢܦܠ ܥܠ ܝܕ ܐܘܪܚܐ. ܘܐܬܕܝܫ. ܘܐܟܠܬܗ
ܦܪܚܬܐ. [6]ܘܐܚܪܢܐ ܢܦܠ ܥܠ ܫܘܥܐ. ܘܡܛܠ ܕܠܝܬ ܗܘܬ ܠܗ
ܛܠܠܬܐ ܒܝ ܘܝܒܫ. [7]ܐܚܪܢܐ ܢܦܠ ܒܝܬ ܟܘܒܐ. ܘܥܒܐ ܥܡܗ
ܘܚܢܩܘܗܝ. [8]ܘܚܪܢܐ ܢܦܠ ܒܐܪܥܐ ܛܒܬܐ ܘܝܗܒܬ ܦܐܪܐ. ܘܥܒܐ
ܘܥܒܕ ܦܐܪܐ. ܚܕ ܒܡܐܐ. ܘܟܕ ܐܡܪ ܗܠܝܢ. ܒܩܠܐ ܪܡܐ
ܐܡܪ ܗܘܐ. ܕܡܢ ܕܐܝܬ ܠܗ ܐܕܢܐ ܕܢܫܡܥ ܢܫܡܥ .܀

col 2 [9]ܘܫܐܠܘܗܝ ܗܘܘ *ܬܠܡܝܕܘܗܝ. ܡܢܘ ܡܬܠܐ ܗܢܐ. [10]ܐܡܪ
ܠܗܘܢ. ܠܟܘܢ ܗܘ ܝܗܝܒ ܠܡܕܥ ܐܪܙܐ ܕܡܠܟܘܬܗ ܕܐܠܗܐ.
ܠܗܢܘܢ ܕܝܢ ܕܒܪܐ ܠܐ ܝܗܝܒ ܠܗܘܢ ܠܡܕܥ. ܡܛܠ ܗܢܐ
ܒܡܬܠܐ ܡܬܐܡܪ ܠܗܘܢ. ܕܟܕ ܚܙܝܢ ܠܐ ܢܚܙܘܢ. ܘܟܕ
ܫܡܥܝܢ ܠܐ ܢܣܬܟܠܘܢ. [11]ܗܢܐ ܕܝܢ ܡܬܠܐ ܐܝܬܘܗܝ. ܙܪܥܐ
ܡܠܬܗ ܗܝ ܕܐܠܗܐ. [12]ܘܗܢܘܢ ܕܥܠ ܝܕ ܐܘܪܚܐ. ܗܠܝܢ ܐܢܘܢ
ܕܫܡܥܝܢ ܡܠܬܐ ܕܐܠܗܐ. ܘܐܬܐ ܒܥܠܕܒܒܐ ܫܩܠ ܠܗ̇ ܡܠܬܐ
ܡܢ ܠܒܗܘܢ. ܕܠܐ ܢܗܝܡܢܘܢ ܘܢܚܘܢ. [13]ܘܗܘܘ ܕܥܠ ܫܘܥܐ.
ܗܠܝܢ ܐܢܘܢ ܕܡܐ ܕܫܡܥܘ ܡܠܬܐ. ܒܚܕܘܬܐ ܡܩܒܠܝܢ
fol 55 v ܠܗ̇. ܘܥܩܪܐ ܠܝܬ ܠܗܘܢ ܒܗ̇. ܘܒܙܒܢ *ܡܗܝܡܢܝܢ. ܘܒܙܒܢ
ܢܣܝܘܢܐ ܡܬܬܥܠܝܢ. [14]ܘܗܘܘ ܕܢܦܠ ܒܝܬ ܟܘܒܐ. ܗܠܝܢ ܐܢܘܢ
ܐܝܠܝܢ ܕܫܡܥܘ ܡܠܬܐ. ܘܒܝܨܦܬܐ ܐܢܘܢ ܘܒܥܘܬܪܐ ܕܥܠܡܐ.

---

4. *No* § *in S*   ܡܬܟܢܫ *S*   ܐܡܪ] ܠܡܐܡܪ ܫܪܝ *S*   5 ܙܪܥ] + ܗܘܐ *S*
6 ܢܦܠ] *so also S*   ܠܗ] *om. S*   7 ܐܚܪܢܐ] *pr.* ܘ *S*   ܘܥܒܐ ܥܡܗ] *om. S*
8 ܘܚܪܢܐ] *C (end of line)*; ܘܐܚܪܢܐ *S*   ܘܝܗܒܬ ܦܐܪܐ] *om. S*   ܕܡܢ ܕܐܝܬ ܠܗ
and ܕܢܫܡܥ ܢܫܡܥ] *S illegible*   9, 10 ܡܬܠܐ....ܠܟܘܢ ܗܘ] *S illegible*
10 ܠܗܘܢ 2°] *S bis*   ܡܬܐܡܪ] ⌈ܐܡܬܪܢܐ⌉ *S*   11 ܡܠܬܗ ܗܝ] *om.* ܗܝ *S*[ed]
12 ܡܠܬܐ ܕܐܠܗܐ] *S illegible, but there is no room for* ܕܐܠܗܐ   ܫܩܠ ܠܗ̇]
S illegible   13 ܘܗܘܘ ܕܥܠ] *S illegible*   ܕܫܡܥܘ] ܕܫܡܥܝܢ *S*   ܘܒܙܒܢ ܢܣܝܘܢܐ]
according to S[ed]*, more is lost before* ܒܙܒܢ *than* ܘ   14 ܗܠܝܢ ܐܢܘܢ] *one illegible word in S*   ܡܠܬܐ] *om. S*   ܐܢܘܢ 2°] *om. S*[vid]   ܕܥܠܡܐ] *om. S*

4 And when there was gathered together a great multitude and *C S*
they that from the cities were coming unto him, he saith to them in
5 similitudes: "Lo, the sower went forth to sow; and when he sowed
some fell by the way-side and was trodden upon, and the birds ate it.
6 And other fell on the rock, and because it had no moisture it failed
7 and withered. Other fell among the thorns, and they sprang up with
8 it and choked it. And other fell in the good land and fruitful, and
sprang up and gave fruit an hundredfold." And when he said these
things, with a loud voice he was saying "He that hath ears that he
should hear, let him hear."

9, 10 And his disciples had asked him: "What is this similitude?" Saith
he to them: "To you is given to know the mystery of the kingdom of
God, but to those without—it is not given to them to know. There-
fore in parables it is said to them, that though they see they may not
11 see, and though they hear they may not understand. Now this
12 similitude is *as follows*: the seed is the word of God; and they by
the way-side--these are they that hear the word of God, and the
enemy cometh *and* taketh it away, *even* the word, from their heart,
13 that they should not believe and live. And that on the rock—these
be they that what *time* they have heard the word quickly with joy
receive it, and they have no root in it; and for a time they believe
14 and in time of temptation they are offended. And that which fell
among thorns—these are they that hear the word, and are in anxiety,
and in the riches of the world and in the pleasantness of living are

---

4 was] is *S* saith] began to say *S* **5** sowed] was sowing *S* **6** it had] there was *S* **7** Other] And other *S* sprang up with it and] *om. S* **8** and fruitful] *so also* E^{125} (*vid*); *om. S* He that hath *and* that he....him hear] *S illegible* **9, 10** this...To you is] *S illegible* to them 2°] *S bis* it is said] ⌜I⌝ say *it S* **12** the word of God] *S illegible, but there is no room for* 'of God' taketh it away] *S illegible* **13** And that on] *S illegible* have heard] hear *S* and in time of temptation] *according to* S^{ed}, *more is lost before* 'in time' *than a simple* 'and' **14** the word] *om. S* the riches of the world] riches *S*

C S ܘܒܒܣܝܡܘܬܐ ܕܒܥܘܬܪܐ ܘܡܬܚܢܩܝܢ. ܘܦܐܪ̈ܐ ܠܐ
ܝܗܒܝܢ. [15]ܘܗܘ ܕܢܦܠ ܒܐܪܥܐ ܛܒܬܐ. ܗܢܘܢ ܐܢܘܢ ܕܒܠܒܐ
ܫܦܝܪܐ ܘܛܒܐ ܫܡܥܝܢ ܡܠܬܐ. ܘܐܚܕܝܢ. ܘܝܗܒܝܢ ܦܐܪ̈ܐ
ܒܡܣܝܒܪܢܘܬܐ. ܀

§A 14 [16]ܡܬܠܐ ܐܚܪܢܐ ܐܡܪ ܗܘܐ. §ܠܐ ܐܢܫ ܡܢܗܪ ܫܪܓܐ ܘܡܟܣܐ
ܠܗ ܒܡܐܢܐ. ܐܘ ܣܐܡ ܠܗ ܬܚܝܬ ܥܪܣܐ. ܐܘ ܒܡܢܪܬܐ
ܡܩܝܡܝܢ. ܐܠܐ ܣܐܡ ܠܗ ܥܠ ܡܢ ܡܢܪܬܐ. ܕܟܠ ܐܢܫ ܕܥܐܠ
¶A ܢܚܙܐ ܢܘܗܪܗ.¶ [17]ܠܝܬ ܓܝܪ ܡܕܡ ܕܟܣܐ *ܕܠܐ ܢܬܓܠܐ. ܘܐܦܠܐ
col 2 ܕܡܛܫܐ ܕܠܐ ܢܬܝܕܥ ܘܢܐܬܐ ܠܓܠܝܐ. [18]ܚܙܘ ܡܢܐ ܫܡܥܝܬܘܢ.
ܡܢ ܕܐܝܬ ܠܗ ܓܝܪ ܢܬܝܗܒ ܠܗ ܘܢܬܘܣܦ ܠܗ. ܘܗܘ ܕܠܝܬ ܠܗ.
ܐܦ ܗܘ ܡܕܡ ܕܣܒܪ ܗܘܐ ܕܐܝܬ ܠܗ ܢܫܬܩܠ ܠܗ ܡܢܗ. ܀

[19]ܘܐܬܘ ܗܘܘ ܠܘܬܗ ܕܢܩܪܒ ܐܡܗ ܘܐܚ̈ܘܗܝ. ܘܩܝܡܝܢ ܗܘܘ
ܠܒܪ. ܘܠܐ ܡܫܟܚܝܢ ܗܘܘ ܕܢܚܙܘܢܗ. ܡܛܠ ܟܢܫܐ ܕܐܢܫܐ.
[20]ܘܐܡܪܘ ܠܗ ܐܡܟ ܘܐܚܝܟ ܩܝܡܝܢ ܠܒܪ. ܘܒܥܝܢ ܠܡܚܙܝܟ.
[21]ܗܘ ܕܝܢ ܥܢܐ ܘܐܡܪ ܠܗܘܢ܂ ܗܠܝܢ ܐܢܘܢ ܐܡܝ ܘܐܚ̈ܝ. ܐܝܠܝܢ
ܕܫܡܥܝܢ ܡܠܬܗ ܕܐܠܗܐ ܘܥܒܕܝܢ ܠܗ̇. ܀

fol 56 r [22]ܘܗܘܐ ܗܘܐ ܒܚܕ ܡܢ *ܝܘܡ̈ܬܐ ܗܢܘܢ܂ ܣܠܩ ܝܬܒ ܠܗ
ܒܣܦܝܢܬܐ. ܗܘ ܘܬܠܡ̈ܝܕܘܗܝ ܥܡܗ. ܘܐܡܪ ܠܗܘܢ܂ ܢܥܒܪ ܠܗ
ܠܥܒܪܐ ܕܝܡܬܐ. [23]ܘܟܕ ܪܕܝܢ ܗܘܘ ܒܐܠܦܐ ܕܡܟ ܠܗ. ܘܗܘܬ

ܘܡܬܚܢܩܝܢ] ܡܬܚܢܩܝܢ Sed   15 ܘܗܘ...ܛܒܬܐ] ܗܘ ܕܝܢ ܕܒܐܪ̈ܥܐ ܛܒܬܐ S
ܫܦܝܪܐ & ܗܢܘܢ] S illegible   16 ܡܬܠܐ...ܗܘܐ] om. S   ܠܐ ܐܢܫ] S illegible
ܘܡܟܣܐ...ܥܪܣܐ] ܘܣܐܡ ܠܗ ܬܚܝܬ ܣܐܬܐ: ܐܘ ܬܚܝܬ ܥܪܣܐ A (cf Mt v 15)
ܐܘ ܒܡܢܪܬܐ ܡܩܝܡܝܢ] om. S; ܐܘ ܣܐܡ ܠܗ ܒܡܢܪܬܐ ܠܡܫܟܐ A   ܕܟܠ ܐܢܫ]
ܕܟܠ ܡܢ S   ܕܥܐܠ] om. A   ܢܘܗܪܗ] + ܕܫܪܓܐ A   17 ܘܐܦܠܐ] ܘܠܐ S
18 ܘܢܬܘܣܦ ܠܗ] om. S   ܘܗܘ] ܘܡܢ S   ܗܘܐ] om. S   ܢܫܬܩܠ ܠܗ] om. ܠܗ S
19 ܗܘܘ] om. S   ܕܢܩܪܒ] om. S   ܘܩܝܡܝܢ ܗܘܘ ܠܒܪ] om. S
ܕܢܚܙܘܢܗ] ܕܢܬܡܠܠܘܢ ܥܡܗ S (ܡܛܠ illegible)   ܕܐܢܫܐ] om. S
21 ܐܡܝ ܘܐܚ̈ܝ ܗܠܝܢ ܐܢܘܢ S   ܡܠܬܐ ܕܐܠܗܐ S   ܠܗ̇] om. S
22. No § in S   ܗܘܐ] om. S   ܗܢܘܢ] om. S   ܝܬܒ] om. S
ܠܗ] om. S   23 ܗܘܘ] om. S   ܒܐܠܦܐ] om. S   ܠܗ] om. S

15 occupied, and are choked and give no fruit. And that which fell in *C S*
the good land—those are they that with a heart sincere and good
have heard the word and taken hold, and they give fruit in patience."
16 Another similitude he was saying: "§No one lighteth a lamp and §*A* 14
hideth it in a vessel or setteth it under a bed or in a concealed place,
but he setteth it upon the lamp-stand that every man that entereth
17 may see its light.¶ For there is nothing secret that shall not be ¶*A*
revealed, neither *aught* concealed that shall not be known and come
18 into the open. See what ye have heard; for he that hath, it shall be
given to him and added to him, and he which hath not, even that
which he was supposing that he hath shall be taken away from him."
19 And there had come unto him, *even* Jesus, his mother and his
brothers, and they were standing outside, and could not see him
20 because of the multitude of folk. And they said to him: "Thy
mother and thy brothers are standing outside and wishing to see
21 thee." Now he answered and said to them: "These are my mother
and my brothers, that hear the word of God and do it!"
22 And it had come to pass on one of those days Jesus went up *and*
sat in the boat, he and his disciples with him, and he said to them:
23 "Let us cross over to that other side of the lake." And when they
were sailing on the sea he went to sleep. And there was a squall of

---

and are choked] *om.* and *S*[ed] **15** And that which fell] Now that *S* those *&* sincere] *S illegible* **16** Another similitude he was saying] *om. S* No one] *S illegible* and hideth....a bed] and setteth it under a bushel or under a bed *A* (*cf* Mt v 15) or in a concealed place] *om. S*; or setteth it in a hidden place *A*: *cf cod. fuld*, p. 46, 'neque accendunt lucernam et ponunt eam sub modio neque sub lecto neque in loco abscondito neque sub uaso.' every man] every one *S* that....light] that every man may see the light of the lamp *A* **17** neither] and not *S* **18** and added to him] *om. S* he which] he that *S* was supposing] supposeth *S* **19** had come] came *S* *even* Jesus] *om. S* were standing outside and] *om. S* see him] ⌜speak⌝ with him *S* of folk] *om. S* **21** These... brothers] My mother and my brothers are these *S* do it] do *it S* **22** had come] came *S* those days] the days *S* Jesus] he *S* **23** when they were] while *S* on the sea] *om. S*

C S ܥܠܥܠܐ ܕܪܘܚܐ ܒܝܡܬܐ. ܘܐܬܡܠܝܬ ܗܘܬ ܣܦܝܢܬܗܘܢ ܡܢ ܓ̈ܠܠܐ.
ܘܩܪܝܒܐ ܗܘܬ ܠܡܛܒܥ. [24]ܘܩܪܒܘ ܐܥܝܪܘܗܝ ܘܐܡܪܝܢ ܠܗ ܪܒܢ
ܐܒܕܝܢ ܐܢܚܢ. ܘܩܡ ܘܟܐܐ ܒܪܘܚܐ ܘܒܡܚܫܘܠܐ ܕܡ̈ܝܐ.
ܘܗܘܐ ܫܠܝܐ. [25]ܘܐܡܪ ܠܗܘܢ ܐܝܟܐ ܗܝ ܗܝܡܢܘܬܟܘܢ܆ ܗܢܘܢ
ܕܝܢ ܟܕ ܕܚܠܝܢ. ܡܬܕܡܪܝܢ ܗܘܘ ܘܐܡܪܝܢ ܚܕ ܠܚܕ܂ ܡܢܘ ܟܝ
ܗܢܐ ܕܐܦ ܠܪ̈ܘܚܐ ܘܠܝܡܐ ܦܩܕ ܘܡܫܬܡܥܝܢ ܠܗ. ܀
col 2 [26]*ܘܪܕܘ ܗܘܘ ܠܐܬܪܐ ܕܓܕܪ̈ܝܐ. ܗܘ ܕܐܝܬܘܗܝ ܠܘܩܒܠ ܥܒܪܐ
ܕܓܠܝܠܐ. [27]ܟܕ ܢܦܩ ܕܝܢ ܠܐܪܥܐ. ܦܓܥ ܒܗ ܓܒܪܐ ܚܕ ܕܐܝܬ
ܗܘܐ ܒܠܘܗܝ ܫܐܕܐ ܡܢ ܙܒܢܐ ܣܓܝܐܐ. ܘܢ̈ܚܬܐ ܠܐ ܠܒܫ
ܗܘܐ. ܘܒܒܝܬܐ ܠܐ ܥܡܪ ܗܘܐ. ܐܠܐ ܒܝܬ ܩܒܘܪܐ. ܘܟܠ
ܙܒܢܐ ܡܟܐ ܗܘܐ. ܘܡܬܚܫܐ ܗܘܐ ܢܦܫܗ ܒܟܐ̈ܦܐ. [28]ܘܟܕ ܚܙܐ
ܠܝܫܘܥ܂ ܩܥܐ ܘܢܦܠ ܣܓܕ ܠܗ. ܘܒܩܠܐ ܪܡܐ ܐܡܪ. ܡܢܐ ܠܝ
ܘܠܟ ܝܫܘܥ ܒܪܗ ܕܐܠܗܐ ܪܡܐ. ܒܒܥܐ ܐܢܐ ܡܢܟ ܠܐ
ܬܫܢܩܢܝ. [29]ܦܩܕ ܗܘܐ ܠܗ ܓܝܪ ܠܗܘ ܪܘܚܐ ܛܢܦܐ ܠܡܦܩ ܡܢ ܒܪ
fol 56 v ܐܢܫܐ. ܣܓܝ ܓܝܪ ܙܒܢܝܢ ܢܦܩ ܗܘܐ ܠܗ. *ܘܡܬܐܣܪ ܗܘܐ
ܒܫܝ̈ܫܠܬܐ ܘܒܟ̈ܒܠܐ ܕܢܛܪܝܢ. ܘܡܬܒܙܪ ܗܘܐ ܐܣ̈ܘܪܘܗܝ. ܘܡܬܕܒܪ
ܗܘܐ. ܘܡܬܒܕܪ ܗܘܐ ܡܢܗ ܡܢ ܫܐܕܐ ܠܚܘܪܒܐ. [30]ܫܐܠܗ ܕܝܢ
ܝܫܘܥ ܘܐܡܪ ܠܗ ܡܢ ܫܡܟ. ܘܐܡܪ ܠܗ ܠܓܝܘܢ܆ ܡܛܠ ܕܣܓ̈ܝܐܐ
ܐܢܫܝܢ ܒܗ. [31]ܘܒܥܝܢ ܗܘܘ ܡܢܗ ܗܢܘܢ ܫܐ̈ܕܐ ܕܠܐ ܢܦܩܕ
ܐܢܘܢ ܠܬܗܘܡܐ ܘܠܐ ܢܦܩ ܐܢܘܢ܂ [32]ܐܝܬ ܗܘܬ ܕܝܢ ܬܡܢ ܒܛܘܪܐ
ܒܩܪܐ ܚܕܐ ܕܚܙܝ̈ܪܐ ܣܓܝܐܬܐ ܕܪܥܝܢ ܗܘܘ ܬܡܢ. ܘܒܥܝܢ ܗܘܘ
ܡܢܗ ܗܢܘܢ ܫܐ̈ܕܐ ܕܢܦܣ ܠܗܘܢ ܠܡܥܠ ܒܗܘܢ ܒܩܪܐ ܕܚܙܝ̈ܪܐ.

---

24 ܘܐܡܪܝܢ] om. ܘ S   ܘܩܪܝܒܐ ܗܘܬ] ܘܩܪܝܒܝܢ ܗܘܘ S   ܡܢ ܓ̈ܠܠܐ] om. S
25 ܘܠܝܡܐ ܦܩܕ] ⌜ܦܩܕ⌝ ܘܠܝܡܐ S   ܕܡ̈ܝܐ] ܕܝܡܬܐ S   ܪܒܢ] ܪܒܢ ܪܒܢ S
26 ܗܘܘ] om. S   27 ܢܦܩ] ܣܠܩ S   ܚܕ] + ܡܢ ܡܕܝܢܬܐ S
28 ܘܟܕ] ܟܕ S   29 ܓܝܪ 1°] om. S   ܘܟܠ....ܒܟܐ̈ܦܐ] om. S   ܒܫܝ̈ܫܠܬܐ S
ܫܐܕܐ] S illegible (? ⌜ܪ⌝ܘܚܐ)   ܘܡܬܕܒܪ ܗܘܐ] om. ܗܘܐ S   30 ܘܐܡܪ 2°] om. ܘ S
31 ܗܢܘܢ ܫܐ̈ܕܐ] om. S   ܕܠܐ ܢܦܩܕ.....ܢܦܩ ܐܢܘܢ] ܕܠܐ ܢܦܩܘܕ ܠܗܘܢ ܠܡܐܙܠ ܠܬܗܘܡܐ. S
32 ܚܕܐ] om. S   ܬܡܢ 2°] om. S   ܡܢܗ] om. S   ܠܡܥܠ] ܕܢܥܠܘܢ S   ܒܗܘܢ ܒܩܪܐ ܕܚܙܝ̈ܪܐ] ܒܚܙܝ̈ܪܐ S

wind on the lake, and their boat was filled by the waves and it was C S
24 near to sink. And they came near *and* awoke him and say to him:
"Our Lord, we are perishing!" And he arose and rebuked the wind
25 and the storm of the water, and there was a calm; and he said
to them: "Where is your faith?" But they, being afraid, were
wondering and saying one to another: "Who then is this, that even
the winds and the sea he commandeth and they obey him?"
26 And they had sailed to the country of the Gadarenes, which is
27 opposite the other side of Galilee. Now when he went forth to the
land there met him a certain man on whom there had been a devil a
long time, and with no garments was he clothed and in no house was
he dwelling but in a tomb, and always with cries he was crying out
28 and was smiting himself with stones. And when he saw Jesus he
cried out and fell *and* worshipped him, and with a loud voice said:
"What have I to do with thee, Jesus, son of the Most High God? I
29 beseech thee, torment me not." For he was commanding that unclean
spirit to come forth from the man. For a long time had he been
cleaving to him, and he used to be bound with chains and with
shackles that he might be kept, and he used to break his bonds and
30 cut *them*, and was driven by that same devil to the desert. Now
Jesus asked him and said: "What is thy name?" And he saith to
31 him: "Legion, because we are many in him." And those devils
were beseeching him that he would not send them to Gehenna and
32 not cast them out. Now there was there in the hill a certain herd of
many swine that were feeding there, and those devils were beseeching
him that he would permit them to enter into that herd of swine.

---

by the waves] *om.* *S* it was] they were *S* **24** and say] *and* say *S* Our Lord] Rabban, Rabban *S* the water] the lake *S* **25** and the sea he commandeth] he commandeth and the sea *S* **26** had] *om.* *S* **27** went forth] went up *S* a certain man] + from the city *S* and always.... with stones] *om.* *S* **28** And when] When *S* **29** For he] He *S* **30** And he saith] He saith *S* **31** those devils] *so also* E^{75}; they *S* that he would not.... cast them out] that he would not command them to go to the abyss *S*; *cf* 'that he would not send them forth from that country (Mk v 10), and would not send them to Gehenna before the time' E^{75} **32** certain] *om.* *S* feeding there] *om.* there *S* him] *om.* *S* that herd of swine] the swine *S*

C S ܘܐܦܣ ܠܗܘܢ܂ [33]ܘܢܦܩܘ ܫܐ̈ܕܐ ܡܢ ܒܪܢܫܐ ܗܘ ܘܥܠܘ ܒܚ̈ܙܝܪܐ܂
col 2 ܘܐܬܪ̈ܓܬ ܗܝ ܒܠܗ̇ ܒܥܕܪܐ ܠܥܘܡܩܐ܂ *ܘܢܦܠܘ ܒܝܡܐ ܘܐܬܚܢܩܘ܂
[34]ܟܕ ܚܙܘ ܕܝܢ ܗܢܘܢ ܕ̈ܪܥܘܬܐ ܡܕܡ ܕܗܘܐ ܥܪܩܘ܂ ܘܐܫܬܥܝܘ
ܒܡ̈ܕܝܢܬܐ ܘܒܩ̈ܘܪܝܐ܂ [35]ܘܢܦܩܘ ܐܢܫܐ ܕܢܚܙܘܢ ܡܕܡ ܕܗܘܐ܂
ܘܐܬܘ ܠܘܬ ܝܫܘܥ܂ ܘܐܫܟܚܘ ܠܗܘ ܒܪܢܫܐ ܕܢܦܩܘ ܡܢܗ ܗܢܘܢ
ܫܐ̈ܕܐ܂ ܟܕ ܠܒܝܫ ܘܡܢܟܦ ܘܝܬܒ ܠܘܬ ܪ̈ܓܠܘܗܝ ܕܝܫܘܥ ܘܕܚܠܘ܂
[36]ܘܐܫܬܥܝܘ ܠܗܘܢ ܐܝܟܢܐ ܚܝܐ ܒܪܢܫܐ ܗܘ܂ ܘܐܝܟܢ ܕܚܙܘ
ܬܘܒ [37]ܒܥܘ ܗܘܘ ܡܢܗ ܟܠܗ ܟܢܫܐ ܗܘ ܕܓ̈ܕܪܝܐ܂ ܕܢܐܙܠ ܠܗ ܡܢ
ܠܘܬܗܘܢ܂ ܡܛܠ ܕܕܚܠܬܐ ܪܒܬܐ ܐܚܝܕܐ ܗܘܬ ܐܢܘܢ܂ ܗܘ
ܕܝܢ ܣܠܩ ܠܗ ܠܣܦܝܢܬܐ ܘܗܦܟ ܡܢ ܠܘܬܗܘܢ܂ [38]ܗܘ ܕܝܢ ܒܪܢܫܐ
fol 57 r ܕܢܦܩܘ ܗܘܘ* ܡܢܗ ܗܢܘܢ ܫܐ̈ܕܐ܂ ܒܥܐ ܗܘܐ ܡܢܗ ܕܠܘܬܗ
ܢܗܘܐ܂ ܘܫܪܝܗ̇ ܝܫܘܥ ܘܐܡܪ ܠܗ܂ [39]ܗܦܘܟ ܠܒܝܬܟ ܘܠܒܝܬ
ܐ̈ܢܫܝܟ܂ ܘܐܫܬܥܐ ܠܗܘܢ ܐܝܠܝܢ ܕܥܒܕ ܠܟ ܡܪܝܐ܂ ܘܐܙܠ
ܗܘܐ ܘܡܟܪܙ ܗܘܐ ܒܟܠܗ̇ ܡܕܝܢܬܐ ܡܕܡ ܕܥܒܕ ܠܗ ܝܫܘܥ܂
[40]ܘܟܕ ܗܦܟ ܝܫܘܥ ܩܒܠܗ ܟܢܫܐ ܣܓܝܐܐ܂ ܠܗ ܓܝܪ ܣܟܝܢ
ܗܘܘ܂ ܀

[41]ܘܐܬܐ ܓܒܪܐ ܚܕ ܝܘܐܝܪ ܫܡܗ ܗܘܐ܂ ܘܪܝܫ ܟܢܘܫܬܐ ܗܘܐ܂
ܘܢܦܠ ܩܕܡ ܪ̈ܓܠܘܗܝ ܕܝܫܘܥ܂ ܘܒܥܐ ܗܘܐ ܡܢܗ ܕܢܐܙܠ ܠܒܝܬܗ܂
[42]ܒܪܬܐ ܓܝܪ ܝܚܝܕܝܬܐ ܐܝܬ ܗܘܬ ܠܗ܂ ܘܐܝܬܝܗ̇ ܗܘܬ ܐܝܟ
col 2 ܒܪܬ ܬ̈ܪܬܥܣܪܐ ܫ̈ܢܝܢ܂ *ܘܩܪܝܒܐ ܗܘܬ ܠܡܡܬ܂ ܘܟܕ ܐܙܠ ܝܫܘܥ
ܟܢܫܐ ܚܒܨܝܢ ܗܘܘ ܠܗ܂ [43]ܘܐܢܬܬܐ ܚܕܐ ܕܕܡܐ ܗܘܐ ܕܒܗ̇ ܫ̈ܢܝܢ

---

33 ܘܐܬܪ̈ܓܬ ܒܥܕܪܐ ܟܠܗ S 35 ܕܢܚܙܘܢ] ܘܚܙܘ S ܠܒܝܫ] ܡܠܒܫ S
36 ܘܐܝܟܢ ܕܚܙܘ ܬܘܒ] ܘ S 37 ܗܘ 1°] om. S ܪܒܬܐ] om. S ܠܗ 2°] om. S ܘܗܦܟ] ܘܐܙܠ S 38 ܒܪܢܫܐ] om. S ܗܘܘ] om. S ܗܢܘܢ] om. S ܠܗ] om. S 39 ܘܠܒܝܬ ܐ̈ܢܫܝܟ] om. S ܠܗܘܢ] om. S ܡܪܝܐ] ܐܠܗܐ S ܗܘܐ 2°] om. S 40 ܝܫܘܥ] ܡܪܢ S 41. § in S also (sic) ܝܘܐܝܪ] ܝܘܝܪ S ܗܘܐ 1°] om. S ܩܕܡ] ܥܠ S ܡܢܗ] om. S 42 ܝܫܘܥ] om. S

33 And he permitted them; and the devils went forth from that man *C S*
and entered into the swine, and all that herd went direct to a steep
34 place and they fell into the sea and were choked. Now when those
herdsmen saw that which came to pass they fled, and they declared
35 *it* in the cities and in the villages. And the folk came forth that they
might see that which *had* come to pass, and they came unto Jesus and
found that man from whom went forth those devils clad and modest
36 and sitting at the feet of Jesus, and they were afraid. And they
declared to them how that man was saved alive, and they† that saw,
37 again,† were beseeching him, *even* all that multitude of the Gadarenes,
that he would go away from their *neighbourhood*, because great
fear had taken hold of them. Now he went up to the boat and returned
38 from them. Now that man from whom had gone forth those devils
was beseeching him that he might be with him. And Jesus dismissed
39 him and said to him: "Return to thy house and to the house of thy
kinsfolk, and declare to them what things the LORD hath done for
thee." And he was going and was preaching in all the city that
40 which Jesus did for him. And when Jesus returned a great multitude
received him, for for him they were looking.

41 And there came a certain man—Joârâsh his name was; and he
was a chief of the synagogue—and he fell down before the feet of
42 Jesus and was beseeching him that he would enter his house; for an
only daughter he had, and she was about twelve years old, and she
was near to die. And as Jesus was going *thither* the multitude was
43 pressing upon him, and a certain woman whose blood had been

---

33 that herd all went *S* **35** that they might see] and saw *S* clad] clothed *S* **36** that saw, again,] *om. S* **37** all that] all the *S* great] *om. S* returned] went *S* **38** that man] he *S* had gone] went *S* those] the *S* to him] *om. S* **39** and to....thy kinsfolk] *om. S* to them] *om. S* the LORD] God *S* was 2°] *om. S* **40** Jesus] our Lord *S* **41** Joârâsh] *C* (*as* syr.vg); Jorêsh *S* was 1°] *om. S* before] at *S* him] *om. S* **42** Jesus] he *S*

C S ܬܬܐܣܝܐ. ܘܟܠܗ ܩܢܝܢܗ̇ ܐܦܩܬ ܥܠ ܐܣܘ̈ܬܐ. ܘܠܐ
ܐܫܟܚܬ ܕܬܬܐܣܐ ܡܢ ܐܢܫ. ܘܐܬܪܥܝܬ ܒܢܦܫܗ̇ ܘܐܡܪܐ. ܐܦ
ܠܢܚ̈ܬܘܗܝ ܕܝܫܘܥ ܐܠܐ ܐܢܐ ܩܪܒܐ ܐܢܐ ܡܬܐܣܝܐ ܐܢܐ.
⁴⁴ܘܩܪܒܬ ܡܢ ܒܣܬܪܗ. ܘܐܚܕܬ ܒܟܢܦܐ ܕܢܚܬܗ. ܘܡܚܕܐ ܩܡܬ ܡܪܕܝܬܐ
ܕܕܡܗ̇. ⁴⁵ܘܐܬܦܢܝ ܝܫܘܥ ܘܐܡܪ ܡܢܘ ܩܪܒ ܠܝ.. ܘܟܕ ܟܠܗܘܢ
ܟܦܪܝܢ ܗܘܘ. ܐܡܪ ܠܗ ܟܐܦܐ. ܪܒܢ ܟ̈ܢܫܐ ܚܒܨܝܢ ܠܟ ܘܐܠܨܝܢ.
fol 57 v ܘܐܡܪ ܐܢܬ ܡܢܘ ܩܪܒ ܠܝ. ⁴⁶ܐܡܪ ܠܗ ܝܫܘܥ. *ܐܢܫ ܩܪܒ ܠܝ.
ܐܢܐ ܓܝܪ ܝܕܥ ܐܢܐ ܕܚܝܠܐ ܢܦܩ ܡܢܝ. ⁴⁷ܟܕ ܚܙܬ ܕܝܢ ܗ̇ܝ
ܐܢܬܬܐ ܕܐܬܓܠܝܐ ܗܘܐ ܠܓܒܗ. ܐܬܬ ܟܕ ܕܚܝܠܐ ܘܪܬܝܬܐ ܢܦܠܬ
ܩܕܡܬ ܠܗ. ܘܐܡܪܬ ܠܥܝܢ ܟܠܗ ܥܡܐ ܗܘ ܒܥܠܬܗ ܡܛܠ ܐܝܕܐ ܩܪܒܬ
ܩܪܒܬ. ܘܐܝܟܢܐ ܒܪ ܫܥܬܗ ܐܬܐܣܝܬ ܩܕܡ ܟܠ ܐܢܫ ܐܟܘܬܗ.
⁴⁸ܘܗܘ ܕܝܢ ܐܡܪ ܠܗ̇ ܒܪܬܝ، ܗܝܡܢܘܬܟܝ ܐܚܝܬܟܝ ܙܠܝ ܒܫܠܡܐ.
⁴⁹ܘܟܕ ܡܠܠ. ܐܬܘ ܡܢ ܕܒܝܬ ܪܒ ܟܢܘܫܬܐ ܘܐܡܪܝܢ ܠܗ. ܡܝܬܬ
ܠܗ̇ ܒܪܬܟ ܠܐ ܬܥܡܠ ܠܡܠܦܢܐ. ⁵⁰ܟܕ ܫܡܥ ܕܝܢ ܝܫܘܥ ܕܡܝܬܬ
§¶Thos 188 ܐܡܪܘ. ܐܡܪ ܠܗ §ܠܐ ܬܕܚܠ· §ܒܠܚܘܕ ܗܝܡܢܘ ܗܝܡܢ¶ ܘܬܚܝܐ
§¶A21 col 2 ܒܪܬܟ.¶ ⁵¹ܘܟܕ ܐܬܐ ܠܒܝܬܗ *ܕܗܘ ܓܒܪܐ. ܠܐ ܫܒܩ ܠܐܢܫ
ܕܢܥܘܠ· ܐܠܐ ܠܟܐܦܐ ܘܠܝܥܩܘܒ ܘܠܝܘܚܢܢ. ܘܠܐܒܘܗ̇ ܘܠܐܡܗ

---

43 ܘܟܠܗ.....ܐܣܘ̈ܬܐ] om. S   ܘܐܬܪܥܝܬ........ܡܬܐܣܝܐ ܐܢܐ] om. S   44 ܡܢ ܒܣܬܪܗ] so also S   ܕܢܚܬܗ] ܕܠܒܘܫܗ S   ܡܪܕܝܬܐ] ܡܒܘܥܐ ܕܡܪܕܝܬܐ S   45 ܘܐܬܦܢܝ ܝܫܘܥ ܘܐܡܪ] ܘܐܡܪ ܝܫܘܥ S   ܩܪܒ ܠܝ..] The small stop in C is black, and by the first hand   ܚܒܨܝܢ ܠܟ ܘܐܠܨܝܢ] ܐܠܝܨܝܢ ܘܚܒ̈ܨܝܢ ܠܟ S   46 ܐܡܪ ܠܗ ܝܫܘܥ] ܗܢܐ ܝܫܘܥ ܘܐܡܪ ܠܗ S   47 ܕܐܬܓܠܝܐ ܗܘܐ] ܕܐܬܓܠܝ ܗܘ ܗܘܐ ܠܐ S (sic)   ܕܚܝܠܐ ܘ] om. S   ܩܪܒ] ܩܪܒܬܐ S   ܩܕܡ ܟܠ ܐܢܫ ܐܟܘܬܗ] om. S   48 ܐܡܪ] pr. ܗܢܐ ܘ S   49. § in S   ܡܡܠܠ S   ܕܒܝܬ ܪܒ] ܒܝܬܗ ܕܪܒ S   ܬܥܡܠ] ⸢ܬܥܡܠܗ̇⸣ S[ed]   50 ܕܡܝܬܬ ܐܡܪܘ] om. S   ܐܡܪ] pr. ܗܢܐ ܘ S   ܒܠܚܘܕ ܗܝܡܢܘ ܗܝܡܢ] C A; om. ܗܝܡܢܘ S; ܐܠܐ ܗܝܡܢܘ ܗܝܡܢ ܒܠܚܘܕ Thos (cf also Thos[325]: ܠܐ ܬܕܚܠܘܢ. ܐܠܐ ܒܠܚܘܕ ܗܝܡܢܘ ܗܝܡܢܘ)   ܘܬܚܝܐ ܒܪܬܟ] C A; ܘܚܝܐ S   51 ܠܟܐܦܐ S   ܘܠܐܡܗ] C (sic, without the point)

issuing for twelve years, and all her property she *had* spent upon C S
physicians and could not be healed by any one—and she meditated
in herself and saith: "Even if the garments of Jesus I should go *and*
44 touch I should be healed." And she drew near from behind him and
took hold of the skirt of his garment, and the issue of her blood stood
45 *still.* And Jesus turned round and saith: "Who is it touched me?"
And when all of them were denying Kepha saith to him: "Rabban,
the multitudes are pressing upon thee and coming, and sayest thou
46 'Who is it touched me?'" Jesus saith to him: "Some one touched
47 me, for I know that power hath gone forth from me." Now when
that woman saw that not even this escaped him, she came fearful and
trembling *and* fell down *and* worshipped him, and she said in the
sight of all that people for what reason she touched, and how straight-
48 way she was healed †before every one she confessed†. But he said
to her: "My daughter, thy faith hath saved thee alive; go in peace."
49 And while he spake, there came some from the house of the chief of
the synagogue and say to him: "Thy daughter hath died; do not
50 trouble the teacher." Now when Jesus heard that thus they said, he
saith to him: §"Fear not; §only indeed believe,¶ and thy daughter §¶ *Thos* 188
51 will live."¶ And when he came to the house of that man he did not §¶ *A* 21
suffer any one to enter but Kepha and James and John and the father

---

43 and all her.....physicians] *om.* *S* and she meditated.....should be healed] *om.* *S* 44 from] *om.* *S* garment] clothing *S* the issue] *pr.* the fountain of *S* 45 turned round and] *om.* *S* pressing upon thee and coming] hemming *thee* in and pressing upon thee *S* 46 saith] answered and said *S* 47 that not even this escaped him] that even this very thing did not escape him *S*; 'that this also was not hid from him' *E*[80] fearful and] *om.* *S* before...confessed] *om.* *S* 48 said] answered and said *S* 49 he spake] speaking *S* there came some] they came *S* 50 that thus they said] *om.* *S* saith] answered and said *S* only indeed believe] *C A*; *om.* indeed *S*; but indeed believe only *Thos* (*cf also Thos*[325] 'Fear ye not, but only indeed believe' [=Mk v 36]): *E*[89] *has* 'Indeed believe' and thy daughter will live] *C A E*[89]; and she liveth *S*

ܕܛܠܝܬܐ. [52]ܘܟܠܗܘܢ ܐܢܫܐ ܒܟܝܢ ܗܘܘ ܥܠܝܗ ܘܡܪܩܕܝܢ ܗܘܘ. C S
ܐܡܪ ܠܗܘܢ ܝܫܘܥ ܠܐ ܬܒܟܘܢ܆ ܛܠܝܬܐ ܓܝܪ ܠܐ ܡܝܬܬ.
ܡܕܡܟ ܗܘ ܕܡܟܐ. [53]ܗܢܘܢ ܕܝܢ ܓܚܟܝܢ ܗܘܘ ܥܠܘܗܝ. ܕܝܕܥܝܢ
ܗܘܘ ܕܡܝܬܬ ܠܗ. [54]ܘܗܘ ܐܚܕܗ ܒܐܝܕܗ ܘܩܪܗ ܘܐܡܪ ܠܗ.
§ܛܠܝܬܐ ܩܘܡܝ. [55]ܘܗܦܟܬ ܪܘܚܗ. ܘܒܪܫܥܬܗ ܩܡܬ.¶ ܘܦܩܕ §¶A165
ܕܢܬܠܘܢ ܠܗ ܠܡܐܟܠ. [56]ܘܬܡܗܘ ܗܘܘ ܐܒܗ̈ܝܗ. ܘܗܘ ܦܩܕ
ܐܢܘܢ ܕܠܐܢܫ ܠܐ ܢܐܡܪܘܢ ܡܢܐ ܕܗܘܐ.

[1]ܘܩܪܐ ܐܢܘܢ ܝܫܘܥ *ܠܬܪ̈ܥܣܪܬܗ. ܘܝܗܒ ܠܗܘܢ ܚܝܠܐ fol 58r
ܘܫܘܠܛܢܐ ܥܠ ܟܠ ܕܝ̈ܘܐ ܘܫܐ̈ܕܐ. ܘܟܪ̈ܝܗܐ ܠܡܐܣܝܘ. [2]ܘܫܕܪ
ܐܢܘܢ ܕܢܟܪܙܘܢ ܡܠܟܘܬܗ ܕܐܠܗܐ ܘܠܡܐܣܝܘ. [3]ܘܐܡܪ ܠܗܘܢ
ܡܕܡ ܠܐ ܬܫܩܠܘܢ ܠܟܘܢ ܠܐܘܪܚܐ. ܠܐ ܫܒܛܐ ܘܠܐ
ܬܪܡܠܐ. ܘܠܐ ܠܚܡܐ ܘܠܐ ܟܣܦܐ. ܘܠܐ ܬܪ̈ܬܝܢ ܟܘ̈ܬܝܢܝܢ
ܢܗܘܝܢ ܠܟܘܢ. [4]ܘܠܒܝܬܐ ܐܝܢܐ ܕܥܠܝܢ ܐܢܬܘܢ ܬܡܢ ܗܘܘ.
ܘܡܢ ܬܡܢ ܦܘܩܘ. [5]ܘܐܝܠܝܢ ܕܠܐ ܡܩܒܠܝܢ ܠܟܘܢ. ܡܢܐ ܕܢܦܩܝܢ
ܐܢܬܘܢ ܡܢ ܡܕܝܢܬܐ ܗܝ. ܘܐܦ ܚܠܐ ܕܪ̈ܓܠܝܟܘܢ ܦܨܘ.
ܕܬܗܘܐ ܠܗܘܢ ܠܣܗܕܘܬܐ. ܀

[6]ܘܟܕ ܢܦܩܘ ܫܠܝܚܘܗܝ. ܘܡܬܟܪܟܝܢ ܒܩܘ̈ܪܝܐ *ܘܡ̈ܕܝܢܬܐ. col 2
ܘܡܣܒܪܝܢ ܗܘܘ ܘܡܐܣܝܢ ܒܟܠ ܕܘܟܐ. [7]ܘܫܡܥ ܗܪܘܕܣ
ܛܛܪܟܐ ܟܠܗܝܢ ܗܠܝܢ ܕܗܘܝ. ܘܡܬܬܕܡܪ ܗܘܐ. ܡܛܠ ܕܐܡܪܝܢ

---

52 |ܘ◯ܟܠܗܘܢ ܐܢܫܐ·>|] C (*sic*): *there is a fault in the skin*
ܥܠܝܗ ܘܡܪܩܕܝܢ ܗܘܘ] ܘܡܪܩܕܝܢ ܥܠܝܗ S ܐܡܪ ܠܗܘܢ ܝܫܘܥ] ܘܗܘ ܐܡܪ ܠܗܘܢ S ܛܠܝܬܐ ܓܝܪ.....ܕܡܟܐ.] ܠܐ ܓܝܪ ܡܝܬܬ ܕܡܟܐ ܗܝ. S
53 ܥܠܘܗܝ. S (*sic*) 54 ܠܗ] *om.* S ܛܠܝܬܐ ܛܠܝܬܐ ܩܘܡܝ A (*very expressly*): *cf* vii 14 55 ܘܗܦܟܬ] ܘܐܬܬ A ܘܒܪܫܥܬܗ] ܘ A
56 ܢܐܡܪ̈ܘܢ S 1 ܘܩܪܐ ܐܢܘܢ ܝܫܘܥ] ܘܩܪܐ ܕܝܢ S ܚܝܠܐ] ܚܠܝܐ S (*sic*) ܥܠ ܕܝ̈ܘܐ ܘܫܐ̈ܕܐ] ܒܟܠܗܘܢ ܫܐ̈ܕܐ S 2 ܕܢܟܪܙܘܢ] ܠܡܟܪܙܘ S
3 ܫܒܛܐ] ܚܘܛܪܐ S (*cf* Mk vi 8) ܘܠܐ ܬܪ̈ܬܝܢ] ܘܐܦܠܐ ܬܪ̈ܬܝܢ S
4 ܐܢܬܘܢ] + ܠܗ S 5 ܘܐܦ] ܐܦ S ܦܨܘ] ܐܢܬܘܢ ܗܘܘ ܢܦܨܝܢ S ܠܗܘܢ ܠܣܗܕܘܬܐ] ܠܗܘܢ ܣܗܕܘܬܐ S 6. *No* § *in* S ܢܦܩܘ] + ܗܘܘ S
ܘܡܬܟܪܟܝܢ] ܡܬܟܪܟܝܢ ܗܘܘ S ܘܡܣܒܪܝܢ] *om.* ܘ S[ed] 7. § *in* S

52 and the mother of the girl. And all the folk were weeping over her *C S*
and were lamenting. Saith Jesus to them : "Weep ye not, for the girl
53 hath not died ; she is indeed sleeping." Now they were laughing
54 at him, in that they were knowing that she *had* died. And he took
hold of her by her hand and called her and said to her : "§Girl, §*A* 165
55 arise !" And her spirit returned and straightway she arose.¶ And ¶*A*
56 he commanded that they should give her *something* to eat. And her
parents had been astonished, and he commanded them that to no one
they should say what happened.

ix 1 And Jesus called his Twelve and gave them power and authority
2 over all spirits and devils, and to heal the infirm. And he sent them
3 that they should preach the kingdom of God, and to heal. And he
said to them : "Nothing shall ye take for yourselves for the way, no
stick and no wallet and no bread and no silver, nor two coats shall
4 ye have. And whatsoever house ye enter, there be and from thence
5 go forth ; and they that do not receive you—what *time* ye go forth
from that city, even the dust of your feet shake off, that it may be
for them for a testimony."

6 And when his apostles went forth, they go about the villages and
the cities and were announcing *the gospel* and healing in every place.
7 And Herod the Tetrarch heard all these things that came to pass ;

---

52 weeping.... lamenting] weeping and lamenting over her *S* Saith Jesus] And he said *S* for the girl] for she *S* indeed] *om. S* 54 to her] *om. S* 'Girl, girl, arise !' *A* (*very expressly*): *cf* vii 14 55 returned] *A has the word generally used for* 'repented' straightway] *om. A* 1 And Jesus called] Now he called *S* power] *miswritten in S* all spirits and devils] all the devils *S* 2 that they should preach] to preach *S* 3 stick] staff *S* (*cf* Mk vi 8) nor two] and not even two *S* 4 enter] + into *S* 5 shake off] be ye shaking off *S* for them for a testimony] for you a testimony *S* 6 went] had gone *S* they go] they were going *S* and were] *and* were *S*[ed]

C S ܗܘܘ ܐ̈ܢܫܝܢ ܐܡܪܝܢ. ܕܝܘܚܢܢ ܩܡ ܡܢ ܒܝܬ ܡ̈ܝܬܐ. [8]ܘܐܚܪ̈ܢܐ
ܐܡܪܝܢ ܕܐܠܝܐ ܐܬܚܙܝ. ܐ̈ܚܪܢܐ ܐܡܪܝܢ ܕܚܕ ܡܢ ܢܒܝܐ ܩ̈ܕܡܝܐ
ܩܡ ܡܢ ܒܝܬ ܡ̈ܝܬܐ. [9]ܘܐܡܪ ܗܘܐ ܗܪܘܕܣ. ܪܫܗ ܕܝܘܚܢܢ ܐܢܐ
ܦܣܩܬ. ܡܢܘ ܗܢܐ ܕܫܡܥ ܐܢܐ ܥܠܘܗܝ. ܘܨܒܐ ܗܘܐ
ܕܢܚܙܝܘܗܝ. ܀

[10]ܘܗܦܟܘ ܗܢܘܢ ܫ̈ܠܝܚܐ. ܘܐܫܬܥܝܘ ܠܗ ܟܠܡܕܡ ܕܥܒܕܘ.
ܘܕܒܪ ܐܢܘܢ ܒܠܚܘܕܝܗܘܢ. ܘܐܙܠ ܠܐܬܪܐ ܚܘܪܒܐ. [11]ܘܟܕ
fol 58 v ܝܕܥܘ ܟܢ̈ܫܐ. ܐܙܠܘ *ܠܗܘܢ ܒܬܪܗ ܒܪܓܠ· ܘܩܒܠ ܐܢܘܢ.
ܘܡܡܠܠ ܗܘܐ ܥܡܗܘܢ ܥܠ ܡܠܟܘܬܐ ܕܐܠܗܐ. ܘܠܐܝܠܝܢ
ܕܣܢܝܩܝܢ ܗܘܘ ܥܠ ܐܣܝܘܬܐ ܡܐܣܐ ܗܘܐ ܠܗܘܢ. ܀
[12]ܘܟܕ ܩܪܒ ܗܘܐ ܠܡܥܒܕ ܪܡܫܐ. ܩܪܒܘ ܬܠܡ̈ܝܕܘܗܝ، †ܐܥܝܪܘܗܝ†
ܘܐܡܪܝܢ ܠܗ ܒܡܥܪܒܐ ܐܢܚܢ. ܫܪܝ ܠܟ̈ܢܫܐ ܗܠܝܢ ܕܢܐܙܠܘܢ
ܠܩܘ̈ܪܝܐ ܗܠܝܢ ܕ̈ܚܕܪܝܢ ܘܠܟܦܪ̈ܘܢܐ ܕܢܫܪܘܢ ܒܗܘܢ. ܐܘ
ܕܢܙܒܢܘܢ ܠܗܘܢ ܡܙܘܢܬܐ. [13]ܐܡܪ ܠܗܘܢ ܗܒܘ ܐܢܬܘܢ
ܗܒܘ ܠܗܘܢ ܠܡܐܟܠ. ܐܡܪܝܢ ܠܗ ܠܝܬ ܠܢ ܝܬܝܪ ܡܢ ܚܡܫܐ
ܠܚ̈ܡܝܢ ܘܬܪ̈ܝܢ ܢܘ̈ܢܝܢ. ܐܠܐ ܢܐܙܠ ܐܢܚܢ ܢܙܒܢ ܡܙܘܢܬܐ ܠܗܢܐ
col 2 ܟܠܗ ܥܡܐ. [14]ܗܘܝܢ ܗܘܘ ܓܝܪ ܚܡܫܐ ܐ̈ܠܦܝܢ *ܓܒ̈ܪܝܢ. ܐܡܪ
ܠܬܠܡ̈ܝܕܘܗܝ، ܐܣܡܟܘ ܐܢܘܢ ܣ̈ܡܟܝܢ ܣ̈ܡܟܝܢ ܚܡܫܝܢ ܒܣܡܟܐ.

---

7 ܐ̈ܢܫܝܢ ܐܡܪܝܢ] *om.* S   8 ܘܐܚܪ̈ܢܐ] ܐܚܪ̈ܢܐ ܕܝܢ S   ܐ̈ܚܪܢܐ] *pr.* ܘ S   ܡܢ ܒܝܬ ܡ̈ܝܬܐ] *om.* S   9 ܗܘܐ 1°] *om.* S   ܫܡܥܢܐ S   10. *No* § *in* S   ܟܠ ܡܕܡ S   ܒܠܚܘܕܝܗܘܢ] ܒܠܚܘܕܝܗܘܢ S   ܠܐܬܪܐ ܚܘܪܒܐ] ܠܐܬܪܐ ܕܡܬܩܪܐ ܒܝܬ ܨܝܕܐ S (*sic*)   11 ܠܗܘܢ] *om.* S   ܒܪܓܠ] *om.* S   ܥܡܗܘܢ] *om.* S   ܥܠ ܐܣܝܘܬܐ] *om.* ܥܠ S[ed]: (?) *read* ⌜ܥܠ⌝ *for the preceding* ܗܘܘ   12. *No* § *in* S   ܘܟܕ] *om.* ܟܕ S   ܠܡܥܒܕ ܪܡܫܐ] ܪܡܫܐ ܠܡܥܒܕ S   ܬܠܡ̈ܝܕܘܗܝ] ܬܪܬܥܣܪܬܗ S   ܐܥܝܪܘܗܝ] C* (*exp. by* C[corr]); *om.* S: *cf* Joh iv 35. *The intrusive word comes from* Mt viii 25 = Lk viii 24   ܒܡܥܪܒܐ] ܒܡܕܒܪܐ S   ܠܟ̈ܢܫܐ] *om.* ܠ S   ܗܠܝܢ] *om.* S   13 ܗܒܘ] ܗܘ S   ܐܢܬܘܢ] *after* ܗܒܘ ܠܗܘܢ S   ܐܠܐ] + ⌜ܐܢ⌝ S[vid], *but if so it is now illegible*   ܢܐܙܠ ܢܙܒܢ ܐܢܚܢ S   ܟܠܗ ⌜ܥܡܐ⌝ S[vid]   14 ܗܘܘ] *om.* S   ܐܣܡܟܘ...ܒܣܡܟܐ] ܐܣܡܟܘ ܐܢܫ ܣ̈ܡܟܝܢ ܣ̈ܡܟܝܢ ⌜ܚܡܫܝܢ⌝ ܐ̈ܢܫ ܐܣܡܟܘ S

and he was wondering, because some folk were saying "John hath C S
8 risen from among the dead"; and others say "Elijah hath appeared."
Others say: "One of the prophets of old hath arisen from among
9 the dead." And Herod was saying: "The head of John I cut off;
who is this, that I hear these things about?" And he was wishing
that he should see him.

10 And those apostles returned, and declared to him everything that
they *had* done; and he took them alone and went to a desert place.
11 And when the multitudes knew they went away after him on foot,
and he received them and was speaking with them about the kingdom
of God, and them that had need of healing he was healing.

12 And when the day was near to wane his disciples drew near †*and*
awoke him† and say to him: "We are in the desert; dismiss these
multitudes that they may go to these villages round about and to the
hamlets that they may lodge in them, or may find for themselves
13 food." Jesus saith to them: "Yourselves give them *something* to
eat." They say to him: "We have not more than five pieces of bread
and two fishes; but let us go ourselves *and* buy food for all this
14 multitude," for they were become five thousand men. He saith to
his disciples: "Make them sit down *to meat* fifty by fifty men in a

---

7 some folk] they *S* 8 and others] but others *S* Others] And others *S* from among the dead] *om. S* 9 was saying] said *S* 10 them alone] them himself alone *S* to a desert place] to the gate of a city called Beth Saida *S* (*sic*) 11 went away] went *S* on foot] *om. S* with them] *om. S* of 2°] *om.* S^{ed} 12 when] *om. S* to wane] to set *S* his disciples] his Twelve *S* *and* awoke him] *C** (*exp. by* C^{corr}); *om. S*: *cf* Joh iv 35. *The intrusive words come from* Mt viii 25 = Lk viii 24 desert] wilderness *S* in them] *om. S* 13 Jesus] He *S* Give them yourselves *something S* but let us go] except we go S^{vid} buy ourselves food *S* 14 they were] they are *S* Make them sit down *to meat* in companies, fifty by fifty folk in a company *S*

C S 15ܘܥܒܕܘ ܗܟܘܬ. ܘܐܣܬܡܟܘ ܐܢܘܢ ܠܟܠܗܘܢ܆ 16ܘܢܣܒ ܗܘ ܝܫܘܥ
ܚ̈ܡܫܐ ܠܚ̈ܡܝܢ ܘܬ̈ܪܝܢ ܢ̈ܘܢܝܢ. ܘܚܪ ܒܫܡܝܐ ܘܒܪܟ ܥܠܝܗܘܢ܆
ܘܩܨܐ ܘܝܗܒ ܠܬܠܡ̈ܝܕܘܗܝ، ܕܢܣܝܡܘܢ ܩܕܡ ܟ̈ܢܫܐ. 17ܘܐܟܠܘ
ܟܠܗܘܢ ܘܣܒܥܘ. ܘܫܩܠܘ ܩܨ̈ܝܐ ܕܡܕܡ ܕܐܘܬܪܘ ܡܠܝܐ ܬܪ̈ܬܥܣܪ
ܩܘ̈ܦܝܢ. ܘܐܬܬܗܘܢ ܗܘܘ ܐܢܫܐ ܗܠܝܢ ܕܐܟܠܘ ܡܢ ܠܚܡܐ
ܗܘ. ܐܝܟ ܚ̈ܡܫܐ ܐ̈ܠܦܝܢ. ܣܦܪ ܡܢ ܢ̈ܫܐ ܘܛ̈ܠܝܐ. ܀
18ܘܟܕ ܗܘܐ ܒܠܚܘܕܘܗܝ، ܘܬܠܡ̈ܝܕܘܗܝ ܥܡܗ. ܫܐܠ ܐܢܘܢ
fol 59 r ܘܐܡܪ. ܡܢܐ ܐܡܪܝܢ ܥܠܝ ܟ̈ܢܫܐ ܕܐܝܬܝ، 19ܐܡܪܝܢ *ܠܗ. ܐܝܬ
ܕܐܡܪܝܢ ܕܝܘܚܢܢ ܗܘ ܡܥܡܕܢܐ. ܐ̈ܚܪܢܐ ܐܡܪܝܢ ܕܐܠܝܐ ܗܘ.
20ܐܡܪ ܠܗܘܢ ܗܘ ܘܐܢܬܘܢ ܡܢܐ ܐܡܪܝܢ ܐܢܬܘܢ ܕܐܝܬܝ،
ܥܢܐ ܫܡܥܘܢ ܟܐܦܐ ܘܐܡܪ ܠܗ· ܐܢܬ ܗܘ ܡܫܝܚܐ. 21ܘܗܘ
ܟܐܐ ܒܗܘܢ ܘܦܩܕ ܐܢܘܢ ܕܐܢܫ ܠܐ ܢܐܡܪܘܢ܆
22ܘܐܡܪ ܕܥܬܝܕ ܗܘ ܠܗ ܠܒܪܗ ܕܐܢܫܐ ܕܢܚܫ ܣܓܝ. ܘܢܣܬܠܐ
ܡܢ ܩܫ̈ܝܫܐ ܘܪ̈ܒܝ ܟܗ̈ܢܐ ܘܡܢ ܣ̈ܦܪܐ. ܘܢܬܩܛܠ ܘܠܝܘܡܐ ܕܬ̈ܠܬܐ
ܢܩܘܡ. ܀ ܀ ܀
23ܘܐܡܪ ܗܘܐ ܠܟܠ ܡܢ ܕܨܒܐ ܕܢܐܬܐ ܒܬܪܝ، ܢܟܦܘܪ ܒܢܦܫܗ.

---

15 ܐܢܘܢ ܠܟܠܗܘܢ] ܒܟܠܗܘܢ S 16 ܠܗܘܢ S ܘܬ̈ܪܝܢ] ܘܗܘܢ S ⌜ܟܠ⌝ܗܘܢ S^vid (several words here are illegible) ܩܕܡ ܟ̈ܢܫܐ] ܠܟ̈ܢܫܐ S 17 ܩܨ̈ܝܐ ܕܡܕܡ ܕܐܘܬܪܘ ܡܠܝܐ] S almost illegible, but seems to omit ܩܨ̈ܝܐ 17, 18 ܬܪ̈ܬܥܣܪ......ܒܠܚܘܕܘܗܝ] For these words S^ed has

ܬܪ̈ܬܥܣܪ ܩܘܦܝܢܝܢ ܡܢ ܠ * * * * * ⌜ܟܕ⌝ ܗܘܐ ܒܠܚܘܕܘܗܝ	probably to be read	ܬܪ̈ܬܥܣܪ ܩܘܦܝܢ ⌜܀⌝ ⌜ܡ⌝ܨܠ⌜ܐ⌝ ⌜ܟܕ⌝ ܗܘܐ ܒܠܚܘܕ⌜ܘܗ⌝ܝ

i.e. S omits ܘܐܬܬܗܘܢ to end of ver. 17 and begins ver. 18 with ܘܟܕ ܡܨܠܐ ܗܘܐ, but ܡܨܠܐ was accidentally omitted and then inserted between the lines, like ܢܐܬܐ in Lk xii 43 and ܐܡܪܝܢ in Joh xiii 16 ܥܠ ܟ̈ܢܫܐ] * * * ܟܢܫܐ S 18, 19 ܕܐܝܬܝ......ܝܘܚܢܢ ܗܘ] S illegible 20 ܠܗܘܢ ܗܘ ܘܐܢܬܘܢ] S illegible, but there is not space for all the words ܐܢܬܘܢ ܐܡܪܝܢ S 21 ܘܗܘ] om. ܗܘ S 22 ܘܐܡܪ] S illegible ܠܗ ܠܒܪܗ] S illegible ܣܓܝ ܘ] S illegible ܩܫ̈ܝܫܐ ܘܪ̈ܒܝ ܟܗ̈ܢܐ] tr. S ܘܢܬܩܛܠ S ܘܠܝܘܡܐ ܕܬ̈ܠܬܐ] ⌜ܘܒܬܪ⌝ ܬܠܬܐ ܝܘܡܝܢ S 23 ܒܬܪܝ 1°] ܒܐܬܪܝ S

15 company." And they did so, and they made them all sit down *to* C S
16 *meat.* And he took those five pieces of bread and two fishes,
and he looked up to heaven and blessed *God* upon them, and brake
and gave to his disciples that they should set before the multitudes.
17 And all ate and were satisfied, and they took up the fragments
that which they left over, twelve baskets full. And these folk
that ate of that bread were about five thousand, besides women and
children.

18 And when he was alone and his disciples with him, he asked them
19 and said: "What say about me the multitudes that I am?" They
say to him: "There are that say 'It is John the Baptist;' others say
20 'It is Elijah.'" Saith he to them: "And ye, what say ye that I am?"
Simon Kepha answered and said to him: "Thou art the Messiah."
21 And he—he rebuked them and commanded them that this to no one
22 they should say. And he saith "The Son of Man is about to suffer
much and be rejected by the elders and the scribes and the priests,
and be killed and the third day he will rise."

23 And he was saying: "Whosoever willeth to come after me, let

---

16 two] those *S* upon them] upon it S^{vid} (*several words here are illegible*) before the multitudes]...to the multitude *S* 17 the fragments....over] *S almost illegible, but it seems to omit* 'the fragments' 17, 18 twelve baskets....alone] *S appears to omit from* 'And these folk' *to the end of ver.* 17 *and to begin ver.* 18 *with* 'When he was praying alone,' *but the word for* 'praying' *appears to have been inserted between the lines, as in* Lk xii 43 *and* Joh xiii 16 about me] *after* 'the multitudes' S^{vid} 18, 19 that I am....John] *S illegible* 20 he to them: And ye] *S illegible, but there is not space for all the words* 21 he—] *om S* 22 And he saith] *S illegible* The Son] *S illegible* suffer] *S illegible* the priests and the scribes *S* and the third day] ⌜and after⌝ three days *S* 23 after me 1°] in my place *S*: *see Notes,* vol. ii

C S ܘܢܫܩܘܠ ܨܠܝܒܗ ܒܟܠܝܘܡ ܘܢܐܬܐ ܒܬܪܝ. [24]ܡܢ ܕܨܒܐ ܓܝܪ ܕܢܚܐ
col 2 ܢܦܫܗ ܢܘܒܕܝܗ. ܘܡܢ ܕܢܘܒܕ ܢܦܫܗ *ܡܛܠܬܝ، ܢܚܝܝܗ. [25]ܡܢܐ ܓܝܪ
ܢܐܬܪ ܒܪ ܐܢܫܐ ܐܢ ܥܠܡܐ ܟܠܗ ܢܩܢܐ ܘܢܦܫܗ ܢܚܣܪ.
[26]ܡܢ ܕܒܗܬ ܒܝ ܓܝܪ ܩܕܡ ܒܢܝܢܫܐ ܘܒܡܠܝ ܕܕܝܠܝ ܐܢܘܢ.
ܢܒܗܬ ܒܗ ܒܪܗ ܕܐܢܫܐ ܡܐ ܕܐܬܐ ܒܬܫܒܘܚܬܐ ܕܐܒܘܗܝ،
ܘܕܡ̈ܠܐܟܘܗܝ، ܩܕܝ̈ܫܐ. [27]ܐܡܪܢܐ ܠܟܘܢ ܕܝܢ ܒܫܪܪܐܝܬ. ܕܐܝܬ
ܐܢܫܐ ܕܩܝܡܝܢ ܗܪܟܐ. ܕܠܐ ܢܛܥܡܘܢ ܡܘܬܐ. ܥܕܡܐ ܕܢܚܙܘܢ
ܡܠܟܘܬܗ ܕܐܠܗܐ ܕܐܬܝܐ ܒܫܘܒܚܐ.܀
[28]ܘܗܘܐ ܒܬܪ ܡ̈ܠܐ ܗܠܝܢ ܐܝܟ ܬܡ̈ܢܝܐ ܝܘ̈ܡܝܢ. ܘܕܒܪ ܠܟܐܦܐ
ܘܠܝܥܩܘܒ ܘܠܝܘܚܢܢ. ܘܣܠܩ ܠܛܘܪܐ ܠܡܨܠܝܘ. [29]ܘܟܕ ܡܨܠܐ
fol 59 v ܐܫܬܚܠܦ ܚܙܘܐ ܕܐ̈ܦܘܗܝ، *ܘܢܚ̈ܬܘܗܝ، ܚ̈ܘܪܝܢ ܘܡܒܪ̈ܩܝܢ ܗܘܘ
ܐܝܟ ܬܠܓܐ. [30]ܘܗܐ ܬܪ̈ܝܢ ܓܒܪ̈ܝܢ ܡܡܠܠܝܢ ܥܡܗ. ܡܘܫܐ
ܘܐܠܝܐ [31]ܕܐܬܚܙܝܘ ܒܬܫܒܘܚܬܐ. ܘܐܡܪܝܢ ܗܘܘ ܥܠ ܡܦܩܢܗ
ܕܥܬܝܕ ܗܘܐ ܕܢܫܬܠܡ ܒܐܘܪܫܠܡ. [32]ܘܫܡܥܘܢ ܟܐܦܐ ܘܗܢܘܢ
ܕܥܡܗ ܝܩܝܪܝܢ ܗܘܘ ܠܗܘܢ ܒܫܢܬܐ. ܘܟܕ ܐܬܬܥܝܪܘ
ܚܙܘ ܬܫܒܘܚܬܗ. ܘܠܗܘܢ ܬܪ̈ܝܢ ܐܢܫܝܢ ܕܩܝܡܝܢ ܗܘܘ ܠܘܬܗ.
[33]ܘܟܕ ܫܪܝܘ ܠܡܦܪܫ ܡܢܗ. ܐܡܪ ܟܐܦܐ ܠܝܫܘܥ. ܪܒܝ ܫܦܝܪ
ܗܘ ܕܢܗܘܐ ܗܪܟܐ. ܘܢܥܒܕ ܬܠܬ ܡ̈ܛܠܠܝܢ. ܠܟ ܚܕܐ.
ܘܠܡܘܫܐ ܚܕܐ. ܘܠܐܠܝܐ ܚܕܐ. ܘܠܐ ܝܕܥ ܗܘܐ ܡܢܐ ܐܡܪ
col 2 ܗܘܐ. [34]ܘܟܕ ܐܡܪ ܗܠܝܢ. ܗܘܬ ܥܢܢܐ ܘܐܛܠܠܬ *ܥܠܝܗܘܢ. ܘܟܕ
ܚܙܘ ܠܗܠܝܢ ܕܥܠܝܢ ܒܥܢܢܐ ܕܚܠܘ. [35]ܘܩܠܐ ܐܫܬܡܥ ܡܢ ܥܢܢܐ
ܗ̇، ܕܐܡܪ. ܗܢܘ ܒܪܝ، ܘܓܒܝܝ ܠܗ ܫܡܥܘ. [36]ܘܟܕ ܗܘܐ ܩܠܐ

ܨܠܝܒܗ] ܙܩܝܦܗ S   ܒܟܠܝܘܡ] om. S   25 ܢܚܣܪ] ....ܘ ܢܚܣܪ S
26 ܡܢ] pr. ܕ S   ܒܝ ܓܝܪ.....ܕܐܒܘܗܝ] S illegible   ܘܕܡ̈ܠܐܟܘܗܝ]
ܡܠܐܟܐ .* S   27 ܕܐܬܝܐ ܒܫܘܒܚܐ] om. S   28 ܘܣܠܩ] ܘܣܠܩ S
29 ܐܝܟ ܬܠܓܐ] om. S   31 ܒܬܫܒܘܚܬܐ] ܒܫܘܒܚܐ S
32 ܘܫܡܥܘܢ ܟܐܦܐ] ܘܟܐܦܐ S   ܕܥܡܗ. ܝܩܝܪܘ S (sic)   ܒܫܢܬܐ]
om. S   33 ܪܒܝ] ܪܒ S   ܗܘ] om. S   ܬܠܬ] om. S   ܡ̈ܛܠܠܝܢ S (sic)
35 ܗ̇، ܕܐܡܪ] om. S   ܫܡܥܘ] ܕܫܡܥܘ S   ܘܓܒܝܝ] ܓܒܝܐ S

him deny himself and take up his Cross every day and come after C S
24 me. For he that willeth to save his life shall lose it, and he that
25 shall lose his life for my sake shall save it. For what should a man
26 gain, if he should get the whole world and lack his life? For he
that shall be ashamed of me before men and of them that are mine,
the son of a man shall be ashamed of him what *time* he cometh in
27 the glory of his Father and of his holy angels. Now I say to you
truly that there are some that stand here, that shall not taste death
until they see the kingdom of God that cometh in glory."

28 And it came to pass after these words, about eight days *after*,
that he took Kepha and James and John, and they went up to the
29 hill to pray. And while praying, the appearance of his face was
transfigured and his garments become white and were glistening as
30, 31 the snow. And lo, two men speaking with him, Moses and Elijah, that
appeared in glory; and they were saying about his decease that it
32 was about to be accomplished in Jerusalem. And Simon Kepha and
those with him had become heavy with much sleep, and when they
awoke they saw his glory and those two persons that were standing
33 by him. And when they began to separate from him Kepha said to
Jesus: "Rabbi, it is well that we should be here, and we will make
here three dwellings, for thee one and for Moses one and for Elijah
34 one!" And he was not knowing what he was saying. And when he
said these things there came a cloud and overshadowed them; and
35 when they saw these entering into the cloud they were afraid. And
a voice was heard from that cloud, saying: "This is my son and my
36 beloved; hear ye him!" And when there came the voice, Jesus was

---

his cross *S* every day] *om. S* 25 lack] lack and.... *S* (*a word illegible*) 26 the son of a man] *see on* Matt xii 40, Lk xxii 48 of me before men.... ...his Father and of] *S illegible* the holy angels *S* 27 that cometh in glory] *or*, 'that it cometh in glory'; *om. S*: *for* E^{155} *see* Mk ix 1 28 they went] he went *S* 29 as the snow] *om. S* 31 glory] *a synonym is used in S* (*cf ver.* 27) 32 Simon] *om. S* much] *om. S* 33 Rabbi] Rabban *S* here 2°] *om. S*: *cf* Matt xvii 4 34 *&* 36 came] *lit.* 'was' 35 that cloud, saying:] the cloud *S* my son and my beloved] my chosen son *S*

C S ܐܫܬܟܚ ܢܦܫ ܒܠܚܘܕܘܗܝ. ܘܗܢܘܢ ܫܬܘ ܠܗܘܢ܆ ܘܠܚܡ
ܐܢܫ ܠܐ ܐܡܪܘ ܡܛܠ ܕܚܙܘ ܗܘܘ ܒܗܢܘܢ ܡ̈ܫܬܘܬܐ. [37]ܘܒܗܘܢ
ܘܡܟܐ ܬܘܒ ܟܕ ܢܫܬܡ ܡܢ ܦܬܘܪܐ. ܦܩܕ ܒܗ ܒܢܫܐ ܘܦܢܝܐ.
[38]ܘܡܒܪܐ ܚܕ ܡܢ ܒܢܫܐ ܗܘ ܡܕܡ ܘܐܡܪ. ܕܠܘܩܒܠ ܒܒܠܐ ܐܢܫ
ܡܢܝܢ ܐܬܪܫܡ ܥܠ ܒܪ. ܫܬܝܐ ܗܘ ܠܝ. [39]ܘܪܘܚܐ ܗܘܐ ܠܗ.
ܘܡܢ ܬܘܒ ܥܠܝܐ ܐܪܡܝܐ ܠܗ ܘܡܪܬܬ. ܘܠܡܫܢܝܘ ܦܪܘܫܐ ܡܢܗ
fol 60r *ܒܗܐ ܕܫܡܥܬܗ. [40]ܘܡܛܠ ܡܢ ܬܠܡܝܕܘܗܝ ܘܠܐ ܐܫܬܥܝܘ
ܠܐܢܫܘܬܗ ܘܠܡܫܡܫܘܬܗ̇. [41]ܘܡܒܐ ܢܦܩ ܘܐܡܪ. ܐܘܢ
ܫܪܝܬܐ ܡܕܠܬܐ ܘܠܐ ܗܡܢܘ܇ ܒܝܕܐ ܠܐܚܪܬ، ܐܝܟܢܐ
ܠܗܬܐ ܘܐܝܟܢܐ ܡܪܢܐ، ܠܝ ܠܒܪܝ ܠܟܐ. [42]ܘܟܕ ܡܦܪ
ܠܗ ܐܝܬܝܗ ܫܐܕܐ ܗܘ܇ ܘܡܒܥܐ ܗܘܐ ܠܗ. ܘܒܥܐ ܒܗ̇
ܢܦܩ ܒܪܘܚܐ ܗ، ܦܠܓܬܐ܇ ܘܐܘܫܛ ܠܦܠܓܐ ܘܐܫܠܡܗ ܠܐܒܘܗ،.
[43]ܘܐܬܕܡܪܘ ܟܠܗܘܢ ܥܠ ܪܒܘܬܗ ܕܐܠܗܐ. ܘܟܕ ܟܠܗܘܢ ܡܬܕܡܪܝܢ
ܗܘܘ ܥܠ ܟܠ ܕܥܒܕ ܗܘܐ. ܐܡܪ ܠܬܠܡܝܕܘܗܝ، [44]ܘܫܡܥܘ ܐܢܬܘܢ
col 2 ܡ̈ܠܐ ܗܠܝܢ ܒܐܕ̈ܢܝܟܘܢ܆ ܒܪܗ ܓܝܪ *ܕܐܢܫܐ ܥܬܝܕ ܗܘ
ܕܢܫܬܠܡ ܒܐ̈ܝܕܝ ܒܢ̈ܝ ܐܢܫܐ. [45]ܘܗܢܘܢ ܠܐ ܡܣܬܟܠܝܢ ܗܘܘ ܠܗ̇
ܠܡܠܬܐ ܗܕܐ. ܡܛܠ ܕܡܟܣܝܐ ܗܘܬ ܡܢܗܘܢ ܕܠܐ ܢܣܬܟܠܘܢܗ̇.
ܘܗܢܘܢ ܕܚܠܝܢ ܗܘܘ ܕܢܫܐܠܘܢܝܗܝ، ܥܠܝܗ ܥܠ ܗܕܐ ܡܠܬܐ.
[46]ܘܥܠܬ ܗܘܬ ܒܗܘܢ ܡܚܫܒܬܐ ܗܕܐ ܕܡܢܘ ܢܗܘܐ ܪܒ ܒܗܘܢ܆
[47]ܢܦܩ ܕܝܢ ܒܪ ܢܒܐ ܡܢܫ̈ܒܬܗܘܢ. ܐܚܕ ܛܠܝܐ ܚܕ ܘܐܩܝܡܗ
ܠܘܬܗ [48]ܘܐܡܪ. ܡܢ ܕܡܩܒܠ ܛܠܝܐ ܗܢܐ ܒܫܡܝ ܠܝ ܗܘ ܡܩܒܠ܂

---

36 ܠܗܘܢ] *om. S* ܐܢܫ] *so also S* ܗܘܘ] *om. S* 37. § *in S* ܘܒܗܘܢ] *C*, but on an erasure; om. S* ܒܗ] ܒܗܘܢ *S* 38 ܐܬܪܫܡ ܥܠ] ܐܬܪܫܡ ܥܠ. *S (sic)* ܫܬܝܐ] *pr.* ܕ *S* 39 ܘܪܘܚܐ.....ܘܡܢ] ܘܡܢ.....ܘܪܘܚܐ *S* ܠܐܢܫܘܬܗ ܘܠܡܫܡܫܘܬܗ̇] ܠܗ +] ܠܗ ܘܡܒܥܐ *S* 40 ܬܠܡܝܕܘܗܝ] + ܕܝܫܘܥ *S* ܠܡܫܡܫܘܬܗ *S (so I read the photograph)* 41 ܘܡܒܐ] *om.* ܘ *S* ܘܠܐ ܗܡܢܘ] ܕܠܐ ܡܗܡܢܝܢ *S* ܠܝ ܠܒܪܝ ܠܟܐ] ܠܟܐ ܠܒܪܝ ܠܟܐ *S* 42 ܘܡܒܥܐ] ܘܡܒܥܐ *S* 43 ܟܠ ܐܢܫ *S* 44 ܘܫܡܥܘ *S (sic)* 45 ܕܡܟܣܝܐ] ܕܟܣܝܐ *S (sic)* ܗܘܘ ܕܢܫܐܠܘܢܝܗܝ] *so also S* (ܗܝ- *S*[vid]) ܗܕܐ ܡܠܬܐ] *tr. S* 46 ܗܕܐ] *om. S* 47 ܡܢܫ̈ܒܬܗܘܢ] ܡܢܫܒܬܐ ܕܠܒܗܘܢ *S* ܚܕ] *om. S* ܠܘܬܗ] ܠܘܬܗܘܢ *S*

found alone. And they kept silence, and in the sight of no one said C S
37 they aught that they had seen in those days. And on that day again,
while they *were* coming down from the hill, a great multitude met
38 him, and a certain man from that multitude cried and said: "Teacher,
I beseech thee, have compassion on my son! He is my only one,
39 and a spirit cometh over him and of a sudden it casteth him down
and he foameth, and scarcely doth it depart from him what *time* it
40 hath convulsed him. And I besought thy disciples, and they could
41 not heal him and cast it out." And Jesus answered and said: "Ah
generation crooked and without faith! until when shall I be with you
42 and endure you? Bring near to me thy son hither." And while
bringing him near, that devil threw him down and was making him
wallow *on the ground*; and Jesus rebuked that unclean spirit, and
43 healed the lad and delivered him to his father. And all of them
wondered at the greatness of God. And when every one was
44 wondering at all that he was doing, he said to his disciples: "Set ye
these words in your ears, for the Son of Man is about to be delivered
45 into the hands of men." And they were not recognising this word,
because it was kept secret from them that they should not recognise
46 it; and they were afraid to ask him about this same word. And
there had entered among them this thought—who should be greatest
47 among them? Now Jesus, when he knew their thoughts, took hold
48 of a certain lad and made him stand by him, and said: "He that

---

36 had seen] saw *S* 37 again] *C*, but on an erasure; om. S* met him] met them *S* 38 have compassion on my son! He] turn round on me! My son—who *S* 39 and of a sudden] of a sudden and *S* casteth him down] + and doth him hurt *S* 40 disciples] + that they should cast it out *S* heal him and cast it out] help him *S* (*so I read the photograph*) 41 And 1°] *om. S* and without faith] *and* faithless *S* to me thy son hither] hither thy son *S* 42 making him wallow *on the ground*] doing him hurt *S* 43 all of them] every one *S* 45 to ask him] *so also S* 46 this thought] a thought *S* 47 their thoughts] the thoughts of their heart *S* certain] *om. S* by him] by them *S*

C S ܘܡܢ ܕܠܝ ܡܩܒܠ ܠܗܘ ܕܫܕܪܢܝ ܡܩܒܠ. ܐܝܢܐ ܕܙܥܘܪ ܒܪ ܒܟܘܢ
ܐܝܟ ܗܢܐ ܛܠܝܐ ܗܘ ܪܒ· 49 ܘܥܢܐ ܝܘܚܢܢ ܘܐܡܪ ܠܗ. ܚܙܝܢ
fol 60 v ܓܒܪܐ *ܚܕ ܕܒܫܡܟ ܫܐ̈ܕܐ ܡܦܩ ܘܟܠܝܢܝܗܝ. ܥܠ ܕܠܐ ܐܬܐ
ܥܡܢ ܒܬܪܟ· 50 ܐܡܪ ܠܗ ܝܫܘܥ ܠܐ ܬܟܠܘܢ܆ ܡܢ ܕܠܐ ܗܘܐ
ܒܪ ܠܘܩܒܠܟܘܢ ܒܓܒܟܘܢ ܗܘ. ܀

51 ܘܗܘܐ ܟܕ ܡܬܡܠܝܢ ܗܘܘ ܝܘܡܬܐ ܕܡܣܬܠܩܢܘܬܗ. ܐܬܩܢ ܦܪܨܘܦܗ
ܕܢܐܙܠ ܠܗ ܠܐܘܪܫܠܡ. 52 ܘܫܕܪ ܗܘܐ ܡܠܐ̈ܟܐ ܩܕܡ ܐ̈ܦܘܗܝ.
ܘܐܙܠܘ ܘܥܠܘ ܠܩܪܝܬܐ ܚܕܐ ܕܫ̈ܡܪܝܐ ܕܢܛܝܒܘܢ ܠܗ. 53 ܘܠܐ
ܩܒܠܘ ܐܢܘܢ. ܡܛܠ ܕܦܪܨܘܦܗ ܠܐܘܪܫܠܡ ܗܘܐ ܠܡܐܙܠ.
54 ܘܟܕ ܕܝܢ ܚܙܘ ܬܠܡ̈ܝܕܘܗܝ ܝܥܩܘܒ ܘܝܘܚܢܢ. ܐܡܪܘ ܠܗ ܡܪܢ
ܨܒܐ ܐܢܬ ܕܢܐܡܪ. ܕܬܚܘܬ ܢܘܪܐ ܡܢ ܫܡܝܐ ܘܬܫܘܦ ܐܢܘܢ.
col 2 55 ܘܗܘ ܐܬܦܢܝ *ܘܟܐܐ ܒܗܘܢ ܘܐܡܪ ܠܗܘܢ܆ ܠܐ ܝܕܥܝܢ ܐܢܬܘܢ
ܕܐܝܢܐ ܐܢܬܘܢ ܪܘܚܐ. 56 ܒܪܗ ܕܝܢ ܕܐܢܫܐ ܠܐ ܐܬܐ ܠܡܘܒܕܘ
ܢܦ̈ܫܬܐ. ܐܠܐ ܠܡܚܝܘ. ܘܐܙܠܘ ܠܗܘܢ ܠܩܪܝܬܐ ܐܚܪܬܐ. ܀
57 ܘܟܕ ܐܙܠܝܢ ܒܐܘܪܚܐ. ܐܬܐ ܓܒܪܐ ܚܕ ܐܡܪ ܠܗ. ܐܬܐ
ܒܬܪܟ ܠܐܬܪ ܕܐܙܠ ܐܢܬ. 58 ܐܡܪ ܠܗ ܝܫܘܥ ܠܬܥ̈ܠܐ ܢܩ̈ܥܐ
ܐܝܬ ܠܗܘܢ. ܘܠܦܪܚܬܐ ܕܫܡܝܐ ܡܛܠܠܐ. ܠܒܪܗ ܕܝܢ ܕܐܢܫܐ
ܠܝܬ ܠܗ ܐܬܪ ܕܢܣܡܘܟ ܪܫܗ. 59 ܘܐܡܪ ܠܐܚܪܢܐ ܬܐ ܒܬܪܝ.
§A 168 ܐܡܪ ܠܗ ܡܪܝ. ܐܦܣ ܠܝ ܠܘܩܕܡ §ܐܙܠ ܐܩܒܘܪ ܠܐܒܝ ܘܐܬܐ.

---

48 ܕܙܥܘܪ ܒܪ] tr. S   ܒܟܘܢ ܐܝܟ ܗܢܐ ܛܠܝܐ] ܘܛܠܝܐ ܠܟܘܢ S   ܗܘ ܪܒ] ܗܢܐ ܪܒ ܗܘ S   49 ܘܥܢܐ] om. ܘ S   ܚܙܝܢ] pr. ܪܒܢ S   ܓܒܪܐ] om. S   ܥܠ ܕ] ܡܛܠ ܕ S   ܒܬܪܟ] om. S   50 ܠܗ] ܠܗܘܢ S   ܠܘܩܒܠܟܘܢ S   ܒܓܒܟܘܢ] ܥܠܓܒܟܘܢ S   51 ܘܗܘܐ ܟܕ] ܘܟܕ S   ܕܢܣܠܩ S (*cf* Lk ii 15)   ܠܗ] om. S   52 ܘܐܙܠܘ] ܐܬܘ S (*sic*)   ܚܕܐ] om. S   53 ܩܒܠܘ ܐܢܘܢ] ܩܒܠܘܗܝ S   55 ܘܗܘ ܐܬܦܢܝ] om. S   55, 56 ܘܐܡܪ.......ܐܠܐ ܠܡܚܝܘ] om. S   57 ܐܬܐ ܓܒܪܐ.....ܠܗ] ܐܡܪ ܠܗ ܐܢܫ S   58 ܠܬܥܠܐ] pr. ܕܐܦ S   ܡܛܠܠܐ] ܩܢܐ S   ܠܒܪܗ ܕܝܢ] ܘܠܒܪܗ S: *for the construction see Notes*, vol. ii   59 ܬܐ] ܐܬܐ S   ܒܬܪܝ] om. S   ܐܒܝ A[a]   ܘܐܬܐ] om. S; + ܠܘܬܟ A

receiveth this lad in my name, me it is he receiveth ; and he that *C S*
receiveth me, receiveth him that sent me. For he which is least
49 among you, like this lad, he is greatest." And John answered and
said to him: "We saw a certain man casting out devils in thy name,
and we forbade him, on *the ground* that he cometh not with us after
50 thee." Jesus saith to him: "Forbid not, for he that is not against
you is with you."

51 And it came to pass when the days of his going up were fulfilled
52 he prepared his countenance to go to Jerusalem. And he had sent
messengers before his face, and they went and entered a certain
53 village of the Samaritans, that they might prepare for him ; and they
received them not, because his countenance for Jerusalem was set
54 to go. Now when his disciples James and John saw *it*, they said
to him: "Our Lord, wilt thou that we say that fire come down
55 from heaven and consume them?" And he turned round and he
rebuked them, and said to them: "Ye know not of what spirit ye
56 are, for the Son of Man came not to destroy lives but to save *life*."
And they went away to another village.

57 And while they *were* going in the way, there came a certain man
and said to him: "I will come after thee whither thou goest."
58 Jesus saith to him: "The foxes—they have dens, and the birds of
the heaven a dwelling, but the Son of Man, he hath not where to rest
59 his head." And he said to another: "Come after me." He saith to
him: "My Lord, permit me first §to go *and* bury my father, and I §*A* 168

---

48 among you, like this lad] and a lad unto you *S* **49** And 1°] *om. S* We] Rabban, we *S* a certain man] one *S* on *the ground* that] because *S* after thee] *om S* **50** to him] to them *S* with you] for you *S* **51** it came to pass] *om. S* **52** and they went] *and* they came *S* (*sic*) certain] *om. S* **53** them] him *S* **54** say that fire come down] 'say, and fire shall come down...' E^{95} (= syr.vg *and* arm.vg) **55** he turned round and] *om. S* **55, 56** and said.....to save *life*] *om. S* **57** there came....to him] some one said to him *S* **58** saith to him: The foxes—they have] saith to him If the foxes have *S* a dwelling] nests *S* but] yet *S* (*lit.* 'and': *so also* E^{74}, *for which see* Matt viii 20) **59** My Lord, permit] Permit *S* and I will come] *om. S*; + unto thee *A*

C S ⁶⁰ܐܡܪ ܠܗ ܝܫܘܥ ܫܒܘܩ ܡ̈ܝܬܐ ܩܒܪܝܢ ܡ̈ܝܬܝܗܘܢ܆ *ܘܐܢܬ ܙܠ
fol 61 r
¶A ܣܒܪ ܡܠܟܘܬܗ ܕܐܠܗܐ.¶ ⁶¹ܐܡܪ ܠܗ ܐܚܪܢܐ ܐܬܐ ܒܬܪܟ.
ܡܪܝ، ܠܡܦܪܣ ܕܝܢ ܐܦܣ ܠܝ ܐܙܠ ܐܫܐܠ ܠܒ̈ܢܝ ܒܝܬܝ، ܘܐܬܐ·
⁶²ܐܡܪ ܠܗ ܝܫܘܥ· ܠܐ ܐܢܫ ܪܡܐ ܐܝܕܗ ܥܠ ܣܟܬܐ ܕܦܕܢܐ
ܘܚܐܪ ܠܒܣܬܪܗ· ܘܗܘܐ ܬܘܒ ܚܫܝܚ ܠܡܠܟܘܬܐ ܕܐܠܗܐ..
¹ܘܡܢ ܒܬܪ ܗܠܝܢ ܦܪܫ ܐܦ ܠܐܚܪ̈ܢܐ ܫܒܥܝܢ ܘܬܪ̈ܝܢ. ܘܫܕܪ
ܐܢܘܢ ܬܪ̈ܝܢ ܬܪ̈ܝܢ ܩܕܡ ܦ̈ܪܨܘܦܘܗܝ، ܠܟܠ ܐܬܪ ܘܡܕܝܢܬܐ ܕܥܬܝܕ
ܗܘܐ ܠܡܐܙܠ. ²ܐܡܪ ܠܗܘܢ ܚܨܕܐ ܗܘ ܣܓܝܐ ܘܦ̈ܥܠܐ ܙܥܘܪܝܢ.
ܒܥܘ ܗܟܝܠ ܡܢ ܡܪܗ ܕܚܨܕܐ ܐܝܟ ܕܢܦܩ ܦ̈ܥܠܐ ܠܚܨܕܗ.
col 2 ³ܙܠܘ ܗܫܐ ܗܐ ܡܫܕܪ *ܐܢܐ ܠܟܘܢ ܐܝܟ ܐܡܪ̈ܐ ܒܝܢܝ ܕܐܒ̈ܐ.
⁴ܠܐ ܬܫܩܠܘܢ ܠܟܘܢ ܟܝܣܐ ܘܠܐ ܬܪ̈ܡܠܐ. ܘܠܐ ܡܣ̈ܢܐ.
ܘܫܠܡܐ ܕܐܢܫ ܒܐܘܪܚܐ ܠܐ ܬܫܐܠܘܢ. ⁵ܘܠܐܝܢܐ ܒܝܬܐ
ܕܥܐܠܝܢ ܐܢܬܘܢ ܠܗ. ܗܘܝܬܘܢ ܐܡܪܝܢ ܫܠܡܐ
ܠܒܝܬܐ ܗܢܐ. ⁶ܘܐܢ ܐܝܬ ܬܡܢ ܒܪ ܫܠܡܐ ܢܬܢܝܚ ܥܠܘܗܝ،
ܫܠܡܟܘܢ· ܘܐܢ ܕܝܢ ܠܐ ܥܠܝܟܘܢ ܢܗܦܘܟ. ⁷ܘܒܗ ܒܒܝܬܐ
ܗܘܝܬܘܢ ܠܟܘܢ ܐܟܠܝܢ ܘܫܬܝܢ ܡܢ ܕܠܘܬܗܘܢ. ܫܘܐ ܗܘ ܦܥܠܐ
ܦܘܪܥܢܗ. ܘܠܐ ܬܫܢܘܢ ܡܢ ܒܝܬܐ ܠܒܝܬܐ. ⁸ܘܠܐܝܕܐ ܡܕܝܢܬܐ
ܕܥܐܠܝܢ ܐܢܬܘܢ ܠܗ̇ ܘܡܩܒܠܝܢ ܠܟܘܢ܆ ܠܗܘ ܒܟܠ ܡܕܡ ܕܡܬܬܣܝܡ
fol 61 v ܩܕܡܝܟܘܢ܆ ⁹*ܘܐܣܘ ܟܪ̈ܝܗܐ ܕܐܝܬ ܒܗ̇. ܘܗܘܝܬܘܢ ܐܡܪܝܢ
ܕܩܪܒܬ ܠܘܬܟܘܢ ܡܠܟܘܬܗ ܕܐܠܗܐ. ¹⁰ܠܐܝܕܐ ܡܕܝܢܬܐ ܕܝܢ

---

60 ܘܐܡܪ A ܫܒܘܩ] om. S; ܡܪܢ A 61 ܡܪܝ· S (sic) 62. For Ephr. *Overbeck* 127, see *Introd.* vol. ii ܬܘܒ] om. S ܠܡܠܟܘܬܗ S *Cf* ܐܝܢܐ ܕܪܡܐ ܐܝܕܗ ܥܠ ܣܟܬܐ ܕܦܕܢܐ܆ ܘܠܒܣܬܪܗ ܚܐܪ ܠܐ ܡܬܚܫܚ *Thos*[315]: and ܐܢܫܐ ܕܐܪܡܐ ܐܝܕܗ ܥܠ ܣܟܬܐ ܕܦܕܢܐ: ܘܗܦܟ ܗܘ ܕܚܙܐ ܠܒܣܬܪܗ: ܠܐ ܡܬܚܫܚ ܬܘܒ ܠܡܠܟܘܬܐ ܕܫܡܝܐ *Addai*[45] 1 ܐܦ ܠܐܚܪ̈ܢܐ] ܡܢ ܬܠܡܝܕܘܗܝ ܐܚܪ̈ܢܐ S ܫܒܥܝܢ ܘܬܪ̈ܝܢ] *so also Thos*[176] *and Addai*[5]
2 ܗܟܝܠ] om. S 3 ܘܙܠܘ ܗܫܐ] ܐܙܠܘ S ܗܐ] + ܐܢܐ S ܒܝܢܝ] S *illegible*
4 ܬܫܩܠܘܢ & ܕܐܢܫ] S *illegible* 5 ܗܢܐ] om. S 6 ܘܐܢ 1° & 2°] om. ܘ S
7 ܘܗܘ ܫܘܐ] + ܓܝܪ S ܦܘܪܥܢܗ] ܐܓܪܗ S 8 ܠܗ̇] om. S 10 ܕܝܢ] om. S

60 will come." Jesus saith to him : "Leave the dead to bury their dead, *C S*
61 and thou go *and* announce the kingdom of God."¶ Another said to ¶*A*
him : "I will come after thee, my Lord, but first permit me to go and
62 shew *it* to the sons of my house, and I will come." Jesus saith to
him : "No one putteth his hand on the ploughshare and looketh
behind him, and becometh again fit for the kingdom of God."

X 1 And after these things he separated others also, seventy and two,
and sent them two by two before his face to every place and city that
2 he was about to go. He saith to them : "The harvest *is* much, and the
labourers few ; beseech ye therefore the Lord of the harvest so that
3 he may send forth labourers for his harvest. Go now ; lo, I send you
4 as lambs among wolves ! Take for yourselves no purses and no wallets
5 and no shoes, and a greeting to no man in the way shall ye give. And
whatever house first ye enter into, be saying 'Peace *be* in this house.'
6 And if there is there a son of peace, your peace shall rest upon it ; but
7 if not, upon you it shall return. And in the same house be ye eating
and drinking of their *store* : the labourer is worthy of his food ; and
8 do not remove from one house to the next. And whatever city ye
enter into and they receive you, eat everything that is set before you,
9 and heal the sick that are therein, and be saying 'The kingdom of
10 God hath drawn nigh upon you.' But whatever city ye enter into

---

60 Jesus] He *S*; And our Lord *A* saith (*so* syr.vg)] said *A* 62 again] *om. S* *For the whole verse, cf* 'My hand have I put on my ploughshare, and behind me I have not turned' *Thos*[315]; *and* 'The farmer that putteth his hand on the ploughshare, if so be that he looketh behind him, the furrows cannot be straight before him' *Addai*[45]. *Thus there is no Syriac evidence for the reading of* D lat[vt] Clem.Al *in this verse* 1 others also] from his disciples others *S* seventy and two] *so also Thos*[176] *and Addai*[5], *with E*[59,160] *and* Ephr.*arm* (*on* 1 Cor xv 7; 2 Cor viii 23, xi 15) 2 therefore] *om. S* 3 now] *om. S* among] *S illegible* 4 Take *and* no man] *S illegible* 5 peace] *or*, 'greeting' (*as* Matt x 13) this house] the house *S* 6 And if] If *S* 7 the labourer] *pr.* for *S* food] reward *S* 8 into] *om. S* 10 But whatever] Whatever *S*

CS ܕܥܠܝܢ ܐܢܬܘܢ ܠܗ̇ ܘܠܐ ܢܩܒܠܘܢܟܘܢ ܒܗ̇. ܦܘܩܘ ܘܐܡܪܘ
ܒܫܘ̈ܩܝܗ̇. [11]ܘܗܘܐ ܐܦ. ܚܠܐ ܕܕܒܩ ܒܪ̈ܓܠܝܢ ܢܦܨܝܢ ܐܢܚܢܢ ܠܟܘܢ.
ܒܪܡ ܕܝܢ ܗܕܐ ܕܥܘ. ܕܩܪܒܬ ܠܗ ܡܠܟܘܬܗ ܕܐܠܗܐ. [12]ܐܡܪܢܐ
ܠܟܘܢ. ܕܠܣܕܘܡ ܢܗܘܐ ܢܝܚ ܒܝܘܡܐ ܕܕܝܢܐ ܛܒ ܡܢ ܕܠܗ̇،
ܡܕܝܢܬܐ ܀

[13]ܘܝ ܠܟܝ ܟܘܪܙܝܢ. ܘܝ ܠܟܝ ܒܝܬ ܨܝܕܐ. ܕܐܠܘ ܒܨܘܪ ܘܒܨܝܕܢ
ܗܘܘ ܚܝܠܐ ܕܗܘܘ ܒܟܝܢ. ܟܒܪ ܕܝܢ ܒܣܩܐ ܘܒܩܛܡܐ ܬܒܘ.
col 2 [14]ܒܪܡ ܠܨܘܪ ܘܠܨܝܕܢ ܢܗܘܐ ܢܝܚ ܒܝܘܡܐ *ܕܕܝܢܐ. ܝܬܝܪ ܡܢ
ܕܠܟܝ. [15]ܘܐܦ ܐܢܬܝ، ܟܦܪܢܚܘܡ ܠܐ ܥܕܡܐ ܠܫܡܝܐ ܬܬܪܝܡܝܢ.
ܐܠܐ ܥܕܡܐ ܠܫܝܘܠ ܬܬܚܬܝܢ. [16]ܡܢ ܕܠܟܘܢ ܫܡܥ ܠܝ ܗܘ ܫܡܥ.
ܘܡܢ ܕܠܟܘܢ ܛܠܡ ܠܝ ܗܘ ܛܠܡ. ܘܡܢ ܕܠܝ ܛܠܡ ܠܡܢ ܕܫܕܪܢܝ ܛܠܡ.
ܘܡܢ ܕܠܝ ܫܡܥ ܠܡܢ ܕܫܕܪܢܝ ܫܡܥ ܀

[17]ܘܗܦܟܘ ܗܘܘ ܗܢܘܢ ܫܒܥܝܢ ܕܫܕܪ ܒܚܕܘܬܐ ܘܐܡܪܝܢ. ܡܪܢ
ܘܐܦ ܫܐ̈ܕܐ ܡܫܬܥܒܕܝܢ ܠܢ ܒܫܡܟ. [18]ܐܡܪ ܠܗܘܢ ܝܫܘܥ.
ܚܙܐ ܗܘܝܬ ܠܗ ܠܣܛܢܐ ܕܢܦܠ ܐܝܟ ܒܪܩܐ ܕܢܦܠ ܡܢ ܫܡܝܐ.
[19]ܗܐ ܝܗܒ ܐܢܐ ܠܟܘܢ ܫܘܠܛܢܐ. ܕܬܗܘܘܢ ܕܝܫܝܢ ܚܘ̈ܘܬܐ
fol 62 r ܘܥܩܪ̈ܒܐ. *ܘܟܠܗ ܚܝܠܗ ܕܒܥܠܕܒܒܐ. ܘܡܕܡ ܠܐ ܢܗܪܒܟܘܢ.
[20]ܒܪܡ ܒܗܕܐ ܠܐ ܬܚܕܘܢ ܕܫܐ̈ܕܐ ܡܫܬܥܒܕܝܢ ܠܟܘܢ. ܐܠܐ
ܚܕܘ ܒܫܡ̈ܗܝܟܘܢ ܕܐܬܟܬܒܘ ܒܫܡܝܐ. [21]ܘܒܗ̇ ܒܫܥܬܐ ܐܪܘܙ ܒܪܘܚܐ

ܠܗ] C (sic) ܘܐܡܪܘ ܒܫܘ̈ܩܝܗ̇] ܒܫܘ̈ܩܝܗܘܢ ܘܐܡܪܘ S 11 ܘܗܘܐ]
ܕܗܘܐ S ܠܗ] C (sic) ܡܠܟܘܬܐ S 12 ܕܠܡܕܝܢܬܐ ܗܝ. S
13 ܕܗܘܘ ܒܟܝܢ] ܕܒܟܝܢ ܗܘܘ S 14 ܕܕܝܢܐ] ܗܘ S 15 ܘܐܦ ܐܢܬܝ]
om. ܐܦ S ܐܠܐ] om. S ܬܬܚܬܝܢ] so also S 16 ܡܢ ܕܫܡܥ ܠܟܘܢ S
ܠܝ ܗܘ ܛܠܡ. ܘܡܢ ܕܠܝ ܛܠܡ] om. S 17 ܫܒܥܝܢ] ܫܒܥܝܢ ⌜ܘܬܪ̈ܝܢ⌝ S^ed: syr.palest
here has ܫܒܥܝܢܬܐ ܘܐܡܪܝܢ] om. ܘ S^ed ܘܐܦ] om. ܘ S ܠܢ ܒܫܡܟ]
so also S: the extra line indicated in S^ed is a mistake 18 ܝܫܘܥ] om. S
ܠܗ] om. S ܕܢܦܠ 2°] om. S 19 ܝܗܒܢܐ S ܘܟܠܗ] ܘܐܦ S
A 131 has ܗܐ ܝܗܒܬ ܠܟܘܢ ܫܘܠܛܢܐ. ܕܬܕܘܫܘܢ ܚܝܠܗ ܕܒܥܠܕܒܒܐ, but the
phrase ܫܘܠܛܢܐ ܕܬܕܘܫ ܚܘ̈ܘܬܐ ܘܥܩܪ̈ܒܐ occurs A 105 20 ܒܪܡ] + ܕܝܢ S
ܕܫܐܕܐ S ܕܐܬܟܬܒܘ] ܕܐܬܟܬܒܘ S 21 ⌜ܐ⌝ܪܘܙ S^ed

and they shall not receive you therein, go forth and say in its streets *C S*
11 'Lo, even the dust that cleaveth to our feet we shake off; but
nevertheless know this, that the kingdom of God hath come nigh!'
12 I say to you that for Sodom it shall be tolerable in the day of
judgement more than for that city.

13 "Woe to thee, Korazin! woe to thee, Beth Saida! for if in Tyre
and in Sidon had happened the mighty works that have happened in
you, then perchance in sackcloth and in ashes they had repented.
14 Nevertheless for Tyre and for Sidon it shall be tolerable in the day
15 of judgement rather than for you. And thou also, Kapharnahum!
not unto heaven shalt thou be uplifted, but unto Sheol shalt thou go
16 down. He that heareth you, me it is he heareth; and he that
defraudeth you, me it is he defraudeth; and he that defraudeth me,
defraudeth him that sent me; and he that heareth me, heareth him
that sent me."

17 And those seventy that he sent had returned with joy, and they
say: "Our Lord, even the devils are subject to us in thy name."
18 Jesus saith to them: "I have been seeing Satan, that he fell as
19 lightning that falleth from heaven. Lo, I give you authority that ye
should be treading on serpents and scorpions and all the power of
20 the enemy, and nothing shall injure you. Nevertheless in this do not
rejoice, that the devils are subject to you, but rejoice in your names
21 that are written in heaven." And in the same hour he exulted in the

---

and say in its streets] in their streets and say *S* 11 Lo] *S*; And lo *C* 13 that in you have happened *S* 14 the day of judgement] that day *S* 15 also] *om. S* but] *om. S* shalt thou go down] *so also S* 16 me it is he defraudeth; and he that defraudeth me] *om. S* 17 seventy] + and two *S*[ed], *but the reading is not quite clear* and they say] *om.* and *S*[ed] to us in thy name] *so also S* 18 Jesus] He *S* that falleth] *om. S E*[116] 19 I give] 'I have given' *A E*[116] all the power] the power also *S* (*not E*[116]) *A* 131 *has* 'Lo, I have given you authority that ye should tread on the power of the enemy', *but the phrase* 'authority that we should tread on serpents and scorpions' *occurs A* 105 20 But nevertheless *S* that 2°] *or*, 'that they' are written] have been written *S* *Cf E*[206] 'That your names are written in heaven among the angels'

C S ܕܩܘܕܫܐ ܘܐܡܪ. ܡܘܕܐ ܐܢܐ ܠܟ ܐܒܐ ܡܪܗ ܕܫܡܝܐ
ܘܕܐܪܥܐ. ܕܟܣܝܬ ܗܠܝܢ ܡܢ ܚ̈ܟܝܡܐ ܘܡܢ ܣ̈ܘܟܠܬܢܐ. ܘܓܠܝܬ
ܐܢܝܢ ܠܛ̈ܠܝܐ. ܐܝܢ ܐܒܝ ܕܗܟܢܐ ܗܘܐ ܨܒܝܢܐ ܩܕܡܝܟ. [22]ܟܠ
ܡܕܡ ܐܫܬܠܡ ܠܝ ܡܢ ܐܒܝ. ܘܠܐ ܐܢܫ ܝܕܥ ܡܢܘ ܒܪܐ ܐܠܐ
ܐܢ ܐܒܐ. ܘܠܐ ܡܢܘ ܐܒܐ ܐܠܐ ܐܢ ܒܪܐ. ܘܠܡܢ ܕܨܒܐ
col 2 ܒܪܐ ܕܢܓܠܐ ܠܗ. [23]ܘܐܬܦܢܝ ܠܘܬ ܬܠܡܝܕܘܗܝ ܘܐܡܪ *ܠܗܘܢ܆
ܛܘܒܝܗܝܢ ܠܥ̈ܝܢܐ ܕܚܙܝܢ ܡܕܡ ܕܚܙܝܬܘܢ܆ [24]ܐܡܪܢܐ ܠܟܘܢ
ܕܣ̈ܓܝܐܐ ܢܒ̈ܝܐ ܘܡ̈ܠܟܐ ܨܒܘ ܕܢܚܙܘܢ ܡܕܡ ܕܚܙܝܢ ܐܢܬܘܢ
ܘܠܐ ܚܙܘ. ܘܠܡܫܡܥ ܡܕܡ ܕܫܡܥܝܢ ܐܢܬܘܢ ܘܠܐ ܫܡܥܘ.
[25]ܘܟܕ ܐܡܪ ܗܠܝܢ. ܩܡ ܥܠܘ. ܢܡܘܣܝܐ ܚܕ ܕܡܢܣܐ ܗܘܐ ܕܢܢܣܝܘܗܝ.
ܐܡܪ ܠܗ ܡܠܦܢܐ ܡܢܐ ܐܥܒܕ ܕܐܪܬ ܚ̈ܝܐ ܕܠܥܠܡ. [26]ܐܡܪ
ܠܗ ܝܫܘܥ ܒܢܡܘܣܐ ܐܝܟܢܐ ܟܬܝܒ. ܘܐܝܟܢܐ ܩܪܝܬ. [27]ܐܡܪ
ܠܗ ܕܬܪܚܡ ܠܡܪܝܐ ܐܠܗܟ ܡܢ ܟܠܗ ܠܒܟ. ܘܡܢ ܟܠܗ ܚܝܠܟ.
ܘܡܢ ܟܠܗ ܢܦܫܟ. ܘܡܢ ܟܠܗ ܪܥܝܢܟ. ܘܠܩܪܝܒܟ ܐܝܟ ܢܦܫܟ.
fol 62 v [28]ܐܡܪ ܠܗ *ܝܫܘܥ ܬܪܝܨܐܝܬ ܐܡܪܬ. ܗܠܝܢ ܥܒܕ ܘܬܚܐ ܐܢܬ܂
[29]ܗܘ ܕܝܢ ܨܒܐ ܗܘܐ ܠܡܙܕܩܘ ܢܦܫܗ܂ ܐܡܪ ܠܝܫܘܥ ܘܡܢܘ
ܩܪܝܒܝ. [30]ܐܡܪ ܠܗ ܝܫܘܥ܂ ܓܒܪܐ ܚܕ ܢܚܬ ܗܘܐ ܡܢ ܐܘܪܫܠܡ
ܠܐܝܪܝܚܘ. ܘܢܦܠ ܒܐܝ̈ܕܝ ܓ̈ܝܣܐ. ܘܐܫܠܚܘܗܝ ܘܡܚܘܗܝ.
ܘܫܒܩܘܗܝ ܒܝܬ ܡܝܬ ܠܚܝ. ܘܐܙܠܘ ܠܗܘܢ܂ [31]ܘܓܕܫ ܟܗܢܐ ܚܕ
ܢܚܬ ܗܘܐ ܒܐܘܪܚܐ ܗܝ ܘܚܙܝܗܝ ܘܥܒܪܗ. [32]ܘܐܦ ܠܘܝܐ ܟܕ
ܡܛܐ ܗܘ ܕܗܘܬܐ ܚܙܝܗܝ ܘܥܒܪܗ. [33]ܫܡܪܝܐ ܕܝܢ ܚܕ ܟܕ ܪܕܐ
ܗܘܐ ܒܗ̇ ܒܐܘܪܚܐ ܘܡܛܐ ܠܘܬܗ܂ ܚܙܝܗܝ ܘܐܬܪܚܡ ܥܠܘܗܝ.

ܡܪܗ] *C* S; a corrector of C has added a dot in red over the* ܗ   ܕܟܣܝܬ] *S illegible*   22 ܡܢ ܐܒܝ] ܡܢ ܐܒܐ *S*   ܘܠܐ ܐܢܫ ܝܕܥ ܡܢܘ ܒܪܐ] ܘܡܢܘ ܝܕܥ ܠܒܪܐ *S*   ܐܢ 1°] *om. S*   ܘܠܐ ܡܢܘ ܐܒܐ] ܘܡܢܘ ܝܕܥ ܠܐܒܐ *S*
23 ܡܕܡ] ܡܕܐ *S*   ܕܚܙܝܬܘܢ] ܕܚܙܝܢ ܐܢܬܘܢ *S*   24 ܠܟܘܢ] + ܓܝܪ *S*
ܕܫܡܥܝܢ ܐܢܬܘܢ] ܕܐܢܬܘܢ ܫܡܥܝܢ *S*   25 ܘܟܕ] ܟܕ *S*   26 ܩܪܝܬ] ܩܪܐ ܐܢܬ *S*
27 ܐܡܪ ܠܗ] *pr.* ܗܘ ⌜ܕܝܢ⌝ ܥܢܐ ܘ *S*   ܟܠܗ ܚܝܠܟ *and* ܟܠܗ ܢܦܫܟ] *tr. S*
30 ܝܫܘܥ] *om. S*   ܘܢܦܠ ܒܐܝ̈ܕܝ ܓ̈ܝܣܐ] ܘܢܦܠ ܒܓ̈ܝܣܐ *S*   31 ܗܘܐ] *om. S*
32 ܘܐܦ] ܘܗܟܢܐ ܐܦ *S*   33 ܒܗ̇ ܒܐܘܪܚܐ] ܒܐܘܪܚܗ   ܘܡܛܐ] *om.* ܘ *S*

Holy Spirit and said: "I give thanks to thee, Father, Lord of C S
heaven and of earth, that thou hast kept secret these things from the
wise and from the understanding and hast revealed them to children;
22 yea, my Father, that so was the will before thee. Everything hath
been delivered unto me from my Father, and no one knoweth who
the Son is save the Father, neither who the Father is save the Son,
23 and he to whom the Son shall be willing to reveal *it*." And he
turned round unto his disciples and said to them: "Happy is it for
24 the eyes that see that which ye have seen! I say to you that many
prophets and kings have wished that they might see that which ye
see, and they have not seen; and to hear that which ye hear and they
25 have not heard." And when he said these things, there drew near a
certain teacher of law that was standing *by* to tempt him. He saith
to him: "Teacher, what shall I do that I may inherit life eternal?"
26 Jesus saith to him: "In the law how is it written, and how hast thou
27 read?" He saith to him "Thou shalt love the LORD thy God from
all thy heart and from all thy power and from all thy soul and from
28 all thy mind, and thy neighbour as thyself." Jesus saith to him:
29 "Rightly hast thou said; these things do, and thou dost live." Now
he was wishing to justify himself; saith he to Jesus: "And who is
30 my neighbour?" Jesus saith to him: "A certain man was going
down from Jerusalem to Jericho and fell into the hands of the
robbers, and they stripped him and beat him and left him between
31 dead and alive, and went away. And a certain priest chanced to
have been coming down in that way, and he saw him and passed by
32 him. And a Levite also when he arrived at that place saw him and
33 passed by him. But a certain Samaritan, when he was journeying in
that same way and *had* arrived by him, saw him and had compassion

---

21 Father.... earth] 'heavenly Father' E^{116} that.... secret] *S illegible* 22 from my Father] from the Father *S* no one *to end of ver.*] who knoweth the Son but the Father, and who knoweth the Father save the Son, and he to whom the Son shall be willing to reveal him? *S* (*not* $E^{117,216}$) 23 that which] what *S* have seen] see *S* 24 I say] *pr.* For *S* 25 And when] When *S* 26 hast thou read] readest thou *S* 27 He saith] ⌜But⌝ he answered and said *S* power.... soul] *tr.* *S* 30 Jesus] He *S* and fell.... robbers, and they] and the robbers fell *on him* and *S* 31 to have been] to be *S* 32 a Levite] *pr.* so *S* 33 in that same way] on his way *S* and.... by him, saw] arrived by him *and* saw *S*

34ܘܐܬܩܪܒ ܘܚܒܫ ܡܚܘ̈ܬܗ· ܘܢܣܟ ܥܠܝܗܝܢ ܚܡܪܐ ܘܡܫܚܐ. C S
col 2 *ܘܐܪܟܒܗ ܥܠ ܚܡܪܗ. ܘܐܝܬܝܗ ܠܦܘܬܩܐ ܘܬܪܣܝܗ. 35ܘܠܨܦܪܗ
ܕܝܘܡܐ ܐܦܩ ܬܪܝܢ ܕܝܢܪܝܢ ܝܗܒ ܠܦܘܬܩܝܐ. ܘܐܡܪ ܬܪܣܝܘܗܝ،
ܘܡܢܐ ܕܡܦܩܬ ܝܬܝܪ ܕܢܦܩ ܠܟ ܬܘܒ ܦܪܥ ܐܢܐ ܠܟ. 36ܡܢܘ
ܡܢ ܗܠܝܢ ܬܠܬܐ ܡܬܚܙܐ ܠܟ ܕܗܘܐ ܩܪܝܒܐ ܕܗܘ ܕܢܦܠ ܒܝ̈ܬ
ܓ̈ܝܣܐ. 37ܐܡܪ ܠܗ ܗܘ ܕܐܬܪܚܡ ܥܠܘܗܝ، ܐܡܪ ܠܗ ܝܫܘܥ. ܠܟ
ܘܐܦ ܐܢܬ ܗܟܢܐ ܗܘܝܬ ܥܒܕ .܀.

38ܘܟܕ ܐܙܠܝܢ ܗܘܘ ܒܐܘܪܚܐ. ܥܠ ܠܩܪܝܬܐ ܚܕܐ. ܘܐܢܬܬܐ ܚܕܐ
ܕܫܡܗ̇ ܡܪܬܐ ܩܒܠܬܗ ܒܒܝܬܗ̇. 39ܘܐܝܬ ܗܘܬ ܠܗ̇ ܚܬܐ ܕܫܡܗ̇
fol 63 r ܡܪܝܡ. ܘܐܬܬ ܝܬܒܬ *ܠܘܬ ܪ̈ܓܠܘܗܝ ܕܡܪܢ. ܘܫܡܥܐ ܗܘܬ
ܡ̈ܠܘܗܝ. 40ܡܪܬܐ ܕܝܢ ܒܝܫܐ ܗܘܬ ܒܬܫܡܫܬܐ ܣܓܝܐܬܐ.
ܘܐܬܬ ܐܡܪܐ ܠܗ. ܡܪܝ، ܠܐ ܟܐܒ ܠܟ ܥܠ ܕܚܬܝ، ܫܒܩܬܢܝ
ܒܠܚܘܕ، ܕܐܫܡܫ· ܐܡܪܝ ܠܗ̇ ܡܥܕܪܐ ܠܝ. 41ܐܡܪ ܠܗ̇ ܡܪܢ ܡܪܬܐ
ܡܪܬܐ ܝܨܦܬܝ، ܘܦܠܝܓܐ ܕܠܐ ܐܢܬܝ ܠܬܠܬܝ ܥܠ ܣܓܝܐܬܐ.
42ܚܕܐ ܗܝ ܕܝܢ ܡܬܒܥܝܐ. ܡܪܝܡ ܡܢܬܐ ܛܒܬܐ ܓܒܬ ܠܗ̇ ܘܠܐ
ܬܫܬܩܠ ܡܢܗ̇ ·܀·

1ܘܟܕ ܡܨܠܐ ܗܘܐ ܕܝܢ ܒܕܘܟܬܐ ܚܕܐ. ܒܬܪ ܕܫܠܡ ܩܠܝܠ ܡܢ
ܨܠܘܬܗ. ܐܡܪ ܠܗ ܚܕ ܡܢ ܬܠܡܝ̈ܕܘܗܝ، ܡܪܢ ܐܠܦܢ ܠܡܨܠܝܘ
ܐܝܟܢܐ ܕܝܘܚܢܢ ܐܠܦ ܠܬܠܡܝ̈ܕܘܗܝ. 2ܐܡܪ ܠܗܘܢ ܐܡܬܝ،
col 2 *ܕܡܨܠܝܢ ܐܢܬܘܢ ܗܟܢܐ ܗܘܝܬܘܢ ܐܡܪܝܢ. ܐܒܘܢ ܕܒܫܡܝܐ ܢܬܩܕܫ.
ܫܡܟ. ܘܬܐܬܐ ܡܠܟܘܬܟ. 3ܘܗܒ ܠܢ ܠܚܡܐ ܐܡܝܢܐ ܕܟܠܝܘܡ.

---

34 ܘܐܬܩܪܒ] ܘܩܪܒ S   ܘܚܒܫ] ܚܒܫ S   ܡܚܘ̈ܬܗ] ܡܚܐܘ̈ܬܗ S (sic): *cf* Mk iii 11 *and Notes*, vol. ii   ܘܢܣܟ] ܘܐܪܡܝ S   ܥܠܝܗܝܢ] *so also* S   ܡܫܚܐ ܘܚܡܪܐ S   35 ܝܗܒ] *pr.* ܘ S   ܬܘܒ] *after* ܕܡܦܩܬ *in* S   ܕܢܦܩ ܠܟ] + ܚܠܦܘܗܝ S   36 ܩܪܝܒܗ S   39 ܕܡܪܢ] ܕܝܫܘܥ S   ܡ̈ܠܘܗܝ] ܡܠܬܗ S   40 ܣܓܝܐܬܐ] *om.* S   ܕܐܫܡܫ] ܠܡܫܡܫܘ S   41 ܐܡܪ ܠܗ̇] ܥܢܐ ܝܫܘܥ. ܘܐܡܪ ܠܗ S   ܝܨܦܬܝ ܘܦܠܝܓܐ........ܡܬܒܥܝܐ] *om.* S   42 ܘܠܐ] ܕܠܐ S   1 ܕܝܢ] *om.* S   ܚܕܐ] S *illegible (? om.)*   ܩܠܝܠ] *om.* S   2 ܘܐܡܪ S   ܐܒܘܢ ܕܒܫܡܝܐ] ܐܒܐ S: *for Thos*[313], *see on* Matt vi 9—13

34 on him. And he drew nigh and bound up his wounds and poured upon *C S*
them wine and oil, and made him ride on his ass and brought him to
35 an inn and nourished him. And on the morrow of the day he paid
out two denars *and* gave *them* to the innkeeper, and said: 'Nourish
him; and what *time* I have returned, that which it doth cost thee
36 again I will repay thee.' Which is it of these three appeareth to
thee that he was the neighbour of him that fell into the hands of the
37 robbers?" He saith to him: "He that had compassion on him."
Jesus saith to him: "Go, and thou also so be doing."

38 And while they were going in the way he entered a certain village,
and a certain woman whose name *was* Martha received him in her
39 house; and she had a sister whose name *was* Mary, and she came
40 *and* sat at the feet of our Lord and was hearing his words. Now
Martha was occupied in much serving, and she came *and* saith to
him: "My Lord, carest thou not for me, that my sister hath left me
41 alone to serve? Say to her to help me." He saith to her: "Martha,
Martha, †my anxiety† and perturbation for me thou hast about many
42 things; but one thing is required. Mary the good part hath chosen
for herself, and it shall not be taken away from her."

xi 1 Now when he was praying in a certain place, after he departed a
little from his prayer, one of his disciples said to him: "Our Lord,
2 teach us to pray, as John taught his disciples." He saith to them:
"Whensoever ye are praying, be saying: Our Father in heaven, thy
3 name be hallowed. And thy kingdom come. And give us the con-

---

34 drew nigh] drew near *S* and bound] *and* bound *S* poured] put *S* oil and wine *S* **35** *and* gave] and gave *S* again] *after* 'returned' *in S* cost thee] + for him *S* **39** our Lord] Jesus *S* E^{98} his words] his word *S* **40** much] *om. S* for me] *so also* E^{98} **41** He saith] Jesus answered and said *S* my anxiety.....required] *om. S*: *see Notes*, vol. ii **42** and it] that *S* **1** Now when] When *S* certain] *S illegible* (? *om.*) a little] *om. S* **2** He] And he *S* Our Father in heaven] Father *S*: *for* $Thos^{313}$, *see on* Matt vi 9—13

⁴ܘܫܒܘܩ ܠܢ ܚܛܗܝܢ. ܘܐܦ ܚܢܢ ܢܫܒܘܩ ܠܟܠ ܕܚܝܒ ܠܢ. ܘܠܐ C S
ܬܥܠܢ ܠܢܣܝܘܢܐ. ܐܠܐ ܦܨܢ ܡܢ ܒܝܫܐ. ⁵ܘܐܡܪ ܠܗܘܢ ܡܪܢ.
ܡܢܘ ܡܢܟܘܢ ܕܢܗܘܐ ܠܗ ܪܚܡܐ. ܘܢܐܙܠ ܠܘܬܗ ܒܦܠܓܘܬ
ܠܠܝܐ. ܘܢܐܡܪ ܠܗ ܪܚܡܝ ܐܫܐܠܢܝ ܬܠܬ ܓܪ̈ܝܨܢ. ⁶ܡܛܠ
ܕܪܚܡܝ ܐܬܐ ܠܘܬܝ، ܡܢ ܐܘܪܚܐ. ܘܠܝܬ ܠܝ ܡܕܡ ܕܐܣܝܡ
ܩܕܡܘܗܝ. ⁷ܘܗܢܐ ܡܢ ܠܓܘ ܘܢܐܡܪ ܠܗ ܠܐ ܬܗܪܢܝ. ܡܛܠ
ܕܬܪܥܐ ܐܚܝܕ ܗܘ. ܘܛ̈ܠܝܐ ܥܡܝ ܒܥܪܣܐ. ܠܐ ܡܫܟܚܢܐ
fol 63 v ܕܐܩܘܡ *ܐܬܠ ܠܟ. ⁸ܐܡܪ ܐܢܐ ܠܟܘܢ ܕܐܢ ܡܛܠ ܪܚܡܘܬܐ
ܠܐ ܢܩܘܡ ܢܬܠ ܠܗ. ܡܛܠ ܚܨܝܦܘܬܗ ܢܩܘܡ ܘܢܬܠ ܠܗ ܟܡܐ
ܕܡܬܒܥܐ ܠܗ. ⁹ܘܐܦ ܐܢܐ ܐܡܪܢܐ ܠܟܘܢ ܫܐܠܘ ܘܢܬܝܗܒ
ܠܟܘܢ܆ ܩܘܫܘ ܘܢܬܦܬܚ ܠܟܘܢ܆ ¹⁰ܟܠ ܐܢܫ ܓܝܪ ܕܫܐܠ ܢܣܒ.
ܘܟܠ ܕܒܥܐ ܡܫܟܚ. ܘܟܠ ܕܢܩܫ ܡܬܦܬܚ ܠܗ. ¹¹ܐܝܢܐ ܕܝܢ
ܡܢܟܘܢ ܕܐܒܘܗܝ، ܒܪܗ ܠܚܡܐ. ܠܡܐ ܗܘ ܟܐܦܐ ܡܘܫܛ
ܠܗ. ܐܘ ܐܦ ܢܘܢܐ ܢܫܐܠܝܘܗܝ، ܕܠܡܐ ܚܠܦ ܢܘܢܐ ܚܘܝܐ ܡܘܫܛ
ܠܗ. ¹²ܐܘ ܐܦ ܒܪܬܐ ܢܫܐܠܝܘܗܝ، ܕܠܡܐ ܥܩܪܒܐ ܡܘܫܛ ܠܗ.
¹³ܘܐܢ ܐܢܬܘܢ ܕܒ̈ܝܫܐ ܐܢܬܘܢ܆ ܝܕܥܝܢ ܐܢܬܘܢ ܡܘ̈ܗܒܬܐ
ܛܒ̈ܬܐ ܠܡܬܠ ܠܒ̈ܢܝܟܘܢ܆ ܟܡܐ ܡܝܬܪܐܝܬ ܐܒܘܟܘܢ ܡܢ ܫܡܝܐ. col 2
ܢܬܠ ܪܘܚܐ ܩܕܝܫܬܐ ܠܐܝܠܝܢ ܕܫܐܠܝܢ ܠܗ. ·:·
¹⁴ܘܗܘܐ ܟܕ ܡܦܩ ܗܘܐ ܫܐܕܐ ܡܢ ܚܪܫܐ. ܘܟܕ ܢܦܩ ܗܘ
ܫܐܕܐ ܡܠܠ ܗܘ ܚܪܫܐ. ܘܐܬܕܡܪܘ ܗܘܘ ܟܢ̈ܫܐ ܗܢܘܢ܆

---

4 ܘܫܒܘܩ S ܘܫܒܘܩ ܚܢܢ ܢܫܒܘܩ] ܐܝܟ ܫܒܩܝܢ ܐܦ S ܐܠܐ ܦܨܢ ܡܢ ܒܝܫܐ] om. S 5. § in S ܕܗܝܡܢܘܬܐ] ܕܐܝܬ S 6 ܕܪܚܡܝ] ܕܪܚܡܐ S ܐܬܐ ܠܘܬܝ] ܚܕܐ ܠܝ S 7 ܘܗܢܐ] ܘܗܘ ܗܢܐ S ܘܢܐܡܪ] ܘܐܡܪ S ܘܛ̈ܠܝܐ] so also S^vid: ܒܢܝܐ S^ed ܠܐ ܡܫܟܚ ܐܢܐ S (but ܐܡܪܢܐ ver. 8)
8 ܢܩܘܡ 1°] om. S ܡܛܠ 2°] pr. ܘ S^ed: the ܘ does not shew on the photograph ܚܨܝܦܘܬܐ S ܠܗ ܟܡܐ] ܠܗ. ܟܡܐ S 9 ܩܘܫܘ] pr. ܒܥܘ ܘܬܫܟܚܘܢ S
10 ܕܢܩܫ] ܕܡܩܫ S (sic): cf xiii 25. For A 443, see on Matt vii 8
11 ܠܚܡܐ]......ܐܘ ܐܦ ܢܘܢܐ ܢܫܐܠܝܘܗܝ] ܢܘܢܐ S ܠܗ ult.] om. S 12 ܘܐܦ] ܐܦ S 13 ܡܝܬܪܐܝܬ] ܝܬܝܪ S ܡܢ ܫܡܝܐ] ܕܒܫܡܝܐ S^ed ܢܬܠ] pr. ܕ S^ed ܪܘܚܐ ܩܕܝܫܬܐ] ܛܒܬܐ S 14 ܗܘ ܫܐܕܐ] om. ܗܘ S ܗܢܘܢ] om. S

4 tinual bread of every day. And forgive us our sins, and we also will *C S*
forgive every one indebted to us. And make us not enter into
5 temptation, But deliver us from the Evil One." And Jesus said to
them: "Which is there of you who shall have a friend, and he shall
go unto him in the middle of the night and say to him, 'My friend,
6 let me borrow three loaves, because my friend hath come unto me
7 from the way, and I have nothing to set before him'; and he will
answer from within and say to him, 'Do not injure me, because the
door is shut and the children are with me in the bed, I cannot rise
8 *and* give to thee.' I say to you If because of friendship he will not
rise *and* give to him, because of his importunity he will rise, and give
9 him as much as is required for him. And I also, I say to you: Ask,
and it shall be given to you; knock, and it shall be opened to you.
10 For every man that asketh receiveth, and every one that seeketh
11 findeth, and every one that knocketh—it is opened to him. Now which
of you whose son shall ask him for bread—doth he hand him a stone?
Or if for a fish he should ask—doth he instead of a fish give him a
12 serpent? And if for an egg he should ask—doth he hand him a
13 scorpion? And if ye that are evil know good gifts to give to your
sons, how much rather the Father from heaven will give a holy Spirit
to them that ask him?"

14 And it came to pass when he was casting out a devil from a deaf-
mute, that when that devil went forth that deaf-mute spake. And

---

4 we also will forgive] we also ourselves forgive *S* But.....Evil One] *om. S* 5 shall have] hath *S* 6 my friend] a friend *S* come unto me] *suddenly* visited me *S*: *cf* Matt xvii 15 7 he will] he—he will *S* and the children] *so also* S^{vid}: the sons S^{ed} 8 rise *and*] *om. S* because 2°] *pr.* yet S^{ed}: *for the construction see* ix 58 *and Introd.* vol. ii his] *om. S* 9 knock] *pr.* seek, and ye shall find *S* 10. *For A* 443 *see on* Matt vii 8 11 for bread.... he should ask] for a fish *S* him *ult.*] *om. S* 12 And if] If *S* 13 from heaven] ⌜in⌝ heaven S^{ed} (*the decisive letters being illegible*) a holy Spirit (*cf* Lk ii 25, 26)] good things *S* 14 that devil] the devil *S*

C S [15]ܘܐ̈ܢܫܝܢ ܡܢ ܦ̈ܪܝܫܐ ܐܡܪܘ. ܒܒܥܠܙܒܘܒ ܪܫܐ ܕܫ̈ܐܕܐ ܡܦܩ
ܗܢܐ ܫ̈ܐܕܐ. [16]ܐ̈ܚܪܢܐ ܕܝܢ ܟܕ ܡܢܣܝܢ ܗܘܘ ܠܗ ܐܬܐ ܡܢ
ܫܡܝܐ ܫܐܠܝܢ ܗܘܘ ܠܗ. [17]ܗܘ ܕܝܢ ܟܕ ܝܕܥ ܡܚܫܒܬܗܘܢ ܐܡܪ
ܠܗܘܢ܆ ܟܠ ܡܠܟܘ ܕܬܬܦܠܓ ܥܠ ܢܦܫܗ̇ ܬܚܪܒ܂ ܘܒܝܬ ܥܠ ܒܝܬܐ
ܕܥܠ ܒܝܬܐ ܡܬܦܠܓ ܢܦܠ ܠܗ. [18]ܘܐܢ ܣܛܢܐ ܥܠ ܢܦܫܗ
fol 64 r ܐܬܦܠܓ ܐܝܟܢܐ ܬܩܘܡ *ܡܠܟܘܬܗ. ܕܐܡܪܝܢ ܐܢܬܘܢ ܕܒܒܥܠܙܒܘܒ
ܡܦܩ ܐܢܐ ܫ̈ܐܕܐ. [19]ܘܐܢ ܕܝܢ ܐܢܐ ܒܒܥܠܙܒܘܒ ܡܦܩ ܐܢܐ
ܫ̈ܐܕܐ ܡܢ ܒ̈ܢܝܟܘܢ܂ ܒܡܢܐ ܡܦܩܝܢ ܠܗܘܢ܆ ܡܛܠ
ܗܢܐ ܗܢܘܢ ܢܗܘܘܢ ܠܟܘܢ ܕ̈ܝܢܐ܂ [20]ܐܢ ܕܝܢ ܒܨܒܥܐ
ܕܐܠܗܐ ܡܦܩ ܐܢܐ ܫ̈ܐܕܐ. ܡܛܠ ܩܪܒܬ ܥܠܝܟܘܢ ܡܠܟܘܬܗ
ܕܐܠܗܐ. [21]ܐܡܬܝ ܕܝܢ ܕܚܣܝܢܐ ܟܕ ܡܙܝܢ ܢܛܪ ܕܪܬܗ ܒܫܝܢܐ ܗܘ
ܩܢܝܢܗ. [22]ܐܢ ܕܝܢ ܢܐܬܐ ܡܢ ܕܚܣܝܢ ܡܢܗ ܘܢܙܟܝܘܗܝ܆ ܘܢܫܩܘܠ
ܙܝܢܗ ܗܘ ܕܬܟܝܠ ܗܘܐ ܥܠܘܗܝ܆ ܘܐܦ ܬܠܝܠܗ ܡܦܠܓ ܠܗ.
[23]ܡܢ ܕܠܐ ܗܘܐ ܥܡܝ ܠܘܩܒܠܝ ܗܘ. ܘܡܢ ܕܠܐ ܟܢܫ ܥܡܝ
ܡܒܕܪܘ ܡܒܕܪ ܀

col 2 *[24]ܪܘܚܐ ܛܢܦܬܐ ܡܐ ܕܢܦܩܬ ܡܢ ܒܪ ܐܢܫܐ. ܐܙܠܐ ܡܬܟܪܟܐ
ܒܐܬܪ̈ܘܬܐ ܕܡ̈ܝܐ ܠܝܬ ܒܗܘܢ ܕܬܬܢܝܚ ܠܗ̇ ܢܝܚܐ. ܘܟܕ ܠܐ
ܕܠܐ ܐܫܟܚܬ ܐܡܪܐ. ܐܗܦܘܟ ܐܙܠ ܠܒܝܬܝ ܡܢ ܐܝܟܐ
ܕܢܦܩܬ. [25]ܘܡܟܐ ܕܐܬܬ ܘܐܫܟܚܬ ܕܡܟܢܫ ܘܡܨܒܬ. [26]ܐܙܠܐ ܕܒܪܐ
ܥܡܗ̇ ܫ̈ܒܥ ܐ̈ܚܪܢܝܢ ܕܒܝܫܝܢ ܡܢܗ̇. ܘܥܠܝܢ ܘܡܥܡܪܢ ܒܗ̇. ܘܗܘܝܐ
ܐܚܪܝܬܗ ܕܗܘ ܓܒܪܐ ܒܝܫܐ ܡܢ ܩܕܡܝܬܗ. ܀

---

15 ܡܦܩ] ⌜ܡܦܩ⌝ ܗܢܐ ܫ̈ܐܕܐ | ** ܫܐܕܐ *S*^ed (? *om.* ܗܢܐ, *with nothing lost*)
16 ܫܐܠܝܢ ܗܘܘ ܠܗ] *before* ܐܬܐ ܡܢ ܫܡܝܐ *S* 17 ܟܕ] *om.* *S*^ed 18 ܐܬܦܠܓ *S*
19 ܕܝܢ.....ܡܦܩܝܢ ܠܗܘܢ] *S illegible* 20 ܡܠܟܘܬܐ *S* 21 ܕܚܣܝܢܐ]
om. ܕ *S* 23 *After* ܡܒܕܪܘ *comes an illegible word in S: probably it is* ܠܝ,
as in ℵ*L boh aeth 24. *No* § *in S* ܬܬܟܪܟ *S*^ed ܡܬܟܪܟܐ]
+ܡܢ ܥܠܡܐ *S* ⌜ܒܗܘܢ⌝ ܒܗܘܢ] *S*^ed ܡܢ 2°] *om.* *S*^ed 25 ܘܡܟܐ] *om.* ܘ *S*
ܘܐܫܟܚܬ] *om.* ܘ *S* 26 ܐܙܠܐ] *pr.* ܗܝܕܝܢ *S* ܫ̈ܒܥ] *om.* *S* ܕܒܝܫ]
om. ܕ *S*^ed ܒܪ ܐܢܫܐ *S*

15 those multitudes had wondered; and some of the Pharisees said: *C S*
"By Beelzebub the chief of the demons this *fellow* doth cast out
16 devils." But others, tempting him, for a sign from heaven were
17 asking him. Now he when he knew their meditation said to them:
"Every kingdom that shall be divided against itself shall be desolated,
18 and every house that against a house is divided falleth. And if Satan
against himself hath been divided, how will his kingdom stand, that ye
19 *should* say that by Beelzebub I cast out devils? But if I by Beelzebub
cast out devils from your sons, your sons—by what do they cast them
20 out? Therefore they shall be for you judges. But if by the finger
of God I cast out devils, henceforth the kingdom of God hath drawn
21 nigh upon you. Now whensoever the strong man armed keepeth
22 his court, in tranquillity is his property; but if there shall come one
that is stronger than he and shall overcome him, he will take away
his armour which he trusted in, and his plunder also he divideth for
23 himself. He that is not with me is against me, and he that gathereth
not with me scattereth indeed.

24 "The unclean spirit, what *time* it hath come forth from a man,
goeth travelling about in places where there is no water, that it may
find for itself ease; and what *time* it hath found none it saith: 'I will
25 return *and* go to my house from whence I came forth.' And what
26 *time* it hath come and found *it* swept and garnished, it goeth *and*
taketh seven other spirits worse than itself, and they enter and dwell
therein, and the last *state* of that man becometh worse than his
first *state*."

---

those] the *S* 15 Beelzebub] Beelzebul $E^{75,160,206}$: *cf* Matt xii 24 16 were asking him for a sign from heaven *S* 17 when he knew.... said] knew.... *and* said *S* 18 hath been] shall be *S* 19 But.... cast them out] *S illegible* 23. *At the end of the verse is an illegible word in S: probably we should read* 'scattereth ⌜me⌝ indeed', *as in* ℵ*L boh aeth 24 travelling about] + suddenly *S* from whence] *om.* from *S* 25 And what] What *S* and found] *and* found *S*: *for the construction see Notes*, vol. ii 26 it goeth] *pr.* then *S*

CS 27ܘܟܕ ܐܡܪ ܗܠܝܢ. ܐܢܬܬܐ ܚܕܐ ܡܢ ܓܘ ܟܢܫܐ. ܒܩܠܐ ܪܡܐ
ܐܡܪܬ ܠܗ. ܛܘܒܝܗ ܠܟܪܣܐ ܕܫܩܠܬܟ. ܘܠܬ̈ܕܝܐ ܕܐܝܢܩܬܟ.
fol 64 v 28ܐܡܪ ܠܗ̇ ܝܫܘܥ. ܛܘܒܝܗܘܢ ܠܐܝܠܝܢ *ܕܫܡܥܝܢ ܡܠܬܗ ܕܐܠܗܐ
ܘܢܛܪܝܢ ܠܗ̇.܀

29ܘܟܕ ܡܬܟܢܫܝܢ ܗܘܘ ܟܢ̈ܫܐ. ܫܪܝ ܠܡܐܡܪ. ܫܪܒܬܐ ܗܕܐ
ܫܪܒܬܐ ܗܝ ܒܝܫܬܐ. ܐܬܐ ܒܥܝܐ ܘܐܬܐ ܠܐ ܬܬܝܗܒ ܠܗ̇.
30ܐܠܐ ܐܝܟܢܐ ܕܗܘܐ ܝܘܢܢ ܐܬܐ ܠܢܝܢܘܝ̈ܐ. ܗܟܢܐ ܐܦ ܒܪܗ
ܕܐܢܫܐ ܠܫܪܒܬܐ ܗܕܐ. 31ܡܠܟܬܐ ܕܬܝܡܢܐ ܬܩܘܡ ܒܕܝܢܐ ܥܡ
ܫܪܒܬܐ ܗܕܐ ܘܬܚܝܒ ܐܢܘܢ̈. ܕܐܬܬ ܡܢ ܥ̈ܒܪܝܗ ܕܐܪܥܐ.
ܕܬܫܡܥ ܚܟܡܬܗ ܕܫܠܝܡܘܢ. ܘܗܐ ܕܝܢ ܡܢ ܫܠܝܡܘܢ ܗܪܟܐ.
32ܓܒܪ̈ܐ ܒܢ̈ܝ ܢܝܢܘܐ ܢܩܘܡܘܢ ܒܕܝܢܐ ܥܡ ܫܪܒܬܐ ܗܕܐ
ܘܢܚܝܒܘܢܗ̇. ܕܬܒܘ ܠܗܘܢ ܒܟܪܘܙܘܬܗ ܕܝܘܢܢ. ܘܗܐ ܕܝܢ ܡܢ
ܝܘܢܢ ܗܪܟܐ..

col 2
§A 14 §*33ܠܐ ܐܢܫ ܡܢܗܪ ܫܪܓܐ ܘܣܐܡ ܠܗ ܬܚܝܬ ܣܐܬܐ. ܐܘ
ܒܐܬܪܐ ܛܫܝܐ. ܐܠܐ ܣܐܡ ܠܗ ܠܥܠ ܡܢ ܡܢܪܬܐ. ܕܐܝܠܝܢ
¶A ܕܥܐܠܝܢ ܢܚܙܘܢ ܢܘܗܪܗ.¶ 34ܫܪܓܗ ܕܦܓܪܐ ܥܝܢܐ ܗܝ. ܐܡܬܝ
ܕܥܝܢܟ ܗܟܝܠ ܬܗܘܐ ܦܫܝܛܐ ܐܦ ܦܓܪܟ ܟܠܗ ܢܗܝܪ ܗܘ.
ܐܢ ܕܝܢ ܥܝܢܟ ܬܗܘܐ ܒܝܫܐ ܐܦ ܦܓܪܟ ܟܠܗ ܚܫܘܟ ܗܘ.
35ܬܗܘܐ ܗܟܝܠ ܙܗܝܪ ܕܠܡܐ ܢܘܗܪܐ ܕܒܟ ܚܫܘܟ ܠܗ. 36ܘܐܢ
ܢܘܗܪܐ ܕܒܟ ܚܫܘܟ ܗܘ. ܚܫܘܟܟ ܒܡܐ ܢܗܘܐ.܀

27, 29. ܘܟܕ *begins a line but apparently not a* § *in S*   28 ܕܫܡܥܝܢ] ܕܫܡܥܘ S
29 ܘܐܬܐ] *om.* ܘ S   ܠܗ̇] ܠܗܘܢ ܠܫܪܒܬܐ S   30 ܐܠܐ] + ܐܬܐ ܕܝܘܢܢ ܢܒܝܐ S
ܐܝܟܢܐ] + ܓܝܪ S^vid   32 ܢܝܢܘܐ] ܢܝܢܘܝ̈ S^ed, *but cf* Matt xxvii 65
33 ܬܚܝܬ ܣܐܬܐ. ܐܘ] *om.* S; + ܬܚܝܬ ܥܪܣܐ. ܐܘ A : *see* Lk viii 16
ܒܐܬܪܐ ܛܫܝܐ] ܒܛܫܝܐ S; *pr.* ܣܐܡ ܠܗ A   ܕܐܝܠܝܢ.....ܢܘܗܪܗ]
ܕܟܠ ܐܢܫ ܢܚܙܐ ܢܘܗܪܗ ܕܫܪܓܐ A   34 ܟܠܗ 2°] *om.* S   35 ܚܫܘܟ ܠܗ]
ܚܫܘܟ ܗܘ S   36. ܐܦ ܦܓܪܟ ܗܟܝܠ ܟܠܗ ܕܠܝܬ ܒܗ ܫܪܓܐ
ܕܒܢܘܗܪ ܗܘܐ ܚܫܘܟ. ܗܟܢܐ ܟܠܗ ܕܫܪܓܟ ܗܘܐ ܢܗܪ ܒܢܘܗܪ ܠܟ. S

27 And when he said these things a certain woman from the midst *C S*
of the multitude with a loud voice said to him: "Happy is it for the
womb that carried thee, and for the breasts that gave thee suck!"
28 Jesus saith to her: "Happy is it for them that hear the word of
God and keep it!"

29 And when the multitudes were gathering together he began to
say: "This generation is an evil generation; a sign it seeketh and a
30 sign shall not be given to it, save as Jonah was a sign to the Ninevites,
31 so the Son of Man also to this generation. The queen of the South
will stand up in judgement with this generation and will make them
guilty, in that she came from the other sides of the earth that she
might hear the wisdom of Solomon, and lo, a greater than Solomon is
32 here! The men-folk of Nineve will stand up in judgement with this
generation and will make it guilty, in that they repented at the
preaching of Jonah, and lo, a greater than Jonah is here!

33 "§No one lighteth a lamp and setteth it under the bushel or in a §*A* 14
concealed place, but he setteth it on the lamp-stand, that they which
34 enter in may see its light.¶ For the lamp of the body is the eye: ¶*A*
whensoever thine eye therefore shall be single, thy whole body also is
35 light; but if thine eye be evil, thy whole body also is dark. Be thou
36 therefore wary lest the light in thee should be darkened. And if the
light in thee is dark, thy darkness—how great it will be!"

---

28 hear] have heard *S* 29 seeketh and a sign] seeketh—a sign *S* to it] to them of heaven *S* 30 save] + the sign of Jonah the prophet *S* as] *pr.* for S^{vid} 33 under the bushel or] *om.* *S*; + under the bed or *A*: *see* Lk viii 16 *and cod. fuld.* (*Ranke*, p. 46) in a concealed place] in *aught* concealed *S*; *pr.* setteth it *A* that they....its light] that every one may see the light of the lamp *A* 34 whole 2°] *om.* *S* 35 should be] be *S* 36.] Thy body also, therefore, what *time* there is in it no lamp that shineth, becometh darkened; so, what *time* thy lamp becometh bright, it shineth for thee (*or*, 'maketh thee shine') *S*. *This recasting of ver.* 36 *is also found in the Latin* MSS *f q*: *see Notes*, vol. ii

C S 37ܘܒܥܐ ܗܘܐ ܡܢܗ ܦܪܝܫܐ ܚܕ ܕܢܫܬܪܐ ܠܘܬܗ. ܘܥܠ ܐܣܬܡܟ.
fol 65 r 38ܘܚܙܐ ܗܘܐ ܦܪܝܫܐ ܗܘ ܐܡܪ ܒܪܥܝܢܗ. *ܕܠܡܢܐ ܠܐ ܥܡܕ
ܡܢ ܩܕܡ ܫܪܘܬܗ. 39ܐܡܪ ܠܗ ܡܪܢ. ܐܢܬܘܢ܂ ܦܪ̈ܝܫܐ ܒܪܗ ܗܘ
ܕܟܣܐ ܘܕܦܝܢܟܐ ܡܕܟܝܢ ܐܢܬܘܢ܂ ܘܓܘܟܘܢ ܡܠܐ ܚܛܘܦܝܐ
ܘܒܝܫܘܬܐ. 40ܚܣܝ̈ܪܝ ܪܥܝܢܐ ܠܐ ܗܘܐ ܡܢ ܕܥܒܕ ܕܠܒܪ ܘܐܦ
ܕܠܓܘ ܗܘ ܥܒܕ. 41ܐܠܐ ܡܕܡ ܕܐܝܬ ܠܟܘ ܡܢܟܘܢ ܗܒܘܗܝ,
ܙܕܩܬܐ. ܘܗܐ ܟܠ ܡܕܡ ܕܟܐ ܗܘ ܠܟܘܢ܂ 42ܐܠܐ ܘܝ ܠܟܘܢ
ܦܪ̈ܝܫܐ ܘܣܦܪ̈ܐ. ܕܡܥܣܪܝܢ ܐܢܬܘܢ ܢܢܥܐ ܘܦܓܢܐ ܘܟܠܗܘܢ
ܝܪ̈ܩܘܢܐ. ܘܥܒܪܝܢ ܐܢܬܘܢ ܥܠ ܕܝܢܐ ܘܥܠ ܚܘܒܐ ܕܐܠܗܐ.
ܗܠܝܢ ܕܝܢ ܥܒܕܬܘܢ ܘܗܠܝܢ ܕܝܢ ܠܐ ܫܒܩܬܘܢ ܀
col 2 43ܘܝ ܠܟܘܢ ܣܦܪ̈ܐ ܘܦܪ̈ܝܫܐ. ܕܪܚܡܝܢ ܐܢܬܘܢ *ܡܘ̈ܬܒܐ ܩܕܡܝܐ
ܒܟܢܘ̈ܫܬܐ. ܘܫܠܡܐ ܒܫܘ̈ܩܐ. 44ܘܝ ܠܟܘܢ ܕܐܝܬܝܟܘܢ ܩܒ̈ܪܐ.
ܘܒ̈ܢܝ ܐܢܫܐ ܡܗܠܟܝܢ ܠܥܠ ܡܢܗܘܢ ܘܠܐ ܝܕܥܝܢ. 45ܘܥܢܐ ܚܕ
ܡܢ ܣܦܪ̈ܐ ܘܐܡܪ ܠܗ. ܡܠܦܢܐ. ܟܕ ܗܠܝܢ ܐܡܪ ܐܢܬ ܘܐܦ ܠܢ
ܡܨܥܪ ܐܢܬ. 46ܐܡܪ ܠܗ ܐܦ ܠܟܘܢ ܘܝ ܣܦܪ̈ܐ. ܕܡܛܥܢܝܢ ܐܢܬܘܢ
ܡܘܒܠܐ ܝܩܝܪܬܐ. ܘܣܝܡܝܢ ܐܢܬܘܢ ܥܠ ܟܬܦܬܐ ܕܒ̈ܢܝ ܐܢܫܐ.
ܘܐܢܬܘܢ ܐܦܠܐ ܒܚܕܐ ܡܢ ܨܒ̈ܥܬܟܘܢ ܩܪܒܝܢ ܐܢܬܘܢ ܠܗܝܢ.
47ܘܝ ܠܟܘܢ ܕܒܢܝܢ ܐܢܬܘܢ ܩܒ̈ܪܐ ܕܢܒ̈ܝܐ. ܕܐ̈ܒܗܝܟܘܢ ܩܛܠܘ
ܐܢܘܢ. 48ܡܛܠ ܣܗܕܝܢ ܐܢܬܘܢ ܘܡܫܬܘܕܝܢ ܐܢܬܘܢ ܒܥܒܕܐ
fol 65 v ܕܐ̈ܒܗܝܟܘܢ܂ ܘܐܢܬܘܢ *ܒܢ̈ܝܐ ܐܢܬܘܢ ܕܗܢܘܢ ܩܛ̈ܘܠܐ.

---

37 ܘܥܠ] ܥܠ *is illegible in S, and the construction of ver.* 38 *suggests* ܘܟܕ *here*
38 ܘܚܙܐ ܗܘܐ......ܒܪܥܝܢܗ] ܐܬܕܡܪ *S* (*sic*)   ܡܢ] *om. S*   39 ܡܪܢ] ܡܥܡܕ *S*   ܐܢܬܘܢ܂ *C* (*sic*), *with a red point*   ܒܪܗ ܗܘ] + ܡܢ ܒܪ *S*   40 ܘܐܦ] ܐܦ *S*   41 ܙܕܩܬܐ] *pr.* ܒ *S*   42 ܘܟܠܗܘܢ *S, as often*   ܘ ܦܪ̈ܝܫܐ] *om. S*   ܗܠܝܢ ܕܝܢ.....ܫܒܩܬܘܢ] ܗܠܝܢ ܘܠܐ ܗܘܐ ܕܬܫܒܩܘܢ ܘܐܦ ܗܠܝܢ ܠܐ ܬܥܒܕܘܢ *S*
43. *Cf also* Mt xxiii 6 ff   ܘ ܦܪ̈ܝܫܐ] *om. S*   44 ܩܒ̈ܪܐ] + ܕܠܐ ܚܙܝܢ ܐܢܬܘܢ *S*   ܡܢܗܘܢ] ܡܢܗܘܢ *S*   ܝܕܥܝܢ] + ܐܢܬܘܢ *S*   45 ܘܐܦ] ܐܦ *S*
46 ܘܝ] + ܠܟܘܢ *S*   ܕܡܛܥܢܝܢ ܐܢܬܘܢ] ܕܡܛܥܢܝܢ ܐܢܬܘܢ ܠܒ̈ܢܝ ܐܢܫܐ *S*   ܘܣܝܡܝܢ....ܐܢܫܐ] *om. S*   ܐܦܠܐ] *om. S*   ܩܪܒܝܢ] ܠܐ ܡܬܩܪܒܝܢ *S*
48 ܘܐܢܬܘܢ ܒܢ̈ܝܐ.....ܩܛ̈ܘܠܐ] ܕܗܢܘܢ ܩܛܠܘ ܐܢܘܢ ܘܐܢܬܘܢ ܒܢܝܢ ܐܢܬܘܢ *S*

37 And a certain Pharisee had besought him that he would breakfast *C S*
38 with him; and he entered *and* sat down *to meat*. And that Pharisee
had begun saying in his mind "Wherefore hath he not baptized
39 himself before his breakfast?" Our Lord saith to him: "Ye
Pharisees *indeed*! It is the outside of the cup and of the dish ye
40 cleanse, and your inside is full of extortion and evil. Ye lacking in
mind! Hath not he that made what *is* outside made what *is* inside
41 also? But that which is inside of you give *as* alms, and lo, every-
42 thing is clean to you! But woe to you scribes and Pharisees! Ye
that tithe mint and rue and all herbs, and pass over judgement and
the love of God. Now these ye have done, but these have ye not left?
43 "Woe to you scribes and Pharisees! Ye that love the honourable
44 seats in the synagogues, and greeting in the streets. Woe to you, ye
45 that are graves, and men walk upon you and know *it* not!" And
one of the scribes answered and said to him: "Teacher, when these
46 things thou sayest us also thou dost insult." He saith to him: "To
you also woe, ye scribes! Ye that take up heavy burdens and lay
them on the shoulders of men, and ye yourselves not even with one of
47 your fingers touch them. Woe to you, ye that build the graves of the
48 prophets whom your fathers killed! Hence ye bear witness to and
make confession of the deed of your fathers, and ye—ye are the sons

---

37, 38 and he entered.... breakfast?"] and ⌜when⌝ he sat down *to meat*, he wondered wherefore he had not baptized himself before his breakfast. *S* (*sic*), *but* 'when' *is illegible* 39 Our Lord] Jesus *S* It is] For it is *S* 41 *as* alms] in alms *S* 42 scribes and] *om. S* Now these..... left? (*cf* Mt xxiii 23)] These it behoved that they should be done and these also not be left! *S* 43. *For A* 269, *cf* Mt xxiii 6 ff, *and see* Diat[ar] xl 41 scribes and] *om. S* 44 graves] + that are not seen *S* upon you] upon them *S* know] ye know *S* 46 also woe] also—woe to you *S* take up] lade men with *S* and lay..... men] *om. S* not even] *om. S* touch] do not draw nigh to *S* 48 and ye.... the murderers] in that they killed them, and ye—ye build *S*

C S [49]ܡܛܠ ܗܢܐ ܚܟܡܬܐ ܕܐܠܗܐ ܐܡܪܬ. ܐܫܕܪ ܒܗܘܢ ܢܒܝܐ
ܘܫ̈ܠܝܚܐ. ܡܢܗܘܢ ܢܩܛܠܘܢ ܘܢܪܕܦܘܢ. [50]ܕܢܬܬܒܥ. ܕܡܐ
ܕܟܠܗܘܢ ܢܒܝܐ ܕܐܬܐܫܕ· ܗܐ ܡܢ ܕܐܬܒܪܝ ܥܠܡܐ. ܒܕܪܐ
ܗܢܐ ܫܪܒܬܐ. [51]ܡܢ ܕܡܗ ܕܗܒܝܠ ܘܥܕܡܐ ܠܕܡܗ ܕܙܟܪܝܐ ܒܪ
ܒܪܟܝܐ. ܗܘ ܕܐܬܩܛܠ ܒܝܢ ܡܕܒܚܐ ܠܗܝܟܠܐ. ܐܡܝܢ ܐܡܪܢܐ
ܠܟܘܢ ܕܢܬܬܒܥ ܡܢܗ ܡܢ ܫܪܒܬܐ ܗܕܐ.܀ ·

[52]ܘܝ ܠܟܘܢ ܣ̈ܦܪܐ ܕܫܩܠܬܘܢ ܩܠܝܕܐ ܕܐܝܕܥܬܐ. ܐܢܬܘܢ
ܠܐ ܥܠܬܘܢ ܘܠܐܝܠܝܢ ܕܥܐܠܝܢ ܟܠܝܬܘܢ. [53]ܘܟܕ ܐܡܪ ܗܘܐ ܗܠܝܢ
col 2 ܠܘܩܒܠܗܘܢ ܠܥܝܢ ܟܠܗ ܥܡܐ. ܫܪܝ ܡܬܟܬܫ *ܗܘܐ ܠܦ̈ܪܝܫܐ
ܘܣ̈ܦܪܐ. ܘܕܪܫܝܢ ܗܘܘ ܥܡܗ ܥܠ ܣܓܝ̈ܐܬܐ. [54]ܘܒܥܝܢ ܗܘܘ
ܠܡܐܚܕ ܥܠܘܗܝ ܥܠܬܐ ܕܢܫܟܚܘܢ ܢܐܟܠܘܢ ܩܪ̈ܨܘܗܝ. [1]ܘܟܕ
ܟܢܫ ܥܠܘܗܝ ܟܢܫܐ ܣܓܝܐܐ. ܐܝܟܢܐ ܕܢܕܘܫܘܢ ܚܕ ܠܚܕ. ܫܪܝ
ܗܘܐ ܠܡܐܡܪ ܠܬܠܡ̈ܝܕܘܗܝ. ܠܘܩܕܡ ܐܙܕܗܪܘ ܡܢ ܚܡܝܪܐ
ܕܦ̈ܪܝܫܐ ܕܐܝܬܘܗܝ، ܡܣܒ ܒܐ̈ܦܐ. [2]ܠܝܬ ܓܝܪ ܡܕܡ ܕܟܣܐ
ܕܠܐ ܢܬܓܠܐ. ܘܠܐ ܕܡܛܫܝ ܕܠܐ ܢܬܝܕܥ· [3]ܐܝܠܝܢ ܓܝܪ ܕܒܚܫܘܟܐ
ܐܡܪܬܘܢ ܒܢܘܗܪܐ ܢܫܬܡܥܢ· ܘܡܕܡ ܕܒܬ̈ܘܢܐ ܒܐܕ̈ܢܐ
ܠܚܫܬܘܢ ܥܠ ܐ̈ܓܪܐ ܢܬܟܪܙ ܀

fol 66 r [4]ܐܡܪܢܐ ܠܟܘܢ ܕܝܢ ܪ̈ܚܡܝ. ܠܐ ܬܕܚܠܘܢ ܡܢ ܐܝܠܝܢ *ܕܩܛܠܝܢ
ܦܓܪܐ. ܘܡܢ ܒܬܪܟܢ ܡܕܡ ܠܐ ܡܫܟܚܝܢ ܠܡܥܒܕ. [5]ܐܚܘܝܟܘܢ
ܕܝܢ ܡܢ ܡܢܘ ܬܕܚܠܘܢ. ܕܚܠܘ ܡܢ ܗܘ ܕܡܢ ܒܬܪ ܕܩܛܠ ܫܠܝܛ
ܠܗ ܠܡܪܡܝܘ ܒܓܗܢܐ. ܐܝܢ ܐܡܪܢܐ ܠܟܘܢ ܕܡܢ ܗܢܐ ܘܠܐ
ܠܡܕܚܠ· [6]ܫܬ̈ܝܢ ܨ̈ܦܪܝܢ ܡܙܕܒܢܢ ܒܐܣܪ. ܘܚܕܐ ܡܢܗܝܢ ܠܐ ܛܥܝܐ

---

49 ܐܫܕܪ] *pr.* ܕ *S*   50 ܕܢܬܒܥ *S* (*and in ver.* 51)   ܗܐ] *so also S*
51 ܘܥܕܡܐ] *om.* ܘ *S*   ܒܪ ܒܪܟܝܐ] *om. S*   ܒܝܬ *S*   ܡܢܗ ܡܢ] ܡܢ ܐܢܫ *S*
52. *No* § *in S*   ܘܠܟܘܢ *S*   ܕܝܕܥܬܐ *S*   53 ܠܘܩܒܠܗܘܢ *S*   ܘܠܦ̈ܪܝܫܐ *S*
54 ܕܢܫܟܚܘܢ ܢܐܟܠܘܢ ܩܪ̈ܨܘܗܝ] *om. S*   1 ܕܢܕܘܫܘܢ *S* (*sic*)   ܠܘܩܕܡ] *om. S*
2 *Cf* ܘܠܝܬ ܡܕܡ ܕܟܣܐ. ܕܠܐ ܠܥܠ ܒܪܫܐ ܢܬܓܠܐ *A* 443   3 ܒܢܘܗܪܐ]
ܒܢܘܗܪܐ *S*   4. *No* § *in S*   5 ܐܚܘܝܟܘܢ *S*   ܡܢ ܡܢܘ] ܡܢ ܡܢ *S*   ܐܝܢ]
ܐܝ *S* (*sic*)   ܘܠܐ] *om. S*   6 ܫܬ̈ܝܢ] + ܓܝܪ *S*   ܒܐܣܪ] ܒܬܪܝܢ ܐܣܪ̈ܝܢ *S*

49 of those, the murderers! Therefore the wisdom of God hath said: *C S*
'I will send among them prophets and apostles; some of them they
50 will kill and persecute, that the blood of all the prophets may be
requited that hath been shed, lo, from *the time* that the world was
51 created unto this generation, from the blood of Habel even unto the
blood of Zacharia son of Barachia, him that was killed between the
altar and the Temple.' Amen, I say to you that it will be requited
from this same generation.

52 "Woe to you, scribes, that have concealed the keys of knowledge!
Ye yourselves have not entered, and them that are entering ye have
53 hindered." And when he was saying these things against them in the
sight of all the people it began to be displeasing to the scribes and
54 Pharisees, and they were disputing with him about many things, and
were seeking to take hold of a pretext against him, that they might
xii 1 be able to accuse him. And when a great multitude was gathered
unto him, so as to trample one on the other, he had begun to say to
his disciples: "First beware of the leaven of the Pharisees, which is
2 respect of persons. For there is nothing secret that shall not be
3 revealed, nor *aught* concealed that shall not be known. For what
things in the darkness ye have said in the light shall be heard, and
that which in the inner chambers in the ears ye have whispered on
the roofs shall be preached.

4 "Now I say to you, my friends: Be ye not afraid of them that kill
5 the body, and afterwards nothing are able to do. But I will shew
you of whom ye shall be afraid; be afraid of him who after he killeth
hath authority to cast into Gehenna—yea, I say to you that of him it
6 behoves to be afraid. Five sparrows are sold for a farthing, and not

---

50 lo] *so also S* 51 even] *om. S* son of Barachia] *om. S* (*E*[211]) this same] the hands of this *S* 52 have concealed] *This may be read as a present tense: cf* 'Woe to you, lawyers, for ye hide the key' *E*[211] 53 Pharisees] to the Pharisees *S* 54 that they might....accuse him] *om. S* 1 First beware] Beware *S* 2 *Cf* 'And there is nothing secret that shall not to every man be revealed' *A* 443 3 light] daylight *S* 5 that & it behoves] *om. S* 6 Five] For five *S* a farthing] two farthings *S*

C S ܩܕܡ ܐܠܗܐ. 7ܐܦ ܣ̈ܥܪܐ ܓܝܪ ܕܪܫܟܘܢ ܡܢܝܢ ܐܢܝܢ
ܠܗ. ܠܐ ܗܟܝܠ ܬܕܚܠܘܢ. ܡܛܠ ܕܡܢ ܣܓܝܐܐ ܕܨ̈ܦܪܐ ܛܒ
ܡܝܬܪܝܢ ܐܢܬܘܢ. 8ܐܡܪܢܐ ܠܟܘܢ ܕܝܢ ܕܟܠ ܕܢܘܕܐ ܒܝ ܩܕܡ
ܒ̈ܢܝ ܐܢܫܐ. ܐܦ ܒܪܗ ܕܐܢܫܐ ܢܘܕܐ ܒܗ ܩܕܡ ܡܠܐ̈ܟܘܗܝ
col 2 ܩ̈ܕܝܫܐ. 9ܘܐܝܢܐ ܕܢܟܦܪ *ܒܝ ܩܕܡ ܒ̈ܢܝ ܐܢܫܐ. ܢܟܦܪ ܒܗ ܩܕܡ
ܡܠܐ̈ܟܘܗܝ ܕܐܠܗܐ. 10ܘܟܠ ܕܢܐܡܪ ܡܠܬܐ ܥܠ ܒܪܗ ܕܐܢܫܐ
ܢܫܬܒܩ ܠܗ. ܡܢ ܕܥܠ ܪܘܚܐ ܕܝܢ ܕܩܘܕܫܐ ܢܓܕܦ ܠܐ ܢܫܬܒܩ
ܠܗ. 11ܡܐ ܕܡܩܪܒܝܢ ܠܟܘܢ ܕܝܢ ܠܟܢ̈ܘܫܬܐ ܩܕܡ ܐܪ̈ܟܘܣ ܘܫ̈ܠܝܛܢܐ.
ܠܐ ܬܐܨܦܘܢ ܕܐܝܟܢܐ ܬܦܩܘܢ ܪܘܚܐ. ܐܘ ܡܢܐ ܬܡܠܠܘܢ.
12ܪܘܚܐ ܓܝܪ ܕܩܘܕܫܐ ܬܠܦܟܘܢ ܒܗ̇ ܫܥܬܐ ܡܕܡ ܕܘܠܐ
ܕܬܐܡܪܘܢ. ○○ ○○○○ ○○

13ܘܐܡܪ ܠܗ ܓܒܪܐ ܚܕ ܡܢ ܗܘ ܟܢܫܐ. ܡܠܦܢܐ. ܐܡܪ ܠܐܚܝ
ܦܠܓ ܥܡܝ ܐܪܥܐ ܘܝܪܬܘܬܐ. 14ܗܘ ܕܝܢ ܐܡܪ ܠܗ. ܓܒܪܐ ܡܢ
fol 66 v ܐܩܝܡܢܝ ܥܠܝܟܘܢ ܕܝܢܐ. 15ܘܐܡܪ ܠܟܢܫܐ. ܐܙܕܗܪܘ *ܡܢ ܟܘܠܗ̇
ܥܘܠܬܐ. ܡܛܠ ܕܠܐ ܗܘܐ ܒܡܘ̈ܬܪܢܐ ܕܢܟܣܐ ܣ̈ܓܝܐܐ ܗܘܝܢ
ܚܝ̈ܐ ܠܒ̈ܢܝ ܐ̈ܢܫܐ. ܀

16ܘܐܡܪ ܗܘܐ ܡܬܠܐ ܗܢܐ ܠܬܠܡܝܕܘܗܝ. ܓܒܪܐ ܚܕ ܥܬܝܪܐ
ܐܥܠܬ ܗܘܬ ܠܗ ܐܪܥܗ ܥܠܠܬܐ ܣ̈ܓܝܐܬܐ. 17ܘܡܬܚܫܒ ܗܘܐ
ܒܢܦܫܗ ܘܐܡܪ. ܡܢܐ ܐܥܒܕ ܕܠܝܬ ܠܝ ܐܝܟܐ ܕܐܟܢܘܫ
ܥܠܠܬܝ. 18ܐܣܬܪܘ ܒܝܬ ܩܘ̈ܫܝ ܘܐܒܢܐ ܐܘܪܒ ܐܢܘܢ. ܘܐܟܢܘܫ
§*A* 381 ܒܗܘܢ ܥܠܠܬܝ. 19§ܘܐܡܪ ܠܢܦܫܝ. ܕܗܘܐ ܛܒ̈ܬܐ ܣܓܝ̈ܐܬܐ

---

7 ܠܗ] *om. S* ܣܓܝܐܐ ܕܨ̈ܦܪܐ] ܨܦܪܐ ܣܓܝܐܐ *S* ܛܒ ܡܝܬܪܝܢ] ܝܬܝܪܝܢ *S* 8 ܕܝܢ] ܓܝܪ *S* ܩ̈ܕܝܫܐ] ܕܐܠܗܐ *S* 9.] *om. S* 11 ܘܫ̈ܠܝܛܢܐ] *so also S* ܕܐܝܟܢܐ] ܐܝܟܢܐ *S* ܬܡܠܠܘܢ] ܬܐܡܪܘܢ *S*
Cf A 415: ܐܡܬܝ ܕܡܩܪܒܝܢ ܠܟܘܢ ܩܕܡ ܐܪ̈ܟܘܣ ܘܩܕܡ ܫ̈ܠܝܛܢܐ (ܫܠܝܛܢܐ *A*[b]).
For the rest of the quotation see Lk xxi 12 ff 12 ܓܝܪ] ܕܝܢ *S* ܕܘܠܐ] *om. S*
13 ܘ ܓܒܪܐ] *om. S* 14 ܡܢ] ܡܢܘ *S* 15 ܣ̈ܓܝܐܐ] *om. S*
16 ܘܐܡܪ ܠܗܘܢ ܡܬܠܐ ܗܢܐ. *S* 18 ܐܣܬܪܘ] *pr.* ܐܠܐ ܘܠܐ ܠܝ ܕ *S*
ܐܘܪܒ] *pr.* ܘ *S* 19 ܘܐܡܪ ܠܢܦܫܝ *S* (*not A*) ܕܗܘܐ] + ܠܟܝ *A*

7 one of them is lost before God; for even the locks of the hair of *C S*
your head are numbered by him. Be therefore not afraid, because
8 ye are much more than the multitude of sparrows. Now I say to you
Every one that shall confess me before men, the Son of Man also will
9 confess him before his holy angels; and he which denieth me before
10 men, there will be a denial of him before the angels of God. And
every one that shall say a word against the Son of Man, it shall be
forgiven him; but he that against the Holy Spirit shall blaspheme, it
11 shall not be forgiven him. Now what *time* they bring you up to
the synagogues before the ruling powers and authorities be ye not
12 anxious as to how ye shall make excuse or what ye shall speak, for
the Holy Spirit will teach you in that hour that which it behoves
that ye should say."

13 And a certain man from that multitude said to him: "Teacher,
say to my brother that he should divide with me the land and the
14 inheritance." But he said to him: "Man, who set me up over you
15 *to be* a judge?" And he said to the multitudes: "Beware ye of all
covetousness; because not in the superfluity of much wealth is life
to the sons of men."

16 And he was saying this similitude unto them: "A certain rich
17 man—his land had brought in to him much produce. And he was
thinking in himself and said, 'What shall I do, in that I have
18 not where that I may store my produce? I will pull down my
granaries and build *and* enlarge them, and I will gather in them
19 my produce.' §And he saith to his soul 'Lo, many good things are §*A* 381

7 by him] *om. S* much more] better *S* 8 Now] For *S* his holy angels] the angels of God *S* 9.] *om. S* 11 as to how] what *S* speak] say *S* *Cf A* 415: 'Whenever they bring you up before the ruling powers and before authorities...' *For the rest of the quotation see* Lk xxi 12 ff 12 for] but *S* it behoves that] *om. S* 13 the land and] *om. S* 15 much] *om. S* 16 And he said to them this similitude *S* 18 I will 1°] But it behoves me that I should *and*] and *S* 19 And I will say to my soul *S* (*not A*) Lo] + quoth he *A*

C S ܣܝ̈ܡܝܢ ܠܟܝ ܠܫ̈ܢܝܐ ܣܓ̈ܝܐܬܐ. ܐܬܢܝܚܝ ܘܠܥܣܝ، ܘܐܫܬܝ،
ܘܐܬܒܣܡܝ. ²⁰ܐܡܪ ܠܗ ܐܠܗܐ ܚܣܝܪ ܪܥܝܢܐ. ܗܐ ܒܗܢܐ
col 2 ܠܠܝܐ ܢܦܫܟ ܬܒܥܝܢ ܠܗ ܡܢܟ. ܘܗܠܝܢ *ܕܛܝܒܬ ܠܡܢ ܢܗܘܝܢ. ²¹ܗܟܢܐ
¶A ܗܘ ܡܢ ܕܣܐܡ ܠܗ ܣܝ̈ܡܬܐ ܘܒܐܠܗܐ ܠܐ ܥܬܪ¶ ·:·
²²ܘܐܡܪ ܠܬܠܡ̈ܝܕܘܗܝ، ܡܛܠ ܗܢܐ ܐܡܪ ܐܢܐ ܠܟܘܢ ܠܐ
ܬܐܨܦܘܢ ܕܢܦܫܟܘܢ ܡܢܐ ܬܐܟܠܘܢ ܘܐܟܠܐ ܕܦܓܪܐ ܡܢܐ
ܬܠܒܫܘܢ. ²³ܢܦܫܐ ܓܝܪ ܝܬܝܪܐ ܗܝ، ܡܢ ܣܝܒܪܬܐ ܘܦܓܪܐ ܡܢ
ܠܒܘܫܐ. ²⁴ܐܬܒܩܘ ܒܥܘ̈ܦܐ ܕܠܐ ܙܪܥܝܢ ܘܠܐ ܚܨܕܝܢ. ܘܠܝܬ
ܠܗܘܢ ܬܘ̈ܢܐ. ܘܐܦܠܐ ܒܝܬ ܡܘ̈ܢܐ. ܘܐܠܗܐ ܡܬܪܣܐ
ܠܗܘܢ. ܟܡܐ ܗܟܝܠ ܐܢܬܘܢ ܡܝܬܪܝܢ ܡܢܗܘܢ. ²⁵ܐܝܢܐ ܓܝܪ
ܡܢܟܘܢ ܟܕ ܝܨܦ، ܡܫܟܚ ܠܡܘܣܦܘ ܥܠ ܩܘܡܬܗ ܐܡܬܐ
ܚܕܐ. ²⁶ܐܢ ܕܝܢ ܐܦ ܠܐ ܙܥܘܪܬܐ ܡܫܟܚܝܢ ܐܢܬܘܢ ܠܡܥܒܕ.
fol 67 r ܡܢܐ *ܝܨܦܝܢ ܐܢܬܘܢ ܥܠ ܫܪܟܐ. ²⁷ܐܬܒܩܘ ܒܫܘ̈ܫܢܐ ܕܕܒܪܐ
ܐܝܟܢܐ ܠܐ ܥܡܠܝܢ ܘܠܐ ܙܩܪܢ. ܘܐܡܪ ܐܢܐ ܠܟܘܢ ܕܐܦ ܠܐ
ܫܠܝܡܘܢ ܒܟܠܗ ܬܫܒܘܚܬܗ ܐܬܟܣܝ ܐܟܘܬܗܝܢ. ²⁸ܐܢ ܕܝܢ
ܠܥܡܝܪܐ ܕܚܩܠܐ ܕܝܘܡܢܐ ܐܝܬܘܗܝ، ܚܩܠܐ. ܘܡܚܪ ܡܢ
ܘܢܦܠ ܒܬܢܘܪܐ ܐܠܗܐ ܡܠܒܫ. ܟܡܐ ܗܟܝܠ ܝܬܝܪܐܝܬ ܠܟܘܢ
ܙܥܘܪ̈ܝ ܗܝܡܢܘܬܐ. ²⁹ܠܐ ܗܟܝܠ ܬܒܥܘܢ ܡܢܐ ܬܠܒܫܘܢ
ܘܡܢܐ ܬܫܬܘܢ. ܘܡܢܐ ܬܬܟܣܘܢ. ܘܬܬܒܢܘܢ ܒܗܠܝܢ.
³⁰ܗܠܝܢ ܓܝܪ ܟܠܗܝܢ ܥܡ̈ܡܐ ܗܘ ܕܐܪܥܐ ܒܥܝܢ ܠܗܝܢ. ܐܒܘܟܘܢ

ܣܝ̈ܡܝܢ] ܣܝܡܠܝ S (sic) A Ephr (see Notes, vol. ii) ܐܬܢܝܚܝ] pr. ܢܦܫܝ A (Ephr)
ܘܠܥܣܝ] ܘܐܟܘܠܝ A Ephr ܘܐܫܬܝ] om. A 20 ܚܣܝܪ ܪܥܝܢܐ] ܕܠܐ ܠܒܐ A
ܗܐ] om. S ܗܠܝܢ.....ܢܗܘܝܢ] ܗܢܐ ܡܕܡ.....ܢܗܘܐ A Ephr 21 ܗܟܢܐ]
pr. ܘܡܢ ܒܬܪܟܢ ܐܡܪ. ܕ A ܗܘ] om. S A 22 ܕܢܦܫܟܘܢ] ܕܢܦܫܐ S
24 ܡܬܪܣܐ] C Thos[194] (see on Matt vi 26, 30); ܡܦܪܢܣ S ܡܢܗܘܢ]
ܡܢ ܦܪܚܬܐ S 27 ܕܕܒܪܐ] om. S ܐܝܟܢܐ ܕܠܐ S ܐܬܟܣܝ]
ܠܒܫ S 28 ܠܥܡܝܪܐ ܕܚܩܠܐ] ܒܥܡܝܪܐ S ܡܢ ܘ] om. S ܗܟܝܠ]
om. S 29 ܘܬܬܒܢܘܢ ܒܗܠܝܢ] om. S 30 ܕܐܪܥܐ] ܕܥܠܡܐ S

laid up for thee for many years; take thine ease and eat and drink *C S*
20 and be merry.' God saith to him: '*Thou* lacking in mind! lo, in
this night thy life they require of thee; these things that thou hast
21 made ready—whose will they be?' So is he which layeth up for
himself treasures and in God is not rich¶." ¶*A*
22 And he said to his disciples: "Therefore I say to you, Be not
anxious for your life what ye shall eat, neither for the body where-
23 with ye shall be clothed; for the life is more than the food and
24 the body than the clothing. Consider the ravens that they sow
not nor reap, and have no store-chambers, nor granaries—and
God nourisheth them; how much therefore are ye more than
25 they! For which of you, though anxious, can add on to his
26 stature one cubit? But if not even a little thing ye can do, why
27 are ye anxious about the rest? Consider the lilies of the plain
how they spin not nor weave, and I say to you that not even
28 Solomon in all his glory was covered like them. But if the grass
of the hills that to-day is on the hills and to-morrow is withered
and falleth into the furnace God doth clothe, how much rather there-
29 fore for you, O lacking in faith? Do not therefore seek what ye
shall eat and what ye shall drink and wherewith ye shall be
30 covered, and be occupied in these things; for all these things the
peoples of the earth seek after, but your Father knoweth that for

---

laid up] stored up *S* (*sic*) *A Ephr* (*see Notes,* vol. ii) for thee] *or,* 'by thee' take] *pr.* my soul *A* (*Ephr*) eat] eat (*different word*) *A Ephr* and drink] *om. A* 20 lacking in mind] senseless *A* (*lit.* 'without heart') lo] *om. S* these things that....they] this which.....it *A Ephr* 21 So] *pr.* And afterwards he said *S* 22 your life] the life *S* 24 nourisheth] *C Thos*[194] (*see on* Matt vi 26, 30); sustaineth *S* than they] than the birds *S* 27 of the plain] *om. S* covered] clad *S* 28 the grass of the hills] grass *S* is withered and] *om. S* therefore] *om. S* 29 and be occupied in these things] *om. S* 30 the earth] the world *S*

ܕܝܢ ܝܕܥ ܕܐܦ ܠܗܘܢ ܡܬܒܥܝܢ. [31]ܐܢܬܘܢ ܡܟܝܠ ܒܥܘ ܡܠܟܘܬܗ C S
ܕܐܠܗܐ. ܘܗܠܝܢ ܡܢ ܩܕܡ ܢܬܘܣܦ ܠܗܘܢ ܀
*[32]ܠܐ ܬܕܚܠ ܓܙܪܐ ܙܥܘܪܐ. ܕܨܒܐ ܐܒܘܗܘܢ ܕܢܬܠ ܠܗܘܢ col 2
ܡܠܟܘܬܐ. [33]ܙܒܢܘ ܟܠܗܝܢ ܕܐܝܬ ܠܗܘܢ ܘܗܒܘ ܙܕܩܬܐ. ܘܥܒܕܘ
ܠܗܘܢ ܟܝܣܐ ܕܠܐ ܒܠܝܢ. ܘܐܦ ܣܝܡܬܐ ܕܠܐ ܚܣܪܐ ܒܫܡܝܐ.
ܐܬܪ ܕܠܐ ܓܢܒܐ ܡܩܪܒ. ܘܐܦܠܐ ܣܣܐ ܡܚܒܠ. [34]ܘܐܬܪ
ܕܣܝܡܬܗܘܢ ܬܗܘܐ ܘܐܦ ܠܒܗܘܢ ܬܡܢ ܢܗܘܐ. [35]ܢܗܘܘܢ
ܐܣܝܪܝܢ ܚܨܝܗܘܢ ܘܡܢܗܪܝܢ ܫܪ̈ܓܝܗܘܢ. [36]ܘܬܗܘܘܢ ܕܡܝܢ
ܠܐܢܫܐ ܕܡܣܟܝܢ ܠܡܪܗܘܢ ܐܡܬܝ ܢܦܢܐ ܡܢ ܒܝܬ ܡܫܬܘܬܐ.
ܕܡܐ ܕܐܬܐ ܘܢܩܫ ܒܬܪܥܗ ܢܦܬܚܘܢ ܠܗ. [37]ܛܘܒܝܗܘܢ
ܠܥܒ̈ܕܐ ܗܠܝܢ ܐܝܠܝܢ ܕܢܐܬܐ ܡܪܗܘܢ ܢܫܟܚ ܐܢܘܢ ܟܕ ܥܝܪܝܢ.
ܐܡܝܢ *ܐܡܪܢܐ ܠܗܘܢ ܕܢܐܣܘܪ ܚܨܘܗܝ. ܘܢܣܡܟ ܐܢܘܢ fol 67 v
ܘܢܫܡܫ. [38]ܘܐܢ ܒܡܛܪܬܐ ܡܨܥܝܬܐ ܢܐܬܐ ܘܢܫܟܚ ܐܢܘܢ ܟܕ
ܥܝܪܝܢ. ܛܘܒܝܗܘܢ ܕܢܫܟܚ ܐܢܘܢ ܘܢܫܡܫ. ܐܘ ܐܢ ܒܡܛܪܬܐ
ܕܬܪ̈ܬܝܢ ܐܘ ܕܬܠܬ ܢܐܬܐ ܘܢܫܟܚ ܐܢܘܢ ܟܕ ܥܝܪܝܢ. ܛܘܒܝܗܘܢ
ܠܗܘܢ܂ [39]ܗܕܐ ܕܝܢ ܕܥܘ. ܕܐܠܘ ܝܕܥ ܗܘܐ ܡܪܐ ܒܝܬܐ
ܒܐܝܕܐ ܫܥܬܐ ܐܬܐ ܓܢܒܐ. ܠܐ ܫܒܩ ܗܘܐ ܕܢܬܦܠܫ ܒܝܬܗ.
[40]ܐܦ ܐܢܬܘܢ ܗܘܘ ܡܛܝܒܝܢ. ܕܒܫܥܬܐ ܕܠܐ ܣܒܪܝܢ ܐܢܬܘܢ
ܢܐܬܐ ܒܪܗ ܕܐܢܫܐ. [41]ܐܡܪ ܠܗ ܟܐܦܐ. ܡܪܝ، ܠܢ ܗܘ ܐܡܪ
ܐܢܬ ܠܗ ܡܬܠܐ ܗܢܐ. ܐܘ ܐܦ ܠܟܠܢܫ. [42]ܐܡܪ ܠܗ ܡܪܢ.

---

31 ܡܟܝܠ] ܟܝܠ * S: *the first letter has been erased* (sic)   ܡܢ ܩܕܡ] *om.* S
32. *No* § *in* S   ܕܨܒܐ] ܕܐܨܛܒܝ S   33 ܘܐܦ] ܘ S   ܓܢܒܐ ܡܩܪܒ] ܓܢ̈ܒܐ ܓܢܒܝܢ S   ܘܐܦܠܐ] ܐܦ ܠܐ S   34 ܬܗܘܐ] *om.* S   ܘܐܦ] ܐܦ S   36 ܐܡܬܝ] *pr.* ܕ S   ܢܦܢܐ] *cf* ܟܕ ܦܢܐ ܡܢ ܒܝܬ ܡܫܬܘܬܐ *Thos*[315]   ܒܬܪܥܗ] ܡܚܕܐ S   37 ܗܠܝܢ ܐܝܠܝܢ] ܗܢܘܢ S   ܡܪܗܘܢ] *after* ܐܢܘܢ S   ܘܢܫܡܫ] ܘܢܥܒܪ ܢܫܡܫ ܐܢܘܢ S   38 ܒܡܛܪܬܐ ܡܨܥܝܬܐ ...... ܘܐܢ] *om.* S; *cf* ܢܛܪܬܐ ܡܛܪ̈ܬܐ ܡܨܥܝܬܐ. ܘܬܠܝܬܝܬܐ ܘܬܠܝܬܝܬܐ *Thos*[315]   ܘܢܫܟܚ 2°] *om.* ܘ S   ܟܕ ܥܝܪܝܢ 2°] ܗܟܢܐ S   39 ܐܬܐ] + ܗܘܐ S   40 ܐܦ] ܘܐܦ S
41 ܟܐܦܐ S   ܠܟܠ ܐܢܫ S (*as often*)   42 ܡܪܢ] ܝܫܘܥ S

31 you also they are required. Ye, henceforth, seek ye the kingdom of *C S*
God, and these things over above shall be added to you.
32 "Fear not, little flock, to whom your Father willeth to give the
33 kingdom. Sell everything that ye have and give alms, and make for
yourselves purses that wear not out and a treasure also that is not
exhausted in heaven, where no thief arriveth nor moth corrupteth;
34 and where your treasure shall be your heart also shall be there.
35, 36 Let your loins be girt and your lamps lighted, and ye be like folk
waiting for their lord whensoever he shall withdraw from the
wedding-feast, that what *time* he hath come and knocked straightway
37 they may open to him. Happy is it for those slaves, they whose lord
shall come *and* find them watching; amen, I say to you that he will
gird his loins and make them sit down *to meat* and serve *them*!
38 And if in the first watch he come and find them watching, happy is it
for them, whom he will make sit down *to meat* and will serve; or if
in the second watch or the third he come and find them watching,
39 happy is it for those! But this know ye, that if the master of the
house were to know at which hour the thief would be coming, he
40 would not suffer that his house should be broken through. Ye also,
be ye ready, for in an hour that ye know not will come the Son of
41 Man." Kepha saith to him: "My Lord, to us dost thou say this
42 similitude, or to every one also?" Our Lord saith to him: "Which

---

31 henceforth] *or*, 'then'; *S partly illegible* (*sic*) over above] *om. S* 32 willeth] hath been pleased *S* 33 also] *om. S* no thief arriveth] no thieves thieve *S* 34 shall be 1°] *is S* 36 withdraw] *cf* 'till he withdraw from the wedding-feast' *Thos*[315] straightway] immediately *S* 37 they] *om. S* serve *them*] come over *and* serve them *S* 38 in the first watch......; or if] *om. S*; *cf* 'I have watched my first watch and the second and the third' *Thos*[315] and find them watching 2°] *and* find them so *S* 39 would be] were *S* 40 Ye also] And ye also *S* 42 Our Lord] Jesus *S*

C S col 2 ܐܢܐ ܗܘ ܫܠܝܚܐ ܕܡܫܝܚܐ *ܘܫܒܝܚܐ ܘܡܠܟܐ. ܕܡܫܝܚܘܗܝ,
ܡܪܗ ܕܟܠ ܥܒܕܘܗܝ. ܕܢܬܠ ܠܗܘܢ ܦܪܘܩܐ ܒܝܕܗ. [43]ܠܟܠܗܘܢ,
ܠܗܘ ܕܒܥܐ ܒܗ ܢܐܬܐ ܡܪܗ ܢܫܒܩܘܗܝ, ܕܥܒܕ ܗܟܢܐ.
[44]ܫܪܝܪܐܝܬ ܐܡܪ ܐܢܐ ܠܟܘܢ ܕܡܫܝܚܘܗܝ, ܥܠ ܒܗܠܗ ܡܢܗܘܢ.
[45]ܐܝܟ ܕܡܢ ܢܐܡܪ ܗܘ ܥܒܕܐ ܒܠܒܗ. ܕܡܪܝ, ܡܗܘܪ ܠܡܐܬܐ.
ܘܫܪܐ ܠܡܣܟܢܐ ܠܥܒܕܐ ܗܢܘܢ ܘܠܫܘܦܪܗܬܐ. ܘܠܡܠܒܫ ܘܠܡܫܬܝܬܐ
ܘܠܡܪܘܐ. [46]ܘܢܐܬܐ ܡܪܗ ܕܥܒܕܐ ܗܘ ܒܫܘܒܚܐ ܕܠܐ ܣܟܪ.
ܘܒܫܥܬܐ ܕܠܐ ܝܕܥ. ܘܢܦܠܓܝܘܗܝ. ܘܢܣܡ ܡܢܬܗ ܥܡ ܐܝܠܝܢ
ܕܠܐ ܡܗܝܡܢܝܢ. [47]ܥܒܕܐ ܕܝܕܥ ܨܒܝܢܐ ܕܡܪܗ ܘܠܐ ܬܐܒ ܠܗ
fol 68 r ܐܝܟ ܨܒܝܢܗ. ܢܠܩܐ *ܡܚܘܬܐ ܣܓܝܐܬܐ. [48]ܘܗܘ ܕܠܐ ܝܕܥ
ܘܥܒܕ ܡܕܡ ܕܫܘܐ ܠܡܚܘܬܐ ܢܠܩܐ ܡܚܘܬܐ ܙܥܘܪܬܐ. ܟܠ
ܕܝܬܝܗܒ. ܠܗ ܓܝܪ ܣܓܝ ܝܬܒܥ ܒܐܝܕܗ. ܘܠܗܘ ܕܐܬܓܠܠ
ܠܗ ܣܓܝ ܡܬܦܪܥܐ ܢܬܒܥܘܢܝܗ, [49]ܢܘܪܐ ܗܘ ܓܝܪ ܐܬܬ
ܕܐܪܡܐ ܒܐܪܥܐ. ܘܗܟܢܐ ܓܒܐ ܐܢܐ ܐܠܘ ܡܢ ܒܝܬ ܫܒܬ·
[50]ܘܡܫܡܫܢܘܬܐ ܐܝܬ ܠܝ ܕܐܫܡܫ. ܘܡܫܡܫܐ ܐܠܝܨ ܐܢܐ ܒܥܒܕܐ
ܕܚܬܢܐ. [51]ܘܒܪܡ ܐܬܘܢ ܕܫܡܥܝܢ ܐܬܬ ܕܐܫܡܫ ܒܐܪܥܐ.
ܐܡܪ ܐܢܐ ܠܟܘܢ ܕܠܐ. ܐܠܐ ܦܠܓܘܬܐ. [52]ܡܢ ܗܫܐ ܓܝܪ
ܢܗܘܘܢ ܚܡܫܐ ܒܒܝܬ ܚܕ. ܢܬܦܠܓܘܢ ܬܠܬܐ ܥܠ ܬܪܝܢ.
col 2 ܘܬܪܝܢ ܥܠ ܬܠܬܐ. [53]ܢܬܦܠܓ ܐܒܐ ܥܠ *ܒܪܗ. ܘܒܪܐ ܥܠ

ܘܫܒܝܚܐ ܘܡܠܟܐ] *om. S* ܕܡܫܝܚܘܗܝ S^{ed} ܒܥܒܕܘܗܝ] ܒܛܝܒܘܬܗ *S*
43 ܠܟܠܗܘܢ] *om. S* ܢܐܬܐ] *inserted between the lines by the first hand in S: cf* Joh xiii 16 44 ܕܡܫܝܚܘܗܝ] ܕܫܠܝܚܘܗܝ *S* ܒܗܠܗ ܡܢܗܘܢ] ܒܟܠ ܕܐܬܐ ܠܗ *S*
45 ܗܢܘܢ] *om. S* 46 ܝܕܥ] ܣܟܪ. *S* ܘܢܦܠܓܝܘܗܝ ܘܢܣܡ ܡܢܬܗ]
ܘܢܦܠܓܘܢܝܗ ܡܢܬܗ ܘܢܣܝܡܘܢܝܗ *S (? for* ܢܦܠܓܝܘܗܝ *&* ܢܣܝܡܘܢܗ*)* ܐܝܠܝܢ] ܗܢܘܢ *S*
48 ܣܓܝ. ܣܓܝ *S* ܘܠܗܘ] *so also S* ܢܬܒܥܘܢܗ *S* 49 ܘܗܟܢܐ ܓܒܐ ܐܢܐ]
ܘܗܟܢܐ ܕܓܒܝܐ *S (sic, ? for* ܘܗܟܢܐ ܕܓܒܝܐ*)* 50 ܘܡܫܡܫܢܘܬܐ] *om.* ܘ *S*
ܕܚܬܢܐ] ܕܚܬܢܘܬܐ *S: for the meaning see* Joh iii 29, *and cf Thos*[216] (ܠܐ ܡܨܝܢ
ܢܚܙܘܢ ܢܘܗܪܗ ܐܠܐ ܒܢܝܐ ܗܢܘܢ ܕܒܗ ܐܬܚܬܢ: ܢܘܗܪܐ ܓܝܪ ܡܬܚܙܐ ܠܗ.)
51 ܕܐܫܡܫ] ܕܐܫܡܫܐ *S* 53 ܢܬܦܠܓ] *om. S*

is the one in authority faithful and wise and good that his lord will *C S*
set up over his slaves, that he may give them *their* ration *of food* in
43 its time? Happy is it for that slave when his lord shall come *and*
44 find him doing so! Truly I say to you that he will set him up over
45 all his property. But if that slave shall say in his heart 'My lord
delayeth to come,' and he begin to beat those slaves and the maid-
46 servants and to eat and drink and be drunken, then the lord of that
slave will come in a day that he doth not expect and in an hour that
he doth not know, and will divide him and set his portion with them
47 that are not faithful. The slave that knoweth the will of his lord
and prepared not for him according to his will shall be flogged with
48 many stripes, and he which knoweth not and doeth that which is
worthy of stripes shall be flogged with few stripes; for every one to
whom much shall be given, much will be required at his hand, and
to him that they have committed much, the more will they require of
49 him. For a fire I have come to lay in the earth, and how I would, if
50 already it had been kindled! And a baptism I have that I should
be baptized with, and how much I am in a strait until it be brought
51 to an end! Suppose ye that tranquillity I have come to make in the
52 earth? I say to you Nay, but divisions. For from now there will
be five in one house—they will be divided three against two, and two
53 against three; the father will be divided against his son and the son

---

one in authority] *or* 'official' and wise and good] *om. S* *Cf* 'Who is *the* overseer, *the* faithful servant good and wise' E^{218} slaves] fellow-servants *S* 43 that slave] that one *S* shall come] *inserted between the lines by the first hand in S*: *cf* Joh xiii 16 44 set him up] give him authority *S* all his property] all that he hath *S* 45 those slaves] the slaves *S* 46 then] *lit.* 'and': *for the construction, see Notes*, vol. ii doth not know] is not aware *S* divide] *cf* 'He will cut him asunder and will separate him' E^{218} (*see Notes*, vol. ii) divide him and set his portion] divide† his portion and set †it† *S* (*but as it stands S reads* 'divide him *as* his portion and set him') 49 how I would] what (*or* 'when') he would *S* (*sic*): *the addition of a stroke would make the clause run* 'And what I would *is*—if it had been already kindled!' 50 And 1°] *om. S* brought to an end] *For the meaning of the Syriac word see* Joh iii 29 *and cf* $Thos^{216}$ ('Nothing strange hath that accursed [serpent] shewn but the nature whereby he hath been brought to an end, for fire doth make an end of him') 51 make] lay *S* 53 will be divided] *om. S*

C S ܐܒܘܗܝ. ܐܢܬܬܐ ܥܠ ܒܪܬܗ̇. ܘܒܪܬܐ ܥܠ ܐܡܗ̇. ܘܚܡܬܐ ܥܠ
ܟܠܬܗ̇. ܘܟܠܬܐ ܥܠ ܚܡܬܗ̇.܀

[54] ܘܐܡܪ ܗܘܐ ܠܟܢ̈ܫܐ. ܡܐ ܕܚܙܝܬܘܢ ܥܢܢܐ ܕܣܠܩܐ ܡܢ
ܡܥܪܒܐ. ܐܡܪܝܢ ܐܢܬܘܢ ܕܡܛܪܐ ܗܘܐ ܘܗܘܐ ܡܚܕܐ. [55] ܘܡܐ
ܕܢܫܒܐ ܬܝܡܢܐ. ܐܡܪܝܢ ܐܢܬܘܢ ܕܚܘܪܢܐ ܗܘܐ ܘܗܘܐ.
[56] ܢܣ̈ܒܝ ܒܐ̈ܦܐ ܦܪܨܘܦܐ ܕܫܡܝܐ ܘܕܐܪܥܐ ܝܕܥܝܢ ܐܢܬܘܢ
ܠܡܒܩܝܘ. ܘܙܒܢܐ ܗܢܐ ܘܐܬܝܬܗ ܠܐ ܒܚܝܢ ܐܢܬܘܢ. [57] ܘܡ̈ܢܦܫܬܟܘܢ
ܠܐ ܕܝܢܝܢ ܐܢܬܘܢ ܩܘܫܬܐ. [58] ܡܐ ܕܐܙܠ ܐܢܬ ܥܡ ܒܥܠ
fol 68 v ܕܝܢܟ ܠܘܬ ܐܪܟܘܢܐ. ܥܕ ܥܡܗ ܐܢܬ ܒܐܘܪܚܐ* ܗܒ ܠܗ
ܗܘܝܘ ܕܬܬܦܪܩ ܡܢܗ. ܕܠܡܐ ܢܫܚܒܟ ܠܘܬ ܕܝܢܐ. ܘܕܝܢܐ
ܢܫܠܡܟ ܠܫܠܛܢܐ. ܘܫܠܛܢܐ ܢܪܡܝܟ ܒܝܬ ܐܣܘܪܐ. [59] ܐܡܪܢܐ ܠܟ
ܕܠܐ ܬܦܘܩ ܡܢ ܬܡܢ ܥܕܡܐ ܕܬܦܪܘܥ ܫܡܘܢܐ ܐܚܪܝܐ ·܀· ܀

[1] ܘܒܗ ܒܥܕܢܐ. ܐܬܘ ܐ̈ܢܫܝܢ ܘܐܡܪܘ ܠܗ ܥܠ ܓ̈ܠܝܠܝܐ.
ܗܢܘܢ ܕܦܝܠܛܘܣ ܚܠܛ ܕܡܗܘܢ ܥܡ ܕܒ̈ܚܝܗܘܢ܆ [2] ܥܢܐ
ܘܐܡܪ ܠܗܘܢ ܝܫܘܥ. ܣܒܪܝܢ ܐܢܬܘܢ ܕܗܠܝܢ ܓ̈ܠܝܠܝܐ ܚܛܝܝܢ
ܗܘܘ ܝܬܝܪ ܡܢ ܟܠܗܘܢ ܓ̈ܠܝܠܝܐ ܕܗܟܢܐ ܚܙܝ ܠܗܘܢ܆ [3] ܐܡܪܢܐ
ܠܟܘܢ ܕܠܐ. ܐܠܐ ܐܦ ܐܢܬܘܢ ܐܠܐ ܬܬܘܒܘܢ ܗܟܢܐ
col 2 ܬܐܒܕܘܢ ܟܠܟܘܢ܆ [4] ܘܗܢܘܢ ܬܡܢܬܥܣܪ ܕܢܦܠ *ܥܠܝܗܘܢ
ܡܓܕܠܐ ܒܫܝܠܘܚܐ ܘܩܛܠ ܐܢܘܢ܆ ܣܒܪܝܢ ܐܢܬܘܢ ܕܚܛܝܝܢ ܗܘܘ
ܝܬܝܪ ܡܢ ܟܠܗܘܢ ܒ̈ܢܝ ܐܢܫܐ ܕܥܡܪܝܢ ܒܐܘܪܫܠܡ. [5] ܐܡܪܢܐ

ܐܢܬܬܐ] ܐܡܐ *S*   54. *Perhaps no § in S*   ܘܐܡܪ] *om.* ܘ *S*
ܐܡܪܝܢ] *pr.* ⌜ܒܪܡܫܬܐ⌝ *S*ed (*cf* Lk v 25)   55 ܕܚܘܪܢܐ] *C S* (*sic*), *also* Ephr v 320 B: *see Introd.* vol. ii   56 ܝܕܥܝܢ ܐܢܬܘܢ] ܝܕܥܝܢ ܐܢܬܘܢ ܕܬܒܩܘܢ *S*
57 ܘܡ̈ܢܦܫܬܟܘܢ] ܠܡܢܐ ܡܢ ܢܦܫܟܘܢ *S*   58 ܡܐ ܕ] ܟܕ *S*   ܒܥܠ] *om. S*
ܐܢܬ ܒܐܘܪܚܐ] *tr. S*   ܗܘܝܘ] ܥܒܕܗ *S* (= ἐργασίαν)   ܘܕܝܢܐ ܢܫܠܡܟ] ܘܢܫܠܡܟ *S*   59 ܕܬܦܪܥ *S*   1 ܐ̈ܢܫܝܢ] ܐܢܫܐ *S*   ܘܐܡܪܘ] *om.* ܘ *S*
ܓ̈ܠܝܠܝܐ] ܓܠܠܝܐ *S* (*and in ver.* 2: *cf* xvii 11)   2 ܝܫܘܥ] *after* ܥܢܐ *S*   ܚܙܝ ܠܗܘܢ] ܗܘܐ ܐܢܘܢ *S*   3 ܬܬܘܒܘܢ] ܬܬܒܘܢ *S*   ܗܟܢܐ] *pr.* ⌜ܐܢܬܘܢ⌝ *S*ed
4 ܒܐܘܪܫܠܡ *S*

against his father, the wife against her daughter and the daughter C S
against her mother, and the mother-in-law against her bride and the
bride against her mother-in-law."

54 And he was saying to the multitudes: "What *time* ye have seen
a cloud coming up from the west, ye say 'Rain is *coming*'; and it
55 is so. And what *time* the south *wind* bloweth, ye say 'A sirocco is
56 *coming*'; and *so* it is. Respecters of persons! the countenance of
the heaven and of the earth ye know *how* to prove; this time and
57 its signs do ye not observe? And in yourselves ye judge not verity.
58 What *time* thou goest with thy adversary unto the ruler, while yet
with him thou art in the way give him his profit that thou mayest
be quit of him, lest he make thee guilty before the judge, and the
judge deliver thee up to the officer, and the officer cast thee into
59 prison. I say to thee Thou wilt not go forth from thence, till
thou repay the last mite."

xiii 1 And in that same time there came some folk and said to him
about the Galileans—those whose blood Pilate mingled with their
2 sacrifices. Jesus answered and said to them: "Suppose ye that
these Galileans were sinners more than all the Galileans, that thus it
3 chanced to them? I say to you Nay; but ye also, if ye will not
4 repent, thus will ye perish all of you. And those eighteen on whom
fell the tower in Shiloah and killed them, suppose ye that they were
5 sinners more than all the men that dwell in Jerusalem? I say to

---

the wife] the mother *S* 54 And he] He *S* ye say] *pr.* straightway *S* 55 a sirocco] *C S* (*sic*). *This rare word is used here also in* Ephr v 320 B: *see Introd.* vol. ii 56 observe] wish to prove *S* 57 And in yourselves] Wherefore of yourselves *S* 58 What *time*] While yet *S* with him] *om. S* his profit] his work *S* (= ἐργασίαν) the judge 2°] he *S* 1 and said] *and* said *S* 2 chanced to them] befel them *S* 3 thus will ye] ye yourselves thus will S^{vid}

C S ܠܗܘܢ ܕܠܐ. ܐܠܐ ܐܦ ܐܢܬܘܢ ܐܠܐ ܬܬܬܘܒܘܢ ܗܟܢܐ
ܬܐܒܕܘܢ ܀ ○ ○

[6]ܘܐܡܪ ܗܘܐ ܡܬܠܐ ܗܢܐ. ܠܓܒܪܐ ܚܕ ܐܝܬ ܗܘܬ ܠܗ ܬܬܐ
ܒܟܪܡܗ. ܘܐܬܐ ܒܥܐ ܒܗ̇ ܦܐ̈ܪܐ ܘܠܐ ܐܫܟܚ. [7]ܐܡܪ
ܠܦܠܚܐ ܗܐ ܬܠܬ ܫ̈ܢܝܢ ܗܐ ܡܢ ܕܐܬܝܬ ܐܢܐ ܒܥܐ ܐܢܐ ܒܗ̇
ܦܐ̈ܪܐ ܒܬܬܐ ܗܕܐ ܘܠܐ ܡܫܟܚ ܐܢܐ. ܦܣܘܩܝܗ̇ ܠܡܢܐ
ܡܒܛܠܐ ܐܪܥܐ. [8]ܐܡܪ ܠܗ ܗܘ ܦܠܚܐ. ܡܪܝ، ܫܒܘܩܝܗ̇ ܐܦ
fol 69 r ܗܕܐ ܫܢܬܐ. ܥܕ *ܐܦܠܚܝܗ̇ ܘܐܙܒܠܝܗ̇. [9]ܘܐܢ ܥܒܕܐ ܦܐ̈ܪܐ
ܘܐܠܐ ܠܡܚܪ ܬܦܣܘܩܝܗ̇ ○○ ○○ ○○ ○○

[10]ܘܟܕ ܡܠܦ ܗܘܐ ܒܫܒܬܐ ܒܚܕܐ ܡܢ ܟܢܘ̈ܫܬܐ. [11]ܘܐܝܬ ܗܘܬ
ܬܡܢ ܐܢܬܬܐ ܚܕܐ ܕܐܝܬ ܗܘܬ ܠܗ̇ ܪܘܚܐ ܫ̈ܢܝܢ ܬܡܢܥܣܪܐ.
ܘܟܦܝܦܐ ܗܘܬ ܘܠܐ ܡܫܟܚܐ ܗܘܬ ܕܬܬܦܫܛ ܠܓܡܪ. [12]ܘܚܙܗ̇
ܝܫܘܥ ܘܩܪܗ̇ ܘܐܡܪ ܠܗ̇. ܐܢܬܬܐ ܫܪܝܬܝ ܡܢ ܟܘܪܗܢܟܝ. [13]ܘܣܡ
ܐ̈ܝܕܘܗ، ܥܠܝܗ̇. ܘܒܪ ܫܥܬܗ ܐܬܦܫܛܬ ܘܩܡܬ̇. ܘܡܫܒܚܐ
ܗܘܬ ܠܐܠܗܐ. [14]ܘܥܢܐ ܪܒ ܟܢܘܫܬܐ ܟܕ ܡܬܚܡܬ ܗܘܐ ܥܠ
ܕܡܐܣܐ ܗܘܐ ܝܫܘܥ ܒܫܒܬܐ ܘܐܡܪ ܠܟ̈ܢܫܐ. ܫܬܐ ܐܢܘܢ
col 2 ܝܘ̈ܡܝܢ ܕܒܗܘܢ *ܘܠܐ ܠܡܦܠܚ. ܒܗܘܢ ܗܘܝܬܘܢ ܐܬܝܢ
ܘܡܬܐܣܝܢ ܘܠܐ ܒܝܘܡܐ ܕܫܒܬܐ ○ [15]ܥܢܐ ܝܫܘܥ ܘܐܡܪ ܠܗ.
ܢܣܒ ܒܐ̈ܦܐ. ܚܕ ܚܕ ܡܢܟܘܢ ܠܐ ܫܪܐ ܬܘܪܗ ܐܘ ܚܡܪܗ
ܡܢ ܐܘܪܝܐ ܒܝܘܡܐ ܕܫܒܬܐ ܘܐܙܠ ܡܫܩܐ ܠܗ. [16]ܗܕܐ ܕܝܢ
ܕܒܪܬܗ ܗܝ ܕܐܒܪܗܡ. ܕܐܣܪܗ̇ ܐܟܠ ܩܪܨܐ ܗܘܐ ܬܡܢܥܣܪܐ

---

5 ܐܢܬܘܢ] + ܟܠܟܘܢ *S* (*sic*) 6 ܒܟܪܡܗ] *pr.* ܕܢܨܝܒܐ *S* ܒܗ̇] ܠܗ *S*[ed]
7 ܐܢܐ ܐܬܐ ܕܐܬܝܬ ܡܢ ܗܐ] ܐܬܐ *S*[ed] (? *for* ܐܬܝܬ) ܒܥܐ *S* (*sic*)
ܒܗ̇] *om.* *S* ܦܣܘܩܝܗ̇] *pr.* ܐܠܐ *S* ܡܒܛܠ *S*[ed] 8 ܐܡܪ ܠܗ]
pr. ܘ ܥܢܐ *S* ܘܐܙܒܠܝܗ̇] *om.* ܘ *S* 10 ܗܘܐ] *om.* *S* 11 ܬܡܢ] *om.* *S*
13 ܘܒܪ ܫܥܬܗ] ܘܒܪ ܫܥܬܐ *S*[ed] (*cf* xii 54) 14 ܕܫܒܬܐ] ܕܫܘܒܬܐ *S*[ed]:
cf x 17, xx 29 15. *Possibly a § in C and in S* ܒܝܘܡܐ ܕܫܒܬܐ] *after*
ܘܐܡܪ ܠܗ *S* 16 ܗܕܐ ܕܝܢ ܕܒܪܬܗ] ܘܒܪܬܗ *S* ܕܐܒܪܗܡ] ܕ *illegible in S*
ܐܟܠ ܩܪܨܐ] ܣܛܢܐ *S*

you Nay; but ye yourselves also, if ye will not repent, thus will ye *C S*
perish."
6 And he was saying this similitude: "A certain man, he had a
fig-tree in his vineyard, and he came *and* sought on it fruit and
7 found none. He saith to the husbandman: 'Lo, *it is* three years,
lo, since I have been coming *and* seeking on it fruit, on this fig-tree,
and I find none; cut it down, wherefore doth it cumber the ground?'
8 That husbandman saith to him: 'My lord, suffer it this year also, till
9 I shall have tilled it and dunged it: and if it hath brought forth
fruit, *well*; and if not, next season thou shalt cut it down.'"
10 And when he was teaching on the sabbaths in one of the
11 synagogues, there was there a certain woman that had had a spirit
eighteen years, and she was bowed and could not stretch herself out
12 at all, and Jesus saw her and he called her and said to her: "Woman,
13 thou art loosed from thy infirmity." And he laid his hands on her,
and straightway her stature was stretched out; and she was
14 glorifying God. And the chief of the synagogue answered, being
made furious for that Jesus was healing on the sabbath, and said to
the multitudes: "Six are the days in which it is fitting to work; in
them be coming and being healed, and not on the sabbath-day."
15 Jesus answered and said to him: "Respecter of persons! Each one
of you—doth he not loose his ox or his ass from the manger on the
16 sabbath-day, and go *and* give him to drink? Now this *woman*, that
is a daughter of Abraham, whom the Accuser hath bound, lo,

---

5 yourselves also] + all of you *S* (*sic*) 6 in his vineyard] *pr.* planted *S* $E^{166\ (not\ 184)}$ on it] for himself S^{ed} 7 lo.... coming] coming S^{ed} (*read* 'I come') on it] *om. S* cut it down] *pr.* but *S* 8 saith] answered and said *S* and 1°] *and S* 10 he was] *om. S* 11 there was there] there was *S* 15 on the sabbath-day] *after* 'to drink' *in S* 16 Now.... Abraham] And that daughter of Abraham *S* the Accuser] Satan *S*

C S ܫ̈ܢܝܢ. ܠܐ ܘܠܐ ܗܘܐ ܕܬܫܬܪܐ ܡܢ ܗܢܐ ܐܣܘܪܐ ܒܝܘܡܐ
ܕܫܒܬܐ. [17]ܘܟܕ ܗܠܝܢ ܐܡܪ ܗܘܐ. ܒܗܬܝܢ ܗܘܘ ܟܠܗܘܢ ܐܝܠܝܢ
ܕܩܝܡܝܢ ܗܘܘ ܠܘܩܒܠܗ. ܘܟܠܗ ܥܡܐ ܚܕܐ ܗܘܐ ܒܟܠܗܝܢ
ܬܕܡ̈ܪܬܐ ܕܗܘܝܢ ܗܘ̈ܝ ܒܐܝܕܗ. ܀ ܀

fol 69 v [18]*ܘܐܡܪ ܗܘܐ ܠܡܢܐ ܕܡܝܐ ܡܠܟܘܬܐ ܕܐܠܗܐ ܘܠܡܢܐ
ܐܕܡܝܗ. [19]ܕܡܝܐ ܠܦܪܕܬܐ ܕܚܪܕܠܐ ܕܢܣܒ ܓܒܪܐ ܐܪܡܝܗ
ܒܓܢܬܗ. ܘܪܒܬ ܘܗܘܬ ܐܝܠܢܐ. ܘܐܩܢܬ ܦܪܚܬܐ ܕܫܡܝܐ
ܒܣ̈ܘܟܝܗ ܀

[20]ܬܘܒ ܐܡܪ ܠܡܢܐ ܐܕܡܝܗ ܡܠܟܘܬܐ ܕܐܠܗܐ. [21]ܕܡܝܐ
ܠܚܡܝܪܐ ܕܢܣܒܬ ܐܢܬܬܐ ܘܛܡܪܬ ܒܬܠܬ ܣܐ̈ܝܢ ܩܡܚܐ.
ܥܕܡܐ ܕܟܠܗ ܚܡܥ. [22]ܘܪܕܐ ܗܘܐ ܒܩܘ̈ܪܝܐ ܘܒܡ̈ܕܝܢܬܐ.
ܘܡܠܦ ܗܘܐ. ܀

[23]ܘܟܕ ܐܙܠ ܠܐܘܪܫܠܡ. ܐܬܐ ܚܕ ܘܡܫܐܠ ܗܘܐ ܠܗ ܘܐܡܪ.
ܡܪܝ، ܐܢ ܙܥܘ̈ܪܝܢ ܐܢܘܢ ܕܚܝܝܢ. ܐܡܪ ܠܗ ܝܫܘܥ܂ [24]ܐܬܟܬܫܘ
ܠܡܥܠ ܒܬܪܥܐ ܐܠܝܨܐ. ܐܡܪܢܐ ܠܟܘܢ ܓܝܪ ܕܣ̈ܓܝܐܐ ܢܒܥܘܢ
col 2 ܠܡܥܠ *ܘܠܐ ܢܫܟܚܘܢ. [25]ܡܢ ܫܥܬܐ ܕܢܩܘܡ ܡܪܐ ܒܝܬܐ
ܘܢܐܚܘܕ ܬܪܥܐ. ܘܬܩܘܡܘܢ ܡܢܒܪ ܘܢܩܫܝܢ ܒܬܪܥܐ.
ܘܬܐܡܪܘܢ ܡܪܢ ܡܪܢ ܦܬܚ ܠܢ. ܘܥܢܐ ܘܢܐܡܪ ܠܟܘܢ ܠܐ ܝܕܥ
ܐܢܐ ܠܟܘܢ ܐܝܡܟܐ ܐܢܬܘܢ܂ [26]ܗܝܕܝܢ ܬܫܪܘܢ ܠܡܐܡܪ. ܩܕܡܝܟ
ܠܟܘܢ ܘܐܫܬܝܢ. ܘܒܫ̈ܘܩܝܢ ܗܠܟܬ. [27]ܗܝܕܝܢ ܢܐܡܪ ܠܟܘܢ܂ ܐܡܝܢ
ܐܡܪܢܐ ܠܟܘܢ ܕܠܐ ܝܕܥܢܐ ܠܟܘܢ ܐܝܡܟܐ ܐܢܬܘܢ܂ ܦܪܘܩܘ

17 ܐܡܪ ܗܘܐ ܗܠܝܢ S (*followed by an illegible half line*) ܘܟܠܗ ܥܡܐ] S *illegible* 18 ܘܐܡܪ] *om.* ܘ S 19 ܘܪܒܬ ܘܗܘܬ] S *illegible* ܒܣ̈ܘܟܝܗ] S *illegible* 20 ܡܠܟܘܬܐ] ܠ̈ܡܠܟܘܬܐ S[ed] 21 ܚܡܥ] S *illegible* 23 ܚܕ] *pr.* ܓܒܪܐ S ܘܡܫܐܠ] *om.* ܘ S ܘܐܡܪ] + ܠܗ S 24 ܠܡܥܠ 2°] + ܒܗ S 25 ܡܢ ܫܥܬܐ] + ܓܝܪ S ܡܪܐ ܒܝܬܐ] ܒܝܬܐ | ܡܪܗ S, *but the* ܒ *is illegible* ܘܢܩܫܝܢ] ܘܡܩܫܩܫܝܢ S (*sic*): *cf* xi 10 ܡܪܢ 2°] *om.* S ܐܝܡܟܐ] *pr.* ܡܢ S 26 ܗܠܟܬ] ܐܗܠܟܬ S 27 ܗܝܕܝܢ ܢܐܡܪ ܠܟܘܢ] ܘܐܡܪ S ܐܝܡܟܐ] *pr.* ܡܢ S

eighteen years, was it not fitting that she should be loosed from this *C S*
17 bond on the sabbath-day?" And when these things he was saying,
all they that were standing up against him were confused, and all
the people were rejoicing at all the marvels that were coming to pass
by his hand.
18 And he was saying: "To what is the kingdom of God like, and
19 to what shall I liken it? It is like to a grain of mustard, that a man
took *and* cast it in his garden, and it grew up and became a tree,
and the birds of the heaven nested in its branches."
20 Again he saith: "To what shall I liken the kingdom of God?
21 It is like to leaven that a woman took and hid in three bushels of
22 meal until the whole should be leavened." And he was journeying
through the villages and the cities, and was teaching.
23 And while going to Jerusalem one came and was asking him and
saying: "My Lord, are they few that live?" Jesus saith to him:
24 "Fight *thou* to enter by the strait gate; for I say to you Many will
25 wish to enter and will not be able. From the hour that the master of
the house shall arise and shall shut the gate, and ye be standing
outside and knocking at the gate, and saying 'Our Lord, our Lord,
open to us,' he will answer and say to you 'I know you not whence
26 ye are.' Then ye will begin to say: 'Before thee we have eaten and
27 drunk, and in our streets thou hast walked.' Then he will say to
you: 'Amen, I say to you I know you not whence ye are; depart

---

17 he was saying these things *S* (*followed by an illegible half-line*) and all the people] *S illegible* **18** And he] He *S* **19** and it grew up and became] *S illegible* in its branches] *S illegible* **21** should be leavened] *S illegible* **23** one] a certain man *S* and was] *and* was *S* saying] + to him *S* **24** to enter 2°] + thereby *S* **25** From] For from *S* our Lord 2°] *om. S* he will answer] *lit.* 'and he will answer': *cf* xii 46 whence] *pr.* from *S* **26** walked] taught *S* **27** Then he will say to you] And he will say *S* whence] *pr.* from *S*

C S ܠܗܘܢ ܡܢܗ. ܟܠܗܘܢ ܒܬܪ ܐܬܢܝܚܘܢ ܦܬܓܡܐ ܕܒܥܘܬܐ. ²⁸ܬܘܒ
ܢܗܘܐ ܒܟܠܐ ܘܢܗܘܐ ܫ̈ܢܐ. ܟܕ ܬܚܝܘܢ ܠܐܒܪܗܡ ܘܠܐܝܣܚܩ
ܘܠܝܥܩܘܒ. ܘܠܟܠܗܘܢ ܢܒܝܐ. ܒܡܠܟܘܬܐ ܕܐܠܗܐ. ܘܐܢܬܘܢ
fol 70 r ܬܗܘܘܢ ܡܦܩܝܢ *ܠܒܪ. ²⁹ܘܢܐܬܘܢ ܡܢ ܡܕܢܚܐ ܘܡܢ ܡܥܪܒܐ.
ܘܡܢ ܬܝܡܢܐ ܘܡܢ ܓܪܒܝܐ. ܘܢܣܬܡܟܘܢ ܒܡܠܟܘܬܗ ܕܐܠܗܐ.
³⁰ܘܐܝܬ ܐܚܪ̈ܝܐ ܕܢܗܘܘܢ ܩܕ̈ܡܝܐ. ܘܩ̈ܕܡܝܐ ܐܚܪ̈ܝܐ. .·.
³¹ܘܒܗܘ ܒܝܘܡܬܐ ܗܘ ܩܪܒܘ ܐ̈ܢܫܐ ܡܢ ܦܪ̈ܝܫܐ ܘܐܡܪܝܢ
ܠܗ. ܦܘܩ ܙܠ ܠܟ ܡܟܐ. ܡܛܠ ܕܗܪܘܕܣ ܒܥܐ ܠܡܩܛܠܟ.
³²ܐܡܪ ܠܗܘܢ ܙܠܘ ܐܡܪܘ ܠܗ ܠܬܥܠܐ ܗܢܐ. ܗܐ ܡܦܩ
ܐܢܐ ܫܐ̈ܕܐ. ܘܐܣܝܘܬܐ ܡܫܠܡ ܐܢܐ ܝܘܡܢܐ ܘܡܚܪ. ܘܠܝܘܡܐ
ܕܬܠܬܐ ܡܫܬܠܡ ܐܢܐ. ³³ܒܪܡ ܘܠܐ ܠܝ ܕܝܘܡܢܐ ܘܡܚܪ.
ܘܠܒܬܪ ܡܚܪ ܐܙܠ̈ܐ. ܡܛܠ ܕܠܐ ܡܫܟܚܐ ܕܢܒܝܐ ܢܐܒܕ ܠܒܪ
col 2 ܡܢ *ܐܘܪܫܠܡ. ³⁴ܐܘܪܫܠܡ ܐܘܪܫܠܡ ܕܩܛܠܬ ܠܢܒ̈ܝܐ. ܘܪܓܡܬ
ܠܐܝܠܝܢ ܕܐܫܬܠܚܘ ܠܘܬܟܝ. ܟܡܐ ܙܒ̈ܢܝܢ ܨܒܝܬ ܠܡܟܢܫܘ ܠܒ̈ܢܝܟܝ.
ܐܝܟ ܬܪܢܓܠܬܐ ܕܟܢܫܐ ܦܪ̈ܘܓܝܗ ܬܚܝܬ ܓܦ̈ܝܗ ܘܠܐ ܨܒܝܬܘܢ܆
³⁵ܗܐ ܫܒܝܩ ܠܟܘܢ ܒܝܬܟܘܢ ܚܪܒ܇ ܐܡܪܢܐ ܠܟܘܢ ܕܠܐ
ܬܚܙܘܢܢܝ ܒܥܠܡܐ ܕܢܐܬܐ ܝܘܡܐ ܕܬܐܡܪܘܢ܆ ܒܪܝܟ ܗܘ ܕܐܬܐ
ܒܫܡܗ ܕܡܪܝܐ. ¹ܘܗܘܐ ܟܕ ܠܒܝܬܐ ܕܚܕ ܡܢ ܪ̈ܫܐ ܕܦܪ̈ܝܫܐ.
ܕܢܐܟܘܠ ܠܚܡܐ ܒܝܘܡܐ ܕܫܒܬܐ. ܘܢܛܪܝܢ ܗܘܘ ܗܘܘ ܕܢܚܙܘܢ
ܡܢܐ ܥܒܕ. ²ܘܓܒܪܐ ܚܕ ܗܕܪܘܦܝܩܘܣ ܐܝܬ ܗܘܐ ܩܕܡܘܗܝ. ³ܥܢܐ
fol 70 v ܝܫܘܥ ܘܐܡܪ ܠܣܦܪ̈ܐ ܘܠܦܪ̈ܝܫܐ. ܕܐܢ ܫܠܝܛ *ܠܡܐܣܝܘ ܒܫܒܬܐ

28 ܒܡܠܟܘܬܐ] C*, but on an erasure; ⌜ܒܡܠܟܘܬܗ⌝ S^ed ܘܐܢܬܘܢ....ܠܒܪ] om. S 29 ܬܝܡܢܐ....ܓܪܒܝܐ] tr. S 30 ܘܐܝܬ] ܘܗܐ ܐܝܬ S 31 ܙܠ] ܐܙܠ S 32 ܠܬܥܠܐ ܗܢܐ] ܗܘ ܠܬܥܠܬܐ S ܝܘܡܢܐ] ܝܘܡܢܐ S (sic) 33 ܘܠܐ] + ܗܘ S ܐܙܠ̈ܐ] ܐܙܠ S 34. § in S ܕܩܛܠܬ ܢܒܝܐ S ܠܡܟܢܫ ܒܢܝܟܝ S ܬܪܢܓܠܬܐ S ܒܢܝܗ̇] ܦܪ̈ܘܓܝܗ S 35 ܠܟܘܢ 1°] om. S ܚܪܒ] om. S ܐܡܪܢܐ] pr. ܘ S ܝܘܡܐ] om. S 1. § in S (sic) ܕܢܚܙܘܢ] ܗܘܘ ܢ S^ed, but from the photograph I read ⌜ܕܢܚܙܘܢ⌝ ܥܒܕ] ܢܥܒܕ S 2 ܚܕ] om. S ܗܕܪܘܦܝܩܘܣ S 3 ܕܐܢ] ܐܢ S ܠܡܐܣܝܘ ܒܫܒܬܐ] tr. S

28 ye from me, for ye are all workers of falsehood.' There shall be the C S
weeping and the gnashing of teeth, when ye shall see Abraham and
Isaac and Jacob and all the prophets in the kingdom of God, and ye
29 shall be cast out. And they shall come from the east and from the west
and from the south and from the north, and shall sit down *to meat* in the
30 kingdom of God. And there are last that shall be first, and first last."
31 And in those same days there drew near some of the Pharisees
and say to him: "Go forth, go away hence, because Herod wisheth
32 to kill thee." He saith to them: "Go, say ye to him, to this fox, 'Lo,
I am casting out devils and my cure I finish to-day and to-morrow,
33 and the third day I am *myself* finished. Nevertheless it behoves me
that to-day and to-morrow and *the day* after to-morrow I should
journey, because it cannot be that a prophet perish outside Jeru-
34 salem!' Jerusalem, Jerusalem, that killest the prophets and stonest
them that were sent unto thee, how many times have I wished to
gather thy sons as the hen that gathereth her young under her
35 pinions—and ye would not! Lo, your house is left to you desolate.
I say to you Ye shall not see me until the day come that ye shall
xiv 1 say 'Blessed is he that cometh in the name of the LORD.'" And
when he entered the house of one of the chiefs of the Pharisees to
eat bread on the sabbath-day, they were keeping *watch* that they
2 might see what he would do. And a certain man with the dropsy
3 there was before him. Jesus answered and said to the scribes and to
the Pharisees, *asking* "Whether it be lawful to heal on the sabbath,

---

28 and ye....cast out] *om. S* **29** south....north] *tr. S* **30** there] *pr.* lo *S* **32** to this fox] to that vixen *S* to-day] †the† day *S* (*sic*) **33** journey] go *S* **34** killest....stonest] *for the rendering, cf* syr.vg *and see Introd.* vol. ii pinions] wings *S* **35** to you 1°] *om. S* desolate] *om. S* I say] *pr.* and *S* the day come] it come *S* **1** that they might see] *so also S* (*as I read the photograph*); themselves S^{ed} **2** certain] *om. S* **3** on the sabbath to heal *S*

ܐܘ ܠܐ. ⁴ܘܗܢܘܢ ܫܬܝܩܝܢ ܗܘܘ. ܘܗܘ ܐܚܕܗ ܘܐܣܝܗ. *C S*
ܘܫܪܝܗ. ⁵ܘܐܡܪ ܠܗܘܢ ܡܢܘ ܡܢܟܘܢ ܕܢܦܠ ܒܪܗ ܐܘ
ܬܘܪܗ. ܐܘ ܚܡܪܗ ܒܒܐܪܐ ܒܝܘܡܐ ܕܫܒܬܐ. ܘܠܐ ܡܚܕܐ
ܢܓܕ ܡܣܩ ܠܗ. ⁶ܘܠܐ ܐܫܟܚܘ ܠܡܬܠ ܠܗ ܦܬܓܡܐ ܥܠ
ܗܠܝܢ .o.

⁷ܘܐܡܪ ܗܘܐ ܡܬܠܐ ܗܢܐ. ܠܘܬ ܗܢܘܢ ܕܡܙܡܢܝܢ ܗܘܘ.
ܘܓܒܝܢ ܗܘܘ ܪ̈ܫ ܡܣ̈ܡܟܐ. ܐܡܪ ܠܗܘܢ ⁸ܐܡܬܝ، ܕܡܙܕܡܢ ܐܢܬ
ܠܡܫܬܘܬܐ. ܠܐ ܬܐܙܠ ܬܣܬܡܟ ܒܕܘܟܬܐ ܩܕܡܝܬܐ. ܕܠܐ
ܢܗܘܐ ܬܡܢ ܡܢܘ ܕܡܝܩܪ ܡܢܟ. ⁹ܘܢܐܬܐ ܗܘ ܡܢ ܕܠܟ ܘܠܗ
col 2 ܩܪܐ. ܘܢܐܡܪ ܠܟ ܕܗܒ ܕܘܟܬܐ ܠܗܢܐ. *ܘܗܝܕܝܢ ܟܕ ܒܗܬܬ
ܐܢܬ ܬܣܬܡܟ ܒܕܘܟܬܐ ܐܚܪܝܬܐ. ¹⁰ܐܠܐ ܡܐ ܕܐܙܕܡܢܬ. ܙܠ
ܐܣܬܡܟ ܒܕܘܟܬܐ ܐܚܪܝܬܐ. ܕܡܐ ܕܐܬܐ ܗܘ ܡܢ ܕܙܡܢܟ.
ܢܐܡܪ ܠܟ ܪܚܡܝ ܐܬܥܠܐ ܠܥܠ. ܘܬܗܘܐ ܠܟ ܬܫܒܘܚܬܐ
§¶A80, 189 ܩܕܡ ܡܣ̈ܡܟܐ ܟܠܗܘܢ. §¹¹ܟܠ ܓܝܪ ܕܢܪܝܡ ܢܦܫܗ ܢܬܡܟܟ.
§A388 ܘܟܠ ܕܡܟܝܟ ܢܦܫܗ ܢܬܪܝܡ.¶ §¹²ܘܐܡܪ ܗܘܐ ܐܦ ܠܡܪܐ
ܐܚܫܡܝܬܐ. ܡܐ ܕܥܒܕ ܐܢܬ ܫܪܘܬܐ ܐܘ ܐܚܫܡܝܬܐ. ܠܐ
ܬܩܪܐ ܪ̈ܚܡܝܟ. ܘܐܦ ܠܐ ܠܐܚ̈ܝܟ. ܘܠܐ ܠܐܚ̈ܝܢܝܟ. ܘܠܐ
fol 71 r ܠܫ̈ܒܒܝܟ ܐܝܠܝܢ ܕܥܬܝܪ̈ܐ ܐܢܘܢ܆ ܕܠܡܐ ܐܦ ܗܢܘܢ *ܢܩܪܘܢܟ.

ܐܘ ܠܐ] *om. S*   4 ܫܬܝܩܝܢ] *so also S*   5 ܒܪܗ ܐܘ] *om. S*
ܡܚܕܐ] *om. S*   7. *No § in S (see facsimile to the Syndics' Edition)*
ܪ̈ܫ ܡܣ̈ܡܟܐ] ܪ̈ܫ ܡܣܡܟܐ *S (sic)*   8 ܕܡܙܕܡܢ] ܕܡܙܡܢ *S*   ܬܐܙܠ] *om. S*
ܬܣܬܡܟ] + ܠܟ *S*   ܕܠܐ] ܕܠܡܐ *S*   ܬܡܢ] *pr.* ܡܟܝܠ *S*   ܡܢܘ] ܡܢ *S*
9 ܕܗܒ] *om.* ܕ *S*   ܕܘܟܬܐ] ܐܬܪܐ *S*   10 ܐܣܬܡܟ] + ܠܟ *S*
ܐܚܪܝܬܐ *S^ed (mea culpa)*   ܡܢ] *om. S*   ܬܫܒܘܚܬܐ *S*   ܟܠܗܘܢ] *om. S*
11 ܟܠ ܕܢܪܝܡ ܓܝܪ *S*   ܟܠ] + ܡܢ *A* 80   ܓܝܪ] *om.* $A^2/_2$
ܢܦܫܗ ܢܪܝܡ] ܡܬܪܝܡ $A^2/_2$ 12 ܗܘܐ ܐܦ] *om. A*   ܚܫܡܝܬܐ $A^{a\,2}/_2$
ܡܐ] ܕܐܡܬܝ *A*   ܐܢܬ] *pr.* ܐܢܬ *S*, now expunged (see facsimile)*
ܫܪܘܬܐ ܐܘ] *om. S*   ܠܐ̈ܚܝܟ *S* A^b ܘܐܦ ܠܐ ܠܐܚ̈ܝܢܝܟ]
om. A   ܘܠܐ 1°] ܐܘ *A*   ܐܚ̈ܝܢܝܟ A^a ܘܐܦ ܠܐ *A*   ܫ̈ܒܒܝܟ *A*
ܐܝܠܝܢ ܕܥܬܝܪ̈ܐ ܐܢܘܢ] ܥܬܝܪ̈ܐ *S A*   ܕܠܡܐ] ܕܕܠܡܐ *S*; ܕܠܐ *A*

4 or no?" And they were silent. And he took hold of him and *C S*
5 healed him and dismissed him, and he said to them: "Which is
there of you whose son or whose ox or whose ass shall fall into a
well on the sabbath-day, and he doth not immediately draw *and* take
6 him up?" And they could not give him an answer about these
things.

7 And he had said this similitude unto those that were bidden and
were choosing the chief *place at* entertainments. He said to them:
8 "Whensoever thou art bidden to a wedding, do not go *and* sit down
to meat in the honourable place; that there be not there one who is
9 more honourable than thou, and he come that hath bidden thee and
him and say to thee 'Give place to this one,' and then ashamed thou
10 wilt sit down *to meat* in the last place. But what *time* thou hast
been bidden, go *and* sit down *to meat* in the last place, that what
time he hath come which hath bidden thee he may say to thee: 'My
friend, come up above,' and thou shalt have glory in the eyes of all
11 the guests. §For every one that shall uplift himself shall be humbled, §¶*A* 80, 189
12 and every one that shall humble himself shall be uplifted."¶ §And he §*A* 388
was saying to the lord of the supper also: What *time* thou makest a
breakfast or a supper, do not call thy friends nor even thy brothers
nor thy relations nor thy neighbours that are rich, lest they also may

---

or no] *om. S* 5 whose son or] *om. S* immediately] *om. S* 8 go *and*] *om. S* sit] + thyself *S* that there be not] lest there be *S* there one] one bidden there *S* 9 place 1°] room *S* 10 sit] + thyself *S* which] that *S* all] *om. S* 11 For] *om.* $A^2/_2$ every one] Whosoever *A* 80 uplift himself] be uplifted $A^2/_2$ 12 was saying] *om. A* also] *om. A* What *time*] Whenever *A* thou] *written twice by S** a breakfast or] *om. S* nor even thy brothers] *om. A* nor 2°] or *A* nor 3°] + even *A* neighbours that are rich] rich neighbours *S A* lest] else *A*

ܘܢܗܘܐ ܠܟ ܦܘܪܥܢܐ. [13]ܐܠܐ ܡܐ ܕܥܒܕ ܐܢܬ ܫܪܘܬܐ. ܩܪܝ، C S
ܠܡܣ̈ܟܢܐ ܘܠܡܚ̈ܓܪܐ ܠܡܟܐ̈ܒܐ ܘܠܥܘ̈ܝܪܐ. [14]ܘܛܘܒܝܟ ܕܠܝܬ
ܠܗܘܢ ܕܢܦܪܥܘܢ. ܘܢܗܘܐ ܦܘܪܥܢܟ ܒܢܘܚܡܐ ܕܙܕ̈ܝܩܐ.¶ ¶A
[15]ܘܟܕ ܫܡܥ ܗܘܐ ܗܠܝܢ ܚܕ ܡܢ ܗܠܝܢ ܕܣܡܝܟܝܢ ܗܘܘ. ܐܡܪ
ܠܗ ܛܘܒܘܗܝ، ܠܡܢ ܕܐܟܘܠ ܫܪܘܬܐ ܒܡܠܟܘܬܗ ܕܐܠܗܐ. [16]ܐܡܪ
ܠܗ ܡܪܢ. ܓܒܪܐ ܚܕ ܥܒܕ ܗܘܐ ܐܚܫܡܝܬܐ ܪܒܬܐ. ܘܩܪܐ
ܠܣ̈ܓܝܐܐ. [17]ܘܫܕܪ ܥܒܕܗ ܒܥܕܢܐ ܕܚܫܡܝܬܐ ܕܢܐܡܪ ܠܗܘܢ
ܕܡܙܡܢܝܢ ܕܐܬܘ. ܗܐ ܠܟ ܟܠ ܡܕܡ ܡܛܝܒ. ܗܘ.
col 2 [18]ܘܫܪܝܘ ܗܘܘ ܡܢܚܕܐ ܠܡܫܬܐܠܘ. ܐܡܪ ܠܗ ܩܕܡܝܐ* ܩܪܝܬܐ
ܙܒܢܬ. ܘܐܠܝܨ ܐܢܐ ܕܐܦܘܩ ܐܚܙܝܗ. ܒܥܐ ܐܢܐ ܡܢܟ
ܫܒܘܩܝܢܝ. [19]ܘܐܚܪܢܐ ܐܡܪ ܚܡܫܐ ܙܘܓܝܢ ܬܘ̈ܪܐ ܙܒܢܬ. ܘܐܙܠ
ܐܢܐ ܕܐܒܩܐ ܐܢܘܢ. ܒܥܐ ܐܢܐ ܡܢܟ ܫܒܘܩܝܢܝ. [20]ܘܕܬܠܬܐ
ܐܡܪ ܐܢܬܬܐ ܢܣܒܬ. ܠܐ ܡܫܟܚܢܐ ܕܐܬܐ. [21]ܘܐܬܐ ܗܘ
ܥܒܕܐ ܐܡܪ ܗܠܝܢ ܠܡܪܗ. ܗܝܕܝܢ ܪܓܙ ܡܪܐ ܒܝܬܐ. ܘܐܡܪ
ܠܥܒܕܗ. ܦܘܩ ܒܥܓܠ ܠܫܘܩܐ ܘܠܫܒܝܠܐ ܕܡܕܝܢܬܐ. ܘܐܥܠ ܠܟܐ
ܠܡܣ̈ܟܢܐ ܘܠܡܚ̈ܓܪܐ. ܘܠܡܟܐ̈ܒܐ ܘܠܥܘ̈ܝܪܐ. [22]ܘܐܡܪ ܥܒܕܐ
ܡܪܝ، ܗܘܐ ܗܘܐ ܡܕܡ ܕܦܩܕܬ. ܘܬܘܒ ܐܝܬ ܐܬܪܐ ܒܣܡܟܐ.
fol 71 v [23]ܐܡܪ *ܡܪܐ ܠܥܒܕܗ. ܦܘܩ ܠܐܘܪ̈ܚܬܐ ܘܠܣܝ̈ܓܐ ܘܠܦܪ̈ܓܠܐ. ܘܥܒܕ

ܦܘܪܥܢܐ (ܦܪܥܢܐ S)] + ܗܢܐ SA   13 ܡܐ] ܐܡܬܝ A
ܫܪܘܬܐ] ܐܫܪܘܬܐ S; om. A   ܠܡܣ̈ܟܢܐ......ܘܠܥܘ̈ܝܪܐ]
ܠܡܣ̈ܟܢܐ ܘܠܡܚܓ̈ܪܐ ܘܠܡܟܐ̈ܒܐ ܘܠܡܫܠ̈ܡܢܐ ܘܐܚܪ̈ܢܐ ܣܓ̈ܝܐܐ S;
A ܠܡܣ̈ܟܢܐ ܘܠܡܕܘ̈ܓܠܐ ܘܠܡܣ̈ܝܐ ܘܠܚܓ̈ܝܣܐ. ܘܠܐܝܠܝܢ ܕܠܝܬ ܠܗܘܢ.
14 ܕܙܕ̈ܝܩܐ] ܥܡ ܙܕ̈ܝܩܐ A   15. § in S   ܗܠܝܢ 1°] om. S   ܗܠܝܢ 2°] ܗܢܘܢ S
ܠܗ] ܠܗܘܢ S   16—24. *For the allusions in Thos*[315] *and* A 106, 107, *see Introd.* vol. ii   16 ܡܪܢ] ܝܫܘܥ S   ܘܩܪܐ] + ܗܘܐ S   ܠܣ̈ܓܝܐܐ] C (*end of line*); ܠܣܓܝܐܐ S   17 ܥܒܕܗ] *om.* S   18 ܘܐܠܝܨ ܐܢܐ] ⌜ܠܝ⌝ ܘܐܠܝܨ S
20 ܘܕܬܠܬܐ] ܐܚܪܢܐ S   21 ܡܪܐ] *pr.* ܗܘ S   ܦܘܩ] *pr.* ܕ S
ܘܠܥܘ̈ܝܪܐ] + ܘܠܡܚ̈ܓܪܐ S   22 ܥܒܕܐ] *pr.* ܗܘ S   23 ܡܪܐ] *om.* S

13 call thee and thou have repayment. But what *time* thou makest a C S
supper, call the poor and the blind and the halt and the suffering,
14 and happy is it for thee that they have not wherewith they
may repay thee; and thy repayment shall be in the rising of the
15 righteous."¶ And when one of them that were sitting *at meat* had ¶A
heard these things he said to him: "Happy is it for him that shall
16 eat breakfast in the kingdom of God!" Our Lord saith to him:
17 "A certain man had made a great supper and called many, and
he sent his slave at the season of the entertainment that he might
say to those bidden that they should come, 'for lo,' *quoth he*,
18 'everything is ready.' And they had begun immediately to excuse
themselves. The first saith to him: 'A field have I bought, and I
19 need to go forth *and* see it; I beseech thee, excuse me.' And
another saith: 'Five yoke of oxen have I bought, and I go to prove
20 them; I beseech thee, excuse me.' And a third said: 'A wife I
21 have taken; I cannot come.' And that slave came *and* said these
things to his lord. Then the master of the house was wroth, and he
said to his slave: 'Go forth quickly to the streets and lanes of the
city, and bring in hither the poor and the crippled and the suffering
22 and the blinded.' And the slave said: 'My lord, lo, that which thou
didst command has been *done*, and still there is room at the enter-
23 tainment.' Saith the lord to his slave: 'Go forth to the highways
and to between the hedges and make them come in, that my house

repayment] this repayment *S A* 13 what *time*] whenever *A* a supper] *it A* the poor....the suffering] the poor and the blinded and the crippled and the suffering and the rejected and many others *S*; the poor and the ignorant and the blind and the halt and them that have not *A* 14 of the righteous] with the righteous *A* 15 them] those *S* these things] *om. S* to him] to them *S* **16—24.** *For the allusions in Thos*[315] *and A* 106, 107, *see Introduction*, vol ii 16 Our Lord] Jesus *S* called] *pr.* had *S* 17 'for lo'] 'Lo' *S* 18 I need] it is needful for me *S* 20 And a third] Another *S* 21 the poor] + and the rejected *S* 22 that thing which *S* 23 the lord] he *S*

C S ܕܢܥܠܘܢ ܕܢܬܡܠܐ ܒܝܬܝ܀ ²⁴ܐܡܪ ܐܢܐ ܠܟܘܢ ܓܝܪ ܕܐܢܫ ܡܢ
ܗܠܝܢ ܐܢܫܐ ܕܩܪܝܢ ܗܘܘ ܠܐ ܢܛܥܡܘܢ ܐܫܬܘܬܝ܀
²⁵ܘܟܕ ܐܙܠܝܢ ܗܘܘ ܥܡܗ ܟܢܫܐ. ܐܬܦܢܝ ܐܡܪ ܠܗܘܢ܆ ²⁶ܡܢ
ܕܐܬܐ ܠܘܬܝ، ܘܠܐ ܣܢܐ ܠܐܒܘܗܝ ܘܠܐܡܗ܂ ܘܠܐܚܘܗܝ،
ܘܠܐܚܘܬܗ. ܘܠܐܢܬܬܗ ܘܠܒܢܘܗܝ. ܐܦ ܠܢܦܫܗ. ܬܠܡܝܕܐ ܠܐ
ܡܫܟܚ ܕܢܗܘܐ ܠܝ. ²⁷ܘܡܢ ܕܠܐ ܫܩܠ ܙܩܝܦܗ ܘܐܬܐ ܒܬܪܝ،
ܬܠܡܝܕܐ ܠܐ ܡܫܟܚ ܕܢܗܘܐ ܠܝ. ²⁸ܡܢܘ ܓܝܪ ܡܢܟܘܢ ܕܨܒܐ
ܕܢܒܢܐ ܡܓܕܠܐ. ܘܠܐ ܠܘܩܕܡ ܝܬܒ ܡܬܚܫܒ ܢܦ̈ܩܬܗ.
col 2 ܕܐܢܗܘ ܕܐܝܬ *ܠܗ ܠܡܫܠܡܘܬܗ. ²⁹ܕܠܐ ܐܢ ܢܣܝܡ ܫܬܐܣܬܐ
ܘܠܐ ܐܫܟܚ ܕܢܫܠܡ. ܟܠ ܕܚܙܝܢ ܢܗܘܘܢ ܡܒܙܚܝܢ ܒܗ ³⁰ܘܐܡܪܝܢ.
ܗܢܐ ܓܒܪܐ ܫܪܝ ܕܢܒܢܐ ܡܓܕܠܐ. ܘܠܐ ܐܫܟܚ ܕܢܫܠܡ.
³¹ܐܘ ܡܢܘ ܡܠܟܐ ܕܐܙܠ ܠܡܬܟܬܫܘ ܥܡ ܡܠܟܐ ܐܚܪܢܐ. ܘܠܐ
ܠܘܩܕܡ ܡܬܪܥܐ. ܕܐܢ ܡܫܟܚ ܒܥܣܪܐ ܐ̈ܠܦܝܢ ܠܡܐܪܥ. ܠܗܘ
ܕܐܬܐ ܥܠܘܗܝ، ܒܥܣܪܝܢ ܐ̈ܠܦܝܢ. ³²ܘܐܠܐ ܥܕ ܪܚܝܩ ܡܢ ܒܝܬ
ܡܪܘܬܐ. ܡܫܕܪ ܐܝܙܓܕܐ ܘܒܥܐ ܡܢܗ ܥܠ ܫܠܡܐ. ³³ܗܟܢܐ ܟܠ
ܐܢܫ ܡܢܟܘܢ ܕܠܐ ܫܒܩ ܟܠܗ ܩܢܝܢܗ. ܬܠܡܝܕܝ، ܠܐ ܡܫܟܚ
ܕܢܗܘܐ. ³⁴ܛܒܐ ܗܝ ܡܠܚܐ܂ ܐܢ ܕܝܢ ܡܠܚܐ ܬܦܟܗ ܒܡܢܐ
fol 72 r *ܬܬܡܠܚ܂ ³⁵ܠܐ ܠܐܪܥܐ ܐܝܠܐ ܐܦܠܐ ܠܙܒܠܐ. ܐܠܐ ܠܒܪ
ܡܫܬܕܝܐ. ܡܢ ܕܐܝܬ ܠܗ ܐ̈ܕܢܐ ܕܢܫܡܥ ܢܫܡܥ܀

---

24 ܗܠܝܢ] ܗܢܘܢ S ܐܫܬܘܬܝ] ܡܢ ܐܫܬܘܬܐ S 25 ܟܢܫܐ]+ܣܓܝܐܐ S
ܐܡܪ] *pr.* ܘ S 26 ܐܦ] ܘܐܦ S ܬܠܡܝܕܐ] ܬܠܡܝܕܝ S ܠܝ] *om.* S
For the whole verse, cf A 263:— ܡܢ ܕܠܐ ܣܢܐ ܠܝ ܝܬܝܪ ܡܢ ܕܠܐܒܘܗܝ ܘܠܐܡܗ
ܘܝܬܝܪ ܡܢ ܢܦܫܗ ܬܠܡܝܕܐ ܠܐ ܡܫܟܚ ܠܡܗܘܐ ܠܝ 27.] *om.* S (*from homoeoteleuton: cf Tischendorf*[loc]) 28 ܢܦ̈ܩܬܗ] *so also* S ܕܐܢܗܘ ܕܐܝܬ]
ܕܐܢ ܐܝܬ S 29 ܢܣܝܡ] ܣܡ S 30 ܡܓܕܠܐ] *om.* S 31 ܐܘ] C*,
but on an erasure 32 ܡܢ ܒܝܬ ܡܪܘܬܐ] *om.* S;
cf ܡܠܟܐ ܢܚܝܢܐ ܥܕ ܡܐܪܥܐ ܪܚܝܩ ܡܫܕܪ ܐܝܙܓܕܐ ܘܒܥܐ ܫܠܡܐ *A* 302
34 ܬܦܟܗ. S (*sic*) 35 ܐܝܠܐ ܐܦܠܐ ܠܙܒܠܐ] ܘܠܐ ܠܙܒܠܐ ܐܝܠܐ S
ܠܒܪ ܡܫܬܕܝܐ] *tr.* S

24 may be filled; for I say to you that none of these folk that were *C S*
called shall taste my supper.'"
25 And while multitudes were going with him he turned *and* said
26 to them: "He that cometh unto me and hateth not his father and
his mother and his brothers and his sisters and his wife and his
27 sons—*yea*, himself also—a disciple he cannot become of mine. And
he that doth not take up his Cross and come after me—a disciple he
28 cannot become of mine. For which is there of you that would build
a tower, and doth not first sit down *and* reckon the cost of it, if so
29 be that he have *wherewith* to finish it? Else, if he shall lay the
foundation and have not been able to finish, all that see *it* will be
30 mocking at him, and saying: 'This man began to build a tower and
31 was not able to finish.' Or what king is there that goeth to fight
with another king, and doth not first meditate if he be able with ten
thousand to meet him which cometh against him with twenty thou-
32 sand; and if not, while yet he is far from the battle-field he sendeth
33 ambassadors and beseecheth him for peace. So every man of you
that doth not leave all his property—my disciple he cannot become.
34 Excellent is salt; but if salt lose its savour, wherewith shall it be
35 salted? Neither for the land is it of use, nor for the dung-heap;
but it is thrown away. He that hath ears to hear, let him hear!"

---

24 these] those *S* my supper] of the supper *S* 25 multitudes] *pr.* great *S* *and*] and *S* 26 himself] *pr.* and *S* a disciple] my disciple *S* of mine] *om. S* *For the whole verse, cf* 'He that loveth not me more than his father and his mother and more than himself, a disciple he cannot become of mine' *A* 263; *and* 'He that loveth me not more than himself...' E^{98} 27.] *om. S* 28 of it] *so also S* if so be that] if *S* 29 shall lay] have laid *S* 30 a tower] *om. S* 32 from the battle-field] *om. S*; *cf* 'The wise king while yet the battle is far off sendeth ambassadors and beseecheth for peace' *A* 302 35 Neither for the land nor for the dung-heap is it of use *S*

C S ¹ܘܡܟ̈ܣܐ ܘܚ̈ܛܝܐ ܡܬܩܪܒܝܢ ܗܘܘ ܠܗ ܕܢܫܡܥܘܢܗ. ²ܘܦ̈ܪܝܫܐ
ܘܣ̈ܦܪܐ ܪܛܢܝܢ ܗܘܘ ܘܐܡܪܝܢ. ܗܢܐ ܓܒܪܐ ܠܚ̈ܛܝܐ ܡܩܒܠ
ܘܐܟܠ ܥܡܗܘܢ. ³ܐܡܪ ܠܗܘܢ ܗܘ ܡܬܠܐ ܗܢܐ. ⁴ܡܢܘ
ܡܢܟܘܢ ܕܐܝܬ ܠܗ ܡܐܐ ܥܪ̈ܒܝܢ. ܘܐܒܕ ܚܕ ܡܢܗܘܢ ܠܐ
ܫܒܩ ܬܫܥܝܢ ܘܬܫܥܐ ܒܛܘܪܐ. ܘܐܙܠ ܒܥܐ ܠܗܘ ܕܐܒܕ ܥܕܡܐ
ܕܢܫܟܚܝܘܗܝ. ⁵ܘܡܐ ܕܐܫܟܚܗ ܣܐܡ ܠܗ ܥܠ ܟܬܦܬܗ. ܘܚܕܐ
⁶ܘܐܬܐ ܠܒܝܬܗ. ܘܩܪܐ ܠܪ̈ܚܡܘܗܝ ܐܦ ܠܫ̈ܒܒܘܗܝ ܘܐܡܪ ܠܗܘܢ.
col 2 ܚܕܘ ܥܡܝ* ܕܐܫܟܚܬ ܥܪܒܝ ܕܐܒܝܕ ܗܘܐ. ⁷ܐܡܪܢܐ ܠܟܘܢ
§A 142 ܕܗܝ ܕܗܟܢܐ ܬܗܘܐ§ ܚܕܘܬܐ ܒܫܡܝܐ ܥܠ ܚܕ ܚܛܝܐ ܕܬܐܒ.
ܝܬܝܪ ܡܢ ܬ̈ܫܥܝܢ ܘܬ̈ܫܥܐ ܙܕ̈ܝܩܝܢ ܕܠܐ ܡܬܒܥܝܐ ܠܗܘܢ
¶A §A 14 ܬܝܒܘܬܐ.¶ ⁸ܐܘ ܐܝܕܐ§ ܗܝ ܐܢܬܬܐ ܕܐܝܬ ܠܗ̇ ܥܣܪܐ ܙ̈ܘܙܝܢ.
ܘܬܘܒܕ ܚܕ ܡܢܗܘܢ ܠܐ ܡܢܗܪܐ ܫܪܓܐ ܘܡܟܢܫܐ ܒܝܬܐ.
¶A ܘܒܥܝܐ ܠܗ ܒܟܝܠܐܝܬ ܥܕܡܐ ܕܬܫܟܚܝܘܗܝ.¶ ⁹ܘܡܐ ܕܐܫܟܚܬܗ
ܩܪܝܐ ܠܪ̈ܚܡܬܗ ܘܠܫ̈ܒܒܬܗ. ܘܐܡܪܐ ܠܗܝܢ ܚܕܝܢ ܥܡܝ ܕܐܫܟܚܬ
ܙܘܙܝ ܕܐܒܝܕ ܗܘܐ. ¹⁰ܐܡܪܢܐ ܠܟܘܢ ܕܗܟܢܐ ܬܗܘܐ ܚܕܘܬܐ
ܩܕܡ ܟܠܗܘܢ ܡ̈ܠܐܟܐ ܕܐܠܗܐ. ܥܠ ܚܕ ܚܛܝܐ ܕܬܐܒ܀
fol 72 v *¹¹ܐܡܪ ܗܘܐ ܠܗܘܢ ܬܘܒ. ܠܓܒܪܐ ܚܕ ܐܝܬ ܗܘܘ ܠܗ ܬܪ̈ܝܢ
ܒ̈ܢܝܢ. ¹²ܐܡܪ ܠܗ ܙܥܘܪܐ. ܐܒܝ ܗܒ ܠܝ ܦܠܓܘܬܐ ܕܡܛܝܐ ܠܝ

---

1. *No § in S* ܠܗ] ܠܘܬܗ *S* 2 ܓܒܪܐ] *om. S* 3 ܗܘ] *om. S*
4 ܡܢܘ] ܡܢܐ *S*^ed ܘܬܫܥܐ] *so also S* ܒܛܘܪܐ] ܒܛܘܪ̈ܐ *S*
ܕܐܒܕ] ܕܐܒܝܕ *S* 4, 5 ܕܢܫܟܚܝܘܗܝ ⁵ܘܡܐ] *It is evident from the crowding together of these words that no stop was intended between them by the scribe of C*
5 ܣܐܡ] ܫܩܠ *S* 6 ܐܦ] ܘ *S* ܠܗܘܢ] *om. S* ܕܐܒܝܕ *S*^ed
7 ܕܗܝ] *om. S* ܕܬܐܒ] ܕܬܝܒ *A*^b ܝܬܝܪ ܡܢ] ܐܘ ܥܠ *S* ܘܬܫܥܐ *S*^ed
ܡܬܒܥܝܐ ܠܗܘܢ] ܚܣܝܢ ܥܠ *S A* 8 ܘܬܘܒܕ] ܘܬܘܐܒܕ *S (sic)* ܠܐ]
pr. ܘ *A* ܘܡܟܢܫܐ] ܘܡܫܚܐ *S A* ܒܟܝܠܐܝܬ] ܒܚܝܠܐܝܬ *S*
ܘܡܟܢܫܐ....ܕܬܫܟܚܝܘܗܝ] ܘܡܟܢܫܐ ܙܘܝܬܗ ܕܐܘܟܒܬ. *A* 10 ܠܟܘܢ] *om. S*
Cf A 150: ܘܚܕܘܬܐ ܗܘܝܐ ܠܡ̈ܠܐܟܐ ܫܡܝܐ ܥܠ ܚܛܝܐ ܕܬܐܒ ܡܢ ܒܘܠܗ
11 ܗܘܐ] *om. S* ܬܘܒ] *om. S* ܠܓܒܪܐ] ܓܒܪܐ *S* 12 ܠܗ] ܗܘ *S*
ܐܒܝ] ܠܐܒܘܗܝ. *S* ܦܠܓܘܬܐ] ܡܢܬܐ *S*

XV 1 And the toll-gatherers and sinners were drawing near to him that *C S*
2 they might hear him, and the scribes and the Pharisees were
murmuring and saying: "This man receiveth sinners and eateth with
3, 4 them." He saith to them himself this similitude: "Which of you
that hath an hundred sheep and one of them be lost, doth not leave
the ninety and nine in the open country and go *and* seek that which
5 was lost until he find it? And what *time* he hath found it, he layeth
6 it on his shoulders and rejoiceth, and cometh to his house, and calleth
his friends and his neighbours too, and saith to them: 'Rejoice with
7 me, that I have found my sheep that was lost.' Now I say to you
that so §there will be joy in heaven over one sinner that doth repent, §*A* 142
more than *over* ninety and nine righteous for whom is not required
8 repentance.¶ Or §what woman that hath ten drachmas and she lose ¶*A* §*A* 14
one of them, doth not light a lamp and brush the house and seek
9 it carefully until she find it?¶ And what *time* she hath found it she ¶*A*
calleth her friends and her neighbours, and saith to them: 'Rejoice
10 with me, that I have found my drachma that was lost.' I say to you
that so there will be joy before all the angels of God over one sinner
that repenteth."

11 He was saying to them again: "A certain man—he had two
12 sons. The younger saith to him: 'My father, give me the inheritance

---

1 to him] unto him *S* 2 This man] This *fellow S* 3 himself] *om. S* 4 the open country] the wilderness *S* 5 layeth] taketh *S* 6 too] *om. S* to them] *om. S* 7 Now] *om. S* doth] shall *A*[b] more than *over*] *more* than over *S* for whom is not required] who have no need of *S A* 8 doth not] *pr.* and *A* brush] sweep *S A* carefully] diligently *S* and seek..... find it] and seek her drachma that she lost *A* 10 to you] *om. S* *Cf A* 150: 'And joy cometh unto the watchers of heaven when a sinner repenteth from his wickedness' 11 was saying] saith (*or*, 'said') *S* again] *om. S* 12 to him: 'My father, give...] to his father: 'Give... *S* inheritance] portion *S*

CS ܡܢ ܒܝܬܟ· ܘܦܠܛ ܠܗܘܢ ܒܠܗ ܡܫܝܚܐ· [13]ܘܡܢ ܒܬܪ ܡܬܚܢܢܘܬܐ
ܡܠܝܠ· ܒܪܝ ܗܘ ܒܪܗ ܕܚܘܪܐ ܒܠܚܘܕ ܕܟܦܠܚܘܗܝ. ܘܐܝܠ
ܠܐܬܪܐ ܕܝܫܘܥ. ܘܬܡܢ ܒܪܝ ܡܫܝܚܐ ܒܡܥܒܪܬܐ ܐܝܠܝܢ ܕܠܐ
ܩܠܝܢ· ܡܛܠ ܕܝܫܘܥ ܗܘܐ ܦܪܝܫܐܝܬ ܒܡ ܕܐܬܬܐ. [14]ܘܒܪ ܠܒܪ ܥܠ
ܡܕܡ ܕܐܝܬ ܠܗ. ܘܗܘܐ ܚܒܝܒܐ ܒܒܝܬܐ ܒܐܬܪܐ ܗܘ· [15]ܐܝܠ
ܢܦܩ ܠܗ ܠܘܬ ܡܢ ܒܪ ܐܬܪܐ ܗܘ. ܘܒܝܬܗ ܠܡܪܬܐ ܠܡܪܒܐ
ܫܪܝܪܐ. [16]ܘܡܬܬܪܓܡܢ ܗܘܐ ܠܡܐܟܠ ܡܢ ܫܪܒܬܐ ܗܘܢ
col 2 ܕܡܠܟܐ ܕܐܟܠܝܢ *ܗܘܘ ܫܪܝܪܐ· ܘܠܐ ܐܝܟ ܢܦܫ ܗܘܐ ܠܗ·
[17]ܘܒܪ ܐܬܐ ܠܘܬ ܢܦܫܗ ܐܡܪ· ܒܟܡܐ ܐܓܝܪܐ ܐܝܬ ܒܝܬܐ ܒܝܬ
ܐܒܝ ܕܣܒܪ ܠܗܘܢ ܠܚܡܐ. ܘܐܢܐ ܐܒܕ ܐܢܐ ܗܪܟܐ ܡܢ
ܟܦܢܐ. [18]ܐܠܐ ܐܩܘܡ ܐܙܠ ܠܘܬ ܐܒܝ ܘܐܡܪ ܠܗ. ܐܒܝ ܚܛܝܬ
ܒܫܡܝܐ ܘܩܕܡܝܟ. [19]ܘܠܐ ܫܘܐ ܐܢܐ ܡܟܝܠ ܕܒܪܟ ܐܬܩܪܐ.
ܥܒܕܝܢܝ ܐܝܟ ܚܕ ܡܢ ܐܓܝܪܝܟ. [20]ܘܩܡ ܐܬܐ ܠܘܬ ܐܒܘܗܝ.
ܘܥܕ ܗܘ ܪܚܝܩ. ܚܙܝܗܝ ܐܒܘܗܝ، ܘܐܬܪܚܡ ܥܠܘܗܝ. ܘܪܗܛ
ܢܦܠ ܥܠ ܨܘܪܗ ܘܢܫܩܗ. [21]ܘܐܡܪ ܠܗ ܒܪܗ. ܐܒܝ ܚܛܝܬ
ܒܫܡܝܐ ܘܩܕܡܝܟ. ܘܡܟܝܠ ܠܐ ܫܘܐ ܐܢܐ ܕܒܪܟ ܐܬܩܪܐ.
Berl 1r [22]*ܐܡܪ ܐܒܘܗܝ ܠܥܒܕܘܗܝ. ܐܦܩܘ ܐܣܛܠܐ ܪܝܫܝܬܐ
ܐܠܒܫܘܗܝ. ܘܣܝܡܘ ܥܙܩܬܐ ܒܐܝܕܗ. ܘܐܣܐܢܘܗܝ ܡܣܐܢܐ.
[23]ܘܐܝܬܘ ܩܛܘܠܘ ܥܓܠܐ ܗܘ ܕܦܛܡܐ. ܢܐܟܘܠ ܘܢܬܒܣܡ.
§¶A 142 [24]§ܕܗܢܐ ܒܪܝ، ܡܝܬܐ ܗܘܐ ܘܚܝܐ. ܘܐܒܝܕܐ ܗܘܐ ܘܐܫܬܟܚ.¶
ܘܫܪܝܘ ܠܡܬܒܣܡܘ. [25]ܗܘܐ ܒܪܗ ܩܫܝܫܐ ܒܚܩܠܐ ܗܘܐ. ܘܟܕ
ܐܬܐ ܩܪܒ ܠܘܬ ܒܝܬܐ. ܫܡܥ ܩܠ ܙܡܪܐ ܘܪܘܩܕܐ. [26]ܘܩܪܐ

ܒܝܬܟ] ܡܫܝܚ S   ܘ- ܒܠܗ] S illegible   13 ܘܡܢ ܒܬܪ] om. ܡܢ S
ܒܡܥܒܪܬܐ....ܩܠܝܢ] om. S   14 ܚܒܝܒܐ] om. S   15 ܒܪ ܗܘ ܐܬܪܐ S (sic): cf Duval *Gram. Syr.* § 357 *f*   16 ܘܡܬܬܪܓܡܢ] om. ܘ S   ܠܡܐܟܠ....ܫܪܝܪܐ] ܡܢ ܗܘܢ ܚܪܘܒܐ ܕܐܟܠܝܢ ܗܘܘ ܚܙܝܪܐ ܕܒܠܥܐ ܒܪܗܘܢ S   17 ܘܟܕ] ܟܕ S
ܐܓܝܪܐ S   21 ܘܡܟܝܠ] om. ܘ S   22. *Here begins one of the Berlin leaves of C*
ܠܥܒܕܘܗܝ C (sic)   23 ܘܐܝܬܘ S (sic)   24 ܕܗܢܐ ܒܪܝ] tr. A

that cometh to me from thy house.' And he divided to them all his *C S*
13 property. And after a few days that younger son of his gathered
together everything that came to him and went to a far country, and
there he scattered his property in foods which are not fitting, because
14 he was living wastefully with harlots. And when he exhausted
everything that he had, and there was a mighty famine in that
15 country, he went *and* attached himself to one of the men of that
16 country. And he sent him to a field to tend swine, and he was
longing to eat of those husks of the sea that the swine were eating,
17 and no one was giving to him. And when he came unto himself he
said: 'How many hired men are now in my father's house for
18 whom bread aboundeth, and I perish here of my hunger? But I will
arise *and* go unto my father and I will say to him: My father, I have
19 sinned against heaven and before thee, and I am not worthy hence-
forth that I should be called thy son; make me as one of thy hired
20 men.' And he arose *and* came unto his father; and while yet he was
far off his father saw him and had compassion upon him, and he
21 ran *and* fell on his neck and kissed him. And his son said to him:
'My father, I have sinned against heaven and before thee, and hence-
22 forth I am not worthy that I should be called thy son.' Saith his
father to his slaves: 'Bring forth quickly the best robe *and* clothe
23 him, and set a ring on his hand and provide him with shoes, and
24 fetch *and* kill that fatted calf; let us eat and be merry, §for that this §*A* 142
my son was dead and is alive, and was lost and hath been found.'¶ ¶*A*
25 And they began to be merry. And that elder son of his was in the
field, and when he came *and* drew near unto the house he heard a sound
26 of singing and music. And he called one of the lads and asked him:

---

house] property *S* them all] *S illegible* **13** in foods.... fitting] *om. S* **14** mighty] *om. S* **16** and (*after* 'swine')] *om. S* to eat of.... eating] of those pods that the swine were eating to fill his belly *S* **17** And when] When *S* **21** and henceforth] *om.* and *S* **22.** *Here begins one of the Berlin leaves of C*

ܠܚܕ ܡܢ ܛܠܝܐ ܘܐܙܠܗ. ܡܢܘ ܗܢܐ ܘܠܐ ܕܗܡܪܐ ܥܡܟ ܐܢܐ. *C S*
[27]ܘܐܡܪ ܠܗ ܐܚܘܟ ܐܬܐ. ܘܩܛܠ ܐܒܘܟ ܟܠܒܐ ܗܘ ܕܦܛܡܐ
ܕܒܪ ܣܠܝܩ ܡܠܟܗ. [28]ܘܪܓܙ ܘܠܐ ܨܒܐ ܗܘܐ ܠܡܥܠ. ܘܢܦܩ
col 2 ܐܒܘܗܝ، ܘܒܥܐ ܗܘܐ ܡܢܗ. [29]ܐܡܪ ܠܗ ܠܐܒܘܗܝ*، ܗܐ
ܟܡܐ ܫ̈ܢܝܢ ܦܠܚ ܐܢܐ ܠܟ ܒܥܒܕܘܬܐ. ܘܠܐ ܥܒܪܬ ܥܠ ܦܘܩܕܢܟ.
ܘܡܡܬܘܡ ܓܕܝܐ ܚܕ ܠܐ ܝܗܒܬ ܠܝ ܕܐܬܒܣܡ ܥܡ ܪ̈ܚܡܝ.
[30]ܘܗܢܐ ܒܪܟ ܟܕ ܦܪܣ ܡܣܟܢ ܥܡ ܙ̈ܢܝܬܐ. ܢܟܣܬ ܠܗ ܥܓܠܐ
ܗܘ ܕܦܛܡܐ. [31]ܐܡܪ ܠܗ ܒܪܝ، ܐܢܬ ܒܟܠܙܒܢ ܥܡܝ ܐܢܬ. ܘܟܠܡܕܡ
ܕܝܠܝ ܕܝܠܟ ܗܘ. [32]ܠܡܒܣܡ ܕܝܢ ܘܠܡܚܕܐ ܘܠܐ ܗܘܐ ܠܝ. ܕܗܢܐ
ܐܚܘܟ ܡܝܬܐ ܗܘܐ ܘܚܝܐ. ܘܐܒܝܕܐ ܗܘܐ ܘܐܫܬܟܚ ○○ ○○. ○○
[1]ܘܐܡܪ ܗܘܐ ܬܘܒ ܢܫܘܥ ܠܬܠܡ̈ܝܕܘܗܝ، ܓܒܪܐ ܚܕ ܥܬܝܪܐ
ܐܝܬ ܗܘܐ. ܘܐܝܬ ܗܘܐ ܠܗ ܪܒܝܬܐ. ܘܐܬܐܟܠܘ ܩܪ̈ܨܘܗܝ
ܡܕܡܘܗܝ، ܐܡܪܝܢ ܕܡܦܣܝܢ ܣܘܦ. *[2]ܘܩܪܝܗ، ܡܪܗ ܘܐܡܪ ܠܗ. *Berl* IV
ܡܢܘ ܗܢܐ ܕܫܡܥ ܐܢܐ ܥܠܝܟ. ܬܐ ܗܒ ܚܘܫܒܢܐ ܕܪܒܝܬܟ.
ܠܐ ܓܝܪ ܡܟܝܠ ܐܝܬ ܕܬܗܘܐ ܪܒܝܬܐ ܬܗܘܐ ܠܟ. [3]ܐܡܪ ܗܘ
ܪܒ ܒܝܬܐ ܒܠܒܗ. ܡܢܐ ܐܥܒܕ ܕܡܪܝ، ܫܩܠ ܠܗ̇ ܪܒ ܒܝܬܘܬܐ
ܡܢܝ. ܕܐܦܠܘܚ ܠܐ ܡܫܟܚܢܐ. ܘܠܡܫܐܠ ܒܗܬܬܐ. [4]ܝܕܥܬ ܡܢܐ
ܐܥܒܕ. ܕܡܐ ܕܢܦܩܬ ܡܢ ܪܒ ܒܝܬܘܬܐ ܢܩܒܠܘܢܢܝ ܒܒ̈ܬܝܗܘܢ.
[5]ܘܩܪܐ ܗܢܐ ܠܚܕ ܡܢ ܚ̈ܝܒܐ ܕܡܪܗ. ܘܐܡܪ ܠܩܕܡܝܐ ܟܡܐ
ܚܝܒ ܠܡܪܝ. [6]ܐܡܪ ܠܗ ܡܐܐ ܡ̈ܬܪܝܢ ܡܫܚܐ. ܐܡܪ ܠܗ ܣܒ
ܟܬܒܟ ܘܬܒ. ܒܥܓܠ ܟܬܘܒ ܚܡܫܝܢ. [7]ܘܡܢ ܒܬܪܗ ܐܡܪ

---

26 ܘܠܐ ܕܗܡܪܐ ܥܡܟ ܐܢܐ] *om.* S   27 ܘܐܡܪ] *om.* ܘ S   ܗܘ] *om.* S
ܐܟܠܗ S   29 ܐܡܪ] *pr.* ܘ ܒܟܐ S   31 ܐܢܬ 1°] *om.* S   32 ܘܠܡܚܕܐ]
after ܘܠܐ ܗܘܐ S   ܠܝ] *om.* S   1 ܢܫܘܥ] *om.* S   ܪܒ|ܒܝܬܐ S
2 ܬܐ] ܐܬܐ S   ܚܫܒܢܐ S   ܕܬܗܘܐ ܪܒܝܬܐ ܬܗܘܐ ܠܟ]
ܬܗܘܐ ܪܒܝܬܐ ܕܬܗܘܐ ܠܟ S (*sic*)   3 ܪܒ ܒܝܬܐ] C, *the word* ܪܒ *ending
the line*   ܡܢܐ] *after* ܠܗ *in* S   ܕܐܦܠܘܚ] ܘܕܐܫܬܐܠ S (*sic*)   4 ܝܕܥܬ]
so also S   5 ܘܩܪܐ ܗܢܐ] ܘܩܪܐ S   ܠܚܕ ܡܢ] C S (*sic*), *for* ܠܚܕ ܚܕ ܡܢ
ܚܝܒ] ܐܢܬ | ܚܝܒ S   6 ܐܡܪ ܠܗ ܣܒ ܟܬܒܟ] *om.* S   ܘܬܒ ܒܥܓܠ ܟܬܘܒ]
ܘܬܒ ܥܓܠ ܘܟܬܘܒ S   7 ܘܡܢ ܒܬܪܗ] ܘܒܬܪܗ S (*sic, nothing lost*)

27 'What is this sound of singing I hear?' And he saith to him: 'Thy C S
brother hath come, and thy father hath killed that fatted calf, for
28 that he hath received him whole.' And he was wroth, and was
not willing to enter, and his father went forth and was beseeching
29 him. He saith to him, to his father: 'Lo, how many years I do for
thee bondservice and I have not transgressed thy commands, and
never one kid hast thou given to me, that I might be merry with my
30 friends; and this thy son, when he hath wasted thy property with
31 harlots—thou hast slaughtered for him that fatted calf!' He saith
to him: 'My son, thou at all times art with me, and everything of
32 mine is thine; but to be merry and to rejoice it was fitting for thee,
for that this thy brother was a dead *man* and is alive, and was a lost
man and hath been found.'"

xvi 1 And Jesus was saying again to his disciples: "A certain rich
man there was, and he had a steward and he was accused before him
2 as having squandered his property. And his lord called him and
said to him: 'What is this that I hear about thee? Come, give a
reckoning of thy office, for thou canst not be any more steward to
3 me.' That steward saith in himself: 'What shall I do, for that my
lord taketh away the stewardship from me. Work I cannot, and to
4 beg I am ashamed. I have known what I shall do, that what *time* I
have gone forth from the stewardship they may receive me in their
5 houses.' And he sent *and* called one of the debtors of his lord, and
6 he said to the first: 'How much owest thou to my lord?' He saith
to him: 'An hundred firkins *of* oil.' He saith to him: 'Take thy
7 bill and sit down quickly and write them fifty.' And afterwards he

---

26 sound.... I hear] *om.* *S* 27 And he] He *S* 29 saith] answered and said *S* 31 thou...art] at all times thou art *S* 32 and to rejoice ...for thee] it was fitting and to rejoice *S* (*om.* 'for thee,' *as also* E^{163}) 1 Jesus] he *S* 3 from me the stewardship *S* Work I cannot] And dig I cannot *S* 5 sent *and*] *om.* *S* one of] *C S*, *not* 'each one of' 6 He saith to him: 'Take thy bill] *om.* *S* and sit..... write] And he sat down quickly and wrote *S*

(C) S col 2 ܠܐܚܪܢܐ.* ܘܐܢܬ ܟܡܐ ܚܝܒ ܐܢܬ ܠܡܪܝ. ܐܡܪ ܠܗ ܡ̈ܐܐ
ܟܘܪ̈ܝܢ ܚܛܐ. ܐܡܪ ܠܗ ܡܟܠ ܒܟܬܒܟ ܘܟܬܘܒ ܐܢܬ ܬܡܢܐܝܢ
ܟܘܪ̈ܝܢ. [8]ܘܫܒܚ ܡܪܢܐ ܠܪܒ ܒܝܬܐ ܕܥܘܠܐ ܕܚܟܝܡܐܝܬ ܥܒܕ.
ܒ̈ܢܘܗܝ ܓܝܪ ܕܥܠܡܐ ܗܢܐ ܚܟܝܡܝܢ ܐܢܘܢ ܒܫܪܒܬܗܘܢ ܗܕܐ
§A388 ܡܢ ܒ̈ܢܘܗܝ ܕܢܘܗܪܐ. [9]ܘܐܢܐ ܐܡܪܢܐ ܠܟܘܢ §ܥܒܕܘ ܠܟܘܢ
ܪ̈ܚܡܐ ܡܢ ܡܡܘܢܐ ܗܢܐ ܕܥܘܠܐ. ܕܡܐ ܕܚܣܪ ܢܩܒܠܘܢܟܘܢ
¶A ܒܡ̈ܛܠܠܝܗܘܢ ܕܠܥܠܡ.¶ [10]ܡܢ ܕܒܩܠܝܠ ܓܝܪ ܡܗܝܡܢ ܐܦ ܒܣܓܝ
ܡܗܝܡܢ ܗܘ. ܘܡܢ ܕܒܩܠܝܠ ܥܘܠ ܐܦ ܒܣܓܝ ܥܘܠ ܗܘ. [11]ܐܢ
ܒܗܘ ܒܡܡܘܢܐ ܕܥܘܠܐ ܠܐ ܡܗܝܡܢܝܢ ܐܝܬܝܟܘܢ܂ ܫܪܪܐ ܡܢܘ
ܡܗܝܡܢ ܠܟܘܢ. [12]ܘܐܢ ܒܕܠܐ ܕܝܠܟܘܢ ܠܐ ܡܗܝܡܢܝܢ ܐܝܬܝܟܘܢ܂
¶C ܕܝܠܟܘܢ ܡܢ ܢܬܠ ܠܟܘܢ ܀¶
[13]ܠܝܬ ܓܝܪ ܥܒܕܐ ܕܡܫܟܚ ܠܬܪܝܢ ܡܪ̈ܘܢ ܕܠܐ ܠܚܕ
ܢܣܢܐ ܘܠܐܚܪܢܐ ܢܪܚܡ ܐܘ ܠܚܕ ܢܝܩܪ ܘܠܐܚܪܢܐ ܢܒܣܐ ܠܐ
ܡܫܟܚܝܢ ܐܢܬܘܢ ܠܐܠܗܐ ܠܡܦܠܚ ܘܠܡܡܘܢܐ.
§A133 [14]ܘܗܘܐ ܟܕ ܫܡܥܘ ܦܪ̈ܝܫܐ ܗܠܝܢ ܟܠܗܝܢ §ܡܡܝܩܝܢ ܗܘܘ ܒܗ
¶A ܡܛܠ ܕܪ̈ܚܡܝܢ ܗܘܘ ܟܣܦܐ.¶ [15]ܐܡܪ ܠܗܘܢ ܐܢܬܘܢ ܐܢܘܢ
ܕܡܙܕܕܩܝܢ ܢܦܫܗܘܢ ܩܕܡ ܒ̈ܢܝ ܐܢܫܐ ܐܠܗܐ ܕܝܢ ܝܕܥ ܠܒܘܬܟܘܢ
ܕܡܕܡ ܕܪܡ ܒܝܬ ܒ̈ܢܝ ܐܢܫܐ ܛܢܦ ܐܠܗܐ ܢܕܕ ܗܘ ܀ ܀ ܀
[16]ܢܡܘܣܐ ܘܢܒܝܐ ܥܕܡܐ ܠܝܘܚܢܢ. ܡܢ ܗܝܕܝܢ ܡܠܟܘܬܗ ܕܐܠܗܐ
ܡܣܬܒܪܐ ܘܟܠ ܐܢܫ ܠܗ ܡܬܚܣܢ. [17]ܦܫܝܩ ܗܘ ܕܝܢ ܕܫܡܝܐ

S ܘܫܒܘܩ ܡܫܚܐ ܫܒܘܩ ܐܡܪ ܠܗ ܡܟܠ....ܘܟܬܘܒ] S ܠܗ ܠܡܪܝ]
ܟܘܪ̈ܝܢ 2°] om. S 8 ܡܪܢܐ] so I read the photograph of S: ܡܪܝܐ S^ed
S ܘܚܟܝܡܝܢ ܐܢܘܢ ܒܢܘܗܝ ܕܥܠܡܐ ܗܢܐ ܒ̈ܢܘܗܝ ܓܝܪ....ܐܢܘܢ]
ܒܫܪܒܬܗܘܢ] so also S 9 ܘܐܢܐ] ܘܐܦ ܐܢܐ S ܗܢܐ] om. S
ܒܡ̈ܛܠܠܝܗܘܢ] so also S 10 ܗܘ 1°] om. S 11 ܒܗܘ] washed out in C:
cf Lk xx 17, xxii 70, xxiii 3, Joh xi 37 ܒܡܡܘܢܐ C ܡܗܝܡܢܝܢ ܐܝܬܝܟܘܢ]
ܡܗܝܡܢܝܢ ܗܘܝܬܘܢ S ܫܪܪܐ] pr. ܠ S 12 ܡܗܝܡܢܝܢ ܐܝܬܝܟܘܢ]
ܡܗܝܡܢܝܢ ܐܫܬܟܚܬܘܢ S ܡܢ] ⌜ܡܢܘ⌝ S^ed (cf xv 4) 13. No § in S
For A 181, see on Mt vi 24 14 ܡܛܠ....ܟܣܦܐ] before ܡܡܝܩܝܢ ܗܘܘ ܒܗ in A
16 ܡܬܚܣܢ] S (sic)

saith to another: 'And thou, how much owest thou to my lord?' (*C*) *S*
He saith to him: 'An hundred cors *of* wheat.' He saith to him:
8 'Receive thy bill and write them eighty cors.' And the lord praised
the steward of wickedness in that he did wisely, for the sons of this
9 world are wiser in this their generation than the sons of light. And I
myself say to you §Make for yourselves friends from this mammon of §*A* 388
wickedness, that what *time* it hath been exhausted they may receive
10 you into their eternal dwellings.¶ For he that in little is faithful ¶*A*
in much also is faithful, and he that in little is wicked in much also
11 is wicked. If forsooth with the mammon of wickedness ye are not
12 faithful, the truth who doth entrust to you? And if with what is not
yours ye are not faithful, your own who will give to you?¶ | ¶*C*
13 "For there is no slave that can serve two lords; else the one he
will hate and the other he will love, or the one he will endure and
the other he will despise: ye cannot serve God and mammon."
14 And it came to pass when the Pharisees heard all these things
15 §they were mocking at him, because they loved silver.¶ He saith §¶*A* 133
to them: "Ye are they that justify themselves in the eyes of men;
now God knoweth your hearts, that that which is high among men
is filthy before God.
16 "The law and the prophets until John—henceforth the king-
17 dom of God is announced, and every one to it is pressed. Now it
is easier that heaven and earth should pass away than one letter

---

7 to my lord] to him *S* He saith to him: 'Receive......cors'] And he sat down immediately and wrote them eighty *S* 8 the lord] the LORD *S*[ed] for.....wiser] and wiser are the sons of this world *S* 9 I myself] + also *S* this] the *S* 11 forsooth] *washed out in C*: *cf* Lk xx 17, xxii 70, xxiii 3, Joh xi 37 mammon] mâmôlâ *C* (*instead of* mâmônâ) are not] have not been *S* 12 are not] have not been found *S* 13. *For* *A* 181, *see on* Mt vi 24 14 because....silver] *before* 'they were mocking at him' *in A* 16 kingdom of God] kingdom of heaven *E*[57] (*in an allusion*)

ܘܐܪܥܐ ܢܥܒܪܘܢ ܐܘ ܐܬܘܬܐ ܚܕܐ ܡܢ ܢܡܘܣܐ ܬܥܒܪ S
¹⁸ܟܠ ܐܢܫ ܕܫܪܐ ܐܢܬܬܗ ܘܢܣܒ ܐܚܪܬܐ ܡܓܪ ܓܐܪ ܘܗܘ
ܕܢܣܒ ܫܒܝܩܬܐ ܡܓܪ ܓܐܪ
¹⁹ܓܒܪܐ ܚܕ ܕܥܬܝܪܐ ܐܝܬ ܗܘܐ ܡܬܠܒܫ ܗܘܐ ܐܪܓܘܢܐ
ܘܒܘܨܐ ܠܒܫ ܘܟܠܝܘܡ ܡܬܒܣܡ ܗܘܐ ²⁰ܘܡܣܟܢܐ ܚܕ ܐܝܬ
ܗܘܐ ܕܫܡܗ ܠܥܙܪ ܘܪܡܐ ܗܘܐ ܠܘܬ ܬܪܥܗ ²¹ܘܡܬܪܓܪܓ ܗܘܐ
ܕܢܣܒܥ ܒܪܣܗ ܡܢ ܡܕܡ ܕܢܦܠ ܗܘܐ ܡܢ ܦܬܘܪܗ ܕܗܘ
§A 383 ܥܬܝܪܐ ܘܐܦ ܟܠܒ̈ܐ ܐܬܝܢ ܗܘܘ ܡܠܚܟܝܢ ܫܘ̈ܚܢܘܗܝ ²²§ܘܗܘܐ
ܘܡܝܬ ܗܘ ܡܣܟܢܐ ܘܐܘܒܠܘܗܝ ܡܠܐܟܐ ܠܥܘܒܗ ܕܐܒܪܗܡ
ܘܡܝܬ ܗܘ ܥܬܝܪܐ ܘܐܬܩܒܪ ²³†ܘܪܡܣܐ ܒܫܝܘܠ† ܐܪܝܡ ܥܝܢܘܗܝ
ܟܕ ܡܫܬܢܩ ܘܚܙܐ ܗܘܐ ܠܐܒܪܗܡ ܡܢ ܪܘܚܩ ܘܠܠܥܙܪ ܒܥܘܒܗ.
²⁴ܘܩܪܐ ܘܐܡܪ ܐܒܝ ܐܒܪܗܡ ܐܬܪܚܡ ܥܠܝ. ܫܕܪ ܠܠܥܙܪ ܕܢܨܒܥ
ܪܝܫ ܨܒܥܗ ܒܡܝܐ ܢܩܘܪܪ ܠܝ ܠܫܢܝ ܕܗܐ ܡܫܬܢܩ ܐܢܐ
ܒܫܠܗܒܝܬܐ ܗܕܐ ²⁵ܐܡܪ ܠܗ ܐܒܪܗܡ †ܒܪܝ† ܐܬܕܟܪ ܕܩܒܠܬ

---

19 *Cf* A 181 ܥܬܝܪܐ ܕܐܪܓܘܢܐ ܠܒܝܫ ܗܘܐ....ܢܦܠ ܒܬܫܢܝܩܐ

19—31. *The story of Dives and Lazarus is given in* A 381—384 *as below*:—

A 381, 382 ܘܬܘܒ ܚܘܝ ܬܘܚܬܐ ܐܚܪܬܐ ܒܥܬܝܪܐ ܕܐܬܒܣܡ ܒܥܠܡܗ. ܘܗܘܐ ܛܠܘܡ ܒܥܘܠ. ²⁰ܘܡܣܟܢܐ ܕܪܡܐ ܗܘܐ ܥܠ ܬܪܥܗ. ²¹ܘܡܐܒ ܗܘܐ ܘܡܬܪܓܝܓ ܕܢܣܒܥ ܒܪܣܗ. ܡܢ ܡܕܡ ܕܢܦܠ ܗܘܐ ܡܢ ܦܬܘܪܗ (Aª ܦܬܘܪ̈ܘܗܝ) ܕܗܘ ܥܬܝܪܐ. ܘܐܡܪ. ܕܠܐ ܐܢܫ ܝܗܒ ܗܘܐ ܠܗ. ܘܐܡܪ ܕܐܦ ܕܟܠܒ̈ܐ ܐܬܝܢ ܗܘܘ ܘܠܚܟܝܢ ܫܘ̈ܚܢܘܗܝ.

A 383 ܘܐܡܪ ܒܚܪܬܗ ܕܬܫܥܝܬܐ. ²²ܕܗܘܐ ܘܡܝܬ ܗܘ ܥܬܝܪܐ. ܘܐܬܩܒܪ. ²³ܘܪܡܐ ܗܘܐ ܒܬܫܢܝܩܐ. ܘܐܦ ܗܘ ܡܣܟܢܐ ܡܝܬ ܘܐܘܒܠܘܗܝ ܡܠܐܟ̈ܐ ܠܥܘܒܗ ܕܐܒܪܗܡ.

23 ܘܪܡܣܐ] S (*sic*), *but the* ܪ *is not quite clear*

(*A* 383 *cont.*) ܘܐܪܝܡ ܥܝܢܘ̈ܗܝ ܗܘ ܥܬܝܪܐ ܡܢ ܓܘ ܫܝܘܠ ܘܡܢ ܬܫܢܝܩܐ. ܘܚܙܐ ܠܐܒܪܗܡ ܘܠܠܥܙܪ ܒܥܘܒܗ (Aᵇ ܒܥܘܒܗ). ²⁴ܘܩܪܐ ܒܩܠܐ ܪܡܐ ܘܐܡܪ. ܐܒܝ ܐܒܪܗܡ ܪܚܡ (Aª ܐܬܪܚܡ) ܥܠܝ. ܘܫܕܪ ܠܠܥܙܪ ܕܢܐܬܐ ܢܨܒܘܥ. ܘܢܛܠ ܠܝ ܠܫܢܝ ܡܢ ܡܘܡܢܐ ܕܐܫܠܗܒ ܐܢܐ ܓܘܗ.

24 ܢܩܘܪܪ] S (*sic*)   25 ܒܪܝ] A *Ephr* ('*Quotations*,' p. 71); ܒܪܡ S (*sic*)

18 from the law pass away. Every one that dismisseth his wife and S
taketh another doth indeed commit adultery, and he which taketh
a divorced woman doth indeed commit adultery.
19 "A certain man that was rich was clothed in purple and fine
20 garments, and every day was making merry; and a certain poor man
21 there was, whose name *was* Lazar, and he was lying by his door and
was longing to fill his belly from that which was falling from the
table of that rich man, and the dogs also were coming *and* licking his
22 sores. §And it came to pass that that poor man died, and the angels §*A* 383
carried him to the bosom of Abraham; and that rich man died
23 and was buried and †cast† in Sheol he lifted up his eyes, being
tormented, and he was seeing Abraham from afar and Lazar in his
24 bosom. And he called and said: 'My father Abraham, have compassion on me, and send Lazar that he may dip the tip of his finger
in water *and* cool for me my tongue, for lo, I am tormented in this
25 flame!' Abraham saith to him: '†My son†, remember that thou

---

19 *Cf A* 181: 'The rich man that in purples was clad.... fell into torment'

19—31. *The story of Dives and Lazarus is given in A* 381—384 *as below*:—

A 381, 382 And again he shewed another demonstration about a rich man that made merry with his goods, and the end of him was in Sheol. [20]And *he told of* a poor man that was lying at his door, [21]and was desirous and craving that he might fill his belly with that which was falling from the table (tables A^a) of that rich man, and he said 'No man was giving to him.' And it saith there 'The dogs were coming and licking his sores.'

A 383 And he said in the end of the matter [22]It came to pass that that rich man died and was buried [23]and was lying in torment, and that poor man also died and the angels carried him to the bosom of Abraham.

23 †cast† in Sheol] *S not quite legible, nor is the construction clear*

A 383 (*cont.*) And that rich man lifted up his eyes from the midst of Sheol and from the torment and he saw Abraham, and Lazar in his lap (in his bosom A^b). [24]And he called with a loud voice and said: 'My father Abraham, have compassion on me, and send Lazar that he may come *and* help me and moisten for me my tongue from the burning, for that I am in a strait exceedingly!'

25 †My son†] *A Ephr* E^{175} (*expressly*); Nevertheless *S* (*sic*)

S [C] ܛܒܬܟ ܒܚܝܝܟ ܘܗܟܘܬ ܐܦ ܠܥܙܪ ܒܝܫܬܗ ܘܗܫܐ ܗܪܟܐ
ܡܬܒܝܐ ܘܐܢܬ ܡܫܬܢܩ ܐܢܬ [26]ܘܒܟܠܗܝܢ̈ ܒܢ ܗܠܝܢ ܒܝܢܬܢ
ܗܘܬܐ ܪܒܬܐ ܫܘܚܐ ܒܝܢܝ ܘܠܟܘܢ ܕܐܝܠܝܢ ܕܨܒܝܢ ܕܢܥܒܪܘܢ
ܡܟܐ ܠܘܬܟܘܢ ܠܐ ܢܫܟܚܘܢ ܘܐܦܠܐ ܕܡܢ ܬܡܢ ܢܥܒܪܘܢ
ܠܘܬܢ [27]ܐܡܪ ܡܕܝܢ ܒܒܥܐ ܡܢܟ ܐܒܝ ܕܬܫܕܪܝܘܗܝ ܠܒܝܬ ܐܒܝ
[28]ܚܡܫܐ ܓܝܪ ܐܚܝܢ ܐܝܬ ܠܝ. ܕܢܣܗܕ ܐܢܘܢ ܕܠܡܐ ܐܦ
ܗܢܘܢ ܢܐܬܘܢ ܠܕܘܟܬܐ ܗܕܐ ܕܬܫܢܝܩܐ [29]ܐܡܪ ܐܒܪܗܡ
ܐܝܬ ܠܗܘܢ ܡܘܫܐ ܘܢܒܝܐ ܢܫܡܥܘܢ ܐܢܘܢ [30]ܐܡܪ ܠܗ
ܠܐ ܐܒܝ ܐܒܪܗܡ ܐܠܐ ܐܢ ܐܢܫ ܡܢ ܡܝܬܐ ܢܐܙܠ ܠܘܬܗܘܢ
ܬܝܒܝܢ [31]ܐܡܪ ܠܗ ܐܢ ܠܡܘܫܐ ܘܠܢܒܝܐ ܠܐ ܫܡܥܝܢ ܐܦܠܐ
¶A ܐܢ ܐܢܫ ܡܢ ܡܝ̈ܬܐ ܢܐܙܠ ܡܗܝܡܢܝܢ ܠܗ¶ ○ ○ ○
[1]ܘܐܡܪ ܗܘܐ ܠܬܠܡܝܕܘܗܝ, ܠܐ ܡܫܟܚܐ ܕܠܐ ܢܐܬܘܢ ܡܟܫܘ̈ܠܐ.
§C ܒܪܡ ܘܝ, | §ܠܗܘ ܕܒܐܝܕܗ ܢܐܬܘܢ ܡܟܫܘ̈ܠܐ. [2]ܦܩܚ ܗܘܐ ܠܗ
Berl 2 r ܐܠܘ ܪܚܝܐ ܕܚܡܪܐ ܬܠܝܐ ܒܨܘܪܗ ܘܡܫܬܕܐ ܒܝܡܐ. ܐܘ ܕܢܟܫܠ
§A35 ܠܚܕ ܡܢ ܗܠܝܢ ܙܥܘ̈ܪܐ. [3]ܐܙܕܗܪܘ ܒܢܦܫܟܘܢ: §ܐܢ ܣܟܠܐ
ܐܚܘܟ ܒܟ, ܟܐܝ ܒܗ. ܐܢ ܬܒ ܫܒܘܩ ܠܗ. [4]ܘܐܢ ܫܒܥ ܙܒܢܝܢ
ܒܝܘܡܐ ܣܟܠܐ ܒܟ. ܘܫܒܥ ܙܒܢܝܢ ܢܬܦܢܐ ܠܘܬܟ ܘܢܐܡܪ ܠܟ
¶A ܕܬܐܒ ܐܢܐ. ܫܒܘܩ ܠܗ¶ ··܀··

ܗܪܟܐ ܡܬܒܝܐ] ܒܒܝܬ ܡܢܝܚ A Ephr ('*Quotations*,' p. 71): *see Introd.*, vol. ii
A 383 (*cont.*) [25]ܐܡܪ ܠܗ ܐܒܪܗܡ. ܒܪܝ. ܕܟܪ (A^a ܐܬܕܟܪ) ܕܩܒܠܬ ܛܒܬܟ
ܒܚܝܝܟ. ܘܠܥܙܪ ܩܒܠ ܒܝܫܬܗ. ܘܗܫܐ ܗܘ ܒܒܝܬ ܡܢܝܚ. ܘܐܢܬ ܡܬܕܒܪ ܠܟ. [26]ܘܥܠ
ܕܫܘܬܐ ܪܒܐ ܐܝܬ ܒܝܢܝ ܘܠܟܘܢ. ܘܠܐ ܡܢܟܘܢ ܡܨܝܢ ܠܡܐܬܐ ܠܘܬܢ.
ܘܐܦܠܐ ܡܢ ܠܘܬܢ. [27]ܐܡܪ ܠܗ. ܘܒܥܐ ܕܠܐ ܐܒܝ ܒܥܐ ܐܢܐ ܡܢܟ.
ܕܬܫܕܪ ܠܒܝܬ ܐܒܝ. [28]ܚܡܫܐ ܓܝܪ ܐܚܝܢ ܐܝܬ ܠܝ. ܢܐܙܠ ܢܣܗܕ ܠܗܘܢ ܘܠܐ
(A^a ܕܠܐ) ܣܠܩܘܢ. ܘܢܐܬܘܢ ܐܦ ܗܢܘܢ ܠܗܢܐ ܬܫܢܝܩܐ. A 384 [29]ܘܐܡܪ ܠܗ
ܐܒܪܗܡ. ܐܝܬ ܠܗܘܢ ܡܘܫܐ ܘܢܒܝܐ. ܢܫܡܥܘܢ ܠܗܘܢ. [30]ܐܡܪ ܠܗ ܠܐ
ܐܒܝ ܐܒܪܗܡ. ܐܠܐ ܢܐܙܠ ܐܢܫ ܡܢ ܡܝܬܐ ܠܘܬܗܘܢ ܘܬܝܒܝܢ. [31]ܐܡܪ
ܠܗ ܐܒܪܗܡ. ܐܢ ܠܡܘܫܐ ܘܠܢܒܝܐ ܠܐ ܫܡܥܝܢ. ܐܦܠܐ ܐܢ ܐܢܫ ܡܢ
ܡܝܬܐ ܢܐܙܠ ܠܘܬܗܘܢ ܡܗܝܡܢܝܢ ܒܗ.

27 ܕܬܫܕܪܝܘܗܝ] S (*sic*)

1 ܡܟܫܘ̈ܠܐ 2°] *om.* S   2 ܘܡܫܬܕܐ] ܘܫܕܝܐ S   ܕܢܟܫܠ] ܢܟܫܠ S (*sic*)
3 ܣܟܠܐ] ܣܟܠ S   ܟܐܝ] ܟܐܐ S (*sic*)   4 ܒܟ] *om.* S
ܘܫܒܥ] ܘܗܠܝܢ ܫܒܥ S   ܠܟ] *om.* S   *Vv.* 3 *&* 4 *appear thus in* A 35:—
[3]ܐܢ ܢܣܟܠ (A^a ܢܣܟܠ) ܒܟ ܐܚܘܟ ܫܒܘܩ ܠܗ. [4]ܘܐܦ (A^a ܐܦ) ܫܒܥ
ܙܒܢܝܢ ܢܣܟܠ ܒܟ ܒܝܘܡܐ ܚܕ ܫܒܘܩ ܠܗ.

didst receive thy good things in thy life, and likewise Lazar also his *S* [*C*]
evil things ; and now here he taketh his ease and thou art tormented.
26 And with all these same things a great gulf is set between us and
you, that they that wish to cross over hence unto you should not be
27 able, nor from there cross over unto us.' He saith : 'Why then I
28 beseech thee, my father, that thou send him to my father's house, for
I have five brothers ; that he may bear witness unto them, lest they
29 also come to this place of torment.' Saith Abraham : 'They have
30 Moses and the prophets ; let them hear them.' He saith to him :
'Nay, my father Abraham, but if one from the dead should go unto
31 them they would repent.' He saith to him : 'If Moses and the
prophets they hear not, neither if one from the dead should go
would they believe him.' "¶ ¶*A*
xvii 1 And he had said to his disciples : "It cannot be that offences
should not come, nevertheless woe | §to him by whose hand the §*C*
2 offences come ! It were profitable for him if an ass's millstone should
be hanged about his neck and he be sunk in the sea, rather than
3 that he should offend one of these little ones. Beware in yourselves :
§if thy brother have sinned, rebuke him ; if he have repented, forgive §*A*35
4 him, And if seven times in the day he sin against thee, and seven
times he turn round unto thee and say to thee 'I repent,' forgive him."¶ ¶*A*

---

here......ease] thou dost beseech him *A Ephr* : *i.e.* ὅδε παρακαλεῖται

A 383 (*cont.*) [25]Abraham saith to him : 'My son, recollect (remember *A*[a]) that thou didst receive thy good things in thy life, and Lazar received his evil things ; but to-day thou dost beseech him, and he doth not help thee [26]because a great ditch is between us and you, and from you they cannot come unto us nor from us unto you.' [27]He saith to him : 'And inasmuch as it is not *so*, my father, I beseech thee that thou send to my father's house, [28]for I have five brothers ; let him go *and* bear witness to them and they will not (that they may not *A*[a]) sin and come themselves also to this torment.'

A 384 [29]And Abraham said to him : 'They have Moses and the prophets ; let them hear from them.' [30]He saith to him : 'Nay, my father Abraham, but let one from the dead go unto them and they would repent.' [31]Abraham saith to him : 'If Moses and the prophets they hear not, neither if one from the dead should go unto them would they believe in him.'

1 the offences 2°] they *S* 2 sunk] thrown *S* that he should] *om. S* 3 have sinned] should sin *S* rebuke] rebuked *S* (*sic*) 4 against thee] *om. S* and seven] and these seven *S* to thee] *om. S* *Vv.* 3 *&* 4 *appear thus in A*35 :—'[3]If thy brother trespass against thee, forgive him ; [4][and] even if seven times he trespass against thee in one day, forgive him.'

C S §¶A 21 [5]ܘܐܡܪܝܢ ܠܗ ܫ̈ܠܝܚܐ ܠܡܪܢ. §ܐܘܣܦ ܠܢ ܗܝܡܢܘܬܐ.¶ [6]ܐܡܪ
ܠܗܘܢ ܐܠܘ ܐܝܬ ܗܘܐ ܒܟܘܢ ܗܝܡܢܘܬܐ ܐܝܟ ܦܪܕܬܐ
ܕܚܪܕܠܐ. ܐܡܪܝܢ ܗܘܝܬܘܢ ܠܬܘܬܐ ܕܥܩܪܐ ܡܢ ܗܪܟܐ ܘܡܬܢܨܒܐ
col 2 ܗܘܐ. ܘܠܬܘܬܐ ܕܐܬܥܩܪ ܘܐܬܢܨܒ ܒܝܡܐ *ܘܡܫܬܡܥ ܗܘܐ
ܠܟܘܢ܁ [7]ܡܢܘ ܡܢܟܘܢ ܕܐܝܬ ܠܗ ܥܒܕܐ ܕܕܒܪ ܦܕܢܐ ܐܘ
ܕܪܥܐ ܥܢܐ. ܘܡܐ ܕܥܠ ܡܢ ܩܪܝܬܐ. ܠܡܐ ܐܡܪ ܠܗ ܒܪܫܥܬܗ
ܥܒܪ ܐܣܬܡܟ. [8]ܐܠܐ ܐܡܪ ܠܗ ܛܝܒ ܠܝ ܡܕܡ ܕܐܚܫܡ.
ܘܐܣܘܪ ܚܨܝܟ ܫܡܫܝܢܝ. ܥܕܡܐ ܕܐܠܥܣ ܘܐܫܬܐ. ܘܒܬܪ ܟܢ
ܘܐܦ ܐܢܬ ܬܠܥܣ ܘܬܫܬܐ. [9]ܠܡܐ ܛܝܒܘܬܐ ܕܥܒܕܗ ܐܚܝܕ
ܥܒܕܐ ܗܘ. ܕܥܒܕ ܐܝܠܝܢ ܕܦܩܕ ܠܗ. [10]ܗܟܢܐ ܐܦ ܐܢܬܘܢ ܡܐ
ܕܥܒܕܬܘܢ ܐܝܠܝܢ ܕܦܩܝܕܝܢ ܠܟܘܢ܁ ܐܡܪܝܢ ܐܢܬܘܢ ܐܝܟܢ
ܥܒ̈ܕܐ ܒ̈ܛܝܠܐ. ܡܕܡ ܕܚܝܒܝܢ ܗܘܝܢ ܠܡܥܒܕ ܥܒܕܢ.܀
Berl 2 v [11]ܘܟܕ ܐܙܠ ܗܘܐ ܠܐܘܪܫܠܡ. ܘܥܒܪ ܗܘܐ *ܒܝܬ ܫܡ̈ܪܝܐ ܠܓ̈ܠܝܠܐ
ܠܐܪܢܘܗ. [12]ܘܟܕ ܥܐܠ ܗܘܐ ܠܩܪܝܬܐ ܚܕܐ. ܘܗܘܐ ܦ̈ܓܥܐ
ܐܬܝܢ ܓܒ̈ܪܐ ܥܣܪܐ ܡܢ ܪܘܚܩܐ. [13]ܘܐܪܝܡܘ ܩܠܗܘܢ ܘܐܡܪܝܢ
ܠܗ. ܝܫܘܥ ܪܒܢ ܐܬܪܚܡ ܥܠܝܢ. [14]ܟܕ ܚܙܐ ܐܢܘܢ ܐܡܪ ܠܗܘܢ܁
ܙܠܘ ܚܘܘ ܢܦܫܟܘܢ ܠܟܗ̈ܢܐ. ܘܟܕ ܐܙܠܝܢ ܐܬܕܟܝܘ. [15]ܚܕ ܡܢܗܘܢ
ܕܝܢ ܟܕ ܚܙܐ ܕܐܬܕܟܝ. ܗܦܟ ܠܗ ܘܒܩܠܐ ܪܡܐ ܡܫܒܚ ܗܘܐ

---

5 ܫܠܝܚܘܗܝ S   ܠܡܪܢ] ܠܝܫܘܥ S   6 ܐܡܪ] pr. ܘ ܗܘܐ S
ܐܡܪܝܢ] ܐܡܪܬܘܢ S   ܐܝܬ ܗܘܐ ܒܟܘܢ] ܐܝܬ ܒܟܘܢ S (sic)
S ܡܢ ܗܪܟܐ + ܕܐܬܥܩܪ] ܠܬܘܬܐ ܗܢܐ S   ܠܬܘܬܐ] ... ܘܠܬܘܬܐ
ܘܡܫܬܡܥ] om. ܘ S   For A 21, see on Mt xvii 20   7 ܡܢܘ] pr. ܘ S
ܕܥܠ] ܕܥܐܠ S   ܩܪܝܬܐ] ܚܩܠܐ S (sic): cf vv. 31, 36, and the parallel case of ܐܠܐ Mt xiv 22 C   ܒܪܫܥܬܗ] ܒܫܥܬܐ S   8 ܐܦ ܐܢܬ] om. ܘ S
9 ܕܦܩܕ] ܕܦܩܕܗ S   10 ܥܒ̈ܕܐ] om. S   11 ܗܘܐ 2°] om. S   ܠܓ̈ܠܝܠܐ]
ܠܓ̈ܠܝܠܐ S (or ܠܓܠܝܠܐ): the final ܐ is clear   ܠܐܪܢܘܗ] om. S
12 ܘܗܘܐ] ܘܗܘܐ ܦܓܥܘ S   14 ܟܕ] ܘܟܕ S   ܘܟܕ ܐܙܠܝܢ] om. ܘ S[ed]
15 ܚܕ ܡܢܗܘܢ] ܘܚܕ ܡܢܗܘܢ S   ܗܦܟ] + ܗܘܐ S   ܪܡܐ] ܪܒܐ S

5, 6 The apostles say to him, to our Lord : §" Add to us faith."¶ He *C S*
saith to them : " If there were in you faith as a grain of mustard, ye §¶*A* 21
would be saying to a hill that it should remove from hence and it
would remove, and to a mulberry-tree 'Be rooted up and be planted
7 in the sea.' and it would obey you. Which is there of you that hath
a slave driving the plough or tending the flock, and what *time* he
hath come in from the field doth he say to him straightway : 'Pass
8 through *and* sit down *to meat*' ? But he saith to him : 'Make ready
for me something that I may sup, and gird thy loins *and* serve me
until I shall have eaten and drunk, and afterwards thou also shalt eat
9 and drink.' Doth that slave hold a favour for himself that he hath
10 done the things which he commanded him ? So ye also, what *time* ye
have done what things are commanded you, ye say : 'We are slaves
and riffraff ; that which we were bound to do we have done.' "
11 And when he was going to Jerusalem and was passing through
12 between the Samaritans and the Galilaeans to Jericho, and when he
13 was entering a certain city, lo, ten men, lepers, stood from afar and
they lifted up their voice and say to him : " Jesus, Rabban, have
14 compassion on us ! " When he saw them he saith to them : " Go,
shew yourselves to the priests." And while they were going they
15 were cleansed. Now one of them, when he saw that he was cleansed,
16 returned and with a loud voice was glorifying God, and he fell on his

---

5 The apostles] His apostles *S* our Lord] Jesus *S* 6 saith] answered and said *S* there were in you] there be in you *S* (*sic*) would be saying] would have said *S* to a hill......tree] to this mulberry-tree *S* rooted up] + from hence *S* and it] *om.* and *S* *For A* 21, *see on* Mt xvii 20 7 Which] And which *S* field] *S has a word for* 'field' *here which is in* syr.vg, *but is elsewhere avoided by S and C* (*e.g. in vv.* 31, 36 : *cf* Mt xiv 22 *C*) straightway] immediately *S* 9 he commanded] is commanded *S* (*sic*): *probably a mere error of the scribe* 10 riffraff] *lit.* 'sweepings'; *om. S* (= aeth) 11 was 2°] *om. S* the Galilaeans] *C S* (*sic*): *see Notes,* vol. ii to Jericho] *om. S* 12 stood] were standing *S* 14 When] And when *S* And while] While *S*[ed] 15 Now] And *S* returned] had returned *S* loud] great *S*

C S ܠܐܠܗܐ. [16]ܘܢܦܠ ܥܠ ܐ̈ܦܘܗܝ، ܩܕܡ ܪ̈ܓܠܘܗܝ، ܕܝܫܘܥ ܘܡܘܕܐ
ܗܘܐ ܠܗ. ܘܗܘ ܗܢܐ ܓܒܪܐ ܫܡܪܝܐ ܗܘܐ. [17]ܐܡܪ ܝܫܘܥ
ܗܠܝܢ ܥ̈ܣܪܐ ܗܘܝܢ ܗܘܘ ܕܐܬܕܟܝܘ. ܬܫܥܐ ܐܝܟܐ ܐܢܘܢ.
col 2 [18]ܚܕ ܡܢܗܘܢ ܕܝܢ ܠܐ *ܐܫܬܟܚ ܕܗܦܟ ܠܡܬܠ ܬܫܒܘܚܬܐ
ܠܐܠܗܐ. ܐܠܐ ܗܢܐ ܕܡܢ ܥܡܐ ܗܘ ܢܘܟܪܝܐ. [19]ܐܡܪ ܠܗ ܙܠ
ܗܝܡܢܘܬܟ ܐܚܝܬܟ ⊙ ○ ○ ○ ○ ○ ○
[20]ܘܫܐܠܘܗܝ، ܦ̈ܪܝܫܐ ܘܐܡܪܝܢ ܠܗ. ܐܡܬܝ، ܐܬܝܐ ܡܠܟܘܬܗ
ܕܐܠܗܐ. ܐܡܪ ܠܗܘܢ ܠܐ ܐܬܝܐ ܡܠܟܘܬܗ ܕܐܠܗܐ ܒܢܛܘܪ̈ܬܐ.
[21]ܘܠܐ ܢܐܡܪܘܢ ܗܐ ܗܪܟܐ ܗܝ، ܐܘ ܗܐ ܬܡܢ ܗܝ. ܗܐ
ܓܝܪ ܡܠܟܘܬܗ ܕܐܠܗܐ ܒܝܢܬܟܘܢ ܀
[22]ܘܐܡܪ ܗܘܐ ܠܬܠܡܝ̈ܕܘܗܝ، ܢܐܬܘܢ ܝܘܡ̈ܬܐ ܕܬܬܪܓܪܓܘܢ
ܕܬܚܙܘܢ ܠܚܕ ܡܢ ܝܘܡ̈ܬܐ ܕܒܪܗ ܕܐܢܫܐ ܘܠܐ ܬܚܙܘܢ܀ [23]ܘܐܢ
fol 73 r ܢܐܡܪܘܢ ܠܟܘܢ ܕܗܐ ܗܪܟܐ ܗܘ ܘܗܐ ܬܡܢ *ܗܘ· ܠܐ
ܬܐܙܠܘܢ ܘܠܐ ܬܪܕܦܘܢ܀ [24]ܐܟܢܐ ܓܝܪ ܕܒܪܩܐ ܒܪܩ ܡܢ
ܪܩܝܥܐ ܕܫܡܝܐ ܘܡܢܗܪܐ ܠܬܚܘ̈ܬܗ· ܗܟܢܐ ܢܗܘܐ ܝܘܡܗ ܕܒܪܗ
ܕܐܢܫܐ. [25]ܠܘܩܕܡ ܕܝܢ ܥܬܝܕ ܗܘ ܕܢܚܫ ܣ̈ܓܝܐܬܐ. ܘܕܢܣܬܠܐ
ܡܢ ܫܪܒܬܐ ܗܕܐ. [26]ܘܐܝܟܢܐ ܕܗܘܐ ܒܝܘܡ̈ܝ ܢܘܚ. ܗܟܢܐ
ܢܗܘܐ ܒܝܘܡ̈ܬܗ ܕܒܪܗ ܕܐܢܫܐ. [27]ܕܐܟܠܝܢ ܗܘܘ ܘܫܬܝܢ. ܘܢܣܒܝܢ
ܗܘܘ ܢܫ̈ܐ ܘܡܗܒܝܢ ܗܘܘ ܠܓܒ̈ܪܐ. ܥܕܡܐ ܠܝܘܡܐ ܕܥܠ ܢܘܚ.

---

16 ܓܒܪܐ] *om.* S 17 ܐܡܪ ܝܫܘܥ] ܥܢܐ ܝܫܘܥ ܘܐܡܪ ܗܘܐ S (*sic vid.*) ܗܠܝܢ ܥ̈ܣܪܐ ܗܘܝܢ ܗܘܘ] ܥܣܪܐ ܗܘܝܢ ܗܠܝܢ S (*sic, see Notes*, vol. ii) ܬܫܥܐ ܐܝܟܐ ܐܢܘܢ] ܐܝܠܝܢ ܐܝܟܐ ܬܫܥܐ S 18 ܕܝܢ] *om.* S ܐܫܬܟܚ ܕܗܦܟ] ܗܦܟ S 19 ܐܡܪ ܠܗ] S *illegible* 20 ܐܡܪ ܠܗܘܢ] *pr.* ܘ ܥܢܐ S 21 ܢܐܡܪܘܢ] ܐܡܪܝܢ S ܗܐ 1° & 2°] *om.* S 22. *No* § *in* S ܠܚܕ] ܚܕ S ܝܘܡ̈ܬܐ 2°] ܝܘܡ̈ܬܗ S 23 ܕܗܐ] *om.* ܕ S ܗܘ 2°] *om.* S. *Here begin again the London leaves of C* ܬܪܕܦܘܢ] ܬܪܗܛܘܢ S (*written* ܬܪܛܘܢ : *cf* Mk xii 1) 24 ܐܟܢܐ] ܐܝܟܢܐ S ܪܩܝܥܐ] ܫܡܝܐ S ܘܡܢܗܪܐ] *om.* ܘ S ܠܬܚܘ̈ܬܗ] ܠܬܚܬܗ S 25 ܠܘܩܕܡ] *pr.* ܡܢ S 26 ܒܝܘ̈ܡܬܐ ܕܢܘܚ S ܒܝܘܡ̈ܬܗ] ܒܝܘܡ̈ܬܐ S 27 ܘܡܗܒܝܢ ܗܘܘ] *om.* ܗܘܘ S

face before the feet of Jesus and was giving him thanks; and that C S
17 same leper was a Samaritan. Saith Jesus: "These were ten that have
18 been cleansed; the nine—where are they?" But not one of them
hath been found that returneth to give glory to God, save this one
19 that is of a strange people. He saith to him: "Go, thy faith hath
saved thee alive."

20 And the Pharisees asked him, and say to him; "When cometh
the kingdom of God?" He saith to them: "The kingdom of God
21 cometh not by observings, and they will not say 'Lo, here it is,' or
'Lo, there it is'; for lo, the kingdom of God among you!"

22 And he was saying to his disciples: "The days will come that
ye will long to see one of the days of the Son of Man, and
23 ye will not see *it*. And if they shall say to you 'Lo, there he is'
and 'Lo, here he is'—let them not lead you astray and do not go.
24 For just as the lightning lighteneth from the uttermost parts of
heaven even unto the ends thereof, so will be the day of the Son of
25 Man. But first he is about to suffer in many things and be rejected
26 by this generation. And as it was in the days of Noah, so will it be
27 in the days of the Son of Man, that they were eating and drinking
and were taking wives and were giving *wives* to men, until the day

---

16 same leper] same *one S* **17** Saith Jesus] Jesus answered and was saying *S* These were ten] Ten are these *S* (*sic, see Notes,* vol. ii) the nine—where are they] where are the nine *S* **18** But......returneth] Hath not one of them returned...? *S* **19** He saith to him] *S illegible* **20** saith] answered and said *S* **21** will not say] do not say *S* Lo 1° *&* 2°] *om. S* among you] *cf* 'The kingdom of God is in your heart..not by days of observing' *E*[209] *and* 'in your heart—which he spake of himself who was standing in the midst of them' *E*[211] **23** he is 2°] *om. S* *Here begin again the London leaves of C* let them.... astray] do not run *S* **24** just as] as *S* even] *om. S* ends] uttermost part *S* (*lit.* 'head') **27** were giving] *om.* were *S*

C S ܠܥܠܡܐ. ܘܐܬܐ ܛܘܦܢܐ ܘܚܒܠ ܐܢܘܢ ܠܟܠܗܘܢ: [28]ܗܟܢܐ
ܐܝܟܢܐ ܕܗܘܐ ܒܝܘܡܝ ܠܘܛ. ܕܐܟܠܝܢ ܗܘܘ ܘܫܬܝܢ. ܘܙܒܢܝܢ ܗܘܘ
col 2 ܘܡܙܒܢܝܢ. ܘܢܨܒܝܢ ܗܘܘ ܘܒܢܝܢ. [29]ܘܒܝܘܡܐ ܕܢܦܩ *ܠܘܛ ܡܢ
ܣܕܘܡ. ܐܡܛܪ ܢܘܪܐ ܡܢ ܫܡܝܐ ܘܐܘܒܕ ܐܢܘܢ ܠܟܠܗܘܢ:
[30]ܗܟܢܐ ܢܗܘܐ ܒܝܘܡܐ ܕܡܬܓܠܐ ܒܪܗ ܕܐܢܫܐ. [31]ܒܗܝ ܕܝܢ
ܫܥܬܐ ܡܢ ܕܥܠ ܐܓܪܐ ܗܘ ܠܐ ܢܚܘܬ ܕܢܫܩܘܠ ܡܐܢܘ̈ܗܝ. ܡܢ
ܒܝܬܐ. ܘܡܢ ܕܒܩܪܝܬܐ ܗܘ ܠܐ ܢܬܗܦܟ ܠܒܣܬܪܗ. [32]ܘܐܬܕܟܪܘ
ܠܐܢܬܬܗ ܕܠܘܛ. [33]ܡܢ ܕܢܒܥܐ ܕܢܚܐ ܢܦܫܗ ܢܘܒܕܝܗ. ܘܡܢ ܕܢܘܒܕ
ܢܦܫܗ ܢܚܝܝܗ. [34]ܐܡܪܢܐ ܠܟܘܢ ܕܝܢ ܕܒܗܘ ܠܠܝܐ ܢܗܘܘܢ
ܬܪ̈ܝܢ ܒܚܕܐ ܥܪܣܐ. ܚܕ ܢܬܕܒܪ ܘܚܕ ܢܫܬܒܩ. [35]ܘܢܗܘܝܢ ܬܪ̈ܬܝܢ
ܛܚ̈ܢܢ ܒܚܕܐ ܪ̈ܚܝܐ ܐܟܚܕܐ. ܚܕܐ ܬܬܕܒܪ ܘܚܕܐ ܬܫܬܒܩ.
fol 73 v [36]ܘܢܗܘܘܢ ܬܪ̈ܝܢ ܒܩܪܝܬܐ. ܚܕ ܢܬܕܒܪ *ܘܚܕ ܢܫܬܒܩ. [37]ܐܡܪܝܢ
ܠܗ ܠܐܝܟܐ ܡܪܢ: ܐܡܪ ܠܗܘܢ ܐܝܟܐ ܕܦܓܪܐ ܬܡܢ ܢܬܟܢܫܘܢ
ܢܫܪ̈ܐ ⊙

[1]ܐܡܪ ܠܗܘܢ ܬܘܒ ܐܦ ܡܬܠܐ ܗܢܐ. ܕܢܗܘܘܢ ܡܨܠܝܢ
ܒܟܠܙܒܢ ܘܠܐ ܗܘܬ ܡܐܢܐ ܠܗܘܢ: [2]ܕܝܢܐ ܚܕ ܐܝܬ ܗܘܐ
ܒܡܕܝܢܬܐ ܚܕܐ. ܕܡܢ ܐܠܗܐ ܠܐ ܕܚܠ ܗܘܐ. ܘܡܢ ܒܢ̈ܝ ܐܢܫܐ
ܠܐ ܡܬܟܚܕ ܗܘܐ. [3]ܘܐܪܡܠܬܐ ܚܕܐ ܐܝܬ ܗܘܬ ܒܗ ܒܗܝ
ܡܕܝܢܬܐ. ܘܐܬܝܐ ܗܘܬ ܠܘܬܗ ܙܒܢ̈ܐ ܣܓܝ̈ܐܐ. ܘܐܡܪܐ
ܠܗ ܬܒܥܝܢܝ ܡܢ ܒܥܠܕܝܢܝ. [4]ܘܠܐ ܨܒܐ ܗܘܐ. ܘܒܬܪܟܢ ܐܡܪ
ܒܢܦܫܗ ܗܘ ܕܝܢܐ. ܐܢ ܡܢ ܐܠܗܐ ܠܐ ܕܚܠ ܐܢܐ. ܘܡܢ

ܠܥܠܡܐ] ܠܥܠܡܘܬܐ *S* 28 ܗܟܢܐ ܐܝܟܢܐ] ܘܐܝܟܢܐ *S* ܒܝܘܡ̈ܬܗ ܕܠܘܛ *S*
ܘܢܨܒܝܢ ܗܘܘ ܘܒܢܝܢ] *om. S* 29 ܢܘܪܐ] + ܘܟܒܪܝܬܐ *S* 31 ܕܢܫܩܘܠ]
ܠܡܫܩܠ *S* 33 ܢܚܝܝܗ] ܢܚܝܗ *S* 34 ܕܝܢ] *om. S* 35 ܐܟܚܕܐ] *om. S*
37 ܠܐܝܟܐ] ܠܐܝܠܟܐ *S* ܢܬܟܢܫܘܢ] ܢܬܟܢܫܘܢ *S*vid 1 ܒܟܠ ܙܒܢ *S*
ܕܢܗܘܘܢ....ܠܗܘܢ] ܘܢܗܘܘܢ ܡܨܠܝܢ ܘܠܐ ܬܡܐܢ ܠܗܘܢ *A* 75, 487: *but cf*
ܘܡܢ ܚܒܝܒܝܢ ܚܝ ܕܦܠܓ ܠܗ ܠܐ ܗܘܬ ܡܐܢܐ ܠܡ *A* 392 2 ܚܕܐ] *om. S* ܒܢ̈ܝ] ܒܪ *S*
3 ܚܕܐ] *om. S* ܐܝܬ ܗܘܬ] ܐܝܬ ܗܘܐ *S* (*sic*) ܙܒܢ̈ܐ ܣܓܝ̈ܐܐ] *om. S*
4 ܘܒܬܪܟܢ] *om.* ܘ *S* ܗܘ ܕܝܢܐ] *om. S*

that Noah entered the Ark, and the Flood came and took them all *C S*
28 away. So *also*, as it was in the days of Lot, that they were eating
and drinking and were buying and selling and were planting and
29 building, and in the day that Lot went forth from Sodom it rained
30 fire from heaven and destroyed them all, so will it be in the day that
31 the Son of Man is revealed. Now in that hour he that is on the roof
let him not go down that he may take up his things from the house,
32 and he that is in the field let him not turn behind; and remember ye
33 the wife of Lot. He that willeth to save his life shall lose it, and he
34 that shall lose his life shall find it. Now I say to you that in that night
there will be two *men* in one bed, one will be taken and one will be
35 left; and there will be two *women* grinding at one mill together, one
36 will be taken and one will be left; and there will be two *men* in the
37 field, one will be taken and one will be left." They say to him:
"Whither, our Lord?" He saith to them: "Where the body *is*, there
will be gathered together the vultures."

xviii 1 He saith to them again this similitude also, that they should be
2 praying at all seasons and that it should not weary them. "A certain
judge there was in a certain city, that of God was not afraid and for
3 men had no reverence; and a certain widow there was in that same
city, and she was coming unto him a long while and saying to
4 him: 'Requite me of my adversary.' And he was not willing. And
afterwards that judge said in himself: 'Though of God I am not

---

the Ark] the ark *S* (*as in* Mt xxiv 38) 28 So *also*, as] And as *S* and were planting and building] *om.* *S* (= *one line of the* MS) 29 fire] + and brimstone *S* 31 that he may take up] to take up *S* 33 find it] save it alive *S* 34 Now] *om.* *S* 35 together] *om.* *S* 1 that they should...... weary them] 'Be praying and it shall not weary you' *A* 75, 487: *but cf* 'And when we do well, let it not weary us' *A* 392 2 a certain city] a city *S* men] man *S* 3 certain] *om.* *S* a long while] *om.* *S* 4 And afterwards] Afterwards that judge] he *S*

C S col 2 ܒ̈ܢܫܐ ܠܐ ܡܬܚܫܒ ܐܢܐ. ⁵ܘܗܕܐ *ܐܬܪܥܠܬܐ ܒܥܠܝܟܘܢ ܡܠܐܟܐ ܠܝ.
ܐܬܒܟܝܢܗ ܕܠܐ ܒܥܠܝܟܘܢ ܬܗܘܐ ܐܬܬܐ ܡܗܪܐ ܠܝ. ⁶ܘܐܡܪ ܡܢܝ
ܫܡܥܘ ܡܢܗ ܐܡܪ ܕܢܐ ܒܗܠܐ. ⁷ܐܠܗܐ ܗܘܐ ܠܗ ܐܠܐ ܠܐܬܪܬܐ
ܢܒܕܐ ܬܒܥܬܐ ܠܩܪ̈ܝܘܗܝ. ܕܚܙܐ ܠܗ ܒܐܣܟܡܐ ܘܒܠܝܐ. ܘܐܡܪ
ܪ̈ܘܫܐ ܒܡܫܘܢ ⁸ܐܡܬܪܬܐ ܠܗܘܢ ܕܢܒܕܐ ܬܒܥܬܗܘܢ ܒܡܠܝ.
ܒܪܡ ܢܐܬܐ ܡܢ ܒܪܗ ܕܐܢܫܐ ܘܢܥܒܕ ܗܫܒܘܬܐ ܥܠ
ܐܪܥܐ. ○○ ○○ ○○
⁹ܘܐܡܪ ܗܘܐ ܬܠܬܐ ܗܢܐ. ܠܗܘܠ ܐܢܫܐ ܕܐܬܒܥܠܝܢ ܥܠ
ܢܦܫܗܘܢ ܕܙܕܝ̈ܩܐ ܐܢܘܢ. ܘܒܫܡ ܗܘܘ ܥܠ ܦܬܓܡܐ. ¹⁰ܬܪ̈ܝܢ
fol 74 r ܓ̈ܒܪܝܢ ܣܠܩܘ ܠܗܝܟܠܐ ܠܡܨܠܝܘ. ܚܕ ܦܪܝܫܐ ܘܐܚܪܢܐ *ܡܟܣܐ.
¹¹ܘܗܘ ܦܪܝܫܐ ܩܐܡ ܗܘܐ ܒܝܢܘܗܝ, ܠܢܦܫܗ ܘܩܐܡ ܡܨܠܐ ܗܘܐ.
ܡܘܕܐ ܐܢܐ ܠܟ ܐܠܗܐ ܕܠܐ ܗܘܝܬ ܐܝܟ ܫܪܟܐ ܕܐܢܫܐ
ܚܛܘ̈ܦܐ ܘ̈ܥܘܠܐ ܘ̈ܓܝܪܐ. ܘܠܐ ܐܝܟ ܗܢܐ ܡܟܣܐ. ¹²ܐܠܐ
ܨܐܡ ܐܢܐ ܬܪ̈ܝܢ ܒܫܒܬܐ. ܘܡܥܣܪ ܐܢܐ ܟܠܡܕܡ ܕܩܢܐ ܐܢܐ.
¹³ܘܗܘ ܕܝܢ ܡܟܣܐ ܩܐܡ ܗܘܐ ܡܢ ܪܘܚܩܐ. ܘܠܐ ܡܬܪܢܐ ܗܘܐ
ܐܦܠܐ ܥܝܢܘܗܝ, ܢܪܝܡ ܠܫܡܝܐ. ܐܠܐ ܡܚܐ ܗܘܐ ܥܠ ܚܕܝܗ
ܘܐܡܪ. ܐܠܗܐ ܐܬܪܚܡ ܥܠ ܚܛܝܐ. ¹⁴ܐܡܪ ܐܢܐ ܠܟܘܢ
ܕܢܚܬ ܠܒܝܬܗ ܗܢܐ ܡܟܣܐ ܙܕܝܩ ܡܢ ܗܘ. ܥܠ ܐܝܟ ܓܒܪ
col 2 ܕܪܡ ܢܦܫܗ ܢܬܡܟܟ. *ܘܟܠ ܕܡܟܟ ܢܦܫܗ ܢܬܬܪܝܡ ·○· ○ ○

ܒ̈ܢܫܐ] ܒܪ ܐܢܫܐ S 5 ܒܥܠܝܟܘܢ 1°] ܕܡܢܟܘܢ S ܒܥܠܝܟܘܢ 2°] ܒܒܐܪܬܐ S ܬܗܘܐ ܐܬܬܐ] ܬܐܬܐ S ܡܗܪܐ ܠܝ] ܬܐܚܕܝܢ S 6 ܘܐܡܪ ܡܢܝ] ܐܡܪ ܫܡܥ S ܒܗܠܐ] ܕܒܗܠܐ S 7 ܘܐܡܪ] ܘܡܐܡܪ S 8 ܘܢܥܒܕ] om. ܘ S 9 ܠܗܘܠ S, as often ܕܙܕܝ̈ܩܐ] ܕܙܕܝܩܝܢ S 11 ܘܗܘ] ܗܘ S ܗܘܐ 1°] om. S ܘܩܐܡ ܡܨܠܐ ܗܘܐ] ܡܨܠܐ S (sic) ܚܛܘ̈ܦܐ ܘ̈ܥܘܠܐ] ܚܛܘܦܐ ܐܘ ܥܘܠܐ ܐܘ ܓܝܪܐ S 13 ܘܗܘ] C*, but on an erasure ܠܐ ܡܬܪܢܐ (so also Ephr. Overbeck 28)] ܠܐ ܨܒܐ S ܐܦܠܐ] pr. ܕ S ܥܠ 2°] ܥܠ S 14 ܠܒܝܬܗ ܗܢܐ] tr. S ܘܟܠ ܕܡܟܟ] ܘܕܡܟܟ S; for A 189, see Lk xiv 11

5 afraid and for men I have no reverence, yet this widow at all times *C S*
doth fatigue me—I will requite her, else at all times she will be com-
6 ing *and* injuring me.'" And our Lord said: "Hear ye what saith
7 the wicked judge; God therefore—will he not rather do requital for
his chosen that call to him by day and by night, and be lenient
8 with them? I say to you that he will do their requital quickly.
Nevertheless, will then the Son of Man come and find faith on the
earth?"

9 And he was saying this similitude against folk that trust in them-
10 selves that they are the righteous and were disdaining many. "Two
people went up to the Temple to pray, one a Pharisee and the other
11 a toll-gatherer. And that Pharisee was standing by himself, and
these things was he praying: 'I thank thee, God, that I have not
been as the rest of the folk, the extortioners and the wicked and the
12 adulterers, and not as this toll-gatherer; but I fast twice in the week
13 and I tithe everything that I possess.' Now that toll-gatherer was
standing from afar, and was not daring *that* even his eyes he should
lift up to heaven, but he was beating on his breast and saying: 'God,
14 have compassion on a sinner!' I say to you that this one went
down to his house justified more than that one; for every man that
shall uplift himself shall be humbled, and every one that shall humble
himself shall be uplifted."

---

men] man *S* 5 at all times 1°] that thus *S* at all times 2°] at the last *S* be coming] come *S* injuring me (*or*, 'annoying me')] take hold of me *S*: *see* 1 Cor ix 27 arab^{sin} *and Notes*, vol. ii 6 And our Lord said] Saith Jesus *S* the wicked judge] the judge of wickedness *S* 7 and be lenient] and he is lenient *S* 8 and find] *and* find *S* 9 the righteous] righteous *S* 11 And that] That *S* was standing] standeth *S* and.... praying] *and* prayeth *S* and the wicked and the adulterers] or the covetous or the adulterers *S* 13 not daring (*so also* Ephr. *Overbeck* 28)] not willing *S* *that*] that *S* on] on me *S* 14 every one that] *he* that *S*; *for A* 189, see Lk xiv 11

C S 15 ܘܡܩܪܒܝܢ ܗܘܘ ܠܗ ܐܦ ܝܠܘ̈ܕܐ ܕܢܩܪܘܒ ܐܢܘܢ܂ ܘܟܕ ܚܙܘ
ܬܠܡܝܕܘܗܝ، ܟܐܝܢ ܗܘܘ ܒܗܘܢ܂ 16 ܘܗܘ ܝܫܘܥ ܐܡܪ ܠܗܘܢ܂
ܫܒܘܩܘ ܝܠܘ̈ܕܐ ܕܢܐܬܘܢ ܠܘܬܝ، ܘܠܐ ܬܟܠܘܢ ܐܢܘܢ. ܐܝܠܝܢ
ܓܝܪ ܕܐܝܟ ܗܠܝܢ ܐܢܘܢ ܕܝܠܗܘܢ ܗܝ، ܡܠܟܘܬܐ ܕܫܡܝܐ.
17 ܐܡܝܢ ܐܡܪ ܐܢܐ ܠܟܘܢ܂ ܕܡܢ ܕܠܐ ܢܩܒܠ ܡܠܟܘܬܐ ܕܐܠܗܐ
ܐܝܟ ܗܢܐ ܝܠܘܕܐ. ܠܐ ܢܥܘܠ ܠܗ ܀
18 ܘܫܐܠܗ ܗܘܐ ܚܕ ܡܢ ܪ̈ܫܐ ܕܦܪ̈ܝܫܐ ܘܐܡܪ ܠܗ. ܡܠܦܢܐ
ܛܒܐ ܡܢܐ ܐܥܒܕ ܕܐܝܪܬ ܚܝ̈ܐ ܕܠܥܠܡ. 19 ܐܡܪ ܠܗ ܝܫܘܥ·
fol 74 v ܡܢܐ ܩܪܐ ܐܢܬ ܠܝ ܛܒܐ. *ܘܡܢܐ ܡܫܐܠ ܐܢܬ ܠܝ ܥܠ ܛܒܬܐ.
ܠܝܬ ܛܒܐ ܐܠܐ ܐܢ ܚܕ ܐܠܗܐ. 20 ܦܘܩ̈ܕܢܐ ܕܝܢ ܝܕܥ ܐܢܬ
ܠܗܘܢ، ܐܢ ܨܒܐ ܐܢܬ ܠܚܝ̈ܐ ܠܡܥܠ· ܠܐ ܬܓܘܪ· ܘܠܐ
ܬܩܛܘܠ. ܘܠܐ ܬܓܢܘܒ. ܘܠܐ ܬܣܗܕ ܣܗܕܘܬܐ ܕܫܘܩܪܐ. ܝܩܪ
ܠܐܒܘܟ ܘܠܐܡܟ. 21 ܐܡܪ ܠܗ ܗܠܝܢ ܟܠܗܝܢ ܢܛܪܬ ܐܢܝܢ
ܗܐ ܡܢ ܕܛܠܝܐ ܐܢܐ. 22 ܟܕ ܫܡܥ ܝܫܘܥ ܐܡܪ ܠܗ ܚܕܐ ܬܘܒ
ܚܣܝܪܐ ܠܟ. ܙܒܢ ܟܠ ܡܕܡ ܕܐܝܬ ܠܟ ܘܗܒ ܠܡܣ̈ܟܢܐ.
ܘܬܗܘܐ ܠܟ ܣܝܡܬܐ ܒܫܡܝܐ. ܘܬܐ ܒܬܪܝ. 23 ܗܘ ܕܝܢ ܟܕ ܫܡܥ
ܗܠܝܢ ܟܪܝܬ ܠܗ. ܛܒ ܥܬܝܪ ܗܘܐ ܓܝܪ. 24 ܟܕ ܚܙܐ ܝܫܘܥ
col 2 ܕܟܪܝܬ ܠܗ. ܐܡܪ. *ܐܝܟܢܐ ܥܛܠܐ ܗܝ، ܠܐܝܠܝܢ ܕܐܝܬ ܠܗܘܢ
ܢܟܣܐ ܕܢܥܠܘܢ ܠܡܠܟܘܬܐ ܕܐܠܗܐ. 25 ܕܠܓܡܠܐ ܗܝ، ܦܫܝܩ ܠܡܥܠ
ܒܢܩܒܐ ܕܡܚܛܐ. ܐܘ ܠܥܬܝܪܐ ܕܢܥܘܠ ܠܡܠܟܘܬܗ

15. *No § intended in S, apparently* ܕܢܩܪܘܒ ܐܢܘܢ] ܕܢܣܝܡ ܐܝܕܗ ܥܠܝܗܘܢ *S* ܘܟܕ ܚܙܘ......ܒܗܘܢ] ܘܟܐܝܘ ܒܗܘܢ ܬܠܡܝܕܘܗܝ *S* 16 ܘܗܘ.....ܠܗܘܢ] ܐܡܪ ܠܗܘܢ ܝܫܘܥ *S* ܕܢܐܬܘܢ] ܐܬܝܢ *S* ܐܝܠܝܢ ܓܝܪ] *pr.* ܕ *S* 17 ܢܩܒܠ] ܡܩܒܠ *S* ܕܐܠܗܐ] ܕܫܡܝܐ *S* ܗܢܐ] *om. S* 18 ܕܦܪ̈ܝܫܐ] *om. S* *For A* 392, *see* Matt xix 16 ff, Mk x 17 ff 19 ܘܡܢܐ ܡܫܐܠ.....ܛܒܬܐ] *om. S* 20 ܐܢ......ܠܡܥܠ] *om. S* ܘܠܐ ܬܓܢܘܒ] *om.* ܘ *S* 21 ܠܗ] *om. S* ܟܠܗܝܢ] *om. S* ܗܐ....ܐܢܐ] *before* ܢܛܪܬ ܐܢܝܢ *S* 22 ܙܒܢ *S* (*sic*) 23 ܗܠܝܢ. *S* ܠܗ. ܛܒ] *C* (*usual red point*); ܠܗ ܛܒ· *S* ܥܬܝܪ] + ܛܒ *S* 24 ܝܫܘܥ] *om. S* 25 ܦܫܝܩ] ܦܫ *S*[vid]: *cf* Matt xii 33 ܕܢܥܘܠ] *om. S*

15 And they had brought near to him even babes that he might bless C S
16 them, and when his disciples saw *it* they were rebuking them. And
he, Jesus, saith to them: "Suffer the children that they should come
unto me and forbid them not; for they that are *such* as these, theirs
17 is the kingdom of heaven. Amen, I say to you He that shall not
receive the kingdom of God as this child, he shall not enter it."
18 And one of the chiefs of the Pharisees had asked him, and saith
to him: "Good Teacher, what shall I do that I may inherit life
19 eternal?" Jesus saith to him: "Why callest thou me Good? And why
dost thou ask me about the Good One? There is none good save
20 one,—God. Now the commandments, thou knowest them: if thou
dost wish to enter life, 'Thou shalt not kill' and 'Thou shalt not commit adultery' and 'Thou shalt not thieve' and 'Thou shalt not bear
21 false witness,' 'Honour thy father and thy mother.'" He saith to him:
22 "These all—I have kept them, lo, from when I was a child!" When
Jesus heard, he said to him: "One thing yet is lacking to thee; sell
everything that thou hast and give to the poor, and thou shalt have
23 treasure in heaven, and come after me." Now he when he heard
24 these things, it grieved him, for exceedingly rich he was. When
Jesus saw that it grieved him, he saith: "How difficult it is for them
25 that have wealth to enter the kingdom of God! For it is readier for
a camel to pass through the eye of a needle than a rich man to enter

15 bless them] lay his hand on them *S* and when....rebuking them] and his disciples rebuked them *S* 16 And he] *om. S* that they should come] to come *S* 17 shall not 1°] doth not *S* of God] of heaven *S* this child] a child *S* 18 of the Pharisees] *om. S* *For A* 392, *see* Matt xix 16 ff, Mk x 17 ff 19 And why....the Good One] *om. S* 20 if....enter life] *cf* Matt xix 17 (*&* E^{168}); *om. S* and 2°] *om. S* 21 to him] *om. S* all] *om. S* lo,....child] *before* 'I have kept them' *in S* 23 grieved...he was] grieved him exceedingly, for rich he was exceedingly *S* 24 it is] *om. S* 25 to enter] *om. S*

CS ܕܐܠܗܐ. [26]ܘܐܡܪܝܢ ܗܘܘ ܐܝܠܝܢ ܕܫܡܥܘ. ܡܢܘ ܡܫܟܚ ܠܡܚܐ.
[27]ܐܡܪ ܠܗܘܢ. ܐܝܠܝܢ ܕܠܘܬ ܒ̈ܢܝ ܐ̈ܢܫܐ ܠܐ ܡܫܟܚܢ ܠܡܗܘܐ.
ܠܘܬ ܐܠܗܐ ܕܝܢ ܡܫܟܚܢ. [28]ܐܡܪ ܠܗ ܟܐܦܐ. ܗܐ ܐܚܢܢ
ܫܒܩܢ ܟܠ ܡܕܡ ܕܐܝܬ ܠܢ ܘܐܬܝܢ ܒܬܪܟ. [29]ܐܡܪ ܠܗ ܝܫܘܥ.
ܐܡܝܢ ܐܡܪ ܐܢܐ ܠܟܘܢ ܕܡܢ ܕܫܒܩ ܒܝܬܐ. ܐܘ ܐ̈ܒܗܐ. ܐܘ
ܐ̈ܚܐ. ܐܘ ܐܢܬܬܐ. ܐܘ ܒ̈ܢܝܐ. ܡܛܠ ܡܠܟܘܬܐ ܕܐܠܗܐ. [30]ܢܣܒ ܚܕ
fol 75 r ܒܡܐܐ ܒܙܒܢܐ *ܗܢܐ. ܘܒܥܠܡܐ ܕܐܬܐ ܢܐܪܬ ܚ̈ܝܐ ܕܠܥܠܡ ◎
[31]ܘܕܒܪ ܠܬܪ̈ܥܣܪܬܗ ܘܐܡܪ ܠܗܘܢ. ܗܐ ܣܠܩܝܢ ܚܢ ܠܐܘܪܫܠܡ.
ܘܡܫܬܠܡܢ ܟܠܗܝܢ ܐܝܠܝܢ ܕ̈ܟܬܝܒܢ ܒܢܒ̈ܝܐ ܥܠ ܒܪܗ ܕܐܢܫܐ.
[32]ܡܫܬܠܡ ܓܝܪ ܠܥܡ̈ܡܐ ܘܢܒܙܚܘܢ ܒܗ ܘܢܨܥܪܘܢܗ. ܘܢܪܩܘܢ
ܒܐ̈ܦܘܗܝ. [33]ܘܢܢܓܕܘܢܗ ܘܢܩܛܠܘܢܗ. ܘܠܝܘܡܐ ܕܬܠܬܐ ܢܩܘܡ.
[34]ܘܗܢܘܢ ܚܕܐ ܡܢ ܗܠܝܢ ܠܐ ܐܣܬܟܠܘ. ܐܠܐ ܡܟܣܝܐ
ܗܘܬ ܡܢܗܘܢ ܡܠܬܐ. ܘܠܐ ܐܫܬܘܕܥܘ ܐܝܠܝܢ ܕܐܬܡܠܠ
ܥܡܗܘܢ ○ ○ ○

[35]ܘܟܕ ܩܪܒ ܗܘܐ ܠܡܥܠ ܠܐܝܪܝܚܘ. ܥܘܝܪܐ ܚܕ ܡܣܟܢܐ ܝܬܒ
ܗܘܐ ܥܠ ܝܕ ܐܘܪܚܐ ܘܚܕܪ. [36]ܘܟܕ ܫܡܥ ܩܠ ܟܢܫܐ ܕܥܒܪ.
col 2 ܡܫܐܠ ܗܘܐ *ܕܡܢܘ ܗܢܐ. [37]ܐܡܪܝܢ ܠܗ ܝܫܘܥ ܢܨܪܝܐ ܥܒܪ.
[38]ܘܩܥܐ ܘܐܡܪ ܝܫܘܥ ܒܪܗ ܕܕܘܝܕ ܐܬܪܚܡ ܥܠܝ. [39]ܘܐܝܠܝܢ ܕܐܙܠܝܢ
ܗܘܘ ܩܕܡܘܗܝ ܕܝܫܘܥ ܟܐܝܢ ܗܘܘ ܒܗ ܕܢܫܬܘܩ ܠܗ. ܘܗܘ
ܝܬܝܪܐܝܬ ܩܥܐ ܗܘܐ. ܒܪܗ ܕܕܘܝܕ ܐܬܪܚܡ ܥܠܝ. [40]ܘܩܡ ܗܘ
ܝܫܘܥ. ܘܦܩܕ ܗܘܐ ܕܢܝܬܘܢܝܗܝ. ܘܟܕ ܩܪܒ ܠܘܬܗ. ܫܐܠܗ
[41]ܘܐܡܪ ܠܗ. ܡܢܐ ܨܒܐ ܐܢܬ ܐܥܒܕ ܠܟ. ܐܡܪ ܠܗ ܡܪܝ
ܕܢܬܦܬܚܢ ܥ̈ܝܢܝ ܘܐܚܙܝܟ. [42]ܐܡܪ ܠܗ ܚܝ ܗܝܡܢܘܬܟ ܐܚܝܬܟ.

---

27 ܕܝܢ] *om.* S   ܡܫܟܚܢ 2°] + ܕܢܗܘܘܢ S   29 ܠܟܘܢ] ܠܟ S   ܕܡܢ] ܕܠܝܬ S   30 ܢܣܒ] *pr.* ܗܠܐ S   ܕܐܬܐ] ܕܥܬܝܕ S   31 ܚܢ] ܐܚܢܢ S
32 ܒܐ̈ܦܘܗܝ] *so also* S   35 ܩܪܒ ܗܘܐ] + ܕܝܢ S   ܠܡܥܠ] *om.* S
39 ܩܥܐ ܗܘܐ] + ܘܐܡܪ S   40 ܗܘܐ] *om.* S   ܕܢܝܬܘܢܗ S   41 ܐܥܒܕ]
pr. ܕ S   ܕܢܬܦܬܚܢ ܥ̈ܝܢܝ ܘܐܚܙܝܟ] ܕܐܚܙܐ S   42 ܐܡܪ ܠܗ] + ܝܫܘܥ S

26 into the kingdom of God." And they were saying that heard: "Who *C S*
27 can live?" He saith to them: "The things that with men cannot be,
28 but with God they can." Kepha saith to him: "Lo, we have left
29 everything that we have and have come after thee." Jesus saith to
him: "Amen, I say to you He that hath left house, or parents, or
30 brothers, or wife, or sons, for the kingdom of God's sake, shall take
an hundredfold in this time and in the world to come shall inherit
life eternal."

31 And he took his Twelve and said to them: "Lo, we go up to
Jerusalem, and all things are to be fulfilled that are written in the
32 prophets about the Son of Man; for he is to be delivered up to the
peoples, and they will mock at him and insult him and spit in his
33 face and scourge him and kill him, and the third day he will rise."
34 And they not one of these things understood, but the word was kept
secret from them and they did not recognise the things that were
spoken with them.

35 And when he was near to enter Jericho a certain blind man was
36 sitting by the way-side and begging. And when he heard the sound
37 of a multitude passing by he was asking "Who is this?" They
38 say to him: "Jesus the Nazarene is passing by." And he cried out
39 and said: "Jesus, son of David, have compassion on me!" And they
that were going before Jesus were rebuking him that he should be
silent; and he the more was crying out: "Son of David, have com-
40 passion on me!" And he, Jesus, stood and was commanding that
they should bring him. And when he drew near unto him he asked
41 him and said to him: "What wouldest thou I should do for thee?"
He saith to him: "My Lord, that my eyes may be opened and I may
42 see thee." He saith to him: "See, thy faith hath saved thee alive."

---

27 but] *om. S* can] can be *S* 29 to you] to thee *S* He that] There is none *S* 30 shall take] that shall not take *S* an hundredfold] 'sevenfold' E^{83} (*quoted out of the order of the Diatessaron*) to come] about to be *S* 35 And] Now *S* enter] *om. S* 39 crying out] + and saying *S* 40 was commanding] commanded *S* 41 I should do] *pr.* that *S* that my eyes.... see thee] that I may see *S* 42 He] Jesus *S*

C S ⁴³ܘܒܪܫܥܬܗ ܚܙܐ. ܘܐܬܐ ܗܘܐ ܒܬܪܗ ܘܡܫܒܚ ܗܘܐ ܠܐܠܗܐ.
ܘܟܠܗ ܥܡܐ ܕܚܙܐ ܫܒܚܘ ܠܐܠܗܐ. ܀܀܀

fol 75 v *¹ܘܟܕ ܥܠ† ܘܥܒܪ ܒܐܝܪܝܚܘ. ²ܓܒܪܐ ܚܕ ܕܫܡܗ ܙܟܝ. ܘܪܒ
ܡܟ̈ܣܐ ܗܘܐ. ܘܥܬܝܪ ܗܘܐ. ³ܘܒܥܐ ܗܘܐ ܠܡܚܙܝܗ ܠܝܫܘܥ·
ܘܠܐ ܡܫܟܚ ܗܘܐ. ܡܛܠ ܕܒܩܘܡܬܗ ܙܥܘܪ ܗܘܐ ܙܟܝ.
⁴ܘܪܗܛ ܩܕܡܘܗܝ. ܘܣܠܩ ܠܬܬܐ ܦܓܡܝܬܐ ܕܢܚܙܝܘܗܝ. ܡܛܠ
ܕܗܒܘܬ ܥܒܪ ܗܘܐ ܝܫܘܥ. ⁵ܘܟܕ ܥܒܪ ܝܫܘܥ ܚܙܝܗܝ· ܐܡܪ
ܐܣܬܪܗܒ ܢܚܘܬ ܙܟܝ. ܝܘܡܢܐ ܓܝܪ ܒܒܝܬܟ ܘܠܐ ܠܝ ܕܐܗܘܐ.
⁶ܘܐܣܬܪܗܒ ܢܚܬ ܘܩܒܠܗ ܚܕܝܐܝܬ. ⁷ܘܟܕ ܚܙܘ ܗܠܝܢ ܟܠܗܘܢ
ܪ̈ܛܢܝܢ ܗܘܘ. ܕܠܘܬ ܓܒܪܐ ܚܛܝܐ ܥܠ ܕܢܫܪܐ. ⁸ܘܩܡ ܙܟܝ ܘܐܡܪ
§A 392 col 2 ܠܡܪܢ܂ §ܗܐ ܡܪܝ, ܦܠܓܘܬ ܢܟ̈ܣܝ, ܝܗܒ ܐܢܐ *ܠܡܣ̈ܟܢܐ. ܘܟܠ
ܕܓܠܙܬ ܚܕ ܒܐܪ̈ܒܥܐ ܦܪܥ ܐܢܐ. ⁹ܐܡܪ ܠܗ ܝܫܘܥ ܝܘܡܢܐ
¶A ܗܘܘ ܚܝ̈ܐ ܒܒܝܬܐ ܗܢܐ.¶ ܘܐܦ ܗܢܐ ܒܪܗ ܗܘ ܕܐܒܪܗܡ.
¹⁰ܘܐܬܐ ܓܝܪ ܒܪܗ ܕܐܢܫܐ ܕܢܒܥܐ ܘܢܚܐ ܠܡܕܡ ܕܐܒܝܕ ܗܘܐ. ܀
¹¹ܘܟܕ ܫܡܥܝܢ ܗܘܘ ܗܠܝܢ. ܐܘܣܦ ܠܡܐܡܪ ܡܬܠܐ· ܡܛܠ
ܕܩܪܝܒ ܗܘܐ ܠܡܥܠ ܠܐܘܪܫܠܡ. ܘܣܒܪܝܢ ܗܘܘ ܕܒܗ, ܥܕܢܐ
ܥܬܝܕܐ ܗܘܬ ܕܬܬܓܠܐ ܡܠܟܘܬܗ ܕܐܠܗܐ. ¹²ܐܡܪ ܠܗܘܢ

---

43 ܕܚܙܐ ܫܒܚܘ] ܚܙܐ ܘܝܗܒ ܫܘܒܚܐ *S* 1 ܥܠ] *S*; ܥܠܗ *C* ܘܥܒܪ ܒܐܝܪܝܚܘ *S* 2 ܓܒܪܐ] *pr.* ܘ *S* ܕܫܡܗ] + ܗܘܐ *S* 3 ܠܝܫܘܥ] + ܡܢܘ *S* ܡܫܟܚ ܗܘܐ] + ܡܛܠ ܥܡܐ *S* ܙܟܝ] *om.* *S* 4 ܩܕܡܘܗܝ] ܠܩܕܡܘܗܝ *S* ܠܬܬܐ ܦܓܡܝܬܐ] ܠܬܐ̈ܢܐ *Diatessaron*: *the Cambridge* MS *of Ishô‘dâd* (*Harris*, p. 19) *has* ܠܬܐܢܐ, *but there is no seyâmê in the corresponding section of Barsalibi* (B.M. *Add.* 7184, *fol.* 108 *b*) 4, 5 ܝܫܘܥ. ܘܟܕ ܥܒܪ ܝܫܘܥ] *S illegible, but from the space it probably omitted* ܝܫܘܥ *in both places, or read* ܝܫܘܥ. ܘܟܕ 5 ܐܡܪ] + ܠܗ *S* 6 ܢܚܬ] + ܙܟܝ *S* 7 ܗܠܝܢ ܟܠܗܘܢ] ⌜ܗܘܘ⌝ *S*^ed^ ܪ̈ܛܢܝܢ ܗܘܘ] + ܘܐܡܪܝܢ *S* 8 ܠܡܪܢ] ܠܝܫܘܥ *S* ܝܗܒ ܐܢܐ] *C* *A*ᵃ; ܝܗܒܢܐ *S* *A*ᵇ (*as often*) ܚܕ ܒܐܪ̈ܒܥܐ] *after* ܦܪܥ ܐܢܐ *A* 9 ܐܡܪ] *pr.* ܘ *A* ܝܫܘܥ] ܡܪܢ *A* ܘܐܦ] ܡܛܠ ܕܐܦ *S* 10 ܠܡܕܡ] ܡܕܡ *S* ܕܐܒܝܕ ܗܘܐ] ܕܐܒܝܕ *S* 11 ܠܡܥܠ] *om.* *S* ܕܡܬܓܠܝܐ ܗܝ *S*

43 And straightway he saw, and he was coming after him and was *C S*
glorifying God. And all the people that saw *it*, glorified God.

xix 1, 2 And when †he† entered and passed through Jericho a certain
man whose name *was* Zacchaeus—and he was a chief of the toll-
3 gatherers and was rich—and he was wishing to see Jesus and could
4 not, because in his stature Zacchaeus was little. And he ran before
him and went up a wild fig-tree that he might see him, because thus
5 Jesus was passing by. And when Jesus passed by he saw him.
Saith he: "Hasten *and* come down, Zacchaeus, for to-day in thy
6 house it behoves me to be." And he hastened *and* came down and
7 he received him gladly. And when they saw these things, all of them
were murmuring that with a man *who was* a sinner he entered to
8 lodge. And Zacchaeus stood and said to our Lord: §"Lo, my Lord, §*A* 392
the half of my wealth I give to the poor; and all that I have
9 defrauded, fourfold I repay!" Jesus saith to him: "To-day hath
life been in this house,¶ and this one also is a son of Abraham." ¶*A*
10 And *he said* "The Son of Man hath come that he might seek
and save alive that which had been lost."

11 And when they were hearing these things he went on to say a
similitude, because he was near to enter Jerusalem and they were
supposing that in that hour the kingdom of God was about to be

---

43 that saw.... God] saw and gave glory to God *S* 1 †he† entered] *S*; they entered *C* (*by a slip*) through] *om. S* 2 a certain man] *pr.* 'and' *S* (*as in* Lk xiii 10, 11 *S C and elsewhere*) *was*] was *S* 3 Jesus] + who he was *S* could not] + because of the multitude *S* Zacchaeus] he *S* 4 before him] *lit.* 'preceded him'; in front *S* (= εἰς τὸ ἔμπροσθεν) a wild fig-tree] *according to Syriac commentators the Diatessaron had here a certain rare word for the* 'wild-fig' *which also occurs in the name* 'Bethphage' 4, 5 Jesus.... Jesus] *S illegible, but from the space it probably read* 'he' *for* 'Jesus' *in both places, or omitted* 'Jesus passed by' *in ver.* 5 5 Saith he] + to him *S* 6 And he 1°] And Zacchaeus *S* 7 saw these things, all of them] had seen, they S^{ed} (*partly illegible*) murmuring] + and saying *S* 8 our Lord] Jesus *S* I give.... I repay] *C S A*; 'I will give.... I will repay' E^{180} 9 Jesus] And our Lord *A* and] because *S* 10 had been] was *S* 11 enter] *om. S*

C S ܓܒܪܐ ܚܕ ܒܪ ܛܘܗܡܐ ܪܒܐ. ܐܙܠ ܠܐܬܪܐ ܪܚܝܩܐ
fol 76 r ܠܡܣܒ ܡܠܟܘܬܐ ܘܠܡܗܦܟ. 13 ܘܩܪܐ ܠܥܣܪܐ ܥܒ̈ܕܘܗܝ. *ܘܝܗܒ
ܠܗܘܢ ܥܣܪܐ ܡ̈ܢܝܢ. ܘܐܡܪ ܠܗܘܢ ܐܬܬܓܪܘ ܒܗܘܢ ܥܕ
§¶A 10, 171 ܐܬܐ ܐܢܐ. 14 ܘܒ̈ܢܝ ܡܕܝܢܬܗ ܣܢܝܢ ܗܘܘ ܠܗ. §ܘܫܕܪܘ ܐܝ̈ܙܓܕܐ
ܒܬܪܗ ܘܐܡܪܝܢ ܠܗ. ܠܐ ܨܒܝܢ ܚܢܢ ܕܢܡܠܟ ܥܠܝܢ ܗܢܐ.¶ 15 ܘܟܕ
ܢܣܒ ܡܠܟܘܬܐ ܘܗܦܟ. ܐܡܪ ܕܢܩܪܘܢ ܠܗ ܠܗܢܘܢ ܥܒ̈ܕܘܗܝ
ܕܝܗܒ ܗܘܐ ܠܗܘܢ ܟܣܦܐ. ܕܢܕܥ ܡܢܐ ܐܬܬܓܪܘ. 16 ܘܐܬܐ
ܩܕܡܝܐ ܘܐܡܪ. ܡܪܝ ܡܢܝܟ ܥܣܪܐ ܡ̈ܢܝܢ ܐܘܬܪ. 17 ܐܡܪ ܠܗ
ܐܝܘ ܥܒܕܐ ܛܒܐ ܕܒܩܠܝܠ ܐܫܬܟܚܬ ܡܗܝܡܢ. ܬܗܘܐ ܫܠܝܛ
ܥܠ ܥܣܪܐ ܟܪ̈ܟܝܢ. 18 ܘܐܬܐ ܕܬܪ̈ܝܢ ܐܡܪ ܠܗ. ܡܪܝ. ܡܢܝܟ
col 2 ܚܡܫܐ *ܡ̈ܢܝܢ ܥܒܕ. 19 ܐܡܪ ܠܗ ܐܦ ܠܗܘ ܘܐܦ ܐܢܬ ܬܗܘܐ
ܫܠܝܛ ܥܠ ܚܡܫܐ ܟܪ̈ܟܝܢ. 20 ܘܐܬܐ ܐܚܪܢܐ ܘܐܡܪ. ܗܐ ܡܢܝܟ
ܗܘ ܕܐܝܬ ܗܘܐ ܠܘܬܝ. ܟܕ ܣܝܡ ܒܣܘܕܪܐ. 21 ܕܕܚܠܬ ܓܝܪ ܡܢܟ
ܕܓܒܪܐ ܐܢܬ ܩܫܝܐ. ܕܫܩܠ ܐܢܬ ܡܕܡ ܕܠܐ ܣܡܬ. ܘܚܨܕ
ܐܢܬ ܡܕܡ ܕܠܐ ܙܪܥܬ. 22 ܐܡܪ ܠܗ ܡܪܗ ܡܢ ܦܘܡܟ ܐܕܘܢܟ
ܥܒܕܐ ܒܝܫܐ ܕܠܐ ܡܗܝܡܢ. ܝܕܥ ܗܘܝܬ ܠܝ ܕܓܒܪܐ ܐܢܐ
ܩܫܝܐ. ܘܫܩܠ ܐܢܐ ܡܕܡ ܕܠܐ ܣܡܬ. ܘܚܨܕ ܐܢܐ ܡܕܡ
ܕܠܐ ܙܪܥܬ. 23 ܐܡܬܘ ܠܐ ܐܪܡܝܬ ܟܣܦܝ ܥܠ ܦܬܘܪܐ· ܘܐܢܐ
fol 76 v ܕܝܢ ܐܬܝܬ *ܬܒܥܬ ܕܝܠܝ ܒܪ̈ܒܝܬܗ. 24 ܘܐܡܪ ܠܗܢܘܢ ܕܩܝܡܝܢ

---

12 ܒܪ ܛܘܗܡܐ] so also S: cf ܓܒܪܐ ܒܪ ܛܘܗܡܐ ܪܒܐ. ܐܙܠ ܕܢܣܒ
ܡܠܟܘܬܐ ܘܢܗܦܘܟ A 10 & ܡܠܟܐ ܒܪ ܛܘܗܡܐ ܪܒܐ. ܕܐܙܠ ܠܡܣܒ
ܡܠܟܘܬܐ A 288   13 ܠܥܣܪܐ] ܥܣܪܐ S   14 ܘܒܢܝ ܡܕܝܢܬܐ S
ܘܫܕܪܘ...ܠܗ] ܘܩܡܘ ܫܕܪܘ ܒܬܪܗ ܐܝܙܓܕܐ ܘܐܡܪܝܢ A 10; ܘܐܡܪܝܢ ܕ A 171
ܠܐ ܨܒܝܢ.....ܗܢܐ] ܠܐ ܢܗܘܐ ܥܠܝܢ ܗܢܐ ܡܠܟܐ A 2/2 (ܗܢܐ ܥܠܝܢ A^b 171)
15 ܘܟܕ ܢܣܒ ܡܠܟܘܬܐ] om. S   ܠܗܢܘܢ] om. ܠ S   ܟܣܦܐ] S illegible
(⌜ܟܣܦܐ⌝ ⌜ܡܢܘ⌝ S^ed, but there is only room for one word)   17 ܐܝܘ] ܐܘ S (sic)
ܕܒܩܠܝܠ] so also S   18 ܕܬܪ̈ܝܢ] ܐܚܪܢܐ S   ܐܡܪ] pr. ܘ S   19 ܠܗܘ] ܠܗ S
ܘܐܦ] ܐܦ S   20 ܐܚܪܢܐ] pr. ܘܗܘ S   ܗܐ] pr. ܡܪܝ S   22 ܡܪܗ] om. S
ܒܝܫܐ] om. S   23 ܐܡܬܘ] ܠܡܢܐ S

12 revealed. He saith to them: "A certain man, a member of a great *C S*
family, went to a far country to receive a kingdom and to return.
13 And he called his ten slaves and gave them ten pounds and said
14 to them: 'Have use of them until I come.' And the men of his city
were hating him, §and they sent ambassadors after him and say to §¶*A* 10, 171
15 him: 'We would not that this *man* should reign over us.'¶ And when
he received the kingdom and returned he said that they should call
to him those slaves of his to whom he had given the silver, that he
16 might know what they had traded. And the first came and saith:
17 'My lord, thy pound ten pounds hath gained.' He saith to him:
'Well *is it,* good slave, that in little thou hast been found faithful;
18 thou shalt be set in authority over ten towns.' And the second came
and saith to him: 'My lord, thy pound five pounds hath made.'
19 He saith to him, to that one also: 'And thou also shalt be set in
20 authority over five towns.' And another came and saith: 'Lo, thy
21 pound which was with me, laid in a cloth! For I was afraid of thee,
in that thou art a hard man that takest up that which thou didst not
22 lay down, and reapest that which thou didst not sow.' His lord saith to
him: 'From thine *own* mouth will I judge thee, evil slave *and* faith-
less. Thou didst know me that I am a hard man and take up that
23 which I did not lay down and reap that which I did not sow. How
is it thou didst not put my silver into the bank, and I then had come
24 *and* required mine own with usury?' And he said to those standing

---

12. *Cf* 'A man, a member of a great family, went that he might receive a kingdom and return' *A* 10 *&* 'A king, a member of a great family, that went to receive a kingdom' *A* 288 14 his city] the city *S* and they sent...to him] and they sent after him ambassadors and say *A* 10; and they said *A* 171 We....over us] This *fellow* shall not be over us a king $A^{2}/_{2}$ 15 when...returned he said] he returned *and* said *S* what] *S illegible* 18 the second] another *S* *and* saith] and saith *S* 19 that one] him *S* And thou] Thou *S* 20 another] that other *S* Lo] My lord, lo *S* 22 His lord] He *S* evil....faithless] faithless slave *S* 23 How is it thou didst] Wherefore didst thou *S*

C S ܠܘܬܗ. ܣܒܘ ܡܢܗ ܡܢܝܐ. ܘܗܒܘܗܝ، ܠܗ̇ܘ ܕܐܝܬ ܠܘܬܗ
ܥܣܪܐ ܡ̈ܢܝܢ· [26]ܐܡܪܢܐ ܠܟܘܢ ܓܝܪ ܕܟܠ ܐܢܫ ܕܐܝܬ ܠܗ
ܢܬܝܗܒ ܠܗ ܘܢܬܬܘܣܦ ܠܗ· ܘܡܢ ܕܠܝܬ ܠܗ ܐܦ ܗܘ ܕܣܒܪ̇
ܕܐܝܬ ܠܗ ܢܬܢܣܒ ܡܢܗ· [27]ܒܪܡ ܕܝܢ ܐܝܬܘ ܠܗܪܟܐ ܠܗܘܢ
ܒ̈ܥܠܕܒܒܝ. ܐܝܠܝܢ ܕܠܐ ܨܒܘ ܕܐܗܘܐ ܥܠܝܗܘܢ ܡܠܟܐ. ܘܩܛܠܘ
ܐܢܘܢ ܩܕܡܝ. [28]ܘܟܕ ܐܡܪ ܗܠܝܢ ܢܦܩ ܡܢ ܬܡܢ.
ܘܟܕ ܣܠܩ ܗܘܐ ܠܐܘܪܫܠܡ. [29]ܘܡܛܐ ܠܒܝܬ ܦ̈ܓܐ ܘܠܒܝܬ ܥܢܝܐ.
ܘܡܛܐ ܠܘܬ ܠܛܘܪܐ ܕܡܬܩܪܐ ܕܒܝܬ ܙ̈ܝܬܐ. ܫܕܪ ܠܬܪ̈ܝܢ ܡܢ
col 2 *ܬܠܡܝܕܘܗܝ. [30]ܘܐܡܪ ܠܗܘܢ ܙܠܘ ܠܩܪܝܬܐ ܗܝ ܕܠܘܩܒܠܢ· ܘܟܕ
ܥܠܝܢ ܐܢܬܘܢ ܗܐ ܡܫܟܚܝܢ ܐܢܬܘܢ ܥܝܠܐ ܟܕ ܐܣܝܪ. ܕܐܢܫ
ܠܐ ܪܟܒ ܥܠܘܗܝ. ܫܪܘ ܐܝܬܐܘܗܝ. [31]ܘܐܢ ܐܢܫ ܡܫܐܠ ܠܟܘܢ
ܠܡܢܐ ܫܪܝܢ ܐܢܬܘܢ ܠܗ. ܐܡܪܘ ܠܗ ܠܡܪܗ ܡܬܒܥܐ. [32]ܘܐܙܠܘ
ܘܐܫܟܚܘ ܗܟܢܐ. [33]ܘܟܕ ܫܐܠܘ ܐܢܘܢ̣ [34]ܐܬܦܢܝܘ ܐܢܘܢ
ܦܬܓܡܐ ܕܠܡܪܗ ܡܬܒܥܐ. [35]ܘܐܝܬܝܘܗܝ، ܠܥܝܠܐ ܠܘܬ ܝܫܘܥ.
ܘܐܪܡܝܘ ܥܠܘܗܝ، ܡܪ̈ܛܘܛܝܗܘܢ. ܘܐܪܟܒܘܗܝ، ܠܝܫܘܥ. [36]ܘܟܕ ܪܕܐ
ܗܘܐ. ܦܪܣܝܢ ܗܘܘ ܡܪ̈ܛܘܛܝܗܘܢ ܒܐܘܪܚܐ. [37]ܘܟܕ ܩܪܒ
fol 77 r *ܠܡܚܬܬܐ ܕܛܘܪܐ ܕܒܝܬ ܙ̈ܝܬܐ. ܫܪܝܘ ܟܠܗ ܟܢܫܐ ܚܕܝܢ ܗܘܘ
ܘܡܫܒܚܝܢ ܠܐܠܗܐ. ܒܩܠܐ ܪܡܐ ܥܠ ܟܠ ܡܕܡ ܕܚܙܘ.
[38]ܘܐܡܪܝܢ ܗܘܘ ܒܪܝܟ ܗܘ ܡܠܟܐ ܕܐܬܐ ܒܫܡܗ ܕܡܪܝܐ. ܫܠܡܐ
ܒܫܡܝܐ ܘܬܫܒܘܚܬܐ ܒܡܪܘܡܐ. [39]ܐܡܪܝܢ ܠܗ ܐܢܫܐ ܡܢ ܦܪ̈ܝܫܐ

---

26 ܢܬܝܗܒ ܠܗ ܘ] *om.* S ܗܘ] + ܡܕܡ S ܕܣܒܪ] *om.* S 28 ܢܦܩ S[vid]
28[b]. *No* § *in* S[vid] 29 ܠܛܘܪܐ ܕܡܬܩܪܐ ܕܒܝܬ ܙ̈ܝܬܐ] ܛܘܪ ܙܝܬܐ S ܬܪ̈ܝܢ S
30 ܕܠܩܘܒܠܢ S ܐܝܬܐܘܗܝ] ܠܟܐ ܐܝܬܘܗܝ S 31 ܘܐܡܪܘ] *pr.* ܗܟܢܐ S
32.] ܘܐܙܠܘ ܐܫܟܚܘ ܗܟܢܐ ܗܢܘܢ ܕܐܫܬܕܪܘ ܐܝܟ ܕܐܡܪ ܠܗܘܢ S
33, 34.] ܘܟܕ ܫܪ̈ܝܢ ܠܗ. ܠܥܝܠܐ ܐܡܪܘ ܠܗܘܢ ܠܡܪܗ ܡܬܒܥܐ S
35 ܘܐܝܬܝܘܗܝ] ܘܐܝܬܝܘ S ܠܝܫܘܥ] + ܥܠܘܗܝ S 36 ܪܕܐ ܗܘܐ] + ܘܐܬܐ S
ܦܪܣܝܢ] *pr.* ܘ S ܒܐܘܪܚܐ S 37 ܘܟܕ] ܟܕ S ܕܛܘܪܐ ܕܒܝܬ ܙ̈ܝܬܐ]
ܕܛܘܪ ܙܝܬܐ S ܟܢܫܐ] + ܕܬܠܡ̈ܝܕܘܗܝ S ܗܘܘ] *om.* S 38 ܘܬܫܒܘܚܬܐ]
ܘܫܘܒܚܐ S 39 ܦܪ̈ܝܫܐ] ܟܢܫܐ S

by him: 'Take from him the pound, and give it to him with whom C S
26 are the ten pounds.' For I say to you that every man that hath, it
shall be given to him and *more* shall be added to him; and he that
hath not, even that which he supposeth that he hath shall be taken
27 from him. But nevertheless bring ye hither those enemies of mine
which would not that I should be king over them, and kill them
28 before me.'" And when he said these things they went forth from
thence.

29 And when he was going up to Jerusalem and arrived at Beth
Phagge and Beth Ania and arrived by the Mount called *the Mount*
30 of the Olive-orchard, he sent two of his disciples, and said to them:
"Go to that village over against us; and when ye enter, lo, ye will
31 find a colt tied that no one hath ridden on, loose *and* bring it. And
if any one asketh you 'Wherefore are ye loosing it?' say to him:
32, 33 'For its Lord it is required.'" And they went and found *it* so. And
34 when they asked them, they returned them the answer that for its
35 Lord it is required. And they brought the colt unto Jesus and they
36 cast upon it their cloaks and mounted Jesus; and while he was
37 moving along they were strewing their cloaks in the way. And when
they drew near to the descent of the Mount of the Olive-orchard all
the multitude began rejoicing and glorifying God with a loud voice
38 for everything that they saw, and they were saying: "Blessed is the
king that cometh in the name of the LORD! Peace in heaven, and
39 glory in the highest!" Some folk of the Pharisees from among that

---

26 it shall be given to him and] *om. S* he supposeth that] *om. S*
28 they] he *S*[vid] **29** the Mount.... Olive-orchard] the Mount of Olives *S*
30 bring it] + hither *S* **31** say] + thus *S* its Lord] *or*, 'its master': *and so in ver.* 34 **32.**] And those that were sent went *and* found *it* so, as he said to them *S* **33, 34.**] And while loosing the colt they said to them: "For its Lord it is required" *S* **35** Jesus 2°] + upon it *S*
36 moving along] + and coming *S* they were] *pr.* 'and' *S*: *cf ver.* 2
37 And when] When *S* of the Olive-orchard] of Olives *S* multitude] + of his disciples *S* **38.** 'Peace in heaven and glory on earth' *E*[27]
39 the Pharisees] the people *S*

C S ܡܢ ܒܝܢܬ ܗܘ ܟܢܫܐ. ܪܒܝ ܟܐܝ، ܒܗܘܢ ܕܠܐ ܢܩܥܘܢ ⁴⁰ܐܡܪ
ܠܗܘܢ ܐܡܝܢ ܐܡܪ ܐܢܐ ܠܟܘܢ ܕܐܢ ܗܠܝܢ ܢܫܬܩܘܢ
ܟܐ̈ܦܐ ܗܠܝܢ ܢܩܥܘܢ· ⁴¹ܘܟܕ ܩܪܒ ܘܚܙܐ ܠܡܕܝܢܬܐ ܒܟܐ ܥܠܝܗ
⁴²ܘܐܡܪ. ܕܐܠܘ ܒܗܢܐ ܝܘܡܐ ܝܕܥܬܝ، ܕܝܢ ܫܠܡܟܝ. ܐܠܐ ܫܠܡܐ
col 2 ܐܬܟܣܝ، ܠܗ ܡܢ ܥܝ̈ܢܝܟܝ. *⁴³ܢܐܬܘܢ ܕܝܢ ܝܘܡܬܐ ܕܢܚܕܪܘܢܟܝ
ܒܥܠܕ̈ܒܒܝܟܝ. ܘܢܐܠܨܘܢܟܝ ܡܢ ܟܠ ܕܘܟܐ. ⁴⁴ܘܢܣܚܦܘܢܟܝ ܥܠ
§A412 ܐܪܥܐ. ܘܠܒ̈ܢܝܟܝ ܒܓܘܟܝ. ܘ§ܠܐ ܢܫܒܩܘܢ ܒܟܝ ܟܐܦ ܥܠ
¶A ܟܐܦ· ܚܠܦ ܕܠܐ ܝܕܥܬܝ، ܝܘܡܐ ܕܣܘܥܪܬܟܝ.¶ ◌◌◌
⁴⁵ܘܟܕ ܥܠ ܠܗܝܟܠܐ. ܫܪܝ ܠܡܦܩܘ ܠܐܝܠܝܢ ܕܡܙܒܢܝܢ ܒܗ ܙܒܢܐ.
⁴⁶ܘܐܡܪ ܟܬܝܒ ܗܘ ܕܒܝܬܝ، ܒܝܬ ܨܠܘܬܐ ܗܘ ܠܟܠܗܘܢ
ܥܡ̈ܡܐ. ܐܢܬܘܢ ܕܝܢ ܥܒܕܬܘܢܝܗܝ، ܡܥܪܬܐ ܕܠ̈ܣܛܝܐ. ⁴⁷ܘܡܠܦ
ܗܘܐ ܟܠܝܘܡ ܒܗܝܟܠܐ. ܘܪ̈ܒܝ ܟܗ̈ܢܐ ܘܣ̈ܦܪܐ ܘܪ̈ܝܫܐ ܕܥܡܐ
ܒܥܝܢ ܗܘܘ ܠܡܘܒܕܘܬܗ. ⁴⁸ܘܠܐ ܡܫܟܚܝܢ ܗܘܘ ܡܢܐ ܢܥܒܕܘܢ
fol 77 v ܠܗ. ܟܠܗ ܓܝܪ *ܥܡܐ ܬܠܐ ܗܘܐ ܒܗ ܠܡܫܡܥܗ ·܀·
¹ܘܗܘܐ ܒܚܕ ܡܢ ܝܘ̈ܡܬܐ. ܟܕ ܡܠܦ ܗܘܐ ܒܗܝܟܠܐ ܠܥܡܐ.
ܘܡܣܒܪ ܗܘܐ. ܩܡܘ ܥܠܘܗܝ، ܪ̈ܒܝ ܟܗ̈ܢܐ ܘܣ̈ܦܪܐ ܕܥܡܐ ܥܡ
ܩ̈ܫܝܫܐ ²ܘܐܡܪܝܢ ܠܗ. ܐܡܪ ܠܢ ܒܐܝܢܐ ܫܘܠܛܢܐ ܗܠܝܢ ܥܒܕ
ܐܢܬ. ܐܘ ܡܢܘ ܝܗܒ ܠܟ ܫܘܠܛܢܐ ܗܢܐ. ³ܐܡܪ ܠܗܘܢ ܐܦ
ܐܢܐ ܐܫܐܠܟܘܢ ܐܡܪܘ ܠܝ. ⁴ܡܥܡܘܕܝܬܗ ܕܝܘܚܢܢ ܡܢ ܫܡܝܐ
ܗܘܬ ܐܘ ܡܢ ܒ̈ܢܝ ܐܢܫܐ. ⁵ܗܢܘܢ ܕܝܢ ܡܬܚܫܒܝܢ ܗܘܘ ܒܝܢܬܗܘܢ

ܪܒܝ] ܡܠܦܢܐ ܫܦܝܪܐ S ܒܗܘܢ] ܒܬܠܡܝ̈ܕܝܟ S 40 ܐܡܪ] pr. ܘ ܒܢܝܐ S ܗܠܝܢ 2°] om. S 41 ܠܡܕܝܢܬܐ] om. ܠ S 42 ܝܘܡܐ] ܝܘܡܢܐ S ܝܕܥܬܝ ܕܝܢ] tr. S ܫܠܡܐ] om. S 44 ܘܢܣܚܦܘܢܟܝ S ܕܣܘܥܪܬܟܝ] ܕܣܥܘܪܢܟܝ S (sic): A 412 ܠܐ ܬܫܬܒܩ ܒܟܝ ܟܐܦ ܥܠ ܟܐܦ ܕܠܐ ܝܕܥܬܝ ܝܘܡܐ ܕܣܘܥܪܬܗ̇ 46 ܠܟܠܗܘܢ ܥܡ̈ܡܐ] om. S ܕܝܢ] om. S 47 ܘܡܠܦ] so also S ܘܪ̈ܝܫܐ ܕܥܡܐ] so also S 1 ܡܠܦ] pr. ܘ S ܕܥܡܐ] om. S ܥܡ ܩ̈ܫܝܫܐ] ܘܩܫܝܫܐ S 2 ܐܡܪ ܠܢ] om. S ܫܘܠܛܢ] ܫܘܠܛܢܐ S ܫܘܠܛܢܐ ܗܢܐ] tr. S 3 ܐܡܪ] pr. ܘ ܥܢܐ S ܐܫܐܠܟܘܢ] + ܡܠܬܐ. S 4 ܗܘܬ] ܗܝ S 5 ܗܢܘܢ ܕܝܢ] ܘܗܢܘܢ S ܒܝܢܬܗܘܢ] om. S

multitude say to him: "Rabban, rebuke them that they should not C S
40 cry out." He saith to them: "Amen, I say to you If these should
41 be silent these stones would cry out." And when he drew near and
42 saw the city he wept over it, and said "Even if in this day thou
hadst then known thy peace—! But peace hath been hidden from
43 thine eyes. Now the days will come that thine enemies will surround
44 thee and will afflict thee on every side and will overturn thee upon
the ground and thy children within thee, and §they will not leave in §A412
thee a stone on a stone, because thou knewest not the day of thy
greatness!"¶ ¶A

45 And when he entered the Temple he began to put forth those
46 selling in it *their* sale, and said: "It is written 'My House is a
House of Prayer for all the peoples,' but ye have made it a den of
47 robbers." And he was teaching daily in the Temple; and the chief
priests and scribes and the chiefs of the people were seeking to
48 destroy him, and they were not finding what they should do to him,
for all the people were hanging on him to hear him.

XX 1 And it came to pass on one of the days, when he was teaching the
people in the Temple and was announcing *the gospel*, there stood up
against him the chief priests and the scribes of the people with the
2 elders, and they say to him: "Say to us by what authority thou doest
3 these things? or who is it gave thee this authority?" He saith to
4 them: "I also will ask you; say to me—the baptism of John, from
5 heaven was *it*, or from men?" Now they were thinking among them-

---

Rabban] Fair Teacher *S* them] thy disciples *S* 40 saith] *so also* E^{208}; answered and said *S* these stones] the stones *S*; *pr.* yet E^{208} (*cf* Lk ix 58 *S*) 42 in this day] in this to-day *S*; *cf* 'to-day this day of thy peace' E^{207} (*one cod. om.* 'to-day') peace hath] *so also* E^{207}; it hath *S* 44 thy greatness] thy visitation *S* (*wrongly spelt*): *cf* 'There will not be left in her a stone on a stone, for that she knew not the day of her greatness' *A* 412 46 for all the peoples] *om. S* but] *om. S*
1 there stood up] *pr.* 'and' *S*: *cf* xix 2, 36 of the people] *om. S* with] and *S* 2 Say....doest] By what anthority doest thou *S* 3 saith] answered and said *S* ask you] + a word *S* 4 was *it*] is *it S* 5 Now] And *S* among themselves] *om. S*

ܘܐܡܪܝܢ. ܐܢ ܢܐܡܪ ܕܡܢ ܫܡܝܐ ܗܘ، ܢܐܡܪ ܠܢ. ܘܡܢܐ ܠܐ C S
ܗܝܡܢܬܘܢܝܗܝ. 6 ܘܐܢ ܢܐܡܪ ܕܡܢ ܒܢܝ ܐܢܫܐ ܗܘ. ܪܓܡܝܢ ܠܢ
ܟܠܗ *ܥܡܐ. ܡܛܠ ܕܡܦܣܝܢ ܗܘܘ ܠܒܪ ܥܠ ܝܘܚܢܢ ܕܢܒܝܐ ܗܘ. col 2
7 ܐܡܪܝܢ ܠܗ ܠܐ ܝܕܥܝܢ ܐܢܚܢ ܡܢ ܐܝܡܟܐ ܗܘ. 8 ܐܡܪ ܠܗܘܢ
ܝܫܘܥ. ܘܐܦܠܐ ܐܢܐ ܐܡܪܢܐ ܠܟܘܢ ܒܐܝܢܐ ܫܘܠܛܢܐ ܥܒܕ
ܐܢܐ ܗܠܝܢ. ܀

9 ܘܫܪܝ ܕܢܐܡܪ ܠܗܘܢ ܡܬܠܐ ܗܢܐ. ܓܒܪܐ ܚܕ ܢܨܒ ܟܪܡܐ.
ܘܐܘܚܕܗ ܠܦܠܚܐ ܘܥܒܕ ܙܒܢܐ ܣܓܝܐܐ. 10 ܘܒܚܕ ܡܢ ܙܒ̈ܢܐ.
ܫܕܪ ܥܒܕܗ ܠܘܬ ܦܠܚܐ ܕܢܬܠܘܢ ܠܗ ܡܢ ܦܐܪ̈ܘܗܝ ܕܟܪܡܐ.
ܘܡܚܐܘܗܝ ܘܫܕܪܘܗܝ ܟܕ ܣܪܝܩ. 11 ܘܐܘܣܦ. ܘܫܕܪ ܠܥܒܕܗ
ܐܚܪܢܐ. ܘܐܦ ܠܗܢܐ ܨܥܪܘܗܝ. 12 ܘܐܦܩܘܗܝ. 13 ܐܡܪ ܡܪܐ
ܕܟܪܡܐ ܡܢܐ ܐܥܒܕ. ܐܫܕܪ *ܠܒܪܝ ܚܒܝܒܐ. ܟܒܪ ܢܬܟܚܕܘܢ fol 78 r
ܡܢܗ. 14 ܟܕ ܚܙܘܗܝ ܕܝܢ ܦܠܚܐ. ܡܬܚܫܒܝܢ ܗܘܘ ܘܐܡܪܝܢ.
ܗܢܘ ܝܪܬܐ. ܬܘ ܢܩܛܠܝܘܗܝ ܘܬܗܘܐ ܝܪܬܘܬܐ ܕܝܠܢ. 15 ܘܐܦܩܘܗܝ
ܠܒܪ ܡܢ ܟܪܡܐ ܘܩܛܠܘܗܝ. ܡܢܐ ܢܥܒܕ ܠܗܘܢ ܡܪܗ ܕܟܪܡܐ.
16 ܢܐܬܐ ܘܢܘܒܕ ܠܦܠܚܐ ܗܢܘܢ. ܘܢܬܠ ܟܪܡܐ ܠܐܚܪ̈ܢܐ. ܟܕ
ܫܡܥܘ ܕܝܢ ܗܠܝܢ. ܐܡܪܝܢ ܚܣ ܘܠܐ ܢܗܘܐ. 17 ܗܘ ܕܝܢ ܚܪ
ܒܗܘܢ ܘܐܡܪ. ܘܡܢܘ ܟܘ̈ܪ ܗܢܐ ܕܟܬܝܒ. ܕܟܐܦܐ ܕܐܣܠܝܘ
ܒܢܝ̈ܐ. ܗܝ ܗܘܬ ܠܪܫܗ ܕܙܘܝܬܐ. 18 ܟܠ ܐܢܫ ܠܒܪ ܕܢܦܠ ܥܠ
ܗܝ ܟܐܦܐ ܢܬܪܥܥ. ܘܟܠ ܡܢ ܕܬܦܠ ܥܠܘܗܝ ܬܫܚܩܝܘܗܝ.

ܐܢ] *pr.* ܕ *S*   ܘܡܢܐ] *om.* ܘ *S*   6 ܠܒܪ (*after* ܗܘܘ)] *after* ܟܠܗ *S*
8 ܘܐܦܠܐ] *om.* ܘ *S*   9 ܘܐܘܚܕܗ] *pr.* ܘܐܚܕܗ ܣܝܓܐ *S*   10 ܦܐܪ̈ܘܗܝ] ܦܐܪܐ *S*   ܘܡܚܘܗܝ *S*   11 ܠܗܢܐ] ܠܗܘ *S*   12 ܘܐܦܩܘܗܝ] ܘܫܕܪ ܐܚܪܢܐ ܕܬܠܬܐ ܘܐܦ ܠܗ ܒܡܚܘܬܐ ܐܦܩܘܗܝ *S* (*sic*): *the rest of ver.* 12 *is lost in C through homoeoteleuton*   13 ܚܒܝܒܐ] ܚܒܝܒܝ *S* (*sic*)
16 ܢܐܬܐ ܘܢܘܒܕ ܠܦܠܚܐ ܗܢܘܢ] ܠܦܠܚܐ ܒܝܫܐ ܢܘܒܕ ܐܡܪܝܢ *S*   ܕܝܢ] *om.* *S*   ܐܡܪܝܢ ܚܣ ܘܠܐ ܢܗܘܐ] ܝܕܥ ܠܒܪ ܕܡܠܠܗܘܢ ܐܡܪ ܡܬܠܐ ܗܢܐ. *S*
17 ܘܚܪ] ܗܘ ܚܪܐ *S*   ܟܘ̈ܪ] *washed out in C* (*the* ܘ *quite effaced*): *cf* Lk xvi 11, xxii 70   ܠܪܫܗ ܕܙܘܝܬܐ] ܠܪܫ ܙܘܝܬܐ *S*   18 ܟܐܦܐ *S*
ܢܬܪܥܥ] ܢܬܬܪܥܥ *S*   ܬܫܚܩܝܘܗܝ *S*   *For A* 11, *see* Matt xxi 44

selves, and saying: "If we say that it is from heaven, he will say *C S*
6 to us 'And how is it ye did not believe him?'—and if we say
that it is from men, all the people will be stoning us, for they have
7 been persuaded about John that he is a prophet." They say to him:
8 "We do not know from whence it is." Jesus saith to them: "And
neither do I say to you by what authority I do these things."

9 And he began to say to them this similitude: "A certain man
planted a vineyard and let it out to husbandmen and departed for a
10 long time. And at one of the times he sent his slave unto the
husbandmen that they should give him of the fruits of the vineyard.
11 And they beat him and sent him away empty. And he went on and
12 sent another slave of his, and this one also they wounded and put him
13 forth. Saith the master of the vineyard: 'What shall I do? I will
send my beloved son; perchance they will have reverence for him.'
14 Now when the husbandmen saw him they were thinking and saying:
'This is the heir; come, let us kill him and the inheritance will be
15 ours.' And they put him forth out of the vineyard and killed him.
16 What will the lord of the vineyard do to them? He will come and
will destroy those husbandmen, and will give the vineyard to others."
Now when they heard these things they say: "Far be it, and it shall
17 not be!" Now he looked on them and said: "And what forsooth
is this that is written 'The stone that the builders rejected, it hath
18 become the head of the building.' For every man that shall fall on
that stone shall be shattered; and whomsoever it shall fall upon, it

---

And how] How *S* 6 all....for they] they will be stoning us, for all the people *S* 8 And neither] Neither *S* 9 and let it] *pr.* and surrounded it with a hedge *S* 11 this one] that one *S* 12 and put him forth] And he sent another, a third, and him also with stripes they put forth *S* (*sic*): *the rest of ver.* 12 *is lost in C through homoeoteleuton* 13 my beloved son] my son, my beloved *S* (*sic*) 16 He....husbandmen] They say: He will destroy the husbandmen *S* Now when] When *S* they say....not be!] for they knew that about them he said this similitude— *S* (*sic*) 17 And what] What *S* forsooth] *washed out in C*: *cf* Lk xvi 11, xxii 70 building] corner *S* 18 *For A* 11, *see* Matt xxi 44

C S col 2 ¹⁹ܘܒܥܘ ܗܘܘ ܪ̈ܒܝ ܟܗ̈ܢܐ *ܘܦ̈ܪܘܫܐ ܕܢܪܡܘܢ ܥܠܘܗܝ ܐܝ̈ܕܝܐ.
ܒܗ̇ ܒܗ̇ ܫܥܬܐ· ܝܕܥܘ ܗܘܘ ܓܝܪ ܕܥܠܝܗܘܢ ܐܡܪ. ܘܕܚܠܘ
ܡܢ ܥܡܐ. ²⁰ܘܒܬܪܟܢ ܫܕܪܘ ܠܓܫ̈ܘܫܐ ܕܢܬܕܡܘܢ ܒܙܕ̈ܝܩܐ.
ܕܢܐܚܕܘܢܗ ܒܡܠܬܐ ܘܢܫܠܡܘܢܗ ܠܗܓܡܘܢܐ. ²¹ܘܫܐܠܘܗܝ
ܘܐܡܪܝܢ ܠܗ· ܡܠܦܢܐ. ܝܕܥܝܢ ܚܢܢ ܕܬܪܝܨܐܝܬ ܡܡܠܠ ܐܢܬ
ܘܡܠܦ ܐܢܬ. ܘܠܐ ܢܣܒ ܐܢܬ ܒܐ̈ܦܐ ܕܐܢܫ. ܐܠܐ ܒܩܘܫܬܐ
ܡܠܬܐ ܕܐܠܗܐ ܡܠܦ ܐܢܬ. ²²ܫܠܝܛ ܠܢ ܠܡܬܠ ܟܣܦ ܪܫܐ ܠܩܣܪ
ܐܘ ܠܐ. ²³ܘܗܘ ܐܣܬܟܠ ܒܢܟܝܠܘܬܗܘܢ ܘܐܡܪ ܠܗܘܢ. ܡܢܐ
ܡܢܣܝܢ ܐܢܬܘܢ ܠܝ. ²⁴ܚܘܐܘܢܝ ܕܝܢܪܐ. ܨܠܡܐ ܘܟܬ̈ܒܬܐ ܕܡܢ
fol 78 v ܐܢܬ ܥܠܘܗܝ. ܘܚܘܝܘܗܝ. *ܘܐܡܪܝܢ ܠܗ ܕܩܣܪ. ²⁵ܐܡܪ ܠܗܘܢ
ܗܒܘ ܕܩܣܪ ܠܩܣܪ. ܘܕܐܠܗܐ ܠܐܠܗܐ. ²⁶ܘܠܐ ܐܫܟܚܘ ܠܡܐܚܕ
ܡܠܬܗ ܩܕܡ ܥܡܐ. ܘܐܬܕܡܪܘ ܥܠ ܦܬܓܡܗ ܘܫܬܩܘ
ܠܗܘܢ ܀ ○○ ○○ ○○
²⁷ܘܩܪܒܘ ܐܢ̈ܫܝܢ ܡܢ ܙܕܘܩ̈ܝܐ. ܗܢܘܢ ܕܐܡܪܝܢ ܕܠܝܬ ܩܝܡܬܐ.
ܘܫܐܠܘܗܝ ²⁸ܘܐܡܪܝܢ ܠܗ· ܡܠܦܢܐ ܡܘܫܐ ܟܬܒ ܠܢ. ܕܐܢ
ܢܡܘܬ ܐܚܘܗܝ ܕܐܢܫ ܒܗ ܠܝܬ ܠܗ ܒ̈ܢܝܐ. ܘܢܫܒܘܩ ܐܢܬܬܐ.
ܢܣܒ ܐܢܬܬܗ ܐܚܘܗܝ. ܕܢܩܝܡ ܙܪܥܐ ܠܐܚܘܗܝ. ²⁹ܫܒ̈ܥܐ
ܐܚ̈ܝܢ ܐܝܬ ܗܘܘ. ܩܕܡܝܐ ܢܣܒ ܐܢܬܬܐ ܘܡܝܬ ܕܠܐ ܒ̈ܢܝܢ·
³⁰ܘܢܣܒܗ̇ ܐܚܘܗܝ ܠܐܢܬܬܐ ܗܝ. ܐܦ ܗܘ ܡܝܬ ܕܠܐ ܒ̈ܢܝܢ.
col 2 ³¹ܐܦ ܗܘ ܕܬܠܬܐ *ܢܣܒܗ̇· ܘܐܦ ܫܒ̈ܥܬܝܗܘܢ ܢܣܒܘܗ̇.
ܘܡܝܬܘ ܟܕ ܠܐ ܫܒܩܘ ܒ̈ܢܝܐ. ³²ܘܡܝܬܬ ܐܦ ܗܝ ܐܢܬܬܐ.

---

19 ܝܕܥܘ.......ܐܡܪ] *om. S: see ver.* 16 ܘܕܚܠܘ] + ܗܘܘ *S* 20 ܒܙܕ̈ܝܩܐ] *so also S* ܠܗܓܡܘܢܐ] ܠܪܫܐ ܘܠܫܘܠܛܢܐ ܕܗܓܡܘܢܐ *S* 21 ܚܢܢ] ܐܚܢܢ *S* 24 ܚܘܘܢܝ *S* ܘܟܬ̈ܒܬܐ] ܒܟܬ̈ܒܬܐ *S (sic); in C the seyâmê are in red (i.e. they have been added later)* ܕܡܢ] ܕܡܢܘ *S* 26 ܠܡܐܚܕ ܡܠܬܗ] *tr. S* ܦܬܓܡܗ] ܦܬܓܡܐ *S*^ed 27 ܐܢ̈ܫܝܢ] ܐܢܫܐ *S* 28 ܒܗ ܠܝܬ] ܘܠܝܬ *S* ܐܢܬܬܗ ܐܚܘܗܝ] ܐܢܬܬ ܐܚܘܗܝ *S* ܕܢܩܝܡ] *so also S* 29 ܫܒ̈ܥܐ] ܫܘܒ̈ܥܐ *S (sic): cf* Lk xiii 14 ܗܘܘ] + ܠܘܬܢ *S* 30 ܐܚܘܗܝ] ܕܬܪܝܢ *S* ܐܦ] ܘܐܦ *S* 31 ܐܦ ܗܘ] ܘܐܦ *S* ܘܐܦ] ܘܗܟܢܐ *S*

19 shall crush him." And the chief priests and scribes had sought to *C S*
lay hands upon him in that very same hour, for they had known that
20 against them he said *it*; and they were afraid of the people. And
afterwards they sent spies that they might feign being righteous, that
they might take hold of him with a word and deliver him up to the
21 governor. And they asked him and say to him: "Teacher, we know
that rightly thou speakest and teachest, and thou hast no respect of
22 persons for any one, but in verity the word of God thou teachest; is
23 it lawful for us to give head-money to Caesar, or not?" And he
himself perceived their ill-will and said to them: "Why tempt ye
24 me? Shew me a denar; the image and the inscription—whose is it
25 thereon?" And they shewed him and say to him: "Caesar's." He
saith to them: "Give what *is* Caesar's to Caesar, and God's to
26 God." And they were not able to take hold of his word before the
people, and they wondered at his answer and kept silence.
27 And there drew near some folk of the Sadducees, those that say
28 that there is no resurrection, and they asked him and say to him:
"Teacher, Moses wrote for us, that if a man's brother die not having
sons and he leave a wife, his brother shall take his wife that he may
29 raise up seed to his brother. There were seven brothers: the first
30 took a wife and died without sons, and his brother took that woman;
31 he also died without sons. The third also took her, and the seven of
32 them also took her and died, not having left sons. And that woman

---

19 for they....said *it*] *om. S*: *see ver.* 16 were] had been *S* 20 the governor] the judgement and the authority of the governor *S* 24 and the] with the *S* 26 his answer] the answer S^{ed} 28 not having sons] and have no sons *S* his brother shall take his wife] *so also* E^{193}; he shall take his brother's wife *S* 29 seven brothers] + by us *S* 30 his brother] a second *S* he also] *pr.* and *S* 31 The third] And a third *S* and 1°] + thus *S* also 2°] *om. S*

C S §A167 §33ܒܩܝܡܬܐ ܕܐܝܢܐ ܡܢܗܘܢ ܬܗܘܐ. ܗܐ ܓܝܪ ܠܫܒܥܬܝܗܘܢ
ܗܘܬ. 34ܐܡܪ ܠܗܘܢ ܝܫܘܥ. ܒܢܘܗܝ ܕܥܠܡܐ ܗܢܐ ܡܘܠܕܝܢ
§A429 ܘܡܬܠܕܝܢ. ܘܢܣܒܝܢ ܢܫ̈ܐ ܘܗܘܝܢ ܢܫ̈ܐ ܠܓܒܪ̈ܐ. §35ܐܝܠܝܢ ܕܝܢ
ܕܠܗܘ ܥܠܡܐ ܫܘܘ ܠܡܡܛܐ. ܘܠܗ ܩܝܡܬܐ ܕܡܢ ܒܝܬ ܡܝ̈ܬܐ.
ܠܐ ܓܒܪ̈ܐ ܢܣܒܝܢ ܢܫ̈ܐ. ܘܐܦܠܐ ܢܫ̈ܐ ܗܘܝܢ ܠܓܒܪ̈ܐ. 36ܐܦܠܐ
ܠܡܡܬ ܡܫܟܚܝܢ. ܐܫܬܘܝܘ ܠܗܘܢ ܓܝܪ ܥܡ ܡܠܐܟ̈ܐ. ܐܝܟ
¶A429 ܒܢ̈ܝܐ ܕܐܠܗܐ ܒܢ̈ܝܐ ܕܩܝܡܬܐ.¶ 37ܥܠ ܡܝ̈ܬܐ ܕܝܢ ܕܩܝܡܝܢ.
fol 79 r ܘܐܦ *ܡܘܫܐ ܒܪܡܙ. ܟܕ ܡܠܠ ܥܡܗ ܐܠܗܐ ܡܢ ܣܢܝܐ
ܘܐܡܪ. ܡܪܝܐ ܐܠܗܗ ܕܐܒܪܗܡ. ܘܐܠܗܗ ܕܐܝܣܚܩ. ܘܐܠܗܗ
§A420 ܕܝܥܩܘܒ. 38ܘܗܘܐ §ܐܠܗܐ ܠܐ ܗܘܐ ܕܡܝ̈ܬܐ. ܐܠܐ ܕܚܝ̈ܐ.
¶A168 ¶A420 ܟܠܗܘܢ ܓܝܪ ܚܝܝܢ ܐܢܘܢ ܠܗ.¶¶ ܀

---

33 ܠܫܒܥܬܝܗܘܢ] pr. ܐܢܬܬܐ S   33—38. *The words from* Matt xxii 28—32 *in* A 167, 168 *are overlined.*   *For vv.* 33 *and* 34, *A has* ܐܡܪܝܢ ܠܗ. ܕܗܕܐ ܐܢܬܬܐ ܗܘܬ ܕܟܠܗܘܢ (A^a ܠܟܠܗܘܢ). ܒܝܬ ܡܝ̈ܬܐ. ܠܐܝܢܐ ܡܢܗܘܢ ܬܗܘܐ. ܗܝܕܝܢ ܐܡܪ ܠܗܘܢ ܡܪܢ. ܕܛܥܝܢ (om. ܕ A^a) ܛܥܝܢ ܐܢܬܘܢ. ܘܠܐ (A^a ܕܠܐ) ܝܕܥܝܢ ܐܢܬܘܢ ܟܬܒ̈ܐ. ܘܠܐ ܚܝܠܗ ܕܐܠܗܐ.
34 ܐܡܪ ܠܗܘܢ ܝܫܘܥ] ܘܐܡܪ ܝܫܘܥ ܒܢ̈ܝܐ S   35 ܕܝܢ] ܓܝܪ A 167; *om.* A 429   ܠܡܡܛܐ] *om.* S $A^2/_2$ ܠܐ ܓܒܪ̈ܐ ܢܣܒܝܢ ܢܫ̈ܐ. ܘܐܦܠܐ] C A^b167; *om.* S; *om.* ܓܒܪ̈ܐ A^a167; ܐܦܠܐ ܢܣܒܝܢ ܢܫ̈ܐ A 429   ܢܫ̈ܐ ܗܘܝܢ ܠܓܒܪ̈ܐ] C S A^a429; ܠܓܒܪ̈ܐ ܗܘܝܢ ܢܫ̈ܐ A 167, A^b429   36 ܐܦܠܐ ܠܡܡܬ ܡܫܟܚܝܢ] ܡܛܠ ܕܠܡܡܬ ܠܐ ܡܫܟܚܝܢ $A^2/_2$ ܐܫܬܘܝܘ.....ܡܠܐܟ̈ܐ] ܕܐܝܟ (A 429 ܐܠܐ ܐܝܟ) ܡܠܐܟ̈ܐ ܐܢܘܢ ܕܐܠܗܐ (A^b429 ܕܫܡܝܐ) $A^2/_2$ ܐܝܟ ܒܢ̈ܝܐ ܕܐܠܗܐ ܒܢ̈ܝܐ ܕܩܝܡܬܐ] ܐܝܟ ܒܢ̈ܝܐ ܕܩܝܡܬܐ S; ܘܒܢ̈ܝܐ ܕܩܝܡܬܐ A 167; ܘܒܢ̈ܝܐ ܕܐܠܗܐ A 429
37 ܥܠ ܡܝ̈ܬܐ ܕܝܢ ܕܩܝܡܝܢ] ܡܝ̈ܬܐ ܕܝܢ ܕܢܩܘܡܘܢ ܥܠ ܩܝܡܬܐ A   ܘܐܦ] ܐܦ S   ܒܣܢܗ ܐܠܗܐ] *tr.* S   *For* ܘܐܦ.....ܣܢܝܐ, A 167 *has* ܠܐ ܩܪܝܬܘܢ ܒܟܬܒܐ ܕܐܡܪ ܐܠܗܐ ܠܡܘܫܐ ܡܢ ܣܢܝܐ   ܘܐܡܪ. ܡܪܝܐ] ܐܢܐ ܐܢܐ ܕܐܢܐ A   ܐܠܗܗ ܕܐܒܪܗܡ ܘܐܝܣܚܩ ܘܕܝܥܩܘܒ A   38 ܘܗܘܐ] ܕܗܘܐ A^a168 (*om.* A 420)   ܐܠܐ ܕܚܝ̈ܐ] *om.* $A^2/_2$ (*exc.* A^a168)   ܟܠܗܘܢ ܓܝܪ] ܡܛܠ ܕܟܠܗܘܢ A 420 (ܟܠܗܘܢ....ܠܗ *om.* A^a168)

33 also hath died. §In the resurrection whose of them shall she be? *C S* §*A* 167
34 For lo, *wife* of the seven of them she became." Jesus saith to them:
"The sons of this world beget and are begotten, and take wives and
35 become the wives of men, §but they which that world have been §*A* 429
worthy to receive, and that resurrection from among the dead, are
36 not men taking wives, nor women becoming *wives* of men; nor
can they die, for they have been made equal with the angels, as the
37 sons of God, *even* sons of the resurrection.¶ Now concerning the ¶*A* 429
dead that they will rise Moses also hath made clear, when God
spake with him from the Bush and said: 'The LORD, the God of
38 Abraham and the God of Isaac and the God of Jacob'; and lo, §the §*A* 420
God not of the dead, but of the living, for they are all living to ¶*A* 168
him."¶¶ ¶*A* 420

---

33 *wife* of] *pr.* the woman— *S* 33—38. *The words from* Matt xxii 28—32 in *A* 167, 168, *are given in small capitals* *For vv.* 33 *and* 34, *A has*: 'They say to him "Lo, the wife she was of all of them. In the COMING TO LIFE OF THE DEAD whose *wife* of them will she be?" Then said our Lord to them: "MUCH DO YE ERR, AND ('that' A^a) YE KNOW NOT THE SCRIPTURES NOR THE POWER OF GOD."' 34 saith to them] answered and said *S* of this world] *pr.* 'of the times' E^{194} beget and are begotten (*sic*)] *S C*: *see Notes*, vol. ii 35 but] for *A* 167; *om.* *A* 429 worthy to receive] worthy of *S* $A^2/_2$ E^{194} men taking wives, nor] *C* A^b 167; *om.* *S*; *om.* men A^a 167; taking women nor *A* 429 36 nor can they die] because they cannot die $A^2/_2$ for...angels] because AS ('BUT AS' *A* 429) THE ANGELS THEY ARE of God ('IN HEAVEN' A^b 429) $A^2/_2$ as....resurrection] as sons of the resurrection *S*; and sons of the resurrection *A* 167; and sons of God *A* 429 37 concerning....rise] concerning THE RESURRECTION that the dead will rise *A* *For* 'Moses also....the Bush,' *A* 167 has: 'HAVE YE NOT READ *IN THE SCRIPTURE* (= Mk) THAT GOD SAID to Moses from the Bush' and said: 'The LORD,....Jacob'] 'I AM the God of Abraham and of Isaac and of Jacob' *A* 38 and lo] who *is* lo A^a 168 (*om.* *A* 420) but of the living] *om.* $A^2/_2$ (*exc.* A^a 168) for] because *A* 420 ('for all...to him' *om.* A^a 168)

³⁹ܐܡܪܝܢ ܠܗ ܐ̈ܢܫܝܢ ܡܢ ܣ̈ܦܪܐ. ܡܠܦܢܐ ܫܦܝܪ ܐܡܪܬ ܐܢܬ. C S
⁴⁰ܘܬܘܒ ܠܐ ܐܡܪܝܢ ܠܡܫܐܠܘܬܗ ܡܕܡ. ○○○

⁴¹ܘܐܡܪ ܗܘܐ ܠܗܘܢ܂ ܐܝܟܢܐ ܐܡܪܝܢ ܣ̈ܦܪܐ ܥܠ ܡܫܝܚܐ
ܕܒܪܗ ܗܘ ܕܕܘܝܕ܂ ⁴²ܘܗܘ ܕܘܝܕ ܐܡܪ ܒܟܬܒܐ ܕܡ̈ܙܡܘܪܐ.
ܕܐܡܪ ܡܪܝܐ ܠܡܪܝ, ܕܬܒ ܠܝ ܡܢ ܝܡܝܢܝ. ⁴³ܥܕܡܐ ܕܐܣܝܡ
ܒܥܠ̈ܕܒܒܝܟ ܬܚܝܬ ܪ̈ܓܠܝܟ. ⁴⁴*ܐܢ ܗܟܝܠ ܕܘܝܕ ܡܪܝ, ܩܪܐ ܠܗ. col 2
ܐܝܟܢܐ ܒܪܗ ܗܘ. ○○○

⁴⁵ܘܟܕ ܫܡܥ ܗܘܐ ܟܠܗ ܥܡܐ ܐܡܪ ܠܬܠܡܝܕܘܗܝ܂ ⁴⁶ܐܙܕܗܪܘ ܡܢ
ܣ̈ܦܪܐ ܕܨܒܝܢ ܠܡܗܠܟܘ ܒܐܣܛܠܐ. ܘܪܚܡܝܢ ܫܠܡܐ ܒܫ̈ܘܩܐ.
ܘܡ̈ܘܬܒܐ ܪ̈ܫܢܝܐ ܒܟܢܘܫܬܐ. ܘܪܝܫ ܣ̈ܡܟܐ ܒܡܫ̈ܬܘܬܐ. ⁴⁷ܘܐܟܠܝܢ
ܒ̈ܬܐ ܕܐܪ̈ܡܠܬܐ. ܒܥܠܬܐ ܕܡܘܪܟܝܢ ܨ̈ܠܘܬܗܘܢ܂ ܘܗܢܘܢ
ܢܩܒܠܘܢ ܕܝܢܐ ܝܬܝܪܐ. ○.

¹ܘܐܪܝܡ ܥܝܢܘܗܝ, ܘܚܙܐ ܠܥܬܝܪ̈ܐ ܕܪܡܝܢ ܗܘܘ ܩܘܪ̈ܒܢܝܗܘܢ
ܒܝܬ ܓܙܐ. ²ܘܚܙܐ ܐܦ ܐܪܡܠܬܐ ܡܣܟܢܬܐ ܕܐܪܡܝܬ ܫܡ̈ܘܢܐ
ܬܪ̈ܝܢ. ³ܐܡܪ ܩܘܫܬܐ ܐܡܪܢܐ ܠܟܘܢ܂ ܕܗܕܐ ܐܪܡܠܬܐ ܡܣܟܢܬܐ
ܐܪܡܝܬ. *ܝܬܝܪ ܡܢ ܟܠܗܘܢ܂ ⁴ܗܠܝܢ ܓܝܪ ܡܢ ܡܕܡ ܕܝܬܝܪ ܗܘܐ fol 79 v
ܠܗܘܢ ܐܪܡܝܘ ܒܝܬ ܓܙܐ ܩܘܪܒܢܐ· ܗܕܐ ܕܝܢ ܡܢ ܡܕܡ
ܕܚܣܝܪ ܠܗ̇ ܟܠ ܕܩܢܝܐ ܗܘܬ ܐܪܡܝܬܗ. ○○○ ○ ○

⁵ܘܟܕ ܐܡܪܝܢ ܐ̈ܢܫܝܢ ܥܠ ܗܝܟܠܐ ܕܒ̈ܟܐܦܐ ܫܦܝܪ̈ܬܐ ܘܒܩܘܪ̈ܒܢܐ
ܡܨܒܬ. ܐܡܪ ⁶ܚܙܝܢ ܐܢܬܘܢ ܗܠܝܢ. ܢܐܬܘܢ ܝܘ̈ܡܬܐ ܕܠܐ
ܬܫܬܒܩ ܗܪܟܐ ܟܐܦ ܥܠ ܟܐܦ ܕܠܐ ܬܬܣܬܪ. ○○ ○○ ○○
⁷ܘܫܐܠܘܗܝ, ܗܘܘ ܘܐܡܪܝܢ ܠܗ. ܡܠܦܢܐ ܐܡܬܝ, ܗܠܝܢ ܢܗܘܝܢ.
ܘܡܢܐ ܐܬܐ ܗܝ ܕܡܫܪܝܢ ܗܠܝܢ ܕܢܗܘܝܢ. ⁸ܗܘ ܕܝܢ ܐܡܪ ܠܗܘܢ.

---

39. *Perh. no § in S*   ܐ̈ܢܫܝܢ] ܐܢܫܐ S   ܐܡܪܬ ܐܢܬ] ܐܡܪܬ S
42 ܕܡ̈ܙܡܘܪܐ] ܕܡܙܡܘܪܘܗܝ S   43 ܬܚܝܬ] *pr.* ܟܘܒܫܐ S   46 ܒܐܣܛ̈ܠܘܬܐ S
47 ܘܗܢܘܢ] *om.* ܘ S   1 ܗܘܘ] *om.* S   ܩܘܪ̈ܒܢܝܗܘܢ S   2 ܘܐܦ ܐܪܡܠܬܐ]
ܐܦ ܐܪܡܠܬܐ ܚܕܐ S   ܕܐܪܡܝܬ] ܘܐܪܡܝܬ S   3 ܩܘܫܬܐ] ܒܩܘܫܬܐ S
4 ܗܘܐ] *om.* S   ܓܝܪ] *om.* S   5 ܐܡܪ] + ܠܗܘܢ S   6 ܗܠܝܢ] + ܟ̈ܐܦܐ S
ܗܪܟܐ] ܒܗ S   7. *No § in S: perh. none was intended by C**   ܗܘܘ] *om.* S

39 Some of the scribes say to him: "Teacher, well sayest thou!" *C S*
40 And not again did they dare to ask him aught.
41 And he was saying to them: "How say the scribes about the
42 Messiah that he is the son of David? And David himself hath said
in the book of the Psalms 'The LORD said to my Lord Sit down on
43, 44 my right hand, until I lay thine enemies under thy feet.' If therefore
David call him 'my Lord,' how is he his son?"
45 And while all the people were hearing he said to his disciples:
46 "Beware of the scribes that wish to walk in porches, and love
greeting in the streets and the honourable seats in the synagogues
47 and the chief entertainments at suppers, and eat up the houses of
widows in the pretext that they are lengthening their prayers—and
they themselves shall receive the more judgement."
xxi 1 And he lifted up his eyes and saw the rich that were casting
2 their offerings into the treasury; and he saw a poor widow also that
3 cast in two mites. He saith: "The verity I say to you, that this
4 poor widow hath cast in more than all of them; for these of what
was abundant to them cast into the treasury *as* an offering, but this
woman of what is lacking to her—all that she was possessing—
cast in."
5 And when some said of the Temple that with fair stones and with
6 offerings it was adorned, he saith: "See ye these? The days will
come that there will not be left here a stone on a stone that will not
be pulled down."
7 And they had asked him and say to him: "Teacher, when shall
these things be, and what *is* the sign what *time* these things begin
8 to be?" Now he said to them: "See lest ye go astray. For

---

39 sayest thou] hast thou said *S* 42 the Psalms] his Psalms *S* 43 under] *pr. as* the footstool *S* 47 and they] *om.* and *S* 1 that were] *om. S* 2 a poor widow] a certain poor woman *S* that cast] and she cast *S* 3 The verity] In verity *S* 4 was 1°] is *S* into....offering] into the offertory *S* 5 he saith] + to them *S* 6 these] + stones *S* here] in it *S E*[44] 7 had] *om. S*

C S col 2 ܚܙܘ ܕܠܐ ܬܛܥܘܢ. ܣܓܝܐܐ ܓܝܪ ܢܐܬܘܢ *ܒܫܡܝ ܘܢܐܡܪܘܢ
ܕܐܢܐ ܐܢܐ. ܘܙܒܢܐ ܩܪܒ. ܠܐ ܬܐܙܠܘܢ ܒܬܪܗܘܢ܆ ⁹ܘܡܐ
ܕܫܡܥܝܢ ܐܢܬܘܢ ܩܪܒܐ ܘܫܓܘܫܝܐ ܠܐ ܬܬܕܘܠܘܢ. ܥܬܝܕܢ
ܐܝܟ ܓܝܪ ܠܡܗܘܐ ܗܠܝܢ ܠܘܩܕܡܐ. ܐܠܐ ܠܐ ܒܥܓܠ ܡܛܬ
§A 133 ܚܪܬܐ. §¹⁰ܢܩܘܡ ܓܝܪ ܥܡܐ ܥܠ ܥܡܐ ܘܡܠܟܘ ܥܠ ܡܠܟܘ.
¹¹ܘܙܘ̈ܥܐ ܪ̈ܘܪܒܐ ܒܕܘܟܐ ܕܘܟܐ. ܘܡ̈ܘܬܢܐ ܘܟ̈ܦܢܐ. ܘܢܗܘܘܢ
¶A ܕܚ̈ܠܬܐ ܡܢ ܫܡܝܐ.¶ ܘܢܬܚܙܝܢ ܐܬ̈ܘܬܐ ܪ̈ܘܪܒܬܐ. ܘܣ̈ܬܘܐ
ܪ̈ܘܪܒܐ. ¹²ܩܕܡ ܗܠܝܢ ܕܝܢ ܟܠܗܝܢ. ܢܪܡܘܢ ܥܠܝܟܘܢ ܐܝ̈ܕܝܗܘܢ
ܘܢܪ̈ܕܦܘܢܟܘܢ܆ ܘܢܫܠܡܘܢܟܘܢ ܠܟܢ̈ܘܫܬܐ. ܘܠܒܝܬ ܐܣܝ̈ܪܐ.
fol 80 r ܘܢܩܪ̈ܒܘܢܟܘܢ *ܩܕܡ ܡ̈ܠܟܐ ܘܗ̈ܓܡܘܢܐ ܡܛܠ ܫܡܝ. ¹³ܬܗܘܐ
§A 415 ܠܟܘܢ ܕܝܢ ܠܣܗܕܘܬܐ ܗܕܐ. ¹⁴ܘܣܝܡܘ ܒ̈ܠܒܝܟܘܢ܆ §ܕܠܐ ܬܗܘܘܢ
ܡܬܒܛܠܝܢ ܠܡܦܩ ܪܘܚܐ. ¹⁵ܐܢܐ ܓܝܪ ܐܬܠ ܠܟܘܢ ܦܘܡܐ
ܘܚܟܡܬܐ. ܐܝܕܐ ܕܠܐ ܡܫܟܚܝܢ ܕܢܩܘܡܘܢ ܠܘܩܒܠܗ̇ ܟܠܗܘܢ
¶A §A 415 ܒܥܠܕܒ̈ܒܝܟܘܢ܆¶ §¹⁶ܢܫܠܡܘܢܟܘܢ ܐܒ̈ܗܝܟܘܢ ܘܐ̈ܚܝܟܘܢ ܘܐܚ̈ܝܢܝܟܘܢ
ܘܪ̈ܚܡܝܟܘܢ܆ ܘܢܡܝܬܘܢ ܡܢܟܘܢ܆ ¹⁷ܘܬܗܘܘܢ ܣܢܝܐܝܢ ܡܢ ܟܠ
¶A ܐܢܫ ܡܛܠ ܫܡܝ.¶ ¹⁹ܒܡܣܝܒܪܢܘܬܐ ܕܝܢ ܬܩܢܘܢ ܢܦܫܟܘܢ܆ ²⁰ܡܐ

---

9. *For* A 417, *see on* Matt xxiv 6   10, 11.] A 133 *has*: ܢܩܘܡ ܥܡܐ .... ¹¹ܘܢܗܘܘܢ ܟ̈ܦܢܐ ܘܡ̈ܘܬܢܐ. ܘܕ̈ܚܠܬܐ ܡܢ ܫܡܝܐ   11 ܘܡ̈ܘܬܢܐ] + ܒܕܘܟܐ ܕܘܟܐ S   ܘܣ̈ܬܘܐ ܪ̈ܘܪܒܐ] *om.* S   12 ܘܗ̈ܓܡܘܢܐ S   13 ܗܕܐ] *om.* S   12—14.] A *has*: ܘܬܘܒ ܐܡܪ ܕܐܡܪܬ ܕܡܫܠܡܝܢ ܠܟܘܢ ܩܕܡ ܐ̈ܪܟܘܢ ܘܩܕܡ ܫܠܝܛܢܐ (Aᵃ ܫܘ̈ܠܛܢܐ). ܘܩܕܡ ܡܠ̈ܟܐ ܐܚ̈ܪܢܐ (Aᵃ ܘܐܚ̈ܪܢܐ) ܒܠܒܐ. ܠܐ ܬܬܪܢܘܢ ܡܢ ܩܕܡ ܕܐܢܐ ܡܢܐ ܬܡܠܠܘܢ. ܘܐܡܢܐ ܬܦܩܘܢ ܪܘܚܐ.   15 ܐܢܐ ܓܝܪ] ܘܐܢܐ A   ܐܝܕܐ] *om.* A   ܡܫܟܚܝܢ] ܢܫܟܚܘܢ A   ܠܘܩܒܠܗ̇] ܠܡܩܒܠܗ̇ S   ܕܢܩܘܡܘܢ....ܒܥܠܕܒ̈ܒܝܟܘܢ] ܒܥܠܕܒ̈ܒܝܟܘܢ ܠܡܒܟܣܘܢ. ܡܛܠ ܕܠܐ ܗܘܐ ܐܢܬܘܢ ܡܡܠܠܝܢ. ܐܠܐ ܪܘܚܐ ܕܩܘܕܫܐ ܕܐܒܘܟܘܢ ܗܝ ܡܡܠܠܐ ܒܟܘܢ܆ A   16 ܢܫܠܡܘܢܟܘܢ] + ܓܝܪ S (*sic*)   ܐܒ̈ܗܝܟܘܢ ܘܐ̈ܚܝܟܘܢ] ܐܚܝܟܘܢ ܘܐܒܗܝܟܘܢ S; ܐܒܗ̈ܝܟܘܢ ܘܐܚ̈ܝܟܘܢ A   ܘܐܚ̈ܝܢܝܟܘܢ....ܪ̈ܚܡܝܟܘܢ] ܘܩܪ̈ܝܒܝܟܘܢ A   17 ܘܬܗܘܘܢ ܣܢܝܐܝܢ ܡܢ] ܘܢܗܘܐ ܣܢܐ ܠܟܘܢ A   ܟܠܢܫ Aᵇ   18.] + ܘܡܢܬܐ ܚܕܐ ܡܢ ܣܥܪܐ ܕܪܫܟܘܢ ܠܐ ܬܐܒܕ S   ܫܡܝ] + ܕܝܠܝ A   19 ܕܝܢ] ܓܝܪ S   ܢܦܫܟܘܢ] ܢܦܫܬܟܘܢ S

many will come in my name, and will say 'I am he' and 'The time C S
9 hath drawn near'; do not go after them. And what *time* ye hear of
war and tumult, be not afraid; for these things are first about to be,
10 but not yet hath the last arrived. §For people will rise against people §A 133
11 and kingdom against kingdom, and *there will be* great earthquakes in
various places and pestilences and famines, and there will be terrors
from heaven¶ and great signs will be seen and great winter-storms. ¶A
12 Now before all these things they will lay hands on you and persecute
you, and will deliver you up to the synagogues and to prison and
they will bring you up before kings and governors for my name's
13, 14 sake. Now it shall be for you a testimony—*even* this. And set in
your hearts §that ye shall not be teaching yourselves to make excuse, §A 415
15 for I myself will give you a mouth and wisdom such that all your
16 enemies cannot stand up against it.¶ §Your kinsfolk and your ¶A §A 415
brothers and your relations and your friends will deliver you up, and
17 they will put some of you to death, and ye will be hated by every one
19, 20 for my name's sake,¶ but in patience ye shall possess your life. Now ¶A

---

9. *For A* 417, *see on* Matt xxiv 6 10, 11.] *A* 133 *has*: 'People will rise...., [11]and there will be famines and pestilences and terrors from heaven' 11 pestilences] + in various places *S* and great winter-storms] *om. S* 13 *even* this] *om. S* 12—14.] *A has*: 'And again he taught us "Whenever they bring you up before the ruling powers and before authorities and before kings [and] rulers of the world, do not meditate before the time what ye shall speak and how ye shall make excuse"' 15 for] and *A* against it] against you *S* such that....against it] *A has*: 'that all your enemies will not be able to conquer, because not ye are speaking but the Holy Spirit of your Father—it speaketh in you' (*see also* Lk xii 11, 12) 16 Your] For your *S* kinsfolk...brothers] brothers...kinsfolk *S*; parents...brothers *A* your relations.....to death] your family *A* 17 ye...every one] every one will be hating you *A* sake] + even mine *A* 18.] + And not one lock of the hair of your head shall perish *S* 19 but] for *S* life] lives *S*

C S ܕܢܣܬܘܢ ܕܝܢ ܠܐܘܪܫܠܡ ܕܢܕܘܢ ܠܗ ܚܝܠܐ. ܕܗܘ ܕܡܦܪܩ ܠܗ
ܣܘܪܒܗ̇. [21]ܘܐܢܚܢ ܕܣܒܪܝܢ ܗܘܝܢ ܢܦܪܘܩ ܠܦܘܪܩܢܐ. ܘܕܥܠܝܗ̇
col 2 ܢܦܩܘܢ ܡܢܗ̇. ܘܐܝܠܝܢ †ܕܣܒܪ̈ܢܐ ܠܐ *ܢܦܠܘܢ ܠܗ̇. [22]ܡܛܠ
ܕܣܘܟܪܬܐ ܗܘܝܢ ܕܬܘܕܝܬܐ. ܕܢܦܠܘܢ ܥܠ ܡܢܐ ܕܡܬܝܒ. [23]ܘ، ܕܡ
ܠܐܝܠܝܢ ܕܩܛܠܝܢ ܘܠܐܝܠܝܢ ܕܚ̈ܝܝܢ ܒܗܘܢ ܘܡ̈ܬܬܐ. ܢܗܘܐ ܠܒܪ
§A410 ܐܘܠܨܢܐ ܪܒܐ ܒܐܪܥܐ. §ܘܪܘܓܙܐ ܣܓܝܐܐ ܥܠ ܥܡܐ ܗܢܐ.
¶A [24]ܘܢܦܠܘܢ ܒܦܘܡܐ ܕܚܪܒܐ.¶ ܘܢܫܬܒܘܢ ܠܟܠܗܘܢ ܥܡ̈ܡܐ.
ܘܐܘܪܫܠܡ ܬܗܘܐ ܡܬܕܝܫܐ ܡܢ ܥܠܡ̈ܐ ܥܡ̈ܡܐ. ܥܕܡܐ
ܕܢܫܬܠܡܘܢ ܙܒ̈ܢܐ ܕ̈ܥܡܡܐ. [25]ܢܗܘܘܢ ܕܝܢ ܐ̈ܬܘܬܐ ܒܫܡܫܐ
ܘܒܣܗܪܐ ܘܒ̈ܟܘܟܒܐ. ܘܐܘܠܨܢܐ ܒܐܪܥܐ ܘܫܘܫܝܐ ܕ̈ܝܡܐ
ܕ̈ܥܡܡܐ. ܘܩܠܐ ܕܕܡܐ ܠܕܡܝܐ. ܘܓܠܠܐ. [26]ܕܡܦܩܢ ܢܦ̈ܫܬܐ
fol 80 v ܕܒ̈ܢܝ ܐܢܫܐ. ܡܢ ܕܚܠܬܐ ܕܡܕܡ ܕܐܬܐ ܠܡܐܬܐ ܥܠ *ܐܪܥܐ.
ܘܢܬܙܝܥܘܢ ܚ̈ܝܠܐ ܕܫܡܝܐ. [27]ܘܗܝܕܝܢ ܢܚܙܘܢܝܗ̇ ܠܒܪܗ ܕܐܢܫܐ
ܕܐ ܐܬܐ ܒܥ̈ܢܢܐ. ܒܚܝܠܐ ܣܓܝܐܐ ܘܒܫܘܒܚܐ. [28]ܡܐ ܕܫܪܝ،
ܕܝܢ ܗܠܝܢ ܕܢܗܘܘܢ. ܐܬܬܘܡܘ ܘܐܪܝܡܘ ܪ̈ܫܝܟܘܢ. ܡܛܠ ܕܩܪܒ ܠܗ
ܦܘܪܩܢܟܘܢ: ○○ ○○ ○○
[29]ܘܐܡܪ ܗܘܐ ܠܗܘܢ ܡܬܠܐ ܗܢܐ. ܚܙܘ ܠܬܬܐܢܐ ܘܠܟܠܗܘܢ
ܐ̈ܝܠܢܐ. [30]ܕܡܐ ܕܫܪܝܘ ܡܦܪܥܝܢ ܘܚܙܝܢ ܦܐ̈ܪܝܗܘܢ: ܡܬܝܕܥܝܢ
ܐܢܬܘܢ ܕܩܪܝܒ ܠܗ ܩܝܛܐ. [31]ܗܟܢܐ ܐܦ ܐܢܬܘܢ ܡܐ ܕܚܙܝܬܘܢ
ܗܠܝܢ ܕܗܘܝܢ. ܕܥܘ ܕܩܪܝܒܐ ܗܝ، ܡܠܟܘܬܐ ܕܫܡܝܐ .○.

21 ܘܕܒܟܠܗܘܢ̇] C^{corr}; ܘܕܒܟܠܗܘܢ C^* ܕܒܣܘ̈ܪܢܐ] S; *pr.* ܘ C: *cf* syr.vg
22 ܡܛܠ] ܡܛܠ ܕ S 23. § *in* S ܒܫܘܒܩܬܐ ܗܢܘܢ S ܒܐܪܥܐ]
om. S ܘܪܘܓܙܐ] ܘܪܘܓܙܐ ܪܒܐ ܬܗܘܐ A ܣܓܝܐܐ] *om.* S A ܗܢܐ] ܗܘ A
24 ܕܫܒܝܐ] ܕܫܘܒܝܐ S (*sic*), *the* ܘ *cancelled by the dot* ܠܟܠܗܘܢ ܥܡ̈ܡܐ]
ܠܟܠ ܐܬܪ S ܘܐܘܪܫܠܡ] C (*end of line*); ܘܐܘܪܫܠܡ S 25 ܢܗܘܘܢ ܕܝܢ]
ܘܢܗܘܘܢ S ܘܫܘܫܝܐ] ܘܫܘܫܠ S ܕ̈ܝܡܐ ܕ̈ܥܡܡܐ] ܕܝܡܐ S 26 ܕܡܦܩܢ]
ܘܢܦܩܢ S ܘܢܬܙܝܥܘܢ] ܘܢܙܘܥܘܢ S 27 ܢܚܙܘܢܗ S 30 ܡܦܪܥܝܢ]
ܦܪܥܝܢ S 31 ܕܫܡܝܐ] S *illegible, but probably has* ܕܐܠܗܐ

what *time* ye have seen Jerusalem with an army surrounding it, know *C S*
21 that its desolation hath come nigh. And they that are in Judaea let
them flee to the hill-*country*, and they within it let them go forth
22 from it, and they †in the villages let them not enter it; because the
days are *days* of requital, that all what is written may be fulfilled.
23 Now woe to them with child, and to them that are giving suck in
those days! For there will be great distress in the earth §and strong §*A*410
24 wrath against this people, and they will fall by the edge of the sword¶ ¶*A*
and they shall be taken captive to all the peoples, and Jerusalem
will be trampled on by all the peoples until the times of the peoples
25 be accomplished. Now there will be signs in the sun and in the
moon and in the stars, and distress in the earth and irresolution of
26 the peoples, and a sound like that of the sea and a trembling, that
sendeth forth the lives of men for fear of that which is about to
27 come on the earth, and the powers of heaven will tremble. And
then they will see the Son of Man coming in the clouds with much
28 power and with glory. Now what *time* these things have begun to
be, look out and lift up your heads because your redemption hath
drawn nigh."
29 And he was saying to them this similitude: "See the fig-tree
30 and all the trees, that what *time* they have begun putting forth *their*
leaves and giving their fruit ye understand that the summer hath
31 drawn nigh. So ye also, what *time* ye have seen these things coming
to pass, know ye that the kingdom of heaven is near.

---

21 in the villages] *S*; *pr.* and *C* (*a blunder*) 22 what] that which *S* 23 in the earth] *om.* *S*: *cf* 'there shall be anguish unto this people' E^{214} strong wrath] *pr.* there will come *A* strong] *om.* *S A* this] that *A* 24 to all the peoples] everywhere *S* 25 Now] And *S* irresolution] *lit.* 'clasping of the hands' *C*; 'slackness of the hands' *S*: *see* Philoxenus 281^{22} *and Notes*, vol. ii like that] *om.* *S* 26 that sendeth....men] and the lives of men will go forth *S* 31 of heaven] *S illegible, but probably has* 'of God'

32 ܐܡܝܢ ܐܡܪܢܐ ܠܟܘܢ ܕܠܐ ܬܥܒܪ ܫܪܒܬܐ ܗܕܐ. ܥܕܡܐ C S
ܕܗܠܝܢ ܟܠܗܝܢ ܢܗܘܝܢ. 33 ܫܡܝܐ ܘܐܪܥܐ ܢܥܒܪܘܢ܆ ܘܡ̈ܠܝ *ܠܐ col 2
ܢܥܒܪ̈ܢ܆ 34 ܐܙܕܗܪܘ ܕܝܢ ܒܢܦܫܬܟܘܢ܆ ܕܠܐ ܢܐܩܪܘܢ ܠܒ̈ܘܬܟܘܢ
ܒܡܐܟܘܠܬܐ ܕܟܣܘܪܐ. ܘܒܪܘܝܘܬܐ ܕܫܟܪܐ. ܘܒܝܨܦܬܐ ܕܥܠܡܐ.
ܘܢܩܘܡ ܥܠܝܟܘܢ ܝܘܡܐ ܗܘ ܡܢ ܬܚܝܬ ܫܠܝܐ. 35 ܐܝܟ ܦܚܐ
ܓܝܪ ܢܐܬܐ ܥܠ ܟܠܗܘܢ ܐܝܠܝܢ ܕܝܬܒܝܢ ܥܠ ܦܘܡܗ̇ ܕܐܪܥܐ.
36 ܫܗܪܘ ܗܟܝܠ ܒܟܠܙܒܢ. ܘܬܗܘܘܢ ܒܥܝܢ ܕܬܫܘܘܢ ܠܡܥܒܪ ܡܢ
ܗܠܝܢ ܕܥܬ̈ܝܕܢ ܠܡܗܘܐ. ܘܬܬܩܘܡܘܢ ܩܕܡ ܒܪܗ ܕܐܢܫܐ ܀
37 ܘܒܐܝܡܡܐ ܡܠܦ ܗܘܐ ܒܗܝܟܠܐ. ܘܒܠ̈ܠܝܬܐ ܢܦܩ ܗܘܐ
ܒܐܬ ܒܛܘܪܐ ܕܡܬܩܪܐ ܕܒܝܬ ܙܝܬܐ. 38 ܘܟܠܗ ܥܡܐ ܡܩܕܡܝܢ
ܗܘܘ ܠܘܬܗ ܠܗܝܟܠܐ ܕܢܫܡܥܘܢܗ.
*1 ܘܩܪܒ ܗܘܐ ܥܐܕܐ ܕܦܛܝܪ̈ܐ ܕܡܬܩܪܐ ܦܨܚܐ. 2 ܘܒܥܝܢ ܗܘܘ fol 81r
ܪ̈ܒܝ ܟܗܢܐ ܘܣܦܪ̈ܐ ܐܝܟܢܐ ܢܩܛܠܘܢܗ܁. ܕܕܚܠܝܢ ܗܘܘ ܓܝܪ ܡܢ
ܥܡܐ.
3 ܥܠ ܗܘܐ ܕܝܢ ܣܛܢܐ ܒܝܗܘܕܐ ܕܡܬܩܪܐ ܐܣܟܪܝܘܛܐ. ܕܐܝܬܘܗܝ
ܗܘܐ ܡܢ ܡܢܝܢܐ ܕܬܪ̈ܥܣܪ. 4 ܘܐܙܠ ܡܠܠ ܥܡ ܪ̈ܒܝ ܟܗܢܐ
ܘܣܦܪ̈ܐ ܐܝܟ ܕܢܫܠܡܝܘܗܝ ܠܗܘܢ܆ 5 ܘܚܕܝܘ. ܘܐܫܬܘܕܝܘ ܗܘܘ
ܕܢܬܠܘܢ ܠܗ ܟܣܦܐ. 6 ܘܐܫܬܘܕܝ ܠܗܘܢ܆ ܘܒܥܐ ܗܘܐ ܠܗ
ܦܠܚܐ ܐܝܟܢܐ ܕܢܫܠܡܝܘܗܝ ܠܗܘܢ܆ ܠܒܪ ܡܢ ܟܢܫܐ.
7 ܘܟܕ ܡܛܐ ܝܘܡܐ ܕܦܨܚܐ ܕܒܗ ܐܝܬ ܗܘܐ ܥܐܕܐ ܕܢܬܢܟܣ
ܦܨܚܐ. 8 ܫܕܪ ܠܟܐܦܐ ܘܠܝܘܚܢܢ *ܘܐܡܪ ܠܗܘܢ܆ ܙܠܘ ܛܝܒܘ ܠܢ col 2
ܦܨܚܐ ܕܢܐܟܘܠ. 9 ܐܡܪܝܢ ܠܗ ܗܢܘܢ܆ ܐܝܟܐ ܨܒܐ ܐܢܬ ܕܢܛܝܒ.

---

32. *No § in S, apparently* 34. *§ in S* ܕܠܐ] + ܡܬܘܡ *S* 35 ܕܝܬܒܝܢ ܥܠ] ܕܥܠ *S* ܦܘܡܗ̇] ܦ̈ܐܘܡܗ *S* 37. *Perh. no § in S* ܘܒܐܝܡܡܐ *S* ܘܒܠ̈ܠܝܬܐ] ܘܒܠܠܝܐ *S* ܒܐܬ] *pr.* ܘ *S* ܕܢܫܡܥܘܢ *S*^ed 1. *No § in S* 2 ܢܩܛܠܘܢܗ܁] *C (sic)*; ܢܩܛܠܘܢܗ܂ *S* 3. *No § in S* ܐܣܟܪܝܘܛܐ] ܡܣܟܪܝܘܛܐ *S*: *cf* Joh vi 71 5 ܗܘܘ] *om. S* 6 ܘܐܫܬܘܕܝ ܠܗܘܢ] *om. S* ܘܒܥܐ ܗܘܐ] ܘܒܥܝܢ ܗܘܘ *S* ܦܠܚܐ] ܦܚܠܐ *S (sic)* ܡܢ] *om. S* 8 ܙܠܘ] *S illegible, but there is no room for* ܐܙܠܘ 9 ܗܢܘܢ] *om. S* ܐܝܟܐ] *S illegible*

32 "Amen, I say to you that this generation will not pass away until *C S*
33 all these things be. Heaven and earth will pass away, and my words
34 will not pass away. Now beware in yourselves that your hearts do
not become heavy with the eating of flesh and with the intoxication
of wine and with the anxiety of the world, and that day come up
35 upon you suddenly; for as a snare it will come upon all them that
36 sit on the surface of the earth. Be ye wakeful therefore at all times,
and be seeking that ye may be worthy to flee from these things that
are about to be, and that ye may stand before the Son of Man."

37 And in the day he was teaching in the Temple, and in the nights
he was going forth *and* lodging in the Mount called *the Mount* of
38 the Olive-orchard. And all the people were going early unto him
to the Temple that they might hear him.

xxii 1 And the Feast of the Unleavened Bread, called Passover, had
2 drawn near; and the chief priests and scribes were seeking how
they might kill him, for they were afraid of the people.

3 Now Satan had entered into Judas called Iscariot, that was
4 of the number of the Twelve, and he went *and* spake with the
chief priests and scribes so that he might deliver him up to them,
5 and they rejoiced. And they had promised that they would give him
6 silver, and he promised them and was seeking for himself an
opportunity how he should deliver him up to them apart from the
multitude.

7 And when the day of the Passover arrived, on which was the
8 custom that the Passover should be slaughtered, he sent Kepha and
John and saith to them: "Go *and* make ready for us the Passover
9 that we may eat *it*." Those say to him: "Where wilt thou that we

---

34 not] + ever *S*   35 that sit] *om. S*   surface (*lit.* 'mouth')] face *S*: *the phrase* ܥܠ ܦܘܡܗ̇ ܕܐܪܥܐ *also occurs in* Josh. Stylites, p. 26[5]   37 nights] night *S*   *and*] and *S*   3 Iscariot] Scariot *S*: *cf* Joh vi 71   5 had] *om. S*   6 and he promised them] *om. S*   and was....himself] and they were seeking for him *S*   an opportunity] a work *S* (*by a blunder*)   9 Those] They *S*

C S ¹⁰ܐܡܪ ܠܗܘܢ ܗܐ ܡܐ ܕܥܠܝܢ ܐܢܬܘܢ ܠܡܕܝܢܬܐ. ܦܓܥ
ܒܟܘܢ ܓܒܪܐ ܕܫܩܝܠ ܩܠܐ ܕܡ̈ܝܐ. ܙܠܘ ܒܬܪܗ ܠܒܝܬܐ
ܐܝܟܐ ܕܥܐܠ. ¹¹ܐܡܪܘ ܠܡܪܗ ܕܒܝܬܐ. ܪܒܢ ܐܡܪ ܐܝܟܐ ܗܘ
ܒܝܬ ܡܫܪܝܐ. ܐܝܟܐ ܕܐܟܘܠ ܦܨܚܐ ܥܡ ܬܠܡܝܕ̈ܝ. ¹²ܗܘܐ
ܡܚܘܐ ܠܟܘܢ ܥܠܝܬܐ ܚܕܐ ܪܒܬܐ ܕܡܫܘܝܐ. ܬܡܢ ܛܝܒܘ.
¹³ܘܐܙܠܘ ܐܫܟܚܘ ܐܝܟ ܡܐ ܕܐܡܪ ܠܗܘܢ. ܘܛܝܒܘ
ܦܨܚܐ. ܀

¹⁴ܘܟܕ ܗܘܐ ܕܝܢ ܪܡܫܐ. ܐܣܬܡܟ ܗܘ ܘܫ̈ܠܝܚܘܗܝ ܥܡܗ.
fol 81 v ¹⁵ܐܡܪ ܠܗܘܢ܂ *§ܪܓܝܓ ܪܓܬܝ ܕܐܟܘܠ ܥܡܟܘܢ ܦܨܚܐ ܥܕ
§¶ Cyril-lona 574 ܠܐ ܐܚܫ.¶ ¹⁶ܐܡܪܢܐ ܠܟܘܢ ܓܝܪ ܕܡܟܝܠ ܠܐ ܐܟܠܝܘܗܝ. ܥܕܡܐ
ܕܢܫܬܠܡ ܒܡܠܟܘܬܗ ܕܐܠܗܐ ܀

¹⁹ܘܢܣܒ ܠܚܡܐ ܘܐܘܕܝ ܥܠܘܗܝ. ܘܩܨܐ ܘܝܗܒ ܠܗܘܢ. ܘܐܡܪ
ܗܢܘ ܦܓܪܝ. ܕܥܠ ܐܦ̈ܝܟܘܢ ܗܟܢܐ ܗܘܝܬܘܢ ܥܒܕܝܢ ܠܥܘܗܕܢܝ.
¹⁷ܘܢܣܒ ܟܣܐ ܘܐܘܕܝ ܥܠܘܗܝ. ܘܐܡܪ ܣܒܘ ܗܢܐ ܦܠܓܘ
ܒܝܢܬܟܘܢ܂ ¹⁸ܐܡܪܢܐ ܠܟܘܢ ܕܡܢ ܗܫܐ ܠܐ ܐܫܬܐ ܡܢ
ܐܕܫܐ ܗܢܐ ܕܓܦܬܐ. ܥܕܡܐ ܕܬܐܬܐ ܡܠܟܘܬܗ ܕܐܠܗܐ.
²¹ܒܪܡ ܕܝܢ ܗܐ ܐܝܕܗ ܕܡܫܠܡܢܝ ܥܡܝ ܥܠ ܦܬܘܪܐ· ²²ܘܒܪܗ
ܕܐܢܫܐ ܐܙܠ ܐܝܟܢܐ ܕܣܝܡ ܗܘܐ ܥܠܘܗܝ. ܒܪܡ ܕܝܢ ܘܝ ܠܗ
ܠܗܘ ܕܒܐܝܕܗ ܡܫܬܠܡ· *²³ܘܫܪܝܘ ܗܘܘ ܕܢܒܥܘܢ ܒܝܢܬܗܘܢ. col 2
ܕܡܢܘ ܒܗ ܗܘ ܕܗܕܐ ܥܬܝܕ ܠܡܥܒܕ.

---

10 ܥܠܝܢ] ܥܐܠܝܢ S   11 ܐܡܪܘ] pr. ܘ S   ܐܝܟܐ 1°] ܐܝܠܟܐ S   ܥܡ ܬܠܡܝܕ̈ܝ] ܐܢܐ ܘܬܠܡܝܕ̈ܝ S   12 ܛܝܒܘ] + ܠܝ S   13 ܐܫܟܚܘ] pr. ܘ S   ܡܐ] om. S
14. No § in S   ܘܟܕ....ܪܡܫܐ] ܘܟܕ ܗܘܬ ܫܥܬܐ S   ܐܣܬܡܟ] ܐܣܬܡܟܘ S   ܘܫ̈ܠܝܚܘܗܝ] ܘܬܠܡܝ̈ܕܘܗܝ S   15 ܪܓܬܝ] ܪܓܬ ܠܝ S   ܦܨܚܐ] + ܗܢܐ Cyrill   16 ܕܢܫܬܠܡ ܒܡܠܟܘܬܗ] ܕܬܫܬܠܡ ܡܠܟܘܬܐ S
19. No § in S   For A 221, see on Matt xxvi 26—28   ܗܢܘ] pr. ܕ S   ܕܥܠ ܐܦ̈ܝܟܘܢ] + ܡܬܝܗܒ S   17 ܘܢܣܒ] ܘܡܢ ܒܬܪ ܕܐܚܫܡܘ ܢܣܒ S   ܒܝܢܬܟܘܢ] + ܗܢܘ ܕܡܝ ܕܝܬܩܐ ܚܕܬܐ S (= ver. 20ª)   18 ܠܟܘܢ] + ܓܝܪ S   ܐܕܫܐ] ܦܐܪܐ S   ܕܓܦܬܐ] om. S   22 ܐܝܟܢܐ] ܐܝܟ S   ܥܠܘܗܝ] om. S   ܠܗ] om. S   23 ܒܝܢ̈ܝܗܘܢ S (and in ver. 24)   ܒܗ ܗܘ] tr. S

10 make ready?" Saith he to them: "Lo, what *time* ye enter the city C S
there will meet you a man carrying a pitcher of water; go after him
11 to the house which he entereth, say to the master of the house: 'Our
Rabbi saith, Where is the guest-chamber where I may eat the
12 Passover with my disciples?' Lo, he will shew you a certain large
13 upper-room furnished; there make ready." And they went *and*
found even as he said to them, and they made ready the Passover.

14 Now when it was the season he sat down *to meat*, he and his
15 apostles with him. Saith he to them: "§I have indeed longed to eat §¶*Cyril-*
16 with you the Passover before ever I suffer;¶ for I say to you that *lona* 574
henceforth I shall not eat it until it be accomplished in the kingdom
of God."

19 And he took bread and gave thanks over it and brake and gave
to them and said: "This is my body that *is* for you; so be doing for
17 my memory." And he took a cup and gave thanks over it and said:
18 "Take this; divide *it* among you. I say to you that from now I
shall not drink of this produce of the vine, until the kingdom of God
21 come. But nevertheless, lo, the hand of my betrayer *is* with me at
22 the table; and the Son of Man goeth as it hath been set for him, but
nevertheless woe to him—to that one by whose hand he is betrayed!"
23 And they had begun to enquire among themselves *saying* "Who
is it then that is about to perform this?"

---

11 say] *pr.* and *S* with my disciples] I and my disciples *S* 12 ready] + for us *S* 13 *and* found] and found *S* even as] as *S* 14 Now] And *S* season] hour *S* he sat] they sat *S* apostles] disciples *S* 15 the 1°] this *Cyrill* 16 until....God] until the kingdom of God be fulfilled *S* 19. *For A* 221, *see on* Matt xxvi 26—28: Diat[ar] xlv 12—16 *puts* 'So be doing for my memory' (*ver.* 19[b]) *after ver.* 18, *otherwise its order agrees with S* that *is* for you] that for you I give *S* 17 And 1°] + after they supped *S* among you] + this is my blood, the new covenant *S* 18 I say] *pr.* For *S* produce] fruit *S*; 'offspring' *E*[222] (*cf* Mk xiv 25) of the vine] *om. S* 22 for him] *om. S* to him—] *om. S* 23 is it then] then is it *S*

C S ²⁴ܘܗܘܐ ܚܪܝܢܐ ܒܝܢܬܗܘܢ ܕܡܢ ܐܝܬ ܒܗܘܢ ܪܒ. ²⁵ܐܡܪ
ܠܗܘܢ ܡܪܢ. ܡ̈ܠܟܝܗܘܢ ܕܥܡ̈ܡܐ ܡܪ̈ܝܗܘܢ ܐܢܘܢ܆
ܘܐܝܠܝܢ ܕܫ̈ܠܝܛܝܢ ܐܢܘܢ ܘܕܫܦܪ ܒܥܝܢܝ. ܥ̈ܒܕܝ ܛ̈ܒܬܐ ܡܬܩܪܝܢ.
²⁶ܐܢܬܘܢ ܕܝܢ ܠܐ ܗܟܢܐ. ܐܠܐ ܐܝܢܐ ܕܪܒ ܒܟܘܢ ܢܗܘܐ
ܐܝܟ ܙܥܘܪܐ. ܘܐܝܢܐ ܕܪܫܐ ܗܘ ܐܝܟ ܡܫܡܫܢܐ ܘܠܐ ܐܝܟ
ܣܡܝܟܐ. ²⁷ܡܢܘ ܓܝܪ ܪܒ ܕܣܡܝܟ ܐܘ ܕܡܫܡܫ. ܠܐ ܗܐ ܐܢܐ
ܐܝܟ ܡܫܡܫܢܐ ܐܝܬܝ ܒܝܢܬܟܘܢ܆ ²⁸ܐܢܬܘܢ ܕܝܢ ܕܟܬܪܬܘܢ
fol 82 r ܥܡܝ ܒܢܣܝܘܢܝ. ²⁹ܘܐܢܐ ܡܫܬܘܕܐ ܐܢܐ ܠܟܘܢ ܐܝܟܢܐ *ܕܐܫܬܘܕܝ
ܠܝ ܐܒܝ ܡܠܟܘܬܐ. ³⁰ܕܬܐܟܠܘܢ ܘܬܫܬܘܢ ܥܡܝ ܥܠ ܦܬܘܪܝ
§A 432 ܒܡܠܟܘܬܐ. ܘܬܬ§ܒܘܢ ܥܠ ܬܪ̈ܥܣܪ ܟܘܪ̈ܣܘܢ. ܘܬܕܘܢܘܢ
¶A ܬܪ̈ܥܣܪ ܫܒ̈ܛܐ ܕܒܝܬ ܐܝܣܪܝܠ.¶ ³¹ܘܐܡܪ ܡܪܢ ܠܫܡܥܘܢ܆
ܫܡܥܘܢ. ܗܐ ܣܛܢܐ ܒܥܐ ܕܢܪܒܘܒܟܘܢ ܐܝܟ ܕܠܚܛܐ. ³²ܐܢܐ
ܕܝܢ ܒܥܝܬ ܥܠܝܟ ܕܠܐ ܬܚܣܪ ܗܝܡܢܘܬܟ. ܘܐܦ ܐܢܬ ܒܙܒܢ
ܐܬܦܢ ܘܫܪܪ ܠܐ̈ܚܝܟ. ³³ܐܡܪ ܠܗ ܗܘ. ܡܪܝ ܥܡܟ ܡܛܝܒ
ܐܢܐ ܘܐܦ ܠܒܝܬ ܐܣܝ̈ܪܐ ܘܐܦ ܠܡܘܬܐ ܠܡܐܙܠ. ³⁴ܐܡܪ ܠܗ
ܝܫܘܥ܆ ܐܡܪܢܐ ܠܟ ܕܠܐ ܢܩܪܐ ܬܪܢܓܠܐ ܝܘܡܢܐ ܥܕܡܐ ܬܠܬ
ܙܒ̈ܢܝܢ. ܬܟܦܘܪ ܒܝ ܕܠܐ ܝܕܥ ܐܢܬ ܠܝ. ·܀·
col 2 ³⁵*ܐܡܪ ܠܗܘܢ ܟܕ ܫܕܪܬܟܘܢ ܕܠܐ ܟܝܣܐ ܘܠܐ ܬܪ̈ܡܠܐ
ܘܠܐ ܡ̈ܣܢܐ. ܕܠܡܐ ܡܕܡ ܚܣܪ ܠܟܘܢ. ܐܡܪܝܢ ܠܗ ܐܦ
ܠܐ ܡܕܡ. ³⁶ܐܡܪ ܠܗܘܢ ܡܢ ܗܫܐ ܡܢ ܕܐܝܬ ܠܗ ܟܝܣܐ
ܐܘ ܬܪܡܠܐ ܢܫܩܘܠ. ܘܡܢ ܕܠܝܬ ܠܗ ܣܝܦܐ ܢܙܒܢ ܢܚܬܗ

24 ܕܡܢ] ܕܡܢܘ S 25 ܡܪܢ] om. S ܕܫ̈ܠܝܛܝܢ] ܕܫܠܝܛܝܢ S
26 ܘܠܐ ܐܝܟ ܣܡܝܟܐ] om. S 27 ܠܐ ܗܐ] ܠܐ ܗܘ ܕܣܡܝܟ S ܐܢܬܘܢ]
om. S ܒܢܣܝܘܢܝ S 29 ܐܢܐ] om. S ܐܝܟܢܐ] ܐܝܟ S 30 ܦܬܘܪܝ]
ܦܬܘܪܐ ܕܝܠܝ S ܒܡܠܟܘܬܐ] ܒܡܠܟܘܬܝ S ܬܪ̈ܥܣܪ ܫܒ̈ܛܐ]
ܬܪ̈ܬܥܣܪܐ ܫܒ̈ܛܝܢ A (cf Matt xix 28) ܐܝܣܪܐܝܠ S 31. § in S
ܘܐܡܪ ܡܪܢ ܠܫܡܥܘܢ܆ ܫܡܥܘܢ] ܫܡܥܘܢ ܫܡܥܘܢ S ܕܢܪܒܘܒܟܘܢ]
ܕܢܪܒܠܟܘܢ S 32 ܐܬܦܢ] ܐܬܗܦܟ S 33 ܗܘ] om. S ܘܐܦ]
ܐܦ S (in each place) 34 ܝܫܘܥ] om. S ܠܟ] + ܟܐܦܐ S ܬܠܬ ܙܒ̈ܢܝܢ]
om. S ܕܠܐ ܝܕܥ] ܕܝܕܥ S 36 ܡܢ ܕܐܝܬ] om. ܡܢ S ܟܝܣܐ 1°] om. S

24 And there was a contention among them who among them was *C S*
25 the greater. Our Lord saith to them: "The kings of the peoples
are their lords, and they that are in authority and do well are called
26 Benefactors. Now ye *are* not so, but he which is great with you
shall be as the least, and he that is the chief as the servant and not
27 as he that sitteth *at meat*. For who is greater, he that sitteth *at*
meat or he that serveth? Am not I, lo, as the servant among you?
28, 29 Now ye that have continued with me in my temptations—and I *too*,
30 I promise you as my Father promised me a kingdom that ye shall
eat and drink with me at my table in the kingdom, and §ye shall sit §*A* 432
on twelve thrones and shall judge the twelve tribes of the House of
31 Israel."¶ And our Lord said to Simon: "Simon, lo, Satan hath ¶*A*
32 besought that he might sift you as wheat, but I have besought for
thee that thy faith should not fail; and thou also in time turn round
33 and strengthen thy brothers." He saith to him: "My Lord, with
34 thee I am ready even to prison and even to death to go." Jesus
saith to him: "I say to thee Before ever the cock crow to-day
twice, three times thou wilt deny me that thou dost not know me."
35 He saith to them: "When I sent you without purses and without
wallets and without shoes, was aught lacking to you?" They say to
36 him: "Not even aught." He saith to them: "From now he that hath
a purse or a wallet, let him carry *it*; and he that hath not a sword,

---

25 Our Lord] He *S* 26 and not....*meat*] *om. S* 27 Am not....you?] Is it not he that sitteth *at meat*? I *am* as the servant among you *S* 29 I 2°] *om. S* 30 my table] a table, *even* mine *S* the kingdom] my kingdom *S* twelve tribes] twelve families *A* (*as in* Matt xix 28) 31 And.....Simon: Simon] Simon, Simon *S* sift] riddle *S* 32 I have besought] + 'my Father' E^{222} turn round] return *S* 33 and even] —even *S* 34 Jesus] He *S* to thee] + Kepha *S* twice] *om. S* dost not] *om.* not *S* 36 a sword 1°] *om. S* (*not* E^{223})

C S ܘܢܙܒܢ ܠܗ ܣܝܦܐ. [37]ܐܡܪ ܐܢܐ ܠܟܘܢ ܓܝܪ ܕܐܦ ܗܕܐ
ܕܟܬܝܒܐ ܥܬܝܕܐ ܕܬܬܡܠܐ ܒܝ. ܕܥܡ ܥܘ̈ܠܐ ܐܬܡܢܝ. ܘܡܕܡ
ܕܥܠ ܗܘ ܠܡܫܬܠܡܘ ܠܗ. [38]ܗܢܘܢ ܐܡܪܝܢ ܠܗ. ܡܪܢ ܗܐ
ܐܝܬ ܠܢ ܗܪܟܐ ܬܪ̈ܝܢ ܣܝ̈ܦܝܢ. ܐܡܪ ܠܗܘܢ ܣܦܩܝܢ ܩܘܡܘ
ܢܐܙܠ ܀

[39]ܘܢܦܩ ܗܘܐ ܘܐܙܠ ܐܝܟ ܕܡܥܕ ܗܘܐ ܠܛܘܪܐ ܕܡܫܚܬܐ ܕܒܝܬ
fol 82 v ܙܝ̈ܬܐ. ܘܐܙܠܘ ܒܬܪܗ *ܘܐܦ ܬܠܡܝ̈ܕܘܗܝ. [40]ܘܟܕ ܡܛܐ ܠܗ̇
ܠܕܘܟܬܐ. ܐܡܪ ܠܗܘܢ ܨܠܘ ܕܠܐ ܬܥܠܘܢ ܠܒܝܬ ܢܣܝܘܢܐ.
[41]ܘܗܘ ܦܪܫ ܡܢܗܘܢ ܐܝܟ ܡܫܕܐ ܕܟܐܦܐ. ܘܣܡ ܒܘܪ̈ܟܘܗܝ
§A 459 ܘܡܨܠܐ ܗܘܐ [42]ܘܐܡܪ. §ܐܒܝ ܐܢ ܡܫܟܚܐ ܢܥܒܪܝܢ ܟܣܐ
¶A ܗܢܐ.¶ ܐܠܐ ܠܐ ܨܒܝܢܝ ܢܗܘܐ ܐܠܐ ܕܝܠܟ. [43]ܘܐܬܚܙܝ ܠܗ
ܡܠܐܟܐ ܟܕ ܡܚܝܠ ܠܗ. [44]ܘܗܘܐ ܒܙܘܥܐ ܪܒܐ. ܘܡܦܝܣܐܝܬ
ܡܨܠܐ ܗܘܐ. ܘܗܘܬ ܕܘܥܬܗ ܐܝܟ ܬ̈ܠܬܐ ܕܕܡܐ. ܘܢܦܠܐ
ܗܘܬ ܥܠ ܐܪܥܐ. [45]ܘܩܡ ܡܢ ܨܠܘܬܗ. ܘܐܬܐ ܠܘܬ ܬܠܡܝ̈ܕܘܗܝ.
ܘܐܫܟܚ ܐܢܘܢ ܟܕ ܕܡܟܝܢ ܡܢ ܟܪܝܘܬܗܘܢ. [46]ܐܡܪ ܠܗܘܢ
ܡܢܐ ܕܡܟܝܢ ܐܢܬܘܢ. ܩܘܡܘ ܘܨܠܘ ܕܠܐ ܬܥܠܘܢ ܠܢܣܝܘܢܐ ܀
col 2 *[47]ܘܟܕ ܗܘ ܡܡܠܠ ܗܘܐ. ܐܬܐ ܟܢܫܐ ܣܓܝܐܐ. ܘܗܘ ܕܡܬܩܪܐ
ܗܘܐ ܝܗܘܕܐ ܚܕ ܡܢ ܬܪ̈ܥܣܪ. ܐܬܐ ܗܘܐ ܩܕܡܝܗܘܢ. ܘܩܪܒ
ܢܫܩܗ ܠܝܫܘܥ. [48]ܐܡܪ ܠܗ ܝܫܘܥ ܝܗܘܕܐ. ܒܢܘܫܩܬܐ ܡܫܠܡ
ܐܢܬ ܠܗ ܠܒܪܗ ܕܐ̈ܢܫܐ. [49]ܟܕ ܚܙܘ ܕܝܢ ܐܝܠܝܢ ܕܥܡܗ ܡܕܡ

---

37 ܥܬܝܕܐ] *pr.* ܕ *S*   ܠܡܫܬܠܡܘ] ܠܡܫܠܡܘ *S*   38 ܠܗ. ܡܪܢ] ܠܗ ܠܝܫܘܥ *S*   ܐܝܬ ܠܢ ܗܪܟܐ] ܐܝܬ ܗܪܟܐ *S*   ܣܦܩܝܢ] + ܠܟܘܢ *S*   ܩܘܡܘ ܢܐܙܠ] *om.* *S*   39 ܘܐܙܠܘ......ܬܠܡܝ̈ܕܘܗܝ] ܒܬܪܗ ܘܬܠܡܝ̈ܕܘܗܝ *S*   40 ܠܒܝܬ ܢܣܝܘܢܐ] ܠܢܣܝܘܢܐ *S*   41 ܘܗܘ ܦܪܫ] ܘܦܪܫ *S*   42 ܐܒܝ] ܐܒܐ *S*   ܡܫܟܚܐ] *C A* (*cf* Matt xxvi 39); ܨܒܐ ܐܢܬ *S*   ܢܥܒܪܝܢ] + ܡܢܝ *S*   ܐܠܐ 2°] + ܐܢ *S*   43, 44.] *om.* *S*   43 ܡܠܐܟܐ] *so also* Ephr. *Lamy* i 233   45 ܠܘܬ ܬܠ̈'] ܠܬܠ̈' *S*   ܘܐܫܟܚ] *om.* ܘ *S*   46 ܐܡܪ] *pr.* ܘ *S*   ܘܨܠܘ] *om.* ܘ *S*   47 ܘܟܕ] ܘܥܕ *S*   48 ܠܒܪܗ ܕܐ̈ܢܫܐ] ܠܒܪ ܕܐܢܫܐ *S* (*sic*), *perhaps a corruption of* ܠܒܪ ܐܢܫܐ   49 ܐܝܠܝܢ ܕܥܡܗ] ܬܠܡܝ̈ܕܘܗܝ *S*

37 let him sell his garment and buy himself a sword. For I say to you *C S*
This also that is written is about to be fulfilled in me, that 'with the
wicked he was numbered'; and that which is concerning me is to be
38 fulfilled." And they say to him: "Our Lord, lo, we have here two
swords!" He saith to them: "They are sufficient; arise, let us go."
39 And he had gone forth, and went as he was accustomed to the
Mount called *the Mount* of the Olive-orchard, and there went
40 with him his disciples also. And when he arrived at the place he
said to them: "Pray that ye enter not into the region of temptation."
41 And he himself departed from them about a stone's throw, and he
42 set his knees and was praying and saying: "§My Father, if it can be §*A* 459
43 let this cup pass me¶—but not my will be *done* but thine." And ¶*A*
44 there appeared to him an angel strengthening him. And he was in
great care and zealously he was praying; and his sweat was as drops
45 of blood and it was falling on the earth. And he rose from his prayer
and came unto his disciples and found them sleeping from their
46 trouble. He saith to them: "Why sleep ye? Arise and pray that
ye enter not into temptation."
47 And while he was speaking there appeared a great multi-
tude; and he which was called Judas, one of the Twelve, was
48 coming before them and he drew near *and* kissed Jesus. Jesus
saith to him: "Judas, with a kiss dost thou betray the son of
49 a man?" Now when those with him saw that which was about

37 is about] that is about *S* (*sic*): *cf* Matt i 22, xxi 4, *and Notes*, vol. ii fulfilled 2°] finished *S* 38 to him: Our Lord, lo,] to him, to Jesus: Lo *S* we have here] here are *S* sufficient] + for you *S* arise, let us go] *om. S* 39 and there went...also] and his disciples with him *S* 40 the region of] *om. S* 41 himself] *om. S* 42 My Father] Father *S* if it can be] *C A* (*cf* Matt xxvi 39); if thou wilt *S* (*not* $E^{229,231}$) my will] + mine *S* but 2°] save *S* 43, 44.] *om. S*; *for ver.* 44 *cf* 'and his sweat became as *it were* drops of blood' E^{235} 43 an angel] *so also* Ephr. *Lamy* i 233 (i.e. *without* 'from heaven') 45 unto] to *S* and found] *and* found *S* 46 He] And he *S* and] *om. S* 47 while] while yet *S* 48 the son of a man (*see on* Matt xii 40)] *S as it stands is ungrammatical. The original reading of the Version may have been* 'a son of man' (*i.e.* 'a man'): *cf* E^{235} 'Judas, num osculando venis tradere filium hominis? Quo et docet Filium Dei ab eo tradi non potuisse' 49 those with him] his disciples *S*

CS ܕܒܬܪܗ ܠܡܗܘܐ. ܐܡܪܝܢ ܠܗ ܡܪܢ ܢܡܚܐ ܐܢܘܢ ܒܣ̈ܝܦܐ.
50 ܘܡܚܐ ܚܕ ܡܢܗܘܢ ܠܥܒܕܗ ܕܪܒ ܟܗ̈ܢܐ ܘܢܣܒܗ̇ ܐܕܢܗ
ܕܝܡܝܢܐ. 51 ܥܢܐ ܝܫܘܥ ܘܐܡܪ ܒܕܘ ܥܕܡܐ ܠܗܪܟܐ. ܘܩܪܒ
ܠܐܕܢܗ ܘܐܣܝܗ̇. 52 ܘܐܡܪ ܘܐܦ ܠܗܘܢ ܪ̈ܒܝ ܟܗ̈ܢܐ ܘܐ̈ܣܛܪܛܝܓܐ
fol 83r ܕܗܝܟܠܐ ܘܩ̈ܫܝܫܐ. ܐܝܟ ܕܥܠ ܓܝܣܐ ܢܦܩܬܘܢ ܥܠܝ *ܒܣ̈ܝܦܐ
ܘܒܩ̈ܝܣܐ. 53 ܟܠܝܘܡ ܕܥܡܟܘܢ ܗܘܝܬ ܒܗܝܟܠܐ. ܠܐ ܡܘܫܛܝܢ
ܗܘܝܬܘܢ ܥܠܝ ܐ̈ܝܕܝܐ. ܐܠܐ ܗܕܐ ܗܝ ܫܥܬܟܘܢ ܘܫܘܠܛܢܟܘܢ
ܕܚܫܘܟܐ. 54 ܘܐܚܕܘܗܝ ܘܐܝܬܝܘܗܝ ܠܒܝܬܗ ܕܪܒ ܟܗ̈ܢܐ. ܫܡܥܘܢ
ܕܝܢ ܟܐܦܐ ܐܬܐ ܗܘܐ ܒܬܪܗ ܡܢ ܪܘܚܩܐ. 55 ܘܢܘܪܐ ܐܚܕܘ
ܗܘܬ ܡܨܥܬ ܕܪܬܐ. ܘܝܬܒܝܢ ܗܘܘ ܚܕܪܝܗ̇. ܘܝܬܒ ܗܘܐ ܟܐܦܐ
ܒܝܢܬܗܘܢ. 56 ܘܚܙܬܗ ܐܡܬܐ ܚܕܐ ܕܝܬܒ ܠܘܬ ܢܘܪܐ. ܘܚܪܬ
ܒܗ ܘܐܡܪܐ. ܘܐܦ ܗܢܐ ܥܡܗ ܗܘܐ. 57 ܘܗܘ ܟܦܪ ܘܐܡܪ
ܐܢܬܬܐ ܠܐ ܝܕܥܢܐ ܠܗ. 58 ܘܒܬܪ ܩܠܝܠ ܚܙܝܗ̇ ܘܐܦ ܐܚܪܢܐ
col 2 ܘܗܘܡܬ ܐܡܪ. ܘܐܡܪ ܟܐܦܐ ܠܐ ܗܘܝܬ *ܡܢܗܘܢ. 59 ܘܒܬܪ
ܚܕܐ ܫܥܐ ܡܬܚܪܝ ܗܘܐ ܐܚܪܢܐ ܘܐܡܪ. ܫܪܝܪܐܝܬ ܘܐܦ
ܗܢܐ ܥܡܗ ܗܘܐ. ܐܦ ܓܠܝܠܝܐ ܗܘ ܓܝܪ. 60 ܘܐܡܪ ܟܐܦܐ
ܓܒܪܐ ܠܐ ܝܕܥ ܐܢܐ ܡܢܐ ܐܡܪ ܐܢܬ. ܘܒܗ̇ ܒܫܥܬܐ ܥܕ ܗܘ
ܡܡܠܠ. 61 ܘܐܬܦܢܝ ܡܪܢ ܚܪ ܒܗ ܒܟܐܦܐ. ܘܐܬܕܟܪ ܟܐܦܐ

---

50 ܠܥܒܕܗ] *so also S* 51 ܠܐܕܢܗ] *so also S* 52 ܘܐܦ] *om. S* ܠܗܘܢ] + ܕܐܬܘ ܥܠܘܗܝ S ܘܐܣܛܪܛܝܓܐ S ܕܗܝܟܠܐ] *om. S*
54 ܫܡܥܘܢ ܕܝܢ ܟܐܦܐ] ܟܐܦܐ ܕܝܢ S, *beginning a fresh §. A new line in C begins at* ܫܡܥܘܢ 56 ܠܘܬ ܢܘܪܐ] *om. C**: *the words are added in a contemporary hand above the line* ܘܐܦ] ܕܐܦ S 58 ܘܐܦ ܐܡܪ] ܘܐܡܪ ܠܗ ܐܦ ܐܢܬ ܡܢܗܘܢ ܐܢܬ. ܗܘ ܕܝܢ ܐܡܪ ܠܗ ܠܐ ܘܗܘܡܬ.......ܡܢܗܘܢ S ܫܡܥܘܢ ܓܒܪܐ ܠܐ ܝܕܥܢܐ.
59 ܘܒܬܪ ܚܕܐ ܫܥܐ] ܘܗܘܐ ܟܐܝܟ ܫܥܬܐ ܚܕܐ S ܐܦ ܗܢܐ ܫܪܝܪܐܝܬ S ܐܦ] ܘܐܦ S ܓܠܝܠܝܐ] ܓܠܝܠܝܐ S* (*see facsimile*): *cf* Matt xxvi 69, Mk xiv 70 60 ܘܐܡܪ ܟܐܦܐ] ܐܡܪ ܟܐܦܐ S ܓܒܪܐ. S ܐܢܐ ܝܕܥ] ܝܕܥܢܐ S ܐܡܪ ܐܢܬ] ܐܡܪܬ S 61 ܡܪܢ] ܝܫܘܥ S ܟܐܦܐ S

to be they say to him: "Our Lord, shall we smite them with *C S*
50 swords?" And one of them smote the slave of the chief priest
51 and took *off* his right ear. Jesus answered and said: "Enough
as far as this *man*." And he touched his ear and healed it.
52 And he said also to those chief priests and soldiers of the Temple
and elders: "As against a robber have ye come forth against me
53 with swords and with staves! Daily that with you I was in the
Temple ye were not putting forth hands against me, but this is
54 your hour and your authority of darkness." And they took hold
of him and brought him to the house of the chief priest. Now
55 Simon Kepha was coming after him from afar; and a fire was set
in the midst of the court and they were sitting round about it, and
56 Kepha was sitting among them. And a certain maid saw him sitting
by the fire, and she looked on him and saith: "And this *one* also
57 was with him." And he denied and said: "Woman, I know him
58 not." And after a little another also saw him and thus said. And
59 Kepha saith: "I am not of them." And after one hour another was
excited and saith: "Truly this *one* also was with him, for a Galilaean
60 also he is." And Kepha saith: "Man, I know not what thou sayest."
61 And in the same hour the cock crew; and our Lord turned round
and looked on him, on Kepha. And Kepha remembered the word

---

52 also] *om. S* those] + that came against him— *S* of the Temple] *om. S* 54 Simon] *om. S* 56 by the fire] *om. C**: *the words are added in a contemporary hand above the line* And this] This *S* 58 thus said......of them] saith to him: "Thou also art of them." Now he said to him: "Let be, man; I know *him* not" *S* 59 after one hour] it came to pass *in* about one hour *S* excited] *see* Mk viii 12, Joh xi 38 Truly....also 1°] This *one* also truly *S* 60 And 1°] *om. S* know not] am not acquainted with *S* sayest] hast said *S* 61 our Lord] Jesus *S*

ܡܠܬܗ ܕܡܪܢ ܕܐܡܪ ܠܗ. ܕܥܕ ܠܐ ܢܩܪܐ ܬܪܢܓܠܐ ܬܪ̈ܬܝܢ CS
ܙ̈ܒܢܝܢ. ܬܠܬ ܙ̈ܒܢܝܢ ܬܟܦܘܪ ܒܝ. [62]ܘܢܦܩ ܒܟܐ ܡܪܝܪܐܝܬ.
[63]ܘܓܒܪܐ ܕܐܚܝܕܝܢ ܗܘܘ ܠܗ ܠܝܫܘܥ ܡܒܙܚܝܢ ܗܘܘ ܒܗ. ܘܡܚܝܢ
ܗܘܘ ܠܗ. [64]ܘܚܦܘ ܐ̈ܦܘܗܝ، ܘܐܡܪܝܢ ܠܗ ܐܬܢܒܐ ܡܢܘ ܡܚܝܟ.
[65]ܘܬܘܒ ܐܣ̈ܓܝܐܬܐ ܓܘ̈ܕܦܬܐ. †ܡܓܕܦܝܢ ܗܘܘ ܘܐܡܪܝܢ ܥܠܘܗܝ،.
[*66]ܘܟܕ ܢܓܗ. ܐܬܟܢܫܘ ܩܫ̈ܝܫܐ ܘܪ̈ܒܝ ܟܗ̈ܢܐ ܘܣ̈ܦܪܐ. ܘܐܣܩܘܗܝ، fol 83 v
ܠܒܝܬ ܟܢܘܫ̈ܬܗܘܢ܆ ܘܐܡܪܝܢ [67]ܐܢ ܐܢܬ ܗܘ ܡܫܝܚܐ ܐܡܪ
ܠܢ. ܐܡܪ ܠܗܘܢ ܐܢ ܐܡܪ ܠܟܘܢ ܠܐ ܬܗܝܡܢܘܢ܆ [68]ܘܐܢ
ܐܫܐܠܟܘܢ ܠܐ ܡܦܢܝܢ ܐܢܬܘܢ ܠܝ ܦܬܓܡܐ. ܘܐܦܠܐ ܫܪܝܢ
ܐܢܬܘܢ ܠܝ. [69]ܡܢ ܗܫܐ ܠܗ ܢܗܘܐ ܒܪܗ ܕܐܢܫܐ ܝܬܒ ܡܢ
ܝܡܝܢܐ ܕܚܝܠܐ ܕܐܠܗܐ. [70]ܐܡܪܝܢ ܟܠܗܘܢ ܐܢܬ ܗܘ ܟܒܪ ܒܪܗ
ܕܐܠܗܐ. ܐܡܪ ܠܗܘܢ ܐܢܬܘܢ ܐܡܪܝܢ ܐܢܬܘܢ ܕܐܢܐ ܐܢܐ.
[71]ܐܡܪܝܢ ܡܢܐ ܬܘܒ ܡܬܒܥܝܐ ܠܢ ܣܗܕܘܬܐ. ܗܐ ܓܝܪ ܐܢܚܢ
ܫܡܥܢ ܡܢ ܦܘܡܗ· [1]ܘܩܡܘ ܟܠܗ *ܟܢܫܐ. ܘܐܝܬܝܘܗܝ، ܠܘܬ ܦܝܠܛܘܣ. col 2
[2]ܘܫܪܝܘ ܐܟܠܝܢ ܩܪ̈ܨܘܗܝ، ܘܐܡܪܝܢ ܗܘܘ. ܐܫܟܚܢ ܠܗܢܐ ܕܡܗܦܟ
ܥܡܢ. ܘܟܠܐ ܠܢ ܕܟܣܦ ܪܫܐ ܠܩܝܣܪ ܠܐ ܢܬܠ· ܘܐܡܪ ܥܠ
ܢܦܫܗ ܕܗܘܝܘ ܡܠܟܐ ܡܫܝܚܐ. [3]ܐܡܪ ܠܗ ܦܝܠܛܘܣ ܐܢܬ ܗܘ
ܡܠܟܐ ܕܝܗܘܕܝܐ. ܐܡܪ ܠܗ ܐܢܬ ܐܡܪܬ. [4]ܐܡܪ ܦܝܠܛܘܣ ܠܪ̈ܒܝ
ܟܗ̈ܢܐ ܘܠܟܢܫܐ ܗܘ. ܐܢܐ ܡܕܡ ܥܠܬܐ ܠܐ ܡܫܟܚ ܐܢܐ ܥܠ
ܓܒܪܐ ܗܢܐ. [5]ܗܢܘܢ ܕܝܢ ܡܥܠܝܢ ܘܐܡܪܝܢ ܐܙܝܥܗ ܥܡܐ.
ܟܕ ܡܠܦ ܒܟܠܗ ܝܗܘܕ. ܘܫܪܝ ܡܢ ܓܠܝܠܐ ܥܕܡܐ ܠܗܪܟܐ.

---

62 ܒܟܐ] ܠܒܪ ܘܒܟܐ S   ܬܪ̈ܬܝܢ ܙܒܢܝܢ] ܢܘܡܢܝܐ S   ܕܡܪܢ] ܕܝܫܘܥ S
ܡܪܝܪܐܝܬ.] C (*end of line*); ܡܪܝܪܐܐܝܬ. S (*sic*): *cf* xxiii 47   63. *No* § *in S* (*see facsimile*)   ܠܝܫܘܥ] *om.* S   65 ܓܘܕܦ̈ܬܐ S (*sic*)   ܡܓܕܦܝܢ] S; *pr.* ܘ C
66 ܩܫ̈ܝܫܐ] + ܕܥܡܐ S   67 ܬܗܝܡܢܘܢ] ܬܗܝܡܢܘܢܢܝ S   69 ܕܚܝܠܐ] *om.* S
70 ܟܒܪ] *nearly washed out in C*: *cf* Lk xvi 11, xx 17   ܐܢܬܘܢ 2°] *om.* S
71 ܬܘܒ] *om.* S   2 ܗܘܘ] *om.* S   3 ܐܢܬ ܗܘ] + ܟܒܪ S (*sic*): *cf* xxii 70
ܐܡܪ ܠܗ 2°] *pr.* ܘ ܗܢܐ S   ܐܡܪܬ] + ܐܢܐ ܕܐܢܐ S   5 ܡܥܠܝܢ] ܡܥܠܝܢ ܗܘܘ S   ܓܠܝܠܐ] ܓܠܝܠܝܐ S: *cf* xxii 59

of our Lord, that he said to him "Before ever the cock crow twice, *C S*
62 three times thou wilt deny me." And he went forth *and* wept
bitterly.
63 And the men that had taken hold of him, of Jesus, were mocking
64 at him and were smiting him, and they hid his face and say to him:
65 "Prophesy, who is it hath smitten thee?" And again many other
66 things †they were blaspheming and saying against him. And when
day dawned there were gathered together the elders and chief priests
and scribes and they brought him up to the house of their assemblies,
67 and they say: "If thou art the Messiah, say to us." He saith to
68 them: "If I say to you ye will not believe, and if I ask you ye would
69 give me no answer, nor would ye release me. For from now will the
Son of Man be sitting on the right *hand* of the Power of God."
70 They all say: "Art thou forsooth the Son of God?" He saith to
71 them: "Ye yourselves say that I am *he*." They say: "Why yet is
there required for us witness? For lo, we ourselves have heard *it*
xxiii 1 from his mouth." And all the multitude rose up and brought him
2 unto Pilate. And they began accusing him and were saying: "We
have found this *fellow* that he perverteth our people and doth forbid
us, *saying* that head-money to Caesar we should not give; and he
3 saith of himself that he is King Messiah." Pilate saith to him: "Art
thou the king of the Jews?" He saith to him: "Thou hast said *it*."
4 Pilate saith to the chief priests and to that multitude: "I—no cause
5 do I find against this man." But they *were* screaming out and
saying: "He hath troubled the people, teaching in all Judaea; and

---

of our Lord] of Jesus *S* twice] to-day *S* **62** forth *and*] forth outside and *S* **63** of Jesus] *om. S* **65** †they were] *S*; *pr.* and *C* **66** elders] + of the people *S* assemblies] *or*, 'synagogues' **67** believe] + me *S* **69** of the Power] *om. S* **70** forsooth] *nearly washed out in C*: *cf* Lk xvi 11, xx 17 **71** yet] *om. S* **2** were saying] *om.* were *S* King Messiah] *or*, 'an anointed king': *see Notes*, vol. ii **3** Art thou] + forsooth *S*: *cf* xxii 70 saith 2°] answered and said *S* said *it*] said that I am *S* **5** *were* screaming out] were crying out *S*

C S ⁶ܦܝܠܛܘܣ ܕܝܢ ܟܕ ܫܡܥ ܕܐܡܪܝܢ ܕܡܢ ܓܠܝܠܐ. ܫܐܠ ܕܐܢ
fol 84 r *ܡܢ ܓܠܝܠܐ ܗܘ. ⁷ܘܟܕ ܫܡܥ ܕܡܢ ܬܚܝܬ ܫܘܠܛܢܐ ܗܘ
ܕܗܪܘܕܣ ܫܕܪܗ ܠܘܬܗ. ܡܛܠ ܕܐܦ ܗܘ ܕܝܢ ܗܪܘܕܣ ܒܐܘܪܫܠܡ
ܗܘܐ ܒܗܘܢ ܝܘܡܬܐ ܕܦܛܝܪܐ. ⁸ܗܪܘܕܣ ܕܝܢ ܟܕ ܚܙܐ ܠܝܫܘܥ
ܛܒ ܚܕܝ. ܛܒ ܨܒܐ ܗܘܐ ܓܝܪ ܠܡܚܙܝܗ ܡܢ ܙܒܢܐ ܣܓܝܐܐ.
ܡܛܠ ܕܫܡܥ ܗܘܐ ܥܠܘܗܝ. ܘܡܣܒܪ ܗܘܐ ܕܢܚܙܐ ܐܬܐ ܚܕܐ
ܡܢܗ ܕܗܘܝܐ. ⁹ܘܫܘܐܠܐ ܣܓܝܐܬܐ ܡܫܐܠ ܗܘܐ ܠܗ· ܝܫܘܥ ܕܝܢ
ܡܕܡ ܦܬܓܡܐ ܠܐ ܐܦܢܝܗ· ܐܝܟ ܗܘ ܕܠܐ ܗܘܐ ܫܡܥ
ܗܘܐ. ¹⁰ܪ̈ܒܝ ܟܗܢܐ ܕܝܢ ܘܐܣܦܪ̈ܐ ܩܝܡܝܢ ܗܘܘ ܘܐܟܠܝܢ ܩܪ̈ܨܘܗܝ
col 2 ܡܠܝܐܝܬ. ¹¹ܘܒܙܚ ܒܗ ܗܪܘܕܣ *ܘܦ̈ܠܚܘܗܝ. ܘܐܠܒܫܗ ܢܚ̈ܬܐ
ܙ̈ܗܘܪܐ ܟܒܘܫܐ. ܘܫܕܪܗ ܠܘܬ ܦܝܠܛܘܣ. ¹²ܘܒܗ ܒܗ ܝܘܡܐ
ܗܘܬ ܬܪܥܘܬܐ ܒܝܢ ܗܪܘܕܣ ܠܦܝܠܛܘܣ· ܡܛܠ ܕܒ̈ܥܠܕܒܒܐ ܗܘܘ·
¹³ܦܝܠܛܘܣ ܕܝܢ ܩܪܐ ܠܪ̈ܒܝ ܟܗܢܐ ܘܠܐܪ̈ܟܘܢܐ ܘܠܥܡܐ ܟܠܗ
¹⁴ܘܐܡܪ ܠܗܘܢ· ܩܪܒܬܘܢ ܠܝ ܓܒܪܐ ܗܢܐ. ܕܐܡܗܦܟܬܘܢ ܠܝ
ܕܐܙܝܥܗ ܠܥܡܟܘܢ· ܘܗܐ ܐܢܐ ܒܥܒܕܬܗ ܠܥ̈ܝܢܝܟܘܢ ܘܡܕܡ ܠܐ
ܐܫܟܚܬ ܒܬܪܗ. ܡܢ ܐܝܠܝܢ ܕܡܪܫܝܢ ܐܢܬܘܢ ܒܗ. ¹⁵ܘܐܦܠܐ
ܗܪܘܕܣ· ܫܕܪܬܗ ܓܝܪ ܠܘܬܗ ܘܡܕܡ ܕܫܘܐ ܠܡܘܬܐ ܠܐ
ܐܫܟܚ ܒܬܪܗ. ܘܐܦܠܐ ܥܒܕ ܠܗ ܡܕܡ ܕܡܘܬܐ. ¹⁶ܐܪܕܝܘܗܝ
fol 84 v ܗܟܝܠ ܘܐܫܒܩܝܘܗܝ. *¹⁸ܘܩܥܘ ܥܡܐ ܟܠܗ ܒܚܕܐ ܘܐܡܪܝܢ·
ܫܩܘܠܝܗܝ ܠܗܢܐ ܘܫܪܝ ܠܢ ܠܒܪ ܐܒܐ. ¹⁹ܗܘ ܕܡܛܠ ܗܦܟ̈ܘܬܐ
ܘܩܛܠܐ ܪܒܐ ܗܘܐ ܒܗܬ ܐܩܘܪܐ. ¹⁷ܘܡܥܕܕ ܗܘܐ ܦܝܠܛܘܣ
ܕܢܗܘܐ ܫܪܐ ܠܗܘܢ ܚܕ ܐܣܝܪ ܒܥܐܕܐ. ²⁰ܘܬܘܒ ܩܪܐ ܐܢܘܢ

---

6 ܕܡܢ ܓܠܝܠܐ ...... ܓܠܝܠܐ ܗܘ] ܕܡܢ ܓܠܝܠܐ ܗܘ S 7 ܠܘܬܗ] ܠܘܬ ܗܪܘܕܣ S ܕܝܢ] om. S ܕܦܛܝܪܐ] om. S 8 ܗܪܘܕܣ] so also S ܠܡܚܙܝܘܗܝ S (sic) 9ᵇ ܐܝܟ ܗܘ to end of 12.] om. S 14 ܕܐܡܗܦܟܬܘܢ ܠܝ] ܘܐܡܗܦܟܬܘܢ S ܕܐܙܝܥܗ] ܕܡܙܝܥ S ܘܗܐ ܐܢܐ] ܘܐܢܐ S ܠܥܝܢܝܟܘܢ S 15 ܫܕܪܬܗ] pr. ܕ S ܘܡܕܡ] so also S ܘܐܦܠܐ 2°] om. ܘ S 16 ܐܪܕܝܘܗܝ S ܘܐܫܒܩܝܘܗܝ S 18 ܟܠܗ ܥܡܐ ܒܚܕܐ S 19 ܗܦܟ̈ܘܬܐ] C (sic); ܚܛ̈ܝܬܐ S: cf ver. 25, and Introd. vol. ii ܐܩܘܪܐ S 17 ܚܕ ܐܣܝܪ] ܚܕ ܐܣܝܪܐ S ܒܥܕܥܕܐ S

6 he began from Galilee even unto here." Now Pilate, when he heard *C S*
them saying 'From Galilee,' asked whether from Galilee he was.
7 And when he heard that he was from under the authority of Herod,
he sent him unto him, because Herod himself also was in Jerusalem
8 in those days of the Unleavened Bread. Now Herod when he saw
Jesus much rejoiced, for exceedingly he had been wishing to see him
for a long time, because he was hearing about him and was hoping
9 that some sign he would see from him coming to pass; and with
wise words he was asking him *questions*, but Jesus no answer
10 returned him, as if he were not there. Now the chief priests and
11 rulers were standing and accusing him fully; and Herod mocked
him and his men-at-arms *also*, and he clothed him with fair garments
12 in mockery and sent him unto Pilate. And in that same day there
was a reconciliation between Herod and Pilate, because they were
13 enemies. Now Pilate called the chief priests and the rulers and all
14 the people, and he said to them: "Ye have brought up to me this
man that ye say to me that he hath stirred up your people, and lo, I
myself have examined him in your sight and naught have I found
15 about him of the things for which ye blame him; nor *yet* Herod,
for I sent him unto him and naught worthy of death hath he found
about him, neither hath there been committed by him any matter of
16, 18 death. I will chastise him therefore and forgive him." And all the
people gave a cry and say: "Take away this *fellow* and release to us
19 Bar Abba":—him that because of †brigandages†(?) and murders had
17 been cast into prison. And Pilate was accustomed that he should be
20 releasing to them one person at the Feast. And again Pilate called

---

6 'From Galilee,'....he was] 'From Galilee he is' *S* *The words* Galilee *and* Galilaean *are confused in S here and in* Matt xxvi 69, Mk xiv 70, Lk xxii 59 **7** unto him] unto Herod S of...Bread] *om. S* **9**[b] as if he—*to end of* **12.**] *om. S* **14** that ye say to me] and ye say *S* hath stirred] stirreth S lo] *om. S* **14, 15** about him] *lit.* 'after him' (*i.e.* 'in his record') **19** brigandages (?)] *C*; evil things *S*: *cf ver.* 25, *and Introd.* vol. ii **17** one person] one prisoner *S*

C S ܦܝܠܛܘܣ ܘܐܡܪ ܠܗܘܢ ܡܛܠ ܕܨܒܐ ܗܘܐ ܕܢܫܪܝܘܗܝ ܠܝܫܘܥ.
[21]ܗܢܘܢ ܕܝܢ ܩܥܝܢ ܗܘܘ ܘܐܡܪܝܢ ܙܩܘܦܝܗܝ ܙܩܘܦܝܗܝ. [22]ܗܘ ܕܝܢ
ܕܬܠܬ ܙܒܢܝܢ ܐܡܪ ܠܗܘܢ ܡܢܐ ܓܝܪ ܕܒܝܫ ܥܒܕ ܗܢܐ. ܡܕܡ
ܓܝܪ ܕܫܘܐ ܠܡܘܬܐ ܠܐ ܡܫܟܚܐ ܒܗ. ܐܪܕܝܘܗܝ ܗܟܝܠ
ܘܐܫܒܩܝܘܗܝ. [23]ܘܗܢܘܢ ܬܒܥܝܢ ܗܘܘ ܒܩܠܐ ܪܡܐ. ܘܐܡܪܝܢ
col 2 ܠܗ ܕܢܙܕܩܦ. ܘܥܫܢ ܗܘܐ *ܩܠܗܘܢ ܘܕܪ̈ܒܝ ܟܗ̈ܢܐ ܒܥܒܕܝܗܘܢ.
[24]ܘܦܣܩ ܦܝܠܛܘܣ ܕܬܗܘܐ ܫܐܠܬܗܘܢ. [25]ܘܫܪܐ ܠܗܘܢ ܠܗܘ
ܕܡܛܠ ܩܛܠܐ ܘܣܛ̈ܣܝܣ ܗܘܐ ܒܝܬ ܐܣܘ̈ܪܐ ܐܝܟ ܕܫܐܠܘ.
ܘܠܝܫܘܥ ܐܫܠܡ ܠܨܒܝܢܗܘܢ ܀

[26]ܘܟܕ ܡܘܒܠܝܢ ܠܗ. ܐܚܕܘ ܠܫܡܥܘܢ ܩܘܪܝܢܝܐ. ܕܐܬܐ ܗܘܐ ܡܢ
ܩܪܝܬܐ. ܕܢܫܩܘܠ ܙܩܝܦܐ ܘܢܐܬܐ ܒܬܪ ܝܫܘܥ. [27]ܘܐܬܐ ܗܘܐ
ܒܬܪܗ ܣܘܓܐܐ ܕܥܡܐ. ܘܢܫ̈ܐ ܕܡܪܩܕܢ ܗܘܝ ܥܠܘܗܝ,
ܘܐܠܝܢ. [28]ܘܐܬܦܢܝ ܝܫܘܥ ܠܘܬܗܝܢ ܘܐܡܪ ܠܗܝܢ. ܒ̈ܢܬ ܐܘܪܫܠܡ
ܠܐ ܬܒܟܝܢ ܥܠܝ. ܐܠܐ ܒܟܝܢ ܥܠ ܢܦܫܟܝܢ ܘܥܠ ܒ̈ܢܝܟܝܢ.
[29]ܕܐܬܝܢ ܓܝܪ ܝܘ̈ܡܬܐ ܕܒܗܘܢ ܬܐܡܪܢ ܛܘܒܝܗܝܢ ܠܥܩܪ̈ܬܐ.
fol 85 r *ܘܠܟܪ̈ܣܬܐ ܕܠܐ ܝܠܕ. ܘܠܬ̈ܕܝܐ ܕܠܐ ܐܝܢܩܘ. [30]ܘܗܝܕܝܢ ܬܫܪܘܢ
ܠܡܐܡܪ ܠܛܘ̈ܪܐ ܕܦܠܘ ܥܠܝܢ. ܘܠܪ̈ܡܬܐ ܕܚܦܝܢ. [31]ܕܒܩܝܣܐ
ܪܛܝܒܐ ܗܠܝܢ ܥܒܕܝܢ. ܒܝܒܫܐ ܡܢܐ ܢܗܘܐ. [32]ܘܐܬܝܢ ܗܘܘ
ܥܡܗ ܬܪ̈ܝܢ ܐܚܪ̈ܢܝܢ ܥܒ̈ܕܝ ܒܝ̈ܫܬܐ ܕܢܬܩܛܠܘܢ. [33]ܘܟܕ ܐܬܘ
ܠܕܘܟܬܐ ܕܡܬܩܪܝܐ ܩܪܩܦܬܐ. ܙܩܦܘܗܝ ܬܡܢ. ܘܠܗܢܘܢ ܥܒ̈ܕܝ
ܒܝ̈ܫܬܐ ܚܕ ܡܢ ܝܡܝܢܗ ܘܚܕ ܡܢ ܣܡܠܗ. [34]ܘܥܢܐ ܝܫܘܥ ܘܐܡܪ
ܐܒܐ ܫܒܘܩ ܠܗܘܢ ܠܐ ܓܝܪ ܝܕܥܝܢ ܡܢܐ ܥܒܕܝܢ. ܘܦܠܓܘ

---

20 ܕܢܫܪܘܗܝ S ܠܝܫܘܥ] + ܕܠܟܢ ܨܒܝܢ ܐܢܬܘܢ ܕܐܫܪܐ ܠܟܘܢ S
21 ܘܐܡܪܝܢ] om. S ܙܩܘܦܘܗܝ ܙܩܘܦܘܗܝ S (sic) 22 ܒܗ] ܒܬܪܗ S
ܐܪܕܝܗܝ S ܘܐܫܒܩܘܗܝ S 23 ܕܢܙܕܩܦ] om. ܕ S ܘܕܪ̈ܒܝ] ܘܪ̈ܒܝ S
24 ܘܦܣܩ] + ܗܘܐ S ܕܬܗܘܐ ܫܐܠܬܗܘܢ] ܕܢܗܘܐ ܨܒܝܢܗܘܢ S
25 ܘܣܛ̈ܣܝܣ] ܘܒܝ̈ܫܬܐ S: cf ver. 19 ܗܘܐ] pr. ܐܣܝܪܐ S 26. Perh. no § in S ܕܢܫܩܘܠ] C on eras ܒܬܪܗ ܕܝܫܘܥ S 28. § in S ܠܘܬܗܝܢ] om. S 30 ܬܫܪܘܢ] ܬܫܪ̈ܝܢ S 31 ܢܗܘܐ] ܢܥܒܕܘܢ S 32 ܐܚܪ̈ܢܝܢ] om. S
34 ܘܥܢܐ ܝܫܘܥ......ܥܒܕܝܢ] om. S

them and saith to them *thus,* because he was wishing that he should *C S*
21 release Jesus. But they were crying out and saying: "Crucify him,
22 crucify him!" But he for the third time saith to them: "*Why,* for
what evil hath this *fellow* done? For naught worthy of death I find in
23 him. I will chastise him therefore and forgive him." And they were
urgent with loud voice, and say to him that he should be crucified.
And their voice was the stronger and that of the chief priests with
24 them. And Pilate commanded that their petition should be *done.*
25 And he released to them him which because of murders and †heresies†
was in prison, as they asked, and Jesus he delivered up to their will.
26 And while carrying him along they took hold of Simon a Cyrenian
that was coming from the field, that he should take up the cross and
27 come after Jesus. And there was coming after him a number of the
28 people, and women that were lamenting over him and wailing. And
Jesus turned round unto them and said to them: "Daughters of
Jerusalem, weep not for me; but weep for yourselves and for your
29 sons! For the days will come in which ye will say: 'Happy is it for
the barren, and for the wombs that have not borne, and for the breasts
30 that have not given suck!' And then ye will begin to say to the
31 hills 'Fall on us!' and to the heights 'Cover us!' *Seeing* that
with the green wood these things they do, with the dry what will it
32 be?" And there were coming with him two others, evil-doers, that
33 they might be killed. And when they came to the place called The
Skull, they crucified him there and those evil-doers, one on his right
34 and one on his left. And Jesus answered and said: "My Father,
forgive them, for they know not what they do." And they divided his

---

20 *thus*] *om. S* Jesus] + "Whom would ye that I should release to you?" *S* 21 and saying] *om. S* 22 in him] about him *S* (*as in vv.* 14, 15) 23 that...crucified] "Let him be crucified" *S* that of] *om. S* 24 commanded] *pr.* had *S* petition] will *S* 25 heresies] evil things *S*: *cf ver.* 19 was in] was cast into *S* 26 that 2°...take up] *C on eras* 28 unto them] *om. S* 30 ye will begin] *fem. verb in S*; 'they' *for* 'ye' $E^{207(vid)}$ 31 will it be] will they do *S* 32 others] *so also* E^{242}; *om. S* 34 And Jesus.....what they do] *om. S*: *the saying is given in* $E^{117, 256, 265}$, *but in neither case in the Gospel order, and* Diat^{ar} lii 6 *puts it immediately before* Lk xxiii 46

C S ܠܢܚ̈ܬܘܗܝ܆ ܘܢܦܩܘ ܥܠܝܗܘܢ܇ [35]ܘܩܐܡ ܗܘܐ ܥܡܐ ܘܚܙܐ.
ܘܡܡܝܩܝܢ ܗܘܘ ܒܗ ܒܦܘܡܗܘܢ ܘܐܦ ܐܪ̈ܟܘܢܐ ܘܐܡܪܝܢ. ܠܐܚܪ̈ܢܐ
col 2 *ܐܚܝ. ܢܚܐ ܢܦܫܗ ܐܢ ܗܘܝܘ ܡܫܝܚܐ ܓܒܝܗ ܕܐܠܗܐ.
[36]ܘܡܒܙܚܝܢ ܗܘܘ ܒܗ. ܘܐܦ ܐܣܛܪ̈ܛܝܘܛܐ ܡܬܩܪܒܝܢ ܗܘܘ ܠܗ
[37]ܘܐܡܪܝܢ. ܫܠܡ ܠܟ. ܐܢ ܐܢܬ ܗܘ ܡܠܟܐ ܕܝܗܘ̈ܕܝܐ ܐܚܝ
ܢܦܫܟ. ܘܣܡܘ ܗܘܘ ܒܪܫܗ ܟܠܝܠܐ ܕܟܘ̈ܒܐ. [38]ܘܟܬܝܒ ܗܘܐ
ܐܦ ܦܬܩܐ ܘܣܝܡ ܠܥܠ ܡܢܗ. ܗܢܘ ܡܠܟܐ ܕܝܗܘ̈ܕܝܐ ܀ ◦
[39]ܚܕ ܡܢ ܗܢܘܢ ܕܝܢ ܒܝ̈ܫܐ܆ ܥܒ̈ܕܝ ܒܝܫܬܐ ܕܐܨܛܠܒܘ ܗܘܘ ܥܡܗ. ܡܓܕܦ
ܗܘܐ ܒܠܘܗܝ܆ ܘܐܡܪ. ܠܐ ܗܘܝܬ ܡܫܝܚܐ. ܐܚܝ ܢܦܫܟ
ܘܐܚܝ ܐܦ ܠܢ. [40]ܘܒܐܐ ܒܗ ܚܒܪܗ ܗܘ ܐܚܪܢܐ ܘܐܡܪ ܠܗ.
ܐܦܠܐ ܡܢ ܐܠܗܐ ܕܚܠ ܐܢܬ. ܕܗܐ ܐܦ ܚܢܢ ܒܗ ܚܢܢ ܒܕܝܢܐ.
fol 85 v [41]ܘܗܘܐ *ܐܢܚܢ ܐܝܟ ܕܥܒܕܢ ܗܘܝܢ ܗܘ̣. ܘܐܝܟ ܕܥܒܕܢ
ܐܬܦܪܥܢ. ܗܢܐ ܕܝܢ ܐܦ ܠܐ ܡܕܡ ܕܣܢܐ ܥܒܕ ܠܗ. [42]ܘܐܡܪ
ܠܝܫܘܥ ܡܪܝ܆ ܐܬܕܟܪܢܝ ܡܐ ܕܐܬܐ ܐܢܬ ܒܡܠܟܘܬܟ. [43]ܐܡܪ
§A266 §A437 ܠܗ ܝܫܘܥ. §ܐܡܝܢ ܐܡܪ ܐܢܐ ܠܟ ܕܝܘܡܢܐ §ܕܥܡܝ ܬܗܘܐ
¶¶A²/₂ ܒܓܢܬ ܥܕܢ¶¶ [44]ܘܐܝܬܝܗ̇ ܗܘܬ܆ ܐܝܟ ܫ̈ܥܐ ܫܬ. ܘܗܘܐ ܚܫܘܟܐ
ܥܠ ܟܠܗ̇ ܐܪܥܐ ܥܕܡܐ ܠܬܫܥ ܫ̈ܥܝܢ. [45]ܘܥܡܛܐ ܫܡܫܐ. ܘܐܨܛܪܝ܆
ܐ̈ܦܝ ܬܪܥܐ ܕܗܝܟܠܐ ܡܢ ܡܨܥܬܗ. [46]ܘܩܪܐ ܝܫܘܥ ܒܩܠܐ ܪܡܐ
ܘܐܡܪ. ܐܒܐ ܒܐܝ̈ܕܝܟ ܣܐܡ ܐܢܐ ܠܗ̇ ܠܪܘܚܝ ܘܐܫܠܡ.
col 2 [47]ܟܕ ܚܙܐ ܕܝܢ ܩܢܛܪܘܢܐ ܡܕܡ ܕܗܘܐ. ܫܒܚ *ܠܐܠܗܐ. ܘܐܡܪ

---

36 ܘܐܦ] ܐܦ S   ܡܬܩܪܒܝܢ] pr. ܘ S   ܠܗ] ܠܘܬܗ S   37 ܒܪܫܗ] pr. ܐܦ S   38 ܐܦ] om. S   ܦܬܩܐ] so also Ephr. *Lamy* i 667   ܗܢܘ] ܗܢܐ ܗܘ S   39. *No* § *in* S   ܥܡܗ] *om.* S   ܘܐܡܪ] + ܠܗ S   ܘܐܚܝ] *om.* ܐܚܝ S   40 ܗܘ] *om.* S   ܕܚܠ ܐܢܬ] ܕܚܠܬ S   ܐܢܚܢ S (*in each place*)   41 ܗܘ̣] *om.* S   42 ܕܐܬܐ ܐܢܬ] ܕܐܬܝܬ S   43 ܐܡܝܢ] ܐܝܟ ܕܐܡܪ ܦܪܘܩܢ ܠܓܝܣܐ ܡܚܝܢܐ ܕܐܡܝܢ A 266   ܝܘܡܢܐ ܕܥܡܝ] ܕܝܘܡܢܐ ܥܡܝ S Aᵇ266 ; ܕܝܘܡܢܐ ܕܥܡܝ Aᵃ266 ; *cf* ܝܘܡܢܐ ܠܗ ܕܥܡܝ A 437   ܒܓܢܬ ܥܕܢ] C A²/₂ (*also* Ephr. *Lamy* i 667, 669); ܒܦܪܕܝܣܐ S   44 ܫ̈ܥܐ ܫܬ] ܫܬ ܫ̈ܥܝܢ S   46. § *in* S   ܘܐܫܠܡ] ܘܫܠܡ S   47. *No* § *seems intended in* S   ܟܕ ܚܙܐ ܕܝܢ] ܘܟܕ ܚܙܐ S

35 garments and drew lots for them. And the people were standing *C S*
and seeing. And the rulers also were jeering at him with them
and saying: "Others he saved alive; let him save himself alive if he
36 is the Messiah, the Chosen of God." And they were mocking at
37 him. And the soldiers also were drawing near to him and saying:
"Hail to thee! If thou art the King of the Jews, save thyself alive."
38 And they had set on his head a crown of thorns, and there was
written a tablet also and set above him: "This is the King of the
Jews."

39 Now one of those evil-doers that were crucified with him was
blaspheming against him and saying: "Art thou not the Messiah?
40 save thyself alive, and save alive us also!" And his comrade, that
other one, rebuked him and said to him: "Not even of God art thou
41 afraid, seeing that lo, we also—we are in the same judgement? And
lo, we—as we deserve it hath befallen us, and as we have done we
have been repaid; but this one—not even aught disgraceful hath
42 been done by him." And he said to Jesus: "My Lord, remember me
43 what *time* thou comest in thy kingdom." Jesus saith to him: "§Amen, §*A*266
I say to thee to-day that §with me thou shalt be in the Garden of §*A*437
44 Eden."¶¶ And it was about the sixth hour, and there was darkness ¶¶$A^2/_2$
45 over all the land until the ninth hour and the sun was darkened; and
46 the veil of the Temple was rent from the midst of it. And Jesus
called with a loud voice and said: "Father, in thy hands I lay my
spirit." And he delivered *it* up.

47 Now when the centurion saw that which came to pass, he glorified

---

36 And they...also were] And the soldiers also were mocking at him and were *S* to him] unto him *S* 37 head] + also *S* 38 a tablet] *The same word is used in* Ephr. *Lamy* i 667 also] *om. S* the King] *pr.* 'the Messiah' E^{243} 39 with him] *om. S* saying] + to him *S* save alive] *om. S* 40 that other] the other *S* art thou] hast thou been *S* 41 it hath befallen us] *om. S* 42 comest] hast come *S*: *cf* 'remember me in thy kingdom' E^{243} 43 Amen] 'As our Saviour said to him on his right hand Amen...' *A* 266 that (*before* 'with')] *C* A^a266; *before* 'to-day' *S* A^b266: *cf* 'He sware to him With me...' *A* 437. *For the ambiguous evidence of* E^{244f} *and the statement in* Barsalibi, *see Notes*, vol. ii in the Garden of Eden] *C* $A^2/_2$ E^{244f} (*also* Ephr. *Lamy* i 667, 669); in Paradise *S* 46 delivered *it* up] expired *S* 47 Now] And *S*

C S ܫܪܝܪܘܬ ܗܢܐ ܟܢܘܪܐ ܕܕܘܡܐ ܗܘ. ܘܟܠܗܘܢ[48] ܐܝܠܝܢ ܕܐܬܚܙܝܘܗܝ
ܬܡܢ ܘܚܙܘ ܡܕܡ ܕܗܘܐ. ܦܪܫܝܢ ܗܘܘ ܟܠ ܚܙܝܗܘܢ ܘܐܡܪܝܢ.
§¶A271 ܘܝ[§] ܠܝ ܡܢܐ ܗܘ̈ܢ ܘ[¶]ܝ ܠܝ ܡܢ ܚܙܬܗܝܢ. ܘܦܫܩܝܢ[49] ܗܘܘ ܡܢ
ܙܘܥܐ ܟܠܗܘܢ ܒܫܘܒܚܬܗ ܕܡܫܝܚ. ܘܬܢ̈ܝܐ ܐܝܠܝܢ ܕܐܬܝ,
ܒܗܘܢ ܡܢ ܓܠܝܠܐ. ܘܫܪܝ ܗܠܝܢ. ܀

ܘܟܢܘܪܐ[50] ܚܕ ܕܫܒܥܗ ܗܘܐ ܢܩܘܫ. ܒܡܠܘܦܐ ܗܘܐ. ܟܢܘܪܐ
ܕܕܝܢܐ ܘܦܓܥܐ. ܡܢ[51] ܕܡܚܬܐ ܒܢܒܐ ܕܫܘܗܕ. ܘܫܐܪ ܗܘܐ
ܠܬܠܡܝܕܘܬܐ ܕܫܡܝܢܐ. ܗܢܐ ܟܢܘܪܐ ܕܠܐ ܐܚܐ, ܕܒܝܢܘܗܝ ܒܡ
fol 86r ܬ̈ܟܠ ܡܪܝܐ. ܘܗܘ[52] ܗܢܐ ܡܪܒ ܘܫܐܠ *ܦܠܚܘܗܝ ܕܡܫܝܚ. ܘܐܝܬܘܗܝ[53]
ܘܒܪܗ ܒܫܘܪܐ. ܘܦܫܩܗ ܒܝܬ ܡܕܘܪܐ ܢܡܘܣܐ. ܐܝܟܐ ܕܒܙܒܢ
ܐܝܟ ܠܐ ܐܬܡܟܪ ܒܗ. ܘܗܘ[54] ܗܘ ܡܫܟܐ ܒܪܘܟܬܐ ܗܘܬ.
ܘܫܒܩܬܐ ܢܦܫܐ ܗܘܬ. ܘܗܠܝܢ[55] ܢ̈ܫܐ ܕܐܬܝ, ܒܗܘܢ ܡܢ ܓܠܝܠܐ.
ܐܬܝ, ܠܒܝܬ ܡܕܘܪܐ ܒܡܫܡܫܬܗܘܢ ܘܚܝ, ܠܫܠܡܐ ܒܪ ܐܒܠܘܗ̇
ܠܬܡܢ. ܘܗܦܟ[56] ܦܠܚ ܗܘܪܒܐ ܘܡܫܝܚܐ ܕܒܡܫܡܫܢܐ. ܘܫܒܩܬܐ
ܥܠ ܐܝܟ ܕܡܫܝ. [1]ܒܡܫܒܚܬܐ ܕܝܢ ܒܥܘܦܪܐ ܢܒܐ. ܐܬܝ, ܗܘ,
ܠܒܝܬ ܡܕܘܪܐ. ܘܐܝܬ, ܗܘ, ܡܕܡ ܕܦܠܚ. ܘܐܬܝ, ܗܘ, ܒܡܫܡܫ
col 2 ܢ̈ܫܐ ܐܚܪ̈ܢܝܬܐ. ܘܐܡܫܚ[2] ܠܚܐܦܐ ܗ, *ܕܡܬܦܠܠܐ ܡܢ ܒܝܬ
ܡܕܘܪܐ. [3]ܘܥܠ ܘܠܐ ܐܡܫܝܚܗ, ܠܦܓܪܐ ܕܡܫܝܚ. ܘܒܪ[4] ܒܪܢܐ
ܗܘܬ ܠܗܝܢ ܥܠ ܗܕܐ. ܚܙܝ, ܬܪ̈ܝܢ ܐܢ̈ܫܝܢ ܕܦܫܩܝܢ ܠܟܠ ܡ̈ܠܝܗܘܢ.

ܫܪܝܪܘܬ] C (end of line); ܫܪܝܪܐܝܬ S: cf xxii 62 ܗܘ] ܗܘܐ S
48. Cf ܡܟܝܠ ܡܢ ܟܢܘܪܐ ܠܐ ܕܝܠܝ. ܡܟܠܦܐ ܡܢܐ ܢܟܪܝܢ. ܘܝ ܠܝ ܡܢܐ ܗܘ̈ܢ A271; ܗܐ ܟܢܪ ܐܟܠܐ ܠܐ ܕܡܟܘ ܫܘܢ ܕܘܦܫܩܘܢ ܕܒܙܗ ܗܘ ܕܐܠܗܐ. ܠܐ ܗܘܐ ܚܙܒܐ ܕܒܫܘܬܗܘܢ ܡܟܪܝܢ ܗܘܘ. ܐܦ ܠܐ ܗܘܐ ܥܠ ܢܦܫܗܘܢ ܘܬܢܐ ܡܦܠܚܝܢ ܗܘܘ Addai[27] 49 ܒܫܘܒܚܬܗ] ܒܫܘܒܚܬܗ S ܓܠܝܠܐ] *before this word there has been a small erasure in C* 50. *No* § *in S* ܒܡܠܘܦܐ S 52 ܡܪܒ] + ܠܘܬ ܦܠܚܘܗܝ S 52, 53 ܕܡܫܝܚ.....ܐܬܡܟܪ] *S illegible* 53 ܒܗ] *pr.* ܗܘܐ S 54 ܘܗܘ (1°)......ܗܘܬ] ܗܘ ܕܝܢ ܡܫܟܐ ܒܪܘܟܬܐ ܗܘܬ S ܘܫܒܩܬܐ] § *in S (apparently)* 55 ܘܗܠܝܢ ܢ̈ܫܐ] ܗܢܝܢ ܘܢ̈ܫܐ S ܒܡܫܡܫܢܘܬܗܘܢ S ܐܒܠܘܗ̇] *the point in C is in red* 56 ܥܠ] *on eras. in C* 1. § *in S, but apparently not in C* 2 ܗܝ] *om. S* 4 ܚܙܝ] ܐܬܚܙܝܘ S

48 God and said: "Truly this is a righteous man." And all they that C S
happened to be there and saw that which came to pass were beating
on their breasts and saying: "§Woe to us! What hath befallen us?¶ §¶A 271
49 Woe to us from our sins!" And there were standing from afar all
the acquaintance of Jesus, and the women which came with him
from Galilee, and *they were* seeing these things.

50 And a certain man whose name was Joseph—a councillor he was, a
51 man righteous and good, from Ramtha a town of Judaea, and he was
looking for the kingdom of heaven—this man, that was not of equal
52 mind with the accusers, this very one drew near and asked for the
53 body of Jesus. And he took it down and wrapped it in a swathe, and
54 laid it in a hewn tomb which hitherto no one was buried in. And
55 that same day was Friday, and the sabbath was dawning. And these
women that came with him from Galilee came to the tomb on their
footsteps, and they saw the corpse when they brought it in thither.
56 And they returned *and* made ready spices and oil of perfume; and
xxiv 1 on the sabbath they rested, as it is commanded. Now on the first
day of the week, in the early dawn, they had come to the tomb and
had brought that which they prepared; and there had come with
2 them other women. And they found that stone rolled *away* from
3, 4 the tomb, and they entered and found not the body of Jesus. And
when it was grieving them about this, they saw two persons standing

---

is] was *S* 48 Woe.... befallen us?] *Cf* 'Henceforth of the LORD we have not been afraid, the King what will he do to us? (Hosea x 3) Woe to us! What hath befallen us?' *A* 271; *also* 'For lo, if those that crucified him had not known that he was the Son of God, the desolation of their city they would not have proclaimed, nor against themselves would they have let fall the Woes' *Addai*[27], *and* 'Woe was it, woe was it to us: this was the Son of God!'....'Lo, the judgements of the desolation of Jerusalem are come' *E*[245,246]. *See also Notes,* vol. ii 51 was not.... accusers] *Cf* 'was not equal in their counsel and deed with the accusers' *E*[266] *and* Diat[ar] lii 26 52 drew near]+unto Pilate *S* 52, 53 of Jesus.... buried] *S illegible, but must have read* 'had been buried' *for* 'was buried' 54 And.... Friday] ⌜Now⌝ that ⌜day⌝ was Friday *S* 55 these] those *S* 56 rested] *on eras. in C* 2 that] the *S* 4 they saw] there appeared *S*

ܘܡܒܗܪ ܗܘܐ ܠܒܘܫܝܗܘܢ ⁵ܘܕܚܠ. ܘܟܕ ܙ̈ܥܝܢ ܘܚܝܪܢ ܗܘܝ, C S
ܒܐܪܥܐ ܡܢ ܕܚܠܬܗܝܢ. ܐܡܪܝܢ ܠܗܝܢ ܗܢܘܢ ܓܒܪ̈ܐ. ܡܢܐ
ܒܥܝܢ ܐܢܬܝܢ ܚܝܐ ܒܝܬ ܡ̈ܝܬܐ. [6]ܠܝܬ ܗܘ ܗܪܟܐ. ܐܠܐ ܩܡ ܠܗ.
ܥܗܕܝܢ ܡܕܡ ܕܡܠܠ ܥܡܟܝܢ ܟܕ ܗܘ ܒܓܠܝܠܐ. [7]ܘܐܡܪ ܗܘܐ
ܠܗܝܢ. ܕܥܬܝܕ ܗܘ ܒܪܗ ܕܐܢܫܐ ܕܢܫܬܠܡ ܒܐܝ̈ܕܝ, ܐܢܫܐ ܚ̈ܛܝܐ
ܘܢܙܕܩܦ. ܘܠܬܠܬܐ ܝܘ̈ܡܝܢ ܢܩܘܡ. [8]ܘܐܬܥܗܕܝ ܐܢܝܢ *ܠܡ̈ܠܐ ܗܠܝܢ. fol 86 v
[9]ܘܗܦܟܝ ܡܢ ܒܝܬ ܩܒܘܪܐ ܐܡܪܝ ܐܢܝܢ ܡ̈ܠܐ ܗܠܝܢ ܠܚܕܥܣܪ.
ܘܠܫܪܟܐ ܕܬܠܡ̈ܝܕܐ ܗܠܝܢ. [10]ܡܪܝܡ ܡܓܕܠܝܬܐ ܘܝܘܚܢ. ܘܡܪܝܡ
ܒܪܬ ܝܥܩܘܒ. ܘܫܪܟܐ ܕܥܡܗܝܢ. ܗܠܝܢ ܐܡ̈ܪܢ ܗܘܝ ܠܫ̈ܠܝܚܐ.
[11]ܘܡܬܚܙܝܢ ܗܘܝ ܒܥܝ̈ܢܝܗܘܢ ܕܐܝܟ ܕܡܢ ܬܡܗܘܬܗܘܢ ܗܘ ܐܡ̈ܪܢ
ܗܘܝ ܡ̈ܠܐ ܗܠܝܢ. ܘܠܐ ܡܗܝܡܢܝܢ ܗܘܘ ܠܗܝܢ ܀

[12]ܫܡܥܘܢ ܕܝܢ ܩܡ ܘܪܗܛ ܠܩܒܪܐ. ܘܐܕܝܩ ܘܚܙܐ ܟܬܢܐ ܒܠܚܘܕ
ܘܐܙܠ ܠܗ. ܘܡܬܕܡܪ ܗܘܐ ܒܡܕܡ ܕܗܘܐ. [13]ܘܐܬܘܚܕܘ, ܠܬܪ̈ܝܢ
ܡܢܗܘܢ ܒܗ ܒܝܘܡܐ. ܟܕ ܐܙܠܝܢ ܗܘܘ ܠܩܪܝܬܐ ܕܫܡܗ
ܐܡܐܘܣ. ܕܪܚܝܩܐ ܡܢ ܐܘܪܫܠܡ ܐܣܛܕ̈ܘܬܐ *ܫܬܝܢ. [14]ܘܡܡܠܠܝܢ col 2
ܗܘܘ ܚܕ ܥܡ ܚܕ ܥܠ ܗܠܝܢ ܟܠܗܝܢ ܐܝܠܝܢ ܕܓܕ̈ܫ. [15]ܘܟܕ ܗܢܘܢ
ܡܡܠܠܝܢ. ܐܬܐ ܝܫܘܥ. ܩܪܒ ܐܢܘܢ. ܘܡܗܠܟ ܗܘܐ ܥܡܗܘܢ.
[16]ܘܥܝ̈ܢܝܗܘܢ ܐܚܝܕܢ ܗܘܝ, ܕܠܐ ܢܫܬܘܕܥܘܢܝܗܝ. [17]ܐܡܪ ܠܗܘܢ
ܡܢܐ ܐܢܝܢ ܡ̈ܠܐ ܗܠܝܢ ܕܡܡܠܠܝܢ ܐܢܬܘܢ ܟܕ ܡܗܠܟܝܢ
ܐܢܬܘܢ ܀

[18]ܐܡܪ ܠܗ ܚܕ ܡܢܗܘܢ ܕܫܡܗ ܗܘܐ ܩܠܝܘܦܐ. ܐܢܬ ܗܘ ܒܪ
ܢܘܟܪܝܐ ܒܠܚܘܕܝܟ ܡܢ ܐܘܪܫܠܡ. ܕܡܕܡ ܕܗܘܐ ܒܗ ܠܐ ܝܕܥ ܐܢܬ.

---

6 ܠܝܬ ܗܘ] ܠܐ ܗܘܐ S   ܒܚ̈ܝܐ S (*and* ܠܗ̈ܝܢ *vv.* 5 *and* 11)   ܟܕ] ܟܕ S
7 ܐܢܫܐ] *pr.* ܒܢܝ S   9 ܐܡܪܝ] *pr.* ܘ S   ܘܠܫܪܟܐ] ܘܫܪܟܐ S   ܗܠܝܢ 2°] *om.* S   11 ܕܐܝܟ] *om.* ܕ S   ܗܘ] *om.* S   ܗܘܘ 2°] *om.* S   12. *No* § *in* S
ܟܬܢܐ] C; ܟܬ̈ܢܐ S   ܒܡܕܡ] ܡܕܡ S   13. § *in* S, *but apparently not in* C
ܕܪܚܝܩܐ] ܘܪܚܝܩܐ S   15 ܡܡܠܠܝܢ] + ܘܡܒܥܝܢ S   ܩܪܒ] *pr.* ܘ S
16 ܐܚܝܕܢ ܗܘܝ S (*sic*)   ܢܫܬܘܕܥܘܢܝܗ S (*sic*): *cf* Mk ix 32, Lk xxii 2   18. *No* § *in* S, *apparently*   ܒܠܚܘܕܝܟ] *om.* S   ܝܕܥ ܐܢܬ] ܝܕܥܬ S

5 over them, and the clothing of them was flashing and *the women* C S
were afraid; and they bowed their heads and were looking on the
earth from their fear. Those men say to them: "Why seek ye the
6 living among the dead? He is not here, but hath arisen; recollect
7 that which he spake with you while he *was* in Galilee and had said
to you that the Son of Man is about to be delivered up into the
hands of sinful folk and be crucified, and in three days he will rise."
8, 9 And they remembered these words. And they returned from the
tomb *and* said these words to the eleven and to the rest of the
10 disciples, *even* these—Mary Magdalene and Johan and Mary daughter
of James and the rest with them,—these things they were saying
11 to the apostles and they were appearing in their eyes as if from
their stupor they were saying these words, and they were not
believing them.

12 Now Simon arose and ran to the grave, and looked in and saw
the linen cloth*s* only and went away, and he was wondering at that
13 which had come to pass. And he appeared to two of them in the
same day while they were going to a village whose name *is* Emmaus,
14 that is distant from Jerusalem sixty stadia. And they were speaking
15 one with the other of all these things which had chanced. And
while they were speaking, Jesus came up with them and was walking
16 with them; and their eyes were held that they should not perceive
17 him. He saith to them: "What are these words that ye are
speaking, being sad?"

18 Saith to him one of them, whose name was Cleopa: "Art
thou then a stranger by thyself from Jerusalem, that with
that which hath come to pass therein thou art not acquainted?"

---

6 while] while yet *S* 7 folk] men *S* 9 *and* said] and said *S* to the rest] *om.* to *S* *even* these] *om. S* 11 they were 2°] *om. S* 12 cloth*s*] cloth *C*; cloths *S* at] *om. S* (*sic*) 13 that is] and is *S* 15 speaking] + and enquiring *S* 18 by thyself] *om. S* art not] hast not been *S*

C S ¹⁹ܐܡܪ ܠܗܘܢ ܡܢܐ. ܐܡܪܝܢ ܠܗ ܥܠ ܝܫܘܥ ܢܨܪܝܐ ܗܘ
ܕܗܘܐ ܓܒܪܐ ܢܒܝܐ. ܘܐܫܬܟܚ ܒܚܝܠܐ ܘܒܥܒ̈ܕܐ ܘܒܡܠܬܐ.
fol 87 r ܩܕܡ ܐܠܗܐ ܘܩܕܡ *ܟܠܗ ܥܡܐ. [20]ܘܐܫܠܡܘܗܝ ܪ̈ܒܝ ܟܗ̈ܢܐ
ܘܩܫܝܫܝ ܠܕܝܢܐ ܕܡܘܬܐ ܘܙܩܦܘܗܝ. [21]ܘܐܚܢܢ ܣܒܪܝܢ ܗܘܝܢ ܕܗܘܝܘ
ܥܬܝܕ ܗܘܐ ܕܢܦܪܘܩܝܗ̇ ܠܐܝܣܪܝܠ. ܘܗܐ ܬܠܬܐ ܝܘܡ̈ܝܢ ܗܐ
ܡܢ ܕܗܠܝܢ ܟܠܗܝܢ ܗܘܝ. [22]ܐܦ ܢܫ̈ܐ ܡܢܢ ܐܙܠ ܗܘ̈ܝ ܠܒܝܬ
ܩܒܘܪܐ ܐܬܪ ܕܩܝܡ ܗܘܐ. [23]ܘܟܕ ܠܐ ܐܫܟܚ ܦܓܪܗ. ܐܬܝ̈
ܐܡܪ̈ܢ ܠܢ ܕܚܙܘܐ ܕܡ̈ܠܐܟܐ ܚܙܝ ܬܡܢ. ܘܬܡܗ̈ܢ ܘܐܡܪ̈ܢ ܥܠܘܗܝ,
ܕܚܝ ܗܘ. [24]ܘܐܦ ܐܢܫܐ ܡܢܢ ܐܙܠܘ ܗܘܘ ܠܒܝܬ ܩܒܘܪܐ. ܘܐܫܟܚܘ
ܗܟܢܐ ܐܝܟ ܕܐܡܪ̈ ܢܫ̈ܐ. ܐܠܐ ܠܗ ܠܐ ܚܙܘ .܀
[25]ܗܝܕܝܢ ܐܡܪ ܠܗܘܢ ܝܫܘܥ. ܐܘ ܣܟ̈ܠܝ, ܗܝܡܢܘܬܐ ܘܝ̈ܩܝܪܝ,
col 2 *ܠܒܐ ܠܗܝܡܢܘܬܗ. ܡܢ ܟܠܗܝܢ ܐܠܝܢ ܕܡܠܠܘ ܢܒ̈ܝܐ. [26]ܠܐ ܗܘܐ
ܗܠܝܢ ܚܫ̈ܐ ܗܘܐ ܕܢܣܝܒܪ ܡܫܝܚܐ. ܘܕܢܥܘܠ ܠܬܫܒܘܚܬܐ. [27]ܘܫܪܝ,
ܗܘܐ ܠܡܐܡܪ ܠܗܘܢ ܡܢ ܡܘܫܐ ܘܡܢ ܟܠܗܘܢ ܢܒ̈ܝܐ.
ܘܡܦܫܩ ܗܘܐ ܠܗܘܢ ܥܠ ܢܦܫܗ ܡܢ ܟܠܗܘܢ ܟܬܒ̈ܐ. [28]ܘܩܪܒܘ
ܠܩܪܝܬܐ ܗ̇ܝ, ܕܐܙܠܝܢ ܗܘܘ ܠܗ̇. ܘܗܘ ܐܬܚܫܒ, ܠܗܘܢ ܐܝܟ
ܕܠܕܘܟܐ ܪ̈ܚܝܩܐ ܐܙܠ ܗܘܐ. [29]ܘܐܠܨܘ ܗܘܢ ܒܥܝܢ ܗܘܘ ܡܢܗ
ܕܢܗܘܐ ܠܘܬܗܘܢ. ܡܛܠ ܕܪܡܫܐ ܗܘܬ ܠܡܚܫܟ. ܘܥܠ ܥܡܗܘܢ
ܐܝܟ ܕܠܘܬܗܘܢ ܢܗܘܐ. [30]ܘܟܕ ܐܣܬܡܟ ܢܣܒ ܠܚܡܐ ܘܒܪܟ.
fol 87 v ܘܩܨܐ ܘܝܗܒ ܠܗܘܢ. [31]ܘܒܗܕܐ *ܐܬܦܬܚ ܗܘܝ, ܥܝ̈ܢܝܗܘܢ
ܘܐܫܬܘܕܥܘܗܝ, ܘܗܘ ܐܫܬܩܠ ܠܗ ܡܢܗܘܢ. [32]ܘܐܡܪܝܢ ܗܘܘ ܚܕ
ܠܚܕ. ܠܐ ܗܘܐ ܠܒܢ ܝܩܝܪ ܗܘܐ ܒܐܘܪܚܐ. ܟܕ ܡܦܫܩ ܠܢ ܟܬܒ̈ܐ.
[33]ܘܩܡܘ ܒܗ̇ ܒܫܥܬܐ ܘܗܦܟܘ ܠܐܘܪܫܠܡ. ܘܐܫܟܚܘ ܠܚܕܥܣܪ

---

20 ܘܩܫܝܫܝ] ܘܩܫܝܫܐ S 21 ܕܢܦܪܘܩܝܗ S 22 ܐܦ] ܘܐܦ S
23 ܘܐܡܪ̈ܢ] ܘܐܡܪܝܢ S 24 ܗܘܘ] om. S ܐܝܟ] + ܡܐ S 25 ܐܘ]
ܘܐ S ܗܝܡܢܘܬܐ] ܒܗܝܡܢܘܬܐ S ܟܠܗܝܢ] pr. ܗܠܝܢ S 26 ܠܬܫܒܘܚܬܐ]
ܠܬܫܒܘܚܬܗ S (sic) 29 ܕܢܗܘܐ ܠܘܬܗܘܢ] ܢܗܘܐ ܠܘܬܗܘܢ ܐܝܟ S
31 ܘܒܗܕܐ] so also S ܐܬܦܬܚ] so also S ܗܘܝ] om. S

19 He saith to them: "What?" They say to him: "Concerning Jesus C S
the Nazarene, who was a man *that was* a prophet, and was found with
power and with deeds and with word before God and before all
20 the people. And the chief priests and our elders delivered him
21 up to the judgement of death, and they have crucified him. And
we were hoping that it was he was about to redeem Israel; and lo,
22 *it is* three days, lo, since all these things have come to pass! Some
23 women also of ours had gone to the tomb where he was laid, and
when they found not his body they came saying to us 'Angels
we have seen there, and we have been astonished'; and *the women*
24 say of him that he is alive. And some folk also of ours had gone
to the tomb and they found *it* so, as the women said, but him
they saw not."
25 Then said Jesus to them: "Ah lacking of faith and heavy of
heart to believe! From all the things that the prophets have spoken,
26 was not the Messiah about to endure these things and to enter
27 glory?" And he had begun to say to them from Moses and from all
the prophets, and was interpreting to them about himself from all
28 the Scriptures. And they drew near to the village which they were
going to; and he appeared to them as if to a far place he was going,
29 and they began beseeching him that he would be *staying* with them,
because it was near to grow dark. And he entered with them as if
30 with them he would be *staying*. And when he sat down *to meat* he
31 took bread and blessed, and brake and gave to them. And at once
their eyes had been opened and they recognised him; and he
32 himself was taken away from them. And they were saying one
to the other: "Was not our heart heavy in the way while he
33 *was* interpreting to us the Scriptures?" And they arose in the
same hour and returned to Jerusalem, and they found the eleven

---

20 our elders] the elders *S* 22 Some] And some *S* 23 'Angels... astonished, and *the angels* say of him that he is alive' *S* 24 had gone] went *S* as] + what *S* 25 Ah] O *S* faith] mind *S* the things] these things *S* 26 glory] his glory *S* 29 that.... *staying* with them] so that with them he should be *staying* *S* 31 had been] were *S*

(C) S ܟܕ ܟܢܝܫܝܢ. ܘܠܐܝܠܝܢ ܕܥܡܗܘܢ. ³⁴ܟܕ ܐܡܪܝܢ. ܫܪܝܪܐܝܬ ܩܡ ܡܪܢ
ܘܐܬܚܙܝ ܠܫܡܥܘܢ. ³⁵ܘܐܦ ܗܢܘܢ ܐܫܬܥܝܘ ܠܗܘܢ ܐܝܠܝܢ ܕܗܘܝ
ܒܐܘܪܚܐ. ܘܐܝܟܢܐ ܐܬܝܕܥ. ܟܕ ܩܨܐ ܠܚܡܐ ܀
³⁶ܘܟܕ ܗܢܘܢ ܡܡܠܠܝܢ ܗܘܘ. ܐܫܬܟܚ ܩܐܡ ܒܝܢܬܗܘܢ. ܘܐܡܪ
ܠܗܘܢ ܫܠܡܐ ܥܡܟܘܢ. ³⁷ܘܗܢܘܢ ܐܬܕܠܚܘ ܘܐܬܪܗܒܘ. ܘܣܒܪܝܢ
col 2 ܗܘܘ ܕܪܘܚܐ *ܚܙܝܢ ܗܘܘ. ³⁸ܗܝܕܝܢ ܐܡܪ ܠܗܘܢ ܝܫܘܥ. ܡܢܐ
ܡܬܕܠܚܝܢ ܐܢܬܘܢ. ܘܥܠ ܡܢܐ ܣ̈ܠܩܝܢ ܡܚܫ̈ܒܬܐ ܥܠ ܠܒܘܬܟܘܢ.
³⁹ܚܙܘ ܐܝ̈ܕܝ ܘܪ̈ܓܠܝ. ܘܓܘܫܘ ܚܙܘ ܕܐܢܐ ܐܢܐ. ܠܪܘܚܐ ܓܝܪ
ܒܣܪܐ ܘܓܪ̈ܡܐ ܠܝܬ ܠܗ. ܐܝܟܢܐ ܕܚܙܝܢ ܐܢܬܘܢ ܕܐܝܬ ܠܝ.
⁴¹ܘܟܕ ܥܕܡܐ ܠܗܫܐ ܠܐ ܡܗܝܡܢܝܢ ܡܢ ܕܚܕܘܬܗܘܢ ܘܡܢ
ܬܗܪܗܘܢ. ܘܡܬܬܗܪܝܢ ܗܘܘ. ܐܡܪ ܠܗܘܢ ܐܝܬ ܠܟܘܢ
ܬܢܢ ܡܕܡ ܠܡܐܟܘܠ. ⁴²ܘܗܢܘܢ ܝܗܒܘ ܠܗ ܡܢܬܐ ܡܢ ܢܘܢܐ ܕܛܘܝܐ.
ܘܡܢ ܒܪܘܬܐ ܕܕܒܫܐ. ⁴³ܘܟܕ ܢܣܒ ܐܟܠ ܗܘܐ ܠܥܝ̈ܢܝܗܘܢ.
¶C ܘܫܩܠ ܡܕܡ ܕܐܬܪ ܝܗܒ ܠܗܘܢ. ⁴⁴ܐܡܪ ܠܗܘܢ. ܗܠܝܢ ¶ܡ̈ܠܐ
|ܡܡܠܠ ܗܘܝܬ ܥܡܟܘܢ ܟܕ ܠܘܬܟܘܢ ܕܢܫܬܠܡ ܟܠ ܡܕܡ
ܕܟܬܝܒ ܥܠܝ ܒܐܘܪܝܬܐ ܕܡܘܫܐ ܘܒܢܒܝܐ ܘܒܡܙܡܘܪ̈ܐ. ⁴⁵ܘܗܝܕܝܢ
ܦܬܚ ܪܥܝܢܗܘܢ ܠܡܫܬܟܠܘ ܟܬܒܐ. ⁴⁶ܘܐܡܪ ܠܗܘܢ ܕܗܟܢܐ
ܗܘ ܘܠܐ [ܗܘܐ ܕܢܚܫ] ܡܫܝܚܐ [ܘܕܢܩܘܡ] ܡܢ ܒܝܬ ܡܝܬܐ
ܠܬܠܬܐ ܝܘܡܝܢ. ⁴⁷ܘܢܬܟܪܙ ܒܫܡܗ ܬܝܒܘܬܐ ܘܫܘܒܩܢܐ ܕܚ̈ܛܗܐ
ܒܟܠܗܘܢ ܥܡ̈ܡܐ ܘܫܘܪܝܐ ܡܢ ܐܘܪܫܠܡ. ⁴⁸ܘܐܢܬܘܢ ܐܢܘܢ

---

33 ܕܥܡܗܘܢ] + ܘܐܬܚܙܝ S (*sic*): *cf* Lk ix 12 *C** 37 ܚܙܝܢ ܗܘܘ] *om.* ܗܘܘ S
38 ܘܥܠ ܡܢܐ] ܘܠܡܢܐ S 39 ܚܙܘ 2°] *pr.* ܘ S ܠܝܬ ܠܗ. ܐܝܟܢܐ *and*
ܐܢܬܘܢ ܕܐܝܬ] *S illegible, but it quite clearly omits ver.* 40, *like C*
41 ܥܕܡܐ ܠܗܫܐ *and* ܡܗܝܡܢܝܢ ܡܢ] *S illegible* ܘܡܢ ܬܗܪܗܘܢ] *only*
ܗܘܢ *is legible in S* ܘܡܬܬܗܪܝܢ *S* ܐܡܪ] *pr.* ܬܘܒ *S* ܠܡܐܟܘܠ]
ܠܡܐܟܠ *S* 42 ܘܡܢ ܒܪܘܬܐ ܕܕܒܫܐ] *om. S* 43 ܗܘܐ] *om. S*
ܠܥܝܢܝܗܘܢ *S* ܘܫܩܠ.....ܝܗܒ ܠܗܘܢ] *om. S* 46 ܗܘܐ ܕܢܚܫ *and* ܘܕܢܩܘܡ]
S illegible

34 gathered together and those with them, saying: "Truly our Lord (*C*) *S*
35 hath risen, and hath appeared to Simon." And they also declared
to them what things befel in the way, and how he was known
when he brake the bread.

36 And while they were speaking, he was found standing among
37 them; and he said to them: "Peace *be* with you!" And they
trembled and were alarmed, and were supposing that a spirit they
38 were seeing. Then said Jesus to them: "Why do ye tremble? and
39 for what *reason* come up thoughts over your hearts? Lo, see my
hands and my feet, and touch *and* see that it is I! For a spirit
41 flesh and bones hath not, as ye see that I have." And while not yet
believing from their fear and from their joy, and they were being
42 astonished, he saith to them: "Have ye here aught to eat?" And
43 they gave him a portion of fish broiled, and of honey-comb. And
when he took he was eating before their eyes, and he took up that
44 which was over *and* gave to them. Saith he to them: "These words¶ ¶*C*
| I was speaking with you while by you, that everything would be
accomplished that is written of me in the Law of Moses and in the
45 prophets and in the Psalms." And then he opened their mind to
46 understand the Scriptures. And he saith to them "Thus it [was]
fitting [that] the Messiah [should suffer and that he should rise]
47 from among the dead in three days; and in my name shall be
preached repentance and forgiveness of sins in all the peoples, and
48 the beginning *shall be* from Jerusalem. And ye are the witnesses of

---

33 with them] + and he appeared *S* (*sic*): *cf* Lk ix 12 *C** 37 were seeing] *were* seeing *S* 38 for what *reason*] wherefore *S* 39 *and* see] and see *S* hath not, as ye] *S illegible, but it quite clearly omits ver.* 40, *like C* 41 not yet believing from] *S illegible* and from their joy] *only* 'their' *is legible in S* saith] + again *S* to eat] *S has the more usual word for* 'to eat' 42 and of honey-comb] *om. S* 43 was eating] ate *S* and he took up....gave to them] *om. S*: *see Notes,* vol. ii 46 should suffer.....rise] *S illegible, but from the space the reading is certain*

S ܣܗܕܐ ܕܗܠܝܢ ⁴⁹ܘܐܢܐ ܐܫܕܪ ܠܟܘܢ ܫܘܠܚܢܗ ܕܐܒܝ ܗܘܘ
ܐܢܬܘܢ ܒܡܬܢܝܚܘܬܐ ܒܡܕܝܢܬܐ ܕܬܠܒܫܘܢ ܚܝܠܐ ܡܢ ܪܘܡܐ ⁵⁰ܘܐܦܩ
ܐܢܘܢ ܒܡܕܝܢܬܐ ܠܒܝܬ ܥܢܝܐ ܘܐܪܝܡ ܐܝܕܘܗܝ ܘܒܪܟ ܐܢܘܢ܂
⁵¹ܘܟܕ ܒܪܟ ܐܢܘܢ ܐܬܦܪܫ ܡܢܗܘܢ ⁵²ܘܗܢܘܢ ܗܦܟܘ
ܠܐܘܪܫܠܡ ܒܚܕܘܬܐ ܪܒܬܐ ⁵³ܘܡܒܪܟܝܢ ܗܘܘ ܒܟܠ ܥܕܢ ܒܗܝܟܠܐ
ܠܐܠܗܐ ܀ ܀

ܫܠܡ ܐܘܢܓܠܝܘܢ

○ ○ ܕܠܘܩܐ ○ ○ ○ ○

ܐܘܢܓܠܝܘܢ ܕܡܦܪܫܐ

---

51. *Cf Addai* 6:
ܘܟܕ ܫܠܡ ܙܒܢܐ ܕܗܠܘܟܗ. ܐܬܦܪܫ ܠܘܬ ܐܒܘܗܝ. ܘܝܬܒ ܥܡܗ ܒܫܘܒܚܐ.

The word ܐܬܦܪܫ *may have been chosen here by the translator because it stood in the corresponding passage of the Diatessaron, where however it seems rather to represent* [Mk] xvi 19. *In* [Mk] xvi 19 *C has* ܐܬܥܠܝ, *and* syr.vg *in the Gospels and in* Acts i 9 *has* ܣܠܩ *or* ܐܣܬܠܩ.

NOTE

The Subscription after S. Luke comes at the end of a leaf; the leaf that followed, containing Joh i 1—25, *is missing. In C the Gospel of S. Luke stands last, S. John's Gospel beginning on the next column to that which contains the end of S. Mark.*

49 these things. And I myself will send upon you the promise of my *S*
Father; wait ye in the city, until ye be clothed with power from on
50 high." And he brought them out unto Beth Ania, and he lifted up
51 his hands and blessed them. And when he blessed them he was
52 lifted up from them. And they returned to Jerusalem with great joy,
53 and were blessing at all times in the Temple God.

[*Subscription in S*]

HERE ENDETH THE EVANGEL OF LUKE.

EVANGEL OF JOHN.

---

51. *Cf Addai* 6: 'And when he fulfilled the will of his Begetter, he was lifted up unto his Father, and sat down with him in glory.'

The combination of Lk xxiv 51 *with* [Mk] xvi 19 *is found also in* Diat[ar] lv 13.

NOTE

The Subscription after S. Luke comes at the end of a leaf; the leaf that followed, containing Joh i 1—25, *is missing. In C the Gospel of S. Luke stands last, S. John's Gospel beginning on the next column to that which contains the end of S. Mark.*

C
fol 39 r
col 2

*ܢܘܢ· ܐܘܢܓܠܝܘܢ. ܕܝܘܚܢܢ ܢܘܢ··

§¶A13 §1ܒܪܫܝܬ ܐܝܬܘܗܝ ܗܘܐ ܡܠܬܐ.¶ ܘܗܘ ܡܠܬܐ ܐܝܬܘܗܝ ܗܘܐ
ܠܘܬ ܐܠܗܐ. ܘܐܠܗܐ ܐܝܬܘܗܝ ܗܘܐ ܗܘ ܡܠܬܐ. 2ܗܢܐ
ܐܝܬܘܗܝ ܗܘܐ ܒܪܫܝܬ ܠܘܬ ܐܠܗܐ. 3ܟܠܡܕܡ ܒܗ ܗܘܐ.
ܘܠܒܪܘܗܝ ܐܦ ܠܐ ܚܕܐ ܗܘܬ. ܗܘ ܕܝܢ ܡܕܡ ܕܗܘܐ 4ܒܗ
ܚܝܐ ܐܝܬܝܢ ܘܚܝܐ ܐܝܬܝܗܘܢ ܢܘܗܪܐ ܕܒܢܝ ܐܢܫܐ. 5ܘܗܘ
§§A13, 330 ¶A330 §§ܢܘܗܪܐ ܒܚܫܘܟܐ ܡܢܗܪ ܗܘܐ.¶ ܘܚܫܘܟܐ ܠܐ ܐܕܪܟܗ.¶ ·o·
¶A13 6ܗܘܐ ܒܪܢܫܐ ܕܐܫܬܕܪ ܡܢ ܐܠܗܐ. ܫܡܗ ܗܘܐ ܝܘܚܢܢ. 7ܗܢܐ
fol 39 v ܐܬܐ ܠܣܗܕܘܬܐ ܕܢܣܗܕ ܥܠ ܢܘܗܪܐ. *ܕܟܠ ܐܢܫ ܢܗܝܡܢ
ܒܐܝܕܗ. 8ܠܐ ܗܘܐ ܗܘ ܢܘܗܪܐ. ܐܠܐ ܣܗܕܐ ܗܘ ܕܢܘܗܪܐ.
9ܐܝܬܘܗܝ ܕܝܢ ܢܘܗܪܐ ܕܫܪܪܐ. ܕܡܢܗܪ ܠܟܠ ܒܪ ܐܢܫ ܕܐܬܐ
ܠܥܠܡܐ. 10ܒܥܠܡܐ ܗܘܐ. ܘܗܘ ܥܠܡܐ ܒܗ ܗܘܐ. ܘܥܠܡܐ
§¶A13 ܠܐ ܝܕܥܗ. 11§ܠܕܝܠܗ ܐܬܐ ܘܕܝܠܗ ܠܐ ܩܒܠܘܗܝ.¶ 12ܐܝܠܝܢ ܕܝܢ
ܕܩܒܠܘܗܝ، ܝܗܒ ܠܗܘܢ ܫܘܠܛܢܐ ܕܒܢܝܐ ܕܐܠܗܐ ܢܗܘܘܢ
ܐܝܠܝܢ ܕܒܫܡܗ ܡܗܝܡܢܝܢ. 13ܐܝܠܝܢ ܕܠܐ ܒܕܡܐ ܘܠܐ ܡܢ ܨܒܝܢܐ
ܕܒܣܪܐ. ܘܠܐ ܡܢ ܨܒܝܢܐ ܕܒܪ ܐܢܫܐ. ܐܠܐ ܡܢ ܐܠܗܐ
§¶A120, 167 ܐܬܝܠܕܘ.† 14§ܘܡܠܬܐ ܦܓܪܐ ܗܘܬ ܘܐܓܢܬ ܒܢ.¶ ܘܚܙܝܢ ܫܘܒܚܗ
col 2 ܐܝܟ *ܫܘܒܚܐ ܕܝܚܝܕܝܐ ܕܡܢ ܐܒܐ. ܟܕ ܡܠܐ ܛܝܒܘܬܐ
ܘܩܘܫܬܐ.

---

1 A13 ܘܐܦ ܡܠܬܗ ܘܡܐܡܪܗ ܕܒܪܐ ܡܫܝܚܐ ܗܘ. ܐܝܟ ܕܟܬܝܒ ܒܪܫ 1
ܣܦܪܗ ܕܝܘܚܢܢ: ܕܒܪܫܝܬ ܐܝܬܘܗܝ ܗܘܐ ܡܠܬܐ.
A167 ܐܝܟ ܕܟܬܝܒ. ܕܒܪܫܝܬ ܥܠܝܐ ܗܘܐ ܕܗܘ ܡܠܬܐ.

2. *Cf* A12 ܡܢ ܪܫܝܬܐ ܠܘܬ ܐܒܘܗܝ ܐܝܬܘܗܝ ܗܘܐ

13 ܐܬܝܠܕܘ] ܐܬܝܠܕ *C*: *the same error is found in some* MSS *of* syr.vg

14 ܘܐܓܢܬ ܒܢ] *cf* Ac v 15 ܐܦ ܛܠܠܗ ܬܓܢ ܥܠܝܗܘܢ

i 1 §In the beginning He was the Word ;¶ and He, the Word, was §¶*A* 13
2 with God; and He, the Word, was God. This *same* was in the
3 beginning with God. Everything came to pass in Him, and apart
from Him not even one thing came to pass. Now life is that which
4, 5 came to pass in Him, and life is the light of men; and He, §§the §§*A* 13, 330
light, in the darkness was shining,¶ and the darkness apprehended ¶*A* 330
it not.¶ ¶*A* 13
6 There was a man that was sent from God—his name was John.
7 This *same* came for witness, that he might bear witness of the light,
8 and that every one might believe through him; he was not the light,
9 but a witness of the light. Now He is the light of truth, that shineth
10 for every man that hath come into the world. In the world He was,
11 and the world itself was in Him, and the world knew Him not. §To §*A* 13
12 His own He came and His own received Him not;¶ but those that ¶*A*
received Him, He gave them authority that they should become sons
13 of God, those that in His name believe, those that not in blood and
not from the will of the body and not from the will of man but from
14 God are born. §And the Word became a body and it sojourned §¶*A* 120, 167
among us,¶ and we saw His glory as the glory of an only *one* from
the Father full of grace and truth.

---

1 'And also the Messiah is the Word and Speech of the LORD, as it is written in the beginning of the gospel of our Life-giver "In the beginning He was the Word"' *A* 13; 'As it is written "In the beginning was a Voice Which is the Word"' *A* 167 2. *Cf* 'From the beginning with His Father He was' *A* 12; 'from' *also appears in* E^{5} 3, 4. *Or*, 'Now that which came to pass, in it is life'; *cf* 'And what came to pass, by him (*or*, 'by it') was life' E^{5} 9 hath come] *or*, 'cometh' 14 sojourned among us] *or*, 'cast its influence in us': *cf* Ac v 15, *where the same word is used of S. Peter's shadow*

[15]ܘܝܘܚܢܢ ܐܣܗܕ ܥܠܘܗܝ، ܘܩܥܐ ܘܐܡܪ. ܗܢܐ ܗܘ ܕܐܡܪܬ C [S]
ܗܘܝܬ ܕܒܬܪ، ܐܬܐ ܘܗܘܐ ܠܗ ܩܕܡܝ. ܡܛܠ ܕܩܕܡܝ ܗܘ ܡܢܝ.
[16]ܘܡܢ ܡܠܝܘܬܗ ܐܚܢܢ ܟܠܢ ܢܣܒܢ ܐܚܝܢ. ܘܛܝܒܘܬܐ ܚܠܦ
ܛܝܒܘܬܐ. [17]ܕܢܡܘܣܐ ܒܝܕ ܡܘܫܐ ܐܬܝܗܒ· ܘܛܝܒܘܬܐ ܘܫܪܪܐ cf A 28
ܒܝܕ ܝܫܘܥ ܡܫܝܚܐ ܗܘܐ. [18]ܠܐܠܗܐ ܡܢ ܡܬܘܡ ܐܢܫ ܠܐ
ܚܙܝܗ، ܝܚܝܕܝܐ ܒܪܐ ܕܗܘ ܒܥܘܒܗ ܕܐܒܘܗܝ، ܗܘ ܐܫܬܥܝ ܠܢ. cf A 115
[19]ܘܗܕܐ ܗܝ، ܣܗܕܘܬܗ ܕܝܘܚܢܢ. ܟܕ ܫܕܪܘ ܠܘܬܗ ܡܢ ܐܘܪܫܠܡ.
*ܟܗ̈ܢܐ ܘܠܘ̈ܝ ܒܫܘܐܠܐ ܘܠܘ̈ܝܐ. ܘܫܐܠܝܢ ܠܗ ܐܢܬ ܡܢ ܐܢܬ· fol 40 r
[20]ܘܐܘܕܝ، ܘܐܡܪ ܕܐܢܐ ܠܐ ܗܘܝܬ ܡܫܝܚܐ. [21]ܘܐܡܪܝܢ ܠܗ ܘܠܡܢܐ
ܢܒܝܐ ܐܢܬ. ܐܡܪ ܠܗܘܢ ܠܐ. [22]ܐܡܪܝܢ ܠܗ ܘܡܢ ܐܢܬ. ܐܡܪ
ܠܢ ܕܢܬܠ ܦܬܓܡܐ ܠܗܢܘܢ ܕܫܕܪܘܢ: ܡܢܐ ܐܡܪ ܐܢܬ ܥܠ
ܢܦܫܟ· [23]ܐܡܪ ܐܢܐ ܩܠܐ ܕܩܪܐ ܒܡܕܒܪܐ. ܬܩܢܘ ܐܘܪܚܐ
ܠܡܪܝܐ. ܐܝܟܢܐ ܕܐܡܪ ܐܫܥܝܐ ܢܒܝܐ. [24]ܘܡܫܕܪܝܢ ܗܘܘ [25]ܘܐܡܪܝܢ
ܠܗ. ܡܢܐ [§]ܗܟܝܠ ܡܥܡܕ ܐܢܬ ܐܠܐ ܗܘܝܬ ܐܢܬ ܡܫܝܚܐ. §S
ܐܦܠܐ ܐܠܝܐ. ܐܦܠܐ ܢܒܝܐ. [26]ܐܡܪ ܠܗܘܢ ܝܘܚܢܢ. ܐܢܐ
*ܡܥܡܕ ܐܢܐ ܒܡ̈ܝܐ. ܒܝܢܬܟܘܢ ܕܝܢ ܩܐܡ ܗܘ ܐܢܫܐ ܕܐܢܬܘܢ col 2
ܠܐ ܝܕܥܝܢ ܐܢܬܘܢ ܠܗ· [27]ܗܘ ܕܐܬܐ ܒܬܪ، ܗܘ ܕܠܐ ܫܘܐ
ܐܢܐ ܕܐܫܪܐ ܥܪ̈ܩܐ ܕܡܣܢܘܗܝ، [28]ܗܠܝܢ ܡܛܠ ܒܝܬ ܥܢ̈ܝܐ.
ܒܥܒ̈ܪܘܗܝ، ܕܝܘܪܕܢ ܢܗܪܐ. ܐܝܟܐ ܕܡܥܡܕ ܗܘܐ ܝܘܚܢܢ.
[29]ܘܠܝܘܡܐ ܐܚܪܢܐ ܚܙܐ ܠܝܫܘܥ ܟܕ ܐܬܐ ܠܘܬܗ. ܘܐܡܪ ܗܐ
ܐܡܪܗ ܕܐܠܗܐ. ܗܐ ܡܢ ܕܫܩܠ ܚܛܝܬܗ ܕܥܠܡܐ. [30]ܗܢܘ ܕܐܡܪܬ
ܥܠܘܗܝ، ܕܒܬܪܝ ܐܬܐ ܓܒܪ، ܘܗܘܐ ܠܗ ܩܕܡܝ. ܡܛܠ ܕܩܕܡܝ
ܗܘ ܡܢܝ. [31]ܘܐܢܐ ܠܐ ܝܕܥ ܗܘܝܬ ܠܗ. ܐܠܐ ܡܛܠ ܕܢܬܝܕܥ
ܠܐܝܣܪܝܠ· *ܡܛܠ ܗܢܐ ܐܬܝܬ ܐܢܐ ܕܒܡ̈ܝܐ ܐܥܡܕ. [32]ܘܐܣܗܕ fol 40 v

---

17 A 28 ܬܘܒ ܒܬܪܟ. ܕܫܪܪܗ ܕܢܡܘܣܐ ܒܝܕ ܝܫܘܥ ܗܘ̣ܐ.
18 Cf A 115 ܒܠܚܘܕ ܝܚܝܕܝܐ ܡܚܘܝܐ ܠܗܘܢ ܝܚܝܕܝܐ ܕܐܝܬ ܒܥܘܒܐ ܕܐܒܘܗܝ
25 ܐܢܬ 2°] om. S   ܐܦܠܐ 2°] ܘܐܦ ܠܐ S   28 ܢܗܪܐ] om. S   ܐܝܟܐ S
29 ܠܝܫܘܥ ܕܐܬܐ S^ed   ܗܐ ܡܢ] so also S   30 ܕܐܡܪܬ] ܗܘܝܬ ܕܐܡܪܬ S
(so I read the photograph)   31 ܡܛܠ ܗܢܐ] om. S

15 And John bare witness of him, and cried out and said: "This is C [S]
he that I had said that after me he cometh and *yet* he was before me,
16 because he is first *compared* with me." And from his fulness we all
17 receive, and grace for grace; in that the law through Moses was
given, and grace and truth through Jesus the Messiah came to pass. *cf* A 28
18 God—never hath any one seen Him; an only *one*, a Son from the *cf* A 115
19 bosom of his Father, he hath declared ***Him*** to us. And this is the
witness of John when they sent unto him from Jerusalem Jews
and chief priests and Levites, and they ask him: "Who art thou?"
20, 21 And he confessed and said "I am not the Messiah." And they
say to him: "And art thou not the prophet?" He saith to them:
22 "No." They say to him: "And who art thou? Tell us, that we
may give an answer to those that sent us. What sayest thou of
23 thyself?" He saith: "I *am* the voice that calleth in the wilderness,
24 'Prepare a way for the LORD,' as said Isaiah the prophet." And they
25 were sending and saying to him: "Why §therefore dost thou baptize, §S
26 if thou art not the Messiah, nor Elijah, nor the prophet?" John
saith to them: "I baptize with water, but among you standeth that
27 one which ye know not, he that cometh after me, the thongs of whose
28 shoes I am not worthy to unloose." These things he spake in Beth
Abrê on the other side of the river Jordan, where John was baptizing.
29 And the next day he saw Jesus coming unto him, and he said:
"Lo, the Lamb of God! Lo, he that taketh away the sin of the
30 world! This is he of whom I said that a man cometh after me and *yet*
31 he was before me, because he is first *compared* with me. And I
myself did not know him; but because he should be known to Israel,
therefore have I myself come that with water I should baptize."

---

17 'Again it is written The truth of the law was through Jesus' *A* 28; *cf* 'Through Moses *is* the law...but the truth of it *is* through Jesus our Lord' E^{36} 18 *Cf* 'All the solitaries—the Only one from the bosom of his Father maketh them glad' *A* 115; 'but the Only one, which *is* in the bosom of the Father... E^{3}: *immediately below E has* 'He was begotten from the bosom of his Father' 19 *Or*, 'when the Jews and....the Levites sent unto him from Jerusalem' 21 *init.*] E^{37} *has* 'They say unto him, Art thou Elijah? He saith, No.' 28 river] *om. S* 29 Lo, he that taketh] *so also S*; that cometh to take $E^{41, (43, 101)}$ 30 I said] I had said S^{vid} 31 therefore] *om. S*

(C) S ܝܘܚܢܢ ܘܐܡܪ. ܚܙܝܬ ܠܪܘܚܐ ܕܐܝܟ ܝܘܢܐ ܢܚܬܬ ܡܢ ܫܡܝܐ
ܘܩܘܬ ܥܠܘܗܝ. [33]ܘܐܢܐ ܠܐ ܝܕܥ ܗܘܝܬ ܠܗ. ܐܠܐ ܡܢ ܕܫܕܪܢܝ
ܠܡܥܡܕܘ ܒܡ̈ܝܐ. ܗܘ ܐܡܪ ܠܝ. ܕܐܝܢܐ ܕܚܙܐ ܐܢܬ ܕܢܚܬܐ
ܪܘܚܐ ܘܩܘܝܐ ܥܠܘܗܝ. ܗܘ ܗܘ ܡܥܡܕ ܒܪܘܚܐ ܕܩܘܕܫܐ.
[34]ܘܐܢܐ ܚܙܝܬ ܘܐܣܗܕܬ ܕܗܢܘ ܓܒܝܗ ܕܐܠܗܐ.
[35]ܘܠܝܘܡܐ ܚܪܢܐ ܩܐܡ ܗܘܐ †ܝܘܚܢܢ†. ܘܬܪ̈ܝܢ ܡܢ ܬܠܡ̈ܝܕܘܗܝ
ܠܘܬܗ. [36]ܘܚܪ ܒܝܫܘܥ ܟܕ ܡܗܠܟ. ܘܐܡܪ ܗܐ ܡܫܝܚܐ. ܗܐ
ܐܡܪܗ ܕܐܠܗܐ. [37]ܘܟܕ ܫܡܥܘ ܗܢܘܢ ܬܠܡ̈ܝܕܘܗܝ ܕܝܘܚܢܢ.
col 2 *ܐܙܠܘ ܠܗܘܢ ܒܬܪܗ ܕܝܫܘܥ· [38]ܘܐܬܦܢܝ ܗܘ ܝܫܘܥ ܘܚܙܐ
ܐܢܘܢ ܕܐܬܝܢ ܒܬܪܗ. ܐܡܪ ܠܗܘܢ ܡܢܐ ܒܥܝܢ ܐܢܬܘܢ·
ܐܡܪܝܢ ܠܗ ܪܒܢ ܐܝܟܐ ܗܘܐ ܐܢܬ· [39]ܐܡܪ ܠܗܘܢ ܬܘ ܘܬܚܙܘܢ·
ܘܗܢܘܢ ܐܬܘ ܒܬܪܗ ܘܚܙܘ ܐܝܟܐ ܕܗܘܐ. ܘܠܘܬܗ ܗܘܘ
ܝܘܡܐ ܗܘ. ܘܐܝܬ ܗܘܝ ܐܝܟ ܫܥ̈ܐ ܥܣܪ· [40]ܘܚܕ ܡܢܗܘܢ ܡܢ
ܗܠܝܢ ܬܠܡ̈ܝܕܘܗܝ ܕܝܘܚܢܢ· ܐܢܕܪܐܘܣ ܫܡܗ ܗܘܐ. ܐܚܘܗܝ
ܕܫܡܥܘܢ ܟܐܦܐ. [41]ܘܗܘ ܐܢܕܪܐܘܣ ܚܙܐ ܠܫܡܥܘܢ ܟܐܦܐ.
ܘܐܡܪ ܠܗ ܐܫܟܚܢܝܗܝ ܠܡܫܝܚܐ. [42]ܘܕܒܪܗ ܘܐܬܐ ܠܘܬ ܝܫܘܥ·
¶C ܘܚܪ ܒܗ ܝܫܘܥ ܘܐܡܪ¶ ܠܗ ܐܢܬ ܫܡܥܘܢ ܒܪܗ ܕܝܘܢܐ
ܬܗܘܐ ܡܬܩܪܐ ܟܐܦܐ ܕܡܬܬܪܓܡ ܝܘܢܐܝܬ ܦܛܪܘܣ ܀
[43]ܘܠܝܘܡܐ ܐܚܪܢܐ ܨܒܐ ܠܡܦܩ ܠܗ ܠܓܠܝܠܐ ܘܐܫܟܚ ܠܦܝܠܝܦܘܣ
ܘܐܡܪ ܠܗ ܡܪܢ ܬܐ ܒܬܪܝ. [44]ܗܘ ܕܝܢ ܦܝܠܝܦܘܣ ܐܝܬܘܗܝ ܡܢ
ܒܝܬ ܨܝܕܐ ܗܘܐ ܡܢ ܡܕܝܢܬܗ ܕܐܢܕܪܐܘܣ ܘܕܫܡܥܘܢ. [45]ܘܦܝܠܝܦܘܣ
ܐܫܟܚ ܠܢܬܢܐܝܠ ܘܐܡܪ ܠܗ ܦܝܠܝܦܘܣ ܠܢܬܢܐܝܠ ܗܘ ܕܟܬܒ

32 ܕܢܚܬܬ S   ܕܐܝܟ ܝܘܢܐ] S illegible   33 ܒܡ̈ܝܐ] om. S   35 ܐܚܪܢܐ S   ܝܘܚܢܢ] S; ܫܡܥܘܢ C   36 ܒܝܫܘܥ] ܒܡܪܢ S   ܡܫܝܚܐ. ܗܐ] ܐ⌜ܡܪ⌝ܐ ܚܝܐ S^ed: photograph illegible   37 ܫܡܥܘܗܝ S   ܬܠܡ̈ܝܕܐ S   ܕܝܘܚܢܢ] ܠܝܘܚܢܢ ܟܕ ܡܡܠܠ S   ܕܝܫܘܥ] om. S   38 ܗܘ ܝܫܘܥ....ܒܬܪܗ] ܡܪܢ S (om. rell.)   ܘܐܡܪ S   ܐܝܠܟܐ S   39 ܐܬܠܟܐ S   ܥܡܟܐ ܒܛܘܪܐ S (cf Mk ix 2)   40 ܡܢܗܘܢ] om. S   ܗܠܝܢ] ܗܢܘܢ S   ܟܐܦܐ] om. S   41 ܟܐܦܐ] ܐܚܘܗܝ ܗܘ ܡܬܩܪܐ. S   ܠܗ] + ܐܚܝ S   42 ܝܫܘܥ] ܡܪܢ S (in each place)

32 And John bare witness and said: "I saw the Spirit that as a dove (C) S
33 descended from heaven and remained upon him. And I, I knew
him not; but he that sent me to baptize with water, he said to me
'That one which thou seest that the Spirit cometh down and re-
34 maineth upon him, it is he baptizeth with the Holy Spirit.' And I
myself saw and have borne witness that this is the Chosen of God."
35 And the next day †John† was standing, and two of his disciples
36 by him. And he looked on Jesus while walking, and said: "Lo,
37 the Messiah! Lo, the Lamb of God!" And when those disciples of
38 John heard, they went away after him, *even* Jesus. And Jesus
himself turned round, and saw them coming after him *and* saith to
them: "What seek ye?" They say to him: "Rabban, where art
39 thou *staying*?" He saith to them: "Come and ye shall see." And
they came after him and saw where he was *staying*, and were with
40 him that day. And it was about the tenth hour. And one of these
same disciples of John, Andrew was his name, the brother of Simon
41 Kepha. And he, Andrew, saw Simon Kepha and saith to him:
42 "We have found the Messiah." And he took him and came unto
Jesus. And Jesus looked on him and said¶ | to him: "Thou Simon ¶C
son of Jona, thou shalt be called Kepha"; which is interpreted in
Greek 'Petros.'
43 And the next day he wished to go forth to Galilee and he found
44 Philip. And our Lord said to him: "Come after me." Now Philip,
his kin was from Beth Saida, from the city of Andrew and of Simon.
45 And Philip found Nathaniel, and Philip said to him, to Nathaniel:

---

32 as a dove] *S illegible* 33 with water] *om. S* 35 John] *S*; Jesus *C* 36 Jesus] our Lord *S* the Messiah! Lo] *S illegible* 37 And when those disciples heard John speaking *S* *even* Jesus] *om. S* 38 And Jesus...after him *and* saith] And our Lord turned round and saith *S* 40 these same] those *S* Kepha] *om. S* 41 Kepha] his brother on that day *S* to him] + My brother *S* 42 Jesus] our Lord *S* (*in each place*)

ܥܠܘܗܝ ܡܘܫܐ ܘܢܒܝܐ. ܐܫܟܚܢܝܗܝ ܕܝܫܘܥ ܗܘ ܒܪܗ ܕܝܘܣܦ S
ܕܡܢ ܢܨܪܬ. [46]ܐܡܪ ܠܗ ܢܬܢܐܝܠ ܡܢ ܢܨܪܬ ܡܫܟܚ ܡܕܡ ܕܛܒ
ܠܡܗܘܐ ܐܡܪ ܠܗ ܦܝܠܝܦܘܣ ܬܐ ܘܬܚܙܐ [47]ܘܚܙܝܗܝ، * * *

[*The leaf of S which contained* Joh i 47—ii 15 *is missing.*]

For ver. 51 *see note.*

[16]ܘܐܡܪ ܗܘܐ ܠܗܢܘܢ ܕܡܙܒܢܝܢ ܝܘܢܐ ܫܩܘܠܘ ܗܠܝܢ ܡܢ ܗܪܟܐ
ܘܠܐ ܬܥܒܕܘܢܝܗܝ ܠܒܝܬܗ ܕܐܒܝ ܒܝܬ ܬܐܓܘܪܬܐ [17]ܟܕ ܗܠܝܢ ܥܒܕ
ܐܬܕܟܪܘ ܬܠܡܝܕܘܗܝ ܕܟܬܝܒ ܕܛܢܢܐ ܕܒܝܬܟ ܐܟܠܢܝ [18]ܐܡܪܝܢ
ܠܗ ܝܗܘܕܝܐ ܡܢܐ ⸢ܗܝ،⸣ ܐܬܐ ܗܕܐ ⸢ܕ⸣ܡܚܘܐ ܐܢܬ ܠܢ ܕܗܠܝܢ
ܥܒܕ ܐܢܬ [19]ܥܢܐ ܡܪܢ ܘܐܡܪ ܠܗܘܢ ܣܬܘܪܘ ܗܝܟܠܐ ܘܠܬܠܬܐ
ܝܘܡܝܢ ܐܩܝܡ ܠܗ [20]ܐܡܪܝܢ ܠܗ ܠܐܪܒܥܝܢ ܘܫܬ ܫܢܝܢ ܐܬܒܢܝ
ܗܝܟܠܐ ܗܢܐ ܘܐܢܬ ܠܬܠܬܐ ܝܘܡܝܢ ܒܢܐ ܐܢܬ ܠܗ [21]ܗܘ ܕܝܢ
ܥܠ ܗܝܟܠܐ ܕܦܓܪܗ ܐܡܪ ܗܘܐ. [22]ܟܕ ܩܡ ܕܝܢ ܡܢ ܒܝܬ ܡܝܬܐ
ܐܬܕܟܪܘ ܬܠܡܝܕܘܗܝ، ܕܗܠܝܢ ܐܡܪ ܗܘܐ ܘܗܝܡܢܘ ܠܟܬܒܐ
ܘܠܡܠܬܐ ܕܐܡܪ ܡܪܢ ܀

[23]ܘܟܕ ܗܘܐ ܒܐܘܪܫܠܡ ܒܥܐܕܐ ܕܦܨܚܐ ܕܦܛܝܪܐ ܘܗܝܡܢܘ
ܠܡܪܢ ܣܓܝܐܐ ܡܛܠ ܕܚܙܝܢ ܗܘܘ ܐܬܘܬܐ ܕܥܒܕ ܠܗܘܢ [24]ܗܘ
ܕܝܢ ܡܪܢ ܠܐ ܡܗܝܡܢ ܗܘܐ ܠܗܘܢ ܢܦܫܗ [25]ܘܠܐ ܡܬܒܥܐ
ܗܘܐ ܕܐܢܫ ܢܣܗܕ ܥܠ ܒܪܗ ܕܐܢܫܐ ܗܘ ܓܝܪ ܝܕܥ ܠܒܐ
ܕܒܪ ܐܢܫܐ ܡܢܐ ܐܝܬ [1]ܘܐܝܬ ܗܘܐ ܕܝܢ ܬܡܢ ܓܒܪܐ ܡܢ
ܦܪܝܫܐ ܫܡܗ ܗܘܐ ܢܝܩܕܡܘܣ· ܘܗܘ ܗܘܐ ܓܒܪܐ ܐܪܟܘܢܐ ܗܘܐ
ܕܝܗܘܕܝܐ [2]ܐܬܐ ܠܘܬ ܡܪܢ ܒܠܠܝܐ ܘܐܡܪ ܠܗ ܪܒܝ ܝܕܥܝܢ
ܐܢܚܢ ܕܡܢ ܐܠܗܐ ܐܫܬܕܪܬ ܠܟ ܡܠܦܢܐ ܡܛܠ ܕܠܐ ܐܢܫ ܡܫܟܚ
ܗܠܝܢ ܢܣܐ ܠܡܥܒܕ ܐܠܐ ܡܢ ܕܐܠܗܐ ܥܡܗ [3]ܐܡܪ ܠܗ ܡܪܢ
ܐܡܝܢ ܐܡܪܢܐ ܠܟ ܕܐܢ ܐܢܫ ܠܐ ܡܬܝܠܕ ܡܢ ܕܪܫ ܠܐ
ܡܫܟܚ ܕܢܚܙܐ ܡܠܟܘܬܗ ܕܐܠܗܐ [4]ܐܡܪ ܠܗ ܢܝܩܕܡܘܣ ܐܝܟܢܐ
ܡܫܟܚ ܕܢܬܝܠܕ ܓܒܪܐ ܣܒܐ ܕܠܡܐ ܡܫܟܚ ܬܘܒ ܠܟܪܣܗ ܕܐܡܗ

---

51 *A* 385 ܬܚܙܘܢ ܫܡܝܐ ܟܕ ܦܬܝܚܝܢ. ܘܡܠܐܟܘܗܝ ܕܐܠܗܐ ܟܕ ܢܚܬܝܢ ܘܣܠܩܝܢ
ܠܘܬ ܒܪܗ ܕܐܢܫܐ. (*A*[a] ܣܠܩܝܢ ܘܢܚܬܝܢ)

1 ܗܘܐ] *S* (*sic*) ܢܝܩܕܡܘܣ

"He that Moses and the prophets wrote of—we have found him, that S
46 he is Jesus the son of Joseph from Nazareth." Nathaniel saith to
him: "From Nazareth can aught of good come forth?" Philip saith
47 to him: "Come and thou shalt see." And [our Lord] saw him * *

[*The leaf of S which contained* Joh i 47—ii 15 *is missing.*]
For ver. 51 *see note.*

ii 16 and he was saying to those selling doves: "Take away these
things from hence, and do not make the House of my Father a
17 house of merchandise." When he did these things his disciples
remembered that it is written "The zeal of thine house hath eaten
18 me up." The Jews say to him: "What [is] this sign [that] thou
19 shewest us, that thou doest these things?" Our Lord answered and
said to them: "Pull down the Temple and in three days I will raise
20 it up." They say to him: "In forty and six years was this Temple
21 built, and dost thou in three days build it?" Now he of the Temple
22 of his body was saying *this*, but when he arose from among the dead
his disciples remembered that these things he had said, and they
believed the Scriptures and the word that our Lord said.

23 And when he was in Jerusalem in the days of the Feast of
unleavened bread, many believed our Lord because they were seeing
24 the signs that he did to them, but our Lord was not trusting himself
25 to them, and it was not required that any one should bear witness of
iii 1 any one's deed, for he knew the heart in man, what it is. Now there
was there a man of the Pharisees, his name was Nicodemus, and
2 this same man was a ruler of the Jews. He came unto our Lord by
night and said to him: "Rabbi, we know that from God thou hast
been sent to us *as* a teacher, because no one can do these miracles
3 save he that God is with." Our Lord saith to him: "Amen, amen,
I say to thee If one be not born anew, one cannot see the kingdom
4 of God." Nicodemus saith to him: "How can an aged man be born?
Can he really again enter the womb of his mother and anew be

---

47 'Lo, indeed a scribe, an Israelite, in whom is no guile' E^{50}
51 'Ye shall see the heavens opened, and the angels of God descending and ascending by the Son of Man' A 385 ('ascending and descending' A^{a})
20 build it] raise it up E^{182}: *cf* Matt v 14 **23** many] *lit.* 'and many': *cf* Lk xiii 10, 11

ܠܟܠ ܘܡܕܪܫ ܠܡܬܠܡܕܘ [5]ܐܡܪ ܠܗ ܡܪܢ ܐܡܝܢ ܐܡܝܢ [C] S
ܐܡܪܢܐ ܠܟ ܕܐܢ ܐܢܫ ܠܐ ܡܬܝܠܕ ܡܢ ܪܘܚܐ ܘܡܝܐ. ܠܐ
ܡܨܐ ܠܡܥܠ | §*ܠܡܠܟܘܬܐ ܕܐܠܗܐ. [6]ܡܕܡ ܕܝܠܝܕ ܡܢ ܒܣܪܐ §C fol 41 r
ܒܣܪܐ ܗܘ. ܡܛܠ ܕܗܢ ܒܣܪܐ ܝܠܕ. ܘܡܕܡ ܕܝܠܝܕ ܡܢ ܪܘܚܐ
ܪܘܚܐ ܗܘ. ܡܛܠ ܕܐܠܗܐ ܪܘܚܐ ܗܘ. ܘܗܢ ܐܠܗܐ ܐܬܝܠܕ.
[7]ܘܠܐ ܬܬܕܡܪ ܕܐܡܪܬ ܠܟ. ܕܘܠܐ ܗܘ ܠܟܘܢ ܠܡܬܝܠܕܘ
ܡܢ ܠܥܠ· [8]ܪܘܚܐ ܐܬܪ ܕܨܒܝܐ ܢܫܒܐ. ܘܩܠܗ ܗܘ ܒܠܚܘܕ
ܫܡܥ ܐܢܬ. ܐܠܐ ܠܐ ܡܢ ܐܝܡܟܐ ܐܬܬ ܝܕܥ ܐܢܬ· ܘܠܐ
ܠܐܝܟܐ ܐܙܠܐ. ܗܟܢܐ ܐܝܬܘܗܝ، ܟܠ ܐܢܫ ܕܡܬܝܠܕ ܡܢ ܪ̈ܘܚܐ
ܘܡܢ ܪܘܚܐ. [9]ܥܢܐ ܢܝܩܕܡܘܣ ܘܐܡܪ ܠܗ. ܐܝܟܢܐ ܡܫܟܚܐ ܗܕܐ
ܠܡܗܘܐ. [10]ܥܢܐ ܝܫܘܥ ܘܐܡܪ *ܠܗ. ܐܢܬ ܗܘ ܡܠܦܢܗ ܕܐܝܣܪܝܠ col 2
ܘܗܠܝܢ ܠܐ ܝܕܥ ܐܢܬ. [11]ܐܡܝܢ ܐܡܝܢ ܐܡܪܢܐ ܠܟ. ܕܡܕܡ
ܕܝܕܥܝܢ ܐܢܚܢ ܡܡܠܠܝܢ ܐܢܚܢ· ܘܡܕܡ ܕܚܙܝܢ ܐܢܚܢ ܡܣܗܕܝܢ
ܐܢܚܢ. ܘܣܗܕܘܬܢ ܠܐ ܡܩܒܠܝܢ ܐܢܬܘܢ. §[12]ܐܢ ܥܠ ܐܝܠܝܢ §A 173
ܕܒܐܪܥܐ ܐܝܟ ܐܡܪܬ ܠܟܘܢ ܘܠܐ ܡܗܝܡܢܝܢ ܐܢܬܘܢ: ܐܝܟܢܐ
ܐܢ ܥܠ ܐܝܠܝܢ ܕܒܫܡܝܐ ܐܝܟ ܐܡܪ ܠܟܘܢ ܬܗܝܡܢܘܢ.¶ ¶A
§[13]ܠܐ ܐܢܫ ܣܠܩ ܠܫܡܝܐ ܐܠܐ ܗܘ ܕܢܚܬ ܡܢ ܫܡܝܐ. ܒܪܗ §A 173
ܕܐܢܫܐ ܗܘ ܕܐܝܬܘܗܝ، ܗܘܐ ܒܫܡܝܐ.¶ [14]ܘܐܝܟܢܐ ܕܐܪܝܡ ܡܘܫܐ ¶A
ܚܘܝܐ ܒܡܕܒܪܐ. ܗܟܢܐ ܘܠܐ ܠܡܬܬܪܝܡܘ ܠܒܪܗ ܕܐܢܫܐ.
[15]ܕܟܠ *ܐܢܫ ܕܡܗܝܡܢ ܒܗ ܢܗܘܘܢ ܠܗ ܚ̈ܝܐ ܕܠܥܠܡ. [16]ܗܟܢܐ fol 41 v

---

5 ܠܡܠܟܘܬܗ S   6 ܡܛܠ ܕܗܢ ܒܣܪܐ ܝܠܕ] om. S   ܗܘ ult.] + ܚܝܐ S
ܘܗܢ ܐܠܗܐ ܐܬܝܠܕ] om. S   7 ܠܟ. ܕܘܠܐ ܗܘ] om. S   ܠܡܬܝܠܕܘ]
+ ܠܟܘܢ S   ܡܢ ܠܥܠ] om. S   8 ܗܘ] exp. S^corr   ܒܠܚܘܕ] om. S
ܠܐܝܠܟܐ S   ܐܝܬܘܗܝ....ܕܡܬܝܠܕ] ܐܟܘܬ ܐܝܠܝܢ ܕܝܠܝܕܝܢ S   ܘܡܢ]
om. ܡܢ S   9 ܥܢܐ.....ܠܗ] ܢܝܩܕܡܘܣ ܐܡܪ ܠܗ S (sic)   10 ܥܢܐ....ܠܗ]
ܐܡܪ ܠܗ ܡܪܢ S   ܕܐܝܣܪܐܝܠ S   11 ܐܡܝܢ 2°] om. S   12 ܐܢ 1°]
+ ܟܢ A   ܥܠ....ܐܝܟ ܐܡܪ ܠܟܘܢ A   ܬܗܝܡܢܘܢ A   13 ܠܐ] pr. ܘ S
ܐܠܐ] + ܐܢ A   ܕܐܝܬܘܗܝ ܡܢ ܫܡܝܐ S   14 ܕܐܪܝܡ] + ܗܘܐ S
ܘܠܐ] + ܠܗ S   ܠܒܪܗ] so also S   15 ܐܢܫ] ܡܢ S   ܒܗ] + ܠܐ ܢܐܒܕ ܐܠܐ S

5 born?" Our Lord saith to him: "Amen, amen, I say to thee If one [C] S
is not born from spirit and water one cannot enter | §the kingdom of §C
6 God. That which is born from flesh is flesh, because from flesh it is
born; and that which is born from spirit is spirit, because God is a
7 spirit, and from God it hath been born. And do not wonder that I
8 said to thee that it behoves you to be born from above. The wind—
where it will it bloweth, and its voice it is only thou hearest, but not
from whence it hath come dost thou know, nor whither it goeth;
9 so is every man that is born from water and from spirit." Nicodemus
10 answered and said to him: "How can this be?" Jesus answered and
said to him: "Art thou the teacher of Israel, and these things knowest
11 thou not? Amen, amen, I say to thee that that which we know
we are speaking, and that which we see we bear witness of, and our
12 witness ye receive not. §If of the things which are on earth I have §*A*173
said to you and ye believe not, how if of the things which are in
13 heaven I shall say to you will ye believe me?¶ §No one hath gone ¶*A* §*A*173
up to heaven save he that came down from heaven, the Son of Man
14 that was in heaven.¶ And as Moses lifted up the serpent in the ¶*A*
15 wilderness, so it behoves the Son of Man to be lifted up, that every
16 man that believeth in him should have life eternal. For so God was

---

6 because from flesh it is born] *om.* *S E*[189] because God is a living Spirit *S*; *E*[189] *does not quote this clause* and from God it hath been born] *om.* *S* 7 to thee that it behoves you] to you *S* from above] *om.* *S* 8 wind] *or*, 'spirit' (*and so elsewhere, wherever the sense permits*) only] *om.* *S* so is every man that is] so are they that are *S* from *ult.*] *om.* *S* 9 answered and said] saith *S* 10 Jesus....said] Our Lord saith *S* 11 amen 2°] *om.* *S* 12 If 1°] For if *A* I shall say to you] *before* 'of...heaven' *A* me] *om.* *A* 13 No one] And no one *S* that was in heaven] *C A*; that is from heaven *S*; *the verse is quoted without this clause in E*[168,187,189] (*cf also* Joh vii 29 *S*) 14 Moses had lifted up *S* 15 every man] whosoever *S* should have] *pr.* should not perish but *S*

ܓܝܪ ܐܚܒ ܐܠܗܐ ܠܥܠܡܐ. ܐܝܟܢܐ ܕܠܒܪܗ ܝܚܝܕܐ ܢܬܠ· C S
ܕܟܠ ܐܢܫ ܕܡܗܝܡܢ ܒܗ ܢܗܘܘܢ ܠܗ ܚܝܐ ܕܠܥܠܡ. [17]ܠܐ ܓܝܪ
ܫܕܪ ܐܠܗܐ ܒܪܗ ܠܥܠܡܐ ܕܢܕܘܢܝܘܗܝ ܠܥܠܡܐ. ܐܠܐ ܕܥܠܡܐ
ܒܗ ܢܚܐ. [18]ܡܢ ܕܡܗܝܡܢ ܒܗ ܠܐ ܡܬܕܝܢ. ܘܡܢ ܕܠܐ ܕܝܢ ܡܗܝܡܢ
ܡܚܝܒ ܗܘ. ܕܠܐ ܗܝܡܢ ܒܫܡܗ ܕܒܪܗ ܕܐܠܗܐ ܚܝܐ. [19]ܗܢܐ ܗܘ
ܕܝܢ ܕܝܢܐ ܕܢܘܗܪܐ ܐܬܐ ܠܥܠܡܐ. ܘܥܠܡܐ ܝܬܝܪܐܝܬ ܪܚܡ
ܠܚܫܘܟܐ. ܝܬܝܪ ܡܢ ܕܠܢܘܗܪܐ. ܡܛܠ ܕܒܝܫܝܢ ܗܘܘ ܥܒ̈ܕܘܗܝ.
[20]ܡܢ ܕܣ̈ܢܝܬܐ ܓܝܪ ܥܒܕ ܣܢܐ ܠܢܘܗܪܐ. ܘܠܐ ܐܬܐ* ܠܢܘܗܪܐ. col 2
ܕܠܐ ܬܗܘܐ ܡܟܣܢܘܬܐ ܠܥܒ̈ܕܘܗܝ. [21]ܗܘ ܕܝܢ ܕܥܒܕ ܩܘܫܬܐ.
ܐܬܐ ܠܘܬ ܢܘܗܪܐ. ܕܢܬܝܕܥܘܢ ܥܒ̈ܕܘܗܝ. ܕܒܐܠܗܐ ܥܒܝܕܝܢ ܀
[22]ܒܬܪ ܗܠܝܢ ܢܦܩ ܝܫܘܥ ܘܬܠܡ̈ܝܕܘܗܝ. ܠܐܪܥܐ ܕܝܗܘܕ. ܘܬܡܢ
ܡܬܗܦܟ ܗܘܐ ܥܡܗܘܢ ܘܡܥܡܕ ܗܘܐ. [23]ܐܦ ܝܘܚܢܢ ܡܥܡܕ
ܗܘܐ ܒܥܝܢ ܢܘܢ ܕܥܠ ܓܢܒ ܫܠܝܡ. ܡܛܠ ܕܡ̈ܝܐ ܣ̈ܓܝܐܐ
ܐܝܬ ܗܘܘ ܬܡܢ. ܘܐܬܝܢ ܗܘܘ ܐܢܫܐ ܘܡܥܡܕܝܢ. [24]ܠܐ ܓܝܪ
ܥܕܡܐ ܠܗܫܐ ܢܦܠ ܗܘܐ ܝܘܚܢܢ ܒܝܬ ܐܣ̈ܘܪܐ ·܀· ·܀·
[25]ܗܘܬ ܗܘܬ ܕܝܢ ܒܥܬܐ ܒܝܢܬ ܬܠܡ̈ܝܕܘܗܝ ܕܝܘܚܢܢ. ܥܡ
ܝܗ̈ܘܕܝܐ ܥܠ ܬܕܟܝܬܐ. [26]ܘܐܬܘ ܠܘܬ* ܝܘܚܢܢ ܘܐܡܪܝܢ ܠܗ. ܪܒܢ. fol 42 r

---

16 ܝܚܝܕܗ S   ܢܬܠ] ܝܗܒ S (sic)   ܕܟܠ ܡܢ ܕܡܗܝܡܢ S
ܢܗܘܘܢ...ܕܠܥܠܡ] ܠܐ ܢܐܒܕ ܐܠܐ ܚܝܐ ܕܠ̈ܥܠܡ ܐܝܬ ܠܗ S   17 ܠܒܪܗ S
ܠܥܠܡܐ] om. S   ܕܢܕܘܢܝܘܗܝ S   18 ܕܝܢ] om. S   ܕܡܗܝܡܢ] + ܒܗ S
ܡܚܝܒ ܗܘ] ܕܝܢ S   ܥܠ ܕܠܐ S   ܕܒܪܗ ܕܐܠܗܐ ܚܝܐ] ܕܒܪܐ ܒܚܝܪܐ S (sic)
19 ܗܢܐ ܗܘ ܕܝܢ] ܗܘ S   ܕܐܬܐ ܢܘܗܪܐ S   ܝܬܝܪܐܝܬ] om. S
ܕܠܢܘܗܪܐ S   ܗܘܘ] om. S   20 ܟܠ ܡܢ S   ܠܐ....ܠܥܒ̈ܕܘܗܝ]
ܕܠܐ ܢܬܝܕܥܘܢ ܥܒ̈ܕܘܗܝ S   21 ܗܘ ܕܝܢ] ܘܡܢ S   ܩܘܫܬܐ] ܫܪ̈ܪܬܐ S (sic)
ܐܬܐ] ܡܬܩܪܒ S (sic)   ܠܘܬ ܢܘܗܪܐ] so also S   ܕܢܬܝܕܥܐ ܒܥܒܕܗ S (sic)
ܥܒܝܕܝܢ] ܥܒܝܕ S (sic)   22 ܒܬܪ] pr. ܘܡܢ S   ܢܦܩ ܝܫܘܥ] ܐܬܐ ܠܗ ܡܪܢ S
ܠܐܪܥܐ ܕܝܗܘܕ] ܠܝܗܘܕ S   22, 23 ܡܬܗܦܟ....ܗܘܐ. [23]ܐܦ ܝܘܚܢܢ]
ܥܡܕ ܗܘܐ. ܘܡܥܡܕ ܥܡܗܘܢ. [23]ܘܐܦ ܝܘܚܢܢ S (sic)   ܒܥܝܢ ܢܘܢ] ܒܥܝܢ ܢܘܢ S
ܐܝܬ ܗܘܐ ܬܡܢ ܦܓ̈ܥܐ S
24. ܡܛܠ ܕܠܐ ܢܦܠ ܗܘܐ ܥܕܡܐ ܠܗܫܐ ܒܝܬ ܐܣܝܪܐ ܝܘܚܢܢ S
25 ܒܝܢܬ....ܝܗ̈ܘܕܝܐ] ܠܘܬ ܡܢ ܬܠܡ̈ܝܕܘܗܝ ܕܝܘܚܢܢ ܥܡ ܝܗܘܕܝܐ S

loving to the world as to give his only Son, that every man that *C S*
17 believeth in him should have life eternal. For God sent not his Son
to the world that he should judge the world, but that the world in
18 him should live. He that believeth in him is not judged, but he that
believeth not is guilty, in that he believed not in the name of the
19 only Son of God. Now this is the judgement that the light came to
the world, and the world *all* the more loved the darkness rather
20 than the daylight, because its deeds were evil. For he that doeth
hateful things hateth the light, and cometh not to the light, that
21 there be not reproof for his deeds. But he that doeth verity cometh
unto the daylight, that his deeds may be seen that in God they are
done."

22 After these things Jesus went forth, and his disciples, to the land
23 of Judaea and there was abiding with them and was baptizing. John
also was baptizing in Ain Yôn by the side of Salem, because much
water there was there, and folk were coming to him and being
24 baptized; for not yet had John fallen into prison.

25 Now there had been a dispute among the disciples of John with
26 the Jews about cleansing. And they came unto John, and say to

---

16 to give] to send *S* (*sic*); *om.* E^{258} his Son, his only *one*, *S* that whosoever shall believe *S* should have life eternal] should not perish but have life ⌜eternal⌝ *S* 17 to the world] *om.* *S* 18 but] and *S* believeth not] + in him *S* guilty] judged *S* in that] on *the ground* that *S* the only Son of God] the approved Son *S* (*sic*) 19 Now this] This *S* *all* the more] *om.* *S* the daylight] the light *S* were] are *S* 20 he that] whosoever *S* that.... his deeds] that his deeds be not seen *S* 21 But] And *S* verity] truth *S* (*sic*) cometh.... daylight] draweth near unto the daylight *S* (*sic*) deeds] deed *S* they are done] it is done *S* (*sic*) 22 After] And after *S* Jesus went forth] our Lord went away *S* the land of] *om.* *S* was abiding.... baptizing (*v.* 23)] was dwelling. And there dwelt with them [23]John also; he was baptizing *S*: *see Notes*, vol. ii 23 Ain Nôn *S* (= Diat$^{ar\,(cod\,A)}$ vi 6) 24. Because he, John, had not fallen yet into prison *S* 25 among.... the Jews] of one of the disciples of John with a Jew (*or*, 'the Jews') *S*

ܗܘ ܕܥܡܟ ܗܘܐ ܒܥܒܪܐ ܕܝܘܪܕܢܢ. ܘܐܢܬ ܐܣܗܕܬ ܥܠܘܗܝ. C S
ܗܐ ܐܦ ܗܘ ܡܥܡܕ. ܘܟܠܗܘܢ ܐܢܫܐ ܠܘܬܗ ܐܬܝܢ. 27 ܐܡܪ
ܠܗܘܢ ܝܘܚܢܢ. ܠܐ ܡܫܟܚ ܒܪ ܐܢܫܐ ܠܡܣܒ ܐܦܠܐ ܡܕܡ.
ܐܠܐ ܐܢ ܝܗܝܒ ܠܗ ܡܢ ܫܡܝܐ. 28 ܐܢܬܘܢ ܕܝܢ ܣܗܕܘ ܠܝ
ܕܐܢܐ ܐܡܪܬ ܕܠܐ ܗܘܝܬ ܡܫܝܚܐ. ܐܠܐ ܫܠܝܚܐ ܐܢܐ
ܩܕܡܘܗܝ. 29 ܡܢ ܕܐܝܬ ܠܗ ܓܝܪ ܟܠܬܐ ܗܘܝܘ ܚܬܢܐ. ܘܪܚܡܗ
ܕܚܬܢܐ ܗܘ ܡܢ ܕܩܐܡ ܘܨܝܬ ܠܗ. ܘܚܕܘܬܐ ܪܒܬܐ ܚܕܐ.
ܡܛܠ ܩܠܗ ܕܚܬܢܐ. ܗܕܐ ܗܟܝܠ ܚܕܘܬܝ ܗܐ ܡܬܡܠܝܐ ܗܝ.
30 ܠܗ ܗܘ *ܓܝܪ ܘܠܐ ܠܡܪܒܐ ⌜ܘܠܝ⌝ ܠܡܒܨܪ. 31 ܗܘ ܓܝܪ ⌜ܕܡܢ⌝ ܠܥܠ col 2
ܐܬܐ ܠܥܠ ܡܢ ⌜ܟܠ⌝ ܗܘ. ܘܗܘ ܕܡܢ ⌜ܐܪܥܐ⌝ ܗܘ ܡܢ ܐܪܥܐ
ܗܘ ⌜ܘܡܢ⌝ ܐܪܥܐ ܗܘ ⌜ܡܡܠܠ⌝· ܘܗܘ ܕܡܢ ⌜ܫܡܝܐ⌝ ܐܬܐ. 32 ܡܕܡ
⌜ܕܚܙܐ⌝ ܘܫܡܥ ܡܣܗܕ ⌜ܘܣܗܕܘܬܗ⌝ ܠܐ ܟܠ ܐܢܫ ⌜ܡܩܒܠ⌝· 33 ܐܝܢܐ
⌜ܕܩܒܠ⌝ ܕܝܢ ܣܗܕܘܬܗ ⌜ܚܬܡ⌝ ܕܐܠܗܐ ⌜ܫܪܝܪܐ⌝ ܗܘ. 34 ⌜ܐܝܢܐ ܓܝܪ
⌜ܕܐܠܗܐ⌝ ܫܕܪܗ ⌜ܡ̈ܠܐ⌝ ܕܐܠܗܐ ܡܡܠܠ· §ܠܐ ⌜ܗܘܐ⌝ ܓܝܪ §A 123
⌜ܒܟܝܠܬܐ⌝ ܝܗܒ [ܪܘܚܐ] ܐܒܐ ⌜ܠܒܪܗ⌝. 35 ܐܠܐ ⌜ܪܚܡ ܗܘ⌝ [ܠܗ] ⌜ܘܟܠ
ܡܕܡ ܝܗܒ ⌜ܒܐܝ̈ܕܘܗܝ⌝·¶ 36 ܡܢ ⌜ܕܡܗܝܡܢ⌝ ⌜ܒܒܪܐ⌝ ܐܝܬ ⌜ܠܗ⌝ ܚ̈ܝܐ ¶A
⌜ܕܠܥܠܡ⌝. ܘܡܢ ⌜ܕܠܐ⌝ ܡܗܝܡܢ *⌜ܠܒܪܐ⌝ ܠܐ ܚܙܐ ܚ̈ܝܐ. ⌜ܐܠܐ⌝ ܪܘܓܙܗ fol 42 v
ܕܐܠܗܐ ⌜ܩܘܐ⌝ ܥܠܘܗܝ.܀

---

26 ܘܟܠܗܘܢ ܐܢܫܐ] ܘܣ̈ܘܓܐܐ S   27 ܝܗܝܒ] ܐܬܝܗܒ S
28 ܕܐܡܪܬ ܕܐܢܐ ܠܐ S   ܩܕܡܘܗܝ] pr. ܕܝܢ S   29 ܡܢ 1°] pr. ܡܛܠ ܕ S
ܓܝܪ] om. S   ܗܟܝܠ] after ܗܝ S   30 ܓܝܪ] om. S   31—iv 6^a *inclusive*] *C is here mutilated; for fuller details see App.* I. *Doubtful words are supplied in square brackets.*   31 ܗܘ ܓܝܪ] ܡܛܠ ܕܗܘ ܕܝܢ S   ܘܗܘ 1°] ܘܐܝܢܐ S
ܡܢ ܐܪܥܐ] ܒܐܪܥܐ S   ܗܘ ܡܡܠܠ] *om.* ܗܘ S   ܘܗܘ 2°] ܘܐܝܢܐ S
ܐܬܐ] + ܠܥܠ ܡܢ * S (*vv.* 32, 33^a, *are illegible, but there is not space for all the words if S read* ܠܥܠ ܡܢ ܟܠ ܗܘ *at the end of ver.* 31)   33 ܕܫܪܝܪܐ ܐܠܗܐ ܗܘ S^{ed}
34 ܐܝܢܐ ܓܝܪ] ܡܛܠ ܕܐܝܢܐ S   ܫܕܪܗ] ܫܠܚ S   ܡ̈ܠܐ] + ܗܘ S
ܠܐ ܗܘܐ ܓܝܪ] *pr.* ܕ S; *om.* ܓܝܪ A   ܪܘܚܐ] A; ܐܠܗܐ S (*cf* vi 46)
ܠܒܪܗ] *om.* S   *Cf also* ܡܛܠ ܕܠܐ ܗܘܐ ܒܟܝܠܬܐ ܝܗܒ ܠܗ ܐܠܗܐ ܪܘܚܐ
A 122 *and* Ephr. *Lamy* i 267   35 ܐܠܐ ܪܚܡ ܗܘ ⌜ܠܗ⌝] ܐܠܐ ܠܒܪܗ * * S;
ܐܠܐ ܪܚܡܗ A   ܘܟܠ ܡܕܡ ܝܗܒ ܒܐܝ̈ܕܘܗܝ] ܘܝܗܒ ܟܠ ܒܐܝ̈ܕܘܗܝ S;
ܘܐܫܠܡ ܟܠ ܒܐܝ̈ܕܘܗܝ A   36 ܘܡܢ] ܘܐܝܢܐ S   ܪܘܓܙܐ S^{ed}

him: "Rabban, he that was with thee on the other side of the Jordan *C S*
and thou didst bear witness of him, lo, he also baptizeth, and all the
27 folk unto him are coming!" John saith to them: "A man cannot
28 even take aught, save if it be given to him from heaven. But ye,
bear witness to me that I said that I am not the Messiah, but am an
29 apostle before him. For he that hath the bride, he is the bride-
groom; and the friend of the bridegroom, he that standeth and
listeneth to him and with great joy rejoiceth because of the voice of the
bridegroom—this therefore my joy, lo, it is brought to an end!
30, 31 For him it behoves to increase and me to diminish. For he that
cometh from above is above all, and he that is from the earth is from
the earth and from the earth he speaketh; and he that from heaven
32 cometh—that which he seeth and heareth he beareth witness of, and
33 his witness not every man receiveth. But he which hath received his
34 witness hath sealed that God is true. For he which God hath sent
speaketh the words of God, §for not by measure did the Father give §*A* 123
35 [the Spirit] to his Son, but he loveth him and everything hath he
36 given into his hands.¶ He that believeth in the Son hath life eternal, ¶*A*
and he that believeth not the Son will not see life, but the wrath of
God will remain upon him."

---

26 all the folk] many *S* 27 be given] hath been given *S* 29 For] Because *S* therefore] *at the end of the verse in S* brought to an end] *For the rendering, see on* Lk xii 50 30 For him] Him *S* 31 For] Because *S* he that 2° *&* 3°] he which *S* from the earth 2°] in the earth *S* cometh 2°] + *is* above * *S* 34 For 1°] Because *S* sent] *S has a synonym: see* Matt xi 2 for 2°] *om. A* ⌜the Spirit⌝] *A*; *C is mutilated*: *cf* 'Because not by measure hath his Father given him the Spirit' *A* 122 *and* Ephr. *Lamy* i 267 34b, 35. *S is here partly illegible: as it stands it reads* 'For not by measure gave God the Father [35] but to his Son [he was loving] and hath given all into his hands' *Cf also* 'And not by measure gave he to his Son' E^{105} 35 given] delivered *A* 36 and he that] and he which *S*

C S ¹ܟܕ ܝܕܥ ܕܝܢ ܝܫܘܥ ܕܫܡܥܘ ܦܪ̈ܝܫܐ ܕܣܓܝܘ ܬܠܡܝ̈ܕܘܗܝ. ܘܡܥܡܕ
ܗܘܐ ܝܬܝܪ ܡܢ ܝܘܚܢܢ. ²ܘܠܐ ܗܘܐ [ܗܘ] ܝܫܘܥ ܡܥܡܕ ܗܘܐ
ܐܠܐ ܬܠܡܝ̈ܕܘܗܝ. ³ܘܫܒܩܗ̇ ܠܝܗܘܕ ܘܐܙܠ ܠܗ ܬܘܒ ܠܓܠܝܠܐ.
⁴[ܡܒܥܝܐ] ܗܘܬ ܠܗ [ܕܝܢ] ܕܢܥܒܪ ܠܗ ܒܝܬ ܫܡܪ̈ܝܐ. ⁵ܘܐܬܐ
ܠܡܕܝܢܬܐ ܚܕܐ ܕܫܡܪ̈ܝܐ ܕܡܬܩܪܝܐ ܗܘܬ ܫܟܝܪ. ܩܪܝܒܬ ܩܪܝܬܐ
ܗ̇ ܕܝܗܒ ܗܘܐ ܝܥܩܘܒ ܠܝܘܣܦ ܒܪܗ. ⁶ᵃܐܝܬ ܗܘܐ ܕܝܢ ܬܡܢ
ܡܥܝܢܐ ܕܡ̈ܝܐ ܕܝܥܩܘܒ. ܘܐܬܐ ܝܫܘܥ ܝܬܒ ܠܥܠ ܡܢܗ
col 2 ܕܡܥܝܢܐ. [ܐܝܟ] ܕܠܐܝܫ ܡܢ *ܒܗܠܟܐ ܕܐܘܪܚܐ. ⁸ܘܬܠܡܝ̈ܕܘܗܝ
ܥܠܘ ܗܘܘ ܠܡܕܝܢܬܐ ܗܝ ܕܢܙܒܢܘܢ ܠܗܘܢ ܣܝܒܪܬܐ. ⁶ᵇܘܗܝ ܗܘ
ܝܫܘܥ ܝܬܒ. ܐܝܬ ܗܘ, ܐܝܟ ܫ̈ܬܐ ܫܥܝܢ. ⁷ܘܐܬܬ ܗܘܬ ܐܢܬܬܐ
ܚܕܐ ܡܢ ܫܡܪܝܢ ܕܬܡܠܐ ܡ̈ܝܐ. ܐܡܪ ܠܗ̇ ܝܫܘܥ ܗܒ ܠܝ ܡ̈ܝܐ
ܐܫܬܐ. ⁹ܐܡܪܐ ܠܗ ܗ̇, ܐܢܬܬܐ ܫܡܪܝܬܐ. ܗܐ ܝܗܘܕܝܐ ܐܢܬ.
ܐܝܟܢܐ ܫܐܠ ܐܢܬ ܠܝ ܡ̈ܝܐ ܠܡܫܬܐ. ܕܗܐ ܐܢܐ ܐܢܬܬܐ ܫܡܪܝܬܐ
ܐܢܐ. ܝܗܘ̈ܕܝܐ ܓܝܪ ܠܐ ܡܬܚܫܚܝܢ ܥܡ ܫܡܪ̈ܝܐ. ¹⁰ܐܡܪ ܠܗ̇
ܝܫܘܥ. ܐܠܘ ܝܕܥܐ ܗܘܝܬ ܡܘܗܒܬܗ ܕܐܠܗܐ. ܘܡܢܘ ܗܢܐ
ܕܐܡܪ ܠܟܝ ܗܒ ܠܝ ܐܫܬܐ. ܐܢܬܝ, ܫܐܠܐ ܗܘܝܬ ܠܗ. ܘܝܗܒ
fol 43 r ܗܘܐ *ܠܟܝ ܡ̈ܝܐ ܚ̈ܝܐ. ¹¹ܐܡܪܐ ܠܗ ܗ̇, ܐܢܬܬܐ. ܡܪܝ, ܐܦܠܐ
ܕܘܠܐ ܐܝܬ ܠܟ. ܘܒܪܐ ܥܡܝܩܐ ܗܝ. ܐܝܡܟܐ ܐܝܬ ܠܟ ܡ̈ܝܐ

1 ܟܕ ܕܝܢ ܝܕܥ S   ܝܫܘܥ] ܡܪܢ S   ܕܣܓܝܘ ܬܠܡܝ̈ܕܘܗܝ]
S ܝܬܪ [ܣܓܝܘ   ܘܡܥܡܕ] S illegible   S^ed * * | ܕܬܠܡܝ̈ܕܐ ܣܓܝܐܐ
2 ܘܠܐ] ܡܛܠ ܕܠܐ S   ܡܥܡܕ [ܗܘ] ܒܠܚܘܕ ܡܪܢ S
4 ܡܒܥܝܐ] ܒܥܐ ܗܘܐ ܕܢܥܒܪ ܒܐܬܪܐ ܕܫܡܪ̈ܝܐ S ......ܫܡܪ̈ܝܐ
5 ܘܐܬܐ] ܐܬܐ ܗܘܐ S (sic)   ܠܡܕܝܢܬܐ ܚܕܐ] ܠܩܪܝܬܐ ܚܕ S
ܕܡܬܩܪܝܐ ܗܘܐ S   ܩܪܝܒܬ] ܠܘܩܒܠ S   6ᵃ ܘܐܝܬ ܗܘܐ (om. ܕܝܢ) S
ܝܫܘܥ] ܡܪܢ S   ܘܝܬܒ S   ܐܝܟ] S illegible   8 ܘܬܠܡܝ̈ܕܘܗܝ S: cf Matt xi 2
ܗܘܘ] + ܠܗܘܢ S   ܠܗܘ ܠܡܕܝܢܬܐ S   6ᵇ ܝܫܘܥ] ܡܪܢ S
ܐܝܟ] om. S   7 ܗܘܬ] om. S   ܘܐܡܪ S   ܝܫܘܥ] ܡܪܢ S   ܡܢ S
9 ܗܐ] + ܐܢܬ S   ܕܗܐ ܐܢܐ ܫܡܪܝܬܐ ܐܢܐ] om. S   ܝܗܘ̈ܕܝܐ ܓܝܪ]
ܡܛܠ ܕܝܗܘ̈ܕܝܐ S   10 ܝܫܘܥ] om. S   ܗܘܝܬܝ S   ܡܘܗܒܬܐ S
ܗܘܝܬܝ S   11 ܗܝ ܐܢܬܬܐ] om. S   ܡܪܝ] om. S   ܐܝܡܟܐ] pr. ܡܢ S

iv 1 Now when Jesus knew that the Pharisees heard that his disciples C S
2 were many, and *that* he was baptizing more than John,—not that
3 Jesus [himself] was baptizing, but his disciples—then he left Judaea
4 and went away again to Galilee. [Now] it was [arranged] for him that
5 he should pass through the country of the Samaritans; and he came
to a certain city of the Samaritans that was called Shechem, near
6a that field which Jacob had given to Joseph his son. Now there was
there Jacob's spring of water, and Jesus came *and* sat over the
spring, [so] that he might rest himself from the fatigue of the road.
8 And his disciples had entered that town that they might buy for
6b themselves food; and when Jesus sat down it was about the sixth
7 hour, and a certain woman had come from Samaria to draw water.
9 Jesus saith to her: "Give me water to drink." That Samaritan
woman saith to him: "Lo, thou art a Jew; how askest thou me for
water to drink, *seeing* that, lo, I am a Samaritan?" For the Jews
10 have no dealings with the Samaritans. Jesus saith to her: "If thou
hadst known the gift of God, and who is this that said to thee 'Give
me to drink,' thou hadst asked him and he would have given thee
11 living water." That woman saith to him: "My Lord, not even a
bucket hast thou and the well is deep; whence hast thou living water?

---

1 Jesus] our Lord *S* that his disciples were many] * * of (? *om.*) many disciples *S* 2 not that....baptizing] because not only was our Lord baptizing *S* 4—5a.] When he was passing by a place of the Samaritans [5]he had come *S* (*sic*): *cf* Diat[ar] xxi 8 5 city] town *S* near] opposite *S* 6a Now] And *S* Jesus] our Lord *S* *and*] and *S* 6b Jesus] our Lord *S* about] *om. S* 7 had come] came *S* Jesus saith] And our Lord saith (*or*, 'said') *S* 9 *seeing*.....Samaritan] *om. S* For] Because *S* 10 Jesus saith] He saith *S* 11 That woman saith] She saith *S* My Lord] *om. S* whence] *pr.* from *S*

C S ܫܬܝܐ. [12] ܕܠܡܐ ܐܢܬ ܪܒ ܐܢܬ ܡܢ ܐܒܘܢ ܝܥܩܘܒ· ܕܗܘ ܝܗܒ
ܠܢ ܒܐܪܐ ܗܕܐ. ܘܐܦ ܗܘ ܡܢܗ̇ ܐܫܬܝ. ܘܒܢܘ̈ܗܝ ܘܒܥܝܪܗ. [13] ܐܡܪ
ܠܗ̇ ܝܫܘܥ. ܟܠ ܕܢܫܬܐ ܡܢ ܗܠܝܢ ܡ̈ܝܐ ܬܘܒ ܨܗܐ. [14] ܘܟܠ
ܕܢܫܬܐ ܡܢ ܡ̈ܝܐ ܐܝܠܝܢ ܕܐܢܐ ܐܬܠ ܠܗ ܬܘܒ ܠܐ ܨܗܐ
ܠܥܠܡ. ܐܠܐ ܡ̈ܝܐ ܗܢܘܢ ܕܐܬܠ ܠܗ ܢܗܘܘܢ ܒܗ ܡܒܥܐ
ܕܡ̈ܝܐ ܠܚ̈ܝܐ ܕܠܥܠܡ. [15] ܐܡܪܐ ܠܗ ܐܢܬܬܐ ܗ̇ܝ. ܡܪܝ ܗܒ ܠܝ
col 2 ܡܢ ܗܠܝܢ ܡ̈ܝܐ. *ܕܠܐ ܗܘܝܬ ܨܗܝܐ ܘܐܬܝܐ ܕܠܝܐ ܡܢ ܗܪܟܐ.
[16] ܐܡܪ ܠܗ̇ ܝܫܘܥ. ܙܠ ܩܪܝ ܠܝ ܠܒܥܠܟܝ ܘܬܝ ܠܗܪܟܐ. [17] ܐܡܪܐ ܠܗ
ܠܝܬ ܠܝ ܒܥܠܐ. ܐܡܪ ܠܗ̇ ܝܫܘܥ ܫܦܝܪ ܐܡܪܬܝ. ܕܠܝܬ ܠܝ ܒܥܠܐ.
[18] ܚܡܫܐ ܓܝܪ ܒ̈ܥܠܝܢ ܗܘܘ ܠܟܝ. ܘܗܘܢܐ ܕܐܝܬ ܠܟܝ ܗܫܐ ܠܐ
ܗܘܐ ܒܥܠܟܝ. ܗܕܐ ܫܪܝܪܬܐ ܐܡܪܬܝ. [19] ܐܡܪܐ ܠܗ ܗ̇ܝ ܐܢܬܬܐ.
ܡܪܝ ܚܙܝܐ ܐܢܐ ܕܢܒܝܐ ܐܢܬ. [20] ܐܒ̈ܗܝܢ ܒܗܢܐ ܛܘܪܐ ܣܓܕܘ.
ܘܐܢܬܘܢ ܕܝܢ ܐܡܪܝܢ ܐܢܬܘܢ ܕܒܐܘܪܫܠܡ ܗܘ ܒܝܬ ܣܓܕܬܐ.
[21] ܐܡܪ ܠܗ̇ ܝܫܘܥ· ܐܢܬܬܐ ܗܝܡܢܝܢܝ ܕܐܬܝܐ ܫܥܬܐ. ܕܠܐ
fol 43 v ܒܗܢܐ ܛܘܪܐ. ܐܦܠܐ *ܒܐܘܪܫܠܡ ܬܣܓܕܘܢ ܠܐܒܐ. [22] ܐܢܬܘܢ
ܣܓܕܝܢ ܐܢܬܘܢ ܠܡܕܡ ܕܠܐ ܝܕܥܝܢ ܐܢܬܘܢ ܘܐܢܚܢܢ ܣܓܕܝܢ
ܐܢܚܢܢ ܠܡܕܡ ܕܝܕܥܝܢ ܐܢܚܢܢ. ܕܚ̈ܝܐ ܡܢ ܝܗܘܕܝܐ ܐܢܘܢ. [23] ܐܠܐ
ܐܬܝܐ ܫܥܬܐ ܘܗܫܐ ܐܝܬܝܗ̇. ܕܣ̈ܓܘܕܐ ܫܪܝܪܐ ܢܣܓܕܘܢ
ܠܐܒܐ ܒܪܘܚܐ ܘܒܫܪܪܐ. ܘܐܦ ܐܒܐ ܓܝܪ ܐܝܟ ܗܠܝܢ ܗܘ
ܣ̈ܓܘܕܐ ܒܥܐ. [24] ܐܠܗܐ ܓܝܪ ܪܘܚܐ ܗܘ· ܘܐܝܠܝܢ ܕܣܓܕܝܢ ܠܗ
ܒܪܘܚܐ. ܘܠܡܣܓܕ ܠܗܘܢ ܘܠܐ ܠܐܝܠܝܢ ܕܒܪܘܚܐ ܘܒܫܪܪܐ
ܣܓܕܝܢ ܠܗ. [25] ܐܡܪܐ ܠܗ ܗ̇ܝ ܐܢܬܬܐ. ܝܕܥܐ ܐܢܐ ܕܡܫܝܚܐ

---

12 ܝܥܩܘܒ ܐܒܘܢ S   13 ܝܫܘܥ] ܡܪܢ S   14 ܐܝܠܝܢ] om. S   ܬܘܒ] om. S   ܕܐܬܠ] ܐܢܐ ܕܝܗܒ S   ܕܡ̈ܝܐ] + ܕܕܝܠܝ S   15 ܗ̇ܝ ܐܢܬܬܐ S   ܠܝ] + ܐܢܬܬܐ S   16 & 17 ܝܫܘܥ] ܡܪܢ S   18 ܡܛܠ ܕܚ̈ܡܫܐ (om. ܓܝܪ) S   19 ܗ̇ܝ ܐܢܬܬܐ] om. S   ܢܒܝܐ] pr. ܕ S   20 ܕܝܢ] om. S   21 ܝܫܘܥ] ܡܪܢ S   ܗܝܡܢܝ S   ܐܦܠܐ] ܘܠܐ S   22 ܠܡܕܡ] ܠܡܐ S (in both places)   23 ܐܠܐ] + ܗܐ S   ܐܝܟ] om. S   ܗܘ] ܐܢܘܢ S   24 ܐܠܗܐ.....ܠܗܘܢ ܘܠܐ] om. S   ܘܠܡܣܓܕ C[1] on erasure   ܐܝܠܝܢ S   25 ܠܗ] om. S   ܝܕܥܐ ܐܢܐ ܕ] ܗܐ S

12 Canst thou be greater than our father Jacob, he that gave us this *C S*
13 well, and he also drank of it, and his sons and his flock?" Jesus
saith to her: "Every one that shall drink of this water will thirst
14 again, and every one that shall drink of the water which I will give
him will not thirst again for ever, but that water which I will give
15 him will be in him a spring of water to life eternal." That woman
saith to him: "My Lord, give me of this water, that I be not thirsty
16 and come drawing from hence." Jesus saith to her: "Go, call to
17 me thy husband and come hither." She saith to him: "I have
no husband." Jesus saith to her: "Well saidst thou 'I have no
18 husband,' for five husbands hast thou had, and this one that thou
19 hast now is not thy husband; this thou hast said true." That
20 woman saith to him: "My Lord, I see, thou art a prophet. Our
fathers in this hill worshipped, but ye say that in Jerusalem is the
21 House of Worship." Jesus saith to her: "Woman, believe me that
the hour cometh, when not in this hill neither in Jerusalem shall they
22 worship the Father. Ye worship that which ye know not, and we
23 worship that which we know, for life is from Judah; but the hour
cometh and now it is, when the true worshippers shall worship the
Father in spirit and in truth, for the Father also—*such* as these for wor-
24 shippers he seeketh. †For God is a spirit, and those that worship him
in spirit, and to worship for them it behoves,† *even* those that in spirit
25 and in truth worship him." That woman saith to him: "I know that

---

12 Jacob our father *S* 13 Jesus] Our Lord *S* 14 which 1°] that *S* again] *om. S* I will give 2°] I give *S* to life] *pr.* flowing *S* 15 this water] + to drink *S* (*not* E^{141}) 16 *&* 17 Jesus] Our Lord *S* 18 for] because *S* 19 That woman saith] She saith *S* thou] *pr.* that *S* (E^{141}) 20 but] and *S* Jerusalem] + only E^{143} 21 Jesus] Our Lord *S* me] *om. S* neither] and not *S* *For* 'Woman, believe me.... when' E^{143} *has* 'Verily, I say unto thee' 22 that which] what *S* (*in both places*) 23 but] + lo *S* *such*....for] these are the *S* 24 For God.... behoves] *om. S* 25 to him] *om. S* I know that] Lo *S* E^{141}

C (S) ܐܬܬܐ. ܘܡܢܐ ܕܐܬܬܐ ܗܘ ܡܟܪܗ ܠܝ ܒܟܠ ܡܕܡ. 26ܐܡܪ ܠܗ̇
col 2 ܝܫܘܥ· ܐܢܐ *ܐܢܐ ܕܡܫܠܠ ܐܢܐ ܒܟܒܪ. 27ܘܒܪ ܗܘܝܘܢ
ܡܫܠܠܝܢ· ܐܬܘ ܬܠܡܝܕܘܗܝ، ܘܡܬܕܡܪܝܢ ܗܘܘ ܕܒܟܝܐ ܐܢܬܬܐ
ܡܫܠܠ ܗܘܐ· ܡܐܡܪ ܕܝܢ ܠܐ ܐܡܪܘ ܠܗ ܕܐܘ ܡܢܐ ܒܟܬ
ܐܘ ܡܪܢܐ ܐܡܪ ܗܘܝܬ ܠܗ̇· 28ܘܗ̇ܝ، ܐܢܬܬܐ ܫܒܩܬܗ̇ ܩܘܠܬܗ̇
ܘܐܙܠܬ ܗܘܬ ܠܡܕܝܢܬܐ. ܘܐܡܪܐ ܠܐܢܫܐ 29ܬܘ ܚܘ ܠܓܒܪܐ
ܕܐܡܪ ܠܝ ܟܠ ܡܕܡ ܕܥܒܕܬ. ܕܠܡܐ ܗܘܝܘ ܡܫܝܚܐ. 30ܘܢܦܩܘ
ܡܢ ܡܕܝܢܬܐ. ܘܐܬܝܢ ܗܘܘ ܠܘܬܗ. 31ܬܠܡܝܕܘܗܝ، ܕܝܢ ܒܥܝܢ ܗܘܘ
ܡܢܗ ܕܢܐܟܘܠ ܥܡܗܘܢ ܠܚܡܐ. 32ܐܡܪ ܠܗܘܢ: ܐܝܬ ܠܝ
fol 44 r ܡܐܟܘܠܬܐ ܕܐܟܘܠ ܐܢܐ ܕܐܢܬܘܢ *ܠܐ ܝܕܥܝܢ ܠܗ̇. 33ܐܡܪܝܢ
ܗܘܘ ܚܕ ܠܚܕ· ܠܡܐ ܕ ܐܢܫ ܐܝܬܝ، ܠܗ ܡܕܡ ܠܡܐܟܠ·
34ܐܡܪ ܠܗܘܢ ܗܘ ܝܫܘܥ· ܡܐܟܘܠܬܝ، ܕܝܠܝ ܕܐܥܒܕ ܗܘ ܨܒܝܢܗ
ܕܗܘ ܕܫܕܪܢܝ. ܘܐܫܠܡܝܗ̇، ܠܥܒܕܗ· 35ܠܐ ܐܢܬܘܢ ܐܡܪܝܢ
ܐܢ̈ܬܘܢ ܕܐܪ̈ܒܥܐ ܐܝܬ ܝܪ̈ܚܝܢ ܘܐܬܐ ܚܨܕܐ· ܗܐ ܐܡܪܢܐ
cf Thos 315 ܠܟܘܢ ܕܐܪܝܡܘ ܥܝܢ̈ܝܟܘܢ ܘܚܙܘ. ܕܐܪ̈ܥܬܐ ܚܘܪ ܘܡܛܝ
ܠܚܨܕܐ· 36ܘܡܢ ܗܫܐ ܚܨܕܐ ܐܓܪܐ ܢܣܒ. ܘܟܢܫ ܦܐܪ̈ܐ ܠܚܝ̈ܐ
§¶A443 ܕܠܥܠܡ. ܘ§ܙ̈ܪܘܥܐ ܘܚܨܘܕܐ ܐܟܚܕܐ ܢܚܕܘܢ:¶ 37ܒܗܕܐ ܓܝܪ
¶S ܐܝܬܝܗ ܡܠܬܐ ܕܫܪܪܐ. ܕܐܚܪܢ ܗܘ ܙܪܥ ܘܐܚܪܢ ܗܘ ܚܨܕ·¶
col 2 38ܘܐܢܐ ܫܕܪܬܟܘܢ ܠܡܚܨܕ ܡܕܡ ܕܠܐ *ܗܘܐ ܐܢܬܘܢ ܠܐܝܬܘܢ

ܗܘ] om. S   ܡܟܪܗ ܠܝ ܒܟܠ ܡܕܡ] ܢܛܠ ܒܟܠ ܡܕܡ S   26 ܝܫܘܥ]
ܡܪܢ S   27 ܡܫܠܠ ܗܘܐ] ܡܫܠܠ ܘܡܫܠܠ ܗܘܐ S (cf vii 26)   ܒܟܒܪ] ܒܟܒܬ S
28 ܫܒܩܬ S   ܘܐܙܠܬ ܗܘܬ] ܘܪܗܛܬ S   ܠܐܢܫܐ] om. S   29 ܕܠܟܠܐ]
ܠܟܠܐ S   30 ܘܢܦܩܘ......ܠܘܬܗ] ܘܟܠ ܕܫܡܥܘ ܢܦܩܘ ܗܘܘ ܠܘܬܗ S
31 ܡܢܗ......ܬܠܡܝܕܘܗܝ] ܬܠܡܝܕܘܗܝ ܕܝܢ ܗܘܘ ܒܥܝܢ S   32 ܕܐܟܘܠ] now washed
out in C   ܐܢܬܘܢ + [ܝܕܥܝܢ S   34 ܗܘ ܝܫܘܥ] om. S   ܡܐܟܘܠܬܝ S
ܨܒܝܢܗ] so also S   ܘܐܫܠܡܝܗ̇ S   .ܠܥܒܕܗ S   35 ܐܢܬܘܢ 2°] exp. Ccorr
(ܐܢ̈ܬܘܢ·)   ܐܝܬ ܝܪ̈ܚܝܢ + [ܝܪ̈ܚܝܢ S   ܚܘܪ ܕܐܪ̈ܥܬܐ] ܚܘܪ ܐܪ̈ܥܬܐ S;
cf ܐܡܪ ܐܢܐ ܠܟܘܢ ܕܐܪ̈ܥܬܐ ܚܘܪ ܘܡܛܝ ܠܚܨܕܐ ܘܡܢ ܗܫܐ ܚܨܕܐ ܚܘܪ ܘܡܛܝ Thos[315] : see Notes, vol. ii
37 ܗܘ ܘܐܚܪܢ] ܘܐܚܪܢܐ S (as elsewhere). In the preceding clause ܕܐܚܪܢ is at
the end of a line in C

the Messiah cometh, and what *time* he hath come he will make C (*S*)
26 clear to us everything." Jesus saith to her: "I am he that am
27 speaking with thee." And while they *were* speaking his disciples
came, and they were wondering that with a woman he was speaking,
but they did not indeed say to him either 'What †sought she†?' or
28 'What wast thou saying to her?' And that woman had left her
29 water-jar and gone to the city, and she saith to the folk: "Come, see
a man that said to me everything that I have done; can he be the
30 Messiah?" And they went forth from the city and were coming unto
31 him. Now his disciples were beseeching him that he should eat bread
32 with them. He saith to them: "I have meat to eat which ye know
33 not of." They say one to another: "Can then some one have
34 brought him something to eat?" He, Jesus, saith to them: "My
own meat *is* that I should do the will of him that sent me and fulfil
35 the work. Say ye not, that there are four months and harvest
cometh? Lo, I say to you Lift up your eyes and see that
36 the lands are white and have arrived at harvest, and already *cf Thos* 315
the reaper receiveth wage and gathereth fruit to life eternal, and
37 §the sower and the reaper together shall rejoice.¶ For in this §¶*A*443
is the word of truth, that one doth sow and another doth reap.¶ ¶*S*
38 And I have sent you to reap that which not ye have toiled

---

he will make clear to us] he will give *S* E^{141} (+ to us *E*) 26 Jesus] Our Lord *S*; 'He' E^{141} 27 speaking 2°] standing and speaking *S* E^{140}; *cf* Joh vii 26 sought she] soughtest thou *S* 28 had] *om.* *S* gone] ran *S* to the folk] *om.* *S* 30 And every one that heard was going forth unto him *S* 31 Now] And *S* him] *om.* *S* 34 He, Jesus, saith] He saith *S* the work] his work *S* 35 four] + other *S* see the lands that they are white *S*; *cf* 'My fields are white and have arrived at harvest, and already let me receive my reward' *Thos*[315]: see *Notes*, vol. ii

C ܒܗ· ܐܠܐ ܐܚܪ̈ܢܝܢ ܕܠܐܝܘ· ܘܐܢܬܘܢ ܥܠܬܘܢ ܥܠ ܥܡܠܗܘܢ
ܕܗܠܝܢ. [39]ܘܡܢ ܡܕܝܢܬܐ ܗ̇ܝ ܫܡܪ̈ܝܐ ܗܝܡܢܘ ܒܗ ܡܢ ܣܓ̈ܝܐܐ·
ܡܛܠ ܦܘܬܓܡܗ̇ ܕܗܝ ܐܢܬܬܐ. ܕܐܡܪܐ ܗܘܬ ܕܟܠ ܡܕܡ
ܕܥܒܕܬ ܐܡܪ ܠܝ. [40]ܘܟܕ ܐܬܘ ܠܘܬܗ ܗܢܘܢ ܫܡܪ̈ܝܐ. ܒܥܝܢ ܗܘܘ
ܡܢܗ ܕܢܗܘܐ ܠܘܬܗܘܢ؛ ܘܗܘܐ ܠܘܬܗܘܢ ܬܪ̈ܝܢ ܝܘܡ̈ܝܢ. [41]ܘܣܓ̈ܝܐܐ
ܗܝܡܢܘ ܒܗ. ܡܛܠ ܡܠܬܗ. [42]ܘܐܡܪܝܢ ܗܘܘ ܠܐܢܬܬܐ ܗ̇ܝ. ܡܟܝܠ
ܠܐ ܗܘܐ ܡܛܠ ܡܠܬܟܝ ܡܗܝܡܢܝܢ ܐܢܚܢܢ ܒܗ. ܐܢܚܢ ܓܝܪ
ܫܡܥܢ ܡܢܗ. ܘܝܕܥܝܢ ܕܫܪܝܪܐܝܬ ܗܢܘ ܡܚܝܢܗ ܕܥܠܡܐ ·܀·
[43]*ܡܢ ܒܬܪ ܗܠܝܢ ܬܪ̈ܝܢ ܝܘܡ̈ܝܢ· ܢܦܩ ܡܢ ܬܡܢ ܝܫܘܥ ܠܓܠܝܠܐ. fol 44 v
[44]ܘܗܘ ܓܝܪ ܝܫܘܥ ܣܗܕ ܗܘܐ ܕܢܒܝܐ ܒܡܕܝܢܬܗ ܠܐ ܡܬܝܩܪ.
[45]ܘܟܕ ܐܬܐ ܩܒܠܘܗܝ ܓ̈ܠܝܠܝܐ. ܟܕ ܚܙܘ ܡܕܡ ܕܥܒܕ ܒܐܘܪܫܠܡ
ܒܥܐܕܐ. ܘܐܦ ܗܢܘܢ ܓܝܪ ܐܬܘ ܗܘܘ ܠܥܐܕܐ. [46]ܘܐܬܐ
ܗܘܐ ܬܘܒ ܠܩܛܢܐ ܕܓܠܝܠܐ. ܐܬܪ ܕܥܒܕ ܗܘܐ ܡ̈ܝܐ ܗܢܘܢ
ܚܡܪܐ ·܀·
ܘܐܝܬ ܗܘܐ ܒܟܦܪܢܚܘܡ ܥܒܕ ܡܠܟܐ ܚܕ ܕܒܪܗ ܟܪܝܗ ܗܘܐ.
[47]ܟܕ ܫܡܥ ܕܝܫܘܥ ܐܬܐ ܡܢ ܓܠܝܠܐ ܠܝܗܘܕ· ܐܬܐ ܠܘܬܗ.
ܘܒܥܐ ܗܘܐ ܡܢܗ ܕܢܚܘܬ ܘܚܝܐ ܠܒܪܗ· ܡܛܠ ܕܡܝܬ ܗܘܐ
ܠܡܡܬ. [48]ܐܡܪ ܠܗ *ܝܫܘܥ. ܐܢ ܐܬ̈ܘܬܐ ܘܬܕܡܪ̈ܬܐ ܠܐ ܚܙܝܬܘܢ col 2
ܠܐ ܬܗܝܡܢܘܢ؛ [49]ܐܡܪ ܠܗ ܥܒܕ ܡܠܟܐ ܡܪܝ، ܚܘܬ ܥܕܠܐ
ܢܡܘܬ ܠܗ ܛܠܝܐ. [50]ܐܡܪ ܠܗ ܝܫܘܥ· ܙܠ ܠܒܝܬܟ ܗܐ ܒܪܟ
ܚܝܐ. ܘܗܝܡܢ ܗܘ ܓܒܪܐ ܒܡܠܬܗ ܕܝܫܘܥ· [51]ܘܟܕ ܐܙܠ ܐܪܥܘܗܝ،
ܥܒ̈ܕܘܗܝ، ܘܦܓܥܘܗܝ. ܘܐܡܪܘ ܠܗ ܕܒܪܟ ܚܝܐ. [52]ܘܫܐܠ ܐܢܘܢ
ܕܒܐܝܕܐ ܫܥܬܐ ܗܘܐ ܫܦܝܪ. ܐܡܪܝܢ ܠܗ ܐܬܡܠܝ ܒܫܒܥ ܫ̈ܥܝܢ
ܫܒܩܬܗ ܐܫܬܐ. [53]ܘܝܕܥ ܐܒܘܗܝ، ܕܒܗ̇، ܫܥܬܐ ܕܐܡܪ ܠܗ ܝܫܘܥ
ܕܒܪܟ ܚܝܐ. ܘܗܝܡܢ ܗܘ ܘܒܝܬܗ ܟܠܗ. [54]ܗܕܐ ܗܝ، ܐܬܐ
ܕܬܪ̈ܬܝܢ ܕܥܒܕ ܝܫܘܥ· ܟܕ ܐܬܐ ܡܢ ܝܗܘܕ ܠܓܠܝܠܐ.

46 ܥܒܕ ܡܠܟܐ] *A* 20: *cf* Matt viii 5 47 ܘܚܝܐ] *C* (*sic*), *but possibly an error for* ܘܢܚܐ: *Gr.* καὶ ἰάσηται, *but* 'et saluaret' *c e*

at, but they that have toiled; and ye have entered upon the labour *C*
39 of those." And from that city many believed on him of the
Samaritans, because of the testimony of that woman that was saying:
40 "Everything that I have done he said to me." And when those
Samaritans came unto him they were beseeching him that he would
41 be with them, and he was with them two days. And many believed
42 on him because of his word, and they were saying to that woman:
"Henceforth not because of thy word do we believe in him, for we
ourselves have heard from him and know that truly he is the Life-
giver of the world."

43 After those two days Jesus went forth from thence to Galilee,
44 for Jesus himself had borne witness that a prophet in his city is not
45 honoured. And when he came the Galilaeans received him, when
they saw that which he did in Jerusalem at the Feast; for they also
46 had come to the Feast. And he had come again to Câtnê of Galilee,
where he had made that water wine.

And there was in Kapharnahum a certain courtier whose son was
47 infirm. When he heard that Jesus was come from Galilee to Judaea
he came unto him, and was beseeching him that he should go down
48 and see his son, because he was near to die. Jesus saith to him:
49 "If miracles and signs ye see not, ye will not believe." The courtier
saith to him: "My Lord, come down before ever the lad die."
50 Jesus saith to him: "Go to thy house; lo, thy son liveth!" And
51 that man believed in the word of Jesus. And while going his
slaves met him and announced to him, and said to him "Thy son
52 liveth." And he asked them at what hour he became well. They
53 say to him: "Yesterday at the ninth hour the fever left him." And
his father knew that *it was* at that hour that Jesus said to him
54 "Thy son liveth"; and he believed, he and all his house. This is
the second sign that Jesus did, when he came from Judaea to
Galilee.

---

46 courtier] *lit.* 'king's slave.' *For the quotation in A* 20 *see* Matt viii 5

C [S] fol 45 r ¹*ܒܬܪ ܗܠܝܢ ܗܘܐ ܗܘܐ ܥܐܕܐ ܕܝܗ̈ܘܕܝܐ. ܘܣܠܩ ܗܘܐ ܝܫܘܥ
ܠܐܘܪܫܠܡ. ²ܘܐܝܬ ܗܘܐ ܒܐܘܪܫܠܡ ܕܘܟܬܐ ܚܕܐ ܕܡܥܡܘܕܝܬܐ
ܕܡܬܩܪܝܐ ܥܒܪܐܝܬ ܒܝܬ ܚܣܕܐ· ܘܐܝܬ ܒܗ̇ ܚܡܫܐ ܐܣ̈ܛܘܢ.
³ܘܪܡܝܢ ܗܘܘ ܒܐܣ̈ܛܘܐ ܗܠܝܢ ܟܢ̈ܫܐ ܕܟܪ̈ܝܗܐ. ܘܥ̈ܘܝܪܐ ܘܚ̈ܓܝܪܐ
ܘܝܒ̈ܝܫܐ· ⁵ܘܐܝܬ ܗܘܐ ܬܡܢ ܓܒܪܐ ܚܕ ܕܬܠܬܝܢ ܘܬܡܢܐ ܫ̈ܢܝܢ
§S ܟܪܝܗ ܗܘܐ. ⁶ܘܟܕ ܚܙܝܗܝ, §ܝܫܘܥ ܕܪܡܐ. ܝܕܥ ܕܙܒܢܐ ܣܓܝܐܐ
ܐܝܬ ܠܗ. ܐܡܪ ܠܗ ܨܒܐ ܐܢܬ ܕܬܬܚܠܡ ܫܪܪ. ⁷ܐܡܪ ܠܗ ܡܪܝ,
ܠܝܬ ܠܝ ܐܢܫ ܕܡܐ ܕܐܬܬܙܝܥܘ ܡ̈ܝܐ ܢܚܬܢܝ ܠܡܥܡܘܕܝܬܐ.
col 2 ܘܟܕ ܐܢܐ ܐܬܐ ܐܚܪܢ ܡܢ *ܩܕܡܝ ܢܚܬ. ⁸ܐܡܪ ܠܗ ܝܫܘܥ·
ܩܘܡ ܫܩܘܠ ܥܪܣܟ ܘܗܠܟ ܘܙܠ ܠܒܝܬܟ· ⁹ܘܒܗ̇ ܒܫܥܬܐ
ܐܬܚܠܡ ܓܒܪܐ ܗܘ ܘܗܠܟ. ܘܗܘ ܗܘ̇ ܝܘܡܐ ܫܒܬܐ ܗܘܬ.
¹⁰ܐܡܪܝܢ ܠܗ ܝܗ̈ܘܕܝܐ. ܫܒܬܐ ܗܝ, ܠܐ ܫܠܝܛ ܠܟ ܕܬܫܩܘܠ
ܥܪܣܟ. ¹¹ܐܡܪ ܠܗܘܢ ܗܘ ܗܘ ܕܐܚܠܡܢܝ. ܗܘ ܐܡܪ ܠܝ ܕܫܩܘܠ
ܥܪܣܟ ܘܗܠܟ. ¹²ܐܡܪܝܢ ܠܗ ܡܢܘ ܗܢܐ ܓܒܪܐ ܕܐܡܪ ܠܟ
ܕܫܩܘܠ ܥܪܣܟ ܘܗܠܟ. ¹³ܘܗܘ ܕܐܬܐܣܝ, ܠܐ ܝܕܥ ܗܘܐ ܡܢܘ·
ܗܘ ܓܝܪ ܝܫܘܥ ܥܛ ܗܘܐ ܠܗ ܡܢ ܕܘܟܬܐ ܠܣܓܝܐܘܬܗ̇. ܡܛܠ
ܟܢܫܐ ܕܐܢܫܐ. ¹⁴ܒܬܪ ܗܠܝܢ ܐܫܟܚܗ ܗܘܐ ܝܫܘܥ. ܠܗܘ ܕܐܬܐܣܝ,
fol 45 v ܒܗܝܟܠܐ· *ܘܐܡܪ ܠܗ. ܗܐ ܚܠܝܡ ܐܢܬ ܬܘܒ. ܠܐ ܬܚܛܐ.
ܕܠܡܐ ܢܗܘܐ ܠܟ ܕܒܝܫ ܡܢ ܩܕܡܝܐ. ¹⁵ܘܐܙܠ ܓܒܪܐ ܗܘ ܘܐܡܪ

---

6 ܝܫܘܥ] ܡܪܢ S   ܕܪܡܐ] om. S   ܕܙܒܢܐ] ܕܒܙܒܢܐ S   ܠܗ]
+ ܕܐܪܡܐ S   7 ܕܐܬܬܙܝܥܘ S   ܢܚܬܢܝ] ܢܪܡܝܢܝ S   ܘܟܕ] ܐܠܐ ܟܕ S
ܐܚܪ̈ܢ] C (end of line) S (sic)   8 ܝܫܘܥ] ܡܪܢ S   ܘܙܠ ܠܒܝܬܟ] om. S
9 ܘܒܗ̇ ܒܫܥܬܐ] so also S   ܘܗܠܟ] pr. ܘܫܩܠ ܥܪܣܗ S
10 ܐܡܪܝܢ ܠܗ ܝܗ'] ܘܟܕ ܚܙܘܗܝ ܝܗܘܕܝܐ ܐܡܪܝܢ ܠܗ S   ܫܒܬܐ ܗܝ] om. S
11 ܐܡܪ 1°] pr. ܘ S   ܠܗܘܢ] + ܗܘ ܕܐܬܚܠܡ S   ܗܘ ܗܘ] ܡܢ ܗܘ S
12.] om. S (from homoeoteleuton)   13 ܘܗܘ ܕܐܬܐܣܝ] ܘܗܘ ܓܒܪܐ S
ܗܘ ܓܝܪ ܝܫܘܥ] ܡܛܠ ܕܡܪܢ S   ܡܛܠ ܟܢܫܐ ܕܐܢܫܐ] ܡܢ ܣܓܝܐܐ S
14 ܒܬܪ] ܡܢ ܒܬܪ S   ܗܘܐ] om. S   ܝܫܘܥ] ܡܪܢ S   ܠܗܘ ܕܐܬܐܣܝ] om. S
ܬܚܛܐ] ܬܗܘܐ S   ܡܢ ܩܕܡܝܐ] ܡܢ ܗܘ S   15 ܓܒܪܐ ܗܘ S

V 1 After these things there had been a Feast of the Jews, and Jesus *C* [*S*]
2 had gone up to Jerusalem. And there was in Jerusalem a certain
place of baptism called in Hebrew Beth Hesda; and there are in it
3 five porches. And there were lying in the porches a number of infirm
5 and blind and withered and crippled *folk*. And there was there a
6 certain man that thirty and eight years had been infirm, and when
§Jesus saw him lying he knew that he *had* had a long time *there*. §*S*
7 He saith to him: "Wouldest thou become sound?" He saith to
him: "My Lord, I have no man who, what *time* the waters have
been troubled, will bring me down to the baptism, and while yet I am
8 coming another before me goeth down." Jesus saith to him: "Arise,
9 take up thy bed, and walk *and* go to thy house!" And in the same
hour that man was made whole and he walked. And that same day
10 it was the sabbath. The Jews say to him: "It is the sabbath; it is
11 not lawful for thee to take up thy bed." He saith to them: "He
that made me whole, he said to me 'Take up thy bed and walk.'"
12 They say to him: "Who is this man that said to thee 'Take up thy
13 bed and walk'?" And he that was healed did not know who it was,
for Jesus had removed from the place elsewhere because of the multi-
14 tude of people. After these things Jesus had found him that was
healed in the Temple, and said to him: "Lo, thou art whole; sin not
15 again, lest there chance to thee a worse than the former *one*!" And

---

3, 4. *For E*[146], *see Notes*, vol. ii 6 Jesus] our Lord *S* lying] *om. S* time] while *S* *there*] *pr.* lying *S* 7 bring me down to] cast me into *S* (*not E*[145]) and] but *S* 8 Jesus] Our Lord *S* *and* go to thy house] *om. S*; *E*[146] *has once* 'to thy house' 9 and he] + arose, took up his bed and *S* 10 The Jews...him] And when the Jews saw him they say to him *S* It is the sabbath] *om. S* 11 He saith to them] And he that was made whole saith to them *S* He that] He which *S* 12.] *om. S* (*but not E*[146]) 13 he that was healed] that man *S* for Jesus] because our Lord *S* because of the multitude of people] away from the press *S*; *cf* 'for Jesus when he beheld the multitude [of the people] withdrew himself from that place' *E*[147] 14 Jesus] our Lord *S* had] *om. S* that was healed] *om. S* chance] be *S* than the former *one*] than that *S* (*or*, 'than him'); *cf* 'lest thou have need of some one else' *E*[147]

C S ܠܝܗ̈ܘܕܝܐ. ܕܝܫܘܥ ܗܘ ܗܘ ܕܐܚܠܡܢܝ. [16]ܘܡܛܠܬܗ ܪܕܦܝܢ ܗܘܘ
ܝܗ̈ܘܕܝܐ ܠܝܫܘܥ. ܥܠ ܕܠܡܢܐ ܥܒܕ ܗܠܝܢ ܒܫܒܬܐ. [17]ܗܘ ܕܝܢ
ܝܫܘܥ ܐܡܪ ܠܗܘܢ. ܐܒܝ ܥܕܡܐ ܠܗܫܐ ܥܒ̈ܕܐ ܥܒܕ. ܡܛܠ
ܗܢܐ ܘܐܦ ܐܢܐ ܥܒܕܢܐ. [18]ܝܗ̈ܘܕܝܐ ܕܝܢ ܡܛܠ ܗܕܐ ܡܠܬܐ
ܒܥܝܢ ܗܘܘ ܠܡܩܛܠܗ. ܠܐ ܒܠܚܘܕ ܡܛܠ ܕܫܪܐ ܗܘܐ ܫܒܬܐ.
ܐܠܐ ܡܛܠ ܕܠܐܠܗܐ ܐܒܝ ܐܡܪ ܗܘܐ. ܘܡܫܘܡ ܗܘܐ ܢܦܫܗ
col 2 ܥܡ ܐܠܗܐ. [19]ܐܡܪ ܠܗܘܢ ܝܫܘܥ. ܐܡܝܢ ܐܡܝܢ *ܐܡܪܢܐ
ܠܟܘܢ. ܕܠܐ ܡܫܟܚ ܒܪܐ ܡܕܡ ܡܢ ܨܒܘܬ ܢܦܫܗ ܠܡܥܒܕ.
ܐܦܠܐ ܡܕܡ ܕܠܐ ܚܙܐ ܠܐܒܘܗܝ ܕܥܒܕ. ܐܠܐ ܡܢܐ ܕܐܒܘܗܝ
ܥܒܕ ܘܐܦ ܒܪܐ ܒܗ ܡܬܕܡܐ. [20]ܐܒܐ ܓܝܪ ܪܚܡ ܗܘ ܠܒܪܗ.
ܘܟܠܡܕܡ ܕܥܒܕ ܡܚܘܐ ܠܗ. ܕܗܘ ܢܥܒܕ. ܘܕܬܬܕܡܪܘܢ ܡܢ ܗܠܝܢ
ܥܒ̈ܕܐ ܡܚܘܐ ܠܗ. ܘܠܐ ܬܬܕܡܪܘܢ ܕܐܡܪܬ ܠܟܘܢ.
[21]ܐܝܟܢܐ ܓܝܪ ܕܐܒܐ ܡܩܝܡ ܡܝ̈ܬܐ ܘܡܚܐ ܠܗܘܢ. ܗܟܢܐ
§¶A 123, 276 ܐܦ ܒܪܐ ܡܚܐ ܠܐܝܠܝܢ ܕܨܒܐ ܒܗ. §[22]ܐܒܐ ܓܝܪ ܠܐܢܫ
ܠܐ ܕܐܢ. ܐܠܐ ܟܠܗ ܕܝܢܐ ܠܒܪܗ ܝܗܒܗ.¶ [23]ܕܟܠ ܐܢܫ
fol 46 r ܢܝܩܪ ܠܒܪܐ *ܐܝܟܢܐ ܕܡܝܩܪ ܠܐܒܐ. ܘܡܢ ܕܠܒܪܐ ܠܐ ܡܝܩܪ
ܐܦܠܐ ܠܐܒܐ ܕܫܕܪܗ ܡܝܩܪ. [24]ܐܡܝܢ ܐܡܝܢ ܐܡܪܢܐ ܠܟܘܢ.
ܕܡܢ ܕܫܡܥ ܡܠܬܝ, ܘܡܗܝܡܢ ܠܡܢ ܕܫܕܪܢܝ. ܐܝܬ ܠܗ ܚܝ̈ܐ
ܕܠܥܠܡ. ܘܠܕܝܢܐ ܠܐ ܐܬܐ. ܡܛܠ ܕܫܢܝ ܠܗ ܡܢ ܡܘܬܐ ܠܚܝ̈ܐ.

ܕܐܚܠܡܢܝ] ܕܐܚܠܡܗ S (cf ver. 18)   16 ܘܡܛܠܬܗ] ܘܡܛܠ ܗܕܐ S
ܠܝܫܘܥ] ܠܡܪܢ S   17 ܝܫܘܥ] ܡܪܢ S   ܘܐܦ] ܐܦ S   ܥܒܕ ܐܢܐ S
18 ܡܛܠ 1°] C on eras   ܐܒܝ] ܐܒܘܗܝ S (cf ver. 15)   ܘܡܫܘܡ] ܘܡܫܘܐ S^ed
19 ܝܫܘܥ] ܡܪܢ S   ܐܡܝܢ 2°] om. S   ܨܒܘܬ] om. S
ܐܦܠܐ......ܕܥܒܕ.] ܐܠܐ ܡܕܡ ܕܚܙܐ ܠܐܒܘܗܝ ⸢ܕܥܒܕ ܗܘ⸣ ܥܒܕ S
ܐܠܐ ܡܢܐ ܕܐܒܘܗܝ ܥܒܕ] ܐܝܠܝܢ ܓܝܪ ܕܥܒܕ ܐܒܘܗܝ ܥܒܕ S
ܘܐܦ ܒܪܐ ܒܗ ܡܬܕܡܐ] ⸢ܗܠܝܢ⸣ ܐܦ ܒܪܐ ܒܗܝܢ ܥܒܕ S^ed   20 ܗܘ] om. S
ܕܗܘ ܢܥܒܕ] om. S   ܘܬܬܕܡܪܘܢ S   20, 21 ܘܠܐ....ܕܐܒܐ ܡܚܝܐ] S illegible
22 ܓܝܪ] om. A   ܠܒܪܐ A^a 276   23 ܢܝܩܪ....ܐܦܠܐ] S illegible
ܡܝܩܪ 2°] om. S at end of ver. (? supply it before ܠܐܒܐ)   24 ܡܛܠ ܕ] ܐܠܐ S

that man went and said to the Jews that 'it was Jesus that made *C S*
16 me whole.' And because of it the Jews were persecuting Jesus, as to
17 why he did these things on the sabbath. Now Jesus said to them:
18 "My Father yet doeth deeds, therefore I also do *them*." But the Jews
because of this word were seeking to kill him, not only because he
was loosing the sabbath, but because he was calling God 'my Father,'
19 and was comparing himself with God. Jesus saith to them: "Amen,
amen, I say to you The Son cannot do anything from his own self,
nor anything which he hath not seen his Father do, but whatsoever
20 his Father doeth the Son also imitateth him. For the Father
loveth his Son, and everything that he doeth he sheweth him that he
may do *it*, and more than these deeds he sheweth him. And do not
21 wonder that I have said *it* to you; for as the Father maketh alive
the dead and raiseth them, so the Son also maketh alive those that
22 believe in him. §For the Father will judge no one, but all judgement §¶*A* 123, 276
23 he will give to his Son,¶ that every man may honour the Son as he
honoureth the Father; and he that doth not honour the Son, neither
24 the Father that sent him doth he honour. Amen, amen, I say to you
He that heareth my word and believeth him that sent me, he hath
life eternal, and into judgement he cometh not, because he hath

---

15 me] him *S* (*not* E^{147}); *cf ver.* 18   16 because of it] therefore *S* Jesus] our Lord *S*   17 Jesus] our Lord *S*   18 'my Father'] his Father *S* E^{147}; *cf ver.* 15   comparing himself] making himself equal S^{ed} $E^{147,148}$ 19 Jesus] Our Lord *S*   amen 2°] *om. S*   his own self] himself *S*   nor anything.... do] but that which he seeth his Father ⌜do he⌝ doeth *S*   but whatsoever....him] for the things which his Father doeth, ⌜these⌝ the Son also like him doeth S^{ed} 20 that he may do *it*] *om. S*   20, 21 And do not...maketh alive (1°)] *S illegible*   22 For] *om. A*   his Son] the Son A^{a}276   23 may honour..... neither] *S illegible*   24 because] but *S*

C (S) §A 156, 167 ¶S ¶A

25 ܐܡܝܢ ܐܡܝܢ ܐܡܪܢܐ ܠܟܘܢ܆ §ܕܐܬܝܐ ܫܥܬܐ¶ ܘܐܦ ܗܫܐ
ܐܝܬܝܗ܂ ܕܐܦ ܡ̈ܝܬܐ ܢܫܡܥܘܢ ܩܠܗ ܕܒܪܗ ܕܐܠܗܐ ܘܢܚܘܢ܆¶
26 ܐܝܟܢܐ ܓܝܪ ܕܠܐܒܐ ܐܝܬ ܚܝ̈ܐ ܒܩܢܘܡܗ. ܗܟܢܐ ܝܗܒ ܐܦ
ܠܒܪܐ ܕܢܗܘܘܢ ܐܝܬ ܠܗ ܚܝ̈ܐ ܒܩܢܘܡܗ. 27 ܘܐܫܠܛܗ ܥܠ ܕܝܢܐ
col 2 ܕܒܪܗ ܗܘ ܕܐܢܫܐ. 28 ܘܠܐ ܬܬܕܡܪܘܢ ܒܗܕܐ. *ܕܗܐ ܟܠܗܘܢ
ܐܝܠܝܢ ܕܒܩܒ̈ܪܐ ܐܢܘܢ܆ ܢܫܡܥܘܢ ܩܠܗ ܕܐܠܗܐ ܘܢܚܘܢ
29 ܘܢܦܩܘܢ܆ ܘܐܝܠܝܢ ܕ̈ܥܒܕܘ ܛܒ̈ܬܐ ܐܢܘܢ ܢܦܩܘܢ ܠܩܝܡܬܐ
ܕܚܝ̈ܐ. ܘܐܝܠܝܢ ܕܥܒܕܘ ܒ̈ܝܫܬܐ ܐܢܘܢ ܢܦܩܘܢ ܠܩܝܡܬܐ ܕܕܝܢܐ.
30 ܠܐ ܡܫܟܚ ܐܢܐ ܡܕܡ ܡܢ ܨܒܘܬ ܢܦܫܝ ܠܡܥܒܕ. ܐܠܐ
ܐܝܟܢܐ ܕܫܡܥ ܐܢܐ ܕܐܢ ܐܢܐ. ܘܕܝܢܝ ܟܐܢ ܗܘ. ܠܐ ܓܝܪ
ܒܥܐ ܐܢܐ ܨܒܝܢܝ. ܐܠܐ ܒܥܐ ܐܢܐ ܨܒܝܢܗ ܕܡܢ ܕܫܕܪܢܝ.
31 ܐܢ ܐܢܐ ܡܣܗܕ ܐܢܐ ܥܠ ܢܦܫܝ. ܣܗܕܘܬܝ ܠܐ ܗܘܬ
ܫܪܝܪܐ. 32 ܐܚܪܢ ܗܘ ܣܗܕ ܥܠܝ. ܘܝܕܥܝܢ ܐܢܬܘܢ ܕܫܪܝܪܐ ܗܝ
ܣܗܕܘܬܗ ܕܐܣܗܕ ܥܠܝ. 33 ܐܢܬܘܢ ܫܕܪܬܘܢ ܠܘܬ ܝܘܚܢܢ.
fol 46 v ܘܐܣܗܕ *ܒܫܪܪܐ. 34 ܐܢܐ ܕܝܢ ܠܐ ܗܘܐ ܡܢ ܒܪ ܐܢܫܐ ܢܣܒ
ܐܢܐ ܣܗܕܘܬܐ. ܐܠܐ ܗܠܝܢ ܐܡܪ ܐܢܐ ܕܐܢܬܘܢ ܬܚܘܢ.
35 ܗܘ ܫܪܓܐ ܗܘܐ· ܕܝܩܕ ܘܡܢܗܪ. ܐܢܬܘܢ ܕܝܢ ܨܒܝܬܘܢ
ܕܬܫܬܒܗܪܘܢ ܕܫܥܬܐ ܒܢܘܗܪܗ. 36 ܐܢܐ ܠܝ ܕܝܢ ܣܗܕܘܬܐ
ܪܒܬܐ ܡܢ ܕܝܘܚܢܢ. ܥܒ̈ܕܐ ܓܝܪ ܕܝܗܒ ܠܝ ܐܒܝ ܕܐܫܠܡ ܐܢܘܢ.
ܗܢܘܢ ܥܒ̈ܕܐ ܕܥܒܕ ܐܢܐ ܣܗܕܝܢ ܥܠܝ ܕܐܒܐ ܫܠܚܢܝ. 37 ܘܐܒܐ
ܕܫܠܚܢܝ ܗܘ ܣܗܕ ܥܠܝ. ܠܐ ܩܠܗ ܡܢ ܡܬܘܡ ܫܡܥܬܘܢ܆ ܘܠܐ
ܚܙܘܗ ܚܙܝܬܘܢ. 38 ܘܠܐ ܡܠܬܗ ܡܩܘܝܐ ܒܟܘܢ· ܡܛܠ ܕܒܐܝܢܐ
ܕܗܘ ܫܕܪ ܐܢܬܘܢ ܠܐ ܡܗܝܡܢܝܢ ܐܢܬܘܢ܆ 39 ܒܨܘ ܠܟܬܒ̈ܐ
col 2 *ܕܒܗܘܢ ܣܒܪܝܢ ܐܢܬܘܢ ܕܚܝ̈ܐ ܠܥܠܡ. ܘܗܢܘܢ ܟܬܒ̈ܐ

---

25 ܫܥܬܐ] *S illegible*; ܬܫܥܬܐ $A^2/_2$ ܘܐܦ] ܐܦ A 156; *om.* ܘܐܦ ܗܫܐ ܐܝܬܝܗ A 167 ܕܒܪܗ ܕܐܠܗܐ] ܕܒܪܗ ܕܐܢܫܐ $A^2/_2$ ܘܢܚܘܢ] *om.* A 167; + ܘܢܦܩܘܢ ܡܢ ܩܒܪ̈ܝܗܘܢ $A^2/_2$ (*cf ver.* 28) 32 ܐܚܪܢ] *end of line in C*; *cf* Joh iv 37

25 removed from death to life. Amen, amen, I say to you §The hour C (S)
cometh,¶ and even now it is, that the dead also shall hear the voice §A 156, 167
26 of the Son of God and shall live.¶ For as the Father hath life in ¶S ¶A
his own person, so hath he given to the Son also that he should have
27 life in his own person, and he hath set him in authority over judge-
28 ment, *seeing* that he is the Son of Man. And do not wonder at this,
for lo, all they that are in the graves shall hear the voice of God and
29 shall live and come forth, and they that are doers of good shall be for
the resurrection of life and they that are doers of evil shall be for
30 the resurrection of judgement. I cannot do anything from my own
mind, but as I hear I judge, and my judgement is upright. For I
31 seek not my will, but I seek the will of him that sent me. If I bear
32 witness of myself my witness is not true. It is another beareth
witness of me, and ye know that true is his witness that he hath
33 witnessed of me. Ye have sent unto John and he hath witnessed
34 in truth, but I—not from man do I take witness, but these things
35 I say that ye may live. He was a lamp burning and shining, but
36 ye wished to make your boast for the hour in his light. But I
have witness that *is* greater than John's, for the deeds that my
Father gave me that I might fulfil them—those deeds that I do
37 bear witness of me that the Father hath sent me; and the Father
that sent me, he beareth witness of me: his voice never have
38 ye heard, nor the vision of him have ye seen, nor doth his word
abide in you, because in the one that he hath sent ye believe not.
39 Search the Scriptures by which ye hope that ye will live for ever,

---

25 cometh] *S illegible*; will come $A^2/_2$ and even now it is] *om.* *A* 167 Son of God] Son of Man $A^2/_2$ and shall live] *om.* *A* 167; + and shall come forth from their graves $A^2/_2$ (*cf ver.* 28) **27, 28.** *For the punctuation, see Notes*, vol. ii **34** 'Not that I receive witness from men' E^{151} (*and* arm.vg); *for the construction, cf* Joh xii 6 **36, 37** sent] *cf* Matt xi 2

C [S] ܥܠ ܗܘ ܦܬܓܡ. ܗܢܘܢ ܕܦܩܕܝܢ ܐܢܬܘܢ ܕܬܥܒܕܘܢ ܐܝܬ
ܠܗܘܢ ܫܢܐ. ܗܢܘܢ ܦܬܓܡ ܥܠ. [40]ܘܠܘܬܝ, ܠܐ ܙܕܩ ܐܢܬܘܢ
ܕܬܐܬܘܢ܇ ܕܢܗܘܘܢ ܠܗܘܢ ܫܢܐ. [41]ܫܘܒܚܐ ܡܢ ܒ̈ܢܝ ܐܢܫܐ
ܠܐ ܢܣܒ ܐܢܐ. [42]ܐܠܐ ܝܕܥܬܟܘܢ ܕܚܘܒܐ ܕܐܠܗܐ ܠܝܬ
ܒܟܘܢ. [43]ܐܢܐ ܐܬܝܬ ܒܫܡܗ ܕܐܒܝ ܘܠܐ ܡܩܒܠܝܢ ܐܢܬܘܢ
ܠܝ. ܘܐܢ ܐܚܪܝܢ ܢܐܬܐ ܒܫܡ ܢܦܫܗ ܠܗܘ ܬܩܒܠܘܢ܇ [44]ܐܝܟܢܐ
ܡܫܟܚܝܢ ܐܢܬܘܢ ܠܡܗܝܡܢܘ. ܕܫܘܒܚܐ ܚܕ ܡܢ ܚܕ ܡܩܒܠܝܢ
ܐܢܬܘܢ. ܘܫܘܒܚܐ ܕܡܢ ܚܕ ܐܠܗܐ ܠܐ ܒܥܝܢ ܐܢܬܘܢ܇ [45]ܠܡܐ
fol 47 r ܣܒܪܝܢ *ܐܢܬܘܢ ܕܐܢܐ ܗܘ ܐܟܠ ܩܪ̈ܨܝܟܘܢ܇ ܡܘܫܐ ܗܘ
ܐܟܠ ܩܪ̈ܨܝܟܘܢ܇ ܗܘ ܕܒܗ ܡܣܒܪܝܢ ܐܢܬܘܢ܇ [46]ܐܠܘ ܓܝܪ
§S ܒܡܘܫܐ ܗܝܡܢܬܘܢ ܗܘܝܬܘܢ܇ [§]ܘܐܦ ܒܝ ܡܗܝܡܢܝܢ ܗܘܝܬܘܢ܇
ܗܘ ܓܝܪ ܥܠ ܗܘ ܟܬܒ. [47]ܘܐܢ ܕܝܢ ܒܟܬ̈ܒܘܗܝ, ܕܗܘ ܠܐ
ܡܗܝܡܢܝܢ ܐܢܬܘܢ܇ ܐܝܟܢܐ ܠܡ̈ܠܝ ܡܗܝܡܢܝܢ ܐܢܬܘܢ ܀

[1]ܒܬܪ ܗܠܝܢ. ܐܙܠ ܝܫܘܥ ܠܥܒܪܐ ܕܝܡܬܐ ܕܓܠܝܠܐ ܕܛܒܪܝܘܣ.
[2]ܘܐܙܠ ܒܬܪܗ ܟܢܫܐ ܣܓܝܐܐ. ܡܛܠ ܕܚܙܝܢ ܗܘܘ ܐܬ̈ܘܬܐ
ܕܥܒܕ ܗܘܐ ܥܠ ܟܪ̈ܝܗܐ. [3]ܘܣܠܩ ܗܘܐ ܝܫܘܥ ܠܛܘܪܐ. ܘܬܡܢ
ܝܬܒ ܗܘܐ ܥܡ ܬܠܡܝܕܘܗܝ. [4]ܘܩܪܝܒܐ ܗܘܬ ܦܨܚܐ ܥܐܕܐ
col 2 *ܕܝܗܘ̈ܕܝܐ. [5]ܘܐܪܝܡ ܥܝܢܘܗܝ ܝܫܘܥ. ܘܚܙܐ ܟܢܫܐ ܣܓܝܐܐ
ܕܐܬܐ ܠܘܬܗ. ܘܐܡܪ ܠܦܝܠܝܦܘܣ ܐܝܟܢܐ ܢܙܒܢ ܠܚܡܐ
ܕܢܐܟܠܘܢ ܗܠܝܢ ܐܢܫܐ. [6]ܗܘ ܕܝܢ ܐܡܪ ܡܢܣܐ ܗܘܐ ܠܗ ܫܐܠܗ.
ܗܘ ܓܝܪ ܝܕܥ ܗܘܐ ܡܢܐ ܥܬܝܕ ܠܡܥܒܕ. [7]ܐܡܪ ܠܗ ܦܝܠܝܦܘܣ.
ܕܡ̈ܐܬܝܢ ܕܝ̈ܢܪܝܢ ܠܚܡܐ ܠܐ ܣܦܩ ܠܗܘܢ ܟܕ ܩܠܝܠ ܩܠܝܠ
ܢܣܒܘܢ. [8]ܐܡܪ ܠܗ ܚܕ ܡܢ ܬܠܡܝܕܘܗܝ., ܐܢܕܪܐܘܣ ܫܡܗ
ܗܘܐ. ܐܚܘܗܝ, ܕܫܡܥܘܢ ܟܐܦܐ. [9]ܐܝܬ ܬܢܢ ܛܠܝܐ ܘܐܝܬ ܥܠܘܗܝ,

46 ܘܐܦ] ܐܦ S   ܥܠ ܗܘ] om. ܗܘ S   47 ܕܝܢ] om. S   ܠܡ̈ܠܝ]
ܒܡ̈ܠܝ ܕܝܠܝ S   1 ܐܙܠ ܠܗ ܡܪܢ S   ܕܛܒܪܝܘܣ S   3 ܘܣܠܩ ܠܗ ܡܪܢ S
4. ܘܩܪܝܒ ܗܘܐ ܒܥܐܕܐ ܕܦܨ̈ܚܐ ܕܝܗܘ̈ܕܝܐ S: see Notes, vol. ii
5 ܝܫܘܥ] ܡܪܢ S   ܟܢܫܐ ܣܓܝܐܐ ܕܐܬܐ S   ܘܐܡܪ] ܐܡܪ S
ܠܗܠܝܢ ܐܢܫܐ ܕܢܐܟܠܘܢ S   8 ܐܢܕܪܐܘܣ ܫܡܗ ܗܘܐ] ܐܢܕܪܐܘܣ ܕܫܡܗ S
9 ܐܝܬ ܬܢܢ....ܥܠܘܗܝ] ܐܝܬ ܬܢܢ. ܛܠܝܐ ܚܕ ܥܠ S

and those Scriptures—of me it is they bear witness. Those that *C* [*S*]
40 ye hope that by them ye have life, they bear witness of me, and
41 unto me ye are not willing to come, that ye may have life! Glory
42 from men I take not; but I have known you, that the love of
43 God is not in you. I have come in the name of my Father and ye
receive not me; and if another should come in his own name, him
44 ye will receive. How can ye believe, that receive glory one from the
45 other, and the glory that *is* from the One God ye seek not? Can ye
suppose that I am your accuser? Moses is your accuser, he in whom
46 ye hope. For if in Moses ye had believed, §in me also ye would have §*S*
47 believed, for he of me hath written. But if in the Scriptures of
him ye believe not, how will ye believe my words?"

vi 1 After these things Jesus went to the other side of the Lake of
2 Galilee, *the Lake* of Tiberius, and there went after him a great
multitude because they were seeing the signs that he was doing on
3 the infirm. And Jesus had gone up to the hill and there was sitting
4 with his disciples. And Pasek, the Feast of the Jews, was nigh.
5 And Jesus lifted up his eyes and saw the great multitudes coming
unto him, and he said to Philip: "Whence shall we buy bread,
6 that these folk may eat?" Now he as if tempting him asked him,
7 for he was knowing what he was about to do. Philip saith to him
"Two hundred denars *worth of* bread would not suffice for them,
8 though they should eat each a little." Saith to him one of his
9 disciples, Andrew was his name, the brother of Simon Kepha: "There
is here a lad and he hath on him five loaves of barley and two

---

47 But if] And if *S* my words] in words of mine *S* 1 Jesus went] our Lord went away *S* Tiberias *S*[vid] 3 And our Lord went up *S* 4 And Pasek....nigh] And nigh was the Feast of the Unleavened Bread of the Jews *S*: *see Notes*, vol ii 5 Jesus] our Lord *S* multitude *S* and he said] he saith *S* that....eat] for these folk that they may eat *S* 8 Andrew was his name] whose name *was* Andrew *S* 9 There is....on him] A certain lad hath on him here *S*

ܣܥܪ ܠܬܢܝ̈ܢ ܕܡܩܕܘܢܐ. ܘܩܐܡ ܢܩܝܦ. ܐܠܐ ܗܠܝܡ ܡܚܒܐ C S
ܚܟܝ̈ܢ ܠܗܠܝܢ ܟܠܗܘܢ. [10] ܐܡܪ ܗܘ ܡܘܒܕ. ܘܠܐ *ܐܫܟܚܢܘ fol 47 v
ܐܢܘܢ ܠܐܘܢܐ ܦܩ̈ܕܝܢ. ܒܦܩܕܐ ܕܝܢ ܦܠܚ ܗܘܐ ܒܗ
ܒܕܘܟܬܐ ܗܝ. ܘܐܫܬܦܟܘ ܐܢܫܐ ܡܚܢܢܐ ܣܓ̈ܝܐܐ ܬ̈ܠܝܦܝܢ.
[11] ܘܣܠܩ ܡܘܒܕ ܠܫ̈ܡܬܪܐ ܗܘܢ ܘܒܪܟ. ܘܡܢ ܠܗܘܢ ܕܦܩܕܝܢ.
ܘܗܒܢܐ ܘܐܦ ܒܠ ܢܩܝܐ ܒܒܝܐ ܕܝܒܘ. [12] ܘܒܪ ܦܠܒܘ ܐܡܪ
ܠܦܠܝܦܘܣ. ܒܢܫܘ ܡܕܝܢܬܐ ܡܕܝܢ ܕܐܬܪܘ. ܕܐܠܡܪ ܡܕܝܢ ܠܐ
ܢܐܒܕ. [13] ܘܒܢܫܘ ܘܡܠܘ ܬܪܥܘܪ ܡܦܝܣܝܢ ܕܩܝܪܝܐ. ܡܢ ܫ̈ܒܥܐ
ܠܝܘܡܝܢ ܕܦܠܒܐ. ܡܕܝܢ ܕܐܬܪܘ ܡܢ ܗܘܢ ܕܐܒܠܘ. [14] ܗܘܢ ܕܝܢ
ܐܢܫܐ ܒܪ ܚܝܠ ܐܝܬܐ ܗܕܐ ܕܒܝܬ. ܐܡܪܝܢ ܗܘܘ. ܥܪܒܐܬ
ܗܢܐ ܗܘ ܢܒܝܐ ܕܐܝܬܝܗ ܠܒܠܒܐ. [15] ܘܫܒܩ ܗܘܐ ܡܘܒܕ *ܕܒܝܬ col 2
ܗܘܘ ܕܢܫܦܩܘܢ ܘܢܒܕܘܢ ܒܠܒܐ. ܥܒܕ ܐܢܘܢ ܘܒܪܝܡ ܠܗ
ܬܒܕ ܠܦܝܪܐ ܒܠܡܘܢܗܘܢ. [16] ܒܕ ܗܘܐ ܕܝܢ ܪܡܫܐ. ܢܦܩܬ ܗܘܘ
†ܬ̈ܠܡܝܕܘܗܝ، ܠܢܗܪܐ. [17] ܘܐܡܪܝܢ ܒܦܝܣܘܬܐ. ܘܐܬܝܢ ܗܘܘ ܠܚܒܪܐ
ܕܡܠܬܐ ܕܡܦܩܪܣܘܢ. ܘܡܫܒܚܬ ܗܘܬ ܠܗ. ܘܠܐ ܐܬܬܐ ܠܬܠܗܘܢ

---

10. § in S   ܠܗܠܝܢ ܒܩܠܗܘܢ ܡܢܐ ܚܟܝܡ [ܗܠܝܢ......ܟܠܗܘܢ S
S ܐܡܪ ܠܗܘܢ ܐܡܫܟܚܐ ܐܢܫܐ [ܐܡܪ ܗܘ ܡܘܒܕ......ܦܩܕܝܢ.
[ܘܐܫܬܦܟܘ.....ܬ̈ܠܝܦܝܢ   S ܒܗ ܒܐܬܪܐ [ܒܗ ܒܕܘܟܬܐ ܗܝ
S ܐܡܪ ܠܗܘܢ ܘܠܐ ܐܫܟܚܢܐ ܐܢܫܐ ܒܠ ܢܘܪܐ
ܡܘܒܕ] so also S   S ܘܒܪ ܐܫܟܚܢܐ ܐܢܘܢ ܗܝܕܝܢ ܥܡܠ [ܘܥܠܠ 11
[ܘܒܪܟ.......ܕܝܒܘ.   S ܗܘܢ ܣܓ̈ܝܐܐ ܠܢܝ̈ܢ ܘܩܪܝܡ ܢܩܝܦ [ܠܫ̈ܡܬܪܐ ܗܘܢ
[ܐܡܪ ܠܦܠ' 12   S ܘܐܬܐ ܠܥܒܪܐ * ܘܡܠܝܟ ܠܬܠܡܝܕܘܗܝ * * * *
so also S   ܡܕܝܢ 1°] om. S   ܕܐܬܪܘ S   ܕ [ܕܐܠܡܪ S
13 ܘܒܢܫܘ] + ܡܢ ܐܢܘܢ ܕܐܬܪܘ ܕܒܢܫܘ S   [ܕܩܝܪܝܐ] om. S
ܡܦܝܣܝܢ ܕܐܬܪܘ ܣܓܝ ܠܬܢܝ̈ܢ ܕܡܩܕܢܐ ܘܩܐܡ ܢܩܝܦ [ܡܢ ܫ̈ܒܥܐ to end of ver.
S ܢܦܩܝܢ ܗܘܘ ܗܘܘ ܕܝܢ ܠܬܪ̈ܥܐ ܕܐܒܠܘ ܗܘܘ ܡܢ ܠܫܒܬܐ ܗܘܐ ܐܠܝܦ ܣܓܝܐܐ
14 ܐܢܫܐ] ܗܘ S   ܗܘܘ] om. S   ܗܘ ܥܪܒܐܬ S   15 ܘܫܒܩ ܗܘܐ....ܗܘܘ]
S ܗܘ ܕܝܢ ܡܘܒܕ ܡܕܝܢ + [ܒܠܒܐ   ܕܢܒܕܘܢܗܘܢ S   [ܘܢܒܕܘܢܗܘܢ   ܘܐܬܪܘܢܗܘܢ S   ܗܘܘ
[ܒܠܡܘܢܗܘܢ   [ܥܒܕ] pr. ܘ S (sic)   ܘܒܪܝܡ] ܘܗܠܝܢ S   ܬܒܕ] om. S
pr. ܗܘ S   16 ܒܕ ܗܘܐ ܕܝܢ [ܒܕ ܗܘܐ] ܘܒܕ ܗܘܐ S   [ܢܦܩܬ ܗܘܘ ܬܠ'
ܢܦܩܬ ܗܘ ܬܠ' C; ܢܦܩܬ ܬܠ' S   17 ܕܐܡܪܬܐ] om. S   ܠܦܝܣܘܬ S   [ܘܐܡܪܝܢ
ܕܐܝܬ ܕܘܡܒܪ S   + ܗܘܐ [ܐܬܬܐ S

10 fishes, but these—what will they do for all these?" Jesus saith: "Go, C S
make the folk sit down *to meat* companies by companies." Now the
green grass was plentiful in that same spot, and the folk sat down *to*
11 *meat* in number five thousand. And Jesus took up those pieces of
bread and blessed, and gave to those that sat *at meat,* and so also for
12 the fishes as much as they would. And when they were satisfied, he
said to his disciples: "Gather the fragments, whatever have remained
13 over, that nothing at all may be lost." And they gathered and filled
twelve baskets of fragments from the five pieces of barley-bread,—
14 those which remained over from them that ate. Now the folk, when
they saw this sign that he did, were saying: "Truly this is the prophet
15 that cometh to the world." And Jesus had known that they were seek-
ing that they should snatch him away and make him a king: he left
16 them and fled again to the hill alone. Now when it was evening his
17 disciples †had gone down† to the sea, and sat in the boat and were
coming to the other side of the lake †of† Kapharnahum. And it

---

but...all these?] but for all these what will they do? *S* 10 Jesus saith....by companies] He saith to them: Make the folk sit down *to meat S* spot] place *S* and.....thousand] He saith to them: Go, make the folk sit down *to meat* on the herbage *S* 11 And Jesus took up] And when they made them sit down *to meat,* then did Jesus take up *S* those pieces of bread] those five pieces of bread and two fishes *S* and blessed.....they would] and gazed up to heaven * * and divided to his disciples * * * *S* (*rest illegible*); *cf* Diat[ar] xviii 38—40 12 whatever] that *S* at all] *om. S* 13 they gathered] + them, the fragments that remained over of them *S* of fragments] *om. S* from the five *to end of ver.*] the superabundance of those five loaves of barley and of those two fishes. Now the men that had eaten of that bread had been five thousand *S* 14 this sign] that sign *S* were saying] say *S* This is truly *S* 15 And Jesus.....seeking] And they had meditated *S* and make] to make *S* a king] + but Jesus knew *S* he left] *pr.* and *S* fled] went up *S E*[134] again] *om. S* alone] *pr.* he *S* 16 Now] And *S* had gone down] went down *S*; *C has* 'he went down and his disciples' 17 of the lake] *om. S* of Kaph.] *C*; to Kaph. *S* And] because *S*

ܝܫܘܥ. ¹⁸ܘܪܘܚܐ ܩܫܬ ܗܘܬ ܠܗ̇ ܒܝܡܐ. ܘܐܫܬܓܫܬ ܥܠܝܗܘܢ C S
ܡܚܬܐ. ¹⁹ܘܕܒܪܘܗ̇ ܗܘܘ ܠܣܦܝܢܬܐ ܐܣ̈ܛܕܘܬܐ ܥ̈ܣܪܝܢ ܘܚܡܫܐ
ܐܘ ܬܠܬܝܢ. ܘܚܙܘ ܠܝܫܘܥ ܟܕ ܡܗܠܟ ܥܠ ܡ̈ܝܐ. ܘܟܕ ܩܪܒ
ܠܘܬ ܣܦܝܢܬܐ. ܕܚܠܘ. ²⁰ܗܘ ܕܝܢ ܝܫܘܥ ܐܡܪ ܠܗܘܢ ܐܢܐ
ܐܢܐ. ²¹ܘܨܒܝܢ ܗܘܘ *ܕܢܣܒܠܘܢܝܗ ܒܣܦܝܢܬܐ. ܘܒܗ̇ ܒܫܥܬܐ ܗ̇ܝ fol 48 r
ܣܦܝܢܬܐ ܩܪܒܬ ܗܘܬ ܠܘܬ ܐܪܥܐ. ܗ̇ܝ ܕܐܙܠܝܢ ܗܘܘ ܠܗ̇ ܀

²²ܘܠܝܘܡܐ ܐܚܪܢܐ ܗܘ ܟܢܫܐ ܕܒܥܒܪܐ ܗܘܐ ܕܝܡܐ· ܕܚܙܐ
ܕܣܦܝܢܬܐ ܐܚܪܬܐ ܠܝܬ ܗܘܐ ܬܡܢ· ܐܠܐ ܐܢ ܚܕܐ ܕܥܒܪܘ
ܒܗ̇ ܬܠܡܝܕܘܗܝ. ܕܝܫܘܥ· ܘܝܫܘܥ ܠܐ ܗܘܐ ܥܡ ܬܠܡܝܕܘܗܝ
ܗܘܐ ܒܣܦܝܢܬܐ. ²³ܘܟܕ ܐܬܝ̈ ܣ̈ܦܝܢܐ ܐ̈ܚܪܢܝܬܐ ܡܢ ܛܒܪܝܘܣ
ܠܐܬܪ ܕܐܟܠܘ ܠܚܡܐ· ²⁴ܘܚܙܘ ܕܠܐ ܗܘܐ ܬܡܢ ܝܫܘܥ ܘܐܦ
ܠܐ ܬܠܡܝܕܘܗܝ. ܢܚܬܘ ܠܗܘܢ ܠܣܦܝܢܬܐ. ܘܐܬܘ ܗܘܘ
ܠܟܦܪܢܚܘܡ. ܘܒܥܝܢ ܗܘܘ ܠܗ ܠܝܫܘܥ· *²⁵ܘܟܕ ܕܝܢ ܐܫܟܚܘܗܝ, col 2
ܒܥܒܪܐ ܕܝܡܐ. ܐܡܪܝܢ ܠܗ ܪܒܢ ܐܡܬܝ, ܐܬܝܬ ܠܗܪܐ. ²⁶ܐܡܪ
ܠܗܘܢ ܝܫܘܥ· ܐܡܝܢ ܐܡܝܢ ܐܡܪܢܐ ܠܟܘܢ· ܕܠܐ ܗܘܐ
ܡܛܠ ܕܚܙܝܬܘܢ ܐܬ̈ܘܬܐ ܒܥܝܬܘܢܢܝ. ܐܠܐ ܡܛܠ ܕܐܟܠܬܘܢ
ܠܚܡܐ ܘܣܒܥܬܘܢ. ²⁷ܠܐ ܬܦܠܚܘܢ ܡܐܟܘܠܬܐ ܕܐܒܕܐ. ܐܠܐ
ܦܠܘܚܘ ܡܐܟܘܠܬܐ ܕܡܩܘܝܐ ܠܚ̈ܝܐ ܕܠܥܠܡ. ܐܝܕܐ ܕܒܪܗ
ܕܐܢܫܐ ܢܬܠ ܠܟܘܢ. ܠܗܢܐ ܓܝܪ ܚܬܡ ܐܠܗܐ ܐܒܐ. ²⁸ܐܡܪܝܢ

18.] S ܘܐܫܬܓܫܬ ܥܠܝܗܘܢ ܝܡܐ ܘܪܘܚܐ ܪܒܬܐ ܢܫܒܐ ܗܘܬ
19 ܘܕܒܪܘܗ̇.....ܘܚܡܫܐ] S ܘܟܕ ܪ̈ܕܘ ܥܣܪܝܢ ܘ̈ܚܡܫܐ ܐܣܛܕܘܬܐ   ܠܝܫܘܥ] + ܕܐܬܐ S   ܘܟܕ ܩܪܒ] pr. ܥܠܝܗܘܢ S, preceded by an illegible line (? ⌜ܘܨܒܐ ܗܘܐ ܕܢܥܒܪ⌝ ܥܠܝܗܘܢ cf Mk vi 48)   ܠܘܬ ܣܦܝܢܬܗܘܢ S
ܕܚܠܘ] S ⌜ܩܥܘ⌝ ܡܢ ܕܚܠܬܗܘܢ   20 ܐܢܐ ܐܢܐ] + ܠܐ ܬܕܚܠܘܢ S
21 ܘܨܒܝܢ..ܕܢܣܒܠܘܢܝܗ] S ܘܟܕ ܢܣܒܘܢܝ   ܘܒܗ̇ ܒܫܥܬܐ] ⌜ܒܫܥܬܐ⌝ S^ed ܗ̇ܝ ܣܦܝܢܬܐ S   ܩܪܒܬ] om. S   22.] S illegible (exc. ܘܠܝܘܡܐ)
23, 24] * * ܣܦܝܢܐ ܐܬܝ̈ ܡܢ ܛܒܪܝܘܣ ܠܐܬܪ ⌜ܕܐܟܠܘ ܠܚܡܐ ²⁴ܘܐܬܘ⌝ S ܠܟܦܪܢܚܘܡ ܠܥܒܪܐ ܕܝܡܐ ܘܒܥܝܢ ܗܘܘ ܠܗ   25 ܕܝܢ] om. S
ܒܥܒܪܐ ܕܝܡܐ] om. S   ܐܡܬܝ & ܠܗܪܐ] S illegible   26 ܐܡܝܢ 2°] om. S
ܒܥܝܬܘܢܢܝ] ⌜ܬ⌝ܒܥܘܢܢܝ S   27 ܡܐܟܘܠܬܐ S (in both places)   ܦܠܘܚܘ S
S ܐܝܕܐ ܕܢܬܠ ܠܟܘܢ ܒܪܗ ܕܐܢܫܐ

18 had become dark and Jesus did not come unto them, and the wind *C S*
19 had risen violently and the lake was agitated against them. And
they had brought the boat twenty-five or thirty stadia, and they saw
Jesus walking on the water, and when he drew near unto the boat
20, 21 they were afraid. But Jesus said to them: "It is I." And they
were willing that they should receive him in the boat, and in the
same hour that boat had drawn near unto the land that they were
going to.

22 And the next day that multitude which was on the other side of
the lake, which saw that there was no other boat there save the one
that the disciples of Jesus crossed over in and Jesus was not with
23 his disciples in the boat—and when other boats came from Tiberius
24 to where they ate the bread and they saw that Jesus was not there nor
his disciples,—they went down to the boat and had come to Kaphar-
25 nahum and were seeking Jesus. Now when they found him on the
other side of the lake they say to him: "Rabban, when camest thou
26 hither?" Jesus saith to them: "Amen, amen, I say to you Not
because ye saw signs have ye sought me, but because ye ate bread
27 and were satisfied. Do not work for the meat that perisheth, but
work for the meat that remaineth for life eternal, which the Son of
28 Man giveth you, for this hath God the Father sealed." They say

---

did not] had not *S* 18.] And the lake was agitated against them and a great wind was blowing *S* 19 And they had brought the boat] And when ⌜they had sailed⌝ *S* Jesus] + coming *S* and when he drew near] *pr.* ⌜and he was wishing to pass⌝ by them *S* the boat] their boat *S* they were afraid] ⌜they cried out⌝ from their fear *S*: *Words between* ⌜ ⌝ *are illegible and supplied by conjecture*; *cf* Mk vi 48 20 It is I] + fear not *S* 21 And they.... receive him] And when they took him *S* and in the same hour] in ⌜the⌝ hour S^{ed} had drawn near unto] was at *S* 22.] *illegible in S* 23, 24] * * boats came from Tiberius, where ⌜they ate the bread. [24]And they came⌝ to Kapharnahum to the other side of the lake and were seeking him *S* 25 Now] And *S* on the other side of the lake] *om. S* Rabban & hither] *illegible in S* 26 amen 2°] *om. S* have ye sought me] will ye seek me S^{vid} 27 giveth] will give *S*

ܠܗ ܡܢܐ ܢܥܒܕ ܕܢܦܠܘܚ ܒܥܒܕܐ ܕܐܠܗܐ. [29]ܐܡܪ ܠܗܘܢ C S
ܝܫܘܥ. ܗܢܐ ܗܘ ܥܒܕܐ ܕܐܠܗܐ. ܕܬܗܝܡܢܘܢ ܒܡܢ ܕܫܕܪ
ܗܘ. [30]ܐܡܪܝܢ ܠܗ ܡܢܐ ܗܟܝܠ ܐܬܐ ܥܒܕ *ܐܢܬ ܕܢܚܙܐ fol 48 v
ܘܢܗܝܡܢ ܒܟ ܡܢܐ ܦܠܚ ܐܢܬ [31]ܐܒܗܝܢ ܡܢܢܐ ܐܟܠܘ ܒܡܕܒܪܐ
ܐܝܟ ܕܟܬܝܒ ܕܠܚܡܐ ܡܢ ܫܡܝܐ ܝܗܒ ܠܗܘܢ ܠܡܐܟܠ
[32]ܐܡܪ ܠܗܘܢ ܝܫܘܥ ܐܡܝܢ ܐܡܝܢ ܐܡܪܢܐ ܠܟܘܢ ܕܠܐ ܗܘܐ
ܡܘܫܐ ܝܗܒ ܠܟܘܢ ܠܚܡܐ ܡܢ ܫܡܝܐ ܐܠܐ ܐܒܐ ܝܗܒ
ܠܟܘܢ ܠܚܡܐ ܕܩܘܫܬܐ ܡܢ ܫܡܝܐ [33]ܠܚܡܗ ܓܝܪ ܕܐܠܗܐ
ܢܚܬ ܡܢ ܫܡܝܐ ܘܚܝ ܗܘ ܘܡܬܝܗܒ ܠܥܠܡܐ [34]ܐܡܪܝܢ ܠܗ
ܡܪܢ ܒܟܠ ܙܒܢ ܗܒ ܠܢ ܠܚܡܐ ܗܢܐ [35]ܐܡܪ ܠܗܘܢ ܝܫܘܥ
ܐܢܐ ܐܢܐ ܠܚܡܐ ܕܚܝܐ ܡܢܘ ܕܐܬܐ ܠܘܬܝ, ܠܐ ܢܟܦܢ ܘܡܢ
ܕܡܗܝܡܢ ܒܝ ܠܐ ܢܨܗܐ ܠܥܠܡ [36]ܐܠܐ *ܐܡܪܬ ܠܟܘܢ col 2
ܕܚܙܝܬܘܢ ܐܢܬܘܢ ܘܠܐ ܡܗܝܡܢܝܢ ܐܢܬܘܢ [37]ܟܠ ܡܢ ܕܝܗܒ ܠܝ
ܐܒܝ ܠܘܬܝ, ܢܐܬܐ ܘܡܢ ܕܠܘܬܝ, ܢܐܬܐ ܠܐ ܐܦܩܘܗܝ, [38]ܕܢܚܬܬ
ܡܢ ܫܡܝܐ ܠܐ ܗܘܐ ܕܐܥܒܕ ܨܒܝܢܝ ܐܠܐ ܕܐܥܒܕ ܨܒܝܢܗ
ܕܐܒܐ ܕܫܕܪܢܝ [39]ܗܢܘ ܕܝܢ ܨܒܝܢܗ ܕܡܢ ܕܫܕܪܢܝ ܕܟܠ ܡܕܡ
ܕܝܗܒ ܠܝ ܠܐ ܐܘܒܕ ܡܢܗ ܡܕܡ ܐܠܐ ܐܩܝܡܝܘܗܝ, ܒܝܘܡܐ
ܐܚܪܝܐ [40]ܗܢܘ ܓܝܪ ܨܒܝܢܗ ܕܐܒܝ ܕܟܠ ܐܢܫ ܕܚܙܐ ܠܒܪܐ

---

29 ܗܢܐ ܗܘ] ܗܢܘ S^vid 30 ܗܟܝܠ] *om.* S ܐܢܬ 1°] *foll.* 48v *&* 49r *in C were passed over by the hand that added the red dots, so they are almost entirely without punctuation. See the Facsimile*, vol. ii ܡܢܐ ܦܠܚ ܐܢܬ] *om.* S
31 ܠܡܐܟܠ] *om.* S 32 ܐܡܪ ܠܗܘܢ ܝܫܘܥ] *om.* S ܐܒܐ] ܗܘ ܐܒܝ S
ܠܚܡܐ 2°] *after this word is an erasure in C, with* ·<· *over it prima manu to fill up the line* ܕܩܘܫܬܐ] ܕܫܪܪܐ S; ܕܩܘܫܬܐ C*, *but on eras* 33 ܢܚܬ] *pr.* ܕ ܐܬܝܗܒ S ܘܚܝ ܗܘ ܘܡܬܝܗܒ] ܘܚܝܐ ܝܗܒ S 34 ܠܚܡܐ ܗܢܐ] ܡܢ ܗܢܐ ܠܚܡܐ S 35 ܝܫܘܥ] *om.* S ܡܢܘ] ܡܢ S ܠܥܠܡ] ܠܥܠܡ S 36 ܕܚܙܝܬܘܢ ܐܢܬܘܢ] ܕܚܙܝܬܘܢ S 37 ܐܒܝ] ܐܒܐ S ܐܦܩܗ S^ed (*? read* ܐܦܩܗܝ) 38 ܕܐܒܐ] ܕܐܒܝ S 39 ܕܝܢ ܨܒܝܢܗ ܕܡܢ ܕܫܕܪܢܝ] *om.* S ܕܟܠ ܡܕܡ] ܕܡܢ ܟܠ ܡܕܡ S ܡܢܗ] ܐܦܠܐ S 40 ܗܢܘ ܓܝܪ] ܡܛܠ ܕܗܢܘ S ܨܒܝܢܗ.....ܘܡܗܝܡܢ ܒܗ] ܨܒܝܢܗ | ܕܡܗܝܡܢ ܒܒܪܐ S

to him: "What shall we do, that we may work for the deeds of *C S*
29 God?" Jesus saith to them: "This is the deed of God, that ye
30 should believe on him that he hath sent." They say to him: "What
sign therefore doest thou, that we may see and believe on thee?
31 What dost thou work? Our fathers, they ate manna in the wilder-
ness, as it is written 'Bread from heaven he gave them to eat.'"
32 Jesus saith to them: "Amen, amen, I say to you Not Moses gave
you bread from heaven, but the Father will give you bread of verity
33 from heaven. For the bread of God hath come down from heaven,
34 and it is alive and is given to the world." They say to him: "Our
35 Lord, at all times give us this bread." Jesus saith to them: "I am
the bread of life; whoso cometh unto me shall not hunger, and he
36 that believeth in me shall never thirst. But I have said to you that
37 ye see and ye do not believe. Whosoever my Father giveth me unto
me will come, and he that unto me will come I will not put him
38 forth, *seeing* that I have come down from heaven not that I should
do my will, but that I should do the will of the Father that sent me.
39 Now this is the will of him that sent me, that everything which he
hath given me—I should not lose from it anything, but should raise
40 it up in the last day. For this is the will of my Father, that
every man that seeth the Son and believeth in him have life

---

30 therefore] *om. S* What dost thou work?] *om. S* **31** to eat] *om. S* (*not E*[136]) **32** Jesus saith to them] *om. S* the Father (*see on* Matt vi 4)] it is my Father *who S* verity] truth *S* **33** hath come down] *pr.* it is that *S* and it is alive and is given] and life it giveth *S* **34** this bread] of this bread *S* **35** Jesus saith] He saith *S* never thirst] not thirst for ever *S* **36** see] have seen *S* **37** my Father] the Father *S* **38** the Father] my Father *S*; *om. E*[234] **39** Now... sent me] This *it* is *S* everything which] from all that *S* from it] even *S* **40** For] Because *S* the will of... in him] the will of †him that believeth in the Son *S* (*sic*); *something must have fallen out in these verses*

C S ܘܡܗܝܡܢ ܒܗ ܐܝܬ ܠܗ ܚܝܐ ܕܠܥܠܡ ܘܐܢܐ ܐܩܝܡܝܘܗܝ ܒܝܘܡܐ
fol 49 r ܐܚܪܝܐ ⁴¹ܝܗܘ̈ܕܝܐ ܕܝܢ ܪܛܢܝܢ ܗܘܘ ܥܠܘܗܝ ܕܐܡܪ *ܕܐܢܐ ܐܢܐ
ܠܚܡܐ ܕܢܚܬ ܡܢ ܫܡܝܐ ⁴²ܘܐܡܪܝܢ ܗܘܘ ܠܐ ܗܘܐ ܗܢܐ
ܝܫܘܥ ܒܪܗ ܕܝܘܣܦ ܘܐܚܢܢ ܝܕܥܝܢ ܐܚܢܢ ܠܐܒܘܗܝ ܐܝܟܢܐ
ܐܡܪ ܕܐܢܐ ܡܢ ܫܡܝܐ ܢܚܬܬ ⁴³ܐܡܪ ܠܗܘܢ ܝܫܘܥ ܠܐ
ܬܪܛܢܘܢ ܚܕ ܥܡ ܚܕ ⁴⁴ܠܐ ܓܒܪ ܐܢܫ ܡܫܟܚ ܕܢܐܬܐ ܠܘܬܝ
ܐܠܐ ܐܢܐ ܕܢܓܕ ܠܗ ܐܒܐ ܕܫܕܪܢܝ ܘܐܢܐ ܐܩܝܡܝܘܗܝ ܒܝܘܡܐ
ܐܚܪܝܐ ⁴⁵ܟܬܝܒ ܓܝܪ ܒܢܒܝܐ ܕܢܗܘܘܢ ܟܠܗܘܢ ܡܠ̈ܦܐ ܕܐܠܗܐ
ܟܠ ܡܢܘ ܕܫܡܥ ܗܟܝܠ ܡܢ ܐܒܐ ܘܝܠܦ ܐܬܐ ܠܘܬܝ ⁴⁶ܠܐ
ܗܘܐ ܡܛܠ ܕܚܙܐ ܐܢܫ ܠܐܒܐ ܐܠܐ ܡܢ ܕܠܘܬ ܐܠܗܐ
col 2 ܐܝܬܘܗܝ ܗܘ ܗܘ ܚܙܐ *ܠܐܒܐ ⁴⁷ܐܡܝܢ ܐܡܝܢ ܐܡܪܢܐ ܠܟܘܢ
ܕܟܠ ܡܢ ܕܡܗܝܡܢ ܠܐܠܗܐ ܐܝܬ ܠܗ ܚܝ̈ܐ ܕܠܥܠܡ ⁴⁸ܐܢܐ ܐܢܐ
ܠܚܡܐ ܕܚ̈ܝܐ ܕܢܚܬ ܡܢ ܫܡܝܐ ⁴⁹ܐܒ̈ܗܝܟܘܢ ܐܟܠܘ ܠܚܡܐ
ܒܡܕܒܪܐ ܘܡܝܬܘ ⁵⁰ܗܢܘ ܕܝܢ ܠܚܡܐ ܕܢܚܬ ܡܢ ܫܡܝܐ ܕܢܐܟܘܠ
ܐܢܫ ܡܢܗ ܘܢܡܘܬ ⁵¹ܐܢܐ ܐܢܐ ܠܚܡܐ ܚܝܐ ܕܢܚܬ ܡܢ ܫܡܝܐ
ܕܡܢ ܕܢܐܟܘܠ ܡܢ ܠܚܡܐ ܗܢܐ ܢܚܐ ܠܥܠܡ ܘܠܚܡܐ ܐܢܐ
ܕܐܢܐ ܐܬܠ ܦܓܪܝ ܗܘ ܕܥܠ ܐ̈ܦ ܚܝܘܗܝ ܕܥܠܡܐ.

⁵²ܘܢܨܝܢ ܗܘܘ ܝܗܘ̈ܕܝܐ ܚܕ ܥܡ ܚܕ ܘܐܡܪܝܢ ܗܘܘ ܐܝܟܢܐ
ܡܫܟܚ ܗܢܐ ܕܢܬܠ ܠܢ ܦܓܪܗ ܠܡܐܟܠ ⁵³ܐܡܪ ܠܗܘܢ ܝܫܘܥ
fol 49 v ܐܡܝܢ ܐܡܝܢ ܐܡܪ *ܐܢܐ ܠܟܘܢ. ܕܐܠܐ ܬܐܟܠܘܢ ܦܓܪܗ ܕܒܪܗ
ܕܐܢܫܐ ܘܬܫܬܘܢ ܕܡܗ. ܠܝܬ ܠܟܘܢ ܚ̈ܝܐ ܒܟܘܢ· ⁵⁴ܘܡܢ ܕܐܟܠ

ܘܐܩܝܡܝܘܗܝ S (sic)   41 ܥܠܘܗܝ] ܥܠ S   42 ܗܘܘ] om. S
ܗܢܐ ܠܐ ܗܘܐ S   ܒܪ ܝܘܣܦ S   ܐܚܢܢ] om. S   ܕܐܢܐ ܡܢ] ܕܡܢ S
ܢܚܬܬ] ܢܚܬ S   43 ܝܫܘܥ] om. S   44 ܓܒܪ] om. S   45 ܡܢܘ] ܡܢ S
ܗܟܝܠ] om. S   ܘܝܠܦ] + ܡܢܗ. S   46 ܗܘ 2°] om. S   ܠܐܒܐ 2°]
ܠܐܠܗܐ ܐܒܐ S (cf iii 34)   47 ܕܟܠ ܡܢ] ܕܡܢ S   ܕܠܥܠܡ] om. S
48 ܕܢܚܬ ܡܢ ܫܡܝܐ] om. S   49 ܠܚܡܐ] ܡܢܢܐ S   ܒܡܕܒܪܐ] ܒܚܘܪܒܐ S
50 ܕܝܢ] om. S   ܘܢܡܘܬ] ܘܠܐ ܢܡܘܬ S   51 ܕܡܢ] ܘܡܢ S   ܗܢܐ] om. S^vid
52 ܘܐܡܪܝܢ ܗܘܘ] om. ܗܘܘ S   53 ܘܐܡܪ S   ܕܐܠܐ] ܕܐܢ | ܠܐ S
54 ܘܡܢ ܕܐܟܠ] ܡܢ ܕܐܟܠ ܕܝܢ S

41 eternal, and I will raise him up in the last day." Now the Jews were *C S*
murmuring against him that he said "I am the bread that came
42 down from heaven," and they were saying: "Is not this Jesus the son
of Joseph, and we ourselves know his father? How saith he 'I from
43 heaven have come down'?" Jesus saith to them: "Do not murmur
44 one with another; for no one can come unto me save he which the
Father that sent me draweth, and I will raise him up in the last day.
45 For it is written in the Prophet 'They shall be all taught of God';
whosoever heareth therefore from the Father and learneth cometh
46 unto me. Not because any one hath seen the Father save he that
47 is with God—he hath seen the Father. Amen, amen, I say to
48 you Whosoever believeth God hath life eternal. I am the bread of
49 life that came down from heaven; your fathers, they ate bread in
50 the wilderness and died; but this is the bread that came down from
51 heaven that a man may eat of it and die. I am the living bread that
came down from heaven, that he that shall eat of this bread may live
for ever, and the bread which I will give is my body, that *is* on behalf
of the life of the world."

52 And the Jews were striving one with the other, and were saying:
53 "How can this *man* give us his body to eat?" Jesus saith to them:
"Amen, amen, I say to you Except ye shall eat the body of the Son
54 of Man and shall drink his blood ye have not life in you, and he that

---

41 against him that] on *the ground* that *S* **42** were saying] say *S* This *one*, is he not Jesus, Joseph's son *S* I....come down] that from heaven he hath come down *S* **43** Jesus saith] He saith *S* **44** for] *om. S* **45** therefore] *om. S* learneth] + of him *S* **46** the Father 2°] God the Father *S* (*cf* iii 34) **47** Whosoever] He that *S* eternal] *om. S* **48** that came down from heaven] *om. S* **49** bread] manna *S* wilderness] desert *S* **50** but] *om. S* and die] *C* E^{137}; and not die *S* **51** that he...may] and he...shall *S* this bread] the bread S^{vid} **52** were saying] saying *S* **53** Jesus] *pr.* And *S* **54** and he that] but he that *S*

ܦܓܪܝ، ܘܫܬܐ ܕܡܝ. ܐܝܬ ܠܗ ܚܝܐ ܕܠܥܠܡ. ܘܐܢܐ ܐܩܝܡܝܘܗܝ، C S
ܒܝܘܡܐ ܐܚܪܝܐ. [55]ܦܓܪܝ، ܫܪܝܪܐܝܬ ܡܐܟܘܠܬܐ ܗܘ. ܘܕܡܝ
ܫܪܝܪܐܝܬ ܡܫܬܝܐ ܗܘ. [56]ܡܢܘ ܕܐܟܠ ܦܓܪܝ، ܘܫܬܐ ܕܡܝ ܒܝ
ܡܩܘܐ ܘܐܢܐ ܒܗ. [57]ܐܝܟܢܐ ܕܫܕܪܢܝ ܐܒܐ ܚܝܐ. ܘܐܢܐ ܚܝ
ܡܛܠ ܐܒܐ. ܡܢ ܕܢܐܟܠܢܝ ܢܗܘܐ ܚܝ ܡܛܠܬܝ. [58]ܗܢܐ ܗܘ
ܠܚܡܐ ܕܢܚܬ ܡܢ ܫܡܝܐ. ܠܐ ܗܘܐ ܐܝܟ ܗܘ ܕܐܟܠܘ
ܐܒ̈ܗܝܟܘܢ ܘܡܝܬܘ. ܡܢܘ ܕܡܢ ܗܢܐ ܠܚܡܐ ܢܐܟܘܠ ܚܝܐ
ܠܥܠܡ. [59]ܗܠܝܢ ܐܡܪ *ܒܟܢܘܫܬܐ. ܟܕ ܡܠܦ ܒܟܦܪܢܚܘܡ. [60]ܘܣ̈ܓܝܐܐ col 2
ܡܢ ܬܠܡ̈ܝܕܘܗܝ، ܟܕ ܫܡܥܘ. ܐܡܪܝܢ ܗܘܘ ܩܫܐ ܗܝ، ܡܠܬܐ
ܗܕܐ. ܡܢܘ ܡܫܟܚ ܠܡܫܡܥܗ̇. [61]ܝܕܥ ܕܝܢ ܒܗ ܝܫܘܥ ܕܪ̈ܛܢܝܢ
ܬܠܡ̈ܝܕܘܗܝ، ܥܠ ܗܕܐ. ܐܡܪ ܠܗܘܢ ܗܕܐ ܡܟܫܠܐ ܠܟܘܢ
[62]ܐܢ ܕܝܢ ܬܚܙܘܢ، ܠܒܪܗ ܕܐܢܫܐ ܟܕ ܣܠܩ ܠܐܬܪ ܕܐܝܬܘܗܝ،
ܗܘܐ ܡܢ ܩܕܝܡ. [63]ܪܘܚܐ ܗܝ، ܕܡܚܝܐ ܐܘ ܦܓܪܐ ܠܐ ܡܕܡ
ܐܗܢܝ. ܡ̈ܠܐ ܕܐܢܐ ܡܠܠܬ ܥܡܟܘܢ ܪܘܚܐ ܐܢܝܢ ܘܚ̈ܝܐ ܐܢܝܢ.
[64]ܐܠܐ ܐܝܬ ܡܢܟܘܢ ܐܢܫܝܢ ܕܠܐ ܡܗܝܡܢܝܢ. ܝܕܥ ܗܘܐ ܓܝܪ
ܝܫܘܥ ܡܢ ܩܕܝܡ ܡܢ ܕܡܫܠܡ ܠܗ. [65]ܐܡܪ *ܠܗܘܢ ܡܛܠ ܗܢܐ fol 50 r
ܐܡܪܬ ܠܟܘܢ ܕܠܐ ܐܢܫ ܡܫܟܚ ܕܢܐܬܐ ܠܘܬܝ، ܐܠܐ ܐܢ
ܝܗܝܒ ܠܗ ܡܢ ܐܒܐ. [66]ܡܛܠ ܗܕܐ ܣ̈ܓܝܐܐ ܡܢ ܬܠܡ̈ܝܕܘܗܝ،
ܐܙܠܘ ܠܗܘܢ ܡܢ ܠܘܬܗ. ܘܠܐ ܡܗܠܟܝܢ ܗܘܘ ܥܡܗ. [67]ܐܡܪ
ܝܫܘܥ ܠܬܪ̈ܥܣܪܬܗ. ܕܠܡܐ ܘܐܦ ܐܢܬܘܢ ܨܒܝܢ ܐܢܬܘܢ
ܠܡܐܙܠ ܠܟܘܢ. [68]ܐܡܪ ܠܗ ܫܡܥܘܢ ܟܐܦܐ. ܡܪܝ، ܠܘܬ ܡܢ

ܦܓܪܗ....ܕܡܗ S   ܐܩܝܡܘܗܝ S   55 ܡܐܟܘܠܬܐ S   56 ܡܢܘ]
ܡܢ S   ܡܩܘܐ] ܗܘ S   57 ܐܒܐ 2°] ܐܒܝ S   ܕܢܐܟܠܢܝ]
ܕܢܐܟܠ ܦܓܪܝ S   ܡܛܠܬܝ S   58 ܡܢܘ] ܡܢ S   ܢܐܟܠ S
59 ܒܟܦܪܢܚܘܡ ܒܟܢܘܫܬܐ ܟܕ ܡܠܦ ܗܘܐ S   60 ܟܕ ܫܡܥܘ] om. S
ܡܫܟܚ] pr. ܕ S   ܗܕܐ ܡܠܬܐ S   ܡܢܘ] ܡܢ S   61 ܕܪ̈ܛܢܝܢ] + ܗܘܘ S
ܥܠ ܗܕܐ] om. S   62 ܬܚܙܘܢ S   63 ܪܘܚܐ ܗܘ S   ܕܡܚܝܐ] + ܦܓܪܐ S
ܐܘ] ܐܢܬܘܢ ܕܝܢ ܐܡܪܝܢ ܐܢܬܘܢ S   ܡܕܡ ܠܐ ܡܗܢܐ S   ܕܐܢܐ ܡܠܠܬ]
ܕܡܠܠܬ S   ܐܢܝܢ 2°] om. S   64 ܐܢܫܝܢ] om. S   65 ܐܢ] om. S
66 ܗܕܐ] + ܡܠܬܐ S   ܡܢ ܠܘܬܗ] om. S   67 ܝܫܘܥ] om. S

eateth my body and drinketh my blood hath life eternal and I C S
55 will raise him up in the last day. My body truly is meat and my
56 blood truly is drink; whoso eateth my body and drinketh my blood,
57 in me he remaineth and I in him. As the living Father sent me and
I am alive because of the Father, he that shall eat me shall be alive
58 because of me. This is the bread that came down from heaven, not
as that which your fathers ate and died; whoso of this bread shall
59 eat shall live for ever." These things said he in the synagogue while
60 teaching in Kapharnahum, and many of his disciples when they
61 heard were saying: "Hard is this word; who can hear it?" Now
Jesus, when he knew that his disciples *were* murmuring at this, said
62 to them: "Doth this offend you? But *what* if ye shall see the Son
63 of Man going up whither he was from of old? It is the spirit that
giveth life or the body hath nothing profited; the words that I
64 myself have spoken with you are spirit and are life. But there are
some of you which believe not." For Jesus was knowing from of old
65 him that should betray him. He saith to them: "Therefore I have
said to you that no one can come unto me, except it be given him
66 from the Father. Because of this many of his disciples went away
67 from *being* with him, and were not walking with him. Jesus saith to
68 his Twelve: "Can even ye be willing to go away?" Simon Kepha
saith to him: "My Lord, unto whom shall we go? The word of life

---

my body....my blood] his body....his blood *S* 56 whoso] he that *S* he remaineth] he is *S* 57 the Father] my Father *S* eat me] eat my body *S* 58 whoso] he that *S* 59 in Kaph in the synagogue while he was teaching *S* 60 when they heard] *om. S* 61 *were*] were *S* at this] *om. S* 63 It....profited] He is the Spirit that giveth life to the body, but ye say 'The body nothing profiteth' *S* myself] *om. S* are 2°] *om. S* 64 which] that *S* 66 of this] + word *S* from....him] *om. S* 67 Jesus saith] He saith *S*

C S ܢܐܙܠ. ܡܠܬܐ ܕܚܝܐ ܕܠܥܠܡ ܐܝܬ ܠܟ. [69]ܘܚܢܢ ܗܝܡܢܢ ܘܝܕܥܢ
ܕܐܢܬ ܗܘ ܒܪܗ ܕܐܠܗܐ. [70]ܐܡܪ ܠܗܘܢ ܝܫܘܥ. ܠܐ ܗܘܐ
ܐܢܐ ܓܒܝܬܟܘܢ ܠܟܠܟܘܢ: ܘܗܘܐ ܐܦ ܡܢܟܘܢ ܚܕ ܣܛܢܐ
col 2 ܗܘ. [71]ܐܡܪ ܗܘܐ ܕܝܢ ܥܠ ܝܗܘܕܐ ܒܪ ܫܡܥܘܢ *ܐܣܟܪܝܘܛܐ.
ܗܢܘ ܓܝܪ ܥܬܝܕ ܗܘܐ ܠܡܫܠܡܘܬܗ ܚܕ ܡܢ ܬܪܥܣܪ ܀

[1]ܒܬܪ ܗܠܝܢ ܡܗܠܟ ܗܘܐ ܝܫܘܥ ܒܓܠܝܠܐ. ܠܐ ܓܝܪ ܐܝܬ ܗܘܐ
ܠܗ ܫܘܠܛܢܐ ܠܡܗܠܟܘ ܒܝܗܘܕ. ܡܛܠ ܕܝܗܘܕܝܐ ܒܥܝܢ ܗܘܘ
ܠܡܩܛܠܗ . . .

[2]ܘܩܪܒ ܗܘܐ ܥܐܕܐ ܕܝܗܘܕܝܐ ܕܡܛܠܠܐ. [3]ܘܐܡܪܘ ܗܘܘ ܠܗ
ܐܚܘܗܝ. ܫܢܐ ܠܟ ܡܟܐ ܘܙܠ ܠܝܗܘܕ. ܕܢܚܙܘܢ ܬܠܡܝܕܝܟ
ܥܒܕܐ ܕܥܒܕ ܐܢܬ. [4]ܠܝܬ ܓܝܪ ܐܢܫ ܕܥܒܕ ܡܕܡ ܒܛܘܫܝܐ ܘܒܥܐ
ܕܢܗܘܐ ܒܓܠܝܐ. ܐܢ ܗܠܝܢ ܥܒܕ ܐܢܬ ܚܘܐ ܢܦܫܟ ܠܥܠܡܐ.
[5]ܒܗܕܐ ܓܝܪ .ܠܗܕܡܝܢ ܐܦܠܐ ܐܚܘܗܝ ܗܝܡܢܘ ܗܘܘ ܒܗ. [6]ܐܡܪ
fol 50 v ܠܗܘܢ *ܝܫܘܥ. ܙܒܢܝ ܕܝܠܝ ܠܐ ܡܛܐ. ܕܝܠܟܘܢ ܕܝܢ
ܙܒܢܟܘܢ ܒܟܠܙܒܢ ܡܛܝܒ ܗܘ. [7]ܘܠܐ ܡܫܟܚ ܥܠܡܐ ܠܡܣܢܝܟܘܢ:
ܠܝ ܕܝܢ ܣܢܐ ܠܝ ܥܠܡܐ. ܡܛܠ ܕܡܣܗܕ ܐܢܐ ܥܠܘܗܝ. ܕܥܒܕܘܗܝ
ܐܢܘܢ ܒܝܫܝܢ. [8]ܐܢܬܘܢ ܣܩܘ ܠܥܐܕܐ ܗܢܐ. ܐܢܐ ܠܐ
ܣܠܩ ܐܢܐ ܠܥܐܕܐ. ܡܛܠ ܕܠܐ ܥܕܡܐ ܠܗܫܐ ܫܠܡ ܙܒܢܐ
ܕܝܠܝ. [9]ܟܕ ܗܠܝܢ ܐܡܪ. ܦܫ ܠܗ ܒܓܠܝܠܐ. [10]ܘܟܕ ܣܠܩܘ ܐܚܘܗܝ،
ܗܝܕܝܢ ܐܦ ܗܘ ܣܠܩ ܠܥܐܕܐ. ܠܐ ܒܝܢ ܒܓܠܝܐ ܐܠܐ ܒܛܘܫܝܐ.

---

69 ܘܚܢܢ] ܐܚܢܢ S^{ed} ܒܪܗ ܕܐܠܗܐ] *pr.* ܡܫܝܚܐ *S*   70 ܝܫܘܥ] *om. S*
ܗܘܐ] ܘ *S*   71 ܒܪ ܫܡܥܘܢ] *om. S*   ܐܣܟܪܝܘܛܐ] ܡܣܟܪܝܘܛܐ *S*;
(ܐ)ܣܟܪܝܘܛܐ *A* 404: *see Notes*, vol. ii   ܗܢܘ ܓܝܪ] ܡܛܠ ܕܗܘ *S*
ܬܪܥܣܪܬܐ *S*   1 ܒܬܪ] *pr.* ܡܢ *S*   ܠܐ ܓܝܪ] ܡܛܠ ܕܠܐ *S*
ܐܝܬ ܗܘܐ ܠܗ ܫܘܠܛܢܐ] ܨܒܐ ܗܘܐ *S*   ܠܡܗܠܟܘ] + ܒܝܢ ܓܠܝܠܐ *S*
2 ܘܩܪܒ] ܘܗܘܐ ܥܐܕܐ ܩܪܝܒ *S*   3 ܘܐܡܪܘ....ܐܚܘܗܝ]
ܘܩܪܒܘ ܐܚܘܗܝ ܠܫܡܥܘܢ ܘܐܡܪܘ ܠܗ *S*   ܘܙܠ] *om. S*   4 ܒܛܘܫܝܐ *S*
ܘܒܥܐ] + ܗܘ *S*   6 ܙܒܢܝ] *after* ܡܛܐ *S*   ܡܛܝܒ] *om. S*   7 ܠܝ 2°] *om. S*
8 ܠܥܐܕܥܐ *S* (*om.* ܗܢܐ)   ܣܠܩܢܐ *S*   ܠܥܐܕܥܐ ܗܢܐ *S*   ܙܒܢܐ ܕܝܠ]
ܙܒܢܝ *S*   9 ܐܡܪ ܗܠܝܢ *S*   10 ܘܟܕ] ܘܡܢ ܒܬܪ ܕ *S*   ܣܠܩ ܐܦ ܗܘ *S*
ܒܝܢ] *om. S*   ܒܛܘܫܝܐ] ܒܛܘܫܝܐ· *S* (*sic*)

69 eternal thou hast; and we ourselves have believed and known that *C S*
70 thou art the Son of God." Jesus saith to them: "Have not I myself
71 chosen you all? And lo, even out of you one is Satan!" Now he
was saying *this* of Judas, son of Simon Iscariot, for he was about to
betray him, *being* one of the Twelve.

vii 1 After these things Jesus was walking in Galilee, for he had
no authority to walk in Judaea, because the Jews were seeking to
kill him.

2 And the Feast of the Jews, *the Feast* of Tabernacles, had drawn
3 near. And his brothers had said to him: "Remove hence, and go to
4 Judaea, that thy disciples may see the deeds that thou doest; for
there is no one that doeth anything in concealment and wisheth that
it should be in the open. If these things thou doest, shew thyself to
5 the world." For till then not even his brothers had believed in him.
6 Jesus saith to them: "My time till now hath not arrived, but yours
7 —your time is at every season ready. And the world cannot hate
you, but me—the world hateth me, because I bear witness of it that
8 its deeds are evil. Go ye up to this Feast; I go not up to the Feast,
9 because not yet the time for me is accomplished." When he *had*
10 said these things he stayed in Galilee. And when his brothers went
up, then he also went up to the Feast, not openly but in concealment.

---

69 and 1°] *om.* S^{ed} the Son of God] *pr.* the Messiah *S* 70 Jesus saith] He saith *S* And lo] Lo *S* 71 son of Simon] *om. S* Iscariot] *C* (*sic*); Scariot *S*: *cf* Lk xxii 3, *where C has* 'Iscarioṭa' *as here, and see Notes*, vol. ii for] because *S* 1 for he had no authority] because he was not willing *S* to walk] + openly *S* 2 And] + at that time *S* had drawn near] was near *S* 3 *init.*] And his brothers drew near to Jesus and said to him *S* and go] *om. S* 4 wisheth] + himself *S* it] *or*, 'he' 6 Till now hath my time not arrived *S* ready] *om. S* 7 me 2°] *om. S* 8 this] the *S* the Feast] this Feast *S* E^{167} the time for me] my time *S* 10 And when] And after *S*

C S [11]ܫܘܕܥܐ ܕܝܢ ܒܟܝܢ ܗܘܘ ܠܗ ܒܚܕܕܐ. ܘܐܡܪܝܢ ܗܘܘ ܐܟܚܕܐ
col 2 ܗܘ. [12]ܘܪܦܛܐ ܦܓܥܐܐ ܐܝܬ ܗܘܐ ܚܠܡܘܗܝ، ܒܒܥܐ. ܘܐܝܬ ܗܘܘ*
ܕܐܡܪܝܢ ܕܪܦܛܐ ܗܘ. ܘܐܝܬ ܗܘܘ ܕܐܡܪܝܢ ܠܐ ܗܘܐ ܪܦܛܐ.
ܐܠܐ ܡܪܦܛܐ ܒܥܐ ܗܘ. [13]ܐܝܟ ܕܝܢ ܒܫܒܛܠܐ ܠܐ ܡܡܠܠ
ܗܘܐ ܚܠܡܘܗܝ، ܡܛܠ ܕܫܠܝܬܐ ܕܫܘܕܥܐ..

[14]ܘܒܪ ܦܠܓܘ ܫܢ̈ܝܬܐ ܕܒܕܒܐ ܕܬ̈ܠܬܐ. ܘܠܡ ܫܡܥ ܠܡܫܠܡܐ.
ܘܡܠܟ ܗܘܐ. [15]ܘܡܬܕܟܪܝܢ ܗܘܘ ܫܘ̈ܕܥܐ ܘܐܡܪܝܢ. ܐܡܟܢܐ
ܫܒܩ ܗܢܐ ܦܐܪܐ ܕܠܐ ܠܦ· [16]ܐܡܪ ܠܗܘܢ ܫܡܥܘܢ. ܘܠܘܩܒܠ
ܠܐ ܗܘܐ ܕܠܦ. ܐܠܐ ܕܡܢ ܕܐܒܪܢ· [17]ܘܡܢ ܕܝܓܪܐ ܕܠܒܒܗ ܓܒܝܗ.
ܫܒܩ ܘܠܘܩܒܠ ܗܢܐ ܐ̱ ܡܢ ܐܠܗܐ ܗܘ. ܐܘ ܐܢܐ ܡܢ ܓܒܘܬ
fol 51 r ܢܦܫܝ ܡܡܠܠ ܐܢܐ. [18]ܡܢ ܕܡܢ ܓܒܘܬ ܪܚܡܘܗܝ ܚܙܐ *ܡܡܠܠ·
ܫܘܒܚܐ ܕܢܦܫܗ ܒܥܐ· ܘܡܢ ܕܫܘܒܚܐ ܕܡܢ ܕܫܕܪܗ ܒܥܐ. ܫܪܝܪ
ܗܘ ܘܥܘܠܐ ܠܝܬ ܒܗ· [19]ܠܐ ܗܘܐ ܡܘܫܐ ܫܡܥ ܠܗܘܢ
ܐܘܪܚܬܐ. ܘܠܐ ܐܝܟ ܡܟܝܟܘܢ ܢܛܪ ܦܘܩܕܢܗ· ܠ ܠܡܟܝܟܐ ܒܟܝܢ
ܐܚܝ̈ܘܗܝ ܠܡܡܠܠܘ. [20]ܐܡܪܝܢ ܠܗ ܫ̈ܒܛܐ ܕܗܘܐ ܐܝܬ ܒܢ· ܡܟܢ
ܒܟܐ ܠܡܡܠܠܘ· [21]ܐܡܪ ܠܗܘܢ ܫܡܥܘܢ· ܚܕ ܒܒܕܐ ܒܒܕܬ
ܠܒܢܝܗܘܢ ܘܠܟܠܗܘܢ ܡܬܕܟܪܝܢ ܐܚܝ̈ܘܗܝ. [22]ܡܛܠ ܗܢܐ ܡܘܫܐ
ܫܡܥ ܠܗܘܢ ܠܘܬܪܬܐ. ܠܐ ܗܘܐ ܡܛܠ ܕܒܟܝܢ ܗܘ، ܡܢ ܡܘܫܐ·
ܐܠܐ ܡܛܠ ܕܡܢ ܐܬ̈ܘܡܝܗܘܢ ܗܘ،. ܘܒܝܡܢܘܬܐ ܕܫܒܛܬܐ ܠܘܬܪܝܡ
col 2 ܐܚܝ̈ܘܗܝ ܒܪܝܫܐ. [23]ܘܐܦ ܒܪܝܫܐ ܡܬܛܪ ܫܒܛܬܐ *ܕܠܐ ܢܫܪܬܐ

11. § *in S* ܫܘܕܥܐ ܕܝܢ] ܘܫܘܕܥܐ *S* ܠܗ] + ܬܡܢ *S* ܒܚܕܚܕܐ *S*
ܚܠܡܘܗܝ] *S (sic)* ܦܓܥ] ܦܓܥܐܐ ܐܝܬ 12 *S (sic)* ܐܠܗܐ ܗܘ] ܐܟܚܕܐ
S (sic) ܒܒܥܐ ܗܘ ܦܓܥܐܐ ܕܐܬ̈ܐ ܗܘܐ ܠܒܒܕܐ] ܒܒܥܐ *S* ܡܛܠܠܬܗ
S ܕܫܠܝܢ ܗܘܘ ܡܢ ܒܥܐ] ܕܫܠܝܬܐ ܕܫܘܕܥܐ 13 *S* ܪܦܛ] ܪܦܛܐ *S* ܕܪܦܛ] ܕܪܦܛܐ
14. *No* § *in S* 16 ܫܡܥܘܢ ܠܗܘܢ ܐܡܪ] ܐܡܪ ܠܗܘܢ ܫܡܥܘܢ ܘܐܡܪ *S*
17 ܘܡܢ] ܡܢ *S* ܐܘ ܐܢܐ] ܘܐ̱ *S* ܢܦܫܝ] ܪܚܡܘ *S* 18 ܚܙܐ] *om. S*
ܕܢܦܫܗ] ܠܢܦܫܗ *S* ܠܝܬ ܒܗ] ܒܠܒܗ ܠܝܬ *S* 19 ܘܠܐ ܐܝܟ ܡܟܝܟܘܢ]
ܠܡܟܝܟܐ] *so also S* ܦܘܩܕܢܗ] ܒܒܝܢ ܐܚܝ̈ܘܗܝ *S* ܢܛܪ] ܘܢܛܪ ܡܟܝܟܘܢ ܠܗ *S*
ܒܟܝܢ] ܡܟܝܢ *S* 20 ܡܟܢ] ܡܢ *S* 21 ܠܒܢܝܗܘܢ *S* 23 ܘܐܦ] ܐܦ *S* ܒܪܝܫܐ
ܒܪ ܐܝܟ *S (sic)* ܫܒܛܬܐ] ܒܫܒܛܬܐ ܕܫܒܛܬܐ *S* ܕܠܐ] *pr.* ܡܛܠ *S*

11 Now the Jews were seeking him at the Feast, and were saying: *C S*
12 "Where is he?" And much murmuring there was over him among
the people; and there were some saying "He is a good man," and
there were some saying: "He is not a good man, but *one who* leadeth
13 the people astray." Now no one openly was speaking of him for
fear of the Jews.

14 And when the days of the Feast of Tabernacles were half *gone,*
15 Jesus went up to the Temple and was teaching. And the Jews were
wondering and saying: "How knoweth this *man* letters who hath
16 not learnt?" Jesus saith to them: "My teaching is not mine, but
17 his that sent me; and he that willeth to do his will knoweth this
teaching, whether it be from God or *if* I from my own self do speak.
18 For he that speaketh from his own mind seeketh the glory of him-
self, and he that seeketh the glory of him that sent him, he is true
19 and wickedness is not in him. Did not Moses give you the Law, and
none of you keepeth its commandments? Me wherefore are ye
20 seeking to kill?" Some say to him: "A demon there is in thee!
21 Who is seeking to kill thee?" Jesus saith to them: "One deed I
22 did before your eyes, and ye all wonder. Therefore Moses gave you
circumcision—not because it is of him, of Moses, but because it is of
23 your fathers—and on the sabbath-day ye circumcise a man. And if a
man be circumcised on the sabbath that the law of Moses should not

---

11 Now] And *S* seeking him] + there *S* **12** over him] because of him *S* the people] that great multitude that had come to the Feast *S* a good man] good *S* (*in each case*) **13** for fear of the Jews] because they were afraid of the people *S* **16** saith] answered and said *S* **17** and] *om.* *S* or *if*] and if *S* self] mind *S* **18** For he] He *S* glory for himself *S* in him] in his heart *S* **19** none] not one *S* keepeth] are doing *S* (*sic*) wherefore] why *S* **23** And if] If *S* a man] *so also* *S* sabbath] sabbath-day *S* that 1°] because *S*

C S ܣܓܘܕܐ ܕܗܟܢܐ· ܒܠ ܪ̈ܚܡܝܢ ܐܢܬܘܢ̄ ܕܠܟܠܗ ܒܪܢܫܐ ܐܣܠܝܒܬ
ܒܗܘܟܐ ܕܫܒܬܐ. [24]ܠܐ ܬܗܘܘܢ̄ ܕܡܢܝܢ ܦ̈ܘܡܝܢ. ܐܠܐ
ܕܝܢܐ ܒܐܝܢܐ ܕܗܘܐ· [25]ܘܐܡܪܝܢ ܗܘܘ ܐܢܫܐ ܡܢ ܩ̈ܕܡ ܐܘܪܫܠܡ.
ܠܐ ܗܘܐ ܗܢܐ ܗܘ ܕܒܥܝܢ ܗܘܘ ܠܡܩܛܠ. [26]ܘܗܐ ܒܝܢ ܒܓܠܐ
ܘܐܦ ܘܡܡܠܠ· ܘܐܢܫ ܡܕܡ ܠܐ ܐܡܪ ܠܗ. ܒܪܡ ܫܪܝܪܐܝܬ
ܝܕܥܘ ܩ̈ܫܝܫܝܢ ܕܗܢܐ ܗܘ ܡܫܝܚܐ. [27]ܐܠܐ ܠܗܢܐ ܗܘ ܝܕܥܝܢ
ܚܢܢ ܠܗ ܡܢ ܐܝܟܢܐ ܗܘ· ܘܡܫܝܚܐ ܐܡܬܝ ܕܐܬܐ. ܠܐ ܐܢܫ
ܝܕܥ ܡܢ ܐܝܟܢܐ ܗܘ. ··o··

fol 51 v [28]ܘܐܪܝܡ ܗܘܐ ܝܫܘܥ ܩܠܗ ܒܗܝܟܠܐ· ܟܕ *ܡܠܦ ܘܐܡܪ. ܠܝ
ܝܕܥܝܢ ܐܢܬܘܢ̄. ܘܡܢ ܐܝܟܢܐ ܐܢܐ ܝܕܥܝܢ ܐܢܬܘܢ̄. ܡܢ ܨܒܘܬ
ܢܦܫܝ ܠܐ ܐܬܝܬ. ܐܠܐ ܫܪܝܪ ܗܘ ܡܢ ܕܫܕܪܢܝ. ܗܘ ܐܢܐ
ܕܐܢܬܘܢ̄ ܠܐ ܝܕܥܝܢ ܐܢܬܘܢ̄ ܠܗ. [29]ܐܢܐ ܕܝܢ ܝܕܥ. ܐܢܐ
ܠܗ ܕܠܘܬܗ ܐܢܐ. ܘܗܘ ܫܕܪܢܝ. [30]ܘܒܥܘ ܗܘܘ ܠܡܐܚܕܗ. ܘܠܐ
ܐܢܫ ܐܪܡܝ ܥܠܘܗܝ ܐ̈ܝܕܝܐ. ܡܛܠ ܕܠܐ ܐܬܬ ܗܘܬ ܫܥܬܗ.
[31]ܘܣ̈ܓܝܐܐ ܡܢ ܟܢܫܐ ܗܝܡܢܘ ܗܘܘ ܒܗ. ܘܐܡܪܝܢ ܗܘܘ ܡܢܐ
ܕܐܬܐ ܡܫܝܚܐ ܕܠܡܐ ܕܝܬܝܪ̈ܢ ܡܢ ܗܠܝܢ ܐ̈ܬܘܬܐ ܕܥܒܕ ܗܢܐ
ܥܒܕ. [32]ܘܫܡܥܘ ܦ̈ܪܝܫܐ ܕܪ̈ܛܢܝܢ ܥܠܘܗܝ ܟܢܫܐ. ܘܫܕܪܘ ܪ̈ܒܝ
col 2 ܟ̈ܗܢܐ ܘܦ̈ܪܝܫܐ ܕܢܐܚܕܘܢܗ. [33]ܘܐܡܪ *ܝܫܘܥ ܩܠܝܠ ܐܚܪܢ̄

ܒܠ ܪ̈ܚܡܝܢ] ܒܪ ܚܝܡ S (sic)   ܕܠܟܠܗ S   25 ܗܘܘ] om. S   26 ܒܓܠܝܐ S
ܘܐܦ ܘܡܡܠܠ] so also S   ܫܪܝܪܐܝܬ ܝܕܥܘ] ܝܕܥܝܢ ܫܪܝܪܐܝܬ S
ܕܗܢܐ S   27 ܐܝܢ S   28 ܩܠܗ ܝܫܘܥ S   ܒܗܝܟܠܐ. ܟܕ ܡܠܦ]
ܟܕ ܡܠܦ ܗܘܐ ܒܗܝܟܠܐ S   ܘܐܢܬܘܢ S   ܐܢܬܘܢ] ܗܘ ܐܢܐ ܕܐܢܬܘܢ   29 ܕܝܢ]
so also S   ܥܠܘܗܝ] pr. ܡܛܠ S   ܐ̈ܝܕܝܐ] ܐܝܕܗ S   ܫܥܬܗ] ܫܥܬܐ S
30 ܗܘܘ] om. S   31 ܘܣ̈ܓܝܐܐ] C (sic, end of line); ܣ̈ܓܝܐܐ ܕܝܢ S
ܡܢ ܟܢܫܐ] om. S   ܗܘܘ] om. S   ܒܗ] + (sic) ܡܢ ܗܘ ܟܢܫܐ S
ܡܫܝܚܐ ܟܕ ܢܐܬܐ S   ܕܠܡܐ] ܠܡܐ S   ܗܠܝܢ] om. S   ܕܥܒܕ] ܕܥܒܕ S
ܥܒܕ] ܥܒܕ S   32. § in S   ܦ̈ܪܝܫܐ] ܦ̈ܪܝܫܐ ܘܪ̈ܒܝ ܟ̈ܗܢܐ S
ܕܪ̈ܛܢܝܢ ܥܠܘܗܝ] ܕܪ̈ܛܢܝܢ S   ܪ̈ܒܝ....ܘܦ̈ܪܝܫܐ] ܠܚܫܐ S (sic)   ܕܢܐܚܕܘܢܗ S (sic)
33 ܘܐܡܪ] ܐܡܪ ܠܗܘܢ S   ܐܚܪܢ̄] end of line in C; cf Joh iv 37

be loosed, against me do ye murmur that I made the man all whole on C S
24 the sabbath-day? Do not be judging by faces and faces, but judge
25 upright judgement." And some of the people of Jerusalem were
26 saying: "Is not this he that they were seeking to kill? And lo,
openly he standeth and speaketh, and no one saith aught to him!
27 Perchance our elders truly knew that this is the Messiah. But this
man—lo, we know him from whence he is; and the Messiah whenever he cometh, no one knoweth from whence he is."

28 And Jesus had lifted up his voice in the Temple, teaching and
saying: "Me ye know, and from whence I am ye know; from my
own self I have not come, but true is he that sent me, he which
29 ye know not. But I know him, that with him am I and he hath
30 sent me." And they had sought to take hold of him, and no one laid
31 hands upon him, because his hour had not come. And many from
the multitude had believed in him; and they were saying: "What
time the Messiah cometh, can *it be* that more than these signs that
32 this *man* hath done he will do?" And the Pharisees heard that
folk murmured concerning him, and the chief priests and Phari-
33 sees sent to take hold of him. And Jesus said: "A little more

---

against me...murmur] on me do ye look *askance* *S* (*sic*): *cf* Deut xxviii 54, 56 26 truly knew] know truly *S* 28 in the Temple, teaching] when he was teaching in the Temple *S* he which ye] and him ye *S* 29 that] because *S* am I] was I *S* sent] *synonym in S* 30 had] *om.* *S* 31 And 1°] Now *S* from the multitude] *om.* *S* had] *om.* *S* in him] + from that †town† *S* (*mistake for* 'multitude') The Messiah what *time* he cometh *S* these signs] the signs *S* done....do] shewed....shew *S* 32 the Pharisees 1°] *pr.* the chief priests and *S* murmured concerning him] *were* murmuring *S* the chief priests.....sent] they sent guards *S* 33 And Jesus said] Jesus saith to them *S*

C S ܙܒܢܐ ܥܡܟܘܢ ܐܢܐ. ܘܐܙܠ ܐܢܐ ܠܝ ܠܘܬ ܡܢ ܕܫܕܪܢܝ.
[34]ܘܬܒܥܘܢܢܝ ܘܠܐ ܬܫܟܚܘܢܢܝ. ܘܐܝܟܐ ܕܐܢܐ ܐܙܠܢܐ ܐܢܬܘܢ
ܠܐ ܡܫܟܚܝܢ ܐܢܬܘܢ ܠܡܐܬܐ. [35]ܐܡܪܝܢ ܝܗܘܕܝܐ ܚܕ ܠܚܕ.
ܠܐܝܟܐ ܟܝ ܐܙܠ ܗܢܐ ܕܠܐ ܡܫܟܚܝܢ ܐܢܚܢ ܠܗ. ܠܡܐ ܟܝ
ܠܙܪܥܐ ܕܐܪ̈ܡܝܐ ܐܙܠ ܡܠܦ. ܕܠܐ ܡܫܟܚܝܢ ܐܢܚܢ ܠܗ. [36]ܐܘ
ܡܢܐ ܗܝ ܡܠܬܐ ܗܕܐ ܕܐܡܪ ܕܬܒܥܘܢܢܝ ܘܠܐ ܬܫܟܚܘܢܢܝ.
ܘܐܝܟܐ ܕܐܢܐ ܠܐ ܡܫܟܚܝܢ ܐܢܬܘܢ ܠܡܐܬܐ ܀
[37]ܘܒܝܘܡܐ ܪܒܐ ܕܥܐܕܐ ܩܐܡ ܗܘܐ ܝܫܘܥ ܘܩܥܐ ܘܐܡܪ.
§A 64, 455 §ܡܢ ܕܨܗܐ ܢܐܬܐ ܠܘܬܝ, ܘܢܫܬܐ.* ¶ [38]ܟܠ ܡܢ ܕܡܗܝܡܢ ܒܝ ܐܝܟܢܐ
Berl 3 r ¶A ܕܐܡܪ ܟܬܒܐ. ܢܗ̈ܪܘܬܐ ܕܡ̈ܝܐ ܚ̈ܝܐ ܢܪܕܘܢ ܡܢ ܟܪܣܗ. [39]ܗܕܐ
ܕܝܢ ܐܡܪ ܥܠ ܪܘܚܐ ܕܥܬܝܕܝܢ ܗܘܘ ܠܡܩܒܠܘ ܐܝܠܝܢ ܕܡܗܝܡܢܝܢ
ܗܘܘ ܒܗ. ܒܕܡܐ ܓܝܪ ܠܗܘ ܙܒܢܐ ܠܐ ܐܬܝܗܒܬ ܗܘܬ ܪܘܚܐ.
ܡܛܠ ܕܠܐ ܥܕܠ ܗܘܐ ܒܕܡܐ ܠܗ, ܫܒܚܬܐ ܫܘܒܚܐ ܝܫܘܥ.
[40]ܘܐܢܫܐ ܡܢ ܟܢܫܐ ܕܫܡܥܘ ܡ̈ܠܘܗܝ, ܐܡܪܝܢ ܗܘܘ. ܕܫܪܝܪܐܝܬ
ܗܢܐ ܗܘ ܢܒܝܐ. [41]ܐܚܪ̈ܢܐ ܐܡܪܝܢ ܗܘܘ ܗܢܐ ܗܘ ܡܫܝܚܐ.
ܐܚܪ̈ܢܐ ܐܡܪܝܢ ܗܘܘ ܐܡܟܢܐ ܡܢ ܓܠܝܠܐ ܐܬܐ ܡܫܝܚܐ. [42]ܠܐ
col 2 ܗܘܐ ܗܟܢܐ ܟܬܝܒ. ܕܡܢ ܙܪܥܗ ܕܕܘܝܕ *ܢܗܘܐ. ܘܡܢ ܒܝܬ ܠܚܡ
ܩܪܝܬܐ ܕܠܗ ܕܕܘܝܕ ܐܬܐ ܡܫܝܚܐ. [43]ܘܗܘܬ ܗܘܬ ܦܠܓܘܬܐ
ܒܟܢܫܐ ܡܛܠܬܗ. [44]ܘܐܢܫ ܗܘܘ ܡܢܗܘܢ ܕܨܒܝܢ ܗܘܘ ܕܢܐܚܕܘܢܗ.

ܙܒܢܐ] *om. S*   ܠܝ] *so also S*   34 ܘܠܐܬܪ *S*   ܐܢܬܘܢ 1°] *om. S*   35 ܚܕ ܠܚܕ] ܒܝܢܬܗܘܢ ܠܚܒܪܗܘܢ *S*   ܕܠܐ] *so also S*   36 ܐܘ ܡܢܐ] ܘܡܢܐ *S*   ܗܕܐ] *om. S*   ܕܬܒܥܘܢܢܝ ܘܠܐ ܬܫܟܚܘܢܢܝ] ܕܐܙܠ ܐܢܐ ܘܠܐ ܡܫܟܚܝܢ ܐܢܬܘܢ ܠܝ. *S*   ܘܐܝܟܐ] ܘܐܝܟܐ ܕܐܢܐ *S*   ܕܐܢܐ] + ܐܙܠܢܐ *S*   37. *No § in S*   ܡܢ] ܟܠ *A* 2/2   ܠܘܬܝ] *om. A* 455   ܘܢܫܬܐ.] *the point is in S also. Here begins one of the Berlin leaves of C*   39 ܗܘܘ 1°] *om. S*   ܕܡܗܝܡܢܝܢ ܗܘܘ] ܕܗܝܡܢܘ *S*   ܒܕܡܐ ܠܗ، ܫܒܚܬܐ] *om. S*   ܫܘܒܚܐ ܝܫܘܥ] ܝܫܘܥ ܫܘܒܚܗ *S*   40 ܘܐܢܫܐ] ܐܢܫܐ ܕܝܢ *S*   ܡ̈ܠܘܗܝ] *om. S*   ܕܫܪܝܪܐܝܬ] *om.* ܕ *S*   40, 41 ܗܘ ܢܒܝܐ.....ܗܘ ܡܫܝܚܐ] ܗܘ ܡܫܝܚܐ *S*   41 ܐܚܪ̈ܢܐ 2°] *pr.* ܘ *S*   ܗܘܘ 2°] *om. S*   42 ܢܗܘܐ] + ܡܫܝܚܐ *S*   ܩܪܝܬܐ] *so also S*   ܡܫܝܚܐ] *om. S*   44 ܡܢܗܘܢ] ܐܚܪ̈ܢܐ *S*   ܕܢܐܚܕܘܢܗ] ܠܡܐܚܕܗ *S*

34 time I am with you, and I go away unto him that sent me. And ye *C S*
will seek me and will not find me, and where I go ye cannot come."
35 The Jews say one to the other: "Whither then goeth this *man* that
we *shall* not find him? Can he then be going teaching to the seed
36 of the Gentiles, that we *shall* not find him? Or what is this word
that he saith "Ye will seek me and will not find me, and where I
am ye cannot come"?

37 And on the great day of the Feast Jesus was standing and crying
out and saying: "§He that thirsteth, let him come unto me and §¶*A* 464,
38 drink;¶ whosoever believeth in me as saith the Scripture: 'Rivers 455
39 of living water shall issue from his belly.'" Now this he said of
the Spirit that they were about to receive that were believing in
him; for until that time the Spirit had not been given, because
40 Jesus until that hour had not received glory. And some from the
multitude that heard his words were saying "Truly this is a
41 prophet." Others were saying: "This is the Messiah." Others were
42 saying: "How cometh the Messiah from Galilee? Is it not thus
written, that from the seed of David he will be, and *that* from
43 Beth Lehem village, David's *town*, cometh the Messiah?" And
there had been a division in the multitude because of him;
44 and there were some that were wishing to take hold of him,

---

time] *om. S* **34** where] whither *S* **35** one to the other] among themselves *S* **36** Or] And *S* this word] the word *S* Ye will seek me and will not find me] I go and ye *will* not find me *S* where] *pr.* that he saith *S* I *am*] I go *S* **37** He that] Every one that $A^2/_2$ unto me] *om.* $A^1/_2$ (*not* E^{196}) and drink;] *both S and C have a stop here, and the quotation in* E^{196} *ends at this point. Cf Robinson's* Perpetua, p. 98. **39** were about] are about *S* were believing] believed *S* until that hour] *om. S* glory] his glory *S* **40** And] Now *S* his words] *om. S* **40, 41** a prophet......This is] *om. S* **41** Others 2°] And others *S* were saying 2°] say *S* **42** he will be] the Messiah will be *S* cometh the Messiah] he cometh *S* **44** some] others *S*

C S ܐܠܐ ܠܐ ܐܢܫ ܐܘܫܛ ܥܠܘܗܝ ܐܝ̈ܕܝܐ. ⁴⁵ܘܗܦܟܘ ܗܢܘܢ ܕܫ̈ܡܫܐ
ܠܘܬ ܪ̈ܒܝ ܟܗܢܐ ܘܦܪ̈ܝܫܐ. ܘܐܡܪܝܢ ܠܗܘܢ ܗܢܘܢ ܦܪ̈ܝܫܐ.
ܐܝܟܐ ܠܐ ܐܝܬܝܬܘܢܝܗܝ. [46]ܐܡܪܝܢ ܠܗܘܢ ܕܫ̈ܡܫܐ. ܠܐ ܡܢ ܡܬܘܡ
ܡܠܠ ܒܪ ܐܢܫܐ ܡܕܡ ܕܡܡܠܠ ܓܒܪܐ ܗܢܐ. [47]ܐܡܪܝܢ ܠܗܘܢ
ܦܪ̈ܝܫܐ. ܕܠܡܐ ܐܦ ܐܢܬܘܢ ܡܛܥܝܐ ܛܥܝܢ ܐܢܬܘܢ. [48]ܡܢ ܟܝ
Berl 3 v ܡܢ ܪ̈ܫܢܐ ܐܘ ܡܢ ܦܪ̈ܝܫܐ ܗܝܡܢܘ ܒܗ. [49]ܐܠܐ ܐܢܘܢ *ܥܡܐ
ܐܝܢܐ ܕܠܐ ܝܕܥ ܐܘܪܝܬܐ ܕܠܝܛܝܢ ܐܢܘܢ. [50]ܐܡܪ ܠܗܘܢ
ܢܝܩܕܝܡܘܣ ܗܘ ܕܐܬܐ ܗܘܐ ܠܘܬܗ ܒܠܠܝܐ. [51]ܕܠܡܐ ܠܢܡܘܣܢ
ܐܘܪܝܬܐ ܕܝܢܐ ܠܒܪܢܫܐ ܒܥܠܐ ܢܫܡܥ ܡܢܗ ܘܢܕܥ ܡܢܐ ܥܒܕ.
[52]ܐܡܪܝܢ ܕܠܡܐ ܐܦ ܐܢܬ ܡܢ ܓܠܝܠܐ ܐܢܬ. ܒܨܝ ܘܚܙܝ ܕܢܒܝܐ
§¶A 14, 330 ܡܢ ܓܠܝܠܐ ܠܐ ܩܐܡ. [12]ܬܘܒ ܐܡܪ ܗܘܐ ܠܗܘܢ ܝܫܘܥ. §ܐܢܐ
ܐܢܐ ܢܘܗܪܗ ܕܥܠܡܐ.¶ ܡܢ ܕܒܬܪܝ ܐܬܐ ܠܐ ܡܗܠܟ ܒܚܫܘܟܐ
ܐܠܐ ܡܩܒܠ ܠܗ ܢܘܗܪܐ ܕܚܝ̈ܐ. [13]ܐܡܪܝܢ ܠܗ ܦܪ̈ܝܫܐ ܐܢܬ
ܥܠ ܢܦܫܟ ܡܣܗܕ ܐܢܬ. ܠܐ ܗܘܬ ܫܪܝܪܐ ܣܗܕܘܬܟ. [14]ܐܡܪ
col 2 ܠܗܘܢ ܝܫܘܥ *ܐܢ ܐܢܐ ܡܣܗܕܢܐ ܥܠ ܢܦܫܝ ܫܪܝܪܐ ܗܝ
ܣܗܕܘܬܝ. ܡܛܠ ܕܝܕܥ ܐܢܐ ܡܢ ܐܝܟܢܐ ܐܬܝܬ ܘܠܐܝܟܐ ܐܙܠ
ܐܢܐ. ܐܢܬܘܢ ܕܝܢ ܠܐ ܝܕܥܝܢ ܐܢܬܘܢ ܠܐ ܡܢ ܐܝܟܢܐ

---

45 ܕܫ̈ܡܫܐ] S ܡܫܡܫܢ ܗܘܐ ܠܟܗܢܘܬܐ   ܐܘܫܛ] S ܘܠܐ   ܐܠܐ] ܠܐ
ܗܢܘܢ ܦܪ̈ܝܫܐ] S ܗܢܘܢ ܕܗܘܐ ܠܘܬ ܦܪ̈ܝܫܐ   ܪ̈ܒܝ.....ܘܦܪ̈ܝܫܐ] S ܘܐܬܘ +
47 ܦܪ̈ܝܫܐ] S ܕܡܡܠܠ   S ܡܬܚܬܘܡ 46   S ܐܝܬܝܬܘܢܝܗܝ   S ܒܗܢܐ ܘܦܪ̈ܝܫܐ
S ܛܥܝܬܘܢ ܠܡ̈ܛܥܝܢ] ܛܥܝܢ ܐܢܬܘܢ   S ܠܡܐ] ܕܠܡܐ   S ܠܕܝܫܐ ܗܢܘܢ +
49 ܘܥܡܠܐ] S ܗܡܢܘ] ܗܝܡܢܘ S^{ed} ܪܫܢܐ] ܪ̈ܫܢܐ   S ܒܗ] 1° ܡܢ 48
S ܐܬܐ] ܕܐܬܐ   so also S] ܢܝܩܕܝܡܘܣ 50   om. S] ܕܠܝܛܝܢ ܐܢܘܢ S^{ed} ܥܡܝܐ
51 ܠܒܪܢܫܐ] S ܠܢܡܘܣܢ ܐܘܪܝܬܐ ܕܠܡܐ   ܕܠܡܐ] ܠܢܡܘܣܢ ܐܘܪܝܬܐ 50, 51
S ܠܡܐ] ܕܠܡܐ   S ܠܗ] + 52 ܐܡܪܝܢ S^{ed} ܕܢܫܡܥ   S ܒܪ ܐܢܫܐ

After ܡܢ, *which is in the middle of a line, there is no stop in C* viii 12. § *in S*
ܗܘܐ] *om. S* ܐܢܐ 2°] *after* ܢܘܗܪܗ *A* 330 ܕܚܝ̈ܐ] ܘܚܝ̈ܐ C^{ed}, *but Mr Glover says the first letter is smudged* 13 ܦܪ̈ܝܫܐ] ܦܪ̈ܝܫܐ S ܐܢܬ 1°] *pr.* ܕ S
ܐܢܬ 2°] *om. S* ܠܐ] *so also S* 14 ܐܢ] ܐܦܢ S ܡܢ 1°] *om. S*
S ܘܠܐܝܟܐ   ܐܢܬܘܢ ܕܝܢ] S ܘܐܢܬܘܢ   ܠܐ ܝܕܥܝܢ ܐܢܬܘܢ] *om. S*
ܡܢ 2°] *om. S*

45 but no one laid hands upon him. And those guards returned *C S*
unto the chief priests and Pharisees, and those Pharisees say to
46 them: "How is it ye have not brought him?" The guards say
to them: "Never spake a human being aught that this man
47 speaketh." The Pharisees say to them: "Can ye also be indeed
48 going astray? For who of the chiefs or of the Pharisees have
49 believed in him, save the mob which knoweth not the Law, that
50 are cursed?" Nicodemus saith to them, he that had gone unto
51 him by night: "Can the Law judge a man at the first, before ever
52 we have heard from him, and known what he doeth?" They
say: "Canst thou also be from Galilee? Search and see that a
viii 12 prophet from Galilee hath not arisen." Again Jesus had said to
them: "§I am the light of the world;¶ he that after me cometh §¶*A* 14, 330
walketh not in darkness, but findeth for himself the light of life."
13 The Pharisees say to him: "Thou of thyself bearest witness; not
14 true is thy witness." Jesus saith to them: "If I bear witness of
myself true is my witness, because I know from whence I have come
and whither I go; but ye know not, neither from whence I have

---

but] and *S* laid] was able to lay *S* **45** returned] + and came *S* unto...and Pharisees] unto those priests and unto the Pharisees *S* those Pharisees] the priests and Pharisees *S* **46** speaketh] spake *S* **47** to them] to them, to those guards *S* be...going] have...gone *S* **49** the mob] *S illegible* that are cursed] *om. S* **50** gone] come *S* by night] + at the first *S* **51** at the first] *om. S* **52** They say] + to him *S* arisen] *no stop in C after this word* viii **12** had] *om. S* of life] and life C^{ed}, *but the* MS *is not clear* **13** Pharisees] Jews *S* not true] *so also S (and* E^{86}*)* **14** If] Even if *S* from 1°] *om. S* but] and *S* know not] *om S* from 2°] *om. S*

ܐܬܝܬ ܘܠܐ ܠܐܝܟܐ ܐܙܠܝܢ. [15]ܐܢܬܘܢ ܕܝܢ ܐܝܟ ܕܠܒܪ ܐܢܫܐ (C) S
ܗܘ ܕܚܙܝܢ ܐܢܬܘܢ܆ ܘܐܢܫܐ ܠܐܢܫ ܠܐ ܕܐܢ ܐܢܫܐ. [16]ܘܐܢ
ܕܐܢ ܐܢܫܐ ܕܚܙܐ ܫܪܪܐ ܗܘ. ܡܛܠ ܕܠܐ ܗܘܝܬ ܒܠܚܘܕܝ.. ܐܠܐ
ܐܢܐ ܘܡܢ ܕܫܕܪܢܝ. [17]ܘܐܦ ܒܐܘܪܝܬܟܘܢ ܟܬܝܒ. ܕܣܗܕܘܬܐ
ܕܬܪܝܢ ܓܒܪܝܢ ܫܪܝܪܐ ܗܝ. [18]ܐܢܐ ܐܢܐ ܕܣܗܕ ܐܢܐ ܥܠ ܢܦܫܝ.
ܘܐܒܐ ܕܫܕܪܢܝ ܣܗܕ ܥܠܝ. [19]ܐܡܪܝܢ ܠܗ ܐܝܟܘ¶ | ܐܒܘܟ. ܐܡܪ ¶C
ܠܗܘܢ ܠܝ ܠܐ ܝܕܥܝܢ ܐܢܬܘܢ܆ ܐܦܠܐ ܠܐܒܝ. ܐܠܘ ܠܝ ܝܕܥܬܘܢ.
ܐܦ ܠܐܒܝ ܝܕܥܝܢ ܗܘܝܬܘܢ܆ [20]ܗܠܝܢ ܡܠܠ ܒܒܝܬ ܓܙܐ. ܘܒܗܝܟܠܐ
ܘܠܐ ܐܢܫ ܐܚܕܗ ܗܘܐ ܡܛܠ ܕܠܐ ܐܬܬ ܗܘܬ ܫܥܬܗ ܀
[21]ܬܘܒ ܐܡܪ ܠܗܘܢ ܫܡܥܘ ܐܢܐ ܐܙܠ ܐܢܐ ܠܝ. ܘܬܒܥܘܢܢܝ.
ܘܬܡܘܬܘܢ ܒܚܛܗܝܟܘܢ ܘܠܐܬܪ ܕܐܢܐ ܐܙܠ ܐܢܐ ܐܢܬܘܢ ܠܐ
ܡܫܟܚܝܢ ܐܢܬܘܢ ܠܡܐܬܐ. [22]ܐܡܪܝܢ ܝܗܘܕܝܐ †ܠܡܐܬܐ† ܗܘ [ܒܬܪܗ]
ܕܢܩܛܘܠ ܢܦܫܗ ܕܐܡܪ ܕܠܐ ܡܫܟܚܝܢ ܐܢܬܘܢ ܠܡܐܬܐ ⸢ܠܐܝܟܐ⸣
ܕܐܙܠܢܐ. [23]ܐܡܪ [ܠܗܘܢ] ܫܡܥܘ ܐܢܬܘܢ ܡܢ ܬܚܬܝܐ ܐܢܬܘܢ
ܘܐܢܐ ܡܢ ܥܠܝܐ ⸢ܐܢܐ⸣ ܐܢܬܘܢ ܡܢ ܗܢܐ ܐܢܬܘܢ ܥܠܡܐ
ܘܐܢܐ ܠܐ ܗܘܝܬ ܡܢܗ. [24]ܐܡܪܬ ܠܟܘܢ ܕܬܡܘܬܘܢ ܒܚܛܗܝܟܘܢ
ܐܢ ܠܐ ܡܗܝܡܢܝܢ ܐܢܬܘܢ ܕܐܢܐ ܐܢܐ ܬܡܘܬܘܢ ܒܚܛܗܝܟܘܢ
[25]ܐܡܪܝܢ ܠܗ ܐܢܬ ܡܢ ܐܢܬ ܐܡܪ ܠܗܘܢ ܫܡܥܘ ܪܫܐ ܕܐܡܠܠ
ܐܢܐ ܥܡܟܘܢ. [26]ܣܓܝ ܐܝܬ ܠܝ ܕܐܡܠܠ ܥܠܝܟܘܢ ܘܕܐܕܘܢ
ܐܠܐ ܡܢ ܕܫܕܪܢܝ ܫܪܝܪ ܗܘ ܘܐܢܐ ܕܫܡܥܬ ܡܢܗ ܡܡܠܠ ܐܢܐ
ܒܥܠܡܐ. [27]ܘܠܐ ܝܕܥܘ ܕܥܠ ܐܒܐ ܐܡܪ ܠܗܘܢ ܀
[28]ܬܘܒ ܐܡܪ ܠܗܘܢ ܫܡܥܘ ܟܕ ܬܪܝܡܘܢܝܗܝ، ܠܒܪܗ ܕܐܢܫܐ ܗܝܕܝܢ
ܬܕܥܘܢ ܕܐܢܐ ܐܢܐ ܘܡܕܡ ܡܢ ܨܒܘܬ ܢܦܫܝ ܠܐ ܥܒܕ ܐܢܐ
ܐܠܐ ܐܝܟܢܐ ܕܐܠܦܢܝ ܐܒܐ ܗܟܘܬ ܡܡܠܠ ܐܢܐ. [29]ܘܡܢ ܕܫܕܪܢܝ

ܠܐܝܠܝܢ S   15 ܕܠܒܪ ܐܢܫܐ] ܕܠܒܪܢܫܐ S   ܘܐܢܫܐ] om. ܘ S
16 ܐܢܐ 1°] om. S   17 ܘܐܦ] om. ܐܦ S   18 ܘܐܒܐ] ܘܐܒܐ S
19 ܐܝܟܘ] ܗܘ ܐܝܠܝܢ S   21 ܫܡܥܘ] S (sic)   22 ܠܡܐܬܐ] ܠܡܐܬܐ S[ed]
ܕܠܐ] S (sic)   ⸢ܠܐܝܟܐ⸣] S[ed]; ? ⸢ܠܐܬܪ   22, 23 ܕܐܙܠܢܐ ܐܡܪ] S (sic)

15 come nor whither I go. But ye according to what is man's do judge; (*C*) *S*
16 and I, no one do I judge. And if I judge, my judgement is true,
17 because I have not been alone, but I and he that sent me. And
in your Law also it is written that the witness of two men is true:
18 I am *one* that bear witness of myself, and my Father that sent
19 me beareth witness of me." They say to him: "Where is¶ | thy ¶*C*
Father?" He saith to them: "Me ye know not, neither my
Father; if me ye had known, my Father also ye would have
20 known." These things he spake in the Treasury and in the Temple,
and no one had taken hold of him, because his hour had not come.
21 Again Jesus saith to them: "I go away and ye will seek me, and
22 ye will die in your sins; and whither I go ye cannot come." The Jews
say: "†Can it be that† he [is about] to kill himself, that he saith
23 'Ye cannot come whither I go'?" Jesus saith [to them]: "Ye are from
beneath, and I am from above; ye are from this world, and I am
24 not from it. I said to you 'Ye will die in your sins'; if ye believe
25 not that I am he, ye will die in your sins." They say to him: "Who
art thou?" Jesus saith to them: "The chief *is*, that I should speak
26 myself with you, *seeing* that I have much that I should speak
concerning you and judge, but he that sent me is true, and what
27 things I have heard from him I speak in the world." And they
knew not that concerning the Father he said *this* to them.
28 Again Jesus saith to them: "When ye shall lift up the Son of
Man, then ye shall know that I am he, and nothing of my own self
29 I do, but as the Father hath taught me even so I speak. And he

---

15 what is man's] what is of the body *S* and] *om. S* **17** also] *om. S* **18** my Father] the Father *S* **22** Can it be that] wherefore S^{ed}: *the two readings only differ by one stroke* he is about] *illegible in S*

ܥܡܝ ܗܘ ܘܠܐ ܫܒܩܢܝ ܡܛܠ ܕܐܢܐ ܡܕܡ ܕ˹ܫܦ˺ܪ ܠܗ ܥܒܕܢܐ S
ܒܟܠܙܒܢ [30]ܘܟܕ ܗܠܝܢ ܡܡܠܠ ܗܘܐ ܣܓܝܐܐ ܗܝܡܢܘ ܒܗ [31]ܗܝܕܝܢ
ܐܡܪ ܝܫܘܥ ܠܗܘܢ ܠܝܗܘܕܝܐ ܕܗܝܡܢܘ ܒܗ ܐܢ ܐܢܬܘܢ
ܬܩܘܘܢ ܠܘܬ ܡ̈ܠܝ ܫܪܝܪܐܝܬ ܬܠܡܝ̈ܕܝ ܐܢܬܘܢ· [32]ܘܬܕܥܘܢ
ܫܪܪܐ ܘܗܘ ܫܪܪܐ ܢܚܪܪܟܘܢ [33]ܐܡܪܝܢ ܠܗ ܙܪܥܗ ܐܢܚܢ
ܕܐܒܪܗܡ ܐܢܚܢ * * * ܡܢ ܡܬܘܡ ܠܥܒܕܘܬܐ ܠܐ ܦܠܚܢ
ܠܢ ܐܝܟܢܐ ܐܡܪ ܐܢܬ ܕܬܗܘܘܢ ܒܢ̈ܝ ܚܐܪܐ [34]ܐܡܪ ܠܗܘܢ
ܡܪܢ ܐܡܝܢ ܐܡܝܢ ܐܡܪܢܐ ܠܟܘܢ ܕܡܢ ܕܥܒܕ ܚܛܝܬܐ
ܥܒܕܐ ܗܘ· [35]ܘܥܒܕܐ ܠܐ ܡܩܘܐ ܠܥܠܡ ܗܘ ܒܒܝܬܐ ܒܪܐ ܕܝܢ
ܒܒܝܬܐ ܠܥܠܡ ܗܘ [36]ܘܐܢ ܒܪܐ ܢܚܪܪܟܘܢ ܫܪܝܪܐܝܬ ܬܗܘܘܢ
ܒܢ̈ܝ ܚܐܪܐ [37]ܝܕܥܢܐ ܕܙܪܥܗ ܐܢܬܘܢ ܕܐܒܪܗܡ ܘܒܥܝܢ ܐܢܬܘܢ
ܠܡܩܛܠܢܝ ܡܛܠ ܕܡܠܬܝ, ܠܐ ܢܩܦܐ ܒܟܘܢ [38]ܐܢܐ ܡܕܡ ܕܚܙܝܬ
ܠܘܬ ܐܒܝ ܥܒܕ ܐܢܐ ܘܐܦ ܐܢܬܘܢ ܡܕܡ ܕܚܙܝܬܘܢ ܠܘܬ
ܐܒܘܟܘܢ ܥܒܕܝܢ ܐܢܬܘܢ [39]ܐܡܪܝܢ ܠܗ ܐܒܘܢ ܕܝܠܢ ܐܒܪܗܡ
ܗܘ ܐܡܪ ܠܗܘܢ ܐܢ ܒܢܘܗܝ, ܐܢܬܘܢ ܕܐܒܪܗܡ ܥܒܕܘܗܝ,
ܕܐܒܪܗܡ ܥܒܕܘ [40]ܗܫܐ ܕܝܢ ܗܐ ܒܥܝܢ ܐܢܬܘܢ ܠܡܩܛܠܢܝ
ܠܓܒܪܐ ܕܫܪܪܐܝܬ ܡܡܠܠ ܥܡܟܘܢ ܐܝܕܐ ܕܫܡܥܬ ܡܢ ܐܠܗܐ
ܐܒܪܗܡ ܗܕܐ ܠܐ ܥܒܕ [41]ܐܠܐ ܐܢܬܘܢ ܥܒܕܝܢ ܐܢܬܘܢ
ܥܒܕܐ ܕܐܒܘܟܘܢ ܐܡܪܝܢ ܠܗ ܐܢܚܢ ܠܐ ܗܘܐ ܡܢ ܙܢܘܬܐ
ܗܘܝܢ ܚܕ ܗܘ ܐܒܐ ܐܝܬ ܠܢ ܐܠܗܐ [42]ܐܡܪ ܠܗܘܢ ܝܫܘܥ
ܐܠܘ ܐܠܗܐ ܗܘܐ ܐܒܘܟܘܢ ܡܚܒܝܢ ܗܘܝܬܘܢ ܠܝ ܐܢܐ ܓܝܪ
ܡܢ ܐܠܗܐ ܢܦܩܬ ܐܬܝܬ ܘܠܐ ܗܘܐ ܡܢ ܨܒܘܬ ܢܦܫܝ ܐܬܝܬ
ܗܘ ܫܕܪܢܝ [43]ܡܛܠ ܡܢܐ ܡܠܬܝ, ܠܐ ܡܫܬܘܕܥܝܢ ܐܢܬܘܢ ܠܐ ܓܝܪ
ܡܫܟܚܝܢ ܐܢܬܘܢ ܫܡܥܝܢ ܠܗ [44]ܐܢܬܘܢ ܕܝ̈ܢ ܕܒܥܝܢܐ ܐܢܬܘܢ
ܘܪܓܬܗ ܗܘ ܕܐܒܘܟܘܢ ܨܒܝܢ ܐܢܬܘܢ ܠܡܥܒܕ ܗܘ ܕܡܢ ܪܫ

33 ܘܡܢ | * * S^{ed}; ? *read* ܡܢ | ˹ܘܠܐܢܫ˺ 42 ܐܬܝܬ] S^{ed}: *photograph illegible*
44 ܐܢܬܘܢ ܕܝ̈ܢ ܕܒܥܝܢܐ ܐܢܬܘܢ] *S* (*sic*)

that sent me is with me, and he hath not left me, because that which *S*
30 pleaseth him I myself do at all times." And when these things he
31 was speaking, many believed in him. Then said Jesus to those Jews
that believed in him: "If ye will continue by my words truly my
32 disciples ye are, and ye will know truth and the truth will free you."
33 They say to him: "The seed of Abraham are we [and to no one]
ever is bondservice done by us. How sayest thou 'Ye will be
34 free-men'?" Our Lord saith to them: "Amen, amen, I say to you
35 He that doeth sin is a slave, and the slave—he remaineth not for
36 ever in the house, but the son is in the house for ever; and if the
37 son free you, truly ye will be free-men. I know that ye are the seed
of Abraham, and ye seek to kill me because my word goeth not forth
38 in you. I, that which I have seen by my Father I do; and ye also,
39 that which ye have seen by your father ye do." They say to him:
"Our father, even ours, is Abraham." He saith to them: "If ye are
40 the sons of Abraham, do the deeds of Abraham. But now, lo, ye
seek to kill me—a man that truly speaketh with you what he hath
41 heard from God! Abraham did not this. But ye do the deeds of
your father." They say to him: "Not from adultery are we;
42 we have one Father—God." Jesus saith to them: "If God had
been your father, ye would have been loving to me, for I from
God have gone forth *and* come, and not from my own self have
43 I come—he sent me. For what *reason* my word do ye not recognise?
44 For ye cannot hear it. But ye that are evil, and the desire of your
father it is ye wish to do—he that from the beginning was a man-

---

33 ⌜and to no one⌝ ever] * * and never S^{ed} 44 *Cf* 'Our Saviour said to them: Ye are sons of Cain, and not sons of Abraham' *A* 331 & 'Ye are the sons of Satan that from the beginning is a manslayer' E^{196}

S ܩܛܠ ܐܢܫܐ ܗܘܐ §ܘܒܫܪܪܐ ܠܝܬܘܗܝ، ܘܒܗ ܫܪܪܐ ܠܝܬ¶ ܘܡܟܐ
§¶Thos 312 ܕܡܡܠܠ ܕܓܠܬܐ ܡܢ ܕܝܠܗ ܡܡܠܠ. ܡܛܠ ܕܕܓܠܐ ܗܘ ܘܐܒܘܗܝ.
[45]ܐܢܐ ܕܫܪܪܐ ܡܡܠܠ ܐܢܐ. ܠܐ ܡܗܝܡܢܝܢ ܐܢܬܘܢ ܠܝ [46]ܡܢܘ
ܡܢܟܘܢ ܡܟܣ ܠܝ ܥܠ ܚܛܝܬܐ ܘܐܢ ܫܪܪܐ ܡܡܠܠ ܐܢܐ
ܠܡܢܐ ܠܐ ܡܗܝܡܢܝܢ ܐܢܬܘܢ ܠܝ [47]ܡܢ ܕܡܢ ܐܠܗܐ ܗܘ ܠܒܪ
ܡܠܬܐ ܕܐܠܗܐ ܫܡܥ ܡܛܠ ܗܢܐ ܠܐ ܫܡܥܝܢ ܐܢܬܘܢ ܠܗ
ܡܛܠ ܕܠܐ ܗܘܝܬܘܢ [48]ܐܡܪܝܢ ܗܘܘ ܝܗܘܕܝܐ ܠܐ ܫܦܝܪ
ܐܡܪܝܢ ܐܢܚܢ ܕܫܡܪܝܐ ܐܢܬ ܘܕܝܘܐ ܐܝܬ ܒܠܒܟ [49]ܐܡܪ ܠܗܘܢ
ܝܫܘܥ ܒܠ ܕܝܘܐ ܠܝܬ ܠܝ ܐܠܐ ܠܐܒܝ ܡܝܩܪܢܐ ܘܐܢܬܘܢ ܡܨܥܪܝܢ
ܐܢܬܘܢ ܠܝ. [50]ܘܐܢܐ ܠܐ ܒܥܐ ܫܘܒܚܐ ܕܢܦܫܝ ܐܝܬܘܗܝ، ܡܢ
ܕܒܥܐ ܘܕܐܢ· [51]ܐܡܝܢ ܐܡܝܢ ܐܡܪܢܐ ܠܟܘܢ ܕܡܢ ܕܡܠܬܝ،
ܢܛܪ ܡܘܬܐ ܠܐ ܢܛܥܡ ܠܥܠܡ· [52]ܐܡܪܝܢ ܠܗ ܝܗܘܕܝܐ ܗܫܐ
ܗܘ ܝܕܥܢ ܕܫܪܝܪܐܝܬ ܕܝܘܐ ܐܝܬ ܒܠܒܟ ܐܒܪܗܡ ܟܒܪ ܡܝܬ.
ܐܢܬ ܐܡܪ ܐܢܬ ܕܡܢ ܕܡܠܬܝ، ܢܛܪ ܠܐ ܢܛܥܡ ܡܘܬܐ. [53]ܠܡܐ
ܐܢܬ ܪܒ ܐܢܬ ܡܢ ܐܒܪܗܡ ܘܡܢ ܢܒܝܐ ܕܡܝܬܘ ܐܢܬ ܡܢ ܥܒܕܬ
ܢܦܫܟ [54]ܐܡܪ ܠܗܘܢ ܝܫܘܥ ܐܢ ܐܢܐ ܡܫܒܚ ܐܢܐ ܢܦܫܝ ܠܐ
ܗܘܐ ܡܕܡ ܫܘܒܚܝ ܐܝܬܘܗܝ، ܐܒܐ ܕܡܫܒܚ ܠܝ ܗܘ ܕܐܡܪܝܢ
ܐܢܬܘܢ ܕܐܠܗܢ ⌜ܗܘ⌝ [55]ܐܢܬܘܢ ܠܐ ܝܕܥܬܘܢܝܗܝ، ܐܢܐ ܝܕܥ
ܐܢܐ ܠܗ. ܘܐܢ ܐܡܪ ܕܠܐ ܝܕܥܢܐ ܠܗ· ܗܘܐ ܐܢܐ ܠܝ
ܕܓܠܐ ܐܟܘܬܟܘܢ ܐܢܐ ܕܝܢ ܝܕܥܢܐ ܠܗ ܘܡܠܬܗ ܢܛܪ ܐܢܐ.
[56]ܐܒܪܗܡ ܡܣܟܐ ܗܘܐ ܕܢܚܙܐ ܝܘܡܝ. ܘܚܙܐ ܘܚܕܝ، [57]ܐܡܪܝܢ
ܠܗ ܝܗܘܕܝܐ ܒܪ ܚܡܫܝܢ ܫܢܝܢ ܠܐ ܗܘܝܬ. ܘܐܒܪܗܡ ܚܙܝܬ
[58]ܐܡܪ ܠܗܘܢ܂ ܐܡܝܢ ܐܡܝܢ ܐܡܪܢܐ ܠܟܘܢ ܕܥܕܠܐ ܢܗܘܐ
ܐܒܪܗܡ ܐܢܐ ܐܝܬ ܗܘܝܬ [59]ܗܝܕܝܢ ܫܩܠܘ ܟܐܦܐ ܠܡܫܕܐ ܒܗ
ܘܝܫܘܥ ܡܛܫܝܐܝܬ ܢܦܩ ܠܗ ܡܢ ܗܝܟܠܐ ○ ○ ○

ܘܒܫܪܪܐ ܠܝܬܘܗܝ] S (sic): cf ܘܥܠ ܫܪܪܐ ܠܐ ܐܩܝܡܗ. ܡܛܠ ܕܫܪܪܐ ܠܝܬ ܒܗ Thos[312]   46 ܠܝ ult.] so I read the photograph: om. S[ed]   54 ܕܐܠܗܢ] S (sic) ܗܘ ult.] S*(vid), but erased by S[corr] : cf Joh x 36   57 ܚܡܫܝܢ S

slayer, §and in the truth he is not and in him the truth is not,¶ and *S* §¶*Thos*
what *time* he speaketh a lie from his own he speaketh, because he is 312
45 a liar and his father,—I that speak the truth, ye believe me not.
46 Which of you reproveth me for sin? And if truth I speak, wherefore
47 do ye not believe me? For he that is from God heareth the word of
48 God; therefore ye hear it not, because ye are not†." The Jews
were saying: "Do we not well say that thou art a Samaritan, and a
49 demon is upon thee?" Jesus saith to them: "Upon me there is no
50 demon, but my Father I honour and ye insult me. And I seek not
51 the glory of myself; there is one that seeketh and judgeth. Amen,
amen, I say to you He that keepeth my word, death he shall not
52 taste for ever." The Jews say to him: "Now we know that truly a
demon is upon thee, for Abraham is dead; dost thou say 'He that
53 keepeth my word shall not taste death'? Canst thou be greater than
Abraham and than the prophets that have died? Thou—whom
54 makest thou thyself?" Jesus saith to them: "If I glorify myself,
nothing were my glory; there is the Father that glorifieth me, he that
55 ye say is our God. Ye have not known him; I know him, and if I
should say that I know him not I should become untruthful like you.
56 But I know him and his word I keep. Abraham was delighted to
57 see my day, and he saw and rejoiced." The Jews say to him:
58 "Fifty years old thou art not, and Abraham hath seen thee?" He
saith to them "Amen, amen, I say to you that before ever Abraham
59 came to be, I was." Then they took up stones to throw at him,
and Jesus secretly went forth from the Temple.

---

he is not] *S* (*sic*): *cf Thos*[312], *where 'the Enemy' is said to have asked our Lord Who He was*, 'and of the truth He informed him not (*lit.* upon the truth He did not set him), because the truth is not in him.' **47.** *One line has been dropped by the scribe of S* 57 hath seen thee] hast thou seen *E*[197] 58 I was] *so also E*[197]

[1]ܘܟܕ ܥܒܪ ܚܙܐ ܣܡܝܐ ܚܕ݂ ܕܣܡܝܐ ܗܘܐ ܡܢ ܟܪܣܗ ܕܐܡܗ S
[2]ܫܐܠܝܢ ܠܗ ܬܠܡܝܕܘܗܝ، ܕܡܢ ܐܢܫ ܚܛܐ ܗܢܐ ܐܘ ܐܒܘܗܝ، ܕܟܕ݂
ܣܡܝܐ ܐܬܝܠܕ݂. [3]ܐܡܪ ܠܗܘܢ ܠܐ ܗܘ ܚܛܐ ܐܦܠܐ ܐܒܘܗܝ،
ܐܠܐ ܕܢܬܚܙܘܢ ܒܗ ܥܒ̈ܕܐ ܕܐܠܗܐ [4]ܘܠܝ ܘܠܐ ܠܡܥܒܕ݂ ܥܒ̈ܕܐ
ܕܡܢ ܕܫܕܪܢܝ ܥܕ݂· ܐܝܡܡܐ ܗܘ ܐܬܐ ܕܝܢ ܠܠܝܐ ܕܒܗ ܐܢܫ ܠܐ
ܡܫܟܚ ܠܡܥܒܕ݂. [5]ܟܡܐ ܕܒܥܠܡܐ ܗܘ. ܐܢܐ ܓܝܪ ܢܘܗܪܗ ܐܢܐ
ܕܥܠܡܐ [6]ܟܕ݂ ܐܡܪ ܗܠܝܢ ܪܩ ܥܠ ܐܪܥܐ ܘܓܒܠ ܛܝܢܐ ܡܢ ܪܘܩܗ
ܘܫܘܦ ܠܗ ܥܠ ܥܝ̈ܢܘܗܝ، ܕܗܘ ܣܡܝܐ [7]ܘܐܡܪ ܠܗ ܙܠ ܐܫܝܓ
ܐܦܝܟ ܒܡܥܡܘܕܝܬܐ ܕܫܝܠܘܚܐ. ܘܟܕ݂ ܐܫܝܓ ܐܦܘܗܝ، ܐܬܦܬܚ.
ܥܝ̈ܢܘܗܝ، [8]ܘܟܕ݂ ܚܙܘܗܝ ܫܒ̈ܒܘܗܝ، ܘܐܝܠܝܢ ܕܚܙܐ ܗܘܐ ܠܗܘܢ̇
ܕܚܕܪ ܗܘܐ. ܐܡ̈ܪܝܢ ܠܐ ܗܘܐ ܗܢܐ ܗܘ ܕܚܕܪ ܗܘܐ [9]ܐܝܬ
ܕܐܡ̈ܪܝܢ * * ܗܘ· ܘܐܝܬ ܕܐܡ̈ܪܝܢ ܕܡܕܡܐ ܕܡܐ ܠܗ. ܐܡܪ
ܠܗܘܢ ܗܘ ܣܡܝܐ ܐܢܐ ܐܢܐ [10]ܐܡܪܝܢ ܠܗ ܕܐܝܟܢܐ ܐܬܦܬܚ.
ܥܝ̈ܢܝܟ [11]ܐܡܪ ܠܗܘܢ ܗܘ ܓܒܪܐ ܕܫܡܗ ܝܫܘܥ ܥܠ ܥܝ̈ܢܝ
ܛܝܢܐ ܘܐܡܪ ܠܝ ܙܠ ܐܫܝܓ ܐܦܝܟ ܒܡܥܡܘܕܝܬܐ ܕܫܝܠܘܚܐ
ܘܐܙܠܬ ܐܫܝܓܬ ܘܐܬܚܙܝ، ܠܝ. [12]ܐܡܪܝܢ ܠܗ ܘܐܝܟܐ ܗܘ ܐܡܪ
ܠܗܘܢ ܠܐ ܝܕܥܢܐ [13]ܕܒܪܘܗܝ، ܠܗܘ ⌜ܕ⌝⌜ܐܬܐܣܝ⌝ ܘܐܝܬܝܘܗܝ، ܠܘܬ
ܦܪ̈ܝܫܐ [14]ܘܗܘ ⌜ܗܘ⌝ܐ ⌜ܝܘܡ⌝ܐ ܫܒܬܐ ܗܘܬ [15]ܘܬ⌜ܘ⌝ܒ ܫܐܠܘܗܝ،
ܦܪ̈ܝܫܐ ܐܝܟܢܐ ܐܬܦܬܚ ܥܝ̈ܢܝܟ ܐܡܪ ܠܗܘܢ ܛܝܢܐ ⌜ܥܠ⌝ ܥܝ̈ܢܝ
⌜ܘ⌝⌜ܦ⌝ܬܚ ܐܢܝܢ * * * ܘܐܝܬ * * * [16]ܡܢܗܘܢ * * * ܘܐܡܪܝܢ
* * ܓܒܪܐ ܡܢ ܐܠܗܐ * * * ܫܒܬܐ ܠܐ ܢܛܪ ܘܓܒܠ ܗܘ
ܛܝܢܐ ܐܚܪ̈ܢܐ ܕܝܢ ܐܡܪܝܢ ܗܘܘ ܐܝܟܢܐ ܡܫܟܚ ܓܒܪܐ ܚܛܝܐ ܗܠܝܢ
ܐܬܘܬܐ ܠܡܥܒܕ݂. ܘܦܠܓܝܢ ܗܘܘ ܚܕ݂ ܥܠ ܚܕ݂ ܕܗܘܝܐ * * ܐ [17]ܘܐܡܪܝܢ
ܠܗܘ ܕܐܬܐܣܝ ܐܢܬ ܡܢܐ ܐܡܪ ܐܢܬ ܥܠܘܗܝ، ܐܡܪ ܠܗܘܢ ܐܢܐ
ܐܡܪ ܐܢܐ ܕܢܒܝܐ ܗܘ [18]ܘܠܐ ܗܝܡܢܘܗܝ، ܠܗ ܝܗܘܕܝܐ ܕܣܡܝܐ
ܗܘܐ ܘܚܙܐ ܠܐܒܘܗܝ، ܘܠܐܡܗ [19]⌜ܘܐܡܪܝܢ⌝ ܐܢ ⌜ܗ⌝ܢܘ ܒܪܟܘܢ
ܠܐ ܐܢܬܘܢ ܐܡܪܝܢ ܕܟܕ݂ ܣܡܝܐ ܐܬܝܠܕ݂. ܐܝܟܢܐ ܕܝܢ ܚܙܐ ܗܫܐ

---

9 ܕܐܡܪܝܢ 1°] *the illegible word looks like* ܒ   13 ܕܐܬܐܣܝ & 14 ܗܘܐ ܝܘܡܐ & 15 ܘܬܘܒ] *so I read the photograph*

ix 1 And while passing by he saw a certain blind man, that had been *S*
2 blind from the womb of his mother. His disciples ask him which
3 one sinned, this *fellow* or his kinsfolk, that he was born blind? He
saith to them: "Neither he sinned, nor his kinsfolk, but that the
4 deeds of God might be seen in him. And me it behoves to do the
deeds of him that sent me while yet it is day, but the night cometh
5 in which no one can do *aught* as long as it is in the world; for I am
6 the light of the world." When he said these things he spat on the
earth and formed clay from his spittle and took *it* up *and* smeared
7 *it* upon the eyes of that blind man, and he saith to him: "Go, wash
thy face with a baptism of Shiloah"; and when he washed his face
8 his eyes were opened. And when his neighbours saw him and those
by whom it had been seen that he was begging, they say: "Is not this
9 he that was begging?" some say * " * it is he"; and some say "It
is indeed like him." The blind man saith to them: "I am he."
10, 11 They say to him "How were thine eyes opened?" He saith to
them: "The man whose name is Jesus smeared upon them clay, and
said to me 'Go, wash thy face with a baptism of Shiloah'; and I
12 went *and* washed, and I *could* see." They say to him: "And where
13 is he?" He saith to them: "I know not." They took him that was
14 healed and brought him unto the Pharisees. And that same day was
15 the sabbath. And again the Pharisees asked him: "How were thine
eyes opened?" He saith to them: "Clay [he smeared] upon them
16 and opened them * * *" * * and [were] saying: "The man
from God [is not, because] the sabbath he keepeth not and he
formed clay." But others were saying: "How can a man *that is*
a sinner do these signs?" And they were dividing one against the
17 other * *. And they say to him that was healed: "Thou, what
sayest thou of him?" He saith to them: "I say that he is a prophet."
18 And the Jews did not believe him that he had been blind, and they
19 sent to his father and his mother [and they say:] "If this is your
son, say ye not that he was born blind? But how seeth he now?"

---

4 'And I must work the works of my Father that sent me' *E*[197]
7 'Go, wash thy face' *E*[199]

²⁰ܥܢܘ ܕܝܢ ܐܒܗܘܗܝ، ⌜ܘ⌝ܐܡܪܝܢ ܝܕܥܝܢ ܐܢܚܢ ܕܗܢܐ ܒܪܢ ܘܕܟܕ S
⌜ܣ⌝ܡܝܐ ܐܬܝܠܕ. ²¹ܐܝܟܢܐ ܕܝܢ ܚܙܐ ܗܫܐ ܐܘ ܡܢܘ ܦܬܚ ܠܗ
ܠܥܝܢܐ ܠܐ ܝܕܥܝܢ ܐܢܚܢ. ܗܘ ܐܦ [ܗܘ] ܡܪܒܝܘܬܗ، ܗܘܐ.
ܡܢܗ ܡܫܐܠܝܢ ܐܢܬܘܢ ܠܡܕܒܪ. ²²ܗܠܝܢ ܐܡܪܘ ܐܒܗܘܗܝ، ܡܛܠ
ܕܕܚܠܝܢ ܗܘܘ ܡܢ ܝܗܘ̈ܕܝܐ ܦܣܩܘ ܓܝܪ ܗܘ̈ܝܐ ܘܦܪܝܫܐ ܕܡܢ
ܕܐܡܪ ܕܡܫܝܚܐ ܗܘ ܢܦܩܘܢܝܗܝ. ²³ܡܛܠ ܗܢܐ ܐܡܪܘ ܐܒܗܘܗܝ،
ܕܠܗ ܫܐܠܘ. ²⁴ܘܩܪܘ ܬܘܒ ܠܗܘ ܕܐܬܐܡܣ ܘܐܡܪܝܢ ܠܗ ܗܒ
ܠܐܠܗܐ. ܐܢܚܢ ܓܝܪ ܝܕܥܝܢ ܐܢܚܢ ܕܗܢܐ ܓܒܪܐ ܚܛܝܐ ܗܘ
²⁵ܐܡܪ ܠܗܘܢ ܗܘ ܕܐܬܐܡܣ ܐܢ ܚܛܝܐ ܗܘ ܠܐ ܝܕܥܢܐ.
ܚܕܐ ܕܝܢ ܝܕܥܢܐ. ܕܣܡܝܐ ܗܘܝܬ. ܘܡܛܠܬܗ ܗܐ ܚܙܐ ܐܢܐ.
²⁶ܐܡܪܝܢ ܠܗ [ܡܢܐ ܥܒܕ ܠܟ ܐܝܟܢܐ] ܐܦܬܚ ²⁷[ܐܡܪ ܠܗܘܢ]
ܚܕܐ ܕܝܢ ܐܡܪܬ ܠܟܘܢ ܘܫܡܥܬܘܢ ܡܢܐ ܬܘܒ ܡܫܬܐܠܝܢ
ܐܢܬܘܢ ܠܝ. ܐܘ ܠܡܐ ܬܠܡܝ̈ܕܐ ܨܒܝܢ ܐܢܬܘܢ ܠܡܗܘܐ ܠܗ
²⁸ܗܢܘܢ ܕܝܢ ܨܚܝܘܗܝ، ܘܐܡܪܝܢ ܠܗ ܐܢܬ ܗܘ ܬܠܡܝܕܗ ܐܢܬ
ܘܐܢܚܢ ܬܠܡܝ̈ܕܐ ܐܢܚܢ ܕܡܘܫܐ. ²⁹ܘܝܕܥܝܢ ܐܢܚܢ ܕܥܡ ܡܘܫܐ
ܐܠܗܐ ܡܠܠ ܠܗܢܐ ܕܝܢ ܠܐ ܝܕܥܝܢ ܐܢܚܢ ܡܢ ܐܝܟܢܐ ܗܘ.
³⁰ܐܡܪ ܠܗܘܢ ܗܘ ܕܐܬܐܡܣ ܒܗܕܐ ܠܡܬܕܡܪܘ ܒܗ ܕܐܢܬܘܢ
ܠܐ ܝܕܥܝܢ ܐܢܬܘܢ ܠܗ. ܡܢ ܐܝܟܢܐ ܗܘ. ܘܥܝ̈ܢܝ ܕܝܠܝ ܦܬܚ.
³¹ܘܝܕܥܝܢ [ܐܢܚܢ ܕܐܠܗܐ ܒܡܠܐ ܕܚ̈ܛܝܐ] ܠܐ ܫܡܥ. ܐܠܐ ܠܡܢ
ܕܕܚܠ ܡܢܗ ܘܥܒܕ ܨܒܝܢܗ ܠܗܘ ܫܡܥ. ³²ܘܗܐ ܡܢ ܥܠܡܐ
ܕܗܘܐ ܒܥܠܡܐ ܠܐ ܐܫܬܡܥ ܕܐܬܦܬܚ ܥܝ̈ܢܐ ܕܡܢ ܐܡܗ
ܣܡܝܐ ܗܘܐ. ³³ܗܢܐ ܐܠܘ ܠܐ ܡܢ ܐܠܗܐ ܗܘܐ. ܐܝܟܢܐ ܥܒܕ
ܗܕܐ. ³⁴ܐܡܪܝܢ ܠܗ ܐܢܬ ܟܘܠܟ ܒܚ̈ܛܗܐ ܐܬܝܠܕܬ ܐܢܬ ܡܠܦ
ܐܢܬ ܠܢ. ܘܐܦܩܘܗܝ، ܠܒܪ. ³⁵ܘܫܡܥ ܝܫܘܥ ܕܐܦܩܘܗܝ،
ܘܟܕ ܐܫܟܚܗ ܝܫܘܥ ܐܡܪ ܠܗ ܐܢܬ ܡܗܝܡܢ ܐܢܬ ܒܒܪܗ
ܕܐܠܗܐ. ³⁶ܐܡܪ ܠܗ ܗܘ ܕܐܬܐܡܣ ܡܢܘ ܡܪܝ، ܕܐܗܝܡܢ ܒܗ.

20 ܘܐܡܪܝܢ] *om.* ܘ S^{ed} 21 [ܗܘ] *Hole in S* 26, 31 *In S the upper corner of fol.* 138 (69) *is torn away, together with nearly two lines of the outer column*

20 But his parents answered ⌜and⌝ say: "We know that this *is* our son, S
21 and that he was born blind; but how he seeth now, or who gave him
power to see we know not. Lo, he also is of age; from him ye can
22 know." These things said his parents because they were afraid of the
Jews, for the scribes and the Pharisees decreed that him that saith
23 "He is the Messiah" they should expel. Therefore said his parents
24 "Ask him." And they called again him that was healed, and they say to
25 him: "Glorify God, for we know that this man is a sinner." He that
was healed saith to them: "If he is a sinner I know not; but one *thing*
26 I know, that I was a blind man, and because of him, lo, I see!" They
27 say to him [: "What did he to thee? How] did he heal thee?" [He
saith to them:] "But one *thing* I have said to you and ye have heard;
why again do ye *keep* asking me? Or disciples do ye wish to become
28 of him?" But they cursed him, and say to him: "Thou art his disciple,
29 and we are disciples of Moses; and we know that with Moses God
30 spake, but this *one*—we know not from whence he is." He that was
healed saith to them: "At this *we have* to wonder, that ye know him
31 not from whence he is, and my eyes, *even* mine, he opened; and we
know [that God the voice of sinners] heareth not, but him that
32 feareth him and doeth his will, him he heareth. And lo, from the
day when the world came to be it hath not been heard that *the
eyes of* a blind man have been opened that from his mother*'s womb*
33 was blind! This *one*—if from God he had not been, how had he
34 done this?" They say to him: "Thou thine own self in sins
wast born; hast thou come teaching us?" And they put him out.
35 And Jesus heard that they had put him forth, and when Jesus found
36 him he said to him: "Believest thou in the Son of Man?" He that
was healed saith to him: "Who is he, my Lord, that I should believe

S [37]ܐܡܪ ܠܗ ܝܫܘܥ ܚܙܝܬܗ܆ ܘܗܘ ܕܡܡܠܠ ܥܡܟ ܗܘܝܘ. [38]ܐܡܪ
ܡܗܝܡܢ ܐܢܐ ܡܪܝ܆ ܘܢܦܠ ܤܓܕ ܠܗ ∘ ܿ ∘

[39]ܐܡܪ ܠܗ ܝܫܘܥ ܠܕܝܢܗ ܕܥܠܡܐ ܗܢܐ ܐܬܝܬ ܕܐܝܠܝܢ ܕܣܡܝܐ
ܐܢܘܢ ܢܚܙܘܢ܆ ܘܐܝܠܝܢ ܕܚܙܝܢ ܢܣܡܘܢ. [40]ܘܟܕ ܫܡܥܘ ܦܪ̈ܝܫܐ
ܐܝܠܝܢ ܕܥܡܗ ܗܘܘ ܠܗ ܐܡܪܝܢ ܠܗ ܐܢܚܢ ܣܡ̈ܝܐ ܐܢܚܢ.
[41]ܐܡܪ ܠܗܘܢ ܐܠܘ ܣܡ̈ܝܐ ܗܘܝܬܘܢ ܠܝܬ ܗܘܬ ܠܟܘܢ
ܚܛܝܬܐ. ܐܠܐ ܐܡܪܝܢ ܐܢܬܘܢ ܕܚܙܝܢ ܐܢܚܢ. ܡܛܠ ܗܢܐ
ܚ̈ܛܗܝܟܘܢ ܩܝܡܝܢ ܐܢܘܢ܆ [1]ܐܡܝܢ ܐܡܝܢ ܐܡܪܢܐ ܠܟܘܢ ܕܡܢ
ܕܠܐ ܥܐܠ ܡܢ ܬܪܥܐ ܠܕܝܪܬܐ ܕܐܝܬ ܒܗ ܥܢܐ ܐܠܐ ܣܠܩ
ܠܗ ܡܢ ܕܘܟܐ ܐܚܪܢܐ ܗܘ ܓܢܒܐ ܘܓܝܣܐ [2]ܘܐܝܢܐ ܕܡܢ
ܬܪܥܐ ܥܐܠ ܗܘ ܪܥܝܗ ܗܘ ܕܥܢܗ [3]ܢܛܪ ܬܪܥܐ ܦܬܚ ܠܗ
ܬܪܥܐ ܘܥܢܐ ܫܡܥܐ ܩܠܗ ܘܚܘܬܗ ܗܘ ܩܪܐ ܥܢܐ ܒܫܡܗܝܢ
ܘܗܘ ܡܦܩ ܠܗ ܘܡܐ ܕܐܦܩ ܚܘܬܗ ܩܕܡܝܗܝܢ ܐܙܠ ܘܥܢܐ
ܕܠܗ ܒܬܪܗ ܐܙܠܐ ܡܛܠ ܕܝܕܥܐ ܥܢܐ ܩܠܗ [5]ܒܬܪ ܢܘܟܪܝܐ
ܕܝܢ ܠܐ ܐܙܠܐ ܥܢܐ ܐܠܐ ܡܬܦܣܩܐ ܥܢܐ ܡܢܗ ܡܛܠ ܕܠܐ
ܝܕܥܐ ܩܠܗ ܕܢܘܟܪܝܐ. [6]ܗܠܝܢ ܡܠܠ ܥܡܗܘܢ ܝܫܘܥ ܒܦܠܐܬܐ
ܘܗܢܘܢ ܠܐ ܡܣܬܟܠܝܢ ܗܘܘ

[7]ܬܘܒ ܐܡܪ ܠܗܘܢ ܝܫܘܥ ܐܡܝܢ ܐܡܝܢ ܐܡܪܢܐ ܠܟܘܢ ܕܐܢܐ
ܐܢܐ ܬܪܥܗ ܕܥܢܐ [8]ܘܟܠ ܐܝܠܝܢ ܕܐܬܘ ܓܢ̈ܒܐ ܐܢܘܢ ܘܓܝ̈ܣܐ
ܐܠܐ ܠܐ ܫܡܥܬ ܐܢܘܢ ܚܘܬܐ· [§9]ܐܢܐ ܐܢܐ ܬܪܥܗ ܕܥܢܐ. §A195
¶A ܘܡܢ ܒܝ ܕܢܥܘܠ ܢܚܐ ܘܢܥܘܠ ܘܢܦܘܩ ܘܪܥܝܐ ܢܫܟܚ·¶ [10]ܓܢܒܐ
ܕܝܢ ܠܐ ܐܬܐ ܐܠܐ ܕܢܓܢܘܒ ܘܢܩܛܘܠ ܘܢܘܒܕ. ܐܢܐ ܕܝܢ ܐܬܝܬ
ܕܚ̈ܝܐ ܢܗܘܘܢ ܠܗܘܢ ܘܡܘܬܪܢܐ ܢܗܘܐ ܠܗܘܢ܆ [11]ܐܢܐ ܐܢܐ
§A195 §Thos209 ¶A¶Thos ܪܥܝܐ ܛܒܐ §§ܘܪܥܝܐ ܛܒܐ ܢܦܫܗ ܢܣܝܡ ܥܠ ܐܦ ⸢ܥܢܗ.⸣¶¶

---

9 ܕܢܥܘܠ] ܕܥܐܠ *A*   ܢܚܐ *S*   ܘܢܥܘܠ ܘܢܦܘܩ *A*
Cf ܐܢܐ ܐܢܐ ܬܪܥܐ ܕܚ̈ܝܐ. ܕܟܠ ܡܢ ܕܒܝ ܢܥܘܠ. ܢܚܐ ܠܥܠܡ *A* 64
11 ܪܥܝܐ ܛܒܐ ܕܝܗܒ *Thos*[209]   ⸢ܥܢܗ.⸣] *A Thos*[209], *and so I read the photograph of S (not* ⸢ܥܢܐ⸣ ܕܝܠܗ, *as S*[ed])

37 in him?" Jesus saith to him: "Thou hast seen him, and he that *S*
38 speaketh with thee is he." He saith: "I believe, my Lord." And
he fell *and* worshipped him.

39 Jesus saith to him: "For the judgement of this world I came,
that those that are blind might see and those that see might
40 become blind." And when the Pharisees which were near him
41 heard, they say to him: "Are we blind men?" He saith to them:
"If ye had been blind men, ye had had no sin; but ye say 'We
X 1 see,' therefore your sins stand. Amen, amen, I say to you He
that entereth not by the door of the fold in which the flock is, but
2 goeth up by another place, he is a robber and a thief; and he
3 which by the door entereth, he is the shepherd of the flock. The
door-keeper openeth to him the door, and the flock heareth his voice
and his beasts he calleth, *each* sheep by its name, and he bringeth
4 them forth. And what *time* he hath brought his beasts forth before
them he goeth, and the flock that *is* his after him goeth, because the
5 flock knoweth his voice. But after a stranger the flock goeth not,
but the flock separateth itself from him, because it knoweth not the
6 voice of a stranger." These things spake Jesus with them in a
parable, and they were not understanding.

7 Again Jesus saith to them: "Amen, amen, I say to you I am
8 the door of the flock. And all those that have come are the thieves
9 and the robbers, but the beasts have not heard them. §I am the §*A* 195
door of the flock, and by me every one that shall enter shall live, and
10 shall enter and go forth and find pasture.¶ But the thief cometh ¶*A*
not save that he may thieve and kill and destroy; but I have come that
11 they might have life and have abundance. I am the good shepherd,
§§and the good shepherd giveth his life on behalf of his flock¶¶; §*A* 195 §*Thos* 209 ¶*A* ¶*Thos*

---

8 have come] + before me *E*[200] 9 shall enter] entereth *A*
Cf 'I am the door of life, that whosoever by me shall enter may live for
ever' *A* 63 11 'The good shepherd that giveth his life on behalf of his
flock' *Thos*[209]

S

§A225 §[12]ܐܓܝܪܐ ܕܝܢ ܫܡܘܪܐ ܕܠܐ ܗܘܬ ܕܝܠܗ ܒܢܐ ܡܢܐ ܕܢܣܒܐ

¶A ܕܐܒܐ ܕܐܬܬܐ ܥܒܕ ܠܗ ܠܒܢܐ ܘܒܪܬ¶ ܘܐܬܬܐ ܕܐܒܐ ܣܦܩ

ܘܡܒܕܪ [13]ܡܛܠ ܕܐܓܝܪܐ ܩ̇ܘ· ܒܗ. ܘܠܐ ܒܦܠܛ ܠܗ ܒܠܒܗ

[14]ܐܢܐ ܐܢܐ ܙܒܢܐ ܠܓܒܐ ܘܝܗܒ ܐܢܐ ܠܕܝܠܟ ܘܝܗܒ ܠܝ ܕܝܠܝ

ܘܡܬܝܗܒܢܐ ܡܢ ܕܝܠܝ [15]ܐܝܟܢܐ ܕܝܗܒ ܠܝ ܐܒܝ ܘܝܗܒ ܐܢܐ

§A195 ܠܐܒܝ. ܘܢܦܫ ܗܟܢ ܐܢܐ ܥܠ ܐܩ̈ܡܗ ܕܒܢܐ. [16]ܘ§ܐܝܬ ܠܝ ܒܪܬܐ

ܐܚܪܢܐ ܐܠܝܢ ܕܠܐ ܗܘܘ ܡܢܗ ܡܢ ܕܪܬܐ ܗܕܐ. ܘܐܦ ܠܗܘܢ

ܘܠܐ ܠܝ ܠܡܬܠܘ ܐܢܘܢ ܘܐܦ ܗܢܘܢ ܥܠ ܢܫܡܥܘܢ ܘܬܗܘܐ

ܒܢܐ ܒܡܠܗ ܚܕܐ ܘܚܕ ܙܒܢܐ [17]ܘܐܡܪ ܡܛܠ ܗܢܐ ܙܒܢ ܠܝ

¶A ܕܗܟܢ ܐܢܐ ܢܦܫܝ¶ ܕܬܘܒ ܐܫܟܚܗ [18]ܘܠܐ ܐܝܬ ܐܢܫ ܥܡܠ ܠܗ

ܡܢܝ. ܐܠܐ ܐܢܐ ܗܟܢ ܐܢܐ ܠܗ ܡܢܝ ܫܘܠܛܢܐ ܒܪ ܕܐܫܟܚܗܝ،

ܘܬܘܒ ܐܫܟܚܬܗ، ܡܛܠ ܕܗܢܐ ܦܘܩܕܢܐ ܡܩܠܬ ܡܢ ܐܒܝ. [19]ܘܡܢ

ܗܠܝܢ ܡܡܠܠ ܗܘܐ ܗܘܬ ܗܘܬ ܦܠܓܘܬܐ ܒܝܢ ܝܗܘܕ̈ܝܐ [20]ܡܛܠ

ܕܐܝܬ ܡܢܗܘܢ ܕܐܡܪܝܢ ܗܘܘ ܕܕܝܘܐ ܐܝܬ ܒܠܒܗ،. ܘܡܫܢܝܐ

ܥܢܐ ܡܢܐ ܡܢܝܢ ܐܢܬܘܢ ܘܪܕܬܘܢ ܠܗ. [21]ܐܚܪܢܐ ܕܝܢ ܐܡܪܝܢ

ܗܠܝܢ ܩ̈ܠܐ ܠܐ ܗܘ، ܕܕܝܘܐ. ܠܗܟܐ ܕܝܘܐ ܡܟܐܒ ܗܟܢܐ

ܠܡܟܬܒܘ ܀

[22]ܘܗܘܐ ܗܘܐ ܒܙܒܢܐ ܒܐܘܪܫܠܡ ܕܡܬܩܪܐ ܐܬܪ ܒܝܬ ܩܒܘܪܐ.

ܘܫܬܐ ܗܘܐ [23]ܘܡܗܠܟ ܗܘܐ ܫܘܩܐ ܒܐܣܛܘܐ ܕܫܠܝܡܘܢ

ܕܐܝܬ ܒܗܝܟܠܐ [24]* * ܫܪܘܗ، ܡܗܘܕܝܐ ܘܐܡܪܝܢ ܠܗ ܒܥܕܢܐ

ܠܐܡܬܝ، ܢܦܫܢ ܐܝܬ ܢܫܩܠܬ ܐ ܐܢܬ ܗܘ ܡܫܝܚܐ ܐܡܪ ܠܢ

ܦܪܗܣܝܐܝܬ [25]ܐܡܪ ܠܗܘܢ ܝܫܘܥ ܡܛܠ ܐܢܐ ܒܥܝܢܘܢ ܘܠܐ

---

12 ܐܓܝܪܐ] + ܐܝܢܐ *A* ܕܝܢ ܫܡܘܪܐ] *om. A* 13 ܗܘ] *S**; *exp.* S^{corr} 16 ܐܚܪܢܐ.....ܗܕܐ] *om. A* ܘܐܦ 1°] ܐܦ A^a ܠܝ 2°] *om. A*[b] ܐܢܘܢ] + ܠܗܟܐ *A* ܘܐܦ....ܢܫܡܥܘܢ] *om. A* 17 ܕܗܟܢ ܐܢܐ ܢܦܫܝ] ܕܢܦܫܝ ܝܗܒ ܐܢܐ ܥܠ ܐܩ̈ܡܗ ܕܒܢܐ *A* 18 ܫܘܠܛܢܐ *S*; ? *for* ܫܠܝܛܐ
22 ܐܬܪ ܒܝܬ ܩܒܘܪܐ] *Cf* יקר בית עלמא *De Vogüé* i 40, 47, *and see Introd.* vol. ii 23, 24 ܒܗܝܟܠܐ * * ܫܪܘܗ،] *In the gap* S^{ed} *has* * * ܘ̈ܠܐ. *Probably the* MS *had* ܒܗܝܟܠܐ. ܘܟܢܫܘ ܫܪܘܗ، *or* ܒܗܝܟܠܐ ܒܟܘܗ. ܘܫܪܘܗ،

12 §but the hireling, the false one, whose own the flock is not, what S §*A*225
time he seeth the wolf coming leaveth the flock and fleeth,¶ ¶*A*
13 and the wolf cometh *and* snatcheth and scattereth—because he is
14 the hireling in it and careth not for it. I am the good shepherd;
and I know my own, and my own know me and I am known by my
15 own, as my Father knoweth me and I know my Father, and my life §*A*195
16 I lay down on behalf of the flock. And §I have other sheep which
are not of this same fold; and them also it behoves me to bring,
and they also my voice will hear, and all the flock will be one and
17 one shepherd. And my Father because of this loveth me, that I lay ¶*A*
18 down my life¶ that again I may take it. And there is not any one
that taketh it away from me, but I lay it down away from me, for
†I have† authority that I should lay it down and again take it up;
19 because this commandment I have received from my Father." And
while he was speaking these things there had been a division among
20 the Jews, because some of them were saying "A demon is upon
21 him, and he is indeed mad; why stand ye and listen to him?" But
others say: "These words are not *those* of a demon; is a demon
able to open *the eyes of* a blind man?"

22 And it had been the Feast in Jerusalem that is called 'Honour
23 of the Sanctuary,' and it was winter and Jesus was walking in
24 Solomon's Porch, that is in the Temple[. And there gathered]
round him the Jews and say to him: "Till when art thou taking up
25 our breath? If thou art the Messiah, tell us plainly." Jesus saith
to them: "I am speaking with you, and ye believe not; and the

---

12 but] *om. A* the false one] *om. A* whose] he whose *A* 16 which.... fold] *om. A* me] *om.* A^{b} to bring] + hither *A* and they.... hear] *om. A* 17 that I lay down my life] that my life I give on behalf of the flock *A* 22 Honour of the Sanctuary] *A similar phrase is found in Palmyrene inscriptions: see Introd.* vol. ii 23, 24 in the Temple.... round him the Jews] *The former of the suggested restorations is translated in the text: the latter restoration means* 'in the Temple, within it. And the Jews surrounded him'

ܡܗܝܡܢܝܢ ܐܢܬܘܢ܂ ܘܥܒ̈ܕܐ ܕܥܒܕ ܐܢܐ ܒܫܡܗ ܕܐܒܝ ܗܢܘܢ S
ܣܗܕܝܢ ܥܠܝ [26]ܐܠܐ ܐܢܬܘܢ ܠܐ ܡܗܝܡܢܝܢ ܐܢܬܘܢ܂ ܡܛܠ ܕܠܐ
ܗܘܝܬܘܢ܂ ܡܢ ܢܩܘܬܝ ܐܝܟܢܐ ܕܐܡܪܬ ܠܟܘܢ܂ [27]ܥܪ̈ܒܐ ܕܝܠܝ
ܩܠܝ ܫܡܥܝܢ ܘܐܢܐ ܝܕܥ ܠܗܘܢ܂ ܘܗܢܘܢ܂ ܐܬܝܢ ܒܬܪܝ܆ [28]ܘܐܢܐ
ܝܗܒܢܐ ܠܗܘܢ܂ ܚܝ̈ܐ ܕܠܥܠܡ ܘܠܐ ܢܐܒܕܘܢ܂ ܠܥܠܡ ܘܠܐ ܐܢܫ
ܚܛܘܦ ܐܢܘܢ܂ ܡܢ ܐܝܕܝ܆ [29]* * ܕܐܒܐ ܕܝܗܒ ܠܝ ܡܢ ܟܠ ܪܒ
ܗܘ܂ ܘܠܝܬ ܐܢܫ ܕܡܢ ܐܝܕܗ ܕܐܒܐ ܫܩܠ. [30]§ܐܢܐ ܘܐܒܝ ܚܕ §¶A 10, 70, 120
ܐܢܚܢ¶ [31]ܟܕ ܐܡܪ ܗܠܝܢ ܫܩܠܘ ܟܐܦ̈ܐ ܠܡܪܓܡܗ [32]ܐܡܪ ܠܗܘܢ
ܝܫܘܥ ܣܓܝ̈ܐܐ ܥܒ̈ܕܐ ܕܐܒܐ ܚܘܝܬܟܘܢ܂ ܡܛܠ ܐܝܢܐ ܡܢܗܘܢ
ܡܢ ܥܒ̈ܕܐ ܪ̇ܓܡܝܢ ܐܢܬܘܢ܂ ܠܝ [33]ܐܡܪܝܢ ܠܗ ܝܗܘ̈ܕܝܐ ܠܐ
ܡܛܠ ܥܒ̈ܕܐ ܫܦܝܪ̈ܐ ܪ̇ܓܡܝܢ ܐܢܚܢ ܠܟ ܐܠܐ ܡܛܠ ܕܟܕ ܐܢܬ
ܒܪ ܐܢܫܐ ܐܢܬ ܡܓܕܦ ܘܥܒܕ ⌜ܐܢܬ⌝ ܢܦܫܟ ܐܠܗܐ. [34]ܐܡܪ ܠܗܘܢ
ܝܫܘܥ. ܠܐ ܗܘܐ ܗܟܢܐ ܒܢܡܘܣܐ ܟܬܝܒ܂ ܕܐܢܐ ܐܡܪܬ
ܕܐܠܗܐ ܐܢܬܘܢ܂ [35]ܘܠܐ ܡܫܟܚܐ ⌜ܕܬܫܬܪܐ⌝ ܡܠܬܐ ܕܐܠܗܐ
[36]ܠܐܝܢܐ ܕܐܒܐ ܩܕܫܗ ܘܫܕܪܗ ܠܥܠܡܐ ܐܡܪܝܢ ܐܢܬܘܢ܂
ܕܡܓܕܦ ܐܢܬ ܥܠ ܕܐܡܪܬ ܠܟܘܢ܂ ܕܒܪܗ ܕܐܠܗܐ [37]ܐܠܐ
ܥܒܕܢܐ ܥܒ̈ܕܐ ܕܐܒܝ ܠܐ ܬܗܝܡܢܘܢܢܝ [38]ܘܐܢ܂ ܕܝܢ ܥܒܕܢܐ ܘܐܦ.
ܐܢ܂ ܠܝ ܠܐ ܡܗܝܡܢܝܢ ܐܢܬܘܢ܂ ܠܗܘܢ܂ ܠܥܒ̈ܕܐ ܗܝܡܢܘ
ܘܬܕܥܘܢ܂ ܕܐܢܐ ܒܐܒܐ ܐܢܐ ܘܐܒܐ ܒܝ ܗܘ [39]ܘܬܘܒ ܒܥܘ
[ܗܠܝܢ ܓܒܝܢ ܗܘܘ ܝܗܘܕܝܐ ܠܡܐܚܕܗ] ܘܢܦܩ ܠܗ ܡܢ ܒܝܢܬ
ܐܝܕܝܗܘܢ܂ [40]ܘܐܙܠ ܠܗ ܠܥܒܪܐ ܕܝܘܪܕܢܢ ܠܐܬܪ ܕܡܥܡܕ ܗܘܐ
⌜ܝܘܚܢܢ⌝ ܡܢ ܩܕܝܡ · [41][ܘܠܬܗܝܢ] ܐܬܘ ܣܓܝܐܐ ܠܘܬܗ. [ܘ]ܐܡܪܝܢ
ܗܘܘ ܕܝܘܚܢܢ * * * ܐܬܐ ܚܘ * * * * * * * * *
* * * ܐܡܪ ܟܠܗܝܢ ܗܠܝܢ [42]ܘܣܓܝܐܐ ܗܝܡܢܘ ܒܗ ∘ ∘
[1]ܘܗܘܐ ܕܟܪܝܗ ܠܥܙܪ ܡܢ ܒܝܬ ܥܢܝܐ ܐܚܘܗ ܕܡܪܝܡ ܘܕܡܪܬܐ

28, 29 ܐܝܕܝ *is followed in S by a short illegible word* 30 ܚܕ $A^3/_3$ (*exc.* A^a 10) 33 ܐܠܗܐ] *cf* Ex vii 1 syr.vg *and* ܕܥܒܕܢܘܬܗ ܐܠܗܐ ܠܡܪܢ A 273 36 ܕܒܪܗ ܕܐܠܗܐ] S (*sic*): *cf* Joh viii 54

deeds that I do in the name of my Father, they bear witness of me. *S*
26 But ye believe not, because ye are not of my ewes, as I said to you.
27 The sheep *that are* mine hear my voice, and I know them and they
28 come after me and I give them life eternal, and they shall not be
lost for ever, and no one shall snatch them away from my hands;
29 * the Father that gave to me is greater than all, and there is no
30 one that doth snatch away from the hand of the Father: §I and my §¶*A* 10, 70, 120
31 Father—we are one."¶ When he said these things they took up
32 stones to stone him. Jesus saith to them: "Many deeds of the Father
I have shewn you; for which of those same deeds are ye stoning
33 me?" The Jews say to him: "Not for fair deed*s* do we stone thee,
but because being a human being thou dost blaspheme and makest
34 thyself a god." Jesus saith to them: "Is it not thus written in the
35 law 'I have said that ye are Gods'—and the word of God cannot ⌜be
36 loosed⌝? To the one which the Father hath hallowed and sent into
the world say ye 'Thou blasphemest,' on *the ground* that he said to
37 you that *he is* the Son of God? If I do not the deeds of my Father,
38 do not believe me; but if I do *them,* even if me ye do not believe,
believe the deeds themselves, and ye will know that I am in the
39 Father and the Father is in me." Again after [these things the
Jews were wishing to take hold of him] and he went forth from
40 between their hands, and went away to the other side of Jordan to
41 where John was baptizing of old. [And thither] came many unto
him, [and] they were saying "John [no] sign * * * * * *
42 said all these things." And many believed in him.
xi 1 And it came to pass that Lazar from Beth Ania was infirm, the

---

29 *init.*] *S illegible* 33 a god] *The same idiom is in* Ex vii 1 syr.vg, *and cf* 'to make him a god to Pharaoh' *A* 273

[2]ܡܪܢ ܕܝܢ ܗܘܐ ܐܝܬܘܗܝ ܕܐܫܟܚܬ ܪܓܠܐ [ܕܫܡܥ ܘܫܡܥܬ S
ܒܡܫܪܝܗ] ܐܝܟ ܗܘܐ ܕܗܕܐ ܗܘ ܠܒܪ ܕܒܪܝܗ ܗܘܐ [3]ܫܠܝܚ
[ܕܝܢ] ܠܗ ܬܬܝܗܒܢ ܐܝܬܘܗܝ ܠܫܡܥ ܡܢܝ ܗܘܐ ܒܪܝܗ ܗܘ
ܕܝܠܦ ܐܢܬ [4][ܒܪ] ܫܡܥ ܫܡܥ ܐܡܪ [ܗܢܐ] ܒܘܪܗܢܐ ܠܐ ܗܘܐ
ܠܡܘܬܐ ܐܠܐ ⌜ܫܠܡ̈⌝ ܬܫܡܫܬܗ ܕܐܠܗܐ ܕܫܬܡܫ ܒܗ ܒܪܗ
[5]ܗܘ ܕܝܢ ܫܡܥ ܡܫܚ ܗܘܐ ܠܗܠܝܢ ܬܠܬܝܗܝܢ ܐܝܟܐ ܠܡܪܝܡ
ܠܡܪܬܐ ܠܠܒܪ· [6]ܘܡܢ ܕܫܡܥ ܕܒܪܝܗ ܠܒܪ ܗܘ، ܒܠ ܕܒܬܗ
ܬܪܝܢ ܡܘܬܢ [7]ܘܐܡܪ ܠܬܠܡܝܕܘܗܝ، ܬܘ ܢܐܙܠ ܠܝܗܘܕ. [8]ܐܡܪܝܢ ܠܗ
ܬܠܡܝܕܘܗܝ، ܪܒܢ ܗܫܐ ܡܗܘܕܝܐ ܒܥܝܢ ܗܘܘ ܠܡܪܓܡܟ ܘܬܘܒ
ܐܙܠ ܐܢܬ ܠܬܡܢ [9]ܐܡܪ ܠܗܘܢ ܝܫܘܥ ܠܐ ܬܪܬܥܣܪܐ ܫܥܝܢ
ܐܝܬ ܒܝܘܡܐ ܡܢ ܕܡܗܠܟ ܒܐܝܡܡܐ ܠܐ ܡܬܬܩܠ ܡܛܠ ܕܚܙܐ
ܢܘܗܪܗ ܕܥܠܡܐ ܗܢܐ. [10]ܡܢ ܕܒܠܠܝܐ ܕܝܢ ܡܗܠܟ ܡܬܬܩܠ ܡܛܠ
ܕܢܘܗܪܐ ܠܝܬ ܒܗ [11]ܘܒܬܪ ܐܡܪ ܗܠܝܢ ܐܡܪ ܠܗܘܢ [§]ܠܥܙܪ ܪܚܡܢ §A169
ܫܟܒ ܐܠܐ ܐܙܠ ܐܢܐ ܕܐܥܝܪܝܘܗܝ، [¶] [12]ܐܡܪܝܢ ܠܗ ܡܪܢ ܐܢ ¶A
ܕܡܟ ܗܘ ܚܝܐ. [13]ܗܘ ܕܝܢ ܫܡܥ ܥܠ ܕܡܝܬ ܗܘ ܠܗ ܠܥܙܪ
ܐܡܪ ܗܘܐ ܠܗܘܢ ܘܗܘܢ ܣܒܪܝܢ ܗܘܘ ܕܥܠ ܫܢܬܐ ܗܘ
ܐܡܪ [14]ܬܘܒ ܐܡܪ ܠܗܘܢ ܫܡܥ ܦܫܝܩܐܝܬ ܠܥܙܪ ܡܝܬ ܠܗ
[15]ܘܚܕܐ ܡܛܠܬܟܘܢ ܕܬܗܝܡܢܘܢ ܕܠܐ ܗܘܝܬ ܬܡܢ ܐܠܐ
ܗܠܟܘ ܢܐܙܠ ܠܘܬܗ [16]ܐܡܪ ܠܗܘܢ ܬ⌜ܐܘ⌝ܡܐ ܠܚܒܪܘܗܝ،
ܬܠܡܝܕܐ ܬܘ ܐܦ ܐܚܢܢ ܢܐܙܠ ܢܡܘܬ ܥܡܗ [17]ܘܟܕ ܐܬܐ
ܝܫܘܥ ܠܒܝܬ ܥܢܝܐ ܐܫܟܚ ܕܩܒܝܪܗ، ܠܠܥܙܪ ܡܢ ܡܪܒܥܗ،
ܐܪܒܥܐ ܝܘܡܝܢ [18]ܘܗܘܬ ܕܝܢ ܒܝܬ ܥܢܝܐ ܩܪܝܒܐ ܡܢ ܐܘܪܫܠܡ
ܐܣܛܕܝܬܐ ܚܡܫܬܥܣܪ ܕܗܘܝܢ * * * * * [19]ܘܣܓܝܐܐ ⌜ܡܢ⌝
ܝܗܘܕܝܐ ܢܦܩܘ ܠܒܝܬ ܥܢܝܐ ܕܢܒܝܐܘܢ ܠܒܗܝܢ ܠܡܪܬܐ ܘܠܡܪܝܡ
[20]ܘܟܕ ܫܡܥܬ ܡܪܬܐ ܕܫܡܥ ܐܬܐ ܢܦܩܬ ܠܐܘܪܥܗ ܘܡܪܝܡ

4 ⌜ܒܪ⌝] *om.* S^{ed} ܐܡܪ] *pr.* ܘ S^{ed} ⌜ܗܢܐ⌝] ⌜ܠܗܘܢ⌝ S^{ed} 11 ܕܐܥܝܪܝܘܗܝ A^b: *but* A^a *has* ܕܐܥܝܪܘܗܝ (*sic*), *like* S 18 * * ܕܗܘܝܢ] *The words to be supplied look like* ⌜ܒ⌝ܪ⌜ܡܫ⌝ܝܢ ܬܪܝܢ

2 brother of Mary and of Martha. Now Mary is she that washed the *S*
feet [of Jesus and wiped *them* with her hair ;] the brother of her was
3 the Lazar that was infirm. [Now] his two sisters sent *word* to
4 Jesus : "Our Lord, lo, he that thou lovest is infirm !" [When] Jesus
heard he saith[: "This] infirmity is not unto death, but for the
5 glory of God, that his Son may be glorified in him." Now Jesus was
loving to these three, the brother *and sisters,* Mary, Martha, Lazar;
6 and from *the time* he heard that Lazar was infirm he remained in his
7 place two days. And he saith to his disciples : "Come, let us go
8 to Judaea." His disciples say to him : "Rabban, lo, the Jews were
9 seeking to stone thee, and again goest thou thither?" Jesus saith
to them : "Are there not twelve hours in the day? He that walketh
10 by day stumbleth not, because he seeth the light of this world; but
he that walketh by night stumbleth, because the light is not in him."
11 And when he said these things he saith to them : "§Lazar our friend §*A* 169
12 is lying down, but I go that I may awaken him."¶ They say to him : ¶*A*
13 "Our Lord, if he sleepeth he will live." Now Jesus on *the ground* that
Lazar was dead had said *it* to them, and they were supposing that of
14 sleep he said *it.* Again Jesus said to them plainly : "Lazar is dead ;
15 and I rejoice for your sakes, that ye may believe, that I was not there.
16 But walk ye *and* let us go unto him." Thomas saith to them, to his
17 fellow disciples : "Come, let us also go *and* die with him." And
when Jesus came to Beth Ania he found that they *had* buried Lazar
18 four days before. Now Beth Ania was distant from Jerusalem
19 fifteen stadia, which are * * * And many of the Jews went forth
20 to Beth Ania that they might comfort Martha and Mary. And when
Martha heard that Jesus was come she went forth to meet him, and

---

4 ⌜When⌝] *om.* S^{ed} saith⌜: This⌝ infirmity] *so* E^{200}; *in* S^{ed} 'to them' *is supplied instead of* 'This' 5 brother *and sisters*] *lit.* 'brothers' 14 Lazar] + 'our friend' E^{201} 18 which are * *] *The words to be supplied look like* 'two parasangs'

ܦܓܥܬ ܒ⸢ܒ⸣ܝܢܬܐ [21]ܘܐܡܪܬ ܠܗ ܡܪܬܐ ܠܝܫܘܥ ܐܠܘ ܠܟܐ ܗܘܝܬ S
ܠܐ ܡܐܬ ܗܘܐ ܐܚܝ [22]ܐܠܐ ܐܦ ܗܫܐ ܝܕܥܐ ܐܢܐ ܕܡܕܡ
ܕܬܫܐܠ ܠܐܠܗܐ ܝܗܒ ܠܟ [23]ܐܡܪ ܠܗ ܝܫܘܥ ܢܩܘܡ ܐܚܘܟܝ
[24]ܐܡܪܬ ܠܗ ܡܪܬܐ ܝܕܥܐ ܐܢܐ ܕܒܩܝܡܬܐ ܒܝܘܡܐ ܐܚܪܝܐ
[25]ܐܡܪ ܠܗ ܝܫܘܥ ܐܢܐ ܐܢܐ ܩܝܡܬܐ ܘܚܝܐ ܕܡܗܝܡܢ ܒܝ ܐܦ
ܡܐܬ ܢܚܐ [26]ܘܟܠ ܕܚܝ ܘܡܗܝܡܢ ܒܝ ܠܥܠܡ ܠܐ ܡܐܬ
§A 21 ܡܗܝܡܢܬܝ ܗܠܝܢ [§27]ܐܡܪܐ ܠܗ ܡܪܬܐ ܐܝܢ ܡܪܝ ܡܗܝܡܢܐ
¶A ܐܢܐ[¶] ܕܐܢܬ ܗܘ ܡܫܝܚܐ ܒܪܗ ܕܐܠܗܐ ܕܐܬܐ ܠܥܠܡܐ
ܠܥܠܡܐ [28]ܘܟܕ ܐܡܪܬ ܗܠܝܢ ܐܙܠܬ ܡܫܬܐܘܬ ܩܪܬ ܠܡܪܝܡ.
ܘܐܡܪܐ ܠܗ· ܪܒܢ ܐܬܐ ܘܩܪܐ ܠܟܝ. [29]ܘܟܕ ܫܡܥܬ ܡܪܝܡ
ܩܡܬ ܘܐܙܕܠܓܬ ܐܙܠܬ ܠܘܬܗ [30]ܘܗܘ ܝܫܘܥ ܠܐ ܒܕܡܐ
ܠܡܫܐ ܥܠ ܗܘܐ ܠܩܪܝܬܐ ܐܠܐ ܒܗ ܗܘܐ ܒܕܘܟܬܐ ܕܐܪܥܬܗ
ܗܘܬ ܡܪܬܐ [31]ܐܦ ܗܢܘܢ ܕܥܠܝܢ ܗܘܘ ܠܘܬܗ ܕܡܪܝܡ ܟܕ
ܚܙܘ ܕܡܗܬ ܩܡܬ ܢܦܩܬ ܐܙܠܘ ܠܗܘܢ ܒܬܪܗ ܣܒܪܝܢ ܗܘܘ
ܕܠܩܒܪܐ ܐܙܠܐ ܠܡܒܟܐ. [32]ܗܝ ܕܝܢ ܡܪܝܡ ܟܕ ܡܛܬ ܠܘܬܗ ܕܝܫܘܥ
ܢܦܠܬ ܥܠ ܪ̈ܓܠܘܗܝ. ܘܐܡܪܐ ܠܗ ܐܠܘ ܬܢܢ ܗܘܝܬ ܡܪܝ ܠܐ
ܡܐܬ ܗܘܐ ܐܚܝ. [33]ܘܗܘ ܝܫܘܥ ܟܕ ܚܙܗ ܕܒܟܝܐ ܘܚܙܐ
ܠܝܗܘ̈ܕܝܐ ܗܢܘܢ ܕܥܡܗ ܕܒܟܝܢ. ܐܬܥܙ ܒܢܦܫܗ ܘܐܬܕܠܚ ܒܪܘܚܗ
[34]ܘܐܡܪ ܐܝܟܐ ܣܡܬܘܢܝܗܝ. ܐܡܪܝܢ ܠܗ ܡܪܢ ܬܐ ܚܙܝ
[35]ܘܐܬܝܢ ܗܘܝ ܕܡ̈ܥܘܗܝ ܕܝܫܘܥ [36]ܘܟܕ ܚܙܘ ܝܗܘ̈ܕܝܐ ܐܡܪ̈ܝܢ
ܗܘܘ. ܚܙܘ ܟܡܐ ܪܚܡ ܗܘܐ ܠܗ. [37]ܘܐܢܫ ܡܢܗܘܢ ܕܐܡܪ̈ܝܢ
ܗܘܘ ܕܗܢܐ ܕܦܬܚ ܥܝ̈ܢܘܗܝ ܕܗܘ ܕܣܡܝܐ ܗܘܐ ܡܢ ܟܪܣܐ
ܕܐܡܗ. ܠܐ ܟܘܕ ܡܫܟܚ ܗܘܐ ܕܗܢܐ ܕܠܐ ܢܡܘܬ.
[38]ܝܫܘܥ ܕܝܢ ܟܕ ܡܬܥܙܙ ܗܘܐ ܒܢܦܫܗ ܘܠܗ. ܐܬܐ ܠܒܝܬ
ܩܒܪܐ ܘܗܘ ܒܝܬ ܩܒܘܪܐ ܢܩܝܪܐ ܗܘܐ. ܐܝܟ ܡܥܪܬܐ ܘܟܐܦܐ
ܬܪܥܗ ܒܟܐܦܐ. [39]ܐܡܪ ܝܫܘܥ ܫܩܘܠܘ ܟܐܦܐ ܗܕܐ ܐܡܪܐ

A 21 ܐܡܪ ܠܗ̇ ܡܪܢ ܠܡܪܬܐ. ܐܚܘܟܝ ܕܡܗܝܡܢܬܝ ܢܩܘܡ ܐܚܘܟܝ 23 (*followed by ver.* 27)   25 ܩܝܡܬܐ] S^{vid}: *the photograph might be read* ܚܝܝܬܐ, *i.e.* ܘܚܝܘܬܐ   26 ܗܠܝܢ S   37 ܟܘܕ] *cf* Lk xvi 11

21 Mary stayed in the house. And Martha said to Jesus: "If here thou S
22 hadst been, my brother would not have died; but even now I know
23 that what thou askest God he will give thee." Jesus saith to her:
24 "Thy brother shall arise." Martha said to him: "I know that in the
25 resurrection in the last day—." Jesus saith to her: "I am the
resurrection, and he that believeth in me, even if he dieth, will live;
26 and he that liveth and believeth in me for ever dieth not. Believest
27 thou these things?" §Martha saith to him: "Yea, my Lord, I believe¶ §¶*A* 21
that thou art the Messiah, the Son of God, that is about to come to
28 the world." And when she said these things she went silently *and*
called Mary, and saith to her: "Our Rabbi has come and calleth
29 thee." And when Mary heard she leaped up and eagerly went unto
30 him. And he, Jesus, until then had not entered the village, but was
31 in the same place that Martha had met him. Those also that were
comforting Mary, when they saw that thus in amazement she went
forth, went away after her: they were supposing that to the grave
32 she was going to weep. And she, Mary, when she arrived by Jesus,
fell at his feet and saith to him: "If here thou hadst been, my
33 Lord, my brother would not have died." And he, Jesus, when he saw
her weeping and saw those Jews with her weeping, was stirred in
34 himself and was excited in his spirit and said: "Where have ye laid
35 him?" They say to him: "Our Lord, come *and* see." And the
36 tears of Jesus were coming; and when the Jews saw, they were
37 saying: "See how much he was loving him!" And there were some
of them that were saying "This is he that opened the eyes of him
that was blind from the womb of his mother; would he not forsooth
38 have been able to make this *one* that he should not die?" Now
Jesus, though he was excited within himself, came to the tomb; and
that tomb was a hollow like a cave, and its door hidden by a
39 stone. Jesus saith: "Take ye away this stone." Martha saith to

---

23 'Our Lord saith to Martha: If so be thou believest, thy brother shall arise' *A* 21 (*followed by ver.* 27) 25 the resurrection] + and the life E^{202}: *see Notes*, vol. ii 31 in amazement...forth] *lit.* 'she was amazed *and* went forth': *cf* Mk ix 15 38 excited] *see* Mk viii 12, Lk xxii 59

ܠܗ ܡܪܬܐ ܡܪܝ، ܡܟܢܐ ܫܠܝܛ ܠܗ ܠܐܠܗܐ ܕܗܘܐ ܦܪ، ܠܗ. ܡܛܠ S
ܕܐܪ̈ܒܥܐ ܠܗ ܝܘ̈ܡܝܢ. [40]ܐܡܪ ܠܗ ܐܡܪܬ ܠܟܝ ܕܐܢ ܬܗܝܡܢܝܢ
ܬܚܙܝܢ ܫܘܒܚܗ ܕܐܠܗܐ. [41]ܗܝܕܝܢ ܐܢܫܐ ܗܢܘܢ ܕܢܩܝܦܝܢ ܩܪܒܘ
ܒܠܘܗ ܠܐܠܗܐ ܗܘ ܕܝܢ ܫܩܠ ܥܝܢ̈ܘܗܝ، ܠܫܡܝܐ ܘܐܡܪ ܐܒܐ
ܡܘܕܐܢܐ ܠܟ ܕܫܡܥܬܢܝ. [42]ܘܐܢܐ ܝܕܥܢܐ ܕܒܟܠܙܒܢ ܫܡܥ ܐܢܬ ܠܝ
ܐܠܐ ܡܛܠ ܟܢܫܐ ܗܢܐ ܕܐܢܫܐ ܐܡܪܢܐ ܗܠܝܢ ܕܢܗܝܡܢܘܢ
ܕܐܢܬ ܫܕܪܬܢܝ. [43]ܘܟܕ ܗܠܝܢ ܐܡܪ §ܩܥܐ ܒܩܠܐ ܪܡܐ ܘܐܡܪ §A165
ܠܥܙܪ ܦܘܩ ܬܐ ܠܒܪ.¶ [44]ܘܒܗ ܒܫܥܬܐ ܢܦܩ ܗܘ ܡܝܬܐ ܟܕ ¶A
ܡܚܝܕܢ ܐܝܕܘܗܝ ܘܪ̈ܓܠܘܗܝ ܒܦܣ̈ܩܝܬܐ. ܘܡܚܝܕܢ ܐܦ̈ܘܗܝ،
ܒܣܘܕܪܐ. ܗܝܕܝܢ ܐܡܪ ܡܪܢ ܫܪܘܗܝ، ܘܫܒܘܩܘ ܐܙܠ.
[45]ܘܣ̈ܓܝܐܐ ܝܗܘ̈ܕܝܐ ܕܐܬܘ ܠܘܬ ܫܡܥܘ ܡܛܠ ܡܪܝܡ. ܡܢ ܗ،
ܥܒܕܬܐ ܗܝܡܢܘ ܒܝܫܘܥ. [46]ܘܐܢܫ ܗܘܘ ܡܢܗܘܢ ܕܠܐ ܗܝܡܢܘܢ
ܐܠܐ ܐܙܠܘ ܠܗܘܢ ܠܘܬ ܦܪ̈ܝܫܐ ܘܐܫܬܥܝܘ ܠܗܘܢ ܡܕܡ
ܕܥܒܕ ܝܫܘܥ ○ ○ ○ ○

[47]ܗܝܕܝܢ ܪ̈ܒܝ ܟܗ̈ܢܐ ܘܦܪ̈ܝܫܐ ܐܬܟܢܫܘ ܘܥܒܕܘ ܐܦܪܗܣܝܐ ܘܐܡܪ̈ܝܢ
ܗܘܘ ܡܢܐ ܢܥܒܕ ܕܗܢܐ ܓܒܪܐ ܐܬܘܬܐ ܣ̈ܓܝܐܬܐ ܥܒܕ. [48]ܘܐܢ
ܫܒܩܝܢ ܐܢܚܢ ܠܗ ܗܟܢܐ ܟܠܗܘܢ ܐܢܫ̈ܐ ܡܗܝ̈ܡܢܝܢ ܒܗ
ܘܐܬܝܢ ܪ̈ܗܘܡܝܐ ܫܩܠܝܢ ܡܕܝܢܬܢ ܘܥܡܢ [49]ܚܕ ܡܢܗܘܢ ܕܝܢ
ܩܝܦܐ ܫܡܗ ܗܘܐ ܪܒ ܟܗܢܐ ܕܠܗܘܢ ܕܗܝ، ܫܢܬܐ ܐܡܪ
ܠܗܘܢ ܗܘ ܩܝܦܐ ܐܢܬܘܢ ܠܐ ܝܕܥܝܢ ܐܢܬܘܢ ܡܕܡ [50]ܘܠܐ
ܡܬܪ̈ܥܝܢ ܐܢܬܘܢ ܕܦܩܚ ܠܢ ܕܚܕ ܓܒܪܐ ܢܡܘܬ ܥܠ ܐܦ̈ ܥܡܐ
ܟܠܗ. ܘܠܐ ܟܠܗ ܥܡܐ ܢܐܒܕ. [51]ܗܕܐ ܕܝܢ ܡܠܬܐ ܠܐ ܡܢ
ܨܒܘܬ ܢܦܫܗ ܐܡܪܗ ܐܠܐ ܡܛܠ ܕܪܒ ܟܗܢܐ ܗܘܐ ܐܬܢܒܝ
ܡܛܠ ܕܥܬܝܕ ܝܫܘܥ ܗܘܐ ܠܡܡܬ ܥܠ ܐܦ̈ ܥܡܐ [52]ܘܠܐ ܥܠ
ܐܦ̈ ܥܡܐ ܒܠܚܘܕ. ܐܠܐ ܕܐܦ ܒܢ̈ܝܐ ܕܐܠܗܐ ܕܡܒܕܪ̈ܝܢ
ܢܬܟܢܫܘܢ ܠܚܕܐ [53]ܡܢ ܗܘ ܕܝܢ ܝܘܡܐ ܐܬܪܥܝܘ ܗܘܘ
ܠܡܩܛܠܗ ○

---

43 ܩܥܐ] ܩܪܐ A   ܘܐܡܪ om. A^a ܦܘܩ] om. A   46 ܗܝܡܢܘܢ] S (sic)
50 ܡܬܪ̈ܥܝܢ] S (sic)

him: "My Lord, why are they taking away the stone? For lo, he hath *S*
40 stunk, because *there have been* four days for him!" He saith to her:
"I said to thee, that if thou wilt believe thou shalt see the glory
41 of God." Then those folk standing *by* drew near *and* lifted the
stone. But he raised his eyes to heaven, and said: "Father, I thank
42 thee that thou hast heard me; and I myself know that at all times
thou dost hear me, but because of this multitude of people I say these
43 things, that they may believe that thou hast sent me." And when
these things he said, §he cried out with a loud voice and said: "Lazar, §*A* 165
44 come forth, come out!"¶ And in the same hour came forth that ¶*A*
dead man, his hands and his feet wrapped with bandages and his
face wrapped with a napkin. Then said our Lord: "Loose him and
45 suffer *him* to go." And many Jews that came unto Jesus because
46 of Mary from that hour believed in Jesus. And there were some
of them that did not believe, but went away unto the Pharisees and
declared to them what Jesus *had* done.

47 Then the chief priests and the Pharisees gathered together and
made a plot, and they were saying: "What shall we do? For this
48 man doeth many signs; and if we suffer him thus, all folk will be
believing in him, and the Romans will be coming *and* taking away
49 our city and our people." But one of them, Caiapha was his name,
the chief priest of them of that year,—that Caiapha saith to them:
50 "Ye know not anything, nor do ye consider that it is profitable for
us that one man should die on behalf of the whole people and not
51 the whole people be lost." Now this word—not from his own mind
said he it, but because he was chief priest he prophesied, because
52 Jesus was about to die on behalf of the people; and not on behalf
of the people only, but that the sons of God also that are scattered
53 should be gathered into one. Now from that day they had meditated
to kill him.

---

43 cried out] called *A* and said] *om.* A^{a} come forth] *om.* *A*
48 our city and our people] 'our nation, the law, and this place' E^{204}

[54]ܝܫܘܥ ܕܝܢ ܠܐ ܡܗܠܟ ܗܘܐ ܒܦܪܗܣܝܐ ܠܒܝܢ ܝܗܘܕܝܐ ܐܠܐ S
ܐܙܠ ܠܗ ܠܐܬܪܐ ܕܩܪܝܒ ܠ[ܡܕܒܪܐ] ܕܡܬܩܪܐ ܐܦܪܝܡ ܘܬܡܢ
ܡܬܗܦܟ ܗܘܐ ܥܡ ܬܠܡܝܕܘܗܝ.
[55]ܘܗܘܐ ܗܘܐ ܙܒܢܐ ܕܦܨܚܗܘܢ ܕܝܗܘܕܝܐ ܘܣܠܩܘ ܣܓܝܐܐ ܡܢ ܟܘܪ
ܠܐܘܪܫܠܡ ܕܢܕܟܘܢ ܢܦܫܗܘܢ [56]ܘܒܥܝܢ ܗܘܘ ܠܗ ܠܝܫܘܥ
ܘܐܡܪܝܢ ܚܕ ܠܚܕ ܒܗܝܟܠܐ ܣܒܪ̈ܝܢ ܐܢܬܘܢ ܕܟܒܪ ܠܐ ܐܬܐ
ܠܥܐܕܐ [57]ܘܪ̈ܒܝ ܟܗܢܐ ܘܦܪ̈ܝܫܐ ܦܩܕܘ ܕܡܢ ܕܝܕܥ ܠܗ ܢܐܬܐ
ܢܕܥܘ ܠܗܘܢ ܕܢܐܚܕܘܢܝܗ [1]ܘܡܢ ܩܕܡ ܫ̈ܬܐ ܝܘ̈ܡܝܢ ܕܦܨܚܗܘܢ
ܦܢܝܐ ܐܬܐ ܠܗ ܝܫܘܥ ܠܒܝܬ ܥܢܝܐ ܩܪܝܬܐ ܠܘܬ ܠܥܙܪ ܗܘ
ܕܡܝܬ ܗܘܐ ܘܚܝܐ. [2]ܘܥܒܕ ܠܗ ܐܚܫܡܝܬܐ ܬܡܢ ܘܠܥܙܪ ܚܕ ܡܢ
ܡܣܬܡ̈ܟܐ ܗܘܐ ܕܡܣܬܡܟܝܢ ܠܘܬܗ ܡܪܬܐ ܕܝܢ ܒܒܝܬܐ ܗܘܬ
ܡܫܡܫܢܝܬܐ. [3]ܡܪܝܡ ܕܝܢ ܢܣܒܬ ܫܛܝܦܬܐ ܕܠܛܪܐ ܡܫܚܐ ܢܪܕܝܢ
ܦܝܣܛܝܩܘܢ ܠܛܪܐ ܕܣܓ̈ܝܐܝܢ ܕܕܡܘܗܝ, ܘܐܫܦܟܬܗ ܥܠ ܪܫܗ
ܕܝܫܘܥ ܟܕ ܣܡܝܟ ܘܡܫܚܬ ܪ̈ܓܠܘܗܝ, ܘܫܘܝܬ ܒܣܥܪܗ ܘܡܠܐ
ܒܝܬܐ ܟܠܗ ܡܢ ܪܝܚܗ ܕܡܫܚܐ [4]ܘܐܡܪ ܝܗܘܕܐ ܣܟܪܝܘܛܐ ܚܕ
ܡܢ ܬܠܡ̈ܝܕܐ. ܗܘ ܕܗܘ ܡܫܠܡ ܗܘܐ ܠܗ. [5]ܠܡܢܐ ܠܐ ܐܙܕܒܢ
ܡܫܚܐ ܗܢܐ ܒܬܠܬ ܡܐܐ ܕܝܢ̈ܪܝܢ ܘܐܬܝܗܒ ܠܡܣܟܢܐ [6]ܠܝܗܘܕܐ
ܕܝܢ ܠܐ ܗܘܐ ܥܠ ܡܣܟܢܐ ܒܛܝܠ ܗܘܐ ܠܗ ܐܠܐ ܡܛܠ
ܕܓܢܒ ܗܘܐ. ܘܓܠܘܣܩܡܐ ܕܡܣܟܢܐ ܨܝܕܘܗܝ, ܗܘܐ [7]ܟܕ ܫܡܥ
ܝܫܘܥ ܐܡܪ ܠܗ ܫܒܘܩ ܠܗ ܢܛܪܐ ܠܗ ܠܝܘܡܐ ܕܩܒܘܪܝ, [9]ܘܫܡܥܘ
ܐܢܫܐ ܣܓܝܐܐ ܡܢ ܝܗ̈ܘܕܝܐ ܕܬܡܢ ܗܘ· ܘܐܬܘ ܠܘܬܗ ܠܐ ܡܛܠ
ܕܢܚܙܘܢ ܠܝܫܘܥ ܐܠܐ ܠܠܥܙܪ ܗܘ ܕܐܩܝܡ ܡܢ ܒܝܬ ܡܝ̈ܬܐ.
[10]ܘܐܬܪܥܝܘ ܗܘܘ ܪ̈ܒܝ ܟܗܢܐ ܕܐܦ. ܠܥܙܪ ܢܩܛܠܘܢܝܗ, [11]ܡܛܠܬܗ
ܟܝܪ ܕܠܥܙܪ ܦܠܓܐ ܗܡܢܘ ܒܝܫܘܥ [12]ܘܠܝܘܡܐ ܐܚܪܢܐ ܢܦܩ
ܘܐܬܐ ܠܒܪ ܐܬܐ ܘܟܢܫܐ ܗܢܘ ܦܠܓܐܐ ܕܐܬܘ ܗܘܘ
ܠܥܐܕܐ. ܟܕ ܫܡܥܘ ܕܝܫܘܥ ܐܬܐ ܠܐܘܪܫܠܡ [13]ܫܩܠܘ ܣܘ̈ܟܐ
ܕܕܩܠܐ ܘܢܦܩܘ ܠܐܘܪܥܗ. ܘܩܥܝܢ ܗܘܘ ܘܐܡܪܝܢ ܐܘܫܥܢܐ ܕܐܬܐ

---

54 ܠ[ܡܕܒܪܐ]] S illegible   2 ܘܥܒܕ] S (sic)

54 Now Jesus was not walking freely in the sight of the Jews, but S
he went away to a place near to [the wilderness], called Ephraim,
and there was abiding with his disciples.

55 And it had become the time that the Feasts were near, and many
went up from the country to Jerusalem that they might hallow them-
56 selves. And they were seeking Jesus and saying one to the other in
the Temple: "Do ye suppose that perchance he cometh not to the
57 Feast?" And the chief priests and the Pharisees commanded that
he that should see him should come *and* reveal *it* to them, that they
xii 1 might take him. And six days before it would be the Unleavened
Bread came Jesus to the village Beth Ania unto Lazar, him that was
2 dead and lived. And he made for him a supper there and Lazar
was one of the guests that sat down *to meat* with him, but Martha
3 was occupied in serving. Now Mary took a vase of a pound of oil,
nard of good pistic, the price of which was much, and poured it on
the head of Jesus as he sat *at meat*, and anointed his feet and wiped
them with her hair; and the whole house was full of the smell of the
4 oil. And Judas Scariot, one of the disciples, he that was himself
5 betraying him, said: "Wherefore was not this oil sold for three
6 hundred denars and given to the poor?" Now Judas—not for the
poor had he a care, but because he used to thieve and the box for the
7 poor was by him. When Jesus heard, he saith to him: "Suffer her
9 to keep it for the day of my burying." And many folk of the Jews
knew that he was there, and they came thither, not because they
should see Jesus but Lazar, him that he raised from among the dead.
10 And the chief priests had meditated that Lazar also they should kill,
11, 12 for because of Lazar many believed in Jesus. And the next day he
went forth and came to the Mount of Olives; and those many
multitudes that had come to the Feast, when they heard that Jesus
13 cometh to Jerusalem, took up branches of palms and went forth
to meet him. And they were crying out and saying: "Osanna! He

ܒܫܡܗ ܕܡܪܝܐ ܡܠܟܐ ܕܐܝܣܪܐܝܠ [14]ܫܡܥ ܕܝܢ ܙܒܢ ܗܘܐ ܒܠ S
⌐ܣܦܪܐ¬ ܐܝܟ ܕܟܬܝܒ ܒܡܙܡܘܪܐ ܕܢܒܝܐ [15]ܠܐ ܬܬܕܚܠܝܢ ܒܪܬ ܨܗܝܘܢ
ܗܐ ܡܠܟܟܝ ܐܬܐ ܠܟܝ. ܘܪܟܝܒ ܥܠ ܥܝܠܐ ܒܪ ܐܬܢܐ. [16]ܗܠܝܢ
ܡܢ ܩܕܡ ܠܐ ܝܕܥܘ ܬܠܡܝܕܘܗܝ, ܐܠܐ ܟܕ ܩܡ ܡܪܢ ܫܘܒܚܗ
ܐܬܕܟܪܘ ܕܗܠܝܢ ܟܬܝ̈ܒܢ ܗܘ̈ܝ, ܥܠܘܗܝ, ܘܗܠܝܢ ܥܒܕܘ ܠܗ [17]ܘܟܢܫܐ
ܗܘ ܐܝܢܐ ܕܥܡܗ ܗܘܐ ܡܣܗܕܝܢ ܗܘܘ ܐܝܟܢܐ ܕܩܪܐ ܠܠܥܙܪ
ܡܢ ܩܒܪܐ ܘܐܚܝܗ ܡܢ ܒܝܬ ܡܝ̈ܬܐ [18]ܘܟܘܠ ܐܢܫܐ ܗܢܘܢ ܪܗܛܘ
ܠܐܘܪܥܗ ܡܛܠ ܕܫܡܥܘ ܕܐܬܐ ܗܕܐ ܥܒܕ. [19]ܦܪ̈ܝܫܐ ܕܝܢ ܐܡܪ̈ܝܢ
ܗܘܘ ܚܕ ܠܘܬ ܚܕ ܚܙܝܢ ܐܢܬܘܢ ܕܠܐ ܡܘܬܪܝܢ ܐܢܬܘܢ ܡܕܡ ܕܗܐ
ܥܠܡܐ ܟܠܗ ܐܙܠ ܠܗ ܒܬܪܗ ○

[20]ܘܐܝܬ ܗܘܐ ܡܢ ܐܪ̈ܡܝܐ ܕܣܠܩܘ ܗܘܘ ܠܡܣܓܕ ܒܥܐܕܥܐܕܐ
[21]ܘܐܬܘ ܘܐܡܪܘ ܠܦܝܠܝܦܘܣ ܗܘ ܕܡܢ ܒܝܬ ܨܝܕܐ ܕܓܠܝܠܐ
†ܡܪܝ† ܠܝܫܘܥ ܨܒܝܢ ⌐ܐܢܚܢ¬ ܠܡܚܙܐ. [22]ܘܦܝܠܝܦܘܣ ܐܙܠ ܐܡܪ
ܠܐܢܕܪܐܘܣ. ܘܐܬܘ ܬܪܝܗܘܢ ܘܐܡܪܘ ܠܝܫܘܥ. [23]ܐܡܪ ܠܗܘܢ
ܝܫܘܥ ܐܬܬ ܫܥܬܐ ܕܢܫܬܒܚ ܒܪܗ ܕܐܢܫܐ. [24]ܐܡܝܢ ܐܡܝܢ
ܐܡܪܢܐ ܠܟܘܢ ܕܦܪܕܬܐ ܕܚܛܬܐ ܐܠܐ ܢܦܠܐ ܘܡܝܬܐ ܒܐܪܥܐ
ܒܠܚܘܕܝܗ ܗܝ, ܐܢ ܕܝܢ ܢܦܠܐ ܘܡܝܬܐ ܦܐܪ̈ܐ ⌐ܣܓܝܐܐ¬ ܡܝܬܝܐ.
[25]ܡܢ ܕܪܚܡ ܢܦܫܗ ܢܘܒܕܝܗ ܘܡܢ ܕܤܢܐ ܢܦܫܗ ܒܗܢܐ ܥܠܡܐ
ܢܛܪܝܗ ܠܚܝ̈ܐ ܕܠܥܠܡ. [26]ܡܢ ܕܠܝ ܡܫܡܫ ܒܬܪܝ, ܢܐܬܐ ܘܐܬܪ
ܕܐܢܐ ܬܡܢ ܢܗܘܐ ܐܦ ܡܫܡܫܢܝ ܘܡܢ ܕܠܝ ܡܫܡܫ ܢܝܩܪܝܘܗܝ,
ܐܒܐ. [27]ܗܫܐ ܗܐ ܢܦܫܝ ܫܓܝܫܐ ܘܡܢܐ ܐܡܪ. ܐܒܐ ܐܦܨܢܝ ܡܢ
ܗܕܐ ܫܥܬܐ ܐܠܐ ܡܛܠ ܗܢܐ ܐܬܝܬ ܠܗܕܐ ܫܥܬܐ. [28]ܐܒܐ
ܫܒܚ ܫܡܟ ܘܒܗ ܒܫܥܬܐ ܐܫܬܡܥ ܩܠܐ ܡܢ ܫܡܝܐ ܕܐܡܪ
§ܫܒܚܬ ܘܬܘܒ ܡܫܒܚ ܐܢܐ¶ [29]ܘܟܢܫܐ ܕܩܝܡܝܢ ܗܘܘ ܬܡܢ §¶A410

---

14 ⌐ܣܦܪܐ¬] S^ed ; ? ⌐ܐܬܬܐ¬, or ⌐ܒܠܐ¬ 17 ܡܣܗܕܝܢ] S (sic) 21 ܡܪܝ] ܡܪܝܐ S: cf Matt xxii 45 26 Cf ܐܬܪ ܕܐܢܐ ܐܢܐ ܘܐܦ ܐܢܬܘܢ ܬܗܘܘܢ A 197
28 ܫܒܚܬ] pr. ܘܫܡܥ ܐܡܪ ܕ A (cf Joh xvii 4) ܘܬܘܒ] om. ܬܘܒ A

14 that cometh in the name of the Lord, the King of Israel!" Now *S*
Jesus was riding on [an ass], as it is written in Zacharia the prophet:
15 "Fear not, daughter of Zion; lo, thy king is coming to thee and
16 riding on a colt the foal of a she-ass!" These things beforehand
his disciples knew not, but when our Lord received his glory they
remembered that these things had been written of him, and these
17 things did they to him. And that multitude which was with him
were declaring how he called Lazar from the grave and saved him
18 alive from the dead; and all those folk ran to meet him, because
19 they heard that he did this sign; but the Pharisees were saying one
to the other: "Ye see that ye are gaining nothing? For lo, the
whole world goeth after him!"

20 And there were some Gentiles that had come up to worship at
21 the Feast, and they came and said to Philip, him that *was* from Beth
22 Saida of Galilee: "†My Lord, Jesus we wish to see." And Philip
went *and* told Andrew, and the two of them came and told Jesus.
23 Jesus saith to them: "The hour hath come that the Son of Man
24 should be glorified. Amen, amen, I say to you that a grain of wheat,
unless it fall and die in the earth, is alone; but if it fall and die, it
25 bringeth much fruit. He that loveth his life shall lose it, and he
26 that hateth his life in this world shall keep it for life eternal. He
that me will serve, after me let him come, and where I am there
shall be my servant also, and he that serveth me the Father will
27 honour. Now my soul, lo, it is agitated, and what shall I say?
'Father, save me alive from this hour'? But because of this I
28 have come to this hour. Father, glorify thy name!" And in the
same hour was heard a voice from heaven, that said: §"I have §*A*410
29 glorified, and again I am glorifying *it*."¶ And the multitudes that ¶*A*

14 an ⌜ass⌝] *or*, 'a ⌜she-ass⌝'; *or*, 'a ⌜colt⌝': *S illegible* 21 My Lord] 'the Lord' *S* (*sic*): *cf* Matt xxii 45 26 *Cf* 'Where I am ye also shall be' *A* 197 28 I have glorified] *To the quotation of these words is prefixed* 'And Jesus said' *in A*: *cf* Joh xvii 4 again] *om. A*

S ܘܫܒܒܘ ܬܚܘܡܗ ܘܐܡܪܝܢ ܕܪܒܐ ܗܘܐ ܘܐܚܪܢܐ ܐܡܪܝܢ
ܡܠܐܟܐ ܡܛܠ ܕܒܗ ³⁰ܐܡܪ ܠܗܘܢ ܝܫܘܥ ܠܐ ܗܘܐ ܡܛܠܬܗ،
ܐܫܬܡܥ ܗܢܐ ܘܠܐ ܐܠܐ ܡܛܠܬܗܘܢ ³¹ܗܫܐ ܕܝܢܗ ܗܘ
ܕܥܠܡܐ ܗܢܐ ܡܕܒܪܢܗ ܕܥܠܡܐ ܗܢܐ ܡܫܬܕܪܐ ܠܬܚܘܬ ³²ܘܐܢܐ
ܡܢܐ ܕܐܬܪܥܡܬ ܡܢ ܐܪܒܥܐ ܐܟܙ ܒܥܠ ܐܢܫ ܠܘܬܝ، ³³ܗܕܐ ܕܝܢ
ܐܡܪ ܕܢܘܚܐ ܒܐܝܢܐ ܡܘܬܐ ܡܐܬ ³⁴ܘܐܡܪܝܢ [ܗܘܘ] ܠܗ ܐܢܫܐ
ܡܢ ܒܢܝܐ ܐܢܫܝܢ ܫܡܥܢ ܡܢ ܐܘܪܝܬܐ ܕܡܫܝܚܐ ܠܒܠܡ ܡܫܘܐ
ܘܐܡܒܢܐ ܐܡܪ ܐܝܟ ܕܒܬܪ ܗܘ ܕܢܬܘܩ ܒܪܗ ܕܐܢܫܐ ܡܢܘ
ܠܡ ܗܢܐ ܒܪܗ ܕܐܢܫܐ ³⁵ܐܡܪ ܠܗܘܢ ܝܫܘܥ ܩܠܝܠ ܐܢܬܘܢ
§¶A 14, 330 ܢܘܗܪܐ ܥܡܟܘܢ ܐܝܬ §ܗܠܟܘ ܒܢܘܗܪܐ ܥܕ ܐܝܬ ܠܟܘܢ
ܢܘܗܪܐ ܕܠܐ ܢܕܪܟܟܘܢ ܚܫܘܟܐ¶ ܡܢ ܕܡܗܠܟ ܓܝܪ ܒܚܫܘܟܐ
§¶A 14, 330 ܠܐ ܝܕܥ ܠܐܝܟܐ ܐܙܠ ³⁶ܥܕ ܐܝܬ ܠܟܘܢ ܢܘܗܪܐ §ܗܝܡܢܘ
ܒܢܘܗܪܐ ܕܒܢܘܗܝ، ܕܢܘܗܪܐ ܬܗܘܘܢ¶

ܘܟܕ ܗܠܝܢ ܡܠܠ ܝܫܘܥ ܐܙܠ ܐܬܛܫܝ ܡܢܗܘܢ ³⁷ܘܟܠܗܝܢ ܐܬܘܬܐ
[ܥܕ] ⌜ܪ̈ܘܪܒܬܐ⌝ ܥܕ ܠܐ ܗܝܡܢܘ ܒܗ ³⁸ܕܬܬܡܠܐ ܡܠܬܐ ܕܐܫܥܝܐ
ܢܒܝܐ ܕܐܡܪ ܗܘܐ ܡܪܝ، ܡܢܘ ܗܝܡܢ ܠܫܡܥܢ ܘܕܪܥܗ ܕܡܪܝܐ
ܠܡܢ ܐܬܓܠܝ ³⁹[ܘܬܘܒ] ܐܡܪ [ܐܫܥܝܐ ⁴⁰ܕܥܘܪܘ] ܥܝܢܝܗܘܢ
[ܘܐܚܫܟܘ] ܠܒܗܘܢ ܕܠܐ ܢܚܙܘܢ ܒܥܝܢܝܗܘܢ ܘܢܣܬܟܠܘܢ
ܘܢܬܦܢܘܢ ܘܐܐܣܐ ܠܗܘܢ ⁴¹ܗܠܝܢ ܐܡܪ ܐܫܥܝܐ ܟܕ ܚܙܐ
ܫܘܒܚܗ ܘܡܠܠ ܥܠܘܗܝ،

⁴²ܘܐܦ ܡܢ ܪ̈ܫܐ ܕܝܢ ܣܓܝܐܐ ܗܝܡܢܘ ܒܝܫܘܥ ܐܠܐ ܡܛܠ
ܦܪ̈ܝܫܐ ܠܐ ܡܘܕܝܢ ܗܘܘ ܒܗ ܕܠܐ ܢܦܪܫܘܢ ܐܢܘܢ ⁴³ܪܚܡܘ
ܫܘܒܚܐ ܕܒܢ̈ܝ ܐܢܫܐ ܝܬܝܪ ܡܢ ⌜ܫܘܒܚܐ ܕܐܠܗܐ ⁴⁴ܝܫܘ⌝ܥ ܕܝܢ

---

35 ܗܠܟܘ] ܗܝܡܢܘ A 330 ܒܢܘܗܪܐ] om. A²/₂ ܠܟܘܢ] ܠܘܬܟܘܢ Aᵇ14 ܢܗܝܪܐ Aᵃ14 ܕܠܐ ܢܕܪܟܟܘܢ] ܕܒܠܐ ܡܕܪܟ ܠܟܘܢ A²/₂ 36 ܗܝܡܢܘ] ܗܠܟܘ Aᵇ330 ܬܗܘܘܢ] ܬܬܬܡܪܘܢ Aᵇ330 37 ⌜ܪ̈ܘܪܒܬܐ ܥܕ⌝] ܥܕ ⌜ܪ̈ܘܪܒܬܐ⌝ * * Sᵉᵈ
43 ܫܘܒܚܐ 2°] Sᵉᵈ: *it is not legible in the photograph and perhaps should be omitted, as there is no room for it in the line*

were standing there and heard were astonished, and they say: "It S
30 was thunder"; and others say: "An angel spake with him." Jesus
saith to them: "Not because of me was this voice heard, but because
31 of you. Now is the judgement of the world; now the sovereign of this
32 world is thrown down. And I, what *time* I have been lifted up from
33 the earth, will draw every man unto me." Now this he said that he
34 might shew by what death he should die. And some from the
multitude [were] saying to him: "We have heard from the Law that
the Messiah for ever remaineth; and how sayest thou that the Son
of Man is about to be lifted up? Who," *said they*, "is this Son of
35 Man?" Jesus saith to them: "A little more the light is with you;
§walk in the light while yet ye have the light, that the darkness §¶*A* 14,
apprehend you not,¶ for he that walketh in the darkness knoweth not 330
36 whither he goeth. While yet ye have the light §believe in the light, §¶*A* 14,
that sons of the light ye may become."¶ 330

And when Jesus spake these things he went *and* hid himself from
37 them. And *for* all the signs, [though] *such* great ones he did, they
38 believed not on him, that there might be fulfilled the word of Isaiah
the prophet, that had said: "My Lord, who hath believed our report,
39 and the arm of the LORD to whom hath been revealed?" [And again]
40 saith [Isaiah "They have blinded] their eye [and darkened] their
heart, that they should not see with their eyes and should hear and
41 should repent and I should forgive them." These things said Isaiah
when he saw his glory and spake of him.

42 Now of the chiefs also many believed in Jesus, but because of
the Pharisees they were not confessing him, that they should not
43 expel them: they loved the glory of men more than [the glory of
44 God.] But [Jesus] cried out [and said: "He that in me] believeth,

---

35 walk] believe *A* 330 in the light] *om.* $A^{2}/_{2}$ light *ult.*] day-light A^{a}14 that...apprehend] while yet the darkness apprehendeth $A^{2}/_{2}$ 36 believe] walk A^{b}330 become] be called A^{b}330 43 the glory 2°] S^{ed}, *but perhaps it should be omitted*

S ܡܟܐ [ܘܐܡܪ ܡܢ ܕܒܪ] ܡܗܝܡܢ ܠܐ [ܗܘܐ ܒܪ ܡܗܝܡܢ] ܐܠܐ
[ܒܗܢ ܕܫܒܪܢ [45]ܘܗܢ ܕܠ ܣܐ] ܣܐ ܠܗܢ [ܕܫܒܪܢ] [46]ܐܝܟܐ [ܒܪܢ
ܢܗܘܪܐ] ܐܬܝܬ [ܠܗ] ܠܚܠܡܐ ܘܗܢ ܕܡܗܝܡܢ ܒܪ ܠܐ ܢܗܘܐ
ܠܟܠ ܢܗܘܪܐ [47]⌜ܡܢ⌝ ܕܐܡܝܪ ܟ̈ܠܗ ܘܠܐ ܢܛܪ ܠܗܘܢ ܐܝܟܐ ܠܐ
ܕܐܢ ܐܝܟܐ ܠܗ. ܠܐ ܒܪ ܐܬܝܬ ܕܐܕܘܢܝܗ̇ ܠܚܠܡܐ ܐܠܐ
ܕܐܚܝܗ̇ ܠܗ ܠܚܠܡܐ [48]ܡܢ ܕܡܫܬܐܠ ܠܝ ܕܝܢ ܘܠܐ ܡܚܒܠ ܡܠ
ܐܝܬ ܡܢ ܕܕܐܢ ܠܗ ܗ̄ܝ ܡܠܬܐ ܕܡܠܠܬ ܒܟܡܐ ܗ̄ܝ ⌜ܬ⌝ܕܘ⌜ܢ⌝ܝܗ̇
ܒܢܘܡܐ ܐܚܪܢܐ [49]ܕܐܝܟܐ ܒܪ ܡܢ ܡܠ ܠܐ ܡܠܠܬ ܐܠܐ ܐܟܐ
ܕܫܒܪܢ ܗܘ ܦܘܪܢ ܡܟܐ ܕܐܡܠܠ ܘܡܟܐ ܕܐܡܪ [50]ܘܫܒܝܚܐ
ܕܦ̈ܘܪܢܘܗܝ ܫܢܐ ܐܝܟܢ ܕܠܚܠܡ ܘܡܫܒܩ ܕܡܡܠܠ ܐܝܟܐ ܐܝܟ
ܕܦܘܪܢ ܗܘ ܡܡܠܠ ܐܝܟܐ. ܀

[1]ܡܢ ܡܕܡ ܦܠܓܘ̈ܬܐ ܕܝܢ ܚܕ ܗܘܐ ܫܡܥ ܕܐܬܬܬ ܠܗ ܥܒܕܬܗ
ܕܢܫܐ ܡܢ ܗܢܐ ܒܠܡܐ ܠܘܬ ܐܒܘܗܝ ܐܝܟ ܠܚܠܡ ܕܒܗܢܐ
ܒܠܡܐ ܘܒܡܥܐ ܠܐܘܪܚܬܐ ܐܝܟ ܐܝܟܢ [2]ܘܗܘܬ ܐܫܬܡܥܬܐ
ܘܦܠܓܐ ܐܘܪܚܐ ܗܘܐ ܒܠܗܘ ܕܡܗܘܕܐ ܒܪ ܥܡܟܘܢ ܡܦܪܘܫܘܬܐ
ܐܝܟ ܕܢܠܡܝܗ̇: [3]ܘܗܘ ܫܡܥ ܡܠܠ ܕܚܕ ܗܘܐ ܕܒܥܠ ܡܕܡ
ܢܗܒ ܐܒܐ ܒܐܝܪ̈ܘܗܝ. ܘܚܕ ܗܘܐ ܕܡܢ ܠܘܬ ܐܠܗܐ ܐܬܬܐ
ܘܠܘܬ ܐܠܗܐ ܐܙܠ [4]ܡܛܠ ܐܝܟ ܢܣܒܘܗܝ. ܘܫܡܥ ܣܘܕܪܐ ܡܫܐ
ܒܣܘ̈ܟܘܗܝ، [5]ܘܫܡܥ ܡܢܐ ܐܘܪܚ ܒܠܡܐ ܕܫܒܝܚܬܐ ܘܚܪ، ܗܘܐ
ܡܫܡܫ ܟ̈ܠܗܐ ܕܬܠܡܝܕܘܗܝ، ܘܡܫܦܪ ܒܣܘܕܪܐ ܕܡܫܐ ܒܣܘܟܘܗܝ،
§A 226 f. [§6]ܘܟܕ ܡܠܟܐ ܠܘܬ ܥܡܟܘܢ ܒܐܦܐ ܐܡܪ ܠܗ ܥܡܟܘܢ ܐܝܬ
ܡܢܝ، ܟ̈ܠܠ ܡܫܡܫ ܐܝܬ ܠܝ: [7]ܐܡܪ ܠܗ ܫܡܥ ܡܕܡ ܕܒܒܐ
ܐܝܟܐ ܠܟ ܠܐ ܚܕ ܐܝܬ ܡܢ ܒܬܪ ܘܒܐ ܕܝܢ ܬܕܒܪ: [8]ܐܡܪ ܠܗ
ܥܡܟܘܢ ܠܚܠܡ ܠܐ ܡܫܡܫ ܐܝܬ ܠܝ ܟ̈ܠܠ ܐܡܪ ܠܗ ܫܡܥ

---

46 ⌜ܒܪܢ⌝] *or* ⌜ܕܡ⌝; *S illegible* 48 ܕܡܫܬܐܠ] S^{ed} (*photograph illegible except* ܕܡܫ): *? read* ⌜ܕܡܬܚܡܠܐ⌝ *or* ⌜ܕܡܬܚܫܠ⌝ ܕܝܢ] *S* (*sic*) ⌜ܬ⌝ܕܘ⌜ܢ⌝ܝܗ̇] *S* (*sic*) 4, 5 *A has* [5a]ܟܕ ܫܡܥ ܒܪ ܦܘܡ ܡܢܐ ܘܐܘܪܚ ܒܠܡܐ ܕܫܒܝܚܬܐ. [4b]ܘܫܡܥ ܣܘܕܪܐ ܡܫܐ ܒܣܘܟܘܗܝ. [5b]ܘܡܫܦܪ ܕܡܫܡܫ ܟ̈ܠܗܐ ܕܬܠܡܝܕܘܗܝ. [6]ܘܟܕ ܡܠܟܐ

6 ܥܡܟܘܢ 2°] *om. A* 7, 8[a] [7]ܐܡܪ....[8]..ܥܡܟܘܢ] *om. A*

45 not [in me doth he believe] but [in him that sent me; and he that *S*
46 seeth me] seeth him that [sent me. For] I [*as* a light] have come
into the world, and he that believeth in me will not remain in not-
47 light. He that heareth my words and keepeth them not, I do not
judge him; for I came not that I should judge the world, but that I
48 should save the world alive. Now he that asketh me and receiveth
not my words, there is one that judgeth him: that word which I
49 have spoken with him, that will judge him in the last day; for I
from my words have not spoken, but the Father that sent me, he hath
50 commanded me what I should speak and what I should say. And I
know that his commandments are life eternal; and that which I
speak, as he hath commanded me that do I speak."

xiii 1 Now before the Unleavened Bread Jesus had known that his hour
was come that he should remove from this world unto his Father; he
was loving to his own that *were* in this world, and until the last was he
2 loving to them. And it was supper and Satan was lying in the heart
3 of Judas son of Simon Scariot, so that he might betray him. And
he, Jesus, because he was knowing that everything the Father gave
into his hands and was knowing that from God he came and unto
4 God was going, rose up *and* laid aside his garments, and he took a
5 cloth *and* put *it* on his loins, and he took water *and* poured *it* into
a washing-dish, and had begun washing the feet of his disciples
6 and wiping *them* with the cloth which he put on his loins. §And §*A* 226 f.
when he arrived at Simon Kepha, Simon saith to him: "Thou, my
7 Lord, my feet dost thou wash for me?" Jesus saith to him: "That
which I do to thee thou knowest not; but after a time thou wilt
8 know." Simon saith to him: "Never shalt thou wash for me my
feet!" Jesus saith to him: "If I wash *them* not for thee, thou hast

---

46 For] *or,* 'but' **48** asketh] S^{ed} **4, 5** [5a]'For when our Saviour took water and poured *it* into a washing-dish, [4b]and took a cloth *and* put *it* on his loins, [5b](then) he began to wash the feet of his disciples. [6]And when he arrived &c.' *A* **6** Simon 2°] *om. A* **7, 8** Jesus saith....... [8]Simon saith to him] *om. A*

ܐܠܐ ܡܫܝܓ ܐܢܐ ܠܟ ܠܝܬ ܠܟ ܥܡܝ ܡܢܬܐ. 9ܐܡܪ ܠܗ S
ܫܡܥܘܢ ܡܕܝܢ ܡܪܝ، ܠܐ ܪ̈ܓܠܝ ܒܠܚܘܕ ܬܫܝܓ ܠܝ ܐܠܐ ܐܦ
ܐܝ̈ܕܝ، ܘܐܦ ܪܫܝ. 10ܐܡܪ ܠܗ ܝܫܘܥ. ܡܢ ܕܣܚܐ ܗܘ ܠܐ ܣܢܝܩ
ܐܠܐ ܪ̈ܓܠܘܗܝ، ܒܠܚܘܕ ܢܫܝܓ¶ ܡܛܠ ܕܟܠܗ ܕܟܐ ܗܘ ܘܐܦ ¶A
ܐܢܬܘܢ ܕܟܝܢ ܐܢܬܘܢ؛ ܐܠܐ ܠܐ ܟܠܟܘܢ؛ 11ܝܕܥ ܗܘܐ ܓܝܪ
ܡܢ ܕܡܫܠܡ ܠܗ. ܡܛܠ ܗܘ ܐܡܪ ܗܘܐ ܡܠܬܐ. §12ܟܕ ܐܫܝܓ §A227
ܕܝܢ ܪ̈ܓܠܝܗܘܢ ܢܣܒ ܢܚܬܘܗܝ، ܘܐܣܬܡܟ ܐܡܪ ܠܗܘܢ ܝܕܥܝܢ
ܐܢܬܘܢ ܡܢܐ ܥܒܕܬ ܠܟܘܢ 13ܗܐ ܩܪܝܢ ܐܢܬܘܢ ܠܝ ܪܒܢ
ܘܡܪܢ ܘܫܦܝܪ ܐܡܪܝܢ ܐܢܬܘܢ ܐܝܬܝ، ܓܝܪ 14ܘܐܢ ܐܢܐ
ܪܒܟܘܢ ܘܡܪܟܘܢ ܪ̈ܓܠܝܟܘܢ ܡܫܝܓܢܐ ܠܟܘܢ ܟܡܐ ܘܠܐ
ܠܟܘܢ ܕܐܦ ܐܢܬܘܢ ܬܗܘܘܢ ܡܫܝܓܝܢ ܪ̈ܓܠܐ ܚܕ ܕܚܕ.
15ܗܢܐ ܕܝܢ ܛܘܦܣܐ ܕܫܘܬܦܘܬܟܘܢ ܕܐܝܟܢܐ ܕܥܒܕܬ ܠܟܘܢ
ܬܗܘܘܢ ܥܒܕܝܢ¶ ܀:܀ ¶A
16ܐܡܝܢ ܐܡܝܢ ܐܡܪܢܐ ܠܟܘܢ ܕܠܝܬ ܥܒܕܐ ܕܪܒ ܡܢ ܡܪܗ
ܘܠܐ ܫܠܝܚܐ ܕܪܒ ܡܢ ܡܢ ܕܫܕܪܗ 17ܐܢ ܗܠܝܢ ܬܕܥܘܢ
ܘܬܥܒܕܘܢ ܛܘܒܝܟܘܢ 18ܠܐ ܗܘܐ ܥܠ ܟܠܟܘܢ ܐܢܐ ܐܡܪܢܐ.
ܡܛܠ ܕܝܕܥܢܐ ܠܐܝܠܝܢ ܕܓܒܝܬ. ܐܠܐ ܡܛܠ ܕܢܫܬܠܡ ܟܬܒܐ.
ܕܐܡܪ ܕܡܢ ܕܐܟܠ ܥܡܝ ܠܚܡܐ ܐܪܝܡ ܥܠܝ ܥܩܒܗ. 19ܡܢ ܗܫܐ
ܐܡܪܢܐ ܠܟܘܢ ܡܢ ܩܕܡ ܕܠܐ ܢܗܘܐ ܕܡܐ ܕܗܘܐ ܬܕܥܘܢ
ܕܐܢܐ ܐܢܐ 20ܐܡܝܢ ܐܡܪܢܐ ܠܟܘܢ ܕܡܢ ܕܡܩܒܠ ܠܡܢ ܕܡܫܕܪ
ܐܢܐ ܠܝ ܗܘ ܡܩܒܠ ܘܡܢ ܕܠܝ ܡܩܒܠ ܠܡܢ ܕܫܠܚܢܝ ܗܘ ܡܩܒܠ.
21ܘܟܕ ܐܡܪ ܗܠܝܢ ܝܫܘܥ ܐܬܥܝܪ ܒܪܘܚܗ ܘܐܣܗܕ ܘܐܡܪ ܐܡܝܢ

---

9 ܘܐܦ] ܐܦ *A*   10ᵇ, 11.] *not quoted in A*
12ᵃ ܘܟܕ ܐܫܝܓ ܪ̈ܓܠܝܗܘܢ ܕܬܠܡܝ̈ܕܘܗܝ ܢܣܒ *A*   ܘܐܡܪ *A*
ܝܕܥܝܢ......ܠܟܘܢ] *om. A*   13 ܘܫܦܝܪ......ܓܝܪ] ܘܐܝܬܝ *A*   14 ܘܐܢ ܐܢܐ]
ܐܢ ܐܢܐ ܗܟܝܠ *A*   ܪܒܟܘܢ] + ܐܢܬܘܢ *A*   ܕܐܦ] ܕ *A*   15 ܕܝܢ] *om. A*
ܕܫܘܬܦܘܬܟܘܢ] *om.* ܕ *A*   ܕܐܝܟܢܐ] ܕܐܝܟ *A*   ܠܟܘܢ] *om. A*   ܬܗܘܘܢ ܥܒܕܝܢ]
ܗܟܢܐ ܬܥܒܕܘܢ *A*   16 ܐܡܪܢܐ] *above the line in S, but by the first hand*:
cf Matt v 48

9 with me no part." Simon saith to him: "Then, my Lord, not my *S*
feet only shalt thou wash for me, but also my hands and my head too."
10 Jesus saith to him: "He that hath bathed needeth not except to wash
his feet only,¶ because he is all of him clean; and ye also are clean, ¶*A*
11 but not all of you." For he knew who *was* betraying him: because
12 of him said he this word. §Now when he *had* washed their feet §*A* 227
he took his garments and sat down *to meat*. He saith to them:
13 "Know ye what I have done to you? Lo, ye call me 'Rabban' and
14 'our Lord,' and well say ye, for I am *so*. And if I, your Rabbi and
your Lord, wash for you your feet, how much doth it behove you
15 that ye also shall be washing the feet of one another? Now this
type that I have shewn you—that as I have done to you ye shall
be doing.¶ ¶*A*

16 "Amen, amen, I say to you There is no slave that is greater
than his lord, and no apostle that is greater than him that sent
17, 18 him. If these things ye know and do, happy is it for you! Not of
every one do I say *it*, because I know those which I have chosen,
but because the Scripture should be accomplished that saith 'He
19 that eateth with me bread hath lifted up against me his heel.' From
now I say to you before yet it come to pass, that what *time* it hath
20 come to pass ye may know that I am *he*. Amen, I say to you He
that receiveth him that I send, me it is he receiveth; and he that me
21 receiveth, him that sent me he receiveth." And when Jesus said
these things he was troubled in his spirit, and he bore witness

---

10^b, 11.] *not quoted in A* **12** 'And when he washed the feet of his disciples he took' *A* He saith] and said *A* Know ye.... to you] *om. A* **13** and well say ye, for] and *A* **14** And if I] If I therefore *A* also] *om. A* **15** Now this type that] This type *A* to you] *om. A* ye shall be doing] so shall ye do *A* **20** send, sent] *cf* Matt xi 2

S ܐܡܪܢܐ ܠܟܘܢ ܕܚܕ ܡܢܟܘܢ ܡܫܠܡ ܠܝ. ²²ܬܠܡܝܕܘܗܝ، ܕܝܢ ܚܝܪܝܢ
ܗܘܘ ܚܕ ܒܚܕ ܘܡܬܬܕܡܪܝܢ ܕܥܠ ܡܢ ܗܘ ܐܡܪ ²³ܚܕ ܡܢ
ܬܠܡܝܕܘܗܝ، ܕܝܢ ܐܝܢܐ ܕܪܚܡ ܗܘܐ ܝܫܘܥ ܗܘ ܕܣܡܝܟ ܗܘܐ
ܒܥܘܒܗ ²⁴ܪܡܙ ܠܗ ܫܡܥܘܢ ܟܐܦܐ ܕܢܫܐܠܝܘܗܝ، ܥܠ ܡܢ ܐܡܪ
²⁵⌜ܗܘ⌝ ܬܠܡܝܕܐ ܕܪܚܡ ܗܘܐ ܠܗ. ܡܚܕܐ ܢܦܠ ܥܠ ܚܕܝܗ
ܕܝܫܘܥ ܘܐܡܪ ܠܗ ܡܪܝ، ܡܢܘ ܗܢܐ ²⁶ܐܡܪ ܠܗ ܗܘ ܗܘ
ܕܐܨܒܘܥ ܠܚܡܐ ܘܝܗܒܢܐ ܠܗ ܘܨܒܥ ܝܫܘܥ ܠܚܡܐ ܘܝܗܒ
ܠܝܗܘܕܐ ܒܪ ܫܡܥܘܢ ܣܟܪܝܘܛܐ ²⁷ܘܒܬܪ ܠܚܡܐ. ܐܬܥܠܠ ܗܘܐ
ܒܗ ܣܛܢܐ ܐܡܪ ܠܗ ܝܫܘܥ ܡܕܡ ܕܥܒܕ ܐܢܬ ܥܒܕ ܒܥܓܠ
²⁸ܘܬܠܡܝܕܘܗܝ، ܠܐ ܝܕܥܝܢ ܗܘܘ ܥܠ ܡܢܐ ܐܡܪ ²⁹ܗܘܘ ܓܝܪ ܣܒܪܝܢ
ܗܘܘ [ܒܪ] ܡܛܠ ܕܓܠܘܣܩܡܐ ܠܝܕܘܗܝ، ܗܘܐ ܕܝܗܘܕܐ.
ܕܝܫܘܥ ܦܩܕ ܠܗ ܙܒܢ ܕܢܣܒ ܠܥܐܕܐ ܘܡܕܡ ܕܢܬܠ ܠܡܣܟܢܐ.
³⁰ܗܝܕܝܢ ܡܢ ܝܗܘܕܐ ܘܢܣܒ ܠܚܡܐ ܘܢܦܩ ܠܗ ܠܒܪ ܘܒܙܒܢܐ
§Addai 20 ܕܝܢ ܠܠܝܐ ܗܘܐ. ³¹ܘܟܕ ܢܦܩ ܐܡܪ ܝܫܘܥ §ܗܐ ܡܟܝܠ ܐܫܬܒܚ
ܒܪܗ ܕܓܒܪܐ. ܘܐܠܗܐ ܐܫܬܒܚ ܒܗ. ³²ܘܐܠܗܐ ܕܒܗ ܡܫܒܚ
¶Addai ܠܗ¶ ܒܝܕܗ ܡܫܒܚ ܠܗ ³³ܒ̈ܢܝ ܩܠܝܠ ܐܚܪܢ ܥܡܟܘܢ ܐܢܐ
ܘܬܒܥܘܢܢܝ ܐܝܟܢܐ ܕܐܡܪܬ ܠܝܗܘܕܝܐ ܕܐܝܟܐ ܕܐܢܐ ܐܙܠܢܐ ܠܐ
ܡܫܟܚܝܢ ܠܡܐܬܐ ܘܗܘܐ ܐܦ ܠܟܘܢ ܐܡܪܬ ³⁴ܐܠܐ ܕܗܫܐ
§¶A 34 §ܦܘܩܕܢܐ ܚܕܬܐ ܝܗܒܢܐ ܠܟܘܢ ܕܬܗܘܘܢ ܡܚܒܝܢ ܚܕ ܠܚܕ¶
ܐܝܟܢܐ ܕܐܢܐ ܐܚܒܬܟܘܢ ³⁵ܒܗܕܐ ܢܕܥܘܢ ܟܠܗܘܢ
ܕܬܠܡܝܕ̈ܝ، ܐܢܬܘܢ ܐܢ ܚܘܒܐ ܢܗܘܐ ܒܟܘܢ ܚܕ ܠܘܬ ܚܕ.
³⁶ܐܡܪ ܠܗ ܫܡܥܘܢ ܟܐܦܐ ܡܪܝ، ܠܐܝܟܐ ܐܙܠ ܐܢܬ. ܐܡܪ
ܠܗ ܠܐܝܟܐ ܕܐܙܠ ܐܢܐ ܠܐ ܡܫܟܚ ܐܢܬ ܠܡܐܬܐ ܒܬܪܝ ܗܫܐ ܘܒܪܢܐ
ܒܐܚܪܬܐ ܕܝܢ ܬܐܬܐ ܒܬܪܝ. ³⁷ܐܡܪ ܠܗ ܫܡܥܘܢ ܠܡܢܐ ܠܐ

---

22 ܒܗ] *S* (sic), beginning a line. Before* ܒ, *in the margin, are signs of a letter* (ܗ *or* ܘ), *perhaps to indicate* ܚܕܘ ܒܗ   30 ܗܝܕܝܢ] *S (sic)*   31 ܒܪܗ ܕܓܒܪܐ] ܒܪܗ ܕܐܢܫܐ *Addai: see* Matt xii 40   ܘܐܠܗܐ ܐܫܬܒܚ ܒܗ] *om. Addai*
34 ܕܬܗܘܘܢ ܡܚܒܝܢ] ܕܬܚܒܘܢ *A*   36 ܒܐܚܪܬܐ] *S (sic)*

and said: "Amen, I say to you that one of you betrayeth me." *S*
22 Now his disciples were looking one on the other and wondering of
23 whom then he spake. But one of his disciples, he which our Lord
24 loved, he that was sitting *at meat* in his bosom, to him Simon Kepha
25 beckoned that he should ask him of whom he said *it*. That disciple
which Jesus loved fell on the breast of Jesus and said to him:
26 "My Lord, who is this?" He saith to him: "He it is for whom I dip
bread; I give *it* him." And Jesus dipped bread and gave to Judas,
27 son of Simon Scariot; and after the bread Satan had made an entry
into him. Jesus saith to him: "That which thou doest, do quickly."
28, 29 And his disciples did not know of what he said *it*, [for] they were
supposing, because the box was with Judas, that he had in fact
commanded him what he should buy for the Feast and what he
30 should give to the poor. Then Judas arose and took the bread
31 and went forth outside; now the season was night. And when he
went forth Jesus saith: "§Lo, henceforth hath the son of a man been §*Addai* 20
32 glorified, and God hath been glorified thereby; and God that thereby
33 glorifieth him¶ at once glorifieth him. My sons, a little more am I ¶*Addai*
with you, and ye will seek me, as I said to the Jews that where I go
34 they cannot come; and lo, to you also I say *it*! But for now §a new §*A* 34
commandment I give you, that ye should be loving one to another,¶ ¶*A*
35 as I myself have been loving to you. For by this all of them will know
that ye are my disciples, if love be in you one towards the other."
36 Simon Kepha saith to him: "My Lord, whither goest thou?" He
saith to him: "Whither I go ye cannot come at this time, but in the
37 last thou shalt come after me." Simon saith to him: "Wherefore

---

30 Then] *S* (*sic*) 31 the son of a man (*see on* Matt xii 40, Lk xxii 48)] 'the Son of Man' *Addai* and God hath been glorified thereby] *om. Addai* thereby] *or*, 'in him' (*in each place*)

ܡܫܒܚ ܗܘܐ ܕܐܬܐ ܒܬܪܢ. ܘܗܫܐ ܢܦܫ ܐܝܟ ܐܘܢܐ ܬܠܬܝܢ. [38]ܐܡܪ S
ܠܗ ܫܡܥܘܢ ܠܢܦܫܟܝ ܬܥܒܪ ܪܘܡܚܐ. ܐܝܟܢ ܐܡܪܝܢ ܠܟܝ ܕܒܥܠܐ
ܢܦܪܐ ܬܪܥܝܬܐ ܬܪܬܝܢ ܕܬܠܬ ܘܟܬܝܢ ܬܬܦܫܪ ܒ [1]ܘܗܘܝܢ
ܐܡܪ ܫܡܥܘܢ ܠܐ ܢܬܦܪܫܘܢ ܠܟܠܗܘܢ ܘܫܡܥܘ ܒܐܠܗܐ ܘܒܝ
§¶A437 ܘܗ ܡܣܬܟܠܝܢ ܐܢܬܘܢ [§2]ܦܓܪܝܐ ܐܢܘܢ ܐܬܪܘܬܐ ܒܥܬ ܐܡܪ[¶]
§A460 ܘܐܠܐ ܐܡܪ ܗܘܝܬ ܠܟܘܢ [§]ܕܐܬܪܐ ܐܪܥܐ ܕܐܝܠܝܢ ܠܟܘܢ
[3]ܘܐܢ ܐܢܬ ܘܐܬܝܬ ܠܟܘܢ: ܬܘܒ ܐܬܐ ܘܐܬܒܪܟܘܢ ܐܝܟ ܠܘܬܝ،
§A119, 486 [§]ܕܐܬܪܐ ܕܐܝܟܐ ܐܦ ܐܢܬܘܢ ܬܗܘܘܢ [¶¶] ܘܠܐܠܗܐ[4] ܕܐܪܥܐ
¶A3/3 ܝܕܥܝܢ ܐܢܬܘܢ ܘܐܘܪܚܐ ܝܕܥܝܢ ܐܢܬܘܢ: [5]ܐܡܪ ܠܗ ܬܐܘܡܐ
ܡܪܝ، ܠܐ ܝܕܥܝܢ ܐܢܚܢ ܠܐܝܟܐ ܐܙܠ ܐܢܬ ܐܝܟܢܐ ܡܫܟܚܝܢ
ܐܢܚܢ ܠܡܕܥ ܐܘܪܚܐ ܐܝܕܐ ܗܝ، [6]ܐܡܪ ܠܗ ܝܫܘܥ ܐܢܐ ܐܢܐ
ܐܘܪܚܐ ܘܫܪܪܐ ܘܚܝܐ ܠܐ ܐܢܫ ܐܬܐ ܠܘܬ ܐܒܝ. ܐܠܐ ܐ ܢ
ܒܝ [7]ܐܢ ܠܝ ܠܐ ܝܕܥܬܘܢ ܐܦ ܠܐܒܝ ܬܕܥܘܢ ܘܡܢ ܗܫܐ
ܝܕܥܝܢ ܐܢܬܘܢ ܠܗ ܘܚܙܝܬܘܢܝܗܝ. [8]ܐܡܪ ܠܗ ܦܝܠܝܦܘܣ ܡܪܢ
ܚܘܢ ܐܒܐ ܘܣܓܐ ܠܢ [9]ܐܡܪ ܠܗ ܝܫܘܥ ܗܢܘܢ ܟܠܗ ܙܒܢܐ [ܐܢܐ]
ܥܡܟܘܢ ܘܠܐ [ܝܕܥܬܢܝ] ܡܢ ܕܠܝ ܚܙܐ [ܚܙܐ] ܠܐܒܝ ܘܐܝܟܢܐ
§¶A70 [ܐܡܪ] ܐܢܬ ܚܘܢ ܠܐܒܐ [10]⌜[ܠܐ] ܡܗܝܡܢܝܢ [ܐܢܬܘܢ] ⌝[§]ܕܐܢܐ
§C ܒܐܒܐ [ܐܢܐ] ܘܐܒܐ ܒܝ [¶] [ܗܘ [12(§)]ܐܝܟܢ] ܐܝܟܢ ܐܡܪܬ⌜ܐ⌝ [ܠܟܘܢ]
ܕܡܢ ܕܗܝܡܢ [ܒܝ] ܥܒܕܐ ܕܐܢܐ] ܥܒܕ ܐܢܐ] ܗܘ [ܢܥܒܕ]

---

1 ܘܗܘܝܢ] S (*Theol. Litztg.* 1898, col. 440): *cf* Diat[ar] xlv 29 2 ܦܓܪܝܐ A ܐܬܪܘܬܐ] *cf* ܒܪܝܬܐ ܚܕܬܐ ܠܟܠܗܘܢ ܕܐܝܠܝܢ ܐܝܟ ܗܢܐ *Addai*[45], *also* ܠܐܬܪܘܬܐ ܕܐܝܟ ܒܪܐ ܕܐܝܠܝܢ ܠܟܠ ܡܢ ܕܢܦܩ ܠܗܘܢ 3 ܘܐܢ.....ܬܘܒ] ܘܗܘܝܢ A ܠܘܬܝ] *om.* A 5 ܐܘܪܚܐ] S (*sic*): *cf* Mk x 32 8 ܦܝܠܝܦܘܣ] S (*sic*) 10 ⌜ܐܢܐ⌝ ܒܐܒܐ] ܐܢܐ ܒܐܒܝ A[a] (*om.* ܐܢܐ A[b]); *cf* ܢܫܒܚ ܕܐܢܬ ܒܐܒܐ ܘܐܒܐ ܒܟ Thos[216] 10[b], 11.] *omitted in S. Half a leaf of C is here preserved (see Appendix* II), *beginning* ܠܐ ܗܘܐ ܡܢ ܝܒܘܬ ܢܦܫ ܡܡܠܠܐ ܐܠܐ ܐܒܝ ܕܒܝ ܗܘ ܥܒܕ ܥܒܕܐ ܗܠܝܢ [11]ܗܝܡܢܘܢ ܕܐܢܐ ܒܐܒܝ ܐܢܐ ܘܐܒܝ ܒܝ ܗܘ ܘܐܢ ܠܐ ܠܗܐ ܡܗܝܡܢܝܢ ܐܢܬܘܢ ܐܦ ܡܛܠܬܗܘܢ ܕܥܒܕܐ ܗܝܡܢܘ [12]ܐܡܝܢ ܐܡܝܢ....
12 ܗܘ] *pr.* ܐܦ C

cannot I come after thee? Now my life will I lay down for thee!" *S*
38 Jesus saith to him: "Thy life wilt thou lay down for me? Amen, I
say to thee Before ever the cock crow twice, for the third time thou
xiv 1 wilt deny me." And then said Jesus: "Let not your heart be alarmed;
2 believe in God, and in me ye *will* believe. §Many are the places in §¶*A*437
my Father's house;¶ and if not, I would have said to you §that a place §*A*460
3 I go to make ready for you. And if I go and prepare for you, again I
will come and take you unto me, §that where I *am* ye also may be.¶¶ §*A*119, 486
4, 5 And whither I go ye know and the way ye know." Thomas saith to ¶*A*$^{3}/_{3}$
him; "My Lord, we know not whither thou goest; how can we know
6 the way which it is?" Jesus saith to him: "I am the way and the
7 truth and the life; no man cometh unto my Father, save by me. If
me ye have not known, my Father also will ye know? And from now
8 ye know him and have seen him." Philip saith to him: "Our Lord,
9 shew us the Father, and it is enough for us." Jesus saith to him:
"All *this* while [I] am with you, and [thou hast] not [known me?] He
that seeth me [seeth] my Father, and how [sayest] thou 'Shew us
10 the [Father'? Do ye not] believe §that I [am] in the Father and my §¶*A*70
12 Father [is] in me?¶ §[Amen], amen, I say [to you] He that believeth §*C*
[in me], those deeds [that I] do he [will do]; and greater than [these

---

2 places] *cf* 'lo, he is gone to prepare for his worshippers blessed Abodes' *Addai*[45], *but on the same page* 'to the Places that the Son hath gone to prepare for every one worthy of them' 3 And if....again] And then *A* unto me] *om. A* 10 the Father] my Father *A*; *cf* 'Jesus that art in the Father and the Father in thee' *Thos*[216] 10^{b}, 11.] *omitted in S. Half a leaf of C is here preserved, beginning* 'not of my own mind speak I with you, but my Father that is in me doeth these deeds. [11] Believe me that I am in my Father and my Father is in me; and if me ye believe not, even if *only* because of the deeds believe. [12] Amen, amen, *etc.*' 12 he also will do *C*

S ¶C ܘܕܡܬܬܢܝܢ ܡܢ [ܗܠܝܢ] [ܒܒ̈ܪܟܐ¶ ܢܥܒܕ ܕܐܝܟܐ] [ܠܘܬ ܐܝܟ ܐܝܠܝܢ
[13]ܘܡܕܡ ܕܬܫܐܠܘܢ ܒܫܡܝ ܐܥܒܕ ܠܟܘܢ] ܕܢܫܬܒܚ ܐܒܐ ܒܒܪܗ
§C [15]ܐܢ ܡܚܒܝܢ ܐܢܬܘܢ ܠܝ ܦܘܩܕܢܝ §ܛܪܘ. [16]ܘܐܢܐ ܐܒܥܐ ܡܢ
ܐܒܝ ܕܢܫܕܪ ܠܟܘܢ ܐܚܪܢܐ ܦܪܩܠܛܐ ܕܢܗܘܐ ܥܡܟܘܢ ܠܥܠܡ.
[17]ܪܘܚܐ ܕܫܪܪܐ ܕܥܠܡܐ ܠܐ ܡܫܟܚ ܠܡܩܒܠܘܬܗ ܠܐ ܓܝܪ ܚܙܝܗ
ܘܠܐ ܝܕܥܗ ܐܢܬܘܢ ܕܝܢ ܝܕܥܝܢ ܐܢܬܘܢ ܠܗ. ܘܠܘܬܟܘܢ
ܥܡܪܐ ܘܠܘܬܟܘܢ ܬܗܘܐ. [18]ܘܠܐ ܐܫܒܘܩܟܘܢ ܝܬ̈ܡܐ ܐܠܐ
¶C ܐܬܐ ܠܘܬܟܘܢ [19]ܘܩܠܝܠ ܐܚܪܢ ܘܥܠܡܐ ܠܐ ܚܙܐ¶ ܠܝ. ܘܐܢܬܘܢ
ܬܚܙܘܢܢܝ ܘܚܝ ܐܢܐ ܘܐܦ ܐܢܬܘܢ ܬܚܘܢ [20]ܘܒܗܘ ܝܘܡܐ
§¶A8, 70, 120, 484, 486 ܬܕܥܘܢ ܕܐܢܐ ܒܐܒܝ ܐܢܐ ܘ§ܐܢܬܘܢ ܒܝ ܐܢܬܘܢ ܘܐܢܐ
§C ܒܟܘܢ ܐܢܐ¶ [21]ܡܢ ܕܐܝܬ ܠܘܬܗ ܦܘܩܕܢܝ ܘܢܛܪ §ܠܗܘܢ ܗܘ
ܗܘ ܪܚܡ ܠܝ ܘܡܢ ܕܪܚܡ ܠܝ ܘܐܦ ܗܘ ܢܬܪܚܡ ܡܢ ܐܒܝ ܘܐܦ
ܐܢܐ ܐܪܚܡܝܘܗܝ ܘܐܚܘܝܘܗܝ ܢܦܫܝ. [22]ܐܡܪ ܠܗ ܬܐܘܡܐ ܡܪܝ
ܡܢܘ ܕܚܬܝܬ ܐܢܬ ܠܡܚܘܝܘ ܠܝ ܢܦܫܟ ܘܠܐ ܗܘܐ ܠܥܠܡܐ
§A130 ܡܚܘܐ ܐܢܬ ܢܦܫܟ [23]ܐܡܪ ܠܗ ܝܫܘܥ §ܡܢ ܕܠܝ ܪܚܡ ܡܠܬܝ ܢܛܪ
¶A ܘܐܒܝ ܢܪܚܡܝܘܗܝ. ܘܠܘܬܗ ܐܬܝܢ ܐܢܚܢ ܘܐܘܢܐ ܠܘܬܗ ܢܥܒܕ.¶
¶C [24]ܡܢ ܕܠܐ ܪܚܡ ܠܝ ܡ̈ܠܝ¶ ܠܐ ܢܛܪ ܘܡܠܬܐ [ܕܫܡܥܝܢ ܐܢܬܘܢ]
ܠܗ ܗܝ، ܡܠܬܐ ܠܐ ܗܘܬ ܕܝܠܝ ܐܠܐ ܕܡܢ ܕܫܕܪܢܝ [25]ܗܠܝܢ

---

15 ܛܪܘ] *C*; ܘܪܘ * *S* (*sic*) 16 ܐܚܪܢܐ ܦܪܩܠܛܐ] *Cf* Ishô'dâd (*Harris*, p. 86): ܗܝ ܕܐܚܪܢܐ ܦܪܩܠܛܐ ܗ݁: ܐܚܪܢܐ ܡܟܝܟܐ 17 ܕܫܪܪܐ] + ܗܝ *C* ܘܠܘܬܟܘܢ ܬܗܘܐ] ܗܝ ܥܡܟܘܢ *C* ܠܡܩܒܠܘܬܗ̇...ܚܙܝܗ̇...(*vid*) ܝܕܥܗ̇...ܠܗ̇ *C* 18 ܐܫܒܘܩܟܘܢ *C* ܐܠܐ ܐܬܐ ܠܘܬܟܘܢ] *om.* *C* 19 ܩܠܝܠ] *pr.* ܗܐ *C* 20 ܘܒܗܘ] *S* (*sic*) 21 ܕܐܝܬ] ܕܡܚܒ *C* ܘܐܦ ܗܘ....ܐܒܝ] ܐܒܐ ܢܪܚܡܝܘܗܝ *C* ܘܐܦ 2°] ܐܦ *C* ܘܐܚܘܝܘܗܝ] ܐܪܚܡܝܘܗܝ *C* ܘܐܦ ܐܚܘܝܘܗܝ *C* 22 ܬܐܘܡܐ] *S* (*sic*); ܝܗܘܕܐ ܬܐܘܡܐ *C* ܕܠܡ ܚܬܝܬ *C* (*om.* ܠܝ *before* ܢܦܫܟ) ܗܘܐ] *om.* *C* ܡܚܘܐ ܐܢܬ ܢܦܫܟ] *om.* *C* 23 ܕܪܚܡ ܠܝ *C* ܐܬܝܢ ܐܢܚܢ] ܐܬܐ ܐܢܐ *C* ܢܥܒܕ] ܐܥܒܕ *C* *A* ܡ̇ܢ ܕܡܚܒ ܠܝ ܒܦܘܩܕܢܝ ܢܛܪ ܗܘܢ. ܠܘܬܗ ܐܬܝܢ ܐܢܚܢ ܘܐܘܢܐ ܠܘܬܗ ܢܥܒܕ (ܥܒܕܝܢ A^{b}) 24 ܡ̈ܠܝ] ܡܠܬܝ *C* (*sic*)

13 deeds¶ will he do, because I go unto my Father. And that which ye *S* ¶*C*
shall ask in my name I will do for you,] that the Father may be
15 glorified in his Son. If ye are loving to me, §keep my commandments; §*C*
16 and I myself will beseech my Father that he should send you another,
17 the Paraclete, [that he may be] with you for ever, [*even* the Spirit of]
truth, which the world [cannot] receive, [for it hath not] seen it nor
known it, but ye know it and with you it dwelleth and with you it
18 shall be. And I will not leave you orphans, but I will come unto
19 you. A little more, and the world seeth¶ me not, and ye shall see me, ¶*C*
20 and I am alive and ye also shall live; and in that day ye shall know
21 that I am in my Father and §ye are in me and I am in you.¶ He that §¶*A* 8, 70, 120, 484, 486
hath by him my commandments and keepeth §them, he it is loveth §*C*
me; and he that loveth me, he also is loved by my Father, and I
22 also will love him and will shew him myself." Thomas saith to him:
"Our Lord, what is it that thou art about to shew to us thyself, and
23 not to the world dost thou shew thyself?" Jesus saith to him:
"§He that loveth me, my word he keepeth, and my Father will love §*A* 130
him and unto him we come and an abode with him we will make.¶ ¶*A*
24 He that loveth me not, my words¶ he doth not keep, and the ¶*C*
word [that ye hear]; and that word is not mine, but his that
25 sent me. These things have I spoken with you, while I am by you,

---

15 keep] *C*; *S illegible* 16 another, the Paraclete] *cf* Ishô'dâd (*Harris*, p. 86): "This 'another Paraclete' means 'another Comforter,'" *and* 'another Advocate I send unto you, i.e. Consoler' E^{225} it shall be] it is *C* 18 but I will come unto you] *om. C* 19 Lo, a little more *C* 21 loveth 2°] is loving to *C* he also...my Father] the Father will love him *C* shew] *pr.* also *C* 22 Thomas] *S* (*sic*); Judas Thomas *C* dost....thyself] *om. C* 23 we come] I come *C* we will make] I will make *C* 'He that walketh in my commandments and keepeth my love, unto him we come and an abode with him we will make' *A* 24 my words] my word *C*

ܡܠܠܬ ܥܡܟܘܢ ܟܕ ܠܘܬܟܘܢ ܐܢܐ ²⁶ܗܝ ܪܘܚܐ ܕܝܢ ܦܪܩܠܛܐ S
ܕܫܕܪ ܠܟܘܢ §ܐܒܝ ܒܫܡܝ ܗܝ ܬܠܦܟܘܢ ܟܠ ܡܕܡ. ܗܝ §C
ܬܥܗܕܟܘܢ ܟܠ ܡܐ ܕܐܡܪܬ ܐܢܐ §²⁷ܫܠܡܐ ܫܒܩܢܐ ܠܟܘܢ¶ §¶A 410
ܫܠܡܐ ܕܝܠܝ ܝܗܒܢܐ ܠܟܘܢ ܠܐ ܐܝܟܢܐ ܕܝܗܒ ܥܠܡܐ ܝܗܒܢܐ
ܠܟܘܢ ܠܐ ܢܬܬܪܗܒ ⌜ܠܒܟܘܢ⌝ ܘܠܐ ܢܕܚܠ ²⁸ܫܡܥܬܘܢ ܕܐܢܐ
ܐܡܪܬ [ܕܐܙܠܢܐ] ܘܐܬܐܢܐ [ܠܘܬܟܘܢ ܐܠܘ] [ܪܚܡܬܘܢ]
ܗܘܝܬܘܢ ܠܝ ⌜ܚܕܝܬܘܢ⌝ ܕܐܙ⌜ܠ⌝ܢܐ ܠܘܬ ܐܒܝ ܕܪܒ ܡܢܝ ²⁹ܘܗܫܐ
ܗܐ ¶ܐܡܪܬ ܠܟܘܢ ܥܕ ܠܐ ܢܗܘܐ ܕܡܐ ܕܗܘܐ ܬܗܝܡܢܘܢ ¶C
³⁰ܡܟܝܠ ܠܐ ܐܡܠܠ ܥܡܟܘܢ ܐܬܐ ܗܘ ܓܝܪ ܐܪܟܘܢܗ ܕܥܠܡܐ
ܘܒܝ ܠܝܬ ܠܗ ܡܕܡ. ³¹ܐܠܐ ܡܛܠ ܕܢܕܥ ܥܠܡܐ ܕܪܚܡ ܐܢܐ
ܠܐܒܝ ܐܝܟܢܐ ܕܦܩܕܢܝ ܐܒܝ ܗܟܢܐ ܥܒܕܢܐ. ܩܘܡܘ ܢܐܙܠ
ܡܟܐ. ¹ܐܢܐ ܐܢܐ ܓܦܬܐ ܕܫܪܪܐ ܘܐܒܝ ܗܘ ܦܠܚܐ. ²ܟܠ cf A 288
ܫܒܛܐ ܕܒܝ ܦܐܪܐ ܠܐ ܝܗܒܐ ܢܫܩܠܝܘܗ ⌜ܘܐܝܕܐ⌝ ܕܝܗܒܐ ܦܐܪܐ
ܢܕܟܝܘܗ ⌜ܕܬܬܠ⌝ ܦܐܪܐ ܣܓܝܐܐ * * ³ܘܗܟܝܢ ܕܟܘ ܐܢܬܘܢ ܕܟܝܢ
ܐܢܬܘܢ ܡܛܠ ܡܠܬܐ ܕܡܠܠܬ ܥܡܟܘܢ ⁴ܩܘܘ ܒܝ ܘܐܢܐ ܒܟܘܢ
ܐܝܟܢܐ ܕܫܒܫܬܐ ܠܐ ܡܫܟܚܐ ܕܬܬܠ ܦܐܪܐ [ܡܢ ܢܦܫܗ] ܐ⌜ܠ⌝ܐ
ܗܝܕܐ ܒܓܦܬܐ ܗܟܢܐ ܐܦܠܐ ܐܢܬܘܢ ܡܕܡ ܠܐ ܡܫܟܚܝܢ
ܐܢܬܘܢ ܠܒܪ ܡܢܝ ⁵ܕܐܢܐ ܓܦܬܐ ܘܐܢܬܘܢ ܫܒ̈ܫܬܐ ܡܢ ܕܒܝ
ܗܘܐ ܐܦ ܐܢܐ ܒܗ ܗܘ ܝܗܒ ܦܐܪ̈ܐ ܣܓܝܐܐ
ܡܛܠ ܕܒܠܥܕܝ ܡܕܡ ⌜ܠܡܥܒܕ⌝ ܠܐ ܡܫܟܚܝܢ ܐܢܬܘܢ ⁶ܘܡܢ ܕܠܐ
ܩܘܐ ܒܝ ܡܫܬܕܐ ܠܒܪ ܐܝܟ ܫܒܫܬܐ ܕܝܒܫܐ ܘܡܫܬܕܝܢܐ ܠܒܪ
ܘܠܩܛܝܢ ܘܪܡܝܢ ܠܗ ܒܢܘܪܐ ܕܬܐܩܕ. ⁷ܐܢ ܕܝܢ ܬܩܘܘܢ [ܒܝ
ܘܡ̈ܠܝ ܢܩܘܘܢ ܒܟܘܢ ܟܠ ܡܐ [ܕܨܒܝܢ] ܐܢܬܘܢ [ܠܡܫܐܠ

26 ܗܝ ܬܥܗܕܟܘܢ ܟܠ ܡܐ] *om. C* ܐܡܪܢܐ ܠܟܘܢ *C* 27 ܫܠܡܐ 1°] + ܕܝܠܝ *A* ܠܐ 1°] + ܗܘܐ *C* 28 ܕܐܢܐ ܐܡܪܬ] ܕܐܡܪܬ ܠܟܘܢ *C* ܠܝ] *so also S* ܚܕܝܬܘܢ] ܚܕܝܢ ܗܘܝܬܘܢ *C*; ܚܕܝܢ ܐܢܬܘܢ *S*ed ܕܐܙܠܢܐ] ܕܐܙܠ ܐܢܐ *C*; ܕܐܬܐܢܐ *S*ed 1 ܓܦܬܐ] ܟܪܡܐ *A* 288 *Ephr Cyrillona*: *see Introd.* vol. ii 5 ܫܒ̈ܫܬܐ] ܓܘܦ̈ܢܐ *A* 288 *Cyrillona*: *cf ver.* 1

26 but that Spirit, the Paraclete that §my Father will send to you in my *S* §*C*
name, it shall teach you everything, it shall remind you of all what
27 I say. §Peace I leave you;¶ peace, *even* mine, I give to you: not as §¶*A*410
the world giveth give I to you. Let not your heart be alarmed,
28 neither let it fear. Ye heard that I myself said [that I go] and come
[unto you; if] ye had [loved] me ye would rejoice that I go unto my
29 Father, who is greater than I. And now, lo,¶ I have said *it* to you, ¶*C*
before ever it happen, that what *time* it hath happened ye may
30 believe. Henceforth I shall not speak with you, for he cometh, the
31 ruler of the world, and in me he hath nothing. But because the world
shall know that I love my Father, as my Father hath commanded me
XV 1 so I do. Arise, let us go hence. I am the vine of truth and my Father *cf A*288
2 is the husbandman. Every vine that in me giveth not fruit will he take
away, and the one which giveth fruit he will cleanse that it may bring
3 forth much fruit. And already ye are clean because of the word that
4 I have spoken with you. Remain in me and I in you; as the shoot
cannot give fruit [of itself if] it be not set in the vine, so neither can
5 ye *do* aught apart from me, in that I *am* the vines and ye the shoots.
He that is in me *and* I also *come to* be in him, he giveth much fruit;
6 because without me nothing can ye do. And he that remaineth not in
me is thrown out as the shoot that withereth and is thrown out, and
7 they pluck and cast it into the fire that it may burn. But if ye remain
[in me and my words remain in you, all what] ye [wish to ask shall be

---

26 it shall remind you of all what] *om. C* I say] + to you *C* 27 Peace 1°] + *even* mine *A* 28 myself] *om. C* would rejoice] would have rejoiced *C* 1 the vine of truth] 'the vineyard of truth' *A* 288 *Ephr Cyrillona*: *see Introd.* vol. ii 5 shoots] 'vines' *A* 288 *Cyrillona*: *cf ver.* 1 *and see Introd.* vol. ii

S ܢܗܘܐ ܠܗܘܢ ⁸ܒܗܕܐ ܡܫܬܘܕܥܝܢ ܐܒܐ ܕܦܬ̈ܓܡܐ] ܘܠܓܒܪܐ ܬܬܠܘܢ
ܐܢܬܘܢ ܘܬܗܘܘܢ ܬܠܡܝܕܝ، ⁹ܐܝܟܢܐ ܕܐܫܕܪܢܝ ܐܒܐ ⌜ܐܢܐ⌝
ܐܫܕܪܬܟܘܢ ܗܘܘ ܒܐܘܪܚܬܝ، ¹⁰ܐܢ ܬܛܪܘܢ ܦܘܩܕܢܝ ܬܗܘܘܢ
ܒܚܘܒܝ ܐܝܟܢܐ ܕܢܛܪܬ ܦܘܩܕܢܘܗܝ، ܕܐܒܝ ܘܩܐܡ ܐܢܐ ܒܚܘܒܗ
¹¹ܗܠܝܢ ܡܠܠܬ ܥܡܟܘܢ ܕܚܕܘܬܝ، ܬܗܘܐ ܒܟܘܢ ܘܬܬܡܠܐ
§¶A12, 34, 256 ܚܕܘܬܟܘܢ §¹²ܗܢܘ ܦܘܩܕܢܝ ܕܬܚܒܘܢ ܚܕ ܠܚܕ¶ ܐܝܟܢܐ ܕܐܢܐ
ܐܚܒܬܟܘܢ ¹³ܚܘܒܐ ܕܪܒ. ܡܢ ܗܢܐ ܠܝܬ ܕܒܪ ܐܢܫ ܢܣܝܡ
ܢܦܫܗ ܚܠܦ ܪܚܡܘܗܝ، ¹⁴ܐܢܬܘܢ ܪܚܡܝ ܐܢܬܘܢ ܐܢ ܬܥܒܕܘܢ
ܟܠ ܕܡܦܩܕ ܐܢܐ ܠܟܘܢ ¹⁵ܠܐ ܡܟܝܠ ܩܪܐ ܠܟܘܢ ܥܒ̈ܕܐ
§A389 ܡܛܠ ܕܥܒܕܐ ܠܐ ܝܕܥ ܡܢܐ ܥܒܕ ܡܪܗ §ܪ̈ܚܡܝ ܕܝܢ ܩܪܝܬܟܘܢ
¶A ܡܛܠ ܕܟܠ ܕܫܡܥܬ ܡܢ ܐܒܝ ܐܘܕܥܬܟܘܢ.¶ ¹⁶ܘܠܐ ܗܘܐ
ܐܢܬܘܢ ܓܒܝܬܘܢܝ. ܐܠܐ ܐܢܐ ܓܒܝܬܟܘܢ ܘܣܡܬܟܘܢ
ܕܬܗܘܘܢ ܐܙܠܝܢ ܡܝܬܝܢ ܦܐܪ̈ܐ ⌜ܘ⌝⌜ܢܦܩܘܢ⌝ ܦܐܪܝܟܘܢ ܕܐܡܬܝ،
ܕܫܐܠܝܢ ܐܢܬܘܢ ܡܕܡ ܠܐܒܝ ܒܫܡܝ ܢܬܠ ܠܟܘܢ ¹⁷ܗܕܐ ܕܝܢ
ܡܦܩܕܢܐ ܠܟܘܢ ܕܬܗܘܘܢ ܪܚܡܝܢ ܚܕ ܠܚܕ. ¹⁸ܘܐܢ ܥܠܡܐ
§A484 ܣܢܐ ܠܟܘܢ ܕܥܘ ܕܠܝ ܣܢܐ ܡܢ ܩܕܡܝܟܘܢ ¹⁹ܘ§ܐܠܘ ܡܢ
¶A ܥܠܡܐ ܗܘܝܬܘܢ ܥܠܡܐ ܠܕܝܠܗ ܪܚܡ ܗܘܐ¶ ܐܠܐ ܠܐ
ܗܘܝܬܘܢ ܡܢ ܥܠܡܐ ܘܐܢܐ ܓܒܝܬܟܘܢ ܡܢܗ ܡܢ ܥܠܡܐ
ܡܛܠ ܗܢܐ ܣܢܐ ܠܟܘܢ ܥܠܡܐ ²⁰ܘܗܘܝܬܘܢ ܥܗܕܝܢ ܕܐܡܪܬ
§A484 ܠܟܘܢ ܕܠܝܬ ܥܒܕܐ ܕܪܒ ܡܢ ܡܪܗ §ܐܢ ܠܝ ܪ̈ܕܦܘ ܘܐܦ
ܠܟܘܢ ܢܪ̈ܕܦܘܢ؛ ܘܐܢ ܡܠܬܝ، ܫܡܥܘ ܘܢܛܪܘ ܘܐܦ ܕܝܠܟܘܢ
¶A ܢܛܪ̈ܘܢ ¶²¹ܗܠܝܢ ܟܠܗܝܢ ܢܥܒܕܘܢ ܒܟܘܢ ܡܛܠ ܫܡܝ ܕܠܐ ܡܛܠ
ܕܠܐ ܝܕܥܝܢ ܠܡܢ ܕܫܕܪܢܝ. ²²ܘܐܠܘ ܐܢܐ ܠܐ ܐܬܝܬ ܡܠܠܬ
ܥܡܗܘܢ ܠܝܬ ܗܘܐ ܠܗܘܢ ܚܛܗܝܢ. ܗܫܐ ܕܝܢ ܠܝܬ ܠܗܘܢ
ܥܠܠܐ ܥܠ ܐܦ ܚܛܗܝܗܘܢ؛ ²³ܡܛܠ ܕܡܢ ܕܠܝ ܣܢܐ ܐܦ ܠܐܒܝ
ܣܢܐ ²⁴ܘܐܠܘ ܥܒ̈ܕܐ ܠܐ ܥܒܕܬ ܒܝܢܬܗܘܢ ܕܐܚܪܢ ܠܐ ܥܒܕ

12 ܕܬܚܒܘܢ] ܕܬܪܚܡܘܢ $A^3/_3$; *cf ver.* 17   15 ܕܝܢ] *om. A*   20 *The clauses are transposed in A* 484; *cf also A* 414

8 to you. In this is the Father glorified, that] much [fruit] ye shall *S*
9 bring forth yourselves, and ye shall be my disciples. As the Father
hath been loving to me I have been loving to you; remain in my
10 affection. If ye keep my commandments ye will remain in my love,
as I have kept the commandments of my Father and remain in his love.
11 These things have I spoken with you, that my joy may be in you and
12 your joy may be complete. §This is my commandment, that ye be §¶*A* 12, 34, 256
13 loving one to the other¶ as I have been loving to you. Love greater
than this is there not, that a man lay down his life for his friends;
14, 15 ye are my friends if ye do what I am commanding you. Not hence-
forth do I call you slaves, because the slave knoweth not what his
lord doeth; §but my friends I have called you, because all that I have §*A* 389
16 heard from my Father I have made known to you.¶ And it is not ¶*A*
ye have chosen me, but I have chosen you and set you that ye should
be going *on* bringing forth fruit and your fruit should remain, that
whenever ye ask anything of my Father in my name he giveth *it* you.
17, 18 Now this I command you that ye should be loving one another. And
19 if the world hateth you, know that me it hated before you. And §if §*A* 484
of the world ye had been, the world its own would have loved;¶ ¶*A*
but ye are not of the world, and I have chosen you from the world,
20 therefore the world hateth you. And be recollecting that I said
to you There is no slave greater than his lord. §If me they §*A* 484
have persecuted, you also they will persecute; and if my word they
21 have heard and kept, yours also they *will* keep.¶ All these things ¶*A*
they will do with you because of my name, *even* mine, because
22 they know not him that sent me. And if I had not come *and*
spoken with them, they would have had no sins; but now they have
23 no excuse for their sins, because he that hateth me hateth my
24 Father also. And if deeds I had not done in their sight that

---

12 be loving to] love $A^{3}/_{3}$; *cf ver.* 17 15 but] *om. A* 20 *The clauses are transposed in A* 484; *cf also A* 414

ܐܝܢ܆ ܠܝܬ ܗܘܘ ܠܗܘܢ ⸢ܫ̈ܠܗܝܢ⸣ ܗܫܐ ܕܝܢ ⸢ܚܙܘܢ⸣ ܘܠܝ ܣܢܝܢ S
ܘܠܐܒܝ ܗܢܝܢ [25]ܐܠܐ ܕ⸢ܬ⸣ܬܡܠܐ ܡܠܬܐ ܕܟܬܝܒܐ ܒܢܡܘܣܗܘܢ܆
ܕܗ⸢ܝ⸣ܡܢܘܢ ܡܓܢ [26]ܡܐ ܕܝܢ ܕܐܬܐ ܦܪܩܠܛܐ ܕܡܫܕܪܢܐ ܠܟܘܢ ܡܢ
ܠܘܬ ܐܒܝ ܪܘܚܐ ܕܫܪܪܐ ܕܡܢ ܩܕܡ ܐܒܝ ܢܦܩܐ ܗܘ ܢܣܗܕ ܥܠ
[27]ܐܦ ܐܢܬܘܢ ܣܗܕܝܢ ܐܢܬܘܢ ܕܡܢ ܩܕܡ ܥܡܝ ܗܘܝܬܘܢ
[1]ܗܠܝܢ ܕܝܢ ܡܠܠܬ ܥܡܟܘܢ ܕܠܐ ܬܬܟܫܠܘܢ܆ [2]ܢܦܩܘܢܟܘܢ ܓܝܪ
ܡܢ ܒܢܘܫܬܗܘܢ ܘܬܐܬܐ ܫܥܬܐ ܕܟܠ ܕܢܩܛܠܟܘܢ ܢܣܒܪ
ܕܐܠܗܐ ܦܠܚ [4]ܗܠܝܢ ܡܠܠܬ ܥܡܟܘܢ ܕܡܐ ܕܐܬܬ ܫܥܬܐ
ܬܥܗܕܘܢ ܕܐܡܪܬ ܠܟܘܢ ܗܠܝܢ ܕܠܐ ܐܡܪܬ ܠܟܘܢ ܡܢ
ܩܕܡ ܡܛܠ ܕܥܡܟܘܢ ܗܘܝܬ [5]ܗܫܐ ܕܝܢ ܕܐܙܠܢܐ ܠܘܬ ܡܢ
ܕܫܕܪܢܝ ܠܐ ܐܢܫ ܡܢܟܘܢ ܡܫܐܠ ܠܝ ܠܐܝܟܐ ܐܙܠ ܐܢܬ
[6]ܡܛܠ ܕܐܡܪܬ ܠܟܘܢ ܓܝܪ ܗܠܝܢ ܘܐܬܬ ܟܪܝܘܬܐ ܘܡܠܬ
ܠܒܘܬܟܘܢ [7]ܐܠܐ ܐܢܐ ܫܪܪܐ ܐܡܪܢܐ ܠܟܘܢ܆ ܕܦܩܚ ܠܟܘܢ
ܕܐܢܐ ܐܙܠ ܡܛܠ ܕܐܢ ܐܢܐ ܠܐ ܐܙܠܢܐ ܦܪܩܠܛܐ ܠܐ ܐܬܐ
ܠܘܬܟܘܢ. ܡܐ ܕܐܙܠܬ ܕܝܢ ܡܫܕܪܢܐ ܠܟܘܢ ܦܪܩܠܛܐ [8]ܡܐ
ܕܐܬܐ ܕܝܢ ܗܘ ܢܟܣܘܗܝ, ܠܥܠܡܐ ܒܚ̈ܛܗܘܗܝ, ܘܥܠ ܙܕܝܩܘܬܗ
ܘܥܠ ܕܝܢܐ. [9]ܘܥܠ ܚ̈ܛܝܐ ܕܠܐ ܗܝܡܢܘ ܒܝ [10]ܘܥܠ ܙܕܝܩܘܬܐ
ܕܝܢ ܕܠܘܬ ܐܒܝ ܐܙܠܢܐ ⸢ܘ⸣ܡܟܝܠ ܠܐ ܬܚܙܘܢ ܠܝ ܐܢܬܘܢ ܠܝ [11]ܥܠ
ܕܝܢܐ ܕܝܢ ܕܐܪܟܘܢܗ ܕܥܠܡܐ ܗܢܐ ܕܝܢ ܗܘ [12]ܥܘܕ ܐܝܬ
ܠܝ ܠܡܐܡܪ ܠܟܘܢ ܐܠܐ ܠܐ ܡܫܟܚܝܢ ܐܢܬܘܢ ܠܡܫܩܠܘ
ܫܡܥܝܢ [13]ܡܐ ܕܐܬܬ ܕܝܢ ܪܘܚܐ ܕܫܪܪܐ ܗܝ, ܬܕܒܪܟܘܢ ܒܟܘܠܗ
ܫܪܪܐ. ܡܛܠ ܕܠܐ ܬܡܠܠ ܡܢ ܪܥܝܢ ܢܦܫܗ ܐܠܐ ܟܠ ܕܬܫܡܥ
ܗܘ ܬܐܡܪ ܘܥܠ ܟܠ ܡܐ ܕܐܬܐ ܬܣܒܪܟܘܢ [14]ܗܘ, ܬܫܒܚܢܝ
ܡܛܠ ܕܡܢ ܕܝܠܝ ܬܣܒ ܗܝ, ܘܬܣܒܪܟܘܢ [15]ܡ⸢ܕ⸣ܡ ܕܐܝܬ ܠܐܒܝ
ܕܝܠܝ ܗܘ ܡܛܠ ܗܢܐ ܐܡܪܬ ܠܟܘܢ ܕܡܢ ܕܝܠܝ ܬܣ⸢ܒ⸣. ܘܬܣܒܪܟܘܢ
[16]ܩܠܝܠ ܘܠܐ ܬܚܙܘܢܢܝ ܘܬܘܒ ܩܠܝܠ ܘܬܚܙܘܢܢܝ ܕܐܙܠ ܐܢܐ ܠܘܬ
ܐܒܝ [17]ܘܐܡܪ̈ܝܢ ܬܠܡܝܕܘܗܝ, ܚܕ ܠܚܕ: ܡܢܐ ܗܝ, ܗܕܐ ܕܐܡܪ

---

24 ܚܙܘܢ] * * ܚܙܘ S^{ed} 25 ܕܢܬܡܠܐ S^{ed} ܕܗܝܡܢܘܢ S^{ed} 5 ܐܙܠ] S (*sic*) 10 ܘܡܟܝܠ] ܘܡܗܟܝܠ S^{ed} 15 ܡܕܡ] ܕܡܕܡ S^{ed}

no other hath done, they would have had no sins; but now S
they have seen [me], and me they hate and my Father they hate—
25 but because the word should be accomplished that is written in
26 their Law, *namely* 'They have hated me for naught.' But what
time the Paraclete cometh that I am sending to you from my Father,
the Spirit of truth that from before my Father goeth forth, he shall
27 bear witness of me. Ye also bear witness, ye that from of old with
xvi 1 me have been. Now these things have I spoken with you that ye
2 be not offended. For they will send you forth from their synagogues,
and the hour will come that he that shall kill you will suppose that
4 to God he is doing service. These things have I spoken among you,
that what *time* the hour hath come ye may recollect that I said to
you these things that I said not to you from of old, because I was
5 with you. But now that I go unto him that sent me, no one of you
6 asketh me 'Whither goest thou?' For because I have said to you
7 these things, grief hath come and hath filled your hearts. But I—the
truth I tell you—it is profitable for you that I go, because if I go not
the Paraclete cometh not unto you, but what *time* I have gone I send
8 you the Paraclete. Now what *time* he hath come he will reprove the
world in its sins and about his righteousness and about judgement,
9 10, and about sinners that they believed not in me, and then about
righteousness that unto my Father I go and henceforth again ye do
11 not see me, but about judgement that the ruler of this world is judged.
12 Much have I to say to you, but ye are not able to take *it* to-day;
13 but what *time* the Spirit of truth hath come, it shall lead you into all
truth, because it will not speak from the mind of its *own* self, but all
that it shall hear that will it say, and about all what cometh it will
14 announce to you. And it will glorify me, because from mine it will
15 take and will announce *it* to you. That which my Father hath is
mine, therefore I have said to you that from mine it will take and
16 will announce *it* to you. A little and ye will not see me, and
17 again a little and ye will see me, for I go unto my Father." And his
disciples say one to the other: "What is this that he saith 'A little

ܕܥܠܝܠ ܘܠܐ ܬܚܙܘܢܢܝ ܘܬܘܒ ܥܠܝܠ ܘܬܚܙܘܢܢܝ ܘܕܐܡܪ ܕܐܙܠ S
ܐܢܐ ܠܝ ܠܘܬ ܐܒܝ. 18ܡܢܘ ܒ ܗܢܐ ܥܠܝܠ ܕܐܡܪ 19ܝܕܥ ܕܝܢ
ܝܫ ܗܢܐ ܒܥܝܢ ܗܘܘ ܠܡܫܐܠܘܬܗ ܐܡܪ ܠܗܘܢ ܡܒܥܐ
ܒܥܝܢ ܐܢܬܘܢ ܠܗܕܐ ܕܐܡܪܬ ܠܟܘܢ ܕܥܠܝܠ ܘܠܐ ܬܚܙܘܢܢܝ
ܘܬܘܒ ܥܠܝܠ ܘܬܚܙܘܢܢܝ 20ܐܡܝܢ ܐܡܝܢ ܐܡܪ ܐܢܐ ܠܟܘܢ
ܕܬܒܟܘܢ ܘܬܐܠܘܢ ܘܬܬܥܝܩܘܢ ܘܥܠܡܐ ܢܚܕܐ ܐܢܬܘܢ
ܬܐܓܦܘܢ ܐܠܐ ܒܪܘܬܟܘܢ ܠܚܕܘܬܐ ܬܗܘܐ. 21ܐܢܬܬܐ
ܡܐ ܕܝܠܕܐ ܟܪܝܐ ܗܝ, ܠܗ ܡܛܠ ܕܡܛܐ ܝܘܡܐ ܕܡܘܠܕܗ ܘܡܐ
ܕܝܠܕܬ ܒܪܐ ܠܐ ܥܗܕܐ ܐܘܠܨܢܗ ܡܛܠ ܚܕܘܬܐ ܕܐܬܝܠܕ ܒܪ
ܐܢܫܐ ܒܥܠܡܐ. 22ܘܐܦ ܐܢܬܘܢ ܗܫܐ ܟܪܝܐ ܠܟܘܢ ܬܘܒ
[ܕܝܢ ܐܚܙ]ܟܘܢ ܘܢܚܕܐ ܠܒܟܘܢ ܘܚܕܘܬܟܘܢ ܠܐ ܐܢܫ ܢܣܒ
ܡܢܟܘܢ 23ܘܒܗܘ ܝܘܡܐ ܡܕܡ ܠܐ ܬܫܐܠܘܢ ܡܢܝ ܐܡܝܢ
ܐܡܝܢ ܐܡܪܢܐ ܠܟܘܢ ܕܟܠ ܡܐ ܕܬܫܐܠܘܢ ܠܐܒܝ ܒܫܡܝ
ܢܬܠ ܠܟܘܢ 24ܥܕܡܐ ܠܗܫܐ ܠܐ ܫܐܠܬܘܢ ܒܫܡܝ ܫܐܠܘ
ܘܬܣܒܘܢ ܕܬܗܘܐ ܚܕܘܬܟܘܢ ܡܫܡܠܝܐ. 25ܗܠܝܢ ܡܠܠܬ
ܥܡܟܘܢ ܒܦܠܐܬܐ ܐܬܝܐ ܕܝܢ ܫܥܬܐ ܕܒܓܠܝܐ ܐܫܘܕܥܟܘܢ
ܥܠ ܐܒܝ 26ܒܗܘ ܝܘܡܐ ܬܫܐܠܘܢ ܒܫܡܝ ܘܠܐ ܐܡܪܢܐ ܠܟܘܢ
ܕܐܢܐ ܐܒܥܐ ܡܢ ܐܒܝ ܥܠ ܐܦ̈ܝܟܘܢ 27ܐܠܐ ܗܘ ܐܒܝ ܪܚܡܟܘܢ
ܕܐܢܬܘܢ ܪܚܡܬܘܢܢܝ ܘܗܝܡܢܬܘܢ ܕܡܢ ܠܘܬ ܐܠܗܐ ܢܦܩܬ
28ܐܬܝܬ ܠܥܠܡܐ ܘܬܘܒ ܐܙܠ ܐܢܐ ܠܘܬ ܐܒܐ 29ܐܡܪܘ ܠܗ
ܬܠܡܝܕܘܗܝ, ܗܐ ܐܦ ܗܫܐ ܦܪܝܣܐܝܬ ܡܡܠܠ ܐܢܬ ܘܦܠܐܬܐ
ܐܦܠܐ ܚܕܐ ܐܡܪܬ ܠܝ 30ܗܫܐ ܝܕܥܝܢ ܐܚܢܢ ܕܟܠ ܡܕܡ ܝܕܥ
ܐܢܬ ܘܠܐ ܣܢܝܩ ܐܢܬ ܕܠܐܢܫ ܬܫܐܠ ܒܗܕܐ ܡܗܝܡܢܝܢ ܐܚܢܢ
ܕܡܢ ܐܠܗܐ ܐܫܬܕܪܬ 31ܐܡܪ ܠܗܘܢ ܝܫܘܥ ܗܫܐ ܗܐ
ܡܗܝܡܢܝܢ ܐܢܬܘܢ ܠܝ 32ܗܐ ܐܬܝܐ ܫܥܬܐ ܘܐܬܬ ܕܬܬܒܕܪܘܢ
ܐܢܫ ܠܐܬܪܗ ܘܬܫܒܩܘܢܢܝ ܒܠܚܘܕܝ, ܘܠܐ ܗܘܝܬ ܒܠܚܘܕܝ, ܕܐܒܐ
ܥܡܝ ܗܘ· 33ܗܠܝܢ ܐܡܪܬ ܕܬܗܘܐ ܠܟܘܢ ܒܝ ܫܠܡܐ ܘܒܥܠܡܐ

19 ܒܥܝܢ 1°] ܕܒܥܝܢ S^{ed}

and ye will not see me, and again a little and ye will see me,' and that S
18 he saith 'I go away unto my Father'? What is then this 'A little'
19 that he saith?" Now Jesus knew what they were seeking to ask
him. He saith to them: "Do ye indeed seek this that I said to you
'A little and ye will not see me, and again a little and ye will see me'?
20 Amen, amen, I say to you Ye will weep and wail and groan, and the
world will rejoice; ye will be anxious, but your grief will become joy.
21 A woman what *time* she is giving birth it grieveth her, because the day
of her child-bearing hath arrived, and what *time* she hath given birth
to a son she doth not recollect her distress, because of the joy that a
22 human being hath been born in the world. And ye also now it
grieveth you, [but] again [I shall see] you and your heart will rejoice
23 and your joy no one taketh from you. And in that day nothing shall
ye ask of me: amen, amen, I say to you All what ye shall ask of
24 my Father in my name he will give to you. Until now ye have not
asked in my name; ask and ye shall receive, that your joy may be
25 completed. These things have I spoken with you in parables, but
the hour cometh that openly I will shew you concerning my Father.
26 In that day ye shall ask in my name, and I say not to you that I will
27 beseech my Father on behalf of you, but my Father himself hath
loved you that ye have loved me, and that ye have believed that from
28 God I have come forth *and* come to the world and again I go unto
29 the Father." His disciples said to him: "Lo, now also plainly dost
30 thou speak, and not even one parable hast thou said to us; now
know we that everything thou knowest, and needest not that any
one thou shouldest ask: by this we believe that from God thou hast
31, 32 been sent." Jesus saith to them: "Now, lo, ye believe me; lo, the
hour cometh and hath come that ye will be scattered each to his
place, and ye will leave me alone—and I am not alone, in that the
33 Father is with me. These things have I said that there may be to
you in me peace and in the world there may be to you distress; but

S §¶A 134 ܢܗܘܐ ܠܗܘܢ. ܐܘܠܨܢܐ ܐܠܐ ܠܐ ܬܬܕܘܠܘܢ. §ܐܝܟ ܠܒܪ ܕܒܝܬܗ
ܠܥܠܡܐ.¶ ¹ܗܟܢ ܐܡܪ ܗܠܝܢ ܢܫܒܘܩ ܐܢܫ ܒܝܬܗ، ܠܡܫܡܫܢܘܬܐ
ܘܐܡܪ ܐܦ ܐܬܬܐ ܫܒܘܩܬܐ ܫܒܘܩ ܒܪܢ ܕܒܢܝܢ ܢܫܒܘܩܝܢ ²ܐܝܟܢܐ
ܕܢܫܒܘܩ ܠܗ ܫܘܠܛܢܐ ܥܠ ܟܘܠ ܒܣܪ ܕܟܠ ܡܢܐ ܕܢܫܒܘܩ ܠܗ
ܢܬܠ ܠܗ ܚܝܐ ܕܠܥܠܡ. ³ܗܠܝܢ ܐܢܘܢ ܚܝܐ ܕܠܥܠܡ ܕܢܝܕܥܘܢ
ܕܠܫܘܕܝܢ ܐܝܬ ܐܠܗܐ ܕܫܪܝܪܐ ܘܠܗܝܢ ܕܫܪܪܬ ܠܥܩܒ ܡܫܝܚܐ·
⁴ܐܝܟ ܫܒܝܩܘܬܢ ܒܐܪܥܐ. ܘܡܒܥܐ ܗܘ ܕܢܫܒܘܩ ܠܝ ܕܐܚܒܒ.
ܫܠܡܘܬܗ ⁵ܘܐܦ ܗܫܐ ܗܘ ܠܝ ܫܘܒܩܢܐ ܐܝܬ ܐܟܢ ܡܢ ܠܘܬܟ
ܡܢ ܗܘ ܕܢܫܒܘܩ ܠܝ ܒܕܠܐ ܢܗܘܐ ܥܠܡܐ ⁶ܘܟܠܝܬ ܫܒܩܢ ܠܟܠ
ܐܢܫܐ ܕܢܫܒܘܩ ܠܝ ܡܢ ܥܠܡܐ ܕܕܝܠܟ ܗܘܘ ܘܠܝ ܢܫܒܘܩ ܐܢܘܢ.
ܘܡܠܬܟ ܢܛܪܘ ⁷ܘܗܫܐ ܝܕܥܘ ܕܟܠ ܡܐ ܕܢܫܒܘܩ ܠܝ ܡܢ ܠܘܬܟ
ܗܘ ⁸ܡܛܠ ܕܡܠܐ ܕܢܫܒܘܩ ܠܝ ܝܗܒܬ ܐܢܐ ܠܗܘܢ. ܘܗܢܘܢ ܩܒܠܘ ܐܝܟ
ܡܢܝ ܘܝܕܥܘ ܫܪܝܪܐܝܬ ܕܡܢܟ ܢܦܩܬ ܘܗܝܡܢܘ ܕܐܢܬ ܫܕܪܬܢܝ.
⁹ܘܐܢܐ ܥܠ ܐܦܝܗܘܢ ܒܥܐ ܘܠܐ ܒܥܐ ܥܠ ܐܦܝ ܥܠܡܐ
ܐܠܐ ܥܠ ܗܢܘܢ ܕܝܗܒܬ ܠܝ ܕܕܝܠܟ ܐܢܘܢ. ¹⁰ܘܟܠ ܡܕܡ
ܕܕܝܠܝ ܗܘ ܕܝܠܟ ܗܘ. ܘܡܕܡ ܕܕܝܠܟ ܗܘ. ܕܝܠܝ ܗܘ. ܘܡܫܬܒܚ
ܐܢܐ ܒܗܘܢ. ¹¹ܘܡܟܝܠ ܠܐ ܗܘܝܬ ܒܥܠܡܐ ܘܗܠܝܢ ܒܥܠܡܐ
ܐܢܘܢ. ܘܐܢܐ ܐܬܐ ܐܢܐ ܠܘܬܟ. ܐܒܐ ܩܕܝܫܐ ܛܪ ܐܢܘܢ
ܒܫܡܟ ¹²ܟܕ ܥܡܗܘܢ ܗܘܝܬ ܒܥܠܡܐ ܐܢܐ ܢܛܪ ܗܘܝܬ ܠܗܘܢ
ܒܫܡܟ ܘܠܐ ܐܢܫ ܡܢܗܘܢ ܐܒܕ. ܐܠܐ ܐܢ ܒܪܗ ܕܐܒܕܢܐ
ܕܢܬܡܠܐ ܟܬܒܐ ܕܐܡܪ. ¹³ܗܫܐ ܠܘܬܟ ܐܬܐ ܐܢܐ ܘܗܠܝܢ ܡܡܠܠ ܐܢܐ
ܒܥܠܡܐ ܕܢܗܘܘܢ ⌜ܡܠܝܢ⌝ ܡܢ ⌜ܚܕܘܬܝ⌝، ¹⁴ܐܢܐ ܝܗܒܬ ܠܗܘܢ
ܡܠܬܟ ܘܥܠܡܐ ܣܢܐ ܐܢܘܢ. ܡܛܠ ܕܠܐ ܗܘܘ ܡܢܗ ¹⁵ܠܐ
ܗܘܐ ܕܬܫܩܘܠ ܐܢܘܢ ܡܢ ܥܠܡܐ ܒܥܐ ܡܢܝ ܐܠܐ ܕܬܛܪ
ܐܢܘܢ ܡܢ ܒܝܫܐ ¹⁶ܠܐ ⌜ܗܘܘ⌝ ܓܝܪ ܡܢܗ ܡܢ ܥܠܡܐ ܐܝܟܢܐ
ܕܐܢܐ ܠܐ ܗܘܝܬ ܡܢܗ ¹⁷ܩܕܫ ܐܢܘܢ ܒܫܪܪܟ ܡܛܠ ܕܡܠܬܟ

---

33 ܠܒܪ] *om. A*   16 ܠܐ ܗܘܝܬܘܢ ܡܢ ܥܠܡܐ. ܐܝܟ ܕܐܢܐ ܠܐ ܗܘܝܬ ܡܢܗ *A* 484; *the last clause occurs also in A* 414

xvii 1 fear ye not, §for I have overcome the world."¶ And when Jesus said S §¶A 134
these things he lifted up his eyes to heaven and said: "My Father,
the hour hath come; glorify thy son, that thy son may glorify thee,
2 as thou hast given him authority over all flesh, that all what thou
3 hast given him he may give to it life eternal. This is life eternal,
that they should know thee, that alone art the God of truth, and him
4 that thou didst send, Jesus the Messiah. I have glorified thee in the
5 earth, and the deed which thou gavest me to do I have finished. And
now also give me glory, *even* thou my Father, from thyself, from that
6 which thou gavest me before ever the world was. And I have
revealed thy name to the men that thou gavest me from the world,
seeing that thine they were and to me didst thou give them and thy
7 word they have kept. And now I know that all what thou hast given
8 me is from thyself, because the words that thou didst give to me I
have given to them, and they have received them from me and they
have known truly that from thee I came forth and they have believed
9 that thou hast sent me. And I on their behalf do beseech, and I do
not beseech on behalf of the world, but for them that thou hast
10 given me, *seeing* that thine they are. And everything that is mine is
thine, and that which is thine is mine, and I am glorified in them.
11 And henceforth I am not in the world and these are in the world, and
I come away unto thee; my holy Father, take *and* keep them in thy
12 name. When with them I was in the world I was keeping them in
thy name, and none of them hath perished save the son of perdition,
13 that what was written might be accomplished. Now unto thee do I
come, and these things I speak in the world that they may be full of
14 my joy. I have given to them thy word, and the world hath hated
15 them, because they were not of it. Not that thou shouldest take
them away from the world do I beseech thee, but that thou shouldest
16 keep them from the Evil One; for they are not of this same world,
17 even as I myself am not of it. Hallow them in thy truth, because

33 for] *om. A* 16 'Ye are not of the world, as I myself am not of it' *A* 484; *the last clause occurs also in A* 414

ܫܪܪܐ ܗܝ [18]ܐܝܟܢܐ ܕܐܢܬ ܫܕܪܬܢܝ ܠܥܠܡܐ ܐܦ ܐܢܐ ܫܕܪܬ S
ܐܢܘܢ ܠܥܠܡܐ [19]ܘܥܠ ܐܦܝܗܘܢ ܡܩܕܫܢܐ ܢܦܫܝ ܕܐܦ ܗܢܘܢ
ܢܗܘܘܢ ܡܩܕܫܝܢ ܒܫܪܪܐ [20]ܘܠܐ ܗܘܐ ܥܠ ܐܦ ܗܠܝܢ ܒܥܢܐ
ܡܢܟ ܒܠܚܘܕܝܗܘܢ ܐܠܐ ܐܦ ܥܠ ܗܢܘܢ ܕܡܗܝܡܢܝܢ ܒܝ
ܒܡܠܬܗܘܢ [21]ܕܟܠܗܘܢ ܢܗܘܘܢ ܚܕ ܐܝܟܢܐ ܕܐܢܬ [ܐܒܝ ܒܝ]
ܘܐܢܐ ܒܟ ܕܐܦ ܗܢܘܢ ܢܬ * * ܢ ܕܢܗܝܡܢ ܥܠܡܐ ܕܐܢܬ
ܫܕܪܬܢܝ [22]ܘܐܢܐ ܫܘܒܚܐ ܗܘ ܕܝܗܒܬ ܠܝ ܝܗܒܬ ܠܗܘܢ ܕܢܗܘܘܢ
ܚܕ ܐܝܟܢܐ ܕܐܚܢܢ ܚܕ. [23]ܐܢܐ ܐܗܘܐ ܒܗܘܢ ܘܐܢܬ ܒܝ
ܕܢܗܘܘܢ ܓܡܝܪܝܢ ܠܚܕ ܕܢܕܥ ܥܠܡܐ ܕܐܢܬ ܫܠܚܬܢܝ ܘܐܚܒܬ
ܐܢܘܢ ܐܝܟ ܕܠܝ ܐܚܒܬ [24]ܘܡܕܡ ܕܝܗܒܬ ܠܝ ܨܒܝܢܐ ܕܐܬܪ
ܕܐܢܐ ܐܦ ܗܢܘܢ ܢܗܘܘܢ ܥܡܝ ܚܙܝܢ ܫܘܒܚܐ
ܕܝܗܒܬ ܠܝ. ܕܐܚܒܬܢܝ ܡܢ ܩܕܡ ܕܢܗܘܐ ܥܠܡܐ [25]ܐܒܝ ܟܐܢܐ
ܘܥܠܡܐ ܠܐ ܝܕܥܟ ܐܢܐ ܕܝܢ ܝܕܥܬܟ ܘܗܢܘܢ ܝܕܥܘ ܕܐܢܬ
ܫܕܪܬܢܝ. [26]ܘܐܘܕܥܬ ܐܢܘܢ ܫܡܟ. ܘܐܘܕܥ ܐܢܘܢ ܕܚܘܒܐ ܗܘ
ܕܐܚܒܬܢܝ ܢܗܘܐ ܒܗܘܢ ܘܐܦ ܐܢܐ ܐܗܘܐ ܒܗܘܢ ܀ ܀
[1]ܗܠܝܢ ܡܠܠ ܝܫܘܥ ܘܢܦܩ ܥܡ ܬܠܡܝܕܘܗܝ ܠܥܒܪܐ ܕܪܓܠܬܐ
ܕܩܕܪܘܢ ܛܘܪܐ. ܐܬܪ ܕܐܝܬ ܗܘܬ ܓܢܬܐ ܘܥܠ ܠܬܡܢ ܗܘ
ܘܬܠܡܝܕܘܗܝ. [2]ܝܗܘܕܐ ܕܝܢ ܡܫܠܡܢܐ ܝܕܥ ܗܘܐ ܠܗ ܠܗܿ ܕܘܟܬܐ
ܡܛܠ ܕܙܒܢܝܢ ܣܓܝ̈ܐܢ ܟܢܫ ܗܘܐ ܬܡܢ ܝܫܘܥ ܥܡ ܬܠܡܝܕܘܗܝ
[3]ܝܗܘܕܐ ܕܝܢ ܡܫܠܡܢܐ ܕܒܪ ܒܗ ܐܣܦܝܪ ܘܡܢ ܪ̈ܒܝ ܟܗ̈ܢܐ
ܘܦܪ̈ܝܫܐ ܘܕ̈ܫܝܐ ܘܡܢܝܢܐ ܕܕܒܪܐ ܒܪ ܫܡܥܝܢ ܢܗܘܪܐ ܘܠܡܦ̈ܐܕܐ
ܘܐܬܐ ܬܡܢ [4]ܘܟܕ ܚܙܐ ܝܫܘܥ ܟܠ ܡܕܡ ܕܐܬܐ ܠܘܬܗ ܢܦܩ
ܐܡܪ ܠܗܘܢ ܠܡܢܐ ܒܥܝܢ ܐܢܬܘܢ [5]ܐܡܪܝܢ ܠܗ ܠܝܫܘܥ ܢܨܪܝܐ
ܐܡܪ ܠܗܘܢ ܐܢܐ ܐܢܐ ܘܩܐܡ ܗܘܐ ܕܝܢ ܐܦ ܝܗܘܕܐ ܠܘܬܗܘܢ
[6]ܘܟܕ ܐܡܪ ܗܠܝܢ ܝܫܘܥ ܕܐܢܐ ܐܢܐ ܐܙܠܘ ܠܒܣܬܪܗܘܢ ܘܢܦܠܘ
ܥܠ ܐܪܥܐ. [7]ܘܬܘܒ ܐܡܪ ܠܗܘܢ ܝܫܘܥ ܠܡܢ ܒܥܝܢ ܐܢܬܘܢ

---

21 ܢܬ * * ܢ] *A possible restoration is* ܢܬܝܚܕܘܢ 22 ܗܘ] *S* (*sic*) 26 ܐܢܘܢ] *S* (*sic*) 2 ܣܓܝ̈ܐ] *S* (*end of line*), *cf* Joh vii 31

18 thy word is truth. Even as thou didst send me to the world I also *S*
19 have sent them to the world, and on their behalf I hallow myself that
20 they also may be hallowed in truth. And not on behalf of these do
I beseech thee—these alone, but also on behalf of those that believe
21 from their word, that all of them may become one, even as thou, [my
Father, in me] and I in thee that they also may be * * that the
22 world may believe that thou hast sent me. And I—the glory which
thou gavest me I have given to them, that they may be one even
23 as we are one. I shall be with them and thou with me, that they
may become perfected into one, that the world may know that thou
hast sent me, and I have been loving to them as to me, Father,
24 thou hast been loving. And that which thou hast given to me, I
wish that where I *am* they also may be with me, that they may be
seeing the glory that thou hast given to me, and that thou hast been
25 loving to me from before the world was. My upright Father, and
the world knew thee not, but I knew thee and they knew that thou
26 didst send me; and I have made known to them thy name and will
make them known, that the love wherewith thou hast been loving to
me may be in them, and I also will be in them."

xviii 1 These things spake Jesus and went forth with his disciples to the
other side of the torrent of Cedron, a hill where there was a
2 garden, and he entered thither, he and his disciples. Now Judas
the betrayer used to know that place, because many times used
3 Jesus to gather there with his disciples. Now Judas the betrayer
brought with him a cohort and *some* of the chief priests and Pharisees
and guards and a multitude of the people carrying lanterns and
4 torches, and came there. And when Jesus saw all what had come upon
5 him, he went forth *and* said to them: "What seek ye?" They say to
him: "Jesus the Nazarene." He saith to them: "I am *he*." Now
6 Judas also was standing by them. And when Jesus said these
7 things "I am *he*," they went back and fell on the earth. And again
Jesus saith to them: "Whom seek ye?" They say to him: "Jesus

21 * *] *The suggested restoration means* 'united' 23 sent] *cf* Matt xi 2 26 them 2°] *S* (*sic*) 1 Cedron, a hill] *cf* 'the lake (*or*, fruit-garden) of Cedron the hill, the place where....' Diat[ar] xlviii 1 (*sic*)

ܐܡܪܝܢ ܠܗ ܠܝܫܘܥ ܢܨܪܝܐ. ⁸ܐܡܪ ܠܗܘܢ ܐܡܪܬ ܠܟܘܢ ܕܐܢܐ S
ܐܢܐ ܐܢ ܠܝ ܒܥܝܢ ܐܢܬܘܢ ܫܒܘܩܘ ܐܠܝܢ. ⁹ܕܬܬܡܠܐ ܡܠܬܐ
ܗ̇ ܕܐܡܪ ܗܘܐ ܕܐܝܠܝܢ ܕܝܗܒܬ ܠܝ. ܠܐ ܐܘܒܕܬ ܡܢܗܘܢ
¹⁰ܫܡܥܘܢ ܕܝܢ ܟܐܦܐ ܫܡܛ ܣܦܣܐ ܘܡܚܝܗ̇ ܠܥܒܕܗ ܕܪܒ
ܟܗܢܐ ܘܫܩܠܗ ܐܕܢܗ ܕܝܡܝܢܐ. ܘܫܡܗ ܕܥܒܕܐ ܡܠܟܘ. ¹¹ܘܐܡܪ
ܝܫܘܥ ܠܟܐܦܐ ܐܗܦܟ ܣܦܣܟ ܠܬܢܬܗ ܟܣܐ ܕܝܗܒ ܠܝ ܐܒܝ
ܠܐ ܐܫܬܝܘܗܝ. ¹²ܗܘ ܐܣܦܝܪ ܘܟܠܝܪܟܐ ܘܕܚܫܐ ܕܝܗܘܕܝܐ
ܐܚܕܘܗܝ. ¹³ܘܐܝܬܝܘܗܝ. ܠܘܩܕܡ ܠܘܬ ܚܢܢ ܚܡܘܗܝ. ܕܩܝܦܐ ܕܗܘ
ܗܘܐ ܪܒ ܟܗܢܐ ܕܗ̇ ܫܢܬܐ. ²⁴ܚܢܢ ܕܝܢ ܫܕܪܗ ܟܕ ܐܣܝܪ ܠܘܬ
ܩܝܦܐ ܪܒ ܟܗܢܐ ¹⁴ܗܘ ܕܡܠܟ ܗܘܐ ܠܝܗܘܕܝܐ ܕܦܐܐ ܕܚܕ
ܓܒܪܐ ܢܡܘܬ ܚܠܦ ܥܡܐ. ¹⁵ܫܡܥܘܢ ܕܝܢ ܟܐܦܐ ܘܚܕ ܡܢ
†ܬܠܡܝܕܐ ܡܫܡܫܢܬܗ ܗܘܐ ܕܪܒ ܟܗܢܐ ܡܛܠ ܗܢܐ ܥܠ ܥܡ
ܝܫܘܥ ܠܕܪܬܐ ܀

¹⁹ܪܒ ܟܗܢܐ ܕܝܢ ܡܫܐܠ ܗܘܐ ܠܗ ܠܝܫܘܥ ܥܠ ܬܠܡܝܕܘܗܝ. ܡܢ
ܐܝܢܐ ܗܢܘܢ ܘܥܠ ܝܘܠܦܢܗ. ܐܝܟܢܐ ܗܘ ²⁰ܐܡܪ ܠܗ ܝܫܘܥ ܐܢܐ
ܒܓܠܝܐ ܡܠܠܬ ܥܡ ܥܠܡܐ ܘܒܟܠ ܙܒܢ ܐܠܦܬ ܒܟܢܘܫܬܐ
ܘܒܗܝܟܠܐ ܘܐܬܪ ܕܟܠܗܘܢ ܝܗܘܕܝܐ ܡܬܟܢܫܝܢ ܘܡܕܡ ܒܛܘܫܝܐ
ܠܐ ܡܠܠܬ. ²¹ܗܫܐ ܕܝܢ ܡܢܐ ܡܫܐܠ ܐܢܬ ܠܝ. ܫܐܠ ܠܐܝܠܝܢ
ܕܫܡܥܘ ܡܢܐ ܡܠܠܬ ܥܡܗܘܢ܆ ܗܐ ܗܢܘܢ ܝܕܥܝܢ ܡܕܡ
ܕܡܠܠܬ ²²ܟܕ ܡܠܠ ܗܠܝܢ ܚܕ ܡܢ ܕܚ̈ܫܐ ܕܩܝܡܝܢ ܩܕܡܘܗܝ. ܥܠ ܦܟܗ
ܠܝܫܘܥ. ܘܐܡܪ ܠܗ ܗܟܢܐ ܡܬܦܢܐ ܐܢܬ ܦܬܓܡܐ ܠܪܒܟܗܢܐ.
²³ܐܡܪ ܠܗ ܝܫܘܥ ܫܦܝܪ ܡܠܠܬ. ܠܡܢܐ ܡܚܝܬܢܝ ܀

¹⁶ܫܡܥܘܢ ܕܝܢ ܟܐܦܐ ܩܐܡ ܗܘܐ ܡܢ ܠܒܪ ܥܠ ܘܢܦܩ ܠܗ
ܬܠܡܝܕܐ ܡܫܡܫܢܬܗ ܕܪܒ ܟܗܢܐ ܘܐܡܪ ܠܢܛܪ ܬܪܥܐ ܘܐܥܠܗ

---

10 ܡܠܟܘ] *S* (*sic*): *cf* Bevan's *Daniel*, p. 213, *and* Nehem vi 6; syr.vg *has* ܡܠܟܣ
11 ܣܦܣܟ] *S* (*sic*): ܐܗܦܟ ܣܦܣܟ ܠܬܢܬܗ *Thos*[256] 15 ܬܠܡܝܕܐ] *before this word some words* (*e.g.* ܬܠܡܝܕܐ ܐܚܪ̈ܢܐ ܐܬܐ ܗܘܐ ܒܬܪܗ ܕܝܫܘܥ. ܗܘ ܕܝܢ) *have dropped out in S* ܡܫܡܫܢܬܗ] *so* *S*[vid], *not* ܡܫܡܫܢܘܬܗ

8 the Nazarene." He saith to them: "I said to you that I am *he*; S
9 if me ye seek, let *them* go," that the word which he had said might
be accomplished "Them that thou gavest me, I have not lost *any*
10 of them." Now Simon Kepha drew a sword and smote the slave of
the chief priest and took off his right ear; and the name of the man
11 *was* Malku. And Jesus said to Kepha: "Put back thy sword into
its place; the cup that my Father hath given me, shall I not drink
12 it?" And that cohort and the chiliarchs and the guards of the Jews
13 bound him, and brought him first unto Hanan the father-in-law of
24 Caiapha that was the chief priest of that year. Now Hanan sent him
14 bound unto Caiapha the chief priest, him that had counselled the Jews
that it was fitting that one man should die on behalf of the people.
15 Now Simon Kepha and one of the †disciples† was an acquaintance
of the chief priest, therefore he entered with Jesus into the court.

19 Now the chief priest was asking Jesus about his disciples who
20 they were, and about his teaching what it was. Jesus saith to him:
"I openly have spoken with the world and at all times have taught
in the synagogue and in the Temple and where all the Jews are
gathered together, and nothing in concealment have I spoken.
21 But now why askest thou me? Ask them that have heard what I
have spoken with them; lo, they know that which I have spoken!"
22 When he spake these things one of the guards that were standing
by smote him on his cheek, *even* Jesus, and said to him: "So dost
23 thou return an answer to the chief priest?" Jesus saith to him:
"Well have I spoken; wherefore didst thou smite me?"

16 Now Simon Kepha was standing outside; *then* entered and came
forth to him the disciple *that was* the acquaintance of the chief

---

10 Malku] *S* (*sic*). *This is the original form of the name* (Arab. مَالِكٌ), *of which* Μάλχος *is a Greek equivalent*: syr.vg *has* Mâlêk 11 thy sword] *S* (*sic*): *cf* 'Put back thy sword behind' *Thos*^{256}, *and* 'Put up again thy sword into his place' *E*$^{186, 232, 236}$ 15 disciples] *after this word some words should follow in S, so as to make the verse run* 'Now Simon Kepha and one of the other disciples were coming after Jesus: now that disciple was...' **13—24.**] *The rearrangement of these verses in S does not follow the order of the* Diatessaron, *neither according to the Arabic nor according to the Latin Cod. Fuldensis: see Journ. of Theol. Studies* ii 141.

S ܠܫܡܥܘܢ܂ [17]ܟܕ ܚܙܬܗ ܠܫܡܥܘܢ܂ ܐܡܬܗ ܕܢܛܪ ܬܪܥܐ ܐܡܪܐ
ܠܗ ܠܡܐ ܐܦ ܐܢܬ ܚܕ ܡܢ ܬܠܡܝܕܘܗܝ، ܐܢܬ ܕܗܢܐ ܓܒܪܐ
ܐܡܪ ܠܗ ܠܐ [18]ܘܩܝܡܝܢ ܗܘܘ ܕܝܢ ܬܡܢ ܥܒܕܐ ܘܕܚܫܐ ܘܫܚܢܝܢ
ܗܘܘ ܠܗܘܢ܂ ܢܘܪܐ ܒܕܪܬܐ ܕܟܗܢܐ܃ ܡܛܠ ܕܩܪܝܪ ܗܘܐ
[25]ܘܐܟܙ ܗܘܐ ܕܝܢ ܐܦ ܫܡܥܘܢ܂ ܠܘܬܗܘܢ܂ ܘܫܚܢ ܘܐܡܪܝܢ ܠܗ
ܗܠܝܢ ܐܢܫܐ ⌜ܕܫܚܢܝܢ⌝ ܠܡܐ ܐܦ ܐܢܬ ܚܕ ܡܢ ܬܠܡܝܕܘܗܝ، ܐܢܬ.
ܗܘ ܕܝܢ ܟܦܪ ܘܐܡܪ ܕܠܐ [26]ܘܗܢܐ ܚܕ ܡܢ ܥܒܕܘܗܝ، ܕܪܒ ܟܗܢܐ
ܐܚܝܢܗ ܕܗܘ ܕܦܣܩ ܗܘܐ ܫܡܥܘܢ܂ ⌜ܒܐܦܐ⌝ ܠܗ ܐܕܢܗ ܐܡܪ
ܠܗ ܠܫܡܥܘܢ܂ ܠܐ ܐܢܐ ܚܙܝܬܟ ܥܡܗ ܒܓܢܬܐ [27]ܘܬܘܒ ܟܦܪ
ܫܡܥܘܢ܂ ܕܠܐ ܝܕܥܢܐ ܠܗ ܘܒܗ ܒܫܥܬܐ ܩܪܐ ܬܪܢܓܠܐ ܀ ܀
[28]ܘܟܕ ܢܓܕܘܗܝ ܕܟܪܘܗܝ، ܠܝܫܘܥ ܡܢ ܠܘܬ ܩܝܦܐ ܘܐܥܠܘܗܝ،
ܠܦܪܛܘܪܝܢ ܕܢܫܠܡܘܢܝܗܝ، ܠܗܓܡܘܢܐ ܗܢܘܢ܂ ܕܝܢ ܠܐ ܥܠܘ ܠܦܪܛܘܪܝܢ
ܕܠܐ ܢܬܛܢܦܘܢ܂ ܥܕ ܐܟܠܝܢ ܦܨܚܐ [29]ܘܢܦܩ ܦܝܠܛܘܣ ܠܘܬܗܘܢ܂
ܘܐܡܪ ܠܗܘܢ܂ ܡܢܐ ܡܐܟܠ ܩܪܨܐ ܐܝܬ ܠܟܘܢ܂ ܥܠ ܓܒܪܐ
ܗܢܐ [30]ܥܢܘ ܘܐܡܪܝܢ ܐܠܘ ܠܐ ܥܒܕ ܒܝܫܬܐ ܗܘܐ ܐܦܠܐ
ܡܫܠܡܝܢ ܗܘܝܢ ܠܗ ܠܟ. [31]ܐܡܪ ܠܗܘܢ܂ ܦܝܠܛܘܣ ܡܕܝܢ ⌜ܕ⌝ܒܪܘܗܝ،
ܐܢܬܘܢ܂ ܘܕܘܢܘܗܝ، ܐܝܟ ܢܡܘܣܟܘܢ܂ ܐܡܪܝܢ ܠܗ ܝܗܘܕܝܐ ܠܝ
ܠܐ ܫܠܝܛ ܠܝ ܠܡܩܛܠ * * * * * * * * *

[*The three leaves of S which contained* Joh xviii 31—xix 40 *are missing. For* xix 31ª *and* 36, *see the apparatus.*]

[40]ܠܦܓܪܐ ܕܝܫܘܥ ܘܟܪܟܘܗܝ، ܒܟܬܢܐ ܥܡ ܚܢܛܐ ܗܝ، ܐܝܟ
ܕܐܝܬ ܗܘܐ ܢܡܘܣܐ ܠܝܗܘܕܝܐ ܕܢܬܩܒܪܘܢ܂ [41]ܘܐܝܬ ܗܘܬ

---

25 ⌜ܕܫܚܢܝܢ⌝] ܕܫܚܢ S (*transcript*) 31 ܕܡܒܪܘܗܝ] S (*sic*) xix 31ª *is paraphrased in* syr.vg *as follows* ܝܗܘܕܝܐ ܕܝܢ ܡܛܠ ܕܥܪܘܒܬܐ ܗܘܬ ܐܡܪܝܢ. ܠܐ ܢܒܘܬܘܢ ܦܓܪܐ ܗܠܝܢ ܥܠ ܙܩܝܦܘܗܘܢ ܡܛܠ ܕܫܒܬܐ ܢܓܗܐ.....ܘܒܟܢ 36 ܓܪܡܐ ܠܐ ܢܬܬܒܪ ܒܗ. ܕܟܬܝܒ ܕܫܠܡܬ ܟܠܗܝܢ ܟܬܒܝܬܐ A 225

17 priest and told the door-keeper and let in Simon. When the maid of *S*
the door-keeper saw Simon she saith to him: "Art thou also not one
18 of the disciples of this man?" He saith to her: "No." Now there
were standing there slaves and guards, and they were making for
themselves a fire in the court that they might warm themselves,
25 because it was cold. Now Simon also was standing by them and
warming himself, and they say to him, these folk that were warming
themselves: "Art not thou also one of his disciples?" Now he
26 denied and said "No." And there answered one of the slaves of the
chief priest, a relation of him whose ear Simon Kepha had cut off,
and he saith to Simon: "Did not I see thee with him in the garden?"
27 And again Simon denied, *saying* "I know him not"; and in the same
hour the cock crew.
28 And when *day* dawned they brought Jesus from *the house of*
Caiapha and carried him along to the Praetorium, that they might
deliver him up to the Governor. Now they themselves entered not
the Praetorium, that they might not be polluted while eating the
29 unleavened bread. And Pilate went forth unto them, and saith to
30 them: "What accusation have ye against this man?" They answered
and say: "If he had not been an evil-doer neither should we have
31 been delivering him up to thee." Pilate saith to them: "Why then
lead him away yourselves and judge him according to your law."
The Jews say to him: "For us it is not lawful to kill * * * *

[*The three leaves of S which contained* Joh xviii 31—xix 40 *are missing. For* xix 31[a] *and* 36, *see the apparatus.*]

xix 40 the body of Jesus, and wrapped it in linen cloths with that balm, as
41 it was the law for Jews to be buried. Now there was in that place a

---

28 while eating the unleavened bread] that they might first eat the lamb in holiness *E*[238] xix 31[a] *is paraphrased in* syr.vg (*and* aeth) *as follows:* "Now the Jews, because it was the Friday, say: These bodies shall not pass the night upon their crosses, because the Sabbath is dawning,.... and they besought... ." *The agreement of* aeth *with* syr.vg *makes it almost certain that these authorities have here preserved the text of* syr.vt 36 'The word was accomplished that is written "A bone shall not be broken in him"' *A* 225

ܕܝܢ ܒܕܘܟܬܐ ܗܝ ܓܢܬܐ ܘܒܗ ܒܝܬ ܩܒܘܪܐ ܚܕܬܐ S
ܕܐܢܫ ܠܐ ܐܬܩܒܪ ܗܘܐ ܒܗ [42]ܘܡܣܬܪܗܒܐܝܬ ܡܢ ܬܚܝܬ ܫܠܝܐ
ܣܡܘܗܝ, ܒܒܝܬ ܩܒܘܪܐ ܚܕܬܐ ܕܩܪܝܒ ܗܘܐ ܠܬܡܢ ܡܛܠ
ܕܫܒܬܐ ܢܓܗܐ ܗܘܬ

[1]ܘܠܠܝܐ ܕܢܓܗ ܚܕ ܒܫܒܐ ܟܕ ܚܫܘܟ ܒܨܦܪܐ ܪܒܐ ܐܬܬ
ܡܪܝܡ ܡܓܕܠܝܬܐ ܠܒܝܬ ܩܒܘܪܐ ܘܚܙܬ [ܕܡܬܓܠܓܠܐ] ܟܐܦܐ
ܘܥܡܠܐ ܡܢ ܦܘܡ ܩܒܪܐ [2]ܘܪܗܛܬ ܐܬܬ ܠܘܬ ܫܡܥܘܢ ܟܐܦܐ
ܘܠܘܬ ܗܘ ܬܠܡܝܕܐ ܕܪܚܡ ܗܘܐ ܠܗ ܝܫܘܥ ܘܐܡܪܐ ܠܗܘܢ
ܕܫܩܠܘܗܝ, ܠܡܪܢ ܡܢ ܗܘ ܒܝܬ ܩܒܘܪܐ ܘܠܐ ܝܕܥܢܐ ܐܝܟܐ
ܐܘܒܠܘܗܝ, [3]ܘܢܦܩܘ ܬܪ̈ܝܗܘܢ ܠܡܐܙܠ ܠܒܝܬ ܩܒܘܪܐ [4]ܘܪܗܛܝܢ
ܗܘܘ ܗܘ ܕܝܢ ܬܠܡܝܕܐ ܩܕܡܗ ܠܫܡܥܘܢ ܘܐܬܐ ܠܒܝܬ ܩܒܘܪܐ
[5]ܘܐܕܝܩ ܚܙܐ ܟܬ̈ܢܐ ܗܢܘܢ ܟܕ ܣܝܡܝܢ ܡܚܠ ܕܝܢ ܠܐ ܥܠ ܗܘ
ܠܒܝܬ ܩܒܘܪܐ [6]ܫܡܥܘܢ ܕܝܢ ܟܕ ܡܛܐ ܥܠ ܘܚܙܐ ܟܬ̈ܢܐ
[7]ܘܣܘܕܪܐ ܕܪܝܫܗ ܘܣܝܡ ܠܣܛܪ [8]ܘܗܝܕܝܢ ܥܠ ܐܦ ܗܘ ܬܠܡܝܕܐ
ܠܩܒܪܐ ܘܚܙܐ ܘܗܝܡܢ [9]ܡܛܠ ܕܠܐ ܒܟܬܒܐ ܠܗܢܐ ܝ̈ܕܥܝܢ ܗܘܘ
ܡܢ ܟܬ̈ܒܐ ܕܘܠܐ ܗܘ ܠܡܩܡ ܡܢ ܒܝܬ ܡܝ̈ܬܐ. [10]ܬܠܡܝ̈ܕܐ
ܕܝܢ ܟܕ ܚܙܘ ܗܠܝܢ ܐܙܠܘ ܠܗܘܢ. [11]ܡܪܝܡ ܕܝܢ ܩܝܡܐ ܗܘܬ ܠܘܬ
ܩܒܪܐ ܘܒܟܝܐ. ܘܐܟܡܐ ܕܒܟܝܐ ܐܕܝܩܬ ܠܒܝܬ ܩܒܘܪܐ [12]ܘܚܙܬ
ܬܪܝܢ ܡܠܐܟܐ ܒܚܘ̈ܪܐ ܟܕ ܝܬܒܝܢ ܚܕ ܡܢ ܐܪ̈ܫܬܐ ܕܗܝ
ܕܘܟܬܐ ܕܪܡܐ ܗܘܐ ܒܗ ܝܫܘܥ ܘܚܕ ܡܢ ܐܪ̈ܓܠܐ. [13]ܐܡܪ̈ܝܢ
ܠܗ̇ ܗܢܘܢ ܡܠܐܟܐ ܐܢܬܬܐ ܡܢܐ ܒܟܝܬܝ, ܘܠܡܢ ܒܥܝܬܝ.
§¶A384f. ܐܡܪܐ ܠܗܘܢ ܕܫܩܠܘܗܝ§, ܠܡܪܝ, ܘܠܐ ܝܕܥܢܐ ܐܝܟܐ ܣܡܘܗܝ.¶
[14]ܘܟܕ ܐܡܪܬ ܗܠܝܢ ܐܬܦܢܝܬ ܠܒܣܬܪܗ. ܘܚܙܬܗ ܠܝܫܘܥ ܟܕ ܩܐܡ.
ܘܠܐ ܝܕܥܐ ܗܘܬ ܕܝܫܘܥ ܗܘ. [15]ܗܘ ܕܝܢ ܐܡܪ ܠܗ̇ ܐܢܬܬܐ

---

1 ܕܡܬܓܠܓܠܐ] *S appears to have* ܡܬܓܠܓܠܬܐ, *but this must be a mistake as* ܘܥܡܠܐ *is clear* 2 *Cf below on ver.* 13 13 ܠܡܪܝ̱ *A*
ܘܠܐ ܝܕܥܢܐ ܐܝܟܐ ܣܡܘܗܝ] *so* A^a, *but* A^b *has* ܘܠܐ ܝܕܥܐ ܐܢܐ ܠܐܝܟܐ ܐܘܒܠܘܗܝ; *both* MSS *of A then add*
ܘܦܢܝ ܡܠܐܟ̈ܐ ܐܡܪܘ ܠܗ̇ ܠܡܪܝܡ. ܕܥܡܟ ܠܗ ܘܐܙܠ ܠܘܬ ܡ̇ܢ ܕܫܒܩܗ.

garden and in the garden a new tomb that no man had been buried *S*
42 in, and hastily at once they laid him in the new tomb that was near
there, because the sabbath was dawning.
XX 1 And in the night that *was* dawning into the first *day* of the week,
while yet it was dark in the early morning, came Mary Magdalene to
the tomb and saw the stone †rolled† and taken away from the mouth
2 of the grave, and she ran *and* came unto Simon Kepha and unto that
disciple that Jesus used to love and saith to them "They have taken
away our Lord from that tomb, and I know not where they have
3 carried him." And the two of them went forth to go to the tomb
4 and were running. Now that disciple outwent Simon and came to
5 the tomb, and he looked in *and* saw those linen cloths laid, but
6 enter indeed the tomb he did not. But Simon, when he arrived,
7 entered and saw the linen cloths, and the napkin wrapped up and laid
8 on one side; and then entered also that disciple into the grave, and
9 they saw and believed. Because not yet were they knowing from the
10 Scriptures that he was about to rise from among the dead. Now the
11 disciples when they saw these things went away, but Mary was standing
by the grave and weeping; and as she *was* weeping she looked into
12 the tomb, and she saw there two angels in white sitting one at the
head of the place that Jesus had been lying in and one at the feet.
13 Those angels say to her: "Woman, why weepest thou, and whom
seekest thou?" She saith to them §"They have taken away my §*A* 384 f.
14 Lord, and I know not where they have laid him."¶ And when she ¶*A*
said these things she turned round behind her, and saw Jesus
15 standing, and she was not knowing that it was Jesus. Now he said
to her: "Woman, why weepest thou, and whom seekest thou?" And

---

1 †rolled†] *S appears to have* 'Magdalene,' *but this must be a mistake in the* MS, *as the* 'and' *which follows is clear* 2 *Cf below on ver.* 13
13 my Lord] our Lord *A* where they have laid him] *so* A^a, *but* A^b *has* 'whither they have carried him'; *both* MSS *of A then add* 'And those angels said to Mary He hath arisen and gone unto him that sent him.'

ܡܢܐ ܒܟܝܬܝ، ܘܠܡܢ ܒܥܝܬܝ،. ܗܝ، ܣܒܪܬ ܠܗ ܕܓܢܢܐ ܗܘ. ܐܡܪܐ S
ܠܗ ܡܪܝ، ܐܢ ܐܢܬ ܫܩܠܬܝܗܝ، ܐܡܪ ܠܝ ܐܝܟܐ ܣܡܬܝܗܝ، ܐܙܠ
ܐܫܩܠܝܘܗܝ، [16]ܗܝܕܝܢ ܐܡܪ ܠܗ ܝܫܘܥ ܡܪܝܡ ܘܐܬܗܦܟܬܗ ܘܝܕܥܬܗ
ܘܐܡܪܐ ܠܗ ܪܒܘܠܝ. ܘܪܗܛܬ ܠܩܘܡ ܠܘܬܗ ܕܬܬܩܪܒ ܠܗ [17]ܘܗܘ
ܕܝܢ ܐܡܪ ܠܗ ܠܐ ܬܬܩܪܒܝܢ ܠܝ ܠܐ ܥܕܟܝܠ ܣܠܩܬ ܠܘܬ ܐܒܝ
ܐܠܐ ܙܠܝ ܠܘܬ ܐܚܝ ܘܐܡܪܝ ܠܗܘܢ ܕܗܐ ܣܠܩܢܐ ܠܘܬ ܐܒܝ
ܘܐܒܘܟܘܢ ܘܠܘܬ ܐܠܗܝ ܘܐܠܗܟܘܢ [18]ܘܐܬܬ ܡܪܝܡ ܐܡܪܬ
ܠܬܠܡܝܕܐ ܕܚܙܬܗ ܠܡܪܢ ܘܐܝܠܝܢ ܕܡܠܐ ܠܗ ܐܡܪܬ ܠܗܘܢ ○○
[19]ܘܒܗ ܒܝܘܡܐ ܗܘ ܕܚܕ ܒܫܒܐ ܐܬܪ ܕܗܘܘ ܬܠܡܝܕܐ ܘܐܚܝܕܝܢ
ܗܘܘ ܬܪܥܝܗܘܢ ܡܢ ܕܚܠܬܐ ܕܝܗܘܕܝܐ. ܐܬܐ ܝܫܘܥ ܩܡ
ܒܡܨܥܬܗܘܢ ܘܐܡܪ ܠܗܘܢ ܫܠܡܐ ܥܡܟܘܢ [20]ܘܟܕ ܐܡܪ ܗܘܐ
ܗܝ، ܐܚܘܝ ܐܝܕܘܗܝ، ܘܣܛܪܗ ܘܟܕ ܚܙܘܗܝ، ܬܠܡܝܕܐ ܚܕܝܘ
[21]ܘܬܘܒ ܐܡܪ ܠܗܘܢ ܫܠܡܐ ܥܡܟܘܢ. ܐܝܟܢܐ ܕܫܕܪܢܝ ܐܒܝ
ܡܫܕܪ ܐܢܐ ܠܟܘܢ. [22]ܘܟܕ ܐܡܪ ܗܠܝܢ ܢܦܚ ܒܐܦܝܗܘܢ ܘܐܡܪ
ܠܗܘܢ ܩܒܠܘ ܪܘܚܐ ܩܕܝܫܬܐ [23]ܕܡܢ ܕܬܫܒܩܘܢ ܠܗ
ܚܛܗܘܗܝ، ܢܫܬܒܩܘܢ ܠܗ. ܘܡܢ ܕܬܐܚܕܘܢ ܬܐܚܝܕܝܢ ܚܛܗܘܗܝ،
ܐܚܝܕ ܗܘ ○○○:○○
[24]ܬܐܘܡܐ ܕܝܢ ܚܕ ܡܢ ܬܪܥܣܪܬܐ ܠܐ ܗܘܐ ܬܡܢ ܗܘܐ ܥܡ
ܐܚܪܢܐ ܟܕ ܐܬܐ ܠܘܬܗܘܢ ܝܫܘܥ [25]ܐܡܪܝܢ ܠܗ ܐܬܐ ܡܪܢ
ܘܚܙܝܢܝܗܝ، ܐܡܪ ܠܗܘܢ ܐܠܐ ܚܙܐ ܐ̈ܝܕܘܗܝ، ܘܕܘܟܬ ܩ̈ܒܥܐ
ܗܠܝܢ ܘܐܪܡܐ ܐܢܐ ܨܒܥܝ، ܒܕܘܟܬܐ ܘܐܪܡܐ ∗ ܐܝܕܝ،
ܒܓܒܗ ∗ ∗ ∗ ܕܒܣܛܪܗ ܠܐ ܡܗܝܡܢ ܐܢܐ ·܀· ·܀·
[26]ܘܡܢ ܒܬܪ ܬܡܢܝܐ ܝܘܡܝܢ ܠܘܬ ܒܝܬܐ ܐܚܪܢܐ ܟܢܝܫܝܢ ܗܘܘ
ܬܠܡܝܕܐ ܐܚܝܕܐ ܒܝܬܐ ܘܬܐܘܡܐ ܥܡܗܘܢ ܘܬ̈ܪܥܐ ܐܚܝܕܝܢ
ܗܘܘ ܐܬܐ ܝܫܘܥ ܘܩܡ ܒܡܨܥܬܗܘܢ ܘܐܡܪ ܠܗܘܢ ܫܠܡܐ
ܥܡܟܘܢ [27]ܘܗܝܕܝܢ ܐܡܪ ܠܬܐܘܡܐ ܐܝܬܐ ܨܒܥܟ ܘܚܙܝ ܐ̈ܝܕܝ،
ܘܐܝܬܐ ܐܝܕܟ ܒܓܒܝ، ܘܠܐ ܬܗܘܐ ܚܣܝܪ ܗܝܡܢܘܬܐ.
[28]ܐܡܪ ܠܗ ܬܐܘܡܐ ܡܪܝ، ܘܐܠܗܝ، [29]ܐܡܪ ܠܗ ܝܫܘܥ ܗܫܐ
ܕܚܙܝܬܢܝ ܗܝܡܢܬ ܒܝ ܛܘܒܝܗܘܢ ܠܐܝܠܝܢ ܕܠܐ ܚܙܘܢܝ ܘܗܝܡܢܘ
ܒܝ ·܀·

she supposed that it was the gardener. She saith to him: "My S
Lord, if thou hast taken him away, say to me where thou hast laid
16 him *that* I may go *and* take him away." Then said Jesus to her:
"Mary!" And she perceived him and answered and saith to him:
"Rabbuli!" And she ran forward unto him that she might draw
17 near to him. But he said to her: "Do not draw near to me; not
yet have I gone up unto my Father. But go unto my brothers
and say to them Lo, I go up unto my Father and your Father and
18 unto my God and your God!" And Mary came *and* said to the
disciples "I have seen our Lord"; and the things which he revealed
to her she said to them.

19 And on that same day of the first of the week, where the disciples
were—and their doors were shut for fear of the Jews—came Jesus
and stood among them, and he saith to them: "Peace *be* with you."
20 And when he had said *this* he shewed them his hands and his side;
21 and when the disciples saw him they rejoiced. Again he saith to
them: "Peace *be* with you; as my Father sent me, I send you."
22 And when he said these things he breathed in their faces and said to
23 them: "Receive a holy Spirit; whom ye shall forgive the sins of,
they shall be forgiven him, and whom ye shall shut *your door*
against—it is shut."

24 Now Thomas, one of the Twelve, was not there with the others
25 when Jesus came unto them. They say to him: "Our Lord came,
and we saw him." He saith to them: "Except I see his hands and
the place of these nails and put forth my finger in the places and put
forth my hand in [the] place that *is* in his side I do not believe."

26 And after eight days, on the first *day* of the next week, the
disciples were gathered together in the house and Thomas with them,
and the doors were shut. Jesus came and stood among them, and
27 saith to them: "Peace *be* with you." Then said he to Thomas:
"Put forth thy finger and see my hands, and lay thy hand on my side,
28 and do not be lacking in faith." Thomas saith to him: "My Lord
29 and my God!" Jesus saith to him: "Now that thou hast seen me
hast thou believed in me? Happy is it for them that have not seen
me and have believed in me!"

---

22 a holy Spirit] *cf* Mk xiii 11, Lk ii 25, 26 23 shut] *see Notes*, vol. ii

30ܘܣܓܝ ܐܬܘܬܐ ܐܚܪܢܝܬܐ ܥܒܕ ܝܫܘܥ ܠܬܠܡܝܕܘܗܝ ܐܝܠܝܢ S
ܕܠܐ ܟܬܝܒܢ ܒܟܬܒܐ ܗܢܐ 31ܗܠܝܢ ܕܝܢ ܕܐܬܟܬܒ ܕܬܗܝܡܢܘܢ
ܕܝܫܘܥ ܡܫܝܚܐ ܗܘ ܒܪܗ ܕܐܠܗܐ. ܘܬܗܝܡܢܘܢ ܒܗ ܘܬܚܘܢ
ܒܫܡܗ.

1ܒܬܪ ܗܠܝܢ ܐܬܚܙܝ ܝܫܘܥ ܠܬܠܡܝܕܘܗܝ ܠܘܬ ܝܡܬܐ ܕܛܒܪܝܘܣ
ܐܬܚܙܝ ܠܗܘܢ ܕܝܢ ܗܟܢܐ 2ܟܕ ܟܢܝܫܝܢ ܗܘܘ. ܟܠܗܘܢ ܐܟܚܕܐ.
ܫܡܥܘܢ ܟܐܦܐ ܘܬܐܘܡܐ ܘܢܬܢܐܝܠ ܗܘ ܕܡܢ ܩܛܢܐ ܕܓܠܝܠܐ.
ܘܒܢܝ ܙܒܕܝ ܘܬܪܝܢ ܐܚܪܢܝܢ ܡܢ ܬܠܡܝܕܐ. 3ܐܡܪ ܠܗܘܢ ܫܡܥܘܢ
ܐܙܠ ܐܨܘܕ ܢܘܢܐ. ܐܡܪܝܢ ܠܗ ܐܦ ܐܢܚܢ ܐܬܝܢ ܥܡܟ.
ܘܢܦܩܘ ܣܠܩܘ ܒܣܦܝܢܬܐ ܘܟܠܗ ܠܠܝܐ ܡܕܡ ܠܐ ܨܕܘ. 4ܘܟܕ
ܨܦܪܬ ܐܬܐ ܝܫܘܥ ܩܡ ܥܠ ܝܕ ܝܡܬܐ. ܘܬܠܡܝܕܘܗܝ ܠܐ
ܐܫܬܘܕܥܘ ܕܗܘܝܘ. 5ܐܡܪ ܠܗܘܢ ܛܠܝܐ ܠܡܐ ܐܝܬ ܠܟܘܢ ܡܕܡ
ܠܡܐܟܠ ܒܗ ܐܡܪܝܢ ܠܗ ܠܐ 6ܐܡܪ ܠܗܘܢ ܐܪܡܘ ܡܨܝܕܬܟܘܢ
ܡܢ ܓܒܗ ܕܝܡܝܢܐ ܕܣܦܝܢܬܐ. ܘܡܫܟܚܝܢ ܐܢܬܘܢ. ܘܟܕ ܐܪܡܝܘ
ܐܝܟ ܕܐܡܪ ܠܗܘܢ ܒܗ ܠܡܫܩܠܘܬܗ ܠܡܨܝܕܬܐ ܠܣܦܝܢܬܐ
ܘܠܐ ܐܫܟܚܘ ܡܢ ܣܘܓܐ ܕܢܘܢܐ ܫܩܝܠܐܐ ܕܐܚܝܕܬ. 7ܗܝܕܝܢ
ܐܡܪ ܬܠܡܝܕܐ ܗܘ ܕܪܚܡ ܗܘܐ ܠܗ ܝܫܘܥ. ܠܫܡܥܘܢ ܗܢܐ
ܡܪܢ ܗܘ. ܫܡܥܘܢ ܕܝܢ ܟܕ ܫܡܥ ܕܡܪܢ ܗܘ. ܢܣܒ
ܟܬܘܢܗ ܡܢܐ ܒܚܨܘܗܝ. ܘܢܦܠ ܒܝܡܬܐ ܘܣܚܐ ܗܘܐ ܘܐܬܐ
8ܡܛܠ ܕܠܐ ܪܚܝܩܝܢ ܗܘܘ ܡܢ ܝܒܫܐ ܘܪܟܒܐ ܕܬܠܡܝܕܐ ܐܬܝܢ
ܗܘܘ ܒܣܦܝܢܬܐ ܟܕ ܢܓܕܝܢ ܠܗ ܠܡܨܝܕܬܐ ܗܝ. 9ܘܟܕ ܣܠܩܘ
ܠܝܒܫܐ ܐܫܟܚܘ ܡܫܟܘܗܝ ܕܝܫܘܥ ܓܡܘܪܐ ܕܢܘܪܐ ܘܢܘܢܐ ܟܕ
ܪܡܐ ܥܠܝܗܘܢ ܘܠܚܡܐ ܟܕ ܣܝܡ 10ܐܡܪ ܠܗܘܢ ܝܫܘܥ ܐܝܬܘ
ܡܢ ܗܠܝܢ ܢܘܢܐ ܕܨܕܬܘܢ ܗܫܐ 11ܘܣܠܩ ܫܡܥܘܢ ܢܓܕܗ
ܠܡܨܝܕܬܐ ܠܝܒܫܐ ܟܕ ܡܠܝܐ ܘܐܫܟܚܘܗ ܗܘܘ ܒܗ ܢܘܢܐ ܪ̈ܘܪܒܐ
ܡܐܐ ܘܚܡܫܝܢ ܘܬܠܬܐ ܘܒܗܢܐ ܣܘܓܐ ܒܟܠܗ ܡܨܝܕܬܐ ܗܝ.
ܠܐ ܐܨܛܪܝܬ 12ܐܡܪ ܠܗܘܢ ܝܫܘܥ ܬܘ ܐܫܬܪܘ. ܘܚܕ ܡܢ
ܬܠܡܝܕܘܗܝ ܠܐ ܡܡܪܚ ܗܘܐ ܠܡܫܐܠܘܬܗ ܕܡܢܘ ܡܛܠ

30 And many other signs shewed Jesus to his disciples which are not *S*
31 written in this book; but these that are written *are* that ye may
believe that Jesus is the Messiah, the Son of God, and ye shall
believe in him and be saved alive in his name.

xxi 1 After these things Jesus appeared to his disciples by the Lake [of]
2 Tiberias. Now he appeared to them thus: when they were gathered
all of them together,—Simon Kepha and Thomas and Nathaniel that
was from Câtnê of Galilee and the sons of Zebedee and two others of
3 the disciples. Simon saith to them: "I shall go *and* catch fish."
They say to him: "We also go with thee." And they went up *and*
4 sat in the boat, and in that night nothing did they catch. And when
it dawned Jesus came *and* stood by the side of the lake; and his
5 disciples did not perceive that it was he. He saith to them:
"Children, have ye not aught to eat of?" They say to him: "No."
6 He saith to them: "Cast your net from the right-hand side of the
boat, and ye *will* find." And when they cast as he said to them, they
sought to take up the net into the boat, and they could not from the
7 weight of the many fish that it held. Then said the disciple whom
Jesus used to love to Simon: "This is our Lord!" Now Simon,
when he heard it was our Lord, took his coat *and* put *it* on his
8 loins and fell into the lake and was swimming and coming, because
they were not far from the dry land. And the rest of the disciples
9 were coming in the boat, drawing that net. And when they came up
to the dry land they found in front of Jesus coals of fire and a fish
10 laid upon them and bread set *ready*. Jesus saith to them: "Bring
11 of those fishes that ye have caught now." And Simon went up *and*
drew the net to the dry land *quite* full, and they had found in it
great fishes, an hundred and fifty and three; and with all this weight
12 that net was not rent. Jesus saith to them: "Come *and* breakfast."
And not one of his disciples was daring to ask him who it was,

S ܕܡܗܝܡܢܝܢ ܗܘܘ ܕܗܘܝܘ [13]ܘܢܣܒ ܝܫܘܥ ܠܚܡܐ ܘܢܘܢܐ ܘܒܪܟ
ܥܠܝܗܘܢ ܘܝܗܒ ܠܗܘܢ [14]ܗܕܐ ܗܘܬ ܕܬܠܬܬܐ ܙܒܢܝܢ ܕܐܬܚܙܝ،
ܝܫܘܥ ܠܬܠܡܝܕܘܗܝ، ܒܬܪ ܕܩܡ ܡܢ ܒܝܬ ܡܝܬܐ [15]ܘܟܕ ܠܥܣܘ
ܐܡܪ ܝܫܘܥ ܠܫܡܥܘܢ ܐܢܬ ܫܡܥܘܢ ܒܪܗ ܕܝܘܢܢ ܪܚܡ ܐܢܬ
ܠܝ ܐܡܪ ܠܗ ܐܝܢ ܡܪܝ، ܐܡܪ ܠܗ ܐܪܥܐ ܠܝ ܐܡܪ̈ܝ. [16]ܬܘܒ
ܐܡܪ ܠܗ ܝܫܘܥ ܐܢܬ ܫܡܥܘܢ ܒܪܗ ܕܝܘܢܢ ܪܚܡ ܐܢܬ ܠܝ ܛܒ
ܐܡܪ ܠܗ ܐܝܢ ܡܪܝ، ܐܡܪ ܠܗ ܐܪܥܐ ܠܝ ܢܩܘܬܝ، [17]ܬܘܒ ܐܡܪ
ܠܗ ܝܫܘܥ ܫܡܥܘܢ ܒܪܗ ܕܝܘܢܢ ܪܚܡ ܐܢܬ ܠܝ. ܟܪܝܬ ܠܗ
ܠܫܡܥܘܢ ܥܠ ܕܬܠܬ ܙܒܢܝܢ ܐܡܪ ܠܗ ܝܫܘܥ ܗܟܘܬ ܐܡܪ ܠܗ
ܫܡܥܘܢ ܟܠ ܡܕܡ ܝܕܥ ܐܢܬ ܕܪܚܡ ܐܢܐ ܠܟ ܝܕܥ. ܐܢܬ
ܘܐܡܪ ܠܗ ܐܪܥܐ ܠܝ ܥܢܝ. [18]ܐܡܝܢ ܐܡܪܢܐ ܕܟܕ ܛܠܝܐ ܗܘܝܬ
ܐܣܪ ܗܘܝܬ ܚܨܝܟ ܘܡܗܠܟ ܗܘܝܬ ܠܐܝܟܐ ܕܨܒܐ ܐܢܬ ܘܡܐ
ܕܬܣܐܒ ܬܦܫܛ ܐܝܕܝܟ ܘܐܚܪܢܐ ܢܐܣܘܪ ܠܟ ܚܨܝܟ ܘܢܝܬܝܟ
ܠܐܬܪ ܕܠܐ ܨܒܐ ܐܢܬ. [19]ܗܕܐ ܕܝܢ ܐܡܪ ܕܒܐܝܢܐ ܡܘܬܐ
ܢܫܒܚ ܫܡܥܘܢ ܠܐܠܗܐ ܘܟܕ ܐܡܪ ܗܠܝܢ ܐܡܪ ܠܫܡܥܘܢ
ܬܐ ܒܬܪܝ. [20]ܐܬܦܢܝ ܫܡܥܘܢ ܘܚܙܐ ܠܗܘ ܠܬܠܡܝܕܐ ܕܪܚܡ
ܗܘܐ ܠܗ ܝܫܘܥ ܟܕ ܐܬܐ ܒܬܪܗ ܗܘ ܕܢܦܠ ܥܠ ܚܕܝܗ ܕܝܫܘܥ.
ܒܐܚܫܡܝܬܐ ܘܐܡܪ ܗܘܐ ܠܗ ܡܪܝ، ܡܢܘ ܡܫܠܡ ܠܟ. [21]ܠܗܢܐ
ܟܕ ܚܙܝܗ، ܫܡܥܘܢ ܕܐܬܐ ܒܬܪܗ ܐܡܪ ܠܗ ܘܗܢܐ ܡܪܝ،
ܡܢܐ [22]ܐܡܪ ܠܗ ܝܫܘܥ ܐܢ ܨܒܐ ܕܗܢܐ ܢܩܘܐ ܥܕܡܐ
ܕܐܬܐ ܐܢܐ ܠܟ ܡܢܐ ܠܟ ܕܗܫܐ ܐܢܬ ܬܐ ܒܬܪܝ، ° °

15–17 ܐܡܪ ܠܗ ܝܫܘܥ ܠܫܡܥܘܢ ܟܐܦܐ. ܐܪܥܐ ܠܝ ܐܡܪ̈ܝ ܘܟܪ̈ܝ ܘܢܩܘ̈ܬܝ A195
For ܘܟܪ̈ܝ, A^b *has* ܘܐܡܪ̈ܝ 16 ܢܩܘ̈ܬܝ] *in front of this word in S is some letter, apparently by a later hand*

13 because they were believing it was he. And Jesus took bread *S*
14 and fish, and blessed *God* over them and gave to them. This was the
third time that Jesus appeared to his disciples after he arose from
15 among the dead. And when they *had* eaten Jesus said to Simon:
"Thou, Simon son of Jonan, lovest thou me?" He saith to him:
"Yea, my Lord." He saith to him: "Tend for me my lambs."
16 Again Jesus saith to him: "Thou, Simon son of Jonan, lovest thou
me much?" He saith to him: "Yea, my Lord." He saith to him:
17 "Tend for me my ewes." Again Jesus saith to him: "Simon son of
Jonan, lovest thou me?" It grieved Simon for that three times
Jesus said to him thus. Simon saith to him: "Everything thou
knowest; that I love thee thou knowest!" And he said to him:
18 "Tend for me my sheep. Amen, I say When thou wast young thou
wast girding thy loins and wast walking whither thou wouldest, and
what *time* thou hast grown old thou wilt lift up thy hands and
another will gird for thee thy loins and will thrust thee whither thou
19 wouldest not." Now this he said of by what death Simon should
glorify God. And when he said these things he said to Simon:
20 "Come after me." Simon turned round and saw that disciple whom
Jesus used to love coming after him, him that fell on the breast of
Jesus at the supper and had said to him: 'My Lord, who is betraying
21 thee?' This one when Simon saw coming after him, he saith to him:
22 "And this one, my Lord, what—?" Jesus saith to him: "If I will
that this one should remain until I come, what *is it* to thee? Now
come thou after me."

15—17 'For he said to Simon Kepha: Tend for me my flock and my sheep and my ewes' *A* 195. *For* 'my sheep,' A^b *has* 'my lambs'

[23]ܘܢܦܩܬ ܗܕܐ ܡܠܬܐ ܒܝܬ ܬܠܡܝܕܐ ܕܗܘ ܬܠܡܝܕܐ ܠܐ ܡܐܬ S
ܝܫܘܥ ܕܝܢ ܠܐ ܗܘܐ ܥܠ ܕܠܐ ܡܐܬ ܐܡܪ ܗܘ ܐܠܐ ܕܐܢ
ܨܒܐ ܐܢܐ ܕܢܩܘܐ ܒܥܕܢܐ ܕܐܬܐܢܐ [24]ܗܢܘ ܬܠܡܝܕܐ ܕܐܣܗܕ ܥܠ
ܗܠܝܢ ܘܟܬܒ ܐܢܝܢ ܘܝܕܥܝܢ ܐܢܚܢ ܕܫܪܝܪܐ ܗܝ ܣܗܕܘܬܗ··
[25]ܘܣܓܝܐܬܐ ܐܚܪܢܝܬܐ ܥܒܕ ܝܫܘܥ ܕܐܠܘ ܚܕܐ ܚܕܐ ܡܟܬܒܝܢ
ܡܬܟܬܒܢ ܗܘܝ ܥܠܡܐ ܠܐ ܣܦܩ ܗܘܐ ܠܗܝܢ. ܘ ܘ:ܘ ܘ:

ܫܠܡ ܐܘܢܓܠܝܘܢ ܕܡܦܪܫܐ ܐܪܒܥܐ ܣܦܪܝܢ. ܫܘܒܚܐ ܠܐܠܗܐ ܘܠܡܫܝܚܗ
ܘܠܪܘܚܗ ܩܕܝܫܬܐ ܒܟܠ ܕܗܢܐ ܘܡܥܕܪ ܘܝܗܒ ܚܝܠܐ ܠܟܠ ܚܠܫܐ ܕܟܬܒ
ܐܠܗܐ ܒܪܚܡܘܗܝ ܢܚܘܣ ܥܠ ܚܛܗܘܗܝ ܒܨܠܘܬܗܘܢ ܕܩܕܝܫܐ. ܐܡܝܢ ܘܐܡܝܢ

·⁘· :: ·⁘·

23 And this word went forth among the disciples that that disciple S
was not to die; but Jesus—not for that he was not to die said he
24 *it*, but 'If I will that he should remain until I come—.' This is the
disciple that bare witness of these things and wrote them, and we
know that true is his witness.
25 And many other things did Jesus, that if one by one they were
all written the world would not be sufficient for them.

[*Subscription in S.*]

Here endeth the Evangel of the Separated, Four Volumes. Glory to God and to His Messiah and to His holy Spirit. Every one that readeth and heareth and keepeth and doeth pray for the sinner that wrote: God in his mercy forgive him his sins in both worlds. Amen and Amen.

APPENDIX I.

Joh iii 30—iv 6 *in C.*

The outer margin of *fol.* 42 in *C* has been torn away, carrying with it a considerable piece of the text. It was somewhat difficult to indicate exactly on p. 434 *ff* the position of the words on the lines: the mutilated portion is therefore repeated here, line for line as it is in the MS. Words and letters between ⌜ ⌝ are supplied by conjecture where the text is missing.

fol. 42 r, col 2

ܓܝܪ ܘܠܐ ܠܡܪܒܐ ⌜ܘ⌝ܠܝ
ܠܡܒܨܪܘ. [31]ܗܘ ܓܝܪ ܕܡ⌜ܢ⌝
ܠܥܠ ܐܬܐ ܠܥܠ ܡ⌜ܢ ܟ⌝ܠ
ܗܘ. ܘܗܘ ܕܡܢ ܐܪ⌜ܥܐ⌝
ܗܘ ܡܢ ܐܪܥܐ ܗ⌜ܘ ܘܡܢ⌝
ܐܪܥܐ ܗܘ ܡ⌜ܡܠܠ⌝:
ܘܗܘ ܕܡܢ ⌜ܫܡܝܐ⌝
ܐܬܐ. [32]ܡܕܡ ⌜ܕܚܙܐ⌝
ܘܫܡܥ ܡܣܗܕ ܘܣܗ⌜ܕܘܬܗ⌝
ܠܐ ܟܠ ܐܢܫ ܡ⌜ܩܒܠ⌝:
[33]ܐܝܢܐ ܕ⌜ܩܒܠ ܕܝ⌝
ܣܗܕܘܬܗ ⌜ܚܬܡ⌝
ܕܐܠܗܐ ⌜ܫܪܝܪܐ ܗܘ⌝.
[34]ܐܝܢܐ ܓܝ⌜ܪ ܕܐܠܗܐ⌝
ܫܕܪܗ ܡ̈⌜ܠܐ ܕܐܠܗܐ⌝
ܡܡܠܠ. ܠܐ ܗܘ⌜ܐ ܓܝܪ⌝
ܒܟܝܠܬܐ ⌜ܝܗܒ ܪܘܚܐ⌝
ܐܒܐ ܠܒܪܗ [35]⌜ܐܠܐ⌝
ܪܚܡ ܗ⌜ܘ * * ܘܟܠ⌝
ܡܕܡ ܝܗ⌜ܒ ܒܐܝ̈ܕܘܗܝ⌝
[36]ܡܢ ܕܡܗ⌜ܝܡܢ ܒܒܪܐ⌝
ܐܝܬ ܠܗ ⌜ܚܝܐ ܕܠܥܠܡ⌝:
ܘܡܢ ܕܠܐ ⌜ܡܗܝܡܢ⌝

l. 9. The stroke visible after ܘܣܗܕ is, I believe, nothing more than the right-hand side of the following ܘ

l. 11. Enough of the ܩ is visible to shew that we must read ⌜ܕ⌝ܩܒܠ and not ܕ⌜ܡ⌝ܩܒܠ

l. 12. ܚܬܡ] *so* syr.vg and *S.*

l. 13. ܫܪܝܪܐ] *so* syr.vg: S^{ed} has ܫܪܪܐ

l. 15. After ܡ̈ܠܐ syr.vg and *S* add ܗܘ, but there is hardly room for it in *C.*

l. 17. ܪܘܚܐ] *so* Aphraates 123. The word in *S* is illegible: S^{ed} (Mrs Lewis) has ܐܠܗܐ, but neither Aphraates nor Ephraim (*Lamy* i 267) has ܐܠܗܐ. In syr.vg we find ܐܠܗܐ ܪܘܚܐ

l. 19. We might supply ܠܒܪܗ, or more probably ܠܗ, as ܠܒܪܗ occurs in the previous line.

fol. 42 v, col 1

⌜ܠܒ⌝ܪܐ ܠܐ ܢܚܙܐ ܚܝܐ.
⌜ܐ⌝ܠ⌜ܐ⌝ ܪܘܓܙܗ ܕܐܠܗܐ
⌜ܢܩܘ⌝ܐ ܥܠܘܗܝ .܀
[1]⌜ܟ⌝⌜ܕ⌝ ܝܕܥ ܕܝܢ ܝܫܘܥ
⌜ܕܫܡ⌝ܥܘ ܦܪܝܫܐ
⌜ܕܣܓ⌝ܝܘ ܬܠܡܝܕܘܗܝ.
⌜ܘܡܥܡ⌝ܕ ܗܘܐ ܝܬܝܪ
⌜ܡܢ ܝܘ⌝ܚܢܢ. [2]ܘܠܐ ܗܘܐ
⌜* ܝܫܘ⌝ܥ ܡܥܡܕ ܗܘܐ
⌜ܐܠܐ⌝ ܬܠܡܝܕܘܗܝ
[3]⌜ܘܫܒܩܗ⌝ ܠܝܗܘܕ ܘܐܙܠ
⌜ܠܗ ܬܘ⌝ܒ ܠܓܠܝܠܐ.
[4]⌜ܡܥܒܪܐ⌝ ܗܘܬ ܠܗ
⌜* *⌝ ܕܢܥܒܪ ܒܠ
⌜ܒܝ⌝ܬ ܫܡ⌜ܪ⌝ܝܐ. [5]ܘܐܬܐ
⌜ܠܡܕܝܢܬܐ ܚ⌝ܕܐ ܕܫܡܪܝܐ
⌜ܕܡܬܩܪܝ⌝ܐ ܗܘܬ
⌜ܫܟܝܪ ܩ⌝ܪܝܒܬ ܩܪܝܬܐ
⌜ܗܝ ܕܝܗ⌝ܒ ܗܘܐ
⌜ܝܥܩܘܒ ܠܝ⌝ܘܣܦ ܒܪܗ.
[6]⌜ܐܝܬ ܗܘܐ⌝ ܕܝܢ ܬܡܢ
⌜ܡܥܝܢܐ ܕܡ⌝ܝܐ ܕܝܥܩܘܒ.
⌜ܘܐܬܐ ܝܫܘ⌝ܥ ܝܬܒ
⌜ܠܥܠ ܡܢ⌝ܗ ܕܡܥܝܢܐ.
⌜* * * ܕܠ⌝ܐܝܢ ܡܢ

l. 3. There is no room for ⌜ܢܩܘ⌝ܐ

l. 6. ⌜ܕܣܓ⌝ܝܘ] *cf* Rom v 20 syr.vg.

l. 9 *init.*] There is, I think, just room for ⌜ܗܘ ܝ⌝ܫܘܥ: at least, the space is too long for ⌜ܝ⌝ܫܘܥ alone.

l. 11. ⌜ܘܫܒܩܗ⌝] *so* syr.vg and *S* (*sic*): the five letters exactly fit the space. For the construction ܟܕ....ܘܫܒܩܗ, see Lk xiii 10 *ff*, and *Introd.* vol. ii.

l. 13. ⌜ܡܥܒܪܐ⌝] *so* syr.vg.

l. 14 *init.*] The space is almost too big for ⌜ܕܝܢ⌝ only (*so* syr.vg), but no other word suits. Perhaps there was a blank space, as often in *C*.

l. 16. ܚܕܐ is certain. This shews us that *C* had the fem. ܡܕܝܢܬܐ (as syr.vg), and not the masc. ܟܦܪܐ (as *S*).

l. 25 *init.*] The word to be supplied may be ܐܝܟ or ܡܛܠ. *S* is unfortunately illegible at this point.

APPENDIX II.

Fragments of Joh xiv *from a detached leaf of C.*

These fragments of the text of *C* are contained on the upper half of a leaf now numbered *fol.* 52. They thus consist of the upper half of four columns. For the sake of clearness I kept the corresponding portions of *S* in the text (p. 506 *ff*) putting the readings of *C* in the apparatus at the foot of the page.

It is worthy of notice that there are no stops on *fol.* 52 r. Probably therefore this page and the one that stood opposite it (now lost) were passed over by the punctuator, as in the case of *foll.* 48 v, 49 r. Further details will be found in the description of *C* in vol. ii, chapter 1.

fol. 52 r, col 1

xiv 10 ܠܐ ܗܘܐ ܡܢ ܨܒܘܬ
ܐܡܪ ܡܡܠܠܐ ܥܡܟܘܢ
ܐܠܐ ܐܒܝ ܕܒܝ ܗܘ
ܥܒܕ ܥܒܕܐ ܗܠܝܢ
11 ܗܝܡܢܘܢܝ ܕܐܢܐ
ܒܐܒܝ ܐܢܐ ܘܐܒܝ
ܒܝ ܗܘ ܘܐܢ ܠܝ ܠܐ
ܡܗܝܡܢܝܢ ܐܢܬܘܢ ܐܦ
ܡܛܠܬܗܘܢ ܕܥܒܕܐ
12 ܗܝܡܢܘ ܐܡܝܢ ܐܡܝܢ
ܐܡܪܢܐ ܠܟܘܢ ܕܡܢ
ܕܡܗܝܡܢ ܒܝ ܥܒܕܐ
ܐܝܠܝܢ ܕܐܢܐ ܥܒܕܢܐ
ܐܦ ܗܘ ܢܥܒܕ
ܘܕܝܬܝܪܢ ܡܢ ܗܠܝܢ
ܢܥܒܕ * * *

* * * * * *

fol. 52 r, col 2

xiv 15, 16 ܛܪܘ ܘܐܢܐ ܐܒܥܐ
ܡܢ ܐܒܝ ܕܢܫܕܪ ܠܟܘܢ
ܐܚܪܢܐ ܦܪܩܠܛܐ
ܕܢܗܘܐ ܥܡܟܘܢ ܠܥܠܡ
17 ܪܘܚܐ ܕܫܪܪܐ ܗܝ
ܕܥܠܡܐ ܠܐ ܡܫܟܚ
ܠܡܩܒܠܘܬܗ ܠܐ ܓܝܪ
ܚܙܝܗ ܘܠܐ ܝܕܥܗ
ܐܢܬܘܢ ܕܝܢ ܝܕܥܝܢ
ܐܢܬܘܢ ܠܗ ܘܠܘܬܟܘܢ
18 ܥܒܪܐ ܘܥܡܟܘܢ ܗܝ ܘܠܐ
ܐܫܒܘܩܟܘܢ ܝܬܡܐ
19 ܗܐ ܩܠܝܠ ܐ⌜ܚܪ⌝ܢ
ܘ⌜ܥ⌝ܠܡܐ ܠܐ ⌜ܚܙ⌝ܐ *

* * * * * *

fol. 52 v, col 1

xiv 21 ܠܗܘܢ ܗܘ ܗܘ ܪܚܡ
ܠܝ. ܘܡܢ ܕܪܚܡ ܠܝ
ܢܬܪܚܡ ܡܢ ܐܒܐ. ܐܦ
ܐܢܐ ܐܪܚܡܝܘܗܝ. ܘܐܦ
22 ܐܚܘܐܘܗܝ ܢܦܫܝ. ܐܡܪ
ܠܗ ܝܗܘܕܐ ܣܟܪܝܘܛܐ
ܡܪܝ ܡܢܘ ܕܠܢ ܥܬܝܕ
ܐܢܬ ܠܡܚܘܝܘ ܢܦܫܟ
23 ܘܠܐ ܠܥܠܡܐ. ܐܡܪ ܠܗ
ܝܫܘܥ. ܡܢ ܕܪܚܡ ܠܝ
ܡܠܬܝ ܢܛܪ. ܘܐܒܝ
ܢܪܚܡܝܘܗܝ. ܘܠܘܬܗ
ܐܬܝܢ ܐܢܐ. ܘܐܒܘܢ
24 [ܠܘܬܗ] ܐܡܥܒܕ ܠܗ. ܡܢ
ܡ̈ܠܝ * * *
* * * * *

fol. 52 v, col 2

xiv 26 ܐܡܪ ܒܫܡܝ. ܗܘ
ܢܠܦܟܘܢ ܟܠ ܡܕܡ
27 ܕܐܡܪܬ ܠܟܘܢ܆ ܫܠܡܐ
ܫܒܩ ܐܢܐ ܠܟܘܢ܆
ܫܠܡܐ ܕܝܠܝ ܝܗܒ
ܐܢܐ ܠܟܘܢ܆ ܠܐ ܗܘܐ
ܐܝܟ ܕܝܗܒ ܥܠܡܐ
ܝܗܒ ܐܢܐ ܠܟܘܢ܆ ܠܐ
ܢܬܕܘܕ ܠܒܟܘܢ ܘܠܐ
28 ܢܕܚܠ. ܫܡܥܬܘܢ ܕܐܡܪܬ
ܠܟܘܢ ܕܐܙܠ ܐܢܐ ܘܐܬܐ
ܐܢܐ ܠܘܬܟܘܢ ܐܠܘ
ܪܚܡܝܢ ܗܘܝܬܘܢ ܠܝ
ܚܕܝܢ ܗܘܝܬܘܢ ܕܐܙܠ
ܐܢܐ ܠܘܬ ܐܒܝ ܕܪܒ
29 [ܡܢܝ.] ܘܗܫܐ ܗܐ
* * * * *

APPENDIX III.

Corrigenda for the printed text of S.

The readings of *S* as given in this edition differ in more than 250 places from the text as originally printed in 1894 and supplemented by Mrs Lewis in 1896. These new readings have mostly been ascertained by my own study of the photograph of *S* given by Mrs Lewis to the Cambridge University Library. Besides these there are some corrections made by Mrs Lewis from a fresh perusal of the palimpsest itself at Sinai, and published by her in the *Expositor* for August 1897.

I cannot claim to have re-read the photograph absolutely through, but I have done so for a great part of *S*. The method adopted was to attempt to verify in the photograph every alleged reading of *S* which either by faulty grammar or construction invited suspicion, together with those where a very slight change in the text would make it agree with *C*. In many cases the reading of *S* as edited was correct: these verified readings are recorded in the apparatus to this edition with no special mark and are not repeated here. In other cases the photograph was illegible: these readings are marked here and in the apparatus by the sign "S^{ed}". Where the recorded reading of *S* was found to be incorrect I inserted the true reading with the sign "*S* (*sic*)", or in cases where the true reading agreed with the reading of *C* in the text by the sign "*so also S*". In a few instances *S* (*sic*) was put to readings where the edition gave the correct reading but it might have been supposed that a mistake had been made.

In this *Appendix* I give all the readings of *S* which differ from the Syndics' Edition (1894) as corrected and supplemented by Mrs Lewis's *Some Pages* (1896), the only exceptions being a few instances where the *seyâmê* (¨) marking the plural and dots marking punctuation are visible in the photograph though not represented in the edition. After some hesitation I have also included the readings marked S^{ed} in the apparatus.

Note that in all cases where the symbol S^{ed} is used the photograph is illegible. An upright stroke | marks the beginnings and ends of lines in *S*.

i 2 *for* ܘܐܚܘܗܝ *read* ܘܠܐܚܘܗܝ
ii 16 „ ܛܠܝܐ „ ܛܠܝ̈ܐ
16 „ ܒܒܝܬܠܚܡ. ܘܒܬܚܘܡܗ „ ܒܝܬ ܠܚܡ. ܘܒܬܚܘܡܗ
16 „ ܠܗ (S^{nunc}) „ ܟܠܗ (*so* $S^{*(vid)}$)
20 „ ܕܐܝܣܪܝܠ „ ܕܐܝܣܪܐܝܠ
20 „ ܗܢܘܢ „ ܐܝܠܝܢ
21 „ ܗܘ | ܕܝܢ ܩܡ „ ܘܗܘ | ܩܡ
21 „ ܕܐܝܣܪܝܠ „ ܕܐܝܣܪܐܝܠ
22 „ ܘܐܬܛܫܝ „ ܘܛܫܐ (*sic*)
iv 18* „ ܘܐܚܝܢ ⌜ܕܗܘ⌝ „ ܘܐܚܝܢ ܕܕܒܪ
v 20 *This verse should be printed thus:*

ܕܐܠܐ ܬܬܝܬܪ ⌜ܙܕܝܩܘܬܟܘܢ⌝
ܡܢ ⌜ܣܦܪ̈ܐ⌝ ܘܦܪ̈ܝܫܐ
ܠܐ ܬܥܠܘܢ ⌜ܠܡܠܟܘܬܐ⌝ ܕܫܡܝܐ

viii 21 ܐܡܪ ܠܗ S^{ed}: *in the photograph* ܠܗ *is illegible, and perhaps we ought to read* ܐܡܪ ⌜ܡܪܝ⌝
24 *for* ܥܠܥܠܐ | ܪܒܐ ܒܡܨܥܬܐ ⌜ܘܪܘܪ̈ܒܐ⌝ | ܗܘܬ (S^{ed}), *I have conjectured* ܥܠܥܠܐ | ܕܝܡܐ ⌜ܘܡܫܘܢ̈ܬܐ⌝ ܪܒܐ | ܗܘܬ
28 *for* ⌜ܩܒܘܪ̈ܐ⌝ *read* ⌜ܩܒܪ̈ܐ⌝
32 „ ܢܦܩܘ ܥܠܘ (‘*Some Pages*’) „ ܢܦܩܘ ܘܥܠܘ (*Syndics*’ *Ed.*)
33* *after* ܟܠ ܡܕܡ *add* ܕܕܝܘܢܐ
34 *for* ܚܙܐܘܗܝ S^{ed} *read* ⌜ܚܙܘ̈ܗܝ⌝
34* „ | ܡܢ ܬܚܘܡܗܘܢ | *read* ܡܢ | ܠܬܚܘܡܗܘܢ ⌜ܘܫܠܘ⌝ ܠܡܫܝܢܘܬܐ
ix 10* „ ܘܡܢ ⌜ܬܠܡܝܕܘ̈ܗܝ⌝ *read* ܘܠܘܬ ⌜ܬܠܡܝܕܘ̈ܗܝ⌝
21 „ ܒܢܫܗ „ ⌜ܒܢܦܫܗ⌝
27 „ ܩܡ „ ܘܩܡ
36 ܠܗܘܢ S^{ed}: *perhaps we should read* ⌜ܠܗܝܢ⌝

* See *Expositor* for August, 1897, p. 113 *f.*

xi 3 ܠܐܚܪܢܝܢ S^{ed}: *read* ܠܐܚܪ̈ܢܐ

21 ܨܝܕܘܢ | ܨܘܪ ܘ S^{ed}: *read* ܘܨܝܕܘܢ | ܨܘܪ ܘ (*as C*)

22 ܘܠܨܝܕܘܢ S^{ed}: *read* ܘܠܨܝܕܘܢ. *I feel sure I must have been mistaken in* 1893

24 ܕܠܣܕܘܡ S^{ed}: *read* ܕܠܣܕܡ (*as C*)

xii 6 ܪܒ S^{ed}: *read* ܕܪܒ (*as C*)

22* *This verse begins a fresh paragraph in S, and* ܘܩܪܒܘ *is legible at the end of the second line*

33 ܐܝܠܢ S^{ed}: *read* ܐܝܠܢ

34 *for* ܬܘܬܪܬܐ *read* ܬܘܬܪ̈ܬܐ

xiii 5 ,, ܘܡܛܠ ܕܗܘܝܐ ܗܘܐ (S^{ed}), *I read* ܘܡܛܠ ܕܥܘܡܩܐ ܗܘܐ *from the photograph*

xiv 24 ܘܐܬܛܪܦܬ * * * | ܡܢ ܓܠܐ S^{ed}: *read* ܘܐܬܛܪܦܬ ܒܓܠ̈ܠܝܗ | ܡܢ ܓܠܐ (*or possibly* ܘܐܬܛܪܦܬ ܗܘܬ ܒܓܠܠܝܗ | ܡܢ ܓܠܐ)

xv 16 ܗܟܢܐ ܠܡܢܐ | S^{ed}, *but* ܠܡܢܐ *does not come to the end of the line, a blank space being left*

19 *for* ܘܣܗܕܘܬܐ | ܕܓܢܒܘܬܐ *read* ܘܣܗܕܘܬ | ܓܢܒܘܬܐ

24 ܐܠܐ ܫܠܝܚܢ ܕܐܠܗܐ S^{ed}: *the photograph suggests to me rather* ܐܠܐ ܫܠܝܚ ܕܐܠܗܐ

32 *for* ܘܝܘܡܝܢ *read* ܬܝܘܡܝܢ

xvi 1 ܡܢܣܝܢ S^{ed}: *read* ܘܡܢܣܝܢ (*as C*)

9 ܠܗܘܢ S^{ed}: *read* ܚܡܫܬܗܘܢ (*as C*)

xvii 19 *for* ܐܫܟܚܢ *read* ܐܫܟܚܢ [i.e. ܐܫܟܚܢ]

xviii 9 ,, ܟܕ ܐܝܬ | ,, ܟܕ ܐܝܬ ܠܟ |

9 ,, ܕܬܐܙܠ ,, ܘܬܐܙܠ

13 ܒܗ̇ *in 'Some Pages' is a misprint for* ܒܗ.

15 *for* ܐܢ *read* ܐܢ

19 *A line is here missed out. Read*

ܬܘܒ ܐܡܝܢ ܐܡܪ ܐܢܐ
ܠܟܘܢ ܕܐܢ ܬܪܝܢ ܡܢܟܘܢ
ܢܫܬܘܘܢ ܒܐܪܥܐ ܥܠ
ܟܠ ܨܒܘ

27 *for* ܐܫܬܪܝܗ *read* ܘܐܫܬܪܝܗ

* See *Expositor* for August, 1897, p. 114.

xviii 29 *for* ܐܓܪܪ *read* ܐܓܪܪ

32 „ ܗܐ „ ܗܝ

xxi 38 ܝܪܬܘܬܐ S^{ed}: *perhaps we should read* ܝܪܬܗ *(as C)*

xxii 13 *for* ܐܘܚܕܘܗܝ *read* ܐܚܕܘܗܝ

15 „ ܢܨܕܘ *(misprint)* „ ܚܨܕܘ

16 „ ܬܠܡܝܕܘܗܝ „ ܬܠܡܝܕܘܗܝ *(sic)*

17 „ ܪܫܐ „ ܪܫܐ

18 „ ܡܥܒܕ ܕܝܢ ܡܢܟ „ ܡܥܒܕ ܕܝܢ ܒܢ ܡܢܟ

19 „ ܚܘܐܘܢܝ „ ܚܘܘܢܝ

19 „ ܪܫܐ ܘܐܘܫܛܘ ܠܗ „ ܪܫܐ ܘܐܫܛܘ ܠܗ

24 „ ܒܪܐ „ ܒܢܝܐ

27 „ ܘܐܚܪܬܐ „ ܒܐܚܪܬܐ

28 „ ܒܚܪܬܐ * * | ܠܐܝܢܐ „ ܒܚܪܬ ܒܚܪܬܐ | ܠܐܝܢܐ

30 „ ܕܐܠܗܐ „ ܐܝܟ

31 „ | ܕܡܢ „ | ܕܝܢ ܕܡܢ

xxiii 6 „ ܒܣܡܟܬܐ „ ܒܣܡܟܐ

37 „ ܕܩܛܠܬ ܢܒܝܐ ܘܪܓܡܬ „ ܕܩܛܠܬܝ ܢܒܝܐ ܘܪܓܡܬܝ

37 „ ܠܘܬܟܝ „ ܠܘܬܟ

37 „ ܠܒܢܝܟܝ ܐܝܟ ܕܬܪܢܓܘܠܬܐ „ ܠܒܢܝܟ ܐܝܟ ܬܪܢܓܘܠܬܐ

xxiv 39 „ ܕܒܪܐ | ܕܐܡܬܐ „ ܕܒܪܗ | ܕܐܡܬܐ

43 „ | * ܡܕܡ ܕܝܢ ܗܕܐ * * | „ | ܡܕܡ ܗܘܝܬܘܢ ܘܗܕܐ |

xxvi 10 ܥܒܕܐ ܦܠܚܐ S^{ed}: *? read* ܦܠܚ, *or* ܘܦܠܚܐ

24 *for* ܕܡܫܬܠܡ *read* ܡܫܬܠܡ *(sic)*

34 „ ܒܠܠܐ „ ܒܠܠܐ

50 ܕܐܬܝܬ *S (sic): a photograph taken by Mrs Lewis in* 1902 *shews the initial* ܕ *clearly*

60 | ܐܬ * * ܫ * ܠܚܕܐ | *is clear, as in* S^{ed}: *read* ܠܚܕܐ ܣܗܕܐ ܫܪܪܬܐ

67 ܡܚܠܗܘܢ S^{ed}: *read* ܡܚܘ ܠܗ (*as* Diat[ar] xlix 40)

xxvii 43 ܗܘܐ ܬܟܝܠ | ܗܘ S^{ed}: *? read* ܗܘܐ ܕܬܟܝܠ | ܗܘ ܐܢ

S. MARK

iii 28 *for* ܕܢܓܕܦܘܢ *read* ܕܡܓܕܦܝܢ

29 ,, ܟܠ * * | ܕܝܢ ܕܢܓܕܦ ,, ܟܠ ܕܝܢ | ܕܢܓܕܦ

The last word I thought was ܕܡܓܕܦ, *but Mrs Lewis in* 1902 *considered that* ܕܢܓܕܦ *was legible in the* MS

iv 5 *for* ܥܡܩܗ *read* ܥܡܩܗܘܢ

6 ,, ܕܗܘܐ * * ܘܝܒܫ ,, ܕܗܘܐ ܥܩܪܗܘܢ ܘܝܒܫ

7 ,, ܘܚܢܩܘ | ܥܡܗܐ ,, ܘܚܢܩܘ ܥܡܗ | ܥܡܗܐ

8 ,, ܦܐܪܐ * * * | ܥܬܠܬܝܢ ,, ܦܐܪܐ * * ܘܝܗܒ | ܥܬܠܬܝܢ

9* ,, ܕܫܡܥ * * ,, ܕܫܡܥ ܢܫܡܥ

12 ,, ܢܫܡܥܘܢ | ܘܠܐ ܢܣܬܟܠܘܢ ,, ܘܫܡܥܝܢ | ܠܐ ܢܣܬܟܠܘܢ

17 ,, ܒܢܦܫܗܘܢ ,, ܒܗ

v 13 ,, ܢܦܩ....ܥܠܡ ,, ܢܦܩ....ܥܠ

18 ,, ܗܘ | ܕܫܐܕܐ ,, ܗܘ | ܕܫܐܕܗ

vi 49 ܫܘܢܝܗܝ S^{ed}, *but I feel doubtful whether we should not read* ܫܘܘܗܝ, *as elsewhere*

55* *for* ܒܪܘܗ *read* ܫܪܘ

56 ,, ܘܫܘܩܐ ,, ܒܫܘܩܐ

vii 30 ܘܢܦܩ S^{ed}: *read* ܘܢܦܩܬ

31 *for* ܢܦܩ *read* ܟܕ ܢܦܩ

35 ܐܬܦܬܚܘ S^{ed}: *read* ܐܬܦܬܘ

viii 3 ܘܐܝܟ ܗܘ ܕܫܪܝܐ ܐܢܐ S^{ed}: *? read* ܘܐܝܟ ܗܘ ܕܫܪܝܐ ܠܗܘܢ (*as* syr.vg)

19, 20* *read* | ܐܡܪܝܢ | ܠܗ ܬܪܬܥܣܪ ܐܡܪ | ܠܗܘܢ ܘܟܕ ܫܒܥܐ |

20, 21* ,, | ܕܦܝܫܐ ܫܩܠܬܘܢ ܐܡܪܝܢ | ܠܗ ܫܒܥܐ ܐܡܪ ܠܗܘܢ |

25* *for* | ܟܠ ܚܙܘܗܝ * * | *read* | ܟܠ ܚܙܘܗܝ * * ܐ |

38* ,, ܒܢܝ ,, ܒܒܢܝ

ix 2 ܘܐܬܚܠܦ S^{ed}: *this spelling is probably correct, as it is found here in the better* MSS *of* syr.vg

* See *Expositor* for August, 1897, p. 114*f*.

ix 28 *for* ܕܠܒܪܐ *read* ܕܠܒܪܝܐ

45 ,, ܕܬܐܙܠ ,, ܬܐܙܠ

47 ,, ܕܬܐܙܠ ,, ܬܐܙܠ

x 21 *for* ܢܬܪܬ *read* ⌜ܘܝܫ⌝ܘܥ (*the first letter not quite certain*)

21 ,, ܚܕܝ ܒܗ ܝܫܘܥ ⌜ܐ⌝⌜ܣܓ⌝ܝ ⌜ܠܗ⌝ *read* ܚܕܝ ܒܗ ܣܓ⌜ܝܐ⌝ܝܬ

22* ,, ⌜ܒܪ⌝ ,, ܒܪ

35 ,, ܕܬܒܒܪ ,, ܬܒܒܪ

xi 2 ,, ܕܠܡܘܒܠܗܘܢ ,, ܕܠܡܒܠܗܘܢ

3 ,, ܘܐܬܐܡܘܗܝ ,, ܘܐܬܡܘܗܝ (*sic*)

3 ,, ܠܒܪܐ ,, ܕܠܒܪܗ

13 ⌜ܬܬܐ ܚܝܐ⌝ *S*^ed^ (*photograph illegible, but there is only room for one word*): *read* ⌜ܬܬܐ⌝

20 *for* ܒܥܒܐ (*misprint*) *read* ܒܨܒܥܐ

22 ܗܘ *S*^ed^: *this word is not visible in the photograph* (*? omit*)

23 *for* ⌜ܢ̈⌝ܗܘܐ | ܢܗܘܐ *read* ܕܗܘܐ | ܢܗܘܐ

xii 23 ,, ܗܟܐ ⌜ܕ⌝ܢ⌜ܦ⌝ܫܟܘܢ ,, ܗܟܐ ܕܢܦܫܐ

23(*) ܕܡܢ (*S*^ed^) *is correct, not* ܠܡܢ

23 *for* ⌜ܒܢ̈ܝ⌝ ܥܘܒܕܬܗܘܢ *read* ܗܐ ܒܢܝ ܥܘܒܕܬܗܘܢ

24(*), 25 *The text of S is*

²⁴ܥܢܐ ܝܫܘܥ
ܘܐܡܪ ܠܗܘܢ ܡܛܠ ܗܢܐ
ܗܘ ܛܥܝܢ ܐܢܬܘܢ ܕܠܐ
ܝܕܥܝܢ ܐܢܬܘܢ ܟܬܒܐ
⌜ܐܦ⌝ ܠܐ ܚܝܠܗ ܕܐܠܗܐ
²⁵ܒܢܝܐ ܕܥܠܡܐ ܕܝܢ ܗܢ
ܒܗ ܡܬܬܝܐ ܠܐ ܢܫܐ
ܢܣܒܝܢ ܘܐܦܠܐ ܢܫܐ
ܗܘܝܢ ܠܓܒܪܐ

26 *for* ܕܫܘܫܢ *read* ܕܐܫܘܫܢ

27* ,, | ܘܗܐ ܐܠܗܐ * * | ,, | ܘܗܐ ܐܠܗܐ ܠܐ ⌜ܗܘܐ⌝ |

29 ,, ⌜ܡ⌝ܒܥܝܐ ,, ܡܒܥܝܢ

29* ,, | ܬܬܥܙܠ * * * * | ,, | ܐܬܥܙܠ ܡܕܝܢܐ |

(*The space between the two words is probably blank*)

* See *Expositor* for August, 1897, p. 115.

xii 32 *for* ܐܚܪܝܢ *read* ܐܚܪܢ

33 ,, * * ܬܪ ܗܘ ,, ܕܡܝܬܪ ܗܘ

xiii 15 ,, ܘܠܘ ,, ܘܠܐ

25 ,, ܘܢܘܥܘܢ | ܚ̈ܝܠܘܬܗ ,, ܘܢܘܥܘܢ | ܚ̈ܝܠܘܬܐ (*sic*)

27 ,, ܪ̈ܘܚܐ *read* ܪ̈ܘܚܗ (*so I now read the photograph*)

28 ,, ܕܬܐܢ *read* ܕܬܐܢܗ (*sic*)

xiv 4 ܕܠܡܢܐ S^{ed}: *read* ܕܠܡܢ̈ܐ

5 *for* ܒܫܢܬܗܘܢ *read* ܒܢܝܬܗܘܢ

9 ܗܕܐ S^{ed}: *read* ܗܕ̈ܐ (*with Merx*)

9 *for* ܡܣܒܪܬܐ *read* ܡܣܒܪܬܝ.

12 ,, ܕܬܠܚܡ ,, ܕܬܢܚܡ

13 ,, ܠܗܘܢ ,, ܒܗܘܢ

14 ,, | ܐܬܩܢܘܢ ܐܝܠܢܐ * ܕܒܢ ,, | ܐܝܟ̈ܠܘܗ ܐܝܟܐ ܡܫܪܝ

19 ,, | * * ܫܪܝܘ ܕܬܒܪ ,, | ܫܪܝܘ ܗܬܒܪ

22 ,, ܝܗܒ ,, ܘܝܗܒ

54 ,, ܠܕܪܬܗܘܢ ,, ܒܕܪܬܗ

56 ,, ܣܗܕܐ | ,, ܣܗ̈ܕܐ |

62 ,, ܝܬܒ ,, ܕܝܬܒ

xv 7 ܘܐܣܝܪܐ S^{ed}: *read* ܘܐܣܝܪ

8 *for* ܘܒܥܐ *read* ܘܠܒܐ

11 ,, ܐܦܣܘ ,, ܐܦ̈ܣܘ

16 ܕܕܪܬܐ ܠܓܘ S^{ed}: *read* ܠܓܘ ܕܪܬܐ

23 *for* ܒܒܣܡܝܐ *read* ܒܒܣܡܐ

xvi 2 ,, ܐܬܝܢ ,, ܐܬܝ

4 ,, ܘܐܙܠ ,, ܘܐܬܝ (*sic*)

5 ,, ܘܥܠܘ ,, ܘܥܠ

5 ,, ܘܕܚܠܘ ,, ܘܕܚܠ

7 ܐܡܪܝ ܐܙܠ S^{ed}: *in* 1893 *I read* ܐܙ̈ܠ ܐܡܪ̈ܝܢ *from the* MS

7 ܬܚܙܘܢܗ S^{ed}: *in* 1893 *I read* ܚܙܘܢܗ

8 ܥܒܕܢ S^{ed}: *read* ܥܒܕ

8 ܢܦܩ S^{ed} (*and Mrs Lewis in Expositor for* 1897, p. 115): *the photograph is illegible, but S may have* .ܢܦܩ, *with a dot*

8 *for* ܘܐܙܠ *read* ܘܐܙܠ (*Syndics' Ed., p.* xxxvi)

8 ,, ܕܕܚܠܢ: *my transcript has* ܕܕܚܠ

S. LUKE

i 3* *for* ܕܒܨܝܬ *read* ܕܒܨܬ

80* ,, ܘܡܬܒܪܒܪܐ * * * | ,, ܘܡܬܒܪܒܪܐ ܐܝܬ ܗܘܐ |

ii 8, 9 ܕܢܛܪܝܢ ܗܘܘ *and* ܐܬܚܙܝ *must be wrong, but the photograph is quite illegible.* ܩܐܡ (*v.* 9) *is visible*

12 ܗܐ ܘܗܢܐ S^{ed} *must be wrong: photograph illegible*

15 ܬܘ ܢܬ * * S^{ed}: *read* ܬܘ ܢܪܕ

43 ܒܫܘܬܦܗܘܢ S^{ed}: *read* ܒܬܪܗܘܢ

44 *for* * ܚܕ | ܝܘܡܐ *read* * ܕܚܕ | ܝܘܡܐ

44 ,, ܒܝܕܥܘܗܝ ,, ܒܥܝܢ ܗܘܘ

45 ,, ܘܠܐ ,, ܘܟܕ ܠܐ

52 ,, ܘܩܘܡܬܗ ,, ܘܒܩܘܡܬܗ

iii 1 ܒܫܘܢܬܐ (S^{nunc}): *I thought the first hand of S wrote* ܒܫܘܢܬ (*as C*), *but Mrs Lewis in* 1902 *thought the final* ܐ *was original*

9 *for* ܠܐ *read* ܕܠܐ

23 ,, ܐܝܟ ܕܡܬܬܣܒܪܐ ܒܪܗ ,, ܗܘܐ ܡܫܬܡܥ ܕܒܪܗ (*sic*)

iv 6 ,, ܕܠܟ ܝܗܒ * ܘܠܡܢ ,, ܕܠܟ ܝܗܒ ܘܠܡܢ

28 ,, ܫܡܥܘ ,, ܘܟܕ ܫܡܥܘ

35 ,, ܢܦܩ ,, ܘܢܦܩ

36 ܐܚܕ S^{ed}: *read* ܐܚܕ

40 ܕܡܪܥܐ S^{ed}: *read* ܕܡܪܥܝܢ

40 *for* ܘܟܠܗܘܢ ,, ܟܘܠܗܘܢ

v 1 ܗܘܐ ܟܢܫܐ | ܟܕ ܐܕܫܐ S^{ed}: *instead of* ܟܕ *the line appears to begin with* ܝ *or* ܫ

17 *for* ܘܐܬܝܢ ܗܘܘ *read* ܘܕܐܬܘ

17 ,, ܘܝܗܘܕ ܘܐܘܪܫܠܡ ,, ܕܝܗܘܕ ܘܕܐܘܪܫܠܡ (*sic*)

17 ,, ܘܚܝܠܐ * * * ܕܡܪܢ ,, ܘܚܝܠܐ ܗܘܐ ܕܡܪܢ

18 ,, ܠܗܘܢ | ܘ[18]ܐܢܫܐ ,, ܘܗܐ[18] | ܐܢܫܐ

18 ,, ܒܥܪܣܐ ܓܒܪܐ ,, ܓܒܪܐ ܒܥܪܣܐ

* See *Expositor* for August, 1897, p. 115.

v 18 *for* ܘܒܥܝܢ ܗܘܘ * * * | ܘܢܣܝܡܘܢ ܠܗ *read*
ܘܒܥܝܢ ܗܘܘ ܕܐܢܥܠܘܢ | ܢܣܝܡܘܢܗ

20, 21* *for* ܫܪܝܘ * * * * | *read* ܫܪܝܘ ܘܐܡܪܘ * * |

22 ܒܠܒܝܟܘܢ S^{ed}: *read* ܒܠܒܟܘܢ *or, more probably,* ܒܠܒܘܬܟܘܢ

25 *for* ܘܩܡ ܒܪ ܫܥܬܐ ܗܝ *read* ܘܒܗ ܒܫܥܬܐ ܩܡ

vi 18 ,, ܕܡܬܐܠܨܝܢ *read* ܘܡܬܐܠܨܝܢ (*sic, as Syndics' Ed.*)

23 ,, ܐܬܝܘܢ *read* ܐܬܝܘܢ ܕܝܢ

24 ,, ܒܘܝܐܟܘܢ ,, ܒܘܬܟܘܢ

33 ,, * * * * | * * ܡܢ ܕܡܬܬܦܪܥܝܢ *read* ܠܟܠ ܡܢ ܕܒܥܐ | ܢܬܒܥܘܢ ܕܬܠܒ

34 ,, | * * *read* | ܗܐ

44 ,, ܠܐ ܓܝܪ ܠܩܛܝܢ ܒܘܛܡܐ ,, ܠܐ ܠܩܛܝܢ ܡܢ ܒܘܛܡܐ (*sic*)

vii 14* ,, ܠܐܪܘܢ *read* ܠܐ....ܐ: *the word is probably* ܠܐܪܢܐ (*not* ܠܐܪܘܢܐ)

20 ,, ܠܐܚܪܝܢ *read* ܠܐܚܪܢ, *and in the next line* ܚܝܢ (S^{ed}) *should be* ܐܚܪܝܢ

viii 6 ,, ܢܦܠܘ *read* ܢܦܠ

11 ܡܠܬܗ ܕܐܠܗܐ S^{ed}: *all the letters to the left of* ܬ *are now torn away*

12 | * ܘܐܬܐ ܒܠܒܒܗܘܢ S^{ed}: *the photograph is illegible, but there is no room for* ܡܠܬܐ ܕܐܠܗܐ *before* ܘܐܬܐ *as in C*

19 *for* ܕܢ * * ܘܢ ܒܟܢܫܗ, *the photograph suggests* ܕܢܬܟܠܠܘܢ ܒܟܢܫܗ

41 *This verse begins a paragraph in S*

44 *for* ܘܩܪܒܬ | ܒܣܬܪܗ *read* ܘܩܪܒܬ ܡܢ | ܒܣܬܪܗ

47 ,, ܠܗ ܗܕܐ ,, ܗܝ ܗܕܐ

ix 6 ܡܣܒܪܝܢ S^{ed}: ? *read* ܘܡܣܒܪܝܢ

11 ܕܡܣܬܢܩܝܢ ܗܘܘ S^{ed}: *read* ܕܡܣܬܢܩܝܢ ܠܗ

17, 18 *for a conjectural restoration of S, see* p. 302

28 *This verse begins a paragraph in S*

33 *for* ܡܛܠܠܝܢ *read* ܡ̈ܛܠܠܝܢ

36 ,, ܐܢܫܐ ,, ܐܢܫ

38 ,, ܐܬܦܝܣܐ ܒܟ ,, ܐܬܦܝܣ ܒܟ.

40** ,, ܠܡܦܩܣܘܬܗ ,, ܠܡܦܩܢܘܬܗ

44 ,, ܫܝܡܘ ,, ܣܝܡܘ

* See *Expositor* for August, 1897, p. 115*f.*

** I feel certain myself of ܠܡܦܩܢܘܬܗ, but in this instance I could not persuade Dr Rendel Harris.

ix 45 *for* ܘܗܘܢ ܕܝܠܡ ܟܠܗܡ. *read* ܘܗܘܢ ܕܝܠܡ ⌜ܗܘܘ⌝ | ܕܢܫܬܐܠܘܢ ܟܠܗܡ.

52 ,, ܘܐܙܠܘ *read* ܐܬܘ

x 4* ,, ܠܟܘܢ ܒܢܦܫܐ * * ,, ܠܟܘܢ ܒܢܦܫܐ ܘܠܐ

4* ,, ܬܪܥܠܐ ܘܠܐ * * ,, ܬܪܥܠܐ ܘܠܐ ܒܢܦܫܐ

6** ,, ܐܝܟ ܕܝܢ ܠܐ ,, ܐܝܟ ܕܠܐ (*sic*)

15 ,, ⌜ܬ⌝ܬܚܫ⌜ܡ⌝ ,, ܬܚܫܡ

17 ܐܒܪܗܡ S^{ed}: *read* ⌜ܘ⌝ܐܒܪܗܡ (*as C*)

17 *The extra line indicated at the top of* col. 2 *in 'Some Pages,'* p. 75, *is a mistake*

34 *for* ܟܠܗܘܢ *read* ܟܠܗܡ

xi 6 ܒܢܝܐ S^{ed}: *? read* ܘܛܠܝܐ (*as C*)

7 ܘܒܛܠ S^{ed}: *the initial* ܘ *does not shew on the photograph of* 1902, *and I doubt whether S did not simply read* ܒܛܠ

7 *for* ܣܝܡܘܬܐ *read* ܣܝܡܬܐ (*sic*)

13 ܕܢܛܠ ⌜ܕܒ⌝ܥܒܕܝܐ S^{ed}: *read* ⌜ܡܢ⌝ ܥܒܕܝܐ ܢܛܠ (*as C*)

15 ⌜ܡܢܟܣ⌝ | * * ܥܐܕܐ S^{ed}: *read* ⌜ܡܢܟܣ⌝ | ܥܐܕܐ

17 ܢܕܒ | S^{ed}: *read* ⌜ܒܕ⌝ ܢܕܒ | (*as C*)

23 * * | ܡܒܒܕܪ S^{ed}: *read* ⌜ܠ⌝ | ܡܒܒܕܪ

24 *read* ܪܘܚܐ ܦܠܓܘܬܐ, *and* ⌜ܒܗܘܢ⌝ (*for* ⌜ܒܗܡ⌝)

24 *for* | ܐܗܦܟܬ ܐܙܠ ܠܒܝܬܝ | *? read* | ⌜ܡܢ⌝ ܠܒܝܬܝ ܐܗܦܟܬ |

26 ܒܫܡ S^{ed}: *read* ܕܒܫܡ (*as C*)

32 ܚܝܘ S^{ed}: *? read* ܚܝܘܐ (*as C*)

37 ⌜ܘܒܕ⌝ S^{ed}: *see note on* p. 324

50 *for* ܗܘܐ *read* ܗܐ

xii 19 ,, ܡܫܒܚ ,, ܫܒܚܠ

31 ,, ܗܒܠ (*'Some Pages'*) ,, ⌜ܡܒ⌝ܠ (*as Syndics' Ed.*)

42 ܕܢܣܒܘܗܝ S^{ed}: *the suffix is not clear in the photograph*

54 ܒܪܫܒܬܐ S^{ed}: *read* ⌜ܒܪܫܒܬܗ⌝

55 *for* ⌜ܕܢ⌝ܘ⌜ܣ⌝ܒܐ *read* ܕܒܘܪܢܐ

xiii 3 ܗܒܢܐ ⌜ܐܢܬܘܢ⌝ S^{ed}: *read* ܗܒܢܐ ⌜ܟܠܟܘܢ⌝

5 *for* ܐܠܐ ܬܬܘܟܠܘܢ ܐܢܬܘܢ *read* ܟܠܟܘܢ ܐܠܐ ܬܬܘܟܠܘܢ

6 ܠܗ S^{ed}: *read* ܒܗ (*as C*)

7 ܐܬܐ S^{ed}: *? read* ܐܬܝܐ

* See *Expositor* for August, 1897, p. 116.

** This correction is due to Mrs Lewis, who examined the passage at Sinai in 1902.

xiii	7	*for*	ܘܡܒܠܐ	*read*	ܡܒܠܐ

7 ܡܒ*ܛܠܠ S^{ed}: *read* ܡܒܛܠܠܐ

13 ܘܒܪ ܫܒܚܬܐ S^{ed}: *read* ܘܒܪ ܫܒܚܬܗ

14 ܕܫܒܘܬܐ S^{ed} (*cf* Lk xx 29): *photograph illegible*

19 *for* ܘܐܪܒܝܬܗ *read* ܘܐܪܒܝܬ

20 ܠܡܠܟܘܬܐ S^{ed}: *read* ܡܠܟܘܬܐ (*as C*)

25 ܒܝܬܐ | ܡܪܗ S^{ed}: *the* ܒ *is illegible in the photograph* (i.e. *S may have* ܕܒܝܬܐ | ܡܪܗ)

28 *for* ܘܠܢܒܝܐ *read* ܘܠܐܢܒܝܐ

28 ܒܡܠܟܘܬܗ S^{ed}: *? read* ܒܡܠܟܘܬܐ (*as* C^{nunc})

xiv	1	*This verse begins a paragraph in S*			
	1	*for*	ܗܘܝ	*read*	ܕܗܘܝ (*as C*)
	4	,,	ܫܬܩܘ	,,	ܫܬܩܘ
	10	,,	ܐܚܪܬܐ	,,	ܐܚܪܬܐ
	28	,,	ܢܦܩܬܐ	,,	ܢܦܩܬܗ

xv 4 ܡܢܟܐ S^{ed}: *read* ܡܢܟܘܢ (*as C*)

4 *for* ܘܬܫܒܘܩ *read* ܘܬܫܒܘܩܐ

6 ܕܐܒܕ S^{ed}: *read* ܕܐܒܕ (*as C*)

7 ܘܬܫܒܘܩ S^{ed}: *read* ܘܬܫܒܘܩܐ (*cf ver.* 4)

	12*	*for*	ܠܗ * * * *	*read*	ܠܗܘܢ ܟܠܗ ܢܟܣܘܗܝ
xvi	2	,,	ܪܒܝܬܐ	,,	ܪܒܝܬܐ
	3	,,	ܪܒܝܬܐ	,,	ܪܒ ܒܝܬܐ
	3	,,	ܘܠܡܚܙܪ	,,	ܘܕܐܚܙܪ
	4	,,	ܝܕܥ ܠܝ	,,	ܝܕܥܬ
	7	,,	ܘܡܬܘܡ * * ܐܡܪ	*read* ܐܡܪ	ܘܡܬܘܡ (*nothing lost*)
	8	,,	ܡܪܝܐ	*read*	ܡܪܝܐ (*as C*)
	8	,,	ܒܕܪܗܘܢ ܗܢܐ	,,	ܒܫܪܒܗܘܢ ܗܢܐ
	9	,,	ܠܡܛܠܠܗܘܢ	,,	ܒܡܛܠܠܗܘܢ

12 ܡܢܟܐ S^{ed}: *read* ܡܢܟ (*as C*) *or* ܡܢܟܘܢ

	16	*for*	ܡܬܚܙܝܢ	*read*	ܡܬܚܙܝ
	24	,,	ܘܢܦܘܪ	,,	ܢܦܘܪ
	27	,,	ܕܬܫܕܪܝܘܗܝ	,,	ܕܬܫܕܪܘܗܝ
xvii	2	,,	ܢܦܠ	,,	ܢܦܠ
	6	,,	ܐܝܬ ܠܟܘܢ	,,	ܐܝܬ ܒܟܘܢ

* See *Expositor* for August, 1897, p. 116.

xvii 9* *for* ܠܥܒܕܬܐ ܢܥܒܕܗ | ܐܘܚܕ *read* ܠܥܒܕܬܐ ܕܢܥܒܕܗ | ܐܚܕ

11 *for* ܠܓܠܝ̈ܠܝܐ *I think we should read* ܠܓܠܠܝܐ (*but not* ܠܓܠܝܠܐ)

13* „ ܘܐܪܝܡܘ *read* ܘܐܪ̈ܝܡܘ

14 ܐܙܠܘ | ܒܕ S^{ed}: *? read* ܐܙܠܘ | ܘܒܕ

17 *for* ܘܐܡܪ ܠܗ ܠܐ ܒܥܣܪܐ *read* ܘܐܡܪ ܗܘܐ ܒܥܣܪܐ

xviii 31 „ ܐܚܝܢ „ ܐܚܝܢ

32 „ ܒܐܢܦܘܗܝ „ ܒܐ̈ܦܘܗܝ

xix 7 ܗܘܘ S^{ed}: *? read* ܗܠܝܢ

15 ⌜ܡܢܘ⌝⌜ܡܢܐ⌝ S^{ed}, *but there is only room for one word: read* ⌜ܡܢܐ⌝ (*as C*)

17 *for* ܒܡܠܝܠ *read* ܕܒܡܠܝܠ

28 „ ܢܦܩܘ „ ܢܦܩ

47 „ ܡܠܦ „ ܘܡܠܦ

47 „ ܘܪ̈ܫܝܗܘܢ ܕܥܡܐ „ ܘܪ̈ܫܐ ܕܥܡܐ

xx 12 „ ܘܬܠܬܝܐ „ ܕܬܠܬܝܐ

12 „ ܘܐܦ * ܗܘܢ ܘܫܡܫܘܗܝ „ ܘܐܦ ܠܗ ܒܫܘܡܫܬܐ

20 „ ܒܪܢܫܐ „ ܒܪ̈ܢܫܐ

26 ܒܬܒܥܬܐ S^{ed}: *read* ܒܬܒܥܬܗ (*as C*)

28 *for* ܘܢܣܒ *read* ܕܢܣܒ

xxi 34* „ ܕܠܐ ܢܐܬܘܢ „ ܕܠܐ ܡܬܘܩ ܢܐܬܘܢ

37 ܕܡܫܒܚܘܢ S^{ed}: *read* ܕܡܫܒܚܘܢܗ (*as C*)

xxii 50 *for* ܠܥܒܕܐ *read* ܠܥܒܕܗ

51 „ ܠܐܕܢܐ „ ܠܐܕܢܗ

59 „ ܓܠܝܠܝܐ „ ܓܠܝܠܐ

62, 63 *There is a point after* ܡܪܝܪܐܝܬ *in S, but ver. 63 does not begin a fresh paragraph*

xxiii 3 *for* ⌜ܒܘܕ⌝ *read* ܒܘܕ

8 „ ܗܪܘܕܣ „ ܗܪܘܕܣ

15 „ ܡܕܡ „ ܘܡܕܡ

xxiv 26 „ ܠܬܫܒܘܚܬܗ „ ܠܬܫܒܘܚܬܗ

31 „ ܘܒܩܝܐ „ ܘܒܩܝܐ

31 „ ܐܬܚܙܝ „ ܐܬܚܙܝ

41* „ | * * * * ܗܘܘ „ | * * ܡܬܕܡܪܝܢ ܗܘܘ

* See *Expositor* for August, 1897, p. 116*f*.

S. JOHN.

i 29 *for* |* * * ܕܐܠܗܐ ܗܘ| *read* |ܕܐܠܗܐ ܗܘܐ ܗܢ|

30 „ ܕܐܬܐ ܐܡܪܬ „ ܕܐܡܪܬ ܗܘܝܬ

36 ܐܢܐ ܚܐ S^{ed}: *possibly we should read* ܡܫܝܚܐ

iii 1 *for* |ܢܝܩܘܕܡܘܣ. *read* |ܗܘܐ ܢܝܩܕܡܘܣ.

6 „ ܚܐ „ ܚܝܐ (*see Note*, vol. ii)

9 „ ܢܝܩܘܕܝܡܘܣ „ ܢܝܩܕܡܘܣ

14 „ ܒܪܗ „ ܠܒܪܗ

16 „ ܢܬܠ „ ܫܕܪ

18 „ ܕܒܪܐ ܝܚܝܕܐ „ ܕܒܪܐ ܒܚܝܪܐ

21 „ * * ܪܬܐ „ ܥܒܪܪܬܐ (*? read* ܥܒܕܪܬܐ)

21 „ ܗܘ. ܩܪܒ ܠܢܘܗܪܐ „ ܡܩܪܒ ܠܘܬ ܢܗܪܐ

21 „ ܒܒܗܡ „ ܒܒܗ

31—33 *See notes on* p. 434

34* *for* ܒܟܝܠܐ *read* ܒܟܝܠܬܐ

34* ܐܠܗܐ ܐܒܐ ܐܠܐ S^{ed}: ܐܒܐ *is distinct* (*Mrs Lewis in Expositor*, p. 117), *but there is apparently no decisive evidence against reading* ܪܘܚܐ *for* ܐܠܗܐ

36 ܪܘܓܙܐ S^{ed}: *read* ܪܘܓܙܗ (*as C*)

iv 4, 5[a] *S reads* ܒܗ

ܥܒܪ ܗܘܐ ܒܐܬܪܐ

ܕܫܡܪܝܐ ܐܬܐ ܗܘܐ

6* *for* |* * ܕܝܬܒ *read* |ܐܝܟ ܕܝܬܒ

34 „ ܨܒܝܢܐ „ ܨܒܝܢܗ

v 7 „ ܐܚܪܝܢ „ ܐܚܪܢ

18 ܘܡܫܘܐ S^{ed} (*as* syr.vg): *I suspect we should read* ܘܡܫܘܝܢ (*as C*)

19 ܗܠܝܢ ܐܦ | ܒܪܐ ܐܟܘܬܗ ܥܒܕ S^{ed} (*as* syr.vg): *a comparison with C suggests to me that S has not been correctly deciphered here*

vi 12 *for* ܡܟܝܠ ܐܡܪ * * | ܠܬܠܡܝܕܘܗܝ

read * * ܡܟܝܠ ܐܡܪ | ܠܬܠܡܝܕܘܗܝ

* See *Expositor* for August, 1897, p. 117.

vi 15 *for* ܫܡܥܢ *read* ܘܫܡܥܢ
15* ,, ܘܫܡ ,, ܘܘ[illegible]ܠ
21 ܒܡܣܟܢܘܬܐ S^{ed}: *read* ܒܗ ܒܡܣܟܢܘܬܐ (*as C*)
29 ܗܘܐ ܚܒܪܢܐ S^{ed}: *read* ܗܘ ܚܒܪܢܐ
37 ܐܚܣܢܗ S^{ed}: *read* ܐܚܣܢܘܗܝ
69 ܐܚܝܢ S^{ed}: *read* ܘܐܚܝܢ
vii 10 *for* ܟܠܗ * * | *read* ܟܠܗܝ ·ܘ·
11, 12 ,, ܗܘ ܘܐܙܠܐ ܥܡܗܐܐ ,, ܗܘ ܗܘ ܘܐܙܠܐ ܥܡܗ
12 ,, ܕܡܕܝܢܬܐ ,, ܕܐܬܬܐ
19 ,, ܠܡܣܒܪܘܗܝ ,, ܠܡܣܒܪܘܗ
20* ,, ܒܢܫܐ ,, ܐܢܫܐ
23 ,, ܒܪ ܐܢܫ ,, ܒܪ ܐܢܫ
23 ,, ܒܬܫܝܢ ,, ܒܢ ܫܝܢ
26 *for* ܘܐܢܫ * * ܒܢܝܚܬܐ *read* ܘܡܒܟܠܠ ܘܐܢܫ | ܕܐܡܪ ܒܢܝܚܬܐ
29 ,, ܒܪܐ *read* ܕܝܢ
32 ,, ܕܢܫܐ | ܕܐܬܚܘܝܘ ,, ܠܕܢܫܐ | ܕܐܬܚܘܝܘ
33 ,, ܘܐܙܠܐ ,, ܘܐܙܠܐ ܠܗ
35 ,, ܘܠܐ ,, ܕܠܐ
35 ,, ܐܚܝܢ (1°) ,, ܐܚܝܢ (*sic*)
42 ,, ܡܘܪܬܐ ,, ܡܪܬܐ
49** *for* ܡܢܐ ,, ܒܕܢܐ
50 ,, ܢܦܫܟܝ ,, ܢܦܫܟܝ
50 ,, ܠܡܦܩ ,, ܠܡܦܩ (*sic*)
51 ,, ܕܢܫܒܚ ,, ܢܫܒܚ (*sic*)
viii 13 ,, ܘܠܐ ,, ܠܐ
21 ,, ܐܡܪ ܠܗܘܢ | ,, ܐܡܪ ܠܗܘܢ ܝܫܘܥ |
22 ܠܒܥܒܪܐ S^{ed}: *read* ܠܒܥܒܪܐ
22 *for* ܠܐ *read* ܕܠܐ
22 ܠܐܡܬܐ S^{ed}: ? *read* ܠܐܬܪ
22, 23 *for* ܕܐܙܠ ܐܢܘܢ ܘܐܡܪ *read* ܕܐܙܠܘܢ ܐܡܪ
33 ܘܡܢ ܒܬܘܒ ܡܢܗ | * * * S^{ed}: ? *read* ܒܬܘܒ ܡܢܗ | ܘܠܐܢܫ
44 *for* ܐܬܬܐ ܕܝܢ ܕܡܫܟܐ *read* ܐܬܬܐ ܕܝܢ ܕܝܢ ܕܡܫܟܐ

* See *Expositor* for August, 1897, p. 117.

** The photograph taken by Mrs Lewis in 1902 leaves no doubt that the word began with ܒ.

viii 44 *for* ܘܒܫܪܪܐ ܠܐ * * *read* ܘܒܫܪܪܐ ܠܝܬܘܗܝ
46 ,, ܐܢܬܘܢ ,, ܐܢܬܘܢ ܠܝ
54 ,, ܕܐܠܗܐ ,, ܕܐܠܗܢ
54 ,, ܘܗ ,, ܘܗ *S** (vid), *now erased*
ix 13 ,, ܠܗܘ * * * | ,, ܠܗܘ ⸢ܕܐ⸣ܬܐ⸢ܣܝ⸣ |
13, 14 *for* ܘܗܘ * * * * | ,, ܘܗܘ ܗܘܐ ⸢ܫܒ⸣ܬܐ |
14, 15 ,, ܗܘܬ * * | ,, ܗܘܬ ܘܬܘ⸢ܒ⸣ |
20 ܐܡܪܝܢ *S*[ed]: *read* ⸢ܘ⸣ܐܡܪܝܢ
x 11 *for* ⸢ܚܠܦ⸣ ܕܥܢܗ *read* ܚܠܦܗ.
23, 24 *See the note on* p. 484
28, 29* *after* ⸢ܐܒ⸣ܕ *there is an illegible word of two letters*
36, 37 *for* ܕܐܠܗܐ *** ܐܢܐ *read* ܕܐܠܗܐ ܐܢܐ
xi 4 ܫܡܥ *S*[ed]: *read* ⸢ܟܕ⸣ ܫܡܥ
4 ܘܐܡܪ ⸢ܠܗܘܢ⸣ *S*[ed]: *read* ܐܡܪ ⸢ܗܢܐ⸣
18 *The words to be supplied after* ܕܗܘܐ *look like* ܬܪܬܝܢ ⸢ܦ⸣ܪ⸢ܣܢ⸣
25 ܩܝܡܬܐ *S*[ed]: ܡܬܐ *is certain, but the photograph might be read* ܢܚܡܬܐ
46 *for* ܕܠܐ ܗܢܝܢܘ (‘*Some Pages*’) *read* ܕܠܐ ܗܢܝܢܘܢ (*as Syndics’ Ed.*)
50 ,, ܡܬ * * *read* ܡܬܦܪܝܡ
55* ,, ܪܡܫܐ ,, ܘܥܠܐ
xii 17* ,, ܟܢܫܐ ,, ܘܟܢܫܐ
17* ,, ܕܡܫܬܥܝܢ ,, ܡܫܬܥܝܢ
37 ܐܬܘܬܐ * * * ܪܘܪ⸢ܒ⸣ܬܐ ⸢ܟܕ⸣ *S*[ed]: *? read* ܐܬܘܬܐ ⸢ܟܕ⸣ ܪܘܪ⸢ܒ⸣ܬܐ
43 ܡܢ | ܫܘ⸢ܒܚܐ⸣ ⸢ܕܐܠܗܐ⸣ *S*[ed]: *there is no room for two words here, so that probably we should read here* ⸢ܐܠܗܐ⸣ | ܡܢ *only*
48 ܕܡܫܐܠ *S*[ed]: *only* ܕܡ *is legible in the photograph: ? read* ⸢ܕܡ⸣ܩܒܠܐ *or possibly* ⸢ܕܡܩ⸣ܒܠ
48 *for* ܠܝ *read* ܠܝ ܕܝܢ
48 ,, ܬܕܘ⸢ܢ⸣ ܠܗ ,, ⸢ܬܕ⸣ܘ⸢ܢ⸣ܝܘܗܝ
xiii 22 ,, ܡܢ | ܡܢܘ ,, ܡܢ | ܗܘ (*see note on* p. 504)
23* ,, ⸢ܒܥܘ⸣ܒܗ ,, ܒܥܘܒܗ
29* ,, * * * * ⸢ܕܓ⸣ܠܘܣ ,, ܗܘܘ * * ⸢ܕܓ⸣ܠܘܣ

* See *Expositor* for August, 1897, p. 117 *f.*

xiii 30	*for*	ܒܗ ܕܝܢ	*read*	ܗܝܕܝܢ
32	,,	⸢ܒ⸣ܫܪܐ	,,	ܒܫܪ̈
36	,,	ܒܐܚܪܬܐ	,,	ܒܐܚܪܝܬܐ
38**	,,	ܬܟܦܪ ܒܝ * * * | ܐܟܦܪ	,,	ܬܟܦܪ ܒܝ ܘܗܘܝܬ | ܐܟܦܪ
xiv 8	,,	ܦܠܝܦܘܣ	,,	ܦ⸢ܝ⸣ܠܝܦܘܣ
20	,,	ܘܒܗܘܢ ܗܪܟܐ	,,	ܘܒܗܘ ܗܪܟܐ
22	,,	ܬܗܘܡܐ	,,	ܬܐܘܡܐ
28	,,	ܗܘܝܬܘܢ ܚܕܝܢ |	,,	ܗܘܝܬܘܢ ܠܝ |

28 ܐܚܬܘܢ *S*[ed]: *we must read* ⸢ܚܕ⸣ܝܬܘܢ

28 ܕܐܬܐܬܐ *S*[ed]: *read* ܕܐܙܠܢܐ (*cf C*)

xv 24 * * ܘܫ *S*[ed]: *read* ⸢ܫܘ⸣ܘܝܢ

25 ܕܢܬܡܠܐ *S*[ed]: *read* ܕܬܬܡܠܐ

25 ܕܣܢܐܘܢܝ *S*[ed]: *read* ܕܣ⸢ܢ⸣ܘܢܝ (*as elsewhere*)

xvi 5	*for*	ܐܬܐ	*read*	ܐܙܠ

10 ܘܗܡܟܝܠ *S*[ed]: *read* ܘ⸢ܡܟ⸣ܝܠ

15 ܕܡܕܡ *S*[ed]: *read* ⸢ܡ⸣ܕܡ

19 ܕܡܚܝ *S*[ed]: *read* ⸢ܡ⸣ܚܝ

24*	*for*	ܠܗ⸢ܫܐ⸣ ⸢ܠܐ⸣	*read*	ܠܗܫܐ ܠܐ
xvii 22	,,	ܫܘܒܚܐ	,,	ܫܘܒܚܐ ܗܘ
26	,,	ܐܝܟ	,,	ܐܢܘܢ
xviii 6	,,	ܠܒܣܦܪܗܘܢ (*misprint*)	,,	ܠܒܣܬܪܗܘܢ
10	,,	ܡܠܟܘ⸢ܣ⸣ |	,,	ܡܠܟܘ |
11	,,	ܣܝܦ⸢ܐ⸣ |	,,	ܣܝܦܟ |
15	,,	ܕܟܗܢܘܬܗ	,,	ܕܟܗܢܬܗ

25 * * ܐܡ̈ܪܐ *S*[ed]: *the transcript of Mrs Lewis has* ܐܡܪܐ ܕܫܡܥ *,
i.e. *we must read* ܐܡܪܐ ⸢ܕܫܡܥܘܢ⸣

31	*for*	| ܕܢܡܘܣܟܘܢ	*read*	| ⸢ܕ⸣ܢܡܘܣܟܘܢ
xix 41*	,,	ܡܩܒܪܐ ܕܐܢܫ	,,	ܡܩܒܪܐ ܚܕܬܐ ܕܐܢܫ
42*	,,	ܒܒܝܬ ܡܩܒܪܐ * * ܬܐ	,,	ܒܒܝܬ ܡܩܒܪܐ ܚܕܬܐ
xxi 5	,,	ܠܡܐܟܠܗ ⸢ܒܗ⸣	,,	ܠܡܐܟܠܗ ܒܗ

** See *Theol. Literaturzeitung* for 1898, col. 440.
* See *Expositor* for August, 1897, p. 118.

CAMBRIDGE: PRINTED BY J. AND C. F. CLAY, AT THE UNIVERSITY PRESS.

www.ingramcontent.com/pod-product-compliance
Lightning Source LLC
Chambersburg PA
CBHW081142290426
44108CB00018B/2414
* 9 7 8 1 5 3 2 6 0 8 6 1 2 *